Our Country

Our Country

-»» ««-

The Shaping of America from Roosevelt to Reagan

Michael Barone

THE FREE PRESS
A Division of Macmillan, Inc.
NEW YORK

Maxwell Macmillan Canada
TORONTO

Maxwell Macmillan International
NEW YORK   OXFORD   SINGAPORE   SYDNEY

The Free Press
A Division of Macmillan, Inc.
866 Third Avenue, New York, N.Y. 10022

973.91
B26So
1992

Maxwell Macmillan Canada, Inc.
1200 Eglinton Avenue East
Suite 200
Don Mills, Ontario M3C 3N1

Macmillan, Inc. is part of the Maxwell Communication Group
of Companies.

First Free Press Paperback Edition 1992

Printed in the United States of America

printing number
1   2   3   4   5   6   7   8   9   10

Library of Congress Cataloging-in-Publication Data
Barone, Michael.
    Our country: the shaping of America from Roosevelt to Reagan /
Michael Barone.
    p.   cm.
    Includes bibliographical references.
    ISBN 0-02-901862-5
    1. United States—Politics and government—1933–1945.   2. United
States—Politics and government—1945–   3. United States—History—
1933–1945.   4. United States—History—1945–   I. Title.
E806.B335   1990
973.91—dc20   d89-23736
                                                        CIP

The author and the publisher gratefully acknowledge permission to reprint excerpts from the following
publications:

Dean Acheson, *Present at the Creation*. Copyright © 1969 by Dean Acheson. Reprinted by permission
of W.W. Norton & Company, Inc., New York, New York.

Rowland Evans and Robert Novak, *Lyndon B. Johnson: The Exercise of Power*. Copyright © 1966 by
Rowland Evans and Robert Novak. Reprinted by arrangement with New American Library, a Division
of Penguin Books USA Inc., New York, New York.

"This Land Is Your Land," words and music by Woody Guthrie, TRO– © copyright 1956 (renewed),
1958 (renewed) and 1970 Ludlow Music, Inc., New York, New York. Used by permission.

Nicholas Lemann, "The Unfinished War," *The Atlantic*, December 1988. Reprinted by permission
of the author.

Jonathan Rauch, "Is the Deficit Really So Bad?" *The Atlantic*, February 1989. Reprinted by permission
of the author.

Jules Witcover, *Marathon: The Pursuit of the Presidency 1972–1976*. Copyright © 1977 by Jules Witcover.
Reprinted by permission of Viking Penguin, a division of Penguin Books USA Inc.

To my parents
Charles Gerald Barone and Alice Darcy Barone
and to my daughter
Sarah Barone

-»» «««-

Contents

PART THREE
American Politics 1947–1964
CONFIDENCE

PART FOUR
American Politics 1964–1981
ALIENATION

PART FIVE
American Politics 1981–1988
RESILIENCE

→>>> <<<←

Introduction

O *ur Country* is a political history of the United States from the 1930s to
the 1980s. The narrative begins in 1930, when my parents were 10 years
old, and ends in the month before 1989, when my daughter turned 10. I am trying
to tell a public story, a story of public people and public events. But it is also a
personal story, an attempt to understand how the country I was born and grew
up in became the country I see about me today.

The book is undergirded by three guiding theses. The first is that in the United
States politics more often divides Americans along cultural than along economic
lines, and that the politics of economic redistribution in the 20 or so years after
Franklin Roosevelt's New Deal is an exception that proves the rule. This con-
tradicts the widespread assumption that American politics revolves around questions of economic distribution—over, in the words of the title of a classic political
science book, "who gets what, when, and how."[1] That position is taken not just
by Marxists but by the Progressive historians who began writing a century ago
and whose ideas continue to influence much political writing and thinking today.

Yet over the long run it is plain that politics more often divides us on cultural
lines—along lines of region, race, ethnicity, religion, or personal values. This is
what we should expect in a country which has always been affluent[2] and where
economic upward mobility is the common experience,[3] but where distinctive cultural identities and views are often lasting and tenacious. It is natural that our
relatively enduring cultural origins and attitudes should be more important more
often than our frequently fast-changing economic status. "Twentieth-century
nations frequently display a mixture of ethnic and social class stratification," two
leading authorities write. But "ethnicity . . . recurrently proves the stronger
attraction and the most volatile source of domestic violence."[4]

In America, with its racial diversity, geographic mobility, and immigrant heritage, politics has often been a struggle to define *who is really an American*. Disagreement over what is meant to be an American set Americans fighting each
other in the Civil War, and for years afterward pitted North against South, black
against white, immigrant against pioneer, in partisan politics. Economic issues

have produced spirited political fights, but it was disagreement over who was really an American which intensified feelings to the point of producing the highest rate of voter turnout in the last eight decades in a presidential election—1960— in which 78% of Catholics voted for a Catholic and 63% of white Protestants for a white Protestant.

Of course economic issues have played a role, often an important role, in our politics, and presidential elections often appear to be referenda on the incumbent's stewardship of the economy. And it was fitting that economics would play a bigger role in the depression of the 1930s, when Americans came to believe they could no longer count on the economic growth which through most of their history had made upward economic mobility commonplace and downward economic mobility bearable. But when economic growth returned after World War II, and as the nation became culturally more diverse in the years of long peace, political issues— civil rights, the Vietnam war, drugs, abortion, policy toward the Soviets and the Third World—tended once again to divide Americans more often on cultural than on economic lines.

The second guiding thesis of this book is that in time of war America, like other countries, tends to choose bigger government and cultural uniformity, while in time of peace we tend to want smaller government and cultural diversity.[5] This thesis helps to explain both the vast growth of American government during World War II and the years after and the strong pressures registered in the political system beginning in the late 1970s, after a long period of peace, to reduce or hold down the size of government. It helps to explain why the conformist, "other-directed"[6] America that emerged from the traumas of the depression and World War II and flourished in the 1950s became the culturally diverse, deeply segmented America of the 1970s and 1980s—a country more typical of what one leading historian calls a "segmented society."[7] It helps to explain why our recent history has not moved constantly in one direction or oscillated in predictable cycles.[8] It is seen more usefully as a series of episodes, each one unique, each produced by the particularities of what came before and by the actions of particular human beings: the shaping of America from Roosevelt to Reagan.

So this narrative does not regard, as so many of the popular pro-New Deal histories written from the 1940s to the 1960s did, American political history as a story of progress on the road from nineteenth-century laissez faire and isola-tionism to twentieth-century welfare statism and internationalism. The path is not so straight nor the course so predetermined as that. Nor does this narrative regard, as so many popular histories written in the 1970s and 1980s tend to see, recent American political history as a tale of decline, the story of how a country suffused with pride betrayed its ideals, lost a war, and allowed its economy to wither or crumble.[9] For this country showed enough resilience in the 1980s to produce once again a growing economy and enough strength to win important (and unexpected) foreign policy victories. Some longer run trends can be seen over the past six decades, notably toward greater tolerance of diversity, belief in civil liberties, and support for civil rights. But at least at the margins, these are still lively cultural issues in our politics, and the possibility of reversal cannot be ruled out.

The third guiding thesis is one I did not begin with, but which the writing of this narrative persuaded me was right, and that is that people—individual people— matter. Demographic trends, the great tides of war and peace, the flow of immigrants and settlers across a continent, cultural heritage, religious beliefs, and personal habits: all these things shape the times, in ways which contemporaries are hard put to discern but which are easier to see from the longer view of history. But Tolstoy was wrong when he argued in his epilogue to *War and Peace* that individuals do not matter, and as a trenchant critic noted, Tolstoy's own "genius . . . in the perception of specific properties," and his delineation of the particularities of personal character refute the "universal exploratory principle" he longed to find.[10] It is inconceivable that the history of our country from the 1930s to the 1980s would have been the same without Franklin Roosevelt or Richard Nixon, without such lesser-known but pivotal politicians as Senator Robert Wagner or Senator Arthur Vandenberg, without civil rights leaders like A. Philip Randolph or Martin Luther King, Jr., or labor leaders like John L. Lewis and Walter Reuther, or losing candidates like Adlai Stevenson or Barry Goldwater.

Towering over them all, in my view, is Franklin D. Roosevelt. Just as Lincoln remade his country in the crucible of Civil War, so Roosevelt remade his country in the crucibles of the Depression and World War II. As one perceptive reporter who happened to be a kinsman put it, he "included the excluded," making it clear to all Americans and not just northern white Protestants that this was their country too, and even in the direst moments he exuded an "absolute confidence in the American future" that was an essential ingredient of economic recovery and military victory.[11] Roosevelt had his political setbacks, he had his share of silly ideas and perhaps more, his modus operandi was on occasion so devious as to be dishonest, and in his love of his countrymen he tolerated some failings that later generations would find intolerable. To some he appeared disorganized, slapdash, cheerful to the point of flippancy.

Yet under that carefree exterior was, I am convinced, an iron self-discipline, and beneath his seeming penchant for disorganization was a determination to see that the important goals were achieved. It was not inevitable, in my view, that the dizzying downard spiral of the economy be stopped in March 1933, nor was it inevitable in December 1941 that we would win the war—it was inevitable that we not lose but to win we had to go forward and do some very difficult things. But Franklin Roosevelt led his country out of the downward spiral and to total victory, and part of the secret of his success was that through the air of confidence he always maintained, in private and in public, he made recovery and victory seem inevitable even though they were not.

The United States which emerged victorious from war in September 1945 was a country shaped by Franklin Roosevelt, and if that shape was altered by later leaders and subsequent events, by the long decades of peace and prosperity that followed, then much of the shaping was done by the two of his successors who were his greatest admirers, Lyndon Johnson and Ronald Reagan.[12] Johnson's attempts to follow Roosevelt's example resulted in the Great Society and the Vietnam war. Reagan's attempt to hold down the growth of government and assert American power in the world, the first a very un-Rooseveltian goal and the second very Rooseveltian indeed, owe much of their success to his style of speaking to the nation in Roosevelt's tones and sometimes in his very words. This is apparent in his best lines in the October 1980 and 1984 presidential debates, neither of which was suggested to him by his advisers. "Are you better off than you were four years ago?" he asked in 1980, in an almost exact paraphrase of Roosevelt's fireside chat of June 1934, while his riposte on the age issue—"I am not going to exploit, for political purposes, my opponent's youth and inexperience"—showed a deftness in flicking aside criticism and a use of perfectly timed humor reminiscent of Roosevelt's September 1944 response to the attacks on his little dog Fala. Roosevelt was still magic fifty years later, even though most voters were not alive when he was president.

II

In writing this book I have used as primary sources demographic data, election returns, and public opinion polling results—sources which in my view have not always been studied closely enough by others. And I have relied on the writings—so many of them, including some I disagree with, beautifully written and a pleasure to read and study—of scholars, journalists, participants, and in a few instances on my own personal experiences and interviews. Although I hope that I have been guilty of no more than the minor inaccuracies and errors that may be inevitable in a work of this length, I would be grateful for corrections of fact great and small and even for differences of interpretation and opinion.

I have also drawn on my personal experience. I have been fortunate to have seen this country from various perspectives: from a modest middle-class neighborhood in Detroit and an elite school in a rich suburb, from knocking on voters' doors in muddy New Hampshire and big city ghettoes and from sitting in offices with politicians of the highest rank. I grew up in the Midwest, live in the East and have close friends in all parts of the country. I have traveled extensively through the United States, setting foot so far in 48 of the 50 states and 420 of the 435 congressional districts. I have been trained as a lawyer and have worked as a political consultant and journalist, and I have written, every two years through the 1970s and 1980s, the biennial editions of *The Almanac of American Politics.*[13]

I have been fortunate in many ways that have been helpful in writing this book. First of all I have parents who are people of high morality and intellectual integrity, with backgrounds that taught them much about their country and intellects that enabled them to make sense of what they saw. Their abhorrence of bigotry and stubborn adherence to principle I hope I have come close to matching. Like Mario Cuomo, I must acknowledge that if I can see clearly and far it is at least partly because I stand on the shoulders of giants. I am fortunate, second, in having a daughter whose lively friendliness and brilliant insights enrich my life—and remind me that for many Americans in these fortunately rather uninteresting times politics is "boring" and "dumb."

Professionally, in the three jobs I have held for the last 20 years I have been fortunate in having worked for three people of superior insight and total integrity: the late Judge Wade H. McCree, Jr., of the United States Court of Appeals for the Sixth Circuit; Peter D. Hart of Peter D. Hart Research Associates, Inc.; and Meg Greenfield of *The Washington Post.* I am grateful to Meg Greenfield and to the *Post* for their forebearance in allowing me partial leave during calendar year 1987 and for other indulgences which helped me in the writing of this book from 1986 to 1988. I am grateful also for the fellowship of many other colleagues at the *Post*, and in particular those who were my colleagues as editorial writers over the entire seven years I was there: Stephen S. Rosenfeld, J. W. Anderson, Robert L. Asher, and Patricia Shakow. I also have reason to be grateful to those who have been my colleagues at *U.S. News and World Report* since April 1989, over the rather large number of months during which this book was "virtually finished," especially editors Roger Rosenblatt, Michael Ruby, and Merrill McLoughlin. Far too lengthy to list here are the names of those, in the newsrooms of *The Washington Post* and *U.S. News and World Report*, on the campaign trail from the Savery Hotel in Des Moines to the Sheraton Wayfarer in Bedford, New Hampshire, in gatherings of journalists in Washington and of politicians there and across the land, from whom I have learned things about politics and about America. Their names alone would fill a large part of this book.

Authors love to tell horror stories about agents and publishers, but I have had wonderful experiences at every stage of working on this book. They not only helped me get *Our Country* published; they helped me shape thoughts and themes that at first were too inchoate and disorganized to make a book. As my agent, Raphael Sagalyn worked far harder than his 10 percent could justify in helping me shape my proposal and enabling me to find the publisher that was right for this book. He succeeded: Erwin Glikes of The Free Press was the perfect publisher for this project. He understood better than I did at first what I was trying to say and helped guide me toward saying it—but saying it in my own way. He understands the marketplace, but even more he cares about the message: the ideal publisher. Grant Ujifusa, my co-author on *The Almanac of American Politics*, also helped when he was senior editor at The Free Press; it was Grant who came up with the idea of *The Almanac*, and so to him I owe my whole career as a political writer. Peter Dougherty, who took Grant's office at The Free Press, showed perception and dedication far above the call of duty in critiquing the manuscript and promoting the book—as if it were not my book but his, which in a sense it is. The Free Press also took care to hire two brilliant readers of the manuscript, who saved me from many infelicities. Richard M. Valelly, of the political science department at M.I.T., and copy editor John Elliott, provided a challenging critique of the entire manuscript. Both brought to their work impressive erudition and good-humored common sense from which I hope I have been wise enough to profit.

Managing editor Eileen DeWald brought a fine critical intelligence as well as an unflappable dedication to her work on the manuscript. Just to recount where each of them came from suggests the richness of our country, a richness that I hope *Our Country* reflects: Springfield, Massachusetts; Antwerp, Belgium and Morningside Heights, New York; Worland, Wyoming; West Philadelphia; Arlington, Massachusetts; Scottsville, Virginia; and Brooklyn, New York.

Early and partial versions of the manuscript were read by Gary Cohen, Joel Garreau, Donald Graham, John Herfort, Norman Ornstein, Nelson Polsby, and Steven Stark. Their comments were stimulating, bracing, and encouraging. I benefited greatly during 1988 from the demise of Albert Gore's campaign, which enabled me to hire onetime Gore staffer Jeffrey L. Pasley, future academic and current political savant, as research assistant. Of course the final product must be counted as my own: for all those who have helped me have disagreed with at least something in the book, and some I think have disagreed with a great deal.

But as I write in late 1989, after the rest of this book has been set into type, I must say that the events of 1989—the "Communist meltdown" in the Soviet Union and Eastern Europe, the brutal massacre in Tiananmen Square—provide additional support, beyond anything in the text of *Our Country*, for the proposition that the fundaments of our system—political democracy, economic freedoms tempered by government protections—really are at the basis of any good society. In the long run, from the 1930s through the 1980s, the history of our country—a country that in that period doubled in population and quintupled in gross national product, that destroyed one branch of totalitarianism in the middle 1940s and helped erode another in the late 1980s—has been a history mostly of success and mostly of goodness, and I feel privileged in having the chance to set it out in my own way.

Our Country

PART
ONE

Our Country
1930

1

⇥ ⇤

Republican Chief

From the third-floor study of the Georgian house on Wyoming Avenue, with its view over the rooftops of the other mansions on this hill above Rock Creek Park, Chief Justice William Howard Taft could look up from his desk and see off in the distance the Washington Monument and the Capitol dome. Taft had lived in Washington before, in the White House from 1909 to 1913, and now he lived in a neighborhood of presidents. Just four blocks down 23rd Street, past tall-windowed townhouses and gray stone mansions, was the red brick Georgian house where Herbert Hoover had lived when he was secretary of commerce from 1921 to 1928. Down the hill, only four lots away on S Street, was the Woodrow Wilson house, with the proportions of an Italianate palazzo but Georgian accents, where the invalid former president had lived after he left the White House and from which he had been taken out for his afternoon automobile ride each day until his death in 1924.

It was natural that America's leaders should cluster in a certain quarter of their capital, just as Britain's leaders lived in the square mile around St. James's and those of France along the Avenue des Champs-Élysées. But Washington was not a huge metropolis like London or Paris; it was not buzzing with commerce, nor was it the focus of national railroad networks; it was only the nation's fourteenth city in population; it had a few monumental buildings, but when Taft became chief justice in 1921 most of its neighborhoods were collections of monotonous rowhouses. The Supreme Court Building he planned had not yet been built, the court's sessions were held in an old chamber on the Senate side of the Capitol, and the only office each justice had was in his home. In the early 1920s Taft would work mornings in his study. Then he would descend in the elevator and walk the three miles downhill from his house across downtown Washington, where no building was taller than 130 feet, and then up the hill to the Capitol in time for the court's noon session. Few fences surrounded government buildings; no guards patrolled their vestibules. It was an era when a motorist, caught in the rain with his top down, could pull under the porte cochere of the White House, step inside the door, and be invited in to shake hands with the president.[1]

Yet the men who occupied high positions in this small city knew that they commanded great things. Taft's father, born on a Vermont farm in 1810, had been a pioneer on the Ohio frontier who made his fortune practicing law in

3

Cincinnati, the Queen City of the West; he eventually became President Ulysses Grant's secretary of war, attorney general, and minister[2] to Austria-Hungary and to Russia. His son Will, educated at Yale, had a career that began locally and spanned the globe. As a federal appeals judge in Cincinnati in the 1890s, he had revived the infant Sherman Antitrust Act with a decision prohibiting price-fixing.[3] As President Theodore Roosevelt's civil governor of the Philippines, he had established American hegemony over an Asian archipelago and civilian control over the U.S. Army. As president himself, he had been concerned not only about the tariff and the Interior Department's conservation policies, but about Russian pogroms and the Japanese advance into revolutionary China. Taft traveled the railroad lines that crossed the continent and saw, ominously glaring over oil-streaked waterways, the steel mills and auto factories built and financed by investment bankers and industrialists. His Justice Department had persuaded the Supreme Court—to which he had appointed more members than any president since George Washington—to break up the Standard Oil and American Tobacco monopolies that girdled the globe. Afterwards, while professor of constitutional law at Yale, he had seen his country's leaders create a military force of 3 million men that fought foreign armies in Europe, 3,000 miles away. He had been the chairman of Woodrow Wilson's War Labor Board and a supporter of the Treaty of Versailles.

Taft was considered a member of an almost aristocratic elite, yet he was only a generation removed from a pioneer past. He did not organize torchlight parades, as politicians still did in the 1890s, he did not lift his hand to solicit political contributions, and he did no ward-heeling and poll-watching on election day. Yet he did not scorn the political arena even if he sometimes found it uncongenial to play his assigned role in it. He understood the hurly-burly of local politics, just as he understood the abrasiveness of labor-management relations. When he was at Yale he became friends with New Haven Republican boss I. M. Ullman, and while on the War Labor Board he traveled to Carolina textile mills and upstate New York factories and insisted that workers be paid a "living wage." He never doubted that his Republican party was better fitted to govern than the opposition Democracy, and he was happy to live in a time when the Republicans, though shut out in the South, won most national elections. Nor did he doubt that the highest places in government were properly filled by men of intellectual and social distinction like himself, his mentor and later enemy Theodore Roosevelt, associates and sometime allies like New York lawyers Elihu Root, Henry Stimson, George Wickersham, and Charles Evans Hughes and New England aristocrat-politician Henry Cabot Lodge; such men, except in the South, were found primarily in Republican ranks. Taft regarded himself as a political failure because when Roosevelt ran against him and split the party in 1912, he was defeated for reelection to the presidency. But as an administrator and a judge, Taft was one of the most effective public officials of his time. He made policy and he made government work. He helped to establish rules and ways of doing public business that mostly prevailed.

He was not a believer in laissez faire. He spent most of his professional life in government. He believed in an energetic federal government that set tariffs and broke up large companies, that maintained the power to wage war and to protect its citizens' interests around the world. He did insist, especially when he was a judge, on setting limits to government power. But they were limits that permitted governments to do many things he considered unwise.

"I love judges and I love courts," Taft said,[4] and on the day he signed Chief Justice Edward D. White's commission in December 1910 he lamented, "There is nothing I would have loved more than being chief justice of the United States."[5] The appointment came to him finally when White died in May 1921, two months after the inauguration of a Republican president, Warren G. Harding, whom Taft had carefully supported and praised. As chief justice, Taft did as much to influence American government and daily life in the 1920s as did Harding and his successors, Calvin Coolidge and Herbert Hoover. He quickly established himself as the clear leader of the court, persuading the justices to reach unanimous decisions on many difficult issues and himself dissenting only once in a major case. He used to the utmost his power as chief justice to assign the writing of opinions when he was in the majority, and he took more than his share of the labor—in those days just before the justices had law clerks—of writing decisions himself. His prose was clear and strong, and his opinions were steady. He clarified the reach of the income tax, which had been enacted with his support when he was president; he supported stern federal enforcement of Prohibition (though his wife was a wet), including the use of wiretaps by federal agents. He took a broad view of the government's power to regulate railroads and, in his one major dissent, argued in 1924 against overturning a state law establishing a minimum wage for women and children.

One great unsettled economic and political question in early twentieth-century America was the position of labor unions. As Americans moved from the countryside into the city, leaving the farm for the factory, they increasingly found themselves working not for themselves or their neighbors but for huge industrial corporations. To many observers, individual workers free to make contracts with these giants did not seem fair. Labor union membership rose from less than 1 million in 1900 to nearly 3 million in 1916; it jumped sharply, partly because of Taft's work on the War Labor Board, to 5 million in 1920.[6] What should be the ground rules for unions and employers? Taft always maintained that he was sympathetic to workers' right to organize unions and strike. But, he would go on, labor should enjoy no special privileges or immunities. Unions should not, for example, be allowed to engage in secondary boycotts, encouraging others to refuse to deal with employers the unions had disputes with; he so ruled in 1890 and held to that view all his life.[7] Even more important, unions should be barred from engaging in violence. Taft encouraged federal courts to enjoin strikes and picketing that were violent, or seemed likely to become so, and he ruled unconstitutional a state law allowing picketing except in cases where it caused "irreparable injury." Pickets could accost strikebreakers, he ruled, but "persistence, importunity, following and dogging"—his words move quickly from Latinate abstraction to Anglo-

Saxon grittiness—"become unjustifiable annoyance and obstruction, which is likely soon to savor of intimidation." He thought it quite enough for striking unions to be allowed one picket "for each point of ingress and egress,"[8] and he was under no illusions that strikes in these circumstances would succeed. It seems reasonable to conclude that he thought it would be better if they usually didn't—which is just what happened: union membership fell to 3.4 million in 1930. Federal court injunctions became one of the standard tools of management, so notorious that one of the major pieces of liberal legislation in those years, ultimately passed as the Norris-LaGuardia Act in 1932 and signed by President Hoover, limited federal judges' power to enjoin strikes.

But for Taft the growth of unions was not synonymous with progress, was perhaps antithetical to it. He had seen America grow from a mostly rural nation where most people lived close to subsistence to a mostly urban nation where millions enjoyed standards of living never before enjoyed by even the privileged few. This change had been produced by a wondrous growth of industry and commerce, nurtured by a small but energetic government and made possible by the freedoms, political and economic, that seemed at the heart of the definition of being American. Interfering with these freedoms or vastly changing the size and role of government might be attractive in some momentary crisis, Taft understood, or might commend itself to believers in some radical theory; but to a man who had seen the system work over time, to tamper with it was the height of folly, and the duty of men like himself was to preserve and to strengthen the framework which made this progress possible.

2

→}}} {{{←

Democratic Chief

From the scallop-bordered windows of Tammany Hall, Charles F. Murphy
could see Luchow's, the old German restaurant, across the busy traffic on
Manhattan's 14th Street; and after he walked down the six broad steps in front
of the hall, he could turn right past the Academy of Music,[1] go around the corner
through crowds surging around the IRT and BMT subway stops and S. Klein's
department store with its bargain prices, and look out across the shabby green
expanse of Union Square, the site of May Day rallies and union protests. Tight-
lipped, with cold gray eyes, tactful, unexcitable, Murphy had grown up a few
blocks east in the Gashouse district, full of four-story townhouses jammed with
Irish immigrant families. His own parents sailed thousands of miles from Ireland
in the 1840s, and by the early 1900s their son's power as the nation's foremost
political boss affected millions and radiated outward for hundreds of miles. But
apart from holidays on Long Island and in the resorts of Hot Springs, Virginia,
and French Lick, Indiana (owned by Indiana's Irish-born Democratic boss, Tom
Taggart), he spent almost all his life within the same few blocks between 14th
and 23rd Streets where as a teenager in the 1870s he had driven a crosstown Blue
Line horsecar.[2]

Murphy was a good athlete when he was young; he organized a successful
baseball team and at the age of twenty opened a saloon on 19th Street and Avenue
A. Known and respected by almost every man in the area, he became active in
politics and in 1892 became Democratic leader in New York's 18th Assembly
district. Ten years later, after the ouster of Richard Croker, he became leader of
Tammany Hall—the Democratic county chairman of Manhattan—and the dominant figure in the Democratic politics of New York City, whose five boroughs
had been united only a few years before. New York, with 3.4 million people in
1900, was the largest city in the nation and second only to London among the
cities of the world. And it was changing as rapidly as it was growing. Each day
ships steamed into New York Harbor and unloaded immigrants at Ellis Island,
near the Statue of Liberty, where they were screened before being allowed into
the country. Each day ferries picked up those who had not been rejected by the
immigration authorities and brought them to New York. The city's nineteenth-
century immigrants had been mostly English, Scottish, Irish, and German, and
three-quarters of them spoke English. But in the 1890s New York began receiving

7

hundreds of thousands of Italians, Slavs, and Eastern European Jews, almost none of whom did. The city's population nearly doubled in the first three decades of the century, to 6.9 million in 1930, and it spread out. Already the completion of the Brooklyn Bridge in 1883 had stimulated mass migration from New York (then consisting only of Manhattan) to more open Brooklyn, and the outflow accelerated after the two cities, together with Queens, the Bronx, and Staten Island, were united as Greater New York[3] in 1898. The first subway line was completed in 1904,[4] and in the quarter-century that followed tens of thousands of immigrants moved out from the crowded tenements of Manhattan to the freshly minted and spacious apartment buildings of Brooklyn and the Bronx and even Queens. Manhattan's population fell from 2.3 million in 1910 to 1.9 million in 1930, while that of the Bronx rose from 430,000 to 1.3 million and that of Brooklyn from 1.6 million to 2.6 million in the same twenty years.

Charles F. Murphy's political achievement was to adapt to this change—and build on it.[5] This most taciturn and conservative-tempered of politicians was a brilliant innovator and a splendid judge of men.[6] Murphy insisted on filling public jobs with patronage appointees and demanded that appointees give a percentage of their salaries to the machine. As for government business, he asserted that "when I can do it without violating the law, it is perfectly right to give out contracts to organization men. If I can, I will." Payoffs of policemen and public officials had been an ordinary cost of doing business, but Murphy, ever prudent, kept his political organization out of the police department—though its personnel were mainly Irish and its potential for profit unmatched—and out of the schools as well. Tammany captains ran steamboat excursions to clambakes in College Point, Queens, staged torchlight parades complete with fireworks, provided food baskets and coal to the needy, and knit together masses of people in a huge and threatening city. Murphy was careful to respond to new immigrants—he championed the Jewish pushcart peddlers, for example—and he courted non-immigrant voters as well by sometimes nominating Fusion (that is, anti-machine) candidates on the Democratic ticket and by advancing the careers of first-rate men. He was denounced by Franklin Roosevelt, a first-term state senator from Dutchess County, for backing a party wheel horse for the U.S. Senate in 1911. But ordinarily Murphy valued talent over seniority. When the Democrats won control of the state legislature in the 1910 elections, he selected as Assembly and Senate majority leaders not some deserving old hacks, but two talented young men of immigrant stock, thirty-seven-year-old Alfred E. Smith and thirty-three-year-old Robert F. Wagner.

Murphy had no instinct or incentive to challenge the underlying rules of the society around him. He was a Roman Catholic, not a Marxist, and the Socialists were competitors of his Democrats—their most effective competition in some Jewish and Italian neighborhoods. But he did find himself embracing the cause of economic reform. On Saturday, March 25, 1911, a fire broke out on the top floors of the Triangle Shirtwaist Company factory on Waverly Place, just off Greenwich Village's Washington Square; 147 women workers suffocated or died of injuries from jumping out the windows because there was no fire escape. A young social worker named Frances Perkins happened to witness the fire and the deaths. She served on the staff of the Triangle Commission created by the legislature, of which Wagner was chairman and Smith vice chairman; it recommended limits on work hours for women, prohibition of child labor, workers' compensation for industrial accidents, and health and safety codes for industry. The harsh facts of industrial life at the time, when almost every working family had a member killed in a work accident or by a work-related disease like tuberculosis, provided more political demand for these reforms than did socialist theory. "Certainly there was nothing social minded about the head of Tammany Hall, Charles Murphy," Frances Perkins wrote later, "whom I went to see when legislation on factory buildings was before the state legislature. I went to enlist his support for this legislation. I climbed up the stairs of old Tammany Hall on 14th Street in a good deal of trepidation. Tammany Hall had a sinister reputation in New York, and I hardly knew how I would be greeted, but, as I later learned, a lady was invariably treated with respect and gallantry and a poor old woman with infinite kindness and courtesy. Mr. Murphy, solemn dignity itself, received me in a reserved but courteous way. He listened to my story and arguments. Then, leaning forward in his chair, he said quietly, 'You are the young lady, aren't you, who managed to get the 54-hour bill passed?' I admitted I was. 'Well, young lady, I was opposed to that bill.' 'Yes, I so gathered, Mr. Murphy.' This can safely be taken as understatement. 'It is my observation,' he went on 'that that bill made us many votes. I will tell the boys to give all the help they can to this new bill. Good-by.' "[7]

And so, it can be argued, was born at least one version of the American welfare state—the politics of using government to systematically regulate private enterprise and to redistribute some of the vast income and wealth of a growing capitalist economy to the great mass of citizens. Wisconsin, under Progressive Governor Robert LaFollette, had adopted an income tax and regulatory laws in the decade before the Triangle fire. Farm states farther west experimented with various kinds of prairie radicalism. But New York in the 1910s and 1920s saw welfare-state policies enacted on a larger scale and with the support—and to the electoral benefit—of one of the two traditional American political parties. Charles Murphy's Tammany Hall, Robert Wagner said in 1937, was "the cradle of modern liberalism in America."[8]

Murphy was not a political dictator. He could not get his way automatically. When he began in politics, there were rival machines contending for the allegiance of New York City's voters, and the dominance of Tammany could not be assumed but was a result that skillful men tried to produce and skillful rivals to prevent.[9] Even at the peak of Murphy's powers he could not always persuade the Democratic leaders of Brooklyn or the Bronx to go along with him.[10] He had virtually no influence on the federal government in Washington; and in 1920, though he had been the most powerful Democratic leader in the biggest Democratic state for two decades, he made a telling reply when the campaign manager of presidential nominee James Cox asked him whether he would back the always anti-Tammany Franklin Roosevelt for vice president. "This is the first time a Democratic nominee for the presidency has shown me courtesy," Murphy declared. "That's why I would vote for the devil himself if Cox asked me to."[11] Though he often held court in the private rooms on the second floor of Delmonico's restaurant at Fifth Avenue and 44th Street, he had little contact with or influence on the rich businessmen and lawyers who made up the restaurant's main clientele. Surely he never would have met an old-family aristocrat like Franklin Roosevelt, for instance, if Roosevelt had not gone into politics; and Roosevelt he knew mostly from a distance, as an enemy who led a bloc of upstate Democrats against Murphy's choice for senator in January 1911, who backed Woodrow Wilson against his choices for president in the Democratic convention in June 1912, who ran against his candidate for senator in the state's first primary in September 1914 (and lost, 73%–27%).

For most of his career, moreover, Murphy did not have reliable majorities of the voters behind him. His early successful candidates for mayor, George McClellan in 1903 and 1905 and William Gaynor in 1909, got only 56% and 44% of the vote, respectively; he lost the mayor's office to Fusionist John Purroy Mitchel in 1913, and he was ridiculed statewide for insisting that same year on the impeachment of the Democratic governor, William Sulzer. But as the nation moved toward the Republicans, Charles Murphy's New York became more Democratic. Al Smith was elected governor in 1918, as the Democrats were losing control of Congress, and after a defeat in 1920, Smith won again in 1922, 1924, and 1926, beating strong Republican candidates each time. Tammany-endorsed John F. Hylan was elected mayor of New York City in 1917 and 1921; he was succeeded by Tammany loyalist James J. Walker. And for 1924, Murphy succeeded in persuading the Democrats to hold their national convention in New York's old Madison Square Garden between Madison and Fourth Avenues and 26th and 27th Streets. It would be the first Democratic convention in the city since the party met in the huge third-floor main hall of the then spanking-new Tammany Hall in 1868[12]—a fitting achievement for an American politician who not only was successful in contemporary politics but also, seemingly unwittingly, had done much to create a politics that would sweep the nation for years after he was gone.

3

→)) (((←

Madison Square Garden 1924

William Howard Taft and Charles F. Murphy represented two contending approaches to American politics and two different cultures.[1] Yet both managed to thrive in the United States of the 1920s. One was Republican, Yankee, elitist, and global in outlook; the other Democratic, Irish, self-educated, parochial. One of pioneer stock and one the son of immigrants, they were leaders of the two great streams of population which comprised the American North and West in the years after the Civil War and which in the 1920s still provided almost all the leaders of its national politics.

Other pairs of politicians could be picked out who would put the parties in a different light—Democrat Newton Baker, Wilson's war secretary and a Cleveland corporation lawyer, and Republican James Watson, the salty-tongued, always partisan Hoosier who became Senate majority leader; or Republican Nicholas Longworth, the debonair House speaker from Cincinnati and son-in-law of Theodore Roosevelt, and Democrat John Nance Garner, the red-faced House veteran from the desert wastes of Uvalde, Texas; or any of the pairs of presidential candidates. But Taft and Murphy not only illustrate the range of possibilities; they both blazed political trails for others to follow, setting a standard that would continue to be looked to in the hard economic times no one knew were ahead. Taft, the Republican, believed in an active but limited government, active enough to wage war and in wartime commandeer the manpower and economic capital of the nation, active enough to enforce Prohibition and assist farmers with a network of county agents, but limited in its ability to regulate the terms and conditions of employment and to redistribute income and wealth. For Taft, government was the end always kept in sight, while politics—the traditional American two-party politics, with its patronage and graft, its back-scratching and boodle, its appeals to Civil War and ethnic loyalties—was the necessary but sometimes distasteful means.

As for Murphy, his entry in the *Dictionary of American Biography* notes that "if he had any theory or philosophy of government, if he had political views on any subject, he never expressed them publicly."[2] Government came second; politics was always first. Politics tied together diverse communities, the urban villages

11

that existed in the interstices of the relentless New York street grid; it helped the helpless, regularized the restless, cemented immigrants and proletarians to existing institutions. In fact, there was a theory of government implicit in Murphy's political decisions: it was that of a government actively intervening in the economy and, in the most prosperous of states, redistributing money to help those less fortunate, a government resistant to proclaiming the dominant Protestant Yankee culture as the only true Americanism and ready to honor other cultures and religions as well. But whether Murphy thought of his politics this way, or whether it just grew organically out of New York soil, like the ailanthus trees forcing their way upward through cracks in the city's sidewalks, there is no way to know.

Their biographers do not record that the articulate, good-humored Taft and the reticent, scrupulously proper Murphy ever met. Perhaps they would have if Murphy had not died in April 1924, three months before the Democratic convention in Madison Square Garden. Taft attended five sessions of the convention and, according to one biographer, "enjoyed every minute of it."[3] Such a reaction suggests he developed a taste for politics, for this was the convention which cast 103 ballots before it selected a presidential nominee, which rejected by the exquisitely narrow margin of 543 3/20 to 542 7/20 a plank condemning the Ku Klux Klan, and which witnessed Franklin Roosevelt, on crutches, nominating "the happy warrior of the political battlefield," Al Smith. It was the first convention Taft had ever seen. He had not even appeared at the two Republican conventions which had nominated him for president, for in those days the parties maintained the antique fiction that no one ran for president and that the surprised and reluctant nominee must be notified of his selection weeks later by an august delegation.[4]

In retrospect that year of 1924, when Calvin Coolidge was reelected, seems the high tide of what Warren G. Harding christened "normalcy." Yet Coolidge's victory seemed far from certain earlier in the year, and both parties were split in ways their leaders must have found threatening. In Madison Square Garden a Catholic for the first time was a serious candidate for a major party's nomination, and urban Democrats like Murphy, with their mostly Catholic constituencies, cannot have been pleased to see the bitter and desperate opposition Smith's candidacy inspired—or the Democrats' unwillingness to condemn the anti-Catholic, anti-Jewish Ku Klux Klan. Although the two leaders of the rural Democrats both had progressive records on economic issues, they instinctively thought of the Protestant yeoman farmers of the South and West as the progressive forces in the republic and saw the polyglot huddled masses of the huge cities as a threat. William Jennings Bryan, the party's three-time presidential nominee, who had come out for government ownership of the railroads in 1907 as well as the free and unlimited coinage of silver in 1896, spoke against condemning the Klan. William McAdoo, the southern-born lawyer who had become Wilson's treasury secretary, married the president's daughter, and finally moved to Los Angeles, was ever suspicious of things urban and gloried in his role as spokesman for the poor folks of the colonial South and West. New York, McAdoo said of the place where he had made his fortune, was an "imperial" city, "reactionary, sinister, mercenary, and sordid."[5]

Bryan's and McAdoo's bitter opposition to Smith and what he stood for was a harbinger of the massive defections Democrats would suffer in the South and West when they nominated him in 1928. Yet Smith's forces had enough votes to stop McAdoo from getting the two-thirds majority then required for the nomination. The candidate produced by the deadlock, the brilliant lawyer John W. Davis, satisfied neither side. He was not a Catholic or a machine politician, but he was also not a believing Protestant or an enthusiastic Prohibitionist. Accustomed to representing corporations, he favored less interference in the economy than either McAdoo or Smith, less than almost everyone but the doctrinairely laissez faire Coolidge.[6] To Taft, Davis seemed "too good a candidate for the Democrats to succeed with." And so he was: he got only 29% of the vote.

But Coolidge did not win an overwhelming percentage himself. He ended up with 54%, winning absolute majorities only in the Republican heartland, or roughly the northern swath of the United States.[7] For the Republican party was also split in 1924. Robert LaFollette, twenty years away from his days as Progressive governor of Wisconsin and still stinging from the violent anger he had aroused when he and other Midwestern Progressives voted against the declaration of war on Germany and stood adamantly against the Versailles treaty, was running at age sixty-nine as a Progressive—with the endorsement of the American Federation of Labor and of the Socialist party. LaFollette favored government intervention in the economy, respect for civil liberties, and an isolationist foreign policy. With no chance to win, and handicapped by the electoral vote system, he still managed to take 17% of the vote. He carried only his home state of Wisconsin, but he ran strong—in some places a close second to Coolidge—in the states directly west of Wisconsin and running south to California. He was never a really serious presidential candidate himself; mentally unbalanced, he had suffered breakdowns at critical points in his career; he died just a year after his defeat. But he obviously spoke for a large constituency.

While the LaFollette movement did not sweep America, it did raise for conservatives like Taft and perhaps for traditionalists like Murphy the specter of socialism. They knew that in Europe socialist parties had displaced many of the traditional parties whose constituencies were formed, as the Republicans' and Democrats' were, out of ancient battles and over cultural divides. In January 1924, Britain's King George V had sent for Ramsay MacDonald, head of the Labour party and an opponent of the late war, and asked him to be prime minister. ("What would dear Grandmama have said?" this grandson of Queen Victoria asked his diary.)[8] Socialists had already headed governments in Germany and France, and revolutionary socialists were in power in Russia and had been driven out only with military force in Hungary and Bavaria. "It was a famous victory," Taft wrote a friend after the 1924 election, "and one most useful in the lessons to be drawn from it, one of which is that this country is no country for radicalism. I think it is really the most conservative country in the world. Whenever people get the clear idea that the issue is between radicalism"—and here Taft meant LaFollette, not the Democrats—"and conservatism, as between maintaining the government we have and going to something we know not of, the answer will always be the same." These words have been cited to ridicule Taft for failing to anticipate the "politics of upheaval" of the 1930s.[9] But they may have been less a prediction than a sigh of relief.

Schism in one major party, a branch of the other almost entirely split off from the trunk—the American political system shaped and led by men like William Howard Taft and Charles F. Murphy was not as strong and not as firmly tied to the traditional American politics of the past as appeared on the surface. In a diverse nation there were more political possibilities and political pitfalls than suggested by the stately march through the 1920s of large Republican majorities in the electoral college. From the returns of the 1924 election and even before, that very interested observer Franklin Roosevelt saw other possibilities besides continued Republican dominance, "though the people will not turn out the Republicans while wages are good and markets are booming."[10] There is plenty of evidence that Roosevelt, defeated as his party's 1920 vice presidential nominee and crippled by polio the following year, had already formed his basic political strategy for a new Democratic majority: to begin with the traditional Democratic party, rooted in the South and a few northern cities; to detach from the Republican party the progressive wing represented by LaFollette and, twelve years before, by his cousin Theodore Roosevelt; to add votes from urban Catholics who supported Al Smith in New York gubernatorial elections in the 1920s and would turn out to support him in the presidential election of 1928.

Of this new majority Democratic party Roosevelt saw himself as the only natural leader: a traditional Democrat with ties to the South (from his days in the heavily southern Wilson administration to his sojourns in Warm Springs, Georgia), with a Roosevelt's special appeal in the progressive Northwest, and with a connection (albeit an uneasy one) to a big-city political machine and its immigrant and Catholic constituents. Roosevelt came from the social class and had the world-traveling experience of William Howard Taft; he was used to doing political business, increasingly on a mutually profitable basis, with Charles F. Murphy; he was the single major politician in the 1920s who could link their traditions of pioneer and immigrant in his own experience. Was some such sense of destiny one of the sources of inner strength that enabled Roosevelt to rebound from the polio that struck him in August 1921?

No one in the 1920s anticipated the circumstances in which Franklin Roosevelt would become president. Charles F. Murphy died in his house on Stuyvesant Square in New York in April 1924, more than five years before the stock market on nearby Wall Street would crash in October 1929. William Howard Taft, gravely ill, resigned as chief justice in February 1930, was carried home, and died a month later. Neither saw or foresaw the changes in the American economic and political systems that would follow from economic collapse. Yet the systems that they had supported and worked in endured at least in part. The economic collapse of the early 1930s and the all-out war of the early 1940s naturally inclined people at the time and later to emphasize the discontinuity between the America of the "roaring '20s" and the America of the Depression years that followed—a discontinuity emphasized by the coincidence that the stock market crash and the Japanese attack on Pearl Harbor both came near the beginning of decades. But there were also elements of continuity between the strong, prosperous, growing, confident, and culturally varied America of 1930 and the America that was to follow.

4

⇢⟫⟫ ⟨⟨⟨⟵

Our Country
1930

The United States in 1930 was a vibrant nation sprawling across the vastness of a continent. In contrast to the suspicious, hostile nations jammed together on the continent of Europe, America seemed a peaceful and homogeneous society—English-speaking. Protestant, prosperous, progressive. But, to a greater extent than usually acknowledged, it was a nation of cultural, economic, and political diversity. It contained the richest cities of the world—and millions of disease-ridden, malnourished subsistence farmers. It proclaimed itself a land of freedom and tolerance—and fostered an implacably defended system of racial segregation. Americans believed they had a political system of unique fairness, one in which any boy could hope to grow up to be president. Yet the United States had only recently granted women the ballot, blacks were routinely denied it, and voters in the most recent presidential ballot had rejected by an unmistakably emphatic margin the candidacy of a Roman Catholic.

The Americans of 1930, like those of 1880 and 1980, took the geographical shape of their country for granted. Yet anyone who takes a relief map of the United States, with the political boundaries indicated by dotted lines, and looks at it upside down or on an angle will see that most of the northern and southern boundaries of the United States were not dictated by natural features. In the nineteenth century some Americans wanted their country to expand north and absorb the mostly empty wilderness of British Canada; others wanted to take Cuba and parts of Central America, continuing the southward expansion that incorporated Texas in 1845 and 40% of the land area of Mexico by the Treaty of Guadalupe Hidalgo in 1848.

But by 1930 it struck no one as odd that the United States had expanded instead to the west, cutting across the corduroy ridges of the Appalachians, crossing the vast grass and scrub land called by Zebulon Pike the Great American Desert, passing over the massive barrier of the Rockies and the parched Great Basin to reach the Pacific. Nor did it seem peculiar that a country that crossed such forbidding natural barriers was bounded on the south and north by nothing more formidable than the trickle of the Rio Grande and the vast but navigable Great

Lakes and St. Lawrence River, and by straight lines surveyed across the vast space between the Lake of the Woods and Puget Sound on the north and between El Paso and San Diego on the south. Yet these waters and those dotted lines on maps sealed off the United States effectively from two foreign cultures—3 million French Canadians and 15 million Mexicans—and even impeded easy contact with the 7 million English-speaking Canadians, most of whom lived within 100 miles of the border.

The shape of America in 1930 will seem even more arbitrary if the map has dots indicating the concentration of population. The western half is a huge expanse of mostly mountains and desert, salt flats and rivers evaporating into mountain-rimmed basins—land populated so sparsely that a pilot flying over might look to the horizon and see not a single sign of habitation. Only 13 million Americans lived in the mostly arid lands west of the 100th meridian. On the other side of this line, in the great Mississippi Valley, the density increases. In this vast center of the country in 1930 lived 70 million Americans, who accounted for a larger percentage of the nation's population than has lived there since. The densest concentrations of people are off to the far eastern edge of the map, clustered in urban areas crammed into the narrow coastal margins where English and Dutch explorers had landed and built their first settlements starting more than 300 years earlier. Some 41 million Americans were jammed into the thin strip of land, 100 to 200 miles wide, from the Appalachian chain east to the ocean. These Americans might look out across the Atlantic with some foreboding at events abroad. But most Americans, especially those living hundreds of miles from any ocean, rested secure in the knowledge that their country seemed invulnerable to military attack. Sheltered on two sides by oceans, bordered by friendly Canada to the north, protected by the vast deserts of northern Mexico from any threat to the south more daunting than Pancho Villa's March 1916 raid on Columbus, New Mexico, Americans had little to fear. The United States, with a population of 123 million, was defending its people and its far-flung interests in Panama and the Philippines and Puerto Rico with armed services manned by only 25,000 officers and 227,000 enlisted men. The continental European countries had military drafts extending far back into the nineteenth century. The United States had had a draft in only two of the preceding sixty-five years. It had 4.7 million veterans, almost all of them from World War I, but the organizations they formed, notably the American Legion, were mostly social groups in whose clubhouses men could gather and drink, not quasi-military organizations hostile to civil government as in much of Europe. Politically the veterans' main demand was for more bonuses, even though payments to veterans already made up one-quarter of the federal budget.

II

The United States owed its shape and its concentrations of population less to the logic of geography than to the movements of great streams of newcomers who together created the country. From the beginning of settlement along the Atlantic coast in the seventeenth century until 1890, that movement was primarily, almost inexorably, westward. At first it ran up against formidable barriers. During the colonial era there were relatively few settlers: the 1790 census showed only 3 million Americans, 20% of them slaves. The Indians were often hostile: King Philip's War of 1676 set back westward movement in New England two generations, and the Mohawk Valley west of Albany, New York, was still Indian territory at the time of the Revolution 100 years later.[1] There were political and economic hindrances as well. The British, wary of attacks from the French and eager to appease the Indians, tried to keep colonials east of the Appalachian chain; the patroon system in the Hudson Valley prevented farmers from buying their own land and thus restricted westward movement through the natural avenue from New England and New York City to the Great Lakes and the Mississippi Valley. The mountains everywhere else were a bar; Daniel Boone did not blaze the trail through the Cumberland Gap until 1769.[2] More than 90% of the Americans counted in 1790 lived within 100 miles of the coast.

But the westward impulse was so strong that in the next 100 years American settlement surged across the continent. The great streams of movement were, to the extent geography and politics permitted, straight west, and different regions of the country west of the Appalachians took on the cultures of the former colonies to the east.[3] Because these cultures had been quite distinct from early in the colonial period, there was, as one historian puts it, "no single 'American' pattern of family and community organization."[4] New England Yankees, penned up east of the Hudson for nearly 200 years, shot straight west and in a few decades created the communities of upstate New York, Connecticut's Western Reserve in northeast Ohio, the settlements that became Chicago and northern Illinois and much of Iowa and Kansas. The religiously and ethnically diverse settlers from the middle colonies moved straight west too, carrying the street grid of Philadelphia, the largest city in the country in 1790, to Cincinnati, the largest city in the interior by 1850, and points west all the way to Colorado Springs.[5] And southerners moved west in several roughly parallel streams. Virginians, following Boone, made their way to Kentucky and southern Ohio, Indiana, and Illinois; Kentucky-born Abraham Lincoln was the son of a man born in Virginia. North Carolinians moved to Tennessee, which became the home of three presidents—Andrew Jackson, James Polk, and Andrew Johnson—who were all born in or on the border of North Carolina. Georgians went to the black belts of Alabama and Mississippi; Tennesseans moved southwesterly, to avoid the Indian Territory, to Texas; the Indian Territory that became Oklahoma, when it was opened to settlement in 1889, attracted poor white farmers coming straight west from Mississippi and Arkansas.

Thus were the different cultures and institutions of the different colonies transported westward. "It was an internalized community that individuals carried with them, and it was a replica of this community which they sought as a place to settle."[6] In 1790 slavery was not yet a peculiarly southern institution; slaves made up 8% of the population of New York. Soon the "peculiar institution" was receding southward; but the retreat ended when the Virginia legislature debated but rejected abolition in 1832, and with white southerners slavery moved in a rush westward. In Ohio, Indiana, and Illinois, the first states formed from the old Northwest Territory, two cultures collided. The southerners and Pennsylvanians who settled south of a line roughly following the National Road and were known variously as Buckeyes, Hoosiers, Suckers, or Butternuts (because they wore homespun clothes dyed with butternut juice) developed a corn-hog-whiskey economy, while the New England Yankees north of the line developed a wheat-cattle-sheep-dairy economy; the Butternuts were Baptist, hostile to blacks, and fond of liquor, while the Yankees were Congregationalist and Presbyterian, hostile to slavery and inclined to temperance. The cultures these groups had carried west with them remained distinct even though far from their origins and close to their rivals.[7]

Eventually the slave and free cultures collided in Kansas, directly west of slaveholding Missouri but also in the westward path of migrants from New England and the former middle colonies; the result was civil war.[8] The fight was not just over slavery, though it would not have occurred without slavery, and it certainly was not over economics or the tariff; this was a struggle between two ways of life.[9] After the war, even though millions of Union soldiers had gone south and millions of southerners, white and black, understood that the North's economic prospects were better than the South's, there was relatively little movement up and down the country. Instead the movement was across. Dozens of east-west rail lines competed murderously and eventually went bankrupt, while one major north-south line, the coal-hauling Illinois Central, hummed along busily and made steady profits.[10] Theodore Roosevelt, whose mother was from the South and whose father, to the son's great embarrassment, paid $300 for a substitute to fight for him in the Civil War, spent almost no time on and devoted none of his immense psychic energy to things southern. His lines of interest went east to west, from his base in New York to his ranch in North Dakota; he looked across the seas to the Philippines and Panama, but he had little interest in the American South.[11] Not only before the Civil War, but for years afterwards, the North and South had two separate and distinct labor markets,[12] with little movement between them; the low southern wage rates which classical economics said should attract northern capital and the high northern wage rates which should attract southern labor notoriously failed to do so.

For 100 years after the new nation was created, ours was a country of pioneers always seeking new frontiers. Then, 100 years after the first decennial census, the frontier disappeared. Actually, it dissolved into dozens of little frontiers; as the superintendent of the census of 1890 wrote, "The unsettled area has been so broken by isolated bodies of settlement that there can hardly be said to be a frontier line." Frederick Jackson Turner, the young historian and son of the Wisconsin frontier, wrote in his famous paper delivered at the 1893 Chicago exposition that "[t]his brief official statement marks the closing of a great historic movement. . . . the history of the colonization of the Great West."[13] Yet there remained in 1930, and remained fifty years later, plenty of pockets of unsettled land in the

United States; the entire continental span never filled up as Ohio or Alabama or eastern Kansas and east Texas did.

III

At just about the time the frontier closed, the stream of immigrants crossing the Atlantic Ocean into the nation's great cities was growing larger. Already in 1890 millions of immigrants had come to America, but most—Scots, Germans, Scandinavians—had settled on farmlands. Already there had been massive movements to American cities, but many of those migrants were colonial-stock Americans moving off their farms. But beginning in the 1890s, the numbers of immigrants increased, the sources of immigrants became increasingly eastern and southern Europe, and their destinations became almost exclusively the great cities of the North, where they accounted for the lion's share of the nation's exceedingly rapid metropolitan growth. Throughout decades from 1890 to 1930, about one out of three Americans was of foreign stock—born abroad or having at least one parent born abroad. In 1930, 15% of Americans were foreign-born and a total of 36% were of foreign stock, the highest such figures in American history.[14] Add to their number those with ancestors who had been of foreign stock in 1890, and nearly half the population and more than half the whites were of immigrant stock.[15] What might be called, with just a little poetic license, the Ellis Island immigration—New York being by far the largest entry point—in effect superimposed another America on top of the country already in place. These immigrants inevitably formed new, distinct groups, with cultural attitudes and political behavior different from those of other Americans.

The shifting flow of immigration is apparent from the following table, which shows the number and sources of immigrants arriving in twenty-year periods from 1840 to 1925 (the last period includes twenty-five years, since immigration was halted briefly by World War I and then continued at high rates until 1924, when the second immigration restriction act went into effect).

Immigration (in millions) 1840–1925

Years	TOTAL	Britain	Ireland	Germany	Scandi-navia	Italy	Eastern and Central Europe	Russia
1840–1860	4.2	.7	1.7	1.4	—	—	—	—
1860–1880	4.8	1.1	.9	1.5	.3	—	—	—
1880–1900	8.9	1.1	1.1	2.0	1.1	.9	1.0	.6
1900–1925	17.3	1.1	.6	.7	.8	3.6	3.9	2.7

More than any other country in the world, the United States accepted and even welcomed immigrants from diverse sources. But sudden surges of certain kinds of immigrants often alarmed many Americans. The arrival of millions of Catholic Irish after the potato famine of the 1840s and Germans in the mid-1850s stirred nativist feeling in the years before the Civil War,[16] not surprisingly since 2.8 million immigrants arrived in the 1850s in a country with 23 million people when the decade began. Similarly, the political demand for immigration restriction grew after 1900 when it became apparent that most immigrants were no longer from the now familiar British Isles, Germany, and Scandinavia, but from the more alien cultures of eastern and southern Europe.[17] It was not immediately apparent to Americans that this shift was part of a natural progression. Immigrants seldom came from the least developed or impoverished of countries, but rather from places that had already achieved a certain level of development and whose residents, even if their moves were motivated by famine or other disaster, still came with some hope of being able to cope with the more advanced society. For example, there was virtually no immigration from Scandinavia before 1880, from Italy before 1890, or of Jews from Russia before 1900.[18] These immigrants were not desperate people without skills, not the "huddled masses" Emma Lazarus wrote of in her poem engraved on the Statue of Liberty. As a recent historian of immigration has pointed out, they "tended to be concentrated in the middle and lower-middle ranks of society" and were competent enough in dealing with advanced societies to get themselves across an ocean, through Ellis Island, and into urban neighborhoods or rural districts where they could make a living. In Europe they came typically from places where economic growth had changed ways of life, where railroads had brought in cheap manufactured goods to compete with local products or where growing cities' demands for farm products had stimulated commercial agriculture and made small plots unavailable or unprofitable. Displaced by industrial growth from secure niches in peasant or craft economies, they were able to move to less insecure niches in America; and if the conditions they found in the tenements of New York's Lower East Side or in factories like the Triangle Shirtwaist Company were grim, over the course of the years their experience was typically one of upward social mobility.[19]

In the United States immigrants typically followed well-worn paths, going where their countrymen or neighbors had already moved. Usually they headed to places where commercially viable farmland was available on the market or where economic growth in cities was generating vast numbers of new jobs. The first British immigrants headed into the countryside; later British immigrants, the overflow from English, Welsh, and Scottish industrial cities, worked the coal mines of Pennsylvania or the factories of Ohio. The Irish headed almost entirely into the eastern cities, especially New York and Boston. Before the Civil War they were a presence, though in much smaller numbers, in Philadelphia and Baltimore and even New Orleans; after the Civil War, they also migrated in large numbers to the growing Great Lakes cities, especially Chicago. The first German immigrants populated the midwestern countryside, especially in the counties just north of the main lines of the New Englanders' westward migration, making much of Wisconsin and Iowa and parts of Ohio, Indiana, and Illinois ethnically German before the Civil War. They also congregated in New York and in the inland cities of Cincinnati, Louisville, St. Louis, and Milwaukee, and after the Civil War in the growing industrial cities. Scandinavians clustered almost entirely in the Upper Midwest, in an arc around the heavily Swedish city of Minneapolis; much of the farmland of Minnesota and the Dakotas was heavily Scandinavian. Italians and eastern European Jews, arriving almost entirely after 1890, were concentrated very heavily in New York City and accounted for much of the population growth that enabled it to remain the nation's largest city, despite the surging growth of Chicago. Almost 2 million of New York's 7 million residents in 1930 were Jewish,[20] and another 1 million or so were Italian. Smaller numbers of Italians and Jews settled in Philadelphia, Boston, Chicago, and other industrial cities. From central and eastern Europe, Poles headed to factory cities like Buffalo, Detroit, and especially Chicago; Hungarians clustered notably in Cleveland; Czechs were concentrated in Chicago. Dutch settled in the furniture-manufacturing country around Grand Rapids, Michigan, and Belgians in Detroit.

In 1930, 39 million Americans in a nation of 123 million were of foreign stock. Some 23 million of these were of western, central, and northern European stock—the groups favored by the immigration law of 1924, whose quotas were based on what were calculated to be the proportions of particular nationalities in the American population of 1890. Yet most of them did not blend entirely unnoticed into colonial-stock America. Some 3 million were Irish Catholics, a figure that understates the number of Americans who considered themselves of Irish descent, since many were more than one generation removed from the Irish immigrants of the 1840s and 1850s or were descended (as is one of the author's parents) from an immigrant from Canada who was of Irish descent. Another 4 million were from Scandinavia or Finland, and 8 million Americans of 1930 were of German stock. As in the case of the Irish, the number misses descendants of the numerous early German immigrants.

German-Americans remained a distinctive group, more distinctive sometimes than they liked, for in the anti-German hysteria of World War I they were ridiculed and persecuted, suspected of disloyalty, and accused of opposing and obstructing the war effort. German place names and product names were changed (sauerkraut became "liberty cabbage"), German family names were often changed, and the teaching of German was banned in the schools. Speaking German on the streets— as Americans commonly did in the Volga German communities of North Dakota and the German wards of Milwaukee—was discouraged and even penalized. The proud heritage of liberal Germany—the nation which produced the first modern universities and the first chemical and electrical industries, the first efficient income tax and welfare state measures—was obliterated in the minds of most Americans after April 1917. In the face of these developments, many German-Americans made every effort to shed their German identity.

Altogether in 1930 there were 23 million Americans of northern, western, and central European foreign stock, most speaking plain American English and most Protestant; there were also 14 million of eastern and southern European stock. These included 5 million Italians, 3 million eastern European Jews, 3 million non-Jewish Poles, and 3 million non-Jews from other Eastern European nations.

Far more than any of the other groups, Jews made an impact on elite America. The scholarly ability and business acumen of eastern European Jews gave them by 1920 a large share of the places at the nation's leading universities (from which they were soon excluded by quotas)[21] and astonishing success in businesses like women's clothing, retail stores, and entertainment, where the key to success lay in a sensitive understanding of the tastes and whims of people unlike themselves—the sort of understanding that Jews had needed to survive in an eastern Europe where they were outnumbered and outgunned by capriciously hostile *goyim.*

The immigrants, most spectacularly the Jews but also others who had arrived since 1900, were concentrated in the parts of the United States with the most dynamic economies and the most rapid economic growth. They were, by definition, mobile. The 32% of Americans who were of foreign stock were living in a different country from that in which they or their parents had been born, while in 1930, forty years after the closing of the frontier, 85% of native-stock whites and 84% of blacks and Americans of other races lived in the same one of the nation's nine census regions in which they had been born.[22] Especially striking is the almost total lack of movement across the invisible boundary between the American North and the American South. To cross this border from the low-wage South to the high-wage North, Americans did not need to board a steamer, did not have to survive the scrutiny of officials at Ellis Island, did not have to learn a new language. But from the Civil War until World War I, a period when 27 million immigrants came across the Atlantic to the northern states, only a handful of southern whites and blacks—perhaps 1 million of each—moved across the Mason-Dixon Line. In 1930, 9.4 million of the 11.9 million American blacks—79%—still lived in the South. Fully 95% of foreign-stock Americans lived in the North. The North in 1930 was 43% foreign stock and 3% black. The South in 1930 was 5% foreign stock and 25% black. Very few parts of the United States—the port cities of Baltimore and New Orleans, the border-state river towns of Louisville and St. Louis—had significant percentages of both foreign-stock and black Americans. It was as if the United States were two separate countries: a North in which low-wage labor came from a continuing stream of migrants, to some extent from the local countryside but more often from remote parts of Europe, and a South in which low-wage labor came from whites who felt rooted in a sympathetic culture and blacks who felt rooted because they feared, with considerable basis, that because of racial discrimination they could not get jobs or make a living anywhere else.[23]

IV

Many Americans in 1920 were surprised when the Census Bureau announced that the nation had become more than half urban, an announcement that was a bit misleading, since the bureau's definition of "urban" included any community with a population of 2,500 or more. Consider instead genuine cities, with 50,000 or more people. They accounted for 12 million Americans in 1890 and 43 million in 1930. The difference of 31 million amounted to more than half of the nation's total population increase of 60 million between those years. In contrast, the population of the indisputably rural areas, including communities with fewer than 2,500 inhabitants, had increased only from 41 million to 54 million. They still accounted in 1930 for nearly half the nation's population, 44%. But they had provided only 22% of the nation's population growth for the preceding forty years. America's small towns and farmlands had once been filled with large families whose children tamed the surrounding countryside or moved ever westward. Now, with low birthrates and small families, these once dynamic communities had become the most unchanging part of America, sending an uncomfortably large number of their sons and daughters away to big cities and watching the others settle placidly into the houses their parents and grandparents had built.

Vitality and economic growth were greatest where there were the most immigrants. In 1929 only fourteen states had per capita incomes above the national average, and all of them had above-average proportions of foreign-born. New York, the state with by far the largest percentage of immigrants in its population, also had by far the highest per capita income, 65% above the national average. In contrast, the bulk of the black population was moored in states with exceedingly low income levels. The states with the highest percentages of blacks in their populations were Mississippi and South Carolina, where per capita income levels were 59% and 62% below the national average—in other words, one-quarter the level of incomes in New York. Within the same borders, the America of 1930 contained both a surging advanced economy and the economy of an underdeveloped country.

V

The immigration of the years after 1890 also produced a country with more diversity of religious values and beliefs—a diversity that left many Protestant Americans uncomfortable and fearful that their basic moral beliefs were threatened. The United States by 1930 had long since ceased to be an overwhelmingly Protestant nation. Its 123 million residents included 20 million Roman Catholics and 4 million Jews. The number of Catholics had doubled since 1900; the number of Jews had risen 25% in the ten years before 1927.[24] In fact, the country's Protestant population was anything but homogeneous, and the proliferation of sects reflected differences of beliefs as well as race and regional origin. But the growing numbers of Catholics and Jews—the latter, with immigration shut off and their birthrate dropping, formed a larger share of the American population in the 1930s than they had before or would after—seemed to many Protestant Americans to pose a serious threat to their national traditions. A long tradition in Anglo-American thought, dating back at least to Britain's Glorious Revolution in 1688 and perhaps to Elizabethan times, held that Catholics could never be considered fully loyal to a non-Catholic state and quoted Jesuit authorities who professed that Catholics were entitled to lie and deceive others in the service of their faith. Thus many Protestants sincerely believed that Catholics' first loyalty might be to a foreign power, a power which had historically sought state support of the Catholic Church and state enforcement of what Protestants saw as its authoritarian commands.[25]

It is hard to gauge the depth of people's religious beliefs or even to determine what they really believe in. It is easy enough to read the credos of particular religious organizations, but it is not easy to penetrate into the minds of the ordinary people who walked through tangled woodlands and waded into southern creeks or turned aside from the turmoil of New York's Lower East Side and stepped into the synagogue—to know the combination of dogma and superstition, gospel and folk tradition, which was so important to ordinary people. Yet this generalization can be made. The Americans of 1930 took their religions seriously, and their beliefs sometimes led to cultural conflict. For many, that conflict was symbolized by the Scopes trial of 1925 in Dayton, Tennessee, in which a biology teacher was convicted of violating the state's law forbidding the teaching of evolution. The protagonists were William Jennings Bryan, speaking for the prosecution and insisting on the literal truth of every word in the Bible, and Clarence Darrow, the labor lawyer from Chicago, who mocked him so effectively that while losing the verdict he won the battle of public opinion. Nor was the brief but widespread upsurge of the Ku Klux Klan in the 1920s a triumph for the anti-Negro, anti-Catholic, and anti-Jewish rhetoric of Klan leaders. The KKK won momentary political power and avoided by the narrowest of margins condemnation by the 1924 Democratic convention. But it was largely discredited the next year when David C. Stephenson, head of the Indiana Klan, was convicted of second-degree murder for abducting and raping a young woman who then killed herself.[26] The increased visibility of Fundamentalism in the 1920s may have been the thrashings of an old doctrine trying to survive in an increasingly urbanized, culturally diverse country; the seeds of bigotry and intolerance did not find as fertile soil here as they did in those same years in Europe.

The United States in 1930 was a country of vastly different cultures, whose people barely understood—and lived in some fear of—one another. It was a country whose vast expanse of land had fostered and protected diversity, if only because, as one historian put it, "it invited those people who had differences to solve their problems by separation instead of accommodation."[27] It was a country of noble traditions of tolerance and liberty which was mostly free of the yearnings for goose-stepping unity and conformity that would soon produce such hideous consequences in Europe. It was a country in which widely differing notions of what moral imperatives required had the potential of setting citizen against citizen and group against group. It was a country in which the political system was dominated by two traditional parties largely defined in terms of the issues raised by a war in the previous century; this system, in a society more complex than those old divisions ever contemplated, would suddenly be faced with challenges it had never anticipated and forced to respond to the collapse of an economy the growth of which it had come to take for granted.

5

➤➤➤ ⫷⫷⫷

American Politics
1930

"The impact of the Civil War on American life and American memory can hardly be exaggerated. It is still 'the war,' "[1] wrote one of the most trenchant observers of the United States in the midst of another great war—eighty years after William Tecumseh Sherman's troops had burned Atlanta and marched through Georgia. For the structure of American politics in 1930 was the residue of history.[2] Political preferences followed closely the lines of westward settlement, Civil War divisions, and immigrant influxes. In the older communities the patterns of westward movement were still visible; you could see, in a map showing counties where Calvin Coolidge got more than 60% of the vote in 1924, the path of New Englanders moving west to upstate New York, through northern Ohio and Michigan and northern Illinois, and west through Iowa and Kansas to southern California. Civil War divisions tended to run along the lines of settlement and remained most pronounced in the borderlands between North and South, where brother sometimes really had been pitted against brother and political allegiance had been a matter of prosperity or ruin, life or death.[3] These borderlands included the hilly country north of the Ohio River in Ohio and Indiana and Illinois, the battleground states of Missouri and Kentucky and Tennessee, and the soft Piedmont hills of Maryland and Virginia. They extended even farther southward to scattered pockets of Union and Republican strength—Sampson County, North Carolina; a few Georgia hill counties; Winston County, Alabama.

In the new industrial urban America superimposed over Civil War America in the forty years before 1930, a new set of political divisions arose along the lines created by differing streams of immigration. In the 1920s these allegiances were not uniform nationwide but were more typically responses to local political environments. In New York City, for example, where the Irish had been wooed by Tammany Hall since the days of Andrew Jackson, they voted overwhelmingly Democratic. In Philadelphia, 80 miles away, the Irish like everyone else voted overwhelmingly Republican; all seven of the city's congressional districts voted more than 80% Republican in the 1924 and 1926 House elections, and even with the Catholic Al Smith on the ballot the Republicans held all seven seats in 1928.

26

The fastest-growing cities of the 1920s, Detroit and Los Angeles, voted heavily Republican, whereas there was a lively Progressive tradition in the San Francisco Bay area and in Cleveland. Chicago, with its Yankee founders joined by immigrant millions, had a thriving politics with two competitive and corrupt party machines, each with its own pesky reform wing;[4] the Democrats captured the mayor's office in 1911, 1923, and 1931, and Republican Big Bill Thompson (who threatened to punch King George V in the snoot) won in 1915, 1919, and 1927. In Missouri, St. Louis, with its large German population, voted Republican while Kansas City, full of pro-Confederate "Bushwhackers" like Harry Truman's family, voted Democratic. New Haven, Connecticut, like many other American cities large and small, seemed to have an even-odd pattern, with each successive immigrant group supporting the opposite party from the previous arrivals: the Yankees there were, as everywhere, Republican; the Irish, as almost everywhere, Democratic; the Italians, though this was not true everywhere, Republican; the Jews, also not true everywhere, Democratic.[5] The result was a crazy-quilt pattern of politics, with the two traditional parties characterized by asymmetrical and illogical patterns of support, and few potentially unifying forces. The two-party system and the electoral college tended to produce a neat two-party politics every four years, though not in 1912 or 1924. But in between elections, and in the undignified scuffling to win each party's nominations at its quadrennial conventions, the tendencies were mostly centrifugal.

The survival and continuity of Americans' traditional two parties seem even more remarkable when they are contrasted with the abrupt changes in the structure of politics in most European countries after the trauma of what in 1930 was still called the World War. Britain in 1930 had a Labour prime minister, Ramsay MacDonald; Labour had replaced the Liberals in November 1922 as the main opposition to the Conservatives. In Germany, Adolf Hitler's National Socialist party emerged as a major vote-getter in the September 1930 election; only seven years before, Hitler had led his beer-hall *Putsch* in Munich and had been jailed a year for it. French politics was more similar to its prewar model, with an anticlerical left led by the Radical party and an increasingly vitriolic right which exalted the Church; but France was also the least demographically changed of democracies, with a low birthrate and an aging population. European politics, it can be argued, was more responsive to changes in circumstances and opinion than was American politics—though the results in the years after 1930 were not better.

The portions of the United States most heavily settled by German and Scandinavian immigrants in the years after 1880 produced political patterns which looked at least a little European. Robert LaFollette's Progressive movement in Wisconsin, where he was elected governor in 1900, got its strongest support from German voters, which helps to explain why this domestic reformer voted against American entry into World War I and was a bitter opponent of Woodrow Wilson's Versailles treaty. In Minnesota, Scandinavian votes were the bedrock support of the Farmer-Labor party, which elected Henrik Shipstead to the U.S. Senate over Republican Frank Kellogg in 1922 and elected Floyd Olson governor in 1930. In

North Dakota it was a political organization called the Non-partisan League, rather than a third party, that became the focus of state politics for many years, beginning in 1915; its support was greatest among Norwegians and Volga Germans. These third-party and non-party movements reflected the liberal and socialist traditions of early twentieth-century Germany and Scandinavia: a faith in the rational use of government to regulate and, in some limited instances, supplant private corporations; an abhorrence of war with Germany; a faith in higher learning; and, after the persecution of war opponents in 1917–20, a vigorous support for civil liberties.

The two major American parties, in contrast, drew more of what they stood for from tradition than from ideology. In 1930 they were, by European standards, already old. The Democratic party could trace its lineage back directly to the party organized by Martin Van Buren to reelect Andrew Jackson in 1832; it could argue less convincingly that its beginning was the alliance of Thomas Jefferson and James Madison with certain New York politicians in the 1790s. The Republican party in 1930 had long been known as the Grand Old Party or GOP: it had sprung into existence in 1854 to protest Stephen Douglas's Kansas-Nebraska Act, had elected a Republican speaker of the House in 1857, and had won the White House and control of Congress in 1860. In the process it plunged the nation into civil war and froze national political alignments for decades afterwards. With almost no support in the South, the Republicans lacked a national constituency, but they always favored nationalizing policies. They took advantage of the majorities they gained in Congress when southern Democrats seceded to pass into law their nationalizing platform, using the federal government to shape America: Lincoln's first Congress produced the Homestead Act, the land-grant colleges, and the transcontinental railroad. In Reconstruction the Republicans tried and failed to bring civil rights to the South 100 years before the civil rights revolution of the 1960s. They had more success keeping the United States a high-tariff country (and therefore, they believed, a high-wage country—in the North). Under Theodore Roosevelt and his successors they added to their causes conservation, trust-busting, and Prohibition. They were the nationalist, activist, even busybody party.

The Democrats, drawing on their past, called themselves Jeffersonian and took care to respect local mores and idiosyncrasies, from segregation in the South to the saloon in the North—to the point that they were unable to present a unified front in the 1920s. The Democracy was a party of white southerners and northern Catholics, of Southern Baptist Prohibitionists and immigrant imbibers, of nativists and those who spoke no English, of teeming eastern cities and the wastelands of the Great Basin. Its members had little in common except that most of them were not native-born northern white Protestants, as most Republicans were. And in 1930, when native-born northern white Protestants still seemed the overwhelming majority of Americans (though actually their majority was small and getting smaller), most Democrats still had an uncomfortable if articulate sense that somehow this was not quite their country.

II

Although the two traditional parties had managed to maintain their dominance of American politics for seventy-five years, by 1930 the enthusiasm of those who supported them had for some time been waning. In the 1870s and 1880s, ordinary Americans surged into the streets to march in torchlight parades for the parties, and on election day the white males who were eligible to vote turned out in percentages—always over 72% and in 1876 82%[6]—that have not been equaled in this century. Starting around 1900, as memories of "the war" started to dim, participation and enthusiasm declined. Turnout was lowered in the South by laws designed to keep blacks and (whether incidentally or deliberately) low-income whites from voting. Turnout was lowered in the North by registration laws and citizenship requirements enacted purportedly to reduce fraud and voting by aliens. But turnout declined also through simple lack of enthusiasm, from 73% in 1900 to 65% in 1904 and 1908. The Progressive movement, whose reforms inspired so many intellectuals in the first two decades of the century, seems to have had little attraction for ordinary voters: turnout declined through the period. "We stand at Armageddon, and we battle for the Lord," Theodore Roosevelt declared in 1912, the only presidential election year in which three presidents (past, present, and future) competed. But the contest was evidently of less apocalyptic importance to eligible voters, only 59% of whom turned out at the polls. Turnout dropped in 1920 and 1924 to 49%, as at first only a trickle of the newly enfranchised women ventured to vote. As American politics became more intellectually respectable and less emotionally stirring, it became less and less interesting to ordinary people.[7]

Turnout rose later in the decade, to 57% in 1928, but the level of enthusiasm for parties remained low. Ticket-splitting became increasingly common in the 1920s, especially in the big industrial states. Traditional campaign devices designed to generate enthusiasm among the party faithful were increasingly abandoned. There were no more torchlight rallies, few voters spent sunny afternoons listening to political orators, and the old-fashioned political bosses of the packed tenements and row houses of the big city had to adapt their techniques to the new automobile-scale neighborhoods, with their single- and double-family houses on tree-lined streets ungraced by the corner saloon or grocery. Advertising was becoming more important in campaigns, and candidates and officeholders could use the new media—radio and newsreels at the movies[8]—to speak directly to their constituents. Political appeals were no longer passed along by intermediaries; they were beginning to be made directly, almost personally, to the voters.

III

American politics has been portrayed as an economic struggle over who gets what and why, as a fight between working people and the rich or between the oppressed colonial South and West and the overlords of the East and especially of Wall Street. But the major struggles in American politics in the two decades before 1930 were not over issues that split the nation on economic lines, but over non-economic cultural issues. These were not always partisan issues, though in most cases at least one of the parties was identified strongly with one side of the contest. This identification made sense because the voting bases of the traditional Democratic and Republican parties were primarily cultural; both drew allegiance from Americans who saw them not as promoters of their economic status but as protectors and champions of their way of life. The cultural conflicts that preoccupied America's politics from 1910 to 1930 included:

Racial segregation. In 1930 racial segregation had been established by law in the South for thirty or forty years.[9] This was true even though the Republican party, much more sympathetic to blacks than the Democrats, had controlled the presidency for most of that time. The rest of the nation came to accept this regional custom: Democratic politicians like Woodrow Wilson were outspokenly sympathetic to segregation, while Republican presidents were moving away from any open sympathy with blacks or support for their aspirations.[10] Theodore Roosevelt invited Booker T. Washington to lunch at the White House; Taft made no such gestures; when Harding presided at the dedication of the Lincoln Memorial in 1922, there was a separate reviewing stand for black dignitaries. When Commerce Secretary Herbert Hoover provided aid to flood victims in Mississippi in 1927, he worked diligently to do something for the black sharecroppers he found there— but not to treat them the same as whites.[11]

The World War. There was widespread and bitter opposition to going to war on the side of Britain, especially in the heavily German and Scandinavian states northwest of Chicago; many war opponents were in turn persecuted. After the armistice, antiwar feeling was transformed in many cases into diehard opposition to the Treaty of Versailles and the League of Nations, which were also opposed by many whose only complaint about American entry into the war on Britain's side was that it was tardy. James Cox's overwhelming defeat in 1920 after he had campaigned as an enthusiastic League supporter essentially ended any vocal support for the League in American politics.

Immigration restriction. Before the World War, few people saw immigration restriction as a practical option. Congressional majorities voted against barring immigrants (except for Chinese and other Asians). Presidents Taft and Wilson, who from their position at the top of society understood the contribution immigrants were making to economic growth and had confidence in Americans' capacity to assimilate them, vetoed bills to require them to pass literacy tests. But the war demonstrated that government could exert far more controls over individuals than had seemed likely or desirable in earlier years, and suddenly in the early 1920s immigration restrictions became not just a political possibility but a political imperative. In 1921 and 1924, Congress passed and Presidents Harding and Coolidge signed laws which cut off most immigration from eastern and southern Europe quite suddenly. These laws reflected the anxieties quickly perceived by the visiting French political demographer André Siegfried, who asked, "Will America remain

Protestant and Anglo-Saxon?" and added that Americans were "trying to maintain their unity of spirit by insisting impatiently that their center of gravity still lies in the Anglo-Saxon and Puritan stock."[12] In demographic fact, as Siegfried understood better than most Americans, "the Anglo-Saxon and Puritan stock" was fast becoming a minority in what it had come to regard as its own country. But few politicians felt safe in opposing the immigration laws openly—even Al Smith only grumbled about them—and there was no move whatever to repeal them. Even in the 1930s, when immigration slowed to a trickle, Congress still resisted any measures to allow refugees into the United States.

Prohibition. The war's demonstration of government's great powers also helped produce Prohibition of liquor, wine, and beer. This "noble experiment," as Herbert Hoover called it during the 1928 campaign, remained a matter of continuing debate and a subject of wide variance in local enforcement—it was a dead letter in much of New York City and Chicago, for example. But in January 1930 the weight of public opinion was still very much in favor of retaining Prohibition, and it was not about to be abandoned by the Hoover administration or the country.

IV

Next to these great conflicts, economic issues counted for relatively little in the politics of the times. The antitrust laws were on the books and had been enforced in landmark cases before the World War; the McNary-Haugen farm bill, passed by Congress and vetoed by Presidents Coolidge and Hoover, stirred controversy but split the Congress primarily on regional lines.[13] But macroeconomic fiscal policy, redistribution of wealth, and government spending programs were not major issues for the simple reason that the government neither raised nor spent nor was capable of redistributing much money in the late 1920s. Federal government spending amounted to only 3% of the gross national product, federal revenues to 4%, and most of that went to pay for past wars. Of the federal government's $3.3 billion in outlays in 1930, 22% went to national security, split between the Army and Navy. Another 25% went to veterans' services and benefits, and 21% to interest on the national debt, almost all of it incurred in World War I (though cut in half through the surpluses and deflation of the 1920s). That left only about one-quarter of the budget, well under $1 billion, for all other government functions. Federal taxes did not impinge noticeably on the lives of most citizens. The individual income tax produced a slightly smaller share (28%) of federal revenues in 1929 and 1930 than the corporate income tax—about $1 billion each. Only a small minority of Americans—4 million in 1929 and 3.7 million in 1930, in a nation of 30 million households—paid income tax in these years. The bite of the tax had been vastly reduced by Treasury Secretary Andrew Mellon's cuts in the high wartime tax rates; the cuts reduced rates most sharply on the rich but took half the taxpayers off the rolls and left rates low enough so that those with incomes as high as $10,000—enough to live in a comfortable house with servants—paid a derisory $90 in 1929 and $154 in 1930.

Nor were the state and local governments vastly bigger or more intrusive. Spending by all governments totaled only 12% of the gross national product in 1927,[14] with more than half of that accounted for by local governments. Effectively, if inarticulately, the different levels of government divided major revenue sources among themselves. The individual and corporate income taxes belonged to the federal government, the sales and gasoline and motor vehicle taxes to the states, and the property tax almost entirely to local governments, who relied on that plus charges, fees, and a little state aid for virtually all their revenues.[15] Spending was also neatly arranged. Local governments spent over 90% of their money on schools. State spending was more varied, with the largest amounts on highways (25%), higher education (10%), hospitals (7%), and natural resources (5%). Altogether, all units of government in the prosperous year of 1927 spent some $11 billion in an economy of $90 to $100 billion.[16] The burden of government sat very lightly indeed upon the nation.

Neither party stood in any coherent way for a major increase in the size and scope of that government. Yet ironically, both had a political incentive to consider such change. For to the extent there was a swing vote in the United States in 1930, a bloc not strongly committed to either major party, it was on the left on economics: the LaFollette progressives and prairie radicals, the progressives on the Pacific coast, the Jewish vote in New York. Although inclined to favor a more active government on economic issues, these swing voters were sensitive to violations of civil liberties because of their experience with religious prejudice and the persecution of Germans and opponents of World War I. They were historically Republicans and sometimes supported Progressives or Socialists in the two decades before 1930. But they provided a potential constituency for a Democratic or Republican party that would stand, as neither did in 1930, for a substantially larger and more generous government, for some form of national economic planning, and for encouraging labor unions—though few in either of the major parties' traditional constituencies looked with favor on such proposals. The Democrats were not generally identified with activist government, although Al Smith was in New York, and so were some of the veterans of the Wilson administration. But most Democrats in office were southerners who wanted no interference with that region's peculiar customs, and in 1930 in the Senate economic activist Democrats like Robert Wagner of New York were outnumbered by economic activists who were at least nominal Republicans, like Robert LaFollette, Jr., of Wisconsin, George Norris of Nebraska, and Hiram Johnson of California. Nor were the Democrats especially sympathetic to civil liberties. It was Woodrow Wilson's administration which encouraged persecution of German-Americans and Wilson's attorney general A. Mitchell Palmer who staged the Red Raids of January 1, 1920, and imprisoned Socialist leader Eugene Debs (who was freed from prison by Warren Harding and invited to the White House for lunch afterwards). The swing vote in America in 1930 was on the left and was up for grabs, and it was by no means clear or foreordained which party would win it. But for the moment, in 1930, this vote was not the object of political competition.

V

Nor were there any great signs that the traditional American party system was ready for a change in 1930. On the contrary: the traditional parties seemed to be adapting though sometimes clumsily to the changing country around them. The Democrats were careful not to fight too openly the hopeless battles against Prohibition or for the Versailles treaty; the Republicans were careful not to fight too openly the lost battle against racial segregation; no one was arguing against immigration restriction. The voters were adapting as well. Ticket-splitting, almost unheard of in the nineteenth century when ballots were printed not by the state but by the parties, was more common in the 1920s than it had ever been in American history: large states like New York, Massachusetts, and Ohio elected Democratic governors or senators while voting Republican for president. Southerners and other rural Protestants who had never voted Republican did so when the Democrats nominated a Catholic presidential candidate, while 16% of the electorate in 1924 voted for a candidate—Robert LaFollette—endorsed by the Socialist party. Memory of the Civil War was still strong—as progressive a southerner as Texas Congressman Sam Rayburn still regarded the Confederacy as a noble cause[17]—but it was slowly fading. The United States in 1930 remained a country with a political system not much different from what it had been in 1920 or 1910 or 1900—a steadiness that, in a rapidly growing and changing country, was itself noteworthy. It was a country with several discernibly different political cultures, bound together only loosely by the continuity of two traditional parties which felt themselves beleaguered and yet entered and left the 1920s—as they would enter and leave the 1980s—as the two primary means by which the people of the world's most powerful nation would express their political views.

‑≫≫ ≪≪‑

PART
TWO

American Politics
1930–1947
TURMOIL

6

⇥⟫ ⟪⇤

New Era

Herbert Hoover, who presided over the nation's most dizzying fall in economic statistics, was the most statistic-minded of presidents. He was also one of the least political—and most government-minded. When he received the Republican presidential nomination in 1928, Hoover had never held or won elective office, and he had spent most of his adult years outside the United States. But as head of a wartime agency and with his conspicuous[1] success as commerce secretary in the Harding and Coolidge administrations, he had become a figure of international renown and a leader accustomed to exerting single-handedly the levers of governance. Most Republican politicians were more deeply rooted in the fabric of their nation and their party. They came from small cities or dusty rural crossroads and watched them grow into steam-heated, brick-walled bastions of prosperity—built up, they believed, because of Republican support of free markets and protective tariffs, the sanctity of contract and the provision of internal improvements and land-grant colleges. They had seen the American past, forty years mostly of prosperity and mostly of Republican government, and it worked.

Hoover had different experiences. He remembered how, as an eleven-year-old orphan heading west on the Union Pacific in 1885 to live with his uncle in Oregon, he had been surprised to find that the Rocky Mountains were made of dirt.[2] Left behind were the tree-shaded streams and green grass of his native Iowa. Ahead was a series of barren, dirt-brown landscapes, from his uncle's rural Oregon to the Stanford University campus on the sunny flatlands beneath the spine of mountains running south from San Francisco to the desert of Western Australia where he began his career as a mining engineer ("a terrible place. You cannot imagine the dust," he wrote)[3] and the mining town of Broken Hill ("the dreariest place on earth"), the jungles of northern Burma and the turbulent dusty streets of Tientsin, China, during the Boxer Rebellion. From dirt and rocks and stones he made his fortune. In his twenties and early thirties, the impoverished geology major from Stanford coolly assessed the mineral potential of remote properties, and on his say-so London investors would stake millions—and reap handsome returns. He worked, as one biographer puts it, in "an ordered world in which careful fact-gathering and publication amounted to an ethic,"[4] and from those facts and figures he made decisions which again and again proved right.

They also enabled Hoover, after spending most of his first twenty-seven years at the periphery of Western civilization, to occupy a prominent place at its center. In 1901 he moved to 39 Hyde Park Gate, London. In an office in the City financial district, looking out into air black with soot and at streets choked with horse-carts and omnibuses and trams, he ran his mining business. After the outbreak of World War I in 1914, he organized food relief for Belgium; when the United States entered the war in 1917, he moved to Washington to become the American food administrator. There he set market prices for all American agricultural commodities, organized transportation and distribution, encouraged every household in America to conserve food. Nothing made him angrier than speculators who profited from others' hardship by selling short or sharp operators who violated the rules intended to protect all. Hoover has been painted as the celebrator of free-market capitalism and the values of American business,[5] but he never made a living or met a payroll in the American heartland. His success had taught him to stake everything on his own appraisals based on his knowledge of the numbers, to distrust the workings of the marketplace and to rely instead on his own ability to get the facts and figures and use them to organize and control the economic environment.

In the 1928 election, peace and prosperity, the contentment of the large industrial states that had voted for Coolidge, and the more progressive Hoover's added popularity in the West would probably have brought him victory even if Al Smith's Catholicism had not cost the Democrats electoral votes in the South and the West. But Hoover was eager to move away from Coolidge's laissez faire policies and seemed genuinely concerned about the parts of America that seemed left behind by the growth of the 1920s. "We in America today," Hoover had told the crowd at Stanford's Spanish Colonial quadrangle as he accepted the Republican nomination, "are nearer to the final triumph over poverty than ever before in the history of the land." But prudently he looked to the parts of the country where this triumph still seemed far off. The immigrant-filled cities had been booming these past seven Republican years, his statistics told him; the farmlands had not. Their halcyon days had been in the World War, when as food administrator Hoover had encouraged them to increase production and gotten the federal treasury to guarantee them a price for all they could produce. In the years of peace the higher level of production continued, but prices slumped. A believer in free markets would have just let the farmers move to the growing cities—a movement which had been going on for many years. But Hoover, who was ordinarily not much for sentiment, shared the Jeffersonian prejudice that farming was a morally superior way of making a living, separated as it was from "the insidious forces of moral degeneration which are such corroding influences in the life of our great cities."[6] And he did think that something must be done for the one-quarter of Americans who lived on farms. But what?

One answer was the plan promoted by George Peek and General Hugh Johnson, which was passed by Congress in February 1927 and May 1928 as the McNary-Haugen Act and vetoed both times by President Coolidge. McNary-Haugen would have set domestic prices for crops at "parity" with the pre-World War prices of

1910–16, with surpluses to be sold abroad at world prices and farmers assessed an "equalization fee" for the difference. Hoover opposed McNary-Haugen, but it had near-unanimous support from Republicans as well as Democrats in the Midwest and West. The Coolidge administration needed an alternative.[7] The obvious solution for the former food administrator was a system to hold down production and raise prices. Hoover's experience in administering American food supplies and in managing food relief in Belgium in 1914–17 and in Russia in 1921–23 was that agriculture worked best when prices were stabilized and production organized, but with individual producers left to make their own decisions and not required to follow government orders.[8] For traditional Republicans, on the other hand, the obvious solution to farmers' economic woes was to add farm produce to the list of products protected by the tariff, because they had seen one industry after another grow and prosper behind the shelter of its walls. Hoover and the Republicans opted for both solutions. They campaigned for them in 1928. They made them the new administration's top priorities.

In retrospect it is plain that this strategy led to terrible results. But then it seemed a humane and sensible compromise between a president whose planner's approach set policy on the course of reform in aid of those in need and a party whose reflexes set policy always in the direction of protecting industry and lowering internal taxes. It was a strategy pursued vigorously, if not always shrewdly. When Hoover took office on March 4, 1929, Congress, operating on the antique schedule set by the Founding Fathers, was not scheduled to convene until December. The new president called a special session immediately and set up his marketing and tariff bills. On June 15 he signed the Agricultural Marketing Act which Congress had obediently passed. It created a Federal Farm Board and a $500 million fund to buy up surpluses and finance farm cooperatives; the board could authorize cooperatives to combine in the market and limit production to prop up prices.

The second goal, revision of the tariff, took longer. High tariffs were the "household remedy" of the Republican party.[9] The tariff was an issue that held most Republicans together and won them votes, and Republican politicians could argue that the high tariffs of most of the last seventy years had been accompanied by economic growth, rising wages, and abundance for most Americans. In a low-wage world, they thought, it was folly for a high-wage country to allow its products to be underpriced by imports produced by cheap labor, and they noted that in the 1920s imports had grown faster than exports. They knew that there were political dangers in the tariff. Hoover had not been in Washington, but most Republican congressional leaders had, when the tariff issue had split the party during the Taft administration, twenty years before. They knew what a public fight between tariff reformers and high-tariff stalwarts could do to their party. But the Republicans in 1930 thought they were avoiding the pitfalls on which Taft had stumbled. The 1909 tariff was remembered as a measure primarily to help manufacturers; now the Republicans were advancing a tariff aimed at propping up and stabilizing crop prices. Typical Republican tariff bills revised rates invariably upward; Hoover was insisting on flexible rates which could be revised downward by a nonpolitical tariff commission. "No provision for flexible tariff," he told one group of Republicans, "no tariff bill."[10]

Hoover's views prevailed in the House. There the Republican leadership, under Speaker Nicholas Longworth, were able through their control of the Rules Committee to hold together their majority for just about any measure. They could manipulate even a much smaller majority than their current 267–167 edge, for relatively few of their members came from the progressive strongholds of the Upper Midwest. Yet they knew they would be almost entirely without leverage if the Democrats won control of the House, and they feared, well before the October 1929 stock market crash, that a contraction in speculation would cost them seats in the November 1930 elections. Hoover among others feared such a contraction, which seemed threatened by sharp drops in the stock market in December 1928 and March 1929. The House Republicans remembered the depression—the word was used because it was less scary than "panic"—of 1921–22, and they remembered that the Democrats had gained more than 70 seats in November 1922. This time the Democrats needed just a 50-seat gain for control. The possibility of a Democratic takeover may have heightened the urgency and sharpened the discipline of the House Republicans; certainly it was on their minds. They wanted a new tariff bill, and they passed it in May 1929.

The problem for the Republicans was the Senate. Nominally they were in control by a 56–39 margin over the Democrats, but the balance of power was held by about 15 progressive Republicans. Most came from the Upper Midwest and West, states where Robert LaFollette had run strongly in 1924. They were strong in small states like the Dakotas and so were overrepresented in a chamber where every sparsely populated western state had two senators.[11] Though they clung to the Republican label (except for Henrik Shipstead, elected as a Farmer-Laborite in Minnesota), the progressives dissented from the regular Republicans on almost every policy: they were isolationist on foreign matters, interventionist on economic regulations, against vigorous government action when it threatened civil liberties, and generally hostile to the tariff. Yet some of them wanted tariff protection for the products of their home states, and the original emphasis by Hoover on a tariff for farm products was, as it was intended to be, politically attractive to them.

In the Senate, however, the tariff bill was under the management of the Finance Committee, whose chairman, Reed Smoot of Utah, then in his twenty-seventh year in the Senate, was a staunch believer in protectionism and an opponent of the progressive effort to limit the bill to farm products. After Senate Majority Leader James Watson announced in March that many senators would seek higher industrial tariffs and that he himself would seek higher rates for cement, William Borah of Idaho introduced a resolution in June to limit tariff revision to agriculture. It failed by only a 39–38 margin, and at least 10 of the 18 senators not voting favored it. But in October, when the full Senate began considering the Finance Committee's bill, it began by rejecting a similar amendment overwhelmingly (progressives argued it would prevent the tariff commission from lowering industrial rates) and raised the rates for carbide and casein above the levels proposed by the committee. Casein is a dairy product, and the importance of the dairy industry in Wisconsin led that state's two senators, Robert LaFollette, Jr., and John Blaine, who on other issues were among the strongest free traders in the Senate, to vote with the protectionist side when casein became the issue. This apparent break in the Senate's anti-tariff majority was followed by the first day of the stock market crash.[12]

Throughout the winter the Senate continued to struggle over the tariff bill, known as Smoot-Hawley after Smoot and Willis Hawley, chairman of House Ways and Means. David Reed and Joseph Grundy of Pennsylvania, the state most strongly committed to a high tariff, threatened to oppose the bill on the grounds that its rates were too low; Hoover's goals were to create a tariff commission with rate-fixing authority and to get rid of a Senate-inserted provision for farm export subsidies. Initially he failed: on March 24, 1930, with Progressive and Democratic support, the Senate passed by a 53–31 vote a version of Smoot-Hawley that included high rates on industrial products, a powerless tariff commission, and farm export subsidies. When the bill went to a conference, however, the House stuck fast with Hoover's priorities. On May 3 it voted along party lines against export subsidies, 231–161, and for the tariff commission, 236–154. On May 19 Hoover persuaded the Senate to retreat on the two issues, but it did so by paper-thin margins—43–41 and a 42–42 tie broken by Vice President Charles Curtis. Strong outside pressure had been developing against Smoot-Hawley during these weeks. On May 4 a petition of 1,000 economists, organized by the University of Chicago's Paul Douglas, urged the president to veto the bill. On May 20, Grundy, the president of the Pennsylvania Manufacturers' Association, was defeated in the state's senatorial primary by a solid 49%–33% margin; his opponent was Hoover's labor secretary, James ("Puddler Jim") Davis, former steelworker and longtime national director of the Loyal Order of Moose. By June more than thirty foreign governments had issued formal protests against the bill, and some nations—France, Italy, India, Australia—had already raised their own tariffs.[13] Yet on June 13 the Senate passed Smoot-Hawley, 44–42, with 3 Progressives and 5 Democrats in favor, and other favorable votes had been available if needed. Hoover made a show of deliberating for a few days. But having squeezed out of the Senate the main concessions he had sought, he was in no position politically to do anything but sign the bill. Defensively voicing some misgivings, he did so on June 17.

Congress adjourned less than a month later. Politically and intellectually, Hoover and his Republicans were exhausted. They had achieved their two major priorities: the farm marketing act and the new tariff. Other new laws had established the Veterans Administration, strengthened the Federal Power Commission, reformed the federal prison system, and created a new Federal Criminal Identification Service—the kinds of rational ordering of government services and tidying up of the administrative structure which Hoover loved. The London Naval Treaty had been ratified. And Congress had finally overturned the policy represented by its refusal after the 1920 census to reapportion House seats among the states. This defiance of the Constitution by representatives of the older native-stock states with stagnant populations had been prompted by fear of the rising electoral power of immigrants in the fastest-growing states; it discriminated against the large cities, especially their new sprawling automobile-era neighborhoods—the sites of the fastest economic growth and the most dramatic social change in America. Henceforward reapportionment would occur automatically after each census by a formula written into the law.[14]

The Republicans knew their work was not perfect. But by the traditional standards of American politics they had made a creditable record. They had addressed what seemed in the 1928 campaign to be the major economic problems of the nation. They did not know, and they had some basis for pleading later that they had no reason to know, that they had failed to recognize and address what history would declare was the nation's greatest problem in 1930. Responding to standard political cues, guided by a president whose feel for statistics and what he regarded as scientific knowledge made him seem acutely sensitive to emerging social problems, they had tried to do something for those lagging behind during an era of economic growth—though of course they had also tried to help their own particular constituencies as well. But they had little warrant in past experience or in present circumstance to understand the new problems inherent in the solutions they offered—or to apprehend how their solutions missed entirely their country's real problems.

7

-»» «««-

Depression

The first half of 1930, as economist Joseph Schumpeter looked back on it, was satisfactory; but in the second half "people felt the ground give way beneath their feet."[1] A nation that expected to reach a safe harbor of prosperity after a year of turbulent economic waters instead seemed to be headed farther out on a stormy uncharted sea. In 1930 there were no random-sampling public opinion polls to describe the changes in attitudes among the American public. The crude straw polls and mail polls that did exist tested opinion only on the most easily summed-up issues (Prohibition versus Repeal) and used unrepresentative samples.[2] But the change in opinion can be charted with other numbers.

Unemployment. Few Americans in 1930 remembered how unemployment had shot upward from 3% in 1892 to 12% in 1893 and 1894—a depression that turned the closely competitive two-party system of the post-Civil War era[3] into a stable Republican majority.[4] A large majority of Americans in 1930 did remember how unemployment had risen after the World War, from 1.4% in 1919 to 5% in 1920 and 12% in 1921. They also remembered that it had declined sharply, too, to 7% in 1922 and 2% in 1923. The figures for 1930 were not so different. Unemployment went up from 3% in 1929 to 9% in 1930, and the 4.3 million unemployed that year were actually fewer than the 4.9 million in 1921, although the work force off the farm had grown nearly 20% in those years.[5] Through all of 1930 and into 1931 Americans could plausibly have believed they were experiencing another sharp but limited depression like that of 1920–22. By the end of 1931, it was obvious that such was not the case. Unemployment had risen to 8 million (16%), and by 1932 it averaged 12 million—fully 24% of the work force. Close to another one-quarter of the work force was still on the farm, technically still working but at low wages and with crop prices plummeting below the already low levels of the late 1920s. Prolonged unemployment and severely diminished income were in 1930 unusual experiences for most Americans. But in a few years they became the common experience of the majority. Breadwinners who had believed they were embarked on the glorious adventure of moving upward and growing affluent in a complex urban civilization suddenly found themselves with no means of livelihood and—more important—no hope of one turning up any time soon.

Fertility rates. No statistic probes more deeply into people's personal lives, into the things they care about most, than the fertility rate. This statistic—the annual

43

number of births per 1,000 women aged 15 to 44—had been declining in the United States in the 1920s, in line with the typical pattern in increasingly affluent countries and also in response to the cutoff of immigration. Population growth continued, because of the decline in death rates, as diseases which had once killed hundreds of thousands annually—diphtheria, typhoid, whooping cough, measles, tuberculosis—were being conquered thanks to immunization, other public health measures, and the general rise in real incomes, which gave more Americans access to medical care.[6] American cities in the 1920s, with their efficient sewer systems, abundant pure water, and residential zoning regulations, were, in contrast to nineteenth-century cities, more healthful than the rural landscapes where so many of their residents came from.[7] Fertility fell even more sharply as the economy collapsed. In 1929 and in 1930, there were 89 births for each 1,000 women in the childbearing years; most of those children were conceived before the 1929 crash and all before it became apparent that the depression was not going to end soon. In 1931, the fertility rate dropped to 85, in 1932 to 82, and in 1933 to 76, and it remained at about that level until World War II.[8]

The plummeting fertility rates show how—and when—the depression cut to the quick. The marriage rate had increased in the 1920s, as more and more couples could afford to get married. But this was an era when artificial contraception was not universally available, when it was shunned by the one-fifth of the population who were Catholic, when simple information about it was often not to be had. (It was not so many years before, in 1915, that Margaret Sanger had been carted off to jail for opening a birth control clinic in Brooklyn.) The sharply lower fertility rates of the 1930s thus mean that millions of American couples were abstaining from sex—and that many others were, through poor nutrition or overwork, rendered incapable of fathering or conceiving children. Whether through abstinence or other means, a large proportion of young married Americans were deciding to postpone parenthood, perhaps forever.[9] But the decline in fertility rates lagged behind the rise in unemployment. Fertility did not drop significantly—Americans did not decide in really large numbers not to have children—until it became plain that the depression was not just temporary. Then fertility stayed low even after the economy revived.

Income. The impact of the depression on Americans' income was devastating, although it was not felt immediately. Incomes in 1930 did not drop as sharply as they did in 1931, and they dropped even more sharply in 1932. In percentage terms the drops for the three years were 13%, 21%, and 28%.[10] Total national income was less than half the 1929 level in 1933, and it did not reach the 1929 level again until 1941. But the decline was not spread evenly over the economy. It was less—although very steep—in employee compensation, and for those who were not unemployed a stable or slightly declining wage in a time of lower prices amounted to hardship but not disaster. But many other Americans—a larger percentage in 1930 than ever again—depended for their living not on wages but on profits, and these people were even harder hit. Many were wiped out. Between 1929 and 1933 employees' income fell by 42%, but farm income fell by 58%, business proprietors' income by 63%, and rental income by 63%. The local doctor and grocer typically found themselves living on credit, asking their suppliers to take their notes and waiting for their patients and customers to get enough cash to pay at least part of the balance that was elaborately recorded. The enterprising family who had built several houses and rented them out could not keep up the mortgages and taxes and lost their investment—and their hope for a comfortable old age. The 1920s had been a decade of vast construction, especially of new houses in the rapidly growing, industrial, usually immigrant-filled big cities. In 1930 more than 6% of all income received by Americans came from rentals. Some 60% of that income vanished in the next three years—and unlike farm and business income, it never reappeared.

One of the tragedies of the depression of the 1930s—one of the main reasons it had such a long-lasting political impact—was that it arrested the upward mobility of millions of Americans, particularly in the big cities with their rapidly growing economies, and instead thrust them economically downward. The extended depression produced some destitution, even some starvation. But probably more importantly politically, it destroyed millions of dreams. Americans, accustomed to a country where they could rise by their own exertions, their own sweat and hustle, tended to blame themselves for their economic disasters. But while blaming themselves, they began looking to politicians and government for some control. They did not find it in Herbert Hoover and his Republicans.

II

Herbert Hoover was to some extent a victim of his country's antique political calendar. He conscientiously devised a legislative program in 1928 and 1929 and called Congress into session quickly after his March 1929 inauguration. But this very speed meant that Congress went out of session in the summer of 1930, before almost anyone was convinced that the depression triggered by the stock market crash of October and November 1929 was going to last any longer than the brief depression of 1920–22, and, except for the lame duck session of the old Congress set for December 1930 after the new Congress had been elected a month before the next regular session was not scheduled until December 1931. Hoover and Congress, with 1920–22 fresh in mind, did do several things in the meantime to combat the downturn. In November 1929, just after the stock market crash, they cut taxes—even then the standard stimulus for a faltering economy.[11] In March 1930 they amended the Public Buildings Act to provide for $230 million more in federal building projects, and in April they appropriated $300 million in road construction aid to the states. These were very substantial sums for a government with a budget of some $3.2 billion. Together with the tax cuts, they provided as much stimulus as was customary for a federal government of the magnitude of that day. In the meantime Hoover urged employers not to cut wages while the nation rode out the depression. Similar tactics, urged on President Harding by Commerce Secretary Hoover, had helped to alleviate the effects of the deep but brief depression of 1920–22; and they seem to have had a similar, though sadly temporary, effect in 1930.[12] Congress had passed a veterans' bill which Hoover had vetoed as too expensive. But with this exception, the political opposition and the administration's critics offered up no measure and urged no policy to combat the depression. No one—not even New York's Senator Robert Wagner—was urging direct relief to the unemployed.

When Congress adjourned in July 1930, therefore, Hoover had reason to believe that the depression would not last long[13] and that his programs had addressed it properly. By the time the next regular session of Congress assembled, in December 1931, he had in hand a program of drastic measures which was enacted and which did help. But in the intervening eighteen months—during which Americans had concluded that the depression would not be a brief one—he did nothing that proved reassuring. Mistrusting politicians, fearing that congressmen would vote for demagogic measures that would frighten businessmen away from investing, Hoover declined to call a special session of Congress, and he put off the announcement of his own program until the regular session began. It was too late—only eleven months before the 1932 election, and more months after voters had decided that the depression was not going away.

In his own defense Hoover could have argued that the voters gave him few cues that they wanted more drastic action. The elections of 1930, held more than a year after the stock market crash, did not signal any great change in the political firmament. On the contrary, the voters responded very much as they had in the only other depression election year most of them had known, 1922.[14] The Democrats gained 8 seats in the Senate, enough to narrow the Republican advantage to 48–47 (1 seat was still held by Shipstead of Minnesota). But regular Republicans had long since lost working control of the Senate, and most of the Republican losses came where they might have been expected, in the Civil War borderlands (West Virginia and Kentucky) and in the volatile Great Plains (South Dakota, Kansas, Colorado). The oddest result came in the hurly burly of Illinois, where sixty-seven-year-old J. Hamilton Lewis, with his long pinkish locks and string ties, made a comeback for the seat he had won in 1912 and lost in 1918. Lewis benefited from the rivalry of Republicans Charles Deneen, who had held the seat, and Ruth Hanna McCormick, who had beaten Deneen in the primary, six years after Deneen had beaten her late husband in the 1924 primary. Deneen's reputation was fragrant. In the 1928 Republican primary his ally Diamond Joe Esposito was murdered "in a private little booze feud." Two weeks before the primary, bombs exploded outside Deneen's house and the house of his candidate for Cook County state's attorney (the all-important Chicago prosecutor), immediately prompting the opposition charge, "They did it themselves to gain sympathy."[15] The Democrats' gain of 49 seats in the House was substantial, though less than their gain in 1922, and they raised their total from 167 to a near-majority of 216. But the Republicans retained 218; the other seat was held by a Minnesota Farmer-Laborite. Two-thirds of the Democratic gains came in the Civil War borderlands from West Virginia to Arkansas, the usual place for partisan turnovers in the

House elections of the 1920s. Al Smith's Catholicism had also depressed the normal Democratic vote in these areas in 1928, and the Democrats would have won many of these seats in 1930 whatever the condition of the economy.[16] Only a handful of turnovers were in industrial or immigrant areas.[17]

III

Today 1930 is remembered as the year in which the Democrats began to enjoy their only briefly interrupted (in 1946 and 1952) control of the House. But this future was not apparent the morning after the 1930 election. Speaker Longworth, who used to give Minority Leader Garner a ride to work in the speaker's limousine, wired Garner immediately after the election, "Whose car is it?"[18] The answer was not clear even a year later. As it happened, the normal attrition of deaths, combined with a collapse of confidence in the economy, finally produced a Democratic majority. In July 1931, Congressman Bird J. Vincent died while sailing on the *Henderson* from Hawaii to the mainland. He represented the old lumber mill town of Saginaw, Michigan, the sugar beet and navy bean farmlands and a heavily Republican district that included Owosso, the hometown of future Republican presidential nominee Thomas E. Dewey. The district had been represented for many years by Republican Joseph Fordney, who rose to chair the House Ways and Means Committee, and it had given Vincent 67% of the vote against Democrat Michael Hart in November 1930. But on November 3, 1931, Hart was elected to the vacancy. That gave the Democrats 217 seats. Three days later in San Antonio came the death of long-ailing Henry Wurzbach, the Republican congressman from the 14th district of Texas, which stretched from the hill country north of San Antonio through Texas German farming counties to the hot level farmlands along the Gulf of Mexico. Democratic Governor Ross Sterling, hoping to capture the speaker's office for his fellow Texas Democrat Garner, called a quick special election, and on November 24 the district elected Democrat Richard Kleberg, a member of the family that owned the giant King Ranch. That gave the House an absolute Democratic majority. (Kleberg hired as his chief assistant a twenty-three-year-old teacher from the far northern end of his district named Lyndon Johnson.)[19] There were still two other vacancies in the House, in historically Republican seats in New Jersey and New Hampshire where Democrats had gotten only 34% and 44% of the vote in 1930. Democrats won the special elections for both these seats as well, in December 1931 and January 1932, and those victories together with their earlier win in Michigan were the first signs that they could win elections in the Republicans' Yankee heartland.

So it is possible to pinpoint with some certainty the time that the economic downturn began to have political effects. The evidence of the off-year elections corroborates inferences from the unemployment levels, fertility rates, and income figures. It was not in 1929, not in 1930, not even, it seems, in the first part of 1931; it was not until the fall of 1931 and the early winter of 1932 that the voters were producing, in Republican heartland districts scattered across the country,

Democratic victories of the sort that would transform American politics and government in 1932.

While most Americans were being driven to the conclusion that the depression was something out of the ordinary, Hoover pored over his statistics, pondered the results of the special census of the unemployed he had ordered in 1930, and found little reason still to overcome his qualms about more vigorous government action. In the lame duck session[20] beginning in December 1930, he found himself on the defensive. He proposed legislation to aid victims of the drought in the lower Mississippi Valley—the same part of the country where he had organized flood relief, to a blaze of publicity, as secretary of commerce in 1927. But he ungenerously opposed direct relief to farmers. The man famous for feeding so many millions of foreigners was in the ludicrous position of refusing, out of devotion to an abstract principle, to feed several thousand Americans. Hoover also vetoed the veterans' bonus act passed by Congress in February 1931; it was promptly enacted over his veto. A month later Congress passed Senator George Norris's proposal to use the nitrate plant at Muscle Shoals, Alabama, which the government had owned since World War I, as the nucleus of a regional public power system—a proposal which Norris had been making for years and which later became the basis of the Tennessee Valley Authority. Hoover vetoed that, too. In each case he thought he had good reason for saying no—good reason, that is, in terms of his own principles and the context of standard American politics. But in each case saying no not only made him look hardhearted but also, perhaps more important, made him seem the prisoner rather than the master of events.

So during the eighteen months when Americans reached the sickening conclusion that the depression was not about to end, Hoover seemed to be doing nothing about it. Much of his time was spent responding to foreign economic crises—the collapse of Austria's Kreditanstalt in May 1931 and Britain's devaluation of sterling in September. His responses, notably the June 1931 moratorium on all international debt repayment and war reparations, were positive. But they were not enough to stop the spiraling descent of the economy. International trade was already drying up, in large part because of the Smoot-Hawley tariff. No sooner had he signed the bill in June 1930 than foreign nations began retaliation; by the fall of 1930 foreign trade was only 75% of 1929 levels, by the fall of 1931 barely more than 50%, and by the fall of 1932—after the sustained effects of the collapse of foreign economies and currency devaluations—just 35%.[21]

The Democrats had suffered grievously when President Woodrow Wilson, bedridden by a stroke, seemed to provide no leadership at a time of strikes, bombings, race riots, epidemic disease, and economic gyrations in the fall and winter of 1919. Hoover, who had been in Washington during much of this period and was sympathetic to Wilson, seemed to provide little more positive leadership in the long and electorally decisive months from July 1930 to December 1931. In October 1931 he did take the trouble to attend a baseball game in Philadelphia as a gesture of confidence. But from the austere, tight-lipped Hoover the gesture was unconvincing. During this time Congress became dissatisfied enough with the political calendar mandated by the Constitution—for an eighteenth-century nation where legislators made their way to the capital on sailing ships and in stagecoaches—that in March 1932 it passed and sent to the states the 20th Amendment, which advanced the start of congressional sessions to January 3 and of presidential terms to January 20. The amendment was ratified by the required three-quarters of the states by February 1933. In the meantime, Hoover, the last president to have a Congress to assemble thirteen months after the election in which it was chosen, paid a huge political price for his apparent inertia. But his predicament was tragic, not farcical. The statistics on which he had always placed such reliance provided no guidance for action, only a basis for despair. His experience in international diplomacy and finance led him to concentrate on foreign causes, which produced no solution, though he insisted for the rest of his life that the depression was caused mainly by foreign failings. The government which he had helped to build was only making matters worse and seemed incapable of making them better. No wonder Hoover seemed for months defeated and baffled, even as the country was. No wonder the country wanted something different.

8

-»» ««-

Disorder

Whittps://hen Congress finally did return in the last month of 1931, only eleven months before the next presidential election, Hoover presented it with an activist program—and one which far outshone any of the Democrats' plans. Its centerpiece was the Reconstruction Finance Corporation, to be empowered to lend $10 billion to businesses and, under a Hoover proposal advanced later in the session, a smaller amount to the states for direct relief spending. In addition, Hoover pressed on reluctant Democrats in Congress the banking reform that became the Glass-Steagall Act, separating deposit banking and investment banking, and enabled the Federal Reserve System to loosen credit and expand the badly contracted money supply. He pushed for and got more than $1 billion in additional public works spending, including funds for what became Hoover Dam. He got the Federal Home Loan Bank Board established, to help savings institutions survive. Hoover maintained later, and in some respects the statistics support him, that the economy revived as 1932 went on. But any economic revival was less visible to the public than was the brutal dispersal in July 1932 of the Bonus Army—the 17,000 veterans who had camped out in Washington's Anacostia flats while demanding higher veterans' bonuses—by Army forces commanded by swagger-stick-wielding General Douglas MacArthur. Hoover did not approve of MacArthur's methods. And his opinion that spending on veterans was already high enough—it amounted to more than 20% of a badly unbalanced federal budget—may very well have been shared by most voters. But once again people in need were asking for help and Hoover seemed to be saying no. Next to that vivid picture his active work on such technical programs as RFC and Glass-Steagall seemed pallid.

The congressional Democrats' own response to the economic crisis was less than impressive. John Nance Garner, the new speaker, was a veteran of twenty-nine years in the House but came from a dusty corner of west Texas and was little known nationally. He was a team player who had risen in the Democratic leadership and whose enthusiasm for pork barrel projects was recorded in his saying "Every time one of those Yankees gets a ham, I am going to do my best to get a hog."[1] He cooperated with Hoover on bills to create the Reconstruction Finance Corporation and to get the Federal Reserve to extend more credit. But he wanted to run for president in 1932 and had only a few months to make a record. The issue he chose was the sales tax. The Republicans had failed to balance the budget, he said, and so a federal sales tax must be enacted. In retrospect, a more deflationary and a regressive policy can hardly be imagined, nor is it easy to consider what would have happened to the structure of American government if the federal government had preempted the tax which the states, starved for revenue, were just then seizing on. But suddenly, after the tax had been reported out of the Ways and Means Committee, two congressmen balked. One was Democrat Robert Doughton, a sixty-eight-year-old farmer and banker from the hills of North Carolina who had been a congressman for twenty years. (The reason may have been less ideological than temperamental; Doughton was less progressive than he was obstinate. As chairman of the Ways and Means Committee in 1933–47 and 1949–53, he was called Muley because he refused to set foot on the Senate side of the Capitol and forced Senate conferees over to see him.)[2] The other was the progressive Republican from the heavily Italian East Harlem neighborhood of New York City, Fiorello La Guardia. Abrasive, voluble, articulate, erupting with rage—his first wife had died of tuberculosis and he saw himself as a crusader against urban squalor that produced poverty and disease—La Guardia also knew his facts and was afraid of no one. As quickly as a lightning strike, and just as surprisingly, he and Doughton staged a hearty offensive on the floor and killed the sales tax in March 1932.[3] In its place Garner and the Democrats pushed a series of excise taxes, which were passed and remained in effect through the rest of the 1930s. Garner also pushed a public works bill widely regarded as a pork barrel measure; it was vetoed by Hoover.

Nevertheless, as 1932 went on it was widely expected that the Republicans would be turned out in November and the Democrats voted in. Twenty years before, an unpopular Republican president had gotten opposition in his own party when Theodore Roosevelt came back from Africa and ran against his protégé Taft. But in 1932 Hoover had no serious Republican opponent. The progressives had grown too separate from the bulk of their party in the 1924 LaFollette campaign, in the push for McNary-Haugen, in fights for labor unions and against utility companies. Robert LaFollette, Jr., was too young to run, Hiram Johnson too irascible, and William Borah too much a loner. Gifford Pinchot, a progressive hero since his tilt with Taft's interior secretary two decades before, had won fiercely contested races for governor of Pennsylvania in 1922 and 1930, but he was aging and too brazenly ambitious. So no progressive opposition to Hoover arose. A former senator from Maryland, Joseph I. France, won primaries in Maryland, Oregon, and other states where the president was not on the ballot, but France, a doctor from a small town on the Chesapeake Bay, was not taken seriously as a candidate. Hoover was renominated without opposition in the June convention in Chicago—but only after managers hustled France out of the hall to forestall his plan to nominate former President Coolidge. It was not a nomination much worth having.

In contrast, the race for the Democratic nomination got tighter as the year went on. The day after Franklin Roosevelt was reelected governor of New York in 1930, his political contact man James Farley had told the press, "I do not see how Mr. Roosevelt can escape becoming the next presidential nominee of his party." The only other prominent Democratic officeholder who was not southern or Catholic or too closely tied to a machine was Governor Albert Ritchie of Maryland. So Farley encountered a positive response as he canvassed the country in 1931. But as it became apparent that Hoover would almost surely lose, other Democrats became interested in the nomination. Late in 1931 Al Smith complained to a visitor about his successor in Albany, "Do you know, by God, that he has never consulted me about a damn thing since he has been governor?"[4]—and added that he had decided to run for president again himself. In January 1932, on a national radio hookup, publishing tycoon William Randolph Hearst came out for Garner.[5] Albert Ritchie began running as a favorite son in Maryland, Governor "Alfalfa Bill" Murray in Oklahoma, and Senator J. Hamilton Lewis in Illinois. Newton Baker, Woodrow Wilson's secretary of war and a former mayor of Cleveland, an internationalist who apprently reluctantly abandoned his support of the League of Nations, loomed as a possible candidate acceptable to most party factions.

In April, Roosevelt gave an appeal that later admirers felt foreshadowed his New Deal programs. "These unhappy times," he said in a radio speech, "call for the building of plans that . . . build from the bottom up and not the top down, that put their faith once more in the forgotten man at the bottom of the economic pyramid." To many in a nation hostile to Bolshevism and aware of how revolutions from below had produced tyranny in Europe, this language smacked of demagoguery. Al Smith's reaction was furious: "I will take off my coat and vest and fight to the end any candidate who persists in any demagogic appeal to the masses of working people of this country to destroy themselves by setting class against class and rich against poor." In the weeks just afterward Roosevelt's fortunes as a candidate sunk to their lowest point. In late April he lost 73%–27% to Smith in the Massachusetts primary and beat him only 57%–43% (not a wide margin in a primary) in Pennsylvania. In May Garner won a three-way race in California, with 41% to 32% for Roosevelt and 26% for Smith, and Smith beat Roosevelt 61%–39% in New Jersey. Local factors may have accounted for the results. Most Massachusetts Democrats were Catholics who saw Smith as their champion, and Roosevelt tied his cause there to the scampish Boston Mayor James Michael Curley, who favored him because his adversaries in Boston were for Smith. Hearst lived in California, and his Los Angeles and San Francisco papers were thought to have influence there. The New Jersey primary vote was minuscule and concentrated in heavily Catholic, machine-dominated Hudson County across the river from Manhattan. Yet Roosevelt's apparent appeal for the "forgotten man" may also have hurt his candidacy, and he did not sound that note again in the weeks up to the convention that began in Chicago June 27.

II

Nothing quite resembles an American political convention. In the days when Americans had to travel four days and change trains to get from one coast to another, when the words "long distance call" still turned heads even in the offices of successful businessmen—and when telephone connections were still prone to go dead or were plagued with static, as was the case on one important call from Roosevelt's managers in Chicago to the governor in Albany—most American politicians did not know each other and did not meet except at these week-long gatherings held every four years. The voting public knew the conventions chiefly from colorful reporting like H. L. Mencken's. The first radio broadcast of the proceedings was beamed out of the Republican convention in Cleveland in 1924. Only 5% of American households had radios then; 27% did in 1928, and 61% in 1932. Franklin Roosevelt understood the power of radio as early as 1928.[6] Most other American politicians and political observers found it hard to get away from the assumption that what mattered was what was going on among the politicians in the hall, the corridors, the hotel lobbies, and the smoke-filled rooms. The demonstrations that followed each nominating speech would look utterly devoid of genuine enthusiasm on television two decades hence and required radio announcers to fill vast hours of air with talk when the conventions were first broadcast. But the enthusiasm of the delegates—or the lack of it—was genuine, and in the 1930s politicians looked to the demonstrations as an indicator of how long a candidate could hold the delegates pledged to him and whether he might be forced to deal. The conventions in 1932 and for some years afterwards, made up of men and women drawn from all parts of a vast and diverse country, from utterly autonomous and often hostile state parties, still made decisions and determined the outcome of great political battles. As Democratic delegates and politicoes arrived in Chicago in late June 1932 and looked over the crowd of hats for a porter, they were still uncertain whom their party would nominate and whether he would win.

When Farley arrived at Chicago's Union Station on Tuesday, June 21, and checked into the Congress Hotel, Roosevelt had a clear majority of the delegates. But he was far short of the two-thirds which the Democrats had required for nomination since their first convention in 1832—a rule that gave the South or any other major element in the party a veto over the nomination. It had kept House Speaker Champ Clark of Missouri out in 1912 and helped produce the 103-ballot deadlock between McAdoo and Smith at Madison Square Garden in 1924. That deadlock had produced a Democratic ticket that got 29% of the vote, and this time Smith was determined to stop Roosevelt. His determination was not, however, entirely shared by Garner or Hearst. Hearst feared most of all the nomination of a pro-League internationalist like Newton Baker; Garner, whose record as speaker had been less triumphant than he must have hoped, did not want another deadlock. Roosevelt commanded majorities on credentials and chairmanship votes. But he failed to get two-thirds on the first three nomination ballots,[7] which began after nominating speeches and demonstrations ended at 4 A.M. Friday morning and extended until after 9 A.M. Roosevelt operatives sent out feelers to Garner's forces. But William Randolph Hearst, out in his palatial California estate of San Simeon, may have pulled a string[8] that made Garner, back in his office in the Capitol, decide to support Roosevelt in return for the vice presidency. That evening Sam Rayburn persuaded the Texas delegation, 54–51, to vote for Roosevelt. Then McAdoo, now a California lawyer running at age sixty-nine for the Senate, rose and switched California's votes from Garner to Roosevelt, bringing him over the two-thirds mark.

III

The new nominee was lightly regarded by political commentators and some thought he had no chance to win. Earlier that year Walter Lippmann, who had known Roosevelt since he was assistant secretary of the Navy in the Wilson administration and watched his governorship up close in New York, called him "a pleasant man who, without any important qualifications for the office, would very much like to be President." "No one, in fact, really likes Roosevelt," H. L. Mencken wrote just after he was nominated, "not even his own ostensible friends, and no one quite trusts him." He "is in general far too feeble and wishy-washy a fellow to make a really effective fight."[9] Mencken called him Roosevelt Minor, and many looking over his career felt he had been outshone as assistant secretary of the Navy by his predecessor and cousin Theodore, as governor by his predecessor and patron Al Smith. He seemed to have no clear philosophy. He campaigned against budget deficits and for direct relief for the hungry. He astounded speech-writer Raymond Moley by replying, when asked to choose between contradictory arguments, "Weave the two together." His strongest support for the nomination came from the South and West, most of which the Democrats were sure to carry. In the large industrial states, the Republican base in the 1920s, he seemed not especially strong: he had lost primaries there and he had nearly lost the New York governorship to Republican Albert Ottinger in 1928, though he won reelection resoundingly in 1930. Given the primitive state of political polling and the un-certainty attendant upon all political predicting in this era,[10] Roosevelt could not be regarded as a sure winner, for all Hoover's problems.

But Roosevelt was ahead of the other politicians in two important respects. He understood how to dramatize his cause. And he knew how to present a consistent general theme in appeals to the voters even while he seemed to the experts to be making contradictory and inane proposals.

His mastery of the dramatic gesture was his flight to Chicago to accept the nomination. Defying the tradition that the nominee never appeared at the convention, Roosevelt hopped into a plane in Albany on Saturday morning and, after stops in Buffalo and Cleveland, got into Chicago late in the afternoon. "Let it also be symbolic," he told the cheering convention, "that I broke traditions. Let it be from now on the task of our party to break foolish traditions." It was in the same long speech that Roosevelt said, "I pledge you, I pledge myself, to a new deal for the American people." At least part of that New Deal—the phrase became popular after it was used the next day by political cartoonist Rollin Kirby—would be "planned action." "What do the American people want more than anything else?" Roosevelt asked. "Work and security."

Echoes of the enthusiasm for economic planning of Roosevelt advisors Adolph Berle and Rexford Tugwell would follow. To the Commonwealth Club in San Francisco, Roosevelt said in September 1932, "Our task now is not discovery or exploitation of natural resources, or necessarily producing more goods. It is the soberer, less dramatic business of administering resources and plants already in hand, of seeking to reestablish foreign markets for our surplus production, of distributing wealth and products more equitably, of adapting existing economic organization to the service of the people." Here he was envisioning a powerful government, directing every aspect of the American economy, and not holding out the prospect of economic growth. In his post-convention swing around the Midwest and West he called for "planned use of land," for federal aid to railroads and regulation of utilities. Then Hoover took to the stump in October and called the New Deal a "proposal to alter the whole foundations of our national life which have been builded through generations of testing and struggle. . . . the growth of bureaucracy such as we have never seen in our country . . . the regimentation of men. . . . You cannot extend the mastery of government over the daily life of a people without somewhere making it master of people's souls and thoughts."[11] On grounds of abstract principle, Hoover was on the attack. But on the facts, he was defensive: "Let no man tell you that it could not be worse. It could have been so much more worse that these days now, distressing as they are, would look like veritable prosperity."[12] Roosevelt responded by dropping his more radical rhetoric and stressing Hoover's "centralization" and budget deficits—his sins by traditional Democratic standards. In boxers' terms, Hoover was scoring at least some points.

But through Roosevelt's intellectually inconsistent campaigning ran one consistent and attractive political theme: he would work to bring things under control. Underneath Hoover's intellectually more rigorous speeches was a politically repellent assumption: that things were desperately out of control, and he was doing the best anyone could. This assumption American voters were not prepared to accept.

The importance of the yearning for order and control is illustrated by the thunderous lack of response in November 1932 to the left-wing parties. The Socialists, whose candidate had won 6% of the vote in 1912 and who had endorsed Robert LaFollette when he had won 17% in 1924, ended up with only 2% in 1932; the Communists, less than three-tenths of 1%. Americans wanted no revolution, no upheaval of the social order. Voters in 1932 were seeking not income redistribution or nationalization of resources. Nor were they thinking about a cradle-to-grave welfare state. They were seeking a national leader who could exert some control over a dizzying downward economic spiral. They wanted action to restore confidence in the American economy—to somehow get it working as it had for all of their adult lives—and they wanted some relief in the meantime. Roosevelt's readiness to drop appeals to the left when they came under attack, in both the primary and the general election campaigns, is evidence that they scared voters.

Roosevelt's talk of exerting control was not just rhetorical flourish. As governor of New York, he had taken some action against the depression and toward enlarging the public sector, supporting public hydroelectric power projects and relief for the unemployed. But these suggested only mild departures from Hoover, who favored building Boulder Dam even as he opposed Norris's Muscle Shoals project, and whose RFC was lending the states money for direct relief. The major difference between Roosevelt and Hoover was attitude. Hoover spent most of the crucial years of the depression huddled in the White House, gathering statistics, pondering the probems of international finance, and seldom if ever speaking directly to the people—for it was the custom that presidents were never to be quoted directly, even when they spoke personally to reporters. In contrast, Roosevelt made a point of appearing in public—partly to dispel the rumors that his crippled legs left him unable to work; he spoke in public in full sonorous tones but talked directly to voters in homey language as well. Roosevelt was optimistic, smiling, even jaunty; Hoover was cautious, grim-faced, dour.

Some have interpreted the 1932 election as a turn to the economic left, but the Democrats, who for years had been portraying themselves as Jeffersonian localists competing with the Hamiltonian centralist Republicans and had been supporting policies that left alone the local institutions of their diverse supporters—segregation and the saloon—were arguably on the right on economic issues; their record of backing programs that expanded the federal government and centralized control over the economy was at most spotty. Most of the congressional advocates of government ownership or economic redistribution were progressive Republicans— LaFollette, Norris, LaGuardia.

It may seem surprising that American voters in 1932 were choosing a traditional party not historically identified with policies of the economic left. But that was the response of voters in most of the democracies to the economic downturn of the early 1930s. In Britain a National government made up mainly of Conservatives overwhelmed the Labour party in 1931 by the biggest popular majority achieved in a British election, and was easily reelected in 1935.[13] In France the right held the premiership during most of the decade, and the Popular Front of Leon Blum took power only with the votes of the anticlerical but often pro-free-market Radicals, who modulated its policies and then overthrew it after little more than a year. In Germany the early 1930s saw stunning growth in the strength of the Nazis, not the left.[14] In Canada the New Deal programs advanced by Conservative R. B. Bennett in 1935 resulted in his overwhelming defeat by Liberal Mackenzie King, whose economic policies were similar to those of Republicans in the United States.[15] The Australian Labor party, long the country's strongest, was beaten soundly in 1931 and did not hold power again for years. True, the left did win elections in the Scandinavian countries at this time.[16] But they had in Europe a demographic and political weight comparable to that in North America of Wisconsin, Minnesota, and Saskatchewan, which also went left in the 1930s. On both continents their leftward movement was the exception rather than the rule in the early 1930s.

A yearning for order and stability through the political exertion of control rather than any desire for revolution, change, and uncertainty—this yearning explains the results of these elections and, in the United States, the weakness of the Republicans and the fluctuating fortunes of Roosevelt in the primaries. Elite businessmen and financiers, remembering the Paris mob and the storming of the Winter Palace, feared revolution, but the response of ordinary Americans was "strangely phlegmatic."[17] It was the same desire for government action to produce order and stability that had prevailed twice earlier in the lifetimes of 1932 voters when support collapsed for the party of a president who seemed utterly inactive in a time of crisis. Grover Cleveland's laissez faire response to the deep depression of the 1890s turned the 218–127 House majority his Democrats won in 1892 to a 244–105 Republican majority in 1894—the biggest loss of House seats, in number and percentage, in American history. Woodrow Wilson's incapacity in 1919–20, underlined by the Cox-Roosevelt ticket's decision to run as Wilson supporters, reduced the Democrats from the 49% they got in the 1916 presidential election to 34% four years later—the biggest decline of any party (except when one or both parties split) up until that time. The transformation of Hoover's 58%—41% victory into his 57%–40% loss to Franklin Roosevelt was a repudiation of similar proportions. Now it would be up to the new president to exert control over events and reestablish the order and stability which had seemed so strong only a few years before.

9

-»> «-

New Deal

Gathering speed north of Grand Central Station, the train emerged from the tunnel into grimy Harlem, ran along and over the Harlem River past the apartments of the Bronx rising from muddy streets along the ridges, pushed north at water level along the Hudson River, and on curving tracks raced past Storm King Mountain and the Hudson Highlands into the vast interior of upstate New York. This is the landscape Franklin Roosevelt saw from childhood until the last year of his life: the brown and gray stone of the city, the green of the trees and fields, and always the blue-green-brown ribbon of the river. From the large-paned windows and spacious lawns of the Roosevelt house at Hyde Park, the river was visible; and Roosevelt, a collector of model ships all his life, could see sailboats in summer, steamers in the fall and spring, and the iceboats he loved to speed on in the winter. Water, one of his most perceptive biographers suggests, was the central metaphor of his life. He was a keen sailor who prided himself on being able to pilot a ship through the sound to Campobello Island, his family's summer home off the Maine coast, and who went on cruises when he needed really to relax. In the icy waters off Campobello he caught his polio, and the soothing waters of Warm Springs helped him conquer if not cure it. Three of his favorite projects were hydroelectric power, the St. Lawrence Seaway, and the Tennessee Valley Authority, though none made traditional political sense. (The private utilities could summon up a sizable constituency of small stockholders, the Seaway proceeded through Republican upstate New York and threatened the primacy of the port of New York, and TVA was the brainchild of a Republican senator from Nebraska and gave its greatest benefits to Republican east Tennessee.) Later he even proposed setting up "Seven TVAs" to use river valley basins as centers for comprehensive national planning despite lack of local backing.[1]

Roosevelt's determination was vastly strengthened and his sympathy for victims of hardship greatly enlarged when he was crippled by polio at age thirty-nine. But his political ambition was there before and after. He called himself a farmer, and he desultorily practiced law and became an investor; but politics was the only real work he ever applied himself to, from his election at twenty-eight as state senator for Dutchess County until his death at sixty-three as commander-in-chief of the largest American military force ever assembled. He was a natural leader at childhood games, sunny and genial in temperament, a rich only child tended constantly by loving parents and adoring servants, a boy at the center of a happy world; and he had reason to see himself in the center of the greater world as well. He was a Democrat ancestrally, but cousin to the most famous Republican of his age. He was descended from old colonial Dutch and Yankee stock, yet the large majority of his votes for governor of New York came from the children of immigrants in New York City. Riding the water-level train frequently from New York City to Hyde Park or Albany, Franklin Roosevelt could see himself, as he came through the gap of the Highlands, at the cusp of America—poised between the great cities of the East with their millionaires and mansions, immigrants and tenements, and the vast interior filled with 70 million descendants of pioneers and planters, immigrants and slaves. Coast and interior, North and (thanks to Warm Springs) South, Democrat and Republican, native and immigrant: he was unique among American politicians of his day in his instinctive understanding of the variety of the nation he sought to lead—and his hunger to learn more about every facet of it. He could believe that all of this was his country.

That belief was strengthened by the results of the 1932 election. If the vote represented a rejection of Hoover and the Republicans, it also amounted to a nationwide call, across regional and class and ethnic lines, for Roosevelt and the Democrats. Roosevelt took 88% of the vote in the Deep South, 64% in the Civil War borderlands, and 61% in Wisconsin, Minnesota, and the Dakotas, where no Democrat before had ever won an absolute majority. Only in the heavy industrial area north of the Ohio River and east of Wisconsin and the Mississippi was the election close: Roosevelt won with 52% there. In each region voters moved strongly toward the Democrats,[2] but the shift was especially great in the progressive Northwest. This was a vindication of the strategy Roosevelt had had in the back of his mind throughout the 1920s, to combine the traditional Democratic vote in the South and borderlands with the Catholic–city machine vote in the eastern big cities and the LaFollette-Progressive vote.

The Republicans remained strongest in the Northeast. If New York City is excluded, Hoover actually carried 50%–47%, that part of the United States including Ohio, Delaware, and all the states north of the Mason-Dixon line; even if New York City is included, he ran barely less than even, 46%–50%. The hold of the Republican party on this industrial and commercial heart of the nation, which accounted for 32% of the total vote (38% if New York City is included), was strong enough for it to cast half its ballots for a seemingly inert and utterly failed president. To put it another way, Hoover carried the northeastern third of the votes cast outside New York City but was utterly repudiated in the rest of the country, losing New York 66%–27% and the remaining 62% of the electorate 62%–36%. Republican strategists knew that the depression was an overwhelming liability. But party loyalty and Hoover's arguments against Roosevelt's supposed radicalism seemed to succeed in rallying majorities or near-majorities in the large industrial states.

With the Democratic victory in the presidential race came an overwhelming Democratic sweep in Congress. The Democrats' gains were augmented by two factors. In the Senate they were running against Republicans elected in the Republican landslide year of 1920 and the generally pro-incumbent year of 1926, many of whom were therefore highly vulnerable. In House races they were aided, marginally, by the reapportionment of congressional districts among the states after the 1930 census and by redistricting in some states and the lack of it in others (31 congressmen were elected at large in Missouri, Kentucky, and Virginia, which lost seats in the reapportionment and failed to redistrict; all were Democrats, and Democrats even won one of 9 at-large seats in Minnesota, where they were used to running third).

Democrats gained a 60–35 margin in the Senate—the first majority they had won there in sixteen years. Their 13-seat gain came from all over the country; they lost only a handful of races. Two of the Republican victors, Hiram Johnson in California and Gerald Nye in North Dakota, were identified with the progressive group, and James Davis of Pennsylvania had considerable union backing. Regular Republicans won only in Oregon, by the narrowest of margins in New Jersey, and in the nation's most Republican state, Vermont. Democrats won by large margins in the Deep South and Civil War borderlands and by narrower but still comfortable margins in industrial states like New York, Ohio, and Illinois and more rural states like Indiana, Wisconsin, Iowa, and Kansas.

The Democrats won 55% of the House vote (3 percentage points below Roosevelt's figure) and the Republicans 41% (only marginally above Hoover's). Most of the rest went for candidates on the left: Farmer-Laborites on the prairie, Socialists in New York and Milwaukee. Overall, 310 Democats were elected and only 117 Republicans. Democrats won every seat in the Deep South, every seat but two (in Unionist east Tennessee) in the Civil War borderlands, all but one seat in the Rockies and all but one in the Pacific Northwest, every seat in Indiana and all but a handful in Ohio and Illinois.

Yet the Republicans clung to their base in the industrial states. They held most seats in New England, all but 4 in upstate New York, and large majorities in New Jersey and Pennsylvania and Minnesota. Republicans were still elected in parts of Boston, Buffalo, Pittsburgh, Cleveland, Detroit, and Chicago and in all of Philadelphia. Their party represented a cross-section of urban and rural districts in the Union heartland; the Democrats, half from the South or Civil War borderlands, tended more to represent farmers and small towns.

The most profound effect on both House and Senate was the turnover. For the only time in the twentieth century, the majority of House members were newly elected. In the Senate, the turnover was less, but still substantial, and the Democrats took over leadership positions for the first time since Woodrow Wilson's days. Gone was Majority Leader James Watson; gone was Reed Smoot after thirty years. In their places the Democrats had seasoned and politically shrewd leaders: Carter Glass of Virginia chaired the Appropriations Committee; Pat Harrison of Mississippi, Finance; "Cotton Ed" Smith of South Carolina, Agriculture; Key Pittman of Nevada, Foreign Relations; Joseph Robinson of Arkansas chaired Rules and was the new majority leader. All had firm political bases in the southern countryside and the small factory towns that dotted it, or in isolated western mining towns; all wanted to maintain local customs like racial segregation and to protect local economic institutions—country banks, low-wage industries, silver miners—from national competition and the depression of free markets.

The House Democrats were less well prepared for their new responsibilities. With Garner elevated to the vice presidency, the speaker's chair went to Henry Rainey of downstate Illinois, who was seventy-two when Congress convened and died seventeen months later. Some committee chairmen were highly competent—notably Sam Rayburn of Texas at Interstate and Foreign Commerce and Carl Vinson of Georgia at Naval Affairs—but most were dusty elderly figures from old courthouse towns, who had little legislative dexterity at a time when staffs were minimal and members themselves had to handle most of the details. The few northerners with important chairmanships—William Connery of Massachusetts at Labor, Samuel Dickstein of New York at Immigration and Naturalization—conspicuously lacked working majorities on their committees. Because the Republican leadership had held an iron grip on the levers of power in the House for all but one of the thirteen years leading up to the election of 1932, most House Democrats, unlike their Senate counterparts, had no experience in framing compromises, pushing legislation through to passage, or using parliamentary procedure to obstruct the opposition. Little wonder that talented legislators like Rayburn were bored and discouraged[3] and that some of the most qualified—Cordell Hull, Alben Barkley, James Byrnes—took serious political gambles to run for the Senate. Many of the Democrats who remained in the House seethed with resentment: against northerners who had invaded their state and beaten down what they considered a noble cause, against Wall Street financiers and lawyers who seemed to treat their regions as economic colonies and squeeze all the profit out of them, against the immigrant masses of the big cities whose Catholicism and cultural habits seemed opposed to institutions and mores they held most dear. Not only was the disciplined Republican majority gone from the House. Also gone were the tradition of party discipline and, with few exceptions, the House's capacity for national leadership. The House which had expeditiously set the terms of the Smoot-Hawley tariff and forced the administration and the Senate to accept them was now paying a terrible political price. Henceforth policy leadership would come from the Senate and, increasingly, the executive branch.

In fact, neither the leadership nor the composition of the Democrats in Congress provided many clues as to how the new majority party would govern. Congress was chaotic and unpredictable, suspicious of what had always been regarded as sound policy and liable to vote unexpectedly for measures traditionally deemed impractical or demagogic. The economic depression which no one had predicted and no one knew how to respond to had changed the political characters and rewritten the political sayings. No one was sure what would—or should—happen next.

10

-》》》 《《←

Hundred Days

Ahead of Roosevelt's and the Democrats' smashing victory of November 1932 stretched a period of four months in which Hoover and the divided lame duck Congress remained in charge of government. This was a hiatus nobody wanted. State legislatures meeting in these months ratified the constitutional amendment moving the president's inauguration back from March 4 to January 20 and the convening of Congress to January 3, but they acted too late for Hoover and Roosevelt. The economy, which had showed signs of mild recovery, was in worse condition than ever by winter, and each new crisis brought further discord between the president and president-elect. When the Europeans were unable to pay an installment of war debts due December 15, Hoover was unable to get Roosevelt to agree on a common American position. Then, in February 1933, a banking crisis began in Detroit, the boom town of the 1910s and 1920s. The Union Guardian Trust, installed in a towering new skyscraper with Aztec motifs and an inlaid marble map of Michigan's two peninsulas and eighty-three counties on the wall of the 40-foot ground floor banking area, was tottering near failure, threatening to bring all Michigan's banks down with it. Hoover's RFC refused to lend it money; Henry Ford, the nation's richest man, refused to keep his company's deposits there and threatened as well to take $25 million out of the First National Bank, a block away. So William Comstock, Michigan's new and utterly inexperienced Democratic governor, declared a bank holiday, closing every bank in the nation's fourth-largest city and seventh-largest state. When Hoover called on Roosevelt to agree on a joint statement of policies to restore confidence, Roosevelt, feeling with some justice that he was being asked for a commitment to Hoover's policies after they had been repudiated by the voters, refused.

This interregnum was the subject of political arguments for years. Hoover felt that Roosevelt had undermined confidence in recovery during the campaign and helped produce the banking crisis by declining to cooperate on the foreign debt problem. This explanation was consistent with Hoover's general analysis that foreign rather than domestic causes were primarily responsible for the depth and length of the depression. Hoover's complaints, implicit at the time but made public within two years, were the first of many Republican charges that Roosevelt wielded power unfairly and illegitimately.

But in the meantime Hoover was president and the economy seemed to be shutting down. Banks failed all over the country, and by March 4 banks in thirty-eight states were closed. At dawn on that inauguration day the governors of New York and Illinois, the states with the nation's biggest banks, declared a bank holiday, too. At 10 A.M. the New York Stock Exchange was ordered closed; commodities exchanges in New York and Chicago were closed as well. In the richest nation in the world, one-quarter of the work force was unemployed, national income was barely half what it had been four years before, and money had almost entirely stopped circulating. America seemed in desperate condition as Franklin D. Roosevelt, his leg braces locked, swung himself forward and walked thirty-seven steps to take the oath of office just after noon.[1]

He showed he understood what the nation was feeling, "First of all," he told Americans, "let me assert my firm belief that the only thing we have to fear is fear itself—nameless, unreasoning, unjustified terror." He promised action and called for the nation to act "as a trained and loyal army willing to sacrifice for the good of a common discipline." He would ask Congress to approve his policies, he said, but if it did not, "I shall ask the Congress for the one remaining instrument to meet the crisis—broad Executive power to wage a war against the emergency, as great as the power that would be given to me if we were in fact invaded by a foreign foe." Roosevelt's wife, Eleanor, noted with foreboding that this last statement evoked the greatest applause.[2]

Saturday, March 4 was the first of the famous Hundred Days. Hoover had refused to call Congress into special session, fearful that it would do something to destroy business confidence. Roosevelt was eager to take the risk. On Sunday, March 5, he ordered a national bank holiday and issued the summons to Congress. When it met Thursday, March 9, it passed his banking bill well-nigh unanimously the same day.

Friday, March 10. Roosevelt presented a bill drawn up by budget director Lewis Douglas which cut veterans' benefits by $400 million and federal employees' pay by $100 million. Fully 90 Democrats revolted and voted against it, but with 69 Republican votes it passed the House on Saturday, March 11. It passed its major test in the Senate on Monday, March 13.

Sunday, March 12. Roosevelt delivered his first "fireside chat" over the radio. The subject was banking, and the new president urged the 60 million Americans listening to put money back into the banks. It was a novel use of the medium: most Americans had never heard their presidents talk except in formal speeches or even read their words quoted except in formal texts; yet here was a chief executive talking as if to friends, using simple words to explain a complicated subject, inspiring confidence when the air was filled with fear. When the banks opened on Monday, Americans put more money into them than they took out.

Monday, March 13. At his evening meal on Sunday, Roosevelt said, "I think this would be a good time for beer." So the next day, while the states were busy repealing Prohibition by ratifying the 21st Amendment, Roosevelt urged Congress to legalize 3.2% beer. Opinion had been swinging against Prohibition since 1930, and most Americans looked forward to repeal.

He had accomplished his original agenda, but Roosevelt, pleased with the way the Congress was working, decided to keep it in session. The banks were open; money was circulating again; the corpse of the economy was reviving. His instinct told him that this was a time for action.

Thursday, March 16. Roosevelt put forward the farm bill which ultimately became the Agricultural Adjustment Act. To diminish surpluses, it empowered the government to tax processors of farm products and use the revenue to pay "parity" prices to farmers who agreed to limit production—a significant extension of Hoover's farm board, which made no effort to curb production. The bill passed the House on Wednesday, March 22, by a 315–98 margin; it passed the Senate on May 12, just in time to avert a farmers' strike called by A. C. Townley, leader of North Dakota's Non-partisan League, and others.

Tuesday, March 21. Roosevelt proposed the Civilian Conservation Corps, to employ young men in work camps. It was passed by voice vote. In addition, less than two weeks after his budget-cutting measure, Roosevelt proposed federal grants to the states for direct unemployment relief. This was a big step beyond Hoover's policy, advanced only late in his term, for federal *loans* to the states for relief. Roosevelt's bill used the Reconstruction Finance Corporation to funnel $500 million to the states through a new Federal Emergency Relief Administration. Some fifteen months before, similar measures had been advanced by only a few legislators on the left: veteran progressives George Norris of Nebraska and Fiorello LaGuardia of New York, freshmen like progressive Bronson Cutting of New Mexico and Edward Costigan of Colorado, and Democrat Robert Wagner of New York. But Roosevelt's bill was passed by overwhelming margins in the Senate in ten days and in the House in three weeks.

Wednesday, March 18. Roosevelt called for the first federal regulation of the securities markets. The law which resulted bore the imprint of such diverse forces as Sam Rayburn and Professor Felix Frankfurter of the Harvard Law School; and it was one New Deal measure wholeheartedly supported by Hoover, who always disliked speculators. Its passage was facilitated by the hearings conducted by Ferdinand Pecora, counsel to the Senate Banking and Currency Committee,[3] in which the likes of J. P. Morgan, Jr., were paraded before disapproving senators and upbraided for their misdeeds. The Pecora hearings, which had begun in 1932, spotlighted shocking practices—one bank had given interest-free loans to its officers while refusing to lend customers any more and calling in their margins, and at another the president had sold short the stock of his own bank. These hearings were the first of several major legislative investigations conducted by liberals in the 1930s which captured the attention of the public and helped change public policy; others were the Nye Committee hearings on munitions makers and the LaFollette and McCormack-Dickstein hearings on the violations of civil liberties of labor organizers.

More legislation followed after only the slightest of pauses.

Tuesday, April 10. Roosevelt called for creation of the Tennessee Valley Authority. For a dozen years after World War I, George Norris had fought off attempts to sell the Muscle Shoals Dam and power plant in Alabama because he wanted it used to provide public power instead. Now Roosevelt, who had become a public power enthusiast as governor of New York, was calling for a much vaster project of public power generation, dam building, fertilizer production, and regional planning. The bill creating TVA was signed into law on May 18.

Friday, April 13. The depression had caused hundreds of thousands of previously upwardly mobile Americans to lose the equity in their homes. So Roosevelt proposed a Home Owner's Loan Act, under which mortgage lenders would receive bonds in return for their interest in mortgages which they could otherwise foreclose on. It passed Congress in June. Eventually the Home Owner's Loan Corporation refinanced one-fifth of the mortgaged houses in the United States.

Through all this frenzied activity the administration again and again came forward with detailed drafts of legislation that stood up under scrutiny over the following months and years, and Roosevelt again and again showed himself capable of brilliant political improvisation—with results that shaped American politics for many years to come. He had prepared for the tasks before him better than most knew, assembling diverse groups of experts to come up with new approaches and draft bills. But he also had superb political instincts: he could understand instantly what might suddenly be possible, and achieve it. He also knew how to respond to threats, particularly to the threat of demagogic legislation, which was always a possibility in such unsettled times. Hoover was paralyzed by this threat; Roosevelt was liberated by it.

The first instance of his superb improvisations came on the Glass-Steagall bill. Prompted by revelations before the Pecora committee, this was an uncontroversial measure requiring a complete separation between investment and commercial banks. But Democratic Congressman Henry Steagall, a small-bank advocate from rural Alabama, and Republican Senator Arthur Vandenberg of Michigan, where banks had remained closed for a full month in early 1933, proposed an amendment providing for federal insurance of bank deposits up to $5,000. Senator Carter Glass, father of the Federal Reserve System, was against the amendment; so were most bankers; so was Dean Acheson, acting for the ailing treasury secretary, William Woodin. But Roosevelt decided to accept it, and it soon proved one of the most clearly successful of New Deal reforms.

The second major improvisation was a response to an amendment proposed by Oklahoma Senator Elmer Thomas on Wednesday, April 18. An old-fashioned advocate of free coinage of silver, in the mode of William Jennings Bryan, Thomas wanted to remonetize silver in order to inflate the dollar. It was a popular move. The dollar was significantly deflated as a result of the depression, and it was widely agreed that low prices were a major problem.[4] The western mining states, disproportionately represented in the Senate, were always eager to promote silver. In addition, Bryan and his policies still commanded widespread support from Democrats, who were now, for only the second time in forty years, in a position to make policy; House Speaker Rainey, an Illinois lawyer when Bryan delivered his historic "Cross of Gold" speech in Chicago in 1896, was a Bryanite through and through. A day before Senator Burton Wheeler of Montana had come within 10 votes of getting the Senate to vote for free coinage of silver. Thomas's amendment was just the sort of demagoguery Hoover feared, a partly sentimental, partly selfish resurrection of a policy that purported to make everyone better off and to cost no one anything.

Roosevelt's response was adroit. He used his congeniality to suggest agreement with the amendment when in fact he was of the opposite opinion—an example of the deviousness that came to be widely resented by his critics and fellow politicians but went unnoticed by his ardent followers. He said he would accept the amendment if it was written to give the president discretion rather than directions. "Well, this is the end of western civilization," said budget director Lewis Douglas, an Arizona copper millionaire, former congressman, and believer in the sanctity of contract and the necessity of honoring debts. On Thursday morning, April 19, Roosevelt told reporters gathered in his second-floor bedroom at the White House that the United States was off the gold standard. Two years before, the British had abandoned the gold standard in the midst of great hand-wringing and a crisis that brought the government down. Roosevelt did the same thing cavalierly, as part of a ploy to deflect the silver enthusiasts.

The third instance of improvisation came in Roosevelt's response to the Senate's passage, by a 53–30 vote on Friday, April 6, of Senator Hugo Black's thirty-hour-week bill. This was drastic legislation, which Roosevelt opposed on both economic and constitutional grounds: drastic legally, because previous court decisions seemed to bar even minimum-wage and child labor laws; drastic politically, because it seemed to impinge on the rights of the states and to threaten the separateness of the southern labor market; drastic economically, because it threatened to further limit production which was already too low. But unlike Hoover, Roosevelt did not simply set in his heels against this demagoguery. He felt he must provide an alternative. It was concocted during April by a variety of advisors: Columbia professors Raymond Moley and Rexford Tugwell, the heart of the "brains trust," who wanted controls to hold prices up and production down; Senators Robert Wagner and Robert LaFollette, Jr., who wanted national economic planning; Labor Secretary Frances Perkins, who along with Wagner wanted to strengthen unions; Senator Edward Costigan, who along with others wanted a massive public works program; and Gerard Swope of General Electric and Henry Harriman of the U.S. Chamber of Commerce, who wanted trade associations exempted from the antitrust laws so they could allocate production among their members. What this diverse group had in common was a complete lack of faith in the mechanism of the free market. "There is no invisible hand," Tugwell said. "There never was. We must now supply a real and visible guiding hand to do the task which that mythical, nonexistent, invisible agency was supposed to perform, but never did."[5]

That view was widely shared by a public which had just seen the economy collapse and which even before 1929 had distrusted the workings of markets and yearned for some measure of control. It was a public that tended to share the trustbusters' view of the American economy as a struggle between giant corporations and a large number of isolated individuals who were helpless before them. What neither the experts nor the public appreciated, as Roosevelt hurried to derail Black's thirty-hour bill, was the difficulty of the work their "real and visible and guiding hand" would be asked to do. The nearest thing to a precedent was the War Industries Board of World War I, headed by Bernard Baruch, which William McAdoo, now a senator from California, explicitly cited as a model. It had been created at a time when the pressures for national unity were obvious, the need for extraordinary government interference was clear, and the goal was to channel rather than limit production. But after four years of economic decline, and under the threat of more demagogic proposals, no one urged much caution in applying the model during peacetime.

Roosevelt's National Industry Recovery Act, announced on Thursday, May 17, managed to weave almost all of his advisors' ideas together. Trade associations would be authorized to draft codes fixing prices and setting production quotas, all exempt from antitrust laws. Unions would be entitled to collective bargaining, fortified by the minimum-wage and maximum-hour provisions that would have to be part of those codes. And the government would spend $3.3 billion on public works, a huge sum that seemed especially huge when measured against the budget cuts passed only weeks before.

The legislative response to these proposals was typical of Roosevelt's relations with Congress in his first term. The issue had been raised in the first place by a surprise demagogic initiative in Congress, which in the emergency was ready to pass all sorts of proposals, many of them simply crazy, which had been around for years and had never been given a serious hearing before. The president responded with a bill that combined various kinds of advice he had been given. The House, with its strict rules and its unreadiness to offer its own legislative initiatives, passed his bill quickly. The Senate, with its looser rules and its recent history of never having been controlled by a single leadership, actually examined the substance of the bill and gave the administration some trouble. Progressive trustbusters like William Borah, Burton Wheeler, and Hugo Black were worried that big businessmen would use the codes to extract monopoly profits from consumers. Jeffersonian Democrats like Bennett Champ Clark of Missouri feared that the labor provisions would enable government to interfere with existing arrangements which, to all appearances, suited both sides. But Wagner, who wanted a nationally planned economy and considered the National Industrial Recovery Act "the first step toward it,"[6] piloted the measure through, and the conference report was finally approved by the narrow margin of 46–39 on Wednesday, June 13.

On Saturday, June 16, Roosevelt signed the bill, and Congress went home— exactly 100 days from the day the session began. This 73rd Congress reconvened for its regular session in December, and in 1934 it passed the landmark Securities Exchange Act. It would superintend and meddle with the conduct of administration programs from time to time. But the initiative and, with few exceptions, the power to make decisions had passed from a legislative branch, whose most creative members were progressive Republicans and whose most politically shrewd members were Jeffersonian Democrats, to an executive branch staffed helter-skelter with lawyers and professors, businessmen and protégés of Bernard Baruch and Felix Frankfurter and Yale Law School Professor Jerome Frank, and orchestrated always by an optimistic, impulsive, and brilliantly instinctive politician, Franklin Roosevelt. The country wanted action; it wanted order; it wanted control exerted over the seemingly uncontrollable downward economic spiral. Franklin Roosevelt promised these things, and he delivered.

11

→)) ((←

Blue Eagle

T he Hundred Days built a government capable of intervening more deeply in American life and in the everyday American economy than had been seen in this country since the wartime years of 1917–18. It also created a new kind of political spectacle, one of far-reaching decisions being made by unelected and hitherto unknown administrators, of internal fights within an administration becoming front-page news—a spectacle which affected the daily lives of ordinary people all across America.

All this change occurred against the background of an economy which rallied from the lowest levels of the depression but still failed to achieve the levels of prosperity of the 1920s. In the first three months of the Roosevelt administration, production rose markedly, but on July 19 the stock market lost most of its 1933 gains. The economy rallied more slowly through the fall and winter; by the spring of 1934 it had reached a plateau where it remained until well into 1935. There was plenty of evidence on which New Dealers could base claims that things had improved. But there was also a basis for others to argue that things had not snapped back to normal and had not improved as much as they should have.

Public attention focused on the most far-reaching and controversial administration program, the National Recovery Administration (NRA). Technically, this was just one part of the machinery set up under the National Industry Recovery Act; and when the act was signed, the newly appointed head of NRA, General Hugh Johnson, was disappointed to see the Public Works Administration and its billions placed under the control of Interior Secretary Harold Ickes, who was honest and extremely thorough but did not spend his money fast enough to inflate the economy. Johnson, a grizzled veteran and garrulous Oklahoman, had been Bernard Baruch's deputy in the War Industries Board and believed in cooperation rather than competition. He worked frenziedly to get industries to agree to NRA codes, and he succeeded. Within three months the ten largest industries, led by cotton textiles, agreed, and by early 1934 there were some 700 codes in force.

But he was laboring at what surely was an impossible task. NRA codes were supposed to hold up prices and wages, to prevent further deflation, but they were also supposed to prevent prices from rising too high. They were intended to enable small businesses to maintain competition and prevent monopolies. But NRA officials typically let large companies write codes which pressed smaller competitors between the vise of low prices and high wages. Moreover, Senator Wagner had been careful to write into the law a section, 7(a), guaranteeing workers the right to organize, and many of Johnson's administrators used this as a wedge to force companies to bargain with unions. But this procedure put a few harried officials in the position of supervising collective bargaining agreements for a huge nation.

Johnson understood the difficulties and hoped to surmount them by whipping up public enthusiasm for NRA. The codes would be enforced not by the government, he said, but by "public opinion." As for the violator, NRA would "break the bright sword of his commercial honor in the eyes of his neighbors—and throw the fragments—in scorn—in the dust at his feet. . . . The threat of it transcends any puny penal provision in the law." In other words, Americans would be urged to visit on those who did not cooperate the same kind of active community disapproval they had wreaked on those who did not cooperate with the war effort in 1917 and 1918. So that everyone would know who agreed to observe the NRA codes, Johnson designed a symbol, a blue eagle, in the Art Deco style then in vogue with movie theater designers, German dictators, skyscraper architects, and French ocean liner decorators. At least initially, public enthusiasm was high. In September 1933, 250,000 Americans marched behind NRA's blue eagle in a parade down New York's Fifth Avenue. "Not since 1917," writes one historian, "had the whole nation savored such a throbbing sense of unity, of marching together"[1]— or, he might have added, such dragooning and regimentation and so great a potential for suppression of dissent and nonconformity.

But discontent with NRA soon grew. Americans in 1934 did not have much regard for free markets or much faith in the price mechanism. But they did find it peculiar that dry cleaners were being forced to shut down because they could not pay the wages demanded by the NRA Dry Cleaners code and that neither price competition nor vastly increased production seemed to be resulting from the scheme. Especially in the boom cities of the 1920s, where money had stopped circulating and people who had thought themselves on the way to affluence suddenly feared they could not provide food, clothing, or shelter for their families, millions of ordinary Americans found reassurance in a sense that NRA had exerted control over an economy that was in a runaway downward spiral. But other Americans feared that NRA was holding down production and preventing the recovery that would otherwise occur in the normal course of things—and a minority believed, with Hoover, that recovery was already happening in early 1932 when Roosevelt interrupted it with his irresponsible campaigning, his refusal to cooperate in the interregnum, and his wild proposals and cavalier economic decision-making afterwards.

From the point of view of many producers, NRA looked even worse. In March 1934, Roosevelt told 4,000 members of NRA's Consumer Advisory Board, "You and I are now conducting a great test to find out how the business leaders in all groups of industry can develop capacity to operate for the general welfare." He continued, in Arthur Schlesinger's paraphrase, "That test might succeed even better if business would keep prices down, reduce working hours, and increase wages"[2]—and, he might have added, recognize adversarial labor unions. Such language sounded to critics of the New Deal less like a cooperative effort demanding sacrifice by all and more like the beginnings of a scheme to redistribute income from producers to workers and consumers. And while an argument could be made for some such redistribution—an argument that was made explicitly at the time by Senator Wagner, but not by many others—it is certainly understandable if those who were intended to provide the resources to be redistributed came to bitterly oppose the New Deal. They opposed it all the more if they were convinced, as many were, that the economy would grow faster and the great majority of Americans would do better without government intervention schemes like NRA. And even more if they feared, as a few critics did, the consequences of arousing mass enthusiasm in parades and with symbols and slogans that looked uncomfortably like those in use in Mussolini's Italy, Hitler's Germany, and Stalin's Russia. Johnson did, after all, refer approvingly to Mussolini's fascism in his 1935 memoir.

The fights within the administration over NIRA were echoed by disagreement and occasional disarray on other issues. Major decisions seemed to be made cavalierly. In the spring of 1933, Roosevelt had abruptly and without consultation gone off the gold standard. In the early summer, with a message he wrote out by hand while cruising off the coast of Maine, he torpedoed the London Financial Conference to which he had sent Secretary of State Cordell Hull and 1920 presidential nominee James Cox. In the fall he went on a gold-buying policy that none of his admirers thought had any beneficial effect, and he set the price at which the United States would buy gold by picking lucky numbers. During the winter of 1933–34, Secretary of Agriculture Henry Wallace became notorious for ordering several million piglets killed as part of a drive to hold down production and cut farm surpluses. The presence in the administration of so many intellectuals and academics also became an issue, enchanting some Americans and repelling others who were aghast that government was being run by, in the words of Baltimore *Sun* reporter Frank Kent, "third rate college professors and unsuccessful welfare workers." Attitudes did not divide simply along class or economic lines. Leaders of large corporations and many national institutions like the U.S. Chamber of Commerce were often willing to cooperate with New Deal schemes—and use them to their own advantage. Small-town bankers and businessmen, their ability to command respect and authority threatened by the intervention of New Deal policies into their local communities, tended to hate Roosevelt and all his works.[3] Not only businessmen but a great many Americans of all kinds were worried about an increasingly intrusive federal government, wary of a leader who seemed bent on redistributing wealth and whose next move was unpredictable even by his own highest appointees, at least a little scared of the dim echoes of European coercion and authoritarianism they heard in the Roosevelt program.

Since the middle 1920s, Roosevelt had pursued the strategy of welding to the Democrats' traditional base of strength the progressive wing of the Republican party, personified by his cousin Theodore (who had died in 1919) and represented demographically by the progressive voters of the Midwest and West and by the electorally critical Jews in New York.[4] Up through the 1934 election he deemphasized party ties and campaigned as a non-partisan leader. Except for the traditionally political postmaster general, Roosevelt's old campaign manager James Farley, cabinet members were forbidden to give campaign speeches. Progressive Republicans and third-party candidates were given support in some cases (Roosevelt praised Robert LaFollette, Jr., in a speech in Green Bay, Wisconsin, in August 1934) and benevolent neutrality in others (he did not speak out for or against Farmer-Laborites Floyd Olson and Henrik Shipstead in Minnesota or Fiorello LaGuardia in his 1933 race against Tammany Democrats for mayor of New York City). Like Woodrow Wilson, who declared at the beginning of World War I that "politics is adjourned," Roosevelt sought to use quasi-military coercion and to channel public enthusiasm toward conformity with his policies—but to do so in a non-partisan manner, so as to overstep the traditional party lines and corral the largest possible coalition of Americans.

But party lines were also being breached in another direction. Old-fashioned Jeffersonian Democrats like Senator Carter Glass were already decrying the government's intrusion into more local matters than they had ever feared it would get into, and Frank Kent noted acerbically a little later that the Roosevelt administration had adopted not the proposals of traditional Democrats like John W. Davis but those of the Progressives and LaFollette.[5] Davis himself attacked the New Deal, and John Raskob, a former Democratic national chairman who had financed publicist Charley Michelson's relentless attacks on Hoover, was by 1934 one of the founders of an anti-New Deal organization called the American Liberty League. The animus of these out-of-office Democrats was most pungently expressed by Al Smith a couple of years later. Pointing to the administration's former Republicans, its social workers, its professors, he asked: "Who is Ickes? Who is Wallace? Who is Hopkins, and, in the name of all that is good and holy, who is Tugwell, and where did he blow from? . . . Is LaGuardia a Democrat? If he is, then I am a Chinaman with a haircut." Smith's point was apt, if the argument was about the past: Wallace was originally an Iowa Republican and Hopkins an Iowa-born social worker; Tugwell was a professor and LaGuardia a Republican congressman. But by 1934 they were very much at the center of Franklin Roosevelt's administration, and hence at the center of his new Democratic party.

The party controlling the White House had always lost seats in off-year congressional elections, as the out party capitalized on local grievances against national policies and the in party ran without its leading candidate at the head of the ticket. But looking ahead to 1934, it was possible to forecast almost any result—particularly since there still was no such thing as a reliable public opinion poll. The Democrats would presumably profit from the improvement in economic conditions. But Roosevelt himself was making defensive comments, denying that there really was a "brains trust" and admitting in September 1934 that there must be changes in NRA.[6]

Earlier, in his June 1934 fireside chat, Roosevelt had brilliantly[7] phrased the questions on which he wanted voters to base their choices in November. "The simplest way for each of you to judge recovery lies in the plain facts of your individual situation. Are you better off than you were last year? Are your debts less burdensome? Is your bank account more secure? Are your working conditions better? Is your faith in your own individual future more firmly grounded?" Of all American politicians, Franklin D. Roosevelt had the least firsthand information, because of his wealth and his handicap, about how the ordinary American lived. Yet he also had the surest instinct for what mattered to ordinary voters and an unerring gift for the homey metaphor that cut through the clutter of political debate and went straight to the heart of voters' everyday lives. His opposition was forever taking in abstractions—about free enterprise, rugged individualism, constitutional checks and balances. Franklin Roosevelt spoke of the realities of life in the language of American voters.

The voters spoke his language back. On election day, the Democrats actually gained seats in both the Senate and the House—the first and only such gains in American history by the incumbent party in an off-year election. Even more than a Democratic triumph, it was a victory for New Deal supporters. The few statewide races lost by Democrats were won mostly by New Dealers. Democrats won 24 of 33 Senate races, and others were won by pro-New Deal Republicans Hiram Johnson in California and Bronson Cutting in New Mexico, the Non-partisan League's Lynn Frazier in North Dakota, Farmer-Laborite Henrik Shipstead in Minnesota, and Progressive Robert LaFollette, Jr., in Wisconsin. Republican Arthur Vandenberg, the father of federal bank deposit insurance, won in Michigan, leaving only three old-guard Republicans winning by narrow margins in the rock-ribbed Republican states of Vermont, Maine, and Delaware. Democrats ousted strong Republicans in Pennsylvania and Indiana by narrow margins and in Ohio and Missouri by wide ones.

In governors' races the picture was much the same. Democrats lost narrowly to old-guard Republicans in New Hampshire, Vermont, New Jersey, and Maryland, where the ailing Jeffersonian Democrat Albert Ritchie, whom H. L. Mencken considered a far superior leader to Roosevelt, was pitched out after fourteen years in office. Democrats came close to beating Alf Landon in Kansas and, after a bruising primary, lost in Michigan—both among the strongest of Coolidge states ten years before. Farmer-Laborite Floyd Olson won in Minnesota and Progressive Philip LaFollette in Wisconsin. In California, the old muckraking novelist, socialist, and Prohibitionist Upton Sinclair was pointedly snubbed by Roosevelt because of his wild EPIC (End Poverty in California) scheme, and the inoffensive Republican incumbent, Frank Merriam, was elected instead. Elsewhere Democrats won, even in Maine, Connecticut, and Pennsylvania—all Hoover states in 1932. Pennsylvania was the biggest prize. Previously the race in Pennsylvania had always been decided in the Republican primary, and 1934 saw another hard-fought primary contest, this time between David Reed, the old-guard incumbent, and Gifford Pinchot, the outgoing progressive governor. Reed won the primary but lost the general election to Joseph Guffey, a Democratic wheel horse from the Pittsburgh area and an ally of John L. Lewis's United Mine Workers. George Earle III, an aristocrat from Philadelphia's Main Line, won the governorship and the tens of thousands of patronage jobs it commanded for a Democratic organization that had hardly existed two years before.[8]

In contests for the House, Democrats astounded just about everyone by gaining rather than losing seats. Their gain was modest: they came out of the election with a 319–103 edge over the Republicans, compared with their 310–117 edge in 1932. But combined with the Progressive sweep in Wisconsin and Farmer-Labor victories in Minnesota, these gains represented a real victory for the New Deal. Again, the biggest single change was in Pennsylvania, a gain of 9 seats. This historic bulwark of the Republican party, the key industrial and energy state in the nation, now had a 23–11 Democratic majority in its House delegation. Democrats gained other industrial seats in Massachusetts, Maine, Connecticut, upstate New York, and Los Angeles. Yet they lost 11 seats in the rural Midwest, including 5 in Michigan and the Indiana seat that for thirty-four years afterwards was represented by House Republican leader Charles Halleck (he won it in a January 1935 special election after the Republican who had won in 1934 died). A similar contrast is apparent in a comparison of the districts where the Democratic percentage rose more than 5 points with those where it fell more than 5 points. Democrats made such gains—and they were especially unusual in the off-year election after a presidential landslide—in most Pennsylvania districts and in districts in the Boston area, western upstate New York, West Virginia, northeast Ohio, northernmost Michigan, and the traditionally volatile West: the Rocky Mountains, the Puget Sound and San Francisco Bay areas, Los Angeles County. On the other hand, Democrats sustained losses of similar magnitude in dozens of districts in rural New York, Ohio, Indiana, Illinois, and Michigan; on the Great Plains; in North Carolina; and in Maryland, where the entire party was hurt by Governor Ritchie's defeat.[9]

But the best way to appreciate the genuinely revolutionary nature of the 1934 election results is to divide congressional districts outside the South into two classes: industrial/immigrant districts and rural Yankee districts.[10] In 1934 these two groups of districts went in precisely opposite directions. The overall Democratic share of the vote in House contests in industrial/immigrant districts went up from 51% to 55%, whereas in rural/Yankee districts it fell from 53% to 51%.[11] In 1932 rural/Yankee districts had been more Democratic than industrial/immigrant ones; in 1934, and thereafter, this pattern was reversed. The shifts were particularly striking in the big states of Illinois and Michigan, where the Democratic percentages in industrial/immigrant districts went up 6 and 4 points, respectively, between 1932 and 1934 while those in rural/Yankee districts, which in 1932 had been the same as in the industrial/immigrant ones, went down 4 and 6 points. In other words, in those states city and countryside were voting the same in 1932, while in 1934 the city was 10 percentage points more Democratic than the country.

Such changes are very much the exception rather than the rule in American political history. They are evidence of great surges of opinion moving, among different segments of the population, in precisely opposite directions. The cities and the children of immigrants were moving toward Roosevelt and the New Deal. Outside the South, the countryside and those of Anglo-Saxon stock were moving away from them. The Catholic masses who had thronged to East Coast cities and the workers who had come to the booming coal-steel-auto belt from western Pennsylvania through Michigan and Chicago up to Minnesota's Mesabi Range— the fastest-growing segments of the nation between 1900 and 1930—were moving toward the Democrats. The residents left behind in the small courthouse towns— the slowest-growing part of the nation in those years—were moving toward the Republicans. It would be only a minor simplification to say that Roosevelt's party gained votes where most people worked with mules.

Political analysts looking at presidential election returns have portrayed both of these movements as responses to what came to be called the Second New Deal legislation of 1935—the sudden passage of the Wagner Act, Social Security, and progressive taxes.[12] But both trends are already apparent in the results of November 1934 and were not much changed in 1936, when Democrats rose from 55% to 57% of the House vote in immigrant/industrial districts and stayed steady at 51% in rural/Yankee districts.[13] The Democrats ran well in the rural, Anglo-Saxon areas. But they showed a special appeal in urban and immigrant areas—an appeal which was startling at the time but was sustained for a long time afterwards.

Why? The inquiry must focus on NRA, which was the centerpiece of New Deal policies. NRA had some success in shifting income toward low- and middle-income city-dwellers. More important, it supplied a sense of control for those whose fortunes seemed to be falling uncontrollably down a bottomless hole. Voters in the great cities of America in the years up to 1930 were not so much the starving masses as they were people who had been gathered in from the countrysides of Europe and North America and were advancing economically more rapidly than they had ever thought possible. They were not so much people mired in poverty as people suddenly and cruelly checked in upward mobility. Having grown up in a world where the milk cow, chicken, and vegetable patch guaranteed sustenance in even the toughest times, they found themselves in a world where they depended on paper—paper money and checks, deeds and mortgages—for their food, clothing, and shelter; then all of a sudden they found their paper was worth nothing. For them NRA, with its price and wage regulations, its controls on production and distribution, provided a sense that things were back under control. Its pageantry and hoopla, the conformity it urged citizens to impose on one another, were assurances that the community would not let them starve.

Other New Deal programs helped them as well. The Farm Credit Administration, Home Owners Loan Corporation, and Federal Housing Administration prevented more than a million mortgage foreclosures. Public works programs put family members back on payrolls, as the federal government suddenly and briefly became an employer of last resort. In November 1933, Harry Hopkins, a fast-talking, irreverent, and street-smart idealist known to Roosevelt from his work running social service programs in New York, was given command of the $500 million Federal Emergency Relief Administration—one of the largest federal spending programs up to that time. Most of its money and $400 million from Harold Ickes's Public Works Administration (which was technically part of NRA) went to the Civil Works Administration for labor-intensive public works projects. Hopkins presented his plan for CWA to Roosevelt on November 2, it was approved, and in an unheated office Hopkins set to work. By November 23 he had 800,000 men working on the CWA payroll, a figure that by December 7 had grown to 2 million. They were repairing streets and digging sewers, building playgrounds and painting murals in public buildings. (To avoid charges of make-work, Hopkins forbade street sweeping, snow shoveling, and leaf raking.) By January 1934, CWA had as many as 4.25 million Americans on its payroll—8% of the labor force![14] And when Roosevelt ordered CWA shut down when winter ended, Hopkins did so quickly and efficiently, leaving not a hint of corruption behind.

Hopkins impressed Roosevelt not just with his ability to put millions to work almost overnight but with his utter loyalty to his boss, his ability to build his empire up and his willingness to shut it down. "Why do you keep Hopkins so close to you?" Wendell Willkie asked Roosevelt when visiting him in the White House one day before the 1941 inaugural which Willkie, the 1940 Republican presidential nominee, had hoped would be his. Roosevelt replied, according to Willkie, "Some day you may well be sitting here where I am now as president of the United States. And when you are, you'll be looking at that door over there"— the visual imagery is poignant in light of Roosevelt's disability—"and knowing that practically everybody who walks through it wants something out of you. You'll learn what a lonely job this is, and you'll discover the need for somebody like Harry Hopkins who asks for nothing except to serve you."[15] When Roosevelt had a tough job—setting up another vast work relief program in 1935, channeling aid to Britain in 1940 and to Russia in 1941—he called on Hopkins, and Hopkins helped him get it done.

Even by the winter of 1933–34, relief administrator Hopkins seemed more able than any American since food administrator Herbert Hoover to make government work rapidly to help vast numbers of ordinary citizens. Like Hoover in his food relief days, Hopkins had no doubt that he could outperform free markets and government bureaucracies, and he did. But while Hoover ended his food relief days with a belief, buttressed by his own success in business, that American society gave everyone a fair chance to be rewarded for his merits, Hopkins, after two decades as a social work administrator, concluded that merit had little to do with success. As he told members of one of his arts projects, "It's just an 'Act of God' that you are sitting on one side of this table and I *happen* to be sitting on the other."[16] Hoover's confidence that there was a connection between merit and reward expressed the optimistic temperament of the prosperous 1920s. Hopkins's bleak picture of a society where success was accidental and misfortune unearned reflected the gloom of the once upwardly mobile Americans who had seen their plans shattered and their dreams vanish in the economic disaster of the 1930s.

By the late 1930s, Americans were divided between these views. "Do you think that today any young man with thrift, ability, and ambition has the opportunity to rise in the world, own his own home, and earn more than $5,000 a year?" Elmo Roper asked in a December 1936 poll. Yes, said 40% of those questioned, still upbeat; no, said 34%, down and discouraged; yes, if he's lucky, replied 18%:[17] for the majority, upward mobility still seemed possible, but only a minority thought you could get ahead without luck. Many Americans stubbornly continued to believe that there was a relationship between effort and reward, and New Deal sympathizers tried in vain to prevent them from blaming themselves for their misfortunes.

NRA and work relief and deposit insurance restored confidence among the city-dwellers of America. Once again they could be sure that their pieces of paper would buy the necessities of life—and even some luxuries. The New Deal's popularity in the cities and in industrial/immigrant areas rested not just on an improvement in economic statistics. It rested on people's confidence that they were no longer in danger of being left helpless, unable to feed, clothe, and shelter their families.

In the countryside, the fear was not so great, and the fall from rising prosperity to depression had not been so far. There the interference of NRA and other New Deal programs in the fabric of local life seemed unneeded and was quickly resented. William E. Leuchtenberg, a historian sympathetic to the New Deal, reports that NRA "sought to drive newsboys off the streets and took a Blue Eagle away from a company in Huck Finn's old town of Hannibal, Missouri, because a fifteen-year-old was found driving a truck for his father's business."[18] Accordingly, in the countryside the Democrats began receding slightly from the levels of popularity they had achieved as the alternative to the discredited Republicans in the disastrous year of 1932.

By early 1934, Franklin Roosevelt had already gone a long way toward creating what would be known as the Roosevelt or New Deal Democratic coalition. Campaigning in unusually nonpartisan terms, without the appeals to class divisions that became so central a part of his rhetoric by 1936, he attracted to Democratic candidates and to a few New Deal supporters with other labels majorities that were made up of traditional Democrats, the left-leaning swing voters from the Jewish ghettoes of New York to the German-Americans of the Upper Midwest, and important parts of what had been the majority Republican coalition from the time of William McKinley until the election of Herbert Hoover—notably the working-class voters of the coal-steel-auto belt.

He had forged this coalition even though the centerpiece of his New Deal in November 1934 was NRA—a program which was ruled unconstitutional six months later, which Roosevelt never attempted to revive, and which his admirers hesitate to defend. NRA may have helped check the downward spiral in 1933. But eventually it retarded economic growth, intruded clumsily into the most minute details of everyday economic life, and depended for its effectiveness on a conformism induced by coercion and something akin to vigilantism. NRA has been attacked as "fascism," partly because Hugh Johnson himself compared it to Mussolini's corporate state. But it was a peculiarly American product, the creation of a desperate nation with almost no experience of intrusive government which was drawing on its one recent example of wartime coercion. Its potential for infringement of personal freedoms was not realized in a country that knew itself to be exceedingly diverse and was used to tolerating, though sometimes grudgingly, unusual and even eccentric cultural and economic behavior.

An additional factor for working for tolerance was that both the major elements in the swing vote were sensitive to violations of civil liberties: Jews, because they had long been the targets of bigotry; Germans, because during World War I they had suffered harassment, economic boycotts, and physical violence from those who doubted their patriotism. Franklin Roosevelt, used to campaigning among Jews, aware always that the Progressives were the key to his national majority, was ever sensitive to violations of civil liberties. A president of different character from another constituency—a Huey Long from Louisiana, for example—might have conducted an inherently intrusive program like NRA with a much less tender regard for citizens' basic rights.

The First New Deal—the measures of the Hundred Days and especially NRA— was a political success initially not so much for what it did, but because it did something. It attracted critical support not so much from the downtrodden bottom of American society as from the masses who had been rising up from the middle and then were suddenly cast down. It galvanized a majority of Americans in the vast middle and at the not-so-large bottom not because it promised to redistribute income or wealth or power, but because it imposed a sense of order and control in a country which desperately sought reassurance. It was a major achievement, but it was also a temporary response to exceedingly unusual conditions, a collection of improvised solutions which threatened to raise problems which would lead to different improvised solutions later. It was not—and no one knew this better than Franklin Roosevelt—a permanent thing. Roosevelt's First New Deal had changed American politics and American government, but it was clear that more changes were in store.

12

➤➤➤ ⫷⫷⫷

Economic Politics

T he 1934 election showed that the extended depression and the record of Franklin Roosevelt's administration had changed traditional American political alignments. Old precedents were not followed; old rules of thumb did not apply. In the countryside of America, most voters had stuck with the party loyalties forged in the crucible of the Civil War, but in the great cities and in smaller factory towns, in the industrial America where nearly one half of the nation's people lived, there had been a surge toward Franklin Roosevelt's New Deal Democrats. It was as strong in the middle-class neighborhoods along the boulevards of Brooklyn and northwest Detroit and the flatlands of the Los Angeles basin as it was in the choked alley-wide streets of South Philadelphia or the stolid brick apartment blocks of the West Side of Chicago.

But at the end of 1934 the United States did not yet have an explicitly economic-based politics. Roosevelt had governed and campaigned as an honest broker, a national leader trying to look after everyone's economic interests. In the course of 1935, that position had become unsustainable. Economic circumstances forced him to come up with new policies, and political circumstances forced him to come up with a new political appeal. On the right, powerful forces drawn from the leadership of both traditional parties—the Hoovers and the Smiths—were alarmed by the tendency of Roosevelt's policies and tried to make a stand on abstract principles while they waited for the practical disasters they were sure were ahead. On the left, advocates drawn from the margins of both traditional parties—the Wagners and the LaFollettes—were encouraged by Roosevelt's willingness to experiment and tried to take advantage of the nation's economic plight to advance their own theories of how society should be organized. At the beginning of 1934, Roosevelt had believed that he could win support from both sides without embracing either's solution. By the end of the year, it was only beginning to become apparent that he could not stay on the course he had chosen and could count on nothing but opposition from the right. But he was not quite ready to commit himself to the path to the left.

In the first half of 1935, he made that choice. The result was a set of policies which gave government new powers to redistribute income and wealth and encouraged the establishment of new institutions—a militant union movement, a vastly expanded government bureaucracy—and a politics which divided voters along economic lines to an extent unprecedented in American history.

II

The choice was forced on Roosevelt by the failure of NRA. Politically, NRA was undoubtedly a success in the election of 1934. But economically, it had not succeeded in producing jobs or increasing output.[1] It had stabilized an economy which was spiraling dizzily downward, and it restored confidence in basic economic institutions. But it left the economy operating at an unsatisfactorily low level and hindered rather than stimulated recovery.[2] In his 1934 campaign speeches, Roosevelt liked to use economic statistics and constantly bragged about how much things had improved since 1933. But he understood that statistics cannot clinch a political argument or close a political sale if they don't ring true to the voter. The voters readily agreed with him that things were better than at the trough of the depression. But they were also aware that the economy had come nowhere close to rebounding to the peaks of the late 1920s. Gratitude for the rebound from the trough was enough to give the Democrats an unprecedented victory in 1934. But the voters of 1936 might hold the president responsible if he did not produce a rebound to the levels of 1929.

NRA was not only disappointing economically; it was threatened legally. On January 7, 1935, the Supreme Court struck down its "hot oil" provision, which had prohibited the sale of oil produced in excess of state production quotas set by the Texas Railroad Commission and other state agencies. The purpose of the measure was to prop up oil prices, and it was typical of NRA provisions which were attractive to businessmen; its overturning by an 8–1 vote as an impermissible delegation of legislative power to the executive branch must have alarmed businessmen who benefited from and supported NRA. The National Industrial Recovery Act delegated to hundreds of code authorities, made up of private businessmen and sometimes union leaders, the power to establish economic regulations and to punish infractions civilly and even bring criminal cases. Granting such responsibilities to non-governmental bodies was quite unprecedented in American history—and in fact was not tried again in the five decades following 1935. The administration had avoided a court test of NRA in 1933 and 1934, when it might have been defended more plausibly as an emergency measure. In March 1935 it flinched at the prospect, refusing to appeal an Alabama decision overturning the Lumber Code. But other cases were making their way through the lower courts, including a challenge to the Live Poultry Code, covering kosher chicken butchers in New York.

By this time NRS was in trouble politically as well. It was due to expire in June 1935 and so needed not merely the passive sufferance of Congress but the active support of majorities in both houses. On February 20, Roosevelt called for a two-year reauthorization of the National Industrial Recovery Act, a proposal which had the support of the U.S. Chamber of Commerce and the American

Federation of Labor. Some New Dealers remained deeply distrustful of free markets ("Industrial laissez-faire is unthinkable," said Raymond Moley) and insisted that the economy must continue to be organized by NRA codes. But even as strong a supporter of NRA as its deputy administrator Donald Richberg was making statements suggesting that the agency's goals were unattainable: "private business is not yet adequately organized for collective action and self-discipline."[3] This admission verged on recognition of the obvious: that for all the deficiencies of free markets, centralized regulation in the manner of NRA was unworkable. In Congress progressive Republicans led the battle against reauthorization, charging that big business was wielding NRA as a weapon for smiting its small competitors. Some members also recognized that by setting minimum prices and production limits, it retarded economic growth. NRA was declared unconstitutional by the Supreme Court in the "sick chicken" case on May 27, 1935. But by then it was already a political dead duck.

The problem not only for Roosevelt but for Congress was what to substitute in its place. The protracted depression had destroyed a faith in laissez faire capitalism which was in any case limited during most of the twentieth century in America, where politicians of both parties agreed that antitrust laws, safety and health regulations, and progressive taxation should restrict the operation of free markets. There was little confidence that the economy would revive of itself. Roosevelt's critics on the right called for lower government spending, balanced budgets, and an end to economic experimentation. But for those policies there was little support in the heavily Democratic Congress.

III

Then there were the critics generally considered to be on the left, of whom the most notable was Louisiana's Senator Huey P. Long. Most liberal Democrats and progressive Republicans in Congress were political allies of the Roosevelt administration, sometimes disappointed in what they considered the president's caution and timidity but usually sympathetic and seldom openly critical. Long was different—different from almost any other politician. He came from perhaps the most politically distinctive state: Louisiana, split between a Catholic south and a Baptist north, with a French heritage reflected in a tolerance of corruption and a lack of interest in civil liberties. Louisiana had one of the oldest cities in America and by far the largest metropolis in the South, New Orleans. It also had some of the most isolated countryside and was one of the poorest states in the nation. Brought up in a well-off home in the tiny town of Winnfield in northern Louisiana, Long was not himself deprived. A self-taught lawyer whose ability to sway juries soon made him a good living, he was an inspired speaker, brilliant and funny, never afraid to make himself look ridiculous and always ready to make his opponents do so. In 1928, after a brilliant campaign as a champion of the little man and opponent of the rich, he was elected governor at the age of thirty-five. Thereafter he dominated state government as no American governor ever had, singlehandedly ramming through the legislature any bills he liked, abolishing offices out from under opponents, and channeling vast sums of money to the projects he favored.

What was startling about his career was not his advocacy of "Every man a king"—dozens of small-time American political operators had been promising for fifty years to take money from the rich and give it to the poor. What was startling was that Long actually delivered on his promises. Within eighteen months of his taking office, the marshy and hardscrabble land of Louisiana was crisscrossed with paved roads; his impoverished Louisiana built more miles of roads in his term than any state except rich New York and huge Texas. The skyscraper Capitol and opulent governor's mansion he ordered for Baton Rouge were built within months, and so were the buildings of Louisiana State University. While Charles F. Murphy's Tammany Democrats were creating a welfare state in the richest of states, Huey Long was building roads and bridges and a university and schoolrooms and public health facilities in one of the poorest—and in an astonishingly short time.[4] Long got unalloyed support from the majority of Louisiana voters and bitter and unscrupulous opposition from many others. After-dinner conversation in polite Louisiana circles centered on the question of who would assassinate Huey.

Long had himself elected to the Senate in November 1930 but did not bother taking his seat until January 1932, when he wound up his term as governor; even afterwards he would walk into the legislative chambers back home, insist that his bills be passed without a single change, and always prevail. In Washington he wore pongee suits and pink ties; he kept his hat on while visiting Roosevelt at the White House, and at Hyde Park his loud rudeness prompted so polite a hostess as the president's mother, Sara Delano Roosevelt, to stage-whisper, "Who is that awful man sitting next to Franklin?" Long cared nothing for Senate etiquette and delighted in vicious attacks on powerful senators like Majority Leader Joseph Robinson and Finance Committee Chairman Pat Harrison.[5] His only friends in the Senate were progressives, like the longtime outsider George Norris and the often acerbic Burton Wheeler. With the public, on the other hand, his popularity went far beyond Louisiana: his campaigning elected the widow Hattie Carraway to the Senate seat held by her late husband in Arkansas in 1932, and his speeches and attacks filled the Senate galleries.

In February 1934, Long made a national radio broadcast to announce his Share Our Wealth Society, the latest version of the economic redistribution plans he had championed for years. He called for confiscation of family wealth over $5 million and of income over $1 million a year; the proceeds would be used to provide each family with a $5,000 house and a $2,000 or $3,000 annual income and to fund old-age pensions, free college educations, and a thirty-hour workweek.[6] This was the most elaborate of several wealth-sharing programs echoing in the politics of 1934. Another came from Father Charles Coughlin, the radio priest whose rich, mellifluous voice was broadcast to millions of Americans from the WJR studios at the top of the ornate Fisher Building in Detroit or from his own Shrine of the Little Flower church in suburban Royal Oak. Coughlin, who wanted to inflate the currency with silver, spoke with fury and vitriol, and by 1935 he was turning to the anti-semitism which eventually got him taken off the air by Detroit's Cardinal Mooney. But in the meantime he had one of the largest audiences in radio and was a frequent uninvited visitor at the White House. A milder crusader, Dr. Francis Townsend, from his small retirement home in Long Beach, California, called for a 2% national sales tax to raise money for old-age pensions of $200 a month which would have to be spent within a month. Not far away, in Beverly Hills, Upton Sinclair was winning the 1934 Democratic nomination for governor of California with his EPIC plan to have the government buy land and rent factories where the unemployed could raise their own food and produce their own clothes.[7] Calls for the redistribution of wealth and harebrained schemes for making every man rich had long been heard in American politics. But they had usually been weak and quickly wafted away. In the middle 1930s, however, in a country with an apparently failed economy and a changed political system, they were being heard more loudly than ever before. The new Congress was an unknown quantity, and so was the new electorate which would vote in 1936. Franklin Roosevelt and the Democratic party had obvious political incentives to adopt policies of economic redistribution.

IV

In his 1935 State of the Union message, delivered January 4—for the 22nd Amendment was now in effect, and Congress went into session only eight weeks after it was elected—Roosevelt called for a $4.8 billion work relief program. This was an astonishing sum of money—more than the entire revenue of the federal government in 1933 or 1934. It also represented a huge increase in the federal debt, for Roosevelt proposed to borrow all but $880 million; in effect, this would be a redistribution of money not only from the rich to the poor, but also from the future to the present. And it would vastly increase the public payroll. In the winter of 1933–34, Hopkins's CWA had put more than 4 million people to work, but CWA was temporary and gone by spring. Now Roosevelt seemed to be calling for permanent federal work relief. Yet his rhetoric was defensive. Later in the year pollster Elmo Roper found that 77% of Americans agreed that "the government should see to it that every man who wants to work has a job."[8] But Roosevelt attacked the dole as "a narcotic, a subtle destroyer of the human spirit"; he promised there would be no "leaf raking"; he assured Americans, 75% of whom preferred the government to create jobs than simply give cash payments to the poor,[9] that "the Federal Government must and shall quit this business of relief." But in the meantime there were 10 million Americans still out of work, most of them men able and eager to work; and Roosevelt was determined to put perhaps one third of them on the federal payroll.

Congress and presumably the public were receptive. But in February a combination of conservative senators and allies of labor unions adopted an amendment requiring the government to pay local prevailing wages in its relief programs. This standard would have sharply reduced the number of men who could be given relief, and Roosevelt was willing to kill the bill rather than allow it. In March, however, the Senate reversed itself and passed the bill without the amendment, leaving Roosevelt with almost total discretion in spending almost $5 billion—an unprecedented abdication of authority from Congress to the president. In April work relief became law, a major expansion of the public sector.

The second major administration initiative was the Social Security bill proposed January 17. It included not just old-age insurance, which is what "Social Security" quickly came to mean to most Americans, but also unemployment insurance and aid for dependent children; the latter was then considered a minor item intended to help young widows, who were nearly always financially distressed.[10] Roosevelt had declined to endorse the Dill–Connery old-age insurance and Wagner–Lewis unemployment insurance bills in 1934, but he had set up a committee of cabinet members headed by Labor Secretary Frances Perkins which met starting in the summer of 1934 and hammered out agreement on a bill by the end of the year. Of old New England stock, tied to an unhappy marriage, Perkins shared many of the qualities and attitudes of Eleanor Roosevelt—including unflappable persistence. She looked politically naive and passive, but she was a shrewd assessor of political possibilities and personalities, and she was ready to take the opportunities afforded by the new politics of the 1930s to get government do things which would have been financially easier but politically impossible in the prosperous 1920s. She could get tough when she needed to. When the committee members were deadlocked on unemployment insurance, she wrote later, "finally, one day during Christmas week, 1934, I issued an ultimatum that the Committee would meet at eight o'clock at my house, that all telephone service would be discontinued at my house for the evening, and that we would sit all night, if necessary, until we decided the thorny question once and for all. We sat until two in the morning, and at the end we agreed."[11]

The result was a bill with a curious amalgam of measures. Old-age insurance was to be a compulsory national program, but with benefits depending on the size of "contributions" (the Social Security word for tax) and with some low-wage workers left uncovered. Unemployment insurance was to be a joint federal–state program, with decisions about the level and duration of benefits and taxes to be made, within limits, by the states. Both plans were concessions to the sensibilities of most Americans and of Roosevelt, who hated anything which smacked of "the dole" and preferred old-age pensions which were in some sense earned and unemployment insurance which took account of the vast differences within the American labor market. The payroll tax which financed Social Security was attacked as regressive and seemed sure to drain money out of the economy and into a trust fund in the deflationary 1930s, but Roosevelt insisted on keeping it in, since it gave voters a stake in the program. Roosevelt and the band of experts who put together the program and set up its administration—including leaders like J. Douglas Brown and Arthur Altmyer and young staffers like Robert Ball, Wilbur Cohen, and Robert Myers—were operating on a long-range blueprint to create a peculiarly American form of social insurance, which proved to be permanently rooted in American soil.[12] The bill was changed somewhat in the House Ways and Means Committee (whose most influential member was Fred Vinson, a canny Kentucky Democrat and a Roosevelt loyalist) and passed by a wide margin on April 19. It was reported out of the Senate Finance Committee on May 13, and after languishing without floor action for weeks, finally passed in August.

Initially the taxes and benefits were low, the increase in the size of the American public sector minimal. The first benefits were not paid out till 1940 and were modest compared with the contributions. But Roosevelt nevertheless insisted that the system be financed without resort to general revenues, even in distant future projections; and he insisted on maintaining an expensive bureaucracy to keep track of the amounts individual taxpayers put in so that they could find out how much was in their "account"—thus nourishing, as Republicans pointed out, the illusion that Social Security was insurance. As Roosevelt explained to one administrator, "That account is not useless. That account is not to determine how much should get paid out and to control what should be paid out. That account is there so those sons of bitches up on the Hill can't ever abandon this system when I'm gone."[13] Four years after the system was set up, at a time when other New Deal programs were being scaled back, the financing mechanism was changed to prevent the buildup of huge reserves; in later years, Social Security was expanded again and again, in a process patiently guided by some of those who had helped set up the system. As Franklin Roosevelt intended, a major American institution had been established: in the view of most Americans, their government was enabling them to guarantee themselves a certain measure of security for their old age.

V

While Congress was rushing to pass the work relief bill and pondering Social Security, political controversy started heating up over the airwaves. On the evening of March 4, 1935, some of the nation's most prominent men—Owen Young of General Electric and John L. Lewis of the United Mine Workers, financier Bernard Baruch and New Deal intellectual Rexford Tugwell—climbed out of limousines on New York's Park Avenue and walked in their white ties and tails into the light gray mass of the new Waldorf Astoria Hotel, crowned by forty-seven–story chrome-topped Art Deco towers. After cocktails and an elegant dinner, they sat in the ballroom and watched as General Hugh Johnson, the long-embattled head of NRA, rose to the NBC microphones. Johnson had been busy promoting his forthcoming book *The Blue Eagle From Egg to Earth;* but instead of dwelling on the past and his departure from the administration, he looked to the future and launched an attack on Huey Long and Father Coughlin. They were appealing to an "emotional fringe," offering choices which would lead to "chaos and destruction," entering into an "open alliance" against the president, Johnson warned. "You can laugh at Father Coughlin, you can snort at Huey Long—but this country was never under a greater menace."[14]

Seven years after Franklin Roosevelt had tailored his nominating speech for Al

Smith to this new medium, the rousing radio speech had come to be the basic medium of political communication. Long and Coughlin demanded free time from NBC to respond. The radio priest flinched at taking on Roosevelt explicitly and said he still supported him,[15] but Long was unrestrained in taking the offensive and offering an alternative to Roosevelt's New Deal. Speaking to 25 million people, his largest audience ever, on March 7, Long refrained from the personal attacks he indulged in on the Senate floor and spent 40 minutes explaining his Share Our Wealth plan. Then he began stumping around the country. He spoke to a crowd of 15,000 in traditionally Republican Philadelphia a few days later. He made a whirlwind tour of South Carolina, the most solidly Democratic part of the solid South, later in the month, enrolling 60,000 South Carolinians in Share Our Wealth Clubs and getting 140,000 to check off "I will" on a card asking whether or not they would vote for Huey Long for president—this in a state where only 104,000 people had voted in November 1932. After ramming a batch of laws through the legislature in Baton Rouge and poking fun at administration leaders from the Senate floor, he went on April 27 to the Iowa State Fairground in Des Moines, where he spoke to a crowd of 10,000 and got almost all of them to raise their hands when he asked who believed in Share Our Wealth. "I could win this state in a whirlwind," he said.[16] In February, Long had helped inflict two legislative defeats on Roosevelt, preventing U.S. participation in the World Court and getting the prevailing wage amendment adopted, and had initiated an embarrassing investigation of alleged (and nonexistent) corruption in James Farley's Post Office Department.[17] Now, as he was beginning to dictate a manuscript he called *My First Days in the White House,* Long was giving a dazzling demonstration of his ability to sway voters in almost every significant political region, in the Union Heartland, the Solid South, and the Progressive Northwest—a demonstration which was surely not lost on the man in the White House.

Nor was it lost on James Farley. In 1935, polls conducted among random samples were not yet part of American politics. George Gallup did not publish his first presidential poll until October 1935, and publications and politicians alike relied on straw polls and mail surveys about the accuracy of whose results Farley was intelligently skeptical.[18] Farley was a traditional politician from a small town on the Hudson River, who traveled across the country in the early 1930s allegedly as an officer of the Benevolent and Protective Order of Elks but in fact as the promoter of presidential candidate Franklin D. Roosevelt. He had a brilliant memory for names and kept up one of the largest correspondences in American politics, always signing his name in green ink. This was still a time when long-distance telephone calls were difficult to place and to hear clearly and were not yet standard operating procedure even in a business as important as electing a president. As late as 1936, Farley based his uncannily accurate estimate of the electoral college results on letters "not a week old" from 2,500 political leaders, supplemented only on the last day of the campaign with telephone calls only "to every state leader north of the Mason and Dixon line."[19]

But Farley was open to innovation; and sometime between April 15 and May

15, 1935, he asked a Democratic National Committee statistician, Emil Hurja, to conduct a poll, the results of which convinced him that "the president is weaker that [*sic*] at any time since inauguration."[20] Still, Farley was predicting that if Long did not run, Roosevelt would be elected by a 5-million-vote plurality; if turnout was at 1932 levels, that would mean a 55%–42% margin, a Roosevelt showing 2 percentage points lower than in 1932. Either that poll or one taken around May 24[21] indicated to Farley that Long would win 3 to 4 million votes, 7% to 10% of the total, and would run uniformly in all regions of the country. "It was easy," Farley wrote later, "to conceive a situation whereby Long, by polling more than 3,000,000 votes, might have the balance of power in the 1936 election." Farley said the poll showed Long could take 100,000 votes in New York. "Take that number of votes away from either major candidate, and they would come mostly from our side, and the result might spell disaster."[22] Although the Long poll is sometimes said to have inspired a shift to the left by Roosevelt in May and June 1935, that relationship is unlikely. The results may not have been obtained until after May 15 and may not have been reported to Roosevelt until as late as June 18,[23] and there is no reason to think Roosevelt took the infant science of polling as infallible any more than Farley did. Nor did the results dictate the strategy Roosevelt followed. Farley himself discounted the idea "that the real opposition would come from the "left," and his strategy for handling Long was to give state and city Democratic leaders some patronage jobs in the work relief program Roosevelt was busy setting up in early May.[24] But Roosevelt's instincts probably told him as early as March that Long was threatening to cut into his support, and that he would have to counter that threat. The evidence suggests that he was working hard at doing so well before any of Farley's polls were taken.

By April, Roosevelt was already superintending progress on the Social Security bill, a public utilities holding company bill, and Federal Reserve Chairman Marriner Eccles's bank legislation. These were three of the four bills he designated as "must legislation" in June, in what is taken as the inauguration of the so-called Second New Deal; but in fact all of them had been endorsed by the president in January or February. And beginning April 8 he was also busy organizing, as Congress had given him full power to do, the nearly $5 billion work relief program. That day he ordered continuation of the Civilian Conservation Corps. On May 1 he set up the Resettlement Agency, to be headed by Rexford Tugwell, who wanted to leave the Agriculture Department because Henry Wallace had fired several liberal aides for trying to regulate southern sharecropper arrangements. On May 6 he established the Works Project Administration, to be headed by Harry Hopkins, which starting in November and all through 1936 employed between 3 and 4 million Americans. On May 14 he set up the Rural Electrification Administration, which within a decade brought electricity to most American farms.

The problem Roosevelt faced in May was what to do about NRA, which was scheduled to expire June 16. In March the Senate had come within ten votes of passing, as an amendment to the work relief bill, a rider killing all NRA industrial codes. On May 2 the Senate Labor Committee reported out the Wagner labor bill, a strengthened version of the portions of NRA which encouraged and protected labor unions, over the opposition of the administration, which still clung to the hope that the whole of NRA could be renewed. That same day the Supreme Court, sitting for its last term in the domed, white-columned, mahogany-furnished Old Senate Chamber in the Capitol, heard oral argument in the Schechter Poultry "sick chicken" case. And that same week the U.S. Chamber of Commerce was meeting in its marble-columned fortress-like headquarters across Lafayette Square from the White House. The Chamber had supported NRA for two years. But now it was concerned about "encroachment of government into business fields as a competitor of private enterprise"; and it had whipped itself into a lather of opposition to Hugo Black's 30-hour workweek bill, the Wagner labor bill, and Roosevelt's public utilities holding company bill.[25] Two years before the Chamber had welcomed NRA as a substitute for the 30-hour workweek. Now it appeared that Congress was about to pass the Wagner bill and to gut NRA of the provisions favorable to big business. The response of the Chamber on May 4 was to oppose all of the administration's economic proposals, in particular the renewal of NRA and the Wagner bill.

What the Chamber feared quickly happened. After seven weeks of hearings in the Senate Finance Committee, Chairman Pat Harrison, a canny, long-nosed, pot-bellied Mississippian, brought to the floor on May 14 a bill renewing NRA only until April 1, 1936, long before the 1936 election, and banning price-fixing by businesses except for natural minerals extraction—a sop to the coal industry and John L. Lewis. Two days later the Senate voted on the Wagner bill, which was still opposed by the Roosevelt administration.

VI

This was a bill which would not have come forward except for the persistence, creativity, and political canniness of Robert F. Wagner. An immigrant from southern Germany, who came to New York in 1886 at age nine speaking only German, Wagner was by 1935 one of the most experienced and skillful legislators in American politics. Much of his early success he owed to the Tammany Hall leader he always called, even among members of his family, Mr. Murphy.[26] His early life was rough, but he excelled at school, and his brother, a cook at the New York Athletic Club, got him a job as bellhop there so he could afford to attend City College. He led his class there and at New York Law School, established law practice in his German-American neighborhood of Yorkville around East 86th Street, and was elected to the New York Assembly as a Tammany supporter in 1904 at age twenty-seven. After the Democratic victory of 1910, Murphy, with his keen eye for talent and little regard for seniority, made the thirty-three-year-old Wagner party leader in the state Senate and the thirty-seven-year-old Al Smith speaker of the Assembly. The following year it was Wagner who became chairman and Smith vice chairman of the committee investigating the Triangle Shirtwaist Company fire. The legislation resulting from that fire was one of the beginnings of the American welfare state, and it justified Wagner's description of Murphy's Tammany Hall as "the cradle of modern liberalism in America."

Over the next decade and a half, Wagner met with his political disappointments and personal tragedy. As a German-American, he was passed over for mayor of New York in 1917 when his patriotism was questioned by the supposedly high-minded reformer incumbent, John Purroy Mitchel; and in 1918, Smith rather than Wagner became the Democratic candidate for governor. That year Wagner's wife became paralyzed, and a year later she died. He then left politics to become a judge for eight years—a hiatus which enabled him to raise his son, the future mayor of New York. It was only when Robert Wagner, Jr., was approaching college age that Wagner ran for the Senate, and he won only because a Prohibitionist candidate took upstate votes away from the wet Republican incumbent.

His conviction that government had a responsibility to help the unfortunate was strong. "My boyhood was a pretty rough passage. I came through it, yes. But that was luck, luck, luck! Think of the others!"[27] Yet he never depended on sentiment to sway his colleagues. He was a natural legislator, a pleasant man of unstinting perseverance who could take the most outlandish of proposals and support it year after year, presenting reams of factual evidence in open hearings and asking genially but persistently for support in the lobbies. His views may have been unusual, but he quickly became identified as a member of the Senate's inner club.[28] Politically, he was fearless. Like most senators in those days, he had no higher ambitions (born abroad, he couldn't be president anyway); and he did not care much about his reelection chances. Tammany would take care of him, and he could make plenty of money in private law practice. He did little electioneering and concentrated instead on putting together a brilliant staff. Indeed, he virtually invented the congressional staff. When he became senator in 1927, he hired as his secretary—one of only three staff positions—a twenty-five-year-old Columbia Law School graduate named Simon Rifkind, later a federal judge and then from the 1950s to the 1980s one of the nation's most brilliant legal practitioners. Another secretary was Leon Keyserling, later head of President Truman's Council of Economic Advisers.[29]

"In large part," writes his biographer J. Joseph Huthmacher, "Bob's pleasant demeanor toward his senatorial peers was a natural reflection of his personality, and he manifested the same manner in his relations with friends, newspapermen, and even strangers. Yet when he had an important bill pending, his ingratiating qualities seemed to activate themselves, perhaps unconsciously, to the point where they became a potent element in the lawmaking process. Simon Rifkind remembers being 'fascinated' by the 'transformation' Wagner underwent at those times, and he marveled at the dexterity with which his boss carried out his part, 'like a great actor who has absorbed a role.' The New Yorker would become unusually sociable with his colleagues and uncommonly solicitous about their affairs, inquiring of the key figures about everything ranging from the bills they themselves had introduced to the status of their golf scores."[30] Unlike some later liberals, he was neither politically naive nor personally ascetic. He lived in a high-rise building, his windows almost always cut off from the sun by the buildings on every side, in the Yorkville neighborhood where he had grown up; but it was only two or three blocks from the rich Upper East Side neighborhood which clung to Central Park and not far from Gracie Mansion, the mayor's residence on the East River. He enjoyed golf and the opera and the life of a prosperous New York lawyer who took trips with his son back to his ancestral Germany each summer. "While I was up there," Keyserling recalled, "the press took a vote, and Wagner was voted the best-dressed man in the Senate, the most popular man in the Senate, the ablest man in the Senate, the most useful man in the Senate, and the one most helpful to the press, all at the same time."[31]

Wagner always based his arguments before Congress on facts, scouring the Library of Congress and the recently established Brookings Institution for evidence that government action was needed. He marshaled statistics by the hundreds and could translate them into human terms. He was a brilliant nose-counter, and he knew that in a Senate with ninety-six members he was one of only a half-dozen or so who believed in government economic intervention and civil liberties. In that forum he had to argue his cases on the facts, not the law, on data, not theories. But he knew his law as well as his facts, and his work was always guided by coherent theory. Much more explicitly than Roosevelt and those around him, Wagner believed that the depression resulted from underconsumption in the 1920s, that the Republican tax cuts had given more to the rich than they could usefully invest and less to the great mass of citizens than they needed to be good consumers. He favored a floor under wages, a ceiling on hours, restrictions on child labor, and strong labor unions to help buoy up wages. He believed in government-run social insurance to give citizens security and dignity. He was a Keynesian well before Keynes published his general theory in 1936, and a believer in the Gardiner Means–Adolph Berle thesis—that corporations were run by managers, not owners, and that government and unions should be set up to be countervailing powers to giant corporations and work together to administer the economy—before Means and Berle published *The Modern Corporation and Private Property* in 1932. Where Roosevelt was guided by his improvising instincts, Wagner was guided by his own American vision of countervailing powers and a welfare state. He was the chief sponsor of the National Industrial Recovery Act in 1933, of the Social Security bill in 1934 and 1935, of every major housing bill before Congress for twenty years.

To the task of passing the labor bill Wagner brought an array of arguments. To the progressives he argued that the bill was a strengthening of the Section 7(a) he had inserted into NIRA to promote unionization, without the obnoxious price-fixing and pro-monopoly features of NRA. To the conservatives he argued that the bill would regularize labor–management relations and prevent violent picketing and crippling strikes. The nation had been alarmed in July 1934 when a strike of 12,000 members of the longshoremen's union headed by Communist-sympathizer Harry Bridges led to a general strike in San Francisco, with echoes of class warfare not heard in the United States since the unnerving years after World War I.

Americans began to fear nationwide labor violence as news came in of bloody strikes in Minneapolis and Toledo, Wisconsin and Rhode Island as well. But actually Wagner had been so successful in building a consensus for his bill that in the end he did not have to argue much at all. The key vote came May 16, on an amendment by Millard Tydings, the stylish old-fashioned Democrat from Maryland. It was rejected 50–21, and Wagner had more votes to spare. The Wagner Act, which transformed American labor–management relations, promptly passed the Senate 63–12.

VII

On May 14, after the Senate had passed the makeshift NRA extension and as it was poised to consider the labor bill, Roosevelt spent the evening with six progressive senators and four of his own advisors—Ickes and Wallace, Professor Felix Frankfurter and Boston liberal David Niles, Roosevelt's informal liaison to American Jews—who had ties with the old Progressive movement. Burton Wheeler, Robert LaFollette's running mate on the 1924 Progressive line, attacked Roosevelt for betraying the liberal cause and trying to appease businessmen; Robert LaFollette, Jr., praised the president's "fine legislative program" and said it was the "best answer" to Huey Long.[32] Roosevelt did not follow the progressives' program completely. He took the unprecedented step of going before the House on May 22 to veto the Patman veterans' bonus bill and had the satisfaction of seeing the Senate uphold the veto the next day, even though Congress had overridden both his and Herbert Hoover's vetoes of earlier bonuses. He approved the reporting of the Wagner bill to the floor of the House on May 19, though it probably would have gone forward anyway, and he finally endorsed it explicitly on May 24—not a moment too soon, since it was about to pass.

The next Monday, May 27, came a bombshell. The Supreme Court ruled NRA unconstitutional, and by a 9–0 vote. Schechter Brothers, a kosher butcher in Brooklyn, had violated the act's Live Poultry Code, partly because it prohibited giving customers their choice of chickens (if they wanted fewer than a dozen, they had to be selected at random)[33] and partly because it required Schechter to break the Jewish dietary laws—a classic illustration of how difficult it was to write codes to regulate a complex economy in a huge, diverse country. The court based its ruling on two findings: first, that Schechter wasn't in interstate commerce, and second, that the whole NRA scheme was "delegation running riot." In a carefully staged press conference May 31, Roosevelt emphasized the first ground and called it a "horse and buggy" decision. Pretty much everything, he argued plausibly, is in interstate commerce now. But on delegation, the court had a point—one which was arguably still good law fifty years later.[34] Roosevelt could decry horse and buggy jurisprudence, but he needed to come up with his own design for a modern vehicle.

This he did in June. On June 4, eight days after the Schechter decision, Roosevelt urged Congress not to adjourn (which it was not about to do anyway) but to pass four measures he described now as "musts." One was Social Security, overwhelmingly passed by the House in April and promptly passed by the Senate in June. The second was the Wagner Act, passed in the Senate overwhelmingly in May and then, with Roosevelt's support, passed by voice vote—an astonishingly casual response to such an important matter—by the House in June. The third and fourth were the public utilities holding company bill and the Eccles banking bill; and it was on the precise terms of these measures—of crucial importance in technical legislation of this kind—that most of the suspense hung during the Second Hundred Days, which ended when Congress was adjourned August 27. The final version of the public utility bill, which was fiercely lobbied, did not include the "death sentence" provision requiring breakup of holding companies by 1940, though as things worked out most of the big companies (including Commonwealth Southern, whose chief executive was an Indiana-born Wall Street lawyer named Wendell Willkie)[35] were broken up. The banking bill was mostly rewritten by Senator Carter Glass; and control over the Federal Reserve System was definitely not given to the White House, as Roosevelt would have liked.

Then, on June 19, Roosevelt added a fifth measure to the must list: a progressive tax law, including estate and gift taxes, a graduated corporate income tax, and sharply graduated taxes on high personal incomes. More than any other measure, this one is what made so many rich people consider Roosevelt a traitor to his class. As time went on, Roosevelt became a more and more fervent believer in progressive taxation. Actually, he was not a millionaire himself. His mother kept close control of most of the family money until her death in September 1941, and Roosevelt tied up most of his own small capital in the Warm Springs, Georgia, spa which proved (like almost all his business ventures) to be an unprofitable investment. Roosevelt always had enough money to live in a way he thought proper, to have household help and send his children to the right schools. But his home at Hyde Park was a comfortable, old-shoe country house for a large and noisy family, not one of the marble palaces suited only for formal entertainment like the Vanderbilt and Ogden Mills mansions not far north on the Hudson.[36] If he always dressed in custom-tailored suits and expensive woolen sweaters, they were often tattered and wrinkled. If he enjoyed a cocktail or two before dinner and knew that one "ought not to serve domestic champagne," his kitchen always prepared notoriously bad food.[37] One senses that Roosevelt saw no reason that anyone needed to live more luxuriously than he did,[38] and that he felt incomes and wealth above the levels of his own should be used to help ordinary people, not to make obscene extravagance possible for a few—an opinion which was by no means as widely shared as his impulses to provide help to the destitute and jobs to the unemployed.[39] In any case, the tax bill was his clear answer to Huey Long's cry to Share Our Wealth. After some tinkering by Congress, which cut some taxes but increased the highest individual bracket to 75%, the bill was passed by large margins. The final bit of Second Hundred Days legislation was the Guffey–Snyder bituminous coal bill, which froze into law the old NRA Code as fixed by John L. Lewis and the big mining companies.

In a letter to newspaper publisher Roy Howard in September, after Congress had adjourned, Roosevelt called for a "breathing spell." No more major legislation would be passed by this 74th Congress. Enough had been done already. A new set of national policies had been established, and a new set of national institutions created. And a politics of economic distribution had come into being. These events happened not as the result of some single plan, but not entirely by accident, either. Roosevelt evidently would have liked to continue the cooperative, broker-state approach of NRA. But he began the year committed to a work relief program which would make the federal government the nation's largest employer for the rest of the decade and to a program of social insurance which, when it came to be expanded as its makers hoped, expected, and planned for it to be, provided protection against unemployment and a base of income for old age. He was committed early to measures which would centralize bank regulation and break the power of the big utility holding companies, affecting some of the biggest American financial interests. And when NRA started foundering he was ready to support the Wagner labor bill, which was intended to and did create labor unions as major economic institutions. Finally, he produced America's first peacetime system of progressive taxation.

Roosevelt's decisions produced not only new public policies but a new political strategy. "What Mr. Roosevelt has done," wrote the *Baltimore Sun*'s Frank Kent at the beginning of 1936, "is adopt neither Democratic nor Republican policies, but rather he has taken over the policies of that small group of so-called Progressive Republicans, typified by Senator Norris of Nebraska"—whom Roosevelt conspicuously endorsed, against a Democrat, in 1936—"and Senator LaFollette of Wisconsin."[40] Roosevelt was trying to put together his long-dreamed-of coalition of LaFollette Progressives, Jeffersonian Democrats, and Al Smith Catholics, and add to them the blue-collar workers who had followed John L. Lewis's lead and supported the New Deal in the coal, steel, and auto states in 1934. Roosevelt had won the 1934 off-year election with that coalition by framing the choice as order versus chaos, the stabilization which NRA supplied versus the spiraling downward chaos which seemed to be the natural result of free markets. But for 1936, with chaos vanquished, voters seemed sure to demand something more than order. In May 1935, Roosevelt was abandoned and reviled by business and the rich and was in danger of being outflanked by wealth-redistributors like Huey Long, though the threat from Long abruptly evaporated when he was shot September 8, 1935, in the marble halls of his Capitol in Baton Rouge, and died two days later after his doctors botched his treatment. He had to choose between policies which would produce an economic redistribution and create new economic institutions and policies which would let free markets operate and give established economic powers their way. In May and June 1935, Franklin Roosevelt made his choice and never looked back. The result was a politics of economic conflict which developed immediately afterwards and continued for the next twelve years with a force diminished only by the threat and then the reality of total war.

13

→)) ((←

Rendezvous

The economic politics that emerged from the policy struggles of 1935 resulted in an overwhelming victory for Franklin Roosevelt and his Democrats in the 1936 elections—a victory greater than any American political party had ever won before or would ever win afterward. The Democrats suddenly seemed to be the nation's natural majority party. Yet they never came close to repeating their 1936 victory in Franklin Roosevelt's lifetime and did so only once, nearly three decades later, in the different circumstances of 1964. The 1936 landslide appeared to vindicate Roosevelt's economic politics. But this election, like all elections, was a choice made at a particular time, in circumstances that could never be precisely replicated.

An understanding of 1936 and its sequels requires not only an appreciation of Roosevelt's strengths as a candidate and a leader but also an awareness of the two new forces in American politics which came into being in the 1930s in response to his policies of economic redistribution and over the next two decades did much to determine election outcomes and public policy in the United States. Those two forces were the new conservative movement, ideological and originally bipartisan, and the industrial labor movement. Both arose early in Roosevelt's first term— the right with the formation of the Liberty League in 1934, the unions in response to Section 7(a) of the National Industrial Recovery Act—but both gained great force and momentum from the economic policies embraced by Roosevelt and passed by Congress in the first eight months of 1935.

II

No American politician grew up more distant from his fellow Americans or had a greater interest in them than Franklin Roosevelt. His attempts to recover from polio surely made this once physically vigorous man more compassionate and transformed an affable but originally haughty politician into one intensely curious about his fellow citizens. His cheerfulness may have looked like sheer ebullience and friendliness, but it was the result of an iron self-discipline that he seems to have developed in his battle against polio and which he seldom, if ever, relaxed. Arthur Schlesinger, Jr., in a superb analysis of Roosevelt's character, quotes Rexford Tugwell as saying, "It was part of his conception of his role that he should

94

never show exhaustion, boredom, or irritation," and a career White House employee as saying, "he never failed to present himself as the leading actor on whatever stage was available at the moment."[1] Certainly his curiosity seems to have increased as his personal mobility was reduced. When one former appointee, the wealthy James P. Warburg, criticized his policies in *The Money Muddle,* Roosevelt urged him to write a second edition, but only after he had traveled around the United States in old clothes and a secondhand car, "undertaking beforehand not to speak on the entire trip with any banker or business executive (except gas stand owners), and to put up at no hotel where [he had] to pay more than $1.50 a night."[2] It sounds as if Roosevelt would have liked to have made the trip himself. He enjoyed traveling around the country in trains going under 35 miles per hour, so that he could take in the scenery, and he was always asking about audiences' responses to movies. Roosevelt's opponents approached the 1936 elections speaking in abstractions, about constitutional limitations and individual liberty and free enterprise. Roosevelt approached them speaking in the language of ordinary people about things they had seen firsthand.

And by 1936 the New Deal had made real changes in the lives of millions of Americans. More than 9 million were still unemployed in 1936, but that figure was down from nearly 13 million in 1933, and the number of Americans with jobs had risen from 38 million to 44.5 million—a 16% rise in three years. The new government programs had touched a very large percentage—perhaps a majority—of American families. Four million mortgages had been refinanced by HOLC. Millions of bank accounts were protected by deposit insurance. Over 2.5 million young people had worked in the Civilian Conservation Corps. Harry Hopkins's CWA and WPA had employed, at one time or another, perhaps 10 million Americans. The Agricultural Adjustment Act, ruled unconstitutional in January 1936 and reenacted as a second AAA in February, had touched a large majority of the 25% of American who lived on farms. For two crucial years NRA had raised wages, limited working hours, and promoted membership in independent unions for millions. Social Security would not pay out its first pension until 1940, but it already affected Americans' lives as they realized that they and their parents could depend on some income in their old age. By June 1936, 53% of Americans polled by *Fortune* magazine thought the depression was over or partly over; 40% said they had become better off over the past two or three years, while only 31% said they were worse off.[3] President Hoover's most venturesome and intrusive anti-depression measure, RFC, had a major economic impact during his administration and later. But it touched ordinary people only indirectly and invisibly. In contrast, President Roosevelt's anti-depression measures touched individuals in a very direct way.

The New Deal changed American life by changing the relationship between Americans and their government. In 1930 the federal government consumed less than 4% of the gross national product; except for the Post Office, it was remote from the life of ordinary people. By 1936 the federal government consumed 9% of GNP and through WPA employed 7% of the work force; it was a living presence across the country. Sometimes—especially through NRA—it was an officious intermeddler. But more often, to millions of people, it was a helper and a friend. Americans no longer had reason to fear fear itself. They no longer had reason to fear, as they did when Franklin Roosevelt took office in March 1933, that the currency would stop circulating, that the economy would keep spiraling downward, that having grown used to an ever-rising standard of living, they would suddenly have to worry about the basics of food and shelter. By late 1935, 31% of Americans surveyed by *Fortune* felt that "Roosevelt's reelection is essential for the good of the country," and another 29% conceded that he "may have made mistakes but there is no one else who can do as much good"—a resounding vote of confidence from 60% of the electorate.[4]

III

"In the summer of 1933," said Franklin Roosevelt during the 1936 campaign, "a nice old gentleman wearing a silk hat fell off the end of a pier. He was unable to swim. A friend ran down the pier, dived overboard and pulled him out; but the silk hat floated out with the tide. After the old gentleman had been revived, he was effusive in his thanks. He praised his friend for saving his life. Today, three years later, the old gentleman is berating his friend because the silk hat was lost." So, with a characteristically aqueous metaphor, did Roosevelt explain the vitriolic right-wing opposition he and his New Deal were encountering.

The self-conscious right began to emerge in the summer of 1934, when the Liberty League was formed by old Democrats like Al Smith and John W. Davis and prominent businessmen like Pierre du Pont and E. F. Hutton, even though Roosevelt was still governing and campaigning as a non-partisan national unifier. Such a movement was hardly necessary in the 1920s or earlier, when government intervention in the economy of the dimensions of the New Deal was, outside of wartime, undreamed of. There was no conservative movement in the 1920s any more than there was an *ancien régime* ideology in France before 1789; the premises of the old regime needed defending not when they were taken for granted by almost everyone but after they had been challenged and overthrown by revolution. "The modern right," writes Clinton Rossiter in his study of American conservatism, "is essentially a posture of anti-radicalism, even of anti-progressivism—a many-sided yet integral reaction to the New Deal, its leader, and his political heirs. . . ."[5] Up through 1930 most politicians of both parties had opposed the sort of policies Roosevelt adopted. So it should not have been surprising that old-time politicians of both parties opposed the New Deal. Even before 1935, Roosevelt's policies were opposed by all the living presidential nominees of both parties except his ticket-mate of 1920, James Cox, who was lukewarm in his support. Among the great publishers, they were opposed vitriolically not only by Republican Colonel Robert McCormick of the *Chicago Tribune* but also by Democrat William Randolph Hearst, who had helped clinch the 1932 nomination for Roosevelt but soon turned against him. These leaders reflected much larger constituencies. The traditional American political parties had always included large numbers of affluent as well as impoverished voters in their ranks: the rich in the South were overwhelmingly Democratic, and Franklin Roosevelt's father was far from the only gentleman farmer in the North who belonged to the party of Jefferson and Jackson (who were both rich landowners themselves). Now the rich were swinging heavily to the Republicans; or if they clung, as many southerners did, to their Democratic identification, they expressed a grudging and sometimes bitter attitude toward the president and his administration.

The vigor of this opposition seems to have surprised Roosevelt and still mystifies many of his admirers.[6] Why was the old man so worried about his silk hat? Simple greed? Or a hunger for the respect he had enjoyed in the prosperous 1920s? Surely these were factors, but there were also substantive and disinterested reasons. NRA and other New Deal policies could be seen as an attempt to squeeze profits in order to produce higher wages and lower prices—an attempt to use government's awesome powers to take money belonging to the rich and give it to the poor. Roosevelt in 1934 was interpreting NRA in just that way himself. At a time when states were suspending debtors' obligations to pay their creditors and the prospects for economic growth seemed dim, the rich were alert to any signs that the government was about to redistribute income and wealth. Some of their resistance was simply selfish. They did not want to be left with a smaller share of a shrinking pie. Some of it was animated by principle. They had learned from precept and experience that a free economy, in which government enforced contracts and maintained a sound currency and otherwise left things pretty much alone, produced fabulous economic growth which in the long run helped everyone. They had learned from the British dole that handouts sapped initiative. They had learned from the American and French Revolutions that a currency undisciplined by gold led to economic ruin. They believed the depression was an aberration which soon would end—or would have ended already but for Roosevelt's policies. His critics were chided for not embracing the twentieth century. But they had some reason to say that they and the principles they defended had produced the affluence and freedom of twentieth-century American life.

The fear of a "dictatorship" which they constantly voiced was not just a smokescreen put up by selfish interests. It also represented genuine fear—fear of national control and direction of the economy by an unaccountable and inexperienced central elite. Big businessmen suddenly had to negotiate with labor unions which had never before had demonstrable support from their employees. Local businessmen suddenly found they had to obey national edicts about wages and hours, prices and discounts. "This country does not know what real taxation is," said Harry Hopkins, who knew how to spend taxpayers' money like no one else. Was that "lightly said," as one New Deal sympathizer put it, or a real threat?[7] We know now that America did not go down the same road as Mussolini's Italy, that Roosevelt had in mind nothing like Stalin's Soviet Union, that General Johnson whipping up enthusiasm for the Blue Eagle was not playing Goebbels to his leader's Hitler. But it was not utterly irrational for Americans in the middle 1930s, having seen how much government had changed in response to depression and how it was changing in other economically advanced countries, to look fearfully down the road and try to avoid the dangers they saw lurking ahead.

The conflict between Roosevelt and this new right—which included much of the old Democratic party—looked different from different angles. A national leader successfully improvising, only to be met with selfish opposition: so it seemed to Roosevelt. A dangerous subversion of American principles by a centralized government run by crank theorists, when the country would have been best served, as it always had been, by the leadership of men of proven abilities: so it seemed to his opponents. It was an argument that might have taken place between Charles F. Murphy and William Howard Taft, had they lived past 1930, an argument between a politician who believed in supple improvisation and a statesman who believed in steady adherence to principle. It was an argument between the left-out groups in American society—the unreconciled Confederates and the Catholic immigrants—and an elite which was confident that it continued to represent, as it had for most of the last three decades, the better instincts of those—Protestant, Yankee, Unionist—who in their view were the essence of America. "After all," wrote the *Saturday Evening Post* from its red-brick Georgian skyscraper overlooking Independence Hall in Philadelphia, a city that was still heavily Republican, "it is our country and not a laboratory for a small group of professors to try out experiments that bid fair to result in an explosion and a stink."[8] "Only 100 days"— or 64, or 28, or 3, as election day drew near and the countdown continued—"to save your country," warned the *Chicago Tribune* from its Gothic tower overlooking Lake Michigan and the plains that stretched to the Gulf of Mexico and the Rockies, speaking to a readership concentrated heavily among the descendants of the morality-minded Yankees who had settled northern Illinois and fought a civil war to make the country theirs.

Our country: the debate was bitter not only because it was a fight over money, but also because both sides sensed it was really a debate about whose country it was. Would it be led, the new right asked, by the men and the ideas that had led it so successfully in the seventy years since the election of Abraham Lincoln? Or would it be led by outsiders, by those who had been complainers and critics, by men and women who seemed somehow to be someting less than 100% Americans?

IV

"Heed this cry from Macedonia that comes from the hearts of men!" No one in the hall in Atlantic City could mistake the speaker, his bushy eyebrows and bulldog countenance, his flat midwestern accent booming out in the language and cadence of the King James Bible. He was John L. Lewis, president since 1920 of the United Mine Workers, the largest and most powerful of American labor unions, a man of mighty temper, utterly without fear or self-doubt. He was speaking at the American Federation of Labor convention in October 1935, two months after the adjournment of the Congress that had passed a significant new law favorable to labor organization, and he was calling on the AFL leaders, each of whom represented a specific craft and had spent years guarding his jurisdiction against raids by other unions, to adopt a new course and create a new kind of labor institution. "Organize the unorganized," he boomed out, "and in doing this make the American Federation of Labor the greatest instrument that has been forged in the history of modern civilization to befriend the cause of humanity."

Lewis and his listeners were acutely conscious that the labor movement had waxed and waned in proportion to its support from government. The War Labor Board encouraged union membership, and union rolls swelled to 5 million in the years just after World War I. But in the 1920s the courts, led by Chief Justice Taft, with their injunctions against strikes and restrictions on picketing, discouraged unions, and membership fell to 3.6 million in 1930. As the depression put people out of work, it fell still further, to 2.8 million in 1933;[9] AFL membership fell from almost 3 million to 2.1 million. Much of this drop represented the virtual disappearance of work in the building trades, whose workers together with the railway brotherhoods, the coal miners, and the garment workers had made up the bulk of AFL membership. Then, as NRA encouraged union organization, union membership recovered to 3.7 million in 1934. Even more important, NRA raised the possibility for the first time that the big mass-production industries might be organized. In the 1920s, after the spectacular failure of the steel strike of 1919, the conventional wisdom had held that the big steel, auto, and rubber firms would never permit unions. They paid higher than average wages, and no one doubted their determination to ferret out and fire employees who tried to unionize. There would be many others ready to take their places. But now the 1935 Wagner Act had strengthened the provisions of NRA which encouraged unions, while at the same time it dismantled the industry code authorities which employers had dominated and used to fight unionization. The act created a new National Labor Relations Board, which was authorized to find employers guilty of unfair labor practices but not to inhibit unions in any way, authorized to order employers to bargain with a union which could win a majority in a particular bargaining unit. And what should a bargaining unit be? The building trades and the railway brotherhoods were committed to craft unions, with membership based on skill and position rather than employer and industry. But Lewis, who headed the one major AFL union with a different membership basis, opposed the craft principle and championed what he called industrial unionism, for he saw a chance to organize giant industrial unions that could wield immense economic and political power. He was urging his fellow AFL members to take advantage of this opportunity—and quickly, because many people, possibly including himself, expected the courts to rule the Wagner Act unconstitutional.

AFL President William Green and the craft unionists refused to follow Lewis's advice. As he was walking down the aisle after finishing his speech, Bill Hutcheson of the carpenters' union called him a bastard, and Lewis turned around and punched Hutcheson solidly in the face, drawing blood. That punch marked the splitting of the labor movement. On November 9, 1936, just after Roosevelt's reelection, Lewis met in Washington with four other union leaders—Sidney Hillman of the Amalgamated Clothing Workers, David Dubinsky of the Garment Workers, Thomas McMahon of the Textile Workers, and Charles Howard of the Typographers—and formed a Committee for Industrial Organization. Ostensibly it was part of the AFL, but in 1937 it was expelled and changed its name to the Congress of Industrial Organizations. Lewis was careful not to change the acronym CIO, under which 4 million workers were by then enrolled.

Lewis's organizers had moved first into the steel industry, a natural target because steel companies owned some coal mines and were among the biggest consumers of coal. Their operations, centered in western Pennsylvania and northeastern Ohio, adjoined the huge bituminous coal fields of Pennsylvania and West Virginia. In addition, the companies seemed large and profitable enough to pay impressive wage increases, and their payrolls were large enough to guarantee huge dues if they recognized a union shop. A Steel Workers Organizing Committee was set up under Philip Murray, one of Lewis's UMW vice presidents; it sent out more than 400 organizers to the grimy steel towns along the bottoms of the Monongahela and Mahoning and Cuyahoga rivers and on the sandy flatlands south of Lake Michigan. They met with stern resistance. The companies kept track of employees through hired spies, and their security forces did not hesitate to beat up men they regarded as troublemakers. Union membership was grounds for dismissal. Yet throughout the election year of 1936, the organizers persevered. They knew they faced steep odds. The Wagner bill might be ruled unconstitutional, as NRA had been; the companies might prevail, as they had in the 1920s. But at least some of these unionists must have been encouraged by the hope, which turned out to be fulfilled, that they were creating a new institution which would become a part of the fabric of American life and would play a major role in the economy and politics of their country.[10]

V

On June 27, 1936, as 90,000 people waited at Philadelphia's Franklin Field on a cloudy, moonlit night, Franklin Roosevelt was brought in to deliver his speech accepting his second Democratic presidential nomination. Roosevelt had trained himself to walk in public, balanced on a cane and his son's or bodyguard's arm, in a way which looked natural but in practice required so much effort that sometimes his shirt would be drenched with sweat and his companion's arm bruised where he held it. As he was making his way to the platform, he moved to greet the eighty-four-year-old poet Edwin Markham and suddenly fell and sprawled helpless. "Clean me up," he commanded grimly, while aides shielded him from view. He was lifted up, his leg brace was relocked, and the fallen pages of his speech text were handed back to him at the podium—out of order. He had to reshuffle them as he began speaking, but he managed quickly to get into his oratorical rhythm.[11] There could be no mistaking his message. He attacked "privileged princes" of "economic dynasties" and "the royalists of the economic order," and he used the language of traditional American political rights—the language being used against him—to send a different message: "If the average citizen is guaranteed equal opportunity in the polling place, he must have equal opportunity in the market place." He highlighted his own record and accomplishments. "In those days we feared fear," he said, echoing his first inaugural, but now "we have conquered fear." Nothing more was heard of his party's traditional localist, states' rights positions; nothing about a balanced budget. The contrast drawn now was between the rich and average Americans, between a generous and an inert government. The peroration was rousing. "Governments can err, presidents do make mistakes, but the immortal Dante tells us that divine justice weighs the sins of the cold-blooded and the sins of the warm-hearted in different scales. Better the occasional faults of a government that lives in a spirit of charity than the consistent omissions of a government frozen in the ice of its own indifference. There is a mysterious cycle in human events. To some generations much is given. Of other generations much is expected. This generation of Americans has a rendezvous with destiny."

The Republicans had no such champion and no winning theme. As a party with few incumbent officeholders, they had few natural presidential candidates. The leading prospects at the beginning of 1936 were Alf Landon, the governor of Kansas; William Borah, the seventy-year-old senator from Idaho, the sometimes progressive former chairman of the Senate Foreign Relations Committee; Colonel Frank Knox, the *Chicago Daily News* publisher and outspoken internationalist (the military title was from his Spanish-American War service in Theodore Roosevelt's Rough Riders); and Herbert Hoover, the discredited former president. Landon, a decent and pleasant man who had never served in Congress and had no experience in international issues, won the nomination easily. But the biggest ovation of the convention went to Hoover. Still bitter because of what he considered Roosevelt's sabotage of the recovery he believed he had been engineering in 1932, Hoover was already beginning to try to rewrite history with his 1934 book *The Challenge to Liberty*. His fellow Republicans joined in his fierce denunciation of Roosevelt and all his works. They were used to a politics in which their ideas and their political label gave them, if not an assured national majority, then something very close to it. But in the new America of 1936, what were they offering as an alternative to the Democrats? They could attack New Deal programs like NRA and AAA. But they could not credibly deny that these and other New Deal measures had restored order and ended chaos. They could argue that NRA and huge government deficits and work relief and the Wagner Act were choking off economic growth. But they could not credibly deny that the economy was in a downward spiral during Hoover's administration and that it had moved upward during Roosevelt's. They could make abstract arguments against government regimentation and redistribution of income and dictatorship—arguments that they hoped voters would respond to at least a little because of what was happening in Europe. But these arguments had little impact. The intrusive regulations of NRA were, since

May 1935, a thing of the past. The AAA order to kill baby pigs to prevent overproduction was a memory of the winter of 1933–34. The ominous San Francisco general strike of 1934, which had threatened to spread to Toledo and Minneapolis, seemed unlikely to recur under the new conditions created by the Wagner Act.

So the opposition was reduced to abstract arguments, to claiming that Roosevelt's policies would make things worse, though for most voters they had demonstrably not done so. If you can't win on the law, as the old saying goes, argue the facts; and if you can't win on the facts, argue the law. Roosevelt could argue facts and his opponents were reduced to arguing law—usually a losing argument in elections.[12]

VI

Yet oddly enough, the Democrats were not considered sure winners as the summer went on, and this misperception may have ultimately inflated their majority by inducing the Republicans to persist in their losing strategy. This was the first presidential campaign in which scientific random-sampling polls were conducted on a regular basis.[13] But the results suggest that the sampling techniques had not been perfected. A January poll by George Gallup showed Roosevelt ahead of "the Republican candidate" 50%–43%, with 5% for a third party and 2% for the socialists. Between January and October, Gallup showed Roosevelt ranging between 49% and 51% when paired against Landon and peaking at 53.5% in early June when third-party support was down; throughout that period Gallup showed Landon with 42% to 44% and the third party—which ultimately meant Union Party candidate William Lemke, a congressman from North Dakota who was supported by Father Coughlin—with 5%. Gallup's final poll, published November 1 but taken October 23–28, showed a 54%–43% Roosevelt lead, with 2% for Lemke, indicating movement toward the actual 61%–37%–2% outcome. Clearly, Gallup consistently underestimated Roosevelt's support. One reason may have been erroneous assumptions about turnout, which rose 30% from 1932 in immigrant/industrial districts, where Roosevelt was strong; it rose 20% in rural Yankee districts, where support for Democrats was declining, and 10% in the South, where the huge Democratic percentages held steady. Another reason for the underestimate may have been undersampling of low-income and immigrant-stock voters. Roosevelt's percentages in the late Gallup polls were especially far below his election-day percentages in states with many industrial workers (New Jersey, Ohio, Illinois, Michigan, Wisconsin, California) or miners (West Virginia, Arizona, Montana).

The widespread belief that the election would be close was supported by the lingering assumption of a natural Republican majority in American politics— Republicans had won three of the four last presidential elections by big margins, and maybe they would win again now that more normal times seemed to be returning—as well as by polling results on specific issues. A 59%–41% majority of those surveyed by Gallup opposed AAA a month before it was declared unconstitutional in January 1936; it had majority support only in the South. Fully 70% said it was necessary "at this time to balance the budget and start reducing the national debt," and 80% wanted these goals accomplished by "governmental economies." Americans were reluctant to change the traditional rules of government: the week after AAA was declared unconstitutional Gallup's respondents opposed, 57%–43%, a constitutional amendment to let the federal government "regulate agriculture and industry." Fully 65% thought politics played a part in the handling of relief in their locality, and 55% favored returning to state and local governments the responsibility for caring for people on relief. If they had to choose between conservative and liberal parties, 53% would take conservative. An uncomfortably large minority, 45%, agreed that "the acts and policies of the Roosevelt administration may lead to a dictatorship."[14] These results probably should be discounted to some extent because of the sampling bias against Roosevelt. But of course no one at the time was aware of that.[15] Other polls were farther off than Gallup. A survey mailed out to telephone subscribers and automobile owners by the *Literary Digest,* for example, showed Roosevelt losing in a landslide. The magazine went out of business in the aftermath of this embarrassment, though in past elections, where opinion had not been split so starkly on economic lines, its sampling methods had worked well. *Fortune* was shrewder, sponsoring random-sample surveys which caught the trend of opinion much better. As early as October 1935, it reported that 62% of Americans felt either that Roosevelt's reelection was essential or that despite his mistakes no one else could do as much good, while only 32% believed that most of his usefulness was over or that his reelection would be "about the worst thing that could happen to this country."[16]

Why was Roosevelt ahead? On some issues, voters were with him. More than 80% approved of the CCC, solid majorities favored minimum wage and child labor laws even if they meant amending the Constitution, and three out of four were in favor of labor unions (though those with an opinion tended to prefer craft to industrial unions). But more important, the major issue for the voters was clearly the economy, and in May a 55%–45% majority said the administration's acts were helping rather than hindering recovery. This was close to identical with the preference expressed for Roosevelt over his opponents in the same survey. The polls of that day did not try to measure opinion about candidates' characters. But with the well-known and tested Roosevelt facing the little-known and little-tried Landon, this factor must have been important. Most Americans were confident that the active, confident, ebullient Roosevelt would persevere and take action. They believed that he knew what they faced in everyday life, whereas the Republicans talked of abstract principles. In 1920, Americans had rejected the party of what they saw as a supine president, and now they contrasted Coolidge's inaction and Hoover's caution with Roosevelt's boldness and eagerness to act.

Roosevelt's campaign strategy was all boldness. James Farley was breezily confident, and by October he astounded almost everyone by predicting—correctly, it turned out—that Roosevelt would carry every state but Maine and Vermont.

Roosevelt himself went on the offensive, perhaps stung by criticism from Republicans and former Democrats, disappointed that the silk-hatted gentlemen he had fished out of the pond were screaming at him. In fact, 1936 had not been a year of major changes in policy. Legislatively, Congress enacted the AAA substitute and in June passed the Robinson-Patman Act, intended to protect small retailers against competition from chains.[17] Judicially, the Supreme Court followed up its AAA decision by predictably overturning the 1935 Guffey-Snyder Coal Act, in which John L. Lewis had gotten Congress to reimpose the NRA coal mining code. Even politically, it is not clear that much changed in the course of the year: the polling shows an almost eerie steadiness of opinion. But 1936 was a culmination, in which Franklin Roosevelt summed up the results of six years of economic and political turbulence and framed in an utterly new way the issues before the American voter. It was a rendezvous between the old and new political America.

In the closing weeks of the campaign Roosevelt amplified rather than modulated his message. On October 31 in New York City's Madison Square Garden, he thundered against "old enemies of peace—business and financial monopoly, speculation, reckless banking, class antagonism, sectionalism, war profiteering." It was the language of standard American demagoguery, drawing on fifty years of resentment of the vastly rich and echoing as well the attacks on munitions makers that had been articulated in the Nye Committee hearings in the Senate the year before. Then he went on, "I should like to have it said of my first administration that in it the forces of selfishness and of lust for power met their match. I should like to have it said of my second administration that in it these forces have met their master." That framed the issue as starkly as possible: Roosevelt versus the rich. But the word *master* was surely disturbing to some Americans familiar with newsreels from Europe of posturing dictators and armies on the march.

VII

The new politics that had emerged in the congressional elections of 1934 is apparent from the presidential results of 1936. Gallup's final survey had suggested a Roosevelt electoral vote total around 300—a solid win and a better showing than the Democratic party had made, except for 1932 and the three-cornered race of 1912, since the days of Andrew Jackson. On election day, however, Roosevelt got not 300-odd electoral votes but 523. "As goes Maine," ran the old saw, "so goes the nation"; "as goes Maine," chortled Farley, "so goes Vermont." Roosevelt's share of the popular vote rose from 57% in 1932 to 61% in 1936. Yet in fourteen states the Roosevelt percentage fell, and in only eighteen states did it rise more than the 4% national average. Nine of these were in the West, most of them small; one was North Carolina; the others were clustered in the northeast and around the Great Lakes. They included Connecticut, New Jersey, and Delaware, where the Republicans' hold on many immigrant and industrial voters, still fairly strong in 1932, finally faltered; Roosevelt's own New York, although he still carried almost no counties except Albany between the New York City line and Buffalo;

and the big coal-steel-auto states of Pennsylvania, West Virginia, Ohio, and Michigan.

Looking at local rather than statewide figures, one finds rousing Roosevelt gains over 1932 in almost every major industrial area—New York, Buffalo, Philadelphia, Pittsburgh and all of western Pennsylvania, Cleveland and all of northeast Ohio, the machine tool belt around Cincinnati and Dayton, Detroit and the outstate Michigan auto towns, Chicago, Milwaukee, Minneapolis–St. Paul, Los Angeles, San Francisco Bay. These gains came disproportionately from the lower-income sections. "In every city I visited while doing a postelection survey," reported political journalist Samuel Lubell, "I found that the Roosevelt vote broke at virtually the same economic level, between $45 and $60 a month rent. Below that his pluralities were overwhelming. Above it, they faded away."[18] In some cities, such as New York, this pattern resulted in an across-the-board increase in what had long been Democratic majorities. But in others, like Philadelphia, it represented the unraveling of Republican machines which had been part of the fabric of urban life. In still others, the most notable of which was Chicago, it changed a competitive two-party machine politics into a one-party Democratic machine politics. Overall, party preference based on ethnic tradition was replaced in the cities by an all but uniform preference for the Democrats.

In the countryside, however, this movement toward the Democrats did not occur. In a majority of the nation's 3,000-plus counties, Roosevelt's percentage went down, not up. It declined, for example, in the Civil War borderlands—the typical pattern for a party there four years after a landslide presidential victory. If metropolitan, industrial, and mining counties are excluded, the pattern of voting preference growing out of the Civil War is still plainly visible in the 1936 results— and would be for years afterwards. The New Deal and Roosevelt's class-conscious rhetoric had changed the politics of the cities. They had helped to build the coalition he had always envisioned of traditional Democrats, big-city immigrants, and northwestern progressives—though even in 1936 it was Progressives and Farmer-Laborites, not Democrats, who were elected as Roosevelt allies in Wisconsin and Minnesota. They had not much changed the politics of the small towns and farms—except perhaps to turn some voters away from the president and his party.

Both these patterns are apparent in the congressional results. Democrats achieved an all-time high in House elections, winning 331 seats to 89 for the Republicans, with 13 for other parties. Of the total popular vote in House contests the Democrats won 57% to the Republicans' 40%, an improvement over their 56%–43% margin in 1932. In both years the House vote closely followed the presidential vote (especially if to the Democrats' 57% in 1936 are added the 3% cast for minor-party candidates, most of them left-wing: the 60% total almost matches Roosevelt's 61%). But the rise was uneven. The Democratic percentage went up between 1932 and 1936 from 51% to 57% in immigrant/industrial districts, while it declined from 53% to 51% in rural/Yankee districts. It was stable in the South, at 85%.[19] Moreover, turnout rose 30% in immigrant/industrial districts, compared with 20% in rural/Yankee districts and 10% in the South. The immigrant/industrial districts now accounted for more than half—52%—of the nation's popular vote in House contests, even though these 172 districts accounted for only 40% of the members of the House—a discrepancy due to inequitable districting as well as to the differences in turnout.

These contradictory patterns in city and countryside had profound political results. Within the Democratic party they strengthened the big-city machines and organized labor. John L. Lewis and his CIO could hardly help noticing that the state with the largest percentage increase in its Democratic vote between 1932 and 1936 was Pennsylvania, the premier coal-and-steel state, the number two state in electoral votes, and a state previously always counted as safely Republican. If Lewis and his allies are also given credit for the Democratic surge in West Virginia, Ohio, and Michigan—and they plausibly could be—then it was clear why he considered organized labor to be the central, determining force in American politics. "The CIO was out fighting for Roosevelt," he said after the election, "and every steel town showed a smashing victory for him."[20] Although the United Mine Workers gave the Democrats $500,000, a large percentage of their total campaign budget, even more important were the votes labor seemed to be delivering. For this support Lewis expected to be consulted regularly by Roosevelt, as he believed J. P. Morgan had been consulted by Republican presidents.[21] Throughout the 1930s, in fact until the Supreme Court redistricting cases of 1962–64, the big industrial cities were underrepresented in Congress and state legislatures. Thus organized labor considered presidential elections its most accessible avenue to power, and considered Roosevelt—who eighteen months before the 1936 election had opposed the Wagner Act—its champion.

At the same time, the results weakened Democratic politicians from the Civil War borderlands. Not only was their proportion in the Democratic caucus reduced, but their votes were, for the moment anyway, less needed. The congressional Democrats still drew many of their shrewdest leaders from the borderlands, like Alben Barkley and Fred Vinson of Kentucky. But the electoral strength of these leaders still lay in memories of the Civil War and a rhetorical commitment to states' rights—not to the politics of economic division Roosevelt was emphasizing. Borderlands Democrats were conscious also that Roosevelt was slipping, not gaining in strength, in their constituencies. Politically, they could afford to—perhaps they needed to—oppose the administration. Nor could they welcome the ascendancy of the big-city machines and the unions, whose stands on cultural and economic issues were political poison in their area.

So to the statement that by 1936 the United States had an emerging economic-based politics must be added a major qualifier: by no means everywhere. Traditional voting patterns tended to endure in much of the countryside, which by any measure—income, standard of living, access to electricity and to mass media—contained the poorest parts of the population. Regional differences along lines of Civil War divisions and ethnic migrations persisted: "there are geographical differences in U.S. ways of thinking," pollster Elmo Roper wrote in 1937, "that cut more sharply through the population than do class differences."[22] While new economic-based voting patterns emerged in the cities, moreover, the low-income voters in the cities—the fastest-growing, most dynamic, most advanced parts of the country in the 1910s and 1920s—were not necessarily the poorest of Americans. They were migrants from rural hinterlands across the sea or over the hill whose upward mobility had been abruptly halted, not a proletariat sunk for generations in a mire of hopelessness and misery.

VIII

After the thrashing and turmoil of the first six years of the 1930s, American politics settled into a routine, albeit not an entirely comfortable one. Issues of income distribution and economic power—debate over labor unions, progressive taxation, Social Security, national planning—dominated the political dialogue, together with the overriding issue of the leadership of Franklin Roosevelt. Straight-ticket voting became the norm, in contrast to the increased ticket-splitting of the 1920s. The two parties' entire tickets rose and fell in response to the business cycle and political events. On occasion, most notably in 1940, foreign policy would play a major part in politics and voting, but even then the shifts in party strength were relatively marginal.

So long as Roosevelt delivered order and economic growth and his opponents were unable to demonstrate that they could produce anything but chaos and economic stagnation, the economic politics of his New Deal Democrats was in-vincible. When circumstances changed, however, the political balance became more even. By no means all Americans saw a direct connection between government action and economic conditions,[23] and many voters in 1936 were responding more to the president's personal strengths and his apparent concern for them than to specific items on his policy agenda. For at the same election voters were also choosing a Congress which, while more heavily Democratic than any other Con-gress in history, was by no means committed to every proposal the president might hand down. These independent tendencies proved frustrating to New Dealers within the administration, an articulate and engaging group of people whose talk at the time and writings in later years shaped historians' views of the period. When Congress opposed Roosevelt's policies or their own, they tended to see it as mindlessly stubborn and parochial or as the suborned or unwitting tool of the propaganda of the rich. Part of the explanation for the New Dealers' frustrations after 1936 lay in the imperfections in the political system: unfair congressional and legislative districting, the central place of businessmen in local politics, the southern Democrats' increasing hostility toward the New Deal as it became as-sociated with civil rights.

But the more important part of the explanation can be found by assessing the 1936 results in context. Americans were not voting that year a once-and-for-all-endorsement of the politics of economic redistribution Roosevelt was championing, much less of liberal schemes some of Roosevelt's advisers believed he would adopt if he felt politically able to do so. They were voting for a president and his party for a limited time in a particular set of circumstances, at a time when their policies seemed to be working and their opponents presented no serious alternative. Policies of economic redistribution helped Roosevelt hold together a huge majority which had been created back in 1934 by the different policies of stabilization and control. The 1936 election confounded those of Roosevelt's critics and opponents who had said that Americans would never endorse a politics of economic redistribution. But the results of the elections to follow continually frustrated those New Dealers who assumed that in 1936 most Americans had endorsed every plank in their platform.

14

-»» «««-

Recession

I n late December 1936, some workers at the Fisher Body Plant Number One
in Flint, Michigan, noticed that several dies were being crated for shipment
out of the plant. Three decades before, Flint had been a courthouse town of
13,000; now, with 150,000 people, it was the site of Chevrolet and Buick factories
as well as the Fisher Body plants which produced auto bodies for General Motors,
the largest industrial corporation in the United States. The workers who noticed
the dies being crated were United Auto Workers organizers, operating secretly
in an industry where union men were routinely fired. A month earlier, two young
brothers and UAW organizers. Victor and Walter Reuther, had led a sit-down
strike at the Kelsey-Hayes plant in Detroit, 60 miles south; two days later workers
at a Fisher Body plant in Cleveland had sat down. Worried that management was
maneuvering to maintain production in case of a strike at Fisher Number One,
the workers there promptly sat down, too. Most strikes required large numbers
of pickets to prevent management from keeping the plant operating with non-
striking employees or replacements. But sit-down strikes, the first of which had
been staged at the Hormel meatpacking plant in Austin, Minnesota, in 1933,
required only small numbers of union activists to keep the plant shut down by
seizing crucial machinery and remaining on the premises.

That is what the men at Fisher Number One and organizers at other plants
did. GM refused to negotiate, sought and got a court injunction against the strikers,
and then, after thirteen days, shut off the heat in the plant and tried to bar the
strikers' families and supporters from bringing in food. Violence resulted: the
strikers' auxiliaries skirmished with police, windows were broken, and tear gas
and jets of water from firehoses filled the frigid Michigan air. To Alfred P. Sloan,
the architect of GM's corporate structure, sit-down strikes were "plainly illegal,"
an unlawful seizure of property. But the union leaders believed or hoped that in
the new world of the New Deal and the Wagner Act, this old legal rule would
be overturned as so many others had been. Michigan Governor Frank Murphy,
a New Deal Democrat elected in November 1936, refused to clear the plant and
urged GM executives to negotiate with the CIO's John L. Lewis. A local pro-
management civic group called the Flint Alliance planned to seize the plant itself.
Meanwhile, Roy Reuther, another of the brothers raised by a trade union activist
and German immigrant in Wheeling, West Virginia, stormed another GM plant

and started a sit-down there. After the first injunction was overturned, another was issued, but the strikers refused to leave the plants; and in Detroit, Lewis said he would join them if Murphy sent troops in. Some 125,000 workers in 117 plants were out of work; Franklin Roosevelt and Frank Murphy wanted them back on the job, but not if that meant shedding blood. The two Democrats pressured GM to negotiate, and Murphy shuttled between GM and CIO representatives. On February 11, John L. Lewis strode into the stolid dull-gray GM Building, across Detroit's Grand Boulevard from the Fisher Building where Father Coughlin made his broadcasts, and signed an agreement in which the nation's largest corporation recognized as the bargaining agent for all the workers in the sit-down plants a union which had scarcely existed a few months before.[1]

On March 2, Lewis announced that Myron Taylor, president of United States Steel in Pittsburgh, had agreed to recognize the Steel Workers Organizing Committee (SWOC) as bargaining agent for its workers. Within ten weeks unions had won recognition at the two biggest companies in the two biggest industries in America—two industries long considered totally inimical to unions. But that was not the end of the sit-down strikes or of labor violence. Other companies held out. In May 1937, Walter Reuther and three other UAW organizers were handing out leaflets on an overpass leading from a parking lot to the Ford Rouge plant in Dearborn, Michigan—the plant which Henry Ford had built in 1918 for $1 billion and at which, he boasted, he could take iron ore out of a docked Great Lakes freighter and convert it to an automobile in 36 hours. Suddenly thugs hired by Ford's Harry Bennett appeared and beat the four unionists up. The picture of Reuther with blood streaming down his face and shirt made national news.[2] And on the South Side of Chicago on Memorial Day, SWOC strikers against "Little Steel" were holding a holiday picnic on the grounds of the huge Republic Steel plant near Lake Calumet when Chicago police charged with billyclubs swinging and guns blazing, killing ten people.[3] A year earlier, these unions had been little more than paper organizations. By the end of 1937, the UAW had 200,000 members and the SWOC 300,000. Filled with enthusiastic cadres, flooded suddenly with millions of unexpected dues dollars, committed to economic redistribution, and firmly attached to civil liberties (the LaFollette committee that was then investigating corporate resistance to union organizers regarded the entire issue as one of civil liberties), the CIO unions were a peculiarly American institution—one that thrilled millions of Americans and frightened millions of others. With some key help from Democratic politicians, they were on their way to changing America.[4]

Both the unions and management felt strongly that justice was on their side and that they represented the country's real interests. GM believed its property was being seized by force and violence, that New Deal politicians were shirking their responsibility to enforce the law, that there was no reason to believe the company's workers really wanted to be represented by a union led by what GM called radicals (only 10% of the workers at Fisher Number One were UAW members when the sit-down started), and that the Wagner Act, then being challenged before the Supreme Court, was probably as unconstitutional as the National

Industrial Recovery Act from which it was derived. "They had no right to sit down [at the plant]," claimed Charles Stewart Mott, GM's largest individual shareholder and a member of its board for sixty years, in an interview years later. "They were illegally occupying it. The owners had a right to demand from the Governor . . . [that he] get those people out. It wasn't done."[5] For their part, the leaders of the sit-downs had no doubt that they represented the real interests of the workers, who they said had been prevented from expressing or even understanding these interests by companies always quick to fire union members and hire goons to beat up union organizers. The big vote for Roosevelt in industrial towns, these leaders said, was a better indication of whose side the workers were on. They believed that the companies were defying the Wagner Act; and they hoped that the sit-down, like mass picketing and other union tactics long labeled illegal by judges of the ilk of William Howard Taft, would be vindicated by the courts at a time when judges' opinions on so many issues seemed to be changing (it was: the Wagner Act was upheld in April 1937). In the meantime, they felt an urgency to act. Sidney Hillman, the leader of the garment workers and one of the leaders of the CIO, said that the months right after the 1936 election might be "the last opportunity" to organize industrial workers; he and other organizers were eager to do so while the Wagner Act was still law and while Roosevelt and sympathetic New Deal governors in Pennsylvania, Ohio, and Michigan controlled the military forces which could have broken the strikes.

The sit-down movement did not come from a downtrodden proletariat. Automobiles had been America's most visible boom industry in the twenty-five years up to 1930, and steel had been a growth industry in the 1920s. For all the insistence of managers on applying Frederick Taylor's mechanistic efficiency rules, working conditions in the big factories were no worse than in smaller, more traditional industries, and wages tended to be higher. Then the depression brought huge layoffs in autos and steel in the early 1930s, and by the middle of the decade Roper found a widespread feeling among Americans that labor was not being treated fairly.[6] But anyone with a job in an auto or steel factory in 1936 was making wages well above the national average for manufacturing. While it is easy to understand the desire of many workers for a union that would represent their interests, bargain for higher wages, and limit the unrestrained power of management, it is also easy to understand why many workers were reluctant to join the sit-down strikers, whose leaders tended to be intellectuals like the Reuther brothers. The hold which the UAW later developed over its members probably owed more to its competence in representing their interests after it was recognized as their bargaining agent than to any initial enthusiasm for it. Just as the New Deal Democrats won crucial votes not from the poorest Americans but from those who were moving up on the middle rungs of the economic ladder until the depression cast them down, so the industrial union movement won crucial victories not from the lowliest of American workers but from those who were up into the middle rungs even after the depression's ravages.

Certainly the reaction of most voters was not to identify with the sit-down strikers. Americans seemed no more likely to sympathize with picketing strikers (as 18% did) than with the picketed business as (22% did).[7] In early February, Gallup found that 66% of those with an opinion agreed that GM was right in refusing to negotiate with the sit-downers until they left the plants; 62% agreed that Lewis did not represent a majority of the plants' workers. Roper found that 74% of those he surveyed for *Fortune* wanted the sit-down strikes stopped, though only 20% did "if bloodshed is necessary," an important qualification. As many as 44% of those with an opinion said their sympathies were with "the John L. Lewis group of striking employees" rather than with the employers. But by a 63%–37% margin respondents favored separate craft unions over a single union for all workers in an industry.[8] The political verdict was delayed by the election calendar but seems fairly clear. In April 1937 the Senate voted 75–3 to denounce sit-down strikes as illegal, though it had just voted against banning them in the coal industry. In the 1938 elections Democrats lost the governorships of Michigan, Ohio, and Pennsylvania, and they even lost the House seat for the district that included Flint. The sit-down strikes and CIO unions were widely unpopular, and even in a factory town the Flint Alliance, at least for the moment, seemed more popular than the UAW.

II

"I see millions," cried Franklin Roosevelt, "denied education, recreation, and the opportunity to better their lot and that of their children. I see millions lacking the means to buy the products of farm and factory and by their poverty denying work and productiveness to many other millions. I see one-third of a nation ill-housed, ill-clad, ill-nourished." At his rain-streaked Second Inaugural on January 20, 1937, Roosevelt was making his intentions clear. He wanted to build a stronger, larger federal government to stimulate the economy and redistribute income and wealth. He wanted the nation to go farther down the road it had embarked on in June 1935.

It was against this background that in February 1937 Roosevelt unveiled his proposal to pack the Supreme Court. He was frustrated because the court had ruled unconstitutional so many New Deal laws and because, despite the advanced years of many justices, he had completed a four-year term without having the opportunity to fill a single vacancy—the only president between Woodrow Wilson and Jimmy Carter thus deprived. Some of the court's decisions on New Deal measures may have seemed sensible in retrospect—NRA, for example, was surely "delegation running riot" and had exhausted its political support before the court killed it—but in others the court did seem to invalidate popular legislation by using a definition of interstate commerce which was straight out of horse-and-buggy days. Attempting to preserve a field in which Congress could not act, the court found itself drawing lines which made no sense and making distinctions which seemed to almost all thoughtful people to make no difference: jurisprudence running riot. From the turn of the century through the days of Chief Justice

Taft, the court had sometimes been attacked as an instrument of the rich because the justices had felt a duty to make sure that activist legislation passed by inexpert legislatures did not violate constitutional limitations. But until 1935 the abstract principles enunciated by the court had seldom found their way into political discourse or threatened to overturn widely popular laws which were at the center of political debate. As 1937 began, important laws—the Wagner Act, Social Security, and the second AAA—seemed threatened by the court. Roosevelt evidently felt he must act.

Yet what he did came as a surprise to almost everyone, and the instant reaction of many politicians was negative. One reason was his disingenuousness. He proposed not a constitutional amendment to overturn the Supreme Court decisions he disagreed with, but a simple law to allow him to name up to six new justices, one for each incumbent who failed to retire after reaching the age of seventy. Congress had changed the number of justices in the nineteenth century, and one of the four conservative stalwarts on the court, Justice James McReynolds, had proposed years earlier the appointment of new judges on the lower federal courts when an incumbent refused to retire at seventy. But Roosevelt, concentrating on secrecy, had failed to enlist his normal political allies. Henry Ashurst of Arizona, grandiloquent chairman of the Senate Judiciary Committee, had recently denied vehemently that the president favored packing the court; and Hatton Sumners of Dallas, Texas, chairman of the House Judiciary Committee, told his companions in Vice President Garner's car as they were being driven back to the Capitol after Roosevelt's announcement, "Boys, here's where I cash in." Liberal Democrats like Burton Wheeler and Wyoming's Joseph O'Mahoney, progressive Republicans like Hiram Johnson and George Norris were opposed: these were all politicians whose careers had been imperiled by their devotion to civil liberties, and the proposal to overturn court decisions by political might stuck in their craw. Wheeler, for example, had been savagely criticized when as United States attorney in the turbulent mining city of Butte, Montana, he had refused to cooperate with Attorney General Mitchell Palmer's Red Raids in 1920; he remembered how in "the hysteria of the First World War, I saw men strung up. Only the federal courts stood up at all, and the Supreme Court better than any of them. Not as well as they should have, but better than the others."[9] At a Senate Judiciary Committee hearing in March 1937, Wheeler read a letter from Chief Justice Charles Evans Hughes conclusively refuting Roosevelt's charges of inefficiency and delay in the court's activities.

In fact, the issue was simply whether the court's power to overturn laws should be limited by "dilution" (or the threat of dilution) of its membership. What Roosevelt really wanted, of course, was for the court to change its reasoning and quit overturning New Deal laws. On that issue, public opinion as measured in polls seemed to be with him. But on the procedural question of limiting the court's powers, Americans were dubious. In November 1936, Gallup had found that a 59%–41% majority of those with an opinion agreed that the Supreme Court should be "more liberal in reviewing New Deal measures," but a majority of exactly the same size opposed "limiting the power of the Supreme Court to declare acts of Congress unconstitutional." In February 1937, Gallup showed a 53%–47% majority of those with an opinion opposed "President Roosevelt's proposal to reorganize the Supreme Court"; and a week later, only 38% said Congress should pass the Roosevelt plan, while 23% said it should be modified and 39% said it should be defeated.[10] Even if most of those with no opinion were pro-Roosevelt, as the president himself sensibly assumed,[11] it was clear that the voting public remained unconvinced of the merits of the court-packing proposal.[12]

If the politicians and the public were nonplused, the justices may have been affected. On April 12 the court surprised many by upholding the Wagner Act, with Hughes and Owen Roberts joining the usual liberal bloc of Louis Brandeis, Harlan Stone, and Benjamin Cardozo.[13] On May 18, Justice Willis Van Devanter resigned, and on May 24 the court upheld the Social Security Act. All these events undermined the court-packing bill, since it seemed now that New Deal legislation would be safe without it. Roosevelt still lobbied furiously. But on the day of Van Devanter's resignation the Senate Judiciary Committee defeated it 10–8, and all the energetic efforts of Majority Leader Joseph Robinson, an Arkansas conservative who had been promised the first new seat, availed nothing. On July 14, Robinson suddenly died; court packing had died some time before.

Was the court-packing bill a drastic political mistake? It can be argued that it achieved many of Roosevelt's goals: that without it the Supreme Court might have overturned the Wagner and Social Security acts (it had difficulty distinguishing them from laws it *had* overturned) and the elderly conservative justices would have stayed on the court, threatening any New Deal legislation passed in the second term (Van Devanter was joined in retirement by George Sutherland in January 1938 and Pierce Butler in November 1939). But even if these premises are granted, it is plain that Roosevelt paid a high political price. He split the congressional Democratic party, which despite its huge majorities passed little New Deal legislation in 1937 and 1938. He eroded his own credibility inside Washington and out: plainly he had not been frank about why he wanted the bill. An impression was etched deep in the public mind that Roosevelt was trying to evade all traditional restraints on presidential and political power. Already poll-takers were asking whether Roosevelt should and would seek a third term—not questions usually asked about American presidents who had just won their second.[14] Already people were noticing that "reliefers" gave New Deal Democrats a greater percentage of their votes than did any other group—proof to some that government money was being used to buy Roosevelt votes. Although the percentage of Americans who were pleased that Roosevelt had been reelected in 1936 remained as high as ever, the percentage who wanted to see him and his New Dealers given all the power they wanted had probably fallen well below 50%.

The mystery is why Roosevelt, ordinarily so sensitive to public opinion, failed to understand the public's fears and apprehensions. Perhaps he concluded that the procedural objections to the court-packing plan were no more widely accepted than the abstract arguments made by the Liberty League and the Republicans in

1934, 1935, and 1936. But his very political success made his threats to traditional arrangements more ominous. So did the progress of events in Europe, where dictatorships continued to make gains at the expense of democracy. And so did a subtle, but not unnoticed, shift in the stated goals of the New Deal. In the First and even the Second New Deal—in NRA and AAA, deposit insurance and Social Security and even the Wagner Act—the beneficiaries were the great mass of Americans, landowning farmers and upwardly mobile city-dwellers whose plans had been frustrated and hopes dashed by economic collapse. In the second Roosevelt term the beneficiaries were depicted increasingly as those on the bottom or somewhere near the bottom of the economic ladder—a group with which only a small percentage of the voters identified.

III

The Supreme Court bill was announced February 5, just six days before the agreement between General Motors and the United Auto Workers: the political firmament that winter seemed to be shaking. No one could be sure what American voters wanted or would accept. Just after the 1936 election, Gallup reported that only 15% of those with an opinion wanted the second Roosevelt administration to be more liberal than the first, 50% wanted it more conservative, and 35% wanted it about the same: no mandate here for the new departures suggested in Roosevelt's campaign speeches and his inaugural address. Yet by a 65%–35% margin, respondents said they would "vote for Franklin Roosevelt today." The contrast between Roosevelt's personal popularity level and that of the events and issues he became identified with in 1937 is sharp. A 65% president, so to speak, based his political future on an alliance with a 44% union movement and support of a 47% court-packing proposal.[15] It is no wonder he got into political trouble and undercut his own landslide.

Undercutting the landslide even more was the recession[16] that began in the fall of 1937, the first downturn in the economic cycle since the beginning of recovery from the depths of 1933. Unemployment rose from an annual average of 7.7 million in 1937 to 10.4 million in 1938. That was not as high as the 12.8 million of 1933, but it was still five times higher than any figure in the 1923–29 period, and unemployment would not decline below the 7 million level until after World War II began. The number of Americans with jobs declined from 46.4 million in 1937 to 44.5 million in 1938. Stock market prices fell sharply, and the gross national product dropped from $90 billion to $85 billion.

Arguments about the reason for this drop continue. Some analysts blame the decline in government spending in 1937, which occurred primarily because the veterans' bonus approved by Congress in 1936 over Roosevelt's veto had been spent. Republicans at the time blamed a decline in business confidence, and in fact a sharp drop in stock prices, as in 1929, was the first sign of trouble. The private economy may simply have been ready for a pause after four years of recovery; seldom is economic growth sustained longer than that. Yet for a public which was largely confident that the depression was over,[17] the recession of 1937–38 was an unnerving experience.

Whatever the reasons for what soon became known as the Roosevelt recession, the political consequences were profound. Roosevelt had won elections as the man who brought order out of chaos; now the CIO strikes were undercutting that argument. And he won as the leader who produced economic recovery; now that appeal seemed undercut, too. The failure of the economy to rebound to the levels of 1929 was tolerable so long as it kept growing. But the Roosevelt recession left Americans in doubt as to whether growth could be sustained and whether they could ever again achieve the prosperity and plenty of the 1920s.

Such doubts were exacerbated by Roosevelt's response to the recession. The leader who had improvised brilliantly in 1933, 1934, and 1935, producing one economic solution after another, many of which seemed to help and none of which, except in the view of partisan critics, seemed to hurt—this leader suddenly seemed at a loss. He seemed to have no formula for economic revival. Instinctively, prodded by Treasury Secretary Henry Morgenthau, Jr., he resisted proposals to vastly increase government spending; instead, as he called a special session of Congress for November 1937 he asked for a balanced budget for the year 1938. The leader whose NRA had encouraged businesses to make agreements to fix prices and wages now unleashed Assistant Attorney General Thurman Arnold for an attack on mononpolists and trusts, though it was not at all apparent that industrial concentration had caused the recession. Eventually, in April 1938, he called for a $3 billion spending program. Even so, the administration which had spent $8.4 billion in 1937 spent only $7.2 billion in 1938 and came within $100 million of balancing the budget. The British economic theorist John Maynard Keynes wrote to Roosevelt urging massive federal spending. But Roosevelt adopted almost precisely the opposite remedy—and may have choked off or weakened the recovery that eventually did occur by 1939.[18]

Politically, the Roosevelt recession not only robbed the president temporarily of his advantage on economic issues.[19] More important, it tended to convince both sides that the politics of economic redistribution was a zero-sum game. With a stagnant or contracting economy, if labor was to get a bigger share of the pie, capital would get less; if the relievers were to get more, middle-class taxpayers would get less; if the city-dweller got more, the farmer got less; if the South got more, the North got less. The politics of economic redistribution is often bitter, but it becomes especially fierce when both sides are convinced that the only way to give others more is to give themselves less. For a dozen years after the Roosevelt recession this tension was an important part of American politics. War brought economic growth, but everyone knew the wartime economy was temporary, and only a few believed that the postwar years would be prosperous. Almost everyone expected that the high unemployment and stagnation of the 1930s would return. In this context, the drive to organize American workers in industrial unions, which won its first victories in February 1937, and the drive to centralize governmental power in the executive branch, which had its first expression in the court-packing proposal made public that same month, undermined the popularity of Franklin Roosevelt and of New Deal Democrats more severely than seemed likely in the early summer of 1937, before the recession began, and more seriously than has been appreciated by many who have written about the period since.

IV

What remained of the Roosevelt program helped to alienate many voters and attracted relatively few. The only major bill expanding government that passed in 1937 was the public housing law sponsored by Robert Wagner. The initiative here came entirely from Wagner, who had grown up in the slums of Manhattan, who believed that the private housing market could not provide enough decent housing for Americans, and who looked to European examples and saw that in Britain and Austria, for example, most of the new housing of the 1930s was built by the government. His bill, providing for annual federal subsidies for local public housing projects, was introduced without administration support and opposed in important part by Treasury Secretary Morgenthau and Interior Secretary Ickes. It nonetheless passed both houses in August and became law—another tribute to Wagner's legislative brilliance.[20]

The major administration measure that was passed in 1938, thanks more to the efforts of its congressional supporters than to those of Roosevelt, was the wage-and-hours bill, an attempt to put into general effect the minimum-wage and maximum-hours provisions that had been included in many NRA codes four and five years before. It mandated a 40-cent hourly wage and a 44-hour workweek, which would go down to 40 hours by 1941. These provisions might not have passed muster with the courts before 1937; now they had trouble passing muster with Congress. Many southern representatives feared that a national minimum wage, which was well below prevailing wage rates in the North, would raise the overall level of southern wages, as NRA and WPA had, and thereby destroy the traditional southern economy.[21] But some southern liberals wanted higher wages in their region (at least for whites: the elimination of low-wage field work would eventually spur many blacks to move north).[22] In January 1938, when the wage-and-hours bill was floundering, its chances were buoyed by the result of a special Alabama senatorial primary in which Congressman Lister Hill, who supported the bill, won a 61%–34% victory over Senator Tom Heflin, an old race-baiter who once shot a black man on a Washington streetcar. The next month the president's son James, a White House staffer, conspicuously endorsed Florida's young Senator Claude Pepper in his bid for a full term, and in a May 3 primary Pepper took 58% of the vote against a former congressman and the incumbent governor. Pepper had campaigned hard for the wage-and-hours bill, and his victory was taken as an endorsement of it in territory where it had been thought to be most unpopular. The bill was promptly discharged from the Rules Committee by the signatures of a majority of House members and was passed into law the next month.

The administration had scored another success in February 1938 with the passage of a new Agricultural Adjustment Act which provided for acreage controls, marketing quotas, storage of surpluses, and federal crop insurance—closer government supervision than would have been permitted by the 1934 Supreme Court. But the administration's most venturesome initiatives failed. One was the reorganization bill which would have put into effect the recommendations of the president's Brownlow Committee; the other was the Seven TVAs bill, which would have set up seven regional authorities, defined by river basins, as a basis for a sort of national economic planning. Together these bills amounted to what historian Barry Karl has called a Third New Deal.[23] The Brownlow Committee called for centralizing national political authority by ending the independence of the federal regulatory agencies and creating a permanent planning board in the White House, which would have authority over regional planning boards set up all over the nation. As a resident of the White House who identified with the central government and a son of the Hudson River Valley who instinctively loved to organize programs by watersheds, Roosevelt naturally liked the Seven TVAs plan; and it seemed to meet certain obvious needs for control of natural disasters, such as the floods which had devastated the Ohio River Valley in early 1937 and the Dust Bowl which had been developing in the valleys of the Mississippi's tributaries farther west. But other politicians hated these bills and the ideas they represented. They did not want experts or White House appointees deciding where dams would be built and post offices established: they wanted to make those politically crucial decisions themselves. To them, the idea of national planning seemed increasingly to mean rule by unaccountable intellectuals. Congress kept putting into administration bills provisions cutting the salaries of men like Harry Hopkins and requiring all officials above a certain salary level to be confirmed by Congress. Father Coughlin and newspaper chain owner Frank Gannett campaigned strenuously against reorganization, which was called the "dictator bill" often enough that Roosevelt issued an announcement which included the odd statement, "I have no inclination to be a dictator. I have none of the qualifications which would make a successful dictator." Yet a 45%–44% plurality of Americans agreed that "Roosevelt has too much power."[24] The reorganization bill was passed in 1939 only after it had been stripped of all its revolutionary centralizing features, and the Seven TVAs bill never passed at all.[25]

In fact, the main effect of these proposals was to increase the apprehensions that politicians and many voters already had about the New Deal. In November 1938, when Hopkins's WPA still had 3 to 4 million people on the payroll, he was quoted by Frank Kent as saying that the administration would "tax and tax, spend and spend, elect and elect." Hopkins denied saying anything of the sort, and Kent refused to name his anonymous source (it turned out to be a theatrical producer who was a racetrack companion of Hopkins). But the story struck a chord (Arthur Krock of the *New York Times* told a congressional committee that "it was a most logical statement of what Mr. Hopkins might have said"—a peculiar standard of journalistic integrity),[26] and it became a staple of Republican oratory. Ronald Reagan, a four-time Roosevelt voter, was quoting it in the late 1980s. Hopkins was by no means apolitical: he made political alliances with the likes of Chicago Mayor Ed Kelly; when he was critized for putting Senator Alben Barkley's supporters on the WPA payroll during Barkley's 1938 primary battle in Kentucky, he said, "There is nothing wrong with supporting the political group that will give you the most."[27] The presence of writers, artists, and intellectuals of all sorts on the WPA payroll only strengthened the fears of New Deal opponents that money they had appropriated was creating a giant political machine to be used against them on election day. The ultimate result of these fears was the Hatch Act, passed in July 1939, which prohibited federal employees from becoming involved in political campaigns. Its chief sponsor was Senator Carl Hatch, a conservative Democrat from New Mexico.

In opposing the centralizing policies of the administration, the politicians were not just acting selfishly; to a considerable extent they were reflecting public opinion. The liberal Hopkins, Perkins, and Ickes were consistently among the least popular members of the administration and served as lightning rods of opposition. Roosevelt's apparent attempt to establish Hopkins as a plausible successor, an attempt which included appointing him to a Cabinet position far less powerful than his post as head of WPA, seemed destined for sure failure (only 9% of those surveyed in a 1938 poll agreed he should be "kept in mind for higher office")[28] and in any case ended when Hopkins's health collapsed in August 1939. But it is understandable that voters might have been afraid of a president who wanted close control over national economic planning and a peacetime federal budget which amounted to 10% of the gross national product, and whose faithful lieutenant had close control over a payroll which included 7% of the work force. With this authority bolstered by the support of the CIO unions, whose memberships were growing by the tens of thousands each month, a specter arose which evidently frightened not only most politicians but quite a few voters as well. The Republicans' previously abstract arguments were now given flesh. Americans who were watching newsreels of Hitler's rallies and Mussolini's marches, who feared more than anything involvement in another possibly even more devastating war, were queasy about anything that smacked of dictatorship.[29]

In the 1938 elections these new developments brought new voters to the polls— but not necessarily from the one-third of the nation that was ill-housed, ill-clad, ill-nourished. In the 1936 presidential election the turnout had risen from 40 million in 1932 to nearly 46 million, and that increase came disproportionately in the industrial/immigrant districts—Roosevelt country. Between 1934 and 1938 the turnout in House elections rose from 32 million to 36 million, a rise of similar proportions. Again the increase was much higher in industrial/immigrant districts, where turnout was up 21%; in rural/Yankee districts it rose only 5%, and in the South it fell 23%. But most of the increase went this time to Republican candidates, not Democrats. The Republican party held the ancestral loyalty of many of the poorest Americans—southern blacks who were not allowed to vote, dirt farmers from the chilly potato fields of Maine to the hills of the Cumberland Plateau in central Kentucky and the Ozarks in Missouri—and the level of Democratic support among most of them was dropping already in 1936 and would be lower in the 1940s than it had been in the 1920s. By 1938 policies of economic redistribution and centralization of power were working as much against Roosevelt and New Deal Democrats as for them.

V

The contests between friends and foes of the New Deal began in the primaries. By this time, the administration was being voted against regularly, for different reasons, by many Democrats in Congress—some of them liberals like the vituperative ambitious Burton Wheeler, others old decentralizing Jeffersonians like Virginia's diminutive, bitter Carter Glass. For the Democratic party in the 1930s was still the offspring of the bitterly divided party that had met at Madison Square Garden in 1924 and refused to condemn the Ku Klux Klan. The Democrats who became upset winners in the early 1930s, including the class of senators up for reelection in 1938, were a motley crew—old Wilsonians and local ne'er-do-wells, philosophical radicals and Jeffersonian localists. The party was obviously being fractured along new lines, but no one could be sure just where the lines would cut: southerners tended to be opposed to the wage-and-hours bill and wary of the CIO unions, but by no means all southerners in Congress were hostile to the New Deal in general. Roosevelt, blessed with a large but often unfaithful party, seemed to conclude that unifying Democrats behind the banner of the New Deal was his best strategy. In 1934 he had campaigned above party, as a non-partisan national leader. In 1934 and 1936 he had taken care to help non-Democratic progressives like George Norris, the LaFollette brothers in Wisconsin, the Farmer-Laborites in Minnesota, and Fiorello La Guardia in New York City. Now, in 1938, he seemed bent mainly on making the old Democracy a New Deal party.

He had more success in the primaries than is generally conceded. The triumphs of Lister Hill in Alabama in January and of Claude Pepper in Florida in May were very much Roosevelt victories. In July, at the Latonia Race Track across the Ohio River from Cincinnati, he endorsed Alben Barkley of Kentucky, who in the summer of 1937 had been elected Senate majority leader by one vote over Mississippi's Pat Harrison; Roosevelt had sent him a "Dear Alben" letter recognizing him as acting majority leader after Joseph Robinson's sudden death. The endorsement helped Barkley to a hard-fought win over Governor "Happy" Chandler, an administration critic. In Oklahoma, Roosevelt mentioned his "old friend" Senator Elmer Thomas, whose free-silver bill in 1933 had prompted Roosevelt to go off the gold standard; Thomas won. In Texas he made a point of announcing a judicial appointment obnoxious to Senator Tom Connally, who had opposed the court-packing bill; but Connally, who had beaten a liberal 59%–37% in the 1934 primary, was not up for election again until 1940. Roosevelt's efforts farther west bore less fruit. In Colorado he "elaborately ignored"[30] Senator Alva Adams, another court-packing opponent. In Nevada, Senator Pat McCarran, whose prevailing wage amendment had almost killed the 1935 work relief bill, maneuvered him into shaking hands.

In California he greeted his "old friend" Senator William McAdoo, now seventy-four; McAdoo was opposed by fifty-four-year-old Sheridan Downey, a supporter of the Ham 'n' Eggs movement, which promised the elderly a check for "$30 every Thursday." Adams and McCarran were reelected, while McAdoo lost to Downey.

Not discouraged by these setbacks, Roosevelt took on tougher challenges—and lost. In the red-clay county seat of Barnesville, Georgia, Roosevelt came out against Senator Walter George in front of George himself. When they shook hands, George said, "Mr. President, I want you to know I accept the challenge." He met it, beating the race-baiting Governor Eugene Talmadge and the New Deal candidate Lawrence Camp. The popular vote was 44%–32%–24%, but George won under Georgia's county unit rule system. In South Carolina, Roosevelt backed Governor Olin Johnston against Senator "Cotton Ed" Smith, the incumbent since 1908, who had walked out of a 1936 Democratic national convention session when a black minister gave the invocation. Smith won 55%–45% (though Johnston beat him six years later). Roosevelt's most humiliating loss came against Maryland Senator Millard Tydings, a consistent New Deal opponent. In September he soundly beat Congressman David Lewis, described by one observer as "a pepperpot of a man, a real idealist and a real scholar,"[31] who had gone to work in the coal mines at age seven, worked his way through law school, and as a congressman sponsored the Social Security Act. But Lewis had run twice before for the Senate from his base in the sparsely populated far western panhandle of the state, had lost both times, and was sixty-nine years old, while Tydings, who was forty-eight, had strong support from organization politicoes in Baltimore and the rural counties on either side of Chesapeake Bay. Roosevelt did have one electrifying win late in the primary season, in the 16th district of New York (the East Side of Manhattan). John O'Connor, chairman of the House Rules Committee and a brother of Roosevelt's old law partner, was beaten by pro-labor Democrat James Fay; in the general election Fay again narrowly beat O'Connor, who had been nominated by the Republicans.

The Roosevelt effort did help to defeat important New Deal opponents and to give others closer races than they otherwise had reason to expect. The outcomes depended heavily on the local strength of the contenders. Strong candidates like Barkley and Hill won; weak ones like Camp and Lewis lost. But Roosevelt failed to demonstrate what he had hoped to: that regardless of local and personal factors, New Deal policies commanded a majority constituency in Democratic primary electorates. The particular politics of the South, founded on opposition there to any threat to its low-wage economy, resulted in some New Deal defeats. But New Deal backers lost as well in Colorado and Nevada and Maryland. A common caricature of the Democratic party at this time portrays it as a monolithic political machine, sustained by patronage and loyal to the national party leaders. In a few places it was: in cities like Chicago and Phildelphia and New Haven, Connecticut, and Wilkes-Barre, Pennsylvania, where the appeal of New Deal policies to immigrant-stock and blue-collar voters reliably delivered control of local office to the Democrats. Yet to the extent that the hold of old machines—Democratic as well as Republican—depended on delivery of services and help to the needy, it was weakened by federal work relief programs and other government aid and by the explosive growth of the CIO unions. Elsewhere the caricature of a machine seldom applied. The Democratic party remained as complicated a political organism, as unpredictable a political animal, as it had been in the 1920s when Will Rogers observed that he did not belong to an organized political party—"I am a Democrat."

If the 1938 primaries were a standoff on the issue of the New Deal, so was the general election. It was counted as a New Deal defeat, since the Democrats lost more seats than expected—70 in the House and 7 in the Senate, including major elections in such key states as Pennsylvania, Ohio, Michigan, Wisconsin, and Minnesota. They nearly lost the governorship of New York to Thomas E. Dewey, the gang-busting thirty-six-year-old Manhattan district attorney, and Senator Wagner was reelected by an unimpressive margin. Yet there were still many more Democrats than Republicans in Congress (the Republicans couldn't have recaptured the Senate if they had won every seat up for election, and they couldn't have in 1940, either).

It was not the 1936 Roosevelt landslide, but the more ambiguous result of 1938, that set the pattern that was followed, with relatively minor variations until after World War II was over and Roosevelt was dead. Both parties were frustrated. Although the Democrats fell decisively from their 1932–36 levels of popularity, the Republicans were not able to regain majority status: the Democrats held onto control of both houses of Congress in all these elections, and Roosevelt was reelected with 55% and 53% of the vote in 1940 and 1944. The turmoil of politics in the early 1930s is shown in the sharp increase in the number of Democrats elected to the House, ranging from 220 in 1930 to 331 in 1936, while the Republicans fell from 214 to 89. The numbers stayed within a much narrower range in the next four elections: 261 Democrats in 1938, 268 in 1940, 218 in 1942, 242 in 1944. Only about 20% of the House seats changed partisan hands in any one of these four elections—an unusually low figure. The overall Democratic percentages in House contests were 49%, 51%, 46%, and 51%, and the lowest of these was the result of a turnout that was unusually low because of the war. The Democrats' losses of House seats in 1938 occurred mostly in rural/Yankee districts north of the Civil War borderlands. The turnover was biggest in the large states that were politically marginal in the upcoming presidential election: Democrats lost 4 of the 6 House seats in Connecticut, 4 of 14 in New Jersey, 10 of 34 in Pennsylvania, 13 (including 2 at large) of 24 in Ohio, 6 of 12 in Indiana, 4 of 26 in Illinois, 5 of 20 in California. Republicans made gains in the farm belt and also in some industrial areas shaken by CIO strikes and accompanying violence: the Flint; Rock Island, Illinois; Muncie, Indiana; Canton, Ohio; and Beaver Valley, Pennsylvania, districts. The overall Democratic percentage in industrial/immigrant districts declined from 57% in 1936 to 49%, and in rural/Yankee districts from 51% to a not very competitive 45%. The Democratic caucus in the House elected in 1938 drew 100 of its 261 members from the eleven states of the Old Confederacy and another 39 from border states from Maryland to Oklahoma; together, these made up a majority of the caucus. Of the other Democrats, most were from districts clustered in and around large industrial cities or other industrial areas.[32] While they were more often machine products than New Deal liberals, they tended to support activist and redistributionist economic policies much more than the northern Democrats elected as late as 1930 would have.

In the next three elections the parties traded a few seats here and there, with little overall effect. In 1940, when Roosevelt's interventionist foreign policy helped in the East but hurt in the Midwest, Democrats gained 16 seats and lost only 2 east of Columbus, Ohio, while gaining only 4 (including one from the Progressives) and losing 11 west of Columbus. In 1942 low turnout hurt the Democrats almost everywhere; and they gained only a few scattered seats while losing in much the same pattern as in 1938, though in smaller numbers. In 1944, with turnout stimulated upward by the presidential contest, Democrats gained some 33 scattered seats and lost only 8. By this time politicians could focus fairly easily on the seats likely to be seriously contested. Switches of party control were concentrated in a relatively small number of districts, most of them industrial/immigrant.[33] These were different grounds from those on which the battles in traditional American politics up to 1930 had been fought.

To understand how the political terrain had changed, compare the evenly divided House elected in 1930 with the Democratic House elected in 1940. There is always some distortion in comparing elections: personal factors and local issues decide some races, even when national issues are as overriding a factor as they were in 1940, and district boundaries and the communities within them change. None-theless, the differences between 1930 and 1940 are revealing. Over that period the Democrats gained 75 seats (including newly created seats in California and Michigan) and lost 22. In the industrial/immigrant districts, they won 54 seats in 1940 they had not won in 1930 and lost only 6 they had won a decade earlier. Since the Democrats won only 61 industrial/immigrant seats in 1930, the net gain of 48 represented almost a doubling of their strength in such districts. The coal-steel-auto territory from West Virginia up through Pennsylania and around the Great Lakes to Gary, Indiana, and Minnesota's Mesabi Range accounted for 24 of the gains and only 1 loss. In rural/Yankee districts, Democratic gains outnumbered Democratic losses by 19 to 16. But most of the gains came in the West, where the Democrats had been very weak in the 1920s; there they gained 14 seats and lost only 1. Outside the West, the Democrats gained only 5 rural/Yankee seats and lost 15, most of them in Ohio, Indiana, Illinois, Missouri, and Nebraska. The Democrats also gained 2 seats in the South which the Republicans had captured in the 1920s, in Tidewater Virginia and south Texas.

VI

The frustrations of both parties led to bitterness, and it was exacerbated by the stakes. Great issues seemed at stake in these elections, issues of war and peace and the division of economic rewards in a time of limited growth. The threat of chaos was much more remote than it had been in 1933. But neither party had a macroeconomic policy that convincingly promised economic growth. The Republicans trumpeted a faith in free markets and free enterprise which few voters shared, while the Roosevelt Democrats' tax-and-spend policies did not seem to have produced sustainable growth.[34] Republicans, after the disaster of 1936, learned that they could not credibly promise that their policies would produce growth; Roosevelt, after the recession of 1937–38, seemed to revert to the philosophy expressed in his Commonwealth Club speech of 1932, in which he implied that government could not stimulate growth and should instead allocate resources and wealth.[35] By 1939 Roosevelt's policies of centralization had been rejected, but the tension between the centralism of the Democratic president and the localism of other Democrats and the increasing localism of the once national-minded Republicans remained.

The deadlock over issues of economic distribution which persisted for a dozen years after Roosevelt's landslide reelection in 1936 was bitter not only because Americans perceived that the economy was not growing, but also because they were arguing about more than money. They were arguing as well about who should be seen as the major economic decision-makers: would New Deal officials and industrial union leaders take the place long filled by corporate bosses and small-town businessmen? The conflict was not easily resolved because the two sides were about evenly matched and because it became obscured (though not totally obviated) by the war. American politics, after the turmoil of the half-dozen years after 1930, had reached an equipoise. If Roosevelt's New Dealers and internationalists won every presidential election from 1936 to 1948, they lost most of the congressional elections and failed to win control of most of the big state governments. With such a close balance, those on both sides believed, probably reasonably, that if they tried just a little harder they might prevail. As it happened, neither group did until after their country had won its total victory in the war and begun the greatest economic growth and prosperity it has ever known— developments not only unforeseen but entirely unimaginable by most Americans in the late 1930s.

15

->» «<-

"America Hates War"

merica's position in the world was nonetheless a subject of American politics. Despite the controversy that had attended the entry of the United States into World War I, in 1930 a majority of Americans still believed their country should have fought in what they still called the World War—and believed that their country would not have to fight again. Europe, after all, was far away; no foreign power could threaten the American homeland. Conversely, it was not clear to Americans in 1930 that the United States could prevail in a protracted European struggle. Its troops may have helped turn the tide in France in 1918; but the American expeditionary force had failed to oust the Bolsheviks in Russia in 1920, and everyone feared that another great war would end in the stalemated trench conflict which had taken millions of lives, for precious little territory, from 1914 to 1918. American foreign policy was run by a small elite—by men like William Howard Taft and Franklin Roosevelt—who were convinced that American power had a role to play in world affairs. But American politics was responsive to voters who were uneasy about American engagement abroad and uncertain about American interests there—yet proud of their achievements and occasionally eager to project their example overseas. In their vast continental nation, safe from foreign invasion, they looked out warily across the oceans, dimly aware of the dangers there. But their isolation was not quite complete, their separation from a turbulent and increasingly terrifying world not total.

II

The 1920s were not a decade of isolationism. Although the United States had declined to join the League of Nations, it did join with other nations to limit the size of the great navies, it helped to initiate the Kellogg-Briand peace pact, it was constantly negotiating with European powers toward what seemed peaceful ends. In possession of the Philippines, it had an interest in Asian affairs. Foreign trade boomed, and millions of Americans traveled to Europe. Almost all of these things changed in the 1930s. The collapse of the western economies, which was aggravated by the Smoot-Hawley tariff, dried up international trade: U.S. foreign trade dropped from $9.6 billion in 1929 to $2.9 billion in 1932 and did not reach its former level until the war year of 1942.[1] Foreign travel plummeted. And political

125

developments abroad were unsettling. Adolf Hitler came to power in Germany in January 1933, just as Americans were about to see their banks close their doors and were waiting for Roosevelt to replace Hoover. In March 1934, Hitler renounced the Versailles treaty and announced he would build up Germany's army and air force. In July 1934, Nazis staged an unsuccessful *Putsch* in Austria and assassinated Chancellor Engelbert Dolfuss. In October 1934 terrorists assassinated King Alexander of Yugoslavia and French Foreign Minister Louis Barthou in Marseilles. Americans did not need to be reminded that the assassination of an Austrian leader in what was now Yugoslavia had started World War I just twenty years before.

Americans, engaged mostly from afar in the benign Europe of the 1920s, turned away from the malignant Europe of the middle 1930s.[2] Isolationist tendencies were increased by writings like the article "Arms and the Man," which appeared in the March 1934 *Fortune* and was reprinted in the *Reader's Digest; Merchants of Death,* an April 1934 Book-of-the-Month Club selection; and Walter Mills's *Road to War: America 1914–1917.*[3] And they were further strengthened by the hearings conducted by the Nye Committee, formed in April 1934 to investigate the role of munitions-makers in fomenting war. Congressional committee investigations, pioneered by Senator Thomas Walsh's inquiry into the Teapot Dome scandal in the 1920s and raised to a high political art by Ferdinand Pecora's probe into Wall Street in 1932, became during this period a weapon of liberals, who on many issues were in the minority in Congress. By making news, they brought facts vividly to the attention of ordinary voters in a way that workaday political speeches no longer could. Famous investigations were conducted by Congressmen John McCormack and Samuel Dickstein, who in 1934 looked into "un-American" fascist and Communist organizers, and by Senator Robert LaFollette, Jr., who in 1936 spotlighted the intimidation of union organizers by heavy-handed employers. But the most famous of these investigations was that of the Nye Committee.

Gerald Nye was a senator from North Dakota, where thousands of farmers still spoke with a German accent (or spoke nothing but German) and remembered the persecutions of World War I. A progressive on domestic issues, he was always ready to give government the kind of economic powers it had in North Dakota, where the state government was the proud owner of a bank and a grain elevator. Nye was appalled by the profits of the munitions makers and wanted to nationalize them. That stance was not entirely outside the American tradition: Alexander Hamilton had wanted the government to control arms production, and the federal arsenal at Harper's Ferry which John Brown had seized in 1859 was important because it accounted for such a large share of the nation's arms-making capacity. But it became apparent to Nye, and to his political allies from the North Dakota wheatfields and in the Corinthian-columned Senate Caucus Room,[4] that eliminating munitions-makers' profits was not enough. The conviction was growing in the 1930s that Woodrow Wilson, with his obvious British sympathies, had maneuvered the United States into war in 1917. Doubt was corroding the belief that Germany was uniquely guilty for the outbreak of war, while the impression was becoming widespread that, as John Maynard Keynes had argued in 1920 in *The Economic Consequences of the Peace,* the Versailles settlement was unduly harsh on Germany and that the Allies' insistence on reparations seriously weakened the world economy. As the storm clouds of war arose over Europe, as Italy threatened in 1935 to invade Ethiopia, and as memories grew more vivid of hundreds of thousands of men dying in mud and squalor, Nye and his allies became determined to ensure that the United States remained neutral in any forthcoming European conflicts.

The result was not nationalization but the Neutrality Act of 1935. Franklin Roosevelt encouraged and attempted to guide the Nye Committee. He seemed to share its members' disgust at the evidence it uncovered, and he came out for a neutrality act himself, but one which would give him discretion over whether to embargo arms shipments. Congress, however, wanted a flat embargo. Roosevelt had already lost one foreign policy fight in 1935 after he asked the Senate in January to ratify the treaty recognizing the authority of the World Court. Bitter attacks on the court by Father Coughlin and William Randolph Hearst eroded support in the Senate, and the administration failed to get the required two-thirds majority. Now, in the summer of 1935, with bills for a public utilities holding company, banking regulation, and progressive taxation all pending, Roosevelt did not want to jeopardize Congress by going against the tide on neutrality. The progressives who were staunch supporters of neutrality were also his most committed supporters on most domestic legislation, and he dared not risk engaging them in a fight over foreign policy.[5] Nor was he willing to ask southern and western Democrats who supported his foreign policy to fight a difficult and probably losing battle against isolation when he was delicately wooing them on one domestic issue after another. And so in August 1935, just as the Italian forces were steaming through the Suez Canal on their way to Ethiopia, Roosevelt signed the Neutrality Act. Congress voted twice to renew the Neutrality Act, strengthening it each time. In February 1936 it prohibited loans or credits to nations on either side of a war, and in May 1937 it prohibited U.S. ships from carrying arms to belligerent zones and required that various non-military goods purchased from the United States by belligerents be paid for with cash and shipped in foreign vessels—a policy known as "cash and carry." Roosevelt signed them both, and every indication is that they increased his popularity.

III

In October 1935, during the political lull after the rush of legislation that summer, Mussolini's legions invaded Ethiopia. Americans followed, through muddled news reports, Emperor Haile Selassie's plaintive pleas to the League of Nations and the Italian conquest that was completed in May 1936. But while 80% of those surveyed by *Fortune* said they would be willing to fight if the country were attacked "on our own territory," only 24% said they would so respond to an attack on the Philippines, and by only a narrow 48%–41% margin did Americans favor refusing to trade with "one nation [which] insists on attacking another."[6] In March 1936, Hitler's troops marched without challenge into the forbidden Rhineland. In July 1936 the troops of General Franco rose in rebellion against the leftist Spanish Republic, and the majority of Americans were pleased when the United States joined France in refusing to sell arms to either side, while Germany and Italy supplied Franco's armies and the Soviet Union supplied the Republicans with arms and men. When Congress returned in January 1937, it passed a resolution continuing this evenhanded embargo of an established government and military rebels. Roosevelt followed this policy until the Republic was defeated in June 1939, doing so partly because of pro-Franco sentiment among American Catholics and despite the objections of his liberal ambassador to Spain, Claude Bowers.[7] In July 1937, after Roosevelt lost the court-packing fight, while the CIO was picketing Little Steel, Japan invaded China; in December the Japanese gunned down the American ship *Panay* in the Yangtze River and, a day later, inflicted horrible atrocities as they entered Nanking. The world was already at war—in China, in Spain—and the dictators of Germany and Italy were on the march in Europe and in Africa.

Against this background Roosevelt attempted to rally public opinion in support of an active American role. In October 1937, returning from a tour around the West inspecting government work projects, he went to Chicago—the city whose mayor ten years before, Big Bill Thompson, had threatened to punch King George in the snoot and whose leading publisher, the *Tribune*'s Colonel Robert McCormick, was obsessively anti-British and isolationist. To everyone's surprise, he spoke on foreign affairs. Using one of his homey metaphors, he said, "When an epidemic of physical disease starts to spread, the community approves and joins in a quarantine of the patients in order to protect the health of the community against the spread of the disease." Did this mean common action against Japan, Germany, and Italy? Roosevelt seems to have had in mind some international agreement to isolate these aggressor nations. But when the reaction to the speech proved harshly negative, he quickly foreswore all specific plans. "America hates war," he noted in Chicago. "America hopes for peace. Therefore, America actively engages in the search for peace." But logic does not always govern public opinion, and most Americans were not prepared to believe that lasting peace required the willingness to risk temporary war. "If one foreign nation insists upon attacking another, should the United States join with other nations to compel it to stop?" Gallup asked during the week after the "quarantine" speech. Only 29% of those with an opinion said yes. Americans seemed determined not to fight. Not only had the Neutrality Act been strengthened, but in January 1938 the House rejected by only a 209–198 margin a resolution, sponsored by Indianapolis Democrat Louis Ludlow, which called for a national referendum before any U.S. declaration of war. "It's a terrible thing to look over your shoulder when you are trying to lead— and to find no one there," Roosevelt said later.

This attitude prevailed as Europe moved closer to general war. As Congress was considering the wage-and-hours bill in March 1938, Hitler's troops entered Austria and received an enthusiastic welcome. In mid-September 1938, after

Roosevelt's highly publicized primary defeats in Georgia and Maryland, Hitler precipitated another crisis by demanding territorial concessions from Czechoslovakia. Roosevelt responded with a message September 27 to the leaders of Germany, France, Britain, and Czechoslovakia—a message which had no perceptible effect on the settlement which British Prime Minister Neville Chamberlain reached with Hitler by the end of the month. Most Americans saw that Hitler's aggression was motivated by a desire to conquer Europe, yet 59% still approved the Chamberlain agreement.[8] In March 1939, Hitler marched into Czechoslovakia. Roosevelt's response was an April letter to Hitler and Mussolini seeking a ten-year guarantee of peace. Hitler's reply later in the month contemptuously repudiated his own 1935 naval agreement with Britain and 1935 pact with Poland, and in May he formalized his military alliance with Mussolini's Italy. On August 23, the Hitler–Stalin non-aggression pact was signed in Moscow by Foreign Ministers Joachim von Ribbentrop and Vyacheslav Molotov. Finally, on September 1, German forces invaded Poland in defiance of Britain and France; and by October 1, Poland was overrun—split, actually, between Nazi Germany and Soviet Russia. World War II had begun.

But not for Americans. Roosevelt continually pushed for more military spending and got the total up from $648 million in 1933 to $914 million in 1936 and over $1 billion in 1938—a pittance next to the $60–$80 billion figures of World War II or even the $13 billion of World War I. The number of military personnel on active duty rose equally modestly, from 243,000 in 1933 to 291,000 in 1936 and 334,000 in 1939—far smaller than European or Japanese military forces. Roosevelt made plans to defend the Western Hemisphere against Nazi attacks. But in early 1939 he declined to support changes in the Neutrality Act which would have allowed the United States to discriminate between aggressors and victims. In March 1939, a bill to allow Britain and France to buy and ship American-made arms on a cash-and-carry basis was introduced by Key Pittman, the chairman of the Senate Foreign Relations Committee—a tall, southern-descended, alcoholic Nevadan who spent much of his energy propping up the price of silver. A weakened version of the bill passed the House in early June but did not become law until November 1939, after the war had broken out. Public opinion tended to favor cash-and-carry arms sales, but only as a means of ensuring that the United States would not be drawn into war.[9] There was considerable popular sympathy for Britain, carefully orchestrated by Roosevelt's hosting of King George VI and Queen Elizabeth on a June 1939 visit capped, in American style, by a picnic with hot dogs on the grounds of Roosevelt's house in Hyde Park. But the determination of most Americans to remain isolated from the conflicts of Europe remained unchanged.

IV

With the Hitler-Stalin pact of August 1939 and Hitler's conquest of Poland in September, the two dictators became uneasy partners in physical control of the greater part of the north European plain. Hitler held Germany, Austria,

Czechoslovakia, and most of Poland—territory roughly coextensive with that of the Central Powers in World War I. Unlike the Central Powers, he was allied with Italy and at peace with Russia. After the conquest of Poland, fighting almost stopped: across the Maginot Line, German and French soldiers watched each other celebrate Christmas. But the "phony war" threatened to turn real at any time.

For Americans who have lived past D-Day, it seems obvious how this situation led to the Allied victory in Europe five years later. But at the time it took great imagination to foresee America's role, and by no means everyone considered Hitler a threat that must be opposed. Roosevelt did. With his Anglophile education, his experience in the Wilson administration and the Navy, it was natural for him to look at events as the British did and to see any single power in control of the continent of Europe as a threat. Moreover, like Winston Churchill, he recognized the malevolent nature of Hitler's regime early on. "Practically speaking," he told a gathering of senators in January 1939, "if the Rhine frontiers are threatened the rest of the world is, too."[10] Staunchly agreeing with Roosevelt were most southern Democrats, representing the most bellicose part of the nation: Anglophile Republicans like Henry Stimson, Hoover's secretary of state, and Frank Knox, the Chicago publisher and 1936 Republican vice presidential candidate; and journalists like Walter Lippmann and Dorothy Thompson and *Emporia Gazette* editor William Allen White. But other Americans saw the situation of their country quite differently.

If the Anglo-Saxon Protestants of the East and South formed the demographic base of pro-British feeling, the German-Americans of Wisconsin, Minnesota, and the Dakotas were the demographic base of isolationism. Most of the outspoken isolationist politicians came from this region—one-time Roosevelt allies like Burton Wheeler and Hiram Johnson and Henrik Shipstead and Robert LaFollette, Jr., as well as Roosevelt opponents like Robert Taft and Arthur Vandenberg and Charles Lindbergh (whose father had been an anti-war progressive congressman from Minnesota during World War I) and Colonel McCormick (who served in the Allied Expeditionary Forces himself). But there were isolationists as well on elite eastern campuses, like McGeorge Bundy and Kingman Brewster. Memories of World War I were still fresh, memories of how 600,000 men had been sent up over the trenches to die within hours, all for a few meters of ground, and how German-Americans had been beaten up and their property vandalized at home. Some isolationists sympathized with the Nazis: Father Coughlin, who was finally ordered off the air in 1940 by the new Catholic archbishop of Detroit, and Gerald L. K. Smith, Huey Long's one-time publicist. But men like Taft and Lindbergh had no sympathy with Hitler's Nazis or Mussolini's fascists. Like many observers at the time, they failed to gauge the hideous evil of the Nazi regime, but in their defense it may be said that many of their critics failed to recognize the hideous evil of Stalin's Communist Russia; and if Russia at that time did not seem to have expansionist tendencies, many observers believed Hitler's assertions that his latest acquisition—Austria or the Sudetenland or Czechoslovakia or Danzig—would be his last. Against the viciousness of the Nazis they weighed their fear that American blood might be endlessly drained to no good purpose, as it seemed to them it had been in World War I. It was not always wise, they argued, to intervene against an evil regime; after all, American troops had been withdrawn from Soviet Russia in 1920 when it might still have been possible for them to overthrow the Communist government. Now as 1940 began, it seemed to the isolationists unlikely that American military power could once again break the bloody stalemate that so many expected in Europe.

Many of the isolationists' premises were cruelly undermined by the facts of the struggle that followed. Their judgment of Hitler's intentions and their gauging of the malevolence of his regime proved terribly wrong. But some of their fears had a basis. It surely would have been impossible (or at least far more costly) for the United States and Britain to have invaded Hitler's Europe successfully had it not been for Soviet help, which was anything but assured until Hitler's invasion of Russia in June 1941. And the alliance with the Soviets, though it produced victory, would do so at a high price. The isolationists were closer than the interventionists to understanding that it would prove impossible to liberate Europe from Hitler without allowing half of it to be enslaved by Stalin.

The isolationists were also worried about what war would mean to America at home. Their fears were not all the same. Progressives like Johnson and LaFollette feared that the war would mean the end of progressive reform. Conservatives like Taft and McCormick feared that war would mean statist regimentation and confiscatory taxes. Both sets of fears turned out to have some justification. The centralizing proposals of Roosevelt's "third New Deal" were never revived during the war, little more was heard of the economic statism recommended by the Temporary National Economic Committee, and the organizing drives of the CIO were stalled. But taxes were raised, as they usually are in wartime, to confiscatory levels, most American males of draft age were enrolled in the military, and a command economy was instituted. War, the isolationists were correct in fearing, would change their country in ways they did not want, even as it changed the rest of the world in ways they did not anticipate.

16

→)) ((←

Third Term

N o, no, Dan, I just can't do it," Roosevelt said when Daniel Tobin of the Teamsters urged him to run for a third term in 1940. "I have to have a rest. I want to go home to Hyde Park."[1] On January 22, Harry Hopkins told a friend, the playwright Robert Sherwood, that he was sure Roosevelt would run, but on April 23 he expressed strong doubts about the matter.[2] "Of course I will not run for a third term," Roosevelt had told James Farley in 1939, and as late as July 7, 1940—eight days before the opening of the Democratic convention—he was saying, "Jim, I don't want to run and I'm going to tell the convention so. . . . I am definitely opposed to seeking a third term."[3] He told Cordell Hull on July 3 that he wanted to write a letter to the convention saying he was going back to Hyde Park and that the delegates should choose Hull.[4] Eleanor Roosevelt was left in the dark, although on July 4 she overheard him telling a cousin at Hyde Park, "I am a tired and weary man."[5] Harold Ickes believed Roosevelt was trying up to the last minute to escape renomination. On July 3, Ickes asked him whether New Dealers would be going to Chicago "leaderless and planless. He grinned at me and said he was 'trusting to God.' " But Ickes said he felt in September 1939 that Roosevelt "did intend to be a candidate if he had control of the convention and if the foreign situation had assumed a serious aspect."[6]

No one can know for sure when Roosevelt decided to run for a third term, though he must have made the final decision sometime between Hitler's invasion of France on May 10, 1940, and France's surrender June 16. But he had been laying the groundwork for years. In this process he was helped by the difficulty both parties had in coming up with suitable alternatives. Among the Democrats, one obvious rival was Vice President Garner. But Garner was a southerner, he was seventy-three in 1940, and his opposition to key New Deal measures like court packing made him anathema to many Democrats. Besides which he was, or so John L. Lewis told a congressional committee in July 1939 in one of his marvellously memorable phrases, "a labor-baiting, poker-playing, whiskey-drinking, evil old man." Secretary of State Hull looked like a president and, as a longtime member of Congress and ardent free trader, had support from old-fashioned Jeffersonian Democrats. But he was also a southerner, he turned sixty-nine in 1940, and—a real handicap in an era of radio campaigning—he spoke with a lisp.[7] He had reason to hope that Roosevelt and the party would turn to him as a widely acceptable candidate popular with the public, but he made no move to run. Postmaster General Farley did, and insisted over strenuous opposition on putting his name before the delegates in Chicago. But his governmental experience was limited to the distribution of patronage, and he was a Catholic.

Roosevelt, with varying degrees of openness, promoted various New Dealers as possible candidates, but all fell by the wayside. Harry Hopkins was incapacitated by stomach cancer in August 1939, Frank Murphy, a Catholic and a bachelor, was beaten for reelection as governor of Michigan in November 1938, and Governor George Earle of Pennsylvania lost his Senate bid the same year. Roosevelt was unable to get Robert Jackson, an acerbic upstate New York lawyer who argued New Deal cases ably but had never held elective office, the Democratic nomination for governor in 1938. Paul McNutt, a law professor at Indiana University who had become national commander of the Indianapolis-headquartered American Legion in 1928, been elected governor of Indiana in 1932, and served as governor general of the Philippines in 1937 and 1938, was known mainly for requiring state employees to contribute 2% of their salaries to the Democratic party and for his missteps in Manila; as head of federal welfare and relief programs in 1939, he was taken out of the running by sniping from Ickes and Farley. Other talented Democrats were obviously unsuitable: the governors of New York and Illinois, Hebert Lehman and Henry Horner, were Jewish; Senators Alben Barkley and James Byrnes were southern; and Byrnes had the additional compound disadvantage of having been born a Catholic and having left the faith.

For all the weaknesses of the alternative possibilities, however, it was not clear in early 1940 that Roosevelt could have forced his nomination without a messy fight that would have damaged his chances. Americans had never elected a president to a third term and still seemed reluctant to do so. As late as May 5–10, Roosevelt had only a 48%–44% plurality when matched against Republican Thomas Dewey in the Gallup poll—only marginally better than Hull's 43%–42%, though Roosevelt was clearly a stronger candidate than Garner or Farley.[8] In peacetime a Roosevelt candidacy was chancy; as a wartime leader, he was much stronger.[9] Roosevelt's approval rating had dipped from above 60% in 1937 to the 53–58% range as the Roosevelt recession sank in, and it rose above that level only with the onset of war: to 61% in September 1939 and to the 63–65% range from October 1939 to March 1940. As the "phony war" went on, his rating dipped to 60–61% in March and April 1940. With the invasion of France it jumped to 70% in May— in the usual pattern of Americans rallying around their leaders in a crisis; it dipped to 66% and 63% in late May and June, then rose above 70% and stayed there through 1943.[10] Support for a third term for Roosevelt grew from 34% in April 1940 to 49% in June.[11] In July, just after the two parties' conventions, Gallup found Roosevelt ahead of Republican nominee Wendell Willkie by a margin—not a reassuring result for Roosevelt, since he was universally known and Willkie was not.[12] But at the same time, voters believed by a 54%–27% margin that Roosevelt could "handle our country's foreign affairs better."[13]

War—more precisely, Hitler's successes in the war—made Roosevelt a winning candidate for a third term. In a lightning stroke in April 1940, Hitler's troops occupied Denmark overnight and Norway after only a brief struggle. On May 10, in one of the warmest and sunniest European springs on record, the Wehrmacht wheeled into the Netherlands, Belgium, and Luxembourg, over the northern European plain and, against every expectation, through the hills of the Ardennes toward France. It was the same kind of invasion the world had watched in 1914, and most observers expected the same result: another stalemate in the north of France. Instead the Panzer units broke through and split the Allies. The Netherlands surrendered May 14, Belgium May 28; from May 26 to June 4, 335,000 British and French troops, surrounded on land by the Germans, were evacuated from the French port of Dunkirk—an evacuation which kept the Allies from losing manpower and equipment but which only the eloquence of Winston Churchill could cast as something like a victory. On June 10, Italy joined the war against France. On June 13 the Germans were in Paris and the French government was in flight. On June 16, Marshal Henri Pétain became premier and called for a halt to the fighting in France, clinging to the fiction that he was head of a neutral independent government based in Vichy.

As events moved rapidly, so did Roosevelt. On May 16, as the Nazis advanced, he asked Congress for more money for defense. On June 3, as the last boats were streaming out of Dunkirk and after it became apparent that France was reeling, the War Department agreed to sell the British old arms, munitions, and aircraft— sales which would have been quite illegal under the Neutrality Act before it changed in November 1939. On June 10, just before France fell, Roosevelt said at the University of Virginia that the United States had moved from "neutrality to non-belligerency"; he said of Mussolini's attack earlier that day on the south of France, "the hand that held the dagger has struck it into the back of its neighbor." (Republicans quoted these words for months and years afterwards, to Roosevelt's political detriment in the Italian-American wards of Brooklyn and Newark, Boston and Philadelphia.) Within the next three days Congress voted $1.5 billion for the Navy and $1.8 billion for the Army—huge sums by 1930s standards.

There was irony here: the same American public which had bridled at the thought of aiding allies when their hold on Europe seemed strong were now willing to help just as that hold was completely slipping away. Perhaps the reason was a new clarity of vision: as one backer of the president later explained, "The knowledge that Britain would fight alone and that America would extend all possible aid as a noncombatant clarified the situation in the public mind, at least until the next crisis should arise; and that represented far more clarification of issues than the people had had at any time since Munich."[14] Hitler did not seem such a threat until he had won his terrifying military victories. Yet it was hard to see what Roosevelt's policy could accomplish beyond its immediate and by no means clearly attainable goal of enabling Britain to resist conquest. Charles Lindbergh, still a national hero and now a spokesman for the isolationist organization America First, argued that the United States could protect the Western Hemisphere but was not "strong enough to impose [its] way of life on Europe and Asia." Robert Taft, who thought little better of American chances, was also convinced that war would mean "the practical establishment of a dictatorship in this country through arbitrary powers granted to the President, and financial and economic collapse," along with "the nationalization of all industry and all capital and all labor." In London, Joseph Kennedy thought Britain was finished and favored a peace with Hitler rather than U.S. aid.[15] In its immediate aim Roosevelt's policy did in fact succeed, as the German Luftwaffe failed to destroy the Royal Air Force in the Battle of Britain, which went on from July to September 1940, and the British did not buckle under the intensive bombing of London that followed. But how could Britain ever hope to establish even a beachhead on a continent filled with Hitler's troops, when Germany had Italy as an active military ally, Russia as a friendly collaborator, France as a passive dependency, and Spain and Portugal as congenial neighbors?

As the great foreign correspondents of the era like John Gunther and William L. Shirer cabled in their reports, and as young radio correspondents like CBS's Edward R. Murrow and Eric Sevareid broadcast daily routines over makeshift hookups amid the whine and crash of falling bombs, Roosevelt continued to move rapidly. He was eager to create a bipartisan coalition and to replace lethargic placeholders with energetic men. On June 20, just a week after the Germans entered Paris, he appointed two leading Republicans to high Cabinet positions. The Wall Street lawyer Henry Stimson became secretary of war, a position he had held in Taft's administration (he had also been Hoover's secretary of state), and *Chicago Daily News* publisher Frank Knox, the 1936 vice presidential nominee and one-time Rough Rider, became secretary of the Navy.

II

Besides accomplishing Roosevelt's other purposes, these appointments also overshadowed the opening of the Republican national convention four days later in Philadelphia. Even more than the Democrats, the Republicans had a hard time coming up with plausible alternatives to Roosevelt. They had lost so many elections in the 1930s that they had few seasoned incumbents. Herbert Hoover and Alf Landon were out of office and landslide losers. William Borah died in January 1940. Arthur Vandenberg, twenty years younger than Borah and one of the few Republican senators from a large state who had some seniority, was garrulous and lacked forcefulness; moreover, he had been discredited by his opposition to amending the Neutrality Act and his pooh-poohing of the Nazi threat during the "phony war" period. The Republicans' most obviously talented men were without much high-level experience. Robert Taft had just been elected to the Senate in 1938, and Thomas E. Dewey in 1940 was a thirty-eight-year-old district attorney (admittedly, of the most important county in the nation, New York, and with a racket-busting record that made him a national celebrity). Harold Stassen had just been elected governor of Minnesota in 1938 at age thirty-one. Wendell Willkie was president of the Commonwealth & Southern utility holding company, a businessman with a Wall Street office and a Fifth Avenue apartment, and a Democrat until he switched his party registration in January 1940.[16] He had voted for Roosevelt in 1932 and for New York's Governor Lehman against Dewey as recently as 1938; but he had also sparred with the New Dealers, helping to lead the fight against Roosevelt's public utilities holding company bill (after losing, he sold most of his company's utility holding to the TVA for $78 million). He had genuine roots in small-town Indiana and a knack for the homespun phrase, but he was also a sophisticated political operator, aptly dubbed by Harold Ickes "the barefoot boy of Wall Street."[17]

In those days the outcomes of conventions were not always foreordained. Party leaders and delegates from different states scarcely knew one another and had seldom conferred about the nominees before their trains brought them into the convention city. It was literally at the convention hall and the hotels around it that the communication and bargaining that were the real business of nominating conventions took place. The leading candidate coming into Philadelphia on June 24 was Dewey, who thought he had 450 of the 1,000 delegates. It is a sign of how crude candidates' communication networks were at the time that the estimate of this most systematic and fact-hungry of politicians was off by a lot: he got 360 on the first ballot. Taft had 189, and a surprising 105 went to Willkie, whose candidacy had been nurtured by his friends in the press. Running his campaign was Russell Davenport, who as editor of *Fortune* put Willkie's picture on the cover of the May issue; Henry Luce, publisher of *Fortune, Life,* and *Time,* helped out; so did the Cowles brothers, who owned *Look* and the Minneapolis and Des Moines papers; and some of his strongest support came from the Reids, who owned the *New York Herald Tribune.* Willkie's cause was also helped by his backers— many of them young recent Ivy League graduates—who jammed the galleries at Philadelphia's Convention Hall and screamed "We want Willkie!" The chant went out over America's radios, and on the sixth ballot Willkie won.

He proved to be an engaging candidate and an interventionist one. "I'm not a cagey politician," he would say. "I don't know the arts of that trade. I'm glad I don't," he would go on, proving as he talked that he did. "I have the satisfaction of knowing that the man who is looking for a job is my chief supporter. The big boys may still be hostile, but the man who works with his hands or wants to have a chance to get a job is rooting for me."[18] His bluff friendliness and candor seemed refreshing, and he became the model for the hero in Frank Capra's movie *State of the Union,*[19] but the demand for his candidacy came from events. Hitler's troops had swept into France, and Hitler and Stalin now controlled most of the landmass of Europe. "As if by a sort of prairie fire osmosis," as Gardner Cowles put it, Willkie was chosen because he "looked like the biggest and strongest man around."[20]

Willkie's nomination and Roosevelt's rise in the polls gave evidence of how the war was changing American politics, increasing the strength of the internationalists in the Republican party and the popularity of the incumbent Democratic president. In another indication that the country was moving toward a wartime mentality, Americans were suddenly accepting and even seeking restraints on personal freedom which are taken for granted in war but are resented and often fiercely opposed in peacetime. Late in June, Congress passed a bill for registration of aliens, the Smith Act, which also banned conspiracy to overthrow the government. (It should be remembered that after the Hitler-Stalin pact hostility had increased toward Soviet Russia, which was fighting brave Finland and helping Nazi Germany.) An export control act went into effect in July. That same month Roosevelt requested a huge $4.8 billion budget for defense, and Congress voted $4 billion for a two-ocean Navy—moves made with an eye on Japan, to which Roosevelt had been hostile since its invasion of China and its bombing of the U.S. gunboat *Panay* in December 1937. And that same month, all the while protesting his innocence of ambition, Roosevelt engineered his third nomination for president.

III

Even as the Democratic convention began July 15, Roosevelt was insisting he only wanted to return to Hyde Park and work in the presidential library he was establishing near his house. Yet as long before as March 1939, Harold Ickes had written in his diary that Roosevelt "was giving very careful consideration to the city in which the Democratic National Convention should be held next year. He wants a city where the mayor can be relied on to fill the galleries with New Deal adherents. The Madison Square Garden convention in New York"—the convention Charles F. Murphy arranged for his home city in 1924—"greatly impressed him with what a gallery can do in influencing delegates. In canvassing the situation, he expressed the view that St. Louis and Chicago probably offered the best cities from the New Deal point of view. He ventured to guess that not even Jim Farley had not thought of this detail." Farley, for all his contracts with politicians, was not a good convention manager; he had nearly destroyed Roosevelt's changes in 1932 by trying to abolish the two-thirds rule. "If [Ed] Kelly is reelected as Mayor of Chicago, as he undoubtedly will be," Ickes noted with entire accuracy, "it is the President's intention to send for him and work out plans for the 1940 convention."[21]

Ickes, the cantankerous curmudgeon, as he was often called, had practiced law in Chicago and knew Kelly well—and disliked him. Ickes was an old progressive Republican, a follower of Theodore Roosevelt, and a believer in clean government; Kelly was an ancestral Democrat, a believer in patronage, and a beneficiary of corruption. He was a product, literally, of the sewers. The great city which had grown up in a few decades where the Great Lakes meet the Great Plains drew in millions of people and pigs, millions of tons of iron and coal: it spewed out billions of gallons of sludge and sewage. Just as Chicago built a circulatory system of railroads and subways, so it had to build a system of excretion for its wastes. That system was the Chicago Sanitary Canal, begun in 1890 when there were 1.1 million people in Chicago and completed in 1900 when there were 1.7 million; it breathtakingly reversed the flow of the Chicago River and sent the city's sludge down toward the Mississippi rather than out into the clear waters of Lake Michigan, which provides Chicago's drinking water. The Sanitary District had jurisdiction over 440 square miles; it employed thousands, let contracts in the millions.[22] One of those employees was Edward J. Kelly, a tall, beefy man with a severe look. Well-connected in Democratic politics, Kelly became an engineer without having an engineering degree; and he was shrewd enough to make a favorable impression on Robert McCormick, who saved Kelly's job when McCormick was briefly head of the Sanitary District Board.[23] By the 1920s, Kelly was chief engineer of the Sanitary District, in a position to channel vast sums of money to private contractors. During the Roosevelt administration the Internal Revenue Service investigated his finances in the 1920s, when his government salary had been $15,000; in a civil settlement—no criminal charges were brought—he admitted to receiving some $724,000 in income in years when he was on the public payroll and reporting only $151,000. He paid $105,000 in back taxes and penalties, while his friend Pat Nash, the Democratic chairman of Cook County, paid some $175,000.[24] When Chicago Mayor Anton Cermak died in February 1933 after being shot while sitting next to President-elect Roosevelt in a motorcade in Florida, Nash chose Kelly as mayor. And this man who knew the city from the guts up, in the words of a sympathetic observer, "did little with Chicago, except let things run away from him."[25]

To no big-city machine had the New Deal been more bountiful than Ed Kelly's and Pat Nash's Chicago. Before 1931, the city had been a political battleground, with the mayoralty contested every four years by both the major parties, with key races for state's attorney and, less important, for governor held in the years in between. When the tight-lipped Cermak installed faithful Democratic ward and precinct leaders in every office, no one was under any illusion that they would remain forever. After four or maybe eight good years, they would probably be out—and perhaps be on the way to jail. The popularity of Franklin Roosevelt and the New Deal changed that. Suddenly Chicago was a one-party city, with the Republicans reduced to a helpless minority—as happened in many smaller cities.[26] Ed Kelly could look forward to handing patronage and office down from father to son, from Arthur Elrod (sheriff in the 1930s) to Richard Elrod (sheriff in the 1970s), from Joe Rostenkowski (32nd ward committeeman beginning in 1935) to Dan Rostenkowski (who was still 32nd ward committeeman when as chairman of the House Ways and Means Committee he put together the 1986 tax reform act). The great wealth of the city of Chicago, the miles of bars and storefronts and factories radiating out from the downtown Loop to the prairies—all this became subject to the tolls exacted, as the price of their organizing the great working masses of the city on election day, by the Democratic machine and the mostly Irish politicians who headed it. "We let the Irish have the government, if they let us do what we please," one of the city's rich men put it.[27] Roosevelt was under no illusions about how the machine worked. Explaining his reason for opposing the lakefront convention hall that would be built and named ultimately for Kelly's friend Colonel McCormick, Ickes wrote, "I also told the President that any funds given Kelly would be subject to twenty per cent for graft and he said he was afraid that was true."[28]

Kelly was the man whom Roosevelt enlisted to ensure that he would be drafted at the upcoming convention. But the president was careful never to say so out loud, and no written record survives of the orders he gave. We have only the evidence, some of it conflicting, of how they were carried out. When Roosevelt wanted something put together fast and in a way which, if not entirely according to the rules, would never prove a problem for him later, he turned to Harry Hopkins. As it happened, Hopkins was literally just down the hall. After his long battle with cancer he had come to dinner at the White House on May 10 and, when he seemed not to be feeling well, had been invited by Roosevelt to spend the night; he ended up staying three and a half years and becoming the president's right-hand man during much of the war. On June 27, the day Willkie was nominated in Philadelphia, Hopkins, in the words of his friendly biographer, Robert Sherwood, "went to Chicago to discuss arrangements for the Convention with Mayor Edward J. Kelly. Acting without express instructions from Roosevelt, but also without prohibition, Hopkins was now moving to take charge of the third term nomination himself."[29] We have only Sherwood's word for it that Hopkins had no instructions; neither Roosevelt nor Hopkins lived to write memoirs. But there can be no real doubt that Hopkins knew what Roosevelt wanted. As Sherwood himself notes, speaking generally of Hopkins, "Roosevelt could send him on any mission, to the Pentagon building or to Downing Street, with absolute confidence that Hopkins would not utter one decisive word based on guesswork as to his Chief's policies or purposes. Hopkins ventured on no ground that Roosevelt had not charted." It's hard to resist the conclusion that Roosevelt told Hopkins what he wanted done, and quite easy to believe that neither man ever spoke of that conversation to anyone else.

Hopkins had help. James Byrnes, then a strong Roosevelt loyalist in the Senate, remembers a dinner "about ten days before" the convention in which Roosevelt met with Byrnes, Hopkins, Kelly, Bronx Democratic leader Ed Flynn, and Frank Walker, a longtime Roosevelt supporter and Farley's successor as postmaster general: a gathering of the most loyal of the loyal. Roosevelt as usual said he was reluctant to run and professed to be perplexed. "I must say that I found it hard to credit him with sincerity," wrote Byrnes later, and noted that it was difficult to persuade him to run.[30] Hopkins took a suite in the Blackstone Hotel—the same suite, overlooking Lake Michigan, where in 1920 Warren G. Harding had been picked for the Republican presidential nomination in the proverbial "smoke-filled room." There he and Byrnes commanded the effort to "draft" Roosevelt and kept in touch with the White House through a direct telephone line in the bathroom. Ickes, more scrupulous and on poor terms with Kelly, kept himself in his own room at another hotel, embarrassed that he didn't know what was going on.

Roosevelt's men wanted him renominated by acclamation. They failed because

Farley insisted on a ballot. But they succeeded in all other respects. On the night of Tuesday, July 16, after speakers had been droning on for some time at Chicago Stadium, Alben Barkley got up and read a statement from Roosevelt in which he said that he had no "desire or purpose to continue in the office of president" and that delegates were "free to vote for any candidate." Then came a roar: "We want Roosevelt!" This was literally the "voice from the sewers": Thomas D. McGarry, Kelly's superintendent of sewers, speaking from an underground passage into a microphone wired to reverberate through the entire hall. A thunderous demonstration began, evidence of genuine enthusiasm; yet it was triggered by a ruse. The next day Roosevelt received 946 of the 1,100 votes.[31] On Thursday, however, he had trouble ramming through the vice presidential nomination of his agriculture secretary, Henry Wallace. Wallace's Iowa roots and farming background were thought to be helpful to a candidate whose fortunes were sagging in the isolationist Great Plains. But Wallace—a dreamy, impractical man, a former Republican who believed in reincarnation, theosophy, and food fads—was mistrusted by other politicians. Roosevelt had to threaten to withdraw himself to get him nominated— "for God's sake," Byrnes went around asking delegates, "do you want a president or vice president?"—and when he was nominated he was plainly so unpopular that it was deemed prudent that he give no acceptance speech.[32]

Then over the radio accepting the nomination came the rich tenor voice of the man who had kept his hand so invisible for months. "Lying awake, as I have, on many nights, I have asked myself whether I have the right, as Commander in Chief of the Army and Navy,[33] to call on men and women to serve their country or to train themselves to serve and, at the same time, decline to serve my country in my personal capacity, if I am called upon to do so by the people of my country. In times like these—in times of great tension, of great crisis—the compass of the world narrows to a single fact. The fact which dominates the world is the fact of armed aggression, the fact of successful armed aggression, aimed at the form of government, the kind of society that we in the United States have chosen and established for ourselves." It was, all at the same time, a bold summons to duty of a reluctant nation and the shameless pitch of a political showman. Roosevelt framed the issue for the general election brilliantly, as usual: it was our country versus their countries, the leader of America at home versus the leaders of dictatorships abroad. But again, as usual, he was aware of a moral gap between means and ends that he took great pains to conceal from an audience. He was a leader who could inspire the nation to victory and a politician who could maneuver his way through the most treacherous of waters.

And with breathtaking nerve. For Roosevelt did not play it safe during the toughest campaign of his life. At a time when Americans desperately wanted to avoid war, he hesitantly adopted and then boldly championed two policies—Lend-Lease and the draft—which aligned the United States more closely with Britain and brought it closer to readiness to fight. In his relations with Congress, in his dealings with other politicians, in his campaign speeches, Roosevelt's maneuvers in 1940 concealed much deviousness. He refused to state boldly his conviction that Americans must fight Hitler and to acknowledge his desire to fight along Britain's side; he asserted a confidence which he himself did not feel that his policies would keep America out of war. But Roosevelt nonetheless took action that could leave voters in little doubt that he was the most intervention-minded candidate in the race, actions that committed his nation to an interventionist course no matter who was elected in November.

The draft was not his initiative. The idea was advanced in June 1940, just after the fall of France, by New York lawyer Grenville Clark, an old Roosevelt friend, and some of their other aristocratic veterans who had started the voluntary Plattsburgh military training camps of 1915, long before most Americans were eager to prepare to join World War I. A month later Henry Stimson, another Plattsburgh veteran, persuaded Roosevelt to support the draft. Toward the end of the summer, as Britain was being pounded by German bombs, Willkie was coming back from his ostentatiously long five-week vacation in Rushville, Indiana, and the explicit campaigning was about to begin, Roosevelt suddenly supported the draft itself. He made an effort to be bipartisan. The bill was sponsored by Senator Edward Burke, a Nebraska Democrat who had opposed the court-packing bill, and Congressman James Wadsworth, the upstate New York Republican who had been ousted from the Senate by Robert Wagner in 1926.

Lend-Lease was not passed as legislation until January 1941. But in August 1940, New York lawyer Charles Burlingham and Washington lawyer Dean Acheson, the one-time acting treasury secretary who had resigned over the gold-buying issue, argued in a *New York Times* advertisement that the president already had authority to transfer military equipment to Britain if that served the interests of American defense. Legally, it was a close case at best. But Britain was reeling, and on September 3, Roosevelt announced that the United States was sending fifty destroyers to Britain in return for long-term leases on British military bases in Newfoundland, Bermuda, and the Caribbean. Two weeks later the Selective Service bill was passed; 16 million young American males registered for the draft on October 16, and the first draft number to determine who would be inducted was picked from a fishbowl by Secretary Stimson on October 29, a week before the election. That same month, the Nazis and their allies were marching farther through Europe. Hungary was already their ally, Czechoslovakia their supine possession, Soviet Russia their uneasy comrade. On October 11, German troops were in Rumania. On October 28 the Italians invaded Greece.

Two days later Willkie charged that Roosevelt's election would mean war. To which Roosevelt replied before a cheering crowd in Boston, an especially isolationist town given the hatred of the Irish for the British, "I have said this before, but I shall say it again and again and again: your boys are not going to be sent into any foreign wars." But of course everyone knew that there was a terrible risk of just that. The United States was supplying military equipment to Britain; it was shipping militarily useful goods to Britain in American ships while the Germans were conducting submarine warfare; it was raising an army and a navy; it was cutting off trade with Japan. Any one of these policies could easily trigger war.

Yet despite their fear of war most Americans, the polls showed, favored the lend-lease deal and the draft. Relatively few forthrightly opposed military aid to the British.

Opinion on foreign policy clearly affected the election results. Roosevelt's percentages dropped most sharply from 1936 in the isolationist Midwest, but they actually rose in Yankee precincts in New England and in parts of the bellicose South. Yet overall the election returns reflected more of the economic cleavages that had appeared since 1932 than of the foreign policy cleavages that had emerged in 1939 and 1940. The economic issues represented in the words "New Deal" continued to motivate voters and to leave them poised equivocally between the two major parties. If only 10% of Americans wanted to go further with the New Deal, only 21% wanted it mostly repealed; 14% wanted it kept and 39% wanted it modified.[34] Curiously, one of the architects of economic politics tried to make foreign policy the issue. John L. Lewis had long been an isolationist (and long a Republican, for that matter), and in late October 1940 he announced not only that he was backing Willkie but also that he would resign as head of the CIO if Roosevelt won. Lewis probably believed that he personally had switched the coal-steel-auto belt from Hoover's Republicanism to Roosevelt's New Deal and that now he could switch it back. But he miscalculated. In Boston on October 30, Roosevelt cited Lewis's ploy and the opposition to him not only of Republicans but of Communists—for the Hitler-Stalin pact was still in effect, and the American Communists followed Stalin's lead and fiercely opposed U.S. aid to the "imperialistic" British. Roosevelt warned of "something very ominous in this combination . . . between the extreme reactionary and extreme radical elements of this country."[35] Then, citing a Republican leader who had said that Roosevelt voters were either paupers or members of the Roosevelt family, he declared, " 'Paupers who are not worth their salt'—there speaks the true sentiment of the Republican leadership in this year of grace. Can the Republican leaders deny that this all too prevailing Republican sentiment is a direct, vicious, unpatriotic appeal to class hatred and class contempt? That, my friends, is just what I am fighting against with all my heart and soul." This brilliant attack must have infuriated his opponents, who believed that it was Roosevelt who had begun to rally voters on the basis of their economic status and with the promise of taking other people's money away and giving it to them. But it did touch a genuine chord. "The essence of his achievement," his kinsman Joseph Alsop, the newspaper columnist, later wrote, was that on "a very wide front and in the truest possible sense, Franklin Delano Roosevelt included the excluded."[36] He built a coalition of people who had been persecuted or whose Americanism had been questioned because they were immigrants or southern or factory workers or poor or black or Catholic. "After all, it is *our country,* and not a laboratory for a small group of professors to try out experiments that bid fair to result in an explosion and a stink," the *Saturday Evening Post* had written; only so many days left, the *Chicago Tribune* had warned its readers, "to save *your country.*" "New York City isn't a melting pot, it's a boiling pot," said Manhattan district attorney Thomas E. Dewey. "The heart of this nation is the rural small town."[37] As if in reply, the pro-New Deal singer Woody

Guthrie sang, "This land is your land, this land is my land, from California to the New York islands, from the redwood forest to the Gulf Stream waters, this land was made for you and me" ©. The you and the me were understood to include the sharecropper and the drifter, the Mexican and perhaps even the Negro, the Italian slum-dweller and the Polish factory worker—as well as the typical Anglo-Saxon resident of the prosperous northern small town. Whose country was it? Franklin Roosevelt's vision was broader, more generous, more encompassing: "we are going to make a country," he said in one speech, "in which no one is left out."[38]

The election was a close thing. Both candidates were links between different Americas—Franklin Roosevelt with his roots in the agricultural Hudson Valley and his political base and East 65th Street town house in crowded, bustling New York; Wendell Willkie with his roots in small-town Indiana, and his office on Wall Street and apartment in one of the gray stone buildings facing the Metropolitan Museum on upper Fifth Avenue.[39] Willkie, like Roosevelt, was personable, charming, and articulate, and he seemed more candid—though in retrospect it seems that his constant defiance of political rules was exceedingly shrewd politics. Turnout was a record high, almost 50 million, and the rate of voter participation was at its highest since the days of McKinley and Bryan. Democratic machine and labor organizers helped boost the turnout, but so did anti-Roosevelt feeling in the Yankee heartland and Great Plains: townships in Maine and Vermont and counties in North Dakota and Nebraska cast more votes than they ever have since.

Roosevelt won with 449 electoral votes to 82 for Willkie; he took 55% of the popular vote to Willkie's 45%. Although he won by big margins in the South and most of the West, he captured only 53% or less in most of the big states—Massachusetts, New York, New Jersey, Pennsylvania, Ohio, Illinois, Wisconsin, Minnesota, Missouri, with 209 electoral votes altogether. He lost Michigan, with 19, by only 7,000 votes. The electoral college had a bias toward Republicans, which becomes apparent if the Roosevelt percentage is reduced by exactly 3.7% in every state: that reduction leaves him with 51% of the popular vote, but only 225 electoral votes to Willkie's 306. The same bias appears in Gallup's final preelection poll, which showed Roosevelt with 55% of the popular vote but Willkie ahead in states with 255 electoral votes, just 13 shy of a majority.[40] Roosevelt himself understood that he could easily lose. As the returns poured into Hyde Park on election night, the usually genial president broke into a cold sweat and told his Secret Service bodyguard not to let anybody in the room—"I said 'anybody' "—and the normally optimistic Hopkins seemed "really worried."[41] Only late in the evening did Roosevelt come out onto his porch to accept the congratulations of his Hyde Park neighbors as Hopkins slapped his fist into his palm, confident finally that he and the man he served had accomplished something no one in American politics had ever done before.

The results allowed the backers of both candidates to believe that their man and his party represented the real heartland of America. Democrats could say that Roosevelt had won an overwhelming majority and overlook how close the election really was. Republicans could console themselves, and many did, by saying that Roosevelt was the choice only of people who were somehow not typically American, the candidate of the South, where he won 70% of the vote, and of the big cities, where he won 59%.[42] Most striking, he won New York's 47 electoral votes with only 52% of the vote, winning a whopping 61% in New York City but losing to Willkie 42%–58% outside the city limits. This vision of an entire state being swung by a single polyglot, cosmopolitan city—even one big enough to cast 6½% of the nation's votes—was profoundly disturbing to many Americans, who could not believe that so many city-dwellers voluntarily voted for the Democrats when so few people they knew in their own communities did. Taking away the special case of the South and the suspect category of the big cities left a country where 62% of all American votes were cast. This country went not for Franklin Roosevelt but for Wendell Willkie, albeit by the narrow margin of 25,000 votes out of 31 million.

There was a saving ambiguity about this result. It enabled a nation deeply and bitterly divided over both domestic and foreign issues to be led unified into war. Both sides' claims to truly represent the nation—both sides' claims that this was *our country*—had a plausible basis, and both were similarly shaky.[43] Roosevelt won the presidency, but as a national war leader who had placed important Republicans in his Cabinet and seemed to be admitting that the time for domestic change was past. He was conceding some of the claims of the opposition. He won also with deviousness and trickery, pretending that he did not want to break the tradition against third terms and allying himself with politicians who came literally from the sewers of American life. His opponents could claim that he had promised mothers—"again and again and again," as he said in Boston—that their sons would not be sent to fight foreign wars. But they could not plausibly claim that any significant number of voters had any doubt which candidate most strongly favored aid to the British and was determined to go closer to the brink of war to provide it. Roosevelt's brilliant campaign, at once cynical and idealistic, devious and daring, gave our country as leader a politician who could not claim a great advantage over his opponents in producing order rather than chaos, whose views on economic redistribution and centralization of government power left most Americans uneasy, whose policies no longer seemed reliably to produce economic growth. But this was a country headed reluctantly and fearfully toward war, a country more diverse than was usually portrayed, with a leader who seemed more able than his opponents to mobilize its people and in time of crisis produce action toward a unified purpose.

17

→》》 《《←

Deadlock

T he United States entered 1941 with a president who was determined to bring the country to the defense of Britain and in favor of extending New Deal programs where possible—and with a Congress most of whose members were determined to keep the nation out of war and opposed to any revival of New Deal legislation. Roosevelt's reelection had been widely expected through the fall of 1940, but his lead seemed narrow and was due mostly to the international situation. Many political observers thought that the Republicans would build on the gains they had made in 1938 and might end up taking control of the House.[1] They failed to capture the House, where the Democrats actually gained 7 seats, but they did make gains in the Senate. In House races outside the South, the total vote for Republicans ran ahead of that for Democrats by a 49%–48% margin, though Roosevelt carried the states outside the South 53%–47%—more proof that his victory was personal and depended on confidence in him as a leader in time of war.[2] The Democrats had the satisfaction of seeing their leader at the head of the nation in time of peril and in command of what he had helped to make the strongest of the three branches of government. But Republicans were gaining experience in office and, though bitter at their defeat in the presidential contest, were encouraged by the success of New Deal opponents in congressional races and by the apparent unpopularity of Roosevelt's domestic policies; thus they opposed Roosevelt's policies more obdurately than ever.

The deadlock between an activist president and recalcitrant legislators had begun when Congress rejected Roosevelt's court-packing proposal in 1937; it continued as Congress cut appropriations for Harry Hopkins's WPA, passed the Hatch Act, and refused to give any serious consideration to Roosevelt's Third New Deal proposals—the Seven TVAs, the proposals for national economic planning, the concentration of power in the presidency. The Temporary National Economic Committee, set up in 1938 and expected to recommend aggressive government action against private monopolies and government control of private businesses, issued its final report in April 1941. The report, as one scholar notes, "attracted no serious attention in a nation already preoccupied with war: and the entire episode was soon largely dismissed as a 'colossal dud' or, more charitably, a 'magnificent failure.' "[3] The deadlock continued into World War II and long afterwards,[4] but it was most bitter in the thirteen months from Roosevelt's third election to Pearl Harbor. In late 1940 and early 1941 everyone knew that issues of the greatest import were at stake—issues of war and peace, of the role of government and labor unions in the economy—and each side feared that the other would embark the nation on a perilous course. But neither side was in command of events. Both were frustrated in achieving their goals. Roosevelt and his allies silently abandoned the domestic policy goals they had been seeking and concentrated on maneuvering the country toward war. The Republicans and their allies feared that the halt in the advance of the New Deal was nothing more than a temporary pause; they were uncomfortably aware that the United States could be forced into war by events they had no control over, and that war would promote the concentration of national power in a Democratic executive which they feared. These were months in which totalitarianism was at the high-water mark around the world, when Hitler and Stalin controlled most of the land mass of Eurasia, when Japan seemed to be creating a huge empire, when Britain was embattled and the United States still was largely undefended. What would America do?

II

"Suppose," said Roosevelt in a press conference the month after the election, "my neighbor's home catches on fire, and I have a length of garden hose four or five hundred feet away. If he can take my garden hose and connect it up with his hydrant, I may help him to put out his fire. Now what do I do? I don't say to him before that operation, 'Neighbor, my garden hose cost me $15; you have to pay me $15 for it.' . . . I don't want $15—I want my garden hose back after the fire is over." This was the homey analogy Roosevelt used to justify the Lend-Lease bill, and if it did not precisely fit the factual circumstances, it was persuasive politically. In September 1940, Roosevelt had traded old destroyers to Britain in return for long-term leases on Western Hemisphere bases. But now Britain needed more—new military equipment, new planes and ships, which could be built only in the United States. In a fireside chat December 29, 1940, Roosevelt unveiled the Lend-Lease program and called on America to be "the great arsenal of democracy." "There is far less chance of the United States getting into the war," he argued, "if we do all we can now to support the nations defending themselves against attack by the Axis." Otherwise, he suggested, Germany would vanquish the Eastern Hemisphere and then come over and, as Hitler had suggested he would do, polish off the Western Hemisphere (he began with plenty of admirers in Latin America). But with this desire for self-preservation Roosevelt mixed another motive, a desire to ensure, as he put it to Congress in Janaury 1941, "a world founded upon four essential freedoms": freedom of speech, freedom of religion, freedom from want, and freedom from fear.[5]

Lend-Lease aroused a storm of protest. Joseph Kennedy and Charles Lindbergh testified against it, and America First tried to whip up opposition. But public opinion was on balance favorable; most Americans wanted to help Britain even at the risk of going to war, and they approved of Lend-Lease by a 2–1 margin.[6] The

House, where the rules allowed Democrats led by Speaker Sam Rayburn to bring the bill forward quickly, passed Lend-Lease on February 8, voting mostly along party lines. The Senate Foreign Relations Committee cleared it days later. Most Democrats on the committee stuck with Roosevelt: most northern Democrats had won on his coattails, and southern Democrats were strongly in favor of intervention. But the bill was opposed by most of the Republican committee members, led by Robert Taft, who feared that "if we enter the war today in order to save the British Empire, we will be involved in war for the rest of our lives," and added, "Lending war equipment is much like lending chewing gum. We certainly do not want the same gum back."[7] On the Senate floor the isolationists tried to stall the bill. They were appalled at the almost complete discretion it gave the president in transferring military materiel: once again, as in the Third New Deal legislation, Roosevelt's impulse was to centralize power in the White House. Rayburn and James Byrnes, administration loyalists but also Capitol Hill insiders, got the bill amended to reduce those powers and to give Congress clear control over appropriations.[8] It became law March 11, just after Bulgaria joined the Axis. Roosevelt immediately asked for an appropriation of $7 billion, a huge amount in a country whose whole government was spending less than $10 billion the year before.

In April, Germany invaded Yugoslavia and Greece and quickly overran them despite fierce resistance. The loss of the Balkans threatened Britain's positions in North Africa and the Middle East, the control of the Mediterranean which was the central artery connecting the British homeland with its great imperial possession of India. Yet German U-boats and battle cruisers in the North Atlantic were sinking ships far faster than the British could build them and preventing American help from getting through to Britain. Roosevelt refused to order convoying of merchant ships, which would mean clashes between the U.S. and German navies. Because of deteriorating relations with Japan, he refused to transfer all but a small part of the American fleet to the Atlantic. But though he refused to publicly announce it at the time, he ordered the Navy to patrol the Atlantic as far east as Greenland, the Azores, and the bulge of Africa, and he placed the Danish possession of Greenland under U.S. protection. He authorized the repair of British ships in American docks and the training of British pilots at American airfields. He told Treasury Secretary Henry Morgenthau in May that he was "waiting to be pushed into this situation," and interventionists like Henry Stimson and Harold Ickes concluded that he was hoping some German attack would give the United States an excuse to go to war. So did many other Americans: for all Roosevelt's arguments that an assertive Navy in the North Atlantic reduced the threat of war, there was plenty of reason to believe that it would have the opposite effect—just as similar activity brought the United States into what was becoming known as World War I. But Roosevelt kept making the same argument. On May 27 he made a speech proclaiming "an unlimited national emergency" and pointing to possible German capture of the Azores and Cape Verde Islands as a threat to Brazil and Latin America: "it would be suicide," he said, "to wait until they are in our front yard." Yet he hesitated to take stronger action. Polls showed that most Americans favored convoys for merchant ships and understood that they might lead to war. But polls also showed Americans overwhelmingly opposed to war.[9] Roosevelt concluded, surely correctly, that hatred of war would outweigh their approval of convoying if convoying should lead, as it had in 1917, to war. He understood, as many of the interventionists did not, that it would be impossible to lead a divided nation to victory except at great cost—cost even greater than in World War I—to its basic values and its civility. He may have agreed with Robert Taft up to a point, sensing that a war entered into over great opposition and with serious misgivings would produce the dragooned, totalitarian society which both Roosevelt and Taft, though each would scarcely have admitted it of the other, hated and fought to prevent in their country.

Adolf Hitler did not give Franklin Roosevelt the clear-cut aggression which might have put the United States into the war early in 1941. For Hitler had other things on his mind—things almost no one suspected until June 22, 1941, when hundreds of thousands of German troops surged eastward and invaded Stalin's Soviet Union. At first it appeared that Russia would be overrun as Central Europe, Scandinavia, the Low Countries, France, and the Balkans had been, and not all Americans were sure that the United States should try to help the Communist regime. But Roosevelt sent Harry Hopkins to see Stalin, and Hopkins concluded the Soviets could hold out. As a result, Roosevelt wanted to send aid to Stalin, though because of the distance and the low level of supplies he could not send much. But the American military continued to advance across the Atlantic. In July, 4,000 American Marines landed in Iceland, to the northwest of Britain and across the only sea lane to the Arctic ports of Russia, and the United States adjusted its naval patrol zone so that it covered almost all the Atlantic. This belligerence was not matched in the Pacific, where Roosevelt was trying to mollify a hostile Japan, though in July it seized Indochina from the helpless regime of Vichy France.

At home, Roosevelt was being proved right again and again in his instinct that Americans, who supported measures which risked war when these measures were far away and involved little sacrifice, would oppose them when they began to hit closer to home. Some 400,000 mine workers went on strike in April 1941, and troops had to be sent in to counter a strike at North American Aviation plants in Los Angeles in June. The big automakers insisted on churning out hundreds of thousands of cars on their assembly lines. There was widespread opposition to renewing 1940's one-year draft: soldiers scribbled OHIO ("over the hill in October," when the draft expired) on latrines, and polls showed a bare 51% in favor of renewal. The crucial vote came in the House on August 12, as Roosevelt was meeting Winston Churchill for the first time (in British battleships anchored in the foggy waters of Placentia Bay off Argentia, Newfoundland). After intensive lobbying and rough arm-twisting, after political deals some of which will probably never be known, Rayburn called the roll. The result was a tie. Then, according to one account, "members who wanted to change their votes crowded into the well, with Rayburn watching closely, and as soon as the total favored draft extension, he took the tally sheet from the clerk and pounded his gavel"; hearing no objection, he declared the bill passed 203–202.[10] That quick gavel meant that the United States would have a draft and a conscript army in place when the Japanese struck.

III

"There is no thought of . . . putting the nation, either in its defense or in its internal economy, on a war basis," Roosevelt had said when Hitler's Panzers invaded Poland in September 1939. By the fall of 1941, well before Pearl Harbor, that thought had materialized and been translated into action. But not completely: Roosevelt's efforts over those two years to put the nation on a "war basis" were halting, incomplete, and only partly successful. In May 1940, after the fall of France, he had set up an advisory committee on war production, which included such leaders as William Knudsen, president of General Motors, and Sidney Hillman, head of the Amalgamated Clothing Workers and one of the leaders of the CIO. They had no power: the bluff and affable Knudsen and the shrewd and politically sophisticated Hillman were simply supposed to cajole companies into producing war-related products and to keep workers busy making these products. Their adversaries included business leaders who were hostile to government interference, New Dealers who wanted to break up big corporations rather than enlist them in the war effort, and John L. Lewis's United Mine Workers, who always seemed to be threatening to strike. More advisory committees followed. In March 1941, Roosevelt set up a defense mediation board to settle and prevent strikes. In April he set up an Office of Price Administration and Civilian Supply, intended, in the argot of the early 1960s, to jawbone businesses to hold prices down; it was headed by an energetic, courageous New Deal liberal, Leon Henderson. In May he set up an Office of Civil Defense under Fiorello La Guardia, who was running strongly for his third term as mayor of New York City.

Quickly these agencies and others like them became the targets of caustic criticism. Their leaders were shuffled into and out of power with great regularity; rivalries were pursued with vigor, and the old arguments between New Dealers and their enemies from the big corporations and Congress were replayed with new vehemence. Complaints about inefficiency and bottlenecks and simple stupidity filled the *Congressional Record* and newspaper columns. Most Americans had entered the 1930s suspicious of free markets and finished the decade convinced that government could do things more fairly and efficiently than the private sector, and so in the war years they expected government to accomplish every desirable thing with dispatch. Of course it didn't—and couldn't, and not just because Roosevelt created overlapping lines of authority on organization charts. Command economies are always inefficient, and individuals and especially well-entrenched groups are not usually inclined to give up their concrete advantages for some abstract common good in a society sufficiently complex that it is always possible to argue that a particular parochial advantage actually works to the common good and that to revoke it would in any case be so unjust as to undermine the war effort all by itself. What is surprising in retrospect is not that so much worked badly but that so much worked so well. Nevertheless, a proposal was made in the House for a special committee to investigate the defense program; it was to be headed by Eugene Cox of Georgia, a friend of Speaker Sam Rayburn and a talented conservative who was a bitter opponent of the New Deal. To forestall this move, James Byrnes arranged in February 1941 to have the Senate set up a committee with a similar mandate. Its head was a little-known backbencher who had been a faithful New Deal supporter, though his fidelity had earned him little patronage and no support in his 1940 primary:[11] Harry Truman of Missouri.

As 1941 went on, war seemed nearer and nearer, and American forces became involved in what looked very much like acts of war. In August the U.S. destroyer *Greer* trailed a German submarine and radioed its position to a British plane, which sent torpedoes against it: the submarine shot torpedoes which the *Greer* dodged. In October the destroyer *Kearney,* on convoy, was hit and damaged by a German torpedo. At the end of the month the U.S.S. *Reuben James* was torpedoed and sunk, with the loss of 115 men. In his public statements Roosevelt made much of these skirmishes, without noting the aggressive and provocative nature of the American patrol.[12] For such candor would have undermined his probably not entirely candid argument that his policies were keeping the nation further from war, not getting it dangerously closer. In the Pacific, Roosevelt limited trade with Japan in stages throughout 1941 and froze Japanese assets in the United States in July. Through the fall negotiations with the Japanese continued, to no apparent conclusion.

On the first Sunday morning in December, 183 airplanes were launched from Japanese carriers northwest of Hawaii; after an 80-minute flight they rained down bombs on the American fleet at Pearl Harbor, sinking 19 ships and 265 airplanes and killing 2,403 servicemen. The American Pacific fleet was destroyed. The United States was in the war. On Monday, Roosevelt went to Congress and said, "Yesterday, December 7, 1941—a date which will live in infamy—the United States of America was suddenly and deliberately attacked by naval and air forces of the Empire of Japan." Roosevelt did not disguise the heavy losses. But his determination was clear. "No matter how long it may take us to overcome this premeditated invasion, the American people in their righteous might"—cheers and roars of approval filled the House chamber—"will win through to absolute victory." Only one member of Congress, Representative Jeanette Rankin of Montana, voted against the declaration of war; by eerie coincidence, in her only other term in the House she had been one of the House members who voted against the declaration of war in 1917.[13] But Roosevelt went further than Woodrow Wilson had, coming close to committing his country to winning an unconditional surrender from its enemies—a total victory which would prevent the losers from claiming afterwards, as so many Germans did in the 1930s, that they had not really been beaten in World War I but were victims of a stab in the back. On Thursday,

December 11, though his troops had failed to capture Moscow or crush the Red Army before the onset of the Russian winter, Hitler nevertheless contemptuously declared war on the United States. Roosevelt, attacked in the Pacific, was now able to concentrate the bulk of the American effort in the Atlantic, as he had wanted to do all along.

Americans now seemed unified, but the bitterness of the deadlock months did not entirely disappear. Some of Roosevelt's opponents believed he had had advance knowledge of the Pearl Harbor attack and had allowed it to take place to get the United States into the war. In January 1942 an investigating committee headed by Supreme Court Justice Owen Roberts issued a report which blamed the Army and Navy commanders in Hawaii for their unpreparedness and inattention to warnings. Left unmentioned were that the United States had broken the secret Japanese military codes and that the president knew the Japanese fleet was at sea. He was advised that it was heading south, toward Singapore, and that messages decoded in Washington had been relayed to Pearl Harbor by Western Union, whose messenger was pedaling to the base when it was hit. Although these facts were rumored during the war, Republican nominee Thomas Dewey, at the request of General George Marshall, declined to reveal them during the 1944 presidential campaign. The controversy reerupted in September 1945, after Japan had been defeated, when the code-breaking was disclosed in the *Chicago Tribune* and a congressional committee once again investigated how much the government had known before Pearl Harbor.[14] But for the present the stunning losses suffered by the American fleet, losses intensified by the Japanese sinking of the British ships *Prince of Wales* and *Repulse* in the China Sea December 10, caused Americans not to question the competence of their leaders but, as usual in crisis, to rally around them. Charles Lindbergh, Burton Wheeler, and John L. Lewis declared themselves in support of the war effort, and the America First committee was dissolved. In December, Congress voted an extension of the draft for the rest of the war and a $10.5 billion supplemental defense appropriation. For American politicians and the American people the war was on.

For the next three years and nine months, domestic politics was overshadowed by the war. Most politicians, public officials, journalists, and other Americans generally strained to understand not whether but how it could be won. And if they vigorously disagreed on strategy, and sometimes refused to sacrifice their own advantages for what everyone recalled afterwards as a grand common cause, still they reached the goal they sought—victory. Amid the preoccupation with winning, Americans were giving less thought to how the war was changing their country. Yet it was being changed irrevocably, starting even before Pearl Harbor, by the mobilization for war. And the decisions that were made by politicians, often in back rooms in Washington, out of the glare of the spotlight and with little notice by the voters, set in motion changes that affected the lives of millions of Americans for at least four decades afterwards.

18

⟶⟫⟫ ⟪⟪⟵

Mobilization

I t was a sunny day in September 1942 when the open convertibles drove into the Vancouver, Washington, shipyard, just across the Columbia River from Portland, Oregon, and which Henry J. Kaiser had built just a few months before. This was one of those defense plants that sprang up as if by magic after the war began, ungainly giant steel structures in a country that had seen few factories built since 1930. Although the workers had no reason to expect a special visitor, it quickly became apparent that the broad-shouldered figure in the front car was the commander-in-chief, Franklin D. Roosevelt, 2,700 miles from the White House in Washington. Roosevelt liked to say that, like Antaeus in the Greek myth, he gained strength from contact with the earth, and his train was taking him on a circuit of defense plants. Henry Ford showed him the half-mile-long assembly line at his Willow Run bomber plant (whose production difficulties would lead Navy Secretary Frank Knox to order Ensign Henry Ford II discharged from the Navy in July 1943 so that he could take over control of the failing family company from its eighty-year-old founder). Roosevelt saw propeller shafts being made in Milwaukee's Allis-Chalmers plant, scene of a bitter strike in January 1941. He would go on from the Pacific Northwest to California, to see the Army embarkation plant at Oakland and the Douglas bomber plant in Long Beach.

In Vancouver he saw the launching of a ship whose keel had been laid ten days before—quite a contrast with the 180 days it had taken to build a ship in World War I[1] and only one of Kaiser's many phenomenal achievements. Bald, stocky, born in upstate New York the same year as Roosevelt, Kaiser was a New Deal industrialist, one of the first American capitalists to build a big business on government contracts and government financing, a man who set up his own group medical plan (the Kaiser Permanente group, still thriving in the 1980s) and was quick to recognize unions and grant them high wages. Roosevelt saw in him what he did in Harry Hopkins—a man whose mind was of a similar bent and who got things done. Kaiser had started in the road-paving business on the West Coast in 1914, just as governments were preparing to pay millions to put hard surfaces on the dirt tracks that made up most of the country's roadways. He started sand and gravel and cement businesses and got construction contracts for Boulder Dam, the San Francisco–Oakland Bay Bridge, Bonneville and Grand Coulee Dams, the Mare Island Shipyard, and the Los Angeles Breakwater. John Gunther lists eleven public projects totaling $148 million, and during the war Kaiser built over 700 ships worth some $1.8 billion—phenomenal amounts for the time. He also got the government to finance his plants: five months before his ride in the back seat of Roosevelt's car in Vancouver, the RFC had agreed to lend him $110 million for his steel mill in Fontana, California, and four months after the ride it was completed. After the war the General Accounting Office said Kaiser had put up only $2.5 million and made $190 million in profit on his war work. He took care to hire well-connected lawyers like Tommy Corcoran, a former Roosevelt lobbyist, and he was prepared with appealing arguments about how low his profits really were and how it would be unfair to make him repay all those loans at top dollar. Kaiser built huge steel and aluminum companies when he had government financing; his foray into the automobile business failed when he had to depend on private investors and San Francisco's Bank of America, so that his company was undercapitalized.[2] Kaiser was a spectacular example of how the war changed the economy and the country, creating new big businesses and thousands of jobs, with government providing direction and guidance and favors though not exerting direct control.

II

War always changes a country, enlarging and strengthening its government; uprooting and moving its people, especially the young; drawing down its economic capital and building new productive capacity. And a society which asks young men to give up their lives usually has little compunction about asking the affluent to give up their money. Statistics suggest the upheaval the war caused in Americans' lives. Federal spending, a source of concern to so many Americans when it reached $9.6 billion in 1940, rose to $95 billion in 1945; War and Navy Department spending rose from $1.8 billion in 1940 (a level more than double that in 1933) to $81 billion in 1945. The rest of the budget doubled, from $7.8 billion to $15 billion; and much of this increase was war-related as well. The following table shows the year-by-year growth in overall spending, military spending, and revenue during this period:

	Total Spending[3]	Total Revenue[4]	Military Spending[5]
1940	9.6	6.9	1.8
1941	14	9.2	6.3
1942	34	15	23
1943	79	25	63
1944	94	48	76
1945	95	50	81

Thus, federal spending was ten times higher in 1945 than 1940, military spending forty-five times higher. Revenues were seven times higher but of course did not come close to paying for the war effort; the shortfall was particularly great in 1943. The increasing budget gap meant that the war dipped deep into the pocketbooks of Americans or, after income tax withholding was instituted in 1943, into their paychecks. World War II, not the New Deal, produced big government in America—with steeply progressive taxes and increased interference in the details of people's daily lives.[6]

The war also put more Americans to work and moved more of them around the country than anything that happened in the 1930s. The civilian work force swelled even as the military grew from a skeletal level to the largest armed force in history (with the possible exception of Stalin's Red Army). The number of employed civilians rose from 47 million in 1940—not much above the 46 million level of 1929—to 54 million in 1943 and 1944, while military personnel increased from 458,000 to over 12 million. The following table shows the number of civilian workers and military personnel for each year between 1940 and 1945:

	Civilian Employment[7]	*Military Personnel*[8]	*Total*
1940	47.5	.458	48.0
1941	50.3	1.8	52.1
1942	53.7	3.9	57.6
1943	54.5	9.0	63.5
1944	54.0	11.5	65.5
1945	52.8	12.1	64.9

A country where in 1933 only 38 million people had worked at civilian jobs or served in the military (fewer than in 1916) had work a decade later for 63.5 million, nearly double that number. Women entering the work force accounted for some of this vast expansion, but not all or even most of it. The female labor force increased from 13.8 million in 1940 to 18.4 million in 1944, and even in the peak years only about one-third of adult women held jobs—a level that would be exceeded in the late 1950s, well before the end of the baby boom.[9]

In addition to the more than 12 million Americans who entered the military service, another 20 million, approximately, left their homes to seek work elsewhere during the war years. At the end of the war, the Census Bureau estimated that 15.3 million civilians were living in a different county from the one in which they had been living on Pearl Harbor Day, half of them in a different state and one-quarter of them in another region of the country. Some 7 million people left farms, 5.5 million of them to work in cities and 1.5 million to serve in the military; probably a majority of them never returned. War production areas like Detroit, Chicago, Mobile, Norfolk, San Diego, Los Angeles, San Francisco, Portland, and Seattle were each jammed with more than 100,000 migrants—Los Angeles and Detroit with many more.[10] Almost 1 million blacks migrated during the war years, mostly north and west to cities with big war industries. In the entire decade of the 1940s, net black migration out of the South was almost 1.3 million—more than in the 1920s and 1930s put together, and not much less than the 2.2 million net migration from the South in the years from 1870 to 1940.[11] Altogether, the war years produced the largest internal migration which had ever occurred in American history within such a short time

III

Yet in many respects government intervention in the economy was less intrusive in World War II than in World War I. In the earlier conflict the government took over ownership of the railroads; this time it did not. Nor did it get into the war production business itself; rather, it channeled contracts and provided lavish financing to existing big businesses and proven operators like Henry Kaiser. In the earlier war, which millions of Americans had opposed even while the fighting was going on, the government had encouraged the suppression of German-American culture and even German words in common use and had imprisoned critics of the war, including one elected member of Congress.[12] But after Pearl Harbor no significant group of Americans opposed U.S. entry into World War II—the only war in the nation's history to command such universal support—and the government saw little need to whip the population into a frenzy of patriotism. There was no persecution of German-Americans, while politicians were especially sensitive to the feelings of Italian-Americans, who had been offended by Roosevelt's remark in June 1940 attributing treachery to Mussolini. Italians were a major voting bloc in the closely contested states of New York, New Jersey, Illinois, Pennsylvania, and southern New England, and restraints on Italian aliens were relaxed as early as October 1942. The single glaring exception to this pattern was the treatment of the West Coast Japanese-Americans, herded into inland detention camps in April 1942 and not released until December 1944. The Japanese-Americans were unfamiliar to most Americans and feared and hated by most residents of California, where state attorney general Earl Warren used his support of internment to beat the liberal Democratic incumbent, Culbert Olson, in the 1942 gubernatorial elections.[13] Roosevelt himself and leading members of his administration did not want to stimulate the hysteria they remembered from World War I.[14] They paid respectful attention to the key swing political groups of the time and understood that the war effort might be diminished, not strengthened, by questioning the patriotism of German-Americans in the old Progressive Northwest or by allowing Americans to conclude that the war was being fought because of the opposition of Jews to the Nazis. The Japanese-American internment was a blot. But it was the exception rather than the rule. The war was prosecuted with amazingly little restraint on citizens' civil liberties, thanks in the large part to the sweetness of character and to the political sensitivity of Franklin Roosevelt.

IV

But in domestic policy Roosevelt's character and preferences were not always decisive. The conservative House, busy the week before Pearl Harbor passing a bill to limit unions' powers, voted the next month to give the agriculture secretary a veto over farm price ceilings—a victory for the still numerous farm bloc, which worked to get farmers high prices throughout the war. Unions were less successful in their efforts to get double pay for overtime and Sundays. Congress bridled at the high tax rates Roosevelt proposed in April 1942; it declined to pass an official secrets act; it bitterly resented the policies of Leon Henderson, whose staff at the Office of Price Administration included the likes of John Kenneth Galbraith and Richard Nixon.[15] Automobiles stopped running off assembly lines at the end of January 1942, but gasoline rationing was not put into effect until December. A general price freeze was ordered by OPA in April 1942, with predictable effects: shortages quickly appeared, claims for special exemptions abounded, and black markets began developing (people talked about buying things from "Mr. Black"). Sugar rationing was instituted in April 1942, but widely evaded. Coffee rationing, tried in November 1942, was abandoned (Brazil was producing plenty of coffee). Meat rationing did not go into effect until March 1943, fifteen months after Pearl Harbor.

The common thread running through most of these developments was that Americans, suddenly more prosperous than they had been for more than a decade, resisted and resented attempts at government control of the economy. If they almost unanimously supported the war, they did not wholeheartedly support the war effort—or at least did not always see the need to make the particular sacrifices that Roosevelt or his appointees were asking. Their wishes were reflected in votes in Congress and ultimately in the decision, made or acquiesced in by the president, that the way to mobilize labor and business and the farmer was to allow each to make a hefty profit out of the war effort and that the way to enlist the consumer was to make rationing and restrictions as limited as possible.

V

American political folklore says that foreign policy does not affect election results. But that was obviously not the case in 1940, when polls suggest Roosevelt would have lost if the election had been fought solely on domestic issues, and it does not seem to have been true in the next three elections, either. The commander-in-chief's party did poorly in 1942,[16] when the United States had made little progress toward winning the war. The Democrats did distinctly better in 1944, when American troops had recaptured Paris and the Philippines, and poorly in 1946, when the necessity for wartime mobilization and restrictions was past.

The 1942 election was taken as a repudiation of New Deal policies and of the mobilization efforts at home. Isolationists did well in the primaries,[17] and in the general election Republicans won more votes overall in House races than did Democrats, who lost House and Senate seats in both industrial areas and the countryside. The Republicans gained 46 House seats while the Democrats lost 50, although they retained a 218–208 edge; Democrats lost 10 seats in the Senate. Compared with the last off-year election, in 1938, the total vote for Democratic House candidates fell from 17.6 million to 12.9 million, while that for Republicans fell from 17.0 million to 14.2 million. In addition to diminished enthusiasm for their candidates, the Democrats' totals were probably reduced by the lack of voting by soldiers and the low registration and turnout rates among transplanted war workers. Timing may have been critical. Roosevelt did no campaigning, but he expected the American landings in North Africa to take place before the election; they might have sparked enthusiasm and turnout for the Democrats. But the landings had to be rescheduled because of the weather and took place four days after the election.

This election marked a low point in the oscillations of popularity of New Deal Democrats since the policy and electoral deadlock began in 1937. If it did not represent a conclusive repudiation of New Deal programs and strict economic regulation, as many New Deal opponents argued and hoped, it was further evidence that the 1936 Roosevelt landslide did not automatically translate into New Deal majorities ever after. The results undercut controversial New Dealers even as the circumstances of war were eliminating the need for some New Deal programs. Leon Henderson resigned as head of OPA at the end of the year. The Civilian Conservation Corps, always a favorite of Roosevelt and of the public, was dropped during 1942 as it became clear that young men would be needed for other things. Roosevelt gave the WPA an "honorable discharge" in December 1942. He did little to save the National Youth Administration from being killed by Congress in June 1943; it had been headed by Hopkins protégé Aubrey Williams, a leftish liberal hated on Capitol Hill.[18] The aggressive antitrust action against big companies which had been recommended by the Temporary National Economic Committee in 1941 and acted on before then by Thurman Arnold of the Justice Department's Antitrust Division was rendered moot by wartime production planning efforts; the National Resources Planning Board, headed by Roosevelt's uncle Fred Delano, was killed by Congress in August 1943; the Farm Security Agency, the Rural Electrification Agency, and the domestic branch of the Office of War Information were left as unfunded shells.[19] For the moment it was, in Roosevelt's words, time to retire "Dr. New Deal" and call in "Dr. Win-the-War."

VI

One political casualty of this change was the political figure who was, after Roosevelt himself, most closely identified with New Deal policy in these years, the man who had been plucked by Roosevelt from his Cabinet and made his putative successor in July 1940: Vice President Henry Wallace. Wallace's background was in farm policy. His father, as Republican secretary of agriculture, had supported the McNary-Haugen bill that was vetoed twice by Calvin Coolidge;[20] the younger Wallace inherited *Wallace's Farmer,* a journal with near-universal circulation in Iowa and surrounding states, and he became a successful developer of corn hybrids. As Roosevelt's secretary of agriculture Wallace had supported the drastic supply-management proposals of both AAAs (such as plowing piglets under in the winter of 1933). He sympathized with the liberals in AAA who wanted to destroy the South's sharecropper system, but he acquiesced in their firing in 1934. With his belief in mysticism and reincarnation, he was altogether one of the less politically acute and least politically popular members of Roosevelt's Cabinet, and he was chosen to be vice president in 1940 probably because Roosevelt thought he would be an asset in the isolationist Farm Belt; perhaps he felt he would appeal to the independent-minded liberal vote symbolized by the Progressives of the old Northwest, for which the Willkie-McNary ticket was a plausible competitor.

In any case, Wallace was a cheerful and loyal vice president, eager to advance his own agenda in the confidence that it was the president's. Roosevelt in turn gave him major responsibilities. Previous vice presidents had spent most of their time on Capitol Hill, where Wallace was little known and little liked. After Pearl Harbor, Roosevelt made Wallace operating head of the Board of Economic Warfare. (Actually, his top aide, Milo Perkins, did the operating.) In May 1942, Wallace spoke out in response to Henry Luce's call in *Life* for an "American century," in which American principles—democracy, free enterprise, moral principles similar to those espoused by Luce's missionary parents—would dominate the world. Wallace said that instead "the century which will come out of this war can and must be the century of the common man." He said that "the people's revolution is on the march" and half in jest called for everyone to drink a quart of milk a day— milk for the Hottentots, his critics said. His call for internationalizing American airports and subsidizing air fares inspired Congresswoman Clare Boothe Luce's epithet "globaloney,"[21] which was applied to many of his ideas. Wallace believed that the government should guarantee 60 million jobs in the United States—a figure far above the prewar employment level and widely ridiculed.

In fact, Wallace was much more prescient than many of his critics. His vision of a vibrant American economy stimulated by government and generating vast numbers of jobs closely resembles what actually happened—and what almost no one else anticipated—in the postwar years. His vision of the century of the common man was, as Luce pointed out to him, actually rather similar to Luce's vision of the American century. They both foresaw a militarily powerful, economically productive, and actively generous America uplifting peoples all over the world— a good forecast of what actually happened. Wallace's expansive generosity and faith in the power of government to stimulate economic growth would be thoroughly vindicated. Where Wallace went off the track was in his conviction, perhaps stimulated by the wartime alliance with Communist Russia, that the greatest single goal of government policy, both at home and abroad, should be the redistribution of income and wealth. As a sympathetic historian puts it, "He regarded the nature of the system as less important than the willingness and capacity of a government to deliver social and economic equity to its citizens"[22]—a polite way of saying he cared little for political freedoms as long as income was being redistributed. He was naively unaware of the nature of a Soviet gulag in Siberia which he visited in July 1944,[23] and he seems to have had scant notion of the limits of government capacity or of desirable government action.

Wallace's political downfall came over his attempt to write into Latin American procurement contracts provisions encouraging high wages, decent housing, and better working conditions—a kind of Wagner Act below the border. These were strenuously resisted by those who thought they would hurt the war effort and by Commerce Secretary Jesse Jones, who as RFC chairman was supposed to provide the loans to finance these purchases. Jones was a Houston cotton broker and newspaper publisher of conservative views and notorious ferocity. He once physically threatened *Washington Post* publisher Eugene Meyer, and James Byrnes thought he was going to hit Wallace during one of their meetings. When Jones refused to approve the purchases, he and Wallace disagreed publicly; in July 1943, Roosevelt resolved the dispute by brutally abolishing Wallace's board and ousting Jones from the RFC job but keeping him as commerce secretary.[24] Wallace continued to speak out on issues and remained the designated successor to a president who by March 1944 was sicker than almost anyone knew. But he was a spent political force. He could not have been nominated for president in 1944 by a Democratic convention made up mostly of southerners and big-city bosses; he could even not have been renominated for vice president without the active backing of Roosevelt, which he pretty plainly did not have. His institutional backing was limited to some of the CIO unions, which before 1944 had had limited success in mobilizing voters and little representation at Democratic conventions. Wallace's elevation to high office was evidence of how much the New Deal had changed American politics. But his political predicament as election year 1944 approached illustrated the limits of those changes and showed that the economic redistributionist politics of the Second New Deal had not swept all before it.

VII

One question which almost everyone was uncomfortable answering was how to mobilize the one out of every ten Americans who was black. War demands equality of sacrifice; yet racial segregation was at its high-water mark in the America of the 1930s, and even the leaders most sympathetic to blacks—even the Eleanor Roosevelts and Harold Ickeses—thought it inconceivable that blacks could serve alongside whites in the military and help alongside them in the civilian war effort. One who did find it conceivable was the head of the Brotherhood of Sleeping Car Porters, A. Philip Randolph. Randolph had founded the porters' union in 1925, when none of the railway unions accepted black members. He built it with a core of disciplined, literate members, rooted in every black neighborhood in America, who traveled around the country and acted as "civil rights missionaries on wheels."[25] In April 1941, before Pearl Harbor, the National Negro Council urged Roosevelt to end racial discrimination in the federal government by executive order. Walter White, head of the NAACP, met with Sidney Hillman to pressure him to end discrimination by defense contractors. When they received little response, Randolph then proposed that tens of thousands of Negroes march in Washington on July 1 unless the administration issued an executive order. This was an initiative of breathtaking boldness. In the 1930s it had been considered daring when Ickes, a former head of the Chicago NAACP, integrated the Interior Department cafeteria and when he and Eleanor Roosevelt arranged to have Marian Anderson sing at the Lincoln Memorial after she was barred by the Daughters of the American Revolution from performing at Constitution Hall. Black voters in the North—there were, of course, few black voters in the South—switched from their ancestral Republicanism to Roosevelt's New Deal Democrats during the 1930s,[26] partly because of Herbert Hoover's hostility to blacks and Alf Landon's indifference. Wendell Willkie, on the other hand, was probably the most fervent supporter of civil rights among American politicians; and Thomas Dewey, conscious of the large Jewish as well as black electorate in New York, was also a sincere civil rights backer. Thus, Roosevelt could expect competition for the black vote in the 1940s.[27] Now Randolph was seeking extensive government action to stop discrimination, and in time of international peril.

Randolph sensed, correctly, that the war gave him leverage, that it would create vast numbers of new jobs, and that once blacks were seen to be contributing equally to the war effort and making equal sacrifices the argument that they should not be treated equally would be undermined. "An army fighting allegedly for democracy should be the last place in which to practice undemocratic segregation," Navy Secretary Frank Knox declared in a 1940 meeting with Randolph and White—though Knox stoutly opposed desegregation of his own bailiwick, the Navy.[28] That year Randolph knew that Roosevelt wanted black votes; in 1941 he knew that Roosevelt, who remembered the race riots in World War I and after, did not want to risk the disunity and disorder which seemed likely to result from a black march on Washington. Roosevelt dithered, negotiated, and tried to outbluff Randolph. But on June 25, one week before the march was scheduled to take place, he capitulated, issuing an executive order calling for an end to discrimination in defense industries. This FEPC order had limited powers, but it was nonetheless attacked bitterly by some southern politicians during the war, and proposals to make it permanent were unsuccessful.[29] After 1941, in fact, many black leaders were dissatisfied with the war's apparent lack of effect on the status of blacks, and the administration was worried by "a general anti-white sentiment which makes fertile soil for Japanese propaganda."[30] For as unlikely as such a fear would seem years later, many were concerned that blacks would sympathize more with non-white Japanese than with white Americans; the same Gandhi who provided an example to Martin Luther King, Jr., and other civil rights leaders of the 1960s was in the 1940s pointedly refusing to aid the British war effort in any way, and American leaders were worried that American blacks might follow his example.

Instead the identity of blacks as Americans was strengthened. Gunnar Myrdal's *American Dilemma,* a best seller when it was published in 1944, pointed up the discrepancy between the American ideal of equality and the American practice of segregation. Most northerners, as Myrdal noted, knew little about southern segregation[31] and managed to ignore what they did know. But maintaining this ignorance was becoming more difficult as more than a million blacks migrated to the industrial cities of the North and West during the war. They were attracted by the suddenly abundant jobs, and their departure helped change forever the economy of the rural South by encouraging the government-subsidized cotton planters to develop labor-saving harvest machinery.[32] Wartime riots, the most deadly of which occurred in Detroit in June 1943 when rumors spread that a black had thrown a white off the bridge to Belle Isle Park in the Detroit River, were evidence that racism was still an integral part of American life. But so also was the idea of equality and a feeling for basic human dignity which would help to change life after the war.

VIII

Like that of blacks, the place of the union movement in wartime and postwar America seemed as yet unsettled. The growth of unions in the late 1930s had been prodigious. The CIO unions, which aside from the United Mine Workers had had virtually no members when the Wagner Act was passed in 1935, had 4 million by 1939. Unions enrolled less than 6% of the labor force in 1933. By 1940 the figure was 16% and rising.[33]

For the new unions, this dramatic increase meant the exhilarating prospect of vast economic power and corresponding political influence. Not a few young union leaders, some of them Communist, many more dedicated to democratic ideas, dreamed of using the union movement to reshape all of American society. But for businessmen and the rather large number of voters who sympathized with them, the growth of unionism was threatening. They saw the relentless advance of an institution which could use its numbers in the street and at the polling booth to take away their property and destroy the businesses they had built up and nurtured through the tough years. To many of them, the growth of big unions seemed just one aspect of the increased economic concentration which the war appeared to be encouraging. The government did not propose to take over defense industries or to build weapons itself. But it was becoming the nation's major buyer of goods and services, and it was buying mainly from the large prewar corporations, the only businesses which seemed capable of turning out materials and finished products in the huge quantities needed. Big corporations, as the CIO organizing drives of the late 1930s showed, might resist unions stoutly; but once they were organized and a union shop was required, union membership could rise very quickly, and union leaders gain considerable economic and political power. Almost all Americans believed there was a basic trend toward economic bigness, and now they hoped—or feared—that not only big corporations but big unions would become major American institutions. Would the government require or encourage defense workers to join unions and defense contractors to recognize them?

The most aggressive labor leader remained John L. Lewis. He kept his pledge and resigned as president of the CIO after Roosevelt won the 1940 election, but he remained head of the United Mine Workers and in that capacity became more militant than ever. In April 1941 he called 400,000 coal workers out on strike for higher wages and an end to the differential between wages in the North and those in the South. In September 1941 he led a strike of UMW members in "captive" mines, those owned by steel companies, to demand a union shop—a demand granted by a Roosevelt mediator in a decision which drew little notice because it came down December 7.

Not long afterwards came the most effective aid to union building, the policy of maintenance of voluntarily established membership. Under this policy, adopted in early 1942 by Roosevelt's four-member War Labor Board, union members had to stay members for the life of a union-management contract unless they opted out in the first ten or fifteen days. The policy gave the union leaders the guarantee of steady income which they, like all organization heads, wanted, but it imposed on them during the war a responsibility to suppress wildcat strikes and keep production moving. In the spring of 1943, Lewis sent his Mine Workers out again in quest of a $2-a-day increase (over the wage allowed under the president's stabilization program) and then ordered them back just as Roosevelt was beginning a fireside chat urging them rather plaintively to return. Then they went out again when the $2 demand was rejected. Roosevelt threatened to draft striking miners; he considered seizing the mines; he offered more money. But throughout 1943 trouble with the Mine Workers and with the railway unions continued.[34] Lewis's damage to the war effort inspired Congress to pass the Smith-Connally labor bill, which not only outlawed Lewis's tactics but also provided for secret ballots on strike votes and banned political contributions by unions. Roosevelt vetoed the bill June 25 and saw his veto overridden within 11 minutes in the Senate and within an hour in the House.[35]

Estranged from the AFL and CIO, Lewis had become a kind of lone rogue. But his strikes dramatized the ability of big labor leaders to cripple the nation's economy and the willingness of at least one of them to do so in the direst of circumstances. Union membership continued to rise steadily through the war, from 8.9 million in 1940 to 14.8 million in 1945.[36] Would the union movement, which grew from 6% of the work force in 1933 to 15% in 1940, to 27% in 1945, continue growing in postwar America? Or would its growth be stopped and its powers limited?

IX

Another question facing wartime America was what should be done for veterans. What had been done for them after World War I seemed clearly unsatisfactory. In the earlier war, the government had presented veterans with "adjusted compensation certificates," bonuses which were payable in 1945. But the depression had created political pressure to pay the bonuses sooner. That pressure had led to the bonus marchers' campout in Washington in July 1932 and to congressional passage of generous bonus bills which were vetoed by the president—not Hoover but Roosevelt—in May 1935 and January 1936. The second time Congress overrode the veto, and the resulting stream of more than $1 billion in bonuses may have stimulated the economy and helped Roosevelt win his 1936 landslide. Yet by the

1940s no one thought a bonus bill would be satisfactory. Government, it was agreed, should do things for veterans now rather than promise to pay them money later.[37]

The crucial force in establishing this consensus was the American Legion. As an organization made up of patriotic World War I veterans, it has often been portrayed as a political ally of Republicans, as entrenched in conservatism and insensitive to diversity and civil liberties. But it was genuinely interested in helping the World War II veterans who would so soon outnumber its current members; and in recommending a full set of social services for veterans rather than cash bonuses, it elevated its own role from that of just another lobby making transient demands on politicians to that of a service organization deeply and permanently engaged in former servicemen's lives. The commission on veterans which Roosevelt appointed in November 1942 came up the next year with recommendations which were in line with the American Legion's plan. And by 1944 Congress had passed most of them into law, including disability pensions and death payments, war-risk life insurance, and a system of Veterans Administration hospitals to treat service-related illnesses and injuries. Much attention was devoted to what was assumed would be the veterans' major problem on returning home: finding a job. The legislation provided that veterans were to be given preference in government employment; they were to be given reemployment rights in private industry; there would be a government agency to help them find jobs. Less attention was given to those veterans who wanted to continue their education or specialized training or who wanted to buy homes or businesses—a group assumed to be much smaller than the number who would face unemployment. But the legislation did provide up to four years of education benefits for those veterans qualifying for and interested in them. And it provided federal guarantees of half the amount of a loan used to buy a house, farm, or small business.

This so-called G.I. Bill of Rights (*G.I.* came from *Government Issue,* which was stamped on servicemen's uniforms) was the product of both liberals and conservatives. It was passed by near-unanimous votes and was managed in the House by none other than John Rankin, the Mississippi Democrat whose rancid anti-Semitism was notable even in the 1940s (he called Walter Winchell "that little kike," and after responding to Rankin's attack on "our international Jewish brethren," Congressman Morris Edelstein of New York dropped dead in the House cloakroom).[38] It spawned a new government bureaucracy, the Veterans Administration, but it also gave the American Legion and the Veterans of Foreign Wars a monopoly over representing veterans in appealing adverse VA decisions. It has been described as Franklin Roosevelt's idea of what social programs for everyone should be,[39] but in fact the particular combination of benefits was not similar to that in the New Deal programs Roosevelt had earlier supported or in the plans for postwar America he sketched out in 1944.

The education benefits, which eventually became known by themselves as the G.I. Bill of Rights, turned out to be revolutionary. At the peak, in April 1947, some 1.2 million veterans were enrolled in America's flabbergasted colleges and universities, which in 1940 had had a total enrollment of only 1.5 million.[40] Almost 6.6 million World War II veterans, 46% of the total, applied for some training benefits by 1947; ultimately 7.8 million enrolled. The veterans were jammed into classrooms; they lived in alternately frigid and steaming quonset huts; they enjoyed little of the camaraderie or tomfoolery of the campus life celebrated by F. Scott Fitzgerald. But they learned. The benefits were generous. Not only was all tuition paid, but single veterans received a subsistence allowance of $65 per month and married men one of $90 per month. As a result, hundreds of thousands of veterans who had never seriously considered attending college did so.[41] Most of them graduated and went on to make far more money than they had ever dreamed— and in the process gave the United States the world's best-educated work force.

Similarly, VA housing loans helped transform the United States from a country made up mostly of renters to one made up mostly of homeowners. This conservative Congress approved such generous government spending partly because everyone believed something should be done for veterans and partly because everyone knew that the program was not permanent, that there would not be another war with 14 million men in uniform, and that within a few years the demand for education and housing benefits would subside. This hybrid of a liberal and conservative program did something neither liberals nor conservatives would have done alone. It provided aid to ordinary citizens and it targeted that aid to provide incentives to upwardly mobile behavior. The Americans of the 1930s had been ready to help the helpless, who often turned out to be those who had been moving up the economic ladder when it was suddenly knocked out from under them. Now the war had helped Americans secure the ladder in place, and more—many more— were ready to move rapidly up the rungs once they were given a little boost.

X

If the veterans' program which emerged from the war was the result of cooperation between liberal and conservative forces, the tax structure which emerged from the war was the result of bitter contention between them. The need for new revenue was obvious: spending was skyrocketing and war bond sales were not filling the gap, even when they reached $1 billion a month. The economy was humming, but just as farmers were resisting efforts to put lids on crop prices and union leaders were resisting efforts to put lids on wage increases, so taxpayers were resisting efforts to increase tax rates. And there were more taxpayers every year. The number of individuals filing income tax returns rose from a low of 3.2 million for 1931 to 6.1 million in 1938, 7.1 million in 1939, and, with a slightly higher tax rate and smaller exemptions for dependents, 14.6 million in 1940.[42] Rates were raised and exemptions lowered for both 1941 and 1942, moves which vastly increased the number of taxpayers each year and, with help from the heated economy, raised revenues substantially as well. But ahead were unthinkably huge war expenditures, and in 1943 the government spent more than three times as much as it took in. The following table shows federal spending and revenue and the number of taxpayers for each year between 1940 and 1945:

	Spending[43] (billion dollars)	Revenue[44] (billion dollars)	Taxpayers (million)
1940	9.6	6.9	14.6
1941	14	9.2	25.8
1942	34	15	36.5
1943	79	25	43.5
1944	94	48	47.1
1945	95	50	49.9

Even before the war the tax structure had been progressive: Roosevelt's 1935 tax law had a top tax bracket of 79%. But this rate applied only to income over $5 million. The relatively low revenue requirements of the government in the prewar years made it possible to have a tax structure which was steeply progressive but at the same time did not impinge deeply on the incomes of the majority of affluent Americans. Now the government was reaching into the pocketbooks of Americans who had never been taxed before. The rates were more steeply graduated—up to 88% on income above $200,000 for 1942. But they also started lower down the economic scale: any income over $2,000 was taxed at at least 19%.

Even at these rates the government's cash flow was still poor. One solution, proposed by the Treasury in 1943, was withholding of income taxes from paychecks. But many bridled at having 1943's taxes withheld at the same time that taxpayers had to come up with the cash to pay 1942's. To meet this objection, Beardsley Ruml, treasurer of Macy's department store and chairman of the Federal Reserve Bank in New York City, proposed that the introduction of withholding be accompanied by a one-time forgiveness of 1942 taxes. This course was opposed by Roosevelt and the Treasury Department, which was headed by Henry Morgenthau, Jr., his Dutchess County neighbor and fellow believer in progressive taxes; they felt it would be a windfall to high-income taxpayers. But Congress, listening to voters' rumblings, agreed with Ruml: 75% of 1942 tax liabilities were forgiven, and withholding began July 1, 1943.

For 1944 the Treasury wanted $12 billion in new income tax revenue, and Roosevelt asked for $10.5 billion, plus a $4 billion increase in estate, gift, corporate, and excise taxes.[45] But Congress voted only about $2 billion more and added tax breaks for mining, timber, and other businesses. Angered, Roosevelt vetoed the bill on February 22, 1944. "It is not a tax bill," his message said, "but a tax relief bill providing relief not for the needy but for the greedy." The next day Senate Majority Leader Alben Barkley, for years a faithful Roosevelt follower, rose in anger. Affable, eloquent, popular with men and attentive always to the ladies, Barkley was Roosevelt's eyes and ears in the Senate. But his support of the president was not helping him at home. On everything but purely military issues, Roosevelt's standing in the Civil War borderlands had been ebbing since 1934. Kentucky had just elected a Republican governor in its November 1943 election, and Barkley's Senate colleague was his old rival Happy Chandler. Now Barkley was furious with the president. The veto message was, he said, "a calculated assault on the legislative integrity of every member of Congress." He announced he was resigning as majority leader, and he called for the veto to be overridden. It was, in the House by 299–95 the next day and in the Senate by 72–14 the day after that—the only tax bill passed over a veto in American history. Byrnes, now Roosevelt's war mobilization director after a two-year stint on the Supreme Court, helped draft a mollifying letter to Barkley; Senate Democrats, after a boisterous caucus, unanimously re-elected him as their leader.[46]

To many of his supporters Roosevelt seemed oddly detached through this brouhaha: "the thing for you to do is forget about it and just don't give a damn," he told Byrnes. Was he just too absorbed in wartime planning to respond vigorously to a stunning defeat? Maybe, but in fact the defeat may not have been so stunning. That amount of revenue at stake was marginal; the war effort would proceed whether the government got money from taxes or from borrowing through the bond drive. Roosevelt certainly believed in progressive, perhaps even confiscatory, taxes. But steeply progressive tax rates were already in effect; they had begun with the politically uncontroversial tax bill of 1942, continued through the vetoed bill of 1944, and (though no one then could be sure of this) would go on well into the postwar period. Government revenues in 1944 amounted to about one-quarter of the gross national product: other countries may have taxed their citizens more heavily during the war, but this was a country in which as late as 1930 the federal government had absorbed no more than 4% of GNP.

Liberal and conservative forces together—Franklin Roosevelt working with a Congress which, except for the war effort, had no stomach for increasing the size or power of government—built a steeply progressive tax structure whose coverage reached far down into the middle- and even lower-income groups and whose rates reached far into the income and assets of the affluent and the rich. The 1944 law had an additional feature that proved of great importance: the $500 exemption for each dependent. That was a significant increase over the $350 exemption in the 1942 law, and when combined with the progressive tax rates that began at rather low income levels, it amounted to a generous children's allowance. A single person paid tax of at least 23% on every dollar earned over $500. A married man with a wife and three children didn't pay any tax until his income exceeded $2,500—a figure well above the median family income before 1941 and not far below it by 1944. In effect this wage-earner had a children's allowance of $345, a substantial sum at the time and probably enough to pay the out-of-pocket costs of child-rearing.

This tax structure, together with the boom in employment in the war years, produced a major shift in income distribution—the last such shift before the 1980s in American history. The one-fifth of American families with the highest incomes received 54% of total income in 1929, 52% in 1935–36, and 46% in 1944—fairly small statistical changes that signaled huge shifts in flows of billions of dollars. The share of total income received by the bottom three-fifths rose from 26% in 1929 to 27% in 1935–36 to 32% in 1944.[47] Americans who had gone through the culturally unifying experiences of depression and war had, in the process of change and growth, gone through some significant economic leveling as well.

19

->>> <<<-

Victory

S ince Pearl Harbor, Americans had taken it for granted that their country
would win World War II. Yet while it was obvious that the United States
could not be defeated, it was not always clear how the United States and its allies
would win the unconditional victory over Germany, Italy, and Japan that Franklin
Roosevelt promised in his speech the day after the Japanese attack. Stalemate was
possible, and perhaps even the endless war that Robert Taft and other isolationists
predicted and feared. Inertia would not produce victory, nor would it happen
serendipitously: the United States had to take affirmative action. Roosevelt personally chose the leading military commanders, starting with the auspicious appointment of George Marshall as Army Chief of Staff over 34 more senior officers,[1]
who by common consent were the most gifted and effective collection of military
leaders in American history.[2] He authorized the secret, multi-billion dollar Manhattan Project which produced the atomic bomb that ended the war in Japan in
a way that saved hundreds of thousands of American and Japanese lives. Most
important was the utter and absolute confidence in total victory which Roosevelt
projected at every point during the war. Joseph Alsop, listening to a broadcast of
Roosevelt's day of infamy speech over a static-filled radio in Hong Kong under
Japanese bombardment, remembered that "in these fairly gloomy circumstances,
it never for one moment occurred to me that there might be the smallest doubt
about the outcome of the vast war the President was asking the Congress to declare
in proper form. Nor did I find any other American throughout the entire war
who ever doubted the eventual outcome."[3] Roosevelt made mistakes and errors of
judgment during the war, none more grievous in its consequences than his failure
to overrule the War Department leaders who refused to order the bombing or
disruption of Hitler's death camps, which one scholar has called "the worst failure
of his presidency."[4] But he understood, as Abraham Lincoln did[5] and Lyndon
Johnson would not, that American voters require their wars to be won within a
single presidential electoral cycle, and he knew that one of the ingredients of
absolute victory was the complete and utter confidence that it would be achieved,
even when reasonable men could have doubts it would.[6]

American military strategy was unsubtle but effective: use the industrial might
and massed manpower of the country to overwhelm the enemy. The challenge
was to overcome inertia and make these advantages work fast enough. The first

news was of defeat, as the United States evacuated the Philippines in March 1942. Then came naval victories in the Coral Sea in May and Midway in June and the American landings in Guadalcanal in August. American planes made occasional bombing raids in Europe, but the first advance in the European theater came with the landings in Vichy-controlled North Africa in November 1942. In February 1943 the Germans were defeated after six months of fighting at Stalingrad, and the Red Army began its long advance to Berlin. In May 1943, American troops drove the last Germans and Italians from North Africa. American troops landed in Sicily in July and secured it within one month; in September they crossed into Italy. They were temporarily frustrated when the attempt of Mussolini's replacement, Marshal Badoglio, to surrender the country to the Allies was thwarted by German troops, who opposed the American and British advance bitterly for months. By the end of 1943, however, plans for the final advance had been made. Roosevelt, Churchill, and Stalin met in Tehran in November to agree on the date of the invasion of Western Europe—the long-promised Second Front—and in December, Roosevelt announced that Dwight Eisenhower would command the Allied invasion force. Now victory was beginning to be in sight, though the war would obviously not be over in 1944.

Roosevelt obviously had no intention of relinquishing office while the war was on, yet the results of the 1942 election suggested that his cause was in trouble. Democrats had won only 46% of the nation's votes in House races; Republicans had outpolled them in all the big states of the Northeast and Midwest, from Massachusetts to Missouri and Minnesota. Moreover, turnout was likely to be down in 1944, with so many soldiers away from home and so many war workers displaced from their roots. Roosevelt's response was threefold. He proclaimed a bold new platform. He attempted to stimulate turnout through a law allowing soldiers to vote and through an alliance with the new CIO political action committee formed by Sidney Hillman in the fall of 1943. And he created a bipartisan foreign policy, to support American involvement in a new international organization and remove the issue from electoral politics. By this time Roosevelt's health was rapidly failing. A physical examination in March 1944 disclosed serious heart problems (though the results may not have been communicated to the patient and certainly were not to anyone else); his schedule was reduced to four hours of work a day, two hours of appointments before lunch and two hours of paperwork following his afternoon nap.[7] Yet he was able to see all these initiatives through to completion.

His platform he set out in the January 1944 State of the Union address, a denunciation of "the whining demands of selfish pressure groups" and a call for steeply graduated taxes, government controls on crop prices and food prices, continued controls on wages, and a national service law to prevent strikes and "make available for war production or for any other essential services every able-bodied adult in the nation." He urged a high standard of living for everyone: "true individual freedom cannot exist without economic security and independence." After the war, he said, the government should guarantee everyone a job, an education, and clothing, housing, medical care, and financial security against the risks of old age and sickness. Not much of this platform was set forth in proposed legislation in 1944, and even less of it would have been enacted by the Congress that heard Roosevelt's message. But Roosevelt here committed the Democratic party to the promise of a much larger, much more active government than Americans had seen before. And he introduced the idea that the government, whose anti-depression and war efforts had done so much (mostly inadvertently) to re-distribute income and wealth in America, should have as one of its major goals the further redistribution of income and wealth. He revived the economic issues which had been at the center of American politics from 1935 to 1940, and he announced a new Democratic offensive. From this 1944 State of the Union mes-sage, more than from earlier New Deal efforts and more than from the veterans, housing, and tax bills Congress was considering, came the Democratic platforms of twenty and thirty and forty years later. If Roosevelt paid little attention to his politics of economic redistribution in the years from 1940 to 1943, when the outcome of the war was not assured, then he plainly decided to revive it in 1944, when victory was in sight.

To get political support he looked to young voters, especially soldiers, and to labor union members—Americans arrayed in constituencies assembled, even cre-ated, during his administration. In the same month as his State of the Union speech, Roosevelt called for a federal law allowing soldiers to vote, regardless of state laws. Republicans opposed this because they feared that soldiers would vote heavily for Roosevelt (as those who voted ultimately did) and that they would be coerced into voting by administration officials much as the Republicans feared WPA recipients had been organized into a Democratic voting bloc by Harry Hopkins's minions. Southern Democrats had no objection to reelecting Roosevelt. But they did not want black soldiers to cast votes that would be counted in their home states nor southern electorates expanded by young voters not affluent and well-settled enough to pay their poll taxes. In retrospect, the soldiers' vote bill seems unexceptionable. But at the time it struck hard at the power base of conservative local and state politicians. Because it tended to create national, not local, constituencies, it is not surprising that it was advanced by the country's leading national politician and was beaten in a Congress whose members drew their power from local institutions and constituencies. The bill was amended to give states more of their customary control over who voted, and only 85,000 soldiers ended up casting federal ballots.

The CIO-PAC was the initiative not of Roosevelt and certainly not of other Democratic politicians, but of two aggressive CIO leaders, Philip Murray and Sidney Hillman. Murray, once John L. Lewis's protégé, was the head of the United Steelworkers and had become president of the CIO after Lewis's departure. He supported the war effort and, despite Lewis's tradition of remaining poised to support either party, was strongly committed to New Deal Democrats. Even supposedly pro-labor Republicans had done little for the CIO in Pennsylvania, Ohio, Indiana, Illinois, and Michigan, the states where Murray's union was concentrated. Hillman was head of the Amalgamated Clothing Workers, the men's clothing workers union, whose membership was mostly Jewish and was centered in New York City. In the 1930s he had sponsored union housing projects, driven the racketeers out of the Amalgamated, and in 1936 created New York State's American Labor Party. Under a peculiar New York law, the ALP could endorse major-party candidates and thus add to their totals; and it was created specifically so that Jewish garment-worker voters, suspicious of Irish-run Tammany Hall under the uninspired leaders who followed Charles F. Murphy, could conveniently and easily vote for Democrat Franklin D. Roosevelt for president, Republican Fiorello La Guardia for mayor, and candidates sympathic to them both in off-year contests. The ALP's constituency, beyond the garment-worker core, was largely Jewish, favored government intervention in the economy and income redistribution measures, and opposed Hitler abroad and violations of civil liberties at home. A product of the Popular Front period of the middle 1930s, it had no enemies on the left: Vito Marcantonio, elected in 1938 as an ALP congressman from La Guardia's old district in East Harlem, followed the Communist party line until his defeat in 1950, as did two top ALP labor leaders, Michael Quill of the Transport Workers Union and Joseph Curran of the National Maritime Union.[8] But Hillman's connections were not just with labor or in New York politics. In 1941 he had been appointed with William Knudsen to the Office of Production Management; although he was let go in 1942 when Knudsen was pushed aside, he remained a Roosevelt loyalist anyway.

The political action committee was Murray's idea, but Hillman was filled with ideas of how to run it, and he was picked as its leader the same day it was approved by the CIO executive council in July 1943. Hillman set up headquarters in New York, hired a legal counsel and writers, and persuaded each of the seven biggest CIO unions to donate $100,000. For years American labor activists had dreamed of setting up a workers' party like the Labour party in Britain or the Social Democrats in Continental European countries. But Hillman knew that labor's influence was better wielded as an independent force, usually but not always allied with the Democrats, and not with traditionalist local Democrats but with Roosevelt's New Dealers and his supporters who ran the big-city political machines. Hillman sensed he was filling a vacuum. Traveling in the Great Lakes states in September 1943, "he noticed," according to a biographer, "that the Democratic party's 'grass-roots' organization had 'just about withered away.' The local Democratic leaders did their work in routine fashion and were accustomed to defeat. Something would have to be done about that, he reflected."[9] In fact, most of those Democrats had lost most elections until the 1930s. Except in Chicago and Missouri, Democratic machines were weak or, as in Indiana, resembled more the patronage-oriented political factions found in Civil War borderlands states like Kentucky and Tennessee. Hillman's goal was to register union members, persuade them to vote Democratic, and get them out to vote on election day when turnout threatened to be dangerously low. The obvious target areas included not only the metropolises where CIO membership was concentrated but also the cities where so many war workers had thronged—Detroit, Los Angeles, San Francisco, Portland (Oregon), Seattle. And his plan worked. In 1944 turnout nationally dropped 4% from 1940; it was down 5% in the South and 6% in the rest of the country outside the biggest cities. But it was up in Detroit's Wayne County, in Chicago's Cook County, in the San Francisco Bay area, in Portland, Oregon, and Vancouver, Washington, up 3% in the counties containing the nation's twelve largest cities.[10] Roosevelt's percentage slipped 5 points in the South and 1 point in the rest of the country outside these central cities. But in the cities it was up marginally. The following table shows, in thousands, the results and turnout for each region in 1940 and 1944:[11]

		Roosevelt	Republican	All Candidates
1940	Total	27,313 (55%)	22,348 (45%)	49,900
	South	5,249 (71%)	2,155 (29%)	7,422
	12 Big Cities	6,707 (59%)	4,587 (40%)	11,358
	Remainder	15,357 (49%)	15,606 (50%)	31,120
1944	Total	25,613 (53%)	22,018 (46%)	47,977
	South	4,665 (66%)	2,230 (32%)	7,048
	12 Big Cities	6,945 (59%)	4,708 (40%)	11,699
	Remainder	14,003 (48%)	15,080 (52%)	29,320 ˙

Hillman and his PAC had in effect created political machines where there were none before, doing so by building on the increase in union membership which resulted from the government's maintenance of membership policy.

They created some opposition as well. Hillman managed to evade the Smith-Connally Act's restriction on using union funds in campaigns by claiming the PAC was a purely educational organization, and he refused to submit its records to Martin Dies's House Un-American Activities Committee, which had been busy investigating native leftists since the late 1930s. In May 1944, Dies decided to retire after the PAC had registered hundreds of union members in the oil refinery town of Beaumont in his Texas district, and two other HUAC members were defeated in spring primaries.[12] Earlier, in a March primary with a total turnout of 80,000, Hillman's forces had won control of the American Labor Party in New York, a victory which prompted rival garment-worker unionists David Dubinsky of the International Ladies Garment Workers and Alex Rose of the Hatters to form the Liberal Party. Although both splinter groups would support Roosevelt in the fall, they differed sharply over the place of Communists in politics. The CIO unions had dozens of Communists in leadership positions, and Hillman saw no reason not to work with them. After all, the United States was now an ally of Soviet Russia, and Roosevelt had taken the trouble to pardon the American Communist leader Earl Browder, who had been imprisoned for activities during the period of the Hitler-Stalin pact (when the Communists, in their slavish obedience to Soviet policy, were hostile to the Allied war effort and American attempts to aid it). But Dubinsky and Rose insisted that Communists, loyal to a totalitarian foreign power and committed to lying and dissembling in the service of that power, should not be accepted as allies in American politics. As events turned out, 1944 was the high-water mark of Popular Front politics in the United States and of Communist influence in American politics and organized labor. In 1932 the Communists had made a major effort to win votes, but they had little success despite the support of intellectuals like Edmund Wilson and Lincoln Steffens. In 1936, before Stalin declared the Popular Front, they had opposed Roosevelt again to no practical effect. In 1940 their opposition had been bitter, and Roosevelt had taken note of it in his campaign speech in Boston. But in 1944 he and Stalin were allies, and he was in the embarrassing position of having Earl Browder's, which is to say Stalin's, support.

II

In January 1944, when Roosevelt was setting out his bold program in his State of the Union address, the toughest possible Republican opponent he seemed likely to face in the November presidential election was Wendell Willkie. More than any other Republican, Willkie was a strong competitor for the independent vote, the mostly liberal groups least strongly moored to either of the two traditional parties. Like Roosevelt, he favored progressive taxes, but he wanted them even more progressive; like Roosevelt, he favored civil rights, but his commitment was stronger and unqualified by a need to placate southern Democrats; like Roosevelt, he was convinced that the postwar world needed a strong international organization, and he hoped that the colonies of the world would gain independence and follow the example of America toward generous democracy.[13] These were the themes of his *One World,* the great best seller of 1943, which he had composed after a trip around the world. "Some day you may sit in this place," Roosevelt had told him in January 1941 when he visited the White House, and while Roosevelt was certainly capable of telling people what they wanted most to hear, he may in this case have meant exactly what he said. Certainly Willkie was the only Republican opponent Roosevelt respected and liked.

But the Republican nominee in 1944 was not Willkie, but Thomas E. Dewey. In almost every sense, Dewey could claim to represent the mainstream of his party—and, in his view, of America. His grandfather had been present at the founding of the Republican party in Jackson, Michigan, in 1854. The candidate had grown up in Owosso, Michigan, a prosperous small city on the banks of the Shiawassee River where the furniture store over which he was born stood just a couple of blocks below a whimsical castle where the popular "North Woods" novelist James Oliver Curwood wrote his books. In high school, Dewey was not an outstanding student; at the University of Michigan he was more interested in singing than in his academic studies; even in his first years at Columbia Law School in New York, he considered a career as an opera baritone. His mother, whom he corresponded with regularly almost all his life (as Harry Truman did with his), was a salty character; his wife was from Oklahoma, a singer who met

Dewey when she was one of the judges in a singing contest (he won). But Dewey himself was a champion of the conventional. When he began law practice in New York in 1925, at the height of prosperity, he was entering a profession over-whelmingly Republican, with members who crowded into oak-paneled clubs for lunch; yet he was doing so in the midst of the country's largest, yeastiest, most ethnic metropolis, ruled by Democrats profligate with power and unrestrained by the careful temperament of Charles F. Murphy, who had died the year before. Like William Howard Taft, Dewey came from the interior of the country and became a cosmopolitan citizen of the world, yet saw himself still as the talented and sophisticated but nonetheless faithful representative of the men who in the natural order of the world ran things in the small towns and cities of the American North. He firmly believed that "the heart of this nation is the rural small town" and that "the Republican party is the best instrument for bringing sound govern-ment into the hands of competent men and by this means preserving our liberties."[14] Like his friend the clergyman Norman Vincent Peale or like DeWitt Wallace, the proprietor of the *Reader's Digest,* Dewey used his metropolitan base to exert his influence over the whole country. But like them, he always exerted it in the name and interest of the small towns from which he, like Peale and Wallace, sprang, and which they tried to recreate in the shadow of the city—in Dewey's and Peale's weekend farms in Pawling, 50 miles north of New York, and in the colonial-style *Reader's Digest* headquarters Wallace built near Pleasantville, 30 miles north.

Ever since 1932 most Republicans (including many former Democrats) had bellowed their hatred of Roosevelt's policies and argued, in abstract terms, that these would lead to national ruin. They were behaving increasingly as the minority party—conceding that the Democrats were more popular and that their leader's record was in line with public opinion. But Dewey was more interested in governing than in opposing. Through most of the 1930s he had been a prosecutor: he had been appointed United States attorney for the Southern District of New York when he was thirty, chosen as a special prosecutor by Governor Herbert Lehman in 1935, elected New York County district attorney with support from Mayor La Guardia and from Sidney Hillman and David Dubinsky in 1937; he had made a national reputation prosecuting gangsters and crooked politicians. For Dewey the Republicans, not the Democrats, were the natural majority party in America, and he argued that "it is the job of the majority party to build, not to tear down; to go forward, not to obstruct. It is not the function of a political party to die fighting for obsolete slogans." Having thus abandoned the futile Republican effort to convince voters that Hoover had been right and Roosevelt wrong, he argued, "Let us have the balance . . . to prove that democracy can maintain itself as master of its own destiny, feed its hungry, house its homeless, and provide work for its idle"—echoes of Roosevelt's 1937 inaugural—"without reliance on political rack-eteers." Dewey was nearly elected governor in 1938 and won that office easily in 1942, when New York Democrats were split. He brought to Albany the aggres-siveness he had shown as a prosecutor as well as a tolerance and respect for civil liberties which appealed to the bloc of New York voters not irrevocably committed

to either of the traditional parties. He also brought a caustic temperament, a taste
for the sharp riposte, a contempt for those who disagreed with him, and a dislike
of most of his fellow politicians which was generally reciprocated.

In his time, Robert Taft was called Mr. Republican. But for thirty years
beginning in 1944, Dewey and men he supported—Dwight Eisenhower and
Richard Nixon—won every Republican presidential nomination but one; and
Dewey and Nelson Rockefeller, whose approach to politics though not always to
government was the same,[15] won every election for governor of New York but
one. At the executive level of government and politics, it was Dewey, not Taft,
who was Mr. Republican in postwar America.

Ever since the 1944 election, Dewey's cause that year has been seen as hopeless.
But it did not seem so at the time. Willkie was forced out of the race in April
when he unaccountably gambled his candidacy on that most isolationist, German-
American turf, the Wisconsin primary; General Douglas MacArthur, Wisconsin-
born, won with 75%, and Willkie finished fourth with only 5%. No serious
candidate emerged against Dewey. Former Minnesota Governor Harold Stassen
was serving in the military, and Taft, up for reelection in Ohio, deferred to the
ambitions of the state's governor, John Bricker. Dewey, at age forty-two, was
nominated almost unanimously. In the summer and fall he led or ran even with
Roosevelt in Gallup polls in many states. Willkie did not endorse him before dying
unexpectedly in October at age fifty-two, and Roosevelt spun dreams of party
realignment in which liberal Republicans like Willkie would join the New Dealers
and conservative Democrats would join old-guard Republicans in a conservative
party.[16] In the long run—over the next thirty or forty years—this is approximately
what happened, although not with the result Roosevelt expected: conservative
Republicans, not liberal Democrats, won four out of the five presidential elections
beginning in 1968. In 1944 it was not yet clear that there was a natural New
Deal Democratic majority in presidential elections: Roosevelt's leads in the crucial
big states were never large and sometimes nonexistent. The outcome of the Dewey-
Roosevelt pairing looked much like the results of the 1942 congressional elections
which the Democrats had lost, except that the Democratic percentages, especially
in the big industrial states, were just a bit higher—which enabled the president
to win reelection by a margin of more than 400 electoral votes instead of losing
by less than 100.

III

Roosevelt's turn back to the left in January 1944 was not followed by his party.
The Democratic Congress passed its tax bill over his veto in February, disdained
his soldier's vote bill, and ignored his calls for postwar economic planning. The
number of solid New Dealers in both houses was low—certainly not one-quarter
of the total. Although the big-city machines and southern politicians were happy
enough to support Roosevelt, they had little enthusiasm for his domestic policies,
except when these poured money directly into their coffers. Nor was the liberal

position strong at the party's national convention. Roosevelt's renomination was taken for granted, but even before 1944 it was apparent that the renomination of Henry Wallace was not. Not only was Wallace unpopularly liberal, but he was also widely considered ineffective at governing and impractical in politicking. Democratic National Chairman Bob Hannegan, a St. Louis machine politician, and Treasurer Edwin Pauley, a California oil man, were all but openly organizing against him.

Roosevelt could have dictated a choice but evidently did not want to be seen to have done so. On July 11 in the White House, he gave Hannegan a penciled note saying he favored Harry Truman, the Missouri senator who had chaired the war investigative committee. But days later he told Wallace, "I hope it's the same team again, Henry." Passing over Alben Barkley, who must have angered him by re-signing the Senate majority leadership over the tax bill, he urged James Byrnes, the former South Carolina senator and Supreme Court justice who was now serving as "assistant president," to run. But Byrnes fell out of favor after Ed Flynn, the hot-tempered and reclusive[17] Bronx boss and a former Democratic national chair-man, pointed out that he would be anathema to Catholics because he had been raised a Catholic and then had left the church. (Of course, if he had remained a Catholic, he probably would never have been elected to office in South Carolina.) Sidney Hillman said Byrnes was also unacceptable to labor, and both men said he was unacceptable to black voters.[18] On July 13, Roosevelt wrote to the con-vention chairman that if he were a delegate he would vote for Wallace. But on June 15 he wrote another letter to Hannegan saying that either Truman or Supreme Court Justice William Douglas would be acceptable to him, and he told Hannegan that after making a final choice he must "clear it with Sidney." Truman did not take the hint. He had committed himself to Byrnes and agreed to give his nom-inating speech. So Roosevelt had to give the game away, at least in private, by calling Hannegan in his Blackstone Hotel suite, where he was meeting with Flynn, Ed Kelly, Frank Walker, and Truman. When Hannegan said he hadn't gotten Truman lined up yet, Roosevelt said, "Well, tell the senator that if he wants to break up the Democratic party by staying out, he can; but he knows as well as I what that might mean at this dangerous time in the world." Thus a sick president picked as his successor a man he hardly knew, a politician who had made his way up as a candidate of the corrupt Pendergast machine in Kansas City.

This proved not to be as bad a choice as it easily could have been. Truman was not a college-educated man, but he was widely read; he was not politically naive, but he was not corrupt; he had almost no experience at the top levels of government, except for his work on the war investigating committee—which was valuable preparation indeed. He was poised between the two wings of the Democratic party: never accepted completely by the New Dealers (Roosevelt forces had backed his opponent in the 1940 Senate primary, though Truman had generally been an administration supporter), he was not regarded as part of the southern bloc either. Yet he was generally acceptable to both groups. His mother, who lived until 1949, was an unabashed supporter of the Confederacy, and Truman himself, like most

Americans, accepted racial segregation as normal; yet he was readier than Roosevelt to take political risks and accede to demands for civil rights. His background was in business: his father had been a mule trader—a big business in turn-of-the-century Missouri—and after serving as an officer in World War I, Truman had opened a top-of-the-line haberdashery which failed in the depression of the early 1920s. But he was friendly enough to organized labor to be cleared easily by Sidney Hillman, who had breakfast with him in the Ambassador Hotel in Chicago on June 18. As Hillman sat in the convention hall watching New York switch on the second ballot from Wallace to Truman and lead the break to the new nominee, he told James Reston of the *New York Times,* "We were for Wallace always, but not against Truman."[19] Halfway between North and South, big city and farm, business and labor, Harry Truman was close to the fulcrum point of the Democratic party of 1944.

IV

In September 1944, Winston Churchill visited Franklin Roosevelt at Hyde Park for the last time, after the Quebec Conference. As the two men relaxed and looked out over the broad lawn above the Hudson and the trees not yet beginning to show fall colors, they had cause for satisfaction. Since their first meeting, on the doomed *Prince of Wales* in the bay off Newfoundland in August 1941, they had led their countries from supine retreat to striding victory. On June 6, 1944, Allied troops had staged only the second successful invasion across the English Channel since William the Conqueror in 1066; progress across the great plain of northern Europe had been slow, but it seemed certain that the American and British armies would meet the Red Army and accomplish the total defeat of Nazi Germany. In the Pacific, MacArthur's island-hopping strategy was working, and the invasion of the Philippines was scheduled for the next month. At Hyde Park, Roosevelt discussed again with Churchill the progress which scientists in Los Alamos, New Mexico, were making toward the development of a weapon of extraordinary destructive power, the weapon which would become the atomic bomb, and the two leaders agreed not to share the secret of the bomb with Russia. At lunch Churchill argued, over Eleanor Roosevelt's objections, that the Americans and British must together guarantee the peace. Very quickly the postwar world was coming into being.[20] Around the world soldiers were fighting amid the clangor of metal and machinery, of bursting bombs and screaming engines. But these two aging men, one nearly seventy and the other sixty-two, crippled, and in failing health, could look over the lawns and the Hudson in utter tranquillity, serene in the confidence that they held in their hands the most awesome power in the history of mankind, a power they knew they could wield to defeat the forces of evil.

Roosevelt was still behind in the polls, further behind than one might expect of a successful war leader facing a forty-two-year-old opponent with no foreign policy experience. Fears about his health had been stimulated by the rambling speech he delivered from a battleship in Bremerton, Washington, in August, at the end of his western inspection tour. (In fact, though it was not reported at the time, he had suffered an attack of angina pectoris as he began speaking.) His party was not overwhelmingly popular—pollsters still found more Americans identifying themselves as Republicans than as Democrats—and his domestic policies were not overwhelmingly popular even within his party. Yet none of those round him sensed in him or felt within themselves much apprehension about the outcome of the election, and the large majority of voters were sure he would win.

In fact, Roosevelt had his strategy well set. Dewey, a sophisticated consumer of public opinion polls, a believer in careful organization and factual precision, was making biting speeches around the country charging that the Democrats were running an aging, inefficient, perhaps even corrupt administration. He glossed over his pre-1941 isolationism and took positions on foreign policy which were similar to Roosevelt's; he accepted rather than attacked much of the New Deal. To him the Democrats were a corrupt, incompetent party, too close to labor union leaders and to well-placed Communists who, despite their small numbers, could work from inside government to undermine Americans institutions.

Roosevelt's response was ridicule—and a reminder of the recent past. On September 23, 1944, three days after Churchill left Hyde Park. Roosevelt spoke at a convention of the Teamsters union at Washington's new Statler Hotel, in its ballroom expressly designed for presidential appearances at the annual Gridiron Club dinner. "Well, here we are—here we are again—" he started, over a national radio hookup, "and what years they have been! You know, I am actually four years older, which is a fact that seems to annoy some people. In fact, in the mathematical field there are millions of Americans who are more than eleven years older than when we started to clear up"—an elegant segue from the age issue to the depression—"the mess that was dumped into our laps in 1933." He was running against Herbert Hoover again: "if I were a Republican leader speaking to a mixed audience, the last word in the whole dictionary that I think I would use is that word 'depression.' " And then came a response to a charge by Minnesota Republican Congressman Harold Knutson, a response Roosevelt had been husbanding for weeks: "These Republican leaders have not been content with attacks on me, or my wife, or on my sons. No, not content with that, they now include my little dog Fala. Well, of course, I don't resent attacks, and my family doesn't resent attacks, but Fala does resent them. You know—you know—Fala's Scotch, and being a Scottie, as soon as he learned that the Republican fiction writers in Congress and out had concocted a story that I had left him behind on an Aleutian Island and had sent a destroyer back to find him—at a cost to the taxpayers of two or three or eight or twenty million dollars—his Scotch soul was furious. He has not been the same dog since. I am accustomed to hearing malicious falsehoods about myself—such as that old, worm-eaten chestnut that I have represented myself as indispensable. But I think I have a right to resent, to object to libelous statements about my dog." Of course, Dewey had never said anything at all about Fala. But the mean-spiritedness with which Republican politicians and so much of the press were attacking Roosevelt was resented by the majority of Americans who voted for or just admired him, and the Fala speech underlined Dewey's vitriolic and contemptuous tone. It also fortified it: Dewey responded by attacking harder and more bitterly. And other Republicans trumpeted that the underlying directive of the Roosevelt administration was "Clear everything with Sidney." Republican billboards read, "It's your country—Why let Sidney Hillman run it?"[21] This taunt played on a reasonable fear of Communists and a partisan fear of the industrial unions, but it was also an appeal to anti-Jewish and anti-immigrant feeling which was unworthy of the candidate it was intended to help.

Roosevelt needed one more show of campaigning to persuade voters he was fit for the job, and he provided it on October 21. For four hours that day he was driven in an open car 50 miles through the four big boroughs of New York City, the huge metropolis which had always supported him so overwhelmingly and which on election day would cast 7% of the nation's votes—a greater share than ever before or since. A driving wind poured cold rain on him and plastered his hat and cape to his face, but he was smiling and waving. At Ebbets Field on Bedford Avenue in Brooklyn, he was helped out of his car and paid tribute to Senator Robert Wagner, whose labor law had created the swelling ranks of the CIO unions and who was the key sponsor as well of Social Security and public housing. Passing crowds all along the route, he drove through Queens to Flushing Meadows, the site of the 1939–40 World's Fair which Mayor Fiorello LaGuardia, on the jump seat beside Roosevelt, had helped to put together as a symbol of the city's achievements and to foresee the future even as the world was headed toward war. He traveled over the Grand Concourse, on the spine of the Bronx, lined with sturdy Art Deco apartments, through the borough where the sons and daughters of Irish, Italian, and Jewish immigrants had moved out on the subway lines from the tenements of the Lower East Side and now, under the leadership of Bronx boss and former Democratic national chairman Ed Flynn, delivered 3–1 Democratic margins.

The cold rain continued to pour down on the frail and sickly president as he rolled through Harlem and past Central Park and then down Broadway to the garment district, where the mostly Jewish garment workers, prompted not just by their union leaders but by their own genuine enthusiasm, gave him his most rousing applause. Roosevelt was the choice of more than 80% of Jewish voters in the 1940s, when they saw him as their champion against Hitler. This was a triumphal parade, with cheers and ticker tape, the closest thing to a celebration of victory that this president, who discouraged any monuments to himself and decreed that his gravestone be decorated only with the birth and death dates, ever allowed himself.

There was no question about victory: American troops had landed in Normandy, had liberated Paris, and were sweeping across France toward Nazi Germany; just two days before, American troops returned, in Douglas MacArthur's word, to the Philippines, even as they were island-hopping within secure airfield range of Japan. And there was little question that the place to celebrate this victory was New York. Washington was the place where the commands were given, but New

York, by virtue of its size and diversity, supplied much of the capital and the brains and the manpower to win the war. London was in ruins, Berlin and Tokyo were being bombed to destruction, Moscow was starving, Paris and Rome were shamed. The people cheering Roosevelt in Brooklyn, Queens, the Bronx, and Manhattan were immigrants and the children of immigrants; they spoke in the rapid speech and coarse accents which echoed the din of the metropolis; their fingers were dirty with ink from the *Daily News* and other tabloids and their fingernails were caked with the remnants of grease and mustard from the hot dogs and soft pretzels they bought from stands and chewed as they walked at the city's hurried pace. In Europe's great cities not long before, vast crowds cheered grandiose leaders who in pomp and ceremony hailed their followers' racial purity and called on them to slaughter their inferiors. In New York—the city, which in October 1944 was economically, demographically, and intellectually the greatest city in the world—Franklin Roosevelt was happy to parade as a vulgar politician seeking the votes and acknowledging the cheers of the polyglot masses whom he was content to count as his equals. Together they were celebrating his forthcoming political victory, but even more they were with a sense of wonderment and exultation beginning to understand that their country—the country which had seemed ruined and stagnant just eleven years before—was now the most powerful and prosperous and beneficent country in the world.

That evening, almost as an anticlimax, Roosevelt spoke to the Foreign Policy Association at the Waldorf-Astoria Hotel, appearing on the platform with Henry Stimson, James Forrestal, Herbert Lehman—great New York investment bankers and lawyers of WASP and Irish and Jewish descent who had wielded the power of capital for years and were now wielding the power of the war machine. The next day, which was brighter and sunny, he was in Hyde Park. Driving the specially equipped Ford convertible he could control with his hands, he was photographed with Fala perched in the passenger seat with his paws resting on the door: the country squire, the commander-in-chief of the mightiest military force in the history of the world, the champion of the masses and the master of the great lords of capital who were his subordinates in government.

The 1944 election, more than any other election in the Roosevelt era, was the prototype of American politics to come. To be sure, turnout was low, particularly among those younger voters who were bound to become a much larger part of the electorate in the decades to come; to be sure, the hubbub of electioneering was obscured by the rat-a-tat-tat of news from the front. Yet these factors made 1944 more rather than less paradigmatic. On one level, Roosevelt won overwhelmingly, with 432 electoral votes, carrying 36 states to Dewey's 12. Yet he won only 53% of the popular vote. In the South he won 66%–32%, but this was the last election in which the South would be so solidly Democratic; and even in 1944 there was one sign of southern disaffection with the national Democrats: a conservative group called the Texas Regulars polled 22% of the vote in that previously overwhelmingly Democratic state. Outside the South, Roosevelt won the sixteen largest central-city counties[22] by 59%–40%—an absolutely crucial margin, since in the rest of the country Dewey prevailed by a 52%–48% margin. This pattern has eerie similarities with the 1948 election (in which Truman ran behind Roosevelt in the South and the big cities but ahead of him in some parts of the countryside, and won) and even with the 1960 election (in which John Kennedy carried the big cities 59%–40%, as Roosevelt had, and lost the rest of the non-southern vote by only a bit more than Roosevelt, 47%–53%; the obvious difference was Kennedy's weaker performance in the South).

In 1944 and elections for the next twenty years, the Democrats would be represented by presidential candidates who wholeheartedly favored the New Deal, received strong support from big labor and big-city machines, and retained some traditional support in the South. In those same elections, with the exception of 1964, the Republicans would be represented by candidates who accepted the New Deal, received almost unanimous support from big business, rolled up their biggest percentages in rural areas outside the South and historically Republican parts of the Civil War borderlands, and were able to win some white-collar votes in the South. Both parties would be represented by internationalists, for the 1944 elections saw isolationists defeated in large numbers. Congressman Hamilton Fish, the Hudson Valley Republican whom Roosevelt hated and whom Dewey publicly opposed, was finally beaten. Gerald Nye, the chairman of the Nye Committee hearings on munitions-makers in 1935, was beaten in that most isolationist of states, North Dakota. Robert Taft barely won in Ohio. Two years later, when their seats came up, isolationist senators like Burton Wheeler of Montana and David Walsh of Massachusetts were ousted.

In the elections to come, issues changed; personalities and character made a difference; the facts of war and peace, of recession and prosperity, all affected the outcomes. But the basic picture remained the same. The Democrats were a majority party whose strength lay almost entirely in the South and the big cities. The Republicans were a near-majority party rooted in the countryside and small towns outside the South, communities which seemed to represent the country's views on many issues but still could not prevail overall in national elections.

For both sides this was a frustrating politics. Both questioned the legitimacy of the results. New Deal Democrats were dismayed that the popular majorities for Roosevelt and most succeeding Democratic presidential nominees did not also produce Congresses that would support New Deal measures.[23] Dewey Republicans were dismayed that the support they had from the public on issues and their competence and lack of corruption could not be translated easily into presidential victories. Roosevelt followers pointed to defects in local political processes—the exclusion of black voters in the South, the poll tax, the underrepresentation of big cities in the legislatures, Republican dominance of local business and media—and charged that these unfairly prevented their majorities from being registered in Congress and the capitals of big states. Their specific criticisms had merit, but eradication of these imperfections would not have been likely to produce the New Deal majorities they wanted. Dewey Republicans complained that the corruption of big-city bosses, the seemingly irrational attachment of conservative southern voters to the party that had opposed the Civil War, and the war issue were unfair advantages that kept Roosevelt and later Democrats in office; for Dewey himself, the most frustrating moment of the 1944 campaign may have occurred when General George Marshall (without Roosevelt's knowledge) prevented him from revealing that the Japanese codes had been broken before Pearl Harbor.[24] These complaints, too, had some validity. Without the war, the Republicans probably would have won the presidency in 1940 and 1944; with the collapse of the big-city machines and the realignment of white voters in the South after the civil rights revolution, the Republicans emerged as the stronger party in presidential politics by the late 1960s. Yet it is difficult to share the Republicans' criticisms entirely. Millions of Americans in big cities, especially the ethnic Americans who were seldom celebrated in Republican oratory and the union members whose cause had been fought bitterly by Republicans, voluntarily and strongly wanted to vote for Roosevelt and the Democrats—as hard as this may have been for the Republicans, from their small-town backgrounds and in their high-income suburbs, to believe.

On the surface this was a bitter politics, full of resentments and doubts about the legitimacy of the opposition. But in the years immediately after the war, Democrats and Republicans would settle those arguments which had been at the heart of the post-1935 politics of economic redistribution, and the United States would begin to experience sustained economic growth such as the world had never seen before. The country which Roosevelt's Democrats and Dewey's Republicans had been arguing over was, even as the arguments were being settled, in the process of becoming a very different country altogether.

20

-》》 《《-

Demobilization

Franklin Roosevelt's third vice president was a man almost no Americans knew—and a man who knew very little about the work he might suddenly be called on to do. He came from the major metropolitan area nearest the geographical center of the forty-eight states, Kansas City, but his home was in the small Missouri courthouse town of Independence, a half-dozen miles east of the "up-to-date" skyscrapers clustered on bluffs above the bottomlands where the Kansas River flowed into the Missouri. Harry Truman's roots were in the Civil War borderlands. His Grandmother Young remembered how a Union general had stopped at her Missouri farm in 1861, seizing 15 mules and 13 horses, shooting 400 hogs, and forcing her to make biscuits for the raiders until her fingers blistered, while the future president's mother cringed under the table.[1] Truman, born in 1884, less than twenty years after Appomattox, was a bookish child who loved to play the piano and read widely in American and classical history. After high school he worked as a bank teller and then helped manage his Grandfather Young's family farm in Grandview, 10 miles south of Kansas City. He joined the new Kansas City National Guard unit in 1905.

The Trumans were always in politics. Harry Truman's father, John, was a country road overseer at a time when road-building was just being undertaken seriously by local governments.[2] He was allied with the Goats, the Jackson County Democratic faction which was headed by Alderman Jim Pendergast and opposed by the Rabbits, led by Joe Shannon. (These factions, led by Tom Pendergast and his son and by Frank Shannon, were still contesting elections in Kansas City in 1944.) The Pendergast machine's most famous politician was James Reed. An aggressive prosecutor elected mayor in 1900, he became a U.S. senator in 1910 and served three terms, in which he became known as a fierce and effective opponent of Woodrow Wilson's League of Nations.[3] When the Goats, now led by Tom Pendergast, slated Harry Truman for Jackson County's eastern district judgeship in 1922, Reed was thus a major national politician and Truman merely a former World War I battery captain, a failed businessman (his men's clothing store, across 12th Street from the fancy Muehlebach Hotel, had folded in the 1920–21 depression), and a political dabbler. But for Pendergast, Truman was more important. Reed's Senate seat gave little patronage, but the eastern district judge was one of three county officials who ruled on paving and building contracts.

There were plenty of streets to pave in Jackson County, and local government became a prodigious builder: Pendergast was in the cement business.

He was also a crooked politician, but Truman wasn't. Pendergast was convicted of income tax evasion in May 1939, after 295,000 people had been recorded as having voted in Jackson County in the 1936 election—a total which fell to 239,000 in 1940, when Pendergast was in jail, and which despite population growth was not equaled for the next fifty years. But Truman had no part in vote-stealing and was scrupulously honest in handing out contracts. In the still country-like town of Independence, he lived in a white Victorian house at 219 North Delaware Street which belonged to his wife's family and in which she lived, except for her time in Washington, all the ninety-seven years of her life. And he had his own independent political base in Independence and the surrounding rural areas, among family, friends, and fellow veterans. When he was elected presiding judge of the county in 1926, after two years out of office, he made his own road-building program and insisted on honest bids, though he did employ Pendergast patronage hacks and sometimes paid more for supplies than he might have.[4] But he did so out of loyalty. Truman was always loyal to those who backed him: in early 1945, when he was vice president, he made a point of attending Tom Pendergast's funeral despite wide criticism.

At many points in his career, Truman was poised uneasily between high achievement and petty failure. One of the things which attracted him about being a county judge, for example, was that his salary couldn't be attached by creditors, while his house remained his wife's family's property.[5] He was denied a congressional nomination and had thought he was about to be shunted to "retirement on a virtual pension in some minor county office" in 1934, when Pendergast gave him his backing for U.S. senator.[6] Then he was shunned by fellow senators as a machine hack when he came to Washington, where he backed New Deal programs regularly, even though the Roosevelt administration often gave patronage to his anti-New Deal Senate colleague, Bennett Champ Clark, instead.[7] He was also shunned by Roosevelt and the liberal *St. Louis Post-Dispatch* in his close 1940 primary race, in which Governor Lloyd Stark opposed him—the same Stark for whom he had obtained Pendergast's endorsement four years before. In a state which was clearly trending toward the Republicans in the early 1940s, and after having been reelected by only a 51%–49% margin in 1940, he might well have assumed he was headed for defeat when his seat came up again (the Republicans did win the seat in 1946). It is little wonder that Truman remained loyal to those Missourians—cronies, as they were later called—and those senators who had stuck with him when he was under attack, and to the blacks and Jews who voted heavily for him in his 6,000-vote primary victory.[8]

His support of the New Deal, the trust he developed with other senators, his experience in negotiating public works contracts—all these recommended Truman for the chairmanship of the committee investigating war industries that bore his name. For the vice presidency—and for the presidency—what recommended him was his position at the fulcrum of the Democratic party. His political base was in a giant metropolitan county, but also in a small town and on a farm. He was a Confederate sympathizer who in the 1930s had been willing to appeal for fair treatment of blacks. He was the product of a political machine yet was a man of prickly honesty. He had what Samuel Lubell called a "middle touch": "when he takes vigorous action in one direction it is axiomatic that he will contrive soon afterward to move in the conflicting direction." He was acceptable both to southern senators and to Sidney Hillman. "Only a man exactly like Truman politically," Lubell wrote, "with both his limitations and his strong points, could have been the Democratic choice for Roosevelt's successor."[9]

II

Franklin Roosevelt died on April 12, 1945, in Warm Springs, Georgia. Truman heard the news at the White House, where he had been summoned from Sam Rayburn's hideaway "board of education"[10] office in the Capitol. He had met with Roosevelt only twice since Inauguration Day; he had no knowledge of the contents of wartime negotiations, including the Yalta Conference of February 1945, beyond what was in the newspapers; he had only a hazy idea that a weapon of unusual destructive force was being developed on secret military bases. Naturally his attention for several months was devoted to foreign and military issues. Five weeks before, American troops had crossed the miraculously untouched Remagen bridge over the Rhine, heading east toward the advancing Red Army. Two weeks before, American troops had marched ashore on Okinawa, where the bitter Japanese resistance provided a forecast of what Americans could expect from an invasion of the main islands of Japan. Messages were passing back and forth between the president and Churchill and Stalin; decisions were being made on Poland and the rest of Eastern Europe, on the governance of Germany, on the future of China and the rest of East Asia, which would do more in a few weeks to shape the postwar world than could be done in the next forty years. Planning for postwar America did not seem urgent and might even distract citizens from the still unfinished business of winning the war, for the conflict against Japan seemed certain to last at least into 1946, and possibly longer. But events moved faster than expected. On April 30, Hitler reputedly killed himself in his bunker in Berlin, and Germany surrendered unconditionally a week later. Okinawa was captured in June and the Philippines in July. In mid-July the first atomic bomb was exploded at White Sands near Alamogordo, New Mexico, and Truman, meeting with Churchill and Stalin at the Potsdam Conference, was informed of its success. The Senate agreed to the United Nations Charter on July 28. Atomic bombs destroyed Hiroshima and Nagasaki on August 6 and 9, and Japan surrendered August 14.

III

During this period Harry Truman's job approval rating was as high as any American president's has ever been: 87% in one Gallup poll. The task before him at home was demobilization. Suddenly the huge military forces and defense industries seemed no longer needed; and most Americans, while full of joyous relief at the end of war, assumed that bad economic times were about to return.[11] Almost no one had Henry Wallace's confidence that 60 million Americans could find jobs in a peacetime economy. And the fighters in the politics of economic warfare— the labor unions and giant industrial corporations—were ready to resume their battles for a larger share of what they thought was unlikely to be a larger pie, each convinced that the war had left them at a disadvantage.

Would Truman follow Roosevelt's lead of eighteen months before and push for a much larger federal government and more power for the unions? The answer came in early September, four days after General MacArthur accepted the Japanese surrender on the deck of the battleship *Missouri:* he would. He could have been under no illusion about the popularity of such a course in Congress. As vice president, he had had to twist arms and accept a bill taking all major powers from the job to get his predecessor, Henry Wallace, confirmed as secretary of commerce; and he had seen Aubrey Williams, the brilliant head of the National Youth Administration, denied confirmation for a higher office because of his unpopularity in Congress. But in September 1945, Truman came out for continued government price controls, a full-employment bill, a higher minimum wage, a public-and-private housing bill, a permanent FEPC, and only limited tax cuts. In December 1945 he endorsed national health insurance.

Almost none of this legislation was passed. A full-employment bill did eventually go through, setting up the President's Council of Economic Advisors and containing language which suggested the government should run deficits to maintain full employment. But it was not binding on Truman or his successors.[12] The permanent FEPC was killed by filibustering southerners by February 1946. Taxes were cut by more than the estimated $5 billion Truman had asked.

On labor issues, Truman was under strong pressure from both sides—and continually wavered. In the fall of 1945 the two most visible CIO unions, the United Auto Workers and United Steelworkers, were threatening to go on strike. In October an administration agency said the auto companies could afford to grant a 24% wage raise. Then, in December, Truman called for the provisions of the Railway Labor Act—a thirty-day cooling-off period, a settlement recommended by the government—to be applied to other industries, an extension which the unions stoutly opposed. Next, he said the companies should be required to open their books to the government. To Alfred P. Sloan, Jr., and Charles E. Wilson of General Motors, this was "a regimented economy." But government involvement in these economic disputes between private parties was a fact. Wartime arrangements had already set the example for the next two decades. The wages and fringe benefits won by the huge CIO unions from the huge auto and steel companies were a matter of national concern: they set a pattern followed in the rest of the economy. Much of the politics of the next twenty years would revolve around presidents' intervention in steel and auto strikes.

Thus, although Truman's intervention seemed ham-handed at the time and lowered voters' opinion of his competence, it was almost inevitable. In early 1946 the government recommended settlements which the auto and steel companies rejected. The companies demanded larger price increases and bargained with the government over existing controls. The steelworkers settled February 15; and Walter Reuther, after asking Truman to intervene to get UAW members more money, accepted a similar settlement with General Motors on March 13. But then the United Mine Workers struck the coal fields April 1. At the time most factories and homes depended on coal for fuel, and by May the steel and auto companies were cutting back production and Chicago was cutting back on its use of electricity. On May 13 John L. Lewis sent the coal miners back to work for ten days, but two railroad unions struck May 23, and the miners went out again May 25. Truman went before Congress seeking a law to allow drafting of strikers, but the railroad unions settled as he was speaking and the bill was stopped in the Senate. In June, Truman vetoed the Case bill to restrict union power—a measure similar to the Smith bill passed by the House in 1941 and the Taft-Hartley bill which would be passed in 1947.

Other strikes plagued the economy as well. In fact, 1946 turned out to be the most strike-ridden year in American history. Some 4.6 million workers, more than 10% of those employed, were involved in work stoppages, which totaled 1.4% of total working time—more than double the 0.6% in the next highest years, 1949, 1952, and 1959.[13] Strikes represented a high degree of militance and solidarity among union members, who amounted to more than one-quarter of the work force. But millions of the other three-quarters of Americans were discommoded and had reason to fear that they would be losers in the fight for a bigger share of the pie.

On the issue of controls, Truman also wavered. He withdrew controls on building materials in October 1945, only to reimpose them in December. Meat rationing was ended in December after consumers complained of shortages. When the Office of Price Administration and price controls were about to be phased out in June 1946, he urged Congress to continue them; he vetoed one bill as unsatisfactory, they signed one which withdrew price controls from meat until August 20. As a result, meat flooded the market before that date and was kept off thereafter by producers, who wanted to hold their livestock until controls were lifted for good. An acute meat shortage developed, and a kind of national hunger for meat— "the great gouamba," journalist A. J. Liebling called it. In effect, the meat producers were on strike, and on October 14 Truman capitulated and ordered an end to price controls on meat.

Voters also began to get the impression of disarray in Truman's administration. The new president shunted aside some of the appointees of the old, notably Secretary of State Edward Stettinius, who was next in line for the presidency under the statute then in effect. He was replaced by James Byrnes in July 1945. Stettinius, son of a J. P. Morgan partner and former president of U.S. Steel, had no political constituency, and his removal caused no problems. But such was not the case with Harold Ickes, the "old curmudgeon" who as secretary of the interior and wartime petroleum czar was one of the leading liberals in government. After Edwin Pauley, the California oil man who had been the Democrats' chief fund-raiser in 1944 and one of the chief promoters of Truman for vice president, was nominated to be undersecretary of the Navy, Ickes testified in February 1946 that Pauley had asked him on Roosevelt's funeral train to give coastal states jurisdiction over the oil which lay under their tidelands and said he could raise $300,000 for the party from oil men if Ickes would do so. That testimony derailed Pauley's nomination and ended what might have been an important career in government. He was an able, aggressive man, who was slated to succeed James Forrestal as secretary of the Navy in 1947 and might have succeeded him as secretary of defense two years later. Truman, who had ruled in September 1945 that offshore oil belonged to the federal government, nonetheless had confidence in Pauley. He said Ickes "could be mistaken," and Ickes, who had threatened to resign numerous times in his thirteen years as secretary, made good his threat the next day.

That was one liberal loss. The other was Henry Wallace. Implausibly positioned as commerce secretary (the one thing which may have made the job attractive to him was that it forced Roosevelt to fire his enemy Jesse Jones), Wallace had relatively little to do. As during the war, he advocated close cooperation with the Soviets. Thus in March 1946 he was dismayed by Churchill's "iron curtain" speech in Fulton, Missouri—a speech which Truman effectively endorsed by accompanying Churchill on the trip to his home state.[14] Then in September, when he was scheduled to speak at a political rally in New York, Wallace cleared with Truman a speech which opposed the "get tough with Russia" policy that Truman and Byrnes were pursuing; when he delivered it September 12, Truman denied there was any contradiction. This claim was wholly implausible, and Truman was forced to repudiate Wallace's policies and to ask him to resign September 20. This was a situation that Truman plainly mishandled, a crisis that arose because of his own incompetence.

IV

Opinions of Truman's competence were not high in 1946. His Gallup approval rating dropped from 87% in May 1945 to 43% in June 1946, when it was depressed by his handling of strikes, to 35% in December 1946. The feistiness for which Truman would later come to be admired seemed foolish belligerence. His loyalty to those around him was considered "government by crony." He was proud of his ability to make crisp, quick decisions, but too many of those decisions were plainly wrong—or were reversed soon afterwards. He had lost the loyalty of the labor unions and articulate liberals, even though he backed most of their policies, because he opposed them on some; yet he was gaining no support among countervailing groups of the electorate. No one was making the case for Truman, not even himself. At the advice of the party's National chairman, Bob Hannegan, he did no campaigning whatever for Democratic candidates in the 1946 elections.

"Had enough?" was the Republican slogan in 1946. Enough strikes, enough meatless days, enough wage and price controls which blocked ordinary people from taking full advantage of the unexpected prosperity which followed the war?

Enough inflation, enough high taxes, enough coddling of unions with their radical and sometimes Communist leaders, enough civil rights? Americans in 1946, mistrustful of economic markets, expected government to arrange economic affairs to their satisfaction and then complained when government was unable to perform that impossible task. They wanted the prices of things they bought controlled and the prices of things they sold set free, and then they complained when they weren't able to buy what they wanted and when their wage increases were eaten up by inflation. For all these evils the Republicans had crisp, clear solutions: end price controls, restrict labor unions, lower taxes. By the standards of the late 1930s and early 1940s, American voters should have been content with the peace and prosperity which Democratic governments had delivered. But they were not. Already in July a majority of those polled by Gallup said they would vote Republican in the fall congressional election, although the same voters split virtually evenly on party preference for the 1948 presidential election.[15] They wanted what the Republicans wanted, and what they delivered after they won the 1946 elections.

Turnout was down in 1946, especially in heavily Democratic areas. The party of Franklin Roosevelt was demoralized in the era of Harry Truman. Republicans won 52% of the total vote for House seats, the only time between 1928 and 1988 they exceeded 50%. They won 55% in the races for Senate; they won majorities in the House, in the Senate, and among governors. The Democratic losses in the House came almost entirely in industrial areas, and mostly in big states: 6 in New York, 4 in Connecticut, 10 in Pennsylvania (including all 6 Philadelphia seats), 3 in West Virginia, 2 in Ohio, 3 in Michigan, 4 in Illinois, 3 in Missouri (including Truman's home district in Jackson County), 7 in California, and 3 in Washington. (The Democrats also gained 3 seats, all in industrial areas: Denver; Duluth, Minnesota; and Worcester, Massachusetts.) Almost none of the switches came in the Civil War borderlands, the site of most of the partisan turnovers the last time the House had changed hands, in 1930. Almost all the Democratic seats left outside the South were in urban areas, while the South remained entirely Democratic except for Louisville and 3 Appalachian districts (plus 4 other West Virginia districts).

V

Fifty miles west of Detroit, next to an old airfield along a little creek called Willow Run, Henry Ford had found the land he wanted for his giant bomber plant. The problem was how to get the 42,000 workers he needed there. There was only a trailer park there, and the sleepy college town of Ann Arbor, with few blue-collar workers, a dozen miles to the west. The federal government provided the answers. It built a 50-mile expressway from the city limits of Detroit, where so many workers had been unemployed such a short time ago; and it built temporary housing units, first a dormitory in February 1943, then prefabricated units for families in August 1943—enough for 14,000 workers. The units were monotonous dingy gray row houses; the kitchens had coal stoves and iceboxes; there was just one shopping center. Local real estate interests opposed permanent public housing but built little housing themselves. Who would want it after the war was over?[16]

Willow Run was a particularly glaring example of the housing problems that faced every big war industry center—and would face the growing metropolitan areas in the postwar years. After Pearl Harbor, workers streamed by the tens of thousands into cities and countryside which had seen almost no housing units built over the preceding dozen years. Blacks in particular suffered, as they were channeled into small ghettoes which quickly became overcrowded. But others had problems as well: landlords, able to pick and choose, didn't want tenants with children and raised their rents as much as they dared. The housing problem might be eased after the war by private construction. But home-building in America was a makeshift business, with no big producers and, it seemed, no economies of scale; and most of those who had built those millions of houses in the 1920s were no longer in the business. What should government do?

In the opinion of Senator Robert Wagner, it should do a great deal. Wagner came from New York, a city with a unique housing situation and unique housing problems in the 1930s; in addition, because of his annual trips to Europe before the war, he was probably more familiar with foreign approaches to housing than other American politicians. In New York, housing construction during the 1920s and 1930s had focused on the replacement of "old-law tenements" built before 1910, mostly in Manhattan, with better-ventilated multi-unit buildings, mostly in the outer boroughs of Brooklyn and the Bronx and sometimes even in then bucolic Queens. Most of the replacements had been put up by private builders, many of them small-time operators scrambling to accumulate just a bit of capital for their old age. But the depression had bankrupted many such builders, and under Mayor La Guardia the government had stepped in, tearing down fetid slums—like the one where La Guardia's first wife had contracted tuberculosis and died—and building sturdy, well-lighted new high-rises in their place. This was precisely what governments were doing in Britain and Austria, where the majority of units built in the interwar years were public housing. In the United States outside New York City, in contrast, private operators accounted for almost all new housing units. But not all of these were sold to owner-occupiers. In 1930 most Americans off the farm had been renters, not homeowners, and as foreclosures increased in the early 1930s the percentage of homeowners fell. The problem was financing. Mortgages on homes in the 1920s had typically come due in five to ten years, at which point they had to be renewed, a difficult task if money was tight at the time. These mortgages typically required a down payment of at least 30% and bore interest rates of 6% to 8%; in addition, many buyers required second mortgages.[17] These conditions meant that buying a house was far beyond most families' capacity. The New Deal's FHA program tried to encourage homeowning by guaranteeing mortgages of privately built houses over terms of twenty to twenty-five years, with lower interest rates and no need for refinancing and second mortgages. It had significant but limited success in the second half of an economically troubled decade.

Senator Wagner, wanting to encourage public housing but recognizing that private housing was inevitably a major part of the American scene, put together a housing bill in the fall of 1945 and got that archetypically conservative Republican Robert Taft to co-sponsor it. A civic father of Cincinnati, Taft believed that some housing had to be built which the private sector would not provide, but he wanted to stimulate the private market as well, and he agreed with Wagner and practically everyone else that home-buying should be made easy for veterans. The result was a bill which passed the Senate by voice vote in August 1946 but then was literally torn apart by the private-housing lobby. Housing for veterans was passed as part of a noncontroversial measure in May 1946, but Republicans and southern Democrats on the House Banking Committee bottled up the measure in July and prevented its passage.[18] It had no chance in the Republican Congress in 1947 and 1948. In 1949 the public housing provisions were scaled back, again in the House Banking Committee, to what became known as the urban renewal program, while the private housing market boomed. Although it came close to doing so for a while, the American political process chose not to create a giant public housing program but to set up a financing system which let the vast majority of units be built by private developers and which enabled the large majority of Americans to become homeowners. As with the G.I. Bill of Rights, what had begun as liberal legislation ended up producing a profoundly conservative result.

VI

The 80th Congress came to Washington in 1947 determined to deflate as much as it could of what it considered a bloated central government. Truman anticipated many of its demands. Heeding the cries for meat and other consumer goods, he removed wage and price controls. On the very last day of 1946 he seized on staffer George Elsey's idea to declare an end to hostilities, a declaration whose legal consequences were to rescind many government powers. He proposed a balanced budget. He spoke in conciliatory terms to the Congress. He spent much of his energy on the controversial but not partisan issue of unifying the military services into a single Department of Defense (a measure taken, for the moment, in name only) and on the creation of the National Security Council and the Central Intelligence Agency (which by Truman's decision was kept clearly out of military control). He acquiesced without much demur in the Republicans' tax cut.

But looming above all these issues was that of the place of labor unions in American society. Union membership had risen from 7% of the civilian work force in 1933 to 15% in 1939 and 27% in 1944.[19] Would membership subside from a postwar high, as it had after the last war? Then it had risen from 7% of the civilian work force in 1916 to 12% in 1920, only to fall to 8% by 1923 and 7% in 1930. Or would it continue upward, so that a majority of American workers would be enrolled in unions?

To a conservative Republican like Robert Taft the latter seemed a possible course and certainly not a desirable one. Taft, who in the years after 1937 had seen the unions capture the steel and rubber factories of northeast Ohio, factories considered unorganizable in the 1920s, must have contemplated the possibility that the same thing would happen in the textile mills of the South, in the machine tool shops of Cincinnati, on the building sites and loading docks of hundreds of medium-sized cities and small towns where labor unions were still not a major presence. For those who feared unions, like Taft, just as for those who built them, like Walter Reuther and his brothers, the labor union was not just an economic institution. It was more than a bargaining agent which squeezed a little more pay and somewhat better working conditions out of hard-shelled employers. It was also a social institution which had the potential to mobilize its members for social ends. In the closed shops which characterized the building trades and large factories, only union members could be hired, a system which gave unions control over hiring and, because of their involvement in the grievance procedure, firing. Someone who wanted a job in such a shop had to join the union—and to stay on good terms with its leaders. On their members the unions urged solidarity: "Solidarity Forever" was the marching song of the UAW, sung to the tune that had mobilized so many northern Americans eighty years before, "The Battle Hymn of the Republic." Without solidarity, without a willingness to submerge individual feelings and desires in a common will and common action, the strike threat had no credibility; and with no credible strike threat, the new unions had no leverage over management whatever.

And the new unions were political institutions. Sidney Hillman's CIO-PAC had shown in 1944 the power of unions in elections, even in a war year when the unions were mostly distracted and bereft of so many of their youngest and presumably most enthusiastic members. In most CIO strongholds Roosevelt's percentage had gone up in 1944, while in most of the rest of the nation it went down. The unions, it is true, were hobbled in 1946, when after Hillman's death they put together no effective PAC and when the rash of strikes made them an attractive target for Republicans. But public opinion would not always be so negative toward them, nor were they condemned to leaderlessness: one effect of the 1946 Republican landslide was to stimulate new PAC activity. If the unions were to keep growing, if they were to gain a controlling hold on the economic life and the political opinions of most of their members—of a potential majority of Americans—then the country's political institutions would be dominated by a group of leaders elected only indirectly, responsible to no broader public but the activist constituencies (or local thugs) which kept them in union office. High in the ranks of the CIO as 1947 began were such Communists as general counsel Lee Pressman, a brilliant veteran of the group of left-wingers purged from Henry Wallace's AAA. The UAW's president, R. J. Thomas, was supported by Communists in his battle with Walter Reuther; and Thomas's general counsel, George Crockett, remained a faithful follower of the Communist party line from that time through his service in the House of Representatives in the 1980s.[20] The electrical workers' union UE was Communist-dominated. Hillman's Amalgamated Clothing Workers were not averse to Popular Front alliances with the Communists. And the National Maritime Union's Joseph Curran and the Transport Workers' Michael Quill were Communist party-liners (Quill, under the proportional representation system New York City used then, was elected to the City Council with Communist support). The specter of a growing labor union movement led by social democrats like Walter Reuther was scary to a free-market conservative like Robert Taft; the specter of a growing labor union movement led by Communists[21] and followers of the Communist party line, just as the Cold War was beginning, was scary not only to Taft but to Reuther as well—so much so that he ran against and beat Thomas in the UAW's 1947 election and, once installed in office, ousted Crockett and Thomas's other party-liner appointees.

In this environment there was general agreement that the Wagner Act must be revised. It declared a series of management actions to be unfair labor practices, but it contemplated no possibility that unions could commit unfair labor practices. It allowed the union shop, which had few supporters on Capitol Hill or among voters. During the war, when union leaders (always with the glaring exception of John L. Lewis) eschewed strikes, a Democratic Congress had passed the Smith-Connally Act, restricting unions, only to see it vetoed by Roosevelt. This Republican Congress plainly would pass similar legislation, and it was not at all clear that the new Democratic president, the bitter foe of Lewis and the adversary of some other labor leaders, would veto it.

Control over the contents of the bill rested with Robert Taft, who was not only the dominant Republican in the Senate but also chairman of the Senate Labor Committee. Taft watched while his House counterpart, Fred Hartley, of Newark, New Jersey, shepherded to passage through the tighter procedures of the House a bill containing just about every restriction on union power which management lobbyists could think of. Mass picketing and industry-wide bargaining were outlawed. Unions could not bargain for pension plans, group insurance, and hospitalization insurance—a provision which would have changed much of the fabric of American society over the next forty years. Unions would be made subject to the antitrust laws, whose vague terms arguably made every action they took illegal. Unions could have no part in the administration of pension and welfare funds. None of these provisions, however, emerged in Taft's bill. Oddly, Taft did not have control of his committee (because of the presence of New York freshman Irving Ives and other Deweyites), but he succeeded in shaping the bill on the floor. Its essential provisions were to define unfair labor practices by unions; to ban secondary boycotts and jurisdictional strikes (or try to ban them—definition here proved slippery); and to allow the president to enjoin strikes dangerous to the national economy for an eighty-day cooling-off period, a provision that put the president in the midst of every big steel and auto contract dispute. Unions could not contribute dues funds to federal election campaigns, and so would have to raise voluntary money for organizations like the PAC. They could not have Communist officers. The union shop was outlawed, but unions could bargain for a closed shop (in which new employees had to join the union within thirty days) except in states where the closed shop was prohibited by what would quickly come to be known as right-to-work laws. In this form Taft-Hartley, as the bill became known, passed both houses in June 1947.

To Taft this was a judicious compromise between extremes. To the unions it was a "slave labor act." That label came specifically from the cooling-off period provision, but it also arose generally from a feeling that Taft-Hartley would cut off the growth of labor unions and allow employers to scale back their membership and their bargaining power, as these had been scaled back in the years following World War I. Both the AFL and the CIO sent hundreds of thousands of letters to the White House urging a veto. But Truman, who had so bitterly opposed disruptive strikes, had already come out for modifications of the Wagner Act and gave serious consideration to signing the bill. Inside the White House the chief advocate of a veto was Clark Clifford, a suave young St. Louis lawyer detailed to the White House as a naval aide under the soon-departed Truman crony Jake Vardaman. Clifford, whose social background and personal manner were elegantly genteel, on this as on other major domestic issues urged Truman to support the political left; with Roosevelt aide James Rowe, he wrote a memorandum setting forth a fighting liberal strategy for 1948. Truman followed his advice. Without giving any hint of his views beforehand, he sent a stinging veto message to Capitol Hill and made a radio speech that evening to boot. Taft replied in a radio speech the same night. By then the House had already overridden the veto by a 331–83 margin. The Senate overrode it 68–25 after a threat of filibuster from the leftist cowboy singer Glen Taylor, who had returned from his job in a California defense plant and won an upset victory in the 1944 election in his home state of Idaho.

Taft-Hartley proved to be a surprisingly enduring piece of legislation, which set the terms and conditions of labor-management relations for more than forty years. It fulfilled its backers' hopes and justified its opponents' apprehensions by largely stopping the growth of labor unions: they never organized a significantly higher share of the civilian labor force than they did in the year the bill was passed. In 1947, unions enrolled 26% of the labor force. That number grew marginally to 28% in 1953–54 and 1956–57; it was still 25% as late as 1970, then fell to under 20% in 1980 and to 15% in 1984. Yet Taft-Hartley did not kill the labor movement entirely. Instead, as most of the southern and many of the Rocky Mountain states hurried to pass right-to-work laws, it simply froze into place the regional variations in unionization which existed in 1947. The Northeast, the West Coast, and especially the Great Lakes region, which were essentially the higher-wage parts of the country already, became a heavily unionized America; while most of the rest of the country became an America in which union members were seldom seen. The Carolinas, with their large textile industries, have never had as many as 10% of their workers enrolled in unions. The sharp differences between the southern and northern labor markets had been eroded by New Deal legislation. But they were not ended, and some differences were perpetuated by the combination of Taft-Hartley and regional right-to-work laws.

Unions, especially the CIO unions, remained vibrant institutions socially and politically. They advanced various welfare-state measures both on their home turf and in Washington; for it was in their interest to extend to all of society the benefits—supplemental unemployment, medical insurance—they were winning for their own members, and their leaders, most notably Walter Reuther, also had an unselfish desire to ensure that the benefits of American affluence were generously and broadly distributed throughout the population. These unions also became major forces for racial tolerance and civil rights—causes in which by no means all their members shared the leaders' liberal views. At the same time, the passage of Taft-Hartley by an antilabor Congress in 1947 combined with the successs of Reuther and like-minded anti-Communists in the union elections of that year resulted in the achievement of a goal both sides would have been reluctant to admit was common, the reduction of Communist influence in the labor movement to zero. When Henry Wallace announced his third-party candidacy for president in November 1947, he expected left-leaning and Communist-sympathizing unions to provide his main institutional support. A year earlier such support would have been formidable; by early 1948 it was negligible. The Communists' one chance to achieve significant power in American public life was destroyed before the end of 1947.

Taft-Hartley, far from being a slave labor act, created a kind of equipoise between the unions which existed in 1947 and the managements of the industries they organized. For the next two decades, much of the substance of American politics would revolve around the contract negotiations in these industries, particularly steel. The steel wage settlement was taken as a standard, to be followed in all manner of industries organized and not; and managements backed Republicans and unions Democrats in order to get just a little extra advantage in these negotiations. Politics here did make a difference, but not nearly as great a difference as the rhetoric—"slave labor," "free enterprise"—suggested. Taft-Hartley settled the major conflicts of American economic politics by determining the amounts of leverage which unions and managements would have and by doing so just at the beginning of a period when rising economic growth would make the satisfaction of each side's wants much more easily accomplished. The Democrats promised to repeal Taft-Hartley should they ever again—it seemed a remote possibility in June 1947—get a solid majority in Congress as well as control of the White House. But when they achieved exactly those conditions in 1949, they were unable to summon up the votes to keep their promise. Taft-Hartley—a triumph not just of Taft but of his opponent Wagner, whose act's basic structure remained the key part of the final product—proved to be one of those liberal-conservative compromises, not entirely satisfactory to either side, which enabled Americans to build the prosperous, confident, and increasingly tolerant country that only the dreamiest of optimists—like Henry Wallace, who ended up politically defeated and intellectually frustrated—had ever dared to predict in the difficult years before 1947.

PART
THREE

American Politics
1947–1964

CONFIDENCE

21

→⟩⟩ ⟨⟨←

The Hinge: From Turmoil to Confidence

The year 1947 was a hinge in American history, a time in which the country changed quite markedly from one thing into another. Of course the change did not take place instantaneously nor even entirely within this single calendar year: it can be argued that trends began and old conditions ended a few years before or a few years after the 365 days from January 1 to December 31, 1947. Nevertheless, what is striking is how much change did converge on this one moment in history.

The story of this change begins with economic growth. Almost no one expected growth after World War II. Most sensible people, on both the right and the left, expected a return of the depression, with New Dealers arguing that government was needed to stimulate the economy and to see that ordinary people got a decent living and New Deal opponents arguing, less persuasively given the experience of the 1930s, that government ought to keep its dead hand off the private economy and, more persuasively given the experience of the war years, that it ought to keep its inevitably ineffective regulations out of people's lives. But the postwar era turned out to be one of those occasions when, as Lord Melbourne put it, all the sensible people are wrong and all the damn fools are right. The gross national product in 1947 was $231 billion: in effect the economy was bottoming out, since adjusted for inflation this was the lowest total since 1942. The GNP rose to $258 billion in 1948, paused at $256 billion in 1949—the pause brought back fears of recession and helped Harry Truman and Democratic congressional candidates win in 1948—and then started rising at unprecedented rates: $285 billion in 1950, $398 billion in 1955, $504 billion in 1960, $685 billion in 1965, $977 billion in 1970. And this rise occurred in times (except for the years of the Korean war) of negligible inflation. In the twenty years following 1948 the American GNP, adjusted for inflation, grew at an average rate of 4.0% annually.[1] This was the most awesome economic growth ever seen in human history.

Nor was it economic growth in the abstract. It changed people's lives. Per capita GNP in 1939 was $691—about $1,600 in constant 1958 dollars. Inflation gobbled up some of the wartime increase, but only some; in constant 1939 dollars, per capita income rose from $1,200 in 1939 to over $1,600 in 1942 and nearly $1,900 in 1945. Income per head did not surge immediately after the war, partly because there were quickly more heads and partly because inflation quickened. It stayed between $1,700 and $1,800 in the years on both sides of 1947. But from that trough, which was already 33% above the highest levels of the 1930s and 1920s, it rose steadily to over $2,000 in 1955.[2] Per capita income figures in this period were depressed by the baby boom: all those new children, whose fathers were working so hard and productively to support them, accounted for a great many new heads who for the moment were not producing any income themselves. The rise in median family income in 1967 dollars was therefore sharper, from $4,500 in 1947 to $5,300 in 1953 and nearly $5,900 in 1956—a rise of 30% in less than a decade. Critics of the United States have complained for years that income distribution has never gotten significantly more equal since 1947. That lack of change might be a cause for concern in a society with stagnant income levels. But in a period of historically unprecedented boom, it meant that even the bottom levels of American society were sharing in growth and affluence. Moreover, in this growing America people did not remain in tightly encased economic compartments: there was great economic mobility, in both directions.[3] For people moving upward on the economic ladder, real growth meant affluence beyond all but their wildest dreams. Perhaps more important politically, real economic growth meant that even those downwardly mobile (relatively) on the economic ladder could enjoy (absolute) incomes equal to or above those to which they were accustomed. The political demand for further economic redistribution was undercut by the growth which itself had been stimulated in part by the redistribution effected mostly during the war years.

Another way in which 1947 was a fulcrum of change was that it marked the first year of the baby boom. The median marriage age dropped from 24.3 for men and 21.5 for women in 1940 to 23.7–20.5 in 1947 and kept plummeting to a low point of 22.5–20.1 in 1956: teen-age marriage almost became the norm for American girls in the mid-1950s.[4] In the years before 1940, marriage had to be postponed until a man could support a family, and many never could. Households were filled with bachelor uncles and maiden aunts who were never able to marry and lived in other people's houses their whole lives. Now, after the war, Americans felt freer to marry, and the fact rather than the prospect of marriage became the goad for young men to make a good living. Once married, of course, they were more likely to have children. Many, though not all, societies have seen their birthrates rise in time of war, as if people are eager to replenish the genetic stock that is being worn down—or as if the young men who are soldiers and the young women who are their mates want to preserve some trace of the existence of a person who may soon die. In the United States the birthrate rose marginally in the first years of the war, then ebbed a bit in 1944 and 1945 when so many young men were away in the service. It rose sharply—and quite unexpectedly—in 1946 and 1947, subsided a bit through 1950, then surged upward and remained high through 1964. The table below gives the fertility rate (the number of births per 1,000 women aged 15 to 44) and the total number of births for each year from 1940 through 1968:[5]

Year	Fertility	Births (millions)
1940	80	2.6
1941	83	2.7
1942	91	3.0
1943	94	3.1
1944	89	2.9
1945	86	2.9
1946	102	3.4
1947	113	3.8
1948	107	3.6
1949	107	3.6
1950	106	3.6
1951	111	3.8
1952	114	3.9
1953	115	4.0
1954	118	4.1
1955	118	4.1
1956	121	4.2
1957	123	4.3
1958	120	4.3
1959	119	4.2
1960	118	4.3
1961	117	4.3
1962	112	4.2
1963	108	4.1
1964	105	4.0
1965	97	3.8
1966	91	3.6
1967	88	3.5
1968	86	3.5

We have already seen how the housing market started to boom in 1947. The government helped to provide financing by guaranteeing FHA and VA loans and by stabilizing the banking and savings industries through deposit insurance, and thousands of small entrepreneurs surged in to build dwellings where all these newly married young couples and their infant children could live. And so began the American flight to the suburbs. As already noted, central-city populations seem to have reached their peak, in absolute numbers and as a percentage of the American population, in 1947 or 1948, and mass transit ridership reached its peak in the latter year. Homeownership was rising sharply in these years, starting at 44% of households in 1940 and rising to 55% in 1950 and to 62% in 1960 (by 1983 it was close to 65%).[6] Buying a home was a good investment: the value of owner-occupied residences unadjusted for inflation increased from $87 million in 1940 to $260 billion in 1950.[7]

The new America which was being created could be seen most vividly in the Los Angeles basin. In the 1930s Los Angeles had seemed a kind of never-never land, with colonies of old people from Iowa falling for nostrums like the Townsend Plan and the Ham 'n' Eggs movement and of hangers-on out of the pages of Nathanael West roaming the star-paved streets of Hollywood, where next to a gleaming Art Deco tower would appear a vacant lot. In the early 1940s Los Angeles had been one of the arsenals of democracy, where Douglas, Lockheed, and North American had churned out planes and Henry Kaiser ships. More than half a million Americans had streamed into the basin during the war, swelling its population to 3.5 million. But in 1945 neither movies nor planes seemed to provide an economic base for the future. In eighteen months at the end of World War II, Los Angeles lost 232,000 jobs in defense industries (the number dropped from 300,000 to 78,000), and every expert predicted depression and depopulation for the basin in the postwar years. Exactly the opposite happened. In the decade following the war Los Angeles was the fastest-growing major metropolitan area in the United States. In the years around 1947 it was generating one out of eight new jobs in the United States and building one out of eleven of the country's new houses.[8] Part of the reason was the building of new plants there by big national corporations, like the auto assembly plants which cropped up at the edge of urban settlement. But small operators were the key, as Jane Jacobs has described: "The new enterprises started in corners of old loft buildings, in Quonset huts and in backyard garages. But they multiplied swiftly, mostly by the breakaway method. And many grew rapidly. They poured forth furnaces, sliding doors, mechanical saws, shoes, bathing suits, underwear, china, furniture, cameras, hand tools, hospital equipment, scientific instruments, engineering services, and hundreds of other things."[9]

Los Angeles was the shape of the American future which began almost precisely in 1947. It was a future built by people whose lives had been molded by depression and shaken up by war, people used to being mobilized in a common purpose but eager now to set off on their own—all on the same path. They had been conditioned by depression and war, and by the politics which had grown up almost accidentally in response to these events, to see themselves as a culturally unified nation, with differences only along economic lines—although they had fought the war with racially segregated military services and although ethnic prejudices, particularly anti-Semitism, may have become more obvious in the war years as young men and others were thrown together with people from cultural backgrounds they had never before encountered.[10]

The Americans in the years beginning in 1947 acted with a confidence in the future which the Americans of 1940 had pretty much lost. They married and had children at ages when, a decade before, they would not have dared to make such commitments. They bought houses, although the depression had taught that the value of housing could collapse and equity could be totally wiped out. They moved around the country—not just during the war, but for years afterwards, unconcerned about the risks, confident of the rewards. Americans were confident because they knew their country worked. They had won the war. They had ended the depression. They could listen to Republican orators assure them that only the war had ended the depression and that the New Deal had failed, and they could listen to Democratic orators assure them that the economy could collapse again for ordinary people if Republican policies were reimposed. They could listen and agree with much in both arguments—and be not much concerned about the way the argument, or the political battle, came out. What mattered was the results. In August 1945 they had learned suddenly that the war was over. Some time not long after 1947 they began to understand that prosperity and economic growth were not over and would continue.

As this confidence was growing stronger, the political system was settling the issues still left over from the politics of economic redistribution and scarcity which had begun in 1935. The basic structure of government and the macroeconomy which would prevail until the middle 1960s, and not be greatly altered even then, was mostly in place. Government set the stage for economic growth: by stimulating economic production in the war, by encouraging young men to go to college and young married couples to buy houses, by creating a generous family allowance through the mechanism of a steeply progressive income tax combined with large exemptions, by building roads and schools and water systems. Each of these programs rewarded upward mobility and honored those who worked their way up in society, placed society's stamp of approval on their affluence and their success. These programs had not been at the heart of the New Deal. Some of them were peripheral to the concerns of most New Dealers; some, like the G.I. Bill of Rights sponsored by the likes of the American Legion and John Rankin, were at least partly the products of those by no means entirely sympathetic to the New Deal. Some, like the FHA program which carefully rated residential neighborhoods, with prejudice against ethnic quarters and black ghettoes, would later be criticized severely by New Deal admirers. They were programs which aimed not at servicing a lower class but at building a middle class—and they succeeded. They built a middle class which was affluent, which was mostly tolerant[11] (and would become much more so after the civil rights revolution of the early 1960s), which was culturally diverse (though uncomfortable with that diversity until the 1960s), which was far better educated than any before, which was geographically mobile and much more familiar with regional differences than most Americans were before 1941, which was politically responsible, rejecting (though not always immediately) demagogues from Joseph McCarthy to George Wallace.

Politically, the United States in 1947 was seeing the emergence of a consensus. On the surface of politics, economic battles were still being waged. But the central issues in most of them were settled by midyear. The Taft-Hartley Act set the terms and conditions of the existence of labor unions, enabling those already in place to thrive as bargaining agents and political operators but blocking the growth of unions elsewhere. Government safety nets in the form of minimum wages and

Social Security continued. The more equitable distribution of income and wealth which had been effected by wartime growth and the progressive income tax was frozen into place. Much public attention was focused on epic labor negotiations, especially in the steel and auto industries, which set patterns widely followed throughout the rest of the economy. Presidents intervened in such negotiations on one side or the other, and that intervention was one reason big labor and big business were so interested in the outcome of presidential elections. Congress engaged in constant political warfare over the level of the minimum wage, increases in Social Security benefits, minor adjustments in labor law, the status of tidelands oil, and limited expansion of public power units like TVA: all marginal economic issues, battles fought out at the edges of the national consensus forged by 1947.

Only one major budgetary issue remained unsettled in 1947: the level of the defense budget. It had been sharply cut after the war, and Truman and Marshall, despite popular support in the polls, were not able to get Congress to approve universal military training. This congressional stance on the draft was an example of the Republicans resisting centralization and higher defense spending and the Democrats pushing for these things, a pattern that held true up to and after the 1960 presidential election. But the draft was reinstituted in 1948, in the face of Communist advances in eastern Europe and China, and defense spending rose sharply after the Korean war began in June 1950 and remained high ever after.

During World War II the Roosevelt government had relied for the war effort on big corporations and big labor unions, partly because big units seemed more efficient, partly because a few big units seemed easier to regulate (except for the one headed by John L. Lewis) than many small ones; and in postwar America the big units probably accounted for more of the economy than they ever had before or have since. This concentration was not a bad thing, argued former price controller John Kenneth Galbraith in 1950; big government, big business, and big labor were countervailing powers, which modified one another's excesses and, thanks to economies of scale, generated vast economic growth.[12] In time the big units faltered and stumbled. But what is interesting is how well they did for so long. Autos remained a growth industry through 1964, steel companies were still building big mills (poorly designed, as it turned out); manufacturing employment surged, and manufacturing states like New Jersey, Ohio, and Michigan grew rapidly enough in the 1950s to gain a congressional seat each after the 1960 census. In 1945 the United States produced about half the world's gross national product. Its internal market was by far the richest in the world, and its products and expertise were sought the world over. It was not immediately clear that this situation was temporary, for the economies of western Europe conspicuously failed to recover in the first years after 1945 and most of the rest of the world was economically backward. But while even victorious European countries like Britain struggled without enough food and fuel, the United States was a land of plenty in which the men at the top of the big countervailing institutions planned for expansion.

That the political atmosphere did not become less bitter and the partisan hatreds did not subside in 1947 resulted from two things: no one could be sure yet that the economic issues had been settled, and foreign policy still presented agonizing choices and led to bitter recrimination. Although the 1948 election seemed to be fought and won largely on the old economic issues, Truman's and the Democratic party's impressive victory did little to overturn the economic settlement made by Taft's 80th Congress and its rather conservative predecessors. Instead, events in the years after 1948 made foreign policy again the central focus of American politics, especially presidential politics, arguably for the next twenty years. This focus on foreign policy helps to explain why the Republicans held the presidency so much of this time when the Democrats were clearly the majority party and when Democratic blocs—labor unions, urban ethnics—accounted for a larger share of the nation's voters than they ever did before or have since.

22

-»)) ((«-

Cold War

A fter years of war and danger, postwar Americans were ready to take care of their business at home. They demanded demobilization of the armed forces[1] and a virtual dismantlement of the nation's military establishment by early 1946. They renounced isolationism and voiced support for an active U.S. part in world affairs,[2] including the new United Nations organization, in the hope that the UN could help prevent their country from being drawn into war again.[3] They disliked Soviet Communism and feared that Russia might not be a reliable ally,[4] as Franklin Roosevelt himself seems to have decided before his death in April 1945.[5] But even though they took Harry Truman's and James Byrnes's side against Henry Wallace in September 1946, when Wallace said we regarded Britain as no more our ally than Russia, they did not yet conceive it necessary for their country to maintain large military forces to deter Soviet aggression. After all, Americans had the atom bomb—and the Soviets, thanks to the decisions of Roosevelt, Churchill, and Truman, didn't have it.

The events of 1947 through 1950 changed Americans' view of their place in the world forever. Before World War II their country had been physically invulnerable but militarily weak. After victory in World War II and the emergence of the Cold War with a nuclear-armed Soviet Russia and a Communist China, Americans had a country which was militarily strong but for the first time, they realized with a sinking feeling, also physically vulnerable.

So even as the pitched battle for Taft-Hartley went on, even as Truman waged what seemed to be his doomed reelection campaign of 1948, foreign crises, new and unexpected dangers, and American initiatives seized and held the headlines, as they had in the heady days of 1939, 1940, and 1941.

II

The first crisis came in February 1947, when the government of Great Britain, exhausted after a freezing, hungry winter and shedding its imperial interests in India and elsewhere, informed the State Department that it could no longer provide the anti-Communist governments of Greece and Turkey with protection against internal and external Communist designs. "A highly possible Soviet breakthrough," Undersecretary of State Dean Acheson told congressional leaders in a meeting at the White House, "might open three continents to Soviet penetration." After a long silence, Arthur Vandenberg, the garrulous one-time journalist who had represented Michigan in the Senate since 1928 and now chaired the Foreign Relations Committee, said, "Mr. President, if you will say that to the Congress and the country, I will support you and I believe that most of its members will do the same."[6]

Everyone in the room understood that Vandenberg was the critical figure there and in the Congress. He was at the climax of a long public career distinguished by the articulation of conventional pieties of midwestern Republicanism—and by a sturdy determination to work his way through practical difficulties and come up with sensible solutions. He had grown up poor and Dutch in the prosperous furniture manufacturing city of Grand Rapids, Michigan, which in his youth was attracting the nation's largest concentration of Dutch immigrants. His big break came, Horatio Alger–style, when in March 1906 at age twenty-one he was made managing editor of the *Grand Rapids Herald* by its proprietor, William Alden Smith, a congressman (1895–1907) who was soon to become a U.S. senator (1907–19). By the time Vandenberg was in his thirties, he was a millionaire. As editor, he was an ardent Theodore Roosevelt Republican who wrote books praising Alexander Hamilton and the Federalists and was pleased with the trends of the Republican 1920s.[7] He always supported child labor laws and unemployment compensation. But looking down on Grand Rapids' small cluster of office buildings from the neighborhood of solid Victorian houses where he moved with his new bride months after becoming editor, he also celebrated middle-class values against the jibes of intellectuals. "Save us BABBITT at his best," one of his many editorials read, "interested in his own home—living with his own wife—striving to educate his own children—helping along his church—still believing in a just God—loving his country and his flag—preserving a few ideals—a good citizen and Samaritan."[8] He opposed ratification of the Versailles Treaty without reservations, taking the position of Woodrow Wilson's opponents, and fiercely opposed Communism at home and abroad. Politically, he and Grand Rapids businessman Frank McKay played a leading role in promoting outstate Republican Fred Green against Detroit-based incumbent Alex Groesbeck in Michigan's 1926 gubernatorial primary; Green won handily and went on to win the general election. In 1928, Vandenberg himself became a candidate for the U.S. Senate seat held by Democrat Woodbridge Ferris. When Ferris died in March, Green threatened to appoint someone other than Vandenberg to the seat, but McKay, who had lent Green large sums, put heavy pressure on him, and Vandenberg was appointed.

In the Senate, Vandenberg was never part of the progressive bloc, but he was not a reactionary either. He wanted to preserve the president's power to lower tariffs, he pushed for reapportionment of congressional districts (fast-growing Michigan gained four seats after the 1930 census), he voted against confirmation of John Parker as a federal judge in April 1930 because Parker opposed votes for blacks, and he was the originator of federal bank deposit insurance. He was one of a handful of Republican senators reelected in 1934, the only one from a large industrial state. (Then and ever after, he watched apprehensively and uncomprehendingly the hundreds of thousands of immigrants and factory workers who had made Detroit one of the nation's fastest growing cities between 1910 and 1930.) He opposed most of the Second New Deal and by 1936, prompted by evidence he heard as a member of the Nye Committee, came to believe in strict American neutrality—a move toward isolationism typical of many politicians of the time. If the United States became involved in a European war, he wrote, "we shall swiftly surrender to the equivalent of military dictatorship ourselves and we shall come from the conflict (no matter how victorious) into bankruptcy."[9]

Vandenberg's grandiloquent oratory and stiff manner helped to eliminate him as a serious presidential candidate in 1936, 1940,[10] and 1948. But as the leading spokesman for isolationism, especially after the death of William Borah in January 1940, he came to play an important role in foreign policy. He opposed Selective Service and Lend-Lease and criticized Roosevelt's mobilization of the Navy in the Atlantic and tough bargaining stance against Japan in the Pacific. After Pearl Harbor, Vandenberg remained wary of Roosevelt's policies but inched toward supporting some kind of international role for the United States after the war. In July 1943, after some argument, he supported the administration's participation in the United Nations relief organization without formal Senate approval. In a conference at the Grand Hotel on Mackinac Island, where the world's longest porch overlooks both of Michigan's peninsulas and the straits connecting two of the Great Lakes, he got a conference of "all Republicans" to support a resolution calling for "responsible participation by the United States in a post-war cooperative organization among sovereign nations to prevent military aggression and to attain permanent peace with organized justice in a free world." He ensured that the 1944 Republican platform contained a plank favoring such an organization. In January 1945 he delivered a speech stating that new weapons had made isolationism an unfeasible policy and that the United States should enter into an alliance under terms that allowed the executive to use force without a vote of Congress. Three weeks later Roosevelt, who always reciprocated Vandenberg's mistrust, appointed him to the American delegation to the April 1945 United Nations conference in San Francisco. Thus was born the famous "bipartisan foreign policy."

Although it was Vandenberg and the Republicans he represented who had switched their position, they were not entirely silent partners in the bipartisan enterprise. Dean Acheson, who often dealt with Vandenberg for the administration, describes his "ritual of statesmanship," in which Vandenberg, "faced with a proposal to take a step into the strange and frightening postwar world, invariably began by resisting the proposal. . . . Then followed the period of gestation. The proposal grew and developed within him." Later he would be "convinced but not committed. Before that occurred, one further step remained to be taken. We called it, variously, 'applying the trademark' or 'determining the price.' This meant either stamping the proposal with a Vandenberg brand, or exacting from the administration a concession which he thought politically important."[11] In the Greece and Turkey crisis, Vandenberg's demand that Truman describe the overarching Communist menace was met, and it set the tone that prevailed in the creation of the North Atlantic Alliance over the next several years. Truman promised in March 1947 not just that Americans would aid Greece and Turkey but that "it must be the policy of the United States to support free peoples"—no limit here on time, place, or the kind of assistance—"who are resisting attempted subjugation by armed minorities or by outside pressures." The president had framed what was ever afterwards called the Truman Doctrine; and Congress, in this specific instance, ratified it by wide margins. Even as it was fighting the administration on taxes and labor law the Republican Congress passed aid to Greece and Turkey.

Another foreign policy crisis was also brewing in the spring of 1947. If Greece and Turkey were threatened by the Soviets across the Black Sea, the millions of people on the northern European plain, in the British Isles and Scandinavian peninsulas, and up and down the boot of Italy were threatened with starvation. The American economy, pumped up by government during the war, was now being set free to grow at an unprecedented rate. The European economies, devastated by war, were woefully short of capital—and of food, fuel, clothing, and shelter—and were still stifled by wartime controls and by the unworkable mechanisms of command economies. Marshall, Acheson, Assistant Secretary of State Will Clayton, Navy Secretary James Forrestal, and Commerce Secretary (and wartime ambassador in Moscow) Averell Harriman were all determined that the United States must do something about this situation. From this determination resulted the Marshall Plan, announced in rather delphic terms by Marshall at the June 1947 Harvard commencement: Europeans must come up with a plan for aid, and the United States would help. That same month, at Vandenberg's suggestion, Truman set up a bipartisan committee to develop the policy from the American side. British Foreign Minister Ernest Bevin took the initiative in Europe. Stalin cooperated in July by denouncing the program: thus it would buttress the free nations of western Europe and not the Soviet Union and its satellites. In October, Truman called a special session of Congress and got a stopgap $600 million for aid to Europe. In December he asked for $17 *billion* for a four-year program; by April 1948, less than a year after Marshall's speech and in an election year, the Republican Congress had approved $5 billion.

This was more than 2% of the American gross national product for that year— "perhaps the greatest example of national generosity in history."[12] It was an extraordinary amount to be approved at a time of federal government outlays totaling only about $36 billion a year,[13] on the initiative of a president widely ridiculed as a lame duck, and at the vote of a Congress controlled by a party long committed to an isolationist foreign policy and afflicted with a state of something close to permanent rage at the continued electoral success of the Democrats. It was also a policy and political success. There is no question that the aid and financing it provided gave a critical boost to the economies of western Europe, beginning a period of unparalleled economic growth there. That growth made possible the resurgence of world trade to levels far above those of the 1920s, trade which increased American economic growth as well. Years later Americans would mourn the lost days of 1947, when the United States accounted for half the gross national product of the world. But the American economy could not have increased in real terms as it did if the economies of other nations had not grown robustly as well.

Politically, the Marshall Plan was relatively uncontroversial. It would not have been proposed by a Republican like Robert Taft. But it was fashioned with the help of Vandenberg and endorsed at critical moments by Thomas Dewey and former Minnesota Governor Harold Stassen—all presidential hopefuls for 1948. Similarly, another potentially divisive foreign policy issue, the disposition of Palestine, produced general agreement among American politicians. Taft, always sympathetic to Cincinnati's long-established German Jewish community (Hebrew Union College, the nation's major seminary for Reform Judaism, had been established in this heavily German city in 1875), had long supported the creation of a Zionist state. Thomas Dewey, who had many Jewish aides and faced an electorate in which Jewish voters cast the swing vote, felt the same way. Truman's instincts were all on the side of allowing Jewish settlement in Palestine; and even Henry Wallace, who criticized the Marshall Plan, called strongly for support of the Zionists, consistent with the current Soviet position on the issues. Opposition came from the British and from Anglophiles and Arabists within the State Department. George Marshall felt strongly that American support of partition of Palestine and, when that was rejected by the Arabs, American recognition of the state of Israel would undermine American influence with the Arabs (he felt so strongly that he told Truman in a Cabinet meeting that, if he were to vote—as a professional soldier, he did not—he would vote for the president's opponent on this issue). But Truman, influenced in meetings with Israel's first president, Chaim Weizmann, which were arranged by his old haberdashery partner, Eddie Jacobson, recognized Israel within minutes of its declaration of independence in May 1948.

Meanwhile, the Soviet Union was tightening its hold on eastern Europe and the Red Army was advancing in China. A pro-Soviet government had taken power in Poland in June 1945, causing friction between the United States and the Soviet Union: By early 1948 it had tightened its hold gradually but thoroughly. In Yugoslavia the Communist partisan leader Josip Tito won an election in November 1945 and executed the anti-Communist partisan Draza Mihailovitch in July 1946; Tito, however, proved independent and split irrevocably with Stalin by June 1948. In Albania, Communist Enver Hoxha also took control in November 1945. Bulgaria came under Communist control by March 1946. "From Stettin in the Baltic to Trieste in the Adriatic, an Iron Curtain has descended across the Continent," said Winston Churchill, who had been introduced by Truman, to his audience at Fulton College in Westminster, Missouri, in March 1946. The Truman Doctrine helped to prevent a Communist victory in the civil war in Greece, and in April 1948 the American-supported Christian Democrats won a decisive victory in elections in Italy. But if the Mediterranean was saved, the East was going under. Communist control of Rumania was consolidated in March 1948.

Czechoslovakian Communists, who had won 37% of the vote in the May 1946 election and taken part in the subsequent government, took total control by threatening a coup in February 1948; the next month Foreign Minister Jan Masaryk, son of the nation's founder, died after falling from his office window in what the Communists called a suicide. That same month the Soviets walked out of talks about the future of Germany, on their way to setting up a separate East German Communist state in their zone of military occupation. From May 1947 the Communists gained tighter and tighter control of Hungary through the arrest of Cardinal Mindszenty in December 1948 and a Communist victory in the May 1949 election. In July 1948 the Soviets began their blockade of the American, British, and French zones in Berlin, which was surrounded by Soviet-controlled East Germany. Truman rejected the idea of sending troops down the Autobahn from West Germany to the blockaded zones and began airlifting supplies instead, although it was by no means clear that the airlift would work.

The death of Jan Masaryk and the Berlin airlift made it clear to almost all Americans that a "cold war" had begun. As early as 1946 the large majority of Americans had rejected Henry Wallace's criticisms of Truman's policies and regarded the Soviet regime with loathing and fear. They were ready to take action in response. In June 1948 the Senate passed a Vandenberg-sponsored resolution authorizing the United States to make military alliances outside the Western Hemisphere—a step toward NATO, whoever won in November. Also in June, Congress, which had been so reluctant to vote a peacetime draft in September 1940 and had reauthorized it by a single vote in the House in August 1941, passed a draft law by comfortable margins even though the membership it had now would not have approved the earlier measure.

III

The other problem looming was China. Many Americans had a sentimental attachment to this other continent-sized nation which had clung to its independence against imperial powers and had overthrown its monarchy and become a republic. For nearly 100 years American Protestant missionaries had been working in China, setting up schools and educating a Christian elite. Henry Luce, the proprietor of *Time, Life,* and *Fortune,* had been born the son of missionaries in China; and Chiang Kai-shek, the head of the Kuomintang (KMT) party and nominal head of state in China since 1927, was a Christian whose charismatic wife was a graduate of Wellesley College. But China was not a united nation, and Chiang Kai-shek was never really in control. Since the Taiping Rebellion broke out in 1850, China had been more or less permanently in a state of civil war. Rebels and warlords almost always controlled or threatened one or more provinces, while the Great Powers set up trading enclaves along the coast. So pervasive was the violence and its effect on the economy that China's population, though always huge, has increased at less than the average world rate since the beginning of the nineteenth century.[14] Franklin Roosevelt and Luce both admired Chiang Kai-shek and depicted him as a great national leader: Roosevelt by seeing that he was featured at wartime conferences and by making China one of the five permanent members of the UN Security Council, and Luce by featuring Chiang, his wife, and her relatives prominently in his publications and by saluting what he regarded as their brave fights against first the Japanese and then the Communists. But from 1927 to 1937, Chiang was no more than the leader of one of several contending armies in China, and was in fact once captured by the Communists. And though he styled himself as the leader of national resistance after the Japanese invasion of 1937, he never really assumed that position. He was criticized by the men who became known as old China hands in the U.S. State Department and by General Joseph Stilwell, who commanded American forces in the China theater for part of World War II, for not husbanding his military resources and not using them to fight the Japanese.[15] But this strategy simply represented prudence for a general who was at best one contender in a prolonged civil war—as the fate of his Kuomintang army showed. The KMT and the Communists cooperated warily against the Japanese. But within two weeks of Hiroshima and Nagasaki, the Red Army took advantage of the Japanese collapse to establish control of several northern provinces, despite an August 1945 KMT-Soviet treaty. In December, Truman dispatched George Marshall, who arranged a truce between the KMT and the Communists in January 1946. This was followed by civil war again in April, another truce in May, and renewed fighting in June. In January 1947 the United States explicitly abandoned mediation and Marshall blamed intransigents on both sides. The Nationalists, as the KMT came to be called, made great military gains in March 1947. But their forces grew weaker in the following months, as their armies dwindled and Communists bought American supplies from corrupt local officials. American aid since September 1945 was estimated at more than $2 billion, and another $400 million was allocated for 1948. But the Truman administration eventually decided to stop throwing good money after bad. In January 1949, Peking fell; in July the Nationalists began preparing their withdrawal to Taiwan, which was completed by December. In response, the State Department stopped all aid in August 1949 and released its White Paper on China, blaming the Nationalists' collapse on their inadequacies.

Neither the fall of China nor the rise of NATO was anticipated by most Americans in 1948. But the politicians were already arguing over whether the United States should concentrate its resources and military force in Europe or in Asia. The Truman Doctrine and the Marshall Plan, initiated by the Truman administration and strongly supported by Republicans like Vandenberg and Dewey, amounted to a Europe First policy. The refusal to increase American aid and to even contemplate American military involvement in China amounted to a rejection of the Asia First policy favored, though not necessarily to the point of military involvement, by Republicans like Robert Taft and William Knowland, the young *Oakland Tribune* publisher appointed in 1945 by California Governor Earl Warren to replace Hiram Johnson in the Senate. "The Asian cult was, in fact, almost mystically based," wrote the *New York Times*'s William S. White. "It rested most of all, one thinks, on a strong concept of American nationalism; on long inherited suspicion of the British; on a wish, conscious or not, to have this country go it alone; on an attitude of rejection toward Europe."[16] The Asia Firsters saw America's destiny in the Pacific, as Theodore Roosevelt had when as assistant secretary of the Navy he ordered Admiral George Dewey to sail toward Manila Bay, and as William Howard Taft had when he arrived as America's governor general in the Philippines, and as Secretary of State John Hay had when he proclaimed the Open Door policy toward China in 1900. The Asia Firsters were not always logical or consistent. They ached to give more aid to China, but their arguments that it would have prevented the Communist victory were built more on hope than on assurance; and it was General Douglas MacArthur—an Asia Firster to the core, who from 1938 until 1951 never left Asia and the Pacific, never set foot in the United States—who warned against ever sending American troops to fight a land war in Asia. It is not at all clear that the Asia Firsters would have followed the logic of their beliefs through to military commitment. We can be fairly sure that a President Robert Taft in 1947 would not have initiated a Marshall Plan, but we can also be fairly sure that he would not have sent American troops to fight for Chiang Kai-shek and the Nationalists.

IV

While Americans were faced with unanticipated threats to their country's strength abroad, Americans—more precisely, white southerners—were threatened with unanticipated attacks on their country's customs of racial segregation at home. Legal segregation—the separation of blacks and whites which was enforced by state and local laws, by local custom, and by threats of force and violence—had not been an inevitable development in the United States. For decades after the Civil War, the South, the only part of the country then with a significant black population, had lived without legal segregation; and blacks had even had the right to vote and participated, uneasily to be sure, in politics. The system of segregation which southerners of the 1940s assumed was the norm and which northerners tolerated with averted gaze had actually been created by politicians and others from 1890 to 1910 and, in the words of one historian, only "reached its perfection in the 1930s," by which point it "prevailed throughout the South and in all aspects of life, everywhere one looked."[17]

World War II was the beginning of the end for segregation. The equality of sacrifice demanded of young men of both races pointed up the absurdity of demanding unequal treatment for civilians. Practices which had been accepted unthinkingly started to be examined, and to be questioned. Did it make sense to practice racial discrimination in a war against a foe the essence of whose evil beliefs was racial discrimination? The demand for war workers in northern factories brought millions of Negroes out into states where legal segregation did not exist, though de facto separation of the races was certainly the norm—a northward migration of blacks greater than the total during the half-century before 1930, when so many millions of immigrants had come to America's shores. Yet the result of blacks' wartime experience was frustration, not integration. The armed forces were not integrated during the war: American military leaders feared that race-mixing would cause trouble in the ranks, perhaps mutiny, and make it harder to win the war. And Negroes' experience in the North was in important ways similar to their life in the South. Race riots, in which blacks were more likely to be the victims than the aggressors (though some were aggressors), occurred in war-swollen cities during World War II as they had during World War I and would in northern cities during the Vietnam war.

Yet the national response to the implicit challenge to segregation was perceptibly different from what it had been in the previous war. Roosevelt, to be sure under pressure from the threats of A. Philip Randolph, created a Fair Employment Practices Commission for war industries and endorsed the principle that there should be no racial discrimination in employment. Eleanor Roosevelt was outspokenly sympathetic to civil rights. Gunnar Myrdal's *An American Dilemma* held up the peculiar American institution of segregation to examination and predicted with more prescience than most practical men of the time realized that segregation could be abolished.

Civil rights also became a focus of political competition. Traditionally the Republicans had been the party of civil rights, and if Herbert Hoover had let that tradition lapse, both Wendell Willkie and Thomas Dewey were eager to revive it. Willkie, whose German-American heritage had acquainted him with discrimination in World War I, was probably the most pro-civil rights politician of the 1940s; and Dewey, one of whose grandfathers had been a founder of the Republican party, considered racial and ethnic discrimination repugnant—inefficient as well as unfair. In New York, where Jews as well as blacks formed large constituencies favoring civil rights, Dewey sponsored the nation's most advanced antidiscrimination laws. Franklin Roosevelt succeeded in winning most black votes through his New Deal programs. But he understood, as Willkie and Dewey did, that the black electorate was growing as blacks streamed north and that it was unusually weakly moored to either of the two parties. Harry Truman, who sought black votes actively and credited blacks with his victory in the close 1940 Senate primary,[18] came to understand these facts very well.

He also understood that integration was becoming more acceptable in American life, a fact which was supported by considerable evidence in sports. In the 1936 Berlin Olympics, Jesse Owens had won four gold medals, beating German athletes and enduring a pointed snub by Adolf Hitler. Joe Louis became the heavyweight boxing champion of the world and held the title after defeating the one man who had beaten him, the German Max Schmeling, in 1938. These were American blacks representing their country and triumphing over the champions of a racist Germany.[19] Louis joined the service in the war and became a symbol of the war effort—vivid evidence to American blacks, even though they were segregated at home and in the military, that this was their country, too. "Under the lights at Yankee Stadium," read an Office of War information pamphlet, "*our* champion knocked out the German champion in one round. Sergeant Joe Louis is now a champion in an army of champions. Joe Louis doesn't talk much, but he talks truly. He talks for 13,000,000 Negro Americans, for all American citizens, when he says: "We're going to do our part, and we'll win 'cause we're on God's side.' "[20] Then in October 1945, Branch Rickey's Brooklyn Dodgers announced that Jackie Robinson had been signed by their farm team in Montreal. In 1947 he suited up to play for the Dodgers—the first black in twentieth-century major-league baseball. "I couldn't face my God much longer knowing that His black creatures are being held separate and distinct from His white creatures in the game that has given me all I own," explained Rickey, an ostentatiously pious Methodist teetotaler from an Ohio farm. Robinson had to run a brutal gauntlet, but he persevered and succeeded, and won widespread admiration in the process. As one sportswriter explained, "those who were good enough to fight and die by the side of whites are plenty good enough to play by the side of whites."[21]

The civil rights issue arose in 1948 largely because of the report of the Civil Rights Commission which Truman had appointed in December 1946—and because of a threat of war which had suddenly become more imminent. The commission's report, issued in October 1947, called for most of the civil rights agenda of the next twenty years: an antilynching law, integration of the armed forces, a Fair Employment Practices Commission, abolition of the poll tax, a guarantee of voting rights, elimination of segregation in federally funded programs and schools.[22] In February 1948, Truman delivered the first presidential civil rights address to Congress, not urging all of the commission's recommendations but arguing for more than any president had before. His call evoked cries of anguish from southern Democratic politicians but little response from Congress, where southern Democrats occupied positions of great power and only a few members of either party strongly favored civil rights measures. (There were only two black members, machine stalwart William Dawson of Chicago and the flamboyant preacher Adam Clayton Powell from Harlem).

The one pressing issue was the draft, which was due to go into effect in August. A. Philip Randolph strongly urged Truman to order the integration of the armed services, and in the spring he told the Senate Armed Services Committee that he would "personally pledge . . . to openly counsel, aid and abet youth, both white and Negro, to quarantine any Jim Crow conscription system."[23] Against this threat, the threats to military discipline posed by angry reactions to integration paled in significance—although later those threats were strong enough to persuade Secretary of the Army Kenneth Royall, a North Carolinian, to resign in protest. Politically, Truman had some incentive to forge ahead. Dewey was threatening to reclaim the black vote for the party of Lincoln, and Henry Wallace, a candidate since November 1947, was actively seeking black and Jewish support with the civil rights issue. At the Democratic national convention in Philadelphia in June, the mild civil rights plank proffered by the president's men, in deference to the South, was rejected for a stronger plank after a rousing speech by the young mayor of Minneapolis, Hubert Humphrey.

In response, many southern delegates walked out[24] and two days later nominated two southern governors—Strom Thurmond of South Carolina and Fielding Wright of Mississippi—on a separate States Rights Democratic ticket. Plainly they would carry some southern electoral votes, and Truman might have to fight for some others. But the greater number of votes were at risk outside the South, where Truman's opponents were ready to characterize him as hostile to civil rights. Truman himself spoke privately in the antiblack idiom of his time and seems to have regarded blacks as inferior; he resented the political pressures which he felt had forced him as a senator to vote for antilynching bills. Yet he also had a sense of fair play which he did not hesitate to apply to civil rights issues, even at some political risk, when they were framed in those terms. "We owe the Negro legal equality," he had said in 1940, "because he is a human being and a natural born American."[25] Two weeks after the 1948 convention he issued executive orders banning discrimination in the armed services and in the civil service.

23

→》》 《《←

Whistlestop

T he 1948 presidential election is considered the upset of the century: the picture of Truman holding up the *Chicago Tribune* early edition with the headline "DEWEY DEFEATS TRUMAN" may be the most famous political photograph of all time. It is true that few observers believed Truman could or would win. He himself said he did from June 1948 on, but he may have just been putting on a good front. Statistician and election buff Louis Bean, who projected state percentages on the basis of the 1940 and 1944 returns, the September results from Maine, and current economic indicators, was one of the few pundits to get the result right.[1] But the Truman victory should not have been quite as much of a surprise as it was. True, the Democratic party was split. In November 1947 Henry Wallace had announced his independent candidacy, arguing that Truman was too anti-Soviet and not sufficiently pro-labor and pro-civil rights. But Wallace's potential pool of supporters, as measured by Gallup in early June 1947, was only 13% of the electorate, heavily concentrated among union members.[2] Later that month Truman's veto of Taft-Hartley—a veto which may have been motivated by Truman's or Clark Clifford's noticing the Gallup results—guaranteed him solid and enthusiastic union support, just as his recognition of Israel in May 1948 and his desegregation of the armed services in July 1948 gave him solid Jewish and black support. Southern Democrats were furious with the civil rights program Truman announced in February 1948, and their fury led directly to the separate candidacy of Strom Thurmond. But it was pretty clear early in the fall that Thurmond's electoral vote total would be limited to a few states and that his candidacy would not give any electoral votes to Dewey.

Nor was Truman's strength negligible. He led most potential Republican candidates in polls through most of 1947.[3] His own standing with voters was always mercurial, depending mostly on whether his almost manic decisiveness produced results which were satisfactory or results which were so unsatisfactory as to require more attention and more rapid-fire decisions. But the standings of his party and of the opposition, which were based on a longer experience, stayed more stable. In March 1947, Gallup found that "if hard times return," voters would prefer having Democrats in office to Republicans by a 51%–30% margin, and that if they were asked who was "better handling the problem of keeping wages high," the Democrats were the favorite by a 54%–22% margin.[4] In June 1947 voters

215

with a preference favored a Democrat over a Republican for the presidency by a 55%–45% margin, more than Truman's lead over Dewey at the time.[5] These results, however much one may quibble about the wording and timing of the questions, indicate fairly solid advantages for the Democrats. Most Americans were not buying the Republican argument that the Democrats had mismanaged the economy and that the Republican policies of lower taxes and less government were producing the postwar prosperity. They were still fearful of an economic downturn and convinced that if it came the Democrats would handle the situation better. Truman was well positioned to win the prosperity issue if the economy should turn downward in the fall of 1948—as in fact it did.

Truman's inherent strengths as a candidate were camouflaged by other developments in early 1948. One was the Wallace candidacy. Observers mesmerized by Wallace's claim to represent Franklin Roosevelt's candidacy, and misled by the inaccurate notion that it was Roosevelt's identification with the more extreme of liberal ideas which made him attractive to voters, overestimated the Wallace potential: they took the 7% he was receiving in Gallup's January 1948 poll as a floor for his candidacy rather than a ceiling. But the electoral college gives American presidential politics a dynamic that works powerfully against third-party candidacies without a regional electoral vote base, and Wallace was never able to come close to competing with Truman and Dewey even in his strongest state, New York. It would have been prudent early in 1948 to assume that Truman would end up with about half of Wallace's January support; and if that assumption is made and sampling error is taken into account, the election was actually tied at that point. In fact, in the January Gallup poll Dewey, who led in polls for the Republican nomination except briefly in April after a flurry of Stassen primary victories, led Truman by only 46%–41%. Dewey's lead widened in the spring, but not by much: to 47%–39% in March and 49%–38% in April. But in these surveys Wallace had 7% and 6%. Observers were also misled by Truman's weak showings in the large northern states which had been critical to Roosevelt's victories. But Roosevelt carried most of them only narrowly in 1940 and 1944, and the Wallace vote tended to be concentrated in them, especially in New York.

Finally, as Gallup himself admitted just after the election, the pollsters retired from the scene too soon. They failed to note the clear improvement in Truman's standing in the first weeks of October, and to investigate whether it would continue up through election day. Moreover, they ignored the truth that polls measure attitude only at one point in time, and in their analysis they failed to take intelligent account of sampling error. Gallup for years measured his final poll results against election results, thereby leading readers to expect him to be within 1 percentage point of the election result rather than educating them about error margins and the necessary imprecision of polls. In 1948 he insisted on reporting some poll results to the half of a percentage point when the error margin was plus or minus 4 points, and he ignored the statistically significant possibility that the 49.5%–44.5% Dewey lead he showed in his final poll, conducted October 15–25, could actually have meant that Truman was leading 48.5%–45.5% even at that time![6]

The following table shows the results of the Gallup polls conducted between the two party conventions and election day, as well as the results of the election:

Interview Dates	Truman %	Dewey %	Wallace %	Thurmond %
July 16–27	37	48	5	
August 13–18	37	48	4	2
August 20–25	36.5	48.5	5	
September 2–7	39	46.5	3.5	2
September 10–15	39	46.5	3.5	2
September 23–28	40	46	4	2
October 15–25	44.5	49.5	4	2
ELECTION November 2	50	45	2	2

The actual election results show the Truman surge which was already apparent in Gallup's October 15–25 polling. In fact, Dewey ended up with a percentage not much different from what he had been getting in polls all along. He had never won the support of 50% of those polled, a fact which by itself should have prevented his fellow politicians and the press from assuming that he would surely be elected. Wallace's support predictably fell from the 7% level of January 1948 to the 2% of November; half of his votes were cast in New York, where his support among Jews and others with a genuine left-wing political tradition was still strong enough that some voters could fool themselves into believing that he was a serious candidate.

Truman's inherent strength was hidden as well by the sniping he was receiving from his fellow Democrats. Used to Roosevelt, suspicious (and sensibly so) of many of their copartisans, the Democrats of 1948 were an inherently fractious lot. The announcement of Wallace's candidacy gave Truman opposition on his left, even though the Taft-Hartley veto had given him a strong basis for appealing to the labor vote. In March 1948 his momentary support for delaying partition of Palestine gave his liberal opponents a further opportunity for making inroads against him among Jewish voters, even while the southern Democrats were bellowing with rage over his position on civil rights. It was in that context that New Dealers like Claude Pepper and Hubert Humphrey, CIO unionists like Walter Reuther and James Carey (acting as stalking horses for CIO president Philip Murray), and, most prominently, three of the Roosevelt sons, James, Elliott, and Franklin, Jr., urged the Democrats to nominate Eisenhower. They were joined by the newly created Americans for Democratic Action, formed in 1947. The Eisenhower boomlet was a quixotic enterprise.[7] In 1905 Eisenhower's brother Arthur had been one of Truman's roommates in Kansas City, so Truman had known the family for years; he knew that Eisenhower was a Republican and also knew that he was not interested in running in 1948.[8] Curiously, Dewey, who worked to draft Eisenhower four years later, went to some trouble in 1948 to keep him out of the Republican race, arguing among other things against the involvement of military men in politics.[9] Moreover, Truman's support from most Democratic machine politicans was firm. This was, after all, a president who attended the funeral of his own political patron, Tom Pendergast, even though Pendergast had gone to jail.

This was also a president who adhered pretty faithfully to a policy and political strategy of some originality which put him in a position to win. The strategy was to pursue an activist, anti-Communist international policy, with strong support from all the Republicans who turned out to be important in the presidential election, and to pursue a liberal, future-oriented domestic policy. The foreign policy sparked opposition from the Henry Wallace left, and one plank of the domestic policy—civil rights—sparked opposition from the Strom Thurmond right; but neither could command any substantial backing in the America of 1948, and both ended up strengthening Truman by their opposition. Wallace's opposition convinced urban Catholics and Civil War borderlands residents, both of whom had been dubious about Roosevelt, to support Truman this time. Thurmond's opposition convinced blacks that Truman was genuinely their champion.[10] Truman chose to move left domestically on Taft-Hartley, left on civil rights, left on the series of domestic programs he called for in his State of the Union address in January 1948—national health insurance, a cut in personal income taxes combined with an increase in corporate rates, increases in unemployment compensation and Social Security, price supports for farmers, public works for the West, a jump in the minimum wage from 40 to 75 cents.[11] Truman persisted in this course even when the Roosevelts, the CIO, and ADA were trying to dump him. He campaigned energetically, despite wretched advance work at first, traveling by train and speaking from the rear platform to crowds small and large, speaking extemporaneously after May because he was hopelessly dry when using a text. When Robert Taft at the Union League of Philadelphia accused him of "blackguarding Congress at every whistle station in the West," Truman asked his audiences how they liked being called "whistle-stops"—the label applied to his campaigning ever since.[12]

Truman was not in full command of the Democratic convention at Philadelphia. Claude Pepper's movement to draft Eisenhower was squelched by the general's Shermanesque statement only the Friday before the convention began.[13] On Monday, Alben Barkley's keynote speech, the third of his career, created such a sensation that he became the clear favorite for the vice presidential nomination though he was seventy years old. On Wednesday the liberals pushed through their strong civil rights plank, although Truman had been trying to downplay the issue. Truman's acceptance speech was not delivered until 2 A.M. Friday morning in a still sweltering Convention Hall. In it he announced that on July 26, "what we in Missouri call turnip day" (the old saying went, "On the 26th day of July, sow your turnips, wet or dry"), he would call the Republican Congress into special session and call on it to enact liberal programs—civil rights, price controls, the Wagner-Taft-Ellender housing bill—which Truman had been pushing and which were mentioned in Dewey's Republican platform.[14] Of course the Congress did no such thing, thus providing a basis for Truman's characterization (actually his use of a reporter's characterization) of this most active of Congresses as the "do-nothing 80th Congress." Truman's job approval rating was still not overwhelmingly high. But he did a fine job of framing the issues in terms favorable to his candidacy.

Still, Truman could not have won if he had not been helped by circumstance—especially the circumstance of a sharp drop in farm prices and a general softening of the economy in September and October 1948. Since the depression, polls had always found that voters considered the Democrats the party better able to handle the economy, and suddenly this advantage became relevant, most prominently in the Farm Belt and less noticeably in the central cities as well. A particular problem for Dewey was a Republican farm bill which prevented the government from building new storage facilities which farmers were required to use in order to be eligible for federal farm programs; when harvests proved bigger than expected and crop prices fell, farmers found themselves unable to sell to the government at the higher federal price because no storage space was available.[15] The swing away from Dewey in the heartland is what enabled Truman to win. In most coastal states Dewey increased his 1944 strength by an amount that would have been enough to win if it had been achieved nationwide, since he had won 46% of the vote in 1944 and both Wallace and Thurmond won 2% in 1948. But in the states between the last western ridge of the Appalachians and the Front Range of the Rockies, Dewey's percentages were down except in Michigan (his birthplace), Illinois (the home of the *Chicago Tribune,* though Truman nonetheless carried the state), and Texas (which Truman carried easily). The Dewey vote was down 7 percentage points in Truman's Missouri and in Hubert Humphrey's Minnesota, down 7 points in Governor Robert Kerr's Oklahoma and 6 points in Alf Landon's Kansas, down 1 point in Robert Taft's Ohio and 4 points in the LaFollettes' Wisconsin. As Dewey himself wrote Henry Luce, with the cold clear vision of hindsight, "The farm vote switched in the last ten days, and you can analyze the figures from now to kingdom come and all they will show is that we lost the farm vote which we had in 1944 and that lost the election."[16]

Dewey's above-the-battle strategy, an overreaction to the criticism he had endured for campaigning too bitterly after the Fala speech in 1944, gave Truman the opening to charge that Republicans were going to shut down successful government programs and refuse to protect ordinary citizens when hard times returned. For ordinary citizens did not know that twenty years of prosperity and vibrant economic growth lay ahead. Around 1947 they may have begun to suspect that that was the case, but the slowdown in the fall of 1948 raised just enough apprehension about another recession that a critical number of voters decided to keep the Democrats in for another four years. In October, Truman started attacking Herbert Hoover, even though he had brought the former president back into government to head a commission on reorganization. Then Dewey made a mistake—or, rather, revealed himself. After his train had suddenly lurched backward toward a crowd in downstate Illinois, Dewey exclaimed into the microphone, "That's the first lunatic I have had for an engineer. He probably ought to be shot at sunrise, but I guess we can let him off for no one was hurt." The sudden movement of the train threatened to harm people in the crowd, including a close

Dewey aide; but to the public this was Dewey at his coldest: proud of his own competence, contemptuous of those who did not measure up, keen to prosecute wrongdoers, short-tempered, and insensitive to the feelings of working men. A day or so later Truman pulled into a crowd of trainmen and said, "We have had wonderful train crews all around the country."

In the course of the fall Truman seems to have created an emotional bond with blue-collar and working-class urban whites. With his midwestern origin (generally considered more humble than it was), and with the opposition of Wallace (half of whose votes were cast in New York and most of whose votes were cast by Jews and blacks), he did worse among Jews, blacks, and self-identified intellectuals than Roosevelt had in 1940 and 1944. But he ran better among Catholics and many union members. He skillfully used the opposition from "Wallace and his Communists," a tough but accurate description (Communists did in fact run Wallace's campaign),[17] to increase Democratic percentages among Catholic voters, which helped him carry Massachusetts comfortably and buoyed his showings in many industrial cities. After the convention, organized labor finally swung behind him. The CIO's PAC was reactivated, the AFL created a similar organization, and both of these helped him in the industrial states. Many Wallace supporters, anticipating a Truman loss in any case, wanted to win a large percentage for their candidate to prove that the Democrats couldn't win without their kind of liberal platform. But Truman preempted most of the liberal ground on economic issues and made the chief distinction between himself and Wallace foreign policy, on which Wallace was associated with the Communists at a time when they were becoming increasingly menacing to Americans. The Wallaceites ended up proving the opposite of what they wanted to. They showed conclusively that there was no significant left-wing vote in America in the years after World War II.

Truman was also better positioned to win on the peace issue than observers at the time or later have conceded. True, debate was stifled in the fall campaign because Dewey supported the main items in Truman's foreign policy, and vigorously. His foreign policy expert John Foster Dulles was included from time to time in policymaking councils, and he pointedly refused to make an issue of the Truman Doctrine or the Marshall Plan or of China policy or the administration's general Europe First orientation. He did not want to lend himself to attacks which, if made by Wallace on the left or Taft on the right, might cripple these policies, which he believed were in the national interest and which he fully intended to continue.

As 1948 went on, Truman's foreign policies seem to have gained increasingly strong popular support, support which at least potentially worked to the political benefit of the candidate who was, for all of Dewey's genuine bipartisanship, the man primarily responsible for them. And the year's events kept foreign policy in the foreground of voters' minds. "As always during the second half of 1948, the Berlin blockade and airlift kept alive the danger of war and thus had a potential effect on the campaign," writes Robert Donovan, a student of 1948 as both reporter and historian.[18] The body of Jan Masaryk smashed on the pavement in Prague, the planes streaming constantly into and out of Berlin's Tempelhof Airport: these pictures vividly portrayed the Soviet threat, and the president's responses—forceful, peaceful, successful—had the public's wholehearted approval. Things had not gone wrong in Asia yet; China had not yet fallen, and South Korea had not been attacked. And American draftees had not yet been called to serve in Europe. Dewey could argue that he backed responsible policies and had a competent foreign policy establishment prepared to move into office. Truman could argue that he had made responsible policies and that he employed the most competent array of foreign policy officials in American history. In fact, Truman stumbled on foreign policy issues even during the campaign, at one point undercutting Secretary Marshall's authority in Europe by proposing to send Chief Justice Vinson to Moscow, at another seeming to shift the administration's position on Israel. But an incumbent with a shaky but mostly successful and in some respects brilliant record on foreign policy is more reassuring to voters than a challenger of the most statesmanlike demeanor. Foreign policy issues, it is said, usually play no role in American politics. But it was to foreign policy issues that the Democrats owed their victories in the 1940 and 1944 presidential elections, and foreign policy issues certainly didn't detract from, and may have contributed to, their victory in 1948.

"It was not my victory, but a victory of the Democratic party for the people," said Harry Truman when it became as apparent to his fellow Americans as he claimed it had been to him throughout 1948 that he had been elected president in his own right. In fact, the 1948 election *was* a party victory. It included not only Truman's reelection but also the best Democratic showing in congressional races between the Roosevelt landslide of 1936 and the Eisenhower recession of 1958. Democrats did especially well in the Senate races, winning 56% of the vote nationally; they controlled the new Senate 54–42, a 9-seat gain over 1946. In the House races Democrats led by a 52%–46% margin nationally and won 263 seats, a 75-seat gain over 1946. The national vote yielded almost precisely the same result as the Democrats' 51%–47% lead in 1944 and 51%–46% lead in 1940, and it began to seem that they had a natural majority in congressional races in presidential years, a majority which could be eroded, sometimes significantly as in 1946, by low turnout in the off years. This pattern turned out not to be a continuing one: Democrats tended to do better in off years than presidential years in the 1950s, 1970s, and 1980s. But it reflected the genuine strength of the Democrats as a presidential party in the 1940s, when macro-issues of peace and prosperity were plainly at stake, a strength that continued, though camouflaged by the unpopularity of the Korean war and the popularity of Dwight Eisenhower, into the 1950s and early 1960s.

In the war years the Democrats had run mostly tired old hacks for statewide office and for Congress in the big states. But in 1948 they had many strong candidates, who ran far ahead of Truman and may in fact have brought just enough Democratic voters to the polls to enable him to win: Frank Lausche in Ohio, G. Mennen Williams in Michigan, Adlai Stevenson and Paul Douglas in Illinois, Hubert Humphrey in Minnesota, Robert Kerr in Oklahoma, and (though Truman carried the state easily) Lyndon Johnson in Texas. The political class of 1948 proved as talented and durable as the veteran-dominated class of 1946; it also included Republican Congressman Gerald Ford of Grand Rapids, Michigan, who as Arthur Vandenberg's protégé beat an incumbent isolationist in the primary in this Republican district, and Democratic Congressman Peter Rodino, who replaced Fred Hartley in Newark, New Jersey.

II

If in retrospect Truman's victory still seems something of an upset, an event that requires explaining, no explanation seems necessary for the New Deal strategy—internationalist abroad, redistributionist at home—to which he adhered while under attack from all sides in the first half of 1948. Yet it was not the only course Truman could have taken. He could easily have been an old-fashioned Jeffersonian Democrat, dedicated (as he was) to free trade and an internationalist foreign policy, skeptical of more government involvement in the economy, hostile to labor unions and other nationalizing influences, respectful of local institutions like racial segregation and the separate southern economy. Many of Truman's personal impulses moved him in that direction; many of his natural political allies took that course; many of the men who promoted him for vice president expected him to be more likely than Alben Barkley or James Byrnes to take a Jeffersonian tack. Barkley and Byrnes were, after all, bigger men in the Senate and more faithful lieutenants of the Roosevelt administration; Truman was smaller and less closely allied. Truman could have signed Taft-Hartley in the same spirit he called out soldiers to break John L. Lewis's strikes. He could have refrained from advancing proposals for progressive taxes, additional Social Security, and national health insurance, as Barkley, Roosevelt's opponent on taxes in 1944, might well have. He could have ignored or opposed demands for more civil rights for blacks, as Byrnes, later an opponent of school integration as governor of South Carolina, would have.

But Truman decided to take essentially the New Deal course, for reasons not altogether clear—which is to say that they probably represented some combination of personal conviction and political strategy. His course in turn had great consequences for the Democratic party and for American politics. It spelled an end to the chance of a Jeffersonian Democrat emerging as head of the party. Adlai Stevenson and John Kennedy, naturally cautious men, did not wholeheartedly embrace but most certainly did not dare to oppose openly the bulk of the 1944–48 liberal Democratic presidential platform. Lyndon Johnson, who probably favored it personally all along, was freed by his assumption of presidential office from any political obligation to oppose it. Hubert Humphrey, George McGovern (who as a graduate student supported Wallace for months in 1948 before finally voting for Truman), and Walter Mondale (who was a congressional district campaign manager for Humphrey in 1948, though he was not yet old enough to vote) were all believers in this liberal agenda. Jimmy Carter felt obliged to endorse almost all of it, although some of his campaign rhetoric suggested he did not entirely believe it. But by the late 1970s the Jeffersonian option had long since been foreclosed for a Democrat, by the obvious success and rightness of national civil rights laws and by the party's commitment to national policies of economic redistribution and welfare state protection. That commitment was foreshadowed by Franklin Roosevelt's policies in the late 1930s; it was enunciated in something very close to its permanent form, and it created its own political constituency, in Roosevelt's campaign of 1944; but it was not engrafted deep in the soul of the Democratic party, and identified more with that party than with the Republicans of Thomas E. Dewey, until it was adopted, embraced, and taken to political victory by Harry Truman in 1948.

III

For a moment the Democrats decided with delight—and their opponents decided with a sickening feeling—that America was now a majority Democratic country. A young Democrat like Richard Bolling, a liberal who had been newly elected to the House from Kansas City after a series of political accidents even though he was a member of neither the Goat nor the Rabbit faction, believed that 1948 was the norm and that the Democrats could go on winning elections by wide margins for years.[19] Margaret Truman recalled that her father's happiest months in office, when all political success seemed before him, were from November 1948 until the invasion of Korea in June 1950; Democrats from Truman to Bolling looked forward to "smashing Democratic victory in the fall elections" of 1950.[20]

Truman forwarded to Congress his program: a civil rights bill, repeal of Taft-Hartley, the Wagner-Taft-Ellender housing bill, national health insurance, increases in Social Security, a higher minimum wage, federal aid to education. Civil rights was stymied by southern senators who managed to get enough votes from Republicans to preserve their right to filibuster procedural motions, even when two-thirds of the senators present were willing to vote for cloture of debate. Both houses still contained enough of those who had voted to override Truman's veto of Taft-Hartley to constitute majorities, and labor failed to persuade legislators that many changes in the law were needed. So Taft-Hartley was left unchanged, and Senator Robert Wagner, after two years of health so ill he had remained in New York and never appeared in the Senate after June 1947, finally resigned and let Governor Dewey fill his seat—with John Foster Dulles.[21] National health insurance was rejected in the House Ways and Means Committee. Although the committee did vote minimal increases in Social Security benefits, the measure got to the floor of the House only after Speaker Sam Rayburn threatened to invoke the new "twenty-one-day rule," designed to outflank the conservative-dominated Rules Committee, which ordinarily controlled the flow of legislation to the floor. The House approved the increases, but the Senate declined to act. The Brannan Plan, named for Truman's secretary of agriculture and intended to bolster farm incomes rather than farm product prices, got nowhere.

The battle over the housing bill followed a similar course. In the House Banking and Currency Committee, real estate lobbyists got most of its public housing features removed, leaving an enhanced FHA which helped private housing and an urban renewal program which ended up clearing many slums but took years to build new housing, most of it intended for upper-income tenants.[22] Even this measure was fiercely opposed, not only because it would cost money but because it would allow the federal government to intrude into local matters. On the floor of the House, as Robert Donovan describes it, "Representative Adolf Sabath, Democrat, of Illinois, 83 years old, began the debate by denouncing the 'unholy alliance and coalition' of Republicans and southern Democrats that had blocked public housing legislation in the past. Representative Eugene E. Cox, Democrat, of Georgia, 69 years old, called Sabath a liar and punched him in the mouth. Sabath's glasses fell off, and he swung blindly at Cox until the two men were pulled apart."[23] Cox, first elected to the House in 1924, was a towering bully from south Georgia who had been the leading southern conservative on the Rules Committee since 1938; a crony of Rayburn who sometimes rescued bills from Rules at the speaker's behest, he had a hot temper which often got him into fights.[24] Sabath was elderly but no innocent, a Czech-born politico who had been elected to the House since 1906 from a district in Chicago's river wards, where the vote was manipulated by ward leaders with mob connections: chairman of Rules since 1940, Sabath once faked a collapse and heart attack when Cox threatened to strip away some of his powers.[25] Two such different constituencies as the worn-out cotton lands of south Georgia and the mostly abandoned slum streets of Chicago's river wards could hardly be imagined; little wonder that their representatives, members of the same party who were yoked together by seniority on the Rules Committee, could agree on almost nothing.

The fight over federal aid to education showed the cultural divisions of the Democrats even more vividly. In May 1949 the Senate passed a bill sponsored by Robert Taft which provided federal aid for schools without either authorizing or prohibiting states to aid private as well as public schools. The Taft bill was fiercely opposed by Congressman Graham Barden, a former teacher from New Bern, North Carolina, who feared federal control and hated the idea of aiding Catholic schools. Barden came forward with a bill, embraced quickly by the National Education Association and by Protestants and Other Americans for Separation of Church and State, which gave church schools nothing at all. In June 1949, New York's Francis Cardinal Spellman, never hesitant to demand that the legislature in Albany pass into law church teachings on issues like divorce, called Barden's bill "a craven crusade of religious prejudice against Catholic children." John Lesinski, chairman of the House Education and Labor Committee and congressman from one of the nation's most populous districts, including the industrial suburbs that had grown up around the Ford Rouge complex and other auto and steel plants on the southwest edge of Detroit, called the Barden bill "anti-Catholic and anti-Negro" and refused to give it a hearing in the committee. To these sentiments Eleanor Roosevelt replied in her newspaper column, "Those of us who believe in the right of any human being to belong to whatever church he sees fit, and to worship God in his own way, cannot be accused of prejudice when we do not want to see public education connected with religious control of the schools, which are paid for with taxpayers' money." Private schools, she said, should receive "no tax funds of any kind." In response, Spellman said that "[your] record of anti-Catholicism stands for all to see—a record which you yourself wrote on the pages of history which cannot be recalled—documents of discrimination unworthy of an American mother."[26] The issue obviously touched a nerve. Americans were vaguely disposed to favor federal aid for education at a time when school enrollments were rising rapidly, but they did not think much about the details—unless as Catholics, or as those who feared that Catholic doctrines prevented Catholics from being fully loyal, they thought that the issue raised the question of who is fully an American, whose country it is. In the end, federal aid to education was not enacted until 1965, when Lyndon Johnson's dominance over an overwhelmingly Democratic Congress enabled him to jam it through—and when school enrollments were about to start to fall.

IV

One reason that the Democrats' liberal programs failed was that the political balance in Congress was not what was supposed by the incredibly naive new liberals there. In contrast to old political pros like Wagner, Burton Wheeler, and Robert LaFollette, Jr. (defeated in his 1946 Republican primary by Joseph Mc-Carthy), newly elected liberals like Hubert Humphrey and Paul Douglas had little legislative experience[27] and were not allies of deeply rooted local political machines. Assuming that other Democrats could be dragooned into automatically supporting the programs of Franklin Roosevelt and Harry Truman (and ignoring Roosevelt's and Truman's own mottled record of support for the 1944 and 1948 Democratic platforms), they alienated their colleagues and defeated their own purposes. They also made these mistakes through naive attacks on the way business was done on Capitol Hill. In one of his first initiatives, for example, Humphrey moved to cut the budget of the Committee to Reduce Nonessential Federal Expenditures. Humphrey was correct in assuming that the committee did little and was a non-essential federal expenditure itself; but he failed to realize that it was a pet project of Harry Byrd, a senior, widely respected, and by many colleagues well liked senator, who naturally regarded Humphrey's move as an attempt to humiliate him. In order to take a cheap shot, Humphrey thus for some time squandered any chance he had to advance substantive proposals which could have changed millions of Americans' lives. In fact, the episode reduced his effectiveness in the Senate for years.[28]

The balance in Congress was much more accurately appraised by another but much more experienced new senator, a former congressman and congressional staffer who had also been an avid follower of Franklin Roosevelt—Lyndon Johnson of Texas. Johnson cultivated Richard Russell, an austere bachelor whose mastery of Senate rules and intellectual integrity made him the natural leader of the southern Democrats. Johnson understood what Humphrey and the inexperienced liberals entirely missed: that only a handful out of all the Democratic members of Congress were personally committed to the liberal platform. Few of the southerners believed in or supported it, and even fewer would after the primary defeats of Senators Claude Pepper and Frank Graham in 1950. Democrats from the Civil War borderlands, noticing that in the 1940s their party was no stronger back home than it had been in the 1920s, were not convinced that liberal policies were the road to victory and hung back from completely endorsing them even in an administration headed by Truman of Missouri and Barkley of Kentucky. Big-city Democrats were mostly the cynical or plodding products of political machines or the loyal sons of ethnic groups who were more interested in being accepted culturally as part of the American community than they were in sharing in some form of economic redistribution. The aggressive new CIO unions had few members of Congress they could call their own. Their influence in big-state elections was considerable, but not always decisive. In House races, districting worked strongly against them. The industrial areas where their members predominated tended to be underrepresented; the tiny central-city districts which were reliably Democratic were now underpopulated and responsive to machine leaders and in some cases leaders of organized crime, not to the CIO-PAC; the outer residential neighborhoods in big metropolitan areas, where their members were moving in large numbers, were the most underrepresented part of America, where many districts leaned Republican, where many non-union voters were hostile to the unions, and where any Democrat had difficulty accumulating the seniority needed for power in the House.

Districting laws also effectively prevented the Democrats from ever winning control of the legislatures in states like New York, Pennsylvania, Ohio, Michigan, and Illinois—with the result that admirers of the New Deal became quite uninterested in the old Brandeis and LaFollette tradition of using the states as laboratories of reform. This situation might have changed if the redistricting cases which reached the Supreme Court in 1947 had gone the other way. But the court, led by Justice Felix Frankfurter, declined to enter what Frankfurter called a "political thicket."[29] Frankfurter feared that the court would be attacked politically if it attempted to change the balance of power in legislatures by requiring proportionate representation—a fear that may well have grown out of this Jewish immigrant's awareness that in the largest and most visible of American states, New York, any reform would take power away from upstate Protestants and give it to Jews and Catholics from New York City. Frankfurter's argument that redistricting was beyond the capacity of the court was plainly wrongheaded, as was proved by the effectiveness of the court's one-person-one-vote decisions of 1964; politicians might resent redistricting decisions but short of passing a constitutional amendment they could not obstruct them, since a court can declare invalid all acts of a legislature it rules improperly constituted. Frankfurter's course allowed the parts of the United States which had been losing population for fifty years to retain a disproportionate share of political power and created a politics distorted by underrepresentation of the most vital and politically creative segments of the population. The practical result was that Congress and the major state legislatures would not see large, legislatively competent liberal blocs until after the middle 1960s.

This result left most votes in Congress in the hands of representatives who wanted to maintain local control and who feared the possible national regimentation and enforced uniformity which would result from policies like national health insurance, federal aid to education, and a massive federal public housing program. Northern Republicans and southern Democrats, plus quite a few border-state and even big-city machine Democrats, felt that medical care, education, and housing were matters better left to local, usually conservative-minded doctors, school administrators, and real estate developers than to Washington-based, intellectual-minded New Deal bureaucrats. In the big states, thanks to districting, legislative power was in the hands of men who represented the small-town power blocs which had managed public affairs more or less uninterruptedly since the Civil War, and who wanted nothing to do with the New Deal or the new nationalizing liberal programs.

V

For the Democrats in 1949 and for years afterwards, the center did not hold. Harry Truman was, in Samuel Lubell's words, "the man who bought time," the border-state politico who stood at the center of the party and could reconcile its warring wings. But Truman was unable to get his fellow Democrats to act together on Taft-Hartley, aid to education, housing, or civil rights. The most politically talented border-staters were either figures elevated above the battle, like Vice President Barkley and Chief Justice Vinson; newcomers to the seats of power, like Lyndon Johnson of Texas and Robert Kerr of Oklahoma; or temperamental outsiders, like Estes Kefauver of Tennessee and William Fulbright of Arkansas, both of whom spent much of the second Truman term conducting investigations that were embarrassing to the administration. In 1944 and 1948 the Democratic party had set out what came to be known as a liberal platform, and in 1948 it had come as close as it would for another decade to electing a liberal Democratic Congress. So even before the morale of the Truman administration was sapped by the fall of China, the Hiss case, and the Korean war, the domestic program of the Democrats was effectively stalled. It remained a part of the background of American politics in the 1950s, a platform which Democratic candidates could refer to when they liked and ignore when ignoring it suited their purposes, a platform which was not enthusiastically embraced by the party's next two nominees, the patrician Adlai Stevenson and John Kennedy, and was finally put into effect only under the next border-state Democratic president, Lyndon Johnson.

Cultural splits within the party—between North and South, states' righters and civil rights advocates, Catholics and Protestants, defenders of local power bases and enthusiasts for centralized government—prevented almost any of this liberal economic platform from becoming law or, for the moment, from affecting American life. The demographic base of Americans who identified with economic liberalism was not large enough (and would not have been even with one-person-one-vote districting) to yield national majorities. The cultural divisions which had been the main dividing lines of American politics before 1930 were beginning by 1949 to split apart the New Deal Democratic party which had supposedly been united on economic issues, just as foreign policy issues would split those Democrats after 1950. The politics of economic distribution, whose difficult issues were settled in 1947 and by the continuing prosperity which began just about then, was still the central focus of American politics. But the Democrats' economic coalition, capable of forming a majority every four years in presidential elections, was unavoidably being split in the halls of Congress in the years in between.

24

→》》 《《←

Thunder

The record of the Truman administration in foreign policy was one of stupendous achievement—and of avoidable disaster. The policies of Truman and his second-term secretary of state, Dean Acheson, was a splendid success in Europe and a dismaying failure in Asia. Both success and failure were foreshadowed by developments during the first term. As Truman was being inaugurated in January 1949, the Marshall Plan was starting to revive the economies of western Europe, the Berlin airlift was demonstrating the resolve of the United States to stop the expansion of Soviet power, the Chinese Nationalists were reeling in their civil war against the Communists, and the separate governments of South and North Korea which had been established in August and September 1948 were glaring at each other across their 38th parallel boundary. In April 1949 the United States and eleven other nations signed the North Atlantic Treaty, laying the foundation for NATO. In May the Soviet Union ended its blockade of Berlin, and nine days later the Federal Republic of Germany was established in what had been the American, British, and French zones of occupation. The last 500 American troops in Korea were removed in June. In July the North Atlantic Treaty was approved 82–13 in the Senate. In August the State Department issued its White Paper on China, anticipating the Communist victory and blaming the corruption and incompetence of the Nationalists. The Nationalist flight to Taiwan (or Formosa, as it was then usually called) began in October. Meanwhile, Truman had announced in September that the Russians had set off an "atomic explosion" the month before. The United States had stopped the advance of Communism in Europe. But it had been unable to prevent the loss of the world's most populous country to Communism in Asia. And it no longer had a monopoly in atomic weapons.

The Truman Doctrine asserted that the United States was interested in the fight for freedom, and by implication the fight against Communism, anywhere in the world. Yet in these years just after World War II the United States was not backing up its foreign policy with a large military. Outlays for national defense, which had been $6 billion in the deadlock year of 1941 and reached $81 billion in 1945, fell sharply to $44 billion in 1946 and $13 billion in 1947, a level where they remained in 1948, 1949, and 1950.[1] Outlays for international spending and finance—mostly foreign aid—climbed from $3 billion annually during the war

229

years to $4.6 billion in 1947 and 1948 and $6 billion in 1949, nearly half what the government was spending for defense. With demobilization, the American military establishment shrank dramatically. There were 12 million Americans in the military in mid-1945, 3 million in 1946, and around 1.5 million in 1947 through 1950.[2] This was a smaller military than the 1.8 million of mid-1941, though of course far larger than any peacetime military the United States had seen before (there were 334,000 Americans in uniform in 1939). It seemed to be a military force large enough to deter the Soviet Union from forcible action against Americans or their allies in Berlin, West Germany, Greece, or Italy—at least so long as the United States was the only nation with the atomic bomb. But the atomic weapons of the years just after Hiroshima probably did not seem very threatening to Mao Zedong's Communists in China, with its hundreds of millions of people dispersed across a continent-sized countryside; and the U.S. armed forces would obviously not go very far toward winning a war on the land mass of Asia.

These limits on American military power in China were apparent to many Americans by August 1949, when the White Paper was issued. Since 1947, Asia First politicians of both parties had been urging much more extensive military aid to the Nationalists, but that was resisted by the Truman administration, which argued that most Nationalist arms were surrendered into the hands of the Communists. By August 1949, Gallup found that Americans by a 48%–23% margin expected that China would fall to the Communists, that they did not have a favorable impression of Chiang Kai-shek (35%–21% unfavorable), and that more than 70% could volunteer nothing the United States could do to save China for the Nationalists. Yet the White Paper evoked disapproval from 53% and approval from only 23%.[3] This disapproval is an interesting example of the public's refusal to follow syllogisms through to their logical conclusions. Americans understood why it was impossible to keep Chiang Kai-shek in power; and far from favoring American military intervention in China, they were so strongly against it that not even the most strident of Asia Firsters argued for it. But Americans were nonetheless unhappy with the Communist triumph in China and ready to blame the politicians in power for it. Voters had rewarded Roosevelt and Truman when they pursued foreign policies which were successful. Now voters were prepared to penalize Truman for a policy which plainly was proving unsuccessful. Initially, Americans opposed both recognition of Red China and major military aid to the Nationalists on Formosa, following the president's course in both respects. But Truman's job approval rating declined from a robust 57% in June 1949 and 51% in September 1949 to only 45% in January 1950 and only 37% in May 1950.[4] The steady decline occurred even as the economy rebounded smartly from what turned out to be a minor pause in the fall of 1948 and even though there was no wave of strikes as in 1946.

Truman was also hurt by controversy about military spending—the first intrusion into American politics of issues raised by what President Eisenhower would call "the military-industrial complex." In the years after World War II the military services were fighting for shares of the declining Pentagon budget. The Air Force, convinced despite the contrary evidence of the Strategic Bombing Survey that bomber planes had won World War II, wanted to build a new bomber, the B-36, whose feasibility was attacked by the Navy. For its part, the Navy wanted to build a huge new aircraft carrier called the *United States.* The keel of this vessel was laid in the huge Navy shipyard in Norfolk, Virginia, just as Defense Secretary James Forrestal was leaving office, out of favor for contributing generously to Dewey but not to Truman in 1948 and afflicted with the mental instability which caused him to take his life weeks later. In April 1949 the new defense secretary, Louis Johnson, a Washington lawyer with roots in West Virginia and ambitious for higher office, whose chief recommendation was his service as Truman's chief fund-raiser in 1948, canceled the building of the *United States* in the first of several cost-cutting measures.[5] In September a Navy captain, John Crommelin, complained publicly that the Navy's aircraft program was being "nibbled to death" and its fighting spirit was "going to pot." In October he leaked to the press letters from three top Navy admirals who agreed with him. Congressional hearings followed, in which the admirals stated their case.[6] In the short run, the admirals' revolt lowered opinion of the stewardship of the Truman administration. In the long run, it provided American politicians with an example of the discord and political tumult which could result from efforts to hold down the defense budget. Politically, the better strategy would be to give each branch of the military what it wanted, to avoid the spectacle of public fights and disorderly conduct of the nation's most important public business.[7]

II

"I have here in my hand a list of 205 [State Department employees] who were known to the Secretary of State as being members of the Communist party and who nevertheless are still working and shaping the policy of the State Department." So Senator Joseph R. McCarthy is supposed to have said in January, 1950—there is no transcript or recording, and he lost or mislaid his own notes—to the Ohio County Women's Republican Club in Wheeling, West Virginia, the factory management town on the hilly banks of the Ohio River.[8] McCarthy was an obscure forty-one-year-old[9] senator, swarthy and overweight, an unprepossessing speaker of no significant public achievements whose previous moment in the national spotlight had come as a spokesman for Harold Stassen in his unsuccessful 1948 campaign for the presidency.[10] The next day in Salt Lake City he claimed to have a list of 57 Communists still in the State Department; later in the month he claimed to have a list of 81; later in the year he claimed 10, 116, 121, and 106 names. In fact he had none. To the extent his charges were based on anything at all, they were based on reports of State Department investigations of employees suspected of various forms of misconduct, including Communism, reports submitted to the House Appropriations Committee in 1946 and 1948. Some of McCarthy's numbers were derived simply by subtracting from the number of cases investigated the number of investigated employees who had been fired by the date the report was compiled—two or four years before his Wheeling speech. Yet in February 1950, McCarthy's charges ignited a firestorm of interest around the nation.

The reason lay in the times. Congressional investigators had been busy trying to ferret out Communists in government and other institutions for years, with varying success. Although liberals had developed the congressional investigating committee as a political weapon in the 1930s, conservatives had soon seized on it, starting with Martin Dies's House Un-American Activities Committee in 1939. Dies had used the committee to hector left-leaning administration officials Harry Hopkins, Harold Ickes, and Frances Perkins, much to Franklin Roosevelt's irritation. After Dies was elbowed out of running for reelection in 1944 by threats of labor opposition, his committee came close to being abolished by the House in 1945, when the United States was still an ally of the Soviet Union and Roosevelt and the Democrats had won the 1944 election despite Republican charges that they were supported by the Communists.

But as the Cold War began, it was obvious to many, not just to right-wing nuts, that a domestic Communist threat did exist. And it was a threat: Communists were not just members of a political party, not just social reformers who favored a program a little to the left of Norman Thomas's Socialists. They were adherents, usually in secret, of a party which slavishly followed the orders of Stalin's Soviet Union, which followed every twist and turn of the Soviet line. They were men and women whose allegiance—however unexceptionable (or, as in the case of civil rights, enlightened and farsighted) their views on some of the American issues of the day—was finally to a totalitarian foreign power and not to the democratic United States. Perhaps only 100,000 Americans were Communists; no one could be sure of the number at the time. But it was apparent to many that Communists were seeking and in some cases had won positions of influence in government and labor unions; and a newly expanded government asserting control over all aspects of citizens' lives and a rapidly expanding labor movement controlling workplaces and capable of determining the outcomes of elections could provide plenty of opportunity for conspirators who considered themselves under no obligation to tell the truth and obey ordinary laws and were bent on seizing power any way they could. There were such men and women in America in 1945. Not only were important posts in the CIO held by Communists; so were important posts in government. Allen Weinstein has established as conclusively as it can be that Alger Hiss, a high official in the State Department, was a Communist agent.[11] Harry Dexter White, one of Henry Morgenthau's and Fred Vinson's top appointees in the Treasury, may very well have been a Communist. Interestingly, both men's main work in government was the building of institutions which in the years after 1945 served the highest American interests. Hiss was one of the architects of the United Nations Charter (a famous photograph shows him shaking hands with Truman in April 1945 at the first UN meeting in San Francisco), and White was the American creator of the International Monetary Fund, of which Truman named him as executive director in 1946, and the World Bank.

Most Communists evidently had been eliminated from important government and union positions long before McCarthy's charges. Truman's loyalty program, announced in March 1947, resulted in about 1,200 dismissals and 6,000 resignations from the government during his administration.[12] Probably most, perhaps all, of the names on the lists McCarthy was evidently referring to were out of the government before he spoke in Wheeling. As for the labor unions, anti-Communist unionists won a series of hard-fought elections in the CIO in the years just after the war and cleaned the Communists out immediately afterwards. The most important victory was the election of Walter Reuther as president of the United Auto Workers in 1947, which led to the ouster, among others, of UAW general counsel George Crockett, a close follower of the Soviet line who was eventually elected in the 1980s as a congressman from inner-city Detroit. The CIO even went to the trouble of setting up a separate electrical workers' union, to be headed by CIO central official James Carey, to replace the Communist-dominated UE, which was expelled from the CIO. The Taft-Hartley Act's ban on Communists in union office made some difference also. But the chief fight was internal, within the CIO, and the sure sign of its success was the hearty endorsement by the CIO and all of its major unions of Truman over Henry Wallace in 1948. Communists in the movie industry—at a time when weekly movie attendance was still well-nigh universal—were investigated with great publicity, notably in October 1947, when the House Un-American Activities Committee summoned the screenwriters who became known as the Hollywood Ten and who were ultimately convicted of contempt of Congress, jailed, and blacklisted by the movie industry.

The charges that White and Hiss were Communists, which were made in August 1948 HUAC hearings by Whittaker Chambers, a former Communist turned *Time* magazine writer, came after the issue of what should be done about Communists in government had been rendered moot. Yet they excited great interest nonetheless, especially when Truman unwisely—in a characteristic adoption of a reporter's phrase—dismissed the Hiss investigation as a "red herring." Hiss dramatically confronted Chambers in the committee room and admitted that Chambers may have known him under another name, but he resolutely denied—and denied for more than forty years afterwards—that he had ever been a Communist. (White, by then retired from the International Monetary Fund, also appeared before the committee and died of a heart attack days afterward.) Hiss sued Chambers for slander but then was himself indicted for perjury after Chambers found documents corroborating his charges (the "pumpkin papers") on his Westminster, Maryland, farm. His first trial ended in July 1949 in a hung jury; he was convicted on retrial in January 1950 and sentenced to five years in prison.

Immediately reporters asked Acheson for his reaction. Acheson had barely known Hiss when they were in the State Department together; but he had employed Hiss's brother Donald as his chief assistant, and in 1947 and 1948 Donald Hiss and Acheson had been partners in Washinton's premier law firm. (Acheson's connection with Donald Hiss was evidently what led Adolf Berle, a disappointed

Roosevelt administration official, to charge that Acheson and Alger Hiss were close.) Acheson was the son of an Episcopal bishop, the product of Groton, Yale, and Harvard Law, the picture of Anglophile elegance with his mustache and tailored suits, with his steadfast Europe First foreign policy. He was just the kind of well-born, well-connected gentleman whom awkward, ungraceful, near-fanatic Asia Firsters hated. Alger Hiss, from a shabby-genteel family in Baltimore, a graduate of Johns Hopkins and Harvard Law, clerk to Justice Holmes and a well-connected New Dealer, handsome and socially graceful, made a vivid contrast with the rumpled, ungraceful, intense Whittaker Chambers—and with Richard Nixon, an awkward young man whose father had been a failed storekeeper in small-town California, who had had to pass up a scholarship to Harvard, and who had never been able to get a job with a big Washington law firm or even with the FBI. Acheson felt a strong loyalty to Donald Hiss and while in private practice had counseled and advised Alger Hiss.[13] After Alger was convicted, Acheson still declined to "discuss the legal aspects of the case" and, consistent with his personal code of honor, went on to tell reporters, "Whatever the outcome of any appeal which Mr. Hiss or his lawyers may take in this case I do not intend to turn my back on Alger Hiss. I think every person who has known Alger Hiss or has served with him at any time has upon his conscience the very serious task of deciding what his attitude is and what his conduct should be. That must be done by each person in light of his own standards and his own principles. For me, there is very little doubt about those standards or those principles. I think they were stated for us a very long time ago. They were stated on the Mount of Olives and if you are interested in seeing them you will find them in the 25th Chapter of the Gospel according to St. Matthew beginning with verse 34."[14] Gallant, courageous words— and disastrous for every political cause Acheson held dear. Acheson offered his resignation, but Truman, according to Acheson, "said that one who had gone to the funeral of a friendless old man just out of the penitentiary [Tom Pendergast] had no trouble in knowing what I meant and in approving it." But for many Americans, not all of them partisan Republicans, the issue was not personal loyalty or charity. The secretary of state, amazingly, was offering forgiveness to a man convicted of acting as a Communist agent while holding high office in the State Department.[15] Roosevelt, for whom Acheson had no warm feelings, would have found a way to drop anyone who made such a political mistake; Truman, loyal to a fault and recognizing Acheson's sterling good qualities, kept him on, for which Acheson was forever grateful.

In this climate McCarthy's charges found a receptive audience among the public. A great nation had just been lost to Communism. A high State Department official (never mind that he had left the department four years earlier, in 1946) had been convicted of being a Communist and had been forgiven by the secretary of state (never mind that there were few more durable or effective anti-Communists in American history). These events fitted in, somewhat, with the Asia Firsters' theme that Roosevelt had sold out eastern Europe in the Yalta Conference, with the connivance of men like Alger Hiss. Never mind that they had no way of suggesting how eastern Europe could have been saved when Stalin's armies already occupied it and the United States was rapidly demobilizing its armies, or how Hiss could have been such an evil genius when in fact he played no role at Yalta and only a minor one on other great issues. For many Americans, bad results demanded an evil cause. McCarthy, in Acheson's later summary, "stumbled upon the combination of themes that made him a welcome tool for the conservative Taft-led Republicans."[16] In 1945, Acheson went on, a former secretary of war and Republican senator from New Mexico, General Patrick Hurley, "charged that conspiracy in the State Department had frustrated his efforts in China. Two years after that Congressman Walter Judd of Minnesota had voiced the same suspicions. McCarthy now took this line. China had been lost through the machinations of Soviet sympathizers and agents in the State Department. In this category he placed John Carter Vincent, John [Stewart] Service, Philip C. Jessup, and Dr. Owen Lattimore of The Johns Hopkins University. The last named, he charged, was 'the architect of our Far Eastern policy,' though Dr. Lattimore had never been connected with the Department."[17]

McCarthy was a pathological liar, an uninformed and obscure politician with certain demogogic gifts who latched onto his anti-Communist crusade without much believing in it himself. He did positive harm: to other politicians who were quite innocent of his charges; to thousands of government employees and professors who by any reasonable judgment should not have lost their jobs as they did; to the formation of American foreign policy, which he helped to bias in unrealistic directions; to the American political process, which he debased and degraded. He did no discernible good, except that from the point of view of a Republican partisan he may have marginally improved the party's performance in the 1950 and 1952 elections. McCarthy himself ran behind rather than ahead of the Republican party line in Wisconsin, and the senators he supposedly helped to defeat would surely have lost even if he had done nothing.[18] McCarthyism became a synonym for a style of Communist-hunting which he did not start and never pursued in any serious way, an enterprise whose only valid purpose had already been achieved long before he held up his sheet of paper before the Republicans in Wheeling. His influence reverberated, however, because he had blundered on an issue which was much larger than himself. America, it was thought, had lost a huge nation to Communism, and McCarthy, it seemed for a few moments to many, had the explanation: Communists in the State Department.

"Who lost China?" was a question that echoed through American politics for the next twenty years. The Asia Firsters did have the semblance of a serious argument. "Old China hands" like Vincent and Service, as well as General Joseph Stilwell, who commanded American forces in China in World War II, had made reports to their superiors casting doubt on the ability of Chiang Kai-shek's Nationalists to prevail militarily against the Japanese before August 1945 and the Communists afterwards; and they sometimes seemed to regard Mao Zedong's Communists as benign agrarian reformers with whom the United States could do business. Their assessment of the Nationalists seems shrewd and justified by events; the China Lobby argued, unconvincingly to those who considered the facts but effectively to some who had emotional ties to an American-allied China, that it was a self-fulfilling prophecy, since the Truman administration, acting on it, sent little aid to China. The old China hands' assessment of the Communists seems more dubious. Like many later American liberals looking at underdeveloped countries, the old China hands were repelled by the corruption of existing regimes allied with and seeking help from the United States, and they underestimated the brutality and totalitarian tendencies of the Communists and their allies. The Communist regime subjected China to at least twenty-five more years of internal turmoil, to the Great Leap Forward and the Cultural Revolution, which resulted in the deaths of millions; Mao turned out to be a tyrant comparable in his own country to Hitler and Stalin in theirs. By any standard of human rights, a Nationalist regime, could it have been sustained, would have been far preferable; and sometimes the old China hands seemed to cross the line between anticipating and hailing the Communist victory.

But in the long run, they proved right in their perception that the United States could live with a Communist China, which proved to be less expansionist than almost anyone expected in January 1950. It sent troops to Korea only after U.S. troops marched to its borders. It split with the Soviet Union by the early 1960s. It never made moves to attack Taiwan or even defenseless Hong Kong. It never gave much support to Communists in Vietnam and even ended up, after the American withdrawal, attacking that country—though without much effect.

But from October 1949 until Richard Nixon announced his opening to China in July 1971, it was considered unthinkable for an American politician to favor even diplomatic recognition of what 1970s politicans quickly came to call the People's Republic of China. It was considered obligatory through most of the 1950s to profess belief in what no serious strategist believed, Chiang Kai-shek's ability to reconquer the mainland. It was considered necessary, despite Douglas MacArthur's admonition against fighting land wars in Asia, to be willing to send not just American aid but American troops to any Asian country under Communist attack. The United States fought in Korea and in Vietnam in part because so many Americans were furious that it had not fought in China—even though almost no Americans at the time wanted to or would have supported such a war. Democratic politicians in particular learned the lesson, notably Dean Rusk, who was assistant secretary of state for Asian affairs when the North Koreans invaded South Korea and secretary of state when the United States started sending large numbers of troops to Vietnam.

III

At 4 o'clock in the morning of June 24, 1950, troops of Communist North Korea crossed the 38th parallel boundary into South Korea. Of all the regimes established in the lands occupied by the losers in World War II, none turned out to be as fanatic, as isolated, or as aggressive as the North Korea of Kim Il Sung. Why he attacked the South in June 1950 will probably never be known—a greater mystery than the motives of the leaders of the Peloponnesian War. At the time it was widely assumed that Stalin approved or even instigated the attack. Yet Stalin was cautious about sending Communist troops over boundary lines at every other time in his long tenure as leader of the Soviet Union; he had not encouraged Mao Zedong's advance in China, and South Korea–entirely agricultural, impoverished, near nothing but Japan, to which the Soviets already had a closer approach in the Kurile Islands—was one of the world's less tempting targets. Stalin was on a peace offensive at the time, was boycotting the United Nations to protest its refusal to admit Communist China, was otherwise unprepared for a North Korean offensive. Of course, it is possible that he ordered the attack anyway, but it seems more likely that the impulsive Kim Il Sung was the force behind it.

To this inexplicable and unexpected attack the Truman administration responded with steely determination—and with a series of mistakes which tarred its name and led to the defeat of the Democratic party. The first mistake had been made six months before, in January 1950, when Acheson described the American "defensive perimeter" in Asia as running from the Aleutians to Japan, the Ryukus, and the Philippines; he pointedly excluded Taiwan, lately occupied by the Chinese Nationalists, and South Korea and added that "it must be clear that no person can guarantee those areas against military attack." Critics complained then only about the exclusion of Taiwan. Not until Kim Il Sung's move in June did it occur to them that Acheson's statement may have been an invitation to attack South Korea. In his memoirs Acheson spreads the blame: MacArthur drew the same line in March 1949, the China Lobby in Congress defeated a Korean aid measure in February 1950, politicians acceding to the public demand for demobilization got all but 500 American troops withdrawn from South Korea by 1950, Acheson threatened a response by the United Nations to invasions beyond his perimeter.[19] These are lame defenses. As was made clear in June 1950, the administration would always have responded to an attack. It should have said so.

The second mistake, made on Acheson's initiative and with Truman's typically quick approval over the telephone from Independence, was to call on the United Nations to take action. If the Soviets kept boycotting, the United States had full control over the UN and could use this control to give its own response to the aggression of a Soviet ally (there were no Soviet forces in North Korea, then or later) an international appearance. This strategy would have been frustrated if the Soviets had returned and used their veto in the Security Council, and it made the UN, rather than Congress, the legislative body whose approval Truman sought for the military intervention Acheson and others in the government were preparing from the first day of the invasion. From the years leading up to World War II, Truman and his advisers had drawn the lessons that aggression should be promptly checked and that international organizations should be strengthened and not ignored; and they acted on those lessons immediately and without much question.[20] Truman's course was almost universally approved in the United States. Meanwhile, the American military commitment was immediately broadened. On June

26, Truman approved Acheson's recommendation to send the Seventh Fleet to seal off Taiwan from the mainland of China—a step the administration had steadfastly refused to take for seven months. Steps were also taken to strengthen U.S. bases in the Philippines and to increase U.S. aid to opponents of the Communist insurgents in Indochina.

Unfortunately, Truman's resolute decisions in Washington were followed by the military collapse of the South Korean forces. Truman committed American sea and air forces June 27; Seoul fell June 28. MacArthur recommended sending in U.S. ground troops on June 30 to prevent utter defeat, and the secretary of the Army relayed the request to the president, who approved. Three days before, on June 27, Republican senators had complained about Truman's failure to consult Congress and asked, quite reasonably considering the assurances Truman's treaty-makers had given them, how American forces could be ordered into battle at the call of an international organization but without the affirmative vote of Congress. Truman may have had the better of the legal argument. But his critics, led by Robert Taft, proved correct in a broader sense: a consensus for the war effort could not be sustained without enlisting both parties' support early in the enterprise. That could have been done easily in the last days of June—but was not.

Not until July 19 did Truman ask Congress for another $10 billion, which was not just for Korea but for an increase in American forces elsewhere in the world. This request reflected the administration's steadfast conviction that, in Acheson's words, "the main center of our activity at the present time has got to be in Europe.[21] It also reflected the president's fears that the Soviets, assumed as they must be in worst-case analysis to be the instigators of the attack, would strike elsewhere— Iran, Truman thought, or Berlin or Taiwan. American conventional forces had been reduced to low levels in the postwar demobilization, on the assumption that the American monopoly on atomic weapons would deter the Soviets. But the bomb had not been brandished in the Berlin crisis, and now that the Soviets evidently had atomic weapons, too, it was not brandished in Korea. It was suddenly apparent that American conventional forces had to be increased substantially if American commitments were to be met. In the spring of 1950 Paul Nitze and Acheson had produced and gotten Truman to approve NSC 68, a secret internal document stating that America must arm itself to face military threats from Communism across the globe. After the invasion of Korea, Truman got busy and put it into effect. Outlays for national defenses rose from $13 billion in the fiscal year ending in June 1950 to $22 billion in 1951, $44 billion in 1952, and $50 billion in 1953; with the coming of peace and a new administration bent on saving money, they sank only slightly to a low of $40 billion in 1955 and 1956.[22] Strategically, this expanded budget gave the United States forces to back up most of its commitments; politically, it protected administrations and Congresses against public battles, like the admirals' revolt, for larger shares of scarce funds. Congress followed the lead of the president and set up the large permanent peacetime military establishment, absorbing approximately one-fifth of the American gross national product and employing in uniform and out about 1 in 20 working adults, which the United States had never had before 1950 and has had ever since.

In the meantime the war in Korea was going dreadfully. By August 1, U.S. troops had been withdrawn to a perimeter around Pusan, in the southeast corner of the Korean peninsula. Louis Johnson, the ambitious defense secretary who had followed Truman's cost-cutting defense budgets with enthusiasm, was fired in early September; and George Marshall—widely revered but now under attack from Senator William Jenner, a McCarthy ally, as "a front man for traitors"—was brought back to the Pentagon. New American troops were sent in, and MacArthur led the daring landings on September 15 at Inchon, the port near Seoul. Around this time Truman made another fateful and probably wrong decision: he decided that UN forces should continue north of the 38th parallel but that they must not cross the Yalu River, which formed most of the boundary between Korea and China. There were good arguments for both positions: staying south of the parallel would allow the North Korean army to regroup and attack again, and sending even airplanes across the Yalu risked war with Communist China. But the combined result proved disastrous. By October 26, MacArthur's troops were most of the way up the Korean peninsula, and MacArthur and Truman both expected the fighting to be over by Thanksgiving. Instead, the Chinese Communists started pouring troops in during late October, in numbers vastly and almost fatally underestimated by MacArthur.

IV

Such was the background when Americans went to the polls for the off-year elections in November 1950. The public had supported the initial American commitment, had been elated at the triumph of Inchon, but was now hearing disturbing reports of Chinese troops. Truman's job approval rating, which had fallen after the loss of China, had been 37% in June 1950 and rose only to 46% in July and 43% in August—not stellar marks. By October it was down to 39%, although it may have slipped upward after November 1, six days before the election, when Truman, napping in his bedroom in Blair House, was awakened by shots as Puerto Rican nationalists tried to storm the building and shoot him. (The White House, structurally a ruin, was being rebuilt for almost the whole of his second term.) The efforts of the China Lobby and McCarthy's charges were building in crescendo. McCarthy was called "a fraud and a hoax" by the committee headed by veteran Democratic Senator Millard Tydings, Roosevelt's target in the 1938 purge. But McCarthy continued to make headlines by attacking Owen Lattimore, who had written sympathetically of the Chinese Communists, and Democrats like Tydings, Brien McMahon of Connecticut, and Majority Leader Scott Lucas of Illinois.

Still, the Democratic party was not in great disrepute with the voters. Nationwide, Democrats ran stronger in Senate and House campaigns in 1950 then they had in the last two off-year elections, 1942 and 1946. What was jarring to them was their defeats in big states and prominent races. Tydings was defeated in Maryland after twenty-four years in office, with the help of an utterly fraudulent composite photograph showing him next to Communist Party leader Earl Browder. Scott Lucas was defeated in Illinois by former Congressman Everett Dirksen, an assailant of Truman's Europe First policy and opponent now of the Dewey wing of the Republican party (in part because he had stuck his neck out by opposing his home-state *Chicago Tribune* and supporting Dewey over Taft in 1948). Francis Myers, the Senate Democratic whip, was beaten in Pennsylvania, while Robert Taft, despite an aggressive campaign in heavily unionized Ohio by the CIO-PAC, beat an outclassed Democrat, Auditor "Jumping Joe" Ferguson. Across the country in California, always a strong Roosevelt state, James Roosevelt lost the governor's race by an overwhelming margin to incumbent Earl Warren; and in the race for Democrat Sheridan Downey's Senate seat, Congressman Richard Nixon, the adversary of Alger Hiss, beat Congresswoman Helen Gahagan Douglas, a faithful New Dealer. The only big Democratic wins were their recapture of a Senate seat by Thomas Hennings in Missouri and Herbert Lehman's repeat of his 1949 special election victory in New York—Truman's and Roosevelt's home states.

The voters returned a House with 234 Democrats, fewer than in most of the Roosevelt years and a loss of 29 seats compared with the results of 1948. Democratic losses in the House came mostly in the outer residential areas of big cities and in smaller industrial towns—the parts of America which had grown most rapidly over the last twenty years and where the Democrats had made the biggest electoral gains in the New Deal period. They included no less than 4 districts in outer Chicago; 3 in the industrial ring around Pittsburgh; 2 in greater Buffalo; the Ohio cities of Akron, Canton, and Toledo (the last lost to independent Frazier Reams); and the outer wards and suburbs of Baltimore and St. Louis. These outer rings of metropolitan areas had become the focal point of electoral conflict in American politics and were even more important in presidential elections than in House races, for they were exactly the kind of areas most underrepresented by House districting plans which survived from some antique census or had been drawn with the explicit intent of overrepresenting demographically stagnant or declining rural areas. Those rural areas, once politically volatile, now voted mostly solidly for one party or the other: relatively few Civil War borderlands districts changed hands in 1950, unless one counts the 5 districts in Indiana—always one of the most volatile states in House elections.[23]

Another ominous trend for the Democrats could be seen in primaries in the South, where New Deal candidates lost to opponents who raised the race issue. The most prominent of these losers were Claude Pepper of Florida, who was to be sure no Truman backer (or vice versa)[24] in May and Frank Graham of North Carolina in June (the day of the North Korean invasion). Pepper was associated with all manner of liberal causes; Graham had been a member of Truman's Civil Rights Commission. "Frank Graham favors mingling of the races," read his opponent's poster, distributed five days before the primary runoff;[25] Pepper, opposed by his one-time protégé George Smathers, was allegedly accused of matriculating at college and of having a sister who was a thespian.[26] Liberals had hoped that the 1944 Supreme Court decision outlawing the white primary (which explicitly barred black voters), the growth of labor unions, the popularity of Roosevelt, and moves to abolish the poll tax would help liberals win southern primaries, as they often had before World War II. These hopes were not realized. The national Democrats' support of civil rights in 1948 and Truman's integration of the military solidified southern whites' opposition to integration.[26] The defeats of Graham and Pepper in 1950 sent the message that no politician who showed any sympathy with civil rights could be elected in the South—a message which remained mostly accurate, except for Tennessee, Texas, and some districts at the edge of the region, until 1970.

The Democrats' Senate losses in big states overshadowed their House losses in the outer edges of the cities and the liberal losses in the South. But the latter trends were more ominous for them. The losses they suffered in a time of relative prosperity when the United States seemed on the verge of victory in Korea would be magnified the next time Americans voted, when circumstances were less favorable.

V

Very shortly after the 1950 election, the debacle of the Korean war became clear. On election day Chinese troops suddenly disengaged in Korea, heightening hopes in MacArthur's headquarters and in Washington that the war was won. On November 24, MacArthur launched a new offensive near the Yalu. The next day, some 300,000 previously undetected Chinese troops counterattacked; by November 28 the UN offensive had collapsed and the Americans were in retreat. The United States suddenly found itself at war with an utterly alien foe, led by men of which it knew almost nothing and with whom it was in no communication, backed by virtually unlimited reserves of manpower. On November 30, Truman said in response to questioning that use of the atomic bomb was under consideration and that "the military commander in the field"—MacArthur—"will have charge of the use of weapons, as he always has." But in fact, MacArthur all along had been urging the bombing of the bridges across the Yalu and hot pursuit by American planes of Soviet-made MIGs over Manchuria; Truman forbade both. The decision to go north of the 38th parallel, coupled with the decision not to cross the Yalu, by stimulating the Chinese invasion and denying American forces a chance to respond against China itself, put United Nations forces in peril and raised the possibility of broader and even nuclear war.

Truman's leadership seemed in disarray. British Prime Minister Clement Attlee, worried about a wider war, made a sudden trip to Washington in December. The same day he was meeting with Truman, the president's press secretary, Charles Ross, a friend since they were classmates in Independence High School, suddenly collapsed and died. That night Margaret Truman, a professional singer, gave her first concert in Washington, which received a negative review in the *Washington Post* the next morning. Truman wrote the reviewer, Paul Hume, a letter. "Some day I hope to meet you," it said in part. "When that happens you'll need a new nose, a lot of beefsteak for black eyes, and perhaps a supporter below!" The ensuing publicity contributed to the impression of an unstable, improvising leader. In mid-December, Truman asked for wage and price controls and declared a state of national emergency. But he did not ask Congress for the declaration of war which would have clarified the national purpose.

Instead, what followed in January 1951 was a full-fledged national debate on foreign policy. On one side was Truman, who favored limited war aims in Korea and more Army troops in Europe to deter any further Soviet aggression. He persuaded Dwight Eisenhower to leave the presidency of Columbia University to head the new NATO allied command in Paris. On the other side were Republicans like Henry Luce, whose magazines attacked Truman shrilly for not taking the fight to the Red Chinese, and Robert Taft, who wanted no Army troops sent to Europe, though he did favor using Navy and Air Force units as a deterrent there. This debate represented the fundamental battle between the Europe Firsters and the Asia Firsters, a battle whose origins went back to the basic strategic decisions made immediately after Pearl Harbor. As Samuel Lubell has pointed out, the heartfelt popular support for the Asia First view came primarily from German-Americans and others who felt that the United States had been fighting the wrong enemy on the wrong front in World War II, that instead of fighting Hitler in Europe Americans should have been fighting first Japan and then the Communists in Asia.[27]

Truman's views prevailed in Congress, but his troubles mounted. In January 1951 the Communists drove south in Korea, capturing Seoul and Inchon. In February 1951 a committee headed by William Fulbright, a bookish senator from Arkansas who had been elected to Congress in 1942 at the age of thirty-seven after Governor Homer Adkins had him removed from his post as president of the University of Arkansas, accused high officials of the Reconstruction Finance Corporation of favoritism to Democratic national committee members and their allies. The husband of one White House secretary was revealed to have gotten a fur coat from a favor-seeker—the famous mink coat which joined in Republican lore the deep freeze that General Harry Vaughan, a top Truman aide and crony, had persuaded a government contractor to send Mrs. Truman. The president, ever loyal, defiantly reappointed the implicated RFC officials. Estes Kefauver, a newcomer to the Senate from Tennessee, held hearings on organized crime in New York and showed how crime boss Frank Costello had connections high in Democratic circles. New York Mayor William O'Dwyer, a former policeman and Brooklyn district attorney who had been elected mayor with Democratic machine support in 1945 and 1949, admitted he had appointed men with underworld connections to office and was forced to resign in March 1950—at which point Truman appointed him ambassador to Mexico, where he was safe from subpoena.[28] All of this adversity came on top of the attacks on Vaughan in 1949 for helping the so-called "five percenters" get government contracts for which they extracted a fee of 5% of the amount from their clients. Truman's job rating went down to 25% positive in early 1951 and stayed at about that level, between 23% and 32%, until his last few months in office.

With that unimpressive public support Truman entered his battle against General MacArthur. In March 1951, UN forces succeeded in retaking Inchon and Seoul. But MacArthur and his commander-in-chief had very different ideas of what to do next. MacArthur asked for more troops and wanted to gain total victory—though whether over North Korea or over Communist China too was not clear. He wanted to win or get out. Truman wanted to settle for an armistice line near the 38th parallel: a negotiated peace at the line he had refused to stop at in September 1950. Neither achieved his objective. MacArthur was fired in April 1951 after he issued a statement threatening war against China, which undercut Truman's plans to seek negotiations, and sent a letter to House Republican Leader Joseph Martin calling for the use of Nationalist Chinese troops in Korea, which was against settled administration policy. Truman's strategy was adopted, and UN forces stayed near the 38th parallel while peace negotiations went on. But the Communists refused to settle during the remaining years of the Truman administration.

As Truman's popularity fell, he trailed Eisenhower 64%–27% and the always unpopular Taft 47%–39% in presidential pairings.[29] With news of MacArthur's firing, more than 100,000 angry telegrams flew into Washington, and Gallup found that only 25% of Americans approved and 66% disapproved Truman's action.[30] Yet underlying signs indicated that eventually the decision might be less universally reviled. Educated voters were more likely to approve it than others— the opposite of the usual pattern of approval for a Democratic president. In addition, Americans preferred Eisenhower, who refused to criticize Truman, to MacArthur as a president by a 2–1 margin, and only 36% thought MacArthur would be a good president; by a 47%–24% margin they would rather defend Europe than Asia if pressed to a choice.[31]

Yet for the moment Americans seemed furious. Perhaps one reason was that just as MacArthur's letter to Martin was published, the government announced the indictments of Julius and Ethel Rosenberg for treason for their part in delivering the secret of the atomic bomb to the Soviet Union. From the evidence which was ultimately produced, there was no doubt that the Rosenbergs were Communists and that they attempted to pass along the secret, to which Ethel Rosenberg's brother had some access as a Manhattan Project employee. To the more primitive opponents of the Truman administration, this betrayal by well-placed Jews,[32] coming on top of the betrayal by the well-connected Hiss, made the administration's apparent refusal to allow General MacArthur to win the Korean war inexplicable— unless there had been some grand betrayal. "This country," said William Jenner, "is in the hands of a secret coterie which is directed by agents of the Soviet Union. Our only choice is to impeach President Truman."

After fourteen years outside the country, MacArthur returned to the closest thing in American history to a Roman triumph; ticker-tape parades in San Francisco and an invitation to address a joint session of Congress (extended, oddly, by Martin, but the Democrats dared not withdraw it). This reception was a response partly to heroism, partly to theatrics: if MacArthur had a capacity for dramatizing himself, he had also proved himself a brilliant leader, the initiator of the island-hopping strategy which with few troops and few casualties had put American forces in position to defeat Japan; the brilliant proconsul who created a peaceful, democratic, and economically creative Japan; the innovative tactician who got American forces out of the Philippines and landed them in Inchon. Truman went on television, saying, "I believe that we must try to limit the war to Korea" and "a number of events made it evident that General MacArthur did not agree with that policy." MacArthur's speech eight days later was more dramatic: "You cannot appease or otherwise surrender to Communism in Asia without simultaneously undermining our efforts to halt its advance in Europe." He also said that "war's very objective is victory—no prolonged indecision" and in closing quoted an old ballad: "Old soldiers never die; they just fade away."

MacArthur surely did not expect to fade away, and for the moment the country's heart was with its hero. But over time its head was with its embattled president. The MacArthur firing was the subject of prolonged hearings of the Senate Armed Services and Foreign Relations Committee, chaired by Richard Russell. At fifty-four Russell was already a senior and dominant figure in the Senate, to which he had been first elected in January 1933 at age thirty-five, having previously served a term as governor of Georgia. He was its premier expert on the rules; he was the leader not only of the southern bloc but of all Senate Democrats (he helped choose Scott Lucas and, after his defeat, Ernest McFarland of Arizona as majority leaders, both men he could dominate, and after McFarland lost in 1952 he chose Lyndon Johnson, whom he could not). By the strength of his total absorption in Senate work (he was a bachelor with an austere personal life) and intellectual integrity, he was a force always to be reckoned with. Russell conducted the hearings slowly and painstakingly, barring the press (and the television cameras, which already had been busy broadcasting Kefauver's crime hearings) but releasing partial transcripts each day after they were declassified.[33] Truman's enemies were still rancid with hate: it was in June 1951 that Joseph McCarthy launched his attack on George Marshall, claiming later that Marshall "would sell his grandmother for advantage."[34] At Russell's hearings the military leadership backed up Truman completely, and the principle of civilian control over the military was forcefully reestablished. But the president remained monumentally unpopular. Although peace talks with the Communists began in June 1951, more than half the American casualties in Korea were sustained after the firing of MacArthur, after the Chinese offensive of November and December 1950.

Those casualties help to explain the anger and rage at Truman, his advisors, and his party. "Frustrated by the war," Robert Donovan writes in explaining the reaction to MacArthur's firing, "disgusted over corruption in Washington, worried about alleged subversion in government, and nearly worshipful of MacArthur, people vented their anger as the mood dictated."[35] A nation used to winning, confident of its strength and growth, found itself caught in a bloody stalemate— and caught in part because of mistakes and wrong decisions by the president. This situation was something the Americans of 1951 were not used to. Under Roosevelt's leadership and Marshall's and Eisenhower's and MacArthur's generalships, American forces had made steady progress once engaged in battle in World War II, with casualty rates which were astonishingly low in the Pacific and far below those of other combatants in the European theater of operations. V-E Day came 41 months and V-J Day 45 months after Pearl Harbor: in that time American forces had scoured the Pacific and invaded and taken control of the continent of Europe. In Korea they ended up spending 36 months to maintain a status quo in a small peninsula of little importance to anyone else. Americans were not eager for the war with China which MacArthur recommended, but they had come to expect the victory he said was the only goal of war. They were not used to frustration, and they were angry at seeing young Americans die to meet the carefully calibrated and deliberately limited goals of an administration unwilling to risk nuclear or all-out war.

Another factor not to be discounted in understanding Truman's unpopularity was the fury and rage of Republicans, approaching their twentieth year out of power and convinced they had somehow been cheated out of being America's natural majority party. It was in this atmosphere that Robert Taft approved of what he must have known were baseless attacks by McCarthy: as early as March 1950, Taft said, when McCarthy was challenged on his allegations, that he should "keep talking and if one case doesn't work out he should proceed with another."[36]

25

→》》 《《←

Crusade

A t the beginning of 1952, few Americans had any idea who would be elected president later in the year. The upset of 1948 had left informed observers questioning all conventional wisdom, discounting each prediction, doubting every poll. The best-known representatives of the major parties were also among the most unpopular of American politicians, Harry Truman because of the Korean war and Robert Taft because of his identification with the politics still widely blamed for the depression. Thomas Dewey, twice defeated, had taken himself out of presidential politics. The war seemed to be dragging on endlessly, with negotiations deadlocked over the prisoner issue: Americans did not want to hand back to the Communist Chinese and Koreans those unwilling to return home, who would face a hideous fate. The result, though no one put it this way in public discourse, was that American boys were dying so that Asian boys wouldn't die. Truman's job approval rating stayed at record low levels—25% in January 1952— and his few attempts at resolute action made him look worse. He fired Attorney General J. Howard McGrath in April 1952 for not cooperating with investigations of corruption among federal officials, and when the steel companies were threatened with a strike that month, instead of using the Taft-Hartley Act he had the Army seize the steel mills, an action ruled unconstitutional by the Supreme Court in June. Few times in the nation's history have Americans been more dissatisfied with their political leadership and more ready for a change.

What is amazing is that both political parties, against long-ingrained habits, responded to the clear demand for new leadership with nominees who evoked widespread and deep public enthusiasm: Dwight Eisenhower and Adlai Stevenson. The Republicans, aching for a return to power, spurned their partisan hero Robert Taft for a general of previously unknown political beliefs who had helped put into practice the major foreign policies of the Roosevelt and Truman administrations. The Democrats, after deferring to incumbent presidents for nearly twenty years, rejected both the incumbent and the clear front-runner in the primaries and turned, in a time of foreign crisis, to a little-known one-term governor whose foreign policy experience had been at the middle levels at best. Both decisions turned out to be good ones, producing candidates who maximized their party's vote in November. Oddly enough, to be strong candidates in the fall both men had to pretend to be non-politicians who were uninterested in being nominated,

the products of spontaneous drafts. Yet both of them were actually adroit maneuverers, whose each deft move preserved the illusion of their reluctance while
keeping open the possibility of their candidacies. Eisenhower had to win the
Republican nomination without revealing his disagreement with the party's leaders
on foreign policy, and in a way which kept him from being identified with the
party's unpopular domestic policies, which he mostly favored. Stevenson had to
win the Democratic nomination without appearing to be the handpicked choice
of the president whose unpopular foreign policies he agreed with, and in a way
which obscured his skepticism about the party's popular domestic policies.

II

The 1952 election was not the first time politicians had seen a potential president
in Dwight Eisenhower: in 1948 liberal Democrats like James Roosevelt and Claude
Pepper had tried to get him the Democratic nomination. The commanding general
of the third successful cross-Channel invasion in nine centuries,[1] the victorious
conqueror of western Europe, he was popular not only for his achievements but
also for his personality: the open-mindedness and friendliness symbolized by his
photogenic grin; the calmness and lack of pettiness in all his public appearances,
qualities which masked the volcanic temper and shrewd judgments of character
he showed in private; and the confidence and competence of a man who had never
been considered an intellectual but had written speeches for the eloquent Douglas
MacArthur and plans of battle for the thorough George Marshall. Eisenhower
had a storybook background. One of six talented sons of a family of German
Mennonite stock, he had been reared in Abilene, Kansas. After going off on the
train from Kansas City to West Point in 1911, he spent most of the next thirty
years in backwater military installations or in a small apartment in Washington.
He worked as a major until July 1936 (when he was forty-six) and then as a
lieutenant colonel until September 1941 in small offices in makeshift wooden
buildings in Fort Lewis, Washington, in San Antonio, Texas, and in Manila in
the Philippines. But in the war Eisenhower rose rapidly: his talents for planning
and diplomacy made him Allied commander of the invasions of North Africa in
1942, of Sicily in 1943, and of Normandy in 1944. At a time when Harry Truman
was a moderately well known second-rank senator and Adlai Stevenson was an
aide to the secretary of the Navy, Eisenhower was working directly with Roosevelt
and Churchill, Marshall and de Gaulle. After the war, as chairman of the Joint
Chiefs of Staff, as the author of the best-selling *Crusade in Europe,* as president
of Columbia University and NATO commander in Paris, he was operating at the
highest levels of the American and Allied governments; he played a key role in
carrying out the Truman-Marshall-Acheson foreign policy, with which he was in
solid agreement.

No one knew which political party Eisenhower belonged to. Both major parties'
1948 nominees called on him to head their parties' 1952 tickets, Dewey publicly
endorsing him in October 1950 and Truman (though he thought Eisenhower was

a Republican) privately promising him the Democratic nomination in November 1951. Truman was right: Eisenhower was a Republican but one whose views were not all that well positioned for 1952. He opposed the New Deal more thoroughly than did Taft, while he favored Truman's Europe First views over Taft's Asia First ones: these stances left him poorly positioned with general-election voters on domestic issues and totally unacceptable to the Taft conservatives on foreign issues, which that year were paramount for many of them and seemed the party's strongest asset. The polls made it plain that Eisenhower could win a general election: he led Truman 64%–28% in late March 1952. But it was not at all clear that he could win the Republican nomination. Conservative Republicans mistrusted him on domestic programs and hated his positions on foreign policy: they were convinced that their positions were more popular than before and that Dewey's "me-too" brand of Republicanism had been proved a loser in 1948, because it had failed to turn out Republican enthusiasts. They had candidates with stature, Taft and MacArthur, but these were, inexplicably to the conservatives, unpopular with the voters. On the other wing of the party, the two main contenders of 1948, Dewey and Stassen, were not running, and Earl Warren was clearly too liberal for most Republicans. Eisenhower's political strength depended on his remaining above the battle, avoiding both parochial and unconvincing appeals to the Republican right and also the impression that he was a tool of Dewey and his East Coast backers. Both then and later, Eisenhower cultivated the impression that he was a political novice. His actions (and inactions) and his success would show him to be a supple political operator, threading his way through a political process full of obstacles to success won the way he wanted.

III

In the summer of 1951 a Citizens for Eisenhower organization was formed by Cliff Roberts, L. B. Maytag, and John Hay Whitney, rich and well-connected Republican businessmen; they enlisted the support of politicians like Dewey, Stassen, Senator Henry Cabot Lodge of Massachusetts, and Senator James Duff of Pennsylvania. Lodge, a Vandenberg rather than Dewey supporter in 1948, became the group's campaign manager in November; and on January 6, 1952, he announced that Eisenhower was a Republican and that he would accept the Republican nomination.[2] Although Eisenhower said he was furious, he carefully avoided repudiating Lodge's statement. He felt duty-bound as a military officer not to seek office actively, but he obviously also perceived that it would be politically harmful to appear to do so or to let it seem that he was a tool of the Dewey forces. Like Roosevelt in 1940, he wanted to be drafted and to appear to be drafted, and it was helpful that the draft movement was led by Lodge, Dewey's 1948 adversary, and included Stassen, his 1948 opponent. Eisenhower was deeply moved when aviator Jacqueline Cochran flew to Paris in February 1952 and showed him a film of a "We Want Ike!" rally in Madison Square Garden. And in London, where he attended King George VI's funeral that month, he told General Lucius Clay, Texas oil man Sid Richardson, and "friend of presidents" George Allen that he agreed to their plan that he return to the United States in June to contest with Taft what seemed likely to be the last and crucial 300 delegate votes for the nomination. He was much influenced by the likelihood that unless he ran Taft would win the nomination, an event he saw as having the evil consequence either of keeping the Republican party out of office if Taft lost or of putting an isolationist, Asia first president into office if he won.[3]

The Republican race went pretty much according to Clay's predictions. Eisenhower stayed out of the race yet won most of the primaries. In March he beat Taft 50%–39% in New Hampshire, where turnout was triple that of 1948—a first sign of the genuine popular enthusiasm for Eisenhower. In Minnesota a week later 108,000 Republicans wrote in Eisenhower's name, placing him just behind Stassen, who was supporting him anyway. In early April came contests in the isolationist Midwest: Eisenhower lost Nebraska to Taft by only 36%–30%, saw him run ahead of Warren and Stassen in Wisconsin, and saw him carry Colonel McCormick's Illinois with a rousing 74%. Then, starting in mid-April, Eisenhower, who was still in Paris, won big victories in New Jersey (61%–36% over Taft), Pennsylvania (74% to 15% for Taft as a write-in), Massachusetts (70%–30%), and Oregon (65% to 7% for Taft as a write-in). Taft beat Stassen easily in Ohio and West Virginia but could beat Eisenhower by only 50.3%–49.7% in isolationist South Dakota in early June. The presidential primary had been an American institution since Robert LaFollette's Wisconsin enacted the first one in the first decade of the century. But not until 1948 had a primary determined the party's nominee, and it was not certain that Eisenhower's primary victories in 1952 would make this general, who at the beginning of the year was reluctant to admit he was a Republican, the Republican nominee.

Eisenhower flew from Paris to Washington on June 1, had a friendly meeting with Truman at the White House, and began what was to him the distasteful business of politicking. He reassured Republicans that he was a conservative on domestic issues and skirted the foreign policy issues which would be his greatest strength in a general election campaign. But it was becoming plain that Taft, not Eisenhower, would enter the convention in July with a delegate majority. Hence at the convention the Eisenhower forces challenged the credentials of southern delegations, which were in fact chosen by highhanded behind-closed-doors methods. These methods were standard operating procedure in a region where for years the only active Republicans had been not-very-competent locals hungry for patronage jobs, a group whose ranks had been severely depleted by twenty years of Democratic rule. To make sure the Eisenhower forces won their challenge, Lodge came up with a "fair play amendment," denying the pro-Taft delegations seated by the Taft-controlled national committee the right to vote on the challenge to their credentials. Rejecting all compromises, even one Eisenhower tentatively accepted, Lodge rounded up votes from big delegations (Richard Nixon swung California's vote, against the wishes of Earl Warren, who hoped for the nomination himself); and the fair play amendment, essentially a rejection of Taft, was adopted

658–548. Eisenhower's challenge in Georgia then won 607–531, and he was nominated when convention chairman Joseph Martin recognized Warren Burger of Minnesota, which gave Eisenhower the necessary votes to go over the top. Playing key roles for Eisenhower at the convention were John Minor Wisdom of Louisiana and Elbert Parr Tuttle of Georgia, who as Eisenhower appointees to the Fifth Circuit federal appellate court would play a vital role in the civil rights revolution through decisions to which Eisenhower himself was far from sympathetic.[4]

All these maneuvers took place on television and were watched by a viewing audience amounting to 46% of the voters—the first major TV audience for a convention, and the beginning of the end for the old convention system. For the hoopla and hour-long demonstrations looked foolish on television, and eventually TV reporters took to switching away from boring platform speakers in favor of interviews with politicians whose views really counted, thereby making the delegates the least rather than the most knowledgeable participants in the selection process. Eisenhower, always telegenic, adapted himself to the new medium with one of those gestures which make great television: after winning the nomination, he walked across from his hotel to Taft's and met with him briefly, asked for his cooperation, and posed for the cameras with him. The picture was worth many thousands of words. His goal in this action, argues his biographer Stephen Ambrose, was a matter of the highest political strategy: it set him on "a path that he would follow for the next eight years, a path whose destination was an accommodation with the Old Guard, one based on the Old Guard's acceptance of NATO and all that it implied."[5] In that quest—his only real political goal—he was utterly successful; the American commitment to the European alliance outlasted his presidency by at least three decades.

IV

The Democrats had no logical front-runner. Vice President Alben Barkley would turn seventy-five just weeks after election day (he died in April 1956, before completion of the term). Richard Russell was little known nationally and too closely identified with the segregationist South to be nominated by a party which had passed a civil rights plank at its last convention. Estes Kefauver was well known to the new majority of Americans with televisions because of his work chairing the hearings on organized crime, but he had antagonized the big-city machines and President Truman (and, in those days when insiders screened candidates, was considered unsuitable as an alcoholic and womanizer). The governors of New York, Pennsylvania, and California were Republicans; the governors of Massachusetts and Ohio were Catholics; and Governor Adlai Stevenson of Illinois had been divorced in December 1949. The only Democratic senators from any of these states were Herbert Lehman of New York, a Jew, and Paul Douglas of Illinois, an economics professor. The Truman administration had been filled with talented men with high-level foreign policy experience. But the administration's foreign policy was unpopular, and the only policymaker mentioned as a candidate was the railroad and investment banking millionaire Averell Harriman, who had never sought or won elective office and for all his other talents was a hesitant and unconvincing public speaker.

From this embarrassingly short list of possibilities a consensus arose rather early among party insiders, though not until the convention was it ratified by the delegates and the public, that the nomination should go to Stevenson. He had a fine Democratic pedigree: his grandfather, for whom he was named, had been elected as Grover Cleveland's vice president in 1892, had been William Jennings Bryan's running mate in 1900, and had run for governor of Illinois in 1908. Yet this Adlai Stevenson seemed to many to be a reluctant politician. Diffidence seemed to come to him naturally, as the scion of a rich family, as a mediocre student at best at Princeton and Northwestern Law School, as a corporation and estates lawyer with the firm of Cutting, Moore, and Sidley in Chicago, as the husband of an artsy Chicago heiress. The impression of distance from down-to-earth American politics was strengthened by, in the words of one admirer, "an accent vaguely 'British' or 'Eastern' (actually it reflected his wide-ranging travel during his formative years and had as its chief quality a clipped precision)."[6] Moreover, Stevenson's credentials for the presidency were not overwhelming. He had considerable experience in government jobs, in the AAA between July 1933 and September 1934 and in various foreign policy posts from July 1941, when he became an aide to Navy Secretary Frank Knox, a fellow Chicagoan, to the fall of 1947, when he served on the U.S. delegation to the United Nations. But his experience had been mostly middle-level, and his contacts with major figures fleeting. He had shaken hands with Roosevelt in a railroad car in Chicago in 1932 and handed him a message on a train outside Portland, Maine, in 1941; he had met Eisenhower in Naples in 1944; he had been an assistant (the "official leak," he told one friend) at the opening meeting of the United Nations in San Francisco in 1945. As governor of Illinois he had a creditable record, but not one which by itself would have catapulted him to national attention.

His chief assets were his speechmaking style and his carefully disguised deftness at political maneuver. He insisted throughout his public career on writing his own speeches, invariably polishing them until the last minute; and this once apathetic student and seemingly stodgy lawyer gave speeches which were consistently elegant and simple, humorous and sonorous. And he was careful always to portray himself as a reluctant candidate, the public-spirited patrician dragged after much hesitation into a seedy business whose tone he elevated by his very presence. Although he did elevate the tone of politics, there was less hesitation and certainly less naiveté than appeared on the surface.[7] His underlying determination and shrewdness were apparent from his success at winning the governorship. Beginning in April 1947, Stevenson began encouraging his friends to boost him for the Senate seat which was up in 1948, a seat then held by Republican C. Wayland ("Curly") Brooks, a World War I Marine hero and follower of the *Chicago Tribune*'s editorial line. Stevenson's record in foreign policy posts would be an asset, and so would his background; for the Chicago Democratic machine, led by Colonel Jacob Arvey of the mostly Jewish 24th Ward (one of the most heavily Democratic constituencies in America then and forty years later), was on the lookout for blue-ribbon candidates. Arvey had seen the November 1946 Republican sweep as a threat to his power base in Chicago (Democrats carried 56% of the Cook county vote in House races in 1944, but only 48% in 1946). He quickly persuaded Mayor Ed Kelly to retire[8] and drafted businessman Martin Kennelly to hold the mayor's office for the Democrats in the April 1947 election, which he did even though Republicans won 11 of the 19 aldermanic races decided in runoffs. Then he met with Stevenson, who wanted to run for senator, and with Paul Douglas, a University of Chicago economics professor who had joined the Marines in 1942 at age fifty and who wanted to run for governor. Stevenson was not coy about his intentions in 1947. "There is no sense in being disingenuous about these things," the man who was disingenuous about these things for much of his career told a reporter. "My mind is open. Naturally I'm interested."[9]

In December 1947, Arvey got the Democratic slate-making meeting to slate the blue-ribbon ticket of Douglas and Stevenson—but not for the offices they wanted. War hero Douglas was set to run against war hero Brooks for the Senate. Speech-maker Stevenson was asked to run for governor, a position he knew little about, against incumbent Dwight Green, the keynote speaker of the 1948 Republican national convention. Stevenson hesitated[10] but didn't ignore practical details: he asked Arvey if he would be free to make appointments. "On your major appointments I wouldn't make a suggestion if you asked me to," Arvey said. "On minor appointments—there'd be scores of them—you'd need help. Even there I wouldn't suggest names unless you asked me to. My bet is that you'd ask me, as a practical matter, but it would be your free choice."[11] This disclaimer was a charade. Arvey knew that a blue-ribbon candidate like Stevenson had to be able to say he was free to make all top appointments; he knew as well that the lifeblood of the Chicago machine was the lower appointments which provided steady jobs to precinct captains of every ethnic group from each of the fifty wards, and that of course Stevenson would let him make these appointments. And some higher ones as well: Richard J. Daley, former state legislator and future Chicago major, became Illinois's tax commissioner, and Frank Annunzio, former business partner of syndicate-connected John D'Arco and future congressman, became director of labor. If Stevenson was not unwilling to work with lower-level politicians, he was also loyal to those above him. At the 1948 national convention Arvey was one of the politicians urging Truman to step aside in favor of Eisenhower. Stevenson, however, stayed loyal to the president and steadfastly backed Alben Barkley for vice president, though when he was at the podium Barkley had refused to recognize Stevenson during a credentials fight related to civil rights. (Oddly enough, Stevenson and Barkley were distant cousins: America not so many generations before the 1950s was a small country.) Even as he was elevating the tone of politics, Stevenson understood the rules and was scrupulous about obeying them.

In this light must be seen what has been regarded as Stevenson's hesitancy to run for president in 1952. On a trip to Washington in January of that year, he was summoned to Blair House, where Truman talked of the history of the presidency, asked him to run, and told him he could be nominated. "But he said: No!" Truman reported in his memoirs. "He apparently was flabbergasted"[12]—but surely no more so than Truman had been when Franklin Roosevelt pressed the vice presidential nomination on him in July 1944. Stevenson pleaded his obligation to run for reelection and his duty to his sons, but of course the first was hardly binding and the sons were in college and prep school. This is the kind of statement politicians make in public but seldom in private, and Truman evidently concluded that Stevenson was a political simpleton. In fact, Stevenson was politically shrewd enough to see the futility of running as the handpicked candidate of an exceedingly unpopular president—Truman's Gallup job rating in January 1952 was 25% positive and 62% negative—and was schooled enough in political nicety never to be rude to a president. Therefore, he gave Truman what he surely thought the president would regard as a transparent but polite excuse.[13]

In public Stevenson protested his unavailability. But in private he took care not to make himself completely unavailable. He did not speak publicly of his meeting with Truman, but later that evening one of the men he called to say that he was "very upset" about being offered Truman's support was James Reston of the *New York Times*.[14] He withdrew his name from every primary ballot but Oregon's (where it was put on by decision of the secretary of state), thus avoiding match-ups against the popular Kefauver. He kept organization Illinois Democrats from working for him, but they could not have done much outside the state. When a group of liberal volunteers formed a Draft Stevenson group, he sent a message disapproving of their actions; but he did not cause them to shut up shop, nor did he prevent his friend George Ball from setting up a "Stevenson information center" in his law office to issue press releases and position papers, and he refused to say he would decline the nomination.[15] All these actions and inactions allowed him to portray a draft as genuine if it succeeded and to disown it if it failed. In early March he met secretly with Truman and repeated that he could run only for governor. Then in late March, after Truman had been beaten by Kefauver in New Hampshire 55%–44%, the president announced that he was indeed not going to run for reelection (repeating a promise made when he was riding high, in April 1950). In mid-April, after Kefauver's near-unanimous victories in Nebraska, Wisconsin, Illinois, and New Jersey, Stevenson announced that because he was running for governor he could not accept the nomination for any other office."[16] But the *could* left a certain ambiguity about his intentions, as this careful wordsmith must have known.[17] Like Eisenhower at the same time, Stevenson was maintaining his deniability while advancing his candidacy.[18] This posture would give him the option of running against Taft if he were the Republican nominee, but not against Eisenhower, which was probably his intention all along.[19]

While others—Russell, Harriman, Kerr, Barkley—tested the presidential waters, Stevenson made speeches in Texas, Oregon, and California, the latter two of which were primary states. Days before the convention met in Chicago, Truman decided to support Barkley; the president and most other party politicians would never have allowed the nomination of Kefauver, whose primary victories left him well short of a majority (for most delegates were selected in caucuses, not primaries). But as the Draft Stevenson people plotted to get Stevenson nominated, he decided that of course he would accept a draft. On Monday, the first day of the convention, labor leaders vetoed Barkley as too old; that same day Stevenson gave his welcoming speech, a characteristically graceful and eloquent talk which thrilled the delegates and the television audience. On Thursday efforts to require a loyalty oath of southern delegations were beaten, defusing the civil rights issue; that day Stevenson called Truman to ask whether it would "embarrass" him if Stevenson "allowed [his own] name to be placed in nomination." Of course Truman said no. And on Friday, after a recess for dinner, Stevenson was nominated on the third ballot. It was a deed deftly done. Stevenson had deniability, for he had been genuinely drafted. He had a united party and one which he made no attempt to reform: unlike Kefauver, he did not threaten the big-city bosses; unlike Truman in 1948, he did not allow the convention to split off the South. Moreover, contrary to Truman's plans, he did not owe the nomination to the incumbent president. His strategy could not have worked except that the alternatives each proved unacceptable. But it gave the Democrats as strong a nominee as they could have hoped for.

After the convention, Stevenson continued, in Truman's bitter words, to "dissociate" himself from the president. He fired Democratic national Chairman Frank McKinney and installed his friend Stephen Mitchell instead. He insisted on having his campaign headquarters in Springfield, Illinois, far from Truman's Washington. In reply to an Oregon newspaper editor's letter about "the mess in Washington," he wrote, "As to whether I can clean up the mess in Washington, I would bespeak the careful scrutiny of what I inherited here in Illinois and what has been accomplished in three years."[20] Stevenson broke with Truman's liberal record on domestic issues. He did not support national health insurance, had no desire to revise Taft-Hartley (and had little instinctive sympathy with unions), was unenthusiastic about raising Social Security benefits or the minimum wage, and had little interest in civil rights.[21] In some respects he represented the Democratic road Truman had not taken in 1947 and 1948, a course faithful to the party's historic tradition of an activist foreign policy, free trade, vague sympathy with minorities and underdogs, and deference to local customs and ways of life.

Such a course left Stevenson's candidacy with a certain weakness. On domestic issues he did not press the advantage which Democrats had enjoyed in 1948— partly because of changed circumstances, with wartime inflation rather than Farm-Belt-led depression the economic threat, but partly because of the candidate's own convictions and his party's inability to deliver on its 1944 and 1948 domestic promises. On foreign policy issues Stevenson was inevitably at a disadvantage against Eisenhower. His experience was far less impressive—Eisenhower was arguably the American president best equipped to handle foreign policy on entering office—and his party was associated with an unpopular and, to most Americans, unnecessary war. Unable to promise easy solutions, Stevenson provided in his acceptance speech and afterwards eloquent descriptions of the nation's problems and responsibilities. "The ordeal of the twentieth century—the bloodiest, most turbulent era of the Christian age—is far from over," he warned. "Sacrifice, patience, understanding and implacable purpose may be our lot for years to come. Let's face it! Let's talk sense to the American people! Let's tell them the truth, that there are no gains without pains, that we are now on the eve of great decisions, not easy decisions, like resistance when you're attacked, but a long, patient, costly struggle which alone can assure triumph over the great enemies of man—war, poverty and tyranny—and the assaults upon human dignity which are the most grievous consequences of each."

This was nothing like Truman's extemporaneous excoriations of the Republicans, nor did it have Roosevelt's soaring confidence in total American victory. Stevenson insisted on making a virtue of the unpopularity of his message, which for him in 1952 was the best of political strategies. "Better we lose the election than mislead the people; and better we lose than misgovern the people," he went on, in the spirit which made him so attractive later in the 1950s to intellectuals and highbrows who instinctively criticized American mores and were repelled by the exuberant evidences of American economic growth. But these were Americans for whom Stevenson's greatest attractiveness was that he lost. The Stevenson of 1952 was trying very hard to win (and even to his intimates maintained up to the end of the campaign that he expected to win: in his office pool he bet that he would get 325 electoral votes).[22] He could not plausibly promise an easy end to the Korean war or a quick end to wartime inflation; he could suggest (as his campaign theme song, "Don't Let Them Take It Away," suggested) that the Republicans would repeal the New Deal, but few voters believed that Eisenhower was as hostile to the New Deal as he in fact was, and Stevenson plainly was not much of an economic liberal himself. And so he made a virtue out of necessity and tried to inspire the voters for the task ahead—and leavened his inspirational rhetoric with humor. It was a Lincolnesque combination, delivered in Lincolnian cadences. In his welcoming speech to the Chicago convention, Stevenson reviewed the Democratic achievements of the past twenty years, in which he had had only a modest part, and added that "our Republican friends have said that it was all a miserable failure. For almost a week pompous phrases marched over this landscape in search of an idea, and the only idea they found was that the two great decades of progress in peace, and of victory in war, and of bold leadership in this anxious hour, were the misbegotten spawn of bungling, of corruption, of socialism, of mismanagement, of waste and of worse. They captured, they tied and they dragged that ragged idea here into this hall and they furiously beat it to death for a solid week."

Stevenson was attacked as an "egghead" in the campaign, but in fact he was less an intellectual than a socialite. The only book on his bedside table, his biographer found after his death, was the *Social Register*.[23] Like Lincoln, he was a lawyer and politician who had a way with words, who came to public notice at a crucial time, and who provided his party with a stronger candidate than it imagined when it nominated him. Against any candidate other than Eisenhower, Stevenson would likely have won; and the philosophy and the capacity for leadership he showed in 1952 would likely have made him a successful president, as Eisenhower's different qualities made him successful. His rhetoric was not the scorn of an intellectual for the unschooled, but the response of a citizen to a call for national leadership in a difficult time. This response came from a citizen interested not in criticizing but in governing, and in drawing on his own experience and the collective rhetorical memory of his society to fashion a new way of looking at politics and government. The Adlai Stevenson of 1952 was not a great loser but a man who could have been, who by his own efforts put himself within reach of being, a good winner. By late July, after both conventions, he trailed the still exceedingly popular Eisenhower by only a 47%–41% margin in the Gallup poll— a far better showing than Truman was making against the not-so-popular Dewey at the same point in 1948.

V

The Republicans, who had been so sure that they would win in 1948, were not at all sure they would win in 1952. In the end they did, but when their triumph is examined, it begins to seem more chancy and less sweeping than is generally thought. Eisenhower had a strong personal appeal to voters, but so as it turned out did Stevenson; and Gallup, which after its 1948 experience was careful to track party as well as candidate preference in the presidential race, found that Eisenhower was running only 2 to 4 percentage points ahead of the Republicans as a party. In the congressional races, Democrats ran essentially even with the Republicans both in preelection polls and on election day. In fact, a significant bloc of voters wanted a Republican president but a Democratic Congress—the former presumably to end the war in Korea and tackle other problems Truman had left unsolved, the latter presumably to see that the New Deal was not repealed.

For even as they were losing the election, the Democrats were benefiting from long-term political change. As compared with the last election in which the outcome was widely considered uncertain, 1940, the Democrats were noticeably stronger as a party; Americans' party identification was 41% Democratic and 34% Republican on Gallup's scale in late July 1952, a trough year for the party electorally, as compared with a 41%–38% Democratic edge in July 1940, something closer to a peak year for the Democrats at the polls. Republicans whose party preference went back to the Civil War era or the early twentieth century were dying out; gratitude for the Democrats' work in ending the depression, winning World War II, and providing the basis for economic growth and upward mobility in the years after 1947 was working for the party in the long term even as policies like the Korean war and episodes like the Truman administration scandals were costing votes in the short term. Long-term demography was also working for the Democrats. In the United States, as in most industrialized societies, the less affluent have more children than the more affluent, and people who had become heavily Democratic in the class-based politics which developed starting in 1935 had produced more children than those who were strongly anti-New Deal. By 1952 those children were starting to vote. Demographically, 1952 may well have been the high point of the New Deal coalition: it came just a few years before the peak of labor union membership as a percentage of the work force and just a few years after the peaks of population in America's central cities and of mass transit ridership, both of which occurred around 1948. Blocs of self-consciously ethnic voters may also have reached their maximum size in these years: the Ellis Island immigrants and their children and grandchildren were mostly middle-class now and registered to vote, but in important ways they still felt themselves outsiders in a country which still thought of itself as Anglo-Saxon and Protestant. The migration from South to North, which had begun in great numbers in 1940, produced many new voters in 1952, almost all of them—white and black—Democrats. The South itself remained largely, though no longer solidly, Democratic in presidential politics, and Democrats were at least competitive in every other part of the country except back corners like Maine and Vermont and the row of Plains states from Kansas to the Dakotas.

The Democrats' strength was increased also because 1952 produced one of the sharpest increases in turnout in the history of American presidential elections. Just under 50 million Americans had voted in 1940; in 1944, with millions serving in the armed forces and working in war industries, the total fell to just under 48 million; in the bitter campaign of 1948, it rose only to 49 million. Suddenly, in 1952, 61.5 million voted. That was a rise of 26%, not matched since Al Smith brought so many Catholic immigrants, especially women, and anti-Catholic Protestants to the polls in 1928.

The campaign produced relatively little change in the candidates' standing, with the most newsworthy event being the exposure of the personal expenses fund which supporters had amassed for Eisenhower's vice presidential nominee, the thirty-nine-year-old Richard Nixon. This practice was actually innocuous, certainly not illegal. Stevenson had amassed a similar fund to supplement his aides' salaries. But Nixon was little known to most voters, and among many liberals he was heartily disliked for his redbaiting, his pursuit of Alger Hiss, and his negative campaigns against Jerry Voorhis and Helen Gahagan Douglas. Eisenhower, who hardly knew Nixon, considered dropping him and left him to make his defense on his own. He did so on September 25 in an effective television speech, at once logical and lugubrious, in which he defended his conduct on the merits, called on the Democratic candidates to reveal their personal finances (by implication this call included an infuriated Eisenhower, who had been taxed at specially low rates on his $650,000 advance for *Crusade in Europe*), and said that whatever happened he and his family were not going to return to the giver his daughters' cocker spaniel, Checkers. Eisenhower, waiting to gauge the public response, summoned Nixon to meet him the next day at Wheeling, West Virginia, and greeted him as he came off the plane with the reassuring yet also condescending cry, "You're my boy!"

Eisenhower's lead did increase from July to September, but this rise may just have indicated that the glow of the Democratic convention was wearing off; the pollsters, watching closely for the surges of change they missed in 1948, did not find them this time. What they did find was an increase in positive feelings toward both candidates[24]—an increase that surely contributed to the high turnout. Eisenhower was not hurt, though probably not helped significantly either, by his appearance with Joseph McCarthy in Wisconsin on October 3 and by his deletion from a speech in Milwaukee that day of praise (which he had previously voiced in Denver) for McCarthy's target General Marshall. On the other hand, he probably did gain votes when he said in Detroit on October 26, "I shall go to Korea." At the least, the statement drew attention to his experience in foreign affairs and to the credibility which he, in contrast to Truman and arguably to Stevenson, would have in threatening aggressive moves against the Communists unless they settled at the bargaining table. It may have reinforced as well the attacks made by more conservative Republicans, including Nixon, on the Truman-Acheson policies as "twenty years of treason" and "Dean Acheson's college of cowardly Communist containment."[25] Such language was not just cynical posturing. The attacks on the Yalta Conference as a sellout of "the captive nations of eastern Europe" and the emphasis on the presence of Communists like Alger Hiss in the State Department reflected a genuine dismay at the postwar gains of the Communists, a dismay amplified by the refusal of politicians frustrated by their lack of power to admit that most and probably all of those gains were unavoidable. But all these complaints probably would not have won the election for the Republicans if it had not been for the public anguish over a war in which young Americans were dying to maintain a stalemate and for the reputation and experience of the man who had won the Republican nomination only by stealing the decisive delegates.

The Democrats lost in 1952 because they had the overwhelming disadvantages of responsibility for a war prolonged by mistakes in policy and because the Republicans nominated the one candidate in twentieth-century American history who had presidential stature in the eyes of the voters even before he took office. Even with those advantages, Eisenhower won by 55%–44%, not by the kind of landslide which elected Roosevelt in 1932 or Warren Harding in 1920 over incumbent parties with problems of similar magnitude to those the Democrats had in 1952. The Democrats, who would probably have lost the presidential elections of 1940 and 1944 but for foreign policy issues, ended up losing on foreign policy in 1952. In the less prosperous and optimistic America which most voters lived in in 1940 and remembered in 1944, domestic issues were not decisive for the Democrats. By 1948 and 1952, after the revival of confidence in economic growth and the vast surge of upward mobility which followed the war, domestic issues worked powerfully for the Democrats—powerfully enough to help them to a respectable showing despite the disabling circumstances of 1952. Although Stevenson lost in almost every region of the country, carrying only nine states in the South and the Civil War borderlands, he was competitive in every region but the Great Plains, where a typical farm revolt was swinging the region against the incumbent party.

Nor did Stevenson drag his party down in the congressional elections. Republicans did win control of both houses of Congress, but by exceedingly narrow margins. In the Senate, Republicans gained a majority largely because of upsets like Barry Goldwater's defeat of Majority Leader Ernest McFarland in Arizona— a result that opened the way for Lyndon Johnson to become Senate Democratic leader—and razor-thin margins in small states like Nevada and Wyoming as well as in Michigan and Maryland. In those days when vote-splitting was still rare, the Democratic ticket was strong enough to make possible victories by John Kennedy in Massachusetts (over the often absent Lodge, who was off campaigning for Eisenhower), Stuart Symington in Missouri, Mike Mansfield in Montana, and Henry Jackson in Washington; and Eisenhower's refusal to rebuke McCarthy prompted Oregon's Republican Senator Wayne Morse to leave the party and, two years later, to become a Democrat. These victories kept the Senate easily within reach of the Democrats in the next few elections and gave the party some of its most important leaders of the next two decades. If Stevenson had run as poorly as James Cox in 1920 or Herbert Hoover in 1932, it is unlikely that any of these Democrats would have won.

As for the House of Representatives, Republican gains were due mostly to reapportionment and redistricting. Population outflows cost the Democrats 7 seats (and the Republicans only 1) in the South and the Civil War borderlands, losses that were compensated by only 2 new Democratic seats in Florida. Republican redistricters in New York created 1 new Republican seat in surburban Long Island, eliminated 3 Democratic seats in Brooklyn and Manhattan, enabled Republicans to gain 4 seats from Democrats in Queens, the Bronx, and Staten Island, and prevented the Democrats from winning any seats in the Buffalo area. In California, Republican redistricters ensured that 6 of the state's 7 new seats went Republican, although the Democrats made a net gain of 1 of the old seats. In Pennsylvania and Illinois, which lost seats, and in Michigan and Ohio, which gained or held even, Republican redistricters saw to it that all gains went to the Republicans, except for the Democratic capture of 1 seat each in Philadelphia and Chicago. Aside from redistricting and reapportionment, Republicans made a net gain of only 11 seats from 1950.

But such minutiae were not much appreciated by the public. What they noticed was the short-run result, that the Republicans took control of the federal government in what turned out to be their only across-the-board triumph in the six decades between 1928 and 1988. What they did not know at the time and could not have apprehended was the long-run result of the election of 1952. This contest between two attractive figures new to national electoral politics not only resulted in an end to the Korean war which was poisoning the political atmosphere. What was more important and more permanent, it helped both parties develop a politics which reflected the deep confidence and the surging economic growth of the country which, to its great surprise, had emerged in the years just after 1945 from a country lacerated by depression and war.

26

⟶⟫⟫ ⟨⟨⟵

Republicans

Dwight Eisenhower entered the White House the best-prepared president of the twentieth century. He had worked closely with the great leaders of the world: he knew Winston Churchill intimately, he had worked warily with and sparred with Josef Stalin, he knew the minor French politicians and the Charles de Gaulle who lurked in his farmhouse in Colombey-les-Deux-Eglises, he knew West German Chancellor Konrad Adenauer. He knew the strengths and weaknesses of Marshall and MacArthur and all the generals in Korea. Of domestic American politics, of the great machines of government which had come into existence over the last twenty years, he knew less—but more than most observers thought. He had a closer acquaintance with leading figures in Congress than any other president who had come from the military, and he had a wider acquaintance of foreign countries than any president since Herbert Hoover. At home he had maneuvered his way through American politics and, over tough opposition from Taft and Stevenson, had gotten himself nominated by a party which was not sure it wanted him and elected by voters who were not sure they wanted his party. He quickly developed a shrewd appreciation of Taft's loyalty to party and principle and of his peevishness, and made him his ally; he was from the beginning contemptuous, though at first only privately, of McCarthy and his kind; he surely understood the strength of Sam Rayburn in the House and Richard Russell in the Senate.

What Eisenhower seems not to have brought to the White House was any determination to do for his party what Franklin Roosevelt and Harry Truman in their different ways did for theirs. Roosevelt came to the White House with no clear plan for governing, but with a long-range political strategy clearly in mind: to combine the progressive Republicans from the Old Northwest with the traditional Democratic party in the South and Civil War borderlands and the liberal Democratic party developed in the big cities by machine politicians like Charles F. Murphy and Ed Kelly and Pat Nash. Truman, preoccupied at first by the burdens of governing, chose for 1948 a political strategy of alliance with organized labor, support for civil rights, and extension of New Deal programs. Eisenhower came to office with ideas for a strategy for governing, but with no long-range political strategy to transform the Republicans once again into the nation's natural majority party. He achieved most of his policy goals—ending the Korean war,

261

stamping out inflation, reining in the growth of the federal government, letting the McCarthyite fever burn out, building important parts of the nation's transportation infrastructure like the St. Lawrence Seaway and the Interstate highway system. He secured his own triumphant reelection. But he did not succeed in winning majorities for other Republicans or in permanently remaking the Republican party in his own image.

II

Yet for a moment, in 1953 and 1954, other Republicans dreamed that they were once again the majority, once again the party of American governance in times of, to use the word coined by Republican President Warren G. Harding, normalcy. If they were no longer quite so strong in some of their old citadels in the North like Pennsylvania, they were now capable of winning elections in modern-thinking towns in the South like Roanoke and Charlotte, St. Petersburg and Dallas.[1] If their big-city machines and labor support no longer enabled them to carry Philadelphia or Pittsburgh, Chicago or Detroit, they were strong in the outer reaches of the big cities and in the new suburbs which were in the early 1950s the fastest-growing part of the country. It was not only luck that redistricting helped Republicans win the House in 1952; the population gains registered by the 1950 census and reflected, however inexactly in those days before one-person-one-vote, in redistricting tended to be biggest in places with Republican leanings.

What was the Republican part in 1953, when it took control of all elected branches of government for the first time in twenty-two years? It was a party defined more by what it was against than what it was for. Its two most talented leaders, Thomas Dewey and Robert Taft, were men of great abilities and impressive integrity who were more interested in governing than politicking. Both had been frustrated in their quest for the presidency, and both were about to leave the scene. Dewey had been drafted for one last term as governor of New York in September 1950; he made it clear he wanted no office in the new administration, and he looked forward to entering law practice at age fifty-two after his term expired in December 1954. Taft became Senate majority leader officially in January 1953 as he had de facto in January 1947. But he learned in May that he had cancer and, after passing the leadership along to William Knowland of California, died at age sixty-three in July 1953. Thus gone from the scene were the two Republicans with national stature and a natural instinct not only for governing but for creating an appeal for a party capable of governing.

Other leading Republicans were in no position to fashion a strategy. Richard Nixon was vice president and had an uneasy relation with his chief. Harold Stassen was head of the Mutual Security Administration, the chief administrator of foreign aid—one of the government's largest and most important programs at the time, but one which turned out to be unpopular and a political dead end. Senator Henry Cabot Lodge, after managing Eisenhower's campaign, had been upset in Massachusetts by Congressman John Kennedy, son of Joseph Kennedy, the former

Securities and Exchange Commission head and ambassador to Britain. (Lodge once said, "I always knew if there came a man with an honest, clean record who was also of Irish descent, he'd be almost impossible to beat.")[2] Given the choice of being ambassador to the United Nations or White House chief of staff, Lodge took the UN post, showing the importance people placed on the organization in those days. Governor Earl Warren of California was appointed chief justice when Fred Vinson suddenly died in September 1953. John Bricker, the 1944 vice presidential nominee, was a senator from Ohio who was advancing his proposal to limit the president's treaty-making power, a measure opposed by Eisenhower. The Republican speaker of the House, Joseph Martin, was a sixty-eight-year-old bachelor from a small Yankee town in Massachusetts, a one-time isolationist whose faithfulness to his party was compromised by his friendship and collaboration with the man who twice preceded and twice succeeded him as speaker, Sam Rayburn.[3]

In Congress and in the states, the Republicans seemed split neatly into two groups. Taft Republicans wanted to repeal the New Deal; they had once been isolationists and now wanted an Asia First foreign policy. They tended to be from the Midwest and West (though they included House powers like John Taber of upstate New York, chairman of the Appropriations Committee, a man with such a booming voice that one roar restored the hearing of a Democratic colleague who had been deaf in one ear since birth).[4] Although they held few governorships, they made up most of the Republican ranks in Congress and the state legislatures because the bulk of Republican legislators were elected outside the major metropolitan areas of America. In the House of Representatives elected in 1952, Republicans representing districts outside the major metropolitan areas outnumbered Republicans from districts primarily in those areas by 148 to 72. In contrast, among the 101 Democrats elected outside the South, those from major metropolitan districts outnumbered the rest by 65 to 36.[5] The Republicans did hold more seats (72) than the Democrats (65) even in the major metropolitan areas. But it was apparent that any increases in the tenuous Republican majority must come either in the major metropolitan areas or in the still overwhelmingly Democratic South. The Democrats had only 7 seats in smaller metropolitan areas and only 29 in the non-southern countryside, most of them in solidly Democratic coal-steel-iron districts. As it turned out, the Republicans made only minimal gains in the South in the 1950s and lost seats in the major metropolitan areas. The political instincts of the Taft Republicans were wrong for both areas: the support many (though not all) of them showed toward civil rights hurt them in the South, while their determination to roll back the New Deal frightened voters in the major metropolitan areas, who since the days of NRA in 1933 and 1934 had especially depended on government to maintain their everyday economic existence and to guarantee their long-term upward economic mobility.

The Dewey Republicans wanted to curb New Deal excesses, to hold down deficits and control rather than be controlled by labor union leaders. Internationalists who supported a Europe First policy, they were particularly numerous in the East Coast states, though not unheard of elsewhere, particularly in the

Upper Midwest and parts of the West Coast. They won all Republican presidential nominations from 1940 until 1960; elected the governors of New York, Pennsylvania, and California for most of that period; and controlled major organs of Republican opinion like *Look,* the *New York Herald Tribune,* and Henry Luce's *Time* and *Life,* which aside from their Asia First policy usually favored the Dewey wing.

III

But Taft and Dewey Republicans also had things in common, as can be seen by looking at two congressmen who were positioned right on the cusp between the two groups: Charles Halleck, the House majority leader from Indiana, and Hugh Scott, the former Republican national chairman from Philadelphia. Both men were born in 1900, both were House veterans (Halleck was first elected in 1935, Scott in 1942), and both would eventually lead their parties on Capitol Hill, Halleck as House minority leader from 1959 to 1965 and Scott as Senate minority leader from 1969 to 1977.

When Halleck was first elected to Congress in January 1935, the prospects for his party seemed as bleak as the cold winter bearing down on his home town of Rensselaer, Indiana. These flat plains midway between Indianapolis and Chicago were settled originally by Yankees from upstate New York; they were one of the earliest and most faithful homelands of the Republican party. In courthouse towns like Rensselaer young lawyers and bankers and businessmen, who had known each other from childhood through fraternities at the state university or a small private college and perhaps law school, took it for granted that they would run public affairs. They ran for office and were almost invariably chosen by their humbler small-town and farm neighbors. Such a man was Charlie Halleck, who had served in World War I and then graduated quickly from Indiana University's undergraduate college and law school. He was outgoing, aggressive, a fighter. He needed to be: when he went to the House, he was the only Republican there from Indiana, one of the few from the Great Lakes states. Most of these Republicans found themselves opposing the reauthorization of NRA and the Wagner Act, the growth of WPA and of public power projects: they resisted Roosevelt's attempts to centralize economic regulation and power and fought for the autonomy of the local political and economic leaders like their old fraternity brothers back home on Main Street. They fought against America's involvement in Europe and lamented its lack of aggressiveness in Asia. Not so long before—in 1930, when they passed Smoot-Hawley on straight party lines—the House Republicans had been a disciplined party, self-confident, with their own solutions for the nation's problems. But in the 1930s they became uncertain, disunited, men whose votes the Democrats didn't need and seldom sought. They were no longer making decisions; they were responding to decisions made by others. The men who were the center of attention on Main Street found themselves ignored in Franklin Roosevelt's Washington.

For a man as aggressive as Charles Halleck, this situation was intolerable. In 1940 he became a leading backer of Wendell Willkie, who had been in the same fraternity as Halleck at IU. In the 1944 and 1946 elections he served as head of the Republican House campaign committee, helping to pile up the party's huge majority in the latter year. In 1947 and 1948 he was majority leader in the Republican House, helping to pass Taft-Hartley and the tax cut, opposing price controls and backing the Marshall Plan. But Halleck and other congressional Republicans had a hard time coming up with an attractive political program after 1952, because in so many respects America already resembled what they wanted. Roosevelt's centralizing bills and organized labor's power had been checked by the bipartisan conservative majorities in Congress, which were maintained even in the Fair Deal session of 1949. The private economy was now producing robust economic growth, despite high tax rates and a lack of major governmental stimulus. Far from wishing to beef up American military power, a prime goal of conservatives a generation later, Halleck and his midwestern colleagues were suspicious of a large military establishment and determined to hold defense spending down. For all their natural assurance that they were the natural people to govern the nation, they had essentially a negative platform: they stood against more things than they stood for.

Much the same could be said of Hugh Scott, though he was a leader of the Dewey rather than the Taft wing of the Republicans. Scott's political base was Philadelphia, but he had been born and educated in Virginia and retained to the end of his life the peculiar Virginia accent (closer to the accent of southern Ontario than to any other in the United States); he moved to Philadelphia partly because there was no future in public life for a Republican in Virginia in 1922. Scott was both a party loyalist and a kind of idealist, a partronage lawyer on the Philadelphia district attorney's payroll until his election to Congress and a backer of civil rights measures all his life. He lived in Chestnut Hill, the home of many of Philadelphia's old elite, with its sprawling cobblestone houses on rolling lots, and commuted to the downtown Center City on the Reading Railroad, through narrow-streeted neighborhoods packed tight with old workingmen's houses. When he moved to Philadelphia, all seven of the city's congressional districts were represented by Republicans elected by better than 3–1 margins; by the 1950s he was the last Republican congressman from the city, carrying his district by hairsbreadth margins every two years with the help of the black and Jewish voters he had long cultivated. A man of elegant bearing, he was a collector of Tang dynasty vases and bowls—and was disciplined enough to mask his nervousness when a Senate colleague whose vote he was seeking started tossing one around.[6] Scott was Dewey's choice as Republican national chairman for the 1948 campaign, and he must have expected a major role in a Dewey administration. Instead he became a target of outraged criticism from the Taft wing of the party, even as his political situation at home became more precarious.

What is amazing about Scott is the vehemence and brio with which he maintained his differences with the Democrats on the one hand and Taft Republicans on the other—even though in important respects his differences with each were marginal. The Democrats he disliked as connivers with southern segregationists and cat's-paws of labor union bosses, men who resisted civil rights and threatened America with creeping socialism. Scott was no prudish reformer: as a patronage employee in Philadelphia, he was familiar with the workings of a political machine deeply intertwined with a dirty-under-the-fingernails city, with the local bookie and the complaisant policeman, the well-connected lawyer and the sleek bootlegger. But for him the corruption of the Democrats was more fundamental than that of the Republicans, more threatening to society: they represented the less savory elements, the intellectually less respectable ideas, the more dangerous tendencies. Scott was vehement because he was convinced his kind of Republicans were the natural and best leaders of his country, and yet he saw them squeezed out again and again by the Truman Democrats and the Taft Republicans. For him the natural political competition would have been Dewey Republicans against the kind of Jeffersonian, localist Democrats which Truman decided against being; and he was confident his side could win that competition. But after the upset of 1948, and after Eisenhower only narrowly won the Republican nomination in 1952, he could see that his kind of politics had to struggle mightily—and vehemently—to prevail, and that if it did not prevail it would not survive.

So neither branch of the Republican party in Congress, neither an aggressive Taft-wing Republican like Charles Halleck nor as vehemently partisan a Dewey-wing Republican as Hugh Scott, entered 1953 and 1954, the only two years in more than fifty that Republicans would control both Congress and the executive branch, with any clear program. Coming to power in a year when the New Deal Democratic constituencies in the big cities and the labor unions bulked larger than they ever had or ever would again in American history, when the American public was basically satisfied with the size and scope of government as established during the new Deal and war years and moderated by the Republicans in 1947, the Republicans had only a dim chance to change the country's basic political balance. The best they could do was to govern.

IV

Governing was what came naturally to Dwight Eisenhower. The first order of business was ending the war. In February 1953, Eisenhower let the Chinese know that he wanted an armistice and that if he didn't get it the United States would "move decisively without inhibition in our use of weapons." In other words, he did not consider himself bound by Truman's decisions not to cross the Yalu and not to use atomic weapons. But on Europe he went with the policy of the past administration, passing up an attempt to attack the Yalta agreements by nominating Charles Bohlen, a Roosevelt advisor there, as ambassador to the Soviet Union and going to the trouble in March 1953 of getting Taft to stop McCarthy from trying to defeat the nomination. He did authorize Secretary of State John Foster Dulles to fire some 300 State Department employees deemed security risks (some surely unjustly), and he refused to stop the execution of Ethel and Julius Rosenberg. But mostly he worked to uphold executive branch power and policies as Roosevelt and Truman had. For much of 1953 and 1954 controversy raged over John Bricker's proposed constitutional amendment to limit presidential treaty-making powers. Like the 22nd Amendment, limiting the president to two terms, this issue was a largely symbolic one, a posthumous slap at Franklin Roosevelt. But Eisenhower, one of two presidents over the next forty years who would be covered by the 22nd Amendment, stoutly opposed the Bricker amendment, even though fighting it occupied much of his and the Senate's attention for eighteen months.

The amendment was not the only issue on which Eisenhower firmly opposed old-guard Republicans and followed the policies of Harry Truman and the "wise men" who had formulated his foreign policies after World War II. Another such issue was trade. Eisenhower very much shared in the postwar transatlantic consensus which committed the United States to the establishment of the dollar as a world currency and the promotion of free trade—a consensus which did in fact produce a peaceful, prosperous, democratic North America and western Europe. His views found support in Congress from the Democrats' Sam Rayburn and Lyndon Johnson, both from Texas, who shared the faith in free trade which had been most persistently articulated over the years by another border-state Democrat, former Secretary of State Cordell Hull. Many old-guard Republicans, in contrast, were still believers in the high-tariff policies of William McKinley, Reed Smoot, and Willis Hawley. No sooner did seventy-seven-year-old Daniel Reed, from upstate New York, become chairman of the House Ways and Means Committee in 1953 than he began pressing for higher tariffs. It was all Eisenhower could do to get the Republican Congress to renew for one year at a time a basic trade bill allowing the president to lower trade barriers. After the 1954 elections, when Rayburn became speaker and Jere Cooper of Tennessee chairman of Ways and Means, Congress gave Eisenhower the three-year renewal he wanted.

But the most important event of these early months of the Eisenhower administration was one over which the president had no control: the death in Moscow, on March 5, 1953, of Josef Stalin. Eight years before, Roosevelt had met with Stalin in Yalta and Truman had sat side by side with him in Potsdam; but for the last seven years Stalin had been a menacing figure, an unscrupulous and possibly mad dictator in possession since September 1949 of the atomic bomb, an enemy of freedom and of the United States in central Europe and east Asia. Suddenly he was gone. Americans, including Eisenhower, had no idea who or what would follow Stalin. But they were reasonably sure it would be no worse. The nightmare of the Cold War was eased. The threat of hot war seemed diminished, and the long agony of the Korean "police action" seemed likely to be over soon.

In April 1953, responding to these hopes, Eisenhower delivered a "chance for peace" speech which evoked a favorable response. Despite the skepticism of Dulles and the opposition of South Korean President Syngman Rhee, he moved toward an armistice agreement leaving Korea divided along a jagged line approximating the 38th parallel—the settlement Truman might have had in October 1950 and could not achieve after December 1950. In July 1953 the armistice was reached, and the United States was out of the Korean war.

Domestically, the real crunch Eisenhower faced was on the budget. As a Republican, he wanted it reduced. But how? Foreign aid he believed must be continued. Military spending could be cut after the Korean war was over, but not severely: the United States had expensive commitments in Europe, the Middle East, and the Far East, and Eisenhower was not going to dismantle the NSC 68 defense establishment set up by the Democrats. Domestic spending was a traditional Republican target. But Eisenhower wanted to spend more on Social Security and education, and other domestic programs were not big enough to provide room for cuts. This was the picture Eisenhower painted in April 1953 when Taft pounded the table and urged more cuts.[7] The temptation was to squeeze defense by relying more on atomic weapons and cutting conventional forces. Although Dulles favored this policy, it was mostly resisted by the former NATO commander. There was in fact a standoff. In November 1952, Americans had exploded their first hydrogen bomb, developed at the insistence of Harry Truman and Admiral Lewis Strauss and over the opposition of Manhattan Project director J. Robert Oppenheimer and Atomic Energy Commission director David Lilienthal. In October 1953, Eisenhower announced that the Soviets had the H-bomb as well.

V

The following month, the issue of Communists in government was revived serendipitously. In November 1953, Attorney General Herbert Brownell, a former top Dewey aide, uncovered FBI evidence that Harry Dexter White had been a Communist. This was literally a dead issue—White had died in August 1948—but because the FBI report had been forwarded to Truman, the former president was subpoenaed to testify before HUAC. He refused to appear and denied that White had helped the Communists. White did seem an unlikely Communist, and Brownell's revelation aroused skeptical responses from reporters. But the evidence is strong that he was right: White did supply the Communists with documents.[8] The second charge, that Robert Oppenheimer was a security risk, was definitely false. Oppenheimer had done nothing to compromise U.S. security; the only basis for the charge was that in opposing U.S. development of a hydrogen bomb he was undercutting administration policy. Nevertheless, Eisenhower allowed Strauss to suspend him from government work in the hopes of keeping McCarthy from investigating the case. McCarthy had in fact made a buffoon of himself earlier in the year by allowing his aide Roy Cohn to wander on a feckless tour of U.S. embassies in Europe with the handsome young G. David Schine; it was Schine's induction into the Army and the homosexual Cohn's attempt to get him exempted from ordinary duty that began McCarthy's feud against the Army.

The result was the ludicrous spectacle of the Army-McCarthy hearings, televised from April to June 1954. McCarthy's great grievance was the promotion of a left-wing dentist at Fort Monmouth, New Jersey; the Army's complaint was that Cohn had sought special treatment for Schine. The hearings were conducted by Karl Mundt of South Dakota, a champion in his home state's specialty of high-school-style debating, whose ham-handed partiality to McCarthy made both of them seem ridiculous. In Richard Rovere's words, he left McCarthy "above, or outside, any system of order, of fair play, of decency, or even simulated respect. It was for him to throw the sessions into confusion whenever he chose and for others to make no effort to apply the tests of germaneness and truthfulness."[9] The impression made by the hearings on the public was especially strong because 1954 was the first year a majority of American households, 55%, had television sets: the number had risen rapidly from 9% in 1950 to 23% in 1951, 34% in 1952, and 44% in 1953, and would rise to 64% in 1955, 71% in 1956, 77% in 1957, 82% in 1958, 83% in 1959, and 87% in 1960.[10] For those able to watch, the Army-McCarthy hearings provided a vivid contrast to Estes Kefauver's serious-minded but thrilling exposés of the connections between gangsters like Frank Costello and the Democratic machines of cities like New York and Chicago; they formed an even more vivid contrast with Richard Russell's untelevised hearings on the firing of MacArthur, information about which was limited to sober press releases. They contrasted also with the elevated and eloquent convention and campaign appearances of Dwight Eisenhower and Adlai Stevenson. McCarthy was feared by many politicians, who thought he had beaten Millard Tydings in Maryland in 1950 and William Benton in Connecticut in 1952 (though Tydings probably and Benton surely would have lost anyway). He was detested by those who thought (correctly) that by promoting conformity and punishing unorthodoxy the overeager housecleaning he inspired in the State Department and elsewhere prevented the government from getting good advice and diversity of opinion. He was seen by communities of intellectuals—Hollywood screenwriters and state university professors—as the symbol of an American desire to punish those with even vaguely left-wing views. He was able to terrify Washington for some time not because he had a wide following in the public[11] but because he was utterly unscrupulous, untethered to any truth, unhampered by any sense of fairness, undisciplined by any desire to accomplish any concrete goal, and backed by the Republican party. Not his ambition but his lack of ambition made him dangerous: he cared not at all for the good opinion of other politicians and so was not bound by the rules of civility and fair play that most politicians observe instinctively in their own self-interest. Most politicians know that if they do not play by the rules they will not be dealt into the next hand, but McCarthy didn't seem to care if he was dealt into the next hand. He would stop at nothing because he cared about nothing; and while politicians must have suspected that his claim on the public's attention would not last, they were afraid of being hurt while it did.

But his powers were overestimated. McCarthy himself, an easy winner in 1946 after he beat Robert LaFollette in the Republican primary, was reelected with only 54% of the vote in 1952, while Wisconsin was voting 61% for Eisenhower.

Only three Republican senators, all from sparsely populated western states which traditionally elected Democrats, ran further behind Eisenhower than McCarthy did.[12] In February 1954, Gallup found that the public had a favorable impression of McCarthy by only a 46%–38% margin; in March the percentages were reversed, with 38% favorable and 46% unfavorable; by April 1954, before the hearings began,[13] the 77% who were familiar with the hearings took Army Secretary Robert Stevens's side over McCarthy's by 46%–23%, and by a 43%–17% margin they said McCarthy's support would make them less rather than more likely to support a candidate for Congress. By May, 87% had heard of the hearings; of those, Stevens came out ahead of McCarthy 40%–25%, and respondents had an unfavorable impression of the senator by a 35%–49% margin. In June that impression was unchanged (34%–45%), given the margin of error. By July respondents were saying by a 46%–34% margin that he should be replaced as subcommittee head. The televised hearings, it is generally thought, did McCarthy in. But he had already been repudiated by the voters before they began. By June 30, when Senator Ralph Flanders of Vermont moved to censure McCarthy, his support was limited to a core of Republican Asia Firsters. A committee headed by an uncowed conservative Republican, Arthur Watkins of Utah,[14] voted for censure; so did the whole Senate, in December 1954, by a 67–22 margin.

VI

McCarthy's destruction was an arresting spectacle. But it was less important than Eisenhower's consistent repudiation of the Asia First policy of the Taft Republicans, for whom McCarthy was an unwitting front man. Eisenhower cut American losses in Korea and continued American involvement in NATO. He presented to the world not the truculent face the Asia Firsters would have liked, but the image of a man of peace, in his April 1953 speech a month after Stalin's death and again in his "atoms for peace" speech to the United Nations in December 1953, when he called for international control of nuclear energy. He cut military spending and confined aggressive American military action to covert initiatives, which were successful in Iran in August 1953 and Guatemala in July 1954 without being identified as U.S. operations.

At the same time he steadily deflected pressure from the Asia Firsters for military intervention. In April 1954, Admiral Arthur Radford, chairman of the Joint Chiefs of Staff, recommended U.S. intervention on the side of the French in Vietnam; in May he and others called once again for American forces to relieve the siege of Dien Bien Phu. Eisenhower refused. In June top officials in the administration called for American intervention on the grounds that the Chinese air force was about to be involved. Instead, Eisenhower urged the French to abandon Vietnam and accept a partition with the Communists, as they did in the Geneva conference in July. In September, when Eisenhower was vacationing in his wife's home town of Denver, his top advisers called for an American military response—perhaps even the use of nuclear weapons—when the Chinese Communists began shelling the Nationalist-held islands of Quemoy and Matsu just off the coast. Again Eisenhower declined, as he did in November when American fliers were jailed as spies by the Chinese Communists. "Five times in one year," Stephen Ambrose summarizes, "the experts advised the President to launch an atomic strike against China. Five times he said no."[15] These decisions were made not noisily but quietly; some were known only in the internal counsels of the administration, some justified publicly in press conferences. In an article in *Life* in 1955, John Foster Dulles boasted that the nation had gone three times "to the brink of war," and he was attacked for what the Democrats called brinkmanship. But the important thing was that the nation never went over the brink.

Many Republicans were intensely dissatisfied with Eisenhower's foreign policy. But the Asia Firsters, who had attacked so bitterly Truman's public and explicit decisions to limit the war in Korea, were not able to attack publicly Eisenhower's quieter and implicit decisions not to go to war against China or in Vietnam. And at home they were frustrated by Eisenhower's quiet but resolute refusal to roll back the New Deal. These conservative Republicans had neither appealing arguments nor, after Taft's death and McCarthy's debacle, spokesmen who could command much attention. Nevertheless, they cherished a sour sense of betrayal, the spirit of which comes out in the statement by Robert Welch, founder of the John Birch Society, that Eisenhower was a conscious agent of the Communist conspiracy. Like Eisenhower's aide Arthur Larson, who after leaving government wrote a book extolling "modern Republicanism," the president and the Republicans around him saw as the only path to victory for their party a Europe First policy and acceptance of the New Deal—policies which found much stronger public acceptance in the middle 1950s than they had a dozen years before. But there was never really any possibility of uniting the entire Republican party behind these policies, nor was it entirely clear that even with such unity the Republican party would have generally prevailed when the Democrats' advantages were so great. In any case, it was apparent before the end of the second year of the Eisenhower administration that the Republicans would not displace the Democrats from their position as the stronger of the two major parties.

27

※》》 《《

Desegregation

On the third Monday of May 1954 the Supreme Court finally handed down its decision in the school desegregation cases it had been considering since June 1952. The court, led since the death of Chief Justice Fred Vinson in September 1953 by former California Governor Earl Warren, surprised almost everyone. Not only did it overturn, as expected, the 1896 decision allowing "separate but equal" schools, but its decision that legal segregation of public schools was unconstitutional was unanimous. The court specifically deferred until its next term the fashioning of a remedy, and the public reaction was cautious. In some border states, such as Kansas, where the original *Brown* v. *Board of Education* case was brought, and in the District of Columbia, which was the subject of a separate case, the system of legal segregation was quickly dismantled. White southerners were alarmed but had reason to hope that the court would order nothing more than symbolic integration—the admission of a few blacks to white schools for special reasons, as had been ordered in southern state-supported law schools, for example. Northerners who supported or did not strongly oppose the decision could reflect that integration had proved feasible in the armed services. President Eisenhower, who had hoped the Supreme Court would maintain the old separate-but-equal doctrine, announced only that he would obey the law, declining to say he approved of it.

The *Brown* decision was recognized as momentous at the time; but it was not as central to the progress of civil rights as many since have regarded it, and it was by no means the most effective advance in civil rights. The idea has grown up that American progress in civil rights was made mostly by the courts. But the historical record shows otherwise. The prime movers for civil rights were black Americans, protesting unfair treatment, demanding change, and threatening often dire consequences if change was not made. To those demands politicians responded, as did the courts less often and less effectively. Thus A. Philip Randolph used the threats of a march on Washington in June 1941 and civil disobedience of the draft in July 1948 to get Franklin Roosevelt to establish a Fair Employment Practices Commission and to force Harry Truman to ban discrimination in the armed services; and if the former had a disappointingly limited effect, the latter eventually had the effect of making the military the most integrated segment of American life. Similarly, public pressure from blacks and competition among politicians for pro-civil rights votes helped prepare the way for the Brooklyn Dodgers' Branch Rickey to make Jackie Robinson the first Negro major-league baseball player in April 1947.[1] The major progress in desegregating schools in the 1950s occurred when politicians decided to follow the *Brown* decision voluntarily; not until the late 1960s did the Supreme Court force large-scale integration on unwilling southern school boards. In the meantime, black protests—beginning with the Montgomery bus boycott in December 1955, continuing through the Freedom Rides of May 1961, and culminating in the Selma march of March 1965—moved Democratic administrations to propose and bipartisan majorities in Congress to pass two landmark pieces of legislation: the Civil Rights Act of 1964, which effectively integrated almost all public accommodations and a great many workplaces in the United States, and the Voting Rights Act of 1965, which effectively guaranteed blacks the ballot in the South and removed from the political system the distortion created by the purposeful and sometimes terroristic exclusion of blacks from the polling booth.

The school desegregation decision struck a South that was changing, both politically and economically. It was still low-wage territory, but it no longer formed an utterly separate labor market, cut off from the rest of the United States as if by a steel curtain. On the contrary, hundreds of thousands of southerners, both black and white, were moving north and west every year, providing low-wage labor in the fast-growing parts of the nation as immigrants from southern and eastern Europe had before 1924. The national minimum wage had pushed up southern labor costs, and federal farm subsidies, especially of cotton, had helped to finance the mechanization which was greatly reducing the demand for farm laborers and thus had undermined the sharecropper system. Also, some southern whites were actively encouraging the migration of Negroes northward. They could see the progress of civil rights nationally, and they feared the consequences if blacks got the vote, especially in states like Mississippi (still 49% black in 1940) and South Carolina.

The result was one of the largest internal migrations in American history: in the 1950s about one out of six southern blacks left the South.[2] The total black out-migration from the South was 1.6 million in the 1940s and 1.5 million in the 1950s.[3] This was especially a movement of young people. Every spring, after graduation ceremonies at the black high schools of coastal South Carolina, many students would get up early, dress in their best clothes, pack a lunch of fried chicken, and climb into the bus known as the "chicken bone special," headed for New York or Philadelphia. Mississippi blacks flocked to Chicago, Alabama blacks to Detroit, Louisiana blacks to California, in well-trodden paths where youngsters would seek out family friends and former neighbors to get their start in the new big cities. The South they were leaving behind was becoming less black: a region which was 25% black in 1930 and 24% black in 1940 was 22% black in 1950, 20% black in 1960, 19% black in 1970, and 18% black in 1980.[4] Mississippi changed from 49% black in 1940 to 36% by 1970, South Carolina from 43% black in 1940 to 30% in 1970, in trends which were well-established by 1954.

To white southerners in 1954, desegregation was supposedly unthinkable and disgusting (the word *integration* was not even in common use at the time), and southern customs—of blacks being addressed by first name and showing deference to whites, of total segregation in public facilities and total exclusion of blacks from voting, of beatings and even lynchings as the penalty for any supposed deviation from this unwritten code—remained well established in southern cities as well as the countryside.[5] The old mores were vividly illustrated in August 1956, when Emmet Till, a Chicago seventh-grader visiting relatives in Mississippi, was beaten and killed by whites for the offense of saying "Bye, baby," to a white woman. The whites were tried—something new for Mississippi—and the case attracted national attention, but they were acquitted.[6]

The response of white southerners in the military earlier in the 1950s and in public accommodations and workplaces after the 1964 act shows that integration was accepted far more readily in many settings than had been expected. But the strategy of the civil rights litigators and of the courts ruling on cases brought before them focused on the schoolhouse, and this proved particularly difficult to integrate. Parents are protective of children, and children, especially teen-agers, are apt to reflect in exaggerated form the prejudices and cruelties of those around them. It is possible that if the Supreme Court had insisted on more rapid integration of the schools and if President Eisenhower had backed up this insistence with his own moral authority, it might have been accepted as integration of the military was: but it was not tried. It is important to remember, however, that the white South paused for several years before responding with violent animosity toward school desegregation. The Southern Manifesto opposing desegregation was not promulgated and signed by southern politicians until March 1956, and even then was not subscribed to by Tennessee's Estes Kefauver and Albert Gore and Texas's Lyndon Johnson; the Little Rock crisis, in which Eisenhower sent in federal troops to enforce the integration of Central High School, did not occur until September 1957; Virginia's "massive resistance" program was not established by Senator Harry Byrd and his machine until 1958. Would a more rapid and resolute determination by the courts and the executive branch have made a difference? It is not a question that was much explored then, but the prompt compliance with the public accommodations section of the Civil Rights Act of 1964 and with the Voting Rights Act of 1965 suggests that the answer might have been yes.

II

Politically, the black-led southern civil rights movement that began with the Montgomery bus boycott in December 1955 eventually changed the politics of the South—and of the nation. Before then, both parties had a mild incentive to favor civil rights. The issue was popular among Jewish voters, who formed a significant segment of the electorate in New York and smaller shares in closely contested states like Massachusetts, New Jersey, Pennsylvania, Illinois, and California, and among black voters, who with the internal migrations of the 1940s and 1950s were a fast-growing segment of the electorate in New York, Pennsylvania, Ohio, Michigan, and Illinois. The civil rights plank adopted by the 1948 Democratic convention after Hubert Humphrey's speech cost Truman the electoral votes of South Carolina, Alabama, Mississippi, and Louisiana, which were carried by Strom Thurmond; but Truman won the election, and the 39 electoral votes in these states were far fewer than the 211 in states where civil rights seemed to be a political asset. Aside from the Thurmond states, the South remained heavily Democratic except for Civil War Republican strength along the Appalachian spine and in a few odd counties elsewhere.

Then in 1952 the Eisenhower candidacy made serious inroads in those parts of the South with the greatest recent economic growth and the largest numbers of new residents (though most of them were from other parts of the South; the influence of transplanted Yankees on southern voting patterns was greatly exaggerated). Eisenhower beat Stevenson in Texas (where the Republican's support of state ownership of tidelands oil helped him), Tennessee (with its strong Republican base in east Tennessee), and Florida and Virginia (with their many new residents). He ran strongly throughout the South, which voted far less distinctly from the rest of the country than in any presidential election since Reconstruction. Civil rights were not really an issue: by personal conviction and political calculation, Eisenhower and Stevenson were less pro-civil rights than Dewey and Truman (or Nixon or Kennedy, for that matter), and neither mentioned the subject.

What was happening was that affluent southerners were moving toward supporting the Republicans, as affluent northerners tended to. This movement was noticeable primarily in the urban areas, which contained almost all the affluent population of the South. Eisenhower carried 51 of 126 southern congressional districts: outside Georgia and Alabama, where he was shut out completely, and Mississippi, where he carried 1 of 6 districts, he carried 50 southern districts to Stevenson's 51.[7] Of Eisenhower's 51 southern districts, only 10 elected Republican congressmen in 1952 and 1954; fully 22 did not even have a Republican candidate running in 1954, when Eisenhower's potential had been demonstrated. Republican victories in Charlotte and Roanoke in 1952 and Dallas and St. Petersburg in 1954 thus did not turn out to be harbingers of Republican victories in Newport News, Miami, Fort Lauderdale, New Orleans, Birmingham, Mobile, Little Rock, San Antonio, or Galveston. Instead, in 1954 the Eisenhower districts produced liberal Democratic freshmen who included a future speaker, Jim Wright of Fort Worth, and a future chairman of the Foreign Relations Committee, Dante Fascell of Miami. Incidentally, Republican opposition to one-person-one-vote, which helped them in the rural areas of the North, hurt them in the soon-to-boom cities of the South, as it did in the northern suburbs. Here Eisenhower's comment that the old-guard Republicans were the stupidest people he knew was apt.

So the South was on the verge of becoming a two-party region before the *Brown* decision and the Montgomery bus boycott sparked the reaction which, for a while, made of most white southerners a bloc which consistently supported the most anti-civil rights candidate, oscillating wildly between the parties or supporting independent candidates when necessary. With blacks effectively barred from voting in states where they formed large percentages of the population (Virginia, the Carolinas, Georgia, Alabama, Mississippi, Arkansas, Louisiana) and casting only a small percentage of votes in states where they were less numerous (Kentucky, Tennessee, Florida, Texas), this white anti-civil rights vote became the dominant vote in the South beginning with the Southern Manifesto of March 1956 and the Little Rock crisis of September 1957. In the short run, this vote strengthened local Democrats. Whereas Republicans were hurt by their association with Eisenhower judicial appointees who issued desegregation decisions and by Eisenhower's support (lukewarm as it was) of civil rights laws and his (exceedingly reluctant) dispatch of troops to Little Rock, local Democrats found it easy to dissociate themselves from distant and little-known figures like Stevenson and Humphrey. Thus Republicans found it impossible to extend their 1952 and 1954 successes in the urban affluent South into poorer and more rural districts.

That effect might have continued if Nixon had been elected president in 1960 and had conspicuously supported civil rights legislation as Kennedy did in 1960. After all, Republicans were among the most faithful supporters of civil rights in Congress—not only northeastern liberals like Jacob Javits of New York but border-state moderates like John Sherman Cooper and Thruston Morton of Kentucky and midwestern conservatives like William McCulloch and Clarence Brown of Ohio. But in the long run it was the national Democrats who became most closely associated with civil rights and thus became for a time anathema to most white southern voters.

None of this underlying change was apparent to most practicing politicians in the middle 1950s. The *Brown* decision and the Montgomery bus boycott would change the way millions of Americans lived much more profoundly than would most of the issues the politicians cared about. But for the politicians these great events were irritating digressions from the ongoing course of political affairs, requiring changes in strategy and adjustments in tactics—inexplicable intrusions in an orderly world they thought they understood. The emerging civil rights issue widened the already existing gap between southern and northern Democrats and threatened the local base of many southern Democrats who were leaders in the Congress. At the same time, however, it denied the Eisenhower Republicans any chance at becoming a national majority party, since to do so they had to make gains in the South—gains which, ironically, the success of the Republicans in 1952 and their status as the national incumbent party rendered impossible in the years after *Brown*, Montgomery, and Little Rock.

28

-»» «-

Split Ticket

T he 1954 election seemed to turn on the economy, and specifically on the mild recession, the first in the Republican years. After government spending was reduced at the end of the Korean war, there was a pause in economic growth. But it turned out to be only a pause. It had the good and appreciated effect of bringing down inflation from the wartime levels, and it was pretty much over by election time. In fact, the 1954 election results were nearly a carbon copy of the 1952 results, with one very important difference: the Democrats ran just enough better to capture control of both houses of Congress.

The difference came not in the Civil War borderlands, where changes in House seats had been concentrated in the years before the Second New Deal, but in the borderlands between the central cities and the countryside, the metropolitan frontier in the suburbs. The great upward mobility of Americans which had begun during the war and accelerated after 1947 was changing the country. The sons and daughters of factory workers and immigrants, who had been sent to bed hungry in dingy apartments and unpainted rowhouses during the 1930s, were now moving out into new Cape Cods nine miles out from where they had grown up or into newly laid-out subdivisions, the front steps of the houses still covered with mud, a whole county farther out than they had ever imagined they would live. Outer-city and suburban constituencies which had been filled with the descendants of small-town Protestant Republicans when the war began were now filling up with Catholic and Jewish Democrats; people who revered the Republican party as the voice of Yankee ingenuity and probity were now in danger of being outnumbered by young husbands and wives who may have voted for General Eisenhower but whose political allegiance still went most strongly to Franklin D. Roosevelt. In the images summoned up by Norman Rockwell in his *Saturday Evening Post* covers of the 1950s, America was still a country of small-town Protestants (although Rockwell was himself a strong liberal and produced moving paintings of young blacks desegregating schools). But as the quietly shifting political balance suggested, America was increasingly becoming a country of descendants of the great migrations of 1840–1924, even as they came to occupy the neighborhoods once considered the precincts of "native" Americans.

Nationally the Democrats gained only 21 House seats over 1952, a gain partially offset by the Republicans' gain of 5. But only 6 of the Democrats' gains were in the Civil War borderlands, while 11 of them were in metropolitan and industrial areas. Just north of Boston the seat including the once heavily Yankee suburbs of Malden and Medford fell to Torbert Macdonald, a college roommate of Senator John Kennedy. In the straight grid streets of northwest Detroit, Martha Griffiths, a law partner of Governor G. Mennen Williams, used a house trailer to campaign among housewives and beat Republican Charles Oakman, who had won this new seat two years before. In Union County, New Jersey, just outside industrial Elizabeth, where the divided highway U.S. 22 streaked through a landscape of garish new stores and drive-in restaurants, this bellwether area which had helped elect Democratic Governor Robert Meyner in 1953 proceeded in 1954 to replace liberal Republican Congressman Clifford Case, who ran successfully for senator, with Democrat Harrison Williams, who would later be his Senate colleague for twenty years. Such results in such districts, multiplied in elections for the next ten years, might be called the Democrats' demographic dividend. Franklin Roosevelt won the allegiance in the 1930s of the Americans who had the most children, and as those children moved up in the world and out from their cities they retained a loyalty to Roosevelt's party which was essential to the success of politicians like Kennedy and Macdonald, Williams and Griffiths, Meyner and Williams.

This demographic dividend[1] was particularly notable not only in the major industrial states where Roosevelt had been strong but also in the northern tier of states from New England and upstate New York through the Upper Midwest to the West Coast, an area which from the Civil War up through the 1940s had been the Republican heartland. In the major industrial states Democrats fielded strong candidates in 1954 and won major governorships: Averell Harriman in New York,[2] George Leader in Pennsylvania, Frank Lausche again in Ohio, G. Mennen Williams, who won reelection by a wide margin in Michigan. In the northern tier states the key was the emergence of young liberals of exceptional skill and honesty who essentially created state Democratic parties in their own image. They included Williams; Edmund Muskie, who was elected governor of Maine in 1954; and Hubert Humphrey, who was reelected to the Senate from Minnesota while Orville Freeman was elected governor and Eugene McCarthy and John Blatnik were elected overwhelmingly in what had recently been Republican House seats. In Wisconsin the collapse of Joseph McCarthy's fortunes was accompanied by a surge for the Democrats which yielded 2 new House seats, produced gains of between 7 and 13 percentage points in the other districts, all of which would be won sooner or later by Democrats, and gave a start to the careers of Democrats like William Proxmire, Gaylord Nelson, and Robert Kastenmeier. Chicago and the less affluent and exclusive Cook County suburbs produced a surge in Democratic votes; so did Iowa and the Dakotas. On the West Coast, Democrats made major gains in Oregon and even in some districts in California, where the cross-filing system made gains difficult.

So while the Republicans failed to take much advantage of their window of opportunity in the South, the Democrats were making good use of their demographic dividend in the northern tier and the metropolitan frontier. These areas, where the appeal of Eisenhower's type of Republicanism might have been thought to be strongest, seemed to be generating successful politicians who were liberal Democrats rather than liberal Republicans—a harbinger of the trend which would make this one-time Republican heartland the least reliably Republican part of the country, even as the country was going consistently Republican in presidential elections.[3] In the short run, while the white southern reaction to the civil rights movement was stymying Republicans' chances to make gains in the South, the Democrats' demographic dividend and their crop of young liberal politicians were stymying Republicans' chances to make gains in the northern tier and in major metropolitan areas. These two countervailing trends—for the anti-civil rights Democrats being elected in the South had little if anything in common with the liberal Democrats being elected farther north—frustrated any chance of creating a national Republican majority.

II

This situation reflected not only the greater suppleness and adaptability of the party out of national power, but also the reluctance of the leader of the party in power to challenge the fundamental premises of the New Deal, which underneath the surface of Republican victories had strong popular allegiance. Eisenhower was convinced that he could make no significant change in the nation's basic Democratic party preference. After the 1954 election his brother Edgar upbraided him for pursuing policies no better than Truman's. Eisenhower replied in a bristling letter, "Should any political party attempt to abolish Social Security, unemployment insurance, and eliminate labor laws and farm programs, you would not hear again of that party in our political history." Of the "splinter group" who believe you can do such things, he said, referring to many of his most fervent fellow Republicans, "their number is negligible and they are stupid."[4] These were objections not of principle but of practical politics, in contrast to Eisenhower's quarrel with the Asia First Republicans. Eisenhower seemed to be conceding that the conservative position could not soon command a national majority; and he seemed unable to prevent the realignment of the national parties, outside the South, along the liberal and conservative lines which Roosevelt among others had mused about in the 1940s and had supposed would make the Democrats a permanent majority.

But as events turned out, the liberal label which was so popular when Eisenhower entered politics in 1952 had become highly unpopular by the time he died in 1969. And Eisenhower may have been a better political prophet than he at first appeared. He scorned those who wanted to abolish the regulatory commissions or discourage labor unions, and he told one correspondent, "I must say that if you think you are going to get rid of the graduated income tax, you are certainly planning to live far longer than I am."[5] But in fact those who did live two decades longer than Eisenhower would see the abolition of some regulatory commissions, a sharp decline of the labor union movement, and the abandonment of the steeply graduated income tax in return for elimination of tax preferences in the 1986 tax reform act. Eisenhower knew that he was governing a country in which the experiences of depression and war—the very war that was responsible for his international renown—had built up a demand for an active, intervention-minded government, and he suspected correctly that it would take many years of peacetime before Americans' appetite for big government would be sated. He could hope that his success at governing would create majorities for his party. But he could understand how it might not, and he did not in any case want a complete triumph for the conservative Taft Republicans, whose domestic policies he considered politically unsustainable and whose foreign policy he considered dangerously wrong on the merits. It should be remembered that Eisenhower endorsed Barry Goldwater's candidacy with some force in July 1964, when the Asia First issues had long since been rendered moot, even though others who fancied themselves Eisenhower Republicans refused to back the party's ticket. Eisenhower may have realized that a party which backed the positions he believed in—cutbacks of domestic programs, an assertive Europe First foreign policy—could not win a majority in his lifetime but at the same time hoped that it might do so some time in the future, as it arguably did in the 1980s under the leadership of two Republicans, Ronald Reagan and George Bush, who found it not inconsistent to back Goldwater in the 1960s, Eisenhower in the 1950s, and in Reagan's case, Roosevelt in the 1930s and 1940s.

III

On September 23, 1955, while vacationing in his wife's home town of Denver, the sixty-five-year-old president suffered a heart attack which threatened to change the political firmament. Experienced, popular, able to claim he had achieved peace and prosperity, Eisenhower was a strong candidate for reelection even in a country which had just demonstrated, in only slightly less favorable circumstances, its preference for the Democrats. Even before the heart attack Eisenhower had mused about retiring, though no one can be sure how seriously. Now his candidacy had to be considered doubtful. Press Secretary James Hagerty, a seasoned reporter and brilliant manipulator of news, decreed that full information about Eisenhower's recovery would be given out, including details of the presidential bowel movements. Only a decade before, the physical deterioration of the sixty-two-year-old Franklin Roosevelt had been covered up during the 1944 election by all those around him—as Republicans bitterly remembered. Hagerty's decision set a precedent followed by succeeding presidents, except for the nondisclosure of the various ailments of John Kennedy.

If Eisenhower did not run, who would? The Republicans were left with no strong candidates. Richard Nixon, at forty-two, was limited in experience and abrasively partisan. William Knowland, who had already let it be known that he would run if Eisenhower did not, was an advocate of unpopular policies and a clumsy political maneuverer at best. ("In his case," Eisenhower wrote in his diary, "there seems to be no final answer to the question, 'How stupid can you get?' ")[6] Earl Warren (who, like Knowland, began his public career in Oakland, California) was not about to resign as chief justice. Thomas Dewey was happily making money as the lead partner in a Wall Street law firm.

As for the Democrats, they continued as in the 1930s and 1940s to produce only a few plausible presidential nominees. Adlai Stevenson had shown greater strengths as a leader in 1952 than his résumé entitled anyone to expect. Averell Harriman had as much experience in foreign and domestic policy as anyone on the political scene after Eisenhower. Estes Kefauver was well known as an opponent of crime, political bosses, and big business. But the first two were associated with what not only Eisenhower but most Americans regarded as the foreign policy blunders of the Truman administration, the loss of China and the war in Korea, and Kefauver was regarded by Washington insiders as plainly lacking in presidential stature. Eisenhower was not speaking entirely for himself or expressing only partisan sentiments when he said, "I just hate to turn this country back into the hands of Stevenson, Harriman, and Kefauver."[7]

The president remained in the hospital in Denver until he flew back to Washington on November 11; not until mid-December did he resume working regularly in the White House. In late 1955 most Americans expected he would not run again. The likely nominees seemed to be Stevenson, who had the support of about half the Democrats, and Nixon, who had the support of only about one-quarter of the Republicans in a multi-candidate field but whose strongest rival, Earl Warren, seemed unlikely to run.[8] Stevenson announced his candidacy in November 1955, four days after Eisenhower left Denver; Kefauver announced a month later. The general expectation was that the Democratic nominee would be elected. Stevenson led Nixon 50%–44% and Kefauver led him 48%–45% in Gallup polls in early November; Stevenson's lead widened to 55%–38% in early January 1956, while Nixon was dropping even in polls for the Republican nomination (though no serious rival was emerging).[9] In a country where membership in heavily Democratic labor unions was at its peak and populations in machine Democratic central cities had only just begun to decline, in a country full of newly successful people who credited the Democratic party for their own success as well as for keeping their parents from starvation, in this basically Democratic country, a successful Republican administration seemed about to be replaced by a solidly Democratic government.

But as the weeks went by, Eisenhower's health visibly returned and his determination to keep the Democrats out grew. He summoned up the energy to present a serious legislative program to Congress in January 1956, and he made it plain by his activity that he was not interested in leaving office. Voters' expectations changed: 56% of Americans in early January, 60% in early February, and 72% by mid-February expected him to run. His formal announcement on Leap Year Day, February 29, came as little surprise.

IV

The 1956 elections featured a party system vastly altered from just a half-decade before. As late as 1950, the vast majority of American voters cast straight-ticket ballots, and their choice of party in congressional or even local elections was an accurate gauge of their feelings toward the incumbent president and his party. It had not always been so: in the 1920s Americans were moving toward split-ticket voting, and splits within the parties, notably the split between regular and progressive Republicans, were understood and responded to by the voters. But Franklin Roosevelt's dominance of the political scene, his controversial domestic and foreign policies, tended to organize American politics on straight-ticket two-party lines. The politics of economic redistribution which emerged suddenly in the spring of 1935 did not entirely replace the traditional party alignments dividing voters according to region, race, ethnic group, and cultural attitudes. But it did tidy up political alignments to the point that in strong Democratic years the Democrats carried overwhelming majorities of blue-collar workers and in strong Republican years the Republicans carried overwhelming majorities of professional and affluent voters.

Suddenly in 1952, and more gradually through the 1950s, this situation began to change. In the 1952 election the phrase "I'm voting for the man, not the party" became common as some 5 million Americans, nearly 10% of the electorate, voted for Eisenhower but not for a Republican candidate for the House. In the next three elections, that proclivity toward ticket-splitting was reinforced, as an electorate which throughout gave Eisenhower high job approval ratings still elected Democratic Congresses three times in a row. At the time this ticket-splitting was seen, with considerable justification, as the result of Eisenhower's personal popularity and a persistent New Deal Democratic majority. But the very persistence of ticket-splitting, and the generally high level of satisfaction with the government it produced, tended to erode party allegiances, which in any case were likely to grow less pronounced as the truly divisive issues of war and economic redistribution receded farther into the past.

The losers in the long run were both the major parties: if the Eisenhower landslide of 1956 did not produce an enduring Republican majority, neither did the Johnson landslide of 1964 produce a Democratic majority capable of enduring much longer than the next off-year election (in which Republicans won a majority of votes for the House outside the South). Eisenhower's success did not deprive the Democrats of the ability to win majorities in national elections. But it contributed to depriving them of inevitable national majorities. The party which surely would have won the presidential election of 1952 but for the disasters of China and Korea only barely won the election of 1960 and, after what turned out to be an evanescent triumph in 1964, lost five of the six next presidential elections. Yet the party which won those elections was able to win control of the House not at all and of the Senate only three times in the eighteen elections after what had seemed on its face to be the across-the-board triumph of the Republicans in 1952.

29

➤➤➤ ⋘⋘⋘

Peace and Prosperity

By February 1956, Eisenhower dreaded the prospect of another Republican Congress, where important chairmanships would be held by members of the old guard who opposed the programs he cared most about. He expected the Democrats to regain control of Congress and was careful in his campaigning not to promote the Republican party's chances to pick up seats.[1] In 1954 the Republican party organizations in the South—many of them amounting to paper entities or filled with old-fashioned patronage seekers—had failed to field candidates in many districts Eisenhower had carried, and Republicans had lost seats in the outer reaches and inner suburbs of central cities, the metropolitan frontierland of America. In 1956, when Eisenhower was running more strongly in the South, Republicans had even fewer candidates there and saw several lose by close margins[2] which surely could have been turned around by a stronger party effort. Similarly, no major effort was launched in the urban areas. One reason the Republicans had problems fielding strong candidates was that in late 1955 most politicians assumed Eisenhower would not run again and the ticket would be weak. But even when it became clear in early 1956 that he would run, no major effort was made.

At the same time, no large group of Eisenhower Republican candidates arose out of the local politics in most states. Starting in the 1950s and continuing even through most of the 1970s and 1980s, strong new candidates, politically adept young men and women, often appeared and ran and won in the unlikeliest of constituencies: many more of these self-starting candidates were liberal Democrats than Republicans. In Ohio, state Republican chairman Ray Bliss made a point of cultivating such candidates, running the gregarious plumber Bill Ayres in Akron and holding that basically Democratic seat for twenty years starting in 1950, pushing the radio-voiced Frank Bow in the Canton district, helping war veteran Albert Baumhart in the industrial Lake Erie district west of Cleveland. But few other Republican politicians were so resourceful. The typical Republican congressman remained a small-town lawyer or businessman from a stagnant-population district in that vast crescent which marks the migration of Yankee stock from New England through the Great Lakes states and Iowa and Kansas west to California: typically, he was the product of college fraternities and small-town service clubs. Hardened by twenty years out of power, angry that the majority of his fellow Americans did not seem to share his views, reflexively opposed to all

283

increases in federal spending and suspicious of all American involvements abroad, he felt more attachment to Robert Taft than to Dwight Eisenhower. He had been wrong about all the major issues of the last two decades: wrong when he assumed that free markets would bring the country out of the depression, wrong when he assumed that protective tariffs would ensure American prosperity, wrong when he believed that war in Europe could be avoided, wrong when he believed that America had been betrayed by Communists and enemies within, wrong most of all when he believed that small-town Yankee Protestants were still the typical Americans, that it was still entirely their country.

Eisenhower, whose career after all had prospered with the vast expansion of government and with American involvement in Europe, was prepared to concede the Republican errors on all these issues, though it is not clear how well he appreciated America's cultural variety; but he could find few Republican politicians across the nation willing to follow him and take the personal risk of running for office. It was clear, of course, that Eisenhower was more popular than his party: his job approval rating was hovering around 70% in 1956, while the Republicans were rated as no better than even with the Democrats on "keeping the country prosperous" and had a rather unimpressive edge, 36%–18%, on "keeping the nation out of war."[3] Eisenhower understood that he was the beneficiary of a strong desire to "vote for the man, not the party," that he had won in 1952 largely because of ticket-splitters, that he would win again by running far ahead of his party. This situation evidently suited him: Eisenhower was the only twentieth-century president who made no effort to help his party and even hoped it would not run well.[4] The conservative Republicans who called him a traitor to their party's cause had some reason to do so.

II

Yet Eisenhower was not passive as a leader on policy. His legislative program for 1956 was as aggressive and active a program as any in his years in office— intended, surely, to demonstrate that he had recovered from the heart attack and was on the job again full time. Yet it also provided little or no partisan advantage for Republicans.

One of the first items was deregulation of natural gas prices. Opinion on this issue was split along geographical lines: gas-producing states were for it and gas-consuming states against. Eisenhower's great ally was Senate Majority Leader Lyndon Johnson and their mutual friend Sid Richardson, probably the richest oilman in the 1950s and the founder of the Bass family fortune, which was one of the nation's biggest agglomerations of capital in the 1980s. It was a heavily lobbied bill—too heavily. South Dakota's Francis Case, the fussiest nit-picker in the Senate,[5] announced that he had been offered $2,500 in cash to support the bill, and so switched from his previous support to opposition. The bill passed both houses, but Eisenhower was unwilling to give the impression that such contro-versial legislation, which might cost many consumers money, had been obtained through bribery, and so vetoed it in February 1956 over the vehement objections of Johnson and Richardson.

Veto was also the result of Eisenhower's Soil Bank, a proposal to withdraw highly erodible farmland from production. Conservatives like Agriculture Secretary Ezra Taft Benson were dubious about using money for this purpose. But it had an appeal to Eisenhower, who had grown up in a small, tree-shaded town on the sun-drenched, windblown plains of Kansas, and it addressed the nagging problem of farm surpluses. Farm prices tend to be highest during wartime and to fall thereafter; and in the economic recovery which followed the end of the Korean war, farm prices and incomes fell; production and government subsidies rose, and many families were squeezed off their ancestral land. The Farm Belt was the one part of the economy which was ailing, and the Democrats, remembering their success there in 1948, hoped to make farm issues a centerpiece of their fall campaign. So in Congress they attached to Eisenhower's Soil Bank bill a provision raising subsidies to 90% of parity. In response, Eisenhower vetoed the whole bill in April, hurting himself and his party in the Farm Belt without helping him perceptibly anywhere else.

Eisenhower's big success in Congress in 1956 was the Interstate Highway program, which like the St. Lawrence Seaway was a public works project of the same magnitude as Roosevelt's. Yet he gained little political credit. It seemed counterintuitive to voters to credit the Republicans for a vast public spending project, and in fact Democrats gave it strong support in Congress. Although the federal government financed 90% of the cost of the new roads, it did so mechanically, by funneling gasoline tax revenues to the state highway departments, which were the creatures of state and local politics. There was no visible, and politically manipulative, national impresario of public works as Harry Hopkins had been in the 1930s.

The other two Eisenhower initiatives of 1956 were frustrated by his usual allies, the southern Democrats. To his school construction bill Adam Clayton Powell, the flamboyant congressman-minister from Harlem, attached one of his Powell Amendments banning racial discrimination. Many Republicans supported this provision, and Eisenhower was eager for Powell's endorsement in the fall (which he got); but it prompted southern Democrats to oppose the bill, which died. The other initiative they killed outright: statehood for Hawaii, with its nonwhite majority.

III

"Here, my friends, on the prairies of Illinois and the Middle West we can see a long way in all directions," Governor Adlai Stevenson had said in welcoming delegates to the Democratic convention in Chicago in July 1952. "Here there are no barriers, no defenses, to ideas and to aspirations. We want none; we want no shackles on the mind or the spirit, no rigid patterns of thought, and no iron conformity. We want only the faith and conviction that triumph in fair and free contest." This was the speech that made Stevenson a national figure, and these words were his hearty response to McCarthyism—and a celebration of his country. He recalled that "until four years ago the people of Illinois had chosen but three Democratic governors in a hundred years. One was John Peter Altgeld, whom the great Illinois poet, Vachel Lindsay, called the Eagle Forgotten; he was an immigrant; one was Edward F. Dunne, whose parents came here from the old sod of Ireland; and the last was Henry Horner, but one generation removed from Germany. John Peter Altgeld, my friends, was a Protestant; Governor Dunne was a Catholic; Henry Horner was a Jew. And that, my friends, is the American story, written by the Democratic party here on the plains of Illinois."[6] But after his 1952 defeat, Stevenson's celebration of flesh-and-blood Americans was replaced by criticism and abstractions. "While I am not in favor of maladjustment, I view this cultivation of neutrality, this breeding of moral neuters, this hostility to eccentricity and controversy, with grave misgiving," he told a commencement audience at Smith College in 1955. America, he said, needed "not just better groupers and conformers (to casually coin a couple of fine words) but more idiosyncratic, unpredictable characters."[7] Stevenson the candidate who was striving to win celebrated the American character; Stevenson the candidate who had lost was criticizing the American character. Stevenson's 1952 celebration of nonconformity was a response to McCarthy and to more responsible critics of the Democratic administration who nevertheless insisted on purging from government those who did not share accepted views. It was the voice of a civil libertarian—or of a politician determined to make civil libertarian views prevail. Stevenson's 1955 criticism of conformity was the voice of a cultural critic, of the intellectual gazing out of his book-lined apartment with grave misgivings at the cultural uniformity and proliferating affluent suburbs and gaudy, glittery styles—in furniture, cars, jewelry—of the 1950s. Yet these were the proximate consequences of Democratic policies and Democratic governance which celebrated the ordinary person, praised cultural unity, and made the achievement of material success for the masses its main policy goal.

In the years before Stevenson became a national figure, liberal politicians had celebrated "the people," their unsophisticated language and their average tastes: Franklin Roosevelt had delighted in serving hot dogs to the king and queen of England when they visited Hyde Park in 1939. Elitist tut-tutting at popular culture, to the extent it was identified with any political force, was associated with conservative Republicans, with their exacting Yankee cultural heritage and their plutocratic patronage of high culture and fine arts. Stevenson was the first leading Democratic politician to become a critic rather than a celebrator of middle-class American culture—the prototype of the liberal Democrat who would judge ordinary Americans by an abstract standard and find them wanting. Stevenson himself recognized the hazards of such an attitude for an American politician. When a woman assured him that all the thinking people were for him, he responded, "Yes, but I need to win a majority." "You educated the people through your campaign," another admirer told him. "But," replied Stevenson, "a lot of people flunked the course."[8] It is unthinkable that Franklin Roosevelt would ever have said those things, or that such thoughts would ever have crossed his mind.

Stevenson's attraction to those who thought of themselves as intellectuals and outsiders in American life was apparent even in the 1952 campaign, but it became much more pronounced after he lost. He became the favorite of, and drew into Democratic volunteer efforts, cadres of youngish, highly educated professionals and intellectuals who in their common fervor loved to be thought of as individualists in a nation of conformists. In late September 1952 columnist Stewart Alsop remarked "to a rising young Connecticut Republican"—his brother John, the party's 1962 candidate for governor—"that a good many intelligent people, who would be considered normally Republican, obviously admired Stevenson. 'Sure,' was the reply, 'all the eggheads love Stevenson. But how many eggheads do you think there are?' "[9] At the time Stevenson's appeal was by no means limited to "eggheads," as it came to be by 1960; but the notion of him as an intellectuals' candidate had taken firm root. Certainly he showed from the beginning a diffidence toward traditional campaign tactics, abjuring "false promises" and the like, and a fastidious disdain for rituals like handshaking, arguing that it did not engage voters' minds—and ignoring the obvious fact that in a democracy voting requires an emotional as well as an intellectual response. As James Q. Wilson has written, to the "amateur Democrats" who were drawn into politics by enthusiasm for Stevenson, he "seemed to be a liberal, but then Harry S. Truman and John F. Kennedy were conspicuously more 'liberal,' and neither of them generated the enthusiasm or dedication produced by Stevenson. He was urbane and witty, he often uttered speculative rather than declamatory remarks, he keenly felt the ambiguity of the political situation and the complexity of public issues. He generalized and dealt in abstractions, and his generalities and abstractions were fresher, more polished, less obvious and chauvinistic, than those of his predecessors. . . . To the intellectual reformer, the crucial factor was the conviction that in Stevenson's case, the classical urbanity was genuine and ingrained. . . . The theme that Stevenson was 'genuine' occurred repeatedly in the remarks of these men and women."[10]

The irony is that Stevenson himself was not much of an intellectual or a liberal; if Eisenhower's taste in books ran to westerns, Stevenson did not seem to read books at all, except perhaps the *Social Register*.[11] For his intellectual followers what was attractive was not his platform but his attitude—his irony, his skepticism, his critical detachment from the roaring course of American life. The young, highly educated people who rallied around him were often separated from most other Americans by their ironic attitudes, by their Jewishness or agnosticism, by their lack of connection to the webs of relationships which undergirded many individuals and guided some upward in the big cities of the day, by their rejection of American exceptionalism, the notion that the United States was specially good and decent; they sought from the seemingly diffident Stevenson not so much changes in public policy as validation of their own cultural stance. Certainly he was no brainier than Eisenhower, only more ironic; he was less stirring than

Roosevelt, though arguably more eloquent and in a style better fashioned for the television medium he professed to disdain. He was an indifferent student and less than an omnivorous reader, a product of the Princeton of the F. Scott Fitzgerald era who married one of Chicago's richest heiresses and became one of a dozen or so partners of one of its most elite law firms. His ideas, like those of most politicians, were derivative. But he did not share the liberal economic notions and disdain for businessmen of his own advisors John Kenneth Galbraith and Arthur Schlesinger, Jr. Unlike the Roosevelt of 1944 or the Truman of 1948, he had little desire to build additions onto the existing makeshift American welfare state, he wanted no increase in the power of the unions, and he had no notion whatever that the government should spend money to eliminate poverty. As a candidate for president in December 1955, he agreed that "moderation is the spirit of the times," a stance for which he was understandably attacked quickly by Mennen Williams and Averell Harriman. He was mistrusted, justly, by George Meany and Walter Reuther, the leaders of the AFL-CIO which was formed that month by the merger of the two rival labor organizations. On civil rights, all his instincts, like Eisenhower's, made him sympathize with white southerners, with this difference: Eisenhower looked at desegregation from the perspective of an ordinary parent whose child would have to go to a school with blacks, while Stevenson looked at it from the cooler, more elitist perspective of a southern community leader, a politician or a newspaper editor like so many of his friends, with a responsibility to keep a community quiet and peaceful enough to attract industry. His rival Estes Kefauver may not have been entirely sincere in his support of civil rights; he had opposed civil rights measures earlier in his career. But at least he was taking risks with his political base in Tennessee when he voted for civil rights bills, opposed civil rights filibusters, and with Albert Gore and Lyndon Johnson declined to sign the Southern Manifesto in 1956. Stevenson took no such risks. His base in 1956, in the Democratic convention and in the electoral college, was in the South, and he did nothing to jeopardize it in the course of the campaign.[12] He went so far in February 1956 as to oppose the use of federal troops to enforce school desegregation orders by federal courts—something which had not yet occurred, but which Eisenhower would reluctantly order in Little Rock in September 1957—and he came out in opposition to the Powell amendment. The greatest enthusiasm and most voluble support for Stevenson came from liberal professionals in big cities who fancied themselves intellectuals. But his largest bloc of votes came from ancestral Democrats in the Civil War borderlands, whose cultural attitudes could scarcely be more different.

Even Stevenson's critiques of the Eisenhower foreign policy were not as dazzling as they seemed to his aficionados at the time. They were more often shallow and contradictory. Since the American entry into World War I in 1917, the Democrats had been the more hawkish of the two parties: they represented the most hawkish region of the country, the South, and after the World War I they backed not only the League of Nations but interventionist policies in general more faithfully than did the Republicans. It was Democrats who in the late 1940s pushed unsuccessfully for universal military training, and the Democrats who in July 1950 used the Korean war as a pretext for putting into effect the recommendations of Paul Nitze's NSC 68, creating for the first time a peacetime American military establishment of mammoth size. It was Republicans, Dwight Eisenhower as well as Robert Taft, who wanted to reduce military spending, to rely more on the threat of nuclear weapons and the reality of covert action than on conventional forces, which cost money and tended toward the regimentation of American civilian life. Stevenson echoed the standard Democratic critique of Eisenhower's "New Look" for reductions and nuclear "massive retaliation" policies, but he also accused Eisenhower of being too provocative in the Formosa Straits.

Alarmed by evidence of danger from radioactive fallout, Stevenson called for an end to nuclear weapons testing in April 1956, but without making the sharp distinction between atmospheric tests (which did in fact produce dangerous fallout and were ended by the Test Ban Treaty ratified in September 1963) and underground tests (which were no threat to health but helped to maintain stable deterrence for more than thirty years after Stevenson's proposal). Then in the fall of 1956 he called for an end to the military draft. One policy threatened to undermine the American nuclear deterrent; the other, given the low manpower pool produced by the low birthrates of the 1930s, threatened to undermine the strength of American conventional forces. Thus Stevenson, a solid supporter of the Truman-Acheson hawkish Europe First policy in 1952 (and even of American intervention in Indochina),[13] gained a reputation on foreign policy as what would come to be called a dove. Just as he was the first leading Democrat to apply a critical eye to mainstream American culture, so Stevenson was the first leading Democrat since Wallace to argue for a less assertive foreign and defense policy. In these respects, though certainly not in his attitude toward civil rights, he was a precursor of the Democrats of the late 1960s and 1970s.

IV

It is hard to avoid the conclusion that one of the things which made Stevenson so attractive to so many of his enthusiasts is that he lost, that he was too good a man for what they regarded, judged against the socialism of Scandinavia or the high culture of western Europe or the purportedly virtuous emerging African and Asian nations, as an unsatisfactory country. Yet in 1956 Stevenson still wanted very much to win the presidency of the United States. He announced his candidacy in November 1955, when it was generally expected that Eisenhower could not run again, and he led Richard Nixon, the likeliest Republican candidate, smartly in the polls: 50%–44% just before his announcement, 53%–40% just after, 55%–38% by early January.[14] In fact, 1956 was probably the year Stevenson had intended all along to run. He had probably expected that he would then be completing his second term as governor, and the men who had seemed in early 1952 the likeliest winners of that year's presidential election would be reaching retirement age (Eisenhower turned sixty-six and Truman seventy-two in 1956; Taft would have turned sixty-seven and Barkley seventy-nine had they lived). With the Korean war over and the Truman-era corruption a dim memory, the Democrats could expect that demographic and attitudinal factors—the Democratic dividend from the New Deal investment—would give their party as much underlying strength in the late 1950s as it could ever expect to have.

But then it became plain that Eisenhower would run again. This must have been crushingly disappointing to Stevenson. Eisenhower's popularity was immense: he had a 70% job approval rating and in January 1956 was running ahead of Stevenson in the polls by 61%–35%—a full 23 percentage points better than Nixon was doing. Just adding the names of vice presidential candidates, as the March and May Gallup polls showed, cut 5 points off Eisenhower's support and added 5 points to the Democrats'. It is hard to see what issues Stevenson could have hoped would make a dent in Eisenhower's popularity, how he conceived there was a ghost of a chance to beat him. But he may have felt a responsibility to run, a sense that if anything happened to Eisenhower he had a duty to give the country better leadership than could be expected from the two likeliest alternatives, Nixon and Kefauver. His fears were certainly not without foundation. Eisenhower lived another dozen years, mostly in good health. But he suffered an attack of ileitis in June 1956 and had to undergo surgery, and his prospects for a strong recovery at that point looked chancy.

Stevenson's campaign was beset with other problems. Kefauver not only won the March 13 New Hampshire primary, where Stevenson was not entered, but also beat Stevenson 57%–43% the next week in Minnesota, where Stevenson's support from Senator Hubert Humphrey's and Governor Orville Freeman's Democratic-Farmer-Labor organization had made him the overwhelming favorite. At this point Stevenson started to campaign furiously, but not until the end of the primary period, in the June 5 California contest, did he beat Kefauver convincingly. Kefauver stayed in the race until July 26, sparking talk of a Harriman-Kefauver alliance to stop Stevenson, and even after he withdrew Stevenson faced continued opposition from Harriman (whose governorship was in a larger state and whose foreign policy experience was far superior) up through the convention in August. There he still declined to assert mastery, throwing the vice presidential nomination open. That contest became one of the last times a national convention really decided something: it boiled down to a battle between Kefauver, who won, and the thirty-nine-year-old Senator John Kennedy, the one Democratic senator who had not declared his support for the censure of McCarthy in 1954 (he was not present, assertedly because of his bad back) and the one serious Catholic contender now. In letting the convention choose the vice presidential nominee, Stevenson wanted to contrast the Democrats' openness with the Republicans' one embarrassment, the renomination of the not terribly popular Nixon, who had only lukewarm support from Eisenhower and the open opposition of disarmament coordinator Harold Stassen.[15] But Nixon did not drag the Republican ticket down enough to make the election close.

Moreover, for most of the year voters' eyes were on foreign policy—Eisenhower's greatest strength. Foreign issues were especially prominent in the campaign month of October. That month Hungary rose in revolt and for a few giddy days seemed to shake off Soviet rule—until Red Army tanks came rolling into Budapest. Days later the Israelis, British, and French swept across the Sinai Peninsula and seized the Suez Canal from Nasser's Egypt. Democrats could argue that both events showed weaknesses in Eisenhower policies. Republican campaign oratory and the 1952 Republican platform which promised "liberation" of eastern Europe were proved a fraud when the president did nothing to help the Hungarians—a fraud which may have led many brave men to hopeless fates; and the Suez crisis followed naturally from the refusal of the United States to finance the Aswan high dam on the Nile, a refusal which had prompted Nasser to nationalize the canal. But as usual, crisis worked politically to the advantage of the president.[16] His cool and pacific responses to these emergencies were widely appreciated and belied the Democrats' arguments that he was just a tool of John Foster Dulles—for on the last Saturday of October, as both crises raged, Dulles went to the hospital for emergency cancer surgery. Eisenhower may have lost some support from Jewish voters because of his insistence on a cease-fire in the Middle East and his lack of support for the Israeli seizure of the Sinai. But overall the 52%–39% lead he had in the October 18–23 Gallup poll rose to a 57%–39% lead in the final October 30–November 2 survey. These results, given the error margin in polling, were consistent with the 58%–42% election result.

In retrospect, the strange thing about the election is that it was as close as it was, that the basic strength of the Democratic party and the unpopularity of partisan Republicans like Nixon were enough to keep Eisenhower's percentage below the 61% level by which other popular presidents won reelection. Stevenson exceeded 55% in only three states—Georgia, Mississippi, and Alabama—but his Farm Belt strength was enough to enable him to carry Missouri, the only time in the twentieth century that state has voted for the losing candidate. To the seven states he carried he came close to adding Kefauver's Tennessee, and he won 46% in Minnesota and West Virginia, two states in which Democratic candidates would do well over the next three decades. Except in Utah, Stevenson ran ahead of his 1952 showing in every state west of the Mississippi River and north of the 36°30′ Missouri Compromise line. He made impressive gains on the West Coast, where new migrants (especially the thousands of Jews from Chicago and elsewhere who were moving to Los Angeles) and young liberals were making Stevenson volunteers a major force in the Democratic parties of California and Oregon. The progressive Republican traditions in the Pacific states were atrophying, and the Democrats were the beneficiaries, winning tough Senate races for Wayne Morse (who had finally switched parties) in Oregon and Warren Magnuson in Washington. Stevenson also ran ahead of his 1952 showing in Michigan, where Mennen Williams and Walter Reuther's United Auto Workers were keeping alive and vibrant a class-conscious politics of economic redistribution in a state which had above-average economic growth in the manufacturing boom from 1940 until the middle 1960s. The 1956 election was the last presidential election in which the Farm

Belt was a strong area for the Democrats, as it had been from William Jennings Bryan's time; and it was the first in which the Democrats started to show above-average strength in the tier of states running from northern New England across the Upper Midwest and including the three states on the Pacific coast.

Eisenhower ran farthest ahead of his 1952 showing among Catholic voters, especially in southern Louisiana (where his stands on offshore oil and gas dereg-ulation helped) and in the outer-city neighborhoods of the East and Chicago. Catholics were still a distinctive group in the America of the middle 1950s: they still attended weekly mass conducted in Latin, supported a celibate clergy and large monastic orders, and refrained from eating meat on Friday or using birth control devices. With their large families and their parochial school systems which were not eligible for public aid, clustered in ethnic neighborhoods in big cities and a few rural settlements, they were still defined as different and somehow not completely American. The defeat of Al Smith in 1928, and the obvious anti-Catholic feeling his candidacy had evoked, made them defensive about their Amer-ican-ness. Franklin Roosevelt in the 1930s helped assure them that it was their country, too, but in the 1940s they grew restive with him. Many Irish-Americans opposed his close alliance with Britain; many Italian-Americans resented his con-tempt for Mussolini ("the hand that held the dagger"); many Polish-Americans smoldered over what they considered the sellout of eastern Europe at Yalta. It was more the opposition he received from Henry Wallace and the Communists than the Roosevelt legacy which produced a large Catholic vote for Truman in 1948. In 1952, Eisenhower cut into the Democratic majority of the Catholic vote, but not drastically; in 1956, he made his biggest gains among Catholic voters.

This was the first election in which the Catholic proclivity for supporting incumbent presidents became apparent—and played a major role in shaping the outcome, by giving Eisenhower large majorities in almost all the major industrial states. Respectful of the voice of authority in their church, eager to prove their patriotism and devotion to their country's leaders, American Catholics swung toward incumbent presidents by unusually great margins, not just in 1956 but in 1972, 1976, 1980, and 1984.[17] Interestingly, Hawaii has been similarly incumbent-prone, reflecting the proclivities of the Japanese-Americans who make up one-third of the state's electorate and whose patriotism was questioned and proved under fire in World War II. These are Americans who insist this is their country, too.

In congressional races Eisenhower's lack of effort for his party showed, as the Democrats retained control of both houses of Congress. Republicans did win some important Senate races, especially in New York, where Attorney General Jacob Javits beat New York City Mayor Robert Wagner, Jr. But Democrats won Re-publican seats in Pennsylvania and Ohio. In House races Republicans captured 9 seats in urban and industrial areas, most of them heavily Catholic,[18] but these proved to be ephemeral gains: Democrats won 5 of them back in 1958. Democrats won 5 seats in the Farm Belt on the Great Plains (the South Dakota 1st going to a baldish thirty-four-year-old former minister and college teacher named George

McGovern) and 4 agriculture-conscious seats in California and Oregon,[19] as well as the Nevada at-large seat and a seat in Edmund Muskie's Maine. Virtually no seats changed hands in the Civil War borderlands, once the great battleground for the House. Now the question was how the man whom the public wanted would continue to govern with the party he privately but fairly plainly preferred in control of Congress.

30

-»» «««-

Erosion

I n no previous American election had more incumbents been returned to office than in 1956. President Eisenhower was reelected with, if not quite an overwhelming majority, a large enough one to improve on his impressive 1952 showing. At the same time the Democratic Congress was reelected almost to a man and woman. In part, the congressional results reflected the lack of effort by Eisenhower to help his party win majorities. Moreover, while his strength on foreign policy redounded to his benefit in the closing weeks of the campaign, the rally-round-the-flag impulse aroused by Hungary and Suez may have helped incumbent congressional Democrats, whose leaders had been careful to support the president abroad, rather than congressional Republicans, who on foreign issues were often heard bellowing their opposition to him. The 1956 election marked the first time since the razor-close elections of the 1880s that a president had not carried in a congressional majority of his party with him—and this time the result was not accidental, but the result of widespread and purposeful ticket-splitting. The conservative Republicans' complaint against Eisenhower, that he did not build a strong Republican party, is well founded. But the Republicans won the presidency in seven of the ten elections beginning with Eisenhower's first run in 1952. It is not clear that they could have done so if Americans, so much better disposed to the Democrats than the Republicans for so many of these years, had stayed in the habit of voting straight party tickets.

Presidents who win reelection by a landslide are often expected to get over-confident and make dreadful blunders. But Eisenhower's 58% was not quite a landslide by historic standards; and he did not make any egregious blunders on matters of great importance during his second term, except perhaps his decision to continue reconnaissance flights over the Soviet Union by U-2 planes in the weeks before his scheduled May 1960 summit meeting with Soviet leader Nikita Khrushchev. Nevertheless, the Democrats did gain strength with the public during Eisenhower's second term, not so much because of his blunders as because of an erosion in the nation's confidence and because of the skills of some of the leading Democratic politicians. The Americans of the early 1940s, so grateful for even the limited success of Franklin Roosevelt's attempts to stimulate the economy and so appreciative of his leadership of a militarily weak nation as a world war was breaking out, had become the Americans of the late 1950s, displeased because unemployment was rising and disturbed when the Soviets succeeded in launching a satellite into space several months before the United States did—and seemingly quite forgetful of how their leaders had just ended the seemingly endless Korean war and had stamped out rampant inflation. This muted discontent did not result in significantly lower ratings for Eisenhower in his second term. But it undermined the appeal of his policies and further reduced the already weak appeal of his party.

II

The erosion began with the so-called budget crisis. In January 1957, Eisenhower submitted a $72 billion budget to Congress. In a press conference the same day, Treasury Secretary George Humphrey, a vocal and able conservative who had been head of the M. A. Hanna Company in Cleveland and was one of Eisenhower's favorite cabinet members, predicted "a depression that will curl your hair" unless taxes and spending were cut and said "there are a lot of places in this budget that can be cut."[1] Three days later Eisenhower said he agreed with Humphrey and invited Congress to cut his budget. Whoops of joy went up from old-guard Republicans, while Democrats were bemused. In April, Eisenhower came up with a list of $1.3 billion in cuts. Democrats like Harry Byrd in the Senate and Sam Rayburn in the House were happy to join in the search for cuts and found some additional items, particularly in foreign aid, which lacked any political constituency. In May, however, Eisenhower seemed to endorse the "modern Republicanism" of his 1956 platform by taking the position, abhorred by the conservatives, that the federal government should run deficits in recessions. But what seemed to be wavering may actually have been genuine ambivalence. By January 1958, in any case, Eisenhower was submitting a tighter budget and had the advantage of having forged, in the fights over cuts in 1957, a solidarity among House Republicans which would enable him to have almost every veto upheld, even by the much more Democratic Congress that was elected in 1958.[2]

Also getting headlines during early 1957 was the administration's proposed civil rights bill, prepared by the aggressive, partisan, and pro-civil right attorney general, Herbert Brownell. The House, where Brownell's views were shared by Republicans conscious of their party's Civil War heritage, like William McCulloch and Clarence Brown, passed essentially the administration bill. But in the Senate it fell victim to Lyndon Johnson's craftiness. As a Texas politician, Johnson had been only narrowly elected in 1948 and was uneasily poised between Texas liberals, who mistrusted him, and conservatives (like former Governor Allan Shivers who supported Eisenhower over Stevenson twice), who always had the potential of raising vast sums against him. As a presidential aspirant, Johnson was poised between his natural base of southerners, who followed but did not trust him, and northern liberals, who erroneously considered him opposed to all their measures. For both his Texas and his national ambitions, he needed to pass through a Senate where it could be filibustered a civil rights bill which would be palatable to the South.

His method was to secure an amendment requiring jury trials in voting rights cases and to drop the section giving the attorney general power to bring school desegregation cases. The jury trial amendment sounded like a reaffirmation of basic American principles and had the additional advantage of echoing the argument long made by labor union leaders that judges should not be able to issue injunctions against strikes and that such issues should be determined by juries which might be sympathetic to workers—an argument crowned with success in the 1932 Norris-La Guardia anti-injunction act. But of course white southerners knew full well that southern juries were always all white, and such juries were not likely to cast unanimous votes for conviction in civil rights cases. Johnson carried his jury trial amendments with support from all southerners, a few Republicans, and some western and new senators indebted to him for committee assignments or other favors. Frank Church of Idaho, for example, backed jury trial and in return got approval for the Hell's Canyon Dam, a public power project on the Snake River which was opposed by Eisenhower but had been Church's number one campaign promise when he won his seat at age thirty-two in 1956.[3] The elimination of the attorney general's power was accomplished by getting civil rights supporters like Clinton Anderson of New Mexico and George Aiken of Vermont to sponsor it and by having Richard Russell determine in a talk with Eisenhower that the president would fight not at all for this provision favored by Brownell. Brownell was a protégé of Thomas Dewey, a strong partisan Republican who was also a committed backer of civil rights; Eisenhower, who had made his career comfortably in a segregated Army, had no enthusiasm at all for civil rights. "I have lived in the South, remember," Eisenhower told his secretary; and though he was firm in his belief that Supreme Court decisions ought to be enforced, he favored "the mildest civil rights bill possible."[4] So a strong civil rights bill proposed by a president who did not really support it was weakened—but also passed—by a Senate majority leader who probably did not oppose its strong provisions.

III

The civil rights bill was only one example of Johnson's brilliant performance as majority leader. It was all the more stunning because this was a man still in his forties and without a reliable political base, either in Texas or in the Senate. Although his father had briefly been a state legislator, the family made no great living in the heartbreakingly poor Hill Country of Texas, west of Austin, which had deluded the first settlers with its seeming lushness but had quickly been stripped of grass by cattle and then of soil by rain.[5] But Johnson had incredible drive and intellectual power. Although he attended the teachers' college in San Marcos rather than the University of Texas in Austin, he managed to parlay a job with reactionary Congressman Richard Kleberg, co-owner of the King Ranch, into the leadership of the Texas branch of Aubrey Williams's National Youth Administration. From there he went on to a victory in the April 1937 special election to replace Congressman James P. Buchanan, chairman of the House Appropriations Committee, in the Austin congressional district which included on its western edge the lightly populated county around his home town of Johnson City. He was all of twenty-eight. Johnson ran as a down-the-line supporter of Franklin Roosevelt, backing his court-packing plan when most Texas politicians shunned it. He remained a Roosevelt man in 1940, when he refused Sam Rayburn's plea to pledge his support for John Nance Garner. He ran as a Roosevelt supporter, though with support from some Roosevelt adversaries, in the June 1941 special election which he lost to Governor W. Lee ("Pass the Biscuits, Pappy") O'Daniel by 1,311 votes—just a few more votes would have made him U.S. senator from one of the largest states in the nation at age thirty-two.

Few American politicians have had the driving ambition of Lyndon Johnson; few have had his brains and instinctive understanding of politics and of power. As a New Deal supporter he developed alliances with Harold Ickes and Harry Hopkins and cultivated young Washington insiders like Abe Fortas, James Rowe, Tommy Corcoran, Edwin Weisl, and Eliot Janeway—first-rate men who helped him in all manner of ways for twenty-five and thirty years. After 1941, with an eye on political trends and economic powers back home in Texas, he increasingly voted against the New Deal. He was no friend of the politics of economic redistribution, of the power of labor unions, of the liberal economic platforms of 1944 and 1948. But he retained his friendships and alliances in Washington. He passed up the 1942 Senate race against O'Daniel because he was serving in the Navy, and he spent time getting rich: his wife bought radio station KTBC in Austin in 1943, it was granted the sole television license in Austin in 1952, and Johnson used the profits to buy land, cattle, and oil and built a net worth of over $1 million. But the shrewdness of his move rightward was shown in 1948, when he ran for the Senate nomination against the more conservative Governor Coke Stevenson. The race was close, and the outcome hinged on the count in Duval County, a sagebrush-pocked expanse of south Texas filled with oil wells and with little settlements of Mexicans clustered here and there. It was in Duval County that William F. Buckley, Sr., founding father of the conservative Buckleys, made his first millions. But local politics was controlled by the Parr family, who delivered the vote en bloc. In the 1941 special election George Parr had reported the Duval County results early; in the 1948 primary he reported late and gave Johnson 202 additional votes in one ballot box, enough to produce an 87-vote statewide margin over Stevenson out of 998,000 votes cast. Although the result was naturally challenged in court, Johnson staffer John Connally and lawyer Abe Fortas defended Johnson successfully.

Johnson was finally a senator, at forty. As "Landslide Lyndon" (Scott Lucas's nickname), he seemed unlikely to be a power in the Senate. But Robert Kerr, an older freshman from Oklahoma who was just as ambitious as Johnson and even more determined to enrich himself, got Johnson the formerly meaningless post of Senate majority whip after the incumbent whip, Francis Myers of Pennsylvania, was beaten in 1950.[6] After Majority Leader Ernest McFarland lost to Barry Goldwater in 1952, Johnson found it easy to get Richard Russell's support and became Senate Democratic leader. To the surprise of Russell and almost everyone else, Johnson made this the most powerful post in Congress. A shrewd analyst of measures and men, he maneuvered quietly while the Republicans controlled the Senate, then as majority leader passed his own program in the early months of 1955, though his own preferences on policy were not strong. He had, one scholar writes, "a relative indifference to most policy outcomes coupled with an interest in finding constructive legislative solutions even in the face of considerable disagreement among his colleagues on the substance of policy."[7] A heart attack in July 1955 slowed him down, but only for a while. To all appearances in Washington, Johnson could have hoped to continue as Democratic leader and dominant figure in the Senate for many years—and could not, as a southerner, have hoped for anything else. But he knew that his position in Texas, poised between liberals and conservatives, must always be tenuous. His power in Washington also depended on a convergence of forces which might not always occur: there must be a Democratic majority in the Senate, but not too big a majority or the liberals would take the initiative, though they might not get their own bills passed (this situation in fact developed after the 1958 election); there must be a Republican president, or Johnson would be overshadowed by a Democratic president with a program of his own (as he surely would have been if he had stayed in the Senate in 1960 and Kennedy or another Democrat was elected president); it would help to have an admiring press, led by Johnson's friend and fellow Texan William S. White, who was the *New York Times*'s Senate reporter at the time.

But Johnson was interested not only in being a strong majority leader: he was ambitious to be president. Passing the Civil Rights Act of 1957 did him no political good in Texas and by fraying his ties with Russell did him as much harm as good in the Senate. But it was an indispensable step toward that goal of winning the White House. The bill may not have been an effective one, though the Civil Rights commission it established did present the stark facts of racial segregation to northerners previously disposed to ignore them, and that the assertion that blacks should be able to vote was worth making. But it was effective for Johnson. It showed that he was not a parochial southerner, but a national leader; not an old-fashioned congressional timeserver, but a man who had things he wanted to do and who could get them done.

IV

One month after the Civil Rights Act was passed, a civil rights crisis began making bigger—and uglier—headlines. This was the controversy over the desegregation of Central High School in Little Rock. Some school systems at the edge of the South—Washington, D.C., for example, and Arlington, Virginia, just across the Potomac River—were desegregating without much incident or controversy. But in most southern districts, the NAACP found it hard to persuade black plaintiffs to bring suit; and courts typically assigned only a few token blacks to integrate white schools, often choosing those whose parents stepped forward and volunteered them for what was dauntingly hazardous duty. This token integration was what had been ordered in Little Rock, a small city on the cusp between the almost totally white mountainous regions of north Arkansas and the flat plains of the Mississippi Valley, where heavily black work forces tended cotton and rice fields. In September 1957, Arkansas's Governor Orval Faubus ordered the state National Guard to bar the black students a federal court had ordered admitted into Central High. Faubus's motivation was obvious: he was serving his second two-year term in a state with an anti-third term tradition and two well-established senators. He wanted to remain governor, and indeed he was reelected four more times (and never lost his appetite for the job: he was beaten in comeback attempts in 1970 and 1986). With typical "deliberate speed," the court scheduled a hearing nearly three weeks hence on this blatant defiance of its order. Eisenhower, on vacation in Newport, Rhode Island, negotiated with Faubus a withdrawal of the National Guard; but after a white mob tried to attack the black students, he reluctantly ordered the 101st Airborne in to enforce the desegregation order. He asserted his faith in the basic goodness of Americans and cautioned them that resistance to desegregation hurt the nation's image and helped Soviet propaganda around the world. But the white mobs howled nonetheless around Central High School, where federal troops remained until November 1957 and the National Guard, under federal control, was stationed until June 1958. Faith in the goodness of the country was at least marginally undermined.

At almost the same time, faith in American technological and military superiority was shaken by the Soviet Union's success in orbiting its first satellite, Sputnik, in October 1957. The Eisenhower administration responded defensively, claiming that American satellites could have been orbited earlier if the government had been willing to spend the money and make the effort; and in fact American satellites were put into orbit in January and March 1958. But the Soviet satellite was bigger and required, as news accounts pointed out, more powerful missiles than the U.S. government had thought the Soviets had developed. This revelation had military implications: the Soviet Union had little chance to deliver a devastating nuclear attack on the United States with its bomber force, which could be repelled, but it might be able to do so with missiles, against which there was no defense. The technological implications were also unnerving: the nation which had produced Thomas Edison and Henry Ford, the atomic bomb and the automatic transmission, the electric freezer and the television set, was now being overtaken by a backward totalitarian rival.

To this perceived threat Eisenhower's response was mostly a non-response. He resisted calls for big increases in spending on rockets or on defense generally—calls that came more often from Democrats like Stuart Symington and Lyndon Johnson, who made his support of the space program a major priority, than from frugal Republicans. But Eisenhower did not object to more government encouragement of scientific research and the increased emphasis on science and academics in the schools, a development coinciding with the abrupt collapse of the "progressive" education movement which placed greater stress on "social adjustment" than on academic mastery. This emphasis produced in the short run the

National Defense Education Act and, it can be argued, in the longer run the high school students with the highest standardized test scores in American history (in the class of 1963). Although it was stimulated and financed almost entirely by governments at the state and local level,[8] it found some inspiration and support at the federal level; and these were expressed significantly more vocally by the Democrats' de facto leader, Lyndon Johnson, than by the Republican president who allowed him in 1957 to seize the policy and political initiative.

31

→))) (((←

Setback

The same year that Americans were stunned by Sputnik they were dismayed to find that the economy had fallen into the deepest recession since the end of World War II. By this time the ideas, although not the label, of Keynesian economics had become widely enough disseminated that not only the liberal Democrats but Eisenhower Republicans as well believed that the proper response to a recession was increased government spending. But Eisenhower, after the budget battle of the first half of 1957, was reluctant to conclude that a recession was really beginning until it had become painfully apparent. The gross national product, which had risen every year since 1954, climbed only 1.4% in real terms in 1957 and then fell 1.1% in 1958; per capita income fell 3.1% between 1956 and 1958. Unemployment rose from 2.75 million (4.1% of the labor force) in 1956 to 4.6 million in 1958. That was 6.8% of the labor force, the highest figure since 1941.[1]

The recession struck deeply at the manufacturing industries which had been growing robustly since 1945. It raised the possibility that these industries might go into decline—or that the new jobs they had been steadily producing since 1940 would be replaced by automation. In the years after World War II blue-collar manufacturing jobs had been a source of upward mobility, as payrolls grew because of increased consumer demand, and wages went up thanks to well-publicized bargaining efforts—and occasional strikes—by the big industrial unions. It was possible for a man without much education, without even a high school diploma, to make enough money to maintain his family in more comfort than he had ever experienced or expected. The recession of 1957–58, followed by the less serious (but politically crucial) recession of 1960–61, threatened to cut off this avenue of upward mobility. It cost some workers their jobs, and it sent a signal to young Americans; this kind of work may not prove to be secure. Coinciding with Sputnik, the 1957–58 recession may have helped to persuade many young Americans, just as the first baby boomers were reaching junior high school, that the best avenue upward was to get plenty of education. The typical pattern of life for ordinary young Americans as the 1950s began was for a boy to graduate from high school and spend two years in the service, then to go home, get a blue-collar job, and not too long afterwards get married to a girl, often already pregnant, who had just graduated from high school. This pattern explains the large number of births to teen-agers that was an important component of the baby boom, and the low marriage

301

age: for a brief time most American girls were married before they turned twenty-one, and they were having children not long after—not very long at all in many cases. This life style depended on the existence of jobs which did not require a college education and paid what the labor union movement traditionally called a family wage. Right out of high school and the service, a boy could get a good enough job to support his wife and their children for the rest of the couple's lives.

The basis for this comfortable pattern of life—the continuing supply of lifetime blue-collar jobs—was undermined by the 1957–58 and 1960–61 recessions. In the 1950s manufacturing states like New Jersey, Ohio, and Michigan grew more rapidly than the national average—rapidly enough to gain a congressional seat each when the 1960 census returns came in. In the three decades afterwards none of the heavy-manufacturing states of the Northeast and Midwest again gained population at a rate greater than the national average. By the late 1950s unions like the United Auto Workers, which earlier in the decade had concentrated on enrolling the auto industry's ever-expanding payrolls (auto company employment in Michigan peaked in 1953), were making a heavily publicized push to guarantee workers' jobs—a signal that the growth in jobs in these heavily unionized industries was over, and that young people entering the job market should look to other opportunities. The recessions of course exacerbated this trend. These developments in the blue-collar job market were occurring at a time when young people were receiving from other sources—from the burgeoning of state college systems (nowhere more spectacular than in California), from the increases in white-collar employment, and from the increased emphasis on academics after Sputnik—the following message: get good grades, stay in school, skip the service if you can, don't get married while you're still teenagers. As a result, the blue-collar model of the 1950s became less common and was replaced by a white-collar model: the boy goes to college and graduates, he marries a girl who has gone to college at least for a time, and they postpone childbearing for at least a couple of years as their income levels rise. The new patterns were plainly apparent in the statistics of the early 1960s, which showed the highest test scores in American history, which showed a majority of high school students in California (the nation's largest state by 1963) going on to some form of college, which showed the marriage age rising and the number of births to teenagers dropping sharply—a drop which accounts, more than anything else, for the abrupt end of the baby boom in 1962.

In the long run, therefore, the recession of the late 1950s played at least a marginal role in undermining the blue-collar pattern of life which provided a continuing majority constituency for the Democratic party. In the short run, on the other hand, the recession helped to increase the Democratic majority, as a significant number of Americans felt the props knocked out from under them and, as they had in such situations ever since the 1930s, resolved to call in the Democrats to solve the problem. Other events as well continued to go against the Republican president. In November 1957 he suffered a stroke, from which he recovered— but it underlined the precariousness of his health. In May 1958, on one of Vice President Nixon's much-ballyhooed trips abroad, he was attacked and nearly killed by a mob in Caracas, Venezuela, a country where the United States had expressed little disapproval of the local dictator. In June 1958 scandal touched the Eisenhower White House. Chief of Staff Sherman Adams, a dour, taciturn New Hampshire-man who had scarcely a friend in Washington, was shown to have accepted favors including a vicuña coat from businessman Bernard Goldfine and to have made calls to the Federal Trade Commission to inquire about a case in which Goldfine was involved. Eisenhower pleaded, "I need him"; but in September, Adams resigned—and in the meantime the Democrats had a juicy political issue. In July 1958, Eisenhower ordered the Marines into Lebanon to prevent the breakup of that country and the ouster of its pro-Western government; they remained until October. By this time voters, rather than rallying around the flag, were evidently apprehensive about a new American commitment in an unfamiliar and dangerous part of the world. In this climate of opinion Maine, for the last time in its history, voted in September—a vestige of the days when election day came after the harvest, which of course is early in the far north. Prognosticators had always watched the Maine results ("as goes Maine, so goes the nation"), ordinarily not to see which party won but to see how high or low the winning Republican percentage was. But this time the Republicans did not win. Democrat Edmund Muskie, after two terms as governor, beat incumbent Republican Senator Frederick Payne by a 61%–39% margin, and a Democrat was elected governor to succeed him. To all but the most partisan observers it was apparent that the Democrats were headed for a great national victory in November.

In the meantime, conservative Republicans picked the 1958 elections as a time to go on the offensive. In the industrial states of Ohio and California, as well as in many small states, they sponsored referenda on right-to-work laws—an attempt to break the power of the big unions by denying them the automatic income which came from dues deducted from paychecks. Among those embracing the right-to-work cause was Senate Republican Leader William Knowland; convinced that he must hold executive office to be elected president, he went back home to California to run for governor, in the process elbowing aside incumbent Republican Goodwin Knight, who was forced to run for Knowland's Senate seat instead. The unions counterattacked furiously, arguing that there was nothing wrong with requiring workers to pay a fee for the job the unions did for them when they bargained for higher wages and better working conditions. They campaigned as never before, concentrating on voter turnout—a critical factor in an election in a recessionary off year in which Republican-leaning voters were likely to be downcast and poorly motivated. From the Republican standpoint, the results proved disastrous. Right-to-work was defeated by wide margins in Ohio and California and almost everywhere else. Also defeated were politicians associated with it: in Ohio, Governor William O'Neill and Senator John Bricker were both beaten, the latter by sixty-eight-year-old former Congressman-at-Large Stephen Young;[2] in California, Knowland lost 60%–40% to Democrat Pat Brown, while Knight lost the Senate seat 57%–43% to Congressman Clair Engle.

These were not the only Republican disasters in the 1958 elections. The Democrats ended up with 35 governorships, the Republicans with 14 (Alaska was admitted to the union in July 1958). Democrats gained 13 seats in the Senate, for a 64–34 edge (Alaska cooperated by electing two Democrats), the biggest Democratic margin there since 1942. In House elections Democrats won 56% of the vote—easily the highest figure since 1936—and emerged with a 283–153 majority, better than they had achieved since 1938. From 1938 to 1956 the number of Democrats elected to the House ranged from 211 to 268, except when it dropped to 188 in 1946; it averaged 235. From 1958 to 1986 the number of Democrats elected to the House ranged from 239 to 295, averaging 264—about 30 seats more.

Even more important, the kind of Democrats elected was different. The new Democrats in the Senate were mostly from the northern tier states, were loyal adherents of the liberal Democratic platforms of 1944 and 1948, and were associated with reformist and liberal elements in their party. In addition to Muskie of Maine, Young of Ohio, and Engle of California, they included such men as Harrison Williams of New Jersey, Philip Hart of Michigan, William Proxmire of Wisconsin (reelected after his August 1957 special election victory), Eugene McCarthy of Minnesota, Gale McGee of Wyoming, Frank Moss of Utah, and Howard Cannon of Nevada, along with Alaskans Bob Bartlett and Ernest Gruening. Also sharing these characteristics were a number of first-termers reelected by huge margins, including John Kennedy of Massachusetts, John Pastore of Rhode Island, Stuart Symington of Missouri, Albert Gore of Tennessee, Mike Mansfield of Montana, and Henry Jackson of Washington.

In the House, Democrats made no gains south of Kansas and Louisville, Kentucky (except in the Los Angeles basin). They continued to make some gains in the outer edges of metropolitan areas from Boston to Los Angeles, but most of the seats they captured could be characterized as farm or factory districts. Taken together with their gains in 1956, they won 15 seats in the Great Plains from the prairies of Illinois to the grazing land of Montana. In the short term, this Democratic swing in the Farm Belt represented a response to the free-market farm policies of Agriculture Secretary Ezra Taft Benson and to general economic trends: Prices for farm products, like those for other commodities, tend to fall in periods of economic growth; the technology of labor-saving machinery tends to substitute capital for labor in a high-wage economy like that of the United States; the flow of people off the farm and into the metropolitan areas continued at a rapid pace. These developments convinced many Farm Belt voters that their region was in depression and that it needed permanent government protection against low prices. Such protection would have been supplied by many practical Republican politicians, but not Ezra Taft Benson; the Democrats, ready to offer programs which represented logical extensions of Henry Wallace's AAA and Harry Truman's Brannan Plan, denounced Benson endlessly on the campaign trail. After 1958 the presence of significant numbers of Farm Belt Democrats in the Senate and the House gave congressional Democrats in general an incentive to vote generous farm programs. The Farm Belt members were ready to supply votes Democratic leaders needed on other issues, votes which they found increasingly hard to get from their co-partisans in the South. Farm programs thus became an important ingredient of the glue that held the Democratic party together.

If the Democrats' gains in 15 Farm Belt districts affected the behavior of their party in Congress, all the more so did their gain of approximately 22 factory seats. Most of these districts were outside the large metropolitan areas, away from the Democratic machines dating from the New Deal or earlier; the chief motivating force in Democratic politics in South Bend, Indiana, or Newark, Ohio, or Scranton, Pennsylvania, or Schenectady, New York, came from the labor unions, and especially from the industrial unions of the old CIO, now merged into the new AFL-CIO but still recognizably distinctive in their élan and their reach. These unions thought big. They still represented a large and what had been until 1957 an expanding segment of the American work force. They were gaining for their members higher wages and more generous fringe benefits than non-union workers, especially in the historically low-wage South, were getting. It was in their interest to gain for other workers through politics some of those things they were gaining for their own members through collective bargaining; otherwise they risked pricing union labor out of the market. Hence the AFL-CIO favored a higher minimum wage, though most of its members made far more than the minimum.

It favored higher Social Security benefits and the Medicare program—medical insurance for the elderly through Social Security—which was being advanced by many of the same men who had formulated the original Social Security program in the 1930s and who came forward with important extensions of it in the 1940s. At the time of the 1958 elections, the AFL-CIO was only beginning to become a powerful lobby on Capitol Hill; and its main lobbyist, former Milwaukee Congressman Andrew Biemiller, was frustrated and humiliated by the issue of labor union racketeering. In 1957 and 1958, Senate hearings conducted by Robert Kennedy, the younger brother of Senator John Kennedy, had spotlighted labor union corruption and resulted in, among other things, the expulsion of the Teamsters (one of Franklin Roosevelt's favorite unions) from the AFL-CIO in December 1957 and the indictment of Teamsters' president Dave Beck. In addition, the Senate passed an anti-racketeering bill framed by John Kennedy and North Carolina's Sam Ervin, which the AFL-CIO did not wholly favor but did not vehemently oppose. But the House Education and Labor Committee rejected the Kennedy-Ervin approach and voted instead a bill proposed by two junior members, Georgia Democrat Phil Landrum, a tribune of the always anti-union textile industry, and Michigan Republican Robert Griffin, a contentious son of the Detroit-area working class who had gone to work as a management lawyer in the small outstate Michigan town of Traverse City. Landrum-Griffin, passed in September 1959, promoted union democracy only marginally (after all, conservatives had reason to fear that truly democratic unions might be too militant) and did relatively little to discourage unionization—certainly it had less effect than the tarnishing of the unions' reputations produced by the Senate hearings and Robert Kennedy's book *The Enemy Within*.

But it made an important political difference. Biemiller and the AFL-CIO's heads, George Meany and Walter Reuther, vowed that they would never again be beaten on a labor bill in the House Education and Labor or the Senate Public Welfare Committees. They would make sure that only sympathetic Democrats and Republicans (for there were a fair number of pro-union Republicans, from northern and especially metropolitan and factory constituencies) were ever appointed to these committees, make sure by establishing their unions as key electoral forces in local politics and as a key lobby in Congress—as the 1960s went along, the most important liberal lobby on domestic issues. The 1958 elections gave them, for the first time, the numbers which suggested this strategy, and their experience with Landrum-Griffin in 1959 convinced them that they must follow it. For most of the next twenty years the AFL-CIO was the dominant lobbying group on Capitol Hill, especially in the House of Representatives.

32

-»» «ᖾ-

Candidates

A lthough no one could be sure of it at the time, the 1958 election, not that of 1952, proved the prototype for the future. Once the Korean War was over, the Republicans had failed to capitalize on Dwight Eisenhower's popularity; and the Democrats took advantage of their longer-term popularity which stemmed from the era of Franklin Roosevelt and was amplified by the demographic dividend which they began enjoying in the 1950s and, outside the South, would redound to their benefit even more in the 1960s. The liberal Democrats who were beating Republicans in farm and factory and metropolitan constituencies were not yet able to take control of the House or Senate legislatively; they understood little yet about the legislative process, they lacked competent leaders, and they were opposed on most substantive matters by an increasingly veto-prone president and by Lyndon Johnson and Sam Rayburn. But they were developing a coherent political program— of extending the New Deal through federal aid to education, Medicare, higher minimum wages—and developing bases of political strength on Capitol Hill and around the nation. And the Democrats had one additional advantage: they were developing what turned out to be a dazzling set of national candidates who would dominate the next dozen years of the nation's politics, men of brilliant talent and unquenchable ambition whose political strength came not from the local bases which had produced most of the leading politicians of the 1930s and 1940s, but from national constituencies, assembled and marshaled in Washington. They were the political progeny not of the fragmented local politics which Franklin Roosevelt had grown up with but of the centralized national politics which had grown up with the large central government produced by Roosevelt's New Deal and wartime policies.

II

One of these new national politicians was Lyndon Johnson. His strong suit was effectiveness, and he was quick to respond to Sputnik by creating a special Senate Space Committee and making himself the chairman. (This action also enabled him to steer space spending to Texas, which he did.) He staunchly supported the administration's foreign policy but suggested it wasn't spending enough on defense. On domestic policies he made no pretense of backing the liberal Democrats' welfare state and redistributionist schemes. Rather, he emphasized his constructive efforts on other issues, including civil rights. Johnson was a balancer, a juggler who could keep each ball in the air only as long as he could keep all the other balls moving too. In Texas he was never fully accepted by the conservative political establishment, including the reactionary oilmen who remembered his support for the Franklin Roosevelt whom they, as so-called Texas Regulars, had opposed on the 1944 Texas ballot. Nor was he trusted by the liberals, who nominated their candidate, Frankie Randolph, over Johnson's choice, B. A. Bentsen, for Democratic national committeewoman in May 1956 and elected the unfriendly and suspicious Ralph Yarborough as his Senate colleague in April 1957.

Johnson lacked a workable strategy to get the Democratic nomination in 1960. He was hoping for a deadlock or for the declared candidates to prove their inadequacy, as in 1952. He was also hoping, against all the historical evidence, that his colleagues in the Senate could win convention votes for him: senators, as he was to learn, had little influence with local politicians, who were inclined to regard them as exalted servants, as ambassadors to a distant and not entirely friendly federal government, rather than as masters. After the 1958 elections, he became somewhat more partisan and confrontational. He played a critical role, for example, in his friend Clinton Anderson's successful drive in May 1959 to deny Admiral Lewis Strauss confirmation as secretary of commerce[1] because of Strauss's actions as head of the Atomic Energy Commission, including his 1954 repudiation of J. Robert Oppenheimer. Eisenhower had begun vetoing more of the Democratic Congress's acts, and the new Republican leaders—Everett Dirksen, who succeeded the defeated Knowland as Senate minority leader, and Charles Halleck, who ousted the seventy-four-year-old Joseph Martin as House Republican leader—were more sharply partisan opponents. But although these shifts enabled Johnson to display his Democratic leadership more forcefully, his plans for running depended heavily on his colleagues in the Senate. He did not seem to realize that their power did not translate automatically into national convention delegates. This master of the politics of the Senate and of the South lacked an intuitive understanding of the politics of the rest of the country.

III

Another candidate for 1960 was John Kennedy. The motivating force behind his candidacy was his father. The son of P. J. Kennedy, an East Boston saloon owner and politician, and the son-in-law of John F. Fitzgerald, a one-time congressman and the first Irish Catholic mayor of Boston, Joseph Kennedy went to Harvard, became the youngest bank president in the country, and made his first million by the age of thirty. Yet he never felt accepted in a Boston where the Yankees, descended from Catholic-hating Puritans, built higher barriers and maintained more exclusive institutions than anywhere else in the country; and in 1927 he moved his wife and eight children[2] to New York. Throughout his career Kennedy had an instinct for numbers and an eye for opportunities that others failed to see.

He got into the movie business early, and made money; he got out of the stock market in May 1929, when almost everyone seemed to be getting in; he supported Franklin Roosevelt in May 1932, when most Catholic politicians were backing Al Smith, and was one of the handful of men who contributed $50,000 to Roosevelt's campaign and raised another $150,000 besides.[3] Roosevelt appointed him the first head of the Securities Exchange Commission, where by all accounts he did a superb job. His gall, brains, and cheeriness made him friends and admirers who ranged from his successor, liberal William Douglas, to the *New York Times*'s crusty conservative Arthur Krock, from New Deal wheel horse James Byrnes to New Deal hater William Randolph Hearst. In December 1937, Roosevelt appointed him ambassador to Great Britain: the first Irish-American at the Court of St. James's. But in London his good judgment deserted him. His intense (and prophetic) concern for his children—his "nine hostages to fortune," as he repeatedly referred to them—made him terrified of an outbreak of war in Europe and led him to become a fervent backer of Neville Chamberlain's policy of appeasement of Hitler. This stance left him in the awkward position of representing a president with whom he was in profound disagreement, and he eventually broke publicly with Roosevelt. Yet when he returned home in October 1940 Roosevelt summoned him to the White House, dined with him and Mrs. Kennedy, and mentioned how much he wanted to help the careers of the ambassador's talented sons; Kennedy endorsed Roosevelt's bid for a third term in an October 29 nationwide radio broadcast he insisted on paying for himself.[4] A few days later Kennedy's political career ended when *Boston Globe* reporter Louis Lyons quoted his gloomy appraisal of the world: "Democracy is all done. . . . Democracy is finished in England. It may be here."

He remained intensely, almost maniacally, ambitious for his sons. Crushed when the oldest, Joseph, Jr., was killed when his airplane exploded in 1944, he fastened his ambitions on the next son, John. In 1946 he masterminded John's election to the House from the district which included East Boston, where his own father had lived, and Beacon Hill, where his father-in-law, John Fitzgerald, lived in the old Bellevue Hotel. He masterminded John's election to the Senate in 1952 as well, when the younger Kennedy beat Henry Cabot Lodge, the grandson of the old senator who had narrowly won reelection over Fitzgerald in 1916. As a congressman and senator, John Kennedy was not much of a legislator. Harry McPherson describes him in the Senate thus: "Elegant and casual, he sat in the back row, his knees against the desk, rapping his teeth with a pencil and reading the *Economist* and the *Guardian.* He was treated with affection by most senators, but he was ultimately elusive, finding his way in other worlds outside the chamber. Mythically wealthy, handsome, bright, and well connected, he seemed to regard the Senate grandees as impressive but tedious. In turn, he was regarded by them as something of a playboy, a dilettante."[5]

If Joseph Kennedy had suffered his disabling stroke in 1955 rather than 1961, it is unlikely that his son would have run for president, at least in 1960. The driving ambition came from the father, not the son. One story has it that the younger Kennedy was asked what his father would have said if he had lost in 1960;

he replied without flickering, " 'Joe would have won.' " Three weeks after the 1956 election, four months after the gallant fight in which John Kennedy nearly won the Democratic nomination for vice president, the Kennedy family gathered at the white house in Hyannis Port which they maintained as their summer home and Massachusetts base. After dinner Joseph Kennedy went into the library with his son, and they talked about whether he should run for president in 1960. The senator presented the arguments against, especially the argument that a Catholic could not win; his father knocked them all down, arguing that a Catholic would be an especially strong candidate. He showed again his instinct for numbers: "Just remember, this country is not a private preserve for Protestants. There's a whole new generation out there and it's filled with the sons and daughters of immigrants from all over the world and those people are going to be mighty proud that one of their own is running for president. And that pride will be your spur, it will give your campaign an intensity we've never seen in public life. Mark my words, it's true." And it was. American Catholics, long stamped by their religion and considered by their fellow citizens as somehow less than completely American, yearned to prove that this was their country, too. They were 25% of the electorate,[6] and they would turn out in record numbers and cast 78% of their votes for John F. Kennedy in 1960. In the library in Hyannis Port, John Kennedy, trusting his father's instinct for numbers and acceding as most people did to his wishes, grinned and said, "Well, Dad, I guess there's just one question left. When do we start?"[7]

IV

Joseph Kennedy and Lyndon Johnson seemed to have recognized in each other the same qualities: vast ambition, so strong that they seemed to bend the world to their shape; brilliant intuition and insight, which enabled them to see opportunities visible to few others; dazzling charm, so irresistible that even those who ended up as political adversaries would years later light up and smile in remembering the grace of their presence. These were men who would walk straight ahead into a brick wall, entirely confident that the wall would give way and they would walk right through—and they did. Coming from the petty and impecunious gentry of East Boston and Johnson City, from the opposite geographic and ethnic ragged ends of the ragged Democratic archipelago, they rose early to heights which not one in a thousand in their circumstances would have thought attainable. At twenty-nine Joseph Kennedy was a millionaire, and at twenty-nine Lyndon Johnson was a congressman; before he was fifty Kennedy was the first Irish-American ambassador to the Court of St. James's, and before he was fifty Lyndon Johnson was majority leader of the United States Senate. Both men came from backgrounds— Catholic, southern—that most politicians in the 1930s assumed ruled them out for the presidency; both made the White House their goal, and both in different ways attained it. Both were, in their time, strong supporters and political allies of Franklin Roosevelt: Johnson was having lunch with Roosevelt and Sam Rayburn when Roosevelt picked up the phone and welcomed the returning Kennedy back to the United States in October 1940, making a cutting motion as if to indicate he was doing Kennedy in.[8] Both Kennedy and Johnson built their most important national base in Washington, among the national opinion leaders, the administration insiders who became savvy Washington lawyers, the smart political operatives, the proprietors and reporters of the press, all of whom became uniquely powerful in the nationalized, centralized politics which came into being in Franklin Roosevelt's presidency. And they seemed to like each other. Johnson was happy to please Kennedy by supporting his son for vice president at the 1956 convention and to place him on the Foreign Relations Committee the next year; and Kennedy, in vivid contrast to his son Robert, was strongly in favor of putting Johnson on the ticket in July 1960.[9]

V

Another ambitious Democrat who built a national constituency was Senator Hubert Humphrey of Minnesota. He had thrust himself into the national consciousness in July 1948, when as a thirty-seven-year-old mayor of Minneapolis he made a stirring speech for the minority plank on civil rights at the Democratic national convention. Humphrey's speech seemed to make the difference in getting the convention to adopt the plank, which triggered both the southern walkout and the subsequent pro–civil rights position of the Truman administration: it was just after the convention that Truman ordered the military desegregated. Humphrey himself came from a constituency where legal segregation by race was as unfamiliar and unpalatable as it would be to an American coming of age in the 1980s. Born and raised in a South Dakota town, the son of an ebullient druggist, he went to graduate school and became a teacher but prudently obtained his pharmacist's license. In 1940, at the age of twenty-nine, he came to Minneapolis, the capital of the vast northern plains province which stretches west across the Dakotas to the Rockies, to teach at the University of Minnesota. Draft-exempt for physical reasons, he obtained local jobs with the War Production Administration and the War Manpower Progress Commission. He also got involved in politics, running for mayor unsuccessfully in 1943, helping to merge the weak Democratic and flagging Farmer-Labor parties in 1944, and winning another race for mayor in 1945. Minneapolis was not then the city of clean and orderly politics it later became. It had some of the nation's toughest and most ideological unions, with the Teamsters run by Trotskyites and some CIO locals run by Communists.[10] Humphrey, idealistic but also tough-minded, took on both groups. The Democratic-Farmer-Labor party he helped to create was exactly the sort of coalition of traditional Democrats and progressive non-Democrats which Franklin Roosevelt had encouraged since the 1920s. But because of the rivalry between the Democrats and Farmer-Laborites and the unpopularity in Minnesota of Roosevelt's war policies before Pearl Harbor, it was one of the last such coalitions put together in the country. It was just coming together, and was on the verge of its great breakthrough electoral victory in November 1948, when Humphrey made his civil rights speech in Philadelphia.

Humphrey's election to the Senate in 1948 made him one of the most visible liberal politicians in the country—liberal in the sense that he really believed in Roosevelt's 1944 and Truman's 1948 platforms. Almost no southern and few northern Democratic officeholders, plus a handful of Republican politicians, believed in such an expansion of the public sector: Roosevelt, who may have, was dead; Truman's commitment was forceful but fitful; grizzled professional politicians like Scott Lucas and Sam Rayburn were more interested in getting along with vested interests and adjusting Democrats' quarrels than they were in enacting liberal programs. Humphrey did believe in them and, naively, seemed to believe that almost all other Democrats so believed or could be talked into acting as if they did. He made the error of assuming that the American people believed in the whole liberal platform because they had voted for Roosevelt and that Democratic politicians who did not believe in the whole liberal platform could be made to vote for it by appealing to the people.

But in time Humphrey recovered from the disaster of his early Senate career. His infectious good humor and his lack of self-righteousness compensated for a senatorial tendency to speak at great length. He was a true believer without being a scold, and even Richard Russell was happy to make common cause with him on the one issue they agreed on, farm policy. Humphrey also built a good relationship with Lyndon Johnson, who early on spotted him as the one liberal with whom he could work and through whom he could communicate with others who shared Humphrey's views but not his trust, openness, and willingness to compromise. By the middle 1950s, Humphrey had made a solid legislative record in such diverse areas as agriculture, foreign policy, and civil rights. He opposed root and branch the market-oriented policies of Agriculture Secretary Benson, he supported arms control approaches to the Soviets, and he worked mightily to advance civil rights. He fairly bubbled over with new legislative proposals, some of which seemed faintly crackpot at the time, some of which proved to be as farsighted and durable as the Peace Corps which he proposed in the 1960 campaign.

By the late 1950s, Humphrey had become a plausible candidate for the executive office which, in his view, was the only governmental position from which liberal goals could be accomplished. Moreover, the reformist Democratic parties in the northern tier states and the CIO labor unions, which together formed his natural political base, had grown in power and coherence over the preceding decade. The fall of 1958 was a good season for him: he gained national attention when he went to Moscow and became the first American presidential aspirant to meet with Soviet leader Nikita Khrushchev, who was still largely unknown in the United States; and his politics were vindicated by the results of the off-year election. When he announced his candidacy in December 1959—unprecedentedly early—Humphrey was reasonably confident that there was a large liberal constituency he could appeal to, though polls showed he was not well known and started out with only a small percentage of the Democratic primary vote. He planned to make his appeal in the primaries of Wisconsin, next door to Minnesota and with a similarly reformist Democratic party; heavily unionized West Virginia; and reformist Oregon.

VI

Other major figures in the Democratic party took different courses. Missouri Senator Stuart Symington decided to run, not openly, but as a candidate a dead-locked convention might turn to. With a certain aristocratic dash, with experience as head of Emerson Electric and secretary of the Air Force, with the support of his fellow Missourian Harry Truman, he thought he might be a formidable figure in the back rooms. Other Democrats from the Civil War borderlands did not seem to have the political heft to run. Robert Kerr was by now too heavily identified with his insatiable desire to enrich himself. Estes Kefauver was a spent force, facing a segregationist opponent in his Senate primary in Tennessee (whom he ultimately beat 65%–35%). His colleague Albert Gore, eclipsed by Kefauver in the 1956 vice presidential free-for-all at the convention, made no move to enter the race. The best known national Democrat at this point was Adlai Stevenson. Despite his lack of enthusiasm for the politics of economic redistribution, and because of his diffidence and elegance, he had the heartfelt support of many liberals symbolized by his friend Eleanor Roosevelt. But he had no stomach to run. As long before as 1955 he had told a friend, "Another race like the last one and I will really have had it."[11] In late 1959 he was telling political admirers like Hubert Humphrey and Chester Bowles that he had no plans to run for president again and that they should feel free to take their own course in the race.

VII

The political party whose nomination these men sought was not quite what it had been in 1952 or 1940 or 1932—but it was not fundamentally different. The population of most of America's central cities had declined in the 1950s, but that decline was not widely appreciated because the 1960 census figures had not yet been published. Centralized Democratic machines continued to dominate the public life of New York and Chicago, Philadelphia and Pittsburgh, Cleveland and Buffalo; while gaggles of politicians, unorganized and disunited, struggled for appointments and patronage in Boston and Baltimore, St. Louis and Kansas City. Machines were not found in all big cities. Detroit, Milwaukee, Minneapolis— the cities of the northern tier—had a non-partisan and non-machine politics, as did all the cities of the West Coast. None of the cities of the South bulked large in national politics. But machine politicians still controlled an important share of delegates at Democratic conventions.

So did southern party leaders, usually the incumbent governors. In 1960, al-though some of them were demagogues promising resistance to integration, Luther Hodges of North Carolina, Ernest Hollings of South Carolina, Leroy Collins of Florida, and Frank Clement of Tennessee were more moderate politicians. Northern governors as well expected to dominate their state delegations: G. Mennen Williams of Michigan, Robert Meyner of New Jersey, David Lawrence of Pennsylvania (the longtime boss in Pittsburgh), and Pat Brown of California expected at least this, and every one but Lawrence probably thought of himself, at least privately and if only momentarily, as a possible president. The reform Democratic movements centered in neighborhoods like the Upper East Side and Upper West Side of Manhattan, and their much smaller counterparts among pockets of well-educated liberals elsewhere, did not have as much direct representation;[12] the same was true for ethnics as such; and black politicians were still scarce (there were only four black congressmen at the time: William Dawson of Chicago, Adam Clayton Powell of Harlem, Charles Diggs, Jr., of Detroit, and Robert Nix of Philadelphia). Labor union leaders as such had less representation in the convention: as a major force in turnout and lobbying, they expected to and did receive respect, but they were in no way so tightly woven into the old-fashioned fabric of party politics as to be a major delegate-swinging force. If the bases of all the leading Democratic candidates were essentially national, the delegates they needed to win were characteristically local.

VIII

Whereas the Democratic field was expanded by the talented politicians who survived 1952 and thrived in 1958, the Republican field was winnowed down by the party's failure to produce more national figures in the early 1950s and the defeat or removal from the scene of leading figures like Joseph McCarthy, John Bricker, and William Knowland later in the decade. The Republicans' only conspicuous victors in 1958 were two businessmen-politicians who could not have been more diametrically opposed on most issues, and who were both elected in traditionally Democratic states: Barry Goldwater of Arizona and Nelson Rockefeller of New York. Actually, both were helped by political trends within their states which were not widely recognized at the time, the unpopularity of the Democratic bosses in New York and the migration of Republicans into Arizona.

Of the two Rockefeller attracted most of the attention. He was a scion of the nation's richest family; he was elected, at fifty, governor of the nation's largest state; he seemed to be the prime representative of the internationalist-liberal-East Coast wing of the Republican party which had prevailed at each of the last five national conventions. He also proved to be an adroit, shrewd, and folksy campaigner. Rockefeller's great advantage in New York was the state's nominating system. Unlike most states, New York did not choose candidates for governor or senator by primaries; state party conventions made the choice. The Republican convention typically was wired from the beginning for the winning candidate, and definitely was after the ultra-rich Rockefeller made plain he wanted the nomination: it was a decorous affair, and quiet and reassuring to the voters. The Democratic convention, on the other hand, was usually raucous and could always be portrayed as controlled by the party bosses—the party chairmen of the four large boroughs of New York City, which cast about 60% of the Democratic votes in the state.[13] Either the bosses prevailed and nominated their handpicked candidate, or they failed and the party was split down the middle—either way, the Republicans had an issue. In 1958 it was boss control, as Manhattan leader Carmine de Sapio, who always wore sinister-looking dark glasses because of an eye ailment, insisted on nominating Manhattan District Attorney Frank Hogan for senator. Hogan was by any measure a blue-ribbon candidate: Thomas Dewey's top assistant and choice as his successor, notoriously honest and able. But he was not liberal enough on some issues to suit some party liberals, and his selection was seen as a sign of weakness on Governor Harriman's part. In November he lost to Rochester Congressman Kenneth Keating—able, white-haired, liberal but strongly partisan in the Dewey tradition—by a 51%–48% margin, while Rockefeller beat Harriman 55%–45%.

Rockefeller was not quite a Dewey Republican himself. When Dewey first ran for president, Rockefeller was part of Franklin Roosevelt's State Department, specializing in Latin America. On foreign policy he was if anything even more internationalist than Dewey and Eisenhower, a believer in active engagement not only with Europe, but with Latin America as well. He served as an assistant secretary of health, education and welfare when the department was first created in the early Eisenhower years and was a foreign policy advisor without portfolio during the 1955 Geneva summit; but he eventually left the administration, criticizing it for not spending more on domestic policy and defense. Unlike Dewey, who was a stickler for balanced budgets and economy, Rockefeller was unconcerned with bookkeeping and loved great projects, like the huge state office complex he built south of the state Capitol in Albany.[14] Rockefeller was a tough partisan, always eager to beat the Democrats, but he lacked the vitriolic bitterness which Dewey and other liberal Republicans who unsuccessfully battled Roosevelt and Truman had.

Goldwater too lacked bitterness—or directed it against the "modern Republicans" he felt were betraying the conservative cause rather than against the Democrats, with many of whom he maintained good personal relations. His grandfather, a Jewish immigrant, had started Phoenix's largest department store; Barry Goldwater, raised an Episcopalian, had been elected mayor of Phoenix in 1949 and won an upset over Majority Leader Ernest McFarland in the 1952 senatorial race. Goldwater's political career can be considered a product of the room air conditioner. When he was growing up, the only protection against Arizona's fierce four-month summer heat was awnings and electric fans; after World War II came in contraptions with a fan blowing over ice cubes; finally, in the early 1950s, came the room air conditioner. Phoenix, a city of 106,000 in 1950, was on its way to becoming the center of a sprawling metropolis of more than 2 million by the late 1980s. And it was not just a home for retirees, but a city full of engineers and office employees and investors—people at the cutting edges of the American free-market economy, interested in keeping government out of their affairs.

In such a constituency Barry Goldwater did not stand out but rather fit in perfectly. He never claimed great talents and did not seek personal advancement. But he did stick unswervingly to the conservative label when it was unpopular, and he helped to transform the intellectual, stuffy conservatism of Robert Taft— the credo which Goldwater embraced when he reached the Senate in 1953—with the more populist, expansive conservatism which in the two decades beginning with his presidential candidacy won more political victories than it lost. Taft had been isolationist before World War II, opposed NATO after it, and was usually as cautious about spending money on defense as on any other government program. Goldwater, an Army Air Force officer during the war who (in a pattern common among Capitol Hill aficionados of the military) rose to the rank of general in the Air Force Reserve after years of part-time service, was an enthusiast for all things military, especially for the complex hardware the Air Force generals wanted, the supporter of an expansive and assertive foreign policy. The resolution of the Europe First–Asia First argument in the Eisenhower administration was demonstrated in Goldwater's politics. Earlier conservatives had voted against NATO; Goldwater supported it without question.

Goldwater also helped to move conservatives away from a localist to a nationalist politics. Taft and even Dewey Republicans wanted to vest power in local politicians and notables because they suspected these men shared their own values and they knew that Democratic appointees and bureaucrats in Washington often did not. Goldwater shared their localist assumptions, to the point that he opposed the Civil Rights Act of 1964—the ultimate in interference with local customs. But it was this Civil Rights Act, more than anything else, which undermined the localist position in American politics. Goldwater's refusal to distinguish the issue of civil rights—in which deference to local notables was producing injustices the rest of the nation was no longer willing to tolerate—from issues on which much stronger cases could be made for localism undermined localist politics so thoroughly that by the time conservative Republican presidents came to office they were firmly committed to using the federal government and centralist policies to achieve their ends. By the late 1980s, state and local governments and courts were increasingly in the hands of liberals and Democrats, while the federal government and courts had been staffed for most of recent history by conservative Republicans. This was not a development anticipated or particularly welcomed by Goldwater, but he played a part in bringing it about.

No one, including himself, saw Goldwater as presidential timber. "I'd like to lob one into the men's room in the Kremlin," he liked to say, in that era of Eisenhowerian gravity. But Goldwater's reelection in 1958 and the publication of his book *The Conscience of a Conservative* made him the hero of a growing group of ideological conservatives unhappy with the failure of the Eisenhower administration to roll back the New Deal or the Iron Curtain and wary of what would happen next. They were not able to get Goldwater to run for president in 1960, but they did nominate him and see him take the podium in Chicago and say, "Let's grow up, conservatives! If we want to take this party back, and I think we can some day, let's get to work."[15]

IX

Neither Rockefeller nor Goldwater was under any illusion that Richard Nixon was his kind of Republican. Yet Nixon had roots in both wings of the party. He had, after all, been chosen for vice president after he helped to swing crucial California votes to Eisenhower at the 1952 national convention. Thomas Dewey was one who recommended his nomination and backed him at every stage of his career. But Nixon's first fame had come in 1948 when as a member of the House Un-American Activities Committee he had led the investigation of Alger Hiss. The national attention he won then and when his accusations were vindicated by Hiss's conviction for perjury helped elect him senator from the nation's second-largest state in 1950 at the age of thirty-seven. Yet before he became a candidate for Congress, Nixon had shown little personal political ambition. At Whittier College and Duke Law School in the 1930s he was a hard worker, expressing no more than the opposition to Franklin Roosevelt which was standard among his heavily Republican fellow Quakers. "Never in any way," writes Stephen Ambrose, "was he a rebel." Yet he did find himself then and later torn between conservatism and liberalism. In 1958 he said "I came out of college more liberal than I am today," but when as a young Whittier lawyer he became head of the local Young Republicans, his standard speech was against FDR's court-packing plan. When the war began he took a Washington job with the liberal-laced Office of Price Administration, a position he claimed made him more conservative "about bureaucracy and about what the government could do because I saw the terrible paper work that people had to go through. I also saw the mediocrity of so many civil servants."[16] He was interested but not heavily involved in politics. He thought about running for the California Assembly in 1940 but got no support. A man with little charm, who did nothing to nurture friendships, who had neither money nor much in the way of connections, he seemed ill-suited to a political career and as the war ended considered staying in the Navy, which he had joined in August 1942. But when a local Republican leader wrote him in November 1945 to ask if he was interested in running for Congress in the eastern Los Angeles County district against New Deal Democrat Jerry Voorhis, Nixon hesitated not a minute before responding positively. And so at the age of thirty-three he began a career in which he would be obsessed with politics for more than forty years.

In his spectacular six-year rise from suburban lawyer and one of dozens of "Had enough?" Republican winners in 1946 to vice president of the United States at thirty-nine, Nixon never showed much of a political compass. *Six Crises* suggests he saw himself as responding to events and issues, not shaping them. The accusations against Hiss by Whittaker Chambers came as a surprise to Nixon; he responded usually, but not always, shrewdly and moved ahead. His often-retold redbaiting tactics against his 1950 opponent, Helen Gahagan Douglas, were actually a reaction to her charges that he had voted with Communist party-liner Vito Marcantonio. His maneuvering at the 1952 convention was a brilliant response to a situation which he did not entirely anticipate. Politically, he was a tactician,

not a strategist; an improviser, not a long-range planner; an adventurer who conquered more kingdoms than he could ever have imagined.

He used his vice presidency well. No one imagined that he played any major
role in White House decision-making, but no one imagined either what a distance
Eisenhower maintained from him: Nixon was never invited into the family quarters
of the White House or into Eisenhower's house in Gettysburg, Pennsylvania; he
became close to the Eisenhower family only when his daughter married Eisenhower's grandson David. Nixon was well informed; he spoke lucidly and clearly;
he traveled abroad in high visibility, debating Khrushchev in the kitchen of an
American exhibition in Moscow and barely escaping mob violence in Caracas. If
he infuriated the Democrats with aggressive and sometimes unfair charges in the
1952 and 1954 campaigns, he was speaking in the idiom and within the generally
accepted limits of political debate of the time. In Eisenhower's illnesses he behaved
with appropriate circumspection and care. By the voting public as 1960 began,
Nixon was generally respected, widely admired, often even well-liked. He was a
strong candidate for the Republican nomination, running well ahead of Rockefeller
and Goldwater in polls even before they left the field. In general election surveys,
he was entirely competitive with the leading Democrats. Yet to some extent the
voters were troubled by what seemed to trouble Republicans as different as Rockefeller and Goldwater and Democrats of all kinds. They were troubled by a sense
that Nixon did not really believe anything, that he was just playing out—sometimes
underhandedly, sometimes brilliantly—the hand he had been dealt.

33

⇶ ⇇

Debate

The 1960 campaign year began not on the hustings, nor in the ancestral homelands of any of the candidates, but in a quintessentially Washington location, the ornate Senate Caucus Room on the marble-walled third floor of the Old Senate Office Building, across Constitution Avenue from the Capitol. There on December 30, 1959, Hubert Humphrey announced his candidacy for president; there on January 3, 1960, John F. Kennedy announced his. These were unprecedentedly early announcements, and they were audacious candidacies: young senators with little seniority, without solid bases in old-fashioned local political machines, were not expected to run for president, certainly not openly, and never so many months before the convention. Humphrey did in fact have a substantial local base, but not in any machine which commanded respect outside the boundaries of his home state. His backing rested on the Democratic-Farmer-Labor party of Minnesota, that repository of reformers and labor union intellectuals which had more political soulmates than many hardheaded politicians thought (in the northern tier states of Michigan and Maine, Wisconsin and Oregon), but not enough to get a candidate anywhere close to a convention majority.

Not announcing so early was Richard Nixon. From most perspectives he occupied a commanding position in the race. Throughout 1959 polls found him the favorite of between 56% and 68% of Republicans, compared with 27% in January and 19% in November for Nelson Rockefeller.[1] And in Christmas week Rockefeller, after canvassing big-state Republicans for two months, announced he was not running—the first but not the last time he would withdraw from a race he would later lunge toward entering in a year in which the Republican candidate had a chance to win.[2] His withdrawal made Nixon the choice of 84% of Republicans, the uncontested candidate of the party whose incumbent president had governed the nation skillfully for eight years and who had in January 1960 a job approval rating of 71%.[3]

The Democrats were generally seen, by a 43%–29% margin, as the party more capable of keeping the country prosperous. But the Republicans had the clear advantage on foreign policy issues,[4] and by an overwhelming margin these were more important to voters in 1960 than were domestic matters. Foreign policy books by academics like Henry Kissinger and Herman Kahn were best sellers; foreign policy study groups conferred earnestly across the country; there was a sense that

319

great decisions were in the air, that history was at some turning point, that with the fading of Stalinism in the Soviet Union (as Nikita Khruschev's secret denunciation of Stalin in February 1956 became known), the "winds of change" (Harold Macmillan's January 1960 phrase) in the colonial world, and the entry of the great powers into space, the world was about to change—and that Americans had better be able to stay ahead of and not be left behind by that change. Nixon's foreign travels, his supposed closeness to foreign policy decision-making, and his fluency in public discussions of foreign policy issues made him a plausible inheritor of the advantages Eisenhower had built up for his party on the issues most Americans cared about most. True, voters still preferred a Democratic Congress, and by a rather hefty margin.[5] A country where a plurality regarded themselves as working class rather than middle class still preferred the Democrats' positions on economic issues. But looking ahead from the vantage point of early 1960, the Republicans— which is to say, Richard Nixon—had the clear advantage. The story of the 1960 election is often told, and never since more stirringly than by Theodore H. White, as the triumphant coming to power of John F. Kennedy. But in many ways it is really a story, and this one White tells also, of how Richard Nixon clumsily squandered his chance to govern.

First, Nixon never played the Eisenhower card. Aware that he needed to prove leadership qualities of his own, Nixon was also jealous of Eisenhower's popularity. He knew that he did not enjoy Eisenhower's full confidence, and he was proud of his own abilities. He wanted to win the presidency on his own.[6] Second, Nixon had a set of pet political theories which sounded logical but in fact seem to have been uniformly wrong. He believed, for example, that he had been hurt by Rockefeller's withdrawal, that beating Rockefeller in early primaries would have helped him to become blooded. But in fact the history of post-1960 elections shows that the faster a candidate clinches his party's nomination, the better he fares in the general election.[7] Clinching the nomination early allows a candidate to frame the issues his way and to shape his campaign to please the general electorate, not the peculiar and partisan electorates of early primary states. Nixon also believed it was important for a candidate to avoid peaking too soon, as if voters' views crested and ebbed like ocean waves. (This attitude resembles the theories of stock market chartists who insist that prices go up and down because of the shape of the lines they make on graphs, rather than because of exogenous facts and the mentality of investors.) He seemed to see an election as a form of personal combat, not as an attempt to persuade reasonable but not always attentive voters to accept as the decisive issues those which favored his own candidacy. Hence throughout the campaign he allowed the issues to be framed and the agenda to be set by his adversaries—first Rockefeller, in his frantic attempts to write his own programs into the Republican platform, then his Democratic opponent Kennedy. He talked about his opponents' issues, not his own. From his supporters, in contrast, he would listen to almost no advice. And he seemed to believe that voters scored the election as if they were professional politicians. He feared that voters in small remote states would resent him if he broke his promise to campaign in all fifty states, even after he had the perfectly plausible excuse of having to spend two weeks in the hospital nursing a knee infection: this the kind of complaint which candidates hear from resentful local politicians but ordinarily have the good sense not to give much heed to. Nixon, for all his reputation as a masterful politician, did not understand presidential electoral politics very well.

II

John Kennedy understood—or learned to, in the course of putting together a successful campaign. Kennedy did not begin as an unknown or long-shot candidate. In January 1959, when he was entering his second Senate term at the age of forty-one, he was the favorite of 25% of the Democrats, just marginally behind Adlai Stevenson at 29%; and among self-identified independents (many of them eligible to vote in Democratic primaries because of their party registration or their state's open primary laws) he led Stevenson 28%–22%. No other candidate had the support of more than 10% of Democrats, and this pattern continued throughout 1959. In January 1960, Kennedy led Stevenson 32%–28%, with Johnson trailing far behind. Why was this junior senator so far ahead of his party's two main contenders in the last two elections and its brilliant Senate majority leader? One reason is that Kennedy had attracted favorable notice in his unsuccessful vice presidential run in 1956, in his work on the Senate committee investigating corruption in the Teamsters and other labor unions, and for his book *Profiles in Courage,* which won a Pulitzer Prize. He had help in achieving such notice: his father had courted and befriended the great media barons for three decades, and Kennedy's handsome features, his young wife, his famous and photogenic and phenomenally rich extended family were featured in Luce, Cowles, and Hearst publications, none of them ordinarily sympathetic to Democrats.

Moreover, long before his nomination Kennedy had attracted special support from his fellow Roman Catholics. In April 1959 only 47% of Americans knew Kennedy was Catholic, but 61% of Catholics did, and 52% of Catholics said they might vote for the presidential nominee of the party other than their own if he was a Catholic—significant because almost half of American Catholics had voted for Eisenhower.[8] By November 1959, while Kennedy still trailed Stevenson 24%–18% among Protestant Democrats, he led Stevenson 38%–26% among Catholic Democrats. Joseph Kennedy's numbers were proving right: being a Catholic was worth votes. Moreover, Kennedy was the right kind of Catholic to break through the barrier against a Catholic president. He was aristocratic in bearing and graced with an accent which was unfamiliar to most Americans and sounded vaguely British to many and cultured to most (although it was actually a Jewish accent from Brookline, Massachusetts, where Kennedy had lived the first ten years of his life, an accent not much more socially elevated than the north-of-England accents of the Beatles and other British pop groups which would sound genteel to American ears a few years later). Educated at prep school and Harvard, elevated above any suspicion of corruption or greed by the fact that his father was one of the nation's richest men, enamored of English culture and naturally skeptical in the tradition of English Whigs, Kennedy was free from all the negative stereotypes afflicting Irish Catholics. He was, someone said, what every Irish Catholic woman wanted her grandson to be. He was beating the Yankee Protestants at all their own games—and yet was as indubitably Irish and Catholic as the earthy, New York street-smart Al Smith.

Kennedy, like Johnson, Humphrey, and Symington, knew that he began the campaign for the nomination with no solid geographic base of any great size. He did have a strong demographic base among Catholics, but Catholic politicians in states like New York, Pennsylvania, and Illinois were dubious about the prospect of a Catholic at the top of the ticket: they thought that on balance his religion would cost votes both for himself and for those lower down on statewide ballots, as with Al Smith in 1928, and that his candidacy would openly identify them with Catholicism and thus expose them to bigotry and attack. His initial machine support came from Massachusetts, where no local politicos cared to buck Joseph Kennedy, and from the unfortunately rather small state of Connecticut, where John Bailey, the shrewd and innovative state Democratic chairman from 1946 until his death in 1975, had broken barriers by slating candidates like the liberal Chester Bowles, elected governor in 1948, and the Jewish Abraham Ribicoff, elected governor in 1954 and reelected in a landslide in 1958.[9]

Kennedy realized that he must therefore win delegates on his own. There were two ways to do this. One was to contest presidential primaries; the other was to prospect for delegates under the noses of local party bosses. In 1960, primaries in fifteen states and the District of Columbia elected 584 Democratic delegates out of a total of 1,521—77% of the number needed to nominate. But even as aggressive and well-financed a candidate as Kennedy declined to contest all the primaries. He ran unopposed in next-door New Hampshire on March 8 and then took on Humphrey in his next-door Wisconsin on April 5; after four weeks of campaigning under the leaden skies of wintry Wisconsin, Kennedy carried the six heavily Catholic or industrial congressional districts around Milwaukee and the Fox River Valley and lost the three districts more heavily Protestant and closest to Minnesota plus the one dominated by the pro-Stevenson university town of Madison, for an indecisive 56%–44% victory. In Illinois on April 12 he won as a write-in but made no attempt to slate candidates for delegates; these would be controlled by Chicago Mayor Richard J. Daley and his machine Democrats. Similarly, in Pennsylvania on April 26 he won the "beauty contest" easily as a write-in but left the actual delegate-picking to the locals; he would negotiate later with Governor David Lawrence, as he would with Daley. On April 19 in heavily Catholic New Jersey, he declined to contest the unpledged delegate slate which would be controlled by Robert Meyner, a lame duck in his seventh year as governor but still the dominant power in a state where officials down to the county prosecutor level were gubernatorial appointees. The Massachusetts primary April 26 of course was Kennedy's, and so would be the delegation. On May 3 he stayed out of the District of Columbia, leaving it to Humphrey, whose prominence as a civil rights advocate since the 1948 national convention enabled him to beat Wayne Morse 57%–43%. On the same day he easily won the Indiana primary, which he had not succeeded in getting Humphrey to enter (Humphrey also declined to enter the May 10 contest in Nebraska), but left the larger Ohio delegation to a slate headed by Governor Michael DiSalle—like Daley and Lawrence a Catholic with reservations about a Kennedy candidacy.

The critical Kennedy–Humphrey showdown took place May 10 in West Virginia. Outwardly this 97% non-Catholic state looked like hostile ground, and Joseph Kennedy argued against his son's running there. But by this time John Kennedy and his brother and campaign manager Robert had taken control of the campaign. Joseph Kennedy was given assignments, like courting Bronx boss Charles Buckley and raising money, and he was not shy about giving advice; but the decision on whether it would be followed was made by the candidate.[10] Kennedy led in initial polls in West Virginia, was well known there as he was elsewhere in the country, and enjoyed invaluable campaigning help from Franklin D. Roosevelt, Jr., whose father was still revered in West Virginia and who reminded voters in this bellicose state that Humphrey had sat out World War II with a deferment while Kennedy rescued the survivors of his sunken PT-109 patrol boat in the Pacific. Humphrey's campaign was woefully underfinanced; he ended up spending his grocery money[11] to keep it going to primary day. Later in the 1960s he would become a widely known figure in his own right; but in 1960 his fame was great only among activist liberals, and at no point in the national Gallup Poll did he ever have the support of more than 7% of the Democrats. He was, if not precisely a stalking horse for Johnson or Stevenson, as the Kennedys suspected, then at least a convenient repository for anti-Kennedy or anti-Catholic sentiment. Humphrey's campaign was managed by James Rowe, a law partner and former Roosevelt administration colleague of Tommy Corcoran, both of whom were close friends and allies of Johnson; his chief West Virginia supporter was freshman Senator Robert Byrd, who had gotten a seat on the Appropriations Committee, where he could help his impoverished constituency, with Johnson's help and who made it clear that he would do anything to further Johnson's presidential candidacy, including supporting a man with whose philosophy he had little in common. But these men were no match for the Kennedys, who were able and willing to win both the new way and the old, to buy both television ads and local politicoes. Anti-Catholic feeling did of course exist in West Virginia, rooted in the old Reformation and Glorious Revolution traditions that the first mountaineers had brought with them over the Appalachians in the 1770s.[12] "All other issues were secondary," wrote Theodore White, who quoted a "[l]ittle old lady, under a dripping umbrella in the rain in Sutton, West Virginia ('Home of the Golden Delicious Apple' says the sign): 'We've never had a Catholic President and I hope we never do. Our people built this country. If they had wanted a Catholic to be President, they would have said so in the Constitution.' "[13] Of course what the Constitution said was that no religious test should be applied for office, but the idea was clear: "our people," even in the muddy, greenery-choked mountains of Braxton County, West Virginia, were not going to give up their country without a struggle.

Yet if anti-Catholic feeling had been decisive, Kennedy could not have won. In fact, his assets—not just his glamour and money, but the genuine positive feelings he had succeeded in inspiring and the lesser-known Humphrey had not—gave him a clear advantage apart from the religious issue. And he insisted on confronting this one liability directly, making the primary a contest between tolerance and bigotry. The key was a TV broadcast the Sunday night before the Tuesday primary, in which Franklin Roosevelt, Jr., asked Kennedy questions and the candidate replied that a president must swear to uphold the Constitution, including the separation of church and state, and said, as White recalled it, that if he violated the oath " 'he is committing a sin against God.' Here Kennedy raised his hand from an imaginary Bible, as if lifting it to God, and repeating softly, said 'A sin against God, for he has sworn on the Bible.' "[14] Even White did not fully appreciate Kennedy's sensitivity to cultural idiom: reading and personally interpreting the Bible was a central part of most Protestant faiths, while Catholics at the time, as was well known to scandalized Protestants, were discouraged from interpreting the Bible themselves, often heard it read in Latin, and were encouraged to rely on their priests for knowledge of it. Kennedy's emphasis on the Bible shows he understood the primacy for Protestants of the Book.

By making tolerance his issue, Kennedy won a smashing 61%–39% victory, and Humphrey promptly withdrew from the nomination contest. Kennedy then easily won successive primaries in Maryland on May 17 and Oregon on May 20. But he deferred to local leaders once again in Florida, where Senator George Smathers's slate was elected May 24, and California, where a delegation led by Governor Pat Brown was chosen June 7. Although a Catholic, Brown was not at all an old-fashioned political boss; from the cloudy, stucco-house middle-class Catholic neighborhoods west of Twin Peaks in San Francisco, he had climbed to be district attorney and attorney general in California's non-partisan government and had finally led the Democrats to a crashing across-the-board statewide victory in 1958. His party had no machine politicians and a great many idealistic liberals who ended up supporting Adlai Stevenson, much to Kennedy's and Brown's dismay.

Kennedy's West Virginia victory put him in a position to harvest the victories in non-primary states which he had been sowing for long months. In early June, on the hills of Mackinac Island, overlooking the Mackinac Bridge (only recently opened and then the nation's longest span) which connected Michigan's two peninsulas, Kennedy won Governor G. Mennen Williams's endorsement and thus almost all of the Michigan delegation. Later in the month, on the lawn of Gracie Mansion (New York City's mayoral residence), overlooking the stupendous Triborough and railroad bridges which connected Manhattan with Long Island and the mainland of America, Kennedy received the fealty of Mayor Robert Wagner, Jr., and the Democratic bosses of all of New York state's major counties. (The New Yorkers' endorsement represented less a voluntary decision than the success of efforts by John Bailey and Joseph Kennedy to secure so much support in upstate New York and in the Bronx that the other downstaters would have to come along.) In Colorado and Wyoming and New Mexico and Arizona, Kennedy went underneath their aging lions of the Senate to up-and-coming leaders like Congressman Stewart Udall and Lawyer Byron White and won delegates and sometimes whole delegations away from Johnson. The key final delegations, not delivered publicly until the Sunday and Monday of convention week in July, were Illinois and Pennsylvania. Mayor Daley, a longtime political debtor to Stevenson, was familiar with the local power of Joseph Kennedy, who owned the Merchandise Mart, the biggest piece of real estate in Chicago; Governor Lawrence, a longtime admirer of Stevenson, was aware of the enthusiasm for Kennedy of Philadelphia's new boss, Congressman William Green, Jr., whose heavily Catholic northeast Philadelphia district had long been marginal but would go 62% for Kennedy in November. Once Illinois and Pennsylvania came over, Kennedy had more than 700 delegates. He was so close to the 761 needed to win—and he was so clearly the popular favorite, with about 40% to Stevenson's 21% in a multi-candidate field poll since early April—that the party would have suffered terrific damage if it had stopped him. Considerable maneuvering took place at the convention; and if Kennedy had had only 600 votes, as Johnson's pre-convention delegate count had it,[15] he might have been in trouble. The strategies of Johnson, Stevenson, and Symington—to hang back and wait for a deadlock—would not have seemed so stupid as they have ever since July 1960 had just a few contingencies at the convention gone the other way. But they didn't, and Kennedy became the Democratic nominee.

III

Since the beginning of the Cold War, Americans had worried about Soviet leaders. Stalin, portrayed by politicians and in much of the press after June 1941 as an earthy hero, was seen after March 1947 as a ruthless and cruel despot, unremittingly hostile and increasingly out of touch with reality. The man Harry Truman had met with in Potsdam in July 1945 became a figure of dread mystery: in command of the atomic bomb and vast armies, he was a threat to peace whether acting in his own rational evil interest or utterly irrationally. Americans had seen one madman conquer most of Europe and threaten the rest of the world. They feared that Stalin was another madman, and one with even greater destructive potential. Thus the sense of relief at his death in March 1953 had been almost as great as that at the Korean armistice in June. Yet Stalin's successors were still scary: they had his secret police chief, Lavrenti Beria, executed in July 1953. Although Khrushchev, the eventual winner of the power struggle, was a more human, sometimes even amiable figure, he was also emotional, erratic, bullying, and utterly ignorant of real conditions outside the Soviet Union—a dangerous man in his position.

Some hopeful signs of an end to the Cold War did appear. In July 1955, President Eisenhower met with Khrushchev and Soviet Premier Nikolai Bulganin, plus the leaders of Britain and France, in Geneva, the first such summit meeting in ten years (and the first to be called a summit). In February 1956, Khrushchev delivered his famous denunciation of Stalin at the Twentieth Party Congress—the toughest denunciation of Stalin by a Soviet leader over the next thirty years. But these developments were not followed up by greater cooperation. After the success of Sputnik in October 1957 and the ensuing embarrassments to the U.S. space program, Khrushchev in November 1958 threatened to sign a peace treaty with East Germany granting it control of the access routes to West Berlin unless the West signed an overall German peace treaty within six months. The United States, having promised to maintain the freedom of West Berlin and having striven mightily to do so in the Berlin airlift of 1948–49, could not give in to this ultimatum. A crisis gratuitously and unpredictably provoked by Khrushchev raised the risk of World War III and shadowed U.S.–Soviet relations for the next four years.

For a time the crisis seemed to ease. In July 1959 Eisenhower said that if progress was made at foreign ministers' talks, he would invite Khrushchev to the United States—the sort of invitation that John Foster Dulles, who had resigned in April and died the next month, had always opposed. In fact, Eisenhower's instructions were misinterpreted, the invitation was extended unconditionally, and Khrushchev told Eisenhower he was coming for ten days in September. Shortly thereafter Nixon had his filmed confrontation with Khrushchev in Moscow, and in August the Khrushchev visit—the first visit of a Soviet chief of state to the United States—was announced. Khrushchev's boisterous trip across the country—his tête-à-têtes in Hollywood with Frank Sinatra and Shirley MacLaine, his canceled visit to Disneyland, and his sojourn at the Roswell Garst farm in Coon Rapids, Iowa—provided Americans with a vivid exhibition of his personality, including his coarseness and defensive hostility. When Mayor Norris Poulson of Los Angeles told him, responding to one of his boasts, "You shall not bury us and we shall not bury you!" Khrushchev replied, "I can go, and I don't know when— if ever—another Soviet premier will visit your country. . . . The unpleasant thought sometimes creeps up on me as to whether Khrushchev was not invited here to enable you to sort of rub him in your sauce and show the might of the United States, to make him shake at your knees. If that is so, then if it took me about twelve hours to get here, I guess it will take no more than ten and a half hours to get back."[16] But if such outbursts were alarming, the result after Eisenhower and Khrushchev conferred for two days at the presidential retreat of Camp David[17] was more comforting: Khrushchev dropped his ultimatum, agreed to another summit, and invited Eisenhower to visit the Soviet Union afterward.

Although this encounter raised Americans' hopes for U.S.-Soviet relations, they were sharply lowered in a few weeks in May 1960. On May 1 the Soviets shot down an American U-2 reconnaissance plane piloted by CIA employee Francis Gary Powers, who survived, against his employers' expectations and the American government's best interests. Eisenhower always believed in covert operations and aerial reconnaissance; he had called for an Open Skies agreement at Geneva, and when the Soviets declined he had the CIA build the U-2 in record time. Its first flight was on July 4, 1956, and each flight was approved personally by the president. When Powers was shot down the CIA assumed that he had died, and the U.S. government denied it had intended to fly over Soviet territory. On May 7, however, Khrushchev angrily revealed that the pilot was alive and had the wreckage of the plane exhibited in Moscow's Gorky Park. With the summit due to begin May 16 in Paris, Khrushchev, already there, told French President Charles de Gaulle that Eisenhower must apologize. Eisenhower refused. The summit broke up May 17, Eisenhower's invitation to Moscow was canceled, and the specter of war over Berlin was raised again, all thanks to what even Eisenhower admitted was a mistake: in retrospect, the U-2 flight should not have been ordered so close to the summit, and the U.S. government ought not to have gotten itself caught in lies afterwards.

Kennedy, who won his crucial victory in West Virginia between the announcement of Powers's capture and the scuttling of the summit, went so far as to say that Eisenhower should have apologized, a statement for which he was roundly criticized by Johnson and Nixon. But if Kennedy made a political error, it was more than counterbalanced by the damage done to administration policy by the incident. Eisenhower's job rating remained high: Americans rallied to his side when he was in trouble. But the dashing of their hopes for peace and the humiliation of their president, coming on top of the Soviets' lead in the space race and the spectacle of Eisenhower lying, left Americans feeling their country was suffering in world opinion. Magazines were full of articles echoing Khrushchev's claims that the Soviet economy was growing more rapidly and producing better weapons than the American economy. Western Europe, the beggarly beneficiary of American generosity a decade before, now seemed to be storming ahead, with greater economic growth and more generous welfare state protections. American prestige—a word often used in the campaign year—seemed in decline. By June the Republicans had lost their edge over the Democrats in polls asking which party could better keep the nation out of World War III, and by July, as the Democratic convention met in the sprawling megalopolis of Los Angeles, the Democrats had a 41%–25% edge over the Republicans on maintaining America's prestige in the world.

IV

Americans entering election year 1960 knew, as no Americans entering any other election year between 1928 and 1988 knew,[18] that their incumbent president was not running for reelection. Dwight Eisenhower was sixty-nine, the oldest president in American history and the first barred from being elected to a third term. But neither of the two party nominees chosen to succeed him were strangers to the public by the summer of 1960. Both were, at least to judge from the polls, their party's strongest candidates. Nixon ran ahead of Kennedy in Gallup's August and November 1959 pairings, but Nelson Rockefeller—whom Kennedy always said he considered a tougher candidate—ran significantly behind. Kennedy, for his part, ran only a few points behind Nixon in November 1959 and January 1960, whereas Stevenson ran nearly 10 points behind him (was this one reason Stevenson was reluctant to run?) and in the spring of 1960 Nixon had even bigger leads than this over Johnson and Symington, at times when he was running even with or behind Kennedy. Kennedy and Nixon were helped by their greater name recognition compared with most of the others (though not with Stevenson), and polls cannot project how a little-known candidate will run when voters get to know him better. But the fact is that no other candidate of either party was running stronger than the two men who were nominated.

The Kennedy-Nixon race is often remembered as a battle in which the lead seesawed from one side to the other and turned on massive shifts of opinion. But what is remarkable is how little opinion changed. In Kennedy-Nixon pairings (Kennedy-Johnson–Nixon-Lodge pairings after the conventions) during 1959 and 1960, Kennedy never got less than 43% of the vote and never more than 51%; Nixon varied between 45% and 50%. Gallup showed one 6-point lead for Nixon, 50%–44%, in an apparent uptick just after the Republican convention, and a 5-point lead for Kennedy in March 1960.[19] Almost always the margin between the candidates was less than the 4-point statistical margin of error, as shown in the following table:

Dates	Kennedy %	Nixon %	Undecided %
July 23–28, 1959	48	45	7
August 20–25	46	47	7
November 12–17	43	48	9
January 6–11, 1960	44	47	9
February 4–9	48	48	4
March 2–7	50	45	5
March 30–April 4	51	44	5
April 28–May 3	48	47	5
May 26–31	47	49	4
July 30–August 4	44	50	6
August 11–16	47	47	6
August 25–30	48	47	5
September 9–14	46	47	7
September 28–October 2	49	46	5
October 18–23	49	45	6
October 30–November 3	49	48	3
ELECTION	49.7	49.5	—

A 1980s polling analyst who was presented with these results, being aware of the statistical margin of error and familiar with the limitations of polling especially in 1960 but even three decades later, would say simply that all these numbers are the same. This was a race in which almost all voters were arrayed on one side or the other from the beginning, and few crossed over. But this division was obscured at the time by Gallup's habit of reporting the results with the undecided voters left out, so that a 49%–46% result, indicating no absolute majority for either candidate and a lead within the statistical margin of error, was reported as 52%–48%, which sounded much more like a conclusive majority for one candidate.

The blocs supporting each candidate were defined more by their religion and ethnic origin than anything else, including economic factors. Around May Day, Gallup showed Kennedy ahead of Nixon 48%–47%. Catholics were 75%–20% for Kennedy; Protestants—including blacks and white southerners—were 61%–34% for Nixon.[20] These numbers are almost identical to Gallup's post-election analysis: 50%–50% (the rounded-off versions of Kennedy's 49.7% and Nixon's 49.5%), with Catholics 78%–22% for Kennedy and Protestants 62%–38% for Nixon. This is evidence of impressive stasis—and of an election dividing the country on cultural, not economic, lines. The 1960 election was not a struggle between a Democratic working class and a Republican middle class. It was a struggle between American Catholics, determined to prove this was their country too, and American Protestants, a large number of whom believed fervently that it was their country alone.

Of course, the events of the campaign did make some difference—and so did the management skills of the candidates. Kennedy's campaign was not as flawless or brilliant as legend would have it. But the candidate generally performed well, and sometimes superbly, in public. The more experienced Nixon, in contrast, ran a campaign riddled with avoidable mistakes.

Kennedy stage-managed the Los Angeles convention satisfactorily. His delegate counting was accurate, and he won the nomination at the end of the first ballot as the last state, Wyoming, voted. The next day he dithered behind the scenes before offering the vice presidential nomination to Johnson, who hesitated before accepting it. Two hours later Johnson was jolted when Robert Kennedy came to Johnson's suite in the Biltmore Hotel, two floors directly below Kennedy's, and said Johnson should withdraw. *Washington Post* publisher Philip Graham, who served both as Johnson's advocate and as his trusted intermediary in these negotiations (and handed his reporters limited scoops in the process), managed to reach John Kennedy one final time on the hotel telephone and recorded his response thus: " 'Oh,' said Jack, as calmly as though we were discussing the weather, 'that's all right; Bobby's been out of touch and doesn't know what's been happening.' "[21] From this incident flared much of the mistrust between Lyndon Johnson and Robert Kennedy, the Senate's master and a Senate staffer in the 1950s—a mistrust with grave consequences for the Democratic party. For Johnson, as Graham delphically noted, wanted the vice presidential nomination, realizing that if he failed to take it and Kennedy lost he would be blamed for any failure to carry southern electoral votes and that if Kennedy won he as majority leader would be eclipsed by the Democratic president.[22] Joseph Kennedy favored Johnson for the nomination—and may have made a crucial phone call to his son the nominee between two of Graham's calls.[23] Kennedy's acceptance speech was poorly delivered by a tired candidate before 80,000 people in an acoustically poor setting at the Los Angeles Coliseum; it featured the stagy and not particularly apt phrase "New Frontier,"[24] in a transparent attempt to provide a convenient label associating his program with Roosevelt's New Deal and Truman's Fair Deal. After the Republican convention Kennedy mouldered on the back benches of the Senate where his running mate was majority leader, as President Eisenhower copied President Truman's 1948 inspiration and called the opposition Congress back into session to pass its own platform, knowing very well it would not do so. What is striking from a later vantage point is that a political candidate could attract such crowds (the only time Ronald Reagan saw such a crowd in 1984 was when he appeared at the opening of the Los Angeles Olympics in that same Coliseum) and that Kennedy felt obliged to show up in the Senate. A 1980s candidate would have explained that he had to go off and campaign and was leaving his running mate in charge.

Meanwhile, Nixon had helped to sabotage what should have been his own triumphant nomination at the Republican convention in Chicago two weeks later by flinching in the face of attack from Nelson Rockefeller. Covertly allowing a Draft Rockefeller movement to go forward, the ambitious New York governor insisted on a platform implicitly repudiating Eisenhower's record as insufficiently expansive on the economy, insufficiently assertive in military policy, and insufficiently supportive of civil rights—the first two of these arguments having been made vehemently the week before by the Democrats in Los Angeles. On the Friday before the convention, while the Platform Committee hearings plodded on under the chairmanship of Charles Percy, the forty-year-old Bell & Howell chairman and obviously a future presidential hopeful himself, Rockefeller threatened a floor fight. At that Nixon flew to New York, met all evening with Rockefeller in his apartment at 810 Fifth Avenue (the building in which Nixon himself would live from 1963 until he was elected president in 1968), and reached agreement on what came to be known as the Compact of Fifth Avenue, in which he agreed to support some of Rockefeller's planks. Percy's committee and the regular Republicans were furious, knowing that they had the votes to beat Rockefeller on the floor; President Eisenhower, who had appointed Rockefeller to high positions, fiercely resented what he recognized as criticism of his record; and Barry Goldwater emerged for the first time as a leader in the party, speaking to the convention and calling on conservatives to grow up and take over their party. In the fall the convention's Rockefeller civil rights plank left the Republicans ill-positioned to build on Eisenhower's advances in a South which was becoming much more virulently hostile to civil rights, in response to the demonstrations by the civil rights movement. At the same time, Nixon's unwillingness to lend support to Martin Luther King, Jr., when he was jailed on a trumped-up traffic charge in rural Georgia in October, combined with Robert Kennedy's reflex decision to phone Mrs. King, meant that Republicans lost the bulk of the black vote in the North—a rapidly increasing segment of the electorate, given the continuing northward black migration of 1940–70—and in most of the few places in the South (Richmond, Atlanta, Memphis, Louisville) where blacks voted in significant numbers.

In September, Kennedy faced and met two challenges which could have derailed his candidacy. The first was his speech September 12 before the Greater Houston Ministerial Association, an organization of Protestant clergymen in the city which

Al Smith had been nominated in and then had failed to carry, in the ornate Rice Hotel downtown where balconies jut out over sidewalks to protect walkers, in the innocent days before ubiquitous air conditioning, from the relentless Gulf Coast sun. An intellectually serious argument could be made that faithfulness to Catholic dogma would require a president to accept dictation from a foreign prelate; those who felt no Catholic should be president included not only backwoods preachers and Norman Vincent Peale, the Republican-leaning author of best-selling "inspirational" books, but also the president of Princeton Theological Seminary and the director of Protestants and Other Americans United for Separation of Church and State.[25] Kennedy had to satisfy the ministers in the Houston audience and millions beyond that he would not accept Church dictation, and he did so by taking an extreme position, averring that "no Catholic prelate would tell the President (should he be a Catholic) how to act" and promising to resign the presidency if he could not conscientiously maintain the constitutional separation of church and state. There were no angry assertions from Catholics that Kennedy was being unfaithful to Church dogma. Many Americans in 1960 feared that a Catholic president would insist on federal aid to Catholic as well as public schools, but Kennedy made it plain at Houston and throughout the campaign that he would (as in fact he did) oppose the Church position on this issue. (Abortion and birth control were not on the political agenda: the first was everywhere illegal, and the second received no government assistance.) Kennedy was confident that Catholic voters wanted more to achieve validation of themselves as Americans than to get their way on what were by comparison marginal issues.

Kennedy's Houston speech came just as Nixon was resuming a campaign which had begun inauspiciously when this least physically graceful of politicians struck his kneecap on a car door in Greensboro, North Carolina, and developed an infection which kept him hospitalized from August 29 to September 9. His insistence on nevertheless honoring his acceptance speech pledge to campaign in all fifty states (for Hawaii had been admitted in August 1959) seems even more unnecessary because personal appearances were coming to mean less in a year when most voters came to know the candidates best on television.

V

On the evening of Monday, September 26, inside a squat tan converted sports arena a block from Lake Michigan where CBS's Chicago station had its studios, Kennedy met his second challenge in the pivotal event of the presidential campaign of 1960, the first of his televised debates with Nixon. These encounters occurred only because both candidates were convinced that TV debates would serve their purpose; the section of the Federal Communications Act requiring equal time for minor candidates had to be suspended by Congress, and this could be done in the time available only by agreement of both major parties' candidates. Nixon was convinced by the success of his Checkers speech and by what he considered his superior knowledge that he could make Kennedy look unfit for the job; Kennedy, coolly confident of his mastery of the facts and contemptuous of the opponent who had fawned over his richer, more polished colleague from the day they had come to the House together in 1947,[26] was convinced he could establish himself as the equal of the incumbent vice president.

Kennedy was right. Prepared from practice sessions, rested from a nap, tanned and dapper in a dark gray suit, he was confident, disciplined, and calm. Nixon had spent the day in solitude; haggard from his knee injury and cold and exhausted from the intensive campaign schedule he had insisted on, he was nervous and ill at ease, slouching and sweating. He was dressed in a light gray suit which blended into the studio backdrop; and his heavy beard, as dark as Joseph McCarthy's on television, he toned down only with a hasty application of "Lazy Shave" makeup. Radio listeners, when polled, divided about evenly on who had won, but television viewers—the large majority of voters—thought Kennedy had prevailed. Nixon, who could have run as the natural heir of a successful administration, inexplicably let Kennedy set the terms of the discussion—as if he did not really believe in his own case. When Kennedy said, "I think it's time to get America moving again," Nixon accepted his framing of the issues: "I can subscribe completely to the spirit that Senator Kennedy has expressed tonight, the spirit that America should move ahead." The self-pity Nixon often expressed in campaign speeches came out at one point: "I know what it means to be poor." Kennedy exerted a command over himself, the subject matter, and his opponent which ended any doubts that he was of presidential stature.

There were three more televised debates, but Nixon never regained the initiative he lost on September 26. Kennedy rose to a 49%–46% lead in Gallup's September 28–October 2 poll and stayed at 49% in Gallup surveys through October. The two disagreed predictably on domestic policy; on foreign policy it was Kennedy who backed a more aggressive stance, insisting that the United States defend the Nationalist Chinese islands of Quemoy and Matsu and refusing to rule out the possibility of an overthrow of Fidel Castro's government in Cuba. But the debates probably did not so much win the candidates votes as solidify them, or prevent them from falling away. The strength of Kennedy's candidacy was rooted in the fervent support he received from American Catholics. He attracted huge crowds— from the 1.25 million who met him in New York City to the 30,000 who waited on the green in the brass manufacturing city of Waterbury, Connecticut, until 3 A.M. of the Monday before election day. These were not so much working-class throngs cheering for a new New Dealer or celebrity hounds eager for a glimpse of a star. They were, though no one was comfortable saying it at the time, basically Catholic crowds, cheering with joy that one of their own seemed on his way to being elected president of their country.

Nixon's crowds were smaller and less enthusiastic. He was whipsawed on the civil rights issue, as his running mate Henry Cabot Lodge promised in a speech in Harlem that the Republicans would appoint a Negro cabinet member, while Nixon himself declined to intercede as the Kennedys did when Martin Luther King, Jr., was jailed. Nixon argued unpersuasively that Kennedy would raise taxes and only slightly more persuasively that the nationalistic Kennedy was knocking rather than boosting America. He told lugubrious stories about his family's poverty. His refusal to use or even much to defend Eisenhower miffed the president so much that in an August press conference, when Texas reporter Sarah McClendon and *Time*'s Charles Mohr asked him again and again for an example of a decision Nixon had taken part in or an idea he had suggested, Eisenhower said, "If you give me a week I might think of one. I don't remember"—and promptly ended the press conference. He spoke little more about Nixon until the last week of the campaign.

On election night the naiveté of political projection at the time was apparent when from the earliest Kentucky, Indiana, and Kansas returns the TV networks projected Nixon the easy winner, then from the quickly tabulated Connecticut returns they projected Kennedy the easy winner, and then as more numbers came in they kept counting an increasingly close election, the outcome of which was not clear until 5:35 A.M. Wednesday. The reason for the wildly shifting projections was the religious polarization of the vote. Catholics, who despite their Democratic allegiance had given the divorced socialite Adlai Stevenson only 54% of their votes in 1956, were now 78% for Kennedy; Protestants, who voted 40% for Stevenson, voted 38% for Kennedy—a drop which was even greater among white Protestants (blacks were counted as 58% for Stevenson, 70% for Kennedy). Kennedy ran behind Stevenson's percentages in Georgia (still Kennedy's second-best state), Tennessee, Mississippi, Arkansas, and Oklahoma, and less than 1 percentage point better than Stevenson in Alabama and Missouri (which both Democrats barely carried). But he ran 22 points ahead of Stevenson in Rhode Island, the most heavily Catholic state, 20 points ahead in his home state of Massachusetts, 17 points ahead in Connecticut, 16 points ahead in New Jersey, 14 points ahead in Maine, Vermont, New York, and Maryland, 13 points ahead in New Hampshire.

What is striking in retrospect is not only how close the result was nationally, but how high the interest was and how close the result was in almost every single state. Turnout was a national record—nearly 69 million, representing 64% of those eligible. This figure was higher than the 63% in 1952, the previous peak years, although lower than the percentages of eligible men who had voted before women were enfranchised and especially before 1900, before segregationist schemes in the South and progressive reforms in the North cut turnout among groups who were widely considered unworthy of the franchise. Enthusiasm for the candidates, especially among Catholics for Kennedy; confidence that the changes needed could be accomplished; a rising affluence and the beginnings of enfranchisement of blacks in the Deep South; the closeness of the race—all these factors helped to produce a high turnout. Contributing to the closeness of state-by-state results was a shift in regional party allegiance. The South and West, heavily Democratic in the days of William Jennings Bryan, Woodrow Wilson, and Franklin Roosevelt, were now in the process of trending Republican; the Northeast and the industrial Great Lakes region, so much of which leaned against Franklin Roosevelt in 1932 or 1940, was now trending Democratic. Kennedy won more than 60% of the vote in only three states, Rhode Island, Georgia, and Massachusetts; Nixon won more than 60% in only two, Nebraska and Kansas. In forty of the fifty states the margin was 55%–45% or less.[27] Kennedy's percentages in the eight largest states are instructive: New York 53% (regarded as a comparative landslide), New Jersey 50%, Pennsylvania 51%, Ohio 47% (regarded as a landslide for Nixon), Michigan 51%, Illinois 50%, Texas 51%, California 50%. Analysis of the results within states shows exceedingly sharp differences between the big metropolitan areas, with large Catholic and in some cases Jewish populations, and the countryside, with largely Protestant populations. So concentrated was Kennedy's vote, and so malapportioned against the rapidly growing Catholic edge-of-the-city neighborhoods were House districts, that he carried only 206 of the nation's 437[28] congressional districts—a figure which gauged the weakness of his standing in the new House. Kennedy ran behind Stevenson in 63 House districts, most in the South and border states but ranging as far north in the Civil War borderlands as Gettysburg, Pennsylvania; Bloomington, Indiana; and Ottumwa, Iowa. They included the eastern South Dakota district represented the preceding four years by George McGovern (who, as Kennedy foresaw, narrowly lost the 1960 Senate race to Karl Mundt) and the Fresno and Bakersfield districts in California's Central Valley, which had attracted so many "Okie" migrants in the 1930s. Kennedy gained more than 10 percentage points over Stevenson's 1956 showing in every district in New England, all but one (the Manhattan "Silk Stocking" district) in New York state, and all but one in Pennsylvania. Otherwise, his big gains came mostly in metropolitan blotches across the country's map: greater Baltimore, greater Philadelphia, the northeast Pennsylvania anthracite country, greater Pittsburgh and Erie, northeast Ohio (but not heavily Protestant Akron), metropolitan Detroit and Milwaukee and the Catholic areas around Lakes Huron, Michigan, and Superior, San Francisco and Oakland (but not much of Los Angeles, where Stevenson had been relatively strong), the Cajun and Mexican Gulf Coasts of Louisiana and Texas, south Florida with its northern migrants. These figures provide the firmest possible evidence for the irrefutable argument that the 1960 election split the nation along religious, which is to say cultural, lines, not along lines of economic class.[29]

Shadows were cast on the legitimacy of the result in 1960 and have been ever after. Vote fraud in Chicago's West Side wards could well have accounted for Kennedy's 8,858-vote plurality (out of 4.75 million votes reported cast) in Illinois. But switching Illinois would have reduced Kennedy's electoral vote count only from 303 to 276—leaving him still with a majority. His 2,294-vote plurality in New Mexico could conceivably have been produced by fraud, too, but New Mexico cast only 4 electoral votes. Republicans have also charged that there was vote fraud in Texas. Perhaps there was, but surely not nearly enough to account for the 46,257-vote Democratic plurality. Republicans of this period saw vote fraud everywhere: from their comfortable and overwhelmingly Republican communities, they found it hard to imagine how so many of their fellow citizens in big cities or southern states could voluntarily mark their ballots for the Democrats. But all the available evidence suggests that in the vast majority of cases they did—especially in 1960, when the Catholic vote was 78% and the Jewish vote 81% for Kennedy. Nixon has been portrayed as magnanimous for not contesting the result. But he was, as he himself has generally argued, simply being prudent and responsible. Not only would a contest have taken a long time; it would not have succeeded in overturning the result. Whatever else the 1960 presidential election was, it was not stolen.

34

-»» «««-

Frontier

Let the word go forth from this time and place to friend and foe alike, that the torch has been passed to a new generation of Americans," said the youngest man ever inaugurated as president in the presence of the oldest man ever to serve in the office. The day was cold, and snow was falling heavily on Washington. "Let every nation know, whether it wishes us well or ill," he continued, that we shall pay any price, bear any burden, meet any hardship, support any friend, oppose any foe to assure the survival and the success of liberty." Except for Franklin Roosevelt's brief wartime message, Kennedy's speech was the shortest Inaugural of the twentieth century, and it is remembered best for the phrase "ask not what your country can do for you; ask what you can do for your country."

These words seem out of character to those who see Kennedy as a domestic reformer, a redistributor of income and backer of civil rights, a believer in giving ordinary people entitlements for which they owed nothing. But the Democrat who took the oath of office in January 1961 had campaigned for a more aggressive foreign policy and higher defense spending, and he chose to speak now almost entirely about the Cold War. He deliberately omitted all mention of domestic policy: it sounded partisan, divisive, too much like the campaign, recalled his chief speechwriter, Theodore Sorenson.[1] Preoccupied by Khrushchev's not abandoned 1958 threat to force the West out of Berlin, alarmed by the specter of Communist advance in Laos, aware of the troubles that might follow the Eisenhower administration's severing of diplomatic relations with Fidel Castro's Cuba earlier in the month,[2] Kennedy felt that the country he was about to lead was under siege and that he must somehow create the sense of unity and willingness to sacrifice he remembered from World War II—in a nation comfortable after years of prosperity and uneasy about events abroad. Eisenhower had made peace in Korea and had resisted arguments to go to war in Indochina and the Formosa Straits; to make advances in the Cold War he had relied on covert action, as in Guatemala and Iran, until covert action was discredited by the downing of the U-2. In calling for national commitment and sacrifice, Kennedy was essentially renouncing covert action in favor of overt U.S. involvement. His Inaugural was an overtly Cold War speech by a man determined to be an overtly Cold War president.

Oddly, his chief foreign policy appointees were men he didn't know. He relied heavily on the so-called Wise Men who had performed so brilliantly in the Truman administration, calling for advice from Dean Acheson, Robert Lovett, and John McCloy and appointing to high (though not the highest) positions Averell Harriman, Charles Bohlen, and George F. Kennan.[3] Dean Rusk, a foundation executive and Truman administration veteran Kennedy had never met, was named secretary of state on the recommendations of Acheson and Lovett, who were more impressed with Rusk's faithfulness as a subordinate than his brilliance as a leader.[4] As secretary of defense Kennedy chose Robert McNamara, a man he knew so little that he did not know he was a Republican and a Protestant, a forty-year-old auto executive and management theorist whose forte was developing and following numerical indices and minimizing reliance on the instinct and intuition developed from long experience. He kept on CIA Director Allen Dulles (as he did FBI Director J. Edgar Hoover—they were his first two appointments) and hired as his White House national security advisor, a more important post than ever before, Harvard professor and administrator McGeorge Bundy, whose verbal brilliance was not always matched by the quality of his judgment over a long career.[5]

These men were tested immediately. In one of his debates with Nixon, Kennedy had suggested more aggressive action against Castro in Cuba; Nixon, furious that Kennedy was backing publicly what they both knew the Eisenhower administration was planning covertly, had felt he had to demur. This covert plan became in April 1961 the Bay of Pigs invasion. The plan called for Cuban emigrés trained secretly in Central America to invade Cuba with secret U.S. support and to rally support from inside the country. Kennedy agreed with Eisenhower that Castro was pro-Communist and should be removed, and he saw Cuba as a challenge for his generation in some way analogous to the challenges faced by American leaders a generation before. But five days before the attack, he lost some of his nerve and canceled U.S. air cover. With invaders receiving neither help from inside Cuba (Castro had allowed Cubans who opposed his regime to leave the island) nor protection from American airplanes, the invasion failed dismally and was clearly exposed as a U.S. effort. Kennedy quickly and gamely took the blame, and to his amusement saw his approval ratings shoot up to what would be their all-time high—a classic example of the rally-round-the-flag impulse.

Following defeat in Cuba in April, Kennedy negotiated the neutralization of Laos in May. While Cuba was, as American politicians endlessly repeated, only 90 miles off our shores, Laos, a landlocked nation carved from an upcountry portion of what had been French Indochina, could not have been more distant from the United States. But it was threatened by Communist takeover; and Kennedy, like all Democratic politicians who had lived through the "Who lost China?" years, was exceedingly skittish about allowing himself to be seen as losing an Asian country to Communism. Although his agreement with the Soviets and Chinese, negotiated by Averell Harriman, allowed Americans to claim Laos as non-Communist and to field a covert CIA army there, Kennedy surely doubted that the Communists could be kept out in the long run.

After these tests Nikita Khrushchev indicated his willingness to meet with Kennedy at a summit in June. Admirers of the American president still saw a young, dynamic leader, an idealist who set up the Peace Corps by executive order in March[6] and an adventurer who promised in May that the United States would land a man on the moon by the end of the decade. But many American Republicans and Soviet Communists saw a president who backed down and flinched when presented with the challenge of Communist advance. Khrushchev certainly did. Kennedy visibly blanched in his first meeting with him, and the Soviets contemptuously publicized the agenda they had prepared for the young president. Khrushchev was confident that "we will bury you," in his famous phrase—that Marxist ideas would sweep the Third World and that the Communist countries would outperform the West economically; and it was not so clear that Kennedy disagreed. The Communists were advancing in Cuba, in Laos, possibly in the Congo (where the United Nations was mired down in a quixotic attempt to enforce the power of the central government against a secession in mineral-rich Katanga province).[7]

In August 1961 they advanced in Berlin. For several years East Germans by the thousands had been migrating westward through the border between East and West Berlin. Suddenly on an August weekend the Soviets began building the hideous wall along the border, sealing off their sector and sealing in the East Germans who had not already moved west. Kennedy had made a grim speech on Berlin in July, stressing American determination to risk war to protect West Berlin and calling (as Nelson Rockefeller did, more conspicuously than any other politician) for a vast program of building nuclear fallout shelters. But as the wall went up Kennedy, as was his practice, was out of Washington for the weekend; no one in the American government had any thoughts on how to prevent the Soviets from building it; within days it was a fait accompli, as it would remain until 1989.[8] Kennedy used the Berlin crisis in July to request the sharp rise in defense spending which he had implicitly promised in his 1960 campaign. Defense Department spending in the last three Eisenhower fiscal years hovered in a narrow range, between $44.0 and $45.7 billion. In Kennedy's first full fiscal year, ending in June 1962, it rose to $49.3 million, where it stayed for the next year before rising to $50.7 billion in 1963–64[9]—an increase of 11% in three years.

II

If the New Frontier in its first year was less successful in waging the Cold War than most Americans realized, it was more successful in achieving some of its domestic policy goals than critics thought then or have believed since. Kennedy had the advantage of having on Capitol Hill the support of old speaker Sam Rayburn and of the emerging power of the AFL-CIO. Their first success was the packing of the House Rules Committee in January 1961. The committee's two ranking Democrats, Judge Howard Smith of Virginia and William Colmer of Mississippi, had first been elected in 1930 and 1932, respectively. They had diverged from most other Democrats on domestic policy since the New Deal days, and with the solidly conservative Republicans on the committee they commanded a majority which could—and often did—keep key liberal legislation off the floor. Rules, intended to be a tool of the speaker, had become a tool used against him; and Rayburn, reluctantly and with hesitation,[10] was persuaded to go along with the proposal to add three new members. Although 263 Democrats had been elected to the House in 1960, only 195 of them voted for Rayburn's committee-packing measure. It succeeded, by a 217–212 margin, only through the support of 22 liberal Republicans, including John Lindsay of the Silk Stocking district in Manhattan and William Scranton of the Pennsylvania anthracite-mining district centered on the city named for one of his ancestors.

The Rules Committee vote was a good gauge of liberal strength in the next two Houses. The liberals—and by this time the term clearly meant supporters of the expansive government programs promised as long ago as in the 1944 and 1948 Democratic platforms, augmented by the Medicare proposal of the late 1950s— found their strongest leadership not in the administration (whose lobbyist Lawrence O'Brien had little experience on Capitol Hill) or in the Democratic leadership (Rayburn was dying during much of 1961, and House Majority Leader John McCormack was long past his vigorous and aggressive days) but from organized labor. Lobbyists like Andrew Biemiller put together a coalition on key votes which included virtually every Democrat north of the Potomac and Ohio Rivers (it became notable when Nevada Democrat Walter Baring went off the reservation in 1962 and started voting, apparently out of conviction, against the liberals on almost every issue), key southerners on others, and a critical number of liberal Republicans, most of whose districts had large numbers of union members. Some of the southerners, like Albert Rains, Carl Elliott, and Kenneth Roberts of Alabama, were genuine liberals on economic issues and held key committee positions besides; they asked only that they be excused from voting for any measure with an anti-discrimination amendment in it, like the ones Adam Clayton Powell delighted in offering. In deference to them, Kennedy postponed until after the 1962 elections his pledge to end "with the stroke of a pen" discrimination in federally financed public housing. Other southerners, like Carl Vinson of Georgia, chairman of the Armed Services Committee, were temperamentally team players who were pleased to go along for a decent quid pro quo. As a result of deal-making and comradeliness, the Georgia and Texas delegations often provided key votes for the Kennedy liberals in the House. Labor's lobbyists could do little to threaten most southerners politically, but they could apply such pressure against Republicans in union districts in the North, where the difference between active opposition and indifference if not endorsement by the unions could easily mean the difference between victory and defeat.

In the Senate labor was not so powerful, nor was the administration. Lyndon Johnson hoped to be as powerful a vice president as he had been a majority leader. But when he tried to preside at the first Senate Democratic caucus in January 1961, seventeen Democratic senators voted not to let him—a rebuff which caused him to largely withdraw from Capitol Hill affairs. Johnson ended up spending more time in the West Wing of the White House and less in his enormous office in the Capitol,[11] setting a precedent which later vice presidents would follow. In Johnson's absence, and because of the passive approach of the new majority leader, Mike Mansfield, the leading power in the Senate in the early 1960s was Oklahoma's Robert Kerr. "The uncrowned king of the Senate," as he was called, chaired no major committee and held no leadership position; personally, he was feared rather than liked; in a time when politicians' relationships were liberally lubricated with alcohol, he was a teetotaler. On issues the liberals—most northern Democrats and some Republicans—usually had the votes. But Robert Kerr, through mastery of the subject matter and force of character, usually determined the results.

When Kerr was elected to the Senate in 1948, after one wartime term as governor of Oklahoma and service as the Democratic keynoter at the 1944 convention, he was expecting greater things. Born in a log cabin, he was friendly with Truman and well-connected at the White House. James Webb, Truman's budget director, ran Kerr's Kerr-McGee company during the Eisenhower years (and then became director of the space program under Kennedy and Johnson). Kerr was fearless: in the firestorm after Truman's firing of Douglas MacArthur, he was the first senator to step forward and challenge the Asia Firsters. "Let them put up or shut up," he said. If they truly backed MacArthur,[12] he contended, they should say that "we should either declare war against Red China or do that which would amount to open warfare against her." But Kerr worked so openly and brazenly at enriching himself that he never got serious consideration for national office. As political columnist Stewart Alsop wrote, he "flatly and frequently stated that he was in the Senate to look after his own financial interest—mostly oil and banking—and the interests of constituents similarly situated";[13] he ended up with a net worth of $55 million, nearly $2 million of it in cash in his office safe and lockboxes. He had fine political instincts and a mind capable of mastering legislative detail. "He was incomparably," said one close observer, "the Senate's most powerful and effective debater."[14] But he was also, in the words of two first-rate congressional reporters, "a domineering bully, merciless, almost sadistic in his verbal assaults on a cornered foe."[15] When Bobby Baker, once Johnson's top Senate aide and after 1961 increasingly Kerr's errand boy, failed to hand over some illegally obtained cash, Kerr picked him up and threw him against a wall.[16]

Kerr used his seats on the Public Works and Finance Committees to enhance his power. With Arkansas's John McClellan, he persuaded the Army Corps of Engineers to begin deepening the Arkansas River so that ultimately Catoosa, Oklahoma, became an ocean port. He got the Kennedy administration to give Oklahoma an Area Redevelopment grant twelve times larger than any other in the country. He insisted that Kennedy maintain on the Federal Power Commission a majority sympathetic to his views on oil and gas policy. On Finance he was a key player on trade and tax policy, two major administration concerns, and the co-sponsor of the American Medical Association's alternative to Kennedy's Medicare program, on which he beat the administration on the floor. But Kerr was not above making deals with Kennedy—on his terms. And Kennedy was not above romancing Kerr, going so far as to spend a weekend in October 1961 on Kerr's

52,000-acre ranch, as an aide recounted with fastidious distaste.[17] Kennedy himself seems to have appreciated Kerr's ability and frankness. "I'm going to go up there," he is supposed to have said once, explaining how he would get a bill through, "and kiss Bob Kerr's ass." Kerr remained the most powerful man in the Senate until he died suddenly on New Year's Day 1963.

III

The standard view is that "Kennedy was never able to lead Congress effectively." But in fact his record was not bereft of achievement. Major legislation was passed through the Senate in 1961 and 1962, if only with the support of the likes of Robert Kerr. And in the House the labor-led liberal bloc may not always have commanded majorities on the floor, but it often did when there was no complicating factor of cultural conflict. Such conflicts did scuttle some legislation. The conflict between Protestants and Catholics over aid to Catholic schools destroyed any chance for federal aid to education in these years. The conflict between blacks' desire for civil rights and white southerners' opposition destroyed the chance of any federal aid bill to which a Powell anti-discrimination amendment became attached. But the liberals did pass some important laws in the early 1960s. In May 1961 a measure was passed raising the minimum wage to $1.15 an hour by September 1961 and $1.25 by September 1963–a law which essentially finished the work of undermining the separate low-wage agricultural subsistence economy of the South. An Area Redevelopment Act passed the same month promoted public works in the economically ailing parts of the country, notably in the Appalachian region Kennedy had come to know in the West Virginia primary. And in June a Housing Act attempted to modify the generally unworkable urban renewal programs which had been started by the 1949 act. This legislation did not represent the entire liberal agenda. But it was at least as successful an attempt to expand the role of the federal government as was made in the halcyon days of the Truman administration in 1949 and early 1950, the most successful since World War II. Kennedy, a politician who respected his elders and tended to follow their lead even while proclaiming himself the avatar of a new generation, followed the liberal Democratic lead on domestic policy in the early years of his administration, and with more success than he followed the lead of the Wise Men he so revered in foreign policy.

35

⋙ ⋘

Confrontation

A merican politicians of the early 1960s, men who had come of political age in the era of great depression and world war, still habitually spoke the language of crisis. They had seen how what seemed at the time to be minor mistakes in economic policy had led to an unending downward spiral. They had seen how what seemed at the time to be minor concessions and praiseworthy accommodation had led to a world conflict which appeared, for the agonizing months from June 1940 to December 1941, by no means sure to be won by the forces of freedom. It was natural to regard every pause in economic growth and every feint by a foreign foe as a threat to the American way of life. It was intellectually congenial and politically useful to refer to every such challenge as a crisis—particularly congenial and useful for politicians like John Kennedy and Richard Nixon, Lyndon Johnson and Nelson Rockefeller, who unlike Harry Truman and Dwight Eisenhower, Dean Acheson and John Foster Dulles, had not themselves faced and overcome the great challenge of World War II and the first grim years of the Cold War.

Much of Kennedy's rhetoric—"the long twilight struggle"—sought to summon up enthusiasm and unity in a peaceful, prosperous country for the challenges he thought were ahead. Yet at home he tended to shy away from many confrontational issues, and abroad he shrank from confrontational stances in Cuba, Laos, and Berlin. For 1962 he decided that his major legislative and political initiative would be trade legislation which would reflect the Democrats' traditional free-trade heritage and the special importance placed by the postwar generation of Wise Men on lowering trade barriers and increasing world trade and production. This was not really any longer a partisan issue. Old-guard Republicans who believed fervently in the protective tariff had pretty much died out, and the southern and Civil War borderlands Democrats who had ached for free trade had been replaced in the party's ranks by labor union members who were beginning to think that the best way to prop their wages up above world levels might be through protectionism.[1] With the Democrats' New Deal surge to power in the nation's industrial belt and with the slow unification of the formerly separate northern and southern economies, the foundations of 100 years of trade politics had been undermined.

The trade bill was not controversial legislation publicly. It attracted little adverse comment in the press; and some may consider it the paradigmatic legislation of

342

what disgusted critics called an era of consensus, a time when the major leaders of business and government, of unions and management, championed essentially the same policies, with slightly different trimmings. But of course the bill was in danger of being hacked to death by a variety of local interests determined to protect their own industries. It might have succumbed had it not included a provision for targeted adjustment assistance to firms and workers who lost jobs because of foreign competition; by the 1970s this would become a major feature of American trade laws.[2] The trade bill in fact absorbed much of the time and psychic energy of the leading members of the Kennedy administration in 1962, and its passage was a tribute to their skill—or to the skills of the men to whom they were wise enough to consign its management, de facto Finance Committee head Robert Kerr in the Senate and Ways and Means Committee Chairman Wilbur Mills in the House.

II

The heart of the American economy, taught economist John Kenneth Galbraith in 1950, following the lead of Adolf Berle and Gardiner Means back in 1932, was the large industrial corporation. Big business was so economically powerful, Galbraith argued, that it could control demand for its own products and set price and wage levels utterly at its own whim—except for the countervailing power wielded by the institutions created by Franklin Roosevelt's Second New Deal, big labor and big government. Galbraith was considered an overly leftish liberal by most politicians, and none openly embraced the doctrines of the man he and academically more renowned Harvard economists hailed as the dominant seer of post-1930 economics, John Maynard Keynes. Yet long before John Kennedy took office, American government was performing much of the role Keynes assigned to it. The 1946 law establishing the President's Council of Economic Advisers and the Joint Economic Committee charged them with the task of recommending government fiscal policy to reduce unemployment.[3] Wartime price control acts gave government the responsibility to hold down inflation. Presidents Truman and Eisenhower recognized that the collective bargaining contracts reached in the coal, auto, and steel industries would set precedents which would be followed throughout the economy.

These views were held even more firmly by Kennedy, who, enjoying Galbraith's political support and appreciating his political reputation, named him ambassador to India. Aware as he took office that the nation was mired in the small 1960–61 recession which followed the much deeper 1957–58 one, he wanted to stimulate economic growth by seeing that workers got decent wage rises. But as a Democrat he was sensitive to the charge that his fiscal policies would promote inflation, and he wanted to hold down prices. His response was to issue wage-price guidelines: unions should not seek wage increases above the level of productivity increases.[4] That standard would allow business to gain reasonable profits from its capital investments without having to increase prices. The policy took for granted two desirable economic conditions: negligible inflation and reliable productivity growth.

But in the largest industries the White House could not rely on this automatic formula and so felt obliged to step in to ensure the results it wanted. One such industry was steel, where in late 1961 and early 1962 the steel companies' chief negotiator was negotiating a new contract with the United Steelworkers.

Kennedy's labor secretary, Arthur Goldberg, knew the steel industry well; he had been the United Steelworkers' principal lawyer before his appointment. Goldberg urged a low wage settlement in order to prevent a steel price rise; so did Kennedy, who met in the White House in January 1962 with Steelworkers president David McDonald and United States Steel chairman Roger Blough. With Goldberg as intermediary, the union agreed to a minimal wage and small fringe benefit increase in March. But just ten days later, on April 10, Blough came back to the White House and presented Kennedy with a press release announcing the price increase he thought he had prevented. Goldberg, having urged restraint on his former colleagues, was hopelessly compromised and wrote out his resignation. Kennedy was furious. "My father always told me that steel men were sons-of-bitches," he told his staffers minutes after Blough left, "but I never realized till now how right he was."

Technically the president had no power over steel prices, but he used all the powers of the executive branch his advisors could think of to get the price rise rescinded. Government statisticians wrote reports. Robert Kennedy's Justice Department, with an eye toward deterring other steel companies from following Blough's lead, as they usually did, noisily looked into the antitrust implications. FBI agents woke two reporters at 3 A.M. to ask them questions about a part of the story they had covered. The Defense Department announced it was canceling orders for U.S. Steel products. The administration contacted other companies and urged them to hold the line on prices. In his press conference on April 11, the president expressed cold fury, and he was quoted as saying that his father had said that "businessmen were sons-of-bitches." The Kennedys persuaded Chicago-based Inland Steel to resist the price rise, then other companies to rescind their increases. On April 13, Blough and U.S. Steel capitulated.

The rescission was on its face a resounding victory for an already exceedingly popular president. Kennedy's March 1962 Gallup job approval rating was 79%, and among those who knew about the steel price crisis—as it was inevitably called—opinion of his action was favorable in May by a 58%–22% margin.[5] Yet it was not a victory without costs. Republican politicians criticized Kennedy sharply for overreacting. His anger did indeed seem to guide his policy more than it perhaps should have; his use of the instruments of government was blatantly partisan, and the FBI intrusion on the reporters recalled for many Americans of the day "the knock on the door at midnight," as Justice Felix Frankfurter put it, when the storm troopers came to take someone away. He was seen less as overly partial to the unions—he had after all urged restraint on them, and successfully—than as dangerously hostile to big business, on whose efforts, it was widely supposed, the nation's prosperity hinged. Just weeks later, on May 28, the stock market suffered a sharp decline. Republicans hoped that Kennedy would suffer politically for sapping business confidence, but Americans' outlook remained optimistic, and the recession that many predicted would follow never materialized.

Kennedy's purpose contrary to the apprehensions of businessmen, was not so much to redistribute income from capital to labor as it was to stimulate economic growth and provide more income to be spread around to everyone. In a June 1962 commencement speech at Yale, his alma mater's traditional rival and for years a bastion of Republicanism, he used the occasion to set out his own economic views. He spoke in an explicitly Keynesian vein, and his plans to stimulate the economy aroused some of his Republican and conservative Democratic critics by seeming to approve of deficit spending. But this was no more than the actual, if not the explicit, policy of the last two administrations; and Kennedy rejected the advice of Galbraith and other liberals by deciding to stimulate the economy not by increasing domestic government spending but by lowering tax rates. By August he was tentatively proposing a tax cut—although with typical caution he deferred his actual proposal to January 1963. The high tax rates then in effect, culminating in the nominal 91% rate on income over $300,000, were one of the legacies of World War II. But in the peacetime America of 1962 they were not sustainable; people will accept confiscatory taxes in wartime, when others are dying, but will resist or avoid them in extended times of peace.[6] Even as he was being attacked as a statist and a backer of parasitic unions in their class warfare against the productive forces of business, Kennedy was actually counseling restraint on the unions and was preparing to abandon the dream of the liberals of Franklin Roosevelt's Treasury Department, the dream of building a welfare state by quasi-confiscatory taxation of high incomes and great wealth. The America of 1962, with economic growth which even after repeated recessions and with affluence dispersed widely among the population, was abandoning the policies of economic redistribution which had arisen in the different America before World War II, when almost everyone had seemed to give up on economic growth. Kennedy's economic decisions changed government's task from allocating scarcity into stimulating abundance—even as big-business executives, indoctrinated with the theology of balanced budgets, excoriated the tax cut.

By mid-1962 it was clear that whatever charges his critics hurled, American voters were exceedingly pleased with this president. For his family they felt a fascination unprecedented in American politics. Imitations of the distinctive Kennedy accent became a staple of American humor; and Vaughn Meader's "First Family" record, poking gentle fun at the Kennedys, became a national best seller. The fears that a Catholic president would impose his religion's dogmas on the country evaporated as Kennedy plainly refrained from doing so (notably in federal aid to education, where he opposed giving anything to the Catholic schools) and as the dogmas themselves changed in the Vatican II conference. Just as America was experiencing its first Catholic president, being a Catholic in America was becoming a much less distinctive experience. Catholics no longer abstained from meat on Fridays, the mass was no longer celebrated in Latin, fewer Catholic children attended Catholic schools, and many Catholics started practicing birth control, so that the large families so common in Catholic neighborhoods in the 1950s became rare as the 1960s went on.

Most professional Republican politicians and Republican journals like *Time* and the *New York Herald Tribune* were convinced that Kennedy was weak and vacillating on foreign policy and menacingly partisan at home. But they could find few voters who agreed. In May 1962, Gallup reported that in a rematch of the 1960 election Kennedy would beat Nixon by a 65%–35% margin.[7] Fascination with the Kennedy family, satisfaction with the president's fluency, good humor, and grace—these were all factors which produced record job approval ratings for a president who, in retrospect, would be remembered more fondly for these qualities than for his not negligible but not dazzling roster of specific achievements.

III

On Saturday morning, October 20, 1962, in the hallowed Democratic precincts of the Sheraton-Blackstone Hotel in Chicago, John Kennedy received a telephone call from his brother Robert and immediately decided to cancel his Midwest campaign trip (the press was told he had a cold) and return to Washington to deal with what soon became known as the Cuban missile crisis. It had begun less than a week before, when American U-2s photographed Soviet offensive missiles in Cuba—something which Kennedy had stated his administration would not tolerate and which Senator Kenneth Keating, the liberal but (in the Dewey tradition) partisan Republican from upstate New York, was charging him with having tolerated for some weeks. Now Kennedy had to decide how to respond. His advisors were split between "hawks" and "doves"[8]—backers of an air strike against the missiles and backers of a naval "quarantine" to keep the Soviets from shipping missiles and warheads in. Either response roused fears that the Soviets would retaliate with force and that both sides would escalate to nuclear war.

Some questioned whether any response was needed. "A missile is a missile," Robert McNamara said. "It makes no great difference whether you are killed by a missile fired from the Soviet Union or from Cuba."[9] But ignoring the missiles or agreeing to give up the U.S. base in Guantanamo Bay, Cuba, and U.S. missiles in Turkey and Italy in return for their removal, as Adlai Stevenson suggested, was not a possible option for an administration under attack by the opposition at home and held in contempt by its enemies abroad for showing weakness in the Bay of Pigs, Laos, Vienna, and Berlin. The day after he returned from Chicago, Kennedy decided on the quarantine; and on Monday, October 22, he reported his decision to the nation in a somber television broadcast. On Wednesday, October 24, Soviet ships bearing missiles turned aside before reaching the U.S. naval blockade. "We're eyeball to eyeball," Rusk said to the number two man at State, George Ball, "and I think the other fellow just blinked." But the crisis was not over. On Friday, Kennedy received a conciliatory though scarcely coherent secret letter from Khrushchev; on Saturday, a more official-sounding and bellicose letter was broadcast on Radio Moscow, proposing the joint withdrawal of Soviet missiles from Cuba and obsolete but (in spite of Kennedy's orders) still deployed U.S. missiles from Turkey. Robert Kennedy suggested a "Trollope ploy": like a heroine accepting a marriage proposal in disregard of an intervening message withdrawing it, Kennedy responded favorably to Friday's letter and ignored Saturday's. On Sunday, Khrushchev retreated and agreed to dismantle the missile bases. Kennedy let the Soviets know quietly that the missiles in Turkey would soon disappear. Both sides kept their word—though the United States did not admit at the time that there was any quid pro quo. The Cuban missile crisis, revealed to the public six days earlier, was over.

IV

In the accounts of the Kennedy administration written by insiders, the Cuban missile crisis occupies the central position. It shows a leader inclined to conciliation nonetheless standing up to provocation and prevailing. In any narrative of the administration's foreign policy it operates as the turning point. Before, Kennedy had been on the defensive against the Communists; afterwards, it was the Communists who were on the defensive. In a history of the American psyche it may also be a critical juncture: the moment when Americans were, and were most aware of being, at the brink of nuclear holocaust. And yet it must be doubted whether the missile crisis was a central event politically, at least in the formation of American public opinion. For the threat it posed to the country's existence was one which was familiar to Americans: ever since the beginning of the Cold War, in the years of the inaccessible and increasingly maniacal Stalin and in the years of the emotional, shoe-pounding, bombastic, and patently unrealistic Khrushchev, America and the world had seemed in constant danger of nuclear war—a danger more constant and more omnipresent in the fifteen years from March 1947 to October 1962 than in the twenty-five years after. And if Kennedy's apparent mastery in this crisis surprised some experts and insiders, it seemed to the public to be in character for a leader whose job approval ratings had been exceedingly high almost uniformly throughout 1961 and 1962. His 74% positive rating in the wake of the missile crisis was not an upswing from, but a continuation of, his rating through the preceding eighteen months.[10]

This high approval rating helped the Democrats to make an unusually strong showing in the off-year congressional elections. As soon as the 1962 election results came in, Republican political strategists argued that the Cuban missile crisis had transformed a normal midterm rout of the party in power into a rather unusual victory for it. For this argument there is almost no evidence. Partisan preference in congressional elections was identical all year: 55% Democratic in late June, 56% in early October, and (with spurious precision) 55.5% just before election day, according to Gallup.[11] Satisfaction with administration policy, admiration for Kennedy, and the demographic dividend for the Democrats combined to put the party in a strong position. Moreover, turnout reached a post-1920 high for off-year elections.[12] The surge of enthusiasm which had pushed turnout to record levels in 1960 continued, even as legal requirements for voting generally remained stringent and restraints on voting by southern blacks continued to be maintained by what can only be called a form of terrorism. An optimistic mood—not a mood totally ignorant of threats, but a buoyant sense that threats could be countered and challenges would be met—prevailed through most of the country.

Where the Democrats did lose in the typical pattern of off-year elections was in contests for state office. They lost the governorships of Pennsylvania, Michigan, and Ohio, in two cases to plausible presidential candidates (William Scranton of Pennsylvania and George Romney of Michigan). They lost some of the best-publicized races: Nelson Rockefeller was triumphantly reelected in New York over Robert Morgenthau, the son of Roosevelt's treasury secretary, whose candidacy had been inspired by a Lou Harris poll suggesting that an aristocratic Jewish candidate would run well;[13] Sidney Yates lost to Everett Dirksen in Illinois, though by a narrow margin; Thomas Kuchel, the Earl Warren protégé who was senator from California, was reelected without trouble. But the Democrats also had some sweet victories. California Governor Pat Brown, who had beaten William Knowland four years before by a 60%–40% margin, beat Richard Nixon by 52%–47%—not overwhelming, but impressive considering that Nixon was the heavy favorite. "You won't have Nixon to kick around any more," the former vice president told reporters the morning after, when neither he nor they suspected that he was a future president. In Kennedy's home state of Massachusetts, thirty-year-old Edward Kennedy was elected to his brother's Senate seat (kept warm by interim appointee Benjamin Smith, a family friend), despite a paucity of accomplishments and over the opposition of Attorney General Edward McCormack in the primary and George Cabot Lodge in the general election; Democrat Endicott Peabody was elected governor over incumbent John Volpe by a narrow margin after the Democrats in the last weeks put up Irish green billboards which proclaimed, "President Kennedy supports Peabody."

The great historical rule was that the party in power lost seats in off-year congressional elections. But in 1962 the Democrats did not.[14] Overall, they lost only 2 seats in the House and actually gained 4 in the Senate. Reapportionment and redistricting, under the rules of the time, were a wash. The Democrats won 7 of the 8 House seats California had gained in reapportionment, thanks to the Democratic legislative majorities elected in 1958, and 3 of the 4 new seats in Florida, where New Deal Senator Claude Pepper, defeated in 1950, was elected to the House from the new Miami district. But in states which lost districts like Illinois, New York, West Virginia, and Arkansas, Democrats were the losers. In races not decided by the decennial reshuffle, Democrats gained 7 seats and lost 11, for a net loss of 2, since they retained the Hawaii and Alaska seats which had temporarily increased the size of the House from 435 to 437.[15]

These results represented random flux, with little evidence of party movement at all: incumbents were endorsed at the congressional level even as a majority of the governors seeking reelection were defeated, seemingly without regard to party. The shift in Senate seats looks more significant at first glance. But considering that most of the incumbents had been elected in the heavily Republican year of 1956, the Democratic gain registered in 1962 was nothing more than a reiteration of the feelings expressed in the 1958 and 1960 elections. American voters by 1962 were reasonably comfortable with the Democrats in control of Congress and were disposed to register approval of the Kennedy administration's record. This judgment was based not just on some working-class identification with Kennedy's attack on the steel companies—for in fact his handling of that crisis affected his standing with the voters hardly at all—nor was it a visceral rally-round-the-flag response to the Cuban missile crisis, which seems to have changed almost no votes in the congressional elections. Rather, this ratification of the Democratic party's control of Congress sprang from a general disposition—born in the days of the great depression, strengthened by events since, unshaken by major mistakes on the part of the Democrats—to two patterns of voting: to favor the party of Franklin D. Roosevelt and to give it control of the national government when the nation seemed threatened, as it had since 1957, by economic recession, and to reward the party of an administration which seemed to have a successful record.

At the time the Kennedy Democrats' success in the 1962 elections seemed to reflect their victories in confrontations: not only the foreign policy confrontation of the Cuban missile crisis, but also the domestic confrontation of the steel price controversy. Both were typical of the confrontations which Americans had become used to in the years since World War II: Cold War confrontations between Americans and Soviets and economic redistribution confrontations between management and labor. But these two confrontations proved to be not paradigms of the future, but the last of their kind. Domestically, the approach to the much less publicized trade bill—the consensus-minded alliance of most articulate segments of the political society against those who were not represented or could be dismissed as simply ignorant—would turn out to be typical of public policy initiatives after 1962. Abroad, the simmering problems of Indochina, a matter of great concern to administration policymakers but scarcely visible to the public in November 1962, would turn out not to be susceptible to a solution as neat and seemingly rational as that of the Cuban missile crisis. In retrospect Kennedy's antagonists in both crises seem irrational—the price increases Blough and other steel executives indulged in made their companies increasingly uncompetitive with foreign producers, and the offensive which Khrushchev undertook was beyond the Soviet Union's capabilities—and the threats they posed may not seem so menacing. But at the time they were the cynosures of all eyes, and John Kennedy's response to their initiatives confirmed the high opinion most Americans already had of him and fortified, for a moment, their confidence in their country.

36

-»» «-

Rights

The Cuban missile episode was not the only crisis John and Robert Kennedy had to deal with in the fall of 1962. The other was the effort to enroll James Meredith, a black, at the University of Mississippi in accordance with a federal court order. The Kennedys had not been eager before to intervene in civil rights controversies,[1] despite Robert's telephone call during Martin Luther King's imprisonment in October 1960. They had kept their distance from the lunch counter sit-ins which began in Greensboro, North Carolina, in February 1960;[2] and in their first year in the White House they had tried to discourage the organizers of the Freedom Rides which sought to desegregate interstate bus transportation in the South in the spring of 1961.[3] They accepted state officials' assurances that the Freedom Riders would be protected, only to see news photographs of the buses pulled off to the side of the road and the black riders beaten when southern officials like Alabama's Governor John Patterson and Birmingham safety director Eugene "Bull" Connor refused to provide police protection.[4] The Kennedys' preferred solutions were covert—they got Senator James Eastland to promise that the Freedom Riders would not be beaten in Mississippi,[5] and they were not—and in September 1961 they helped to get the Interstate Commerce Commission to rule that segregation was unconstitutional on interstate motor carriers and in bus terminals.

Personally, John and Robert Kennedy were only mildly sympathetic to the civil rights movement. They could understand why people wanted to be treated equally. But these men who prided themselves on their pragmatism regarded civil rights demonstrators' goals as impractical: they believed, as most Americans then did, that white southerners had never allowed blacks to be treated as equals and would never do so. Politically, they saw civil rights as the one issue which could split asunder the electoral majority produced by the Democrats' demographic dividend, the president's personal popularity, traditional party issues like trade and opposition to big business, and higher defense spending. In the polls John Kennedy was running far ahead of any possible opponents for reelection. But take away the white southerners, who had given him a majority in 1960, and his national majority would be gravely imperiled.

This political intuition was sound, as the electoral history of the next twenty-five years suggests. But the practical assessment was flawed. White southerners had not, in fact, always insisted on racial segregation. As C. Vann Woodward revealed in *The Strange Career of Jim Crow* (which as it happens was published at just this time), rigid southern segregation was not much more than two generations old.[6] A pattern only two generations old could conceivably be changed just as it had been established in the first place—with a lot of trouble and violence and bloodshed—with the difference in this case that the violence would be committed not by those who wanted to change the existing system, but by those who wanted to preserve it.[7] Moreover, the success of the integration of the military might have tipped off American leaders of 1963 to the likelihood that their fellow citizens, once the government clearly insisted on integration, would not cling obdurately to segregation but would accept blacks as equals in the workplace, in places of public accommodation, even in more intimate settings.[8]

But to almost no one, except to some of the most farsighted leaders of the civil rights movement like Martin Luther King, Jr., did that likelihood seem apparent in September 1962, when James Meredith appeared at the University of Mississippi. The institution he was seeking to attend was quintessentially southern. Its flag was the Confederate Stars and Bars, its football team was known as the Rebels, and its admired style was that of the well-dressed, slightly boozed-up fraternity boy with the deep drawl who had little interest in his studies and was primarily concerned with having a wild good time and finding an attractive but demure wife before settling down to run some small town. Oxford, the town where "Ole Miss" was located, had been the home of one of America's great writers, William Faulkner; but among local whites the prevailing attitude toward blacks was one of crude and vicious contempt,[9] and the prevailing style of action was violence. Meredith, who had spent nine years in the Army and had been attending all-black Jackson State College, was a quirky sort himself, who wanted to drive onto campus in his Thunderbird. Governor Ross Barnett, a politician of flagging popularity and feeble intellect, publicly resisted his enrollment even while negotiating his entrance with Robert Kennedy. When Kennedy had Meredith flown onto campus September 30, Barnett refused to use the National Guard to keep the peace and instead made a speech vowing resistance. Overnight two men were killed in Oxford, and Army troops had to be ordered in—the military response for which Democrats had criticized Eisenhower in Little Rock—before peace could be established and Meredith could, the next morning, register for classes.[10]

II

By this time the clashes over James Meredith in 1962 had already made more of an impression on most Americans than had the longer-lasting and potentially more consequential lunch counter sit-ins of 1960 and Freedom Rides of 1961. The reason was television. In the spring of 1962, just at the moment when "for the first time, television had the technology and other resources to compete, on film, with newspapers on a day-to-day basis,"[11] CBS had opened a bureau in Dallas, manned by a former local radio and TV reporter named Dan Rather. Rather went to Ole Miss for Meredith's enrollment, accompanied by a cameraman[12] who provided America's television news viewers with footage the next day of the mob at Oxford. Before the early 1960s, Americans had tended to get their first word of news events from the radio and their first pictures from newspapers. The most emotion-laden photographs often did not appear until the weekly edition of *Life* or the biweekly edition of *Look* arrived. Television in the 1950s had operated much like a magazine in this respect: it took time to transport and develop film, and so the most vivid and moving footage was broadcast on documentaries, often aired long after the events they reported. Live television was reserved for interviews in studios and for the very occasional broadcasts of congressional hearings. The strong political impact of these hearings, from the racketeering investigation led by Kefauver to the Teamster hearings featuring the Kennedys, is an indication of the emotive power of television broadcasting.

But this power had seldom been involved in the early-evening newscasts each network dutifully presented. These 15-minute programs, scheduled well before prime-time entertainment shows, consisted mostly of shots of the anchors reading the news. The most successful newscast in the late 1950s was NBC's program featuring Chet Huntley and David Brinkley, the crisp and laconic team whose presentations at the 1956 national party conventions had made them national favorites and boosted them into the top ratings position.[13] By 1962, however, technology had advanced, with videotape allowing quicker film processing and communication satellites (though at first they were prohibitively expensive) rapid transmission to network headquarters in New York. (Still ahead was the widespread use of the videotape camera, which would permit prerecording and instant playback.)[14] The newscasts began featuring more footage of dramatic activities, and politicians sensitive to the emotive impact of the medium used it to advantage. As the main focus of television network news shifted from documentaries to the early-evening newscasts, plans were made for the expansion of these programs from 15 minutes to half an hour, a change which occurred at CBS and NBC in September 1963.[15] Surveys began to show that Americans were relying more on television than on newspapers for information about the events of the day. The network newscast was about to become the central focus of American politics.

Radio was the great medium of oratory, of the mellow and reassuring tones of Franklin D. Roosevelt and of the angry ranting of Huey Long and Father Coughlin. But on what Marshall McLuhan called the cooler medium of television, dramatic oratory looked merely melodramatic and angry ranting looked threatening.[16] John Kennedy, whose fluent conversational style was well suited to the medium, understood his mastery of it and used it deliberately; he had his regular press conferences televised, for example, and decided to use a live television address to deliver his ultimatum to Khrushchev in the Cuban missile crisis. Meredith's enrollment at Ole Miss in September 1962 and Kennedy's speech on the Cuban missile crisis the following month were examples of events which were brought home and made vivid in Americans' living rooms through the by now universal medium of television[17]—and events which ended successfully. But there were no immediate and satisfying happy endings to the major events which television brought dramatically into Americans' homes in 1963—the police dogs chasing down peaceful civil rights demonstrators in Birmingham, the Buddhist priests setting themselves afire in Vietnam, the murder of the president in Dallas. As a few seconds of film flashed on millions of television screens, Americans' confidence in themselves and their country, in their basic institutions and their country's destiny, was shattered, not to be restored for years to come.

III

Birmingham not long before 1960 could plausibly claim to be the most progressive city in the South. It was industrialized: built beneath a mountain of pure red iron ore, with smoking furnaces, clanging foundries, and some of the biggest steel mills in the United States running up and down between wooden-house neighborhoods in its valleys, their flames and sparks sometimes visible from where the managers and professionals lived in the hills. With 326,000 people in 1950, it was as big as any city between Washington, D.C., and New Orleans. But in the early 1960s Birmingham was becoming known as a violent town. Blacks were publicly beaten, most notably in May 1961 when Police Commissioner Eugene "Bull" Connor (who, quite astonishingly, was also Alabama's Democratic national committeeman) allowed Freedom Riders to be beaten without police intervention. Most Birmingham whites were repelled by Connor's inaction: they voted to abolish his office in November 1962 and elected his opponent in the race for mayor in April 1963. But Connor challenged the first vote in a lawsuit and was still holding office for months after Dr. Martin Luther King, Jr., began "Project C—for Confrontation" in March 1963.

King was only thirty-four years old, but he had been a leader—the most famous and most tested leader—of the southern civil rights movement since the Montgomery bus boycott which began in December 1955.[18] King was a product of Atlanta's black bourgeoisie: his father was the pastor of the Ebenezer Baptist Church, one of the city's leading black churches, and King himself had earned a Ph.D. from Boston University. He could speak in the idiom of the rural black preacher and in the language of the urbane scholar as well. In depth of vision, in steeliness of discipline, in steadiness of nerve, he was easily the greatest of the civil rights leaders, and the self-evident purity of his purpose united blacks behind him and undermined the legitimacy of the whites who opposed his demands. Yet he had terrible vulnerabilities. His closest advisor from the early 1960s, New York lawyer Stanley Levison, had been a supporter of Communist causes in the early 1950s and was identified as a Communist in the 1960s by J. Edgar Hoover, who initiated FBI surveillance and harassment of King which continued until his death in April 1968[19] and produced evidence of personal behavior which would have been exceedingly harmful to King and his cause if it had been revealed (just as evidence of similar behavior by John Kennedy would have been harmful to him and his presidency had it been revealed). Hoover shared the view of pro-Communist blacks like Paul Robeson that the Communists were the only supporters of civil rights. In fact, in the 1930s and early 1940s the Communists had been the only articulate political group in America which recommended the dismantlement of racial segregation; they had, after all, nothing to lose and quite a lot to gain by taking that stand. But Hoover's surveillance of King proved after the fact what seemed sufficiently certain to most observers long before, that there was no Communist influence on King, that his ideas and his actions came from within. King saw himself as a patriot, trying to make his country live up to the better part of his heritage, though it should be added that like many a patriot he believed that major features of life in his country needed to be changed. Even after the successes of the Civil Rights Acts of 1964 and 1965, he came to believe that equality for the races depended on some kind of socialism. Blacks, he felt, could never be made equal by voluntary action and free-market capitalism.[20]

But in Birmingham he was dealing with capitalism—organizing a black boycott of downtown stores to force them to integrate their lunch counters, restrooms, and drinking fountains and to hire black clerks. They had done all these things in the summer of 1962 and then backed down under pressure from Connor.[21] The new mayor and the Kennedy administration tried to persuade King to stop the protests. But Connor got an injunction banning demonstrations by King and others, and in April, on Good Friday, King violated it—and went to jail for two weeks. He and his associates then persuaded hundreds of schoolchildren to demonstrate. On May 3, Connor attacked them with police dogs and firehoses with enough water pressure to rip bark off trees. The images were unforgettable. As the only Birmingham white willing to negotiate with King, David Vann, put it, "in marching only one block they [the demonstrators] could get enough news film to fill all the newscasts of all the television stations in the United States."[22] Southern whites understood the explosive potential of such footage, and many southern stations refused to let network reporters relay film to New York, so that all three networks' reporters agreed informally to let their competitors use the facilities of any local station which would cooperate.[23] Within days, Birmingham businessmen again agreed, behind Connor's back, to integrate lunch counters and hire black clerks.

After the motel where King was staying was bombed and policemen moved in and pummeled blacks, Robert Kennedy persuaded his brother to send federal troops to Fort McClellan, outside Birmingham. The city eventually grew quiet. But on June 11, Governor George Wallace, elected on a "segregation forever" platform the year before, stood literally in the schoolhouse door, posing as if to block the entrance of two black students a court had ordered admitted to the University of Alabama. Deputy Attorney General Nicholas Katzenbach (Robert Kennedy prudently remaining away from the scene) then ordered federal marshals to escort the blacks, and they were admitted. But if Martin Luther King had discovered how to use television to make the protests of blacks irresistibly appealing to the large majority of the American people who were mostly indifferent to segregation when it remained distant but disliked it when forced to face the unpleasant measures needed to maintain it, then George Wallace had discovered how to use television to appeal to the large number—was it a majority?—of Americans who felt that there should be limits to blacks' demands, limits to the extent to which the larger white society should be required to change its behavior and its way of life.

IV

On the television screens of Americans that same month of May 1963 came news of the Buddhist uprisings in Hue, Vietnam, against the country's Catholic leader, Ngo Dinh Diem. In June, a Buddhist monk sat down on an asphalt street, crossed his legs, and allowed himself to be doused with gasoline and set on fire.[24] The photograph of this self-immolation—the first of many—was reprinted countless times in the United States. Of course the issues were local, and the principles of neither party in the dispute were recognizable to most Americans. Yet in the chronological juxtaposition, a certain symmetry between the American South and the Vietnamese South appeared. Local protesters were being oppressed beyond endurance by rulers who depended for crucial support on the government of the United States. The oppression these victims felt was a rebuke to ordinary Americans, to a people whose own confidence in their goodness and deserved success had not for years been challenged, and their government's policies seemed threatened with failure. Vietnam did not loom so large as civil rights then in most Americans' minds, but before May 1963 Vietnam had scarcely loomed in their minds at all. The process of sapping the confidence of the American people in the goodness and success of their system had begun—a process in which the fortuitous coincidence of the advance of television technology and the ripeness of the civil rights revolution and of the Buddhist protest against the Diem government played a major role.

To these challenges John Kennedy responded aggressively. These were the banner weeks of his presidency, when he set courses which mostly prevailed—though he dodged the prickly issue of Vietnam. He set these courses in two speeches delivered in Washington on successive days in June, followed by a memorable foreign trip later that month and a new economic policy announced the following month.

Khrushchev's willingness to back down in Cuba had not yet undermined his standing with the Politburo, and Kennedy set out to get agreements with the Soviets which had previously been unobtainable. In his speech at American University on June 10, he seemed to renounce the language of the Cold War which he had previously found so congenial. "Let us reexamine our attitude toward the Soviet Union," he said. Noting that both sides had an interest in halting the arms race, he called for "general and complete disarmament—designed to take place in stages." Kennedy's willingness to overlook the crude disparagements of the United States in Soviet propaganda and his unwillingness to respond in kind—though American criticism of the Soviet system was, after all, much more justified in fact—signaled a shift in presidential rhetoric which prevailed at least through

1980, and his suggestion that the primary goal of superpower diplomacy must be the reaching of partial arms control agreements remained the guiding spirit of American policy at least as long. The steps he actually took at the time were modest: installation of a "hotline" to the Kremlin and the dispatch of Averell Harriman to Moscow to negotiate a treaty banning above-ground testing of nuclear weapons. Harriman came back in August with a treaty which was ratified by the Senate in September only after the attachment of reservations by an initially skeptical Henry Jackson—another pattern which prevailed in later administrations.

Then on June 11, Kennedy spoke on civil rights over prime time television from the White House, sitting on the rocking chair he used to soothe his ailing back. His foreign policy shift had been the culmination of a month-long process. On civil rights he had shifted since the Birmingham beatings the month before from a posture of hoping the issue would go away (and trying to help it do so) to an aggressive and even audacious response. By now the firehoses and police dogs of May and the defiance of Governor Wallace earlier that very day had forced his hand: if it was risky, for political and policy reasons, to act forcibly and aggressively on civil rights, it was also risky not to act. The television footage of the demonstrations had reduced the abstract and (to most Americans) distant issue of civil rights to a concrete and pressing issue. Why should some Americans not be allowed to live and work and walk down the street where they wanted? Kennedy spoke in the same plain language. "The heart of the question is whether all Americans are to be afforded equal rights and equal opportunities, whether we are going to treat our fellow Americans as we want to be treated," he said. "We cannot say to 10% of the population that you can't have that right; that your children can't have the chance to develop whatever talents they have; that the only way that they are going to get their rights is to go into the streets and demonstrate. I think we owe them and we owe ourselves a better country than that."[25] The issue was what kind of country America was, and to make it a better country Kennedy proposed an omnibus civil rights bill, more sweeping than Congress had ever seriously considered, going far beyond the mild measures Kennedy himself had refused to embrace a few months before. It included a ban on racial discrimination in public accommodations. It provided for federal enforcement of desegregation of public schools and for stronger protections of voting rights. It included, when Kennedy submitted his bill a few days later, a ban on discrimination in employment. It bade fair to change a long-established (though by no means eternal) way of life in the South.

Changes in attitudes, made most visible by responses to the events of the spring of 1963 but apparent also over a much longer period of time, had left the majority of Americans at least mildly favorable to this initiative. Yet there were also grave political risks for Kennedy. The percentage of Americans who believed the administration was moving too fast on civil rights rose from 36% (versus 18% who believed it was not moving fast enough) in May to 41% (versus 14%) in June and 50% (versus 10%) in mid-August, just before the march on Washington in support of the bill. Whites outside the South approved of desegregation of public accommodations by a 55%–34% margin in late June; but white southerners, who were undoubtedly the white voters most concerned about the issue, disapproved by an 82%–12% margin.[26] But there was some fatalism in the southern whites, a vestige perhaps of the experience of bitter defeat which generations had kept alive since Appomattox. By an 83%–13% margin they thought that public accommodations desegregation would actually occur—a more accurate prognostication than the doubts harbored by most practical-minded Washington politicians.

On the surface Kennedy's job approval rating did not suffer, nor did his performance in pairings against Republicans deteriorate substantially. Against Barry Goldwater he prevailed by 60%–36% in May, 60%–34% in June, 59%–35% in July, and 57%–37% in August, as indicated in Gallup polls. But he did show slippage in the South in those pairings,[27] and the small, perhaps not statistically significant decline in his job approval rating, from 64%–24% in May to 59%–28% in October, was attributable almost entirely to a decline among white southerners. Lou Harris, Kennedy's pollster in the 1960 campaign, quit polling for candidates and started public polling in June 1963: his first public survey showed Kennedy's job approval rating at 64% outside the South and 48% in the South.[28] In July, Kennedy's support in the South against Goldwater was below 40%, and it was not much higher against the pro-civil rights Romney or Rockefeller. The southern electoral votes which had been essential to his 1960 election seemed certain to be missing in 1964; and although some formerly Republican votes seemed to be going his way in the northern states, among Catholics and among Protestants who favored civil rights, no politician was entirely comfortable counting on votes which had never gone his party's way before. The southern whites were surely furious, but was there any reason to believe that the northern Republicans were more than mildly and momentarily pleased? Should Kennedy's overall popularity decline significantly—a prospect for which a political strategist should always be prepared— he could conceivably be defeated by losing the entire South, much of the West (where the Democrats had not run well in 1962), and some of the big industrial states of the East and Great Lakes. Americans still preferred a liberal to a conservative party (by a 49%–46% margin),[29] and they still heavily preferred the Democrats on the major foreign policy and domestic issues. But the Democrats' loss of the white South—a key factor in American politics for at least the next twenty-five years—was already apparent. As it happened, Lyndon Johnson won in November 1964 in patterns eerily reminiscent of Kennedy's showings in the polls of September and October 1963: by overwhelming Goldwater in the East and Midwest, where the Democratic percentages were unprecedented even in Franklin Roosevelt's years, and despite losing the votes of whites in most states in the South. But in the summer and fall of 1963 few if any politicians of either party thought that these patterns would prove enduring or that the national Democrats would come out ahead in this reshuffling of political blocs.

Rather, for professional Democrats the losses seemed plain and the gains ephemeral. The political drawbacks became especially visible on Capitol Hill the day after Kennedy's June 11 speech, when the House of Representatives failed to reauthorize the Area Redevelopment Act which had passed easily two years before. All but one of the vote switchers came from southern and border states.[30] The civil rights issue was clearly changing the political landscape more rapidly and drastically than it had been changed since 1933, 1934, and 1935; and few practical politicians are comfortable with a changing political landscape.

V

Kennedy retained his popular support on both foreign and economic policy. His easy fluency and almost flawless grace, the sense of command he radiated on television even when, even by his own admission, he was not in command of his work, powerfully reinforced the voters' perceptions that they were living in a time of increasing peace and prosperity. The U.S. relationship with the Soviets was perceptibly less tense after the Cuban missile crisis than it had been before. The economy, after the 1957–58 and 1960–61 recessions, was perceptibly reviving and growing. After his two great speeches of early June 1963, Kennedy flew off to Europe, where he had been received more rapturously than in some parts of the United States. He had stood up to the Soviets on Berlin and Cuba, it seemed without going to war. Now in the eighteenth year after World War II, it was apparent that there would be no new war, as it had been apparent in the eighteenth year after World War I that a new war was inevitable. He had removed the specter of destruction from Western Europe and the threat of enslavement from West Berlin. In Berlin in July he received his most tumultuous reception. He looked past Checkpoint Charlie, the famous military guard post at the Berlin Wall, into the dreariness of East Berlin, and spoke in front of the city hall. "There are some who say that communism is the wave of the future," he noted. "Let them come to Berlin. And there are some who say in Europe and elsewhere we can work with the Communists. Let them come to Berlin. . . . All free men, wherever they may live, are citizens of Berlin, and, therefore, as a free man, I take pride in the words *'Ich bin ein Berliner.'*" From Berlin he went to Ireland to see his relatives, to England to see his sardonic and skeptical soulmate Harold Macmillan, and to Italy to see the new pope, Paul VI—but not to kiss his ring.

VI

One problem which persisted was Vietnam. In his approval of the Laos settlement, Kennedy had accepted neutralization in the hope of at least delaying and possibly avoiding Communist control. But he was uneasy about adopting this policy as a pattern,[31] if only because he was part of a generation of Democratic politicians who remembered the reaction to the "loss of China." He was clearly "very much disturbed by the picture of the monk on fire"[32]—a vivid example of the impact of visual media–and in summer 1963 was considering abandoning U.S. support of the regime of President Diem. Diem's brother Ngo Dinh Nhu and his wife seemed especially obnoxious; Madame Nhu disdained Buddhist and other protesters with a flair which, for Americans though perhaps not for her, was reminiscent of the disdain for protesting American blacks shown by her precise American contemporary, Bull Connor. In August 1963, when Kennedy was in Hyannisport and many of his top appointees vacationing, a cable went out from the State Department to the U.S. Embassy in Saigon that the president would no longer support Diem.[33]

The precedents of "who lost China?" and McCarthyism were clearly on Kennedy's mind in this period. "If I tried to pull completely now from Vietnam," he told Senator Mike Mansfield, an East Asian expert who did not think pulling out a bad idea, "we would have another Joe McCarthy red scare on our hands, but I can do it after I'm reelected. So we had better make damned sure I *am* reelected."[34] Politically insecure despite his high standing in the polls, Kennedy did not want to be seen as losing Vietnam or even to make a compromise agreement as he had for Laos. One problem he had with Diem and his brother was the hint that they might be making a separate peace with North Vietnam. On September 2, in an interview with Walter Cronkite of CBS which has often been cited as evidence that Kennedy wanted the United States to withdraw from Vietnam for the same reason latter-day opponents of the Vietnam war would, Kennedy was actually responding to those hints of a separate peace. He wanted Diem to propitiate his South Vietnamese opponents: "We hope he comes to see that, but in the final analysis it is the people and the government itself who have to win or lose this struggle. All we can do is help, and we are making it very clear, but I don't agree with those who say we should withdraw. That would be a great mistake."[35] A week later, on September 9, when David Brinkley of NBC asked him if he subscribed to Eisenhower's domino theory, Kennedy said, "I believe it. I think that the struggle is close enough. China is so large, looms so high just beyond the frontiers, that if South Vietnam went, it would not only give them an improved geographical position for a guerrilla assault on the Malays, but would also give the impression that the wave of the future in southeast Asia was China and the Communists. So I believe it."[36]

Kennedy clearly meant to commit the U.S. to keep the South Vietnamese government in power, in part because of a fear of Chinese Communist advances. The question he was unsure about was not whether the United States should stay in or get out of Vietnam; it was whether the United States should support or oppose the Diem government. On that question Kennedy seems to have been genuinely ambivalent, and it was indeed hard to know how to achieve a strong pro-American government. If Diem seemed unable to command loyalty and unity,[37] as so many American critics argued, so did most of his American-sponsored successors. In August he decided (or allowed his administration to decide) to withdraw support from Diem and his family by appointing Henry Cabot Lodge ambassador to South Vietnam and by approving the cable allowing Lodge to indicate his lack of disapproval of a military coup attempt against them. The result was the early November coup which cost Diem and Nhu their lives, and which surely profoundly unsettled many American voters. The assassinations of Diem and Nhu cast a pall—a pall horrifyingly magnified by the assassination of Kennedy three weeks later.

VII

Plans for the civil rights march on Washington scheduled for August 28, 1963, met with considerable resistance even from those who supported its aims. The specter of hundreds of thousands of blacks converging on the nation's capital raised apprehensions about violence among many Americans, by no means all of them bigots. Members of Congress—not just southern segregationists, but northern Democrats and Republicans not strongly committed to civil rights—muttered that they were not going to be intimidated by masses of black marchers. In a meeting with Martin Luther King in late June, a meeting which was also attended by Lyndon Johnson and Robert Kennedy, the president worried that "the wrong kind of demonstration at the wrong time" would defeat the civil rights bill he had refused to support before Birmingham.[38] Never for a moment did either of the Kennedys consider attending the march, nor did any other major politician. The AFL-CIO, probably the most powerful lobby on Capitol Hill, refused to support the march, which George Meany, the one-time Bronx plumber who had succeeded William Green as the head of the AFL and headed the joint labor federation since December 1955, feared would antagonize both his members and his political allies (although Meany's rival Walter Reuther, head of the CIO before the merger, supported the march strongly and backed a march of 125,000 in Detroit in late June). The NAACP supported the march, but pointedly declined to help pay for it.

But as King told Kennedy, "I have never engaged in any direct action movement which did not seem ill-timed. Some people thought Birmingham ill-timed." To which Kennedy responded in his disarmingly self-deprecating way, "Including the Attorney General."[39] In fact, the march was well timed and, even more important, well organized. The elderly but still much-respected A. Philip Randolph was named chairman of the event; he chose Bayard Rustin as his deputy, to organize it, and he and other civil rights leaders widely proclaimed that there would be no civil disobedience. The crowd of 200,000 which gathered around the Reflecting Pool in front of the Lincoln Memorial was not only peaceful but also rapturous as it listened to speeches whose contents had been carefully vetted by Robert Kennedy's top aides. Then it came the turn of Martin Luther King to speak. Moving beyond his prepared text, King extemporized along the same lines he had used in Birmingham in April and Detroit in June: "I say to you, today, my friends, so even though we face the difficulties of today and tomorrow, I still have a dream. It is a dream deeply rooted in the American dream. I have a dream that one day this nation will rise up and live out the true meaning of its creed—we hold these truths to be self-evident, that all men are created equal." In the cadence of black preachers, with a biblical lilt, King talked specifically of the South. "I have a dream that one day on the red hills of Georgia, the sons of former slaves and the sons of former slave-owners will be able to sit down together at the table of brotherhood." "Let freedom ring," he concluded in a grand national vision. "When we allow freedom to ring, when we let it ring from every village and every hamlet, from every state and every city, we will be able to speed up that day when all of God's children—

black men and white men, Jews and Gentiles, Protestants and Catholics—will be able to join hands and sing in the words of the old Negro spiritual, 'Free at last, free at last; thank God Almighty, we are free at last.' " In the idiom of the black Americans whom many of their fellow citizens did not regard as really American at all, King had defined what it meant to be an American more eloquently and lucidly than any other public figure of his generation.

VIII

It has often been argued, and it seemed to be the case at the time, that a major defect of Kennedy's presidency was his failure to get major legislation through Congress. But this criticism is not really supported by the facts—if one stops to reflect how Congress worked at the time. There was a lively expectation (in the minds of some it was dread) that Kennedy would come to office in January 1961, as Roosevelt supposedly had in March 1933, with a long list of legislative proposals which he would dazzle Congress into passing speedily and perfunctorily. Of course this was sentimentalism. Whatever America's problems in January 1961, they were nothing as compared with those in March 1933, when the currency had stopped circulating in large parts of the economy and the economy itself had literally ground to a stop. The foreign policy crises which occupied so much of Kennedy's time required little congressional action. And much of Kennedy's serious legislation did get passed, from area redevelopment to the omnibus trade bill. The argument that Kennedy was unable to get major legislation through Congress rests on two major bills, the tax cut and the civil rights bill, neither of which was passed when he was assassinated in November 1963. But both were in fact well on their way to passage then. All they required was a certain amount of time and the same kind of reasonably competent management the administration had shown all along.

The tax bill was introduced in January 1963, pursuant to Kennedy's promise in August 1962, but the delay in delivery was matched by a hesitancy in contents. After all, the president was promising a tax cut in a year when a $11.9 billion budget deficit was expected, and it was a tenet of orthodox economics that budget deficits were dangerously inflationary and a staple of Republican oratory (at least when Republicans were out of office) that the federal budget should be balanced just as a family budget must be (this latter argument failed to take account of, among other things, the vast but sustainable increase in consumer debt which was occurring). The Constitution gives the popularly elected House the right to initiate all tax bills, and the one proposed by Kennedy went to the House Ways and Means Committee chaired since January 1958 by Wilbur Mills of Arkansas. A lawyer from the mountain town of Kensett, who prided himself on never traveling abroad, Mills had first been elected to the House in 1938. Thanks to the seniority system and the death of Chairman Jere Cooper in December 1957, he had found himself at forty-eight chairman of one of the most powerful congressional committees, perhaps for life.[40]

But Mills was not a simple backwoodsman: he was a graduate of Harvard Law

School, he was a skilled legislative draftsman and political strategist, he was a man who from his first days as chairman combined a desire to write good legislation with a desire to write winning legislation, bills that would prevail on the floor. His Ways and Means had no subcommittees; all staff were appointed by and reported to the chairman. Typically he asked and often he got closed rules limiting amendments of his bills on the floor. Mills took his responsibilities seriously and was neither an obdurate opponent nor a misty-eyed admirer of the economic policies of liberal Democrats. He was the architect of the Kerr-Mills bill, supported by the American Medical Association as the alternative to Social Security-financed Medicare for the elderly, and he more or less single-handedly prevented Medicare from passing in 1959 and 1960 (when it would have been vetoed anyway).

Mills was willing to consider the tax cut and the explicitly Keynesian arguments for it on the merits, and ultimately to report it out. But examining the details of legislation and amending it in line with what he was persuaded were valid objections by business lobbyists took time. By September 1963—by no means forever as these things go—Mills had pushed through on the floor a tax bill with Kennedy's steep income tax rate cuts, with more generous depreciation allowances, and with a new investment tax credit. This was by any reasonable standard a pro-business measure, though it was not recognized as such by the anti-spending and pro-balanced budget chairman of the Senate Finance Committee, Harry Byrd. The bill seemed to be languishing in Finance until Kennedy's death. But in fact pro-Kennedy Democrats on the committee had Byrd's and Minority Leader Everett Dirksen's commitment that the bill would come to the floor by January 1964, and they also had the votes (it passed Finance 12–5 over Byrd's opposition). After Kennedy's assassination, Johnson also cleverly muted Byrd's hostility by cutting Kennedy's $101.5 billion in spending for 1964–65 to under $100 billion; but "on the bill itself," according to a vivid and definitive account, "Johnson's succession to the presidency made not one whit of difference in either its timing or its size, notwithstanding the legend that he saved it from certain death."[41]

As for the civil rights bill, its way to passage was assured by October 1963. By that point the administration had managed to overcome an obstacle created in September when Emanuel Celler, the seventy-five-year-old chairman of the House Judiciary Committee,[42] produced and passed behind closed doors in subcommittee his own version of a bill. Celler, a regular Democrat elected to the House since 1922 by heavily Jewish, oddly shaped districts which snaked through Brooklyn from the brownstones of Bedford-Stuyvesant through the brick apartments of Brownsville to the bungalows on the seaside mudflats of Canarsie and Sheepshead Bay, expanded the coverage of the public accommodations section and extended voting rights provisions to state and local elections. These changes infuriated William McCulloch, the ranking Republican on Judiciary, a Taftish but fervently pro-civil rights Republican from small-town Ohio. They made the bill unpassable, he charged, and they violated Celler's commitment to him. Republicans did not want to seem to be guilty of scaling the bill's provisions back. They still thought of their party, and not the Democrats, as the natural backer of civil rights; and some Republicans hoped that failure to pass a civil rights bill would deny the Democrats any political benefits for supporting civil rights. As the bill came up in committee in October, Robert Kennedy intervened on McCulloch's side, insisting on cutbacks in the committee bill and getting Celler to agree to them. But Celler botched the compromise, at which point all the principals were summoned to the White House to see the president. Finally, crucial commitments were lined up from McCulloch and Charles Halleck, who originally had been cagily noncommittal about whether he would support the administration bill.[43] On October 30 the Judiciary Committee passed a bill which the Republicans could support and which the administration was confident could pass. The Rules Committee, still chaired by Judge Howard Smith, was not eager to report the measure to the floor. But the votes to get it to the floor were there, and so on the Senate side were the votes to overcome a filibuster. The one genuine danger to passage was behind. The passage of the Civil Rights Act of 1964—in the House in February and in the Senate, after some months of filibustering, in July—was inevitable.[44]

So both the tax bill and the civil rights bill were predictably on their way to passage when John Kennedy took his trip to Texas in late November 1963 to try to paper over the feud—a feud based not only on personal mistrust but also on profoundly different ideas about public policy—between Senator Ralph Yarborough and Governor John Connally. This is not to say that the bills would have been passed precisely at the same time and in the same way as they ultimately were if Kennedy had remained president. Lyndon Johnson supplied a decided impetus to the tax bill, and to civil rights he brought the conviction—surprising to many on the outside, but presaged by the speeches he had made publicly and the advice he had supplied privately during his years as vice president—that the whole House bill must be passed through the Senate, that there must be no compromise in the face of the filibuster led by his one-time mentor Richard Russell. Nor is it likely that Kennedy could have run as well in the southern and border states as Johnson did in 1964, though everything in the 1963 polls suggests that he would have run roughly as well in the East, Midwest, and West. But we are running quickly into the realm of impossible speculation, guessing whether Kennedy would have escalated the war in Vietnam as Johnson did, whether he would have been able to forge the sense of consensus which Johnson did, whether he would have shown the shrewdness of legislative tactics which Johnson did. The guess here is that in most respects he would have done pretty much what Johnson did, for contrary to general belief he had always steered the civil rights and tax bills on the way to passage,[45] he had never considered withdrawing from Vietnam and had committed himself to the overthrow of the Diems and to deep involvement with whoever would succeed them, and he was already leading all possible Republican candidates in the large majority of states by margins eerily similar to those Lyndon Johnson won in November 1964.

In any case, Kennedy's assassination played less of a role in changing immediate policy and legislation than in affecting, subtly but overwhelmingly, the national mood.

37

-»> «‹-

Continue

At 12:30 P.M. on Friday, November 22, 1963, while his car was passing Dealey Plaza in Dallas, John Kennedy was shot dead, the top of his head blown off by a bullet fired apparently from the top floor of the Texas School Book Depository. Dallas was a city known in the early 1960s for the rawness of its political expression. In November 1960, Lyndon Johnson and his wife, Lady Bird, campaigning for the Kennedy-Johnson ticket in the ornate lobby of the downtown Adolphus Hotel, had been jostled and nearly beaten by a crowd led by Dallas Congressman Bruce Alger, a Republican first elected in 1954, who was carrying a sign saying "LBJ sold out to Yankee Socialists."[1] In October 1963, Ambassador to the United Nations Adlai Stevenson, after speaking on United Nations Day, had been attacked by eighty picketers as he left the hall, struck on the head by a sign, and spat upon as he got into his car.[2] On November 22, Kennedy had been welcomed to the city with a black-bordered full-page display advertisement in the *Dallas Morning News,* the city's dominant paper, whose publisher, Joe B. Dealey, was a member of the family for whom the plaza was named; sponsored by the *Morning News* and "American-thinking citizens of Dallas," the ad attacked Kennedy for what it characterized as pro-Communist policies. Dallas was not just a Republican city, satisfied with its own free-enterprise success and contemptuous of the lack of success of others. It was a city in which the dominant political tone was pervaded with a sour sense that Kennedy and Johnson somehow lacked legitimacy, that this was not really their country.

Yet it was not a right-wing nut who killed Kennedy, although this was probably the thought that went through most Americans' minds when they heard he had been shot in Dallas. The assassin was quickly identified as Lee Harvey Oswald, who had spent months in the Soviet Union and had been part of a "Fair Play For Cuba" committee. Another thought then occurred to most Americans, the thought that the assassination was part of a conspiracy.[3] Johnson took care to take the oath of office from Judge Sarah T. Hughes[4] on the ground and then ordered Air Force One to fly to Washington, out of any conspiracy's way; in the following five days, Gallup found that only 29% of Americans believed that Oswald had acted on his own, while 52% thought some group or element was also responsible. Such suspicions prompted Johnson to create the special commission to investigate the assassination, headed by Chief Justice Earl Warren.[5]

For a long, unforgettable moment the attention of almost all Americans was on Kennedy's death and his funeral. Almost no American old enough to remember the assassination forgets where he was when he first heard the news. On Friday and Saturday, half the television sets in America were on, watching Walter Cronkite of CBS and the other networks' anchors broadcast the sad news. On Sunday, when the president's body lay in state in the Capitol Rotunda, some 80% of households were tuned in. On Monday, more than 100 million people watched Kennedy's funeral,[6] saw Presidents Hoover, Truman, Eisenhower, and Johnson share the same pew in St. Matthew's Cathedral, saw French President Charles de Gaulle, British Prime Minister Sir Alec Douglas-Home, West German Chancellor Ludwig Erhard, Soviet Deputy Premier Anastas Mikoyan, and Ethiopian Emperor Haile Selassie pay their respects, and saw three-year-old John F. Kennedy, Jr., salute as his father's horse-drawn coffin went by. Once against in 1963 television was bringing literally home to Americans a spectacle of sadness and grief which undercut their confidence in their country and their feeling that America was a land specially blessed.

In the thirty years up to November 1963 only one American president had died— Franklin D. Roosevelt, who, like Abraham Lincoln, died just at the moment of victory in a war in which he had led the nation. There was in retrospect a kind of poetry in these tragedies; and these most partisan of presidents, hated by large numbers of their fellow citizens during their years in office, were transformed into national heroes and, for the large majority of Americans, elevated ever after above politics. John Kennedy's death did not fit this pattern. Unlike Roosevelt and Lincoln he had not led the nation in a war, though he had had his foreign policy successes; his work was not finished, but was plainly in midstream; he did not look like a man worn old by the cares of office. To a country which had never seen a president die so late in his term, had never seen a president driven from office by disgrace, had seen strong presidents handle every crisis that had arisen for the last thirty years, this was an experience utterly shattering, an experience which shook national confidence in ways which were not fully apparent at the time and perhaps have never been fully appreciated.

II

Lyndon Johnson was determined to restore confidence, and by any standard he did a magnificent job. He took scrupulous care to keep Kennedy's top appointees on board, including even Attorney General Robert Kennedy and the entire White House staff, though Kennedy and many staffers had done much to humiliate and undercut him when he was vice president. Even Ted Sorensen, John Kennedy's speechwriter since 1953, did not leave until the end of February 1964. On Monday, November 25, Johnson met with foreign leaders and with the governors of the fifty states. On Wednesday, November 27, he spoke to Congress and, through television cameras, to the nation. He called first for passage of the civil rights bill, then for passage of the tax bill, then for "an end to the teaching and the preaching of hate and evil and violence." In the weeks that followed he brought in his own top staffers, but to a remarkable extent the Johnson government remained the Kennedy government; in this respect Johnson pointedly did not follow the precedent of Harry Truman, who, though much less experienced and knowledgeable about government, had gotten rid of most of Roosevelt's Cabinet and virtually all his White House staff in short order. Johnson maintained a highly visible courtship of Congress, romancing such Kennedy opponents as Richard Russell, Harry Byrd, and Charles Halleck. He made something of a splash by getting a wheat-sale-to-Russia bill through. But his main work with Congress, as he plainly understood, was to follow through on the civil rights and tax bills which had been securely on their way—their long, tortuous way—to passage since October 1963.

Among voters Kennedy's assassination created an overwhelming desire for continuity which worked to the benefit of incumbents in election year 1964. Johnson's competence strengthened those desires and left him with overwhelming political strength. His first Gallup job approval rating, in mid-December 1963, was 79%, with only 3% disapproving. He led Barry Goldwater 75%–20% nationally, 70%–24% in the South, and 91%–6% among Catholics, and was ahead of Richard Nixon 69%–24%.[7] Any political analyst would have had to say that these figures were inflated and could not be entirely sustained. Passage of the civil rights bill might be anticipated to lower Johnson's huge majority in the South down to somewhere near the minority Kennedy had been receiving there. But Kennedy had already been far ahead in the East and Midwest, where most of the electoral votes still were; Johnson, taken down a few notches, would be running at about the point Kennedy was. The analyst who would caution Johnson that these levels of support could not be sustained would have to add that the Democratic president was in an excellent position to win a major victory, regardless of who his Republican opponent was, unless he made some terrible mistake. Much was made at the time of Johnson's policy of governing by "consensus," presumably in contrast to Kennedy's policy of governing by partisan confrontation. But Johnson built his Congressional majorities on Democratic bedrock, and the electoral majority he would finally assemble in November 1964 consisted primarily of the majority Kennedy had already commanded a year earlier plus the extra votes Johnson, as a Texan, was able to win in southern and border states. The election, except for the shouting and the choice of the Republican nominee, was effectively over.

III

Even so, there was wide interest in and furious controversy over the seesaw battle for the Republican nomination. The putative winner as 1963 began had been Nelson Rockefeller, governor of New York and scion of one of the nation's great fortunes, ambitious for this nomination which did not seem especially propitious presumably because it would give him an advantage for the nomination in 1968, when the Democrats might be split by a succession battle between Johnson and Robert Kennedy. The strategists around Rockefeller—the old Dewey Republicans who shopped in men's stores and lunched in men's clubs on or just off

Madison Avenue near Grand Central Station—assumed that it was just a matter of time before Rockefeller took his rightful place in the White House. They looked with contempt on what they regarded as the naive and clumsy policies of John Kennedy, they looked with rancor on Kennedy's alliance with labor unions and big-city machines, and they believed that Rockefeller's policies of exuberantly accepting the New Deal and of robustly increasing defense spending commanded popular support, especially among the critical bloc of liberal-minded voters who had been the swing group in the electorate for the past thirty years. They discounted the polls showing Kennedy far ahead of any Republican and assumed that Rockefeller would have no troubling commanding as an electoral base the 45–47% of the vote which Dewey had won in 1944 and 1948.[8]

Almost certainly they misinterpreted the polls, if only by ignoring them. More important and more immediately, they did not account for the human being behind the candidate. Rockefeller's divorce had cost him a few points in his reelection campaign against Robert Morgenthau in November 1962.[9] Rockefeller's remarriage in early 1963 to a divorced woman who gave up custody of her four children to marry him caused a sudden plunge in his political fortunes. In April 1963 he led the Gallup poll of Republicans' presidential preferences with 43%, followed distantly by Goldwater's 26% and Romney's 13%. Then, when the New York legislature adjourned, Rockefeller announced his remarriage. In early May, Goldwater moved to a 35%–30% lead, in late May to a 38%–28% lead; Rockefeller never rose above 30% again and, after Nixon and Henry Cabot Lodge started appearing in speculation and on Gallup polls after Kennedy's death, his percentage plummeted to 13% and hovered thereafter between 6% and 16%.[10] Eastern establishment Republicans argued that Goldwater was not widely popular, but plainly he had more support than Rockefeller.

During 1963 Goldwater's pluralities rose, to 45%–23%–16% over Rockefeller and Romney in October. Goldwater, a backbencher in the Senate, had little experience and a propensity for saying things like "Let's lob one into the men's room of the Kremlin." He had been elected to the Senate in 1952 as a beneficiary of the Eisenhower landslide but as a follower of Robert Taft: an Asia Firster, a McCarthyite, a Republican who wished to repeal the New Deal from the graduated income tax to Social Security, and who even muttered that the United States needed a higher tariff. His was a backward-looking politics, focusing its resentments on the works of Franklin D. Roosevelt and on unions like Walter Reuther's United Auto Workers—a frequent Goldwater target—which were so plainly the creation of Roosevelt's Second New Deal. Yet in some respects Goldwater was not a conventional Taft Republican. Far from seeking ways to cut the defense budget, he was an enthusiast for Air Force bombers and Pentagon gadgets generally: the old conservative isolationist impulse transformed into a high-technology-minded hawkishness. And far from being rooted in a long-established small town or in the oriental-carpeted legal establishment of some interior American city, Goldwater was from the desert town of Phoenix, in his youth a dusty station stop on a transcontinental railroad and by 1964 a fast-growing, dynamic metropolis. He was unconstrained by traditional standards of behavior: he was not from a verdant neighborhood filled with Georgian mansions or magnificent stone town houses fitted out with Early American or country English antiques, but from a subdivision with cactus-bordered streets, desert-sand front lawns, and stucco houses fitted out with Navajo art and electronic gadgets like Goldwater's own automatic flagpole. Goldwater by 1963 was in the process of transforming himself, consciously or not, from the last Taft conservative to the first Sun Belt conservative.

After November 1963, Goldwater was suddenly overshadowed by Republicans with more experience and gravity. What is interesting is that he was not overshadowed more. In Republican pairings in December, he trailed Nixon by only 29%–27% and led Lodge (16%) and Rockefeller (13%). By early February 1964 Nixon was ahead with 31% to 20% for Goldwater, 16% for Rockefeller, and 13% for Lodge. Rockefeller in March said that Goldwater was outside "the mainstream of the Republican party"; and it could be argued that Goldwater's 20% showing in this poll, when the three leading candidates who could be classified as liberals or moderates were sharing 60%, showed the weakness of conservatism as a force in Republican politics. But voters do not choose by labels, and the history of Republican primaries does not show stable and steady conservative and liberal blocs of voters going back even to 1952 or 1948, much less to the 1912 contests between Theodore Roosevelt and William Howard Taft, as has sometimes been suggested; there was a much larger conservative bloc of voters in 1952, when Robert Taft was a leading candidate, then in 1948 or 1964, when he wasn't. In all these contests Republican voters, like Democrats, responded to the specific qualities of the candidates and their stands on issues.

But Nixon stayed out of the race and Lodge stayed in Saigon, and Republican voters seemed forced in early 1964 to choose between an excessively liberal (and personally besmirched) Rockefeller and an excessively conservative (and naively inexperienced) Goldwater. Eisenhower, who had deeply resented Rockefeller's criticisms of his policies in July 1960 and had no reason to see Goldwater as anything other than a not very bright member of a Republican faction he had long despised, tried in November 1963 to persuade Lodge to run and then in December to get William Scranton, the liberal governor of Pennsylvania, to enter the race.[11] Neither would. Into the vacuum stepped two young political amateurs from Boston, Paul Grindle and David Goldberg, who launched a write-in campaign for Lodge in the New Hampshire primary. Miraculously, in a blizzard raging amid the snow-topped mountains of New Hampshire, the ambassador working in the tropical heat of Asia received 36% of the votes as a write-in, compared with 22% for Goldwater and 21% for Rockefeller, both of whom were on the ballot, and 15% for Nixon, also a write-in (Nixon thus won less than half the votes of his running mate of four years before). Lodge immediately shot up in the Gallup poll of Republicans to 42%, versus 26% for Nixon and, in a pathetic showing for the two declared candidates, 14% for Goldwater and 6% for Rockefeller. The Republican party was in desperate straits, with two especially weak candidates for a nomination which did not seem worth anything.

Through write-ins Lodge won some more primaries in which no serious candidate was listed on the ballot. But delegates have to be sought, and Lodge did not seek them. Rockefeller and Goldwater did. Rockefeller's assets were his money, his total control of the New York delegation, and the presumption among many—though it was repeatedly contradicted by polling data—that he would be a stronger general-election candidate than Goldwater. Goldwater's assets were less visible: the principled, dedicated conservatives who felt that their country had been led in the wrong direction for thirty years and were now desperately afraid, with good reason, that it was about to be led even farther in that direction unless somehow the course of politics could be turned. Their views were generally ignored, articulated only in then obscure publications like William F. Buckley, Jr.'s *National Review.* In February 1963 they organized a Draft Goldwater Committee led by F. Clifton White, a suave operative formerly allied with the Dewey wing of the party in New York. Goldwater conservatives labored in precincts, where places had been left vacant by the retirement or inactivity of the liberal-minded Republican workers of yore; they set up their own organizations and, learning the rules, won control of party organizations even in places where their views commanded little assent; they did not just take over, but also filled with their people the mostly vacant ranks of the Republican party in many states in the Deep South. Motivated by deep beliefs, unencumbered in most cases by personal relationships or past associations, these new Goldwater conservatives went a long way toward taking over the Republican party—and won dozens of delegates who gave them a bedrock of support in the July 1964 convention in San Francisco's Cow palace, which proved far larger than expected.

Both campaigns were motivated by unrealistic expectations: Rockefeller's by the idea that a New York moderate Republican was bound to run as well as Thomas Dewey had, Goldwater's by the idea that there was a hidden conservative vote out there, a vote which had failed to come to the polls when Dewey was a candidate but would come streaming out for Goldwater. Rockefeller's vision was more realistic in light of past politics, but Goldwater's vision was a more accurate forecast of American politics to come. For if the key swing vote in American politics from the 1920s to the 1950s was a self-consciously liberal, even leftish vote, anchored in the Progressive German-American Northwest and among New York and other big-city Jews, the key swing vote in American politics from the 1960s to the 1980s, it would turn out, was a self-consciously conservative vote, anchored in the white South and among ethnic and blue-collar whites in the big metropolitan areas. The ferocity of the battle for this worthless nomination reflected the fact that both Rockefeller and Goldwater Republicans sensed that they were fighting for the future direction of their party, to determine whether this minority party would seek swing votes on the "liberal" left or the "conservative" right.

IV

The result was determined mostly by accident. With Goldwater's conservatives quietly winning more delegates than anyone had expected, and conventional Republicans holding off from endorsing the unpopular Rockefeller, the final contest came down to the Oregon primary May 15 and the California primary June 2. "He cared enough to come" was the easterner Rockefeller's slogan in Oregon, where it enabled him after non-stop campaigning to beat Lodge by a 33%–28% margin and effectively end his candidacy. Goldwater had only 18% and Nixon, his name put on the ballot by Oregon's secretary of state pursuant to state law, only 17%. In California, Goldwater had a stronger base. Southern California's registered Republicans, it turned out, were strongly conservative. Their conservatism was not just the mindless response of rootless yahoos, as eastern sophisticates supposed; there was a sociological basis for it. For these southern Californians had not just seen, but had been part of and had profited from, the most explosive expansion of any metropolitan economy in the nation's history; they had seen how small businesses, mostly with no help from the government (with the conspicuous exception of aerospace and defense contracts), had grown far beyond anyone's dreams, and had created what was probably the most affluent city in history in just a few years. The new migrants into southern California in the 1950s had helped move the Los Angeles area, particularly the heavily Jewish west side, toward Democrats like Adlai Stevenson in the 1950s. But as the prosperity continued, and even though none of the media were articulating or celebrating the achievements of Los Angeles's private sector, the area by the early 1960s was moving to the right. To his consternation Richard Nixon had right-wing opposition in the 1962 gubernatorial primary from Los Angeles area Assemblyman Joseph Shell, who won what was to most observers, and to Nixon, an ominous one third of the votes. Two of the Los Angeles area's Republican congressmen then, Edgar Hiestand and John Rousselot, were members of the John Birch Society, whose leader, Robert Welch, had called president Eisenhower "a dedicated, conscious agent of the Communist conspiracy." Hiestand and Rousselot were beaten by Democratic redistricting plans, but conservative forces made gains in 1963 and 1964 in the Los Angeles basin. Four congressional districts outside the South elected Democratic congressmen in 1962 and Republican congressmen in 1964; one was in Idaho and three were in California.[12] So far as southern Californian Republicans could see, they owed none of their prosperity to easterners, who were trying only to tax it away. It was to these voters that Goldwater appealed when he said, "Sometimes I think this country would be better off if we could just saw off the Eastern Seaboard and let it float out to sea."

If Southern California provided a good base for Goldwater, the birth of Nelson Rockefeller, Jr., the Saturday before the primary moved the critical bloc of votes. Between May 20 and May 29, Rockefeller led in Louis Harris surveys with between 47 and 49% of the vote to Goldwater's 36–40%. On Sunday his lead was reduced to an insignificant 44%–42%, and on Monday the race was 44%–44%. Goldwater won 52%–48%.[13] This result upset the plans of Nixon and Eisenhower, who had expected a Rockefeller victory which would have eliminated both Goldwater (because he would not have won any seriously contested primaries) *and* Rockefeller (because of his unpopularity). But Goldwater's California win, along with the hitherto unheralded success of Clifton White's and other conservatives' delegate-winning efforts, made him suddenly the clear favorite for the nomination.

V

At this moment something more dramatic was happening than the struggle over the Republican nomination: the senate was preparing to conclude the filibuster of the civil rights bill which had begun in March. And as it was doing so, public opinion and the flow of legislation was passing it by. Already in January the 24th Amendment, outlawing the poll tax in federal elections, had been ratified; this measure struck not only at the disenfranchisement of blacks but also at a system that discouraged lower-income whites from voting. Now the major goals of the civil rights movement, it seemed, were about to be achieved.

To those goals a new one was about to be added: Americans suddenly decided they must end or at least significantly reduce poverty in their country. The catalyst for this crusade was *The Other America,* a book written by Michael Harrington, a longtime Socialist and follower of Dorothy Day, editor of the pacifist *Catholic Worker.* Published in 1962, *The Other America* was little noticed until it was reviewed favorably in January 1963 by the veteran (and maverick lefist) writer Dwight Macdonald in the *New Yorker,* at which point it suddenly became widely noticed in Washington—and, most important, in the White House. John Kennedy was moved by its vivid descriptions of the daily lives of poor Americans and its statistical proof that there were still many more poor people in the United States than most politicians had thought. Like most politicians of the time, Kennedy remembered the 1930s and was aware of the economic progress most Americans had made in the 1940s and 1950s. He had seen the percentage of Americans who could be regarded as in some sense poor shrink as first the war and then the unanticipated postwar economic growth enabled ordinary people to achieve a standard of living which was in many cases far beyond their dreams. His working assumption was that poverty was dying out and that as economic growth continued it would disappear. This assumption Harrington challenged. Many more Americans were poor, he argued, than was generally supposed. And many of them—blacks in big cities and southern backwaters, poor whites in Appalachia, people stuck in dead-end jobs—seemed trapped in poverty, unable to escape. After a long period of economic growth, poverty suddenly seemed more rather than less conspicuous,[14] for poverty is more noticeable when economic growth makes it seem avoidable. A rich society, Kennedy and other Americans quickly concluded, should do something about poverty—though it seems likely that Kennedy did not mean to make an antipoverty program the centerpiece of his domestic policy in 1964.[15]

Kennedy had been curious about poverty at least since his campaigning in the West Virginia primary in May 1960, and his Area Redevelopment program of 1961 was aimed partly at that region. One goal of the new antipoverty program would be to set up an Appalachian Regional Commission to spur economic growth and upgrading of job skills in the isolated, insular hollows and hills which stretched from the close-up coal mines of Pennsylvania to the ridges of east Tennessee and the northeast corner of Alabama. Another would be to address juvenile delinquency, a problem Attorney General Robert Kennedy had become fascinated by in 1961 and 1962: why did boys go bad, and what could be done about it? The answer advanced by certain academics was that the boys were not being bad but were responding to the bad conditions—lack of opportunity, general unfairness—they perceived around them. The implication, that the problem was not that the individual was bad but that society was bad, appealed to Robert Kennedy. It stimulated proposals for a comprehensive attack on conditions which seemed to hold people in poverty–amd on the institutions which society had set up during the previous thirty years to help the poor. The idea was in the air that the paternalism of welfare bureaucrats and their nit-picking regulations were holding down welfare recipients, and that the poor needed to take control of their own lives. From this emerged the idea of community action agencies, federally funded entities somehow democratically selected by the poor—no one was sure quite how, since the poor already democratically selected their public officials, usually by ratifying the choices of local political machines—which would operate as an adversary to existing governmental and civic institutions.[16]

Lyndon Johnson, responding to these ideas and perhaps to his own experiences growing up in Texas Hill Country, announced in March 1964 the terms of his own $962 million "war on poverty." The different approaches to poverty were, at Johnson's insistence, woven into a single antipoverty bill, a bill which would have had no chance of passage in normal times because of the way it undercut existing politicians and their allies. Struggling for a rubric to explain the new programs he was championing, Johnson fell upon the phrase "Great Society" and used it to considerable acclaim in a commencement speech at the University of Michigan in May. He pushed the antipoverty program hard through Congress, even as the Senate was going through the theatrical motions of the southerners' filibuster on civil rights. Cots were set up outside the chamber and speeches were given around the clock as the southerners sought to demonstrate—in some but not all cases they also felt obliged out of personal commitment to demonstrate—that they would oppose the bill to the bitter end. But they never had the votes. Johnson had to squeeze hard to get the requisite two-thirds vote to cut off the filibuster; he had to make a showy but not especially meaningful bow to Senate Republican Leader Everett Dirksen (long a compromiser with liberal Republicans and Democrats, despite his conservative reputation) in order to get his help. But the outcome was never really in doubt. The filibuster was broken, and the Senate passed the bill in mid-June. Three days later, three young men—two Jews from New York and one black from Mississippi—who had been part of a summer project to flood Mississippi with civil rights workers were reported missing; fears that they had been murdered were confirmed in August when their bodies were discovered. In the meantime, Lyndon Johnson signed the Civil Rights Act on July 2, thirteen months after it was proposed—not such a long time to pass such revolutionary legislation, but a time in which much in the country had changed. Only a month later, in August, Congress passed the antipoverty program, an attempt–and a much less succesful one—at producing a similarly revolutionary change in American society.

VI

The closing moments of the civil rights battle in Congress were also the closing weeks of the battle for the Republican presidential nomination. It was a time when Republicans like Rockefeller and Romney were genuinely savoring the triumph of a cause which they believed, with some justice, had been pursued over the years more vigorously by their own party than by the opposition. And yet their party was preparing to nominate a man who was poised to vote against the civil rights bill. In their agitation the pro-civil rights Republicans tried to make the electoral arguments that Dewey Republicans had always made, that there was great political advantage in supporting civil rights and little political profit in opposing them. But these arguments were flatly refuted by the polls. The party of John Kennedy and Lyndon Johnson was winning virtually unanimous support from blacks, a level of support which Democrats in only a few states—notably the religiously pro-civil rights G. Mennen Williams in Michigan—had been able to achieve as recently as 1960. It mattered not a whit which Republican was paired against Johnson. At the same time, the Republican party was clearly on the verge of making historically unprecedented gains in the Deep South–greater gains if a candidate like Goldwater was nominated than if one like Rockefeller or Scranton was, but significant gains nevertheless. Once John Kennedy embraced the cause of civil rights as his administration's first priority in June 1963, the die was cast: the Democrats, for all their past ambivalence about civil rights, would now be for both blacks and whites, North and South, the pro-civil rights party; the Republicans, for all their past (though not unanimous or entirely constant) support of civil rights, would be the anti-civil rights party.

That there might be political liabilities for the Democrats in this arrangement was suggested by the results in the presidential primaries. Johnson, shy of being beaten, did not allow his name to be put on ballots. In most states he was nominated by overwhelming percentages of write-ins. But in Wisconsin, Indiana, and Maryland, he arranged for Governors John Reynolds and Matthew Welsh and Senator Daniel Brewster to have their names placed on the ballot as favorite sons, in effect as Johnson stand-ins. George Wallace used this opportunity to show that his opposition to civil rights measures had vote-getting appeal in the North. This he did, winning 34% in Wisconsin, 30% in Indiana, and 43% in Maryland and thereby helping to make "white backlash" a common phrase in American politics. In 1964, this white backlash was not an overpowering force, and in particular it availed Goldwater almost nothing. But Wallace's showings, especially in working-class white neighborhoods, alerted politicians to the possibility that acceding to demands made in behalf of blacks could be politically damaging to northern Democrats, who were now, ineluctably and without exception, associated with civil rights.[17]

VII

The San Francisco convention was the scene of the triumph of the Goldwater conservatives—and one of the causes of their defeat in November. As Goldwater proclaimed the unexceptionable sentiment that "extremism in the defense of liberty is no vice," viewers were reminded of the "extreme" statements he had made in 1963 and 1964; that NATO area commanders should use atomic weapons, that the Tennessee Valley Authority should be sold, that the United States should withdraw its diplomatic recognition of the Soviet Union and withdraw from the United Nations if it admitted Communist China to membership, that the graduated income tax should be abolished and Social Security be made voluntary. Nor did it help the Republican cause in November that Rockefeller was vociferously booed, as if by a mob, when he faced the delegates, or that even Eisenhower was cheered as he denounced sensation-seeking columnists—one of the first examples of an attack on the press by a leader of a party which up to that time had been supported by the large majority of the press. All this hostility and turmoil was profoundly unsettling to Americans, who more than anything else wanted calm and reassurance. Little wonder that in late July, just after the convention was over, a time when there is ordinarily a euphoria for the ticket just nominated, Americans preferred Johnson over Goldwater by a 59%–31% margin, and southerners favored him by 51%–40%. These results—the best Goldwater saw in 1964—were reasonably accurate presagings of the result in November.

Johnson's strategy was to avoid confrontation, to present himself as the embodiment of consensus, and to win overwhelmingly. It was so successful that important steps he took on issues which would be exceedingly divisive in a few years received almost unanimous support in August 1964. It was early in that month that he secured passage of his antipoverty program in Congress, not by overwhelming margins to be sure, but without serious opposition from voters at large. It was also in early August that he presented to Congressional leaders what he said was evidence that two U.S. Navy destroyers patrolling in international waters in the Gulf of Tonkin had been attacked by North Vietnamese PT boats. On August 7, at Johnson's behest, Congress passed the Gulf of Tonkin resolution, giving the president power "to take all necessary measures to repel any armed attack against the forces of the United States and to prevent further aggression." Since 16,000 American "military advisers" were stationed in South Vietnam, and since the Navy and Air Force would continue patrolling the Gulf, possibilities existed for further "armed attack" at almost any time; and "all necessary measures" meant that the president could by himself wage what amounted to war in Vietnam. Yet from this extraordinary grant of power no member of the House and only two members of the Senate—Wayne Morse of Oregon and Ernest Gruening of Alaska, both liberal, contrary-minded old-timers—dissented.

The major suspense of the Johnson campaign was the question of who would be nominated for vice president. Johnson gleefully pointed to polls which suggested that any nominee would cost him (as any vice presidential nominee in 1952 had cost Eisenhower) 5 percentage points in the vote. Sentiment argued for putting the thirty-nine-year-old Robert Kennedy on the ticket; every instinct of Johnson's—the instinct to take revenge on the Kennedy acolytes who had opposed and humiliated him, the instinct to win the office on his own and not with the help of the Kennedys—argued against it. Johnson, never a master of election politics, was nervous about his ability to control the convention he scheduled for August in the shabby, rickety resort town of Atlantic City, New Jersey. He was displeased when Kennedy received almost as many write-ins for vice president as he received for president in New Hampshire. After some missteps, however, Johnson figured out how to finesse the desire many Democrats had to nominate Kennedy. First, in late July he rescheduled the documentary film about John Kennedy from the first day of the convention to the last, the night after the vice presidential nomination. Second, two days later he told Kennedy that he would not be chosen. Finally, a day after that Johnson announced publicly that he would select no one from the Cabinet. This strategy was disingenuous and maladroit, but it worked: everyone conceived Kennedy was out of the running. The obvious candidate then was Hubert Humphrey. But Johnson toyed with choosing Humphrey's Minnesota colleague, Eugene McCarthy, a quieter, more intellectual, more cynical Democrat who had never liked the Kennedys; and on the eve of the choice Johnson brought with him in his helicopter to Atlantic City not only Humphrey but also Thomas Dodd, the strongly anti-Communist senator from Connecticut.

Humphrey's mettle was tested in the controversy over the challenge to the all-white Mississippi delegation by the Mississippi Freedom Democratic Party, an uneasy coalition of civil rights activists, whose leading witness, Fannie Lou Hamer, presented an unforgettable narrative of vicious discrimination against blacks in the delegate selection process. Johnson's initial reaction was to give the MFDP delegation floor passes and an assurance that Mississippi Democrats wouldn't discriminate in the future. But this proposal seemed likely to provoke a floor fight from liberals; and Humphrey (assisted on the details by the young attorney general of Minnesota, Walter Mondale), Walter Reuther, Clark Clifford, and Johnson aide Walter Jenkins were given the assignment of arranging a compromise which would keep the issue off the floor. After much negotiation they succeeded in reaching a settlement which afterwards would seem ludicrous in its attempt to propitiate the segregationists, but which to Johnson and many others at the time may have seemed daring in its refusal to defer entirely to the decisions of segregationist state politicians. Humphrey's mettle was also tested by Johnson's almost pathological caginess; in this, as in lesser nominations, he could not bear to be scooped, he insisted on prolonging suspense to the end, he insisted on maintaining the fiction that he was not responsible for decisions which at the same time he insisted on making.

VIII

Few issues as such surfaced in the campaign, nor were there any climactic events which turned opinion around. Johnson forces made much of the Goldwater Republicans' refusal to repudiate extremists like the John Birch Society and of their candidate's statement that "extremism in the defense of liberty is no vice." Johnson also made much of his support from business leaders who considered themselves Republicans, as if they were the spiritual leaders of millions of voters who had voted Republican for years. But the edge of labor-management animosity, for all of Johnson's involvement in settling strikes, was growing dull; and the polling evidence, showing Democratic percentages just as high fourteen months before the businessmen's endorsements, suggests that they had little if any impact on people's voting.

The efforts of neither campaign made any perceptible difference, with one possible exception. This was the so-called daisy spot, a 60-second television advertisement prepared by New York media master Tony Schwartz for the Johnson campaign. A little girl is shown picking a daisy in Riverside Park in New York,[18] counting "one, two, three, four, five, seven, six, six, eight, nine, nine." Then she looks up, startled, as a man's voice loudly counts down from ten to one and the screen goes black; then an atom bomb is shown exploding, with voice-over from the edited tape of a Johnson speech: "These are the stakes—to make a world in which all of God's children can live, or to go into the dark. We must either love each other, or we must die." Finally the announcer and words on the screen say, "Vote for President Johnson on November 3. The stakes are too high for you to stay home."[19] The spot only ran once, on the September 7 *CBS Monday Night at the Movies,* but it generated a firestorm of reaction and evoked complaints, which persisted twenty-four years later, that somehow it was unfair advertising—which of course it was not. Like all effective political ads, it spoke in shorthand and referred to other things voters knew: Goldwater's statements that he would like to "lob one into the men's room of the Kremlin" and that he would consider using tactical nuclear weapons as a defoliant in Vietnam. There was plenty of room for legitimate argument that Goldwater as president would do things which would unduly risk nuclear war, and the spot was simply a vivid and chilling reminder to the viewer of what nuclear war would mean in human terms. It was also a harbinger of the strength of television as a political medium: how the cool medium could express and arouse emotions better than hot oratory could.

IX

For one period of 24 hours in October, some Americans thought that the result of the election might be in doubt. On October 14 it was revealed that a week earlier Walter Jenkins, one of Johnson's two or three closest aides for twenty-five years, a man of immense power and skill at the White House, a husband and father, had been arrested for engaging in homosexual acts with a man named Andy Choka in the men's room at the YMCA one block west of the White House on G Street. This news raised the possibility, suggested on the stump by Goldwater, that Jenkins had been blackmailed and had compromised American security interests. Johnson's pollster Oliver Quayle found no effect on the election—not surprisingly, since the basic contours of opinion were the same as they had been a year before, when the Democratic nominee was assumed to be Kennedy and he led any Republican—and Johnson, after his wife had already done so, issued a statement sympathizing with Jenkins's personal collapse.

On October 15, Nikita Khrushchev was ousted from power by the Politburo of the Communist party of the Soviet Union. On the same day the Labor party won the British election, making Harold Wilson prime minister in place of Sir Alec Douglas-Home. On October 16 the People's Republic of China exploded its first nuclear bomb. These foreign developments, particularly the ouster of Khrushchev, completely overshadowed the Jenkins scandal. Any doubts Americans might have had about the wisdom of voting to keep Lyndon Johnson in office were quickly resolved. The world was changing—rapidly, alarmingly. Their country had had change—too much change—in its leadership and its way of life. The president, this volcanic man who had not been known in any depth by most voters eleven months before, was for all his eccentricities plainly an exceedingly competent leader. He had skillfully advanced, and in no significant way betrayed, the legacy of the president whom most of the nation's voters—the large majority of the nation's voters outside the South—had been prepared to reelect a year before. In November, when it came time to vote, Americans did what came naturally. They voted for Lyndon Johnson—and for every respectable, visible incumbent in their country, regardless of party.

The election of 1964 was the Democratic landslide which had been presaged in the polls since long before John Kennedy was murdered, but which Republicans for months and even years had not been able to believe would actually happen. What especially shocked the Republicans was that Democrats won not so much because of huge margins in their historic strongholds—though they did roll up such margins in the big cities—but because of victories in areas which had long been rock-ribbed Republican. Lyndon Johnson won with 61% of the vote, the same percentage Franklin Roosevelt had won in 1936. But he ran much better in the large states of the North, carrying hundreds of suburbs and counties which had never voted for a Democratic presidential candidate before. At the same time, he ran much worse in the South, only narrowly carrying four border states and Florida and losing five Deep South states to Barry Goldwater.

The trend in the North was most prominent in New York State. Johnson—scarcely as sympathetic or familiar a figure to New Yorkers as Roosevelt—carried every one of the state's sixty-two counties; Roosevelt had carried thirteen. Johnson won 73% of the vote in New York City, the same as Roosevelt, but he also won 60% in the suburbs, where Roosevelt had won 45%, and 68% in upstate New York, where Roosevelt had won 44%. These were also vivid contrasts with the performance four years before of Kennedy, who had won 63% in New York City, 43% in the suburbs, and 46% upstate (a good showing for this Catholic Democrat in a region by then heavily Catholic but usually Republican). Similar patterns appeared almost everywhere in the East and Midwest. In New England, the most Republican of regions in 1936, Johnson carried even Maine and Vermont and won 76% in Massachusetts. In Pennsylvania he won 65% and lost only two small counties; in mostly suburban New Jersey and Maryland he won by nearly 2–1. Ohio was 63% for Johnson, Michigan 67%, Illinois a bit lower at 59%, for suburban Cook County and the "Collar Counties" beyond—full of those who had succeeded in private enterprise and grown up reading Colonel McCormick's *Chicago Tribune* —gave Goldwater majorities. Johnson carried every northern and western state except Goldwater's own Arizona, where he got 49%. And in only a couple of other non-southern states (Idaho and Nebraska) was the margin close. But California, surprising many, was only 59% for Johnson, less than the national average: this result, like the Goldwater victory in the state's presidential primary, was a sign of some things to come.

In the South, Goldwater won 87% of the vote in Mississippi—a spectacular and totally unprecedented Republican triumph. The unpledged slate of electors chosen in the Democratic primary won only 31% in Alabama, compared with Goldwater's 69%. Johnson got above 40% in South Carolina, Louisiana, and Georgia, and he carried the more northerly states of Virginia, North Carolina, Tennessee, and Arkansas with between 54% and 56%; he won with 51% in Florida. But leaving aside Texas, where home state pride in the president and (perceptible in the returns for Dallas at least) a yearning for expiation for the assassination of his predecessor gave Johnson a whopping 63%, Johnson actually lost the South to Goldwater. Even with Texas included, he ran no better than even among white southerners.

These results represent a sudden reversal of the patterns, ingrained for a century, of Civil War party loyalties. The civil rights issue detached most southern whites from the Democrats and played an important part in detaching northerners— particularly Protestants in the far northern tier of the country—from the Republicans. Were these just momentary changes, responses to particular personalities and events, or were they permanent changes—or changes which could have been sustained over a long period? The advance of southern whites into Republican ranks in presidential elections proved to be permanent. Many were persuaded to vote for George Wallace in 1968, and a larger-than-usual minority voted for Jimmy Carter in 1976. But a Republican preference was established and went at least some way down the ballot. Within twenty-five years every southern state but Mississippi had elected a Republican governor, and every southern state but Mississippi had elected a Republican U.S. senator.[20] The northern movement into the Democratic column appears, at first glance, less permanent. After all, Republicans won most of these states in most of the next five presidential elections. Yet in races for Congress and governorships and even state legislatures, Democrats were often able to win the lion's share of elections.

What 1964 made plain was that the number of Americans willing to consider candidates of either major party was much greater than ever before. It showed a nation which had grown adept at ticket-splitting and a nation in which party identification was less firmly established—in which attachment to the party your ancestors had favored since the Civil War or the party which had represented your side of the labor-management war since the sit-down strikes of 1937 had grown weak enough to be overcome by personal preference for a particular candidate or by a response to a particular contemporary issue. Both the Civil War loyalties dating to the 1850s and the politics of economic redistribution dating to the 1930s had faded in importance.

For 1964 was in important respects not a Democrats' election but an incumbents' election. True, in state legislative and U.S. House races where incumbents had not taken care to become well known, many Republicans were defeated; the Democrats won 57% of the total House vote and ended up with a net gain of 37 seats since 1962, even after losing 12,[21] and a huge 295–140 majority. Yet Republicans who had been working hard for years to hold marginal districts held them in 1964, even when they went overwhelmingly for Johnson. Examples included William Ayres in working-class Akron, Ohio, and William Broomfield in the mostly high-income suburbs of Oakland County, Michigan. Republicans who were defeated were those who had taken their districts for granted, who had not bothered to send out thousands of newsletters and pepper their constituents with favors and otherwise use the prerogatives of office to hold on to their seats. These seats were heavily concentrated in the northern tier states. The use of the power of incumbency to hold onto marginal seats, which had been pioneered by Republicans like Ayres and Broomfield in the 1950s, was discovered by alert Republicans and Democrats in the mid-1960s and by the late 1960s had become the norm among House members, with correspondingly and usually record high incumbency reelection rates in every election from then on, with the limited exceptions of 1974 and 1980.

In gubernatorial races, where incumbents automatically enjoyed high visibility, they did exceedingly well in 1964. Not a single incumbent Republican governor was defeated; and only two Democratic incumbents, John Reynolds of Wisconsin and Albert Rosellini of Washington, fell victim to the discontent over increased taxes which had helped to defeat a majority of the governors who had sought reelection in 1962.[22] Republican Governor John Chafee of Rhode Island was reelected with 61% of the vote even while President Johnson was winning the state with 81% and Democratic Senator John Pastore was taking 83%. In Michigan, Romney had gone to the trouble of sponsoring a law abolishing the lever which allowed voters to cast a straight party ballot with one pull, but the Democrats got enough petition signatures to force a referendum which preserved the lever; even so, Romney was reelected with 56% of the vote, while Johnson carried the state with 67% and Democratic Senator Philip Hart was reelected with 64%.

In senatorial elections the pattern of success for incumbents was much the same. Republican Senator Hiram Fong of Hawaii was reelected with 53% of the vote as Johnson carried the state with 79%. Democratic senators of the class of 1958 were mostly, like Hart, reelected by overwhelming margins. There were a few exceptions. One was in California, where the physically incapacitated Clair Engle had been beaten in a primary by Kennedy's press secretary, Pierre Salinger; although Salinger had grown up in San Francisco, his ties to the state were tenuous, and he was defeated by Republican actor George Murphy in November. This conservative victory proved an important precedent, as did the near-victory (he lost by 48 votes) of Republican Paul Laxalt against Senator Howard Cannon in next-door Nevada. In addition, the liberal Republican electoral formula was showing signs of wear. Hugh Scott held on in Pennsylvania, but Kenneth Keating, vastly resented by the Kennedys for his charges in August and September 1962 that the Soviets were putting missiles into Cuba, found himself opposed by Robert Kennedy in New York. By capitalizing enough on the affection for the Kennedys among Catholics to nearly carry upstate New York and by overcoming Keating's inroads among Jewish and other liberal voters in New York City, the former attorney general carried 1964's best-publicized Senate race by a 53%–43% margin.

Overall, the 1964 election results show a country ready to discard its historic preferences and reelect by an overwhelming margin and across traditional party lines a Democratic administration which, in the opinion of most voters, had performed ably. This readiness to reelect the Democratic president changed only marginally between the supposedly unpopular and conflict-minded John Kennedy in October 1963 and the supposedly universally popular and consensus-minded Lyndon Johnson in November 1964. But the 1964 election results also show a country determined to retain in office any visible and arguably competent leaders at a time when Americans' confidence in their nation's good fortune and even stability was undermined by the totally unanticipated assassination of their young president.

Seen in this light, the Democratic victories of 1964 were not of a type to be easily replicated. The desire to retain incumbents (at a time when most incumbents were Democrats) would not necessarily survive to more placid times or to times when incumbents' policies seemed to work less well. The widespread approval of the performance of this particular administration would not necessarily extend to other administrations whose performance was or seemed different. And the willingness to consider candidates of both parties, the readiness to throw aside ancestral allegiances and the politics of economic class, could work as easily against the Democrats as for them, just as it in fact worked powerfully against the Democrats among white southerners in 1964. Thus the Democrats' victories in 1964 were not the firm foundation of an era of Democratic command but were evidence of changes in the rules, changes which meant that neither party would have a guarantee of dominance or a reliable majority. In the wake of the 1964 election the question was widely asked whether the Republican party would even survive. Yet in retrospect the erosion of party loyalties and the detachment of what would turn out to be a critical group of voters—white southerners—from the Democratic coalition were crucial circumstances which permitted the Republicans to win five of the next six presidential elections. The election which represented the triumph of Lyndon Johnson's Great Society also contained the seeds of the repudiation of that same Great Society and the victory of something rather different from what Johnson and his Democrats had in mind.

PART FOUR

American Politics 1964–1981

ALIENATION

38

→》》 《《←

From Confidence to Alienation

O n the Saturday night after Barry Goldwater was nominated in San Francisco, in July 1964, and less than a month after Lyndon Johnson signed the Civil Rights Act, beneath the glaring signs atop five-story stone buildings on the busy corner of 125th Street and Seventh Avenue in New York's Harlem, the first race riot of the summer of 1964 began. The cause, typically, was obscure: a protester alleging some grievance led a march on a police station around 10 o'clock at night, police attempted to break up the march, bottles were thrown, and within an hour mobs surged up and down Harlem's avenues breaking windows and looting stores. The violence was repeated the next night and for several nights thereafter in Harlem and in Brooklyn's Bedford-Stuyvesant neighborhood. One person was killed and over 100, one third of them policemen, injured. This was the first of the urban riots of the 1960s, in which one incendiary element was the mistrust of white policemen and ghetto blacks for each other and another was the expectation, which grew stronger after each riot, that on hot summer evenings others would be joining in, that the police would lose control and looters would be immune from punishment.

The tension between white policemen and ghetto blacks became common in the years after World War II. Police jobs, like those in so many skilled blue-collar trades, were typically handed down father to son, cousin to cousin, among members of white ethnic groups, often Irish-Americans. Officially, of course, the jobs were open to anyone; but insiders knew when vacancies would open up and could coach others on how to pass the tests, and outsiders—especially blacks[1]—soon learned they were not welcome. So big-city police forces had very few black patrolmen, who would have been able to understand and control black neighborhoods better. Instead, the almost entirely white police forces tried to impose in black ghettos, as they did in white neighborhoods, their own rough-and-ready version of law and order. Used to the street language and cues of white ethnic neighborhoods, these policemen misread the blacks whose neighborhoods they were supposed to patrol. In their own neighborhoods white police typically responded to rowdy but not murderous behavior with a back-alley beating—a response which was considered within the rules, a warning that such behavior should not recur. But to blacks such beatings were racist brutality. In the 1950s such "police brutality"—the term didn't come into common use until the early 1960s—must have been commonplace, but there were few articulate protests and no major urban riots. The civil rights movement, however, helped to teach northern blacks to question the treatment they received, even as the rapid growth of their communities, fueled by continual northward migration, led to rapid dispersion and creation of new black neighborhoods where community institutions were weak and the moral restraints typical of deeply rooted communities were largely absent. Thus black protest over police tactics became an issue in city politics, and the authority of the white policeman on the beat in the black ghetto was no longer seen as legitimate.

The result was the crash of breaking glass and the sound of laughter as television sets and clothes were dragged out of storefronts on Seventh Avenue and 125th Street and Lenox Avenue and on Fulton Street in Brooklyn. The Harlem and Bedford-Stuyvesant riots were not just local events. As Theodore H. White noted, television, "with its insatiable appetite for live drama, found in the riots gorgeous spectacle."[2] Many Americans responded, as they had to the television spectacle of Birmingham, by asking how society had gone wrong. What grievances did these blacks have? How had the police mistreated them? Were they justified by anger at white storekeepers and landlords? Other Americans responded more angrily, rejecting the idea that the police had done anything wrong, outraged at—and perhaps scared by—the violence. This response was the "white backlash," a term invented a year before and popularized in May 1964 as George Wallace was making his surprisingly strong showings in northern Democratic primaries.[3] Eventually in Harlem and Bedford-Stuyvesant the police restored order, and as the weather cooled the expectation that others would riot vanished and the riots themselves vanished too. But Harlem set an example, the very month the Civil Rights Act was signed, which would be matched in city after city in the summers of 1965 and 1967 and the spring of 1968.

II

Between the crowded, dirty streets of Harlem and the spacious green campus of the University of California at Berkeley, sprawled out over the hills above San Francisco Bay, there could hardly be a greater contrast. But they had things in common. Both Harlem and Berkeley voted well-nigh unanimously in favor of Lyndon Johnson over Barry Goldwater in 1964, and both erupted in riot as the campaign was going on. In fact, the explosion at Berkeley was triggered by the campaign. In September 1964 students wanted to set up a table on the Bancroft Strip, the entrance to the university grounds which was across the street from the commercial strip at Telegraph Avenue, to hand out literature and enlist volunteers for the Johnson-Humphrey campaign. Under prodding by the *Oakland Tribune,* owned by former Senator William Knowland, university chancellor Edward Strong prohibited this and all other forms of political activity on campus.

Within three days students formed a United Front, including all manner of political groups, in protest; shortly thereafter, hundreds of students were picketing Sproul Hall under its aegis. When five students were cited for violating university rules, some 500 more, led by a physics student and former civil rights worker named Mario Savio, stepped forward and insisted they too be disciplined; and they were. This action was the beginning of the Free Speech Movement, which in early October, after more nonviolent demonstrators blocked policemen from making arrests, got Strong to agree to cancel the restrictions on political activity on the Bancroft Strip. But then the administration tried to discipline Savio and other leaders in November, leading to more demonstrations, a record number of arrests, a student strike in December, and the firing of Strong by the university Regents—a politically appointed body—in January 1965, after which tables and displays in support of political causes were allowed all over the campus.[4]

The Berkeley demonstrators gave not a moment's notice to the American commitment in Vietnam; they mentioned the civil rights movement only to compare their own grievances, quite implausibly, with those of southern blacks. Their complaints reeked of adolescent angst. Savio evoked his strongest response when he cried that students were treated like IBM cards and didn't have any personal contact with university professors or administrators. These were the cries of elite adolescents angry and bewildered that they had not yet, at twenty-one, gained the power of their elders, quite reached the top levels of society. Savio was moved by his experiences in the civil rights movement and told students that "there appears to be little else in American life which can claim the allegiance of men" and that middle-class life was "flat and stale" and a "wasteland."[5] Of course this indictment ignores—or takes for granted—the affluence, the civil liberties, the widespread tolerance typical by then of American life, and ignores the struggles it took to produce those conditions.

Demographically, these Berkeley rebels were the cutting edge of the giant generation created by the postwar Baby Boom: the freshmen of September 1964 were typically born in 1946, just one year before the boom technically began, and already a year of rising birthrates. Their grievances were those of young people who took the achievements and the personal security of the years 1947–64 for granted—and who found the large institutions which had helped their elders move upward stifling and constricting. Many showed an idealistic desire to improve their country and help those in need, desires which characteristically grow when a society is peaceful and prosperous enough to make the conquest of injustice and poverty seem possible. But there were also in the students' plaints an adolescent yearning for excitement and a failure to understand that the Chinese were uttering a curse, not a blessing, when they wished that someone might live in interesting times.

III

Harlem and Berkeley were evidence that the United States in the middle 1960s, centering on calendar year 1964, was going through one of the hinges in its history, a period of rapid change, a sudden shift in attitudes and behavior which provided the backdrop for the political events in the years to come. This change was not much noticed at the time, especially because in the months and years just after the assassination of John Kennedy in November 1963 Americans were fastening on any symbol of stability and continuity and glossing over or ignoring any evidence of change. To most Americans, Harlem and Berkeley seemed inexplicable. They had trouble imagining what grievances the rioters could conceivably have, these people—blacks and students at one of the nation's greatest universities—who were the intended beneficiaries of recent acts and decisions of a generous government and a well-intentioned country. One thing both groups had in common was that the civil rights revolution had taught them to question the legitimacy of basic American institutions: the legitimacy first of state-imposed racial segregation in the South, then of the rule of almost all-white police departments in northern cities, then—though in retrospect this was hardly comparable—of a faceless and unsympathetic university administration in California.

For many Americans the civil rights revolution, even if it did not much affect their personal lives, affected everything about the way they saw their country. Taylor Branch, then in high school and later the author of a definitive biography of Martin Luther King, recalled, "What happened in Birmingham in 1963—with Bull Connor and the fire hoses and the dogs—called everything I believed into question." King and other civil rights leaders led Branch, he said, to "look at the world from a moral perspective. It occurred to me that the most fundamental political questions were, in fact, moral questions." In college in 1964 "the people I met were already more interested in Vietnam, [but] the civil rights movement was why they cared about Vietnam."[6]

Branch and his Baby Boom generation contemporaries were not the only Americans who learned to look beneath the surface of institutions to their underpinnings, and not in a mood of mellow acceptance but with an almost belligerent skepticism. Americans who had once been concerned mainly with results and substance were now increasingly concerned with methods and process. Not only must ends be good but so must means. The Americans who took pride in and gained confidence from their nation's success in rebounding from the depression and winning the war were now examining the underpinnings of their basic institutions and finding rottenness. Confidence in government, business, labor unions, the press, and almost every other institution in American life declined sharply in the years immediately after the civil rights revolution and John Kennedy's assassination, and did not substantially recover through the 1970s.[7]

In this atmosphere of national self-criticism, the civil rights revolution became the paradigmatic experience of the 1960s. For half a century most white Americans—southerners actively and belligerently, northerners passively and sometimes resignedly—accepted the institution of legal segregation and the brutal, sometimes even terrorist means used to enforce compliance with segregationist mores. It did not shake their faith—it did not even shake the faith of some black Americans—in the decency and goodness of American life. The civil rights revolution forced all Americans to confront the human realities of segregation—by forcing them to look at photographs of the Little Rock children being jeered by mobs and of Freedom Riders' buses burning, to watch on television the firehoses and police dogs directed at the peaceful demonstrators in Birmingham—and convinced most Americans that the system of legal segregation was wrong and must be changed. This was one of the sharpest shifts of opinion in American history. And though it was not fully accomplished by 1964, opinion had already moved further than most practical men of the world had thought it ever could. Dreamy civil rights leaders turned out to be correct when they predicted (or perhaps just hoped) that white southerners would accept integration of public accommodations and transportation, of stores and restaurants and theaters and even schools. Practical politicians were wrong when they said that white southerners meant what they said when they cried "Never!"

In that same month of May 1963 that most Americans watched Bull Connor's police at work on the streets of Birmingham, President Diem's troops in Vietnam shot down Buddhist protesters, and a month later Americans saw the pictures of Buddhist monks immolating themselves in protest against Diem's policies. For years stretching back to the beginnings of World War II, Americans had been accustomed to think well of their country's acts abroad: American soldiers and American aid-givers were saving Europe and Asia first from Hitler's Nazism and then from Stalin's Communism; Americans were feeding the starving and educating children and sending out idealistic young people to teach people in underdeveloped countries how to help themselves. Americans knew that some foreigners scratched "Yankee go home" on their lamp posts and that their country was vitriolically attacked by the Communists. But they wanted to believe that their government, as Franklin Roosevelt had wished, was working to dismantle colonial empires, in the hope that newly liberated peoples would follow the example of this country which, not so long ago, had itself been formed from newly liberated colonies. Now, suddenly, they found the United States on the side of a seemingly unpopular regime—a government which seemed unpopular with its Buddhist citizens for the same reasons the segregationist southern state governments were unpopular with their black citizens, a government which seemed unable to maintain basic standards of civility and decency.

Of course the Kennedy assassination and the events in Birmingham and Hue, Berkeley and Harlem, were not the only forces undermining American confidence. An observer could look back to Sputnik in 1957 and see how Americans' confidence in their technological superiority had been shaken; could see Richard Nixon jeered in Caracas in 1958 and Dwight Eisenhower humiliated in Paris in 1960; could listen to the campaign rhetoric of 1960 which, echoing Nikita Khrushchev's boasts, aroused what turned out to be absurd fears that the economy of the United States was about to be overtaken by that of the Soviet Union.

What is peculiar here is that confidence was undermined in a system which was operating, by most historical standards, very satisfactorily. Ironically, the decline in confidence actually improved the operation of the system—and was, in the case of civil rights, a necessary part in the improvement of the system. Progress in desegregation and integration could not be secured until white Americans were convinced that one important underpinning of their system was rotten. Once they were convinced of this, they began improving the system—but at the same time, to think less well of it—just as they had never really become conscious of poverty until nearly two decades of economic growth had reduced it to an extent which would have astonished any earlier generation. Americans' more critical appraisal of their country was more realistic, more mature perhaps, than the starry-eyed, almost childlike confidence which characterized so many of the years after World War II. But there was a danger that this critical habit of mind could obscure for Americans how they were making their country better—and a danger as well that the country's leaders, who came of age long before the middle 1960s, would not understand this new attitude.

IV

This concern for process as well as substance, for means over and above ends, came in a country which seemed well able to afford it. The United States was peaceful and prosperous. In the aftermath of the Cuban missile crisis the fear of war with the Soviet Union—a fear which was lively and near-universal from March 1947 to Stalin's death in March 1953 and again from Khrushchev's Berlin ultimatum in October 1958 to October 1962—was suddenly vastly reduced. By 1964, Americans had stopped worrying that World War III was imminent.

Economically, the United States was not just momentarily prosperous. In 1964, as Americans looked about them, they saw a country which seemed to have discovered the secret of producing sustained economic growth without inflation or recession. Forgotten by most were the three recessions of the 1950s which had helped elect so many Democrats to Congress; forgotten were the episodes of inflation following on World War II and Korea; forgotten was the uneasy feeling of the late 1950s that the United States was being overtaken economically by the Western Europeans and even by the Soviets. From the shallow recession of 1960–61 the economy grew at rates which afterwards seemed self-propelling. GNP rose 26% (in nominal terms) from 1960 to 1964 and 37% from 1964 to 1968. It almost doubled—increasing 94% in nominal and 48% in real terms—from 1960 to 1970. Between 1958 and 1970, in every year of the 1960s, real GNP per capita increased.[8]

One reason 1964 was a hinge in American history was that about that time most Americans began taking economic growth for granted. If Americans around 1947 concluded that economic growth was once again possible, around 1964 they decided it was more or less inevitable. The business cycle, it seemed, had been abolished. Wise custodians of public policy, using the tools of macroeconomic demand management, could sustain inflationless growth by setting federal spending at a level which would balance the budget if there was full employment and by persuading the Federal Reserve to maintain interest rates at a level low enough to keep the economy from being stifled.[9] The Kennedy-Johnson tax cut, promised in August 1962 but not enacted finally until February 1964, has been credited, surely justly, for much of this growth.[10] But the economy began growing even before the tax cut was proposed and, with the stimulus of Vietnam war spending, continued to grow long after its effect had been felt. Although the cut had the long-run effect of adjusting tax rates downward, in the short run it is not clear that the lower rates did all that much to stimulate investment or growth. After all, growth had been substantial in the seventeen years before 1964 even with marginal tax rates on individuals and corporations which would seem confiscatory by the standards of the 1980s (or 1920s).

Economic growth naturally changed the country which produced it. In the quarter-century up to 1964, millions of blacks and whites had left the South and moved to the great industrial cities of the Great Lakes and the East and West Coasts. Within a few years of the passage of the Civil Rights Acts of 1964 and 1965, the movement of blacks stopped—or, rather, the migration of blacks out of the South was balanced by a migration of blacks back to what in most cases was their native or ancestral region. Around the same time, and with little notice from the public, the migration of Hispanics, especially Mexicans, and of Asians into the United States began to increase—even though the immigration law was changed in 1965 to place restrictions for the first time on immigration from the Western Hemisphere (the continued argument over the terms and conditions under which "guestworkers" should be allowed in to work on American farms turned out to be not as central an issue as was thought by policymakers at the time). This shift back toward the pattern which had prevailed during most of American history, when low-wage labor had come more from other countries than from other parts of the United States, had political implications. The percentages of blacks in the populations of northern states would soon cease rising,[11] as they long since had in the South; and while the rate of black voter participation would keep rising in the South after the first huge increases following the Voting Rights Act of 1965, the rate in the North would tend to decline. The percentages of Hispanics and Asians, whose experiences as minorities and attitudes toward politics did not replicate those of blacks (to the surprise of some, especially liberals), would be rising in some of the largest states, notably California, Texas, Illinois, New York, and Florida.

Much better appreciated at the time was another change: that the United States around 1964 was changing from a blue-collar country to a white-collar country, from a country where most people identified themselves as "working class" to a country where most now identified themselves as "middle class."[12] Before World War II, America had been a country where most jobs required muscle; well over half of employed Americans worked at blue-collar jobs or on farms. After the war, even as the number and proportion of farm jobs fell rapidly, the number of white-collar jobs—by no means all well-paid or glamorous, but requiring more verbal and organizational skills—grew more rapidly than the number of blue-collar jobs;

by 1964 white-collar jobs outnumbered blue-collar jobs, and the gap continued to grow in later years. The following table shows the percentages of white-collar, blue-collar, service, and farm workers in the economy at ten-year intervals from 1930 to 1980:

Year[13]	White-Collar %	Blue-Collar %	Service %	Farm %
1930	29	40	10	21
1940	31	40	12	17
1950	36	40	10	12
1960	40	37	12	6
1970	47	36	13	3
1980	51	32	13	3

It was around 1964 also that the United States changed from a country where most young people had only a high school education to a country where a near-majority of eighteen-year-olds went on to college or some other form of higher education. In 1930 high school graduates had represented only 29% of the total post-school age population; by 1946 the figure was 47%, still under half; by 1961 it had risen to 71%, and it stayed at or above that level, with minor exceptions, in years afterwards.[14] In 1932, only 12% of those who had entered the fifth grade graduated from high school and went on to college; in 1950, after the unusual circumstances of the war and the postwar influx of veterans, this index of college entry had risen only to 20%; in 1964, it was 36% nationwide and over 50% in what had become in 1963 the nation's largest state, California; by the time the turn of the high school class of 1970 came, 46% nationwide were off to college.[15]

These changes had a major impact on people's lives. As discussed earlier, in the 1950s the most common pattern among young blue-collar Americans, and therefore the most common pattern among young Americans generally, was for boys graduating from high school to go off for their two years in the service—for the large military establishment of the 1950s needed large percentages of the pre–Baby Boom age cohorts which were coming of age—and then to return to marry a girl who had just graduated from high school, a girl who was often already pregnant as she went down the aisle. This human drama showed up in statistics, in the probability that an American female in the middle 1950s was already married at age twenty, and in the large number of babies born to women under twenty-one. By the early 1960s, this pattern had suddenly become much less common. The Baby Boom, it is generally agreed, ended quite suddenly in 1962; and the biggest drop in births after that year was among women under twenty-one. By 1964 the birthrate was plummeting further, to a level lower than any since the Baby Boom began in 1947. The following table gives the fertility rate (the number of births per 1,000 women aged 15 to 44) and the total number of births for each year between 1960 and 1981:

Year	Fertility	Births (*millions*)[16]
1960	118	4.3
1961	117	4.3
1962	112	4.2
1963	108	4.1
1964	105	4.0
1965	97	3.8
1966	91	3.6
1967	88	3.5
1968	86	3.5
1969	86	3.6
1970	88	3.7
1971	82	3.6
1972	73	3.3
1973	69	3.1
1974	68	3.2
1975	66	3.1
1976	65	3.2
1977	67	3.3
1978	65	3.3
1979	67	3.5
1980	68	3.6
1981	67	3.6

The change in the early 1960s undoubtedly reflects the increased use of artificial birth control devices in that period by Catholics and the introduction into the marketplace of the birth control pill. The additional sudden and sharp drop in births and fertility rates in the early 1970s undoubtedly reflects the increased availability of abortion.[17] By the end of the 1970s some 1.5 million abortions were being performed every year: some were surely just a substitute for birth control, but others terminated pregnancies which would have continued were abortions not widely available and would have resulted, in many cases, in marriages if the pregnancy had occurred in the legal and cultural environment of the 1947–62 Baby Boom period.

By 1964 most American families enjoyed an affluence which few had dared take for granted as recently as 1947. Per capita income, in constant 1958 dollars, was $1,700 in 1947, $2,000 in 1955, $2,200 in 1960, and $2,400 in 1964—a rise of 43% in just seventeen years. It continued rising rapidly, to $3,000 in 1970, $3,500 in 1976 and $3,800 in 1981.[18] The rise in median household income began lagging behind the growth in per capita income, however, as increasing numbers of Americans used their greater affluence to create new and smaller household units; more couples divorced, and more young or elderly relatives were able to live independently in their own households rather than as dependents in someone else's. Moreover, rises in nominal dollars were, in the years after 1964, increasingly eroded by inflation. Nonetheless the increases were substantial. In the 1950s a $5,000 income was a goal, but far from the norm, for the family of a factory worker; a white-collar employee was considered to be doing very well if he made $10,000. Between 1947 and 1964 median household income rose from $2,700 to $5,700; from 1964 to 1981 it rose further, clearing $10,000 in 1973, $15,000 in 1977, and $20,000 in 1980, to $22,300 in 1981.

Even more important, most Americans were getting close to the evanescent goal of economic security. Most big companies had been increasing their payrolls. Blue-collar jobs in which seasonal and cyclical layoffs were common were becoming a smaller share of the job market than white-collar jobs from which, typically, few people were fired or laid off. The guaranteed annual wage which had long been the goal of the labor movement's most thoughtful leader, Walter Reuther, was in effect achieved by more and more Americans each year. Unemployment compensation in most states maintained an acceptable family income for those who were still subject to layoffs, while medical insurance was becoming common. Social Security benefits, increased in the 1940s and 1950s, provided an income floor for retirement.

This progress toward economic security gave Americans new luxuries, one of which was the ability to turn from the seemingly solved problems of economic production to the still not entirely finished work of economic distribution. This was not the old issue of how to slice the pieces of a pie which stayed the same size, but the new issue of how to make sure that those who seemed to have been left out got a fair share of a pie which seemed to be growing inexorably. "A rising tide," John Kennedy liked to say, "lifts all boats." But the civil rights movement taught that certain Americans faced special barriers and disabilities, and so it seemed plausible that special efforts would be needed to lift them.

If Americans were rich enough as a society to think they could afford to end poverty, they were also affluent enough personally to choose their own personal life style. In the 1940s and 1950s Americans accustomed to wearing their country's uniform in war were comfortable with conforming to an ideal of normality. It was an age when it was a compliment to be regarded as average and when David Riesman's *The Lonely Crowd* described most Americans, not entirely approvingly, as other-directed. But the rioters of Harlem and Berkeley—or the young people listening to the rock music of Elvis Presley and the Beatles—were harbingers of change. For in different ways they were asserting their own particular identity, saying that the things which made them distinctive as blacks or students or teenagers were more important than the things which they had in common with other Americans. A country characterized by cultural uniformity was becoming a country of cultural variety. A country in which even the economic issues which had sharply divided those who regarded themselves as working people from those who regarded themselves as middle class still left most Americans believing they were average and normal, was becoming a country in which the cultural identity and attitudes which characterized dozens of different groups tended to structure political choices and create political conflicts. War tends to produce cultural uniformity; peace and affluence tend to produce cultural variety. In the years after 1964, American politicians used to a culturally uniform nation would have to try to govern in a nation increasingly split between different and often hostile cultural groups.

V

For the Americans of the middle 1940s, listening in grimy New York tenements or the only recently electrified farms of the Tennessee Valley to the soothing voice of Franklin Roosevelt on their radios, it was enough that results were right: America won the war, and they did not worry much that in the course of doing so it fought with a racially segregated army, unjustly interned Japanese-Americans, and allied itself with Stalin's totalitarian Soviet Union. For the Americans of the middle 1960s, watching from tract houses in Levittown or Los Angeles the raging crowds of Harlem and Berkeley and Hue on their televisions, successful ends were taken for granted, and more attention was being paid to the means by which they were attained. This shift helps to explain many disparate developments in American public life in the years following 1964. It illuminates the student rebellions which followed Berkeley and helps to explain the hostile reaction to American involvement in Vietnam, so different from the response a dozen years before to American involvement in Korea. It helps to account for the war on poverty and the whole range of Ralph Nader-inspired consumerist policies. The list goes on, including the reform of the political process after the 1968 Democratic national convention, the environmental movement, the movement toward deregulation.

Americans had grown tired of the messy compromises and practical arrangements (including the political party system extolled by sages like Walter Lippmann, Clinton Rossiter, and D. W. Brogan)[19] which had justified themselves by their results in the past. They were ready for change and even for radical solutions. The economic comfort and moral discomfort of the society—the very opposite of the conditions which had prevailed in 1947, not so long before—generated demands for sharply different and often contradictory policies, for black power and law and order, for honoring the country's ideals and demonstrating against the country's leaders, for a concentration on America's problems at home and a concerted American war effort abroad. The events of the middle 1960s produced a politics which sharply expanded American government and the protections of the makeshift American welfare state and sharply increased the projection of American military power abroad, but at the cost of undermining faith in government action and American power generally.

The two dominant politicians in the decade after 1964, Lyndon Johnson and Richard Nixon, were men of high intellect, driving ambition, and vast experience in postwar American government. Yet both failed to master the new politics or to understand the new country which came into existence in the months and years after the murder of the man who had beaten them both for the presidency in 1960.

Lyndon Johnson brought to the White House a superb understanding of the Senate and the South; he not only understood them as they were but, far more than any other politician, understood what they might be, and how he could bend them to his mastery. He understood the executive branch and the traditional politics of the North less well, and he had little instinctive feel for how the rest of the world worked and how his own country was changing. Misled by the success of incumbent officeholders in 1964, distracted by the encomiums to the eternal strength of the political center which were being offered in the wake of Barry Goldwater's smashing defeat, Johnson approached every issue as a legislative exercise: how to assemble a majority for that new policy here, how to compromise that nagging issue there. And so he assembled majorities for policies which failed to work (like the Community Action programs in the cities of the North, which did little to help the poor and much to undermine Johnson's natural political allies) or which tried to reconcile irreconcilable differences (like the limited war effort in Vietnam, which satisfied neither those who wanted to win nor those who wanted to get out). Johnson's attempts to base policy on conciliation of the leaders of big business and big labor failed to work in a country where voters had less and less confidence in major institutions, and his delight in making deals behind closed doors inspired little confidence in a nation successful enough to be concerned about means as well as ends. Like so many sons of the 1930s who revered the memory of Franklin D. Roosevelt, Johnson felt that a leader must assert the essential purity and goodness of the country even while dealing with the messy and often sordid facts of everyday politics. Roosevelt could do that in the 1930s and 1940s when Americans expected no more of their leaders and were willing to overlook their behind-closed-doors peccadilloes. Johnson could not do the same thing in the more process-minded country of the late 1960s.

Richard Nixon, scarred by his loss to John Kennedy and his humiliation in California two years later, showed some suppleness and sensitivity in adapting to the new political climate. Blocked from any major role in the 1964 campaign, a role which would have been disastrous for any Republican nominee, not burdened with governmental responsibilities in 1965, 1966, and 1967, years when any conceivable course he could have taken would have caused political problems, Nixon was free to learn from his previous mistakes. Yet from his residence on Fifth Avenue, his law practice on Wall Street, and his peripatetic campaigning for Republican candidates in 1966 and for himself in 1967 and 1968, he seems not to have entirely understood how the country had changed—and how those changes made it much more difficult for him to emulate what he evidently saw as the successes of the figures who since 1960 seem always to have been at the center of his thoughts, the Kennedys. He proposed policies and enunciated themes which, with some reason, he thought might serve as the basis for national unity: liberal initiatives like the Family Assistance Program and the winding down of the Vietnam war together with conservative rhetoric on crime and patriotism. Yet in a country where different cultural groups were fighting what amounted in spirit to a civil war, he was able to satisfy neither side. Moreover, no more than Johnson did Nixon have a sense of the country's increasing demand for purer political and governmental processes, as the Watergate scandal—and all the other White House horrors it revealed—eventually showed.

The presidencies of Johnson and Nixon left most Americans angry and alienated from their politicians and from government. These leaders who seemed and were, in pre-1964 terms, vastly competent proved unable to govern satisfactorily in the different times which came after 1964. Their failures added to Americans' dissatisfactions and prolonged the undermining of confidence in the country's basic institutions until well into the late 1970s.

39

–»» «««–

Great Society

Lyndon Johnson spent most of the weeks following his landslide reelection on his LBJ Ranch on the Pedernales River. As the sun cast long shadows from the live oak trees which lined the narrow river and the white ranchhouse not far from its banks, Johnson, exercising in Texas, where he had never been dominant, the power he had amassed in Washington, had time to think of what he wanted to accomplish in the next year—and time to reflect on what he regarded as his inevitable loss in popularity and hence in power. "I was just elected president," he told an audience of administrators from various departments in January 1965, "by the biggest popular margin in the history of the country, 15 million votes. Just by the natural way people think and because Barry Goldwater scared hell out of them, I have already lost about 2 of those 15 million and am probably getting down to 13. If I get in any fight with Congress, I will lose another couple of million, and if I have to send any more of our boys into Vietnam, I may be down to 8 million by the end of the summer." It was essential to take advantage of the moment's opportunity, Johnson insisted,[1] to pass his program.

What was that program? What did Johnson want to add to the tax cut, the Civil Rights Act, and the antipoverty program already passed in 1964? Two items were leftovers from the agenda of President Truman, which the Democrats had been unable to pass since 1949: federal aid to education and Medicare under Social Security. Federal aid for education had long been popular, but had been held up by cultural conflicts pitting Catholics against southerners and liberals opposed to aid to Catholic schools. Now Johnson's top men at the Department of Health, Education, and Welfare—John Gardner, formerly head of the Carnegie Foundation, and Wilbur Cohen, one of the experts who had helped create the Social Security system since the 1930s—put together a package targeting most of the federal aid at school districts with more low-income children and providing some books and materials for Catholic schools. The bill was passed by the House in March 1965 and the Senate in April—speed reminiscent of the Hundred Days of Franklin Roosevelt in 1933.

The passage of Medicare was ensured by a change, reflecting the election results, in the party ratio on the House Ways and Means Committee. Chairman Wilbur Mills, who had opposed financing Medicare from Social Security, now prudently switched positions and went to work on the details of the bill, which was passed

396

in the House in March and the Senate in July. Johnson made a point of flying out to Independence, Missouri, to sign the Medicare bill in the presence of the eighty-one-year-old Truman, who had proposed a similar measure nearly twenty years before.

That visit symbolized the continuity in the Democrats' new programs. Yet neither represented a fully articulated, comprehensive welfare state approach. Medicare protected only the elderly covered by Social Security from only some medical costs; many of its framers saw it as an entering wedge for something like national health insurance, but they had no illusions that that would come soon. As for education, the federal government would still pay for less than 10% of the cost of education nationwide—not a strong enough lever to mold local policy. Commissioner of Education Francis Keppel, a former dean of the Harvard School of Education, promised in April to use the 1964 Civil Rights Act to desegregate schools by the end of 1967. But the government proved utterly unable to live up to that promise, and it stood as evidence of the extravagant ambitions of Great Society officials at a time when the old limits seemed suddenly removed and it was not apparent how high the new ceiling would be.

Other bills represented the same approach as the Kennedy administration's 1961–63 Area Redevelopment Administration: the Appalachian program passed in April 1965 along with a new Economic Development Administration to finance public works programs in economically ailing areas. A major public housing bill—the last to embody faith in the idea that public housing projects could serve a useful purpose for anyone but the elderly—was also passed.

Some Great Society measures melded quickly into the fabric of American life: Medicare, for example, and federal aid to education. Others remained controversial—the Office of Economic Opportunity, set up to wage the war on poverty, for example—and were eventually sloughed off. What is significant politically is that neither the permanent nor the transient measures created affirmative political constituencies. Franklin Roosevelt's Social Security and the Wagner National Labor Relations Act created issues and constituencies which worked politically for the Democrats for years to come. Not so Medicare and federal aid to education, since they never seemed to be under any threat, or OEO, since it was never deeply supported by any group of voters and its efforts to create new political units and constituencies failed.[2] "In getting legislation through Congress without significant change," two leading scholars write, "Johnson did better than Roosevelt. On paper the Great Society not only completed the New Deal but promised to leave it in the shadows. Yet Johnson had the lesser sense of history. . . . [His] myopia led him to create domestic programs without built-in staying power. Evidently he lacked FDR's awareness of how hard it is in America to build something that endures the way you want it. In consequence, many of his social programs fell far short of their marks; some have not survived through the mid-1980s. Others became expensive out of all proportion to his own priorities, let alone those of his successors."[3] For all Johnson's careful description of how his majority would be disassembled by an anticipated and natural course of events, he seemed to speak of it as if it were an object that he might with luck hold on to—rather than an expression of approval of policies, events, and leadership styles for which both he and Kennedy had been responsible over the preceding four years. He acted as if the 1964 verdict signaled a new accretion to a natural Democratic majority, rather than showing how weak party ties had become and how far voters' party preferences could change—in either direction—according to circumstance.

And circumstances, unlike the Congress in 1964 and the first six months of 1965, were something that Lyndon Johnson could not control. From Selma to Saigon, circumstances forced Johnson's hand and led him to actions which turned out to be as momentous—for good and for ill—as any of the Great Society legislation he was so proud of. For it was not as the master legislator, steering bills to passage in Congress, that Johnson made his most important marks in the first six months of 1965, but as commander-in-chief, dispatching American troops to meet challenges created by the initiatives of others. Those initiatives came from, literally, all over the world: from Pleiku, Vietnam, in February; from Selma, Alabama, in March; from (as it was then called) Ciudad Trujillo, the Dominican Republic, in April. To each challenge Lyndon Johnson responded resolutely, dispatching the United States Marines or committing the United States government—with widely varying and, at the time, mostly unpredicted results.

II

In February 1965, McGeorge Bundy, former dean of the faculty at Harvard, co-author of the memoirs of his father-in-law, Henry Stimson, and an incisive memo-writer as Kennedy's and Johnson's national security advisor, went on an inspection trip to Vietnam. On the night of February 7, Viet Cong raiders—South Vietnamese allies of Communist North Vietnam's regular troops—attacked a U.S. Air Force barracks in Pleiku, in the Vietnamese highlands, with mortar fire and hand grenades, killing eight Americans and injuring many more. From Saigon, Bundy joined Ambassador Maxwell Taylor and General William Westmoreland on the phone with Johnson and recommended a response.[4]

The response, long anticipated and planned by Johnson and his advisors, was a policy of carefully limited reprisal bombings of North Vietnam. This seemed profoundly at odds with Johnson's assurances, delivered exuberantly on the campaign trail in Akron, Ohio, in October 1964, that "we are not about to send American boys nine or ten thousand miles away from home to do what Asian boys ought to be doing for themselves." But bombing preserved the illusion that American troops were somehow not seriously involved, although downed servicemen could and did become prisoners of war. Moreover, Johnson's insistence on maintaining personal control ("they can't even bomb an outhouse without my approval")[5] of the number of raids and targets—something he could not conceivably do for ground operations—allowed the administration's policymakers to continue to believe that a steady and graduated use of military power could persuade the other side to back down. This was, after all, what had happened in the Cuban missile crisis, less than three years before, in which Johnson himself and most of his top advisors had been in on the secret strategy meetings, and in which the president stayed in the closest personal control of every operation and the other side did back down.[6] But in Cuba the other side was, for all practical purposes, the Soviets—for Khrushchev ruthlessly ignored Castro's interests—while in Vietnam, as it turned out, the other side was the North Vietnamese led by Ho Chi Minh, who was not controlled by (as the administration's gradual escalators feared) the Chinese or (as they hoped) the Soviets. They worried that the Chinese might pour masses of troops into Vietnam, as they had into Korea, and that the Chinese or the Soviets might resort to nuclear weapons if American military force was escalated too abruptly or successfully.

On Johnson's mind was the fate of the Truman administration after it "lost China": the lesson was that losing an Asian country to the Communists was utter political ruin. Johnson, after all, had been a Washington eyewitness to these events, a Capitol Hill insider who had followed every political turn since he came to the city in December 1931. "I knew that Harry Truman and Dean Acheson had lost their effectiveness from the day that the Communists took over China," he told Doris Kearns later. "I believed that the loss of China had played a large role in the rise of Joe McCarthy. And I knew that all these problems, taken together, were chickenshit compared with what might happen if we lost Vietnam."[7] Johnson expected that in this event an opposition led by Robert Kennedy would attack him for abandoning John Kennedy's commitment to a Catholic regime—a dreadfully bad misreading of American Catholics, who never showed any special identification with their Vietnamese co-religionists, and a misreading as it turned out of Robert Kennedy as well. And throughout the war Johnson was also fearful that American hawks would force an escalation which would produce Chinese infantry or Soviet nuclear attacks. Most of his analysis was baseless. China had occupied a central place in the American consciousness for much of the twentieth century; all but the most ignorant citizens knew it was a continent-sized civilization of the greatest geopolitical importance. Vietnam, in contrast, never much engaged the affections or interest of Americans: it was a small country, economically unimportant,[8] geographically marginal, and culturally uncongenial. If the administration had simply ignored Vietnam, American voters quite possibly would have been uninterested in its fall to the Communists, as they were uninterested in the eventual fall of Laos and Cambodia. Few Americans, whether they supported or opposed American involvement there, paid much attention to Vietnam after the Communist victory in April 1975.

The administration's attraction to the ratchet-like policy of gradual escalation, an attraction typical of Democratic strategists and not shared by most Republican strategists from the 1950s to the 1980s, came from a familiarity with the game-theory approach to nuclear war strategy. In those theories, the key element was to prevent anyone from pushing the nuclear button, and the argument usually rested on a confidence that the other side was reading your signals and an assumption that it shared your sense of rationality and your goals. American strategists assumed that the North Vietnamese would capitulate and agree to negotiations when they reached "the crossover point," that is, when American attrition tactics cost the North Vietnamese more troops than they could replace.[9] But in Vietnam, as it turned out, Ho Chi Minh interpreted gradual escalation accurately as an indication that the Americans would not militarily destroy his country, which by virtue of its economic backwardness and military élan was not susceptible to any other form of destruction. And he assumed accurately that he could sustain the North Vietnamese desire to overrun all of Indochina longer than the Americans could sustain their people's determination to prevent this from happening. Ho Chi Minh knew he could hold out for years and he knew—as Johnson did not—that Johnson needed something better than a stalemate by election year 1968.

The first bombing raids came in February 1965; sustained raids began in March and, except for a few bombing pauses, continued for three years. Although the amount of bombing was slowly stepped up, no attempt was made to truly cripple North Vietnam: the Red River dikes were never systematically bombed in this mostly lowland country; Hanoi and Haiphong were never carpet-bombed; Barry Goldwater and other conservative critics were correct when they charged that an unrestrained bombing program was never tried.[10]

For American politicians, the key variable, because of its obvious impact on voters, was the number of American troops stationed in Vietnam. In the first half of 1963, when David Halberstam was writing the dispatches for the *New York Times* which became the basis for his book *The Making of a Quagmire,* there were some 11,000 American troops in Vietnam, serving ostensibly as advisors to the South Vietnamese. In October the White House announced that 1,000 of these would be withdrawn by January 1964. But the assassinations of Ngo Dinh Diem and Ngo Dinh Nhu intervened, and the possibility of troop withdrawals was forgotten. In February 1965, Westmoreland requested 3,500 Marines—the first U.S. ground troops—to protect the air base at Danang. By March, as a result of various quiet increases, there were 23,000, and by Johnson's unannounced orders they were out patrolling rural areas and seeking contact with the Viet Cong, not just guarding U.S. bases. In April, Johnson offered to de-escalate the U.S. military action and—the characteristic touch of this compromise-prone New Deal politician—to build a Mekong River power project if the North Vietnamese would negotiate. They refused to go to the table until the bombing stopped and the Viet Cong were given positions in the Saigon government, conditions they insisted on until late 1972. After Canadian Prime Minister Lester Pearson called for a bombing pause in April and academics conducted the first "teach-ins" criticizing American involvement in Asia in May, Johnson quietly halted the bombing for six days in May—with no result. In that month, 42,000 Americans were stationed in Vietnam; by late June, the figure was up to 63,000. In late July, Johnson announced that he was increasing American troop strength in Vietnam from 75,000 to 125,000. By June 1966 the total had reached 285,000; by January 1967, 380,000; by January 1968, 550,000.

Eventually General Westmoreland's request in March 1968 for yet another

200,000 troops in response to what appeared to Americans at the time as the success of the Communists' Tet offensive in February persuaded Johnson to reverse his course of escalation and to relinquish office.[11] But nothing like this degree of escalation was contemplated at the beginning. Johnson's insistence on maintaining control over the specifics of the bombing, his frequent pauses, his calls for negotiations beginning in April 1965—all showed his lack of stomach for an aggressive, as opposed to an attritive, strategy and signaled the North Vietnamese that the Americans were not seriously engaged in an effort they could sustain.

III

The Civil Rights Act of 1964, which did so much to integrate public accommodations and workplaces, did little to address one remaining glaring type of racial discrimination practiced in most southern states: the prevention of most blacks, by various legal devices and by physical intimidation, from voting in elections. Without the vote southern blacks had no way of exerting political influence on public officeholders, and in the supercharged political atmosphere in the South after the civil rights issue became prominent in the middle 1950s it became more politically risky for politicians to support policies favored by blacks or perform constituent services which helped blacks. The bars against voting were strongest where blacks were most numerous, as in Mississippi Delta and Alabama Black Belt counties where blacks still made up the majority of adults. As a result of a generation of northward migration, such black-majority constituencies were far less common than they had been in the years before World War II, and in 1965 blacks did not come close to forming a majority in any southern state or in any major southern city. So in the short run it was not apparent that enfranchising blacks would reverse the political results symbolized by Barry Goldwater's huge majorities in the almost all-white electorates of Mississippi and Alabama in 1964. But in the long run, at such time as politics became less racially polarized (and it was already less racially polarized in the states to the north of Mississippi and Alabama), the addition of blacks to the voting rolls would inevitably change the political calculus of the South. It would give practical politicians an incentive to seek the votes of their black constituents and to figure out how to do so without repelling whites. It would integrate politics as the 1964 act integrated public accommodations and workplaces.

In December 1964, Martin Luther King, Jr., went to Stockholm to accept the Nobel Peace Prize. The awarding of the prize to him then, like the establishment of his birthday as a national holiday in 1986, was a recognition of the importance of the civil rights movement of which he was by far the most visible and most visionary leader and an honoring of the movement's achievements as well as his own. Yet King, who had shown that protest outside politics could be more powerful than any purely political action, also understood that without electoral power blacks could never expect to be treated equally as Americans. So on his return from the wintry antique and sleek-modern streets of Stockholm he decided that in 1965 he would lead nonviolent demonstrations of blacks seeking the right to vote, and he chose as his target for January an old industrial town called Selma in the middle of the Black Belt of Alabama.[12] There was no guarantee that King's protests would attract national attention, and at first the shrewd Selma police chief, Wilson Baker, "met nonviolence with nonviolence." The federal government was by no means entirely friendly to King's purpose: outgoing Attorney General Robert Kennedy told Baker, "You know, if you're smart enough, you can beat him [King] at his own game"; and it was in January 1965 that J. Edgar Hoover, no ally of Kennedy to be sure, had his FBI mail King a recording it had made of his private life together with a suggestion that he commit suicide.[13] Voter registrars in Selma continued to process blacks' applications at an agonizingly slow pace, and King's argument that this amounted to a denial of the right to vote was irrefutable. But the efforts to defuse the protests were frustrated when county Sheriff Jim Clark, a hothead who ironically was a political supporter of the populist and non-racist former governor "Kissin' Jim" Folsom, led his men in making viciously violent arrests in January and February, and a black sharecropper was shot by a state trooper while trying to protect his mother from being beaten. Only then did President Johnson declare that "all Americans should be indignant when one American is denied the right to vote"; and when King announced a 54-mile march from Selma to Montgomery for early March, he met with Johnson and was told the administration was drafting a voting rights bill. The marchers were repelled at the Edmund Pettus Bridge outside the Selma city limits by tear gas from Sheriff Clark's men; state troopers beat marchers bloody along Highway U.S. 80. During a second march King with careful orchestration turned the marchers back from the Pettus Bridge, where they faced massed state troopers and a federal court injunction barring them from proceeding; however, a white minister from Boston died after being beaten on the head. In the presence of George Wallace, whom he had summoned from Alabama, Johnson eloquently championed the cause of the demonstrators. Then he went on national television and proclaimed, "It is wrong—deadly wrong—to deny any of your fellow Americans the right to vote in this country." And he adopted the language of the civil rights movement itself: "We shall overcome" the country's "crippling legacy of bigotry and injustice."

The ensuing successful completion of the Selma-to-Montgomery march, together with the rifle-shot murder of Viola Liuzzo, a Detroit housewife who was one of hundreds of volunteers who had come south to help the marchers, helped to ensure the passage of the already well-on-its-way Voting Rights Act of 1965. This was an artful law, with drastic remedies which worked where the more moderate approaches of earlier acts had failed. It suspended the operation of literacy tests and other laws restricting voting in any state or county where less than half the voting-age population actually voted (this provision brought under coverage such uncontemplated jurisdictions as the Bronx and Alaska) and brought federal registrars into such jurisdictions to sign up voters. Johnson framed the issue perfectly—should Americans be allowed to vote?—and his bill won overwhelming support from voters generally and from Republicans as well as Democrats. It passed by overwhelming margins, more easily by far than any earlier civil rights bill, and was signed into law in August. In practice it proved more effective than even its advocates had predicted. In many areas of the South blacks were able in 1966 to register and vote for the first time; they could do so throughout the region, with only the most minor of exceptions, in 1968; and they did so in proportions not much lower than those of southern whites. This change did not mean black control of southern elections, and often it did not mean victories for black-supported candidates (usually, but not quite always, Democrats). But it did mean that blacks had entered irrevocably into the political marketplace in the South as they had in the North, with multifarious consequences too numerous to enumerate and, as time went on and the hard edge of segregation was beveled off into a gentle curve, too subtle to measure.

IV

On the afternoon of Wednesday, April 28, 1965, the U.S. ambassador to the Dominican Republic, a career diplomat named W. Tapley Bennett, cabled Washington that "American lives are in danger" and recommended an immediate landing of U.S. Marines. The Dominican Republic was a desperately poor sugar republic in the Caribbean, its population descended mainly from black slaves since the diseases spread by Christopher Columbus's Spaniards wiped out the indigenous peoples, its politics dominated in the twentieth century by the U.S. Marines and for almost thirty years by the dictator Rafael Trujillo.[14] When Trujillo was assassinated in May 1961, John Kennedy remarked that there were three probabilities open to the country, in "descending order of preference: a decent democratic regime, a continuation of the Trujillo regime, or a Castro regime. We ought to aim for the first, but we really can't renounce the second until we are sure that we can avoid the third."[15] Johnson felt the same way. Four days before Bennett's cable, open warfare had broken out in the capital, Santo Domingo, between Loyalist troops commanded by the regular military and Rebels supporting the dreamy and left-leaning Juan Bosch, who had served as president from February 1963 until he was ousted in a coup the followed September. Bennett and his colleagues feared that Bosch and his Rebels were, if only unwittingly, fronts for Castroite Communists. So did Lyndon Johnson, who ordered the Marines in within minutes after Bennett's cable was rushed to him.

Johnson's rapid response brought him great criticism. He acted without even notifying congressional leaders or the Organization of American States (OAS), much less seeking their support. And he was exercising the kind of naked American power not seen since Franklin Roosevelt withdrew the Marines from various Latin American countries in the 1930s in pursuit of his "good neighbor policy." Liberals were furious: as two perceptive reporters put it, "no decision would so expose him [Johnson] to charges of yielding to panic, of trigger-happy, gunboat diplomacy, of despoiling the American image around the world."[16] American liberals liked the image of Kennedy's Alliance For Progress, the idea that the United States should take the lead in helping Latin Americans to the kind of social democratic polity that the liberals hoped for in their own country (although in fact more Latin countries in Kennedy's years succumbed to dictatorship than embraced the social democratic policies the Kennedy vision suggested). But hopes for such a future were dim in the benighted Caribbean, and Johnson switched from an initial claim that intervention was motivated solely by the need to protect American lives to charges that the Rebel forces were infiltrated by Communists. Both claims may well have been founded on fact—though who could be sure in a backward country where information was seldom reliable?—but neither proved persuasive to Johnson's critics, who saw the first as a smokescreen and the second as a McCarthyite besmirching of a fellow social democrat.

The Dominican Republic crisis was solved quickly and satisfactorily. By late May, OAS forces were patrolling Santo Domingo, and American troops withdrew. In June 1966 a free election was held in which Bosch was defeated by moderate rightist Joaquin Balaguer—not a social democrat but a man capable of maintaining order and respect for civil liberties in a society with little potential for economic growth and a heritage of minimal civility. But in the meantime, Senator William Fulbright, chairman of the Foreign Relations Committee and formerly a Johnson intimate, had made a speech in September 1965, criticizing the president's Dominican policy. Fulbright was a skeptic, an intellectual who opposed civil rights measures because his greatest interest was foreign affairs, a man whose commitment to international understanding and respect for other nations caused him to cavil at any policy which to him reeked of chauvinism.[17] Although he had loyally backed Johnson on the Gulf of Tonkin resolution in August 1964, he was skeptical about whether American bombing and troop escalations in Vietnam could achieve their objects. Fulbright had saluted Kennedy as a president who denied old myths and talked of new realities, by which Fulbright meant that American leaders should not claim that their country embodied all virtue and that the Soviet Union was an empire entirely evil. This relativist frame of mind may have been nurtured by Fulbright's own skeptical or cynical support of segregation (when southerners like Johnson and Tennessee's Estes Kefauver and Albert Gore spurned it), which made more congenial to him the ideas that all power is flawed and all leadership tainted with illegitimacy.

With such ideas Johnson had—or allowed himself to confess—no sympathy. His break with Fulbright over the Dominican Republic presaged their disagreement, and the disagreement of so many other Americans, over Vietnam. As it happened, Johnson certainly had the better of it on the argument over the Dominican Republic. The landing of the Marines prevented what might conceivably have been a Communist takeover, which would have hurt the Johnson administration less politically than it would have hurt the Dominicans practically. The prompt withdrawal of U.S. forces allowed first the introduction of OAS troops and then the operation of electoral democracy, with results which proved widely acceptable. The Dominican Republic crisis turned out to be a benign episode for the Dominicans. For Americans, however, its lessons proved unhelpful. Johnson saw that a leader might receive corrosive criticism for standing up to Communism but that in relatively short order he would be vindicated. Johnson's critics concluded that this president was always at risk of acting impulsively and illiberally on foreign policy—even though in both the Dominican Republic and Vietnam he acted on the advice of the foreign and military policy appointees he inherited from the Kennedy administration which so many of these critics so admired—but that they might make him change his policy by criticizing it. Both sides derived from the Dominican Republic crisis, as they had from the Cuban missile crisis, an unspoken assumption that crises were of short duration and that even subtle shifts in the exercise of American power by policymakers in Washington could determine what would happen on the ground all over the world. All these messages proved dreadfully misleading in the long run in Vietnam. But the Dominican Republic crisis, a crisis over in not much more than a month in a country surely marginal by any measure of American interests, had its effect on American policy and American political debate for months and decades after it was over in June 1965.

V

Lyndon Johnson never seriously considered asking Congress to declare war on North Vietnam. The critical decisions to escalate he made in 1965 were made without the advance approval or knowledge of members of Congress; and crucial decisions, such as the decision to use U.S. troops to patrol the countryside rather than just to protect U.S. bases, were made without any disclosure to Congress. There was some precedent for these omissions. Truman had purposely refused to ask Congress to declare war when North Korea attacked over the 38th parallel. But his purpose was to enhance the role of the United Nations, of which the United States was technically just one member; and his administration suffered losses in politics and of morale by neglecting to get Republicans to endorse its policies early. Franklin Roosevelt more deliberately and deviously tried to conceal from a hostile Congress the degree to which he was aiding the British and courting a hostile response from the Germans and the Japanese in the contentious days between June 1940 and December 1941. But he had proposed the first Lend-Lease exchanges in September 1940 and had his secretary of war (a Republican, to be sure) draw the first draft numbers in October 1940, just a week before the election: Roosevelt, for all his slippery rhetoric about not sending boys to foreign wars, had given voters every reason to understand that he would do things which would seriously risk just that.

Johnson had none of these excuses. His promises in the 1964 campaign had given voters every reason to expect that he would do the opposite of what he was doing. He introduced American troops into what inevitably amounted to combat situations without informing the American public in any way. He seems never to have contemplated the possibility of simply walking away from Vietnam—nor, to be fair, did most of the critics of his policy. They accepted as given the assumption that the United States must not only defend but also set up the government of a nation 10,000 miles from its borders, a densely populated society of different values and predispositions from any which most Americans understood. Although there were skeptics aplenty about escalation at various stages in early 1965—Maxwell Taylor, George Ball, William Fulbright, Frank Church, Clark Clifford, William Bundy—Johnson struggled to wear them down and with his volcanic force of personality usually succeeded. By June reports showed that the bombing was having little impact on North Vietnam. Johnson regarded this information as an indication not that his assumptions were faulty but that further effort was necessary.

More escalation—more American troops—was his response. Yet as the number of American troops in Vietnam increased from 42,000 in May to 75,000 in July, the Communist military position in South Vietnam strengthened because of the weakness of the various governments there and because of North Vietnamese attacks. By July it was obvious that the military situation in Vietnam was going poorly, and Defense Secretary Robert McNamara recommended an increase in troops to 125,000, a calling up of the reserves, and a massive bombing offensive against North Vietnam of the type Johnson had been avoiding. Johnson eventually announced the increase in American troop strength from 75,000 to 125,000—on a noontime broadcast on July 28, as if he hoped that most Americans would miss this news on a summer midday. But he declined then and later the recommendations for larger-scale bombing or for calling up reserves. It was almost as if he were trying to persuade the Soviets and fool Americans into thinking that he was not really waging war.

This July 1965 escalation was the critical decision that sent hundreds of thousands of Americans to Vietnam. The draft had been a part of American life since June 1948, affecting the lives of most young men in the years after high school, especially in the 1950s when they were part of the small age cohorts produced by the low birthrates of the 1930s. In the early 1960s, as young men from the larger age cohorts of the early 1940s turned eighteen, the draft became less demanding, and many young men—fathers, college students, even students who took a year off to travel to Europe—were not called up. Yet it was apparent that any significant increase in American military effort in Vietnam would require drafting more men or calling up the reserves or National Guard (many of whom had signed up to avoid active duty), or both.

Johnson, understanding that either move would discomfit voters, instinctively resisted both steps, as if he were trying to sneak the nation into a war—or, more likely, as if he were trying to disguise how warlike his government's actions were, as Roosevelt had done from June 1940 to December 1941, in the hope that the North Vietnamese would commit some clear act of aggression which would rally the American people to full support of his war effort, as the Japanese had done at Pearl Harbor. The reserves never were called up in Vietnam—leading one to wonder what reserves existed for. The National Guard was called on very little.[18] Draft calls were in fact stepped up. But the system of deferments for both undergraduate and graduate students was maintained, on the kind of quantitative reasoning McNamara always favored: the manpower pool was and would for years be larger than needed, because the first Baby Boomers turned eighteen in 1965 and only 6% of draft-age males were needed for combat;[19] the country would be therefore better off exposing fewer of its brighter young men to the risks of combat.[20] What this reasoning ignored was morale. In peacetime such policies may make sense, but if a nation is to be rallied to fight a war, then the risk of death must be shared equally.[21]

So Johnson decided to wage a war without really saying so to the American people. Until after the November 1966 elections, draft calls were increased only marginally and taxes were not raised. But General Westmoreland was authorized to pursue an ambitious military strategy with U.S. forces fanning out from American-controlled enclaves to use firepower to dominate the countryside and raids to break North Vietnamese supply lines; thousands of peasants were resettled and the Vietnamese economy transformed by the logistic requirements of an American army.

All of these policies were justified by invoking the idea of the golden mean, which had much currency in the middle 1960s—the idea that any policy midway between two extremes was bound to be right. Lyndon Johnson talked constantly of his "consensus" approach to government, and suggested that the age of class warfare economic politics was over. Barry Goldwater's Republican critics (none more vitriolic than journalist Robert Novak)[22] never tired of flailing him for "extremism." There was an assumption that any solution that fell midway between two alternatives was almost certainly correct. Johnson defended his Vietnam policy as a golden mean between two extremes, like George Ball's preference for "an immediate political solution that would avoid deeper U.S. involvement" and Walt Rostow's recommendation of audacity.[23] But in this case the critics were right who said that either extreme was better: win or get out.

VI

As 1965 began, Lyndon Johnson seemed in command of the whole political landscape. As the year went on, he seemed to lose control of events. He responded quickly to attacks in South Vietnam and the Dominican Republic, but the quick success in the latter did not, as it turned out, presage success in the former. He responded brilliantly to the Selma marches and produced the Voting Rights Act. But five days after he signed it into law in August, the Watts riot broke out in Los Angeles. Raising the levels of blacks' expectations and validating their hitherto inarticulate sense of the illegitimacy of society's institutions, the civil rights revolution helped to produce the riots which marred Johnson's second term. Increasingly Johnson was responding to the cues of others rather than making others respond to his.

Inadvertently, he allowed the undermining of the authority—already threatened by events—of major institutions which were props of his administration. The one major piece of legislation he was unable to persuade the overwhelmingly Democratic 89th Congress to pass was repeal of Section 14(b) of the Taft-Hartley Act. This was an attempt by national labor unions to wipe out the right-to-work laws in force in most of the states of the South and the Rocky Mountains; they hoped that repeal would be followed by levels of unionization similar to those in the Northeast, in the Great Lakes states, and on the West Coast. It probably would not have been, but the unions never got the chance to see. Instead, the bill was filibustered when ordinarily liberal Democrats from small states with right-to-work laws (including George McGovern of South Dakota) refused to vote cloture. In the following years the unions were unable to expand their membership in the parts of the country which were growing most rapidly, and they saw their size shrink as a percentage of the work force and, in the case of some national unions, even in absolute terms. In the meantime, Johnson supported auto pollution standards (passed in October 1965) which imposed costs on an industry whose Henry Ford II and Walter Reuther had provided him with handsome consensus support in 1964, and in 1967 he supported a clean air act which threatened to impinge sharply on the pro-Johnson steel and coal industries. The big unions and the big auto and steel companies which had joined to support Johnson's consensus in 1964 were getting little in return.

In his political dealings Johnson was always respectful of the mayors and Democratic leaders of the large cities. Many of his Great Society programs involved injections of federal money into existing local bureaucracies and through regional directors of federal departments who were responsive to local politicians; it was understood that all the regional directors in Chicago, for example, were the appointees of Mayor Richard J. Daley. Yet for all the deference that Johnson paid to state governors and local political bosses, he did not really seem to understand the bases of their power; and when it came to setting up his antipoverty program he undermined it seriously. His Community Action Programs, the centerpiece of the Office of Economic Opportunity, were intended to be and often were parallel structures to local government—elective antipoverty boards and regional offices staffed by people who were scathing critics of local politicians. They threatened the authority of mayors just as more generous welfare payments undermined the already weakened power of political bosses. And Johnson went further. He made a special effort to persuade governors and Congress not to add a governor's veto to OEO projects, an omission which had the practical effect of facilitating federally funded advocacy programs which opposed state and local government policies: these included the Legal Services Corporation and the California Rural Legal Assistance group, which was bitterly opposed by the state's fruit, vegetable, and cotton growers and by its Republican governor elected in 1966, Ronald Reagan. And in 1966 he developed and persuaded Congress to enact the "demonstration cities" program (renamed Model Cities so as not to carry connotations of protest demonstrations); this was a social scientist's dream and a mayor's nightmare, in which the resources of all government aid programs were supposed to be poured into a single favored neighborhood. During this period, demographic forces—the outward movement first of whites and then of blacks from the central cities—were undermining the base of the big-city political machines and bosses, just as economic forces—the faster increase in white-collar than in blue-collar jobs—were undermining the base of the union leaders. But Johnson by omission and action accelerated both processes.

These developments in turn undermined the strength of the Democratic party, on which he was counting for renomination and reelection in 1968. Voters' allegiance to parties was already declining, as the 1964 results had showed, and as the election of John Lindsay, a liberal Republican, to replace Democratic loyalist Robert Wagner, Jr., as mayor of New York in November 1965 demonstrated even more graphically: Lindsay's coalition of blacks, Puerto Ricans, and upper-income whites showed how fluid electorates could be in a ticket-splitting age. The Democrats faced the additional problem that Johnson's Great Society programs gave very little to the ordinary, non-elderly white citizen. The Voting Rights Act helped southern blacks, Medicare was a boon to the elderly, and federal aid to education helped children—but invisibly, through transfers of money from one budget ledger to another. Antipoverty programs by definition did not directly help the very large majority of voters. After World War II the major policies with which Democrats had been identified had directly benefited most Americans. That condition was not true two decades later.

So it seems that Johnson failed to understand what presidents must do to present successful records for themselves and their party to run on. He believed that his macroeconomic policies would bring prosperity without inflation (and they mostly did), and he hoped that his Vietnam policy would succeed: he presumably hoped to run in 1968 as he had in 1964 as the candidate of peace and prosperity. He recognized fairly early on that peace might be beyond his grasp, but he eagerly cited the results of the polls showing that each action he took in Vietnam—each escalation or each offer to negotiate—had the overwhelming support of the American people. Of course it did: this was the rally-round-the-flag response which gives every president, for a moment, widespread support in time of crisis, even when his performance has been as obviously incompetent as John Kennedy's was in the Bay of Pigs fiasco. Johnson, who understood the South and the Senate so well, failed to understand national polls and public opinion. He acted as if voters, once they approved of a course, would feel obliged as politicians do to stick to their original opinions. He had little sense that what matters is how the public responds to the final result of a policy rather than how it responds to each step along the way.

Nor did Johnson, the product of the politics of a one-party state, have a good sense of how a party leader operates. As Evans and Novak put it, he "saw himself at the center of a new 'Era of Good Feelings' similar to the period of one-party rule during the Virginia 'dynasty' between the two Adamses that reached its culmination in the presidency of James Monroe. [Yet who could have been temperamentally more the opposite of the passive Monroe than the hyperactive Johnson?] He regarded his vast majority against Goldwater as a permanent base of support. Partisan, ideological, and factional disputes would give way to serene consensus presided over by Johnson." Evans and Novak find this vision of consensus at odds with the liberal program of the Great Society, and they point out that Congress quickly grew restive with his insistence that it pass the entire program.[24] But the real problem is that Johnson failed to understand that his 1964 majority was a response not just to his post-November 1963 stewardship and achievements but also to the January 1961–November 1964 record of the administration of which he had been (more than folklore remembers) a working and useful part until November 1963 and a masterful leader thereafter. But that record would not be enough for 1968, and Johnson's program for 1965 and 1966 failed to provide anything which was. Johnson had lost control of events by late 1965 because, for all his brilliance, he did not understand his success. He understood too well the world he had grown up in—the world in which you could sneak America into a war but you couldn't lose China, the world in which getting the endorsement of businessmen and big-city bosses got you the mass of Republican and Democratic voters as well—and he failed to understand well enough the world he, prominently among others, had brought into existence.

40

>>> <<<

Guns and Butter

G uns or butter: that was the choice which seemed to face Lyndon Johnson as he prepared his budget and State of the Union message in January 1966. Johnson wanted to expand his domestic spending programs, and he wanted to prosecute aggressively the war in Vietnam—"the center of our concerns," as he called it in the State of the Union message. Yet as a Democrat who sought consensus, who was proud that he had brought his first budget in at under $100 billion when every expert had said it must be higher, Johnson felt that he must discipline spending very carefully. And as a leader who hoped that Americans would not be much discommoded by the war he was prosecuting until after it was over, he was loath to ask for any tax increase. Always given to byzantine maneuver, and not averse to (if not prone to) lying and concealment, Johnson took the extraordinary step of not informing his economic advisors of the amount of spending his military advisors told him his Vietnam war policy would require. He presented a budget which appeared to be close to balancing, and which met the Keynesian requirement of "full employment balanced budget." In fact, in macroeconomic terms it proved successful: the economy kept growing. But it understated the amount of military spending he sought, and it was the pressure of continued military spending which buoyed up the domestic economy.

"There are men who cry out: we must sacrifice," Johnson said in his speech. "Let us rather ask them: whom will they sacrifice? Time may require further sacrifices. If so, we will make them. But we will not heed those who will wring it from the hopes of the unfortunate in a land of plenty. I believe we can continue the Great Society while we fight in Vietnam." In the end, even as 1966 ended, it was becoming apparent that Johnson could not persuade Americans to continue either indefinitely. He would not get the guns necessary to gain victory in the Vietnam war, nor would he get the butter to extend his Great Society programs as far as he wanted. Yet at the same time he got enough guns to enrage those who were coming to oppose the Vietnam war and enough butter to enrage those who hated the Great Society. Johnson's Gallup job approval rating in December 1965, as he prepared his third State of the Union, was 62%–22% positive, and that was his lowest rating of the year. By November 1966, when Democratic representatives and senators were seeking reelection, his rating was down to 48%–37%. On the Vietnam war his rating in November 1966 was only barely positive (43%–40%), and on the Great Society it was negative (32%–44%). A president who had won reelection with 61% of the vote in November 1964 was by the summer of 1966 leading a little-known George Romney by only 48%–44% and, among Democrats, leading Robert Kennedy by an insigificant 40%–38%.[1]

Various events and trends of 1966 helped to weaken Johnson's standing. Inflation gew apace during the year, though at rates which would seem negligible by the late 1970s, as Johnson's attempt to hide war costs and prevent a tax rise backfired politically. Voters, many with fresh memories of the inflations started in Democratic wars and curbed by the Republican 80th Congress and Eisenhower administration, turned against the Democrats on macroeconomic issues.[2] As for the antipoverty programs on which Johnson spent so much political capital, only one—Head Start preschool education—was popular, while the much-vaunted Community Action Programs generated negative headlines and little in the way of positive results in most cities. The requirement of "maximum feasible participation" of the poor guaranteed public controversy and estranged the mayors—otherwise the program's natural allies—from it; the effort to create a parallel political structure in fact only produced elections marked by pathetically light turnout (usually under 3% of eligibles) and won by local hustlers whose eleemosynary desire to help their fellow poor people was understandably usually outweighed by their selfish desire to escape that status themselves.[3] The fact that so many sophisticated people accepted the idea that the poor would be good guides on how to get people out of poverty shows how deeply rooted was the idea, planted by the success of the civil rights movement, that American society was fundamentally flawed, that only its victims truly understood it, and that they had an unlimited moral claim on the resources of the guilty majority.[4]

But dominating the headlines and the increasingly important television newscasts was the Vietnam war. Johnson's much-heralded Christmas 1965 bombing pause, extended into January, was finally ended the last day of the month when the Communists failed to respond as Johnson hoped. In February, on only days' notice, Johnson held a conference with South Vietnamese officials in Honolulu where he agreed to increase U.S. troop strength in Vietnam from 184,000 to 429,000 within the year. This hasty improvisation produced few results but together with massive antiwar protests beginning in March succeeded in overshadowing the new civil rights, education, antipoverty, Cabinet reorganization, and four-year House term bills Johnson had proposed in January—an agenda which turned out to be almost completely unrealized. Johnson's bombing raids on Hanoi and Haiphong in June again failed to get the North to the bargaining table. They were followed by black riots in Chicago in June and in Atlanta in September. In October, Johnson staged a conference in Manila which was more elaborate than the one in Honolulu, with Asian leaders including Philippines President Ferdinand Marcos invited. But the results were no more positive. General William Westmoreland, U.S. Commander in Saigon, claimed to see "light at the end of the tunnel," but was careful to promise no immediate victory.[5]

In the meantime Americans were no longer rallying unquestioningly around the flag but were beginning to be of two minds about the war. By May 1966 they disagreed by only a 49%–36% margin with the statement that sending American troops to Vietnam had been a mistake, and by only a 48%–35% margin did they believe the United States should continue waging war in South Vietnam.[6] For those who remembered the nearly unanimous support for the war effort after Pearl Harbor, and for the Korean "police action" (and in fact the widespread dissatisfaction with the Truman administration's policy had not produced significant support for American withdrawal), this rather close division was startling. The facts that one third of the voters were ready to abandon the war effort and that less than an absolute majority were prepared to say it should be continued were results far out of line with any that Americans had seen since December 1941. All along voters preferred a candidate ready to compromise with the Communists to one pledged to send more troops, and by July 1966 voters' formerly overwhelming preference for Democratic candidates in the upcoming congressional election had changed to a bare plurality for the Democrats, due mainly to their support in the South, where most districts were still not seriously contested by Republicans.[7] By November, when Democrats for the first time in a decade failed to carry a majority of the House vote outside the South, it was apparent that the war was hurting Johnson and his party.

But it is a mistake to classify the voters as strict hawks or doves, to use the terms pundits quickly borrowed from accounts of the Cuban missile crisis. When Gallup tried to understand voters' opinions on Vietnam in April and May 1965,[8] he gave them an array of options, from complete withdrawal to all-out war. The responses, shown in the following table, not only show no consensus; they show a tendency to cluster, at least initially, at the extremes.

Alternative	*Apr. 2–7*	*Apr. 23–28*	*May 13–18*
Withdraw completely from Vietnam	17	13	12
Start negotiations, stop fighting	12	12	16
Continue present U.S. policy	14	13	20
Step up military activity	12	8	4
Go all out, declare war	19	17	17

The current policy was endorsed by no more than one in five Americans. Moreover, later analyses of public opinion showed that the second choice of those who favored one extreme could very easily be the other. For policymakers, especially those as accustomed as the leading members of this administration were to game-theory and quantitative methods of analysis, this pattern seemed illogical and implausible: if voters were at position C on this one-dimensional spectrum, then their second choice should be B or D. But there was more wisdom in the voters' untutored, instinctive responses. They were less interested in endorsing methods than they were in obtaining results. Victory was an acceptable response, and so was withdrawal. What wasn't acceptable, it turned out, was the bloody stalemate produced by the Johnson decisions, each one of which the voters endorsed at the moment it was announced.

That fact should have been reasonably apparent by December 1966. But neither Johnson nor the consensus-minded Washington political community could conceive that any such thing could be true. The memory of Johnson's landslide was too fresh, the talk of the withering away of the Republican party (for its sin of nominating Barry Goldwater) too plausible, the faith in the policies of the center and the golden mean too strong, and the idea that Americans would dissent over a war was too preposterous for a generation with no memory of World War I or previous American wars when such dissent had been commonplace and expected. Standard political analysis at the time liked to concentrate on the facts that the economy was still growing robustly, that the Democrats retained their majority in Congress, that the apparent Democratic hegemony of which the Eisenhower administration suddenly seemed only a fleeting interruption was still in force.

Yet any analysis of the 1966 election results showed the Democrats' strength gravely diminished. In the Senate they retained 64 seats, since there were not too many targets for the Republicans in the crop of seats filled in the 1954 and 1960 equipoise election years. But the 1966 election results showed Democratic Senate candidates pressed in the South and victors in the North in only a few isolated instances where large numbers of Catholic voters stayed faithful to the party of the Kennedys (New Hampshire, New Mexico, Rhode Island), or incumbents prevailed in small western states (Alaska, Montana), or a capable appointee represented a strong local tradition (Walter Mondale in Minnesota). Otherwise Democrats lost, and the strength of the Democrats in the Senate was diminished. In the House the Democrats lost more seats than they had gained in 1964, ending up with 246—only 13 more than the 233 they had won in Eisenhower's landslide year of 1956. And the new House clearly lacked a majority for Great Society measures. The pattern of votes on domestic issues was plainly set: all but one northern Democrat (Baring of Nevada) usually followed the lead of the administration and the AFL-CIO, as did a handful of southern and border state Democrats and about a dozen liberal Republicans representing urban or labor districts. Before November 1966 there were 191 northern Democrats, only 27 short of the House majority of 218; after the November 1966 election, there were 156,[9] 62 votes short of a majority. The Democratic leaders in the House were uninspired and tired: John McCormack, picked by Sam Rayburn to be majority leader back in 1940 and seventy-five years old in 1966, and Carl Albert of Oklahoma, placed on the leadership ladder in 1953 and now slowed down by a heart attack. They could pretty easily round up the 27 votes they needed before November 1966, but they had virtually no chance to round up the 62 votes they needed afterwards.

In the Senate, things were less partisan. Except for Johnson and Robert Taft, there was no tradition of strong partisan leadership. Majority Leader Mike Mansfield's impulse always was to respect other senators' prerogatives. Mansfield's Senate did break Richard Russell's filibuster of the 1964 Civil Rights Act, but liberals like Hubert Humphrey and Jacob Javits took the lead, and Minority Leader

Everett Dirksen—usually more ready to cooperate with Democrats than he liked people to think he would be—played a key role. On other issues Johnson could be thankful that Mansfield did not use his power to impose or advance his views— for Mansfield, a former professor of East Asian history who would serve as Jimmy Carter's and Ronald Reagan's ambassador to Japan, was profoundly skeptical about Johnson's policy in Vietnam. But neither did he squelch the doubts of others— most but not all of them Democrats and liberals—about the war policy; and the Senate, rather than the theoretically more responsive House, became the focal point of political opposition to the war, even as the House was moving toward solid hostility to the Great Society.

But the greatest rebuke to Johnson's politics came in what had become the nation's largest state, California. Governor Pat Brown was Johnson's kind of politician: sympathetic, even sloppily sentimental, toward policies to help the poor and spend government money; respectful and friendly toward existing centers of power, in government, business, and labor; unabashedly patriotic and supportive of his country's cause abroad and of his party's leader at home. As governor, he had achieved great things. He had helped to build California's university and junior college systems into the nation's finest, he had pushed to completion the state's gargantuan water system, and he had completed a vast freeway system. He used government to help provide the human capital and physical infrastructure which made possible the most bounteous economic growth in human history. He had beaten two presidential hopefuls: William Knowland in 1958, Richard Nixon in 1962. Yet in 1966 Brown was in political trouble. Middle-class voters seethed at the threats raised by the Berkeley rebels and the Watts rioters. They bridled at the taxes necessary to support the generous government the Democrats favored. They resented the smug and self-satisfied manipulation of the political apparatus in Sacramento by Brown and his Democratic rival, Assembly Speaker Jesse Unruh, the 300-pound "Big Daddy" who had grown up poor in Texas and been elected from a suburban Los Angeles district in 1954, and who now was busy expanding the staff and expertise of the legislature and ladling out to his allies the vast sums of political money he was able to raise.

But Brown and his strategists had, they thought, one advantage: their chief opponent was a political extremist, a former actor known politically chiefly for the October 1964 national TV broadcast he had made for Barry Goldwater: Ronald Reagan. They feared only that former San Francisco Mayor George Christopher, a moderate, would beat him in the primary. To forestall that possibility, they leaked to columnist Drew Pearson details of Christopher's violations of milk price regulations when he headed a dairy in World War II. "We feared Christopher could take the center away from us in the general election," wrote Brown's chief aide, Hale Champion (who became chief administrator in the 1970s for Harvard University and in the 1980s for Massachusetts Governor Michael Dukakis), "and we didn't think Reagan could. Moreover, while we knew we were behind, we were sure we could count on Reagan to help us overcome our problems." Champion and other Brown strategists assumed they could portray Reagan, as the Democrats had Goldwater, as one who would repeal the New Deal. But Reagan had begun his adult life as a Democrat, voting four times for Franklin Roosevelt and speaking prominently in 1948 for Harry Truman, and he spoke in the idiom of the 1940s movies he had occasionally starred in—movies which had been universally watched, which had appealed winningly to almost every segment of society, and which some critics would argue were the best popular culture since the novels of Charles Dickens. As Champion later recalled, "Reagan almost always refuses to be threatening or to let his opponent make him look threatening. He doesn't attack head-on very often. He much more frequently makes wisecracks or pokes fun. Most of the cracks aren't very fair, and some of them aren't very nice. But they work off the predictable resentments and emotions of his audiences, without requiring him to be harsh or abrasive. He is up there acting pleasant and reasonable while reaching, almost jocularly, for the resentments and emotions that hard times bring to the surface."[10] Reagan beat Christopher by better than 2–1—a classic example of the unwisdom of one party's candidate's trying to select the other party's nominee—and then went on to beat Brown by a rousing 58%–42% margin.[11]

Reagan's victory was seen by some as just another Republican triumph in a state election, like Nelson Rockefeller's come-from-behind win over an outclassed Frank O'Connor in New York or George Romney's landslide win in Michigan, achieved by a wider margin than Democrat Mennen Williams had ever managed and accompanied by Williams's defeat by lackluster Robert Griffin in the Senate race. Others saw the victory of a conservative like Reagan as further evidence of California's wackiness. But it was something more. Reagan showed, in a state which contained one out of ten Americans, that the old rule that conservative Republicans could not win in large industrial states was obsolete. He showed, even as Lyndon Johnson was seeking an ever bigger Great Society, that there was a demand in the political marketplace for a politician who would limit the growth of government. And he showed, even as the Democrats were dabbling with theories about empowering the poor and speculating that they too would riot or commit crimes if they were the victims of racial discrimination, that there was great electoral power in the culturally conservative response of ordinary voters who wanted to see traditional American values honored and traditional American patterns of life followed. Not much of his significance was appreciated at the time, and Reagan's fumbling efforts at governance when he took office seemed to fortify his critics' views that this kind of politician could never govern. But Reagan's victory in California, as support for Lyndon Johnson's guns and Lyndon Johnson's butter was diminishing, turned out to be a harbinger of American politics to come.

41

⇢⟩⟩ ⟨⟨⇠

Upheavals

Just past 3 A.M. on a sticky, hot night in July 1967, Detroit vice squad officers raided a blind pig—the local term for an illegal after-hours bar—in the Economy Printing Company, on Twelfth Avenue just south of Clairmount. A decade and a half before, this had been a middle-class, all-white area, 8 miles north of Detroit's downtown and $1^1/_2$ miles north of the General Motors and Fisher Buildings, just a few blocks from Boesky's, Detroit's best delicatessen. Then in less than two years the neighborhood had changed from all-white to all-black, and now Twelfth was one of Detroit's leading black entertainment and shopping streets. In the years after the neighborhood changed racially, it changed physically as Dutch elm disease began to kill off almost all the trees planted along Detroit's grid of streets in the 1910s and 1920s, so that streets which had stayed cool in the summers of the 1950s and early 1960s were now stickily, uncomfortably hot. In many different ways these tightly packed streets were a less comfortable place to live now that they were filled with the offspring of the 1940s and 1950s migrants from the South than they had been when they were filled with the offspring of 1900s and 1910s migrants from southern Ontario farms and eastern European shtetls. Tipping over blind pigs, arresting proprietors and patrons, was steady business for Detroit's police force, still 97% white although a mayor sympathetic to blacks, Jerome Cavanagh, had been elected in 1961 and reelected in 1965. The Economy Printing Company operation required four paddy wagon rides before the last arrestees were carted off. As they departed, a brick was thrown through the building's back window. The large crowds on Twelfth started throwing more bricks and breaking into storefronts. The Detroit riot, the biggest and bloodiest black riot of the 1960s, had begun.[1]

The riots were explained then and later as if they were political rallies or civil rights demonstrations, justified responses to "unresolved grievances by ghetto residents against local authorities," in the words of the Kerner Commission which was set up after Detroit.[2] But the outbreak of a riot in Detroit tended to refute that explanation, since Cavanagh was as sympathetic to and warmly supported by blacks as Mayor Hugh Addonizio of Newark, where a riot had broken out the week before, was unsympathetic and opposed. Blacks in all American cities had obvious reasons to be dissatisfied with local conditions—and had had even stronger reasons for years before the riots which started in the middle 1960s. In fact, the

417

key to the outbreak and continuation of the looting and destruction of property which were the essence of these riots was the widely shared expectation that others would join in, and in numbers sufficient to render all the rioters immune to any arrest or hindrance from local police or military forces. The Detroit riot spread rapidly in the early morning hours of Sunday, July 23, surviving the attempts of Cavanagh and Michigan Governor George Romney to squelch it by bringing in state police and the ill-trained National Guard (the same Guard which the Johnson and Nixon administrations always declined to send to Vietnam). Smoke rose over the commercial strips in the stillness of the hot, smoggy Sunday afternoon; after nightfall radios in the police commissioner's office reported with the crackle of static first one, then another, then still another square mile or so of ghetto being abandoned by the police and the Guard to those who were setting it aflame. As news came of riots in other cities—"Spanish Harlem is in flames," Cavanagh said; Romney asked, "Is that on the west side of town?"[3]—the mayor and the governor tried to get the Johnson administration to send federal troops. There was resistance. This would be only the third time in history that federal troops had been sent in to quell local insurrection; and President Johnson and Attorney General Ramsey Clark did not want to set a precedent which might, they feared, be followed in dozens of cities. Romney at one point hesitated, postponing the dispatching of federal troops till Monday night. By Thursday, after forty people had been killed, the federal troops succeeded in calming the city by staying in place and refusing to fire back at the first report of hostile snipers; their officers understood that gunshots can be heard a mile away, and there was no confirmation that there ever were any snipers at all.[4]

That same Thursday Johnson appointed the Kerner Commission, which in March 1968 issued a report portraying an America "with two societies—one white, one black," a view which spotlighted the separation of black and white Americans in daily life but which in claiming that the country was headed toward "two separate nations—one black and one white" explicitly discounted the considerable evidence that America had endured and overcome other wide divisions between its peoples. The Kerner Report called for more massive federal programs to help blacks, while others, including the congressman from Twelfth and Clairmount, John Conyers, Jr., were busy seeking to provide a guaranteed annual income by spinning variations of free-market economist Milton Friedman's negative income tax scheme.

II

Yet the majority of voters plainly lacked the stomach for such solutions, and the president himself was unable to come up with any lively proposals for action. Instead, he was finally admitting that the government was fiscally pressed by the demands of war and Great Society together; in January 1967 he finally asked for the tax increase he had spent 1966 deceiving his own economists to avoid. It was little enough sacrifice to ask of an affluent citizenry at a time when some were giving up their lives for their country, but it was resisted all the same. Nor were voters generally favorably disposed to the demands of blacks. The strident demands by House members and constituents in February and March 1967 that Adam Clayton Powell be punished by the House for ethical violations no more serious, though perhaps more flamboyant, than those tolerated when committed by white committee chairmen and the refusal by a 307–116 vote to seat him[5] showed a nasty edge of antiblack feeling. The ridicule by conservative southern congressmen of a bill for rat control showed not only a contempt for government programs but a cruel indifference toward the poor. The shrill cries of racial separatism and revolution from one-time civil rights workers like Stokely Carmichael and H. Rap Brown surely moved many whites toward thinking that black demands were growing increasingly unreasonable and threatening and could not be—should not be—satisfied.

There was a dissonance here between the administration and the people it sought to govern. Administration policymakers and the growing cadres of urban specialists, people who had come of age and lived almost all their adult lives in the years of the politics of economic distribution which had begun so abruptly in May 1935, saw the problem posed by the riots as one largely—or at least in important part—of economics, and the solution as one of redistribution. If antidiscrimination laws were passed, an action Congress had already taken, many of them reasoned that society then needed only to enable blacks to get jobs, and the problem would go away. But at a time when unemployment for blacks was still not much higher than for whites, earnings by blacks were far lower, and the effects of past discrimination were hard to overcome immediately. This situation led some to conclude that the only way to achieve economic equality was for the government to redistribute income and wealth. One who agreed with this conclusion was Martin Luther King, Jr. Despairing of blacks' abilities to compete in a free-market economy even with antidiscrimination legislation in place, discouraged by his failure to make an imprint on life in Chicago as he and his allies had so dramatically in the South, influenced by the Scandinavian countries he had seen while accepting the Nobel Peace Prize, King was embracing socialism. As he had told his cellmate Chuck Fager in Selma as long before as February 1965, "If we are going to achieve real equality, the United States will have to adopt a modified form of socialism."[6]

But most American voters by July 1967 had long since moved away from the politics of economic distribution and found such responses to the riots repugnant and baffling. They saw the divide between blacks and other Americans as cultural, not economic, and they saw the threat not as economic deprivation but as deep-seated disorder. To be sure, there were still labor-management conflicts over wages and prices; the Machinists shut down the railroads in July, provoking legislation to shut down their strike. Then in September the UAW struck the Ford Motor Company not just for higher wages and more generous fringe benefits but for Walter Reuther's dream of a guaranteed annual wage. The Ford picketers marched in front of the Rouge plant where Reuther had been beaten in 1937, but what had once been an act of defiance and bravery, and of determined conflict, was now routine: a ritual without the drama and danger of the rioting which had gone on just a few weeks before as close as a mile away—or of the march that same month on the Pentagon across the Potomac River from Washington. The real conflicts which split American society were no longer economic, and the chief antagonists were no longer the union leaders and the big companies' management.

Certainly voting was increasingly along cultural, rather than economic, lines. The ticket-splitting which had become more common in the Eisenhower years and rampant as millions switched from their traditional parties during the Kennedy years eroded the economic-based coalitions so apparent in national elections from 1936 through the 1950s. By 1960 the biggest dividing factor clearly was not economics, but religion, with Catholics 78% for Kennedy and white Protestants 63% for Nixon. The civil rights issue—a cultural issue par excellence—shifted millions of votes in a period centered on June 1963. White southerners moved to the Republicans; blacks and many white northern Protestants moved (the first permanently, the second temporarily) to the Democrats. The Vietnam war—again, not an economic issue—would also cleave the electorate, particularly the young, although precisely how was not apparent in 1967, when none of the Baby Boomers who were the focus of the draft were eligible to vote.[7]

III

The cleavage between young and old, and between different parts of the huge Baby Boom generation—the young people born in the high birthrate years between 1946 and 1962—was about to become a central focus of American politics. There had been perceptible differences between generations before, as when the young servicemen and war workers were much more likely to vote for their commander-in-chief in 1944 than were other Americans. But never, or so it seemed at the time, had there been an age divide like this. The rising affluence of the postwar years enabled the Baby Boomers to create a market for a popular culture of their own, centered on the rock-and-roll music personified by Elvis Presley beginning in 1955 and the Beatles beginning in 1964.[8] The explicit political content of this music was almost nil, at least until 1967, but it helped to set a generation apart. Rock music had almost no audience among people born before 1940, and parents attacked it with a self-righteous vehemence. This was a culture of the affluent, with a more than faintly rebellious tone, which young people shared with others of their age and with no one else. Other behavior changed with this generation. The birth control pill, introduced in 1960, resulted in greater frequency of pre-marital sex, both monogamous and promiscuous; since venereal diseases had supposedly been conquered, there seemed no reason not to indulge. By the middle 1960s excessive alcohol use, always a problem among students and young unmarried men, was replaced on elite campuses by recreational use of marijuana and LSD and other hallucinogenic drugs. Attitudes literally subversive of social norms or at least of blind faith in American society were fostered by books which won wide audiences, most notably Joseph Heller's *Catch-22,* which hilariously sent up all the pieties of that primary culturally unifying experience of the Baby Boom generation's parents, World War II. *Catch-22* taught not that war was unglamorous and tragic, but that it was ridiculous, that it didn't matter whether you fought for your country or even your buddies, but only whether you survived.

Calendar year 1967 saw the emergence of a self-consciously adversarial counterculture, firmly based in this younger generation and propagated on a very wide scale. Musically, it was expressed most vividly in the sophisticated *Sgt. Pepper* album released by the Beatles in June 1967 and with great sexual explicitness in the songs of the Rolling Stones—the name came from a Bob Dylan song and was also appropriated by the rock-and-counterculture magazine first published by Jann Wenner in San Francisco that year. In the middle 1960s male students had taken to wearing long hair, while their fathers grumbled that they needed to go down to the neighborhood barbershop more frequently. By 1967 young men were growing long locks which were never touched by barbers; they were stared at with hatred, and glared back with contempt. Outré dress became common on campus; and countercultural neighborhoods, redolent with the smell of marijuana smoke, sprang up, most notably in the shabby frame houses of San Francisco's Haight-Ashbury. In every outward manner, the young people of the counterculture were proclaiming their rejection of and contempt for the larger, mainstream American society. Yet their life style—a term beginning to appear in these times—was made possible only by the affluence and tolerance of that society. Only societies as prosperous as America or Western Europe, where a similar counterculture arose in these years, could afford and would permit the flourishing of so many people who were economically parasitic and culturally subversive.

By 1967 the central political focus of these young people—still a minority of even their own age cohorts, to be sure, but a larger minority than most elders were comfortable admitting—was the Vietnam war. The young men were, of course, threatened by the military draft. For those graduating from college in 1967, automatic deferments for graduate study were no longer the rule,[9] and the prospect of drafting undergraduates seemed near. Yet opposition to the war among these young people, even if it coincided more closely with their exposure to the draft than they cared to admit, nonetheless had roots in other experiences—in the counterculture, in the civil rights movement which was of course adversary to so many traditions in American life, in the originally stolidly radical movement begun by Tom Hayden and the other founders of Students for a Democratic Society with their Port Huron Statement of June 1962.[10]

The march on the Pentagon in October 1967 was not the first demonstration against the Vietnam war, nor the last, nor even the most violent. The first student teach-in against the war had been sponsored at the University of Michigan in Ann Arbor in April 1965; the first demonstrations, tentative but fortified by the fury which followed the dispatch of the Marines to Santo Domingo, had begun later that year. Antiwar protests were nonetheless a new phenomenon to most Americans, who had seen nothing like them once U.S. troops were committed in World War II and Korea. The protests, bitter and well-attended, against American intervention in the 18 months between the fall of France and Pearl Harbor had been mostly forgotten or, worse, discredited. But in the climate of opinion after years of successful civil rights demonstrations—demonstrations which were at first condemned by most Americans and then ended up persuading them that a major feature of their society was rotten and must be changed—antiwar demonstrations became first thinkable and then almost inevitable. The march against the Pentagon, chronicled for all time by participant Norman Mailer,[11] was an audacious enterprise, a gathering on the marshy land around the largest office building in the world, where Robert McNamara and his systems analysts worked uneasily with professional military men in planning the war. As the protesters surged around the soldiers guarding the premises, a photographer snapped a long-haired demonstrator placing a flower in the barrel of a G.I.'s rifle: one of the quintessential images of the war at home.

This cultural war between different segments of Americans was nowhere more bitter than among the young American men of draft age. College students were turning against the war and were on no war-related issue more unanimous than in their opposition to drafting college students. They were aware, as a generation brought up just after World War II, that in that earlier war almost all young American men had been asked to serve; and their opposition to the war had the happy effect of giving them an excuse for their own exemption from military service. They were also aware that as the number of American troops in Vietnam shot up over 400,000 there was an increasing demand for American manpower and casualties sharply increased, with 9,500 killed and 20,000 wounded in 1967, as compared to 6,500 killed and 11,000 wounded during the previous seven years; the urgency of opposition to the war perceptibly increased each time the draft law was modified, or when rumors started circulating that it would be. In contrast, young Americans not in college in these years mostly accepted the draft docilely and with only the kind of grumbling traditional among conscripts. It was among these young working-class Americans that the highest casualty rates in Vietnam were recorded. Yet this non-college group was a diminishing segment of the young population, and perceptibly so. Where it had once, as recently as during the Korean war, been the norm for young men to go into the service right after high school, by the middle 1960s it was becoming the norm for young men to go into college instead. Young working-class men had once had, in return for their lower social status and incomes, the consolation of knowing that their behavior was sanctioned and honored as normal and average by a culturally unified society which valued the commonplace. Now they found themselves taking grave risks for which they received little honor or thanks, in a country in which they could no longer think of themselves as representatives of a celebrated majority but were threatened with becoming an unappreciated minority.

Of course, many eighteen-year-olds were not explicitly aware of such demographic trends. But they did know, better than their elders, how the draft laws worked; and in their daily lives they made choices which affected, more than the behavior of the young usually affects, the character and texture of the whole society. The behavior and values of the two classes of young men—the college students who were mostly draft-exempt and the non-students who were mostly draftable—were increasingly different and potentially hostile. The next time a demonstrator came forward with perhaps something more threatening than a flower, would the rifleman fire?

In one other respect the young Americans of the late 1960s affected the future, and in this respect both college and non-college men and women responded to the war in the same way—and in a way totally different from their parents' response to earlier wars. This response was in the birthrate. The American birthrate had risen sharply in World War II, from the low levels of the 1930s up toward the Baby Boom rates of reproduction which were seen after the war; it rose as well during the Korean war, from the already high Baby Boom rates of 1947–51 to the even higher plateau of peak birthrates of the years 1951–57. It was as if young Americans, threatened with death, were determined to replenish their stock— and were optimistic for the future. The young Americans of the 1960s behaved in just the opposite way. The Baby Boom had ended in 1962 and birthrates began dropping, as new methods of birth control—notably the pill—became available, as strictures against birth control ceased to be universally obeyed by Catholics, and as an increasing percentage of young people headed to college and avoided early marriage. With the onset of the Vietnam war, the birth rate not only failed to rise; it plunged far lower, down toward the low, scarcely replenishing levels of the 1970s. It was as if young Americans, baffled by the war in which service was not honored or uniformly demanded, had given up on the future.

An argument can be made that Korea resembled Vietnam more than has generally been appreciated, that in each case the United States was committed to propping up an unpopular quasi-dictatorship in marginal territory in East Asia, that in each case American leaders were unable to show the way to a speedy and conclusive victory.[12] Yet the American response to Vietnam was much different from the American response to Korea—and not just because some of the facts on the ground were different. More important, two very different Americas, just fifteen or twenty years apart, faced and fought these two frustrating wars, and the differences in their responses tell us much about the differences in the countries.

IV

Riots and marches were not the only political events of 1967. This was also the year of Israel's victory in the Six Day War in June and the summit between Lyndon Johnson and Soviet Premier Alexei Kosygin in Glassboro, New Jersey, later that month. It was the year in which Robert McNamara, seemingly acting on his own, announced in September a decision to deploy a limited antiballistic missile system, directed not against the Soviet Union but against China—a decision which would nonetheless set the course for Soviet-American arms control politics for the next two decades, while having almost no effect on American-Chinese relations. It was a year in which the impulse to examine critically and alter significantly the processes which governed American public life reached a high, as Congress, at the prodding of "consumer advocate" Ralph Nader,[13] passed its first air quality act and a consumer product safety proposal in November.

During most of the year the general assumption was that only a liberal Republican could unseat Lyndon Johnson in 1968 and that for all of Johnson's low job approval ratings it would still be exceedingly difficult for a liberal Republican to do so. Goldwater, no longer in the Senate because he had relinquished his seat reluctantly in 1964, was obviously not going to be a presidential candidate again. Ronald Reagan, the new governor of California, looked like an extremist and, as a former movie and television actor, seemed ludicrously inexperienced to analysts east of the Sierra Nevada; also, in September he had to fire his top aide for heading a ring of homosexuals, and for several months afterwards he was politically inactive because of the scandal.[14] In mid-July, when Johnson's approval rating was well below 50%, he was still leading Reagan easily, 51%–39%. Richard Nixon, returned from California to law practice on Wall Street and an apartment at 810 Fifth Avenue literally below Nelson Rockefeller's, was running no better than even against Johnson throughout the year; similar showings were made by Rockefeller, reelected as governor of New York in 1966 by only a 45%–38% plurality after Democrat Frank O'Connor blew a lead. (A footnote to that election which presaged the future: the Liberal party candidate, none other than Franklin D. Roosevelt, Jr., was outpolled by an upstate college professor running under the banner of the Conservative party: even in New York, *conservative* was replacing *liberal* as the preferred political label, only two years after Barry Goldwater's defeat.)

In polls among Republicans, Nixon led, but clearly the most popular Republican in general elections was silver-haired George Romney, just overwhelmingly reelected governor in heavily Democratic and unionized Michigan, a man known for his television commercials criticizing "gas guzzlers" for American Motors in the late 1950s and early 1960s, a devout Mormon and leader in his church. Like other well-known auto executives of the period, he was not exactly the get-things-done manufacturer people thought nor the naif citizen-in-politics he pretended. His forte was public relations, and he had been the head of the Automobile Manufacturers Association in Washington, the industry's chief lobbyist, during World War II. He was less successful as the vice president of Michigan's constitutional convention in 1961 (a more conservative Republican was the president) than he was as candidate with a campaign which used the sophisticated polling of Market Opinion Research (a leading Republican polling firm ever after) and heavy television advertising in a state which, like most states, had never seen such techniques in a non-presidential contest. In the still highly charged class-warfare atmosphere of Michigan's UAW-versus-the-companies politics, Romney managed to win enough ticket-splitters to take 51% of the vote in 1962, to be reelected with 56% despite the Johnson win in 1964, and to win 61% in 1966.

Romney's problem was that he was not well informed about national issues and did not have firmly formed opinions on them.[15] He came out of a political tradition which supposed it was enough to take a stand in the ground between the liberal Democrats on the left and more conservative Republicans on the right, to win primaries by arguing your greater electability in the general election and to win the general election by arguing that you were more practical and less divisive than the Democrat. This was a winning formula when the focus was on economics and the issue was how much welfare-state protection government should provide; it was not a helpful formula, and may have been a downright misleading one, when the issues were foreign or cultural—what to do about Vietnam, or about urban riots. Romney actually led Nixon in head-to-head polls among Republicans through early 1967, by as much as 52%–38%. He tended to corral those whose first choices were Rockefeller or Charles Percy. But Romney may have been injured by the Detroit riot, and he certainly was injured by his performance in the August taping of a Detroit television talk show hosted by an often vitriolic former businessman named Lou Gordon. Asked whether his position on Vietnam hadn't become more pro-administration after a trip there, he said, "Well, you know when I came back from Vietnam, I just had the greatest brainwashing that anybody can get when you go over to Vietnam." Several days later, the story was picked up by the *New York Times* and the national press and Romney was almost literally laughed out of the presidential race. Spoken by another politician, the actual words might not have been so damning; but they pointed directly to the central flaw of the Romney candidacy. By mid-September his first-choice support among Republicans had declined from the 25–30% level to 14%, no higher than Rockefeller and Reagan, and against Nixon one-on-one he was behind 66%–31%. Rockefeller, not wanting to run himself and largely financing the Romney campaign, insisted that his Michigan colleague stay in the race. But a December poll showed Romney behind Nixon 64%–12% in the New Hampshire primary, and to avoid further humiliation he left the race February 28, 1968, two weeks before the primary.[16]

V

The riots and demonstrations culminating in Detroit in July 1967 and the Pentagon in October presented American voters with a deeply disturbing cultural phenomenon: disorder. Intellectuals and writers tend to underestimate ordinary people's desire for order and predictability. They are less concerned in most times with having government change things in ways which enrich and help them than they are in having government behave predictably so that they can get on with their personal lives and business without undue hindrance. To the intellectuals who placed a diagram showing how to make a Molotov cocktail on the cover of the August 24, 1967, *New York Review of Books,* the prospect of change seemed inviting (partly, surely, because they forgot how many books perished in every revolution). To ordinary citizens, most of whom were not aware of the Molotov cocktail cover but had some inkling of the incitement to riot which it represented, change was a subject of dread. The great demand of voters in the depression years of 1932 and 1933 had not been for economic redistribution but for the restoration of order; economic redistribution emerged as a policy from the Roosevelt administration only after the success of policies which restored order and as the result of a series of events which were unpredictable and unpredicted. Similarly, in 1967 and 1968 Americans were looking to their government not for the affirmation of change and the distribution of aid, but for the restoration of predictability and the imposition of rules. They saw around them riots and demonstrations and rising crime rates—all things which they had had no experience of for a quarter century and which they hated. The desire of voters for "law and order," as the phrase had it, was caricatured as a racist desire to beat up on blacks. It did include a nasty punitive element, and some racial prejudice, though no substantial number of Americans even in the South wanted to reimpose legal segregation and most did not want to officially sanction racial discrimination.[17] But a more important force behind the "law and order" rhetoric was an understandable and essentially positive desire to make society work according to widely accepted rules and standards. The November 1967 elections saw some racial divisiveness, and they saw the landmark elections of some blacks—Richard Hatcher as mayor of Gary, Indiana, the first black legislators in some southern states—coming largely along polarized black-versus-white lines. But November 1967 also saw the election of a black mayor in white-majority Cleveland, where Carl Stokes won the Democratic nomination narrowly and persuaded enough white Democrats to stay with him to win a partisan contest—the first of dozens of blacks elected mayors of major American cities over the next two decades.

Political analysts debated whether events had moved voters to the left or the right. Did the Kerner Report which followed the Detroit riots convince voters that expansive government spending programs were needed, or did the riots just persuade voters that the police should crack down on blacks? Did the march on the Pentagon convince voters that the Vietnam war effort was unsustainable and wrong and must be abandoned, or did it convince them that unpatriotic long-haired demonstrators must be suppressed more effectively and the war effort stepped up to reach a hasty conclusion? Cases could be made both ways, and were, with great vehemence. But what could not be denied is that in the wake of these disorders the voters responded negatively to Lyndon Johnson. He received the lowest Gallup job rating of his entire presidency immediately after the Detroit riots (39% approved and 47% disapproved), and it was virtually identical in the poll just after the Pentagon march (38%–50%).[18] He trailed Romney by August and even the not very popular Nixon in October polls. He was far behind Robert Kennedy (39%–51%) in the September poll of Democrats. He was being beaten on both the right and, given Kennedy's public criticism of his war policies and identification with the poor and with blacks, on the left as well. The extremes on the political spectrum, as in early opinion on Vietnam, were stronger than the center: "win or get out" made more sense than fighting half a war. The voters, appalled by the disorder they saw around them, or at least on their television sets, reacted sharply against the president who once seemed to control all around him.

VI

It was in this climate that Allard Lowenstein, an articulate agitator against injustice everywhere from South Africa and Francisco Franco's Spain to North

Carolina and New York, went to Kennedy in September and October 1967 and asked him to run against Johnson. Lowenstein thought that Kennedy was uniquely positioned to take on Johnson and end the war. He could be critical of the American military effort and yet, as a Kennedy, could not be faulted as unpatriotic or unwilling to sacrifice for his country; he could bring together the intellectuals who opposed the war with the blacks who revered him and his late brother (crediting them with the Civil Rights Act, unaware that Johnson had been far more aggressive in pushing it and that the Kennedys were long reluctant and skeptical) and with white working-class Catholics who had emotional ties to the first Catholic First Family. But Kennedy had weaknesses as well as strengths. If he aroused more enthusiasm—more shrieking, impassioned crowds in the streets—than America has seen since 1968, he also aroused bitter opposition. He had always been the ruthless Kennedy, the backroom operator; he had been, briefly, an ally of Joseph McCarthy and, for years, the nemesis of Teamsters President Jimmy Hoffa; he was quoted often as saying in the 1960 election that he didn't care what happened to anyone else as long as his brother was elected. In the years of Johnson's presidency, after Kennedy won his Senate seat in New York,[19] he became almost dreamily devoted to the poor, the black, the underprivileged. His hawkish reputation (never fully justified, as witness his advice in the Cuban missile crisis) was replaced by his criticism of the administration's Vietnam war policy (criticisms not much echoed by his brother Ted).[20] Johnson obviously disliked and distrusted Kennedy, at least since Kennedy had tried to maneuver him out of the vice presidential nomination in 1960; Johnson had vetoed him for that same nomination in 1964. For his part, Kennedy thought Johnson was "mean, bitter, vicious—an animal in many ways. You know, as I say, I think his reaction on a lot of things is correct, but I think he's got this other side of him in his relationship with human beings which makes it very difficult, unless you want to kiss his behind all the time."[21]

Kennedy, skeptical about the war which Johnson had thought he would insist be fought, deeply distrustful of Johnson himself, gave serious thought to running. But understanding that his chances would depend on events far from his control, reluctant to make a race which would risk making him seem more ruthless than ever, he decided not to do it. His candidacy would be seen as a personal vendetta against Johnson, he feared; and perhaps more to the point, almost all his political experienced advisors thought the race was futile: an incumbent president could control a nominating convention, and Democratic discord would only help the Republicans. This conventional analysis was firmly based in precedent. Another Democratic president had appeared ready to run for reelection while in charge of an unpopular, apparently stalemated war—Harry Truman in 1952—but no opponent had arisen within the party to charge that the war effort should be scaled down or abandoned. Henry Wallace's candidacy in 1948, it was thought, had proved conclusively that the anti-Cold War vote in America was about 2%, and the rules for selecting delegates which had made an intraparty challenge by Wallace inconceivable had not changed significantly.[22]

The analysis of those like Lowenstein who wanted Kennedy to run proved better.

They understood that poll questions showing support for the war were less mean- ingful than Johnson's job rating, and they saw that "win or get out" feeling could mean that the support for a dovish candidate could balloon to much greater numbers than were backing dovish positions at the moment. They also understood that beneath the surface continuity, the Democratic party had vastly changed, even in the decade since Joseph Kennedy and his sons had figured out how to win its nomination. The big-city machines, fueled by patronage and supported by de- pendent masses, had flourished in Franklin Roosevelt's presidency but dwindled in Johnson's. Johnson's programs did much to undermine them, and economic and demographic trends did more—economic growth made the masses less dependent on and less grateful to the machines, central-city populations were declining, and big-city turnout would never return to its 1960 peak.[23] Idealistic reformers had taken the place of practical patronage-minded politicoes in many jurisdictions, from Greenwich Village in New York, where a young lawyer named James Lanigan had beaten Tammany boss Carmine DeSapio for district leader in September 1961 and DeSapio's comeback attempt was narrowly foiled by another young lawyer named Edward Koch in September 1963,[24] to California, where the California Democratic Clubs guided by State Controller Alan Cranston made endorsements which often proved decisive in Democratic primaries.

The other major elements of the party in 1960, the southern governors and party leaders, had been thrown on the defensive by their party's unpopularity (they lost Senate seats in 1966 in Tennessee and Texas and came uncomfortably close to losing them in the Carolinas and Oklahoma) and were battening down to survive an independent George Wallace candidacy; they could not hope to deliver their states' primary votes to a northern candidate. As for organized labor, its delegate strength at Democratic conventions had never been great, and still wasn't, outside a few states like Michigan and Ohio. Some criticisms of the reforms made in the Democratic party's presidential selection process after 1968 suggest that a strong, vibrant, functioning structure was wantonly destroyed. But in fact the Democratic party structure in 1968 was, more than almost anyone understood at the time, an empty shell. The process-minded reforms which were to occur in this process- minded age amounted to a recognition that form must follow function, and that a system which was controlled by politicians who could not deliver votes in a general election needed to give way to one which rewarded, if only through a proliferation of primaries, a demonstrated capacity to win votes.

Even as he was talking with Kennedy, Lowenstein was also walking down the marble corridors of the Senate office buildings looking for someone else to run. The Senate at this time had the largest concentration of Vietnam doves in the political system. One reason was constitutional: the Senate has the sole power to ratify treaties and confirm ambassadors, and many senators are drawn into the prestigious business of making—or pontificating on—foreign policy. Another rea- son was the example set by the skeptical and urbane William Fulbright as chairman of the Foreign Relations Committee. Like Fulbright, many other Democrats and a few Republicans had gained or were holding their seats on other issues or themes and were politically free to take a stand which conventional wisdom thought was sure to be unpopular. They included big-state Democrats (Robert Kennedy, Stephen Young of Ohio, who had been reelected at age seventy-four in 1964, Vance Hartke of Indiana), senators from the relatively dovish northern tier states (Abraham Ribicoff of Connecticut, Gaylord Nelson of Wisconsin, Eugene McCarthy of Minnesota, George McGovern of South Dakota, Mike Mansfield of Montana, Wayne Morse of Oregon, Ernest Gruening of Alaska) and Republicans with an appeal to some Democratic voters (Mark Hatfield of Oregon, John Sherman Cooper of Kentucky). They knew that behind the scenes Democrats like Richard Russell and John Stennis of Mississippi had grave reservations about the Johnson policies they felt obliged to support publicly. In contrast, antiwar sentiment made little progress in the House beyond the few embattled liberals who made a stand on minority causes like abolishing the House Un-American Activities Committee (for which thirty or so members voted every two years). Leading House committee members were relatively inarticulate men from low-income Democratic districts— committee chairmen Thomas Morgan from the black country of Pennsylvania and Mendel Rivers from Charleston, South Carolina; next-in-lines Clement Zablocki from the south side of Milwaukee and Melvin Price from the industrial slums of East St. Louis, Illinois—whose every instinct as men who remembered World War II and the loss of China was to support the incumbent Democratic president. Almost every House Republican felt obliged to support the war, as did the unimaginative party leader, Gerald Ford of Michigan, who had gotten his start in politics as a protégé of the bipartisan internationalist Arthur Vandenberg. So Lowenstein, who would run for and win a Long Island House seat in 1968, did not look to the House for a backup to Kennedy, but to the Senate.

His success was limited. Many doves understood that their home state strength would not survive the exposure of a controversial party-splitting national candidacy. Even as sincere a war opponent as George McGovern, who once told senators they had blood on their hands, was reluctant; he was up for reelection in 1968. But Eugene McCarthy pointedly left the door open and, when Kennedy said no in October 1967, promptly agreed to run. Almost unknown nationally, McCarthy was actually an accomplished and skilled politician. He was an authentic Catholic intellectual, schooled at St. John's College in frigid Collegeville, Minnesota; he was a beautiful orator, whose nominating speech for Adlai Stevenson had been the best performance of the 1960 national convention. Elected to the House as part of Hubert Humphrey's liberal anti-Communist Democratic-Farmer-Labor party in 1948, he became a member of the Ways and Means Committee and ate regularly at Sam Rayburn's Texas table in the Members' Dining Room. Yet in 1957 he was a founder of the liberal Democratic Study Group, called McCarthy's Mavericks at the time.[25] He was utterly fearless, debating Joseph McCarthy on a national television hookup in June 1952 when the Republican was charging that the Democrats had lost 450 million Chinese to Communism. "I don't think you can say we have lost them," the junior congressman replied. "We never had them. Of course, it is not our policy to have people. I think that we can say that we have saved much of the world from Communism through the sound foreign policy which the Democratic administration did initiate, and which was given bipartisan support by the Republicans as long as it seemed to be going along very well."[26] McCarthy's response to Vietnam and his performance in the 1968 campaign is foreshadowed in this response: his coolness under attack, his utter self-assurance, his almost droll play with words, his cynicism about his opponents' motives.

McCarthy savored the detail work of the House, but he ran for the Senate in what turned out to be the good Democratic year of 1958, probably with presidential ambitions in the back of his mind.[27] "I should run for president," McCarthy himself quipped, "I'm twice as Catholic as Kennedy and twice as liberal as Humphrey"—and, a reporter added, twice as smart as Symington.[28] He was also a speaker as good as Stevenson and an analyst of other politicians, if not an operator, as acidly insightful as Lyndon Johnson. He was clearly hurt when Johnson publicly passed him over for the vice presidency in August 1964—and Johnson believed that that was why McCarthy was at first skeptical of and ultimately outright opposed to Johnson's Vietnam policy.

But that opposition was consistent with McCarthy's approach to politics. He tempered genuine convictions with a practical prudence: if he was for liberal tax reform generally, he was for leaving the oil depletion allowance alone; if he was for repelling Communism internationally, he became convinced that, as Walter Lippmann was arguing, it was imprudent to try to fight a war on the land mass of Asia to save a country which was really of marginal importance anyway. He did not share the common assumption, which was central to Robert Kennedy, that American society was fundamentally unjust to the poor and the black and that rectifying this injustice must be the central goal of public policy. McCarthy's was a subtle sort of liberalism, cool and calculating, shaded with nuance, less optimistic than Humphrey's, less aggressive than Johnson's, less empathetic than Robert Kennedy's. McCarthy declared his candidacy November 30, then proceeded to address a group of organizers, which Lowenstein, for whose enthusiasm he had some distaste, had assembled in Chicago. Of course he began far behind in the polls, this politician few Americans had heard of: Johnson's job rating was recovering in December 1967 and January 1968, as memories of Detroit and the Pentagon faded a bit and as the war in Vietnam seemed to be progressing, and McCarthy trailed Johson 71%–18% in Gallup's January 1968 poll. But Kennedy had seized the lead over Johnson in October and November, 1967, just after he declined to run[29]—a sign the president was vulnerable. And the first presidential primaries of 1968, as it happened, were in New Hampshire on March 12 and Wisconsin on April 2—states in the far northern tier of the United States, the segment of the country consistently most skeptical about the war and most in favor of withdrawal. The first tests of the 1968 Democratic contest would be on what turned out to be McCarthy's ground.

42

⇥⟫⟫ ⟪⟪⟨

Bullets

On the morning of the last day of January 1968, during the Tet holiday which even in the midst of war both sides had continued to observe, the Vietnamese Communist armies launched attacks on dozens of towns and American bases in South Vietnam and even on the capital city of Saigon. There they stormed the radio station, the presidential palace, and the U.S. embassy. On their evening newscasts, 50 million Americans saw the enemy troops within their embassy, shooting bullets amid dead bodies and rubble; they watched one American soldier lob a pistol to a senior embassy official and the official shoot and kill the last of the Viet Cong invaders—within what everyone had assumed was the safest place for Americans in South Vietnam. After 34 months of active military involvement, a period almost as long as the 36 months of the Korean war or the 44 months between Pearl Harbor and Hiroshima, Americans and their South Vietnamese allies were unable to keep even the embassy safe from ground attack. Nor were the horrors over when the embassy was relieved after 6 hours. The next day Americans saw in their newspapers and on the *NBC Nightly News* the picture of a South Vietnamese general, incensed by the killing of some of his men and their family members, shooting a Viet Cong prisoner in the head. For days afterwards, well into February, they saw the battle continue, most bloodily and protractedly in Hue—the site of the Buddhist demonstrations which had so affected the Americans of May 1963.

The Tet offensive came as a surprise to American commanders in Vietnam and to American voters at home.[1] General William Westmoreland, the commander on the scene, had interpreted a November 1967 Communist attack on the mountain outpost of Khesanh as an attempt to repeat the Vietminh victory over the French at Dienbienphu in May 1954; determined to hold the site, he sent U.S. troops there. They held out, and it had seemed to Americans that the Communists were finally being thrown back. Johnson's Gallup job approval rating had risen to 46%–41% positive in December 1967 and 48%—39% in January 1968—his first positive ratings in six months. He zoomed to over 50% in polls against Romney, Nixon, and Reagan, and a 48%–40% lead over Rockefeller. His long effort to stay the course in Vietnam had seemed to be paying off, militarily and politically. Tet changed all these perceptions. Militarily, it turned out to be the Communist defeat which Westmoreland and Johnson rushed to proclaim even before they could be sure: the Communists' losses were huge and their tangible gains minimal. But as Peter Braestrup has documented in *The Big Story*,[2] the American media treated Tet as a great American defeat, most vividly when *CBS Evening News* anchor Walter Cronkite, the ratings leader and one of the most trusted men in America, in late February came out against continuing the American war effort. Americans' goals were not just military, and their patience with a war which was nearing the length of World War II was growing thin. Affluent and comfortable at home, Americans were dismayed by the vision of the American embassy under attack— and a war with no end in sight.

II

This dismay grew as word began to leak out in newspaper stories, which were soon confirmed, that the generals wanted more troops: in the Senate, Robert Kennedy spoke out against such escalation in early March, and even hawks like John Stennis and Henry Jackson opposed it. Meanwhile, Eugene McCarthy's campaign in New Hampshire, hopelessly behind in January, was beginning to catch fire. As volunteers from college campuses, shorn and neatly dressed ("clean for Gene"), streamed into a McCarthy rally on Saturday, March 9, just three days before the primary, the usually laconic candidate was grinning and the scent of an upset was in the air.[3] The next morning the Sunday *New York Times* reported definitively that with 550,000 Americans already stationed in Vietnam. General Westmoreland had asked for 206,000 more. In fact, that request had already been effectively rejected, as the new defense secretary, Clark Clifford, the Washington "superlawyer" and former Truman aide brought in by Johnson to replace the increasingly dovish McNamara, decided that the war was unwinnable and must be wound down rather than escalated. Clifford had been a hawk, but he quickly became convinced that the troop increase would be politically disastrous and that the war was otherwise unwinnable; as in 1948, he pushed a Democratic president to the left.[4]

Meanwhile, in New Hampshire on March 12 the write-in effort organized for Lyndon Johnson—for as in 1964, Johnson was chary about putting his own name on the ballot—was expected to win overwhelmingly but in fact edged McCarthy out by only a 50%–42% margin. If write-ins cast on Republican ballots are counted, Johnson led McCarthy by a scant 524 votes. New Hampshire, whose registered Democrats were mostly gritty Irish and French-Canadian mill hands, was assumed to be a hawkish state; and as polling data made clear, many of the votes cast for McCarthy were cast by "win or get out" voters whose first choice was the first of those alternatives. But they evidently preferred "get out" to an apparently endlessly escalating, never-ending war.[5] Johnson's Gallup job approval rating sank to 35%–52% negative in March 15–20; his rating on Vietnam was an abysmal 26%–63%. And the next primary, on April 2, was in Wisconsin—historically the home of German-American and LaFollette Progressive isolationism, a state which was one of the four or five most dovish in the country. Suddenly it began to appear that Johnson could be beaten.

This possibility brought Kennedy into the race he had refused to make as recently as October 1967. On the Saturday four days after McCarthy's New Hampshire near-victory, the oldest living Kennedy brother announced his candidacy amid great fanfare and with obvious haste and improvisation. Perhaps he assumed that McCarthy would step aside, or that the better-known candidate could sweep aside the little-known senator who, many felt, had won votes simply as an alternative to Johnson. But McCarthy, a serious politician seriously interested in becoming president, bitterly resented what he considered Kennedy's characteristically ruthless attempt to horn in on his success; and his youthful followers resented it even more. Kennedy could have led a united antiwar majority in the Democratic primaries, the argument went, if he had taken the risk that McCarthy had in November 1967, the risk that events would justify his decision to oppose the incumbent president. But Kennedy, who as recently as January 1968 had said he would not run "under any conceivable circumstances," had refused to take the risk, and McCarthy's enthusiastic supporters felt strongly that he should not get the reward.

Johnson spent the two weeks after Kennedy's announcement contemplating Westmoreland's request for 206,000 more men in Vietnam—and confronting, as well, the political prospects of all of his choices on Vietnam policy. In late March not only Clifford but most of the "wise men" came out against the troop increase. Clifford, long a hawk, was appalled to learn that neither the military nor their civilian superiors had any plan to achieve military victory no matter how many U.S. troops were committed. The Johnson strategy was that American lives would be lost in large numbers until the North Vietnamese leaders began behaving as game theorists said they would. The military, which wouldn't promise victory with an increase, certainly couldn't promise it without one; and the chances that the North Vietnamese would negotiate in response to a bombing halt—the administration had tried seven before, without success—were uncertain. If the policy choices were moving Johnson toward de-escalation, the political choices were pushing him hard in that direction. On March 20, just eight days after New Hampshire and even before the advice from the "wise men," James Rowe—one of Roosevelt's top aides in 1940, a Washington lawyer and insider in the years since, a Johnson loyalist in 1960—delivered a political memorandum. Johnson had become "the war candidate," Rowe said; he must do "something exciting and dramatic" to recapture the peace issue. "Hardly anyone today is interested in winning the war. Everyone wants to get out, and the only question is how."[6] Certainly by March 1968 the polls showed a deep desire for de-escalation. For months pluralities in polls had said that going to war in Vietnam had been a mistake—a judgment which goes against the grain in a nation used to rallying to its leaders in wartime—and in the aftermath of Tet the prospects for the "win" half of "win or get out" seemed at best distant and at worst unreachable. Americans, though still unsympathetic to many antiwar demonstrators and though still preferring to win if possible, preferred to get out once they decided that victory was beyond reach. This stunning change of mind on the part of millions of voters did not mean that they came to accept fully the dovish politicians' views. But it did mean that they had conclusively rejected the leadership of Lyndon Johnson.

One week later, while preparing a televised speech on Vietnam scheduled for Sunday, March 31, two days before the primary in Wisconsin where he was running far behind, Johnson decided to get out—of Vietnam and the presidency. He vetoed troop increases (and the necessary calling up of the reserves and increase in taxes), and he announced at the end, in a peroration that caught even Lady Bird by surprise, "I have concluded that I should not permit the presidency to become involved in the partisan divisions that are developing in this political year. Accordingly, I shall not seek and I will not accept the nomination of my party for another term as your president." Americans were stunned—and mostly delighted. Johnson's Gallup job approval rating rose 13 percentage points, to 49%–40% positive, and approval of his Vietnam war policy increased from 26%–63% to 64%–26%.[7]

III

Johnson's withdrawal left the Democrats, though they were the party in power, in chaos and the Republicans, though they were the out party, seemingly united around a single candidate—the opposite of the usual situation. George Romney's withdrawal from the New Hampshire primary had left Richard Nixon the easy winner there. Then, two weeks later, Nixon was spared serious opposition in upcoming primaries when Nelson Rockefeller surprised just about everyone (none more so than his biggest booster among his fellow Republican governors, Spiro Agnew of Maryland)[8] by announcing that he was not running. Quietly, without much notice from journalists concentrating on the disarray among the party they were accustomed to thinking of as having a natural majority, Nixon was sewing up the Republican nomination and trying out themes for the general election. If he was not the favorite candidate of either the Rockefeller or the Goldwater wings of his party, he was not unacceptable to either; if he was not as popular with general election voters as he had been in 1960, he was being careful not to let his unpopularity increase—in contrast to the leading Democrats.

Among the Democrats, Vice President Humphrey was obviously heir to Johnson's support, what there was of it, but he did not take quick advantage of his situation. Although Johnson had told him of his decision to leave the race, Humphrey kept a date in Mexico the night of March 31, putting him out of the country the night Johnson made his announcement. Kennedy was now an active but still entirely disorganized candidate, spending much of his energy on winning back longtime supporters who had gone to work for McCarthy when Kennedy said he wasn't running. McCarthy's supporters were exhilarated at having forced Johnson out of the race, but in fact they were deprived of what had become their most vulnerable opponent.

And there was another Democrat running: George Wallace. In 1966 he had executed a brilliant political coup in Alabama, evading its one-term limit on governors by running his wife, Lurleen, in his stead; she overwhelmed liberal Richmond Flowers in the primary by 54%–19% and then whipped Republican Congressman Jim Martin, who had won his House seat on Goldwater's coattails, by a 63%–31% margin in the general election. Master of his own state, wildly popular with many southern whites, Wallace had decided by early 1968 to run as a third-party candidate and was directing the arduous process of getting himself on the ballot in all fifty states.[9] He spoke eloquently in the feisty, bantam-rooster, populist idiom of Alabama politics, whose most successful practitioner in the 1940s and 1950s, "Kissin' Jim" Folsom, had railed against the "Big Mules" of Birmingham— the populist name for the state's big economic interests—and promised to build roads and schoolhouses for the little people.

Wallace made such promises, too, and delivered on some of them, but his main platform was opposition to desegregation. There was plenty of irony here. Little in Wallace's career suggests any deep-seated devotion to segregation, and in fact he turned out to be perfectly able to play biracial politics in the 1980s. But he was ambitious and shrewd; and after he was, in his word, "outsegged" in the 1958 gubernatorial primary, he determined that that would never happen again. Another irony was that he was entirely unsuccessful in stopping desegregation. In his first term, his stand in the schoolhouse door—an obvious bit of political theater—failed of its purported purpose; in his second term, the federal government through its new civil rights laws integrated public accommodations and began integrating schools in Alabama; in later terms, he let the entire cause of segregation be lost and repudiated it. Yet he retained his support from most rural and lower-income whites over those years. They were demanding not the achievement of results, but the expression of attitudes; not the preservation of a system which after 1964 clearly could not be preserved, but the continued voicing of resentment and anger and what political analysts were starting to call alienation. At this exploitation of angry feelings Wallace could not be bettered, and he could speak the language if not quite in the accents of North as well as South.

But his core support was in the South, and his candidacy tended to hurt the Republicans and help the Democrats. The national Democrats had lost southern white support when John Kennedy came out for a civil rights act in June 1963, and later Democratic presidential nominees never regained it.[10] In 1967 polls southern whites preferred even Republicans long identified with civil rights, like Romney and Nixon, over Johnson. But when Wallace was added to the mix, the Republicans' leads vanished. Thus a Romney lead of 48%–45% nationally in June 1967 turned into a 39%–41% deficit, with 11% for Wallace; a 47%–44% Johnson lead over Nixon in November 1967, not really statistically significant, balloons when Wallace gets his 12% to 44%–36%.[11] In early April 1968, Wallace got only 9% or 10% in three-candidate polls, but he jumped to the 14% level in May and stayed at least that high through the election, when he got 13.5%. That was enough to enable him to carry five southern states and come close to carrying three others.

None of the other Democrats showed impressive strength when Johnson withdrew. Gallup's three-way April 1968 poll of Democrats gave Humphrey and Kennedy 35% each and McCarthy 23%—an indeterminate result, given the fluidity of primary electorates. In one-on-one pairings the lesser-known McCarthy trailed both Humphrey (48%–37%) and Kennedy (46%–37%), while Kennedy led Humphrey 45%–41%—all narrow, presumably reversible margins. In general election polls Kennedy and McCarthy both trailed Nixon 38%–41%, with 10% for Wallace, while Humphrey ran somewhat worse, 34%–43%–9%. None of the Democratic candidates showed wide popularity, even among Democratic primary voters. And in general election polls these candidates of the party which had won 61% of the vote in November 1964 could not win even 40% in April 1968.

As it turned out, there never was a contest involving all three of these Democrats. Because of the filing deadlines and other rules, Kennedy was not listed on the ballot in any April contest; and Humphrey never ran in any primaries at all. On the Tuesday after Johnson's withdrawal McCarthy beat him in Wisconsin by a 56%–35% margin; almost everyone agreed that McCarthy would have run at least 10 points better if Johnson had still been a candidate.[12] In the next primaries, the Pennsylvania "beauty contest" (delegates were chosen by party caucus) on April 23 and Massachusetts on April 30, McCarthy was the only candidate on the ballot. The only real contests would be between McCarthy, Kennedy, and Johnson surrogates in Indiana on May 7, Nebraska on May 14, Oregon on May 28, and California on June 4.

IV

Early in the evening of Thursday, April 4, just two days after McCarthy's victory in the Wisconsin primary, Martin Luther King, Jr., was killed by a rifle shot while standing on the second-floor balcony of the Lorraine Motel in Memphis, Tennessee. King was in Memphis—that humid, flat, utterly segregated city on the lowlands next to the Mississippi River, just north of the Mississippi state line—to demonstrate in support of striking city garbage collectors. His death led immediately, that same night, to rioting in dozens of cities. None was hit worse than previously quiet Washington, D.C., where Fourteenth Street, just two blocks from the White House and long a shopping street for the city's black majority, was soon in flames. Robert Kennedy, alighting from a plane in Indianapolis, spoke extemporaneously and memorably to blacks there of King's legacy. But in Chicago, Mayor Daley said that police spotting looters should "shoot to kill."

The difference between these two responses reflected deeper differences among Americans—and among those who traditionally voted for the Democratic ticket. The nation had been given an explanation for black rioting when the Kerner Commission report was released in March: the proximate cause was "white racism"; and unless special programs were undertaken to help poor blacks, the country was on the road to becoming "two societies, one black, one white."[13] Yet most Americans rejected the idea of placing the blame solely on the huge white majority, many of whose members had grown up with many disadvantages themselves. That approach seemed to reject the idea that blacks should be held responsible for their personal behavior. If the criminal justice system—the police officers, judges, and juries, most of them still mostly white even in the most heavily black cities—was responding to the increase in crime charted in the statistics since 1964[14] by greater leniency and milder sentences which resulted in stable or declining prison populations nationally, that "softness on crime" was beginning to be a political liability for politicians associated with it. Hubert Humphrey asserted, with typical ebullience, that if he were born in a ghetto he might stage a pretty good riot himself; George Wallace said that he had grown up in a house without indoor plumbing and had lived in poverty himself, but had never started a riot. So Wallace, who had first come to national attention by his playacting at disobeying a court order, now was campaigning as the candidate of "law and order"; Kennedy was campaigning as the former attorney general of the United States, the prosecutor who had sent Jimmy Hoffa to jail; Nixon, by the Oregon primary, was emphasizing his support of "law and order" as emphatically as anyone.[15] Only Humphrey and McCarthy, from Minnesota with its low black population and low crime rates, missed the cue.

As mentioned earlier, however, to dismiss Americans' yearning for "law and order" as simply an expression of racial backlash is to miss much of what was happening. Their plea was not so much for law as it was for order: the natural desire of ordinary people for a reliable, orderly, moral, and safe society in which they can go about their everyday business and live their personal lives. The riots following the death of King came after several years of agitation by men treated by the media as civil rights leaders—Stokely Carmichael urging "black power" and H. Rap Brown crying "Burn, baby, burn!" Other groups were rioting as well. In April and May students at Columbia University occupied the president's office and smoked his cigars, purportedly in protest of plans to build a university gymnasium in a park used by Harlem residents, but also explicitly as representatives of a revolutionary movement, poorly defined but menacing enough to take over the most prestigious university in the nation's largest city. Similar incidents occurred at other colleges, and in May television brought home to Americans the spectacle of French students taking over the city of Paris and bringing the government of Charles de Gaulle to its knees. This was followed by student riots in Northern Ireland and Italy, West Germany and Britain—seemingly a worldwide uprising by the young, destroying or threatening to destroy the institutions people had set their lives by.[16] Echoing Mario Savio in Berkeley in 1964 and the Port Huron Statement of 1962, they professed an aching for "community," which to most adults at the time sounded like romantic adolescent rhetoric from people who were postponing family-formation and refusing to enter into the lively communities which already existed because they sensed, not entirely correctly, that they would not be able to run them immediately. In fact, achieving power through traditional institutions proved relatively easy, as the success of many liberals in 1968 and after showed.

In this disorderly world, the candidacy of Robert Kennedy, which offered so much promise to his fervent supporters, seemed a threat to many others. One reason was his close association with the cause of civil rights and the fervent and near-unanimous support he won from blacks, even against Hubert Humphrey, who had been among America's most prominent advocates of civil rights for twenty years; quite forgotten or unknown was Kennedy's long coolness to the cause and complicity in the wiretapping of Martin Luther King only a few years before. Another was his identification with the downtrodden: when Kennedy attended mass with Cesar Chavez in the Central Valley of California on Easter Sunday 1968, as Chavez was ending a fast, he was identified not just with Chavez's locally unpopular United Farm Workers but also with those who threatened to overturn the established order of things. Kennedy was unpopular also among older liberals who remembered him from the 1950s and among young antiwar activists who resented his earlier refusal to run and his eventual decision to get into the race against McCarthy. In multitudinous ways Robert Kennedy, the brother and political heir of a man who had moved seemingly effortlessly to the top of American politics, seemed to be challenging the basic rules and threatening the underlying order of that same political system.

Despite the lingering popularity of John Kennedy, therefore, his brother was on balance an unpopular candidate. In early May he was trailing Nixon in a three-way poll including Wallace, 32%–42%–15%, while Humphrey and McCarthy were running essentially even, with 36% and 37% to Nixon's 39% and Wallace's 14%.[17] Kennedy did win the Indiana primary May 7, with 42% to 31% for Johnson stand-in Governor Roger Branigan and 27% in this hard-bitten, anything-but-idealistic state for McCarthy.[18] And he won even more impressively in Nebraska a week later, 52%–31% over McCarthy; a large share of Democratic primary votes there were cast by Catholics, and Robert Kennedy evidently still had the same Kennedy magic with them as he had had in upstate New York in 1964 and in gritty Gary the week before. But in Oregon, heavily Protestant and almost all white, McCarthy beat Kennedy 44%–38% on May 28—the first loss a member of the Kennedy family had ever sustained in an American election. Kennedy complained privately that he couldn't get a handle on Oregon: "This state is like one giant suburb."[19] But demographically America in 1968 was on its way to becoming something like "one giant suburb." Kennedy's ability to win votes from both blacks and ethnic whites, hailed by his supporters as a sign that he could unite the nation, showed instead that his popularity was concentrated in the diminishing core of the Democratic constituency.

V

And so the strategy of each of the Democrats was being undercut by events. McCarthy's strategy was to topple Johnson and inherit the nomination as the only alternative to a terminally unpopular president; and if many of his backers saw him as a symbolic figure, he seems at this stage to have seen himself as a future president. But Johnson left the race too early, Kennedy's entry split the antiwar cause (although McCarthy kept more of the antiwar activists than Kennedy's backers had hoped), and Humphrey was far more acceptable to labor and party leaders, most of whom didn't appreciate McCarthy's history of sophisticated accommodation of professional politicians and were repelled by the amateurs and students who made up most of his 1968 campaign. Technically, 40% of the Democratic delegates in 1968 were from primary states, but primaries in some of the big states—Pennsylvania, Ohio, Florida, New Jersey, Illinois—were "beauty contests." Only 19% of the delegates were chosen in primaries, and 81% were chosen otherwise, in procedures where McCarthy had little chance.

Kennedy's strategy was to appeal to the professional politicians as he had on his brother's behalf in 1960. But the bosses were not as strong as they had been, and they did not look on this Kennedy with warmth. "Tip, let me tell you something," Joseph Kennedy once said to Thomas P. ("Tip") O'Neill, John Kennedy's successor as congressman from Cambridge, Somerville, and several wards in Boston. "Never expect any appreciation from my boys. These kids have had so much done for them by other people that they just assume it's coming to them."[20] The old-timers knew that when boss Charles Buckley of the Bronx had been opposed in the 1964 House primary by reformer Jonathan Bingham, a medium-level Kennedy administration appointee, Robert Kennedy supported Bingham—even though Buckley had delivered key votes to John Kennedy in 1960 and, for that matter, to Robert Kennedy at the convention which had nominated him for the Senate in 1964. In June 1966, Kennedy, again interested in appealing to reformers and repulsed by the regulars, endorsed reformer Samuel Silverman over Tammany leader Carmine DeSapio's choice, Arthur Klein, for surrogate of New York County—a wonderful patronage plum, for the Manhattan Surrogate's Court probated all estates, appointed all guardians and trustees and appraisers and bank repositories for every estate in the island where so many of America's richest people live and die.[21] The bosses might support Kennedy out of fear, but when he was winning primaries by less than overwhelming margins and running poorly in general-election polls, they were not much in fear of him.

Humphrey, that most poorly organized of major American politicians, scarcely had a strategy. He was evidently hoping that McCarthy would eliminate Kennedy and that he, as the heir of Johnson, would inherit the nomination. He did some things right. He worked the telephones and prevented most of the leading professional politicians from committing themselves to Kennedy in the week after Johnson's withdrawal. And he assembled a good delegate-hunting operation and relied heavily on his labor union allies to win delegates in big states like Pennsylvania, Ohio, and Michigan. But he avoided primaries and did nothing to help sympathetic slates, like that headed by Attorney General Thomas Lynch in California. And he did almost nothing to raise money. He could not count on the support of Johnson, who bullied him throughout the campaign, especially when he showed any sign of independence on Vietnam. Even his natural ebullience and oratorical skill worked against him. His amiable garrulousness kept him talking longer than even the friendliest of audiences wanted to listen—and much too long for sound bites on the television evening newscasts—and led him to mistakes like physically embracing Georgia's segregationist Governor Lester Maddox.

More important, Humphrey was deaf to the tone of this most tragic year of twentieth-century American politics. He began his formal campaign in late April, in the midst of an unpopular war, just three weeks after the murder of Martin Luther King and the riots in dozens of major cities, by proclaiming his belief in "the politics of joy." Humphrey might be able to win the nomination from old-time leaders who detested his opponents. But this most articulate politician was, quite unlike Adlai Stevenson in 1952, unable to articulate a message and a theme which set him apart from the unpopular Democrat in the White House and provided a basis for his own leadership of the party and nation.

When McCarthy beat Kennedy in Oregon, Humphrey's strategy seemed about to work. Another victory by McCarthy in California a week later would force Kennedy out of the race—he admitted as much publicly—and McCarthy by this time was a pariah to the regular politicians and could win no delegate votes beyond those he captured in primaries or in caucuses in liberal-minded, dovish, non-organization states like Iowa, Vermont, and Colorado. Just as many Republican professionals in 1964 had hoped that Rockefeller would beat Goldwater in California and eliminate them both, so many Democratic professionals in 1968 hoped that McCarthy would beat Kennedy in California and effectively eliminate them both. If Kennedy won, both men would surely remain in the race, bitter enemies. Yet the delegate arithmetic showed that the only way either could conceivably get a majority was to unite virtually all the McCarthy and Kennedy delegates and add to them almost all the delegates from states like New York, New Jersey, Pennsylvania, Ohio, Illinois, and Michigan, many of whom were already committed to Humphrey.[22]

Then, on the night of the California primary, after acknowledging his 46%–42% victory over McCarthy and raising his hand shyly in the "V" salute he adopted from the antiwar marchers, Kennedy walked into the kitchen of the Ambassador Hotel on Wilshire Boulevard in Los Angeles and was shot by Sirhan Sirhan. Two days later he died. With him went any chance that the Democrats could coalesce. Humphrey, deeply stricken with grief, was immobilized for a month; he had expected that if Kennedy lost in California he would have supported Humphrey, and that if he won in California he would have lost gallantly at the convention and ended up as Humphrey's vice presidential nominee.[23] McCarthy seemed stricken in a different way. He could barely say anything positive about his former rival, but became himself dreamier and more disconnected from campaigning, refusing to politick and spending more time reciting poetry with the likes of Robert Lowell. As for Johnson, he impaired his party's chances by insisting that Humphrey toe the line on Vietnam and implicitly threatening to get his delegates in the South to abandon him if he did not. Humphrey, always ready to listen sympathetically and to defer to this man who could not fire him, meekly submitted, never really taking command as Americans expect their presidents to do. It apparently did not occur to Humphrey[24] that Johnson had no real alternative to himself, and that he could have called Johnson's bluff as Adlai Stevenson in effect had called Truman's in 1952. For all his brilliance as a political innovator, Humphrey lacked the steeliness and ruthlessness which Americans want their presidents to bring to the White House and use in behalf of their country.

Another way to gauge the tragedy of 1968 is to compare it with 1952, that other year when an unpopular Democratic president was unable to end a deadlocked Asian war. In 1952 both political parties found candidates who transcended their parties' political difficulties, who sounded inspiring themes, and who showed themselves capable of providing leadership of a quality voters had despaired of finding. In 1968 neither party could find such a man. In 1952 and 1940 the old-fashioned conventions had produced stirring nominees, although not always by means which were entirely presentable; but in 1968 they ended up choosing, by means which were broadcast much more directly to the public, nominees who failed to rise to the occasion as Dwight Eisenhower and Adlai Stevenson had. Richard Nixon and Hubert Humphrey, each with strong advantages in his race for the nomination, had both hunkered down, hoping to win by process of elimination. Neither sounded the inspiring themes or was seen to provide the strong leadership which Americans want in their president. Neither provided the reassuring sense of restoring order which Americans sought in the dispirited, disorderly, bullet-ridden America of 1968.

VI

Richard Nixon, unlike Hubert Humphrey, knew how to speak directly to voters in 1968. His campaign advisor H. R. Haldeman, a Los Angeles advertising man, told him in a remarkably prescient memo that candidates appeal to voters primarily through television and that they should try to deliver only one message each campaign day—the winning campaign tactic over the next twenty years.[25] What Nixon did not know was what exactly to say. Nixon no longer seemed the tattered and discredited man who had told reporters in Los Angeles after he was defeated for governor in 1962 that "you won't have Nixon to kick around any more." He moved to New York in 1963, campaigned actively for Republicans around the country in 1966, and could draw on two decades of experience at the highest levels of American politics and government. To the campaign in 1967 and 1968 he brought less self-pity and more self-discipline than he had in 1952 and 1960. But he was disciplined not just by himself but by his accurate perception of the political circumstances. Even though he had no declared opposition in the primary season, he knew he was hemmed in on either side in the race for the nomination, leaving him little room to stake out positions for the general election.

On one side was Nelson Rockefeller. His seemingly irrational moves—backing the flagging Romney, then deciding to enter the race in March 1968—were dictated by his own inability to win primaries, because of voters' uneasiness about his personal life and his free-spending economic policies. So he waited until most primary deadlines had passed before entering the race April 30. He hoped to argue, as liberal Republicans had since 1940, that he should be nominated because he was more electable than Nixon. But Nixon was running quite well against Democrats in the polls—as well as Rockefeller or better. On the other side was Ronald Reagan, only in his second year as governor of California and with a reputation as a conservative ideologue; he was reluctant to run in primaries, too, and lost to Nixon 65%–20% in Oregon. Reagan, as the next twenty years would show, was better positioned to win the decisive swing vote that oscillated between the parties, now that that vote was no longer LaFollette Progressives and New York Jews but southern whites and northern blue-collar ethnics. But almost no one accepted that argument just four years after the defeat of Barry Goldwater.

Rockefeller and Reagan both tried to swing delegate votes away from Nixon; their operatives ended up cooperating, since there was no overlap between their targets. Nixon's strategy was to hold together his majority up through the convention by arguing the weaknesses of his opponents. It was a negative strategy for a candidate who had been in a position to present himself in 1960 as the positive spokesman of a successful administration; and it kept Nixon, once so much in the spotlight, behind the scenes. Nixon showed a steely coolness as the convention opened in July 1968 in the surreal environment of Miami Beach, from which demonstrators could easily be barred by policing the causeways from the mainland. The Rockefeller candidacy was demolished by the latest Gallup poll, which showed Nixon beating Humphrey 40%–38%, with 16% for Wallace, while Rockefeller was only even with Nixon and was losing more votes to Wallace, 36%–36%–21%.[26] Rockefeller had nearly 300 delegates (out of 667 needed) and could hope for another 182 which belonged to mostly pro-Rockefeller favorite sons like Romney and Ohio Governor James Rhodes, but he could add no more while Nixon was in the race.

Reagan was the candidate with more upward potential, and the South was his obvious hunting ground. But working the caucuses and the floor for Nixon was Strom Thurmond, States' Rights Democrat candidate for president in 1948, a former South Carolina governor and now one of the state's senators, a Democrat turned Republican to support Goldwater in September 1964, and at age sixty-five[27] a man looking for a winner. In June 1968, Nixon had given Thurmond assurances that he would appoint "strict constructionist" judges and ease up on, though not entirely abandon, civil rights enforcement; and those assurances won Thurmond's support and that of many of the southern delegates he canvassed. Clifton White, Goldwater's delegate hunter in 1964 and Reagan's in 1968, believed that switches by just a handful of delegates from Florida, Georgia, Mississippi, and Louisiana would have swung these states' unit-rule votes away from Nixon and prevented his nomination (the unit rule meant that all of a state's votes were cast the way a majority of its delegates voted). That is possible, for Nixon won with just 692 votes, only 25 more than necessary, on the first ballot. Before 1968, such struggles would have taken several ballots, as votes would be held back from one candidate tactically, so he could show gains on a later ballot, and as backers of the different candidates figured out just how many votes they had. But 1968 saw the first serious, in-depth, and accurate independent delegate count, made by CBS News and superintended by off-camera CBS political analyst Martin Plissner. The delegate count made the multi-ballot convention obsolete, since bargainers now could know their strengths and weaknesses long before the roll was called. The tantalizing question, which neither White nor Plissner could answer definitively, is who would have won if Nixon had been stopped—Rockefeller (not likely) or Reagan (more likely, but not assured) or someone else (but who?).

An old convention tradition remained: the post-midnight picking of the vice presidential nominee. Nixon had made no decision before the balloting, had not even winnowed the field down: such disparate characters as Texas Senator John Tower and New York Mayor John Lindsay were in the running. Then around 12:30 Nixon settled on Governor Spiro Agnew of Maryland, the spurned Rockefeller supporter four months before, the Baltimore County executive three years before that, a member of the County Board of Zoning Appeals not long before that—one of the fastest risers in American politics. Agnew had been elected governor on a fluke in 1966 after a perennial nuisance candidate (contractor George Mahoney) campaigning against open housing won Maryland's Democratic gubernatorial primary by a 30.2%–29.8%–27.3% margin. This opponent made Agnew the proper choice of all progressive-thinking Marylanders (and a well-known figure, through the *Washington Post*'s coverage of Maryland politics, to the Washington political establishment), though he showed no steady views on issues local or national. Nonetheless, Agnew had an air of assurance and made a good first impression, and he was a Greek-American in a year when the ethnics who had voted for John Kennedy in such numbers were now visibly deserting the Democrats. Agnew's unclear place on the ideological spectrum—he was counted as a liberal Republican in November 1966 and as late as March 1968 and now sounded more conservative—was also an advantage. But his malleability was less of an asset than his maladroitness proved a liability: this was a man whose first appearance was always his most impressive and who turned out to be a bribe-taking criminal even as he appeared waving with Nixon on Thursday night.

VII

Lyndon Johnson scheduled the 1968 Democratic convention for the week of his sixtieth birthday—making it the latest national convention in American history—and in October 1967 chose to hold it in the city led by one of his most faithful supporters, the Chicago of Richard J. Daley. The decision was characteristic of Johnson—the egoism, the elaborate public deference to an elderly grandee of the Democratic party, the echoes of Franklin Roosevelt's dark days of 1940. Although Chicago made elaborate presentations to get the convention away from its chief rival, Houston, there is some reason to believe that Daley, wary of Martin Luther King's movement in the city, afraid as every big-city mayor was of a black riot, actually did not want the convention.[28] But Johnson, unlike most active politicians and journalists of 1968, vividly remembered 1940, when the president he most admired, beleaguered in wartime and unsure of his party's support, chose to hold the national convention in Chicago because he knew Mayor Ed Kelly, with his loyalty, his organization, and his voice from the sewers, could control the hall and the gallery and thus determine what Americans would hear as the president was renominated. What evidently did not occur to Johnson as he made this decision is that in a television age an organization could not control a convention hall too tightly and that what went on outside the hall could be as important as what went on inside.

The hotels where the convention delegates and the press were housed were arrayed in that great wall of skyscrapers which rise up above Grant Park, the swath of green Daniel Burnham built over the railroad tracks on the shore of Lake Michigan. Here on South Michigan Avenue and Balbo Drive was the Blackstone Hotel, where Harry Hopkins had kept in touch with the White House on one telephone line in the bathroom in July 1940; south of Balbo on South Michigan was the Conrad Hilton, with some 2,000 rooms the nation's biggest hotel and the headquarters of Hubert Humphrey and Eugene McCarthy. The convention hall, the Amphitheater at the Stockyards, was inland, six miles southwest of the Loop: a low-lying building, surrounded by flat concrete pavement, in the mile-square Stockyards compound which Mayor Daley sealed off against all but authorized buses and a few politician's limousines. Riders saw the neighbors, cheery-faced whites in areas similar to the mayor's own nearby Bridgeport, waving signs that said "We Love Mayor Daley."

The demonstrators who came to town chanted, yelled, and screamed very much the opposite message. There were three distinct groups of them. The noisiest and most chaotic were the Youth International Party, or Yippies, names conjured up by their leaders Abbie Hoffman and Jerry Rubin.[29] Their name was a variant on hippies, their spirit was anarchic, and their aim was to make fun of standard politics; they asked for a permit to camp out in Lincoln Park, two miles north of the Loop. and promised those who joined them music, drugs, and places for lovemaking. Not surprisingly, Chicago officials turned them down. On the Friday before the convention they nominated their own candidate for president, a pig named Pigasus. The second group, more serious in demeanor, was the antiwar Mobilization headed by David Dellinger, SDS founder Tom Hayden, organizer Rennie Davis, and other leaders of what had begun as student protest and was now a fractious and self-consciously radical movement dedicated to revolutionary changes in American society.[30] They said they favored "socialism with a human face"—a week after Leonid Brezhnev's Soviet troops had crushed that ideal in Czechoslovakia—and they wanted to lead a nonviolent march from Grant Park to the Amphitheater. City officials refused to let them get near the Amphitheater but granted them a permit for a parade in Grant Park on Wednesday, August 28. Daley, who had ordered his police force to "shoot to kill" rioters after the King assassination in April, made it plain that the city was prepared to arrest and quite possibly to beat up the demonstrators. Like any mayor, he wanted to keep demonstrators out of his city, and his lack of cooperation surely deterred many; so did

McCarthy in early August when he called on his young followers to stay away. The Yippies and the "Mobe" together brought in fewer than 10,000 people in a city with a police force of 11,000 and a state National Guard commanded by a governor (Otto Kerner's interim successor, Samuel Shapiro) who was subservient to Daley. Both forces received extensive training in restrained riot control.

But in this most traumatic of American political years Lyndon Johnson could not control the hall and Richard Daley could not control the streets. The galleries at the Amphitheater were filled with the third group of demonstrators, spectators who booed mention of Johnson's name—it became obvious on Monday night that he couldn't attend or even hold the convention birthday party which had long been planned for him—and sang "The Battle Hymn of the Republic" while the gavel was banging; they had gotten legitimate passes from McCarthy and other anti-Humphrey politicians and delegates to get past the electronic security checkpoints.[31] Johnson could banish the antiwar New York and California delegations to the back of the hall and put Daley's beefy Chicagoans in front of the podium. But the TV cameras were out of his control; and heavy-handed security measures backfired, as when delegates were arrested for having supposedly insufficient identification and when CBS News's Dan Rather, as always at the camera-focus of controversy, was beaten by a guard Tuesday night.

On Monday evening the convention wrangled about credentials and moved against the unit rule. Southerners silently threatened to dump Humphrey for Johnson, and news of a draft movement for thirty-six-year-old Edward Kennedy pervaded the hall. By no stretch of the imagination was he qualified or ready for the presidency; but he was the last Kennedy brother, he could conceivably win the support of Daley (who on Sunday kept the Illinois delegation officially uncommitted for another 48 hours) and of McCarthy (who told Kennedy brother-in-law Steve Smith, by Smith's account, that he might support "Teddy," but "[he] never would have done it for Bobby"),[32] and he had been conspicuously milder in his criticisms of Johnson's Vietnam policy than Robert Kennedy had been. Humphrey had a majority, but he did not have command of it. Through an otherwise obscure functionary named John Criswell, Johnson had control of the microphones, and Humphrey quaked in fear that the South would desert him over his mild concessions on the unit rule or that Johnson would ditch him if he objected to one iota of the Vietnam platform plank the White House had written.[33] Nor did Humphrey have much to say to Daley about how the streets were run: he had written the mayor a letter urging that demonstrators be given a permit to demonstrate, but Daley did not reply[34] to what he must surely have considered a perfunctory request written only for the record. Humphrey did not have the nerve to act on the calculation that no majority could be assembled for anyone else, that the great mass of northern votes would never go to a Lyndon Johnson who could not even attend this convention, that southerners would decide, that they obviously did not want Edward Kennedy, a decision they reached by Tuesday afternoon, even before Kennedy telephoned Humphrey, Daley, and Jesse Unruh on Wednesday morning to tell them he would not accept a draft. "This day," the usually admiring Theodore H. White writes of the day Humphrey was nominated, "Humphrey is not in command either of himself, the convention or anything."[35] Yet the office he was running for was called, among other things, commander-in-chief.

Humphrey's lack of command was apparent in the victory Tuesday for the followers of McCarthy and George McGovern, the South Dakota senator and former next-door neighbor of Humphrey who had become a presidential candidate two weeks before chiefly as a convenience for Robert Kennedy supporters who could not stomach voting for McCarthy. Their victory came over the rules. A commission started by McCarthy supporter Geoffrey Cowan of Connecticut and headed by Governor Harold Hughes of Iowa had prepared a report criticizing Democratic party rules and calling for a party reform commission. It got support from some Humphrey backers and almost all Humphrey opponents and passed 1351.25 to 1209[36]—thus setting in motion the commission which after the 1968 election would make vast changes in the American presidential selection process. The post-civil rights revolution impulse for good means as well as good ends, acceptable process as well as correct results, was perfectly expressed in this initiative.

As the convention wrangling went on Monday night, Chicago police began to clear Lincoln Park of the Yippies. This was not the first violent confrontation associated with the convention—a seventeen-year-old runaway who had allegedly pulled a gun on policemen had been shot the preceding Thursday,[37] the only fatality either week—nor did it get much coverage on television. For the telephone workers were on strike in August 1968, and though they allowed TV equipment to be installed in the Amphitheater, it was impossible to have any live remote cameras anywhere other than at the Conrad Hilton. All film and videotape had to be delivered and edited before it could go on the air.

But even from the hall television coverage was disastrous for the Democrats. On Tuesday night House Speaker Carl Albert lost control of the proceedings when the administration's Vietnam plank was coming up for debate after 1 A.M. Opponents made such an uproar that Daley called for adjournment. This meant that the convention Wednesday had to debate Vietnam, nominate presidential candidates, and vote on them. On Vietnam the vote was rather close, 1567.75–1041.25, with significant line-crossing in the New York and Michigan delegations, where big-county political bosses and United Auto Workers leaders recognized, as evidently Humphrey did not, that the minority plank would help him win the election. But the key event Wednesday came at 7:57 P.M. (dusk in the Chicago summer) opposite the Conrad Hilton as police moved to block the Mobilization from marching. Many policemen showed firm discipline, but others—resenting the demonstrators and what they stood for, goaded by verbal abuse and endangered by flying rocks and bags of urine—lost all control and began beating demonstrators and onlookers with their nightsticks. This was the "police riot" described by the investigative commission headed by businessman Daniel Walker.[38] "The whole world is watching," the crowd chanted, quite correctly, for Michigan and Balbo was the one location in strike-torn Chicago where television cameras and lights were set up. Tear gas was sprayed in Grant Park and wafted over into the ventilating shaft of the Conrad Hilton. As some bloodied victims went into the hotel lobby, others went up to the McCarthy rooms on the fifteenth floor. For the rest of the convention the lobby reeked of the vomit smell of tear gas, and its carpet was stained with blood. The battle of Michigan Avenue was over by 8:30. But it took some time to develop and process the footage; and it was broadcast just after San Francisco Mayor Joseph Alioto nominated Humphrey, taking Cleveland Mayor Carl Stokes's seconding speech off the air. Shots of sickening violence filled television screens, inspiring the usually cool-tempered Connecticut Senator Abraham Ribicoff to say in his McGovern nominating speech, "With George McGovern we wouldn't have Gestapo tactics on the streets of Chicago." Mayor Daley, sitting in the front row of the dais and perhaps not aware himself of how the police had suddenly gone berserk, shouted anti-Semitic slurs at Ribicoff, who looked at him squarely and said, "How hard it is to accept the truth." Against that drama there was little tension in the roll call which nominated Humphrey and none in the sight of him in the Conrad Hilton kissing the television screen as his wife Muriel appeared on it—a gesture at once authentically ebullient, characteristically awkward, and ludicrously insensitive to what Americans had been watching that night.

The violence continued. At 5 A.M. on Thursday morning the police, convinced they had seen objects thrown at them from the Conrad Hilton's fifteenth floor, stormed up to McCarthy's headquarters and beat dozens of his volunteers. Interviewed on the air by Walter Cronkite, Daley defended his policemen by simply ignoring the fact that so many of them had gone amok. McCarthy went across Michigan Avenue to the grass of Grant Park, quoted Robert Lowell, and made it quite clear he was not going to support Humphrey. Meanwhile, Humphrey chose Maine's laconic Senator Edmund Muskie as his running mate over Senator Fred Harris of Oklahoma. Twenty years before Humphrey had made his national reputation as an orator at the Democratic convention. On Thursday night his speech accepting the party's presidential nomination was upstaged by the Robert Kennedy movie (carefully scheduled by Johnson to follow the balloting, as the John Kennedy movie had been four years before), followed by the galleries singing over and over "The Battle Hymn of the Republic." Humphrey called for reconciliation, but in vain. McCarthy's bitter refusal to support him, the revulsion of so many of his opponents at what had happened inside and outside the hall in Chicago, his own refusal to indicate that his Vietnam policy would differ from Johnson's—these blocked all reconciliation and created a bitterness which would pervade internal Democratic party fights for years.

VIII

Richard Nixon entered the fall campaign with an overwhelming advantage. Voters were appalled by the disorders at the Chicago convention; and while polls quickly showed that overwhelming majorities supported Daley and the Chicago police and blamed the demonstrators, they also associated Humphrey with the disorders which he had plainly been unable to prevent. Nixon got a boost from his convention, as nominees usually do, and in a Gallup poll in early August led Humphrey 45%–29%, with 18% for Wallace. Humphrey got no boost from his convention, and in early September Nixon led 43%–31%–19%. Even worse, Humphrey had unaccountably failed in August to produce either a general election campaign plan (political consultant Joseph Napolitan was typing one up in a Hilton suite as the police went berserk)[39] or a fund-raising operation. Not surprisingly, he stayed at these same low levels as late as late September, when Nixon led 43%–28%–21%.[40]

These figures show the weakness of voters' party identification in the late 1960s and the fierceness of their repudiation of Lyndon Johnson's Democrats: the party which had won 61% of the vote just four years before was now getting about 30%. The regulars blamed McCarthy, but he had a point when he said later that he would take the blame for the last 1% by which the Democrats ultimately lost the election if Johnson and Humphrey would take the blame for the other 17% their party lost in those four years. The leaders who delivered votes for Humphrey in the convention—Johnson, the southern governors, the big-city bosses—were incapable of delivering many votes for him in the general election; labor union leaders turned out to be the one conspicuous exception. A strong argument for the pre-1968 system of selecting presidential delegates is that it vested power in those who were sensitive to voters, capable of understanding what they wanted and of delivering their votes, and who had a stake in the outcome. But in the weak-party-identification, high-ticket-splitting environment of the late 1960s, few state and local Democrats were being held responsible for the record of their party's leaders; and thus few had any stake in who was on the ticket. In fact, 1968 would prove to be in some respects a proincumbent year, an election in which voters chose to keep in office familiar faces of both parties: 396 members of the House were returned to office in the nation's 435 congressional districts, the largest number in history up to that time.[41] Voters chose order and continuity where they could find it.

The strategy which Humphrey ultimately developed assumed that American politics still revolved, or could be made to revolve, around economic class interests. The election showed that this strategy left the Democrats well under 50% of the vote. Income redistribution had little constituency: after four years of antipoverty programs most voters assumed that any money redistributed would come from them and go to people who didn't feel like working, and even Humphrey didn't mention the war on poverty much. Nor did he mention the Democrats' record of fiscal management; for the consensus was that the economy, after one of the longest expansions in history, was in danger of serious inflation. He did have some success winning back union members and blue-collar workers who had flirted with voting for George Wallace by reminding them of the low wages and poor working conditions in Alabama—vestiges of the separate regional economy of the South, which as it happened was starting to grow rapidly in the second half of the 1960s.

But the chief problem with Humphrey's economic appeal was that the prosperity produced by twenty-five years of economic growth had left relatively few Americans with a purely economic grievance. In a country of great geographical, economic, and social mobility, sustained economic growth had produced vast increases in real incomes for those who were maintaining or improving their relative socio-economic status and had kept steady the real incomes even of many who were moving downward on the socioeconomic ladder.[42] The programs Democrats had passed to help ordinary people—Social Security, Medicare, FHA, education aid—were so firmly rooted and popular that they seemed in no danger from Richard Nixon's Republicans. Even with a relatively high 61% of the eligible population voting in November, a percentage only slightly reduced from 1960's 64% (and including many low-income southern blacks who had not been allowed to vote eight years before), the majority of voters had come to see themselves not as working class but as middle class. It was not coincidental that 1968 saw a lapse in the Democrats' not very old tradition of starting the campaign with a rally in Detroit's Kennedy (formerly Cadillac) Square. As one UAW leader put it, "How can you get anyone downtown when they're all out at their cottages or on their boats?" "Because of the great leap forward in economics," Democratic election expert Richard Scammon declared, "economic questions have been eliminated in American politics."[43] The Democrats' economic policies no longer won them votes not only because of their failures but perhaps more because of their successes.

More surprising was Nixon's lack of appeal. In all of Gallup's polling throughout 1968, Nixon never topped 45% in a three-way race;[44] the 43.4% he ultimately ended up with was toward the top rather than the bottom of his range. This for a man and party who had won 49.5% eight years before; it was a showing eerily similar to Thomas Dewey's consistently under-50% poll showings in 1948. As Nixon had been before the convention, so now he was squeezed between two opponents. On one side was Wallace, threatening him in the South; on the other was Humphrey, whose possible willingess to end the war more quickly and greater sympathy for civil rights were assets with many of the voters who had supported Lyndon Johnson in 1964. Nixon's longtime support of an assertive Cold War policy made it difficult for him to sound like a dove on Vietnam; his status as a longtime supporter of civil rights, in the Eisenhower administration and at the 1960 national convention, made it difficult for him to steal away Wallace's votes.

Nixon's response was to run a campaign which was criticized then and later for manipulativeness and lack of content, but which forecast reasonably well the major policies of his administration. His strategists shrewdly arranged their campaign schedule to get the candidate on television in the setting they wanted—often as "the man in the arena," spontaneously answering questions from friendly audiences—and were careful to avoid events or statements which would divert attention from the message they intended to send. On Vietnam, Nixon said very little of substance, professing to want to avoid interfering with the negotiations Averall Harriman was conducting in Paris and hinting only that a new president would be able to bring peace.[45] The Democrats later accused him of claiming to have "a secret plan to end the war," but he never said exactly that, and in fact in office he did end up negotiating and de-escalating the war the Democrats had entered and escalated. He decried disorder and disrespect for the law, high crime rates and riots, but said little about what he would do about these, though he did capitalize on Humphrey's 1966 statement that if he lived in a slum he could "lead a mighty good revolt" himself. About domestic economic issues Nixon also remained mostly silent, except for quickly denouncing federal welfare and antipoverty programs and assuring local audiences he supported their pet programs: a reasonable forecast of his various approaches when in office. He adroitly avoided his 1960 mistake of letting the Democrats frame the issues. If he was capitalizing on the Democrats' weakness on issues both foreign and domestic, he was also presenting information on his own positions which was not misleading or inaccurate. If he was avoiding hostile questions from the press and debates with his opponents, he was under no obligation to present his case in an unfavorable forum.

Nixon could argue, as his 1968 strategist Kevin Phillips did,[46] that his mandate was greater than his vote totals suggested, and that the major reason for the decline from his 1960 showing was the Wallace candidacy; he could point out that most (though not quite all) 1967 polls simultaneously testing pairings with and without Wallace showed most of the Wallace vote coming out of the Republican side.[47] If Wallace had not been a candidate, the argument goes, Nixon would have won almost all his votes and would have won the election easily. This is probably true (though some of Wallace's southern voters would have stayed home in a Nixon–Humphrey race). But Wallace was a candidate, and one who helped set the tone for the fall campaign; and most of the time he was taking votes from Nixon. For a while he was even taking votes away from Humphrey: in the summer his vote was increasing even as Nixon's was holding steady, rising from 14% in June to 16% in July, 18% in August, 19% in early September, and 21% in late September.[48] He shot up in the polls as he denounced those who undermined traditional values, "the pointy-headed bureaucrats" by the Potomac and the Supreme Court justices who hobbled the policeman on the beat, the liberals who upset the order in American life and refused to honor its traditions. He was cheered as he threatened that "if any demonstrator lies down in front of my car when I'm president, that'll be the last car he lays down in front of"; and he denounced "Robert Kennedy, the blood-giver" (a reference to his "bleeding heart" liberalism, evidently) and "that socialist Nelson Rockefeller" and "that left-winger George Romney" and said "there's not a dime's worth of difference in any of 'em, national Democrats or national Republicans."[49] He made special inroads among blue-collar workers and union members, inroads made more conspicuous by the fact that he always won much more support from men than from women: two thirds of his November 1968 voters were men. Thus union political operatives tended to overestimate Wallace support in factories where most of the workers were men because they failed to realize that many of the Wallace supporters' wives did not share their views.

There was some irony to Wallace's appeal. He got cheers and votes from people because he "says it as it really is." But the evidence is that while Wallace may have had strong resentments, he had no strong convictions. He had an instinctive ability to speak voters' language, but his convictions were malleable; it was his ambition that was hard. He was running as a third-party candidate not just to send a message but to become president. And for a moment in late September, when his level of support in polls was approaching Humphrey's and Nixon's was stagnant, he may have believed he actually was going to do so. His advisors hoped and expected he would carry all of the South and several border states, that the electoral college would be deadlocked and that perhaps the House would be, too, at least for a time, that Wallace would not settle the contests but would start a third-party movement which would win (through conversions or ousters) congressional seats and status as a major party for 1972. It was not a totally unrealistic scenario. A 21% national showing would have given him four more states and 46 more electoral votes[50] and would have denied Nixon an electoral-vote majority. The House would then have elected an unpopular Humphrey or no one: in the latter case Muskie, who presumably would have been elected vice president by the still heavily Democratic Senate, would become the president—and one clearly without a mandate.

But Wallace's appeal proved unsustainable. This law and order candidate's campaign showed little respect for the law and seemed less and less orderly as the television cameras focused on it, showing pro-Wallace hecklers beating up spectators and crowds raucously cheering the bantam-sized governor's remarks. Wallace's choice in early October of retired Air Force General Curtis Lemay as his running mate may have been less than inspired; Theodore H. White had the brilliant instinct that this was an instance of an enlisted man's candidate embracing the brass.[51] These mistakes, compounded by the tendency of the electoral college's "unit rule" formula to reduce support for any third-party candidacy, ended up eroding Wallace's support; and in October his percentages declined just as noticeably as they had increased from June through September.

IX

What ultimately moved opinion and changed the shape of the election was not economics but the issue of war and peace. On September 30 in Salt Lake City, Humphrey delivered a speech diverging from administration policy on Vietnam. His suggestion was banal and probably would have been vain: a bombing halt in the hopes that the North Vietnamese would make concessions in response, an approach tried at least eight times by Johnson without appreciable success before the Paris peace talks began. But it was the first instance of Humphrey's actually taking command, making his own decision, stating his own policy, doing something other than quiver in terror that Johnson would be angry with him. Immediately thereafter Humphrey began winning support from hitherto hostile Vietnam doves. More important, he began rising in the polls. By mid-October he was behind Nixon only 44%–36%, with 15% for Wallace[52]—a margin still statistically significant but much less than it had been, and with the Wallace vote perceptibly sinking below the threshold at which any reasonably informed citizen could imagine that he was a real contender for the presidency. The Nixon strategists knew that Humphrey was gaining. But they continued on their strategy of declining to debate (presumably because of the 1960 experience), declining to talk specifically about the war, and presenting their candidate in seemingly unrehearsed but actually carefully controlled and favorable environments on television. They were attacked later, notably in Joe McGiniss's book *The Selling of the President,* for conducting a manipulative campaign. But they were simply trying to present their candidate in a favorable light, understanding, as Nixon's opponents and critics did not, that voters' interest in and attention span for political ideas were limited and that their appetite for extensive debate and voluminous issue papers was almost nonexistent.[53]

Finally, it was the peace issue which nearly turned the election away from Nixon and toward Humphrey. In mid-October the North Vietnamese suggested in the Paris peace conference that they would allow the South Vietnamese into the negotiations—a U.S. goal—if the United States "unconditionally" halted bombing. This offer looked like a formula for getting near an agreement, and by Sunday, October 27, some of it began to be reported. By Tuesday, October 29, a week before the election, it was a major news story. On Thursday, Halloween, Johnson ordered the bombing stopped. This clearly helped Humphrey. Despite the much-publicized divergence between his Vietnam policy and Johnson's, when the administration got closer to an agreement Humphrey benefited.[54] In Gallup's Tuesday-through-Saturday polling he trailed Nixon only 42%–40%; Lou Harris had him ahead the Sunday before the election.[55] Then Americans' desire for peace and an end to their war in Vietnam led enough of them to shift to Humphrey in the last days to almost give him a plurality victory in a three-way election.

The Humphrey–Muskie ticket, made up of two men from the northern tier of the country, made gains along the northern tier and on the West Coast as well, as compared with the Democratic ticket eight years before. Humphrey carried Muskie's Maine and Warren Magnuson's and Henry Jackson's Washington, both of which Kennedy had lost to Nixon; he ran far ahead of Nixon in Minnesota and Michigan and only narrowly lost Wisconsin and Ohio; he ran well ahead of Kennedy's percentage in Massachusetts and the rest of New England. The strength of the culturally liberal, militarily dovish Democrats in the northern tier was established, and would be accentuated even more in the showings of later northern tier–dominated tickets: McGovern–Shriver in 1972, Mondale–Ferraro in 1984, and Dukakis–Bentsen in 1988. At the other extreme of the country, Wallace carried 66% of the vote in Alabama and 63% in Mississippi, and with pluralities carried Louisiana, Georgia, and Arkansas as well; he lost South Carolina to Nixon 38%–32%, Tennessee 38%–34%, and North Carolina 40%–31%. Humphrey carried Texas, 41%–40% over Nixon, because of residual loyalty to Johnson. But otherwise almost all of Humphrey's southern votes were cast by blacks, many of them voting for president for the first time thanks to the Voting Rights Act of 1965. In the Deep South fewer than 10% of whites voted Democratic.

Nixon carried, seldom with absolute majorities, what was in between. He won over 50% in only fourteen of the fifty states, most of them in the Rocky Mountains or the Great Plains; others were New Hampshire and Vermont and the Republican machine state of Indiana. In the big states which were so important in the electoral college in close elections, Nixon failed again to win New York and Pennsylvania and Michigan, and he just missed out in Texas; but he won New Jersey, Ohio, Illinois, Florida (where the real competition was Wallace), and California (despite an electric last-weekend appearance by Humphrey). Nixon eked out a victory which would have been enough (but for his own errors) to give him the presidency for eight years. Yet he did not win it on anything like his own terms. He entered office as a remainderman president, a politician whose appeal was to voters who found the alternatives unpalatable. If Nixon's victory was evidence of, in Kevin Phillips's book title, an emerging conservative majority, Nixon had given neither the voters nor, it seems, himself a clear idea of what his kind of conservatism would mean and how it would cement together a majority.

But if Nixon failed to provide optimal leadership in this most traumatic of election years, other politicians of similar talents did worse. Lyndon Johnson failed either to win or get extricated from the Vietnam war, and his antipoverty programs split the Democratic party while doing little to help the poor. Robert Kennedy failed to challenge Johnson when he could have squarely. Eugene McCarthy retreated into sulky petulance when his own chances to win the presidency vanished, without regard to his followers or his cause. Hubert Humphrey failed to take command of his party or even of his own campaign. George Romney lacked the discipline and knowledge to be a persuasive national candidate. Nelson Rockefeller proved that he could neither be elected nor be removed for any length of time from the race for the Republican nomination. Only Ronald Reagan, who mostly kept himself out of a race he surely could not have won, avoided a serious mistake.

43

—⋙ ⋘—

Polarization

I n claiming victory the day after the November 1968 election, Richard Nixon
poignantly recalled the sign he had seen held up by thirteen-year-old Vicki
Cole at the whistle-stop town of Deshler, Ohio, in October: "Bring Us Together."
Even as he denounced black rioters and student demonstrators, he recognized the
yearning for order and harmony in a disorderly and fractious nation. He was also
acutely conscious that he had won with only 43% of the vote, that he was not
most Americans' first choice for president and in many cases not their second or
third or fourth choice. He hoped, and had some reason to hope, he could make
himself and his policies acceptable to a far larger number.

His problem was that the nation was grievously split, between a majority of the
public who wanted to express attitudes generally known as conservative and a
media and policy elite in Washington and university towns and elsewhere who
wanted to express attitudes generally known as liberal. To be sure, when it came
down to actual policies, there was less difference than there was in rhetoric; but
this was a time when to millions of Americans rhetoric was important. To the
conservative majority who had voted for Richard Nixon and George Wallace it
was important to reaffirm the decency of traditional American values and institutions which had been under staccato attack over the last five years. To the
liberal media and policy elite who had scorned Hubert Humphrey even as they
voted for him it was important to affirm the guilt of America in Vietnam and on
race. Richard Nixon seems to have had a clear sense of these two attitudes and
a rational strategy for bringing them together, and he was able to submerge for a
time the visceral hatred for and paranoid suspicion of the articulate liberals which
was such a driving force in this articulate not-so-conservative politician's career.
He had after all won the election and was taking leadership of a government which
except for the liberal Democratic Senate and the Supreme Court was sympathetic
to his own political ideas; he controlled the Executive Branch, and the Democratic
House had weak Democratic leadership and was controlled on most issues by the
conservative coalition of Republicans and southern Democrats.

Nixon, who had lost elections himself and who prided himself on being able to
see things from his adversaries' point of view, many have understood how for many
Americans the 1968 result did not seem a conclusive repudiation of liberalism.
To these Americans, liberalism seemed a victim not of voters' choices made in

response to major events, but of the awful symmetry of the political assassinations of the 1960s. Just as John Kennedy's murder had left a cloud (undeservedly) over Lyndon Johnson's administration, so Robert Kennedy's assassination left a cloud (undeservedly) over Richard Nixon's. Many Americans, not all of them Kennedy supporters and perhaps even including Nixon himself, who retained a fascination for the Kennedys longer than most Americans,[1] thought that Robert Kennedy might well have beaten Nixon, just as his brother had. Other liberals—McCarthy, Romney, Rockefeller—seemed to have been removed from contention by happenstance or personal idiosyncrasy. The ideas were still very strongly implanted that America was a country with a natural Democratic majority and that, in the political scientists' language, if Americans were ideologically conservative, expressing support for their basic system of government and business, they were operationally liberal, favoring an expanded and generous government to help workers and the poor. From the liberals' point of view the narrowness of Nixon's margin over Humphrey was strong evidence that the 1968 result was just a hideous accident. As for Nixon, he had better reason than most of his supporters to know how tenuous his victories in 1968 were: that although he lacked serious opposition during most of the preconvention period, he was nearly squeezed out in Miami Beach by Reagan and Rockefeller; that although he faced a grievously wounded Democratic nominee in the fall, he was nearly squeezed out in November by Humphrey and Wallace.

II

Who was this politician in the middle? Richard Nixon entered the White House at fifty-five as one of the most experienced of American politicians, and one of the most mistrusted. He had been challenged by early and unexpected victories and humiliated by embarrassing and narrow defeats. He was considered by admirers and detractors as a master of political tactics and as a keen strategic political thinker. Yet before his election to Congress in 1946 his interest in politics had been limited, and his giant steps upward in his early career—the Hiss case, his selection as vice president—had resulted mainly from the acts of others. Both tactically and strategically his handling of the 1960 campaign had been gravely flawed, and his campaign for governor of California had suffered from a flaw which usually proves fatal: the candidate did not particularly want the office he was seeking. Nixon's defenders could point out that from August 1948 until November 1962 he had been subject to attacks as relentless and vitriolic as those on any American politician. But he had failed to rise above the attacks and instead continually responded to them. Sounding often the note of self-pity which was so jarring in the 1960 campaign, he sharply attacked his attackers in ways which fired up his conservative supporters in the short run but did little to enable him to frame issues his way in the long run.

Once out of office and removed from the clamor of political debate, in the (for him) tranquil environment of law practice and luxury living in New York City,

Nixon grew more contemplative and reflective, less reactive and more creative as a political thinker. After an initial stumble, he stayed out of the 1964 campaign, which seemed sure to be disastrous for Republicans; out of the national spotlight, he worked hard for congressional candidates in 1966, which turned out to be a very good year for Republicans. Then, displaying greater self-discipline than he had previously shown, following the course he and his campaign advisors set rather than responding to the initiatives of others, he won the presidency in 1968. By that time he had become known as a conservative—a label he was quicker than most Washington observers to understand was an advantage in the race for the Republican nomination and, at the very least, not a disadvantage in a general election. Yet his own views fluctuated within a rather wide range of possibilities which started to the left of Eisenhower Republicanism on some issues (notably civil rights, for Nixon did not share Eisenhower's feeling that it would be best if blacks would just accept second-class status) and stayed to the left of Reagan Republicanism on most others. On foreign policy, Nixon had always been a Europe First internationalist, like Eisenhower, though he had been critical of the Democrats for losing China and not winning in Korea. On domestic policy, he no more than Eisenhower thought it feasible to repeal most parts of the New Deal; and though he called himself a believer in individualism, he had little sense that the tide toward a larger and more intrusive government could be turned. In 1960 he had been arguing that the Republicans would do about the same things as the Democrats, only a little bit less of them and that more efficiently. In 1968, as he carefully avoided specifics on the emotion-charged issues of war, race, and crime, he got closer to suggesting that Republicans would do different things than the Democrats, but was at best ambiguous about what they would be.

Years later Nixon lamented that his Cabinet members had refused to clean out Democratic appointees and vowed that at the beginning of his second term he would make sure they would do so.[2] But early in his administration he seems to have been genuinely eager to "bring us together." When asked about civil rights policy, campaign-manager-turned-Attorney General John Mitchell cryptically said, "Watch what we do, not what we say." Mitchell, whose dour expression, bald forehead, and pensively puffed pipe gave him the appearance of an old-time conservative, was actually an intimate advisor of politicians as a municipal bond lawyer and had been ingenious and unconservative enough to create for that most expansive of governors, Nelson Rockefeller, the independent public authorities which issued "moral obligation" bonds allowing him to evade limits on public borrowing and fund new projects without getting voter approval.[3] Mitchell's association with Nixon dated only from January 1967, when their law firms merged; and his acquaintance with political conservatives outside the Nixon campaign was limited. When he said "watch what we do," the plain implication was that the administration record would be more favorable to civil rights than candidate Nixon's alliance with Strom Thurmond and criticism of rioters suggested.

Writing later, Nixon tried to create the opposite impression. He quoted himself as telling his newly assembled Cabinet, "In effect, we want to reverse the whole trend of government over the last eight years. We may have only four years in which to do it, so we can't waste a minute." And he claimed that he recognized that he was at odds with the cultural trends of the times: "I was ready to take a stand on these social and cultural issues; I was anxious to defend the 'square' virtues. In some cases—such as opposing the legalization of marijuana and the provision of federal funds for abortions, and in identifying myself with unabashed patriotism—I knew I would be standing against the prevailing social winds, and that would cause tension."[4] Yet in fact he did not always stand against them. On the cultural issues, he made little sustained impact. At home, he increased the size and activity of government. In foreign policy, he disengaged from Vietnam and moved toward negotiated arrangements with the Soviet Union and Communist China. In many ways Nixon turned out to be a liberal president, but one who infuriated liberals in the process. Why?

III

To explain the course of the Nixon years, it is necessary to put this enigmatic president into the larger perspective of the government and politics of his time. The Congress Nixon faced was nominally Democratic, but the two houses differed widely in their politics. The House of Representatives was responsive to the AFL–CIO lobby on economic issues but conservative on cultural and especially on foreign issues, thanks partly to the sentiments of voters and partly to the dead hand of the seniority system.[5] Southern Democrats still held the balance of power on roll-call votes; and Nixon was a shrewd enough vote-counter to keep in touch with their more talented leaders, like Joe Waggoner of Louisiana and Sonny Montgomery of Mississippi. The lead positions on foreign policy and military committees tended to be held by either southerners or veteran representatives from big-city districts, both utterly out of touch and sympathy with the antiwar liberals—Mendel Rivers, Mel Price, Thomas Morgan, Wayne Hays of the coal strip-mining country of eastern Ohio. These men had gone into politics in the World War II years, when the memory of isolationism was fresh; their instinct was to support any administration's foreign, defense, and war policies.

There were auguries of the liberal triumphs of the future in the 1969 special elections to fill vacated seats. In the northern tier states, thirty-three-year-old Democrat David Obey, a legislator since he was twenty-four, was elected in April to replace Defense Secretary Melvin Laird in north-central Wisconsin; Democratic veterinarian John Melcher captured the usually Republican district on the eastern plains of Montana in June; Michael Harrington, a fiery antiwar liberal, was elected in September from the Massachusetts North Shore district which for thirty-two years had elected George and later William Bates, father and son, Pentagon stalwarts on the Armed Services Committee. Even in heavily Republican suburbs, Republicans were on the defensive. Barry Goldwater, Jr., was elected in April with only 57% of the vote against Democratic prosecutor John Van de Kamp, later Los Angeles County district attorney and California attorney general; and in November free-market conservative professor Philip Crane won with only 58% in the North Shore Chicago suburban district vacated by Donald Rumsfeld when he became OEO director. A countervailing trend was the razor-thin 49%–48% November victory of Democrat Robert Roe in heavily Catholic Passaic County, New Jersey. Both Nixon Republicans and Wallace third-party boosters were frustrated in the special election in traditionally segregationist west Tennessee, which was won in March by old-fashioned Democrat Ed Jones (48%) over a Wallace-supported American party candidate (24%) and an administration-supported Republican (23%). Special elections usually favor the party out of power (if only because competent in-party politicoes are scrambling for administration jobs); but these results, as it turned out, were good forecasts for the liberal mid-1970s.

With 57 Democrats and 43 Republicans, the Senate in January 1969 was as heavily Republican as it had been since the Eisenhower years. But it was also more liberal than ever. Freshmen Republican conservatives like Robert Dole of Kansas made little initial impression, and elderly Republican conservatives like Carl Curtis and Roman Hruska of Nebraska had few political skills. Freshman Republican moderates, like Oregon's Bob Packwood, who had upset Wayne Morse, and Mark Hatfield, who had beaten a hawkish Democrat in 1966, attracted more attention: they were news. On the Democratic side, the old conservative southerners were dwindling in number. Harry Byrd of Virginia had resigned in November 1965 and been replaced by his son and namesake, who had none of his clout. Richard Russell of Georgia was ailing; Strom Thurmond of South Carolina was a Republican; Spessard Holland of Florida was preparing to retire; Russell Long of Louisiana, brilliant but erratic, was ousted from his position as Democratic whip in a lightning coup in January 1969 by that other scion of a famous political family, Edward Kennedy. Only John McClellan of Arkansas and James Eastland and John Stennis of Mississippi continued undimmed. The Senate was increasingly a cockpit of presidential ambitions. From the Civil War until the 1960 election, senators had been considered unlikely presidential candidates. Their duties gave them no executive experience, they had few accomplishments to point to, and until 1913 they were not even elected by the voters. But Estes Kefauver in 1952 had shown how a well-publicized senator could run and beat the bosses; and in the next two elections Senators Johnson, Kennedy, and Symington, and former Senator Nixon were major candidates. In 1964 the major contenders included Senator Goldwater and former Senator Johnson, in 1968 Senators Kennedy and McCarthy and former Senator Humphrey. In 1969 about one out of five senators harbored or would harbor presidential ambitions, some plausible, some not.[6]

Among the Senate liberals, most of them Democrats but some Republicans, a new political force was rising: the staff. When Senator Robert Wagner hired Simon Rifkind in 1927, he had one more staffer working on substantive issues than most senators did. By the late 1960s senators had literally dozens of staffers, some of them on their own payrolls, some on the payrolls of the committees they headed or of the subcommittees which proliferated so vigorously that almost every Democratic senator headed at least one and some headed half a dozen. Staffers in the late 1960s were typically young, highly educated, without much adult experience in the everyday world and the middle-class neighborhoods where most Americans spent most of their time—they had all the experiences typical of the mostly young Americans who, stimulated by the civil rights revolution, had come to examine critically all American institutions and were quick to come to the conclusion that they were in need of major reform.

Increasingly staffers tended to drive the work of the Senate.[7] No senator could keep up with the minutiae of the programs Congress had been busy voting to set up. But working with like-minded middle-level employees in the executive branch and with one of the increasing number of non-business lobbyists, a few dedicated staffers could, and did. These so-called Iron Triangles maintained support and appropriations for many programs with minimal political appeal. Mostly liberal, staffers pushed through reform legislation for which, without their efforts, there was no perceptible demand—though in some cases, as with consumer laws, when passed it proved popular. And in January 1969 they were poised to oppose anything they considered backsliding or pandering to bigotry by the Nixon administration. Operating often at the subcommittee level, where few members attend hearings and a skillful chairman armed by staffers with talking points and a well-written report can carry all before him, they had many successes during the Nixon years. Not all were publicized. But the power of the staffer was perhaps best symbolized by what happened when Nixon nominated Judge Harrold Carswell of Florida to the Supreme Court seat for which Clement Haynsworth of South Carolina had been rejected. Most Democratic senators were not eager for another confirmation fight. But James Flug, a staffer for Edward Kennedy, was determined to stop Carswell and shopped around until he found a senator, Birch Bayh of Indiana, to lead the forces against him. That the case against Carswell proved strong was Bayh's good luck and Carswell's bad fortune. But without alert action by a staffer, quite unauthorized by any elected politician, this worse than mediocre judge would have found his way to the Supreme Court more or less unopposed. Instead he was defeated by a 51–45 vote in April 1970.[8]

Another source of liberal pressure in the political system came from an arena which fifteen or twenty years before had seemed dominated by adversaries and critics of the New and Fair Deals: the state governments. In 1969 the governors of the big northern tier states were Republicans who were embarking or were about to embark on what would turn out to be record-setting public spending: Nelson Rockefeller; Francis Sargent, who succeeded John Volpe in Massachusetts; William Milliken, who succeeded George Romney in Michigan. Even Ronald Reagan ended up increasing spending far more substantially than he had contemplated and pushed through a major welfare reform bill which increased payments to recipients while cutting the numbers eligible for those payments.[9] This increased spending was fueled by several sources: the new programs set up by the federal government typically required matching state spending; and the central cities, hurt by population loss and dispersion of the affluent to the suburbs, were sloughing off what spending responsibilities they could on the states. Nor was the liberalism of state governments limited to economic issues. Rockefeller and (much to his later regret) Reagan signed liberalized abortion laws which were among the most sweeping of the sixteen such laws passed, in states with 41% of the nation's population, in the five years preceding January 1973. Milliken and Sargent conspicuously favored such laws, in states where there was strong opposition to them not only from prelates of the Roman Catholic Church, which considers abortion murder, but among Democratic legislators with heavily Catholic constituencies. Nixon Republicans were cheered by their party's capture of the two governorships up in November 1969, but both new governors proved to be liberals in the context of their states—William Cahill of New Jersey a big spender, Linwood Holton of Virginia a firm integrationist—and no Republican of similar ilk was nominated for governor in either state for years.

Southern states saw little of this liberal trend until after the election of 1970 (the exception was Arkansas, where Republican Winthrop Rockefeller made support of desegregation politically acceptable). And in the Civil War borderlands and the practical-minded central belt from Pennsylvania to Missouri, liberal forces made less headway. But in every state one influence was present: the redistricting of state legislators. Redistricting had been forced finally by a Supreme Court decision of June 1964, and the efforts of Senator Everett Dirksen to get Congress to propose a constitutional amendment authorizing legislative districts of unequal population was foiled in the Senate. Politically, the result was that certain houses long reserved for one party by old formulas were now opened up to competition, and so tended to attract better members: these included the eternally Republican and outstate-dominated Michigan Senate and the eternally Democratic and northern-dominated California Senate. In the larger and more legislatively active states, the trend was to the Democrats; and the practical effect was to remove any brake on spending from upstate, downstate, and outstate Republican county-seat lawyers.

At the same time, big-city mayors—almost all liberals—remained important figures politically and governmentally. John Lindsay, the glamorous liberal Republican mayor of New York, compared over and over since his first run in 1965 to John Kennedy, considered presidential material despite his clear failure to understand ordinary middle-class Americans, was defeated for renomination in the Republican primary in September 1969; but as the nominee of the moribund Liberal party, the favorite still of the *New York Times,* and the beneficiary of the unfitness of Democrat Mario Procaccino, he was reelected anyway in November. Richard J. Daley was still extremely popular in Chicago. In Los Angeles, Councilman Thomas Bradley, a black former police officer, took 42% of the vote to conservative Mayor Sam Yorty's 26% in the city's first nonpartisan primary in March 1969. But in the runoff Yorty summoned up racial fears and won 54%–46%. Other well-known mayors at this time were articulate liberals like Jerome Cavanagh of Detroit (who retired, squeezed between blacks and anti-black whites, in 1969) and Kevin White of Boston or faithful Democrats like James H. J. Tate of Philadephia and Joseph Alioto of San Francisco. None except Daley and Tate depended on old-fashioned political machines and patronage politics. Others maneuvered adroitly between black and white voting blocs and appealed to voters directly through the mass media of metropolitan newspapers and local television news.

Back in Washington, the Republicans who came in to run the Nixon administration were confronted with a new phenomenon, also predominantly liberal: the public interest organization. Influenced by the success of the civil rights movement, new organizations were sprouting up in these years. Common Cause was set up in a huge direct-mail campaign in September 1970 by John Gardner, the liberal Republican who had been Johnson's secretary of health, education and welfare, and concentrated on reforming the electoral and other political processes. Environmental groups, some headed by charismatic young gurus and others by hard-charging lawyers, opposed dams, strip mining, the Alaska oil pipeline, the cross-Florida barge canal, and all manner of other economic interferences with the environment. And the clusters of organizations started by the reclusive and workaholic Ralph Nader sought such varied goals as auto safety and sterner antitrust laws, deregulation of industries like railroads and trucking where government helped to prop up prices, and increased regulation of industries which make consumer products, from non-prescription drugs to toys. Nader urged free-market principles where government, business, and unions had ganged up to prop up prices and wages; he urged government regulation almost to the point of control where he thought businesses were harming individuals' health or the environment.

All these groups, like the civil rights movement, applied an abstract, neat logic to the concrete and disorderly world they saw around them. They were asking the country to live up to its ideals and were disgusted at the practical arrangements which well-positioned groups had gone along with to get along.[10] In their emphasis on process over results and their concern for theory over facts, in their lack of connection with the vast masses of America (except through the medium of direct mail, which enabled them to find their constituency in a geographically vast and culturally increasingly various country) and their fervent opposition to the traditional lobbying forces which claimed with varying plausibility to represent the interests of those masses, these groups looked something like the Progressive reformers of the years just after the turn of the century. Some of them seemed to have a Republican tinge as well. Common Cause emphasized Gardner's Republican affiliation (though he had never had much to do with Republican politicians), and it was widely publicized that the Ralph Nader group reporting critically on Lyndon Johnson's Federal Trade Commission included Edward Finch Cox, a young lawyer from an old and rich New York family who in June 1971 married President Nixon's daughter Tricia. Many of this report's recommendations were followed by Nixon's FTC director, a former California assemblyman and top aide to Governor Reagan named Caspar Weinberger. But this Republican opening was the exception rather than the rule. The Naderites found most of their political allies in the ranks of the Democrats, and the Democrats found many of their political causes of the 1970s from the agenda of the Naderites.

IV

So Richard Nixon, despite his victory in 1968 and his high—over 60%—job approval ratings in 1969, did have reason to believe that he was operating in a less than hospitable political environment and that the strength of his adversaries was great. And the issues which were central to the political struggles of the time were not the traditional issues of economic redistribution, which had become routinized and drained of emotional content; they were cultural issues which excited Americans' passions far beyond their practical effects. Whose country was this anyway? Was it the country of those who insisted that the Vietnam war was immoral and that established ways of governing were illogical and immoral? Or was it the country of those who in time of disorder, when neighborhoods and families were threatened, stood up and reaffirmed the essential goodness of traditional American ways of doing things? This was a struggle for legitimacy, a struggle in which each side asserted that its view of the nation, and of the 1968 election, was correct and the other's side wrong. The critics of traditional American society felt that they had prevailed in 1968 but had been robbed of their victory. The defenders of traditional American mores felt that they had won and clearly represented the majority. The struggle was bitter because each side had some basis for its belief and because each had reason to fear that the other side was stronger.

What neither side appreciated or could feel sure of was that Americans of such different views could live at peace with each other in the same country. Americans in the late 1960s were used to the cultural unity which had been the norm when the very large majority of Americans shared the experiences of depression and war. They assumed that cultural unity was the natural state of their society, and that one side or the other—the angry critics of American society and its angrier, though less articulate, defenders—must succeed in establishing its cultural attitudes as the sole legitimate ones. The question seemed to be who would impose their life style on others. What neither side fully understood was that they could coexist. America was not just one country any more; it was not even, as the Kerner Commission said, two countries, one black and one white. After more than two decades of mostly peace and mostly prosperity, the United States had become many countries, a land of cultural variety, where people were free to hold sharply different values and develop radically different life styles. Those who cut their hair short and wore flag pins in their lapels could live with those who let their hair and beards grow and wore blue jeans; they could argue, in political forums, over political issues, including the war, but there was no need to resolve their cultural differences, no necessity that one side prevail.

While the divisive political issues persisted and both sides remained wary that the other was invading their space,[11] there were loud cries of discord in the air.

But when the political issues were settled, and as it became clear that different kinds of Americans could live in proximity to one another, the cries would quiet down and the fighters would settle down to cultivating their gardens.

It is against this background that the Nixon years—the president's initial desire to bring Americans together and his subsequent failure to do so—must be seen. For a politician whose whole career had taken place in the culturally unified America which existed in the years after World War II, bringing the country together seemed not only an achievable task, but a desirable one. Those who identified with business and labor might disagree about the amount of the minimum wage or the size of the Steelworkers' settlement; but on the major issues which cut to the quick of people's lives there should be a consensus which would be widely, almost universally, shared, if a politician were wise enough to point the way and well disciplined enough to stay on course. As he entered office, Nixon understood that he had been an unusually divisive figure for most of his career, and he must have retained privately the exquisite sensitivity to the aspersions of his opponents which was so apparent for the first two decades of his career. But during the campaign and the first months of his presidency he avoided expressing those feelings, and during the most calamitous presidential election year in American history he managed to campaign with a dignity and a discipline which no other candidate achieved in 1968.

But was the unity Nixon sought really achievable? Was it possible to unite a country increasingly divided along cultural lines, in which different kinds of Americans reacted to events in quite different, and often diametrically opposed, ways? It is not clear that the answers to these questions in 1969 and the years just after had to be no. But it also seems clear that the task Richard Nixon set himself was more difficult than all his years of experience in politics made it seem.

V

Certainly for his Cabinet Nixon did not choose appointees who seemed inclined "to reverse the whole trend of government." The ranks of experts on public policy contained few admirers of free-market economics or of an assertive foreign policy; in Washington the phrase "conservative intellectual" seemed very much an oxymoron. The incoming Republican president in 1969, as in 1953, looked reflexively to the chief executives of big corporations to handle the top Cabinet jobs. But Nixon appointed several canny politicians as well. If he made the head of the Continental Illinois Bank his first Treasury secretary, he also appointed William Rogers, who had once been a top Nixon staffer and Eisenhower's attorney general, secretary of state; and he had the wit to appoint a politician, Congressman Melvin Laird, as defense secretary and former governors George Romney and John Volpe to domestic positions.

Even more important, for all his conservative talk later Nixon named as his two chief White House policy advisors two Harvard professors whom he hardly knew and whose political associations had been with Rockefeller Republicans and Kennedy-Harriman-Wagner Democrats. For his national security advisor he picked Henry Kissinger, evidently because of his performance in one interview. Like most foreign policy experts, Nixon was familiar with Kissinger's writings, well known since his 1957 best seller *Nuclear Weapons and Foreign Policy;* and he knew that Kissinger was not a unilateral disarmer or a Vietnam dove. The whole thrust of Nelson Rockefeller's foreign policy, which Kissinger had done much to shape, was toward more defense spending. Nixon knew this as an intraparty adversary, from those days in 1959 and 1960 when liberal Republicans like Rockefeller and Democrats like John Kennedy called for big increases in defense spending, which President Eisenhower firmly opposed and conservatives in the Robert Taft tradition were dubious about.

As his chief White House advisor on domestic affairs Nixon chose Daniel Patrick Moynihan, also a Harvard professor and assistant secretary of labor in the Kennedy and Johnson administrations. To be sure, Moynihan was not a stereotypical liberal. In his pungent prose he could quote English lords; but he also could talk of a boyhood in Manhattan's gritty Hell's Kitchen neighborhood, of being brought up by a mother abandoned by her husband, and of enlisting at seventeen in the Navy. If he was a font of liberal ideas, he usually spouted them inconveniently early and in inconveniently unorthodox terms. In the 1950s, for example, he was writing about how the death toll from auto accidents could be reduced—nearly a decade before Ralph Nader was under surveillance from General Motors detectives and published *Unsafe at Any Speed.* In March 1965 he wrote a description of the breakup of black family life in his report *The Negro Family: The Case for National Action,* for which he was roundly excoriated by blacks and liberal whites[12]—almost two decades before the problem of black single-parent underclass families was finally acknowledged to be one of American society's greatest public problems.[13] Nixon was surely correct in seeing in Moynihan as in Kissinger not only a powerful mind but an original one. Most of the policies which later conservatives would excoriate— which they would campaign against—from the Nixon years were the product of Kissinger and Moynihan. What Nixon was apparently hoping was that these two intellectuals, with their professional base and personal connections in Cambridge— the city Nixon regarded above all others as the home of his enemies—could devise policies which would help bring the country together, around a successful Nixon presidency.

VI

It was not to happen, partly because Nixon's adversaries, the liberals in the Democratic party and the media, having been disappointed by the policies of Lyndon Johnson, whom they had strongly backed, were now acutely sensitive to the possibility that they would be deceived in the policies of Richard Nixon, whom they had for years disliked and mistrusted. They bellowed with rage when he undertook an initiative which they opposed, and they watched suspiciously and sullenly when his administration did things which they approved.

An early example was the response to the Santa Barbara oil spill in February 1969, when an underwater oil platform ruptured off the coast of California and the beaches and sea birds of one of America's richest communities were coated with oil. Nixon's interior secretary, Walter Hickel, a former Alaska governor and hotel developer who had been attacked in Congress for being insufficiently interested in preserving the environment, flew over the spill in a helicopter and pledged to stop the drilling in the Santa Barbara Channel. As it turned out, Hickel was probably more aggressive in protecting the environment than Kennedy's and Johnson's interior secretary, Stewart Udall, who had been operating in a climate of opinion in which environmentalism was much weaker. But more vivid, especially to many young voters, than that record was the memory of the newscast footage showing the oil slick and the coated birds, illustrating what damage business was doing to nature.

If the burgeoning environmental movement left a large bloc of voters focused on issues which little concerned the Nixon-Wallace majority, the continuing student demonstrations polarized Americans. Some cheered the springtime rebels as demonstrations broke out in April and May 1969 at Harvard, the City College of New York, and San Francisco State College. Others cheered San Francisco State's president, the beret-capped semanticist S. I. Hayakawa, as he climbed on top of a student sound truck and pulled the plugs on the loudspeakers. A more serious issue which polarized Nixon and his political adversaries was the anti-ballistic missile. In March 1969, when he announced that he was building a bigger ABM system than had been approved by Robert McNamara, Nixon aroused a storm of protest from Democratic arms control experts and from Democratic politicians as well—only a few of whom had murmured any opposition to McNamara's defense buildups over the years. In the end Nixon came very close to the humiliation of having an administration's weapon system voted down by the Senate—something which had not happened since the days of neutrality before World War II. Most northern Democrats, with the conspicuous exception of Henry Jackson, rallied around the arms control experts who believed that building a nuclear defense would undermine the Soviet Union's confidence in its ability to retaliate and hence produce a more unstable world; they were able to win support from most Democrats and many Republicans in the Senate, and in August the administration prevailed on the key ABM vote by a 50–50 tie. Ironically, that was the same month that Nixon started using the word "détente" to describe U.S.–Soviet relations. But neither his opponents nor the media paid anything like the attention they had to the highly visible ABM fight when Nixon began the SALT (strategic arms limitation) talks with the Soviets and signed the Nuclear Non-Proliferation Treaty or when he came out in November 1969 for a treaty limiting chemical and biological weapons—even though each of these represented genuine moves toward arms control beyond Johnson administration policies.

Polarization on domestic issues began in earnest in May 1969, when Nixon was presented with the windfall of a Supreme Court appointment after Justice Abe Fortas, a Johnson intimate, was forced to resign because he had taken money from a foundation headed by Miami businessman Louis Wolfson.[14] The year before, when Johnson had been a lame duck, Fortas's nomination to succeed Earl Warren as chief justice had been sidetracked by the dogged opposition of Michigan's Senator Robert Griffin, who never unearthed any really damaging charges but played on the accurate perceptions that Fortas's liberal jurisprudence was similar to Warren's and that he was close personally and politically to Johnson. As a result Nixon had been able to appoint Warren Burger, a one-time Minnesota political lieutenant of Harold Stassen, in Warren's place. That had not been a controversial appointment, despite Nixon's campaign rhetoric promising a court of "strict constructionists" and despite Burger's own contentious record on the District of Columbia Circuit Court of Appeals, where he had differed sharply from liberal colleagues David Bazelon and J. Skelly Wright.

But now Nixon stirred controversy by his determination to appoint a southern conservative to a seat held for thirty years by Jewish liberals. Nixon's nominee, Clement Haynsworth, was a craftsmanlike judge from South Carolina, untainted by any scandal and possessing a record of nothing more than the perfunctory support for racial segregation which every man of his generation in public life in the Deep South had to express. But South Carolina was Strom Thurmond's state; and so Nixon's critics associated Haynsworth with Thurmond's bitter opposition to civil rights, though Haynsworth was not at all a Thurmond protégé. And a painstaking investigation of his record over the summer provided a basis for a charge that he heard an appeal on a case in which he owned some shares of stock in one of the parties. Improbably and unfairly, the Senate rejected his nomination 55–45 in November. Ironically, in the meantime the eight-member panel now known as the Burger Court continued the trend of the Warren Court's desegregation decisions, calling in an October decision, *Alexander* v. *Holmes County Board of Education,* finally making an effective end of dual systems of black and white schools.

Civil rights also produced polarization, even though Nixon did not reverse national policy despite his campaign rhetoric suggesting a halt to civil rights advances. In October 1969 his labor secretary, George Shultz, even approved a "Philadelphia plan" to integrate the building trades union which required what was called a goal but was pretty clearly intended to be a quota of black membership. The building trades typically had union hiring halls from which contractors, whatever the law said, had to hire their workers. Like police and fire departments, they were father-and-son institutions, in which openings were advertised by word of mouth and coveted positions handed down to friends and relatives: not only were blacks excluded, but so were most whites not part of the in-group. These folkways were tolerated in the confident and economically growing America in the years after World War II; they suddenly started seeming terribly unfair after the civil rights revolution. The building trades were well represented on the AFL–CIO executive board—George Meany himself was from the plumbers' union—and they were well connected in Congress. Despite the Philadelphia plan, Nixon was criticized in many quarters for not enforcing civil rights laws vigorously enough; there was a flurry of protest, for example, when HEW civil rights office head Leon Panetta, then a Republican and after 1976 a Democratic congressman from California, resigned in 1970. But in fact it was under Nixon that first the executive branch and then the Congress explicitly endorsed what amounted to a racial quota (though they were careful not to call it that) to enforce civil rights laws which said that selection according to race was illegal.

VII

Not every event of 1969 was polarizing. In July, Neil Armstrong stepped off the Apollo 11's lunar landing module and became the first man on the moon. Thus was fulfilled John Kennedy's promise, which had seemed so rash when it was made in May 1961, to put a man on the moon before 1970. Obviously most of the work which made the moon landing possible was done long before Nixon became president, but he did get to preside over the event.

Two days before, as the nation was watching Apollo 11 head toward its destination, Nixon's claim on national leadership had been strengthened by a very different event. Senator Edward Kennedy, on a weekend outing in Martha's Vineyard, drove his car off a bridge to Chappaquiddick Island; Mary Jo Kopechne, a twenty-eight-year-old staffer and campaign aide who had been a passenger, was drowned. Kennedy's failure to call the police immediately and his changing stories—some crafted with the help of famous Kennedy wordsmiths—destroyed confidence in the man who, at thirty-six, had come close to being drafted to run for president at the Chicago convention. Before the accident, he had been considered sure to be the Democratic nominee in 1972, and not just by Nixon, who after 1960 was always haunted by the Kennedys. In January he had upset Russell Long for the office of Democratic whip; and in pre-Chappaquiddick polls for the 1972 nomination he led Humphrey and Muskie 45%–21%–17%. He was favorably regarded by 71% of the voters, who by a 47%–34% margin they said they'd like to see him as president some day. Nixon led Kennedy 52%–34% in May, but for an incumbent president to run only just above 50% at a time when his job approval rating was 61%–11% positive was not entirely reassuring.[15] Kennedy's standing in the polls did not entirely collapse after Chappaquiddick; he retained a large following. But Nixon led him 53%–31%, and he ran no better than in the middle, between Humphrey and Muskie, in what amounted to a three-way tie among Democrats, 29%–27%–24%.[16] Although no one could be sure at the time, Edward Kennedy's chances to win the presidency had vanished.

VIII

One of the most startling developments of the first Nixon years was the continued growth of the youth counterculture. It was almost totally unexpected in a society in which each generation of parents resembles the previous one in only one respect: in its assumption that its children will replicate its own experience, an assumption which invariably proves wrong. If the existence of the counterculture was proclaimed most visibly in San Francisco's Haight-Ashbury district in the summer of 1967, its emblematic event was the Woodstock rock festival of August 1969. Some 250,000 people, almost all young, clad in blue jeans (or less), smoking marijuana or using other drugs in many cases, congregated at Max Yasgur's farm in Bethel, New York, to hear a concert originally scheduled for the considerably trendier town of Woodstock, some 50 miles away. Even so, the concert made the name of several entertainers. Woodstock gave its name to a generation.

The counterculture was also on display in the Chicago Seven trial which began in September 1969 and lasted through February 1970. This was a kind of show trial, a case brought against seven men, mostly highly visible—Abbie Hoffman, Rennie Davis, Tom Hayden, David Dellinger, and Black Panther Bobby Seale—for inciting to riot at the 1968 Democratic convention. The defendants, except perhaps for Hoffman, had played only minor parts or none at all in Chicago in 1968; and the rioting there was as much the result of abuse of power by the police. The provocative conduct of radical defense lawyers William Kunstler and Arthur Kinoy, together with the progovernment bias and, worse, ham-handedness of Judge Julius Hoffman, who ordered Seale bound and gagged in the courtroom after several outbursts, combined to make triply polarizing this trial—this woebegone case which never should have been brought by the government, which never should have been defended against so provocatively, and which never should have been mishandled as it was by the judge.

Yet the idea was spreading that the counterculture, which could not even provide sanitary facilities for the instant city it caused to come into existence at "Woodstock," was the wave of the future. The idea was spread most convincingly by Charles Reich, a law professor at Yale known there for his practice of giving all his students A's. In December 1969, the first installment of what became his book *The Greening of America* appeared prominently in the *New Yorker*. "There is a revolution coming," Reich wrote. "It will not be like revolutions of the past. It will originate with the individual and with culture, and it will change the political structure only as its final act. It will not require violence to succeed, and it cannot be successfully resisted by violence. It is now spreading with amazing rapidity, and already our laws, institutions and social structure are changing in consequence. It promises a higher reason, a more human community, and a new and liberated individual. Its ultimate creation will be a new and enduring wholeness and beauty—a renewed relationship of man to himself, to other men, to society, to nature, and to land."[17] What is interesting about this moony Rousseauian theory-spinning, reminiscent with its talk of "community" of the adolescent yearnings at the heart of the Port Huron Statement which Tom Hayden wrote to begin Students for a Democratic Society in June 1962,[18] is that it was taken so seriously by so many sensible grown-ups. *The Greening of America* was a best seller, spoken of in reverent tones, hailed as the harbinger of a new era—when it was nothing more than a fluently written piece of adolescent theorizing.[19]

A "silent majority" of Americans, in Nixon's later phrase, were not persuaded by the Chicago Seven trial or *The Greening of America* that the American political or economic systems were fundamentally rotten. But many Americans were, and those who were not found themselves on the defensive, feeling compelled to defend institutions which had not performed flawlessly—indeed, about whose flaws they had their own complaints—and to counterattack against those they saw as destructive to society as they knew it. And so, well before the end of Nixon's first year in office, the country whose leader said he wanted to "bring us together" was once again, after the briefest and perhaps most deceptive of intervals, deeply and troublingly polarized.

44

->>> <<<-

Incursion

In this increasingly polarized country, Nixon came forward with two major policy initiatives, one foreign and one domestic, each produced by one of the two Harvard professors he had brought into the two highest policy positions in the White House. Both could be considered liberal policies, logical advances of liberal critiques of the Johnson years: the Vietnamization of the Vietnam war and the Family Assistance Plan to provide a guaranteed annual income for the poor. Yet both were opposed, vociferously and with great animosity, by liberals—almost unanimously in the case of Vietnamization, and in just large enough numbers to defeat the program in the case of guaranteed income.

The first was the Vietnamization policy hammered out by Nixon and Henry Kissinger and announced to the public in a much-heralded speech by Nixon on November 3, 1969. Nixon's negotiating position was not strong. He sought from the North Vietnamese the same kind of agreement Johnson had, and got the same results. He began secret bombing of Cambodia in March 1969 to get at North Vietnamese units there, but he declined for months to bomb North Vietnam for fear the Communists would leave the Paris peace talks.[1] His insistence that the United States was committed to the South Vietnamese was undermined by his announcements in June that 25,000 U.S. troops were being withdrawn, in July that the United States would not again send troops to Asia to defend its allies (the so-called Nixon Doctrine), and in September that another 35,000 troops would be withdrawn in December. His stepped-up bombing of North Vietnam in October, accompanied by an ultimatum demanding concessions by November 1, received the same non-response Johnson's bombing had. He was evidently trying to follow the advice both of Defense Secretary Laird, who as a seasoned politician insisted that Americans must be withdrawn from Vietnam, and National Security Advisor Kissinger, who as a geopolitical strategist insisted that the United States should not be seen as having been defeated and must withdraw in a way which would give the South Vietnamese a chance to win—or at least "a decent interval" before they were destroyed. Nixon insisted to Republican congressmen that "I will not be the first president of the United States to lose a war" and pointedly declared that "under no circumstances will I be affected whatever" by the Moratorium protests scheduled for October 15. But these declarations succeeded only in enraging his opponents at home without impressing his opponents in Hanoi.

The Moratorium represented a new escalation of antiwar activity, based on the idea that massive demonstrations would be held the 15th of every month until the war was over. Sympathetic federal and other workers were urged to stay away from work. The organizers believed that antiwar activists had ousted Johnson and had then been cheated of the complete withdrawal from Vietnam which they believed voters had endorsed. So they were determined to make it impossible for Nixon to govern unless he ended the war as promptly as they wished. It was, as Nixon said, an attempt to set national policy "not at the ballot box, but through confrontation on the streets."[2] At the same time, the organizers enlisted the support of many mainstream Democrats, who with Johnson out of office were now free to oppose the war; these included former Paris peace negotiator Averell Harriman, former UN ambassador and Supreme Court Justice Arthur Goldberg, and Coretta Scott King, widow of Martin Luther King, Jr.

As David Broder of the *Washington Post,* the country's premier political reporter for more than two decades, argued, the Moratorium was profoundly antidemocratic, an attempt to bypass the electoral process and to make public policy by mass demonstration. The implications for anyone who remembered the history of Europe in the 1930s were chilling. But few Americans, and none of the men and women in their twenties who organized and marched in the demonstrations, had vivid memories of such events. They believed that the Vietnam war was profoundly immoral and that American involvement had worsened the lives of the Vietnamese; and they were fortified by journalism and books which argued that the mass of South Vietnamese favored the Viet Cong, that the Viet Cong was independent of North Vietnam's Ho Chi Minh, and that Ho Chi Minh was a nationalist not dominated by the Soviets or Chinese, who would rule benignly if his forces were successful—analyses which were all cruelly refuted by events after the final Communist victory in April 1975. The Moratorium supporters scoffed at any analogy between the Vietnamese Communists and Adolf Hitler's Nazis and the argument that Ho Chi Minh should not be appeased any more than Hitler should have been. They tended instead to see themselves in a position analogous to that of Hitler's domestic opponents (one law professor wrote a book entitled *Nuremberg and Vietnam)*[3] and thought they had a duty to oppose an immoral policy of their own government, if necessary using the same technique of protest by civil disobedience which had been so successful in ending the immoral policy of racial segregation just a few years before. Fortifying these feelings was the news of the My Lai massacre, a story exposed not by a major newspaper or magazine but by one of those alternative journals which had sprung up in the late 1960s, in articles by Seymour Hersh, a free-lance investigative reporter who had served briefly as press secretary in Eugene McCarthy's campaign. In late November 1969, My Lai got great national publicity, as the Army charged Lieutenant William Calley—a southerner, clearly not very competent, a symbol for war opponents of all which was wrong with the American military—of leading the massacre of Vietnamese civilians. His trial would go on for months, with extensive television coverage, even as the number of American troops in Vietnam was being reduced.

The first Moratorium went splendidly, attracting hundreds of thousands of supporters around the country as well as support from eminent leaders and many in the news media. Nixon's response on November 3 was to swear that the United States would keep its commitment in Vietnam—and to announce a slow but, as it turned out, steady continuation of the withdrawal of American troops. The South Vietnamese who had put their lives on the line by fighting with Americans ought not to be abandoned instantly, he said; he hoped that given some training and the motivation supplied by the knowledge the Americans were leaving, they might summon up the morale to prevail against the Communists. This speech did not satisfy the antiwar protesters, who planned another Moratorium for November 15. But it did give Nixon solid majorities in Congress on the issue and pleased the "silent majority" he explicitly appealed to. They were pleased as well by the rhetoric composed by combative speechwriter Patrick Buchanan and delivered by Spiro Agnew on November 13, denouncing the instant analyses and bias of the television networks. Gallup reported 77% approval of Nixon's Vietnam policy. Though Americans called themselves doves rather than hawks by a 55%–31% margin, they also opposed immediate U.S. withdrawal from Vietnam by a 74%–21% margin.[4]

The November 15 Moratorium again attracted 250,000 protesters to Washington, and a few burned the American flag. Yet the Moratorium movement quickly lost momentum. In early December the government started a new draft lottery, which theoretically made college students as well as non-students subject to the draft. The student exemption, supposedly intended to maximize the quality of the nation's civilian manpower, made little sense in a time when the casualty rates in Vietnam were small compared with the size of the huge Baby Boom age cohorts coming into draft years; and the differing treatment of college and non-college students in the Johnson years had contributed to the polarization of American society and prevented the growth of any sense that the entire nation was embarked together on a war. At the same time, the fact that students were subject to the draft on leaving school, even at an age which was older than the military preferred for inductees, contributed to the fervor with which students opposed the war. Nixon apparently understood that. One aim of his Vietnamization policy was to reduce draft calls, and the draft lottery was structured in such a way that on its completion most young men in the age group covered could be sure they would not be called.

So the lottery probably contributed to the fact that the December 15 Moratorium elicited a far smaller response than the demonstration the month before; also, the weather was colder, and it was apparent that the government was not to be moved. Nixon, like Johnson, was embarked on a Vietnam policy which was popular at the outset, as Americans literally rallied around the flag. But Nixon knew as Johnson had not that he would be held accountable for success at the end of the quadrennial political cycle—and that success, for most Americans, meant less a victory against Communism than an American extrication from Vietnam. And much earlier than Johnson, Nixon was matched with a hostile though momentarily quiet antiwar movement which was strong not just on campuses but in the Democratic party and in the Senate.

II

Nixon's State of the Union message in January 1970 might have been written by a liberal Democrat. The nation's first priority, he said, was to end the war in Vietnam. The nation also needed to do more to ensure equality of opportunity, said the Nixon who had supposedly waged a southern strategy in 1968; and, he went on in the accents of those critics of process who had come to dominate American public thought on so many issues, the nation needed to be more responsive to citizens' needs. Finally, he said, the nation needed to guarantee a minimum annual income to all its citizens.

Hardly anyone had expected this message from Richard Nixon—or would have expected it from Hubert Humphrey, for that matter. It was widely expected, by supporters and opponents alike, that Nixon would dismantle Great Society programs. But he did not abolish the Office of Economic Opportunity but allowed it to become a launching pad for former Congressman Donald Rumsfeld, a young and aggressive Ivy League graduate from the North Shore suburbs of Chicago. The Model Cities program, an obvious candidate for extinction even if Humphrey had won, was kept by Nixon simply because he feared the response from the media if he abolished it.[5] And Nixon proposed a guaranteed annual income—the only president in American history to do so.

This generous promise, never dreamed of by Johnson, was mainly the work of Daniel Patrick Moynihan. It marked a convergence of ideas coming from two very different directions. On the one hand, supporters of the Great Society were dismayed by the incompleteness of its success. Poverty had been substantially reduced since the middle 1960s, probably more because of economic growth than because of antipoverty programs. But some poverty remained, including a large underclass made up most visibly of black welfare mothers; and the apparatus of community action agencies, designed as parallel political structures to the city governments and any remaining political machines, had obviously failed to produce the idealistic and effective leaders the antipoverty theorists had argued must exist in the ghettos and slums. Government is not a very good agent for changing people's lives, critics like Moynihan said, but it can give them more money. From quite a different source came support for the same idea. Professor Milton Friedman of the University of Chicago, a believer in free markets in an age of Keynesians, had long been regarded by most economists as a crank, a worthy historian of banking and money supply perhaps, but an impossibly impractical advocate of free-market solutions for every problem. Undaunted by this criticism, Friedman applied his free-market ideas to the problem of poverty, arguing that if the government was going to impose an income tax on people with incomes above a certain amount, it should remit money to people with incomes below a certain amount: a negative income tax.

Both Great Society and free-market advocates of the guaranteed income had to answer the question indignantly posed by ordinary voters: if you pay people not to work, won't many more people just not work? The Great Society social scientists devised guaranteed income experiments which they hoped would prove the non-existence of work incentives;[6] Friedman blithely replied that at every income level under his proposal, the market would reward greater work effort, so logically there could be no disincentive. In the White House, Moynihan admitted that the question was troubling. But he went ahead anyway and prepared a Family Assistance Program (FAP) which Nixon publicly unveiled in August 1969. It provided $1,600 a year for a family of four with no income, assistance of more than $1,000 a year to such a family with $2,000 in income, a little less than $1,000 a year to such a family with $3,000 in income—in other words, lower payments as incomes approached the poverty line. Median household income in 1968, by comparison, was $7,400.

Before August 1969, the only members of Congress sponsoring bills for a guaranteed income were those on the far left of the House, like William Fitts Ryan, the Reform Democrat from the Upper West Side of Manhattan, and John Conyers, Jr., an angry critic of existing policies who represented Twelfth Street in Detroit. Now it was the policy of a Republican and supposedly a conservative administration. Nixon understood that his proposal went against the grain of his own constituency, and mused about himself as a twentieth-century American Disraeli, the British Conservative whose Reform bill of 1867 enfranchised more voters than the Liberals would have; in this train of thought he was greatly encouraged by the Anglophile Moynihan, who quotes him as saying, "Tory men and Liberal policies are what have changed the world."[7] In Congress, FAP initially lacked a coherent constituency. The Democrats most prone to redistributing income—Conyers, for one; Eugene McCarthy, desultorily, was another—mistrusted Nixon, noting that he insisted his proposal was not a guaranteed income (once again, Nixon's rhetoric made opponents of those to whose policies he had moved closer than anyone expected). They called for a much higher guaranteed income, and some wanted benefits for families already making as much as $5,500 a year—an extension which would have covered a huge percentage of American families.[8] Republicans were of mixed views. Those based in small towns and rural areas tended to be skeptical, especially the man who turned out to be FAP's greatest obstacle in the Senate Finance Committee: John Williams, a chicken farmer from Millsboro, Delaware. Since the Truman years he had made a name as a nit-picker on corruption issues; and as Moynihan put it, his "prime concern was that citizens derive as little financial gain as possible from government, whether by theft, welfare, bribery, or whatever."[9] The greatest support came from Republican liberals responsive to the giant corporations and great foundations, who were favorable; from some Democrats of similar mind; and from the Republican-leaning media (including *Fortune* and the *Reader's Digest*): from the establishment more than the people.[10] Eager to be generous to the poor, accustomed as the proprietors of major institutions to making decisions which affected great unseen masses of people, unfamiliar in their own daily lives with the poor and the needy, they were prepared to take a chance on a radical untested program which promised in one quick stroke to solve several vexing problems to which they had no other solution.

One result of this pattern of support was that FAP tended to win its strongest allegiance from members whose constituencies got the least direct benefits. The greatest benefits in dollar terms went to the southern states, where incomes and wage levels were still distinctly below the national average, and the least to states like New York and California, which already provided generous welfare benefits under the permissive federal law which gave states this option. That was one reason the National Welfare Rights Organization, its members mostly already welfare recipients in big states, opposed the program bitterly and vociferously, employing tactics which included outright lies and violent occupations of sympathetic congressmen's offices.[11]

Within Congress the chief support for FAP came from the House Ways and Means Committee or, to put it more precisely, from Chairman Wilbur Mills. Since January 1958, when he became chairman, Mills had been writing the nation's tax bills; he had written Social Security legislation and (once he stopped opposing it) Medicare; he was the leading sponsor of the liberalized trade legislation which probably contributed more than it was ever credited for to the economic growth and prosperity of the 1961–69 boom. He was the House's premier legislator on welfare, too, pushing through in 1967 both the so-called Aid for Dependent Children "freeze" and a new work incentive program. He shared the attitude, widespread after the success of the civil rights movement, that poverty was something which just happened to people, that for many Americans there was no reliable connection between effort and reward. "It is not a sin to be poor," Mills said in a November 1969 hearing. "I think it is a sin on the part of all of us to do nothing about it, nothing more than trying to maintain that status in life. And I am convinced from the people that I talk to, who are able-bodied people, that they would much prefer an opportunity to be self-reliant and they seek it."[12] This idea had much support in the welfare bureaucracies of the great cities, which welcomed the efforts of the welfare rights organizations to clog the rolls with new recipients and the sum of whose own individual decisions undoubtedly added many more: AFDC rolls increased 32% in calendar year 1969.[13] On deliberation, Mills led Ways and Means to report the bill favorably by a 21–3 margin in February 1970. The bill was given the closed rule (barring amendments) typically accorded major Ways and Means measures and received support from most Republicans and from San Francisco's Phillip Burton, a welfare expert active in the Democratic Study Group, who criticized benefits as inadequate but still rounded up about 100 liberal Democratic votes. The South was overwhelmingly against it (though it was supported by George Bush of the affluent west side of Houston, a Ways and Means member; he was attacked for this stance by Democrat Lloyd Bentsen when the two ran for the Senate that fall). The House passed FAP 243–155 in April—a Nixon victory as striking as the collapse of the Moratorium a few months before.

The bill speedily went into hearings in the Senate Finance Committee and was speedily killed. Chairman Russell Long, recently deprived of the whip position, protested that FAP would not reform the existing welfare system's encouragements to idleness. Ranking Republican Williams pounced on the "notch," the work disincentives in FAP and existing welfare programs caused by the fact that at some point in any system benefits fall to the point of nonexistence and incomes rise to the point of being taxable. After two days, on April 30, Long announced that HEW Secretary Robert Finch would report back to him with proposals to eliminate the work disincentives in all welfare programs. FAP was stalled; as it turned out, it "could not survive," in Moynihan's words, "a committee dominated by Democrats representing the southern states where FAP would have its greatest impact on the social order, and Republicans representing western states where welfare was a minimal problem, and reform a marginal concern."[14]

III

April 30, 1970, was also the day on which Nixon announced the invasion of Cambodia. For a politician who had been a freshman senator when Douglas MacArthur was fired in April 1951, the idea of crossing an Asian border to get at a Communist enemy's sanctuary had a certain familiarity—and in this case a genuine military utility. North Vietnamese troops were using Cambodia as a base to launch attacks on South Vietnam, and Saigon was only 30 miles from the Cambodian border. The Cambodian government of General Lon Nol, who had ousted the tottering Prince Sihanouk while he was on vacation in France in January 1970, was under attack from the Communist Khmer Rouge who were allied with Sihanouk, now in residence in Peking. Yet Nixon's move came as a surprise in the United States. Just ten days before he had announced that another 150,000 U.S. troops would be withdrawn within the next year. Now it seemed to opponents of the war that it was about to be widened indefinitely. The Cambodian "incursion," like the Tet offensive, raised in the minds of many Americans the prospect of an endless, expanded war, even though Nixon seems genuinely to have seen it as a means to end the war more quickly. Nixon proclaimed that the United States must not act like "a pitiful helpless giant," but in fact the operation itself was relatively small and the results apparently meager.

What was tremendous was the reaction at home. Opinion leaders and students were enraged and protested vociferously, with 200 State Department employees and four members of Kissinger's staff resigning in protest and student strikes springing up on 400 campuses; 100,000 students marched on Washington. Nixon, who could have argued that the incursion was marginal, instead invited confrontation: in one unguarded comment he labeled student protesters as "bums blowing up campuses." On May 4, National Guardsmen sent to the campus of Kent State University in Ohio by Governor James Rhodes (who was running in a close Senate primary days later) opened fire on nonviolent demonstrators and killed four young people. Nixon's press secretary Ron Ziegler said, "When dissent turns to violence, it invites tragedy." Later in May, Nixon paid a dawn visit to the Lincoln Memorial and talked briefly to demonstrators, but to no great effect.[15]

As usual, most voters seemed to rally behind a president who in crisis had made a military decision: Nixon's job rating remained high, disapproval of student protesters was at least as strong as ever. By all those standard measures, Nixon was ahead. But he knew from Johnson's experience that initially popular actions did not remain so if American troops were still in peril and tangible victories not achieved, and he knew that the trend of opinion among the elite—whose vehement opposition to the Cambodia invasion can hardly be overstated—could in time come to be shared by the masses. Nixon talked in his April 30 speech of the possibility of being a one-term president. This was an expression of his standard self-pity, and a betrayal of lack of discipline and thus loss of nerve in the face of strong and unexpected opposition. But there was also some genuine basis for his insecurity about his political prospects.

For the political impact of Cambodia at home was much greater than the military effect in Indochina. The energies which had gone into the extrapolitical Moratorium movement were now directed into electoral political activity: students were organizing to defeat congressmen who supported the invasion. Their first efforts yielded meager results. A notable example was in the 15th District of New Jersey, where Lewis Kaden, a veteran of John Lindsay's New York City administration, went to oppose Democrat Edward Patten, a fat, garrulous, malaprop-prone personification of old-time machine politics. Patten prevailed after running a newspaper ad reprinting the current Manhattan phone directory with Kaden's name and address.[16] But in the long run, the anti-Cambodia movement had the effect of encouraging young antiwar candidates whose ultimate victories determined the tone and substance of House politics nearly two decades later.[17] Northern Democratic senators rallied nearly unanimously to the antiwar cause, and many Republicans joined as well. There was some truth to Nixonites' bitter complaints that the same politicians—notably Hubert Humphrey and Edmund Muskie—who had steadfastly supported a Democratic president when he escalated the war now refused to support a Republican president who was de-escalating it.

Their vehicle for opposition became a series of amendments proposed in the Senate and requiring U.S. withdrawal from Cambodia; these were sponsored by Kentucky Republican John Sherman Cooper, whose courtliness combined the best attributes of his native Cumberland Plateau and his wife's Georgetown salon, and Idaho Democrat Frank Church, who had been elected to the Senate at thirty-two in 1956 from a state by 1970 increasingly hawkish and culturally conservative, and reelected in 1968 only because of the ineptness of his opponent, right-wing Congressman George Hansen. Cooper–Church amendments had about 50 votes in the Senate and one actually passed; but they had no chance in the House.

IV

But the Cambodia invasion was not the only event of the spring of 1970 which marked the creation of a new liberal politics. Just a few days before, on April 22, environmentalists had staged Earth Day: 10,000 young people gathered at the

Washington Monument and applauded politicians like Edmund Muskie, who from his seat on the previously obscure Public Works Committee had sponsored air quality acts in 1963 and 1967 and clean water acts in 1965, 1966, and 1970.[18] Environmental causes had engaged few Americans' interest in the 1960s: they were overshadowed by civil rights and Vietnam for the socially conscious, and others were too busy enjoying the fruits of an affluence which in many cases was unexpected to muse on its effects on nature. But the Santa Barbara oil spill of February 1969 and the first pictures of the earth which came back from the moon landing of July 1969 provided visual evidence of the fragility of the environment of "Spaceship Earth." Environmentalists saw people as using up resources, recklessly ruining their environment; puritanically they insisted on a sparer, more austere life style. "The ecological movement," wrote Moynihan, "depicted a world groaning under the burden of abundance."[19] The environmentalists' insistence on imposing costs on users of resources made sense; but they failed to understand that scarce resources tend to rise in price, at which point people find cheaper substitutes, and that affluence made it easier for a society to meet their demands. But for the moment they were all euphoria, sensing correctly that they were on the verge of changing their society, and mostly as it turned out for the better.

Just a month after Cambodia, in June, Congress passed a law giving eighteen-year-olds the vote in federal elections and therefore in all other elections as well. Proponents expected that college-age voters, furious with Nixon for continuing the war, would vote heavily Democratic; and at least in many college towns, especially on the East Coast, in the Upper Midwest, and on the West Coast, they did.

The summer brought more liberal advances. In July the New York legislature, dominated for years on cultural issues by the Albany lobbyist of the Catholic Church, passed a bill which essentially legalized abortion. The key vote was cast dramatically in the Assembly by George Michaels, a Jew from heavily Catholic Cayuga County who was defeated in the next election; but Nelson Rockefeller signed the bill, and abortion became an ordinary part of life in America's second-largest state and largest city. Later that month Nixon submitted to Congress an executive reorganization plan which set up the Environmental Protection Agency, gathering together in one visible bureaucracy agencies set up in different departments over the years. Attempts to veto this plan failed in Congress in September.

Also in September, the United Auto Workers, under new president Leonard Woodcock (who had succeeded Walter Reuther after he died in a plane crash in May), struck General Motors; after two months on the picket line, members received a settlement both large and largely predictable.[20] Finally, in November, in a lame-duck session after the election, Congress established the Occupational Safety and Health Administration, proposed by Nixon in August 1969 and the number one priority of the AFL–CIO in that Congress; the OSHA bureaucracy soon became the number one target of embittered criticism of government regulation on the part of small businessmen. On substantive policies, foreign and domestic, Nixon either failed to resist or, more often, actively embraced the ideas and goals advocated by his political enemies. Yet in rhetoric and attitude, he managed almost continually to enrage them, in the culturally polarized America which had rapidly come into being in the late 1960s.

V

Richard Nixon's Republican strategy for the 1970 elections was based heavily on the analysis of Kevin Phillips, a young Bronx-born lawyer and assistant to John Mitchell whose knowledge of historical American voting trends has seldom if ever been equaled by an active campaign operative. Even before the 1968 election, Phillips had begun writing his monumental *The Emerging Republican Majority,* in which he argued correctly that Republicans could amass an electoral college majority from the votes of white southerners and what Phillips dubbed the Sun Belt. He also argued that Republicans could add to that coalition northern urban ethnics, including many of the Catholics who had voted so heavily for John Kennedy in 1960. Phillips's analysis explains the 1968 result if the Nixon and Wallace votes are taken together; and in fact, as discussed earlier, most Wallace voters would have chosen Nixon over Humphrey in a two-way race. Moreover, Wallace seemed likely to abandon his third-party strategy. The independent candidate he supported had badly lost the special House election in 1969 in west Tennessee; and at home in Alabama, after his wife died in office in May 1968, he had entered into a fight for his political life with her successor, Albert Brewer, in the May 1970 Democratic primary.[21] Both white southerners and white ethnics, Phillips argued, had been split off from the New Deal Democratic coalition by their dissatisfaction with the cultural liberalism they associated with the Great Society and other liberal trends, by their patriotic instincts and their belief in national and cultural traditions; and the new residents of the burgeoning free-enterprise metropolises of the Sun Belt— the archetypical example of which was Barry Goldwater's Phoenix—provided a new demographic base for the Republicans. Phillips understood long before other observers that the critical swing groups in the electorate were no longer the culturally and economically liberal Jews in the big cities and the Upper Midwest progressives—both groups were by 1968 solidly Democratic—but the southern whites and northern ethnics, who were conservative on cultural though not always on economic issues.

So while Nixon fought for policies which addressed liberal priorities, he sought votes from people who had conservative values. This strategy demanded constant and angry confrontation with the Democrats; and Nixon, personally and through his mouthpiece Spiro Agnew, provided it in the months after Cambodia. Agnew denounced the press as "nattering nabobs of negativism" and Democratic politicians as "radiclibs." The White House political operation sent him out to states where Republicans had chances to win in Senate contests; taken together, these were perhaps the most hotly contested set of Senate elections of the twentieth century. The seats up in 1970 had been swept by one party in each of the preceding four cycles, by the Republicans in 1946 and 1952 and the Democrats in 1958 and 1964.

Republican strategists knew that if they were to have any chance at controlling the Senate in the 1970s they must make major inroads now; the Democrats knew that the focus of their power in the federal government, power to slow a war effort and determine who sat on the Supreme Court, came from their control of the Senate. Republicans made serious challenges, although in a few cases they fizzled well before election day, in all but three seats: hawkish and highly popular Democrats John Stennis, Henry Jackson, and Robert Byrd had no serious competition in Mississippi, Washington, and West Virginia. So strong was the competition that a fair number of the losers—and their wives and children—became important political figures in years hence.[22]

The Democrats, as befitted Will Rogers's party, had no unified strategy. They relied on the skills and shrewdness of their incumbents and their advisors to pick off enough victories to keep the Senate in Democratic hands. Yet they did sound some general themes. Democratic candidates heeded the advice of Richard Scammon and Ben Wattenberg in their 1970 book, *The Real Majority,* to hew to the center, appear pro- not anti-American, and remember that their core constituent was a housewife in Dayton whose brother-in-law was a policeman (the Democrats carried Dayton handily in November). Adlai Stevenson III in Illinois was a case in point. A diffident and less eloquent version of his father, Stevenson, while running for the seat opened up by Everett Dirksen's death in September 1969, took to wearing an American flag pin in his lapel as so many Republicans were doing and hired as his campaign manager the chief prosecutor of the Chicago Seven. But the Democrats also took care to untangle themselves entirely from that still dreadfully unpopular politician of the center, Lyndon Johnson.

For more than thirty years, since the days of Franklin Roosevelt, northern and some southern Democrats had run as candidates of a national party with a national philosophy and with national leaders. Suddenly in 1970, Democrats found themselves running as candidates perhaps vaguely associated with fallen heroes but in no particular way tied to national leaders or, except for a critical attitude toward a Republican president most voters did not entirely trust, linked by common stands on issues. The Democrats were once again, as they had been before 1934, the local party, decentralized and autonomous; the Republicans, as they had been before 1934, found themselves a party of centralized direction and a centralized, though not overwhelmingly popular, leader. In a large country, geographically and ethnically diverse and increasingly culturally divided, a natural advantage in congressional elections accrued to the party most capable of adapting to local political environments; and this party in 1970, and in most of the two decades thereafter, was the Democratic party.

The Democrats were advised by various authors and intellectuals to use the economic issues which were thought to be the major basis for what was considered their natural majority; and some Democrats, particularly in the high-unemployment industrial Midwest, did. But the goal of reassembling the New Deal majority remained elusive, for the economic conditions and attitudes which had produced that majority had mostly vanished. Since the middle 1960s, economic growth and the existence of a stronger safety net—unemployment insurance, welfare and other assistance programs, increasing equity in homes—had made the specter of total economic disaster, which had been commonplace in the 1930s and 1940s and not unknown as late as the recessions of 1957–61, remote from almost all voters' lives. Unemployment was an inconvenience, not a disaster. Moreover, while voting behavior was still correlated with economic status, the connection was becoming more tenuous. Economics still worked powerfully for the Democratic presidential candidate in 1952 and 1956; and it was a serious factor in 1960, although religion and ethnic origin were much more significant. But by 1964 it worked only in the sense that Johnson was credited with the prosperity—class warfare themes were deliberately muted by Johnson—and in 1968 economic issues did not determine the outcome of the election at all. Hubert Humphrey lost the entire South but carried Texas (the lowest-income region in the country and one of its highest-income states); he carried high-income states like New York, Massachusetts, and Michigan. In congressional races by 1968, Democrats were helped less by their association with the politics of economic redistribution than they were by the advantages of incumbency. As the 1970s began, the environment and antiwar issues did much for the Democrats—attracting them votes among the young and inspiring politically adept young people to run—while economic issues had only a limited effect.

Odd factors played a part, as they tend to in ticket-splitting politics. In California, Senator George Murphy, an adept dancer as a movie star, who had been elected in 1964 over John Kennedy's press secretary Pierre Salinger, was beaten by Edward Kennedy's pal Congressman John Tunney—mostly because Murphy was exposed as having accepted salary-like payments from Technicolor, Inc. In Texas one key factor was a referendum on allowing local option on liquor-by-the-drink; this brought out rural Baptists in great enough numbers not to defeat the referendum but to help elect former Democratic Congressman Lloyd Bentsen over Republican Congressman George Bush. For his May primary victory over liberal Ralph Yarborough, Bentsen had run TV ads showing footage of the 1968 Chicago convention—a tactic followed by Nixon Republicans in the fall. But after winning the primary, Bentsen sought labor and black support and after the election denied Spiro Agnew's claim that he was part of a pro-Nixon bipartisan majority. Bush's faithfulness as a Nixon follower sparked rumors in October that if he won he would be substituted for Agnew on the 1972 ticket and led afterwards to his appointment to the array of jobs which would make him a plausible presidential candidate in 1980 even though he had never won an election except in one of the nation's half dozen most Republican congressional districts. In Maryland the issue was gun control, which destroyed the career of Democrat Joseph Tydings, bearer of a great local name and an obvious aspirant to national office.

Three-way races were prominent in 1970. In New York, Agnew's well-orchestrated attack on liberal Republican Senator Charles Goodell (appointed by Rockefeller to Robert Kennedy's place) as the "Christine Jorgenson"[23] of American politics led to a surge of liberals to Goodell, to the detriment of Democrat Richard

Ottinger, and a surge of Nixon supporters to James Buckley, the Conservative party nominee and brother of columnist and *National Review* editor William Buckley. The result: Buckley stunned everyone by winning with 43%, to Ottinger's 37% and Goodell's 20%. In Connecticut, there was a different three-way split. Incumbent Democratic Senator Thomas Dodd, a strong anti-Communist censured on corruption charges, was persuaded to run as an independent; he won 23%, compared with Democratic nominee (and 1968 McCarthy organizer) Joseph Duffey's 34%; the winner was Republican Congressman Lowell Weicker with 42%. In Virginia, Harry Byrd, Jr., took note from the narrowness of his own 1966 primary victory and the primary defeat that year of seventy-nine-year-old Byrd machine stalwart A. Willis Robertson that he could easily lose a Democratic primary. He ran as an independent instead, and from the broader general electorate won an absolute majority against a Democrat and a Republican.

Nevertheless, overall the Democrats won the 1970 Senate races. Republicans beat only two incumbents—Tydings and Albert Gore of Tennessee—and only by narrow margins. They also picked up the open seats vacated by Democrats in Ohio and Connecticut, while losing their seat in California. After the election Democrats had 55 votes in the Senate (including one from Harry Byrd, Jr., who didn't want to lose his committee seats). At least four results needed to have gone the other way for the Republicans to have won control. But the Democrats won seven seats with 54% or less—Indiana, Missouri, New Mexico, Texas, Florida, New Jersey, and California. It is easy to imagine circumstances in which these races would have gone differently, in which Republicans could have picked up the southern seats of Texas and Florida, as they had planned (Tennessee, which they won, and Mississippi and Virginia were the only other possible targets of the southern strategy that year), or in which they could have overcome in the Rocky Mountain states (as they did later in the 1970s) the Democrats' argument (which helped them hold New Mexico, Wyoming, Utah, and Nevada) that incumbents had seniority which helped their states.

But it should be added that "New South" Democratic moderates, freed from association with a national administration, showed unexpected strength in southern gubernatorial races. Democrat John West beat Republican Albert Watson in South Carolina after Watson expressed approval of the burning of a school bus. Democrat Jimmy Carter won in Georgia over an Atlanta newscaster. In Arkansas mellifluous Dale Bumpers beat the two men, Orval Faubus in the primary and Winthrop Rockefeller in the general election, who had been governor for the last sixteen years. Reubin Askew ousted the flamboyant and fatuous Claude Kirk in Florida. Major Republican success in the South came only in Tennessee, and there only by the narrow margins by which Memphis dentist Winfield Dunn was elected governor over Nashville wheeler-dealer and Kennedy ally John J. Hooker, Jr., and Chattanooga Congressman William Brock beat Gore, "the old gray fox"; Gore nearly held on, despite his opposition to the Vietnam war and votes against Judges Haynsworth and Carswell. The refusal of southern whites to vote solidly Republican and the continuing appeal of moderate Democrats in the region show that voters there were not interested in reinstituting legal segregation or in reviving the old fights over racial issues. The enduring preference of southern whites for Republican presidential candidates, which was notable even when Jimmy Carter was the Democratic nominee, apparently resulted not from the opposition to civil rights which had first led them to support Republicans in June 1963 when John Kennedy came out for a civil rights bill, but from their positions on a series of cultural and other non-economic issues, many of them totally unrelated to race, on which they found national Democrats unpalatable and Republicans and moderate southern Democrats acceptable.

The Nixon–Agnew–Phillips strategy of polarizing the electorate was symbolized by Nixon's attempt to swing the election in its final week. He was barnstorming the country, denouncing liberals; and the Republicans purchased national TV time to show a videotape of him speaking in Phoenix. But the tape was fuzzy and Nixon seemed almost to be ranting: the contrast could not have been greater with the disciplined, flawlessly produced Nixon of 1968. The contrast was also great with the Democrats' response: a broadcast, arranged by Geoffrey Cowan and filmed by Robert Squier, of Edmund Muskie speaking calmly and reassuringly from his home in Kennebunkport, Maine. The polarizing strategy worked when it was intended to divide a once-dominant Democratic coalition and to highlight discontents with an incumbent Democratic administration. It worked less well when it was intended to defeat Democrats who were free to adapt to local terrain and to assemble a dominant Republican majority. Nixon's 1968 instinct that the country wanted a leader who could bring it together was sound; and if his inability to do that in 1969 and 1970 was more the result of circumstances and the acts of his political opponents than anything else, he still must be held culpable for his failure to sustain the self-discipline to avoid the divisive and self-pitying note which to voters sounded jarring in a man entrusted with the responsibilities of a national leader. The aggressive, sometimes raucous tone of the Republicans' campaigns did not produce the sense of calm mastery and consensual order that voters were seeking. Franklin Roosevelt with his iron self-discipline always managed to sound like a national leader, even when making partisan attacks. Richard Nixon, his self-discipline already cracking, managed to sound like a negative ranter even while advancing policies which he could fairly claim embodied a creative national consensus.

The strategy had an additional problem: the electorate was rapidly changing. Phillips shrewdly identified and targeted the demographic segments—the cultural fragments of an increasingly culturally fragmented society—which were moving or could be moved away from the Democrats. But he failed to acknowledge that these groups—white southerners angry about desegregation, northern Catholic ethnics angry about the decline of their old neighborhoods, Sun Belt migrants looking for the bedrock values they had left behind—were in most cases, groups of declining demographic importance. In a nation which was increasingly college-educated, white collar, and racially tolerant, the Nixon strategy targeted those who were just the opposite. Moreover, their grievances were changing. White southerners' antagonism to desegregation was greatest among the old; young white southerners were ready to accept integration, though not to embrace the national Democrats on busing or other issues. Northern ethnics had already been moving out into the suburbs and upward on the socioeconomic ladder in great numbers. The mostly conservative-minded Sun Belt migrants of the 1960s were being followed by a younger generation whose attitudes had been shaped by the civil rights, antiwar, and environmental movements: they were seeking not the affirmation of an old code but the enactment of their own new code.[24]

Perhaps the most vivid political result of this generational shift appeared in the legislative elections in Nixon's native state of California. In 1968, Ronald Reagan's Republicans had succeeded in winning control of the California Assembly and Senate for the first time in ten years. In 1970 they hoped to capitalize on Reagan's popularity by holding on to both houses and drawing up redistricting plans which would keep the legislature and California's 43-member House delegation in Republican hands up through 1980. But former Assembly Speaker Jesse Unruh held Reagan to a 54%–46% reelection victory, his closest margin in California ever; and the Democrats recaptured both the Assembly and the Senate. As a result, they held on to the California legislature and congressional delegation for the next two decades—no small victory in American politics and government.

But for all that, the Republicans' attempt to win control of the Senate failed by only a narrow margin. Happenstance, personal weaknesses and strengths of candidates, all made as much difference as Nixon's strategic mistakes. If Nixon had faced a Republican Senate and a conservative-dominated House in the 1970s, much of the partisan rancor of the decade would have been avoided, and quite different policies might have been adopted. Instead, the 1970 election produced a sharply divided, distrustful, adversary government in Washington. Around the country it was a harbinger of what became the atomized congressional politics of the 1970s. In contrast to the off-year elections of 1958, 1962, and 1966, it swung less on national issues and party labels and more on local issues and character. It featured some central direction on the Republican side (some of it very shrewd, some utterly ham-handed) and almost none among the Democrats, except through the medium of shared political consultants, pollsters, media makers, and pundits. It saw conflicting regional trends and a confusing combination of results. It showed that the Democrats were still capable of extracting some political advantage out of recession, especially in the Farm Belt and the industrial regions of the Midwest; but in such regions they won no Senate seats and gained only a handful of House seats—5 in the industrial Great Lakes states, 6 in Farm Belt districts. What the election of 1970 did not see was the emergence of a new Republican majority— or of a new Democratic majority either. Voters, shaken in their belief in leaders, skeptical and questioning about all the nation's major institutions, did not reliably gravitate to either party or any leader. The 1970s had begun.

45

➤➤➤ ⫸⫷

Shock

On K Street, once a boulevard lined with mansions; on side streets once lined with cheap three- and four-story buildings; on Connecticut Avenue, running diagonally northwest from the White House—throughout downtown Washington in the late 1960s and early 1970s construction cranes were towering over sites where sparkling new buildings were going up in record numbers. Almost every new building was 130 feet high, for Washington was the only one of the nation's major cities to retain the height limits which had commonly been imposed around the turn of the century for safety reasons, and most of its new buildings were plain modern boxes in the International Style and entirely filled their sites: if this new Washington had a more human scale than other American downtowns, it was also more monotonous. Huge gaudy developments were represented only by the new government buildings in Southwest Washington, especially that of the new Department of Housing and Urban Development, and by the curving, toothed-balconied Watergate office-apartment complex going up along the Potomac just north of where the John F. Kennedy Center for the Performing Arts was being built on the site of the gasworks which had given that part of town the name Foggy Bottom. Underground workers were tunneling out the first line of the new Metro subway system—one of the nation's most expensive public works projects, heavily subsidized by the federal government for the use of what had become the nation's highest-income metropolitan area. Washington in the Nixon years, even more than in the Kennedy and Johnson years, was a boom town. Bereft of industry, blessed with little commerce, it had never before been one of America's great metropolises. Now it was: the Washington metropolitan area zoomed into the nation's top ten in the 1970 census, growing more rapidly than such Sun Belt metropolitan areas as Dallas–Fort Worth, Atlanta, Miami, and Los Angeles and only slightly less rapidly than Houston.[1] John Kennedy had once described the Washington of the 1950s as a city "of northern charm and southern efficiency." It was a city rigidly segregated by law and custom; it was a city whose only major employer, the federal government, paid low wages and attracted employees considered low in initiative. The Wall Street lawyers and financiers who came to Washington to serve in government lived almost as if they had moved out to the country, giving gracious parties in their old houses but disdaining Washington's few restaurants and driving 40 miles to Baltimore for a good restaurant meal,

485

decrying its dearth of performing arts, mocking its few well-known hostesses. But by the early 1970s Washington was, in all these respects, becoming the cosmopolitan equal if not of New York then probably of any other American city.

The engine behind Washington's growth was the continuing growth of government. Federal civilian employment reached almost 3 million in 1967, 1968, and 1969—the peak peacetime figures in American history—and declined only slightly immediately thereafter.[2] There was only a slight pause in Washington's growth in the early 1970s; even as federal payrolls shrank, the government was increasingly contracting out work to private employers. Giant office developments across the Potomac in suburban Virginia—Crystal City near National Airport, Pentagon City, Rosslyn across Key Bridge from Georgetown—were filled largely with government employees and government contractors' employees. With rising federal pay rates and an increasingly upscale federal work force (for the government had begun to hire more lawyers and fewer unskilled laborers), Washington was becoming the nation's most affluent metropolitan area. It did not contain the nation's largest concentrations of the very rich, but its income levels—especially in Montgomery County, Maryland, northwest of the city—were on average the nation's highest.

In economic growth Washington was sprinting ahead of a nation which had been expanding for a decade. American economic growth was producing a bounteous stream of revenue for the federal government. By the 1968–69 fiscal year, the federal government's receipts were up to $194 billion, a vast increase over the $117 billion of 1964–65 and the $92 billion of 1959–60.[3] Revenue rose as a percentage of gross national product at a time when GNP was rising rapidly. Rising incomes put more and more Americans into higher brackets of a tax system which was, even after the Kennedy–Johnson tax cuts, still steeply graduated (and in which tax avoidance had not yet developed nearly as extravagantly as it would by the late 1970s). At the same time, rising corporate profits boosted receipts from the corporate income tax. Rises in Social Security taxes to pay for higher benefits and for Medicare were accepted with scarcely a murmur of protest. In the recession of the early 1970s there was a pause in the growth in revenues. But there was still plenty of room for domestic spending to rise—the post-Vietnam dividend hoped for in the late Johnson years in fact did occur—because defense spending was down as Nixon withdrew more and more troops from Vietnam. The following table shows the changes in federal spending during this period:

Federal Government Outlays by Category, Fiscal Years
1968–69 and 1971–72
(in billion $, rounded off)

	1968–69	1971–72	% Change
Total Outlays	184	232	+ 26
Social Security			
Trust Funds	43	67	+ 55
Non-Defense	60	87	+ 44
Defense	81	78	− 3

What Elizabeth Drew called the "constantly growing, bipartisan collection of people here—journalists, politicians, politicians' aides, lawyers, lobbyists, government workers, hangers-on, and the geological strata of several administrations' worth of former officials—who make up what is usually referred to as 'Washington' "[4] was almost unremittingly hostile to Richard Nixon, and he to it. This Washington gave Nixon little credit when he acted in line with its own fuzzily liberal instincts and excoriated him when he spoke out against them. If this Washington had been spectacularly unsuccessful in electing its kind of president in 1968, it now dominated opinion in the city's leading paper (the *Washington Post*), in the Senate, in a few odd corners of the House, in the bureaus of the three televison networks, and in the city's fashionable society.

II

Throughout his first term, Nixon seemed to accept many of the premises of his political opponents, acting more often to expand than to contract federal domestic programs. Like Lyndon Johnson, he strove to go beyond the economic class warfare politics of labor-management struggles by seeing that both sides got what they wanted. Unlike Johnson, he did not interfere in major negotiations but rather let both sides go through the motions and emerge with most of what they sought. This apparently painless solution was what eventually resulted from the UAW strike against General Motors from September to November 1970, which produced a big wage increase and a cost-of-living adjustment package for the union and led to higher prices for the company: the assumption was that the consumer would always be willing to pay. Similarly, after a railroad strike which lasted all of two hours in December 1970, Nixon and Congress surrendered to the unions, raising wages far above inflation rates. Again, with help from government regulators, the consumer was assumed to be boundlessly able to pay. Gone were the wage-price guidelines of the Kennedy years, supposedly limiting wage increases to productivity increases; now unions were protecting their members against inflation threats while getting wage and benefit increases well above productivity gains. For inflation was rising to what seemed alarming levels. The Consumer Price Index, which had risen less than 2% a year and nearer 1% most of the years between 1959 and 1965 (and had risen more than 2% in only two years between 1953 and 1965), rose 2.9% in 1966 and 1967, 4.2% in 1968, 5.4% in 1969, and 5.9% in 1970[5]— an alarming trend against the background of the preceding seventeen years, when Americans had come to take stable prices (and rising incomes) for granted.

On fiscal policy Nixon also explicitly accepted his opponents' premises. The budget he announced in 1971 was, as he described it later, "set to balance at full employment and run a deficit to help take up the slack when unemployment was high"—the exact prescription of the Kennedy–Johnson economists. He even proclaimed, "We are all Keynesians now,"[6] just at the point in American history when the problem Keynesian economics was intended to attack, unemployment, was becoming less paramount while the problem it had little to say about, inflation, was becoming endemic, partly because of application of Keynesian principles.

Nixon's other domestic policies were consistent with his Keynesian macroeconomics. The Family Assistance Program had been beaten 10–6 in the Senate
Finance Committee in November 1970. Though Nixon revived it, its chances
looked dim. His major initiative in the January 1971 State of the Union was revenue
sharing: the federal government would give state and local governments sums
determined by population and other formulas. This was the brainchild of economist
Joseph Pechman of the Brookings Institution, who noted that federal revenue
sources, primarily the graduated income tax, and state and local government spending were both growing more rapidly than the economy. The constituencies behind
it were assembled by the national governors' and mayors' organizations.

In March 1971 another of Nixon's major initiatives was rejected by a narrow
margin in the Senate. This was financing for a supersonic transport aircraft, to
be built by the Boeing Corporation. Support for the SST was led by Washington
state's Warren Magnuson and Henry Jackson, committee chairmen who were
brilliant maneuverers and old-time New Dealers; Boeing was one of their state's
leading employers. Opposition was led by William Proxmire of Wisconsin, a Democrat with a liberal reputation but a critic of government spending who issued a
"Golden Fleece" award each month for what he considered the least meritorious
government aid project. Proxmire was helped by a new skepticism among many
liberal Democrats and Republicans about spending on high-technology projects.

In April 1971 the Supreme Court announced its decision in the landmark
Charlotte, North Carolina, busing case. Written by Nixon's appointee, Chief
Justice Burger, for a unanimous court, it allowed extensive busing to be used for
desegregation when the trial judge decided it was appropriate. It did not require
busing in every case but authorized it when it was ordered. In Charlotte, as it
happened, busing was received with less hostility than in many places in the North.
This was a bustling commercial city, envious of the growth and style of burgeoning
Atlanta, which had styled itself "the city too busy to hate" since the late 1950s.
Charlotte parents organized groups to help make the busing work, to welcome
black children bused from black neighborhoods to other areas, and to assure the
white parents whose children were being bused into the southeast that their
children were safe and were being well educated. In Pontiac, Michigan, in contrast,
white parents pulled their children out of the schools and in 1972 staged a march
on Washington. Whites in Pontiac and other parts of the Detroit metropolitan
area were enraged in 1972 by a federal judge's ordering of busing from the suburbs
into the separate Detroit school district. In these cases, the public still believed
in a juridical distinction which the courts were increasingly erasing. Southerners
knew that their school systems had practiced legal segregation, and had come to
accept that rather drastic remedies would be required to end its effect. Northerners
knew that they had never had legal segregation and were unpersuaded that the
decisions made by local school boards which the courts said promoted de facto
segregation were enough to trigger a major busing order. It did seem a bit strained
to say, as the Detroit judge did, that school assignment decisions involving a few
hundred students in the central city should require busing of hundreds of thousands

of students over a metropolitan area of 4 million people. His order, which was never put into effect, was a classic example of an application of logic and theory to the facts of everyday life which, unlike the application of logic which challenged and ended legal segregation in the South, struck most Americans as absurd. Politically, there was no doubt of the response. Busing orders evoked little enthusiasm from black voters and sparked intense opposition among most whites in affected communities, especially in the North.

The strength of the impulse toward government action was shown again in May 1971 when the federal government set up the subsidized Amtrak system to take over ownership and operation of almost all passenger trains in the United States. Long squeezed between an Interstate Commerce Commission which wouldn't allow rate increases and unions which demanded higher wages, the passenger lines typically reported losses; and the nation's biggest passenger train operator, the merged Penn Central, went into bankruptcy in June 1970. But apart from sentimental reasons, there was little cause to subsidize passenger rail traffic outside the one part of the country, the thickly settled Northeast Corridor, where it might be economically profitable. Everywhere else other transportation modes had a competitive edge: jet airplanes would always be quicker than the train, the interstate bus would be cheaper, and outside city centers the passenger car would be more convenient.

Keynesian economics, the SST, busing, Amtrak: all are examples of how the policy ideas of American liberals still had a stranglehold on the work of politicians even while their results proved increasingly unpopular at the polls. Richard Nixon was making war on the liberals on the campaign trail, but he was doing something very much like their work in the White House and the Old Executive Office Building (where Nixon, quite eccentrically, kept a hideaway office). Nixon could find few ideas of how to run a conservative government, while the new Washington which had grown up since he first became a political celebrity in August 1948 pushed hard against any abandonment of liberal goals. In foreign policy as well, there were similar pressures, and similar results.

III

In April 1971, at an international Ping-Pong tournament in Nagoya, Japan, the Chinese team invited the American team to visit China; and the Americans accepted. This exchange was quickly and widely recognized as a momentous event. Ever since the Red Army had conquered mainland China in September 1949, the U.S. government had banned Americans from traveling to China and Chinese communists from coming to the United States. There was to be no contact, no trade, no intercourse with this monstrous and, American governments professed to hope, temporary regime. In the 1950s and early 1960s no American politician had been a more vociferous supporter of this policy than Richard Nixon: "all that we have to do is take a look at the map and we can see that if Formosa falls the next frontier is the coast of California," he said while campaigning for senator in

California in 1950.[7] But from his first months as president Nixon moved toward establishing contact with China, initially without any prodding from and against the instincts of the man who would be credited in some quarters with inspiring the initiative, Henry Kissinger.[8] The Ping-Pong players were feted by Premier Chou En-lai, who called the event "this beginning again of our friendship," and a return invitation was issued. By late April, Nixon had announced the easing of many restrictions on U.S.–Chinese contacts. The public did not know that Kissinger was already planning his secret July trip to Peking, but it was clear some opening to China was in the works. And in July Nixon announced that he would travel to China sometime in 1972.

The reaction of voters, so long assumed to be hostile to any recognition of the Chinese Communists, was overwhelmingly favorable.[9] Only Nixon, it is often said, with his record of opposition to Red China and his criticism of the Democrats for losing China to the Communists, could have made such an opening to Peking. Of course, Nixon did have this advantage over the Democrats. But more important, he was simply shrewder than the Democrats—most of them who remembered from their first years in politics the "Who lost China?" firestorm—in recognizing that American opinion had shifted and that the desire for peace and stability with China was strong and the hope that anti-Communists would reconquer the mainland had long since evaporated. It is true that if a President Humphrey had gone to China as President Nixon did, conservative Republicans would have yelped in complaint and made an issue of it in 1972. But as the polls and the election results showed, the issue would have helped the president, not the complainers, at least if the president had the nerve to stick with his initiative and pursue it as Nixon did.

IV

In June 1971, just before Kissinger's trip to Asia, where he planned to leave reporters behind in Islamabad, Pakistan, and fly to Peking, the *New York Times* printed the first of several installments of the "Pentagon papers." These were documents which had been compiled in the Pentagon at Robert McNamara's direction and concerned the Vietnam war—the sort of raw material which historians need to write detailed histories of policymaking but the policymakers themselves usually keep secret, at least until they write their own memoirs. Even though all of them came from the Johnson years or before, Kissinger wanted to keep them secret; and the Nixon administration got a federal judge to enjoin the *Times* from printing further installments until the issue was resolved in court. Of course other newspapers went after the papers; and thanks to Daniel Ellsberg, a one-time Pentagon and Rand Corporation analyst who photocopied and distributed them out of antiwar fervor, the *Washington Post, Boston Globe,* and *St. Louis Post-Dispatch* got copies and printed them.[10] Injunctions were then sought by the administration in other courts. The Supreme Court took the case on an expedited basis; in July it ruled that in the absence of a British-style official secrets act, the government could not prohibit publication. This was a popular decision: by a 58%–30% margin Americans thought the papers should have been published.[11] As it turned out, publication had little immediate effect on American foreign policy. But the strongest messages in the Pentagon papers—the revelation that McNamara and his subordinate John McNaughton, who had died in a plane crash in July 1967, had come to have serious doubts about the wisdom of escalating the war—buttressed the arguments of those who believed that American escalation was based on incorrect assumptions. It further undermined an already weak (for many, nonexistent) faith in the wisdom of recent American leaders and the workings of major American institutions.

V

The most electrifying appointment of the Nixon administration was the naming of John Connally to be secretary of the Treasury in February 1971. For that job Connally actually had few of the standard qualifications: he had no background in finance, no connections on Wall Street, no experience dealing with the finances and currencies of the major Western allies. What Connally did have was iron self-assurance and an association with the presidents who still overshadowed Richard Nixon in both the public's mind and Nixon's own. Silver-haired and ramrod-straight in his early fifties, Connally was as handsome and self-possessed as Nixon was odd-looking and clumsy. He had served as a top staffer for Lyndon Johnson and as secretary of the Navy in the Kennedy administration; he had been elected governor of Texas in 1962, the same year Nixon lost the governorship of California. Sitting next to President Kennedy, he had been wounded by a bullet on that terrible day in Dallas in November 1963. In the 1968 Chicago convention, as undisputed head of the Texas delegation though he had already announced his retirement as governor, Connally had been the leader of Johnson loyalists, even though he himself was much more conservative than Johnson on domestic policy and a more convinced hawk on foreign policy. In the early 1970s, he had no particular prospects for further elective office[12] and no great connections to Texas wealth (he had been an aide to Fort Worth oilman Sid Richardson, perhaps the richest man in America in the 1950s, but Richardson's wealth and power went to his nephew Perry Bass). But his self-assurance, the quality which had endeared him to patrons as strong-minded and successful as Richardson and Johnson, endeared him as well to that less strong-minded and (in his own mind) less successful patron, Richard Nixon.

By the summer of 1971 it seemed to Connally, as it did to many observers, that the chances of avoiding an inflationary spiral were doubtful—and that if it were not avoided, Nixon's chances of winning reelection in 1972 would be doubtful as well. Nixon's Gallup job approval rating in June and July was only 49%–38%;[13] in hypothetical election pairings in May he had been running behind Muskie (39%–41% with 12% for Wallace) and just barely ahead of Kennedy (42%–41%–10%) and Humphrey (42%–39%–12%).[14] These showings represented no progress

for Nixon since the 1968 election. Moreover, voters' views on the top two issues
were not especially pro-Republican. For inflation they favored as drastic a solution
as wage–price controls by a 50%–39% margin, and by a 61%–28% margin they
preferred withdrawing all American troops from Vietnam by July 1972 to keeping
a residual force of 50,000 there.[15] There still were nearly 200,000 American troops
in Vietnam; and even through recession, inflation was still running around a
threatening 5% a year.

To meet this threat, Connally concocted a new economic program and pushed
it through to approval at an August 1971 meeting of administration economists at
Camp David. Nixon announced the plan in a televised Sunday night speech, but
it was explained in detail on Monday by Connally. The most notable domestic
feature was a 90-day freeze on wages and prices, to be enforced by a pay board,
a price board, and a cost of living council—the beginnings of just the kind of
bureaucracy which Nixon, remembering his days at the OPA price control operation
during World War II, had always inveighed against. Connally also ladled out tax
relief to politically well-placed groups: general income tax relief for the mass of
voters, an investment tax credit for big business, a repeal of the excise tax on cars
in order to help the Big Three auto companies and the UAW get the benefit of
the bargains they had made in November 1970. He imposed a 10% tax on imports,
thus putting a damper on international trade for the first time since World War
II. This feature made the program more palatable to industries—textiles, shoes—
which traditionally saw themselves as threatened by low-price foreign competition.
In the long run, however, what may have been the more important aspect of
Connally's economic program was its international features. The British, who as
usual in these years were trying vainly to support the pound, wanted to convert
$3 billion in dollars to gold. But Connally decided not to fulfill the longstanding
American promise to convert any amount of dollars to gold at a fixed price. This
closing of the "gold window" completely destroyed the system of currency exchange
set up at the Bretton Woods conference in July 1944, which was based on pegging
the dollar to the price of gold. The discipline imposed by this monetary policy was
politically inconvenient for the Nixon administration, and so it was done away
with. The result was a system of floating exchange rates and wildly fluctuating
gold prices which was accompanied by if it did not (and most economists thought
it did) promote severe inflation and retarded economic growth.

Connally's program[16] brought more state direction to economic policy and did
more to undercut the operation of free economic markets than anything done,
except in war, by the Roosevelt, Truman, Eisenhower, Kennedy, or Johnson
administrations. It was the product of a man contemptuous of the workings of
markets and confident that he could single-handedly make correct economic decisions for the nation and the world. Connally had thrived in a Texas which paid
lip service to the principles of the free market but whose great economic fortunes,
including those of Connally's patrons Richardson and Johnson, had much of their
basis in public policies, government regulations, and political favoritism. Connally
was just the latest and one of the most dazzling of the Texas fixers who hated

New Deal policies generally but schemed and took brilliant advantages of the new government apparatus the New Deal had set up. Now this sensibility was brought not to the setting of the oil depletion allowance or the allocation of a Texas broadcasting license, but to the determination of the fundamental rules of international trade and national currency. Connally was like a Texas cowboy in the Palace of Versailles, ignorant of who or what established the building, uncaring about what his spraying bullets might destroy.

VI

Of course in the short run the New Economic Policy was highly popular, as sharp changes in policy almost always are in times of perceived crisis. The policy was approved by a 68%–11% margin in a Gallup poll, and by 45%–10% Americans thought they personally would be better off economically in the next year.[17] Nixon's New Economic Policy increased his popularity and gave him leads, though not impressive ones, over Muskie (42%–36%–11%), Kennedy (43%–38%–10%), and Humphrey (43%–37%–11%). He was even farther ahead of John Lindsay (45%–30%–12%), who switched parties and became a Democrat in August 1971, and whose candidacy was taken seriously only because of his local celebrity in that still important media town, New York. For a moment administration policies seemed to be working. In September, with the sudden retirements of Supreme Court Justices Hugo Black and John Harlan, Nixon was able to appoint two justices of his own, Lewis Powell from the precincts of the establishment of Richmond, Virginia, and William Rehnquist from the mint-new stucco subdivisions of Phoenix and John Mitchell's Justice Department. In foreign policy the Soviets, far from shunning Nixon because of his opening to China and the continued American support of the South Vietnamese, made progress on a SALT agreement and on settling the still-festering Berlin issue. In October, Nixon was able to announce that he would go to Moscow for a summit with Leonid Brezhnev in the election year of 1972, three months after his trip to Peking. The same month the United States also came out for seating China in the United Nations, although UN Ambassador George Bush was unable to round up the votes to keep the Chinese out of the Security Council seat held so anomalously by the Taiwan-based Nationalist government. In November, there were further Vietnam troop withdrawals, leaving 139,000 Americans there—only one quarter of the maximum under Johnson. American casualties were down more than 90% since 1968, and no draftees were being sent to Vietnam anymore—a development which resulted in a perceptibly lower level of antiwar agitation on campuses than in 1968 or in May 1970, when it seemed to war might be widened. Also in November, Nixon announced the so-called Phase II of his wage–price controls, designed to hold inflation down to an annual rate of 2.5%. Nixon's system produced some of the disadvantages but none of the advantages of the wage–price bureaucracies of World War II and Korea years. It would be easy enough for a time to monitor the wage and price behavior of big companies and big government. But the continuing though at the time largely unnoticed vitality of small economic units, and the myriad ways in which fringe benefits could be substituted for wages and products could be modified, meant that in the long run the program could not succeed. Inflation could not be abolished by fiat; the economy would suffer distortions and dislocations when such an effort was tried.

Other ominous developments loomed for those who could see. In December 1971 the British withdrew from the Persian Gulf military forces which had been stationed there since World War II. The Conservative party had criticized the Labor government's January 1968 decision to withdraw, but once in power the Conservatives accelerated the timetable.[18] Though the initial decision had aroused opposition in the Johnson administration, Nixon and Kissinger evidently paid little attention to it: it is mentioned not at all in Nixon's memoirs and only cursorily in Kissinger's.[19] The Western withdrawal from the Gulf was quickly followed by sharp oil price escalations by the Organization of Petroleum Exporting Countries, the cartel led by such Gulf countries as Saudi Arabia, Iran, Iraq, and Kuwait. Americans, still preoccupied with winding down a war in a country which produces rice, were unwilling even to consider stationing military forces in a region which produced the lion's share of the world's oil.

Looking ahead to 1972, Nixon did not see these Middle Eastern developments as looming political problems. Even so, his outlook was not especially favorable. The major policy initiatives of his first two years—Vietnamization, FAP—were dubious political assets. The opening to China and the New Economic Policy were momentarily popular, but it was not clear that that popularity could be sustained. And even while they remained popular, Nixon was showing political weakness. By December 1971 his job approval rating was down to 49%–37%. His core support was clearly less than half the electorate. In primary pairings against Congressman Pete McCloskey, a lawyer from woodsy Portola Valley, in the hills above Stanford on the peninsula south of San Francisco, who had beaten Shirley Temple Black in a December 1967 special election and now was running against the president as a Vietnam dove, Nixon had a 73%–14% lead. But that was vaguely reminiscent of the margins by which Lyndon Johnson had led Eugene McCarthy four years before. In general election pairings Nixon was anything but an overwhelming favorite. In November he had statistically insignificant identical leads over Muskie and Kennedy (44%–41%–10%), though he was farther ahead of Humphrey (47%–37%–10%). His confrontational political stance had clearly helped him make inroads in the South and among less-educated voters, but his liberal policies had produced no political gains and left him with much smaller than normal Republican leads among college-educated and younger voters—both fast-growing segments of the electorate.[20] For all the achievements Nixon could claim, the outcome of the 1972 presidential election was by no means clear as 1972 began.

46

→)) ((←

Majority

L ooking back on the 1972 campaign with author Theodore White on Air
Force One on election day, Richard Nixon named as the first turning
point of his reelection victory the day George Wallace decided to run for the
Democratic nomination and not as an independent in the general election.[1] In
this assessment Nixon surely was correct. Late 1971 and early 1972 polls showed
him not much better than even with leading Democrats if Wallace was in the
race—he led Hubert Humphrey 46%–37%–12% and Edward Kennedy 45%–39%–
10% but was even with Edmund Muskie 42%–42%–11% in the January 1972
Harris poll. But Republican strategists like Kevin Phillips believed that Wallace
was drawing almost all his voters away from Nixon, even if at the time many were
saying that they would support Muskie. With Wallace in the race the Democrats
might well have won the election with something like the 43% which Hubert
Humphrey had gotten in 1968 and which George McGovern might have gotten
in 1972 if he had not made several avoidable mistakes, though it clearly would
have been hard for a Democratic presidential candidate to get the 50% needed to
win a standard two-candidate race. Nixon's own polling[2] showed him running
well ahead in two-way pairings in January, and his job approval in March ballooned
to 59% after his China trip. But he could not be confident his standing would
not decline (he had trailed Muskie in three-way races in Harris polls from November
1970 to June 1971); and all three-way pairings showed him well under 50%,
indicating that a crucial segment of his support was soft.

Wallace's decision to run in the Democratic primaries might have been testimony
to a residual faith even on his part that the Democratic party label was worth
something and was his only possible route to the White House. Or it might have
been the result of a deal. Many observers believed, as one writer put it, that
"Wallace abandoned the idea of a third-party race as part of a deal in which the
Nixon administration dropped a grand jury investigation of campaign funds which
involved Wallace's brother, Gerald."[3] Wallace denied that he had made any such
bargain. But in any case he could see that in comparison with 1968, when the
selection of Democratic delegates had been controlled by governors and party
insiders, he had a better chance to win delegates now, especially in the South,
in the proliferation of primaries which had resulted from the reforms proposed by
the commission originally chaired by George McGovern. The vote against him

would be split—between Muskie, the front-runner in most polls, and Humphrey, who was on the verge of running again,[4] and perhaps also Henry Jackson, ever skeptical of arms control and a critic of busing now, and McGovern, the most fervent and consistent critic of the Vietnam war in the race.

That such different politicians could hope to become the Democratic nominee illustrates the diversity within the Democratic party. And their differences were much less on economics, which they talked little about, than on cultural issues. All agreed that the Vietnam war now needed to be wound down and ended (even as Nixon was winding it down and, as it turned out, ending American involvement in it), but they disagreed on their attitude toward it. For McGovern it was a purely immoral assertion of power; for Wallace, a patriotic cause subverted by Washington and media intellectuals; for Humphrey, a well-intentioned policy which had proved unsuccessful; for Jackson, a war which had been strategically unwise but not supported strongly enough once it was undertaken; for Muskie, a sadly mistaken policy. They differed in their attitudes toward student protesters, toward black protest and welfare rights movements, about the wrongness of drug use. Their followers assumed, probably rightly, that they differed as well about purely cultural matters: how long men should wear their hair and how long mothers should stay at home with their children.

Their impulse, except for Wallace and McGovern, was to brush these issues aside as peripheral, and to insist that as Democrats and the heirs of the New Deal they would concentrate on economic matters. But here they found they had lost the populist high ground to Richard Nixon and John Connally. The economy was growing again in December 1971, unemployment was falling, and Nixon was planning to gun the accelerator for 1972 at least as emphatically as any Democrat would dare to recommend. Wage and price controls were in effect; the dollar was unhinged from gold and other currencies, so there was no way to charge that Americans' standard of living was being depressed to help foreigners. The Republican president, far from trying to scale down Social Security, was vying with Wilbur Mills, briefly a presidential candidate himself, to see who could increase it most: from this competition came the overindexed cost-of-living adjustments and benefit increases which nearly bankrupted the system and required major unpleasant changes in 1977 and 1983. The guaranteed annual income, proposed by Nixon and rejected by a Democratic Congress, was scarcely a viable political vehicle for a Democrat, although McGovern tried. A Democrat could argue that workers should make more money; but until John Connally's controls went into effect unions had been winning record wage and benefit increases, and they were doing well under Connally, too. A more activist government? Nixon had enlivened the Federal Trade Commission, had agreed to the creation of new activist bureaucracies like the Environmental Protection Agency and the Occupational Safety and Health Administration, had integrated the building trades with the Philadelphia plan and presided over the integration of schools in dozens of districts by busing orders. It was hard to think of things the federal government could do which it wasn't already doing under Nixon. The Democrats could argue, with some justice, that the elevation of millions of Americans from working class to middle class had been the achievement of Democratic presidents and Democratic Congresses. But these things had already been achieved, and Richard Nixon had demonstrated that you didn't need to elect a Democratic president to keep them.

In any case, it was obvious that the old economic-based party coalitions (which had never entirely replaced the configurations of support based on cultural factors like region, religion, and ethnic origin) had been reshaped by changes in cultural attitudes. The Democrats, thinking themselves the party of an economic-based majority coalition, were actually a party with less than a majority in national contests, a party made up of diverse and hostile cultural segments, few of which were much interested in economic issues.[5] The Republicans, still often thinking themselves the party of affluent Yankees, had trouble capitalizing on their potentials for gain, as the 1970 elections showed; and their capture of the White House made them less flexible and capable of adaptation to local factors than the protean Democrats in contests for other offices. The two parties were not quite in a position of deadlock: the Democrats' hold on the Senate and the Republicans' hold on the White House were too insecure for that. But in a time when confidence in institutions was low and declining, both were operating from positions of weakness, not strength.

II

Richard Nixon was one politician who was aware that his popularity was limited and his standing with the voters was tenuous, and he was prepared to use every lever at his command to win a second term in which he hoped he might escape from the predicament he found himself in in his first. In retrospect there is a certain symmetry to the Democratic presidential landslide of 1964 and the Republican presidential landslide of 1972: two incumbent presidents won reelection by wide margins. But these two landslides were not identical or even similar phenomena. The Democratic landslide was the voters' settled verdict on the record of an administration, decided upon when John Kennedy was president and maintained and even a little strengthened after Lyndon Johnson succeeded to the office. Nixon's landslide was anything but inevitable. It was not accompanied by any significant Republican gains in congressional or other elections, and it was contingent on events which had not happened and decisions which had not been made in December 1971.

Nixon's awareness of his dire straits was apparent in two decisions he announced in January 1972. First, he said he would withdraw half the remaining U.S. troops left in Vietnam, leaving only 69,000, though he had made no progress in the peace talks. Second, he recommended a budget with a record deficit of $25 billion. These were Democratic policies which, if he had been a challenger out of office, he might well have attacked as retreat abroad and reflation at home. But liberals, concerned to prove Nixon was an evil conservative, were not inclined to charge him with overliberalism.

The Democrats took little notice of what Nixon was doing: they were too absorbed in their own internal contest. The initial favorite for the presidential nomination was Muskie, and his theme in a time of cultural conflict and turmoil was reconciliation: "Trust Muskie." It came naturally to this somber, grave son of a Polish immigrant who was a tailor in a small town in Maine. As a young Democratic lawyer, Muskie had been elected governor in 1954 and 1956 and then senator in 1958 in what had been one of the nation's most heavily Republican states until the growth of the Catholic population in a region where party preference split almost precisely along religious lines. While campaigning for vice president in the gritty factory town of Washington, Pennsylvania, in September 1968, he had been heckled by college students; he had offered one of them, cigarette-puffing, side-burned, Rick Brody, 10 minutes on the podium if he would promise to listen to the candidate for 10 minutes, too. In his 10 minutes Muskie defended the American system by telling his own story and finished by saying, "Don't misjudge the basic good will of this American system." The exchange made all three network newscasts that night and put Muskie on the way to becoming arguably the most popular nominee of 1968. A few days later, in New York, he said, "The great issue in America is whether or not, as in the past, Americans can trust each other." And he would ask, "Who can you trust to hold this wonderful country of ours together as one people and one nation?"[6]

Muskie made his reputation for putting together environmental legislation, beginning in 1963 when it was not fashionable; his achievements included 1963 and 1967 air quality acts and 1965, 1967, and 1970 water quality acts, limiting pollution and providing federal dollars for infrastructure like sewers and water treatment plants.[7] This was not an easy or gentle business. Muskie had to buck major industries and fight his fellow members for jurisdiction; he was a tough, stubborn, sometimes vitriolic negotiator, "the most miserable man in the whole Congress to deal with," said Congressman John Dingell, himself no pushover.[8] But once Edward Kennedy was effectively removed from the race by Chappaquiddick in July 1969, Muskie became the front-runner. On issues, Muskie moved adroitly with other Democrats: the politician who had defended the majority plank on Vietnam in Chicago in August 1968 and voted for Lyndon Johnson's ABM in the Senate was supporting the Moratorium in October 1969 and stoutly opposed Nixon's ABM. He amassed a roster of impressive endorsements from holders of public and party office; and he built a large campaign staff which took up all of the building at 1910 K Street, renumbered 1972 K for the campaign. He led comfortably in preelection polls—but he was ambushed in New Hampshire. First his state coordinator, Maria Carrier, allowed herself to say that Muskie would be the loser if he couldn't carry 50% of the vote in the state next door to his native Maine. Then he was attacked stoutly by publisher William Loeb's stridently right-wing *Manchester Union Leader;* and in early March 1972, when the paper attacked his wife and printed an anonymous letter saying that he had spoken disparagingly of "Canucks"—that is, of French-Canadians, who made up a large share of New Hampshire's registered Democrats—Muskie appeared before the *Union Leader* building and, seeming to cry, denounced Loeb and his newspaper. The effect was devastating: the "crying incident" undercut the idea of Muskie as conciliatory and made him seem volatile and temperamental instead.[9] He won the New Hampshire primary on March 7, but only by a 46%–37% margin over George McGovern, who argued that he had opposed the Vietnam war from the beginning (his slogan, and the name of his campaign manager Gary Hart's post-campaign book, was "Right From the Start"). Muskie no longer seemed the inevitable nominee, and McGovern was now a serious contender on the left.

The same night that television viewers saw Muskie seeming to cry in the snow in New Hampshire, they were watching the majestic procession of Richard Nixon in the People's Republic of China. Nixon was the first American president to see China since Herbert Hoover, who had been there during the Boxer Rebellion of the summer of 1900. In this country sealed off from Americans for twenty-three years Nixon was now penetrating to the innermost sanctum (although he saw no evidence of the then ongoing Cultural Revolution); and the leaders of a nation of 800 million people, armed with nuclear weapons and seemingly unremittingly and irrationally hostile to the United States and its allies for almost a quarter of a century, were suddenly toasting the president of the United States and assuring him that they sought peaceful and even friendly relations. The China trip showed Nixon at his best, as an assured and innovative international statesman; and it spotlighted him at a time when the leading Democrat, thanks partly to Nixon's campaign operatives' Canuck letter, was seen at his worst. Nixon himself was careful not to do anything which looked like campaigning, though he had opposition in New Hampshire from two congressmen. California liberal Pete McCloskey was angry that Nixon had continued the war in Vietnam even at steadily reduced levels, while Ohio conservative John Ashbrook was furious that he was making overtures to China. McCloskey won 19.8% in New Hampshire; but he had set 20% as his goal for continuing the campaign; but he didn't get it, he moved quickly to meet the filing deadline three days later for reelection to the House in California.[10] Ashbrook won 9.7%, his biggest percentage until he got 9.8% in California; his entire performance demonstrated the opposite of his premise, that Nixon couldn't survive the loss of conservatives outraged by his recognition of Red China. Nixon was left with the winning percentage of 68%, which turned out to be his lowest in any primary. He would not be another Lyndon Johnson, forced out of office by the voters of his own party.

III

With Nixon returned from China, preparing for Russia, and effectively re-nominated, the focus shifted to the Democrats and their contest, a week after New Hampshire, in Florida. The major issue in Florida was busing. Governor Reubin Askew, a teetotaling reformer from the Deep South Navy town of Pensacola who had already pushed a major tax reform bill through the legislature, put two busing referenda on the ballot, not to posture against the federal courts but in the hope of reinforcing them. Instead Florida Democrats gave a big plurality of their votes to Wallace and made him once again the center of national political attention. Candidates who had been the subject of national media speculation up through Florida did miserably. Muskie finished fourth with 9% of the vote, Lindsay a pathetic fifth with 7%. Jackson, who emphasized his support of busing, finished third with 13%; Humphrey, who pitched his appeal to Florida's minorities of blacks, union members, and Jews, was second with 19%. Wallace had 42%, not a majority but enough for what was taken as a breathtaking victory.

Operating in the least culturally southern of southern states, Wallace had essentially snatched from the Democratic candidates viable in the North any chance of winning a primary in the South, while at the same time running well enough in the non-Dixie parts of the state to pose a threat in some primary states in the North. Wallace operated without much of an organization, as a brilliant speaker who could capture almost any crowd and who could always attract network camera crews. "Send them a message" was the message he sent, and he was capable of delivering it. "Trust Muskie," on the other hand, was directed at Richard Nixon, intended for the general election, and not capable of being transmitted easily in a primary-season sound bite. Moreover, the traditional sources of power in the Democratic party failed to deliver in this new, primary-heavy system. Muskie's legion of endorsers and Humphrey's fans in labor unions and among black leaders were not able to deliver the constituencies they purported to represent. McGovern, in contrast to his rivals, had few endorsements and was never capable of rousing a crowd. But he did have cadres of activists, veterans of the demonstrations and campaigns against the Vietnam war, young men and women who were impressed by McGovern's early opposition to the war. McGovern was also the only candidate who mastered the new rules. Not only were his volunteers able to identify, persuade, and turn out favorable votes in primaries; they were also capable of maximizing their delegate totals in every caucus system. In addition, they were able, through direct mail as well as solicitations of large givers, to raise large sums under the new campaign finance law which went into effect April 7, 1972. McGovern also used the medium of television better than his rivals. On each primary night, when other candidates were shown before frenzied crowds shouting thanks to faithful helpers, McGovern appeared on the networks' half-hour primary specials in a calm setting and spoke directly to the voters in the next contest. After Florida he said that he shared the disillusion of many Wallace voters about things as they were. There never was much overlap between the Wallace and McGovern constituencies, but he established some linkage.

McGovern avoided the Illinois primary March 21, for the delegates were selected in separate elections which were won by organization candidates. Wisconsin on April 4 was dovish territory, filled with antiwar activists and devoid of old-fashioned machine politicians: McGovern beat Wallace there 30%–22%, carrying even the Polish and German south side of Milwaukee and running far ahead of Humphrey (21%), Muskie (10%), Jackson (8%), and Lindsay (7%). The next big contest was in industrial Pennsylvania, where nearly half the state's households, and probably most of the state's Democratic households, contained a union member. Here the unions helped Humphrey to a 35% victory—the first primary the sixty-one-year-old Humphrey had won in three presidential campaigns. Second place was essentially a tie among Wallace (21%), McGovern (20%), and Muskie (20%). On the same day McGovern beat Muskie in Massachusetts by 53%–21%—at which point Muskie left the race. In the next two weeks Humphrey edged McGovern in Ohio and Wallace in Indiana by tiny margins; Wallace then won Tennessee and over the opposition of former Governor Terry Sanford carried North Carolina 50%–37%—proof, if anyone still doubted it, that the southern Democratic vote was his. Humphrey won 67%, his best percentage of the year, in West Virginia; but McGovern edged him 41%–34% in Nebraska, just south of South Dakota, where both Humphrey and McGovern were born.[11]

Then, on May 15, while campaigning in Laurel, Maryland, Wallace was shot and grievously wounded; he would be paralyzed below the waist for the rest of his life. The immediate political effect was to inflate his percentages in the two primaries the next day. He carried Maryland narrowly and Michigan by a wider margin; more than half the latter state's Democratic votes were cast in the Detroit metropolitan area, and with turnout inflated by the busing controversy Wallace took 51% to 27% for McGovern and only 16% for Humphrey.

Yet even as the spotlight was on Wallace, it was also turning to McGovern, who, it was suddenly apparent, might very well be the Democratic nominee. And in a year when the voters had not irrevocably decided to reelect Richard Nixon, McGovern was initially the object of sympathetic consideration. In March and April 1972 he was behind Nixon 59%–32% and 54%–34% in Lou Harris polls, showings notably weaker than Muskie's and Humphrey's. But these reflected voters' unfamiliarity with him, and in May he had closed the gap to 48%–41%. This is a result of the highest significance: it showed that at least in his initial appearance in the spotlight McGovern did not come off badly and that he might well be the strongest of the conceivable Democratic nominees; it suggested that his positions on issues and his right-from-the-start opposition to the Vietnam war might not be the electoral handicaps so many in Washington imagined; it showed that Nixon, as an incumbent president who was universally known but not supported by 52% of the voters, could very well be beaten.

But nothing was standing still in the spring of 1972. While the Democrats moved out to the West Coast for the climactic primaries in Oregon on May 23 and California on June 6, Nixon took one of the greatest risks of his career by bombing Haiphong Harbor in May, just before his scheduled trip to Moscow. The risk—and how great a risk it was no one could be sure—was twofold: first, that the North Vietnamese would break off negotiations; second and more important, that the Soviets would cancel the summit meeting or reject Nixon's negotiations, as Khrushchev had done to Eisenhower in May 1960 and to Kennedy in June 1961. But Nixon calculated that both adversaries would decide that accepting the bombing was the preferable alternative, and he was proved correct. The bombing did not break off negotiations with the North Vietnamese. Nor did it prompt Brezhnev to cancel the Moscow summit. There Nixon was able to hold out the prospect of a détente with the Soviet Union, a prospect of great value to the

American people in general, and to announce the conclusion of a deal to sell very large amounts of American wheat to the Soviets, an announcement of great value to the chronically disaffected Farm Belt states in particular. More important electorally, Americans were becoming convinced, correctly, that their involvement in the Vietnam war really was, as Nixon had said it was all along, on its way to being concluded.

In the California primary the two leading Democrats debated three times, and Humphrey tore into McGovern by asking him to explain his "demogrant" proposal. This was an idea, crafted by staffers, to produce something like a guaranteed annual income by granting every American the sum of $1,000 a year, to be financed by a progressive tax. McGovern himself was hazy on the proposal, which he said would not really cost anything—as if Social Security, which was also a transfer of money from one set of taxpayers to another set of recipients, did not cost anything either. Alternatively, he said that it would cost those with incomes between $12,000 and $20,000 only an extra $21 a year—a figure taken out of the air. The $1,000 a year plan, as it became known, and his proposal to substantially increase estate and gift taxes were the McGovern staff's response to the not unjustified refrain that their movement was interested primarily in the foreign policy issue of the Vietnam war and subsidiarily in a variety of cultural issues, but not at all in traditional Democratic economic issues. Without any instinctive understanding of the electorate, they set to work on the drawing boards and came up with two proposals which, in theory, did redistribute a great deal of income and wealth.

The trouble was that they turned out to be heavily unpopular with the voters they were supposed to benefit. In an affluent country in affluent times with plenty of upward mobility, most voters seemed to think they were or would be the people from whom McGovern wanted to redistribute income and wealth, rather than the beneficiaries of these redistributions. In California, Humphrey pointed out that single people with incomes of $8,000 would pay more under McGovern's plan, that a family of four with an income of $12,000 would pay $409 more. And he added, his staccato delivery moving rapidly, that McGovern's defense policies would "halt the Minuteman procurement, half the Poseidon procurement, halt the B-1 prototype. Phase out 230 of our 530 strategic bombers. Reduce aircraft carrier force from 15 to 6. Reduce our naval air squadrons to 80 percent. Halt all naval surface shipbuilding. Reduce the number of cruisers from 230 to 130. Reduce the number of submarines by 11." To these specifics McGovern responded in a soothing manner but with no reassuring specifics of his own.[12] His lack of answers cut deeply into his vote in the California primary—and would cut even more deeply into it later.

IV

So by early June 1972 the political fortunes of Richard Nixon were entirely revived. His gamble on the bombing of Haiphong had not destroyed the summit, and he could plausibly claim that peace was on its way in Vietnam and that the

United States had at last become reconciled with both Communist China and the Soviet Union. George Wallace's shooting had reduced to zero the chance that he would run as a third-party or independent candidate in the general election. For reasons not entirely clear, consumer confidence in the economy rose substantially in June: voters evidently decided that prosperity was here to stay. Humphrey and McGovern had destroyed each other's chances by the time of their debates in California, and the decision by Humphrey and his labor allies later in June to vote against giving McGovern the entire 271-vote California delegation he had won under the state's winner-take-all primary law (a law written when California was a much smaller part of the nation than it was in 1972) guaranteed that the two sides would be at war up through the July convention in Miami Beach. Nixon's tenuous 48%–41% lead over McGovern in the May Harris poll was replaced by a solid 54%–38% in June and 55%–34% in early July. In May, Nixon had quite possibly been on the way to losing. By June he was pretty clearly assured of winning.

But this advantage was not apparent to the operatives in charge of the campaign. Reflecting, as every campaign does, the character of the candidate, the 1972 Nixon campaign cut every corner, violated every rule, and took advantage of every loophole it thought it could get away with. It assigned a young lawyer, Donald Segretti, to play "dirty tricks" on the Democrats; his operation produced the Canuck letter which helped to sink Muskie's candidacy. In order to bring the Republican national convention to Nixon's favored site, San Diego, a $400,000 commitment was extracted from ITT's Sheraton hotels; not long afterwards the Justice Department dropped an antitrust case involving other parts of the ITT empire. Incoming Attorney General Richard Kleindienst lied about this in congressional testimony, and ITT lobbyist Dita Beard put on a farcical performance professing illness in a Denver hospital in April and May 1972. Nixon's chief fund-raiser, Maurice Stans, went around to corporate chief executives with lists of federal regulatory and legal matters in which their corporations were involved and recommendations that they contribute $50,000. These were typically not men who had that kind of money in their checking accounts: the unstated but obvious deal implied in Stans's presentation was for the executive to contribute $50,000 or so of the corporation's cash and for the government to refrain from all adverse action. Although corporate contributions were illegal, until April 7 the old campaign finance law applied and cash contributions were legal. In the last two days before April 7, according to later testimony, more than $2 million in cash passed into the Nixon committee's hands.

Finally, there were the activities of the Committee to Reelect the President, headed by John Mitchell and later dubbed CREEP by its adversaries. Nixon's paranoid mentality and contempt for the law had already resulted in violations of criminal law by government officials: a burglary of Daniel Ellsberg's psychiatrist's office, for example, and wiretaps unauthorized by any court on columnist Joseph Kraft. Into CREEP Mitchell allowed the likes of E. Howard Hunt, a former CIA operative, and G. Gordon Liddy, a former Dutchess County, New York, assistant district attorney (and nearly successful candidate for Congress in 1968). They set up a squad including CREEP security chief James McCord and three Cuban-American activists, which burglarized the Democratic National Committee's offices in the Watergate complex on the night of June 16–17, 1972. Why they targeted the DNC was and is unclear, although Nixon, obsessed as always with the Kennedys, seems to have been eager to learn more particulars about an acknowledged relationship between reclusive billionaire Howard Hughes, who had once lent Nixon's brother Donald some money, and Democratic National Chairman Lawrence O' Brien, a former top campaign aide to John Kennedy. McCord and the Cubans were apprehended by an alert security guard and Washington, D.C., police officers. But Hunt and Liddy made their escape from the Howard Johnson's Motor Lodge across the street, and the burglars' connection with the Nixon campaign seemed only bizarre. Nixon was aware at least from June 23 of the involvement of Mitchell and members of his campaign staff—if he was not the instigator of the operation all along, a plausible proposition but one for which hard evidence has never been found; on that day he ordered the CIA to keep the FBI (no longer headed by the sometimes stubborn Hoover, who had died in May), off the investigation. Nixon argued many times that his political opponents used similar tactics. But there is no other recorded instances of an American president using secret agencies of government to cover up the burglary of the opposition party's headquarters.

This was obstruction of justice, criminal behavior. But Nixon, complaining again and again of the injustices other politicians (especially the Kennedys) and the press had done to him, seems to have found that behavior alluring. Characteristically, he insisted on doing at least as badly to his opponents as they had done to him—and characteristically, he failed to appreciate that he was operating in a time when voters were far more sensitive and hostile to violations of procedural rules and infringements on the rights of others than they had been in the days when Robert Kennedy was bearing down on Jimmy Hoffa or Lyndon Johnson was getting leaks about what his opponents were up to.

Nixon did have options other than those he chose. He could have disengaged himself from the scandal in June 1972 by sacrificing the high officials of his campaign who had had some knowledge of it. But that course would have carried at least some political cost, since the story at the time had very low visibility; and any politician hesitates to cause himself political trouble in the short run in order to avoid greater trouble in the long run if he thinks there is a good chance that greater trouble will not occur, or will occur after the election.

V

In June and July 1972, the Watergate incident was obscured by the struggle for control of the Democratic party. McGovern's majority at the convention was tenuous and was threatened by the credentials committee's decision to divide the California delegation proportionately according to votes cast. His opponents surely recognized the high cost of such tactics in a procedure-conscious age and knew that any other nominee would not be regarded as legitimate by many voters and might face a third-party challenge. But they believed that McGovern's views on foreign policy were a genuine danger to freedom and must be challenged and rebuked if at all possible. They could not yet be certain that he would lose to Nixon, and they were correct in thinking that he was genuinely different from Humphrey or Muskie. McGovern, for most of 1948, had supported Henry Wallace rather than Harry Truman, switching to Truman only reluctantly and at the end. He genuinely believed that the United States was as much a threat to peace in the world and democracy in at least some countries as was the Soviet Union and that what amounted to unilateral disarmament by the United States would persuade the Soviets to disarm, too, and even if not, would be desirable nonetheless. George Meany of the AFL–CIO, a staunch supporter of the Cold War, found these views and a McGovern nomination utterly unacceptable (although he would not have vetoed Humphrey or Muskie, even though they were Vietnam doves by then).

In Miami Beach these forces were launched in titanic battle. Competing for a nomination which (as soon became apparent if it was not already) was worthless, they fought as if great things were at stake. The key vote was on the California credentials fight. The McGovern forces, commanded by delegate counter Rick Stearns from a trailer out in the corridors of the hall, had contrived to lose a feminist challenge to the South Carolina delegation so as to avoid a parliamentary precedent which might be fatal in California. Momentarily there was consternation as many observers, including CBS's Walter Cronkite, reported that McGovern had lost control of the hall. But after a rousing speech by California Assemblyman Willie Brown ("Give me back my delegation!"), the 271 California McGovern delegates were seated. The McGovernites next proceeded to oust the Illinois delegates, including Chicago Mayor Richard J. Daley, on the grounds that though popularly elected their ranks included too few women and minority-group members to satisfy the new rules the McGovern–Fraser Commission had written; they seated instead a delegation chosen quite irregularly which included rebel Alderman William Singer and civil rights activist Jesse Jackson. The fetish for their new rules was starting to hurt the McGovernites' cause. It continued to do so. They proceeded to nominate McGovern (the roll call was conducted in a preselected random order, so as not to discriminate on the basis of alphabetic sequence) and then totally botched the vice presidential nomination.

McGovern's own choice for the office was a fellow senator he barely knew, Thomas Eagleton of Missouri, who had been sixth on his original list. Edward Kennedy, after some telephone calls to Hyannisport and back, rejected the nomination; Sargent Shriver could not be reached because he was on a business trip to Moscow; Kevin White was offered the nomination, accepted, and then suffered the indignity of having it withdrawn when he was vetoed by John Kenneth Galbraith as a former Muskie supporter;[13] Senator Gaylord Nelson of Wisconsin, a friend of McGovern and many other politicians, firmly declined as did the next two men. Finally the choice settled on Eagleton, in time to make the McGovernites' self-imposed 4 P.M. deadline for submission of names. The nominations dragged on past midnight, including an appearance in which Senator Mike Gravel of Alaska ludicrously took the platform and, moved to tears, nominated himself. Thus Kennedy's rousing introduction of McGovern—one of the best speeches of his career— and McGovern's acceptance—not as good by a long shot, but one of his best speeches—were not broadcast until around 3 A.M. Eastern time, prime time in Alaska and Hawaii. "Come home, America," McGovern proclaimed—a call for withdrawal from Vietnam (though that had mostly been completed) and from other foreign commitments as well and a call, in his view, for a return to the best of American progressive values.

Eagleton was a fine choice, but for one thing. More articulate, more humorous, from a larger state and a faster political track than McGovern, son of a prominent and politically adept St. Louis lawyer, elected city prosecutor at twenty-seven and state attorney general at thirty-one and still only forty-two in July 1972, a Catholic unburdened with a record on Vietnam during the Johnson years (because he was elected to the Senate only in 1968), he seemed a fine candidate and, whatever the fate of McGovern, a possible future president himself. But only days after the convention, when McGovern was vacationing in South Dakota's Black Hills, Robert Boyd and Clark Hoyt of the Knight newspapers learned that years before Eagleton had been hospitalized twice for depression and had had electroshock therapy. This drastic treatment suggested to many that he lacked the stability Americans want in a possible president. Yet McGovernites had a strong impulse to proclaim a lack of prejudice against anyone with a previous mental illness. Eagleton made no move to get off the ticket; McGovern said he backed him "1,000%." Eagleton proclaimed to a cheering crowd in Honolulu that he would stay on forever. Then McGovern proceeded clumsily, through his designee as Democratic national chairman, a husky-voiced Utah mink farmer named Jean Westwood, to do what he had had to all along and dump him.

The story stayed on the newscasts for days, making McGovern look unprogressive to his own followers and vacillating and unreliable to everyone. His candidacy had become such an obviously lost cause that he had a hard time finding another running mate. Kennedy turned him down again, several times; Senator Abraham Ribicoff of Connecticut refused without hesitation; Humphrey, pursued on the Senate floor and off, refused a "humiliating, debilitating exposure";[14] Reubin Askew, on vacation in the cool North Carolina hills, said no; Muskie, to whose modest house in Bethesda, Maryland, McGovern repaired, took a day to think about it and refused; finally Shriver, not in Moscow this time, checked with Lyndon Johnson, Richard Daley, and Kennedy and accepted. Shriver was a fine choice, and would have been a better one in Miami Beach. He owed his elevation to public office to the fact that he had married Joseph Kennedy's daughter Eunice. But he was a man of culture and good humor, with a touch of Cary Grant-like class and a total lack of pomposity. He had performed ably in every office he held, launching the Peace Corps with an enthusiasm still echoed three decades later, setting up antipoverty programs with no sign of corruption or fraud during his tenure, serving Presidents Johnson and Nixon as ambassador to France when the Vietnam peace talks were taking place in Paris.

So as the Republicans prepared to meet in convention and renominate, with exactly one dissenting vote,[15] Richard Nixon, the McGovern candidacy collapsed. The candidate who was within spitting distance in the May Harris poll was behind 57%–34% in early August, before the full impact of the Eagleton affair hit, and 63%–29% in early September.[16] For the rest of the campaign Harris showed Nixon at 59% or 60% and McGovern fluctuating between 31% and 35%—results which comport with the final result of 61%–38%. In June it had appeared that McGovern was headed toward the same 43% Humphrey had won four years before, distributed slightly differently. The convention and the Eagleton fiasco cost him about 5 percentage points. He ran behind Humphrey's showing most grievously not in the South—where Humphrey was already exceedingly weak except in Texas—but in small factory towns, full of older, tradition-minded, blue-collar Democrats who sensed the cultural divide between their values and McGovern. The events of the fall campaign changed almost nothing, except possibly for the damage done to the Democrats by Nixon TV ads showing John Connally sweeping tin soldiers and ships off a table and denouncing McGovern's defense cuts. Watergate was not a major issue. In June the *Washington Post*'s Bob Woodward and Carl Bernstein— two young reporters from the metropolitan desk assigned to what had first appeared to be a routine crime story—had reported that the arrested burglars had White House consultant E. Howard Hunt's phone number in their notebooks and that $25,000 in cash paid to them could be traced to the Committee to Reelect the President. But that information was little noticed as McGovern's candidacy disintegrated in July. Seven of the Watergate burglars, including Hunt and Liddy, were indicted in September; but trial was set for after the election. In October, by hard-nosed lobbying of Republican members and of Democrats themselves vulnerable to blandishments by special interests or threats of prosecution, the administration roused enough votes to stop House Banking Committee Chairman Wright Patman, a venerable but ineffective populist, from investigating the scandal. In September and October, Woodward and Bernstein wrote spectacular stories reporting that Watergate was part of a massive sabotage campaign financed by a fund controlled by Mitchell and others and that Nixon's chief of staff, H. R. Haldeman, was involved in the scandal. These accusations were denied in thunderous tones by Nixon's press spokesmen and, aside from two stories on the *CBS Evening News,* were mostly ignored by the rest of the nation's media. The effect on opinion, except perhaps in a few scandal-conscious states in the Upper Midwest, seems to have been minimal.

Nor did McGovern's return in October to denunciations of the Vietnam war or Henry Kissinger's slightly premature declaration in late October that a deal had been reached with the North Vietnamese have much effect. Politically none of these developments mattered. To McGovern and many of his fervent antiwar followers, the continuing U.S. involvement in Vietnam from January 1969 to

November 1972 was not just a mistaken policy, but a crime; the offense was not just the number of casualties or the number of draft-age Americans sent over, but the fact that their country continued to be embarked on a deeply immoral enterprise. Their focus was not on what would ultimately happen to the South Vietnamese, for any calculation of that might lead to the conclusion that a victory for the U.S.-backed forces would be preferable to a Communist triumph, but on what the war effort said about the moral character of the United States. The Senate, McGovern had said in one of his early speeches on Vietnam, had "blood on its hands"—a statement which ignored who else might have blood on theirs, and how much. From this perspective, it was not very important that Nixon had reduced U.S. forces in Vietnam down toward zero, that he had virtually ended the draft, that he was prepared to make major concessions to the North Vietnamese and Viet Cong in negotiations. What mattered more was that Nixon had continued the war and had asserted its moral worthiness. Most voters did not share the McGovernites' perspective. For them, U.S. involvement in Vietnam had been a mistake, not a crime; and they were concerned less with the past than with the future. Much more than the McGovernites, they were aware of the facts on the ground. In the fall of 1972 they knew that almost all the U.S. troops had been withdrawn from Vietnam, that no more were going to be sent there, that draft calls had declined from 299,000 in 1968 to 50,000 in 1972; and they cared no more than they had in 1965 about the fate of South Vietnam. Vietnam had been discounted as an issue; what the 1972 presidential election was about was cultural conflict.

For in 1972 there was still a deep divide between what might be called tradition-minded America and trend-minded America, between what columnist Joseph Kraft called Middle America and the part of the country which sympathized with the counterculture. It was not an absolutely neat division, for the large majority of Americans had come to accept the civil rights movement's indictment of racial segregation, and their levels of trust in most insitutions were well below those of the early 1960s.[17] On the other side, the minority who applied intense critical scrutiny to most aspects of American life still celebrated the Bill of Rights and the country's traditions of tolerance. McGovern, despite his flat midwestern accent, his corny manner, and his five children, clearly was seen as part of the adversary culture. Nixon, though he had lived at the sophisticated pinnacles of American public life for more than twenty years, seemed plainly Middle American in his sympathies.

Given this contrast, it is not surprising that Nixon, after hovering at or below 50% in two-candidate polls for several years, won 61% of the vote and McGovern only 38%. The decline in party loyalty, obvious in the 1964 results, continued. Most white southerners had voted for John Kennedy in 1960; only about one in eight voted for McGovern in 1972 (or, outside of Texas, for Humphrey in 1968). That left McGovern with less than one third of the vote in any state of the old Confederacy. He was also weak in traditionally Democratic blue-collar areas, winning less than 40% in states like Maine, New Jersey, Pennsylvania, West

Virginia, Ohio, Indiana, and Missouri. But in the northern tier and along the West Coast—the historic heartland of the Republican party and the Progressive Old Northwest—McGovern was almost competitive with Nixon. He won Massachusetts with 54% of the vote, and without the Eagleton fiasco (and without the busing issue in metropolitan Detroit) he probably would have won Rhode Island (where he got 47%), Humphrey's Minnesota and his own South Dakota (both 46%), Wisconsin (44%), and Michigan (42%) and would have been competitive in Oregon (42%), California (42%),[18] New York (41%), Illinois (41%), Iowa (40%), and Connecticut (40%). These were not an inconsiderable part of the country: together with the District of Columbia, which McGovern of course carried,[19] they contained 201 electoral votes. If he ran far behind Nixon in declining working-class neighborhoods like Long Island City, Queens, he was carrying the glittering and once solidly Republican Upper East Side of Manhattan across the East River. If he was losing votes in smudged-stucco working-class South Gate and Huntington Park outside Los Angeles, he was carrying Beverly Hills and the booming West Side neighborhoods all around. In a nation which was rapidly becoming more affluent and culturally liberated, this trade-off was not necessarily as bad as it would have been in the downscale America of the heyday of Second New Deal economic politics. In important parts of America, McGovern's dovish foreign policy, his cultural liberalism, and his politics of procedural regularity were political assets, attracting new constituencies to his party label. Even the Watergate scandal seems to have had some impact in states like Iowa and Wisconsin, which had always prided themselves on their lack of corruption. These states where McGovern ran relatively well would prove to be growth areas for the Democrats in years to come—and even in 1972.[20]

VI

The Republicans gained almost no political advantage out of their president's landslide in 1972. The Nixon campaign made a deliberate decision not to campaign for Republican candidates. John Connally headed a group called Democrats for Nixon, whose roster included some who might well have been indicted had they not agreed to endorse Attorney General Kleindienst's boss; and he insisted that Nixon direct his appeal primarily to Democrats culturally disaffected with McGovern. To add to that an appeal to vote for other Republican candidates, he argued, would be self-defeating. This advice was almost certainly wrong. McGovern's unattractiveness to such Democrats was so great that Nixon was unlikely to lose many, and he certainly had a large cushion. But once again, as in 1960 and 1968, he squandered the chance to campaign for the ideas and policies he professed privately and in his memoirs to believe in. By hurling epithets against his opponents, he enraged them without rousing his supporters to what he insisted were his causes.

The upshot was that the Republicans gained only a handful of seats in the House and actually lost seats in the Senate. In the House races the reapportionment of seats among the states, though it favored the Republican-leaning Sun Belt, was a wash between the parties, because Democrats controlled redistricting in Florida, Texas, and California. Democrats lost 8 seats and gained 8; Republicans lost 4 and gained 4. In races where redistricting was not a major factor, the Republicans gained 17 seats, but a number of them were won for odd reasons—a popular incumbent retired, a fluke winner two years before was beaten, minority-party candidates split the Democratic vote in 2 southern seats, 2 seats were gained when conservative Democratic incumbents were beaten by liberals in primaries. Suburbanization accounted for 5 of the Republican gains, as the district lines for 1972 followed people out to the more Republican areas they had moved to between 1960 and 1970. In only 6 seats—4 in the South, 2 in the straight-ticket states of Connecticut and Indiana—did Republicans win thanks to Nixon's coattails. And they were balanced by 6 Democratic gains. If the Democrats lost seats in Colorado and Nevada, where environmental-antiwar liberals had beaten conservatives in the primaries, they gained back the Denver seat they had lost the same way two years before (and would gain back the Nevada seat in 1974 as well); and they picked up a Utah seat on similar issues. Otherwise their gains came mostly in northern tier states, and mostly in districts where challengers had prepared the ground by making strong races in 1970. Republicans, depending on a well-financed national party and a president used to giving central direction, generated relatively few good challengers in House races where candidate quality was increasingly crucial. Democratic challengers, on the other hand, inspired by antiwar and environmental issues, were springing up everywhere; the new people whom the old party bosses complained about were even in 1972 winning elections for Democrats, many in places Democrats had never carried before. Richard Nixon may have won a big victory in 1972, but the House in years to come would be dominated by the likes of 1972 Democratic winners Patricia Schroeder of Denver and Gerry Studds of Cape Cod, Massachusetts.[21] Nixon carried 376 of the 435 congressional districts, but Democratic House candidates won half of those seats. Except for 3 in Massachusetts, the 59 McGovern districts, most of them in central cities, all elected Democrats to the House.

In the Senate races the contrast between the northern tier and the South was clear. Republicans gained 4 seats, all south of Washington, D.C. In three of them incumbent Democrats had retired or been beaten in the primary—North Carolina, where Jesse Helms won, Oklahoma, and New Mexico—while in Virginia an incumbent was caught unaware when Republican William Lloyd Scott's campaign used the proceeds of a bank loan guaranteed by a millionaire for a last-minute ad campaign which beat anti-Byrd Democrat William Spong; the loan was of course repaid by the millionaire rather than the campaign (afterwards the law was changed so that guarantees would count as contributions and be subject to the $1,000 contribution limit). But this replacement of moderate Democrats by conservative Republicans was offset by the replacement of conservative Republicans by liberal Democrats in five states and of a moderate Republican by a moderate Democrat in Kentucky. The liberal wins were mostly surprises. In Maine, Congressman

William Hathaway outhustled veteran Margaret Chase Smith. In Delaware, twenty-nine-year-old Joseph Biden showed an ear for voters' alienation and replaced an amiable but tired incumbent who had been persuaded to run by the Nixon campaign in order to prevent a nasty primary fight. In Iowa, Congressman John Culver's aide Dick Clark walked across one of the nation's most dovish states and beat a lackluster incumbent. In South Dakota, one-term Democratic Congressman James Abourezk took advantage of the absence of Senators McGovern (out campaigning) and Karl Mundt (incapacitated by a stroke since 1968) to provide constituency services and make himself an easy winner. In environment-conscious Colorado, which had recently voted to reject the Winter Olympics, Floyd Haskell's late purchase of TV ads surprised and upset Gordon Allott, thus facilitating the journalistic career of columnist George Will, who had been on Allott's staff.

The new Congress, in other words, would be no friendlier and was potentially more hostile to Richard Nixon than either of the two Congresses he had faced in his first term. Nixon may have won big in the electoral college, but he had demonstrated no significant ability to help his friends or hurt more than a few of his enemies in other elections. Nor was he any force at all in the politics of the large states, which had governors who were Democrats or Republicans not beholden to Nixon. He could take some satisfaction in his landslide victory, of course. But he also had reason to feel politically beleaguered.

Even more important, he had paid some heavy prices to ensure this victory. Wage-price controls would prove to be unworkable, and lingering controls on energy prices and rents in big cities would distort the workings of the economy and exact heavy costs by the end of the 1970s. The closing of the gold window and the abandonment of the Bretton Woods system led to ten years of terrifying inflation at home and abroad, and to a serious dampening of economic growth. The acquiescence in the withdrawal of Western military power from the Persian Gulf helped enable the OPEC nations to raise oil prices, at hideous cost to the economies of most of the world. The Social Security increases and the double cost-of-living adjustment which resulted from his competition with Wilbur Mills, policies justified on the unlikely assumption that another baby boom was about to occur, would threaten to bankrupt the Social Security system in 1977 and 1983. The Soviet wheat deal propped up a rotting Soviet economy and produced a boom–bust cycle in the American Farm Belt. Nixon in 1972 took the usual risk which incumbents tend to take and suffered the usual consequences—he pumped up the economy too much, a step which led to a recession a year later—but he did many more harmful things besides, with more lasting and more serious consequences, to secure his reelection.

By his own account he was dissatisfied with much of the work of his first term. He was pleased by his slow extrication of the United States from Vietnam and believed that the South Vietnamese government had a chance to survive, and he certainly took satisfaction from his successful opening to China and summit diplomacy with the Soviet Union. But domestically, he had been successful only when he pushed in liberal directions and had usually failed when he tried to move things the other way. While arousing the anger of the liberals, he had ended up doing much of their work. The president who had come to office decrying government bureaucracy created OSHA and EPA, continued the antipoverty program, and came close to establishing a guaranteed annual income. He appointed a chief justice who sanctioned massive school busing and a secretary of labor who wrote the federal government's first racial quota regulation, the Philadelphia plan. He signed the bill authorizing the eighteen-year-old vote and presided over the most aggressive antitrust enforcement since the days of Thurman Arnold in the Roosevelt administration. Abroad in the land Nixon saw abortion legalized—the Supreme Court decision invalidating all state abortion laws, *Roe* v. *Wade,* was handed down in January 1973, having apparently been delayed until three days after his inauguration as a courtesy by Chief Justice Burger;[22] he saw pornography and prostitution[23] become widely accepted in American life; he saw marijuana become widely prevalent; he saw homosexuality become more open and premarital sex become a commonplace. The counterculture had been beaten decisively in the 1972 presidential election. But in many other ways, in politics, in government, and in everyday American life, it had seen its values prevail, and the values that Richard Nixon purported to represent defeated and humiliated.

47

⟶⟫⟫ ⟪⟪⟵

Watergate

Richard Nixon began his last term in national office not jubilant but full of resentment. He would even old scores and reverse the direction of national policy. He would try to capture control of a federal government which he had twice been elected to lead but which seemed so often frustratingly beyond his grasp. The day after the election he abruptly decreed that every person holding appointive office in the federal government must resign. The entire Cabinet and White House staff were expressly included. Nixon was obsessed with "the Eastern stranglehold on the executive branch and the federal government"[1] and believed, with some basis, that top civil servants and many of his administration's appointees were not sympathetic to his policies; he wanted to staff the government only with those who were. "There are no sacred cows," he told his White House staff the day after the election, and then shifted metaphors. "We will tear up the pea patch."[2]

This upheaval was glaringly out of tone with his reelection campaign, in which he had carefully avoided the Republican label and presented himself as the candidate of the consensus, of the political center: nothing in it prepared the public for the idea that the second Nixon administration would involve great departures from past practice. As in 1960 and 1968, Nixon had not taken the occasion of the campaign to stress his belief in policies which under other circumstances—in resentful comments hurled defiantly from the stump at his opponents or recorded privately in his diary—he professed to support. As a result, once in office he had little support in public opinion and could not call on the political strength inherent in a president who has been elected on an explicit platform.

Even in areas where his policies were political assets, he received little credit after the election. The economic policies which had boosted the economy enough through 1972 were still appreciated by the voters. But in December he kicked the props out from under his generally popular anti-inflation policy by announcing abruptly that wage and price controls would be abandoned. His success in winding down the Vietnam war was widely appreciated. But the winding down took more time and more American action than perhaps voters had counted on. In December, frustrated by the post-election unwillingness of the North Vietnamese to agree to terms he and Henry Kissinger could sell to the South Vietnamese, Nixon ordered intensive bombing of the North, which his critics called "carpet bombing." Soon

513

enough a peace agreement with the North acceptable to the South was produced—"peace with honor" was Nixon's phrase, hurled at his critics. As a result of the agreement, Americans saw the films of returning prisoners of war stepping off planes and running to embrace their wives and children, and they heard accounts of North Vietnamese torture which had been pooh-poohed by the war's opponents and denied by travelers to Hanoi like Tom Hayden and his wife, actress Jane Fonda. Some observers who remembered the politics following the fall of China in 1949 expected another round of recriminations against those who failed to stop Communist aggression. Instead Vietnam seemed to fade out of Americans' consciousness just as it faded off their television screens.

Nixon followed up his abandonment of economic controls with an offensive against the ever-increasing size of government. In January 1973 he proposed a budget with $6.5 billion in cuts from current spending projections for 1973 and $16 billion for 1974. In early February his budget director, Roy Ash—the job was relabeled director of the Office of Management and the Budget—announced that the administration would impound, or refuse to spend, some $8.7 billion authorized and appropriated by Congress in bills signed into law by Nixon. Impoundment was an old procedure, routinely used by an executive branch which was not always able to spend as much as Congress wanted it to. Seldom if ever had it been used to frustrate the purpose of Congress and destroy programs a president didn't want funded—an obvious end run around the Constitution, which provided for a presidential veto but also provided that it could be overridden by two-thirds votes in Congress. But this was clearly Nixon's intention. Congress, deeply distrustful of Nixon as it had come to be distrustful of Johnson, was busy considering what would ultimately become, over Nixon's veto, the War Powers Act, an intended infringement on the president's power to act on his own in foreign policy. It was not hard to predict that attempts by the president to act on his own in the domestic sphere would meet with similar resistance. But shortly thereafter these initiatives and issues were almost immediately forgotten because of the reemergence of an issue voters had known about but mostly paid little attention to in 1972: Watergate.

II

Ordinarily complexity works against the emergence of a political issue. A large cast of characters, tangled stories and conflicting interests, unclear ethical standards and legal precedents—all these were present in the Watergate scandal as it unfolded in early 1973, and all ordinarily make a political controversy impenetrable for ordinary citizens. But with Watergate they all seemed to work in the opposite direction. The cast of characters proved vivid and engrossing; the stories were parsed and compared, almost line by line; debate on the rightness or wrongness of particular acts was pursued not just in the halls of Congress and on television newscasts, but in ordinary homes and workplaces. The participants, once linked by a common interest in keeping things covered up, suddenly had conflicting motives as some spoke out lest they be implicated by others or left, in White House aide

John Ehrlichman's later phrase, "twisting slowly in the wind." Looming over the whole scandal was Richard Nixon. The public which had reelected him so overwhelmingly in November 1972 had even then no great confidence in his integrity. Voters had seen through the years how he was petulant in victory as well as defeat, how he concentrated on getting even with his enemies even when he had the chance to frame issues and set goals for the entire nation.[3] Nixon was respected but not trusted, his strength with the voters would last only as long as his effectiveness remained, and his effectiveness in turn was undermined as it became apparent that he could not be trusted.

The unraveling of the Watergate cover-up began in the Washington courtroom of U.S. District Court Judge John Sirica, where the Watergate burglars went on trial in January 1973. All but McCord and Liddy pleaded guilty, and those two were convicted by the jury. But Judge Sirica, a one-time Republican committeeman in the District of Columbia and a notoriously tough sentencer in criminal cases, was not satisfied that the full story had been told. He was suspicious that the defendants were being promised clemency and money (as indeed they were) for their silence, and he imposed the maximum sentences on them pending resentencing later, with the clear intention of making them talk.

Meanwhile, the Senate was setting up a special Watergate committee, to be chaired by Sam Ervin, with Howard Baker as its ranking Republican. Ervin was a seventy-six-year-old North Carolinian, a former judge and judicial conservative who opposed civil rights laws and the Equal Rights Amendment, a self-proclaimed "country lawyer" who seemed to quiver with hesitation when he spoke. But he was also a devotee of constitutional protections, as he interpreted them, who could declaim as he doubtless had to juries in moonshining cases in his native hills William Pitt's saying that no officer of government, not even the king of England, could cross even the humblest of thresholds without a search warrant issued by a court. A partisan Democrat, Ervin deeply mistrusted Nixon. Howard Baker was from the other side of the Great Smoky Mountains, from the ancestrally Republican hills of east Tennessee. His father had been a congressman from the Knoxville district and had been succeeded briefly by his widow, Howard Baker's stepmother, when he died; Baker himself married the daughter of Senator Everett Dirksen. He could have run for the family House seat in 1964 but had wider ambitions, losing a special election for senator that year, then winning the seat by impressive margins in 1966 and 1972. Forty-eight years old, soft-spoken and articulate in a way which made him as persuasive a television performer as any of his contemporaries, Baker was a partisan Republican, but with his own base in the party and his own ambitions. He was shrewd enough never to allow himself to be used as the tool of Richard Nixon. Nixon understood what he was up against. In February 1973 he declared he would invoke executive privilege and refuse to let his staffers testify before the committee.

The Watergate committee and Judge Sirica's courtroom were not the only venues of investigation. The Senate Judiciary Committee was holding confirmation hearings on the nomination of L. Patrick Gray to be head of the FBI. As acting director since May 1972, he had been in charge of the Watergate investigation which Nixon claimed was so complete. Now he was being questioned about it by hostile committee members Edward Kennedy, Birch Bayh, and Robert Byrd. A conservative on most policy issues, little known except as a detail man in his capacity as Democratic whip, Byrd was a stickler for details.

In mid-March things began crackling. On March 19, McCord wrote a letter to Sirica charging that a cover-up was taking place, that "political pressure" had been put on the defendants to be silent and that perjury had been committed in the trial—a letter which Sirica immediately realized would "break this case wide open."[4] On March 22, Byrd pinned Gray down into admitting that White House counsel John Dean had "probably lied" during the FBI's investigation; Dean, a one-time House Republican staffer who was little known, had conferred with Nixon about the burglary in September 1972 and then, after a long hiatus and unknown to outsiders, began meeting with the president as his closest aide on this issue starting February 27, 1973. On March 26, the Watergate grand jury was reconvened. Stories began to be leaked that Dean and others were implicating Mitchell, Haldeman, and Ehrlichman. On April 17, Nixon claimed that he had begun a new investigation March 21 but revealed no results; those came instead from Dean, who issued a statement saying he would not be a "scapegoat," and Gray, who resigned. On April 30, Nixon announced the resignations of Haldeman and Ehrlichman ("two of the finest public servants I have ever known"), the firing of Dean, and the forced resignation of Kleindienst, who was succeeded as attorney general by Elliot Richardson, a Massachusetts Brahmin, former HEW secretary, and current defense secretary. "Honk if you think he's guilty" bumper stickers began appearing in Washington; in Boston stickers appeared with an outline of Massachusetts, the only state McGovern had won, and the words "We told you so." In early May, there were other revelations at the trial of Daniel Ellsberg for releasing the Pentagon papers: Judge Matthew Byrne revealed that Ehrlichman had dangled the directorship of the FBI as a sort of bribe before him; the burglary of Ellsberg's psychiatrist's office (with tools provided by the CIA) first became known. Meanwhile, Mitchell and Maurice Stans were indicted for perjury and obstruction of justice in connection with contributions to Nixon's reelection campaign by the convicted and fugitive financier Robert Vesco.

Watergate became the focus of American journalism. Television news, ill-suited to covering abstract issues, slow-moving national trends, and complex governmental matters, proved able to handle the concrete facts of burglary, cover-up, lying, and betrayal. It was able to portray much more vividly than print journalism could the characters caught up in the scandal. The Ervin committee hearings, which began May 18, were covered live on television for two months. Ervin's folksy but often incisive questions, Baker's refrain of "What did the president know and when did he know it?," Florida Republican Edward Gurney's dogged defense of Nixon, and Connecticut Republican Lowell Weicker's relentless attacks on him became familiar to most American voters. Nixon's job approval rating plummeted, from 68% in the Gallup poll just after the peace agreement with North Vietnam in January

1973 to 48% in April, 44% in May and June, 39% in July, 36% in August, 33% in September, and 27% in October; never again in his presidency did he rise to the 30% level.

The decline in Nixon's ratings liquidated his political capital with Congress. His assets there had never been great: party loyalty worked against him; he cultivated personal relationships with only a few Republicans and southern Democrats, fewer than a dozen altogether; his own service there had been so brief and so long ago as to be irrelevant. His first political moves after the 1972 election had been alarming to members of both parties; his firing of Cabinet members and other appointees removed some men who had built relationships with Capitol Hill and gave their power to a few White House assistants whom most members of Congress had never laid eyes on; and the impoundment policy was a direct threat to Congress's greatest institutional power, the power of the purse.

Now, with Watergate, a president who, to exaggerate only a bit, was bent on governing without Congress suddenly found he needed Congress very badly. Members had seen in the 1970 and 1972 elections that there were no particular rewards for them in supporting Nixon and that there were seldom grave penalties for opposing him. They didn't like him and they weren't afraid of him. When Kleindienst was forced to resign as attorney general, the Senate exacted from Richardson as the price of his confirmation a commitment to appoint an independent special prosecutor, a roving Watergate investigator with the power of subpoena and no obligation to obey, indeed with considerable incentive to attack, the White House. Richardson's choice for this job was Archibald Cox, a crew-cut Harvard Law School professor who had been solicitor general in the Kennedy administration, an aggressive advocate and a partisan Democrat. When the Senate Watergate committee subpoenaed administration witnesses and documents, Nixon was forced to abandon his claim of executive privilege, thus paying a political price for making the claim but gaining no political benefit from it. On most substantive issues, he was in continuous retreat. His plans for government-by-impoundment failed; Congress in its haphazard way kept control of the budget. The bombing of Cambodia, which he considered necessary to bolster the South Vietnamese regime, he had to abandon in July 1973. The War Powers Act was passed over his veto in November.

Nixon attempted to seize the initiative by freezing the price of retail goods in June and instituting "Phase IV" of his wage and price controls in July. And in foreign policy he pulled off the spectacular feat of having Soviet leader Leonid Brezhnev visit Washington and Nixon's Casa Pacifica in San Clemente, California, in June. But both Phase IV and the Brezhnev visit were overshadowed later in the month by the coolly delivered, detail-packed Watergate committee testimony of John Dean, which implicated Mitchell, Haldeman, and Ehrlichman directly and charged Nixon with authorizing payment of hush money to the Watergate burglars. In mid-July a committee staffer, in a routine interrogation, asked former White House functionary Alexander Butterfield whether Nixon ever taped his conversations. Butterfield replied that an elaborate White House taping system had been set up in the spring of 1971 and had been in operation ever since. Previous presidents going back to Franklin Roosevelt had taped some conversations; Nixon was the first to do so systematically.[5] His public testimony to that effect made a sensation, and both the Ervin committee and Archibald Cox demanded certain tapes. Nixon refused them both. The committee sued. Legal battle was joined. But the political battle Richard Nixon had already lost.

III

Seldom has a month been as full of ominous events in American government and politics as October 1973. On October 6, with complete surprise—for it was Yom Kippur, the highest of Jewish holy days, when literally everything stops in Israel—Egyptian troops invaded the Israeli-occupied Sinai Peninsula and Syrian troops attacked the Israeli-held Golan Heights. The Egyptians made great progress initially—the only Arab attack ever to throw back Israeli troops. On October 10, in the federal courthouse in Baltimore, Vice President Spiro Agnew pleaded guilty to evading taxes on bribes paid to him by Baltimore area businessmen while he was governor of Maryland and vice president. He was given no jail sentence, as part of a bargain which required him to resign his office.[6] On October 15, Richard Nixon and Henry Kissinger—appointed secretary of state the month before—agreed to resupply Israel with military equipment; Israel had still not turned the tide of battle, and the Soviets were supplying the Arabs. On October 20, Nixon ordered Elliot Richardson to fire special prosecutor Archibald Cox for refusing to accept the president's offer of a synopsis of the requested tapes rather than the tapes themselves. Rather than fire Cox, Richardson and Deputy Attorney General William Ruckelshaus resigned. The firing was then done by Solicitor General Robert Bork, the last link in the legal chain of command, who feared chaos at the Justice Department if he refused to act. That same day, the Arab oil-producing countries declared an embargo on oil exports to the United States, in retaliation for its help to Israel, and ordered production cuts as well. On October 22, the United States and the Soviet Union jointly sponsored a Middle East cease-fire which went into effect two days later. On October 23, House Democrats led by Majority Leader Tip O'Neill decided that the House Judiciary Committee should begin hearings on the impeachment of the president.

These developments created a new and different world, the outlines of which could not have been perceived in January 1973 but were indelibly inscribed and beginning to be filled in by January 1974. The fortuitous removal of the plainly incompetent Agnew helped clear the way for the ouster of Nixon. The Yom Kippur war led proximately to the Arab oil embargo and the vast rise in oil prices and general inflation which followed, causing damage to the economy so great that the wage and real income levels reached in 1973 would prove a high point not to be attained again for years afterwards. In foreign affairs, the Yom Kippur war resulted in a more or less continuous involvement of the United States in Middle East diplomacy to a greater extent than ever before. The firestorm of negative response to the firing of Cox—the Saturday Night Massacre, as it immediately became known—led to a sharp leftward lurch in the House and the effective takeover of its leadership by O'Neill and liberal political operators in place of the more conciliatory Carl Albert and generally conservative committee chairmen. Nixon's ambitious plans for conservative governance were utterly dead, the generally liberal initiatives and achievements of his first term (except for the opening to China and the SALT treaty) were almost entirely forgotten, and the triumph of the ideas of his opponents seemed virtually assured.

Agnew's abrupt removal once again gave Congress leverage over Nixon. The 25th Amendment, drafted by Birch Bayh and ratified in February 1967, provided for the first time a way to fill vacancies in the vice presidency:[7] the president would nominate and majorities in each house of Congress must confirm. Nixon's choice was John Connally.[8] He had considered dumping Agnew and putting Connally on the ticket in 1972; he wanted Connally as his successor in 1976; he wanted him in the number two spot now. But it soon became apparent that Connally, who had just switched to the Republican party and was deeply distrusted by politicians on both sides of the aisle, could never be confirmed. Nominating either Nelson Rockefeller or Ronald Reagan would, Nixon thought, split the Republican party—and confirmation of either would install a successor whose presidential stature might seem superior to that of the Watergate-wounded Nixon. So Nixon quickly decided on House Minority Leader Gerald Ford, a stolid conservative elevated to his job over the quicker and more astringent Charles Halleck in January 1965, a plodding speaker who had followed Nixon faithfully on almost every issue, temperamentally a team player who had many friendly relations with Democrats as well as Republicans in the House. Nixon believed he was competent to take over the presidency, and there was no doubt that he would be confirmable—although after the Saturday Night Massacre, Congress examined his credentials and disclosure forms closely, and he was not confirmed until December.

For a few days in October it had appeared that Israel's security might really depend on American assistance, and for a few days it had even seemed possible that the American and Soviet aid to opposite sides in the Yom Kippur war might escalate to a more direct conflict. In the aftermath, both superpowers were drawn into determining terms of settlement. Kissinger had long been excluded from Middle East issues because it was thought that as a Jew he would not be accepted as a suitable mediator. But his skills and his authority were needed, and he was brought in. The American role became greater after Egyptian leader Anwar Sadat expelled Soviet advisors and technicians from his country. The United States, which had friendly relations with the governments of Israel, Egypt, and Jordan and was on speaking terms with the government of Syria, was the only possible mediator. Kissinger's "shuttle diplomacy" concentrated on producing a more stable line of settlement between Israel and Egypt; it provided a precedent for the even more direct and personal intervention later in the 1970s by Jimmy Carter.

In the meantime, the Arab embargo began to drive up oil prices in the United States. The boycott could not keep oil out of the United States. It is among the most fungible of commodities, and the operation of oil markets was by no means suspended. But the world market was vulnerable to pressures producing a sudden rise. World oil prices had been low for years because the cost of marginal production in the vast Saudi Arabian fields was very close to zero. (Prices in the United States were higher because Congress and the Texas Railroad Commission purposely propped them up to provide a good return to American producers.) The first OPEC country to show the ability to use its sovereign powers to raise prices had been Libya in 1971, when it got the Western oil companies bidding against each other for extraction rights there and obtained a high price from Dr. Armand Hammer's Occidental Petroleum. Now, with Western military power removed from the Middle East, the Arab powers aggrieved with Israel and greedy for higher prices felt themselves free to break their contracts; and Saudi Arabia's market power working with spot shortages resulted in sharp increases in the world price. The United States, having acquiesced in Britain's withdrawal from the Persian Gulf in 1971, had no leverage to prevent these.

In the United States politicians and consumer advocates immediately shrieked that the big oil companies were using the embargo as an excuse to jack up prices and reap huge profits, charges which had only a shred of truth. The real problem was that American voters had no stomach whatever for stationing troops in or near countries which produced oil. Lines formed outside gasoline stations not so much because the boycott was effective in making oil scarce but because existing price controls on gasoline meant that supplies were allocated bureaucratically rather than by markets, with inevitable inefficiency. Americans were spending hours lining up to pay close to $1 a gallon for a commodity they were used to purchasing instantly for less than 30 cents—a price which had fallen in real terms over the preceding decade. They were topping off their tanks rather than running them down to empty—a practice which by itself accounted for nearly 1 billion extra gallons at any given time in a nation with 102 million passenger cars. The Americans of 1973 cherished their automobiles almost more than anything else. They spent lavishly on their cars, spent hours a day in them since they chose to live and work in locations far apart, accessible usually only by private automobile; they regarded the freedom and flexibility their cars gave them, and the comfort and glamour they provided, as important, even central, parts of their lives.[9] Many of them, perhaps one out of ten, depended on automobiles for their livelihoods as well. The gas lines were not just an inconvenience; they were threatening to make obsolete a comfortable and cherished way of life. And the government and politicians to whom most Americans of 1973 were accustomed to look for the solution of problems which vexed them could offer no plausible solution this time.

By October 1973 the United States was already heading into a recession, in the familiar pattern which had led to the recessions of the political off-years of 1958 and 1970 and threatened similar harm to the Republican party. But the oil embargo and the resulting inflation and disruption made the recession deeper than it would otherwise have been, and more impervious to the traditional Keynesian remedy of deficit spending by government. For that was limited by inflation, and inflation also began to erode investment returns and work incentives. The drive by labor unions for higher wages in the early 1960s had been transformed into drives first for higher fringe benefits and greater security—not just the security of an assured paycheck rising automatically with inflation, but the security of a comfortable and early retirement. This transformation probably represented some generalized change in personal economic goals, a change which made sense in a time of rising real incomes. And the political as well as the economic system was responding to these desires, notably in the Social Security changes in 1972, when the COLA gave elderly Social Security recipients security against inflation. The result was an economy with many people scrambling for security and few pushing for greater production. Productivity increases trailed off sharply at this time; real wages declined; welfare payments, increased many times in the years before 1973 but left mostly steady in the inflationary years afterwards, reached their peak in 1973.

IV

The political landscape was transformed as well. The Democratic party in Congress and in states across the country was suddenly united under the leadership of men more consistently hostile to the politics which Richard Nixon represented for them than any Democratic leaders before. The Republicans, their liberal wing atrophying, their conservatives demoralized, were not a coherent political force. Electorally, the events of October 1973—especially the Saturday Night Massacre— determined the outcome of the elections of 1974. For Nixon's debacle prompted the candidacy of dozens of smart, aggressive, politically adept Democratic candidates and dissuaded almost all such Republicans from running. In the fluid political environment of the years after 1964, when most voters were not moored to party identification and were open to appeals by candidates with attractive personal qualities and their own specific issue platforms, the critical factor in elections was how many strong challenger candidates a party would field. In 1966 the Republicans were able to field many such challengers and had won many seats whose Democratic incumbents failed to use the advantages of incumbency. By 1972 few House members of either party failed to use incumbency intelligently, and the number of House incumbents returned to office, which had reached a record high in turbulent 1968, when voters were eager to reward familiar figures, remained very high amid the less disturbing and more typical partisan currents of 1970 and 1972.

The Democrats in these years held down their losses in large part because of strong young candidates, motivated by opposition to the Vietnam war, support of environmental causes, and hatred of Richard Nixon. By October 1973 they had many more such strong challengers gearing up to run than the Republicans did;[10] and for all practical purposes decisions had to be made by that time, not so much to meet legally imposed filing deadlines (though Illinois's was as early as December 1973) as to meet practically imposed deadlines for raising money and organizing a campaign staff in an era when party organizations were clearly incapable of running a successful congressional campaign. In the Senate races this discrepancy made little difference, since in the fluid ticket-splitting environment of the 1960s and 1970s both parties were capable of winning Senate elections in every state and most Senate races were seriously contested, whatever the partisan trend of opinion. But in the House races the trend could make a great difference and did in the 1973–74 cycle.

The trend coincided with an internal change in the House. Speaker Carl Albert had said he would retire in 1978, when he would turn seventy. But by 1973 it was apparent that the skills which had helped him round up Democratic votes in the conservative-leaning, southern-dominated House Democratic ranks of the 1950s and early 1960s had either atrophied or had grown irrelevant as he passed age sixty-five. On Vietnam, especially, in his patriotic desire to support the administration of either party Albert was out of line with an increasing number of House Democrats who for idealistic or opportunistic reasons were furious in their opposition to Nixon's policy, even after American troops had left, opposition signaled by their successful campaign to force Nixon to stop the bombing of Cambodia. The House majority leader elevated when Albert became speaker after the 1970 elections was Hale Boggs of Louisiana, an articulate liberal first elected to the House in 1940, who had risked his uptown and suburban New Orleans seat by voting for civil rights and had nearly been defeated in 1968. He was also a foreign policy hawk and an old-fashioned wheeler-dealer in his way of doing business. Boggs was the obvious successor to Albert and seemed likely to be a more able and energetic speaker. But in October 1972 he went to Alaska to campaign for freshman Representative Nick Begich, their plane was lost in the cloudy skies over the mountains of the Alaska panhandle, and his seat was ultimately declared vacant.

That declaration resulted in the elevation to the majority leadership of Tip O'Neill of Cambridge, Massachusetts, the successor to John Kennedy in the House but a very different kind of Irish Catholic Democrat. He was a product of Cambridge the town, not gown, whose only connection to Harvard was a summer job cutting grass and trimming hedges in Harvard Yard, a Democrat whose politics started with finding jobs for his constituents, one by one or through massive government public works programs, and whose opposition to the Vietnam war beginning in September 1967 was prompted not by his Harvard constituents (who were vastly outvoted at a time when the voting age was still twenty-one) but by the arguments of his children around the family dinner table.[11] O'Neill was capable of being a charming talker, but he was a better listener, ambling slowly through the marble halls of the Capitol asking fellow Democrats and an occasional few Republicans "What do you hear?" He had been elected to the Massachusetts House in 1936, when Democrats there were a despised and totally unconsulted minority; he had the satisfaction of becoming the first Democratic speaker in the twentieth century after the 1948 election and showed the skill to dominate that body with only a narrow Democratic majority and an utterly uncooperative Republican opposition of mostly Yankee Protestants who believed that the mostly Irish Catholic Democrats were incapable of governing. In the U.S. House, O'Neill had served on the Rules Committee and seen Chairmen Howard Smith and William Colmer combine with

Republicans to frustrate the majority Democrats. From these experiences he had developed strongly partisan instincts, and an impulse to rule the House not through a coalition of northern Democrats and liberal Republicans with just a few southern Democrats, as the AFL–CIO lobbyists were used to doing, but through a cohesive Democratic party united around such issues as might be available to hold them together. And while the AFL–CIO, out of the hawkish and Cold War convictions of George Meany and other leaders, tried to bludgeon northern antiwar Democrats into line, O'Neill was ready, even before his own conversion on the war, to listen to dovish Democrats and to work with them.

O'Neill was thus disposed to work with the insurgent Democrats led most ably and aggressively by Phillip Burton of San Francisco. An oversized, loud, bellicose, bullying man, with a posture of standing always for the downtrodden and the underdog, Burton had been elected to the House in February 1964 (to replace John Shelley, a labor Democrat who had been elected mayor). In the beginning he seemed doomed to be a hopeless outsider, voting against the Vietnam war and for abolishing the House Un-American Activities Committee. But Burton was also an organizer and was chairman in 1971–72 of the Democratic Study Group, a small band of liberals when it was formed by Eugene McCarthy and others in 1957. Burton dominated the DSG as chairman and afterwards, and under his leadership it prepared the House's best whip notice (written description) of roll call votes and included on its rolls most of the Democrats in the House. Temperamentally an old-fashioned boss who gloried in his role as California redistricter (of Assembly and state Senate as well as U.S. House seats), he was the champion of procedural reform in the House, notably election of committee and subcommittee chairmen and of House leaders and assertion of policymaking power by the Democratic caucus. Burton was not trusted by O'Neill, who was never comfortable with ousting senior members from positions of power; but the reforms Burton was seeking for their consequences O'Neill was coming to accept because of their wide backing among House Democrats. Unlike Sam Rayburn, who had considered the large Democratic House majority produced by the 1958 election troublesome because the new liberals sought measures his old committee chairmen opposed, O'Neill and Burton both wanted to see as many Democrats elected as possible in 1974—Burton because he saw new Democrats as the key to his power in the caucus, O'Neill because he saw new Democrats as the key to his power in the House. So both men and their allies worked to make sure that strong Democratic candidates, who for years had been able to expect little financing except from a handful of labor unions and rich liberals, would have enough money and professional campaigning advice to win.

At the end of 1973, both men were on their way to succeeding. And both were profiting immensely from the disgrace of Richard Nixon. Both had reason to dislike him: O'Neill knew him as a contemporary in the Washington of the 1950s, for whose character he had early developed contempt in poker games;[12] Burton remembered his 1962 gubernatorial campaign, when Nixon had demanded that Pat Brown repudiate Burton, then an assemblyman, for his opposition to HUAC. Now

Nixon and the conservative presidency he only belatedly tried to build were being destroyed, by the president's own misdeeds and miscalculations; and the insurgent, reformist, antiwar House which O'Neill and Burton, in their different and sometimes antagonistic ways, were trying to build was springing into creation. And so it was the House, where Richard Nixon had started his political career and first won national fame, which with its new leadership and its new governing coalition was now, twenty-five years after Nixon's confrontation with Hiss, the chief institutional locus of power against Nixon, poised to oust him from the White House.

48

$\rightarrow$$\gg\!\gg$ $\langle\!\langle\!\langle$$\leftarrow$

Impeachment

A s 1974 began in Muncie, Indiana—the "Middletown" which the pioneering
sociologists Robert and Helen Lynd had studied in the 1920s and 1930s[1]—
Philip Sharp was running for Congress for the third time. As a twenty-eight-year-
old junior faculty member at Ball State University, he had won 49% of the vote
against Republican David Dennis in the recession year of 1970. In 1972, when
George McGovern was winning only 31% in the 10th District, Sharp won a
respectable but still clearly losing 43%. On the cultural divide which split the
nation in the early 1970s, Muncie was clearly on the tradition-minded side: the
factory workers on the south side of town were, if anything, more hostile to the
critical-minded youth than were the professionals and business people of the west
side. Nor was the increasing tilt of the Democratic party to urban, urbane liberals
attractive in Muncie. The last time the 10th had elected a Democratic congressman
was in 1958, when it voted 51% for Randall Harmon, who lost in 1960 when it
was revealed that he had rented out his front porch to the government as his
district office.

Sharp was a different kind of candidate. His roots in the everyday life of Muncie,
for example, were not deep. Born in Baltimore, he had gone to DePauw University
in Greencastle, Indiana, on the other side of Indianapolis from Muncie, and then
to Georgetown and Oxford. Then he worked on the staff of Indiana's Senator
Vance Hartke. Only in 1969 did he join the Ball State faculty, and almost immediately he began running for Congress (although he did get his Ph.D. in 1974).
Politically, Indiana was still one of the most patronage-minded of states, with state
employees required to kick back 1% or 2% of their salaries to the political party
of their boss. Local legislators and county officials in towns like Muncie got into
politics for personal advancement. But most were not much interested in serving
in the U.S. House, which controlled little or no patronage, and Sharp was not
much interested in patronage; so he and the local Democrats got along. In the
early 1970s, Sharp won the enthusiastic support of the United Auto Workers, the
largest union in Muncie, because he was believed to support its positions on national
issues (though in fact he would not vote on economic issues in the utterly reliable
pro-union way almost all northern Democrats had in the years up to 1974). His
money came as much from national as from local sources, from labor and liberal

political action committees and contributors who spotted him as one of the Democrats' many likely winners that year, and who saw that he was able to spend almost precisely as much as the incumbent Dennis.[2]

The political climate in which Sharp's campaign against Dennis was being conducted in January 1974 was totally different from that of January 1973. Then the incumbent Republican president had just successfully extricated America from Vietnam and had a 68 percent positive job rating. Now the same president was defending himself lamely and unconvincingly against charges of covering up a burglary and had a 29 percent positive job rating.[3] Then the economy had seemed to be growing, and inflation seemed tame. Now the economy was plainly in recession, and inflation in the preceding 12 months had been the highest since 1946. Then the affluence, security, and personal choices open to ordinary Americans seemed almost limitless. Now on Kilgore Avenue and Broadway in Muncie, as on main streets everywhere in America, motorists were lining up for gasoline, while out on four-lane U.S. 35 and Interstate 69, where they used to drive at 70 miles per hour or more, they were now limited to 55. The undisputed achievements of the Nixon administration—including its extrication of Israel from the brink of defeat and its facing down of the Soviets in the Middle East in October 1973, in the midst of the Saturday Night Massacre firestorm—elicited no great positive response in Muncie; the shortcomings of Nixon and his administration were the focus of all political attention.

In this environment there was little that Dennis, an articulate, peppery sixty-two-year-old lawyer, could do to advance his political cause. He was surely astounded to find himself, as a member of the Judiciary Committee, considering a motion to impeach the president who had won the votes of forty-nine states only 14 months ago; and there was little doubt that he would use the talents which had served him well for years with juries in Richmond, a city founded by Quakers and still characterized by an unusually articulate and educated population, to defend Nixon at every step and harass the attacking Democrats. Voters in Muncie believed by a wide margin that the country was not going in the right direction but was pretty seriously off on the wrong track.[4] They believed that Nixon should leave office, though more wanted him to resign than to be impeached—a word which in January 1974 still seemed forbiddingly strange to many Americans. They tended to favor the Democrats on energy price controls (because they feared the Republicans were too sympathetic to the hated big oil companies) and on fiscal policy (because of the recession). The cultural divide which had yawned so wide a year or so earlier now seemed less threatening, partly because American involvement in the Vietnam war was over, partly because people with different cultural attitudes were getting used to living together, partly because some of the practices of the trend-minded (casual marijuana use, divorce, abortion) were becoming more common among all segments of society—or at least all segments of the young.[5] So the Democrats were able to benefit from such associations as they had with the trend-minded without losing ground among the tradition-minded.

II

The Muncie district was only one of more than 100 in which Democrats in January 1974 were making serious challenges in Republican-held seats.[6] Events—everything the voters saw on their television newscasts—were moving the Democrats' way. In a November 1973 appearance Nixon had memorably declared, "I'm not a crook." Nine days later his secretary, Rose Mary Woods, had testified that by activating a foot-pedal while stretching to answer a telephone, she had caused the 18½-minute gap on a tape of Nixon speaking with Haldeman three days after the Watergate break-in. The same month Nixon, through acting Attorney General Bork, had replaced special prosecutor Archibald Cox, with his close Kennedy ties, with Leon Jaworski, a Houston lawyer long associated with Lyndon Johnson. In December, Nixon had nominated as his new attorney general Senator William Saxbe of Ohio, a plain-speaking skeptic about Nixon's innocence whose chief virtue from Nixon's perspective was that as an incumbent senator he could be confirmed. In January 1974, Nixon admitted having taken political factors into account in raising milk price supports in March 1971—a transaction for which John Connally would be indicted in July 1974, in Nixon's second-to-last week in office, and acquitted long afterwards. In February, Nixon argued publicly that he couldn't be impeached except for breaking a criminal law. In March, Mitchell, Haldeman, and Ehrlichman were indicted for covering up the Watergate scandal (and as Judge Sirica revealed in June, Nixon was named as an unindicted co-conspirator); Senator James Buckley, the Conservative party nominee elected as a Nixon supporter in 1970, called on Nixon to resign. In April, Nixon agreed to pay $432,000 in back taxes after the huge deductions he had taken for donating his papers to charity were questioned. Also in April, Nixon was subpoenaed by a 33–3 vote of the House Judiciary Committee to turn over tapes and documents already requested; later that month Nixon submitted edited transcripts of the tapes, which the committee rejected as inaccurate. In May, the committee formally began impeachment hearings—a carefully choreographed and presented proceeding in which Nixon's attackers and his defenders as well grappled gravely with the evidence as they were covered live by all three television networks. The same month Jaworski appealed to the Supreme Court his case seeking sixty-four tapes from Nixon.

In the midst of these Watergate headlines, other issues seldom obtruded. When they did, they were bad news for Nixon. In April, for example, inflation exceeded 1% a month—which is to say it reached double-digit figures on an annual basis. Nixon did travel in June, first to the Middle East, where it was announced he was suffering from phlebitis, and then to the Soviet Union, where he was feted by Leonid Brezhnev and appeared before friendly crowds which he could no longer find in the United States.

III

Through all these events the voters were heard from. In February the special election to fill Gerald Ford's Grand Rapids seat was won by Democrat Richard Vanderveen, who called for Nixon's resignation and said Ford ought to be president. It was the first time that a Democrat had won this northern tier seat since 1910. Two weeks before, Democrats had picked up an industrial Pennsylvania seat formerly held by a Republican; weeks later they captured a seat in heavily Republican Cincinnati. Suddenly the top political writers and television network reporters were looking at the special House election in Michigan's 8th District, which included the factory cities of Saginaw and Bay City and the heavily Republican sugar beet and bean fields of the so-called Thumb of Michigan's mitten-shaped Lower Peninsula—the descendant of the district which in another special election in November 1931 had first signaled that the bottom had fallen out politically for Herbert Hoover. Nixon traveled to the district and appeared in a motorcade in the Thumb with Republican candidate James Sparling. But Democrat Bob Traxler won handily. The Democrats were fortunate to have four special elections in or near the northern tier, where hostility to Nixon and liberalism on cultural issues were strongest. But their four victories, together with polls like the Lou Harris result in April showing a plurality in favor of impeachment, refuted the belief by Washington insiders that the American people could not stand to see their president impeached.

Refuting another widely held belief was the conduct of the impeachment hearings by Judiciary Committee Chairman Peter Rodino. Dismissed by Nixon aides as a machine hack ("Rodino is a guy out of Essex County, New Jersey," one of them said. "What else do you need to know?"),[7] little known to most of the press, Rodino was a man of substance and strength: a son of Italian immigrants who became a lawyer and a New Dealer in the 1930s, a politician scrupulously honest (unlike his Newark colleague Hugh Addonizio, who became mayor and then went to jail), a gentle man with a sense of humor and a published songwriter. It was assumed that Rodino, whose district since 1972 had had a black majority, would support impeachment. But he proceeded deliberately, hired a distinguished staff, and let all members have their say; he seems genuinely not to have made up his mind till the end. Nixon's defenders and many others assumed that all the 17 Republicans and all the southern Democrats on the 38-member committee would stay with Nixon; and Walter Flowers, a Wallace supporter when he was in the Alabama legislature, made it plain that he thought supporting impeachment would be politically risky for him. But as the polls and the special elections were showing, the political risk was all on the other side. As the hearings went on, all the southern Democrats seemed critical of Nixon, while many of the uncertain Republicans, led by Tom Railsback of Illinois, started meeting together and working their way through the facts.

Nixon's end in office came quickly in late July and early August. On July 24 the Supreme Court ruled 8–0 that he must turn over the sixty-four tapes to Jaworski. The decision was all the more damning because Nixon's appointees agreed. From July 27 to July 30 the Judiciary Committee voted 27–11 for impeachment, charging obstruction of justice, failure to uphold the nation's law, and refusal to produce subpoenaed material. The decision was all the more damning because even the partisan Democrats were obviously reluctant to take such a grave step—tears welled in the eyes of Rodino and junior member Barbara Jordan as they voted—and because Nixon was repudiated even though he had received an able and spirited defense from Charles Wiggins, a suburban trial lawyer who represented some of Nixon's original House district in the valleys east of Los Angeles, and from others like David Dennis. On August 5 the special prosecutor's office found that a tape made June 23, 1972, showed Nixon ordering Haldeman to have the FBI halt its Watergate investigation: a clear obstruction of justice and a clear indication that Nixon knew about his campaign committee's involvement in the burglary long before he had ever admitted it. Nixon's chief of staff Alexander Haig (a general who was a Kissinger protégé), Charles Wiggins—almost all of his defenders except for members of his family and Vice President Ford, who stood aside from considering the issue—decided that he would be impeached in the House and convicted in the Senate by almost unanimous votes and therefore must resign. On August 8 Nixon announced he would resign and on August 9 he did so, flying off to San Clemente at noon after a tearful last speech focusing, characteristically, on his enemies and filled, characteristically, with self-pity.

Almost the entire American electorate was eager to see him go. For many months in 1973 and early 1974 many well-informed opinion-makers who sympathized with Nixon or some of his administration's aims had argued that Americans could not stand the trauma of having their president—especially one so recently reelected over such bitter opposition—removed from office. But the voters plainly were ready for Nixon to leave long before he did; they were less awed by the lack of precedent for his removal than they were offended by his violations of fundamental laws and his continual lies to cover up the violations. The voting public, far from being divided over Nixon's removal, turned out to be united around it.

This politician who prided himself on his shrewd understanding of voters' preferences plainly failed to understand the rising concern in the late 1960s and early 1970s for process as well as policy, for means as well as ends. His preoccupation with the Kennedys, which may have led him to plan or condone the burglary of Lawrence O'Brien's office, served him poorly in a country where the Kennedy name had lost much of its luster and the Kennedy machine was by this time largely a product of Nixon's imagination. Nixon's political enemies, it is true, judged him by a double standard, damning him as a war criminal and scourge of the poor for policies which were in fact far closer to their own preferences than were the policies of Lyndon Johnson, which in almost every case they had at least meekly supported and often fulsomely praised. In their self-righteousness the liberals were hypocritical in their criticisms of Nixon and self-deluding in their caricature of him as a bleak reactionary. But unlike Franklin D. Roosevelt, Richard Nixon did not have the self-discipline to rise above the strafing of his enemies and to define the issues of his times in his own terms. Even as his policies were succeeding, in just the month when American voters were deciding to give him the landslide victory for which he had always hungered and which he thought would establish his ascendancy over his country, he set his seal of approval on the criminal act which would undo him—and in a way which left very few Americans regretful that he must go.

IV

The new president was a man Americans knew little about. Gerald Ford in August 1974 was the least formidable and least heralded figure to come to the office since Harry Truman in April 1945, with whom he had many things in common. Neither Ford nor Truman had imagined, as recently as ten months before his accession, that he might ever be president. Truman, as an obscure senator who had barely been renominated in 1940, was looking ahead to what surely would have been an unsuccessful campaign for reelection in 1946 when he was tabbed as Roosevelt's running mate in July 1944. Ford, as an obscure House minority leader whose reelection percentage in the Nixon landslide year of 1972 was as low as it had ever been, was looking forward to retiring in 1974 when he was tabbed as Nixon's vice president in October 1973. Neither Ford nor Truman had reason to believe he was his president's first choice or was especially close to the president personally or politically. In Congress both men had been steady partisans whose solid personalities made them friendships across party lines. Both men were brighter than reputed. Truman, widely read in history and a careful observer of contemporaries, was ignorant of many aspects of public policy but was not the country bumpkin he sometimes liked to appear. Ford, described by Lyndon Johnson as too dumb to walk and chew gum at the same time[8] and clearly not gifted with much imagination and flair (*A Ford Not a Lincoln* was the title of a book about him by the perceptive journalist Richard Reeves), was nevertheless always capable of digesting the details and rationale of public policy and was not just the partisan drudge he seemed to the House press galleries.

Politically, Ford occupied the center of his party as Truman occupied the center of his—but with the difference that neither Ford nor most contemporaries understood his position. As the leader of House Republicans since January 1965, Ford was assumed to be part of the conservative wing of his party, the natural leader of a group of men who had made their way from jovial fraternity houses to garrulous small-town service clubs to the chummy ranks of House Republicans without ever entertaining a serious thought about public policy or a serious doubt about the Republican orthodoxy of balanced budgets and free enterprise. Actually, Ford had come to the House because of a Republican split on foreign policy. As a thirty-five-year-old lawyer in Grand Rapids, he had been selected by that city's best-known politician, Senator Arthur Vandenberg, to run in the August 1948 primary as the champion of Vandenberg's new-found internationalism against incumbent Congressman Bartel Jonkman, who still supported Vandenberg's prewar isolationism. As a junior House member Ford could claim to be an Eisenhower Republican: he was a supporter of Eisenhower's Europe First, not Robert Taft's Asia First, foreign policy; and if he was generally opposed to an expansion of government powers, so was Eisenhower. As a Republican leader during the Great Society years, he claimed to represent constructive Republican alternatives to Democratic proposals; few ever got anywhere, but he did not embrace the Goldwater rhetoric of opposing Democratic statism even though his voting record was not inconsistent with that philosophy. After Nixon became president, Ford loyally supported administration policy on the floor. But as the House changed and the old Republican–southern Democrat coalition lost its strength to the new antiwar Democrats, his work increasingly took on the character of a holding action, and not always a successful one; this change may have been one reason he was planning to retire. Another was that after enjoying a long and successful political career and raising a large family, he had never succeeded in putting much money aside. Devotion to duty and a practical approach to everyday life: these things characterized Gerald Ford.

They were both the strength and the weakness of his presidency. Succeeding a president who had been ridiculed when he draped the White House guards in gold braid and excoriated when he claimed absurdly high deductions on his income tax, Ford was hailed as a man who made his own toast in the morning and was in the evening the affectionate father of four high-spirited young adults. He entered office with enormous good will and, after his first reassuring statement, a high job approval rating. "Our long national nightmare is over," he proclaimed on August 9. Yet within a month he made two decisions which fatally weakened his presidency and, in retrospect, made the difference between winning a presidential term in his own right and being rejected by the voters in 1976.

The first of these decisions was his nomination, twelve days after Nixon resigned, of Nelson Rockefeller to be vice president. In some ways Rockefeller was a natural choice. Although he had resigned the governorship of New York in December 1973, he remained one of the most experienced of Republican officeholders, with fifteen years as a governor and with foreign policy experience which went back thirty years to the Roosevelt administration. If he was no intellectual,[9] he was the patron of that distinguished intellect Henry Kissinger, whom Ford inherited as secretary of state. He was certainly far more experienced than the other big-state Republican governor, Ronald Reagan of California, or the man who was Ford's chief alternative choice, George Bush, who was serving a difficult year as Republican national chairman after a not very successful year as UN ambassador.[10] Nixon's own favorite, John Connally, was unavailable even if Ford had wanted him; he was indicted by the Watergate grand jury in the milk price bribe case in late July 1974. And Ford may have felt that as a member of the congressional wing of the Republican party, which was considered by many analysts to be coincident with the conservative wing,[11] he would be balancing his administration by nominating a prominent member of the gubernatorial and reputedly more liberal wing.

If so, he miscalculated. For, by 1974 Ford was regarded by the Republicans' increasingly large conservative wing as a moderate-to-liberal himself. And the liberal wing, which had nominated Willkie, Dewey, and Eisenhower, had now withered to a small band who could not prevent the nominations of Goldwater and Nixon, had only a handful of votes in either house of Congress or at the party's national conventions, and held few governor's offices as well. The Rockefeller nomination led many conservatives to mistrust Ford and helped to guarantee that he would have serious opposition from Reagan in the 1976 primaries. If he had nominated Reagan instead, it seems in retrospect, he might have had some trouble getting the nomination confirmed (although Rockefeller's confirmation took some time, too, because it took time to analyze his financial affairs), but once in office, the ticket would have been routinely nominated in 1976. That would not have guaranteed victory in November, but it probably would have helped.

Ford's second decision was even more momentous. On September 8, just thirty days after taking office, he issued an unconditional pardon of Richard Nixon. His asserted reason was to save the nation the spectacle of a former president on trial and the division he believed this spectacle would cause—though the course of the impeachment year itself suggested very strongly that few ordinary Americans felt traumatized by seeing Nixon get what they thought he deserved. Ford's political supporters also pointed out that any Nixon trial would probably come during or near the 1976 campaign, to the political detriment of Ford and his party; so it was sensible of him to hope to get any damage over with quickly. But the damage proved more severe and more lasting than Ford may have calculated and must have hoped. His own statements at his confirmation hearings, when he had seemed to rule out a pardon, now seemed insincere (or prophetic: he said the people wouldn't stand for it); his press secretary, former *Detroit News* reporter J. F. Ter Horst, resigned in protest. Even worse, his action raised the question of whether Nixon, like Agnew, had extracted before he agreed to leave office a commitment that he would not be prosecuted. Any such commitment would contradict Ford's words on August 9, "If you have not chosen me by secret ballot, neither have I gained office by secret promises," and for many Americans would undermine the legitimacy of his whole presidency. His standing in the polls plummeted sharply and stayed down for most of the rest of his presidency. His Gallup Poll approval rating declined from 71% in mid-August and 66% in early September to 50% late in the month—and never through the rest of his presidency rose significantly above that figure.[12] To quell the widespread suspicion of his motives, Ford agreed to appear in a quite extraordinary session before the House Judiciary Committee in October 1974, where he maintained that "there was no deal, period." But the pardon continued to hurt him politically, every poll showed, through November 1976. Quite possibly Ford would have suffered similar or worse damage if he had not pardoned Nixon and if a trial had taken place in 1976. Most likely there was no good political alternative open to him. His presidency was infected by the way he had come to it.

It was also damaged because it began during a sharp downswing in the business cycle—a downswing which was accompanied, quite uncharacteristically as far as any American voters were concerned, with continuing inflation. November's unemployment rate rose to 6.5%, the highest since the 1958–61 recessions; the Consumer Price Index rose 12% from September 1973 to September 1974. Real wages and real earnings were down sharply. Ford's response, as was foreshadowed by his record in the House, was to hold down spending, for which purpose he quickly began wielding the presidential veto with a gusto not seen since Harry Truman's day.

V

The huge Democratic victories of 1974 were already in train before Ford became president. They were nonetheless of stunning proportions. Including the seats they had won in special elections earlier, the Democrats gained 46 seats over their 1972 total and controlled the House 290–145—enough, theoretically, to override a veto without a single Republican vote. Democratic gains came almost exclusively outside the South and the border states.[13] Particularly striking were their gains in and near the historically Republican northern tier. Democrats now held 9 out of 11 seats in Indiana, 5 out of 6 in Iowa, 7 out of 9 in Wisconsin, 4 out of 9 in outstate Michigan (plus 8 out of 10 in metropolitan Detroit), 17 out of 25 in New England, 6 out of 7 in Washington, all 4 in Oregon, and 15 out of 19 in northern California (and 14 out of 24 in southern California). The only major state in which Democrats were significantly behind Republicans in House members was Ohio, and even there they were picking up. Overall these House results represent a devastating political legacy for the Nixon administration. The Republicans failed to make any significant headway in the South despite the Nixon potential recognized early by Kevin Phillips. In states like South Carolina and Tennessee, Republicans were clearly weaker than they had been in 1968. Meanwhile, the stances which Nixon strategists had hoped would produce gains in the South instead helped to produce losses in the North. Under Nixon the Republicans did a miserable job both of recruiting and of inspiring serious candidates. The contempt which Nixon heaped on the class of educated, articulate young Americans fell on just that age and cultural group which tends to produce most of the self-starting political candidates in American society. So perhaps it was no accident that his party had trouble finding such candidates not only in 1974, but in 1972 and 1976 as well.

Democrats made lesser but still impressive gains outside the House. In the Senate, where their majority was already large, they picked up 4 seats, in Kentucky, Florida, Colorado, and Vermont, which elected a Democratic senator for the first time. The New Hampshire vote turned out to be a virtual tie, over which the Senate wrangled long and hard, but the ultimate rematch in September 1975 was won rather easily by Democrat John Durkin. Nixon–Ford Republicans won almost no Senate races. Republicans with liberal reputations held seats in New York, Pennsylvania, Maryland, and Oregon; Farm Belt incumbents won narrowly in North Dakota, Oklahoma, and Kansas. In Kansas former Republican National Chairman Bob Dole, when asked if he wanted Nixon to help him, quipped that he wouldn't mind having him fly over the state. Dole was one of the first candidates to use his opposition to abortion to advantage in the wake of the *Roe* v. *Wade* decision; he made the point that his opponent, physician-turned-congressman William Roy, admitted that he had performed a few (legal) abortions himself. Only two clearly conservative Republicans won unambiguous victories: Jake Garn in Utah, on the brink of becoming the most Republican state in presidential contests, and Barry Goldwater in Arizona, for his fourth term.

As for governorships, Democrats Jerry Brown and Hugh Carey were elected to succeed Republicans in California and New York; Democrats won in almost every other major state with the exceptions of Michigan and Ohio, where William Milliken and James Rhodes won narrow victories. These Democratic victories seemed likely to have more consequences for government than similar Democratic victories in the 1950s, because now most of the legislatures were controlled by Democrats, too. In the South, the only Republican governor left was Mills Godwin, elected only narrowly in 1973 over populist Democrat Henry Howell, who ran as an independent. Even more than in Washington, around the country Americans had turned to the Democrats. Judging just by the roster of officeholders, six years after the Democrats' disastrous year of 1968 the country was more Democratic than it had ever been—more Democratic than in the presidential landslide years of 1936 or 1964, more Democratic than in the recession years of 1948 and 1958, more Democratic (at least for a moment) than when it was led by its paladins Franklin Roosevelt and John Kennedy.

49

➤➤➤ ⫷⫷⫷

Limits

Americans began 1975 in a world they never anticipated and would not have recognized just three years earlier. So far as they could tell, the events of 1973 and 1974 had been without precedent in their country's history. A criminal president had been driven from office—in a nation which fancied (despite James Buchanan, despite the debacle of Woodrow Wilson) that crises always produced strong leaders and that the normal operations of the political system always produced decent ones. The economy was being ravaged in ways that were totally unfamiliar. Prices were rising at rates most Americans had never experienced, despite the various systems of controls the Nixon administration kept imposing. At the same time, the economy had not only stopped growing but was contracting at a sharper rate than at any time since the 1930s. Real wages and incomes had gone into a decline—and for many Americans would not rise again in years. Gasoline, the cheap commodity which fueled Americans' moves to the suburbs, which made possible their continent-spanning vacations and weekend jaunts, which enabled them to live any social life and enjoy almost any leisure activities they chose—gasoline was suddenly more expensive and, for agonizing months, in short supply, and a 55-mile-an-hour speed limit was imposed on the Interstate highways where Americans were used to driving 75—and all because the United States, the most powerful nation in the world, had lost control of the production and supply of crude oil to a bunch of Persian Gulf sheiks and monarchs.

The country which Americans had been complaining about so recently suddenly seemed to many a lost paradise.[1] Those who had been complaining that constant economic growth had been polluting the environment and using up resources now took to complaining that the lack of economic growth was eliminating upward mobility and preventing blue-collar workers from earning a comfortable living. By the early months of 1973, in the proliferation of polls being conducted publicly for various media and privately for various political candidates, only about 30% of Americans said the country was going in the right direction, while more than 60% said it was pretty seriously off on the wrong track. By early 1974, about 75% of Americans were saying that the country was headed in the wrong direction— a result which was surely wildly out of line with what would have been registered had the question been asked at any time earlier in the twentieth century, even in most of the depression years, when a confidence in the fairness of the system persisted in a large share of the population. This corrosive pessimism was at first considered a response to Watergate. But after Nixon left office and Ford took over, there was, as it turned out, only a momentary sharp rise in the percentage who felt that America was going in the right direction.

The problem for the voters was not just discontent with their leaders—though that was part of it. The problem was that their way of life seemed threatened, the promise of continuing economic growth on which people had based their lives had been broken, the underpinnings of economic security which they had taken for granted had been undermined and it was becoming painfully apparent that the stratagems which had been relied on to provide economic security—rapidly rising wage contracts, Social Security and other cost-of-living adjustments, government aid and intervention programs—were only making the problem worse. The solutions and the theories which had produced economic growth and personal security no longer seemed to work. Neither the Republicans who had presided when they failed nor the Democrats who reaped the immediate political benefits of their failure seemed to have solutions and theories to replace them.

II

Up to California's gleaming white golden-domed Capitol, past its spacious grounds in sunny Sacramento, in January 1975 an austere four-door Plymouth sedan was driven and a thin, unsmiling thirty-six-year-old man, his carefully clipped sideburns just beginning to be flecked with gray, got out to go to work. This was the new governor of California, Edmund G. Brown, Jr., known as Jerry. He owed much of his political success to the name made by his father, who had been elected governor in 1958 over William Knowland 60%–40% and in 1962 over Richard Nixon 52%–47% before he lost in 1966 to Ronald Reagan 58%–42%. But the younger Brown represented a very different kind of politics. Pat Brown believed in using state government to encourage economic development; he was proud of expanding California's water system, bringing water from the underpopulated north to the growing south, and of building hundreds of schools and dozens of junior colleges. California grew to be the nation's largest state during his governorship, and the physical infrastructure and human skills he helped to build contributed vastly to its growth. Pat Brown had fallen prey finally to Californians' suspicion of ever-burgeoning government and impatience with cultural conflict: he could survive the Nixon candidacy in the optimistic, culturally unified times of 1962, but he was swept under by Reagan in the culturally polarized climate generated by the Berkeley rebellion, the Watts riot, and the first demonstrations against the Vietnam war. Yet under Reagan his achievements were not discredited and his government not dismantled. Reagan reluctantly agreed to state income tax withholding in his first term and helped put together a major welfare reform with Democratic Assembly Speaker Bob Moretti in his second. He signed a bill which came close to legalizing abortions, and to his frustration he presided over continually increasing state budgets.[2] He found the political demands for spending on education and highways and even welfare impossible to resist.

Not so Jerry Brown. If his father was a conventional Democratic politician, he was the essence of the unconventional. A bachelor who had spent several years in a seminary and was interested in Zen Buddhism, Jerry Brown had no close political allies and insisted on questioning every rule of thumb in politics—and especially his father's. His name had enabled him to be elected secretary of state in 1970, in which office his major accomplishment was framing a campaign finance reform referendum which was passed by the voters (for in the legislature it had little support and he had little clout). His name had also enabled him to come out first in a strong field in the June 1974 Democratic gubernatorial primary. Reagan's failure to groom a successor (his lieutenant governor, Ed Reinecke, was indicted in April 1974 for lying to Congress about the ITT case) gave him a moderate Republican opponent in the general election, whom he beat by only a 50%–47% margin. Yet once he was in office Brown's iconoclasm made him instantly popular with the post-Watergate California electorate. He slept in an unfurnished apartment rather than in the suburban governor's mansion Reagan had had his friends obtain for his comfort; he rode in the Plymouth from the state car pool rather than in a limousine; he did his own detail work, studying one issue to the exclusion of all others when it interested him; he stayed up working till all hours of the California night, when with Japan just rising and all of Europe and North America asleep, he was practically alone in the world. He questioned every government program: we were in an era of limits, he proclaimed, when we must conserve scarce resources rather than expend them, when (in the title of one of his favorite books) "small is beautiful," when we must approach every problem anew without preconceived assumptions that either more or less government would solve it.

Jerry Brown was operating in a friendly political environment. Reagan's Republicans had captured control of the California legislature in 1968, thus ending Democratic Speaker Jesse Unruh's control of the Assembly. But they lost it back to the determined, politically adept Democrats in 1970, when Unruh ran a surprisingly strong race for governor, losing to Reagan by only 53%–45% despite being pitifully underfunded. In 1972, Democrats gained legislative seats again, thanks partly to Phillip Burton's redistricting but also to increasing cultural liberalism in upper-income areas which enabled, for example, thirty-one-year-old Howard Berman to beat a former Republican Assembly leader in a district in the affluent Hollywood Hills. By January 1975, Democrats controlled the state Senate 24–15 and the Assembly 54–25. The Democratic legislators, unlike Brown, were politicians who had made their own way upward with no help from a famous name, who got along well with other politicians, who were in many cases the creatures of a political culture of lobbyists and legislative staffers which had come into being with Unruh's professionalization of the legislature in the 1960s. They found it difficult to deal with this new governor, but they recognized his popularity and used it to their own advantage. While Brown was preaching the limits of government, they were stretching it farther, making Sacramento, once a sleepy small river town dwarfed by the Capitol dome, into the center of one of the nation's most prosperous and highly educated million-plus metropolitan areas—a western version, out in the flatlands of California's Central Valley, of Washington, D.C.

Jerry Brown and the Sacramento Democrats were representative, in an exaggerated way, of the tendencies of the party and its leading politicians who had come to power in the wake of Americans' repudiation of Richard Nixon and all his works. The leaders were not cheerleaders of big government but skeptics who styled themselves problem-solvers, like Brown and Gary Hart, his Yale Law School classmate and another one-time seminarian (but they were not particular friends),[3] who had transformed himself from George McGovern's campaign manager in 1972 to senator from Colorado in 1974. Those in the legislative ranks were looking for new programs and new reforms to support, but they were united more by their obdurate opposition to what they conceived to be the central programs of hated Republicans like Nixon and Reagan than they were by any concrete positive agenda of their own. They were against economic exploitation of the environment and felt almost a kind of loathing for the evidence they saw in everyday life—the sprawl of suburban subdivisions and shopping malls—of the economic growth of the preceding quarter-century. They felt comfortable in calling for less growth, less exploitation of resources, and were quite blind to the problems—the economic frustrations caused by diminished upward mobility and increased downward mobility—caused by lack of growth. They were hostile to technological innovations they associated with the military and big business (this was long before the personal computer) and were attracted to simple, old-fashioned technologies like the wood stove and the windmill. They seized on the temporary oil crisis of early 1973 as evidence that Americans must discipline their consumption of energy and other resources and assumed that government must set limits on individual consumption because markets could not be trusted to discipline a materialistic older generation. They had opposed the Vietnam war and drew from it the lesson that U.S. military power tends to work against the cause of decency abroad and that the availability of U.S. military capacity tends to lead to its use. These were the politicians who represented with some fidelity the attitudes of the leading edge of the Baby Boom generation, of the college-educated segment[4] of this huge bulge in the population which was just beginning to enter the electorate in large numbers in the early 1970s and was initially heavily supportive of what might be called Trend Democrats—less liberal on economics, more liberal on cultural issues than the traditional, Hubert Humphrey-style Democrats they tended to scorn and distrust.

III

Nowhere in January 1975 were these Trend Democrats as strong as they were in California and Colorado, with their hordes of newcomers and their youthful populations unmoored by tradition and receptive to cultural change. But echoes of these attitudes were apparent almost everywhere, except perhaps in the Deep South, and were certainly registered in Washington. The 75 freshman Democrats elected in 1974 set the tone of the House of Representatives and provided the votes to adopt the reforms long sought by Phillip Burton and Richard Bolling and embraced now by Tip O'Neill. In lightning Democratic caucus meetings in December 1974, even before the new Congress officially assembled, the House Democrats voted in effect to elect all committee chairmen[5] and chairmen of subcommittees as well. Two chairmen, aging populist Wright Patman of Banking and hawkish autocrat Edward Hebert of Armed Services, were promptly ousted; and the message was sent to all chairmen that they must be alert and responsive to the wishes of the majority of the Democratic caucus or they might lose their chairs as well. This was the end of the iron rule of the seniority system, a rule which had only become iron during the speakership of Sam Rayburn.[6] Burton also engineered the abolition of the House Un-American Activities Committee (by getting all its Democratic members but one to resign and by passing a rule disqualifying the other because he was not a lawyer). Unrecorded votes were made much less common, and altogether a new atmosphere prevailed; Carl Albert was still speaker, but he saw the trend of events and retired in 1976. Others saw similar trends. The Democrats held a midterm conference, mandated by their 1972 convention, in Kansas City, Missouri, in December 1974. It was envisioned as a forum in which liberal delegates could hold more conservative officeholders accountable. Instead it became a forum for arguing over the rules for the next convention, especially the implicit quotas which the convention had rather absentmindedly endorsed.[7] Ultimately compromise language was hammered out by party Chairman Robert Strauss, a Texan determined to repudiate the McGovern legacy, and outgoing Ohio Governor John Gilligan, who was a good bit more sympathetic to it; the AFL–CIO leaders were dubious, but Mayor Daley, less principle-bound and more sensitive to trends, went along.

Proposals for redistribution of income and wealth or for major increases in the size and scope of government were the subject of less interest among the Democrats than were abuses of government power at home and abroad. This was the time when Arthur Schlesinger, Jr., the celebrator of strong presidents since *The Age of Jackson* was published in 1938, wrote a book called *The Imperial Presidency,* finding that the office which had been expanded by his heroes Franklin Roosevelt and John Kennedy had been abused by Lyndon Johnson and Richard Nixon.[8] It was a time when newspaper accounts in December 1974 of illegal domestic spying by the CIA were followed quickly by Ford's appointment of a commission headed by Vice President Rockefeller to investigate the subject and by the setting up of a Senate committee under longtime Vietnam dove Frank Church for the same purpose. The War Powers Act had been passed over Nixon's veto; and when Ford called on Congress in March 1975 to approve aid to the beleaguered South Vietnamese government, which was about to be toppled by the Communists, freshman Democrat Congressman Bob Carr, from the Lansing district next to Ford's old Grand Rapids seat, brought the issue up at a Democratic caucus meeting and got a solid vote against—a vote which removed any doubt that South Vietnam would fall.

On Vietnam, on the CIA, on spending and taxing, Gerald Ford was on the defensive. The economy had deteriorated in Nixon's last year to the point that 1974 saw the highest inflation and the highest unemployment rates since 1947. Ford's party had no political strength, and after the Nixon pardon he had only limited moral authority. His one advantage was that the Democrats did not know what they wanted to do with their new power. Trend Democrats like Jerry Brown and Gary Hart and most of the freshmen House members knew what they were against, but they were not sure what they were for. Ford, building on his stolid defense of a set of coherent principles in twenty-five years in Congress, knew what he wanted. He wanted to maintain an assertive internationalist foreign policy, and he would do so except to the extent that Congress expressly forbade it. He wanted to hold down federal spending and taxes and prevent the expansion of government, and he would do that except to the extent that Congress could frustrate him by overriding his vetoes. He vetoed bills as no president since that other product of Congress, Harry Truman, had; for he was used to voting reflexively against Democratic measures, and now his new position, by converting his vote to a veto, gave it much more force than when he had cast it on the floor of the House.

In foreign policy, Ford's pursuit of an arms control agreement with Brezhnev at the Vladivostok conference in November 1974 was a logical sequel to Nixon's policy, which was not surprising inasmuch as Ford kept Kissinger as secretary of state and reposed great trust in him. He continued Kissinger's détente policy, refusing to meet expelled Soviet writer Aleksander Solzhenitsyn in the White House even as Solzhenitsyn's works were beginning to finally sour the European left on the Soviets; and in July 1975 he signed the Helsinki Accords guaranteeing civil liberties in the Soviet bloc, though there was no way to enforce them. He traveled to Peking in December 1975. But his one moment of popularity on foreign policy came in May 1975 when he ordered Marines to repulse a Cambodian attack on the Navy ship *Mayaguez.* The operation itself was botched, and the rally-round-the-flag effect lasted an unusually short time; Ford's job approval rating was buoyed up from 39% to 50% but dropped back down to 45% by summer.[9] Foreign adventures were not popular: this was the one time since the emergence of the Cold War in March 1947 that a significant plurality of Americans favored cutting the defense budget.

On domestic policy he followed a mixed course. The tax cut and rebate he proposed in January 1975 and the unbalanced budget he proposed in February added up to a clearly Keynesian policy of pump-priming in a time of recession—even at some risk of stirring up inflation. Ford even called for $2 billion in public works jobs for the unemployed. In fact, inflation was abating while the gross national product was plunging, and this was the indicated program. But Ford still vetoed many bills which exceeded his guidelines: a $5 billion public works bill in May, a $1.2 billion housing bill in June, a $7.9 billion education bill in July, a $2.7 billion school lunch bill in October. He also announced in May that he would oppose federal aid to keep New York City's government out of bankruptcy—an announcement which prompted the *New York Daily News* headline "FORD TO CITY: DROP DEAD"—although as the city government came under increasing fiscal discipline he ended up supporting bailout legislation by November.

These measures resisted by Ford were mostly responses to emergency or routine continuations of existing programs. The Democrats presented him with nothing like the articulated new approach of Nixon's Family Assistance Plan. They proposed no major changes in the balance between public and private sectors, no grand expansion of government. They had the advantage that Ford seemed to many a bumbler: his unfortunate tendency to fall and bump his head, even the two assassination attempts which he survived in Sacramento and San Francisco in September 1975, made him a figure of fun and a butt of ridicule. Nor did the Republicans have other towering figures: Rockefeller was beleaguered, while Reagan was out of office and approaching sixty-five and seemed to represent an extreme point of view most commentators thought had been thoroughly repudiated in November 1964. But the Democrats themselves were able to elevate no dominant leader. Edward Kennedy was still tarred by Chappaquiddick and took himself out of the 1976 presidential race in September 1974. George McGovern was still held in contempt: retrospective polls showed him still behind Nixon even when Nixon's reputation was near its low point. Hubert Humphrey was tarnished by his loss to McGovern in 1972 and the widespread sense among Democrats that he represented a politics of the past. Senate Majority Leader Mike Mansfield was self-effacing, and Speaker Carl Albert was about to retire even as he seemed about to be pushed aside. Governor Jerry Brown in Sacramento was a distant figure to most Americans, and Governor Hugh Carey in Albany was preoccupied with the city and state fiscal crises. The Democrats' most popular politicians came from small states and so seemed unsuitable as national leaders. As the bicentennial year of 1976 approached, the United States seemed to have a vacuum of leadership, and a populace which more than at any time in a half-century was skeptical of leaders, their motives, and their effectiveness.

50

->>> <<<-

Bicentennial

As the nation's bicentennial year approached, giving an occasion for Americans to reflect on their political traditions, neither political party, looking ahead to the year's presidential election, wanted much to do with its own recent partisan traditions. The Republican party's two most recent nominees, reelected in triumph in 1972, were by 1975 branded as criminals, lucky not to be in jail. Its only other living former nominees were Barry Goldwater and William Miller, the cheerful veterans of the badly defeated 1964 ticket, both of whom were welcome at the convention but would not be its ornaments; Henry Cabot Lodge, who had served as Kennedy's and Johnson's ambassador in Saigon and would not be particularly welcome at the convention; and 1936 presidential nominee Alf Landon and 1944 vice presidential nominee John Bricker, who at eighty-eight and eighty-two could hardly be expected to make the trip and would not be remembered by most delegates and television viewers if they did. All except Lodge had been landslide losers; none except Lodge had played a significant part in national government. It was the Democrats, with Franklin Roosevelt and Truman and Kennedy, who could claim the glorious heroes of the past, not the Republicans, whose Eisenhower was still respected by those who remembered him but not generally revered as a great leader and whose Theodore Roosevelt and Lincoln were only dim memories.

What the Republican party did have was a president whom it had never nominated and who commanded little loyalty from the conservatives who, since 1964, had produced most of its convention delegates. Ford's strengths with general election voters were weaknesses with these partisans. His secretary of state, Henry Kissinger, was almost universally acknowledged as the nation's preeminent expert on foreign policy. But by self-conscious conservatives Kissinger was criticized for an overly cozy détente with the Soviet Union and for negotiating with Panama with a view toward relinquishment of U.S. control of the Panama Canal. His choice as vice president, Nelson Rockefeller, was clearly of presidential stature. But in November 1975, painfully aware of the message implied in the open criticism of him since July by Ford's reelection chairman, Howard (Bo) Callaway (he called Rockefeller Ford's "number one problem"), Rockefeller announced he would not seek the office in 1976. Rockefeller trailed Reagan among Republicans in a head-to-head vice presidential poll,[1] and it was all too clear that this man who had been confirmed by a Democratic Congress could not be nominated by a Republican convention. Ford's cabinet contained as many able luminaries as any in the preceding forty years. But many of its members—Edward Levi at Justice, Carla Hills at HUD, William Coleman at Transportation, Elliot Richardson at Commerce— were regarded as dangerously sympathetic to liberal ideas, and in some cases rightly so. The Ford family seemed attractive to many Americans, especially after Betty Ford's public disclosure that she had breast cancer. But Mrs. Ford also angered conservatives by her support of the Supreme Court's abortion decision, her laissez faire attitude toward marijuana experimentation, and her willingness to condone premarital sex.

And Ford had a conservative opponent for the 1976 presidential nomination. Reagan, just retired as governor of the nation's largest state, allowed a campaign committee to be set up in Washington in July 1975; in fact, Reagan had been determined to run since some time in the spring, regardless of the fate of Rockefeller or the course of Ford's administration. In November, two weeks after Rockefeller took himself out of the race and Ford reshuffled his cabinet, Reagan officially declared. Despite his experience as governor, and despite the voters' usual desire for a president with experience in office, Reagan ran as an outsider, and specifically against Washington. "Our nation's capital," he said, "has become the seat of a buddy system that functions for its own benefit—increasingly insensitive to the needs of the American worker who supports it with his taxes. Today it is difficult to find leaders who are independent of the forces that have brought us our problems—the Congress, the bureaucracy, the lobbyists, big business and big labor."[2] At first Reagan trailed Ford by wide margins in polls,[3] and his candidacy was heavily discounted by Washington insiders and political experts. But he quickly gained ground, trailing the incumbent president by just 53%–42% in January 1976.[4] This anti-Washington candidate very nearly unseated an incumbent president at the Republican convention in Kansas City in August.

II

The anti-Washington theme worked in the Democratic party as well. Even though the 1974 election results had seemed to signal that "Happy Days Are Here Again"—the 1932 Roosevelt campaign theme song which was still played repeatedly at Democratic conventions—the party's best-known figures declined to make the race. Edward Kennedy, by far the front-runner for the nomination, had withdrawn from the race in late September 1974, much to the surprise of political insiders: at forty-two he was more concerned about his personal problems (his son's recovery from cancer, his wife's alcoholism) than about his political prospects. With Kennedy out, the temporary leader for the nomination in the polls was George Wallace; but it was unthinkable that he could win. His past appeals to racism and his support of "segregation forever" made him anathema to the large majority of Democratic politicians and activists and to the majority of Democratic primary voters as well, and his physical condition would probably disqualify him from the presidency even if he should somehow be taken seriously otherwise. Henry Jackson, a stalwart liberal for so many years, was nonetheless totally unacceptable to the Vietnam doves who were now such a large part of the Democratic constituency. Hubert Humphrey was ill and after losses in 1960, 1968, and 1972 had little stomach to try again. And Humphrey's protégé, Walter Mondale, who had been appointed attorney general of Minnesota in 1960 and senator to replace Humphrey in 1964, bowed out in November 1974 after spending two years scouting the campaign trail, saying, "Basically, I found I did not have the overwhelming desire to be president which is essential for the kind of campaign that is required," and adding that he didn't want to spend a whole year "sleeping in Holiday Inns."[5]

That sounded like a quip, but actually it was based on a shrewd analysis of the presidential selection process which had emerged from two Democratic rules reform commissions. Mondale realized that it was necessary to raise large sums of money well before 1976 in order to qualify for federal matching funds early that year, so that he could finance a campaign which could get him from one state to another; and he found that as a candidate who did not inspire fervor among many high-income contributors, he was not the recipient of large flows of money even after Kennedy left the race. Mondale also understood that intensive personal campaigning, door-to-door in early contests in small states like New Hampshire, was required—a schedule difficult to reconcile with the duties of an incumbent senator in Washington. He knew that any campaign would require the efforts of dozens of organizers, who must be recruited one by one. And he knew that his old allies in regular party and labor circles produced relatively few such organizers now and that among the antiwar young people who produced most such organizers, Mondale, as a supporter of Humphrey in 1968 and a quiet opponent of the Vietnam war afterwards, as an organization liberal temperamentally opposed to breaking ranks and operating outside established hierarchies, would have difficulty arousing enthusiasm.

Mondale understood finally that though his prospects were as good as anyone else's, the race was inevitably chancy. He might do well in the precinct caucuses in Iowa, just south of his native Minnesota; but journalists had never taken much notice of them before 1976,[6] though they were the first contests of the year. But the fact that the Democratic electorate in New Hampshire was mostly Catholic and the fierce opposition of the *Manchester Union Leader* to any state sales or income tax—an opposition which had kept New Hampshire the only state with neither tax and was helping to make it the fastest-growing state in the East—worked against a candidate like Mondale, who was the son of a Protestant minister and favored the same kind of generous federal spending programs as his mentor Humphrey. Massachusetts a week later might be more favorable ground; in Florida, a week after that, the only conceivably successful challenger to Wallace would be another southerner. The delegates in Illinois, a week later, would be won by the party machine candidates in every district; North Carolina was scheduled the next week so that former Governor Terry Sanford could show he was a serious candidate by beating Wallace, though he had failed to do so in 1972; Wisconsin in the first week of April and Pennsylvania in the last were the next real possibilities for a candidate like Mondale. In November 1974 the 1976 primary schedule was not finally set and the details not yet clear. But no one could fail to see that there were many possible scenarios, that the process was tortuous, that assembling a majority of convention delegates would be difficult, and that campaigning would be a full-time job, demanding total commitment.

III

"I'm not a lawyer, I'm not a member of Congress, and I've never served in Washington." So ran Jimmy Carter's standard speech as he went around the country in 1975 and early 1976 running for president. A born-again Christian, he invariably pledged, "I'll never tell a lie." By ordinary standards, Carter's qualifications for the presidency were not readily apparent. The son of a farmer who was a prominent citizen of the mostly black community of Archery, outside the town of Plains in rural Sumter County, Georgia, but who would not have been considered affluent in any northern city, Carter grew up in a house with an outhouse and lived in close physical proximity to blacks: he remembered how in June 1938 blacks had listened quietly to the broadcast of the Joe Louis–Max Schmeling fight on the Carters' radio and then, after they returned to their own shacks, had shouted whoops of joy at Louis's victory.[7] His father was a segregationist; but his mother, "Miss Lillian," one of those salty, high-spirited women whom the rural South seems peculiarly to produce, forbade her children to use the word "nigger" and insisted that they treat blacks politely. Carter went away to the U.S. Naval Academy in 1943, graduated in 1946, and served as an officer in Admiral Hyman Rickover's nuclear submarine service until his father's death in 1953, when he retired from the Navy and returned to Plains.

Georgia then still had the unit rule system, in which every county had either 2, 4, or 6 votes in Democratic primaries, so that two or three small rural counties could cancel out Atlanta. The result was that in small counties local gentry like the Carters naturally became involved not only in local politics but in state Democratic primaries as well. Carter himself, after establishing his success as a peanut farmer and warehouse owner, was elected to the state Senate in 1962. He might have been expected to run for the U.S. House seat which opened up in 1966 when Bo Callaway, the surprise Republican winner in 1964, ran for governor. But instead Carter ran for governor himself, perhaps sensing that there was room for him to sneak through between leading candidates Callaway, whose party affiliation was still a serious handicap statewide; Ellis Arnall, the governor in 1943–47, who was an outspoken liberal; and Lester Maddox, who was famed for keeping blacks out of his restaurant. Carter came from the rural counties which still cast the bulk of Democratic primary votes even after the Supreme Court overturned the unit rule system in June 1963, yet he might be acceptable to those who opposed diehard segregationists. His strategy nearly worked. Starting off almost unknown, at age forty-two, Carter won 21% of the primary vote to Arnall's 29% and Maddox's 24%; almost surely he could have beaten either of them in the runoff, and most likely he, unlike Maddox, would have come out ahead of the hapless Callaway in the general election (Maddox won the governorship because Arnall ran as an independent and no one had an absolute majority, a result which threw the election into the Democratic legislature).

In 1970, Carter ran again, pursuing a different strategy. This time his single target from the beginning was former Governor Carl Sanders, a racial moderate who had spent the last four years out of office in Atlanta. Carter circulated a picture of Sanders celebrating with black basketball players and led him in the first primary 49%–38% and in the runoff 59%–41%. In the general election he beat the Republican, an Atlanta television newscaster, by a margin similar to that in the runoff. But in January 1971 he startled his backers, and got himself on the cover of *Time* as the exemplar of the New South Democratic governors, when he said in his inaugural address, "The time for racial segregation is over," and ordered a portrait of Martin Luther King, Jr., hung in the state Capitol. A man genuinely poised between opposites—a rich man from a poor county, a sympathizer with blacks from the heartland of segregation, a native of south Georgia with a certain sophistication from his service in the Rickover Navy—Carter was a protean figure, who could with some legitimacy and some ingenuity portray himself in quite different tones, depending on his political needs of the moment.[8]

Carter decided sometime in 1972 to run for president in 1976; he did so after meeting various presidential candidates on their way through Atlanta and concluding that he was as qualified for the office as any of them. In November 1972 his twenty-eight-year-old aide Hamilton Jordan produced a memorandum detailing the strategy for a Carter candidacy. It saw the need to find running room between Kennedy and Wallace, much as Carter had tried and almost succeeded in 1966 between Arnall and Maddox. Jordan argued that Carter could make better than expected showings against Kennedy in New Hampshire and Wallace a week later in Florida, follow those up with victories in northern states like Wisconsin, win a big northern state like Pennsylvania or Ohio, and run well everywhere.[9] Although he failed to anticipate Kennedy's withdrawal, Jordan understood his weakness (Jordan would be delighted when Kennedy decided to run against an unpopular President Carter in 1980, on the grounds that this was one Democrat Carter could beat);[10] and he shrewdly anticipated the moral climate of 1974–76.[11] He showed a better appreciation than anyone else of the new nominating system caused by the changes in the Democrats' rules, the proliferation of primaries, and the increasingly close focus on the process by newspaper and television reporters who were determined to provide the insights and foreshadow the results in their daily reporting as they had seen Theodore White do in his four *Making of the President* books. Jordan understood the power of the new national media, which in the absence of a group of effective power-broking politicians operated as the main transmitter of information about the effectiveness and viability of different candidates and the gauge of their relative success.[12] Instead of waiting for convention roll calls to see how well different candidates would do, as they had as late as 1960 and 1964, reporters now went out and saw whether they were raising money in the big cities and winning the support of activists in the early caucus and primary states, and so that information that used to become available only after White's books appeared in the year after the election now appeared in newspapers and magazines the year before the election.

IV

Carter followed Jordan's plan. Ineligible to run for a second consecutive term as governor, he got Democratic National Chairman Robert Strauss, a Texas lawyer and fund-raiser with shrewd political instincts and a desire to keep the Mc-Governites from dominating the party without driving them out of it, to name him as "campaign chairman" for the 1974 election, giving Carter an excuse to travel throughout the country that year and make friends with up-and-coming candidates and political operatives. Kennedy's withdrawal in September 1974 robbed him of an obvious target. But the proliferation of northern, Washington-based Democrats who did run provided Carter with a split opposition against which he could readily prevail. He paid particular attention to Iowa, New Hampshire, and Florida and cultivated hundreds of locally active Democrats, helping them in their campaigns, listening gravely to their opinions, staying overnight in their houses, and carefully making his bed in the morning. His positions on issues were just what one might have chosen to appeal to the center of the Democratic spectrum in late 1975. His well-publicized acceptance of civil rights, fortified by signs of genuine conviction (his support from Atlanta Congressman Andrew Young and other blacks, his vote years before to integrate his Plains Baptist church), made him the hope of northern liberals in the battle against Wallace in the South, as well as the choice of many black voters. His reluctance to accept every item on the liberal/labor economic agenda, symbolized by his refusal to endorse the Humphrey–Hawkins bill which purported to guarantee every worker a job, helped him at a time when belief in the ability of government to solve problems was declining. His championing of concepts like executive reorganization and zero-based budgeting, which he claimed to have put into effect in Georgia, made him sound modern and innovative.

Moreover, his Democratic competitors, except for Wallace, ran from bases in Washington at a time when Washington politicians were exceedingly unpopular with voters: Johnson and Nixon, after all, had been experienced Washington politicians. Morris Udall of Arizona, a favorite of liberal Democrats in the House more for his forthright character and good humor than for any aggressiveness and ambition (he had lost a quixotic race to Hale Boggs for majority leader in December 1970), was running as a representative of what he called the "progressive" rather than liberal tradition of the party. Birch Bayh, a narrow winner in Indiana Senate races in 1962, 1968, and 1974, the conqueror in the Senate of the Haynsworth and Carswell nominations, and the framer of the presidential succession constitutional amendment, was already finding his chairmanship of the Judiciary Committee working against him, as he opposed measures to overturn the Supreme Court decision legalizing abortion and to prevent lower courts from ordering school busing. Bayh was running as a candidate experienced in Washington—a deadly appeal in the post-Watergate atmosphere. A similar insider appeal had already doomed Texas Senator Lloyd Bentsen's candidacy even before New Year's 1976: he could raise money, but his well-tailored, tight-lipped demeanor meant that not he but Carter would be the economically moderate, pro-civil rights southerner to win a spot on the national ticket. More hesitant in getting into the race—he skipped Iowa and New Hampshire—was Henry Jackson, the hawkish, domestically liberal senator from Washington state who had served on Capitol Hill for thirty-six years. Also running were Sargent Shriver, whose status as a Kennedy in-law made him seem a lightweight despite his excellent record at the Peace Corps, OEO, and the Paris embassy, and Fred Harris, a cheerful and self-proclaimed populist, whose cultural liberalism and national interests had forced him to abandon his Oklahoma Senate seat in 1972, at age forty-two, and who was stumping New Hampshire.

Against this field Carter's person-to-person campaigning and economic moderation accumulated enough votes to enable him to finish second behind the large number of uncommitteds in Iowa's precinct caucuses in January 1976 and first in tiny New Hampshire's primary in February, with 28% of the vote to 23% for Udall, 15% for Bayh, 11% for Harris, and 8% for Shriver. A week later Jackson's well-financed campaign won in Massachusetts with 22% to 18% for Udall and 17% for Wallace, who had hoped to capitalize on a bitter busing controversy in Boston which had little reverberation because only a small percentage of voters still lived in the central city and only a small percentage of them had children in public schools; Carter won 14% and Bayh 5%. These results eliminated Harris, Shriver, and Bayh. A week later in Florida, Carter took 34% to Wallace's 31%— not all that much below his 42% of four years before, but now a weak second place to a fellow southerner instead of a strong first place over half a dozen Yankees. Carter would surely have done even better had it not been for Jackson's heavy campaigning, stressing his opposition to busing in Dixie-ish north Florida and his support of Israel in the heavily Jewish condominium country of the south, which won him 24%. The Florida result, repeated in North Carolina two weeks later when Carter beat Wallace 54%–35%, effectively ended Wallace's campaign and his career as a presidential candidate and guaranteed Carter near-unanimous support from the remaining delegates to be chosen in the South.

V

The Republican race had only two candidates, and they were surprisingly evenly matched. Although the first polls in 1975 had shown Ford far ahead of Reagan, Reagan's strength increased rapidly. This surge reflected the fundamental popularity of his anti-government, anti-Washington message among Republican primary voters: after all, if Nixon had remained in office, Reagan surely would have been the overwhelming favorite for the nomination. Reagan's generalities were more appealing than his specifics, which started voters wondering whether he might cut programs they benefited from. For example, he was hobbled, although not greatly, when he came out for a proposal to transfer responsibility for $90 billion of federal programs to the states. Nonetheless, in New Hampshire, Ford won only a 49%–48% victory—a good forecast, as it turned out, of the entire primary season vote.[13] Massachusetts and Vermont were, as expected, strongly for Ford—still Yankee Republican country, at least in the primaries. Florida's Republican primary vote was concentrated around St. Petersburg and on the "Gold Coast" from Miami to West Palm Beach and included many retirees; apprehensive about what Reagan might do about Social Security, they voted heavily for Ford and enabled him to carry the state 53%–47%. With strong backing from organization Republicans, Ford carried Illinois 59%–40%, though it is Reagan's native state.

But Reagan fought on in North Carolina, where his campaign was headed by Senator Jesse Helms, a one-time States' Rights Democrat and segregationist (he had worked for Willis Smith's campaign to oust Senator Frank Graham in the June 1950 primary and runoff) who had become well known as a right-wing radio commentator and had won election to the Senate in 1972. Reagan had noticed that crowds cheered loudly when he said he would never give away the Panama Canal—"We built it, we paid for it, and we're not going to give it back"—while the Ford administration was negotiating with the leaders of Panama (where there had been riots back in 1964 over which flags would fly over the canal) to do just that. The canal issue enabled Reagan to pile up large enough margins in the historically Democratic east to overtake Ford's margins in the traditionally Republican mountains in the west and to win 52%–46%. The Republican race, which Ford had seemed about to sew up, was suddenly as wide open, if not as complex, as the Democrats' contest. The emerging Republican majority which Kevin Phillips had predicted in presidential elections, but which seemed to have vanished because of Watergate, was reappearing in this Republican primary—and the issue which raised it was not southern segregation, but American nationalism.

VI

The Democratic race continued in the North. On April 6, Wisconsin held its primary and New York Democrats voted, too, in a primary in which originally only the delegates' names were on the ballot; a late change in the law put their candidate preference on the ballot immediately below their names, so that what started off appearing to be a contest favoring existing organizations ended up resembling an ordinary primary. The three serious candidates still in the race—Carter, Jackson, and Udall—had to decide where to concentrate their scarce resources. Jackson chose New York. He had hoped to bank on organizational support, but he had another advantage now: New York had little history of primary contests[14] and turnout was low; in this environment the relatively highly educated, high-income Jewish voters could form a disproportionate share of the electorate, well over 30%. From 1976 through 1984 the New York Democratic primary became the major electoral contest in which American Jews, always concerned about the fate of Israel and more worried than ever because of Israel's near-loss in the 1973 war, could exert maximum political leverage. Jackson had always supported Israel and was the chief sponsor of an amendment, opposed vigorously by Henry Kissinger, to limit trade with the Soviets until they allowed Jews and others to emigrate; this was less a human-rights issue for Israel than a demographic one, since the Soviet Union was the chief source for new Jewish settlers of this country heavily outnumbered by unfriendly neighbors. Carter chose to concentrate on Wisconsin, where he had been campaigning and whose farm areas he especially hoped to win. Udall chose Wisconsin but made feints at New York; almost pathologically afraid of bankrupting himself, he consistently refused to spend the small extra margins of money which might have turned him from a consistent second-place finisher into a winner. The first exit polls in Wisconsin called him the victor; but when the rural vote came in he trailed Carter by 7,500 votes, for a 36%–37% loss, while in New York Jackson won 38% of the vote to Udall's 25%.

These results set the stage for the climactic contest in Pennsylvania on April 27. Jackson hoped his backing by labor union leaders and some Philadephia politicoes would produce a victory. But he had run out of money by overspending his budget in Massachusetts and Florida, and federal matching funds were cut off after the Supreme Court invalidated some parts of the 1974 campaign finance law and Congress dawdled before repairing it. Carter borrowed heavily himself (some charged he overborrowed) to keep his campaign going; Udall, the liberal who called himself a progressive and ran his campaign as a fiscal conservative, was out of funds in a state with few culturally liberal voters. By this point Carter, with heavy support from southern, born-again Christians, and rural voters, had a following in national polls which placed him about even with Humphrey and far ahead of any other candidate. That popularity, fortified by his bigger campaign budget, enabled him to carry Pennsylvania with 37% of the vote, to Jackson's 25% and Udall's 19%.

Pennsylvania clinched the Democratic nomination for Jimmy Carter, though he was still far short of a delegate majority. The early losses of Harris and Shriver showed that there were no populist or Kennedy constituencies which could beat him. Udall's losses in Massachusetts and Wisconsin showed that the self-conscious liberals were not as large or powerful a bloc as the nomination of McGovern four years before had suggested. Jackson's loss in Pennsylvania proved that organized labor and party machines simply couldn't deliver many votes. The Democratic nomination was open to anyone whose character and ideas seemed interesting enough to attract some votes and whose campaign strategy and tactics took advantage of a complex system to produce victories or at least better than expected showings at each stage of the process.

But now the still little-known Carter himself became a victim of this same process. Humphrey did resist the temptation to run one more time and took himself out of the race in a press conference April 29; one factor may have been the signs of the cancer which killed him in February 1978. Udall kept himself in the race and nearly won in Michigan, where he got votes from liberals and from Wallace supporters unhappy that Carter was supported by Detroit's black mayor, Coleman Young. Frank Church jumped in after his committee investigating the CIA ("a rogue elephant," he called it) issued its report in April; proclaiming himself a western candidate, he beat Carter in Nebraska by 1,400 votes, 38%–38%. Jerry Brown, after 16 months as governor, decided to proclaim the age of limits on a national scale and came into the May contest in Maryland, of all places—where he rounded up support from tattered old politicoes[15] as well as sophisticated suburbanites and beat Carter 48%–37%. In May, Carter won no significant victories outside the South. Yet his well-organized campaign accumulated additional delegates; and when he carried New Jersey and Ohio on the last day of voting, he removed any doubt. Theoretically he could be denied the nomination. But his continuing support in national polls, especially among southern whites and born-again Christians, meant the cost would be so high that no practical politician would want to pay it unless he was convinced that Carter would do dreadful things to the nation. No practical politicians outside Georgia knew Carter well enough to be sure of such a dire judgment. And so within a week of the last primaries he was endorsed by Wallace, Jackson, and Richard J. Daley; and the nomination was his. Between Pennsylvania and the convention various events—his sympathizing with a desire for "ethnic purity" in white neighborhoods, Steven Brill's "Jimmy Carter's Pathetic Lies" article in *Harper's* magazine, the resignation of speechwriter Robert Shrum after only nine days—made many Democrats and others uneasy about Carter. Evidence was accumulating that he was a shrewd professional politician who used the half-truths and occasional untruths which are arguably indispensable to ordinary political life.

But it was too late for the Democrats to find anyone else, and so they decided to make the best of their new leader, celebrating his virtues and overlooking his weaknesses. By July the Democrats nominated their candidate with much more harmony and self-congratulation than the Republicans could summon. In an important way, Carter's nomination symbolized the closing of a divide between North and South, a reconciliation between warring regions, a recognition by the South of the victory of civil rights and a recognition by the North of the basic decency of the South. If Carter's own record on civil rights was far from letter-perfect, if he had campaigned for the Wallace vote in 1970 and done less for civil rights than some others had on other occasions, there was no doubt about his basic good will or his determination that equal rights be not only the law but the way of life of the land. Carter's decision on the vice presidency also showed a desire to close ranks: after interviewing several candidates who had trooped into his house in Plains in front of television cameras, he picked Walter Mondale, a man he had hardly known, the protégé of Humphrey, a welfare state liberal and Washington insider. And the convention ended with a moving piece of theater following Carter's acceptance speech. With George McGovern and Henry Jackson, George Wallace and Hubert Humphrey and even Jerry Brown all on the platform, the Rev. Martin Luther King, Sr., delivered the benediction. "Surely the Lord sent Jimmy Carter"—the southernness of the nickname never seemed more appropriate—"to come on out and bring America back where she belongs." Then the delegates and dignitaries sang the civil rights anthem "We Shall Overcome." So strong was the trend favoring the Democrats that as soon as he became nationally known in March 1976, Carter was running even with Ford; by early May he had a statistically significant lead; as the convention ended, he led by a 62%–29% margin[16]—far larger, quite possibly, than the lead Franklin Roosevelt would have held over Herbert Hoover had polls been conducted in 1932.

VII

The remainder of war for the Republican nomination followed a course reminiscent of the prolonged trench warfare of World War I. Both sides fought hard and neither gained much ground. In May and June, Ford won primaries in West Virginia, Maryland, Michigan, Kentucky, Oregon, Tennessee, Rhode Island, New Jersey, and Ohio—states in which Republicans had established a presence by the time of the Civil War. Reagan won primaries in Georgia, Indiana, Nebraska, Arkansas, Idaho, Nevada, Montana, South Dakota, and California—states in which (with the exception of Indiana) Republican strength dated from some later time.

As a result, the incumbent party was far less harmonious than the others. Ford's lead in delegates was established by the end of the primaries; but it was so narrow that Reagan's manager, John Sears, spent weeks concocting schemes to detach one or another small bloc from the president so as to nominate the former governor. The final scheme, hatched the week before the August convention in Kansas City, was for Reagan to pledge to choose as his vice presidential nominee Senator Richard Schweiker of Pennsylvania. As a suburban Philadelphia congressman from 1960 to 1968, Schweiker had had a conventional, Gerald Ford–like conservative voting record; but as senator from an industrial state since 1968, he had supported the AFL–CIO and opposed the Nixon and Ford administrations on most economic and foreign issues. But Schweiker brought almost no Pennsylvania delegates with him, not even Drew Lewis, his longtime associate and the 1974 Republican gubernatorial nominee.[17] After much pulling and hauling within the Mississippi delegation over whether it would vote by unit rule or not, ultimately Ford prevailed. His own choice for vice president, Senator Robert Dole of Kansas, was made almost haphazardly and at the last minute. Yet Ford's acceptance speech—vibrant, confident, partaking of the spirit of the year's bicentennial celebrations—was outstanding: an indication that despite the polls showing Carter far out in front, this would be a seriously contested election.

VIII

For 1976 was a special year in American history, when pageantry and celebration went at least some way toward dispelling the negative political atmosphere. The Tall Ships—dozens of sailing ships—which graced New York Harbor on July 4, set a patriotic, happy tone which permeated the Democratic convention held in the grimy precincts of Eighth Avenue and 33rd Street two weeks later, which extended to the Republican convention in Kansas City in August, and which was perpetuated by the snappy, positive Ford campaign ads in September and October. The bicentennial celebrations and the "Bicentennial Minute" television ads sponsored by Shell (a British–Dutch company) recalled days when Americans had great leaders. And, it seemed, they provided a contrast with a present when the government was led by a journeyman politician who a few years before had been preparing to retire from an obscure position to no one's regret and when his leading opponents were a former movie actor in his own party and a peanut farmer as the nominee of the other. Only in a political environment where experienced leadership generally was disgraced, by the examples of Lyndon Johnson and Richard Nixon, could such choices be seen as desirable. Only in a country where people had despaired of heroes arising in politics—and where perhaps people had decided there was no need of heroes arising in government—would such choices be accepted as tolerable and appropriate. The voters in fact resisted some possible heroes. The Democrats' convention was so enthralled by the spectacle of black Congresswoman Barbara Jordan addressing it as one keynote speaker as to make the appearance by former astronaut Senator John Glenn as the other seem utterly unremarkable. Astronauts, feted in *Life* magazine in the 1960s, seemed to spark little enthusiasm, at least among Democratic delegates, in the 1970s. No military heroes of any kind emerged from the Vietnam war: the only celebrated fighting men were victims instead, the prisoners of war, some of whom behaved heroically in captivity but none of whom did what heroes in other American wars did—defeat the enemy. The image of the Vietnam veteran as a maladjusted, unstable, violence-prone problem was already starting to emerge; and by the summer of 1976 the ranks of the youngest members of Congress did not include a single one[18] (although John Murtha of Pennsylvania, elected in a February 1974 special election, had served in Vietnam in the Marine Corps while in his thirties). At the same time a few exemplars of the counterculture were doing well in the political arena: SDS and Chicago Seven veteran Tom Hayden made (with the help of money earned by his wife, actress Jane Fonda) a surprisingly strong showing against Senator John Tunney in the June Democratic primary in California. In the backwash of Woodstock, when *MASH,* with its Vietnam-like depiction of the Korean war, was becoming the most popular television show and *Saturday Night Live* was setting the terms of political discussion (as when it lampooned Ford's apparent clumsiness), the only American heroes were antiheroes.

IX

By all standard criteria, the Republican ticket ought to have lost overwhelmingly. The Democrats had a wide edge in party identification (48%–23% in the last Gallup Poll before the election), the voters were still angry at the Republicans for nominating Richard Nixon (and opposed his pardon 55%–33%), the Democrats had nominated a candidate whose southern origin strengthened them in a region they would otherwise have had to write off, and the Republican candidate had no special hold on voters generally or on any segment of the electorate outside his home town of Grand Rapids. Moreover, no great events in the summer or fall of 1976 and no signal accomplishments worked to the political advantage of the incumbent.

Yet the election turned out to be surprisingly close. A contest in which one candidate was scarcely known and party identification was far weaker than twenty years before was inherently volatile. One reason for the closeness was that the voters were not so certain, once they had a chance to look at him up close, that they wanted a candidate who was utterly inexperienced in Washington and about whose basic character and way of doing business they knew nothing at all. However much they said they liked a candidate who carried his own garment bag and eschewed pomp and ceremony, they still recognized that a president had to fulfill certain terrifying responsibilities; and each unknown candidate must meet a burden of proof that he could. Carter's level of support quickly dropped from the 57%–62% of the weeks just after the Democratic convention to the 46%–54% level where it hovered during the rest of the campaign. That percentage made him a serious but not an unbeatable candidate.

The second reason that the Carter margin diminished was the debates between him and Ford. These were only the second series of debates in a presidential election, and the fact that both candidates agreed to them shows that each—Carter because he began unknown, Ford because he began behind—had a special need to show well in this confrontational format. The very fact that Johnson in 1964 and Nixon in 1968 and 1972 had refused to debate—and that Kennedy in 1960 had debated—made the debate format more attractive to both candidates.

The third reason for Ford's near-victory was that he had a better campaign strategy. "We had spent four years thinking, working, and planning to win the nomination," Hamilton Jordan later wrote, "but had given very little thought to the general election." The result was that Carter campaigned furiously but ineffectively, looking "as if he were running for sheriff in fifty states."[19] In contrast, Ford's campaign had carefully prepared a brilliant and original strategy, which concentrated heavily on building a positive feeling not only about the president but also about the country. "I'm feeling good about America," ran the song which strategists Douglas Bailey and John Deardourff commissioned for their Ford commercials. The result was that Ford's percentage rose from 29% in July to 37% in mid-August, over 40% by early October, after the first two debates, and over 45% by the end of the month.[20] And if the Democrats' advantage in party identification continued, the thrust of opinion toward their position on fundamental issues was turning around. The drive for a guaranteed annual income which had seemed so strong when Nixon endorsed it now was plainly waning. The percentage of voters who wanted cuts in defense spending had peaked and was now declining. And though no one recognized it as such at the time, one index of the degree of guilt most Americans felt about racial and economic injustice was shifting: the prison population, stable for twelve years, began sharply rising in 1976.[21] For years judges, juries, prosecutors, local legislators, and the voters who elected them or from whose ranks they were drawn had been unwilling to send enough people to prison long enough to raise prison populations—even though crime rates were rising. Now, quite suddenly, they were sending more people to prison longer. The civil rights revolution had inspired Americans to look critically on all their institutions and had cast doubt on their moral entitlement to penalize the blacks and poor who formed vastly disproportionate percentages of criminal defendants and prisoners. By 1976 they were if anything even more critical of most institutions, but seemed largely free of the guilt they had once felt about punishing criminal acts. The sense that the United States was fundamentally flawed was diminishing among the majority of voters. And Gerald Ford, who campaigned as a cheerful optimist about America, was in a better position to take advantage of that change than Jimmy Carter, who campaigned as a critic of so many aspects of American life.

X

The debates, widely expected to determine the winner of the campaign, probably had less to do with the result than did Ford's paid advertising. Carter approached the first debate on the defensive, after the furor aroused by an interview in *Playboy* magazine in which he had admitted, in the style encouraged by the vogue among the trend-minded for openness, that he had "lust in my heart"—which may have been frank, but seemed hardly presidential. The mid-September debate centered on economic issues, and Carter failed to gain the advantage his party had enjoyed since the 1930s in this area. But the greatest attention was focused on the failure of the sound system 8 minutes before the debate was scheduled to end: for 27 minutes the two candidates stood mute, neither willing to be the first to sit down. Carter's late August lead of 54%–36% was narrowed to 50%–42% in late September. Ford was then thrown on the defensive by charges that he had tried to stop Wright Patman's investigation into Watergate in September 1972 (which, as a faithful partisan, he had), by charges (which never amounted to anything) about irregularities in contributions to his House campaigns, and by the ouster of Agriculture Secretary Earl Butz in early October after the author of the expansive farm programs which followed the Soviet wheat deal made the incredible mistake of telling a racist joke to singer Pat Boone in the presence of the chief unraveler of the Watergate cover-up, John Dean. In the second debate, after Carter attacked détente and Ford attacked Carter's advocacy of defense spending cuts, Ford himself made an incredible mistake by saying, when asked about Poland, that there was "no Soviet domination of Eastern Europe and there never will be in a Ford administration"—an absurd statement on its face, though understandable if one supposes that Ford was defending himself against the charge that the Helsinki agreements amounted to a concession of Soviet domination and misspoke slightly in doing so. Whatever the reason, the statement hurt him, and badly because he took three days—three nights of television newscasts—to back down from his position. It was valuable time lost, in a campaign in which voters were paying attention for only a few weeks.

There followed a debate between Mondale and Dole, the vice presidential nominees, distinguished by Mondale's cool command of the facts and the jab by Dole that "I figured up the other day if we added up the killed and wounded in Democrat wars in this century, it would be 1.6 million Americans, enough to fill the city of Detroit." To Dole, who had been grievously wounded in Italy in April 1945, just three weeks before the end of World War II in Europe, "Democrat wars" was a lively issue; to most Americans in 1976, it was just partisan bitterness, or a reference to a political argument which was long out of date—the bitter debate over foreign policy which on the surface ended abruptly in December 1941 but subterraneanly shaped many voters' opinions through the McCarthy period and after. Before the third debate, on October 22, the candidates' standing had declined to a 47%–41% Carter lead in Gallup: the 12% not committed were evidence of a negative reaction to two candidates whose major initial claim on public sympathy was that they lacked the qualities Americans had for years sought in presidents. The third debate advanced neither candidate's cause much. The heavy Ford TV ad campaign—far bigger than Carter's, because the Democrat had chosen to spend his federal funds differently—increased his vote powerfully in the last two weeks. The candidates' origins—Carter's in the Deep South heartland of the Democracy, Ford's in the Upper Midwest birthplace of the Republican party—worked against recent political trends, in which Republicans had been growing stronger in the South and Democrats in the northern tier. The result was an election which was not only close nationally but also, like the election of 1960, close in most states, so that the commentators' baffled statements in the week preceding the vote that the outcome was not predictable were in fact true.

The results of the 1976 elections looked routine: the majority party kept control of Congress and prevailed 51%–48% in a presidential election whose closeness evoked memories of the 1960 and 1968 results. Yet the volatility of the 1976 race suggests that many other outcomes, some as one-sided as the elections of 1964, 1972, 1980, and 1984, were possible; while the strength and steadiness apparent in the course of the 1960 campaign and, at least in Nixon's percentages, the 1968 campaign as well indicates that some of this similarity is just coincidence. Moreover, under the surface of similar percentages and margins, there were vast movements of different cultural segments of the population. The America of 1976 was very different from the America of 1960, and the changes in cultural patterns—and especially the changes in which cultural issues became important in national politics—help to explain why the years which followed the narrow Democratic victory of 1976 produced such a different result for the two parties than the years which followed the narrow Democratic victory of 1960.

Geographically, the 1960 and 1976 victories looked similar on an electoral college map: Carter and Kennedy both carried most of the South—Carter carried the whole region except for Virginia and Oklahoma—and snared several big states in the Northeast: Massachusetts, New York, Pennsylvania, Maryland. Both narrowly lost California and narrowly carried Texas. But—a telltale sign—other states went differently: Kennedy carried and Carter lost Connecticut, New Jersey, Michigan, and Illinois; Carter carried and Kennedy lost Ohio and Wisconsin; and Carter nearly carried Iowa and Oregon, where Kennedy was not competitive. By religion and race the results were far different. Kennedy carried 78% of Catholics, Carter 57%; Kennedy ran 28% ahead of his national average among Catholics, Carter just 7%. Among white Protestants, in contrast, Kennedy won just 37% of the vote and Carter 45%; and the difference was surely sharper among those who considered themselves born-again (a category not separately tabulated in 1960). The two candidates' percentages among white southerners were not much different, but Carter's represented a sharp rebound from the negligible levels won by Hubert Humphrey and George McGovern. Among blacks Kennedy won 68% and Carter 85%—a movement toward the Democrats which had entirely taken place by the summer of 1963, after Kennedy endorsed the civil rights bill.

In these figures are written the aspirations and hopes, the disappointments and discontents, of cultural groups who had often been regarded and regarded themselves as outsiders in America. Blacks by July 1963 had become solidly attached to the national Democratic party and by July 1964 were repelled by the Republicans. Catholics, their Americanness certified by Kennedy's victory and by the accompanying but coincidental decline in the distinctiveness of American Catholic life styles, had started to behave politically very much like Protestants. White southerners, angry at national Democrats since June 1963 (and beginning to move against them long before, starting in June 1948), were in some cases attracted by Jimmy Carter; the divide here seemed to be economic, with Carter winning over most lower-income white southerners but running just as dismally as any other recent Democratic presidential candidate in affluent precincts.

But outside the South, economic and occupational differences had come to mean much less than differences in cultural attitudes. Trend-minded voters had moved toward the Democrats, even toward a born-again Christian like Carter: this movement helps to explain why he ran better than Kennedy in northern tier, Protestant-majority states like Wisconsin, Minnesota, Iowa, South Dakota, and Oregon.[22] In the southern-accented counties of Ohio, Indiana, and Illinois, below U.S. 40, the old National Road, and in the pro-Confederate parts of rural Missouri, Carter also ran ahead of Kennedy, as he did in every state of the Confederate South except Alabama. But in heavily Catholic areas and—more significant—in areas of rapid population growth from 1960 to 1976, Carter ran well behind Kennedy's percentages, with the biggest drops in libertarian Alaska (in favor of rampant economic growth and legalization of marijuana, all at the same time) and Mormon Utah and southern Idaho (in favor of free-market economic growth and the cultural conservatism of large families and traditional moral values.)[23] Carter's nomination and general election victory symbolized, in a way nothing else could, the reconciliation of the races in the South and the acceptance by white southerners of the civil rights revolution. But his comparative weakness in areas of cultural liberation (like Marin County, California, where he ran behind McGovern) and cultural conservatism (like the Mormon West) was an indication that outside the South his peculiar combination of cultural attitudes was out of line with leading cultural trends.

XI

While the election turned the incumbent party out of the White House, the change in the composition of Congress was almost nonexistent. Democrats and Republicans ended up with the same number of seats in the House as after the 1974 elections—an astonishing retention by the Democrats of their huge majority. Only 2 of 1974's freshmen Democrats—a hapless winner in a heavily Republican downstate Illinois seat and a married man caught trolling for a prostitute in heavily Mormon Salt Lake City—were defeated; 5 other incumbent Democrats and 3 incumbent Republicans were beaten; otherwise there was just the usual flux caused by changes in open seats. The Watergate Democrats who had so changed the composition of the House had also perfected the fine art of using the perquisites of incumbency to win reelection. Significantly for the course of legislation in the next Congress, Carter's coattails were almost nonexistent. Of the nearly 300 seats held or won by Democrats, Carter had a higher percentage of the vote than the congressional candidate in only 24, and there were only 3 congressmen who really owed their seats to his coattails.[24]

Incumbent senators were less lucky in the elections. The voters' dissatisfactions of the hour, finding no outlet in House races, were directed with full force in Senate contests, the large majority of which were seriously contested now that neither party's hold on any single state was unshakable. But the additions and subtractions balanced out, for a net advantage of exactly one seat to the Republicans.[25]

The net result was a government that looked overwhelmingly Democratic. Democrats were convinced that, in the words of Franklin Roosevelt's 1932 campaign song, "Happy Days Are Here Again," while many conservative Republicans looked ahead with anger and anguish to a political future that seemed solidly Democratic. But beneath the surface of the Democratic triumph there were fissures. Carter's victory was more contingent on circumstances than many supposed and the Democrats' hold on Congress due more to institutional advantages than to the popularity of their policies. The Democrats had managed to win an impressive victory. But now they had to show they could govern.

51

-》》》 《《《-

Democrats

T he result of the 1976 election was Democratic government as far as the eye could see. It was almost universally expected that the Democrats would hold onto the executive branch for eight years; it was considered unthinkable that they could lose either house of Congress; their chances of nominating a majority of Supreme Court justices and the large majority of federal judges in the next few years seemed excellent; the state governments were as heavily and solidly controlled by Democrats as at any time in history. The Republican party was, if not defunct, then certainly dispirited. As Democratic politicians gathered on tarmacs to await the candidate's airplane, or sat at banquet head tables to pay homage to the stranger from south Georgia whom they had nominated, they were confident that he would be the next president but less sure about what he would do. The most interesting question in American politics seemed to be what the Democrats would do next.

No one could be sure, for Jimmy Carter seemed determined to do the unexpected. He was determined to pursue new goals and enact new policies which turned out to be quite different from the goals and policies of other leading Democrats in Washington. Carter's acquaintance with Washington Democrats in January 1977 was almost nonexistent;[1] and his top aide, thirty-two-year-old Hamilton Jordan, evidently took pleasure in showing contempt for the Washington insiders whom he had outsmarted in the 1976 campaign—for example, by giving Tip O'Neill's dozen guests inaugural dinner tickets in the last table in the balcony.[2] From his twenty-six-year-old pollster Patrick Caddell, who had become a national figure as George McGovern's pollster four years before, Carter received the advice in December 1976 to keep "campaigning," to do things which symbolized his status as an outsider in Washington and his closeness to the lives of ordinary people, as he had in his campaign.[3] Yet the campaigning which had gotten him into the White House by a narrow margin had had almost no effect on congressional elections. Carter had not campaigned in a way to help other Democrats, or vice versa; there was almost no sense of intertangling obligations of the sorts which have usually bound American political parties together.

Carter symbolized his new approach when he hopped out of his car at the beginning of his inaugural parade and walked the whole mile up Pennsylvania Avenue—intentionally renouncing pomp and ceremony and heralding his iden- tification with ordinary Americans. The next day he issued a pardon of Vietnam-era draft evaders which went beyond the limited forgiveness issued by Gerald Ford. His appointments of Max Cleland, a Georgia veteran who had lost both legs and an arm in Vietnam, as head of the Veterans Administration and of Sam Brown, the Colorado state treasurer and one of the leaders of the Moratorium, as head of Vista, the domestic agency similar to the Peace Corps, were announced the same day and were intended to reconcile opponents of the war and opponents of resistance to it. They may have had some effect, for there was no great backlash on Vietnam, no recriminations like those of the isolationists of the 1930s, no resentments like those of the McCarthyites of the 1905s. His first television speech was a "fireside chat," complete with a blazing fire and the president dressed in a warm sweater; on another broadcast he took questions relayed from viewers by CBS's Walter Cronkite.

II

One of Carter's pet causes was government reorganization. But he had to expend considerable effort to get a general reorganization bill through Congress over the opposition of Jack Brooks, the chairman of the House Government Operations Committee and a tough-talking, cigar-chewing Texan who had voted for the Civil Rights Act of 1964 while representing rural east Texas. Yet it was not clear over the next four years whether reorganization made much political or governmental difference, and Brooks supported almost all of Carter's specific reorganization plans anyway. Zero-based budgeting, a technique Carter had ballyhooed in the campaign, seemed to make little difference.

Sometimes the new Carter policies were counterproductive. The new president antagonized many members of Congress in February 1977 by proposing, without any advance consultation, the cancellation of nineteen water projects. This move was consistent with Carter's concern for the environment and with his managerial style, but it was terrible politics. Congressmen based whole careers on their ability to deliver water projects, which took years to formulate, build, and complete; to have their constituents see them canceled suddenly, without any notice, threatened to undermine their entire political base. Carter's action also showed how little he understood the water-hunger of the parched West: in the Rocky Mountain states and California, he got a competitive 45% of the vote in 1976 but a pathetic 34% in 1980.[4] The Senate voted against Carter's cuts 65–24.

In foreign policy Carter was little more successful. During the campaign Jordan had said that Carter would have failed if Cyrus Vance and Zbigniew Brzezinski— establishment choices—had ended up heading the State Department and the National Security Council. They did. Yet Carter's leading foreign policy initiatives were stymied anyway. His nomination of John Kennedy's top aide, Theodore Sorenson, to be head of the CIA met widespread opposition on Capitol Hill and had to be withdrawn in January 1977. His nomination of Paul Warnke to be head arms control negotiator aroused Henry Jackson, always worried that arms control would weaken the United States relative to the Soviet Union; and he summoned up 40 votes against Warnke's confirmation. This total was not enough to defeat it; but it put, or should have put, the administration on notice that there were more than enough senators opposed to Warnke's approach to prevent a two-thirds vote for ratification of a Warnke-type arms control treaty. As if in response, the administration's first arms control proposal in March took Jackson's approach, calling for much deeper cuts in strategic weapons than Ford and Brezhnev had contemplated in Vladivostok in November 1975. But it was promptly rejected by the Soviets, and the progress toward another arms control agreement—increasingly, since Nixon's SALT I, the foreign policy issue most focused on by domestic politicians—was visibly slowed.

On other foreign issues Carter embraced the view of Vietnam war opponents who felt that American intrusion rather than Communist expansionism was the problem in East Asia. He came close to giving economic aid to North Vietnam in May 1977 and was maneuvering at the same time to withdraw American troops from South Korea. The failure of these moves—and their obvious unwisdom as the years went on, revealing the vicious nature of the Vietnamese regime and the economic dynamism and relative freedom of South Korea and the other East Asian rim countries—was perhaps a harbinger of future Democrats' foreign policy failures.

III

Domestically, Carter gave halfhearted support to the liberal/labor agenda of the middle 1970s, with dismal results. The top item on the AFL–CIO's wish list was "common situs" picketing, a demand by the building trades, then as always an important part of the federation, that any union having a dispute with any subcontractor be able to picket an entire job site; because of the presence of many employers on construction sites, building trades unions would have either more or less ability to picket than most unions, and they wanted more. Common situs picketing had already been passed by Congress, only to be vetoed in January 1976 by Ford; with a Democratic president and just as many Democrats in the House, it seemed a sure thing. Yet the bill was defeated in the House in March 1977 by a 217–205 margin. The setback permanently hobbled the AFL–CIO's lobbying strength and showed that the Watergate-era northern Democrats—so many of whom had been elected from districts which were historically and on economic issues Republican—would not automatically follow union leadership as non-southern congressional Democrats elected in the 1950s and 1960s had.[5]

Nor did the acolytes of Ralph Nader enjoy the dominance over Democratic congressmen they once had. In November 1975 the previous House had passed Nader's centerpiece program, a consumer protection agency which would be licensed to intervene in almost every kind of regulatory and administrative proceeding—an institutionalization of Nader himself. Now, when it was brought forward again, it prevailed in committee in May 1977 by only a 22–21 margin; in November it was yanked off the calendar by Tip O'Neill, who felt it didn't have enough votes to pass; ultimately it was defeated 227–189 in February 1978. This course of events enraged and bewildered its backers, who charged that corporate lobbying had affected the outcome. Of course it had, but what was important is that the younger, Watergate-era Democrats were willing to listen to arguments— substantive as well as political—against legislation which earlier Democrats might have accepted with only perfunctory discussion. Those earlier Democrats, who had gone to college and law school when most articulate opinion was Republican and pro-business, were used to shutting their ears to the honey-voiced blandishments of the other side. These younger Democrats, who had gone to college and law school when most articulate opinion was Democratic and liberal, felt secure enough in their own environment to listen to others—and were sometimes persuaded. For by 1977 the faith that government could solve all problems was vanishing, and both voters and politicians were increasingly skeptical of the efficacy of government action and open to arguments against it.

That decline in faith affected the energy policy Carter presented as his legislative centerpiece in April 1977. Sharp rises in gasoline prices, combined with occasional scarcities attributed to the Arab boycott which followed the October 1973 war, had led even the Nixon and Ford administrations to seek statist remedies at a time when faith in government action was higher. Price controls were left on oil after they were taken off almost everything else. Energy czars were appointed supposedly to allocate supplies and see to distribution of petroleum products. The thought was widespread that Americans—especially poor Americans, whose needs seemed to be the central focus of every public policy question—could not conceivably pay more for gasoline or heating oil and must have their costs held down or subsidized by government. By April 1977 some of these presumptions had been undermined, as the promised solutions failed to appear. Texas and other oil- and gas-producing states, which wanted higher oil prices set by free markets, emerged as a political counterweight to the Northeast, which wanted low prices because of its dependence on home heating oil. On the campaign trail Carter had made a commitment to Oklahoma's Governor David Boren that he would back deregulation of natural gas; once he approached office, however, his commitment on this issue, as on others like abortion, the Humphrey–Hawkins bill, and defense spending cuts, became slippery. His April 1977 energy package was internally contradictory: it included deregulation of new oil and an increase in natural gas prices (favored by the energy-producing states), but it also included taxes on "gas guzzlers" and rebates to small-car buyers and homeowners who used energy-saving devices (favored by environmentalists and Naderites). Free markets and a Department of Energy, deregulation and a corporation to subsidize development of synthetic fuels—these were all parts of the Carter program.

It was passed in the House thanks to the skill of Tip O'Neill, who in his first year as speaker saw his job as passing the Democratic president's program. (It was sometimes hard to figure out what that was: O'Neill was displeased to hear only 10 minutes before the public announcement the news that Carter no longer supported the B-1 bomber which O'Neill, from dovish Massachusetts, had been loyally backing.)[6] O'Neill, correctly gauging that in the post-Watergate House this energy bill could not be bulled through, created a special committee headed by Thomas Ashley of Ohio, which ironed out conflicts between regions and among standing subcommittees; the result was a bill which passed the House by a 244–177 vote. In the Senate, whose rules permitted dilatory tactics without end, action was much slower. The final energy bill which was passed in October 1978 was a rococo compromise, subsidizing synthetic fuels and a coal slurry pipeline, delaying deregulation and setting up different categories of petroleum products subject to different regulations, the defining of which enriched Washington and Texas lawyers until the middle 1980s. The bill postponed the benefits of deregulation while seeming to permit politically damaging price rises.

If the Democrats were divided about what to do on energy, they seemed united about what to do about the economy. The economy had manifestly been in recession at least since October 1973; and if it was recovering in 1976, the growth was too slow and seemed too tenuous to please Keynesian Democrats. At the same time, they feared that stepping too hard on the accelerator would flood the nation's engine with inflation. The result was a proposal for a $50 rebate to every taxpayer. This amount sounded like a lot to economists like Charles Schultze, head of Carter's Council of Economic Advisers, who had been raised in the depression and had grown to adulthood at a time when most Americans made less than $100 a week; $50, their calculations told them, would provide just the right degree of fiscal stimulus for the macroeconomy. But the $50 rebate quickly became another political casualty. To most Americans in early 1977, $50 was not an amount almost equal to a week's paycheck; it was enough to take the family out to the movies and dinner. People and politicians laughed at the $50 rebate, and some of the Keynesians started to think it might overheat the economy; Carter abandoned it in April 1977, one day before the income tax filing deadline. It was quickly forgotten. Yet it was a reminder that in the new American economy which was developing among the country's increasingly culturally liberated and culturally diverse people, the old policies no longer struck a chord and the old rules of thumb would not suffice. And it showed that policies which were based on careful quantifications would not work if they failed to capture voters' imaginations.

IV

The extended recession which followed the 1973 oil shock injured the American economy in many ways. Wage levels reached a peak in 1973 which, by some measures, they did not reach again in the next fifteen years.[7] Productivity, which had risen rapidly in the 1950s and 1960s, grew perceptibly more slowly after 1973 and in some years grew not at all. The inflation sparked by the efficient funneling of billions of dollars to the oil-producing countries and the inefficient recycling of those billions back into productive investment in the developed and developing countries caused a drop in real incomes and a drop in economic production in the United States and its major trading partners. In early 1977, American eyes were focused on the weaknesses of the economy. They missed seeing its greater and truly amazing strengths.

The greatest of these strengths was that the American economy generated record numbers of jobs. The rise in the number of employed Americans in the period 1975–85 was 24%, compared with 20% in 1965–75 and 14% in 1955–65. This growth was entirely appropriate, for the American economy in the 1970s and 1980s had a record number of entrants into the work force. Overall population growth, to be sure, was lower than in earlier decades. But the children of the 1947–62 Baby Boom were now entering the work force. Immigrants arriving in unanticipated numbers were swelling the work force as well, particularly in some of the most economically vibrant parts of the country. And women were entering the work force in large and quite unanticipated numbers. Population grew only 11% in the 1970s, the lowest of any decade in American history except the 1930s. But the work force increased by 28%, compared with 19% in the 1960s and between 13% and 15% each decade from 1930 to 1960. Given this vast increase in the work force, the best one could hope for from a job market is a sizable increase in the number of jobs—jobs which in most cases would not pay high wages (for who wants to pay an inexperienced person top dollar?) but which would provide the opportunity job entrants seek. And the American job market pretty much fulfilled this hope, except during the two hiatuses following the oil shocks of 1973 and 1979. During the years immediately following the shocks, the economy gained half a million jobs a year or fewer. But in the other years of the 1970s and 1980s, the annual gain was about 3 million jobs—a stunning rate.[8]

These new jobs made possible astonishing changes in cultural patterns—and gave individual Americans an unprecedented range of choices in their personal lives. They made possible the vast increase in cultural variety within the nation— or at least they made it congenial and easy to live with. The cultural wars of the late 1960s and early 1970s faded into memory as it became apparent to most Americans that there was plenty of room for them to live together in quite different styles and arrangements.

The biggest cultural change was the entry of unexpected numbers of women into the work force. In retrospect, this was a natural development. When the Baby Boom ended[9] quite abruptly in 1962 and young women started having fewer children (as women in most advanced societies have), it was likely that more women would start looking for jobs. Married women's rate of participation in the work force, never higher than 26% in World War II, was 34% in 1962; two thirds of married women were not in the work force. That percentage rose to 41% by 1970 and 45% in 1975, crossed 50% in 1980, and was 55% by 1986.[10] The percentage of single and divorced women in the work force did not rise as rapidly, and the percentage of women who were not married increased during these years, from 32% of women 18 and over in 1970 to 33% in 1975, 37% in 1980, and 40% in 1985.[11] By no means all of these new women workers were seeking or obtained full-time employment. But their presence in the work force made a difference in personal lives which is hard to overstate. In just a dozen years, from 1962 to 1975, the childbearing rate was cut almost in half. Work force participation by wives rose rapidly and was on its way to coming close to doubling during the longer period from 1962 to 1985. Young women in the 1947–62 period had structured their lives around getting married and bearing children. As marriages started to seem less permanent and childbearing and child-rearing less attractive, they placed increasing reliance on working outside the home to supplement their family income and give them a basis for independence if their marriage should break up and greater leverage within it while it remained intact.

By the middle 1970s this change in personal lives had produced cultural conflict. Believers in traditional religions and practitioners of traditional housewifery resented the new life style and opposed what seemed to be its manifestations in public policy—legalized abortion and the Equal Rights Amendment. On both they seemed at first to be fighting losing battles: the Supreme Court legalized abortion in January 1973, and the Equal Rights Amendment was quickly passed by nearly the required number of legislatures after it was finally sprung from Emanuel Celler's House Judiciary Committee and passed by both houses of Congress. Yet through the 1970s antiabortion groups grew larger and gained converts beyond the Catholics who were originally interested in the issue, and the lobbying of Phyllis Schlafly (ironically, very much a working woman herself, who began each speech by thanking her husband for permission to be there) stopped the progress of ERA in key legislatures in Illinois, Florida, and North Carolina. Efforts by Jimmy and Rosalynn Carter to turn the tide were unavailing, as opponents argued persuasively that the delphic words of the amendment might be interpreted to require policies—such as putting women in military combat—which struck most voters as absurd.

This change in work and living patterns, together with the continued threat of inflation, also undermined the foundations of Keynesian macroeconomic theory. In a work force loaded with new entrants, wage and benefit increases proved more inflationary than theory might suggest. And inflation not only undercut the value of wage increases, it also pushed taxpayers into higher brackets of the progressive tax structure which remained in effect for ordinary people even as it had been rendered nominal by tax avoidance devices and provisions for those with more discretion or control over how they received income. At the same time, wage levels had a less direct effect on incomes than in the past: for many households the size of the paycheck was less important than the number of paychecks coming in. And the number of paychecks depended primarily on personal factors—how many children a couple had, what kind of child care they preferred, whether they stayed married or got divorced, what their attitudes toward traditional gender roles were. These developments made it harder to pump the economy up with fiscal stimulus and harder to hold down inflation. The Keynesian and redistributionist economic policies of the Democrats, which they had come to think of as their political strong suit, had become much less useful in the new economy they found when they returned to power after eight years.

V

New York, the noisiest of American cities, had an even noisier than usual mayoral election in 1977. Since the days when Alfred E. Smith and Robert F.

Wagner and Franklin D. Roosevelt had shown the way to build an American welfare state, New York City voters had demanded and New York City politicians had promised an American version of heaven on earth. New Yorkers would be protected against rises in housing costs, by controlling rents, and against rises in costs for the most elaborate public transit system in the country, by freezing the subway and bus fare (from 1953 to 1966 it remained 15 cents). They would be guaranteed free schooling not only in some of the best elite high schools in the nation but also in the City University system which had produced so many of the city's and the nation's leaders. The honesty of public servants in this most avaricious of cities would be guaranteed by elaborate codes of procedures and cross-checks; their competence would be guaranteed by batteries of examinations; their satisfaction would be guaranteed by liberal pay and pensions and vacations. "I do not propose to permit our fiscal problems to set the limits to our commitments to meet the essential needs of the people of the city," said Mayor Robert Wagner, Jr., a shrewd politician elected with the Democratic bosses' support in 1953 and 1957 and as a reform candidate over their opposition in 1961.[12] His successor, John Lindsay, elected in 1965 when he was in Murray Kempton's phrase "fresh when everyone else is tired," an Upper East Side Manhattan WASP, turned out to be far more profligate than Wagner, borrowing the equivalent of next year's budget to pay for this year's, granting municipal unions huge increases after volcanic confrontations. Meanwhile, large parts of the city—Brownsville in Brooklyn, the South Bronx—were largely abandoned, their streets handed over to teen-age criminals, their rent-controlled buildings left to the city by their bankrupted owners. New York's population dropped by 1 million people in the 1970s, from 8 million to 7 million, almost entirely because of such abandonment—a destruction of lively neighborhoods unparalleled in the nation's history.

By 1975 it was New York City which was bankrupt. Mayor Abraham Beame—amazingly enough, the first Jewish mayor in the city's 300-plus years—had been elected for his bookkeeping ability but turned out to have no idea how far the city was in debt and no sense of how to get it out. City finances were taken over by the state government (which was in fiscal trouble for a while itself) and by a series of makeshift arrangements cobbled together by the likes of investment banker Felix Rohatyn and including municipal union consultant Jack Bigel and union leader Victor Gottbaum. The unions' pension funds bought city bonds when no one else would, the federal government stepped in with loans and guarantees, and so the humiliation of bankruptcy was avoided. But as the 1977 city election approached, the city still had no competent management.

Governor Hugh Carey's candidate for mayor was Mario Cuomo, a Queens lawyer who had won fame mediating a dispute over the placing of a low-income housing project in the middle-class Forest Hills neighborhood back in May and June 1972. Carey called in another Democratic candidate, Edward Koch, the reformer who in 1963 had beaten Carmine de Sapio for Manhattan district leader and had become in 1968 the first Democrat elected to Congress from the Silk Stocking District since 1936. Tall, acerbic, blunt, Koch told Carey in his whiny nasal voice that

Cuomo should run on his slate for the number two post, president of the city council. Uneasily the governor said, "I was thinking about it the other way around."[13] The result of Koch's rejection of this ticket was a four-candidate Democratic field, which also included Beame, still claiming to be a good manager, and Congresswoman Bella Abzug, claiming that she would get the money New York deserved from the federal government. Koch and Cuomo took the position that the city government would have to be restructured—or, in the word that American auto manufacturers were using at the time, downsized. Cuomo brought to the contest a great eloquence, but Koch ended up dominating it by his brassiness. With New York bravado more redolent of the outer boroughs than of Manhattan (though he had been born in Newark and lived his adult life in Greenwich Village), Koch called Beame "incompetent," attacked the municipal labor leaders and invited their insults, campaigned outspokenly in favor of capital punishment and against racial quotas—and won.[14]

New York City's unique primary law provides for a runoff if no candidate gets 40% of the vote in the first Democratic primary; the first contest in September 1977 was almost a dead heat, with 20% for Koch, 19% for Cuomo, 18% for Beame, and 17% for Abzug. In the runoff, after Koch and Cuomo had debated each other constantly, Koch won decisively. This election signaled a new kind of municipal politics in New York, and one not inferior to what preceded it. The fabled ability of the borough Democratic leaders—the famous bosses—to deliver votes turned out to be close to zero. These men had become dispensers of judicial patronage and what other crumbs they could find to a network of greedy hangers-on, but their connection with the voters had become limited indeed. The old dichotomy between regulars and reformers mattered not a whit either. What had become more important was media politics—not just the paid media of television advertisements but the free media of intensive television as well as newspaper coverage. In this particular media politics, talent was rewarded: Koch and Cuomo, clearly able men, emerged from this election which they had entered virtually unknown as the two men who would dominate New York City and (after Cuomo's election as governor in 1982) New York state politics for a decade. Koch's media advisor David Garth had a good message: "After the clubhouse [Beame] and charisma [Lindsay], why not try competence [Koch]?" But the message worked not because of its intrinsic appeal but because after the voters saw Koch they decided it was accurate.

Under Koch the city government retreated from its grandiose dreams and eventually started repairing its rotted underpinnings. The laboratory of American liberalism shut out its lights and opened up again as a rather different kind of institution. Payrolls were cut back, wages frozen (at least technically), services cut back, the subway fare vastly increased, free tuition abolished, and even rent control subjected to some limits. The idea that government could solve all social problems was abandoned in the American city where it had been the strongest. In its place, starting to grow but only slightly visible, was a vibrant private sector. Manhattan real estate prices were in a slump in the bankruptcy-threatened years, enabling some shrewd operators to buy property cheap—notably Donald Trump, son of a Brooklyn and Queens apartment magnate, who after backing Carey in the 1974 primary got state help in redeveloping the old Commodore Hotel into the new Grand Hyatt and got the footing which enabled him to become by the late 1980s one of Manhattan's bigger and certainly its flashiest real estate developers. New York's financial sector had never been ailing (although when Lindsay wanted to put on a stock transfer tax, the Stock Exchange talked of moving to New Jersey), and now it was on the verge of vast growth, growth which would make Manhattan boom again and would reverberate by the middle 1980s into the outer boroughs.

In Washington and on national media the focus in the fall of 1977 was on the failure of most of Jimmy Carter's programs, his inability to produce the tax reform and the welfare reform and the energy program he had talked about, and the embarrassment suffered by this post-Watergate president when his budget director, an affable, able, and overweight Georgian named Bert Lance, was forced to resign because of his failure to disclose personal financial problems.[15] But a greater attention to New York City's problems would have put in sharper focus the limits on government, the increasing skepticism about its efficacy and the increasing concern about its ever-burgeoning cost, which were more dimly apparent in the fumblings and personal drama of the Carter administration.

52

-》》 《《-

Camp David

From the domestic issues which were all he knew and most of what he had campaigned on, Jimmy Carter turned early in his presidency to the foreign policy issues which he began knowing little about and which he had mentioned only infrequently in his campaign. The wonder is not that his foreign initiatives sometimes misfired, but that some of them turned out so well. He brought to his foreign policy some of the sense, widely developed in critics of the Vietnam war, that the era of American domination of the world was—and should be—over. A deserving, virtuous Third World would rise to take America's place, and its indigenous leaders would uplift their formerly oppressed peoples. Through much of the early 1970s most Americans wanted their country's defense spending cut rather than increased, they believed that American intervention almost always caused more harm than good, and they believed that American diplomacy should put more effort into advancing the cause of democracy and something like income and wealth redistribution in countries around the world.[1]

Behind these seemingly naive views there was at least one sound political instinct. Support for American foreign policy could not be sustained over the long haul without some appeal to those abstract ideals which more than sheer territory, more than a shared heritage stretching back before written history, defined the American nation. Henry Kissinger's shrewd *Realpolitik* aroused Americans' admiration, at least so long as he seemed a dashing and romantic figure. But his policies of working with bloodthirsty dictatorships—from rightist regimes in Latin America to the brutal Soviet system of Leonid Brezhnev and the Chinese at what Americans learned later[2] was the peak of the Cultural Revolution—did not provide the spirit of cohesion and common purpose which Kissinger himself knew was essential to the credibility of the ultimate threat to use force, the threat without which American power was easily mocked. Carter sought to fill that void by declaring in February 1977 that "human rights" would be an important factor in determining American foreign policy and by setting up a former Mississippi civil rights supporter, Patricia Derian, as an assistant secretary in the State Department to assert the interest of human rights in every policy area. Naturally there was friction with practitioners of established lines of policy, but there were some worthwhile successes as well.

Some of Carter's foreign policy achievements were products of letting the permanent foreign policy establishment move its own priorities forward. In the spring of 1978 the traditionally Arab-oriented State Department[3] moved forward a sale of F-16 jets to Saudi Arabia which Carter invested much effort in getting through Congress; the department's NATO-oriented European bureaucracy tended to push against too tough a treatment of Turkey after its invasion of Cyprus. Both policies not only lacked, they antagonized, political constituencies in the United States. It was also the career State Department which brought forward the ongoing business of the Panama Canal Treaties. Since the riots of January 1964 in Panama, that country's leaders—members of its few leading families or the commanders of the National Guard—had pressed the United States to relinquish control of the canal it had built between 1903 and 1914. Negotiations were approaching completion in the Ford administration but were not consummated in the election year of 1976; certainly Ford must have noticed that it was Ronald Reagan's repeated declarations that "we built it, we paid for it, it's ours, and we're going to keep it," which produced his victory in the North Carolina primary[4] and which made him a nearly successful challenger of the incumbent president at the Kansas City convention.

Jimmy Carter was convinced that a Panama Canal agreement was needed "to correct an injustice."[5] He was attracted by the competence and charm of Omar Torrijos, the head of Panama's National Guard and effective chief of state; and by September 1977 the two countries had signed a set of treaties. Now came the hard work of getting it through the Senate, where more than the one third of senators capable of blocking any treaty were already on record against its terms and every senator was aware that polls showed voters against the agreement by an overwhelming margin. Gallup's initial survey showed a solid plurality opposed, and even the small segment of voters who could correctly identify the features which preserved U.S. leverage were only equally divided.[6] The Carter administration immediately launched a mammoth lobbying operation, complete with intense personal effort by the president, designed to produce the necessary two-thirds majority. Eventually, in March and April 1978, the Treaties were ratified by just barely the required number of senators. The arguments for them were essentially prudential: if they were not ratified, there was a risk of war in a part of the world where the "colossus of the North" was widely resented; the military and commercial value of the canal was not as great as it once had been; the United States retained the right to defend the canal against attacks by third countries. Intellectually, to senators and even to many voters, these were momentarily persuasive. But to voters in the long haul they proved unpersuasive. Three generations of schoolchildren had learned the canal as a kind of quintessential American success story; we built it where the French had failed, we created the nation of Panama in order to build it, we conquered yellow fever in order to build it. The canal was a living example of American ability and American strength: for many voters, to abandon it was to abandon an important part of America. Of these feelings Carter and most of his advisors were largely ignorant, nor were they at all sympathetic to them.[7] American nationalism was to them nothing more than American colonialism. Progressive policy, as they saw it, consisted of adjusting American views and positions to the imperatives of the rising Third World. They assumed that American voters in this post-Vietnam era would come to see this truth soon enough.

The political aftermath of the canal treaties ratification is proof as solid as one gets in politics that this assumption was wrong. Of the senators who voted to ratify the treaties, nine[8] were defeated in November 1978 or November 1980—some of them heavy favorites to win reelection and probable winners had it not been for the treaties issue. Senate Republican leader Howard Baker's crucial support of the treaties destroyed any chance he had had of winning the Republican presidential nomination in 1980. Ronald Reagan in his 1980 presidential campaign, Jesse Helms in his attempts to defeat Democratic senators in 1978 and 1980 (when his Congressional Club and Terry Dolan's NCPAC raised millions through direct mail to run "independent expenditure" campaigns against liberal Democrats) all got great mileage from the issue. Against this grave political cost, the Panama Canal treaties produced absolutely no political gain—for President Carter, for the Democrats, for Republicans like Baker who provided crucial political support.

II

In the ten years following the publication of Michael Harrington's *The Other America,* the crucial domestic questions in American politics hinged on spending. For the ten years or so after 1973, the crucial domestic questions in American politics hinged on taxes. For forty years almost every critical decision on domestic taxing and spending policies was made in Washington. By the late 1970s some of the most important of these decisions were being made in state capitals—or in state polling places.

One place they were made was in California. And the leading actor was not a trend-minded Democrat like Jerry Brown, but one of those old-fashioned denizens of southern California with a midwestern accent and a booming voice reminiscent of the migrants who had filled the Los Angeles basin in the 1940s and early 1950s, a man with the corny optimism about America and the sour cynicism about government which in varying quantities were the staple of many Los Angeles radio call-in shows, a durable and (until 1978) mostly unsuccessful crusader against taxes and spending named Howard Jarvis. Ronald Reagan had given up the cause of holding down state government spending after the failure of his anti-spending Proposition 1 in November 1973 and his retirement from the governorship a year later. Now Jarvis took as his target local property taxes: the Proposition 13 which he got onto the June 1978 ballot would scale them back and would bar future increases. He had chosen his target shrewdly. Most Californians were homeowners, and most California real property had risen rapidly in value in the inflationary 1970s: this was citizens' one major source of increasing wealth in an uncertain time. But California's efficient and incorruptible assessors were keeping careful track of that wealth, and its high (though not the nation's highest) property tax rates were in effect a tax on assets which were rapidly appreciating but produced no cash income. California politicians almost universally opposed Proposition 13, since it would vastly cut local government budgets, thereby reducing services and increasing demands on state budgets. Even Jerry Brown, with his habit of criticizing bureaucracies, his penchant for promoting austerity, and his taste for puncturing received wisdom, echoed the arguments made by civil servant union leaders and local county supervisors.

Those arguments were rejected resoundingly by the voters, who approved Jarvis's proposition by 65%–35%. The effect on Brown's career was drastic: he quickly positioned himself as an eager implementer of the new law, but the politician whose reputation depended on his faithfulness to principle seemed revealed now as a man with no—or too many—principles, and his popularity plunged. Although he won reelection in November 1978 by making fun of the mistakes of an inept Republican opponent, the governor whose hopeless candidacy had received 59% of the votes in California's 1976 presidential primary received only 4% four years later; in 1982 he lost a Senate race to the little-known mayor of San Diego, Pete Wilson. But Proposition 13 did even greater damage nationwide to the idea that a steady expansion of government was a feature of the modern age, which must be accepted and could not be controlled or reversed. Government services in California were cut back, but not nearly so drastically as Proposition 13 opponents had argued: it turned out that there was fat which could be cut when politicians and bureaucrats were forced to cut. And the cuts which were made did not spawn any countervailing voter movement for more services and taxes. Tax-cutting efforts rapidly spread to other states, with varying success; and their opponents began to suffer defeat. One prominent and unexpected example was another young trend Democrat who had been elected governor in 1974, Michael Dukakis of Massachusetts, who was defeated in his September 1978 primary.

III

In Washington, the political impulses which resulted in the surprise passage of Proposition 13 resulted in similar surprises on domestic legislation. In his 1975–76 campaign Carter had excoriated the American welfare system, decried the nation's lack of national health insurance, and called the tax system "a disgrace to the human race." Most of his Democratic rivals were even more scathing. But in office Carter was unable to produce welfare reform, national health insurance, or tax reform bills which could pass the overwhelmingly Democratic Congress. Welfare reform foundered on the impossibility of coming up with a bill which both contained work incentives and reduced costs. Legislators who had voted for or gone along with great increases in Aid to Families with Dependent Children benefits between 1963 and 1973 were content to let inflation erode the value of these benefits after 1973. On health insurance Carter's proposal was opposed on the one hand by Edward Kennedy and unions led by the United Auto Workers, who wanted a total national health insurance system (and eventually, in Kennedy's case, an issue on which to run against Carter in 1980), and on the other by Republicans and some Democrats who wanted less government involvement in health care and successfully opposed the administration's attempts to impose cost controls on hospitals.

But it was on taxes that the Democrats' efforts were most roundly defeated. Their impulse was to eliminate the loopholes which had grown up in the tax code and were one of the two factors which gravely reduced its nominal progressiveness. The other factor, however, worked against this goal: it was that economic growth and inflation had tended to put the mass of voters into higher tax brackets than they had ever dreamed they would be in. Increasing taxes on the rich by plugging loopholes was technically difficult and politically difficult or impossible; the beneficiaries of some loopholes—notably the deduction for mortgage interest—included a vast majority of voters. The income tax structure had been designed at the beginning of World War II to absorb almost all the income of a very small number of rich people and to take a small part of the income of everyone else. It had been transformed, through the lowering of the top rates in the Kennedy-Johnson years and the growth of loopholes and tax avoidance in a postwar climate in which paying as little as you could did not seem unpatriotic and was not frowned on in any circles, until by the late 1970s most voters were taxed and, in their view, rather heavily taxed. The burden seemed particularly heavy after Social Security taxes were raised in December 1977 to pay for the increased benefit levels which Richard Nixon had produced for the 1972 election but which were based on the dishonest or naive demographic assumptions that immediate rises in economic growth rates back to 1962–69 levels and in birthrates back to 1947–62 levels would produce enough revenues in the short and long runs to fund them. Under these circumstances Congress had political incentives to provide loopholes to the well-placed and to ostentatiously relieve taxpayers from the effects of "bracket creep" by periodic cuts in rates. Carter's call for elimination of most loopholes and a rate structure which would make the periodic cuts less showy meant that there was little support in Congress and no organized constituency outside for his bill.

What there was, as it turned out, was a constituency for lowering rather than raising taxes on those with relatively high incomes. Congressman William Steiger, a Republican from Wisconsin, slight and blond and so young in appearance that when he came to the House after being elected in 1966 at the age of twenty-eight he was mistaken for a page, was generally counted as a liberal; he was open to persuasion on policies to help the poor, he was willing to support culturally liberal positions, he was on good personal terms with Democrats as well as Republicans. But in early 1978 he came up with an original idea on taxes: the maximum tax on capital gains must be lowered from 49% to 25%. In the liberal tax reformers' view, the existing rate already represented a gaping loophole. Capital gains—the amount of appreciation on property sold after being held for at least six months— was already taxed at a lower rate than ordinary income, and this differential had provided the incentive for the creation of various tax avoidance schemes by ingenious accountants, lobbyists, and legislators. But on the Ways and Means Committee, Steiger was able to persuade a majority that the capital gains rate was choking off investment, particularly in high-technology areas; and his argument, assiduously supported by lobbyists, proved persuasive to the House in August 1978 and the Senate in October. A progressive tax reform bill had been converted into a tax cut bill.

And as Steiger and others had predicted, revenues from capital gains taxes promptly increased after Carter signed the bill, as taxpayers took gains which they had avoided taking before because of the high tax rates. Steiger had come upon the truth that in an advanced, complex, free society, in a time of peace when government does not claim a superintending authority over citizens' lives and therefore over their property, most people with significant economic assets can determine the form in which their income is received and can make that determination (and feel no moral obligation not to make it) in a way which minimizes their taxes. Consequently, if a government wants greater economic activity and growth, what it must do is lower taxes, especially on the kind of voluntary transactions which were taxed in 1978 as capital gains.

IV

The greatest achievement of Jimmy Carter's presidency, the Camp David agreement between President Anwar Sadat of Egypt and Prime Minister Menachem Begin of Israel in September 1978, was something probably no other American president since Theodore Roosevelt could have accomplished; and it was accomplished in a way no other president would have attempted and certainly no presidential advisors would have recommended. It was the result of improvisation, for it certainly was not part of the original plan of Carter's Middle East diplomacy. Through most of 1977 he was pushing for a multipower conference which would include the Soviet Union—a proposal which evidently so alarmed Sadat, who had thrown the Soviets out of Egypt and did not want them back in the Middle East, that he took the extraordinary step of proclaiming his desire for peace with Israel and visiting Jerusalem in November. When Sadat and Begin were unable to reach agreement, Carter invited them both to the presidential retreat of Camp David. There, in comfortable wooden cabins on a quarter-square-mile compound on top of a Maryland mountain ridge, Carter personally conducted negotiations for thirteen days, relaying messages from one man to the other (Sadat and Begin seldom met). The president, normally the cynosure of every night's television newscast, put aside all other business, was absent from Washington, imposed a total news blackout on the negotiations—a procedure which would have looked farcical and been politically disastrous had no agreement been reached. But with great negotiating skills and shrewdness, and with the command over detail which served him ill on other occasions but on this one was probably essential to success, Carter got an agreement and was able to parade Sadat and Begin before a joint session of Congress.

For this achievement Carter's job rating jumped from 39%–44% negative in late July 1978 to 56%–30% positive in September.[9] More important and more lasting, the Camp David agreements, by making peace between Israel and the one Arab nation with the manpower to be a genuine military threat in conventional warfare, greatly reduced the danger that the United States would be called on to intervene militarily to rescue Israel from destruction, an intervention which would risk a great-power military confrontation. Carter's skillful negotiation thus substantially reduced the risk of a major nuclear war.

For Carter, Camp David seems to have been a paradigm of how to settle the most important issues. He had tried to assemble a large coalition of adverse interests and hammer out a detailed position on energy—a procedure which worked tolerably well within his administration and the House but not in the Senate. He tried to produce consensus welfare reform and health insurance policy and tax reform by getting experts together and using a knowledge of details to come up with an acceptable compromise, with less success. He had even less success on arms control, where he allowed the internal process to commit his administration to opposite and mutually inconsistent policies. On the Panama Canal Treaties, he mobilized his administration and its allies and used his mastery of detail to achieve success, as he defined it: ratification of the treaties.

But politically there was never much gain for Carter and for the Democratic party of which he was after all the nominal head. The compromise welfare and health and tax policies, even if they had been passed, did not come close to assuaging the discontents which Carter had articulated on the campaign trail; in a complex, mostly affluent society, in which the discontents were exaggerated in the backwash of Vietnam and Watergate, it was not likely that any workable policies could have. Even the energy program seemed more to perpetuate the discontent by emphasizing the problem rather than assuage it by providing a neat, widely acceptable solution. In foreign policy, the Panama Canal Treaties were affirmatively unpopular, a lasting political liability, while Camp David was so transcendently a personal triumph and so plainly a once-in-a-lifetime situation that it added nothing to the luster of the Democratic party and, over the long run, surprisingly little to that of Carter.

It has been said in defense of Carter that the problems he faced were intractable and the practical difficulties of governing overwhelming.[10] Perhaps, but another problem was the dissonance between what pollster Patrick Caddell called Carter's "campaigning" and what Carter actually did to govern once in office. Going into the 1976 campaign, the Democrats had spent eight years passionately denouncing the Richard Nixon whom their divisions had helped to elect, the Vietnam war which their own president had started and the hated Nixon eventually ended, the Watergate scandal which despite their control of Congress they had done little to uncover before the 1972 election, and the iniquitous workings of the American tax, welfare, and health care systems which they far more than the Republicans had put into place.

Their rhetoric was scathing, apocalyptic, aggressive in claiming virtue for the speaker and the audience and in denouncing vice in some unseen possessor of central power. A Harvard student who grew up in the southern port city of Jacksonville, Florida, Caddell listened to George Wallace and advised first his 1972 client George McGovern and then his 1976 and 1980 client Jimmy Carter to appeal to Americans' "alienation"—a common word then in academic discourse. This McGovern did with some positive effect in the 1972 primaries and Carter did with great positive effect in the 1976 primaries and general election. The trouble was that there was no connection between this electioneering strategy and a strategy for governing. No possible set of policies could satisfy the loud sense of grievance the candidates had been evoking or could deliver the combination of all good things which they promised. These things were impossible not so much because of the evil condition of government and the weakness of the nation as because of the opposite situations: the government was never as bad nor the nation as weak as the rhetoric suggested. In the quarter-century following 1963, the United States showed an almost unending capacity for economic growth, though slowed down significantly by exogenous oil shocks and made fitful by inflation; it grew vastly more tolerant and secure in its increasing cultural diversity; it suffered no major war or foreign threat. No politician could improve the country as much as Jimmy Carter's rhetoric promised, because the country was not in such bad shape in the first place.

So even before the oil shock of 1979, even before the Iran hostage crisis, even in the aftermath of Camp David, Jimmy Carter was in political trouble, not because he had failed to do a reasonable job addressing the problems government could handle, but because he had contributed mightily to the sense Americans had gotten that their nation was in terrible shape and that he could do far more to improve it than anyone thought.

V

The 1978 elections stopped short of being a disaster for the Democrats: their losses were marginal and were partly balanced by gains made at the expense of the Republicans. The hurricane of antitax feeling which seemed to follow the passage of Proposition 13 in June seemed fairly well blown out by November. The Democrats' number of House seats declined only from 292, a number which seemed unsustainable anyway, to 277; the Republicans failed to make the big inroads into the Texas and Missouri delegations they had hoped for after an unusually large number of rural-based Democrats retired. In the Senate, the number of Democrats was cut from 61 to 58, a marginal loss, although one with some political significance; for it takes 60 votes to cut off a filibuster, and now the Republicans, if they stuck together, had enough votes to sustain a filibuster indefinitely. The Democrats won majorities of popular votes in both Senate and House seats. Their performance in gubernatorial races was not bad either: they held California, New York, and Florida by wide margins and lost Pennsylvania and Ohio only narrowly, while losing Illinois and Michigan more conclusively. There was one shock, however. By 16,000 votes out of 2.3 million cast, Republican William Clements, a millionaire offshore oil rig outfitter and former deputy secretary of defense, was elected governor of Texas after spending a record $7 million. Clements's big margins came in the affluent parts of the state's big metropolitan areas, west Houston and north

Dallas and their smaller equivalents in San Antonio and Forth Worth. But Clements also made some inroads into traditionally Democratic rural and small-town Texas, which for all the state's metropolitan growth still cast 40% of its votes.[11]

In the Senate races Democrats made 3 of their 5 gains in the heavily urban states of Massachusetts, New Jersey, and Michigan; their other gains, in Oklahoma and Nebraska, were triumphs by popular governors in open seats which told little about opinion on national issues. Republican Senate gains, on the other hand, tended to come in smaller, more rural, and less culturally cosmopolitan states: Maine and New Hampshire in the East, Mississippi in the South, Iowa, South Dakota, and Colorado on the Great Plains; the major exception was half-metropolitan, half-rural Minnesota, where the Democratic-Farmer-Labor party ran into self-inflicted problems and lost both Senate seats to the Independent Republicans. This same trend away from the Democrats outside metropolitan areas was apparent in House races. The Democrats won 10 seats they had lost in 1976: 2 in the New York metropolitan area; 1 in exceedingly affluent and culturally liberal Montgomery County, Maryland, outside Washington; 2 in the Pittsburgh and Miami areas; 2 in outstate Michigan (which had been trending Democratic, except when Gerald Ford was running in 1976, since before the McGovern candidacy); and 3 open seats in Ohio, Florida, and South Dakota. In contrast, the 25 Republican gains, with 1 glaring exception—the Silk Stocking District of Manhattan, which was captured by liberal Republican Bill Green after Edward Koch was elected mayor in November 1977—tended to come in rural or small-town districts or in 4 cases in districts encompassing the least culturally liberal parts of metropolitan areas (eastern Long Island, northeast Philadelphia, the flat suburbs southwest of Houston, and Long Beach, California).

In 1976, Jimmy Carter had run unusually strong for a Democrat in rural and small-town areas, not only in the South but all over the country. Now, after two years of his administration, his party was clearly losing support in such areas. Tradition-minded voters, who had seen the Southern Baptist Carter as their kind of leader and had distrusted a veteran politician like Gerald Ford whose wife trumpeted her support of women's liberation, now seemed disappointed with the work of the Carter Democrats, who had given them few concrete or symbolic victories. On the contrary, Carter clearly tended toward the orientation of the Trend Democrats, as shown by his stands on issues from the Panama Canal to drug legalization. Kevin Phillips's conservative Republican majority was beginning to emerge, even if the Congress and the state governments seemed to remain overwhelmingly Democratic. This trend was generally unnoticed at the time. But in retrospect it goes some way toward explaining Carter's weakness in the 1980 presidential race. The cultural segment of America which was emotionally most inclined to see Jimmy Carter as its kind of American had decided he was not; its members felt at the least disappointed, and in some cases betrayed. In the cultural politics of the late 1970s and early 1980s, the Carter Democrats had, unknowingly, lost their core cultural group, and had nothing to replace it with.

53

→》》 《《←

Malaise

S udden gunshots popping out on the jungle-surrounded landing strip in Guyana: the television cameras' confused footage gave little sense of what was happening, but viewers soon learned the story. California Congressman Leo Ryan, who had flown to Guyana just after the November 1978 election to track down some constituents' relatives who had been attracted to a cult, was shot dead on orders of its leader, Jim Jones, who then ordered all his followers to kill themselves by drinking poisoned Kool-Aid—an order which, with just a couple of exceptions, they obeyed. The incidents at "Jonestown" were sickeningly bizarre, even in a time when the memory was fresh of the kidnapping of newspaper heiress Patricia Hearst in 1974 by a ragtag group of San Francisco Bay Area radicals who called themselves the Symbionese Liberation Army and who had persuaded her to join them in committing armed bank robberies; she had gone to jail just six months before the events in Guyana.

Hearst's captors and Jones and his lieutenants all claimed to be acting on behalf of the poor and the powerless against the oppressors and the powerful; their images reflected, with grotesque distortion, the common pose of protesters beginning just after the great successes of the civil rights revolution, portraying themselves as the vanguard of the next generation of downtrodden against an older generation of rulers. If they exaggerated the powers of those they opposed, they also acted with an adolescent heedlessness of tradition and recklessness of consequences, a hostile indifference to what had come before and an arrogant lack of curiosity about what was to follow. Their pretensions were pathetic; and if the Symbionese Liberation Army was destroyed in a blazing gun battle, Jim Jones's followers literally turned on and destroyed themselves. In the process they began what was for most Americans a hideously disorienting political year, a time in which bizarre violence seemed to rain down on their nation and in which their leaders were unable to exert any control at all over a dizzying spiral of events.

Jim Jones had been a figure, at least at the fringe, of politics in San Francisco before he took his followers to Guyana for salvation. San Francisco had long prided itself on its toleration of unusual life styles, even of those regarded as deviant elsewhere; its American straight-grid streets marching resolutely up and down scenically steep hills housed not only blue-collar Irish and Italians like the big cities back east but also the hippies of the late 1960s and vast communities of gays by the middle 1970s. In this environment successful politicians had no enemies on the cultural left, seeking the backing of an ex-convicts' support group at one point, the various gay political clubs at another, and Jim Jones and his mostly poor black followers at a third. No cult seemed too outré, no cause too far out for the successful politicians of San Francisco to embrace.

Eight days after Jonestown, one of the leaders of San Francisco's liberal political establishment, Mayor George Moscone, and the first openly gay member of the city's Board of Supervisors, Harvey Milk, were gunned down in their offices in San Francisco's monumental City Hall by former Supervisor Dan White, an ex-policeman enraged by the ruin of his own career and the prospering fortunes of the homosexuals and liberals who opposed him. Ironically, White ultimately was found guilty only of manslaughter by a San Francisco jury either unwilling to punish the murderer of homosexual and liberal politicians or of the liberal mindset which tended to find in violent action the involuntary expression of irresistible impulses; he was sentenced to only seven years and eight months in prison and after his release ended up killing himself.

II

The events in Jonestown and San Francisco were soon replaced in the public eye by those in Iran. On New Year's Day 1978, Carter had visited Iran and toasted its shah. Just 364 days later, on New Year's Eve 1978, the shah was about to be driven from power, and the new government forced on him by rioting Iranians had stopped oil exports; in January 1979 the shah left Iran, and on February 1 the octogenarian Ayatollah Ruhollah Khomeini, the Iranian Islamic leader long in exile in Iraq and France, returned to the seething land he was to rule. The sudden cessation of oil exports from Iran, the second largest oil exporter after Saudi Arabia, and of the Iranian government's guarantee of the military stability of the Persian Gulf—a guarantee maintained, pursuant to Henry Kissinger's design, after the British military withdrawal from the Gulf in 1971—meant that the market price of oil must soar, which it did with the help of OPEC. By February 1979, Iranian oil prices were 30% above those of December 1978; OPEC prices rose 14.5% in December 1978 and 24% in June 1979. In the year ending September 1979, gasoline prices in the United States were up 52% and heating oil prices up 73%. Suddenly gas lines started growing in various parts of the United States, as the supplies allotted this or that state by bureaucrats of the new Department of Energy proved inadequate; by June 1979 several states had adopted odd-even gas regulations, with odd-numbered license plates allowed to buy gas on three days and even-numbered ones on three others. The economic effects of this 1978–79 oil shock were significant. To an ever greater degree, income and wealth were redistributed from Western countries like the United States, which knew how to recirculate them to produce economic growth, to the oil-producing kingdoms and theocracies of the Middle East and elsewhere, which wasted a large portion of what they learned to plunder.

III

While the economy was being ravaged and the everyday life of ordinary Americans, anchored in almost every case by the automobile, was being transformed nightmarishly, the television screen was showing one bizarre spectacle after another. Iranian politics, hitherto a matter of little interest, was now covered extensively, with interviews of figures whose names most Americans could not keep straight—Bakhtiar and Banisadr, Ghotzbadeh and Dr. Yasdi (who not long before had been a dentist in Toledo), and, as he left his suburban Paris exile for Tehran, the Ayatollah Khomeini himself. The Soviet bear sat not far above Iran on the map, glaring southward; in Afghanistan, where the Soviet influence was already strong, the American ambassador was murdered in February 1979. Back home, American technology seemed to founder. The nuclear accident at the Three Mile Island nuclear plant in Pennsylvania sent up a scare in March. In May an American Airlines DC-10 crashed just beyond Chicago's O'Hare Airport, leading to doubts about the safety of one of the products of one of America's technologically most successful industries.

In the meantime, as voters and many politicians became more discontented with what they considered the liberal policies of the Carter administration—the Panama Canal treaties, the abortive attempts at welfare and tax reform—many liberal Democratic politicians were becoming estranged from Carter. The liberals came out of a political tradition of seeking economic redistribution by always asking more—more government action in behalf of the poor—with little or no regard to how much more. They assumed that the forces arrayed against them were so powerful that they would not get much and that they would never approach the point at which, they might be prepared to admit when in a theoretical frame of mind, the public sector would start to squeeze the life out of the private sector. But by the late 1970s many Americans thought that point had been reached. Government spending as a share of gross national product had risen from 24% in 1950 and 29% in 1960 to 33% in 1970 and 35% in 1975. The bureaucratic and political forces pulling for more government spending, especially for programs like Social Security which created entitlements for middle-class voters, seemed to be outweighing the forces calling for restraint, like the now defunct demand for a balanced federal budget. To the opponents of liberal programs these trends were obvious and ominous; by the liberals they were studiously ignored.

Instead, in the political climate validated by Carter's "campaigning" rhetoric, every representative of any group which did not receive every bit of what it wanted complained bitterly of its oppression. At the Democrats' December 1978 midterm convention in Memphis, liberals lambasted Carter for what they called his lack of compassion for the poor and Edward Kennedy delivered a speech widely interpreted as the forerunner of a primary challenge of the president. In January 1979 former Congresswoman Bella Abzug was forced off a national commission on women after vociferously criticizing an administration which had tried (and failed) to pass the Equal Rights Amendment; that same month the National Urban

League's Vernon Jordan said that American blacks were "at the brink of disaster" because of budget cuts sanctioned or accepted by the administration. February saw Washington invaded by a "tractorcade" of farmers from the Great Plains, unhappy about crop prices and farming costs which later farm protesters would look back to as the happy benchmark against which they measured further oppression. In March, José Lopez Portillo, in the midst of what would turn out to be a scandalous and economically profligate term as president of Mexico, attacked Carter for not doing enough for his country. By May five congressmen had formed a Draft Edward Kennedy movement to oppose Carter's renomination in 1980. Kennedy did nothing to discourage such activities; and in polls of Democrats he led Carter 58%–35% in a two-candidate race in April, 52%–17% in a multi-candidate race in June, and 66%–30% in a two-candidate pairing in July.[1]

In the clear light of hindsight it becomes apparent that Kennedy's lead was the product of Carter's unpopularity, and that Carter's unpopularity was in turn the product of a sense that the nation's leader had lost control of events. As the barrage of inexplicable disasters at home and abroad continued, as the overthrow of the shah was accompanied by the installation of Khomeini and the apparent advance of the forces of Islamic fundamentalism throughout the "crescent" from the Persian Gulf to the Indian subcontinent, Carter's job rating went on a dizzying downward spiral, in counterpoint to the growth in inflation. The following table shows the progression:[2]

Month	Inflation	Carter Job Rating
May 1978	7.0	43–43
June 1978	7.4	
July 1978	7.7	40–41, 39–44
Aug. 1978	7.8	
Sep. 1978	8.3	56–30, 50–37
Oct. 1978	8.9	52–36
Nov. 1978	8.9	
Dec. 1978	9.0	50–34
Jan. 1979	9.3	50–36, 43–41
Feb. 1979	9.9	
Mar. 1979	10.1	39–50
Apr. 1979	10.5	43–46
May 1979	10.9	37–49
June 1979	10.9	29–56, 29–57[3]
July 1979	11.3	

There is almost a linear relation here: Carter's job rating sagged as inflation rose, rose sharply after Camp David in September 1978, then sagged again as inflation kept rising and other untoward events occurred.

Voters do not watch inflation statistics closely, but they notice, if only subliminally, changes in the costs of items in the world around them. By July 1979 they were clearly noticing not only the sharp rise in gasoline and heating oil prices but also the steady, unrelenting rise in prices generally which produced only the second episode of double-digit inflation (the first lasted from February 1974 to April 1975) since the days just after World War II—which is to say, in most voters' living memory. And the events outside the country, particularly in Iran and the Middle East, which obviously were contributing importantly to the inflation seemed to be spinning out of America's control. At the back of people's minds was the possibility of hyperinflation, of the currency being rendered worthless, of the stories told of the German inflation of the 1920s, when wheelbarrows full of money had to be brought to the market to buy a little food. If the value of money was falling so rapidly, who could say it would not start spiraling downward ever faster? In earlier episodes of double-digit inflation, the voters' retribution had been swift: in 1946 they had given the Republicans their biggest majorities in Congress in 60 years, and in 1974 they had not only crushed the Republicans in congressional elections but created a climate of opinion which tolerated or even encouraged the removal from office of the incumbent president. In the summer of 1979 the economic and political indicators suggested a similar fate for Jimmy Carter and the Democrats unless they could demonstrate a mastery over events and exert some control over the trends which were threatening Americans' way of life.

IV

To this threat Carter's response was to go to the scene of his greatest triumph, Camp David, and to try to engineer some domestic equivalent of the agreement he had fashioned between Menachem Begin and Anwar Sadat. In June 1979 Carter took some major initiatives, announcing his health program and proclaiming the SALT II disarmament agreements at a summit with Leonid Brezhnev. But these failed to seize the public's imagination: the health program was immediately criticized by Republicans on one side and Edward Kennedy on the other; and the SALT II treaty was not only generally anticipated but also vociferously attacked. For July, Carter planned an energy speech. But he had just delivered one in April, and after he went up to Camp David to prepare the talk he canceled it at the last minute and stayed up on the mountain. He had before him a memorandum from Patrick Caddell reciting his perennial theme, the voters' alienation from and disbelief in major institutions, and calling it a national "malaise." Unlike Vice President Mondale, who in a rare lapse from his usual complete loyalty let it be known that he thought Caddell's advice was ludicrous, Carter failed to understand that voters yearning for control to be exerted over events would be appalled by the spectacle of a president canceling a major speech, isolating himself from public view, and declining all public comment while he met with various notables, most of them private citizens, for what he later called "leisurely conversations about our nation, my administration, and the serious problems we faced, including the important subject of energy."[4] The subject often was which members of the administration should be fired—and the president's own shortcomings. Carter's diary makes the process sound like a therapy session: "I spent 90% of my time listening. I worked hard all week, some of the more strenuous work of my life. Also, it's not easy for me to accept criticism and to reassess my way of doing things. And this was a week of intense reassessment."[5]

After 12 days Carter returned to the White House and spoke to the nation on a Sunday night telecast "about the need to have faith in our country—not only in the government, but in our own ability to solve great problems."[6] In effect, he was reading back to the public the responses Caddell had gotten to his poll questions, acknowledging their alienation, empathizing with their asserted sense of power-lessness and their lack of confidence in major institutions. The next day he delivered an energy speech, then ordered all his Cabinet members to submit their resignations and promptly accepted those of Treasury Secretary Michael Blumenthal and HEW Secretary Joseph Califano—two thorns in the side of the Carter White House staff—and Energy Secretary James Schlesinger, who had long wanted to leave; Transportation Secretary Brock Adams announced minutes ahead of the ax that he was leaving. The young Georgians close to Carter, Hamilton Jordan and press secretary Jody Powell, were of course left unscathed. Their unpopularity (despite their considerable abilities) prompted the comment of Texas Congressman Charles Wilson: "Good grief! He's cut down the tall trees and left the monkeys."

The "domestic Camp David" was the prime example of how Carter followed Caddell's advice and insisted on "campaigning" rather than governing. The energy policy which he eventually proposed and got partially through Congress—gradual oil price decontrol with a windfall profits tax—moved in the direction of promoting energy conservation through the price mechanism, but too slowly to produce the political dividends Carter wanted. In the meantime, inflation continued, reaching a peak annual rate of 14.8% in March 1980 and declining only to 12.8% in October, as voters were deciding which candidate to support. Carter was never able to establish the sense that he was in control of events—for the good reason that for the most part he was not.

V

The Democrats' position continued to decline. In September 1979, campaigning for relection in Idaho, Frank Church, in his first year in his long-sought position as chairman of the Senate Foreign Relations Committee, announced the presence of a Soviet brigade in Cuba and thereby caused the hearings on the already faltering SALT II treaty to be suspended. When Church was first elected, in 1956, over an apparently alcoholic[7] and erratic follower of Joseph McCarthy, Idaho was still a state which remembered fondly its support of Franklin Roosevelt and, in an earlier time, William Jennings Bryan, one of those western states which resented the colonial overlordship of the East and found the federal government to be a friend which built irrigation systems and electric power lines and fought the bosses of Wall Street and the speculators of the Chicago Board of Trade. Idaho's Mormons, a majority in the southeastern part of the state as they were in adjoining Utah, felt a sympathy with John F. Kennedy as a fellow sufferer from religious discrimination; with 46% of the vote, Kennedy nearly carried the state in 1960. But after that Idaho moved steadily right. No longer a pauper state in need of federal services, it found itself badgered by federal land regulators and would-be gun controllers; its culturally tradition-minded citizens recoiled from the cultural liberalism they saw on Democratic national convention broadcasts. Idaho gave 49% of its votes to Barry Goldwater in 1964, and by 1968 it was one of the most heavily Republican states in the nation. Although an early Vietnam and arms control dove, Church was reelected in 1968 and 1974, in large part because he worked on water issues on the Interior Committee with Vietnam and arms control hawk Henry Jackson[8] of Washington, keeping cheap water pumping through Idaho's many irrigation canals and keeping it away from the designs of thirsty Californians. Church had run a presidential campaign in 1976 which, while unsuccessful, ended on an upbeat note for him. Yet by 1979 he was plainly in trouble back home. His role on Foreign Relations, where he had helped to pass the Panama Canal Treaties while waiting for the seventy-eight-year-old chairman, John Sparkman, to retire, was proving a liability. Now he seized on what was to him new evidence of the Soviet brigade in Cuba to halt what was in Idaho an unpopular arms control treaty.

The other blow to the Democrats also came from the liberals who claimed to represent the soul of the party: this was the presidential candidacy of Edward Kennedy. The younger brother who had declined to considered for the nomination in 1968, when as a thirty-six-year-old untested in major national affairs he was nonetheless already the one candidate who could have united the party at the convention; whose conduct after the Chappaquiddick incident of 1969 had kept him away from a 1972 nomination which turned out to be worthless; whose surprise decision in September 1974 had kept him from running for the one Democratic nomination in a dozen years which turned out to be favorable for the party—this younger brother of the man who was still the hero-president of a nation 16 years after his death finally decided to run in 1980, a year which turned out to be the most unfavorable for his party in more than a generation. To be sure, the initial polls looked favorable: Kennedy led Carter by 2–1 margins in the summer of 1979. And to be sure, Kennedy seemed gifted with genuine issues: on health care, on welfare, on taxes, he was ready to assert the liberal, economic-redistributionist cause against a president who had trimmed and compromised and given away what Democrats who believed in that cause felt was the heart of their moral case to the nation. Yet when Roger Mudd, interviewing Kennedy in the informal surroundings of Hyannisport in the summer of 1979, asked him why he would run against Carter, Kennedy was unable to come up with an articulate answer.

Nothing in the polls of the summer of 1979 suggested that Kennedy's candidacy would be doomed or even handicapped by Chappaquiddick. Yet as he made the moves to run, as the Mudd interview was aired in November, exactly one year before the election, Kennedy started sinking in the polls. With no evidence that Carter was gaining in support, Kennedy was falling; the issue positions which he may have believed worked in his behalf did nothing to shore up support for his candidacy, while doubts about his personal character eroded it fatally—at almost precisely the time he officially declared. By eerie coincidence, Kennedy officially announced on November 7, just three days after Iranian students seized the United States embassy in Tehran and took the fifty Americans there hostage. Election year 1980 had begun.

54

→》》 《《←

Hostage

Enemies of the United States are well advised to launch attacks on this country on weekends, when its president has repaired to one of his weekend retreats and his high staff members are dispersed all over the country. Pearl Harbor was attacked on a Sunday morning; the Berlin Wall was put into place on an August weekend when John Kennedy was in Hyannisport; the supposed attack on the U.S.S. *Maddox* which triggered the Gulf of Tonkin resolution occurred, if it occurred at all,[1] on another August weekend only three years later; and the seizure by Iranian "students" of the 50 Americans stationed at the U.S. embassy in Tehran took place on the first Sunday of November 1979, when Jimmy Carter was at Camp David and his chief assistant, Hamilton Jordan, was on the Eastern Shore of Maryland at the estate of a Democratic fund-raiser. Jordan was eager[2] to watch that Sunday evening's much ballyhooed prime-time CBS broadcast of the Roger Mudd interview with Edward Kennedy—the interview in which Mudd, a longtime personal friend of the Kennedy family, flummoxed Kennedy into inarticulateness by asking him the not exactly startling question of why he was running for president.

In retrospect, partisans of both Carter and Kennedy might see these events of the day precisely one year before election day 1980 as fatal to their campaigns. Yet even before that, Kennedy had begun to fall in the polls once it became clear he was actually going to run against Carter, who himself had some of the lowest job approval ratings and weakest showings against potential opponents in primary or general elections that pollsters had ever recorded for an incumbent president. Even by November 4, Kennedy's lead over Carter among Democrats was reduced to 54%–32%, and by early December Carter was ahead 48%–40%.[3] Carter's job rating just before the Iran hostage seizure was approaching the all-time low for American presidents: 29%–58% negative according to Gallup in early October 1979, 32%–55% in early November.[4] The two leading Democrats were already reeling before the hostages were seized and the Mudd interview broadcast.

The serendipitous nature of the major decisions of the Carter administration was illustrated not just by the accidental genesis of the "domestic Camp David" but also by the way in which Carter ended up producing a stout anti-inflationary economic policy. The fateful decision, though it was not at all intended, was made in July 1979 when Carter filled the embarrassing vacancy caused by his firing of Treasury Secretary Michael Blumenthal with Federal Reserve Board Chairman

G. William Miller, a politically-minded corporation executive who had cooperated with the Democrats' expansionist policies. That appointment forced Carter to find a new Fed chairman, which he did in the person of Paul Volcker, a cigar-smoking giant of the high intellect and public-spirited probity of top-level European civil servants, who had served in the Treasury in administrations of both parties. Inflation sparked by the 1979 oil shock was blazing, seemingly out of control: the Consumer Price Index, in January 1979 9.3% above the level of 12 months earlier, was by April up 10.5%; by July up 11.3%; and by October up 12.1%. Interest rates were rising past 20%; and it seemed to many Americans that hyperinflation, of the kind Germany had experienced in 1924 and Argentina was experiencing in the 1970s, actually could happen in the United States. In this panic-stricken environment, Volcker in October adopted a new Fed policy targeting not interest rates but the money supply, which was squeezed in a way almost certain to cause a recession on the theory—almost certainly correct—that this was the only way to check inflation.[5]

II

Carter's response to the hostage crisis was effectively determined within two days. At first his advisors thought it was just another incident like one in February 1979 when the embassy had been threatened and then relieved after negotiations with Iranian government officials. But by November 6 the Ayatollah Khomeini had ousted the country's supposedly moderate premier and had personally endorsed the seizure. By any reasonable standard, this action meant that the government of Iran had seized the American embassy—a violation of the iron rule of diplomatic immunity honored by Soviet Russia, by Nazi Germany, by outlaw regimes of every stripe. Under the rules of international law, the United States was entitled to consider itself the object of an act of war and to take steps—up to and including a declaration of war—to end the intolerable situation of its diplomats being held captive. Carter and all his advisors, however, seemed to treat the situation as if a plucky little bank teller and a gaggle of hapless customers were behing held hostage by crazed protesters who had to be mollified and dealt with gently and would probably be worn down eventually by lack of sleep and food. But of course the Iranians were not going to be worn down in a city where they held all military power and where they had suddenly achieved the dream of protesters everywhere: the attention of American and world television cameras. Walter Cronkite began signing off the *CBS News* every night by recounting how many days the hostages had been held; ABC began running a daily late-evening broadcast on the issue, anchored by Ted Koppel, which later became the interview program *Nightline*. Carter's paramount concern for the personal welfare of the hostages, rather than the principle of diplomatic immunity and the power of the United States, led him to send former Attorney General Ramsey Clark, a sympathizer with Third World critics of the United States, to Tehran as an envoy. Hamilton Jordan feared that "an ugly mood will develop in this country," by which he surely meant a demand for a military response to this military attack. For Carter and his advisors any resort to military force was dismissed as too risky and likely to provoke criticism of the United States in the Third World.

In this crisis as in most others, Americans' initial reaction was to rally around their flag and their president, no matter how poorly defended the former or how ineffectual the latter. Carter's job rating rose to 38%–49% negative within two weeks, to 51%–37% positive in less than a month, and to 61%–30% in early December,[6] just before it was proposed that Christmas presents be sent to the hostages, presumably to shame their Islamic fundamentalist captors into letting them go. Of Carter's concern for the hostages' welfare there can be no doubt; for over a year he would make that the paramount concern of American foreign policy. Yet he and his advisors could not have helped noticing that response to the hostage crisis—any response to the hostage crisis, as long as Americans were rallying around the flag—was the single factor elevating his job ratings and giving him wide leads over Kennedy in Democratic primary polls and over the seemingly bedraggled group of potential Republican candidates in general-election pairings. On economic issues, on other foreign policy issues, most voters thought Carter was not doing a good job. The Iranian hostage crisis looked like the one issue which could keep his candidacy alive.

III

By standard criteria the Republican field was not awesome. The best-known candidate was Ronald Reagan, a former movie actor who would turn sixty-nine in February 1980—the oldest previous president, Dwight Eisenhower, had left office not long after he turned seventy—and who had not held public office since retiring as governor of California in 1974. Two senators, Minority Leader Howard Baker and 1976 vice presidential candidate Robert Dole, were running; but neither was of national stature. Baker was hobbled by his support for the Panama Canal treaties, anathema to so many Republican activists and primary voters; and Dole was running a pathetically disorganized campaign which would net him exactly 597 votes in the 1980 New Hampshire primary. Better known was John Connally, the favorite of Richard Nixon and, with his forceful manner and utter confidence, the darling of many corporate CEOs (chief executive officers: an acronym just coming into wide use). But Connally had never run for office as a Republican before and was mistrusted by Republicans in his native Texas; and he had never developed the knack of appealing to ordinary people, as opposed to big shots looking for an impressive acolyte. The overwhelmingly Democratic House threw forward some possible Republican presidential contenders, two from Illinois. John Anderson, whose increasingly moderate stands on issues had nearly cost him his House leadership position in 1976 and nearly resulted in his defeat in the 1978 primary, had decided to retire from the House in 1980 and, with nothing to lose, was running as a Republican critical of many conservative programs. But he had the overwhelming problem of being a candidate who was becoming more liberal in a party which was becoming more conservative: even if he survived initial contests, once the race came down to one-on-one contests he must surely lose, given the strong conservative views of Republican primary voters. Philip Crane, a conservative of strong convictions and good looks, would have fewer problems on the issues. But he turned out to have a weak intellect and little follow-through. Jack Kemp, the former Buffalo Bills quarterback elected from a suburban Buffalo district in 1970, had become a genuine leader on national policy in 1978 when he persuaded almost every elected Republican to endorse his 30% tax rate cut— 10% a year for each of three years. But Kemp, having gotten Reagan enthusiastic about his plan, wasn't running himself.

The other significant Republican candidate was an odd duck: George Bush, son of a partner in Brown Brothers Harriman investment banking firm and senator from Connecticut, himself a former congressman and failed Senate candidate in Texas, a favorite of Nixon who had been UN ambassador when Communist China was seated in the Security Council over U.S. objections, Republican national chairman when the party reached the nadir of the Watergate years, U.S. envoy in Peking when Henry Kissinger controlled China policy from Washington, and CIA director for less than a year just after the agency had been chastened by the Church committee reports. In each of these jobs he had been dutiful but, even by his own account, scarcely commanding; at the CIA his most important achievements had been authorizing an assessment of the Soviet Union by a group of hard-liners from outside the agency known as Team B and—what he mentions in his memoir—taking up jogging.[7] What Bush had going for him was energy—"Up for the 80s" was his slogan, and he campaigned 329 days in 1979[8]—and a superb campaign organization, headed by his Houston lawyer friend James Baker, who had managed Gerald Ford's 1976 campaign and had won 46% of the vote against Democrat Mark White in the race for attorney general of Texas in 1978.

With his Eastern establishment background, Bush looked to many like a liberal Republican, a lineal descendant of the WASP aristocrats accustomed to shopping in Madison Avenue men's stores and exercising at Madison Avenue men's clubs, a reader of the *New York Herald Tribune* and reliable supporter of liberal Republicans from Wendell Willkie and Thomas Dewey through Dwight Eisenhower to Nelson Rockefeller and, while he was still a Republican, John Lindsay. The same prep schools and Ivy League colleges which had been considered the incubators of the reactionaries in the 1930s were now considered the natural breeding grounds of welfare state enthusiasts, civil rights supporters, and foreign policy doves. And in 1979 and 1980, Bush, a product of Phillips Academy and Yale, certainly did not share either the enthusiasm for tax cuts of Jack Kemp and his allies or the hostility to abortion, sexual permissiveness, and non-traditional mores of the new Religious Right which was becoming activated in Republican politics—a key development, as it turned out, in 1980s politics, and one with almost as many reverberations as the political activation of CIO union organizers and members had in the politics of the 1940s and 1950s.

Iowa's precinct caucuses, the scene of Jimmy Carter's first victory in January

1976, when they were only spottily reported, were now recognized as the first major contest of 1980; and there Bush's solid organization and his liberal appearance appealed to activists of a party still full of well-intentioned liberal Republicans. After Reagan, alone among Republicans, declined to attend the debate sponsored by the *Des Moines Register,* Bush sprinted ahead of him and won an upset victory on caucus night, January 21. John Anderson's third-place finish kept him in the race; Baker, Connally, and Dole ran dismally. Bush suddenly became the favorite in the New Hampshire primary February 26. But Reagan's solid conservatism gave him a base in this state which had resisted income and sales taxes in the 1960s and 1970s when every other state adopted one or the other and now was experiencing the fastest economic and population growth east of the Rockies and north of the Potomac. (William Loeb and his *Manchester Union Leader* forced every candidate for state office to "take the pledge" not to support any broad-based tax.) He began pulling ahead of Bush in mid-February and then outfoxed him in what had been billed as a Reagan–Bush debate sponsored by the *Nashua Telegraph,* with costs paid by Reagan. Reagan privately invited the other Republicans, who paraded in while Bush sat still, as if paralyzed; and when the editor cut off Reagan's audio the former actor responded, in lines echoing Spencer Tracy's in Frank Capra's 1948 movie *State of the Union,* "I paid for that microphone, Mr. Breen." Characteristically, Reagan got the detail of the man's name wrong and the larger message right. On February 26 he won 50% of the vote to 23% for Bush, 13% for Baker, and 10% for Anderson.

Among the Democrats, the New Hampshire primary signaled the defeat of the hapless campaign of Edward Kennedy. He had lost 2–1 in Iowa, though the Democratic caucuses there attracted many unionists and foreign policy doves who might have been thought his base constituency; he lost 47%–37% in New Hampshire (with 10% for Jerry Brown), most of which was part of his home-state Boston media market. Kennedy did win in Massachusetts a week later, but he was then overwhelmed not only in southern states but on March 18 by a 65%–30% margin in Illinois, where most of the Democrats were blacks and ethnics. Doggedly, for no clear motives except perhaps a hatred of Carter (who had found reason to postpone indefinitely the posthumous presentation of a medal voted by Congress for Robert Kennedy) and a desire to serve as a kind of tribune for the poor and helpless (though most of them insisted on voting for Carter), Kennedy persevered. He managed to win some victories only when his backers argued that he would not be nominated anyway and when Carter made an error, as in the March 25 contest in New York, where Secretary of State Cyrus Vance's testimony on Middle Eastern policy had angered Jewish voters concerned about Israel. But at no point was Kennedy ahead in delegates; nor was he ever, in national polls or in the sequence of contests, in a position to defeat Carter for the nomination.

The Republican race was more complicated. Anderson's opposition to the Kemp-Roth tax cut proposal (named for Kemp and his Senate co-sponsor), his pro-choice position on abortion, and his comments on foreign policy—in the Iowa debate he became perhaps the last American politician to publicly regret his support of the

Gulf of Tonkin resolution and Lyndon Johnson's Vietnam war effort—made him seem the liberal some Republicans and many in the press had been missing in recent contests. He came in a close second to Bush in Massachusetts, ran only slightly behind Reagan in Vermont, and won 37% to Reagan's 48% in Illinois. But these near-victories were illusory indicators of strength. The ranks of Republicans in New England contained more liberals than elsewhere, and Illinois was Anderson's home state; he had no support whatever in the South, increasingly an important Republican region, and little in the West; he had negligible support from party activists in non-primary states; and his 22% in Wisconsin, with its progressive Republican tradition, compared with 24% for Bush and 32% for Reagan, made it clear that he had no chance to prevail in Republican contests generally. He was left in early April to decide whether to continue a hopeless primary race or run as a third-party candidate in the general election, hoping to pick up support from his Republican and Kennedy's Democratic constituencies.

IV

The headlines during this campaigning period were dominated more by foreign disasters than electoral politics. Over Christmas 1979, Soviet troops had invaded Afghanistan, where a pro-Soviet government was being bloodily replaced by a Soviet puppet. Jimmy Carter, who in the first months of his administration had decried "inordinate fear of Communism" and in June 1979 had embraced and kissed Leonid Brezhnev at a summit meeting, now said "the action of the Soviets made a more dramatic change in my opinion of what the Soviets' ultimate goals are than anything they've done in the previous time I've been in office." Carter made no military response, but he did call for the American athletes not to participate in the 1980 Summer Olympics in Moscow and embargoed U.S. grain shipments to the Soviet Union. Nor did Carter make any military response to Iran's continued hostage holding. Instead he tried to negotiate, through Ramsey Clark (who was not allowed into Iran at all) and through various foreign intermediaries, some of whom Hamilton Jordan began meeting with secretly and in disguise. Great efforts were made to keep the shah out of the United States, to avoid provoking the Iranians—as if they were not provoked already. Grave retribution was promised if the Iranians should harm the hostages—as if they were not already harmed by being held captive. No serious consideration was given to what Ronald Reagan said he would have done after one or two weeks: "there comes a time when a government has got to be willing to set a date for their release and to let them know privately what the option will be if they are not released as of that date."[9] Yet a combination of a deadline and a threat is what eventually worked: in December 1980, President-elect Reagan signaled the Iranians that he might take military action by calling them "barbarians" and "criminals," at which point negotiations became more intense; and the hostages were released within hours of Reagan's inauguration.

But throughout 1980 there were flurries of hope, in the Carter White House and out, that a deal was about to be made and the hostages about to be released. Hopes were never higher than on the morning of April 1, the day of the Wisconsin primary, when Carter went on television live at 7:20 to announce a "positive step," that the Iranian government was taking custody of the hostages from their captors— as if the Iranian government had not been the essential force keeping them in captivity at least since the second day after the embassy was seized. In the short run this announcement helped Carter follow a 59%–41% loss in New York with a 56%–30% win in Wisconsin. But the fact that it was followed by no significant progress had the opposite long-run effect: it persuaded not only his opponents but many ordinary voters to discount his claims that the crisis was about to be solved, especially those made just before the election, and gave credibility to Republicans' apprehensions that Carter would produce an "October surprise" to secure his reelection. Thus the sudden flurry of hostage negotiations the weekend before the election availed Carter nothing politically.

Having renounced force for almost six months, Carter suddenly resorted to military action on April 24—and failed. The military rescue attempt by a commando force sculpted out of disparate units (so that every military service would have its part), provided with insufficient material, and operating under micromanagement from various military headquarters and the White House predictably did not work. Secretary of State Cyrus Vance, who had opposed any use of force, resigned. Carter, having botched the military solution, refused to try again, choosing to credit reports (which were later refuted) that the hostages were dispersed around Iran. In the short run the incident seemed to make little difference politically. Carter led Reagan 49%–43% in early April and 47%–43% just after the rescue attempt.[10] But of course neither of these was a convincing lead for an incumbent president (who had been ahead 60%–31% two months before) against a sixty-nine-year-old challenger with no experience in national office and a reputation as a political extremist.

V

By April 1980 the nominees of the two major parties were assured and the third-party candidacy of Anderson was launched; yet the races for both parties continued. Bush soldiered on, winning an occasional primary, as in Michigan, until James Baker, convinced that otherwise Bush would forfeit his chance for the vice presidency, persuaded him in June to withdraw. Kennedy, with no chance at all of displacing the loyal Walter Mondale, soldiered on as well. He championed the cause of government intervention in the economy, calling for much more massive government jobs programs, a national health insurance system, a set of wage and price controls, and succeeded only in proving conclusively that these policies, even as they were churned out by activists-turned-lobbyists, could no longer command the allegiance of many voters. For five months, from March to August, he persevered in a hopeless candidacy, to reach the one forum in all of American politics which was most favorable to his style and his message: the featured speech, crafted by brilliant speechwriters and delivered with a force and verve all his own, before an enthusiastic hall of political partisans cheering on his every sentence. Kennedy had delivered such a speech in July 1972, introducing George McGovern; his five months of futile campaigning earned him the right to deliver another, at Manhattan's Madison Square Garden in August 1980.

As for the live candidates, none of them was running especially strong. Carter's job rating sagged terribly during the spring, declining to 32%–56% negative by June and never recovering. As the hostage crisis continued and he failed to obtain a satisfactory solution, attention focused on other issues, to disastrous effect: in March and April the Consumer Price Index was up 15% over the previous year's levels, while the economy, thanks to Paul Volcker's fiscal policies, was rapidly moving into recession by the second quarter of 1980. By late June, Carter trailed the elderly, untested Reagan in the polls, and the incumbent president never regained a significant lead (except perhaps momentarily). The Republican convention, which featured a flurry of speculation about a Reagan–Ford "co-presidency" before Reagan came onto the podium and announced his selection of Bush as his running mate, gave Reagan a mild boost in the polls. The Democratic convention, dominated by Kennedy's electrifying speech and by Carter's futile pursuit of Kennedy around the podium in quest of the traditional hands-clasped-high photograph, gave Carter no boost at all.

John Anderson, having no convention and, as increasingly became clear, no chance of winning, saw his share of the vote evaporate from the 24% Gallup recorded in a three-way poll June 13–16 to 9% in early October and the 7% he ultimately won in November. The liberal Republican constituency to which he appealed had long since atrophied, while those Democrats unhappy that Carter was not expanding government rapidly enough could find little warrant in Anderson's current rhetoric or past actions that he would. Anderson's rhetoric seemed well-positioned to appeal to a growing segment of the electorate which might be termed libertarian—it was cautious about government intervention in the economy, opposed to military assertiveness abroad, supportive of liberation-minded life styles. But Anderson's past record was inconvenient: it turned out that he had always supported the Vietnam war and in his early years in Congress had introduced a bill to have the United States declared a Christian nation. The question of whether he was to be included in presidential debates vexed the sponsoring League of Women Voters, who said at one point that their decision would be based on the polls. He did debate Reagan in September, when Carter declined to join them, but was not invited to the final debate, which took place October 28.

When the candidates were preparing for that final, late appearance, it still seemed possible Carter might win. Damaging stories which had stayed on evening newscasts for days—his brother Billy's dealings with the government of Libya, a special prosecutor's investigation into utterly baseless charges that Hamilton Jordan used cocaine—were resolved or had at least disappeared. Doubts about Reagan's age and ability remained. But underlying Carter's lead in the pollsters' pairing questions was fundamental dissatisfaction with his policies. This same dissatisfaction was apparent in the standing of several highly visible liberal Democratic senators who had won, often easily, in 1974 and earlier but were now trailing or in trouble in the polls: Birch Bayh of Indiana, Frank Church of Idaho, John Culver of Iowa, Warren Magnuson of Washington, Gaylord Nelson of Wisconsin. The buffetings the United States and its allies had absorbed abroad undermined the case for the Democrats' conciliatory foreign policy, aimed at avoiding superpower confrontations and Vietnam-like embroilments. The battering the American economy was taking after the 1979 oil shock undermined the case, strong since 1933, for the Democrats' claim to be the party which knew best how to produce prosperity and economic growth. Unmentioned by any politician was the argument that both these trends sprang from, or were gravely exacerbated by, the same cause, the American refusal to maintain a military presence in the Persian Gulf after the British withdrawal in 1971, a refusal prompted by American leaders' determination not to risk another Vietnam.

From the Democratic convention until the October 28 debate both Carter and Reagan fluctuated between 39% and 45% in Gallup polls, a relatively narrow range which showed dismayingly low support for the incumbent and a degree of strength for the challenger about equal to that enjoyed by Richard Nixon in the 1968 campaign. But Nixon was running as a highly experienced candidate against a non-incumbent, while Reagan was running as a little-experienced challenger of an incumbent. Voters decided long before the conventions that they would like to get rid of the incumbent; the question they pondered during the campaign is whether the challenger would disqualify himself. They waited to give their answer until the last week; and as it happened, their decision-making process focused on the debate Carter had finally agreed to. Preparation for and reaction to the debate made up most of the week's political news; if there had been no debate, voters would have made up their minds on some other basis.

In the debate Reagan demonstrated he was not unqualified. He was, indeed, more at ease, more congenial, more confident than the incumbent: "There you go again!" he responded quickly to one Carter charge. Carter, coached by Patrick Caddell, clumsily inserted appeals to particular constituency groups which would, the Democrats hoped, together produce a plurality, and made the argument— much favored by those who perceived an "era of limits"—that the United States faced insoluble economic and foreign problems and should just get used to less than totally satisfactory solutions. It was an appeal reminiscent of Herbert Hoover's lame argument that no one could have done very well in the hard times of the 1930s.

Reagan, in contrast, spoke in the language of Franklin Roosevelt. Even after his turn against the graduated income tax and toward conservatism in the 1950s, even after he changed his party registration to Republican after the 1960 election, Reagan remained an ardent admirer of the man for whom he had enthusiastically cast his first four votes for president. William Leuchtenberg, in chronicling Roosevelt's continuing influence on American politics, notes that when "a historian interviewed Roosevelt's successors as the FDR centenary approached, he found Ford listless, Carter guarded, but Reagan so chockful of enthusiasm that in the midst of a busy White House schedule he went on talking about FDR beyond the allotted time and 'with the most obvious fondness.' Reagan, David McCullough concluded, 'sees Roosevelt as his "kind of guy,"—confident, cheerful, theatrical, larger than life.' "[11]

Thus Reagan modeled his own leadership style on the leader who for him always remained the ideal of an American president—and whom he startled his audience and the press by citing in his July 1980 acceptance speech. Reagan even spoke in Roosevelt's language. "Though he left the party of Roosevelt, he refused to abandon the words and phrases which provided a shared language and a common bond with his fellow citizens," writes his definitive biographer, Lou Cannon. Cannon points out that the standard Reagan speech wound up with the phrase "rendezvous with destiny," lifted from Roosevelt's 1936 acceptance speech, and that all his "speeches were peppered with other borrowings from Roosevelt, whose words and memories stoked hidden fires of approval and patriotism among American working men and women."[12] And Reagan's masterstroke at the end of the October 28 presidential debate was an echo of Roosevelt once again. Reagan's critics have always described him as a man programmed by others, but none of those prepping him for the 1980 debate had any recollection of how Roosevelt had used his June 1934 fireside chat to frame the issue for that year's elections. Reagan did. "It might be well," said Reagan in his closing statement, almost precisely echoing Roosevelt's appeal, "if you would ask yourself: Are you better off than you were four years ago? Is it easier for you to go and buy things in the stores than it was four years ago? Is there more or less unemployment in the country than there was four years ago? Is America as respected throughout the world as it was? Do you feel that our security is as safe, that we're as strong as we were four years ago?" The homey metaphors, the combination of appeal to self-interest and to the interests of the nation, the stressing of the concrete and absence of any abstract argumentation—all these were lessons Reagan learned from Roosevelt.

Like Roosevelt, Reagan connected with the voters. His peroration framed the issue cleanly: was the Carter administration a success? His performance resolved doubts about his competence. His standing in the polls surged in the days after the debate. Gallup had him at 39% in one survey October 24–27 and at 42% in another October 25–27, then after the debate at 44% October 29–30 and 47% October 30–November 1. A last-minute flurry of negotiations on Iran, looking very much like the "October surprise" the Republicans had been predicting, seems to have had little effect, or at least no positive effect for Carter: the voters who had been rallying to his support when the crisis began, hoping for good results, were now punishing him because he had failed to produce those results.[13] Carter had instinctively used the hostage crisis as a campaign issue. But in the end voters responded not to how he campaigned but to how he governed.

VI

For most political analysts the results seemed unbelievable. On election day, November 4, just one week after the debate, Ronald Reagan got 51% of the vote to 41% for Jimmy Carter and 7% for John Anderson. This was the biggest repudiation of an American president since Herbert Hoover lost in 1932, and perhaps the most stunning and surprising too. Even more surprising, the Republicans gained 13 Senate seats, winning almost every closely contested seat (in some cases with candidates who ran ahead of Reagan), and won control of the Senate for the first time since 1952 and only the third time since Hoover's defeat. In House elections the Republicans did not do quite so well, but they still gained 33 seats as compared with their 1978 performance; and in House elections outside the South they won more votes than the Democrats for the first time since 1968. The Democrats, who four years before had held the Senate by a 62–38 margin, were now behind 53–47, while their margin in the House was reduced from the overwhelming 292–143 which had first elected Tip O'Neill speaker in January 1977 to a narrower 243–192 which seemed likely to deprive O'Neill of working control of the chamber.

In the shocked precincts of Washington there was talk at the time that Reagan did not really have a mandate from his victory, that voters had just rejected Carter for ineptness, that the ideas which had guided the Carter administration had not been repudiated, that national and international problems were so intractable that no one could solve them and that this next president like those before him would be rejected in turn by an electorate unsophisticated enough to expect more.[14] Certainly Carter, like Hoover before him, had been removed from office because voters sensed that he could not keep things under control. But in both cases voters undoubtedly concluded that the reasons for losing control involved not just the president himself, but also his policies. Certainly 1980 was not just a referendum on Carter: Republican candidates for Senate and House ran essentially even with Reagan nationwide. The Republicans won a larger percentage of votes in House races and just as many House seats in 1980 off Reagan's 51% of the vote as they had in 1972 off Richard Nixon's 61%. They gained 13 Senate seats off Reagan's percentage but had lost 2 Senate seats off Nixon's. Improved performance by Republican campaign committees and a commitment to party victory by the ticket leader help to explain the difference. But it is also apparent that ideas were at work. The 1980 result was not an accident. It showed that most American voters wanted limits on the growth of government at home, a more assertive foreign policy abroad, and some greater honoring of traditional moral values in their basic institutions.

─≫≫ ≪≪─

PART
FIVE

American Politics
1981–1988
RESILIENCE

55

→⟩⟩ ⟨⟨←

From Alienation to Resilience

To drivers coming into Detroit on the Willow Run Expressway, the most prominent object on the table-flat landscape was a giant tire, with the Goodyear logo above and a meter showing the number of automobiles produced that year. In the years after the oil shock of 1979, the meter told a melancholy story—and a misleading one. For it measured only production by American automakers in the United States and so ignored—as American automakers were wont to do—foreign producers and import sales. On New Year's Eve 1978,[1] as the Ayatollah Khomeini was preparing to leave his dreary Paris exile for Tehran, the meter on the Willow Run Expressway showed 9.2 million American cars produced—the highest level in history.[2] But that was not quite as good news as it seemed to the Detroiters driving by. Well over 90% of them were driving American cars; but in the nation as a whole in 1978, import sales had risen to 2 million, 18% of the total. Auto industry analysts had the habit of focusing on the share of U.S. producer sales which was held by each of the Big Three automakers. But even as the industry was having its biggest year, the market share of all three major producers was shrinking or was threatened by the European and especially the Japanese producers. The trend was accelerated when, because of rapidly rising oil prices, total car sales in the United States fell from 11.3 million in 1978 to 10.7 million in 1979, 9.0 million in 1980, 8.5 million in 1981, and 8.0 million in 1982. The good news for U.S. automakers was that "voluntary restraint" agreements with the Japanese held imports to the 2.2–2.4 million level from 1979 to 1984. The bad news was that sales of cars made in the United States by American companies fell from 9.3 million in 1978 to 8.3 million in 1979, 6.6 million in 1980, 6.2 million in 1981, and 5.8 million in 1982.

The result was massive unemployment, especially in Michigan, where the auto industry was still centered, and nearby Ohio and Indiana; auto industry employment fell by 250,000 from 1979 to 1982. The Big Three auto companies, though still among America's largest industrial corporations, were tottering on the brink of collapse—something almost no expert had thought possible a few years before. By September 1979, Chrysler was insolvent and was kept from bankruptcy only

599

through a government-guaranteed loan, lobbied through Congress by Michigan's Senator Donald Riegle and Congressman (and later Governor) James Blanchard, Chrysler's Lee Iacocca and the UAW's Douglas Fraser.[3] Ford's North American operations lost $7 billion from 1979 to 1982; the company was kept going only by its European profits.[4] In 1980 even General Motors lost money. The American automakers had been hailed not long before as master managers who could, with sophisticated market research and brilliant advertising, sell any level of production they wished to sustain at any price they wanted to command: John Kenneth Galbraith wrote that a big corporation was "large enough to control its markets."[5] But their market research, churning out frequent surveys showing fractional changes in this month or that, failed to detect the slow but steady changes in demand which were readily perceived by Japanese producers; and their corporate strategists, who had risen to their eminence in years when the American domestic market had overshadowed all others, failed to appreciate the potential of foreign competitors or to foresee that the biggest growth in demand might come in fast-growing economies abroad. Americans, it turned out, did not need a new American-made car every two years. The two-car family, in a country where the size of households was shrinking, was not about to become the three-car family. And consumers were not willing to pay a premium for cars they did not particularly want in order to pay auto workers wages and fringe benefits 60% above the manufacturing average. Plainly the Big Three no longer had control of their markets.

For many years the Big Three automakers and the United Auto Workers had been the symbols of the success of big organizations in American economic life. The industry they produced stood as a symbol of the American can-do spirit; and its orderly progression of brands, from the low-priced Chevrolet and Ford and Plymouth to the high-priced Cadillac and Lincoln and Chrysler,[6] provided a metaphor for a culturally uniform society in which people seemed differentiated mainly by economic status, the sort of society which most Americans liked to think they lived in through the three decades after 1935. But in the culturally diverse America of the late 1970s and early 1980s, the idea of brandishing your economic status by your choice of car was increasingly unappealing;[7] and it was Japanese rather than American executives who were the first to understand consumers' desire for diverse vehicles—affordable sports cars, small city cars, and the like—and their desire for cars that were well built and easy to maintain.

Thus the collapse and permanent shrinking of what for 60 years had been America's most vibrant big industry did not occur just because its leaders failed to anticipate the second oil shock; it collapsed and shrank because they—UAW leaders as well as Big Three executives—failed to understand their country and how it was changing. In this failure they were not alone. After long years of economic growth and success, after decades in which the big units of American society—big corporations, big unions, big government—had been growing or at least remaining big, these units tended to have as their first goal their own self-perpetuation, seeking help through the political process to fend off change which would force them out of their comfortable ways.[8] Their very success, sustained too long, tended to breed failure.

The leaders of these big units failed to understand at least two important things. One was that consumer wants were changing as America was becoming a culturally more diverse country. The other was that the United States was increasingly becoming part of the world economy, benefiting from the strengths of its trading partners but also subject to their competition and to the discipline exerted by international markets and currency rates which, in an electronic age, were increasingly beyond control by governments. Neither of these changes was much appreciated by businessmen, politicians, or journalists in the 1970s. But their consequences were becoming apparent to ordinary citizens. The standard paradigms which members of the American elite used to understand and explain events—analyses of the leaders of big American units, a focus on domestic markets and domestic elections—clouded rather than clarified their understanding. And the "malaise" which many Americans felt at the beginning of the 1980s reflected a general failure to understand how the world around them was changing, and why—and how the things which were going wrong could be made right again.

II

As Americans prepared to watch a sixty-nine-year-old movie actor replace a fifty-six-year-old peanut farmer as their president, the sense was widespread that their system—the economy, the government, even the cultural norms of personal lives—were not working satisfactorily. Inflation at home and frustration abroad had almost all Americans telling pollsters that the nation was pretty seriously off on the wrong track and had many saying that things had never before been so dreadful. Much of this rhetoric was obviously overblown: the United States in the early 1980s was not Central Europe in the late 1930s. This lamentation was not a measured assessment of objective conditions but an emotional response to unanticipated change. Americans who had come to take economic growth for granted, and to criticize its ill effects, now feared that growth had come to an end, replaced by unpredictable inflation. Americans who had come to take their country's military might for granted, and to try to restrain it from being exerted, now saw their country stymied and threatened by Communists or Third World revolutionaries, from Central Europe to Central America, from Afghanistan to Angola to Iran. Americans who had ordered their lives according to what had seemed to be appropriate rules now found the results were not what they expected. And Americans who had grown up in a country whose economy was organized by decisions of big units had a hard time understanding the new country that was coming into being. The new trends are apparent in where Americans chose to live. In the 25 years beginning around 1940, most job growth in America had come in the big units of the economy—in the major corporations (especially the unionized corporations) and the big government which had come into existence to fight and win World War II and, against most expectations, had continued their surging growth afterwards. But from the middle 1960s to 1981, and for the rest of the decade as well, the big generators of economic growth were not big units but small units, not big corporations and government but small businesses, as invisible individually and even collectively to Washington policymakers and analysts as the big units remained visible. During this later period population growth tended to occur in states where such small-unit growth was particularly vigorous as well as in states whose opportunities for leisure activities made them attractive to those like retirees and the unattached young free to choose where they wanted to live. Big-unit growth had occurred without regard to local tax levels; in fact, big-unit decision-makers tended to prefer environments where high taxes produced high levels of public amenities and well-educated work forces (and big government at the state and local level of course depended on high taxes). Small-unit growth turned out to be responsive to tax rates; small-unit decision-makers sought out low-tax havens like New Hampshire and Arizona and avoided high-tax Massachusetts and New York so assiduously that population growth there all but stopped in the 1970s. The table on pages 604–605 shows the changes in population between 1940 and 1987 for each state and region.

The big-unit growth of 1940–65 was concentrated, even after the war years, in the states with major defense industries and installations in World War II. The migration of southern blacks to northern industrial cities, which began quite suddenly around 1940 because of New Deal changes in southern farm economies and wartime demand for factory labor, continued until around the time the Civil Rights Act of 1964 was passed and riots started breaking out in northern ghettoes. During this period the West Coast's population more than doubled, increasing by 13 million; there was significant growth in Michigan and, outside the central cities, in the "Megalopolis" corridor from the Fairfield County, Connecticut, suburbs of New York to the Fairfax County, Virginia, suburbs of Washington. In contrast, after 1965 growth was concentrated in places where big units did not dominate—in the Pacific Rim (the 1980s name for the West Coast); the Oil Patch (the 1980s name for the big oil-producing states of Texas, Louisiana, and Oklahoma); and the Atlantic Coast South, where small-unit decision-makers were willing to accept weak public infrastructure in return for low taxes and wage levels and in vacationlands—Florida, southern California, Arizona and Colorado, the northern reaches of New England and Michigan.

For despite the two oil shocks of the 1970s and the recessions which followed, despite the long-run trend toward an ever-higher statistical level of unemployment, immigrants, who had shunned the United States in the stagnant 1930s, came in the 1970s in great (and, since so many came illegally, uncounted) numbers—only to be cited as another problem to be solved. Numerically immigrants accounted for only a minority of the growth after 1965. But it is significant that the mostly Latin and Asian immigrants of 1964–81, like the mostly Eastern and Southern European immigrants of 1890–1924, headed for California and Texas and growing metropolitan areas elsewhere (and not just because they are close: Los Angeles is more than 1,000 miles from where almost all Mexicans but those in the border towns live). These were the places which were generating the most rapid economic growth—and places where the immigrants helped to generate some of that growth themselves.

The result was that even as birthrates reached record lows, the labor force increased in the 1970s at a greater rate than in any other decade since 1900–10; and except for the years of recession the American economy generated an average of almost 3 million jobs a year from the early 1970s on. For the periods 1971–73, 1975–79, and 1983–88, there was an annual average of 2.8 million new jobs— that is, net increase in employed members of the work force. In contrast, in the non-recessionary years 1961–69, the economy averaged 1.5 million new jobs a year and never generated more than 2 million.[9] Real wages reached a peak in 1973 which they would not reach again until the late 1980s. But with the proliferation of fringe benefits and the effect of income tax "bracket creep," many workers or their unions were choosing to take gains in the form of health and retirement benefits, which worked as hedges against inflation; so wage levels tended to understate real incomes. The task the American economy had been given by demographics and changing cultural attitudes was to find jobs for the millions of Baby Boomers, women, and (many fewer in numbers) immigrants who were swelling the labor force at record rates. What is surprising is not that the economy failed to produce jobs for some of them but that it succeeded in producing jobs for so many. To be sure, many of these in the 1970s were entry-level jobs paying low wages; and the efforts of these new workers were resulting in relatively small increases in output, thus almost halting the increase in statistical productivity after 1973. But it is not clear that the American economy could have produced the larger productivity gains seen in Western Europe, where the labor force in these years was not increasing at all; the choice in the United States was between lower productivity and much higher unemployment.

Much of this job growth was invisible, because the big units which Americans had been accustomed to regarding as the bulk of the economy were growing slowly if at all,[10] and public policies which had been devised to regulate the growth of a big-unit economy were not working well in the small-unit economy which had grown up in its place. Keynesian economic management did not work so well in an economy in which large numbers of jobs were being generated and at the same time unemployment rates were being boosted above historic levels by the existence of relatively generous jobless benefits; its assumption that unemployment is the central problem for macroeconomic policy makers resulted again and again in overstimulation of the economy followed by stepped-up inflation. Nor in a small-unit economy could wages be expected to follow the patterns of the auto and steel union–management bargains; these industries, using accumulated political clout and relying on what they had been told was their power to manage and even create demand for their products, raised their wages far above what most other businesses could or would offer—and far above, it turned out, what was sustainable in a world market where they had competition from abroad. Wage and price controls performed poorly in an economy in which small units could evade them by increasing

STATES, POPULATION 1940–1987 (estimated)

State	Population (000s)			Change 1940–87	1940–87	Percentage Change 1965–87	1940–65
	1987	1965	1940				
UNITED STATES	243,400	193,426	132,165	111,235	84	26	46
EAST	56,078	52,354	38,727	17,351	45	7	35
Maine	1,187	997	847	340	40	19	18
New Hampshire	1,057	676	492	565	115	56	37
Vermont	548	404	359	189	53	36	13
Massachusetts	5,855	5,502	4,317	1,538	36	6	27
Rhode Island	986	893	713	273	38	10	25
Connecticut	3,211	2,857	1,709	1,502	88	12	67
New York	17,825	17,734	13,479	4,346	32	1	32
New Jersey	7,672	6,767	4,160	3,512	84	13	63
Pennsylvania	11,936	11,620	9,900	2,036	21	3	17
Delaware	644	507	267	377	141	27	90
Maryland	4,535	3,600	1,821	2,714	149	26	98
Dist. of Columbia	622	797	663	–41	–6	–22	20
MIDWEST	59,538	54,224	40,144	19,394	48	10	35
Ohio	10,784	10,201	6,908	3,876	56	6	48
Indiana	5,531	4,922	3,428	2,103	61	12	44
Illinois	11,582	10,693	7,897	3,685	47	8	35
Michigan	9,200	8,357	5,256	3,944	75	10	59
Wisconsin	4,807	4,232	3,138	1,669	53	14	35
Minnesota	4,246	3,592	2,792	1,454	52	18	29
Iowa	2,834	2,742	2,538	296	12	3	8
Missouri	5,103	4,467	3,785	1,318	35	14	18
Kansas	2,476	2,206	1,801	675	37	12	22
Nebraska	1,594	1,471	1,316	278	21	8	12

South Dakota	709	692	643	66	10	2	8
North Dakota	672	649	642	30	5	4	1
WEST	49,699	32,204	14,378	35,321	246	54	124
Montana	809	706	559	250	45	15	26
Idaho	998	686	525	473	90	45	31
Wyoming	490	332	251	239	95	48	32
Colorado	3,296	1,985	1,123	2,173	193	66	77
New Mexico	1,500	1,012	532	968	182	48	90
Arizona	3,386	1,584	499	2,887	579	114	217
Utah	1,680	991	550	1,130	205	70	80
Nevada	1,007	444	110	897	815	127	300
California	27,663	18,585	6,907	20,756	301	49	169
Oregon	2,724	1,937	1,090	1,634	150	41	78
Washington	4,538	2,967	1,736	2,802	161	53	71
Alaska	525	271	73	452	619	94	271
Hawaii	1,083	704	423	660	156	54	66
SOUTH	78,084	54,680	38,916	39,168	101	43	41
West Virginia	1,897	1,786	1,902	−5	−0	6	−6
Virginia	5,904	4,411	2,678	3,226	120	34	65
North Carolina	6,413	4,863	3,572	2,841	80	32	33
South Carolina	3,425	2,494	1,900	1,525	80	37	31
Georgia	6,222	4,332	3,124	3,098	99	44	39
Florida	12,023	5,954	1,897	10,126	534	102	214
Alabama	4,083	3,448	2,833	1,250	44	18	22
Mississippi	2,625	2,246	2,184	441	20	17	3
Tennessee	4,855	3,798	2,916	1,939	66	28	30
Kentucky	3,727	3,140	2,846	881	31	19	10
Arkansas	2,388	1,894	1,949	439	23	27	−3
Louisiana	4,461	3,496	2,364	2,097	89	28	48
Texas	16,789	10,378	6,415	10,374	162	62	62
Oklahoma	3,272	2,440	2,336	936	40	34	4

fringe benefits rather than nominal wages or by altering their products or services rather than changing their nominal prices. Policies which had worked admirably to stimulate growth and raise incomes in the big-unit economy of 1940–64 were plainly not working in the small-unit economy of 1964 and after. The method of managing by careful attention to quantitative measurements, well adapted to mobilizing national resources in World War II and stamping out large quantities of standardized consumer goods after the war, turned out to be poorly adapted to anticipating the changing and various tastes of a segmented, fragmented market or to winning a war in which intangibles of morale and determination proved to be more important than quantitative measures of bombing loads or body counts.[11]

For the failure of big-unit policies to work well in a small-unit economy was a matter not just of mechanics but of mentalities. The Americans who were mobilized for war in the early 1940s remained disposed for mobilization long afterwards. The big units of society—big corporations and unions, the big-city school systems which enrolled a huge proportion of the nation's children and the military services which unexpectedly remained big after the war—performed well, eliciting good work from hundreds of thousands of seemingly ordinary individuals. The notion of being united in a common purpose, of striving together rather than just seeking one's own advantage, of working loyally for an organization in the confidence that this loyalty would be rewarded—these attitudes of solidarity and conformity came naturally to Americans who had, they believed, seen rampant individualism result in the collapse of their economy and common effort result in total victory for their country. When some were called on to give their lives, others were willing to defer their ambitions in order to work for a big corporation or give up most of their income in order to pay near-confiscatory income taxes. Of course there was cynicism under the veneer of cooperation, and cheating, but taken as a whole the America which won the war and grew so robustly afterwards was a culturally unified, cooperation-minded society.

But by the middle 1960s the mentality of mobilization had largely vanished. The Vietnam war would be fought not by an entire age cohort, but by those not able or willing to take advantage of the easy outs available to the affluent and studious. Nominally high income tax rates were lowered by the Kennedy–Johnson tax cuts and were increasingly avoided by those in a position to take advantage of proliferating tax shelters; anyone who didn't, the feeling came to be, was a chump. The ideal of cultural uniformity, the mentality which elevated the average and ordinary and ridiculed the unusual and eccentric, was quickly yielding to an explosion of cultural variety. Americans no longer felt united by common purposes. They were part of an increasingly fragmented country, in which one citizen had no significant claims on another.

So when a Gerald Ford pinned a "Whip Inflation Now" button on his lapel or a Jimmy Carter called his energy policies "the moral equivalent of war," Americans tended to snicker: the idea of common action was absurd. In an economy where inflation was endemic and tax avoidance a way of life, and where the profusion of small units gave more and more people the opportunity to evade big-unit commands and controls, the idea of common effort came to seem absurd—and yet the sense remained that only by some form of common effort could the problems of inflation at home and ineffectiveness abroad be solved. Hence the paradox of widespread despair in a country which was, by any historical standard, peaceful, prosperous, and tolerant. Americans from 1964 to 1981 had been twisted and contorted by events which seemed unpredictable and out of control. Would they be resilient enough to withstand those shocks without deformation, to get back into shape to confront the public woes besetting them?

III

"This time the lady with all the answers has no answers at all." With those words Ann Landers, the country's most popular advice columnist, announced to her readers that her husband was seeking a divorce—and promised to say nothing more about it after that day's column. Since 1955, Landers had been the most sensitive gauge of Americans' moral attitudes and critic of their personal behavior; she had managed to uphold traditional moral standards and yet adapt gracefully as those standards changed. Now in her own personal life she was exhibiting the same inability to live up to what had been expected standards which she read about from so many of her readers.

Her predicament was not atypical as Americans passed through the hinge period around 1981. If inflation produced uncertainty in Americans' economic lives, changing patterns of living produced uncertainty in their personal lives—with effects which proved to have an even greater impact on electoral politics. "In a matter of a few years," wrote pollster Daniel Yankelovich in 1981, "we have moved from an uptight culture set in a dynamic economy to a dynamic culture set in an uptight economy."[12] If the impulse for common effort and big-unit allegiance of World War II and the years afterwards had waned by the middle 1960s, so had the impulse toward what had been seen in those years as an ordinary family life, with a breadwinner husband and several children. Actually, such lives were anything but universal before 1945. In the years before World War II, and especially the depression decade of the 1930s, many Americans could not afford to have several—or any—children or even to get married. It was the growing economy of the 1947–64 period which allowed more people to get married, and at earlier ages: finally almost all Americans were free to get married and start families.

Then, as the years went by, increasing numbers of Americans felt free not to have children and even to remain or become unmarried, as economic growth made those options attractive or feasible and changing or diverging moral attitudes made them widely acceptable. The fertility rate dropped sharply twice, from 118 in 1960 to a plateau of 86–88 in 1967–70 and then to 69 in 1973, after which the rate remained in the 65–68 range through the late 1980s.[13] The first drop occurred after the birth control pill was introduced in 1960 and Catholic attitudes toward birth control were liberalized in the wake of the Vatican II conference (before, most had obeyed the church's teaching against artificial methods of contraception;

afterwards, increasing numbers ignored it). The second drop occurred after state legislatures started liberalizing abortion laws and continued until the Supreme Court in January 1973 essentially struck down all restrictions on abortion during the first three months of pregnancy.[14] The divorce rate, after some upswings after 1945 as wartime marriages were dissolved, remained between 9 and 11 per 1,000 married couples from 1948 until 1967. Then it rose sharply to 22 in 1978 and stayed at a plateau of 21–23 through the middle 1980s.[15] The proportion of married women working outside the home increased by about 50% in these same years, from 36% in 1966 to 48% in 1978; the number continued rising, somewhat more slowly, to the 55% range in the middle 1980s.[16]

These changes coincided with, but were not necessarily caused by, the emergence of the women's liberation movement from the publication of Betty Friedan's *The Feminine Mystique* in 1963 and the launching of *Ms.* magazine in 1972. The movement began by concentrating on the plight of women like Friedan, educated and affluent but raising more children in a house with fewer servants than someone familiar with affluent life styles of the 1920s or 1930s would expect. The changes in behavior, in contrast, were evident in a much broader segment of the population. As contraception became more common and effective, births by teenage mothers and early marriages decreased rapidly even though premarital sex became more common. The unspoken compact of the postwar nuclear family seems to have been broken by both sides at about the same time, in the late 1960s and early 1970s: the compact that men would stay married and support their wives and children, and that women would bear several children and work full-time at homemaking. As the stigma against and restrictions on divorce dissolved,[17] husbands began to wander; as the fertility rate declined, wives found jobs, hedging their bets against the possibility that their husbands would no longer provide a comfortable living for them. In the process Americans said they were seeking "self-fulfillment." But many found their new unconnectedness a problem rather than a solution.

The changes in Americans' sexual and family lives had economic and political consequences. The economic consequences, unrecognized in the flurry of self-congratulatory feminist rhetoric, were often terrible for women, especially those women who were divorced and left with children.[18] For many Americans the key to economic success was not the size but the number of paychecks coming into each household; and a major component of the increasing inequality of household incomes beginning around 1981, an increase noted with disapproval by political liberals, was the prosperity of two-income families and the straitened circumstances of households headed by a single woman. If, Americans had stayed married in the years after 1968 at the same rate as they had in 1948–67, the income disparity would have been less: the cultural liberal's goal of greater choice in marital status undercut the economic liberal's goal of lessening inequality of incomes.

The political result of the shifting relationship between the sexes was the so-called gender gap which became apparent in the 1980 election and remained apparent through the 1980s. Feminists correctly noted that women were significantly less likely to vote for Ronald Reagan and for Republicans identified with him than were men. In their hurry to argue that Reagan was on the wrong side of the gender gap and would suffer severe political consequences, however, they looked at the gap from the wrong perspective themselves: they failed to foresee that he and his party would win most of the major elections of the 1980s because, one might say, of their especially strong support from men. Closer examination of polls, in fact, shows that the difference in many elections was not so much between men and women as it was between married women, who voted much like men, and unmarried women. There surely was a perceptible and probably growing vote made up of well-educated but not necessarily high-income women, a large percentage of them single or divorced, many in social service or government jobs, which was strongly anti-Reagan and anti-Republican on both feminist and economic issues. And there was a much more muted tendency on the part of women generally to be skeptical about Reagan's changes.

But this was not the first gender gap in American political history. In previous close presidential elections, women had tended to vote for the candidate of the incumbent party who seemed less willing to take risks which might lead to war: pluralities of women had backed Richard Nixon in 1960, Hubert Humphrey in 1968, and Gerald Ford in 1976. Women had been much less likely than men to vote for the raucous and bellicose George Wallace. The common thread here seems to be not that women are more leftist than men, but that they tend to be more averse to risk. In France and Italy, after all, there have been large gender gaps since women got the vote after World War II, with the women on the right, favoring the party of church and tradition, and the men on the left, favoring socialist parties and anticlerical skepticism; it was women in Italy who voted against legalizing abortion and men who voted for it (and in the United States, too, most polls showed slightly larger percentages of women opposing abortion). In the United States in the 1980s, the risk-averse position was to protect the makeshift welfare state which had come into being over the last 50 years against attacks from Reagan Republicans who wanted to partly dismantle it. And this posture was surely especially attractive to single women in straitened economic circumstances who also had a grievance against Reagan's cheery cultural conservatism.

The gender gap was only one example of the cultural divides which shaped political attitudes and preferences around the year 1981. When Times Mirror (the parent company of the *Los Angeles Times*) and the Gallup organization went about dividing up the electorate into eleven groups for purposes of analyzing the 1988 campaign, most of the questions they used to define those groups were about cultural issues, such as degree of religious faith and belief in America's superiority to other nations, rather than economic issues.[19] They developed the new methodology because it was plain that the old categories—income groups, ethnic groups, even voters grouped by party identification—were not catching important differences of and changes in opinion. It has been asserted that the 1980 and 1984 Reagan elections divided Americans more sharply along lines of economic class than had any other presidential election in recent decades.[20] But these assertions are misleading since they depend on comparisons with atypical years (1984 with

1956, when Adlai Stevenson ran worse than most Democrats of his era among blue-collar and Catholic voters), because they ignore the obvious cultural chasms which are apparent from the exit poll data, and because they brush over the considerable extent to which cultural attitudes (willingness to divorce, for example, or valuation placed on money making in choice of career) had come to determine economic status in an economically affluent and culturally diverse country. Only in the South in the 1980s was presidential voting clearly along economic lines, and even there the low-income support for the Democrats was largely the product of their culturally based near-unanimous support from blacks. In the East and in some midwestern states, there was no pattern at all along income lines, an absence which is understandable when voters are analyzed according to education. Those with grade school educations were heavily Democratic, but most were either elderly or black or both. Those who had graduated from college and gone no further voted heavily Republican, but those who had gone to graduate or professional school— a group that includes all doctors and lawyers and most teachers and social workers, but not so many salesmen and engineers—tended to vote much more often for the Democrats. The difference between these groups, between businessmen and engineers on the one hand and lawyers, doctors, and professors on the other, was not so much in economic status as in cultural attitudes, with the former being more culturally conservative and the latter more liberal. But the final proof of the importance of culture over class appeared in the results. The Democrats won precious few elections in the late 1970s and the 1980s by appealing for economic redistribution. The Republicans won many elections by campaigning on shared cultural values.

But what is most striking about the cultural gaps which explain American politics around 1981 is the comparative lack of bitterness between the different groups. In the late 1960s and early 1970s, when one cultural segment of America was fighting a war which another segment believed it should lose, when there were riots breaking out on campuses and in ghettos and when the length of a haircut could split a family, cultural divisions cut deep. Americans then were used to a culturally uniform society, and each segment seemed desperately trying not only to prevent its own life style from being suppressed but also to make it prevail generally. In the late 1970s and early 1980s, when economic circumstances were bleaker and American power seemed on the defensive abroad, these problems absorbed people's attention and cultural divisions seemed more bearable. Americans had discovered that they now had a culturally diverse society in which they were mostly free to live and let live, and they brought their cultural agendas into politics only when they felt their personal space was somehow being infringed on (as proponents of legalized abortion did in 1968–73 and opponents did after 1973 when they felt that widespread abortion amounted to mass murder).

Ronald Reagan and his Republicans did indeed trim back the growth of America's makeshift welfare state, and they did inaugurate new economic and foreign policies—all in significant departure from the 1970s. But most of the dire consequences predicted for these changes failed to occur; and positive consequences, some expected and some not, in time began to appear. Culturally, the changes in the 1980s were more subtle. But that subtlety was what one might have expected under an administration headed by Reagan, who despite his cheery appeals to traditional values was also a divorced man who had made his living in show business for three decades and who remained as personally tolerant and unbigoted as when he had been in his own phrase, a "bleeding-heart Roosevelt–Truman liberal" in the 1940s. Finally, the country turned out to be in not as bad shape as the Americans of 1981 supposed. The Iran hostage crisis proved readily soluble. Underneath surface difficulties, the American economy and American military power remained massive and strong. In the 1980s Americans found that their country was stronger and more resilient than most of them had thought.

56

Cuts

T he key political player in the early months of the Reagan administration, David Stockman, was an improbable choice for anyone's Cabinet, a thirty-four-year-old former divinity student who had served two terms as a minority party congressman from the conservative flatlands of southwest Michigan. But Stockman had made the most of the years he had spent as a Capitol Hill staffer at a time when staffers were becoming public policy entrepreneurs, the drafters of the talking papers which congressman or senators would read from after striding late into a committee hearing and of the committee reports which congressmen would sign without reading and lawyers and judges would later cite as evidence of what Congress had really meant, regardless of what the law it had passed actually said. His first big political breaks came when, as a student at Harvard Divinity School, he got a position as house-sitter with Daniel Patrick Moynihan, commuting then from Cambridge to his job in the Nixon White House, and when David Broder, his instructor in a seminar at Harvard's Kennedy School of Government, recommended him as a staffer for moderate Republican Congressman John Anderson, a recommendation seconded by Moynihan.[1] That the bulk of young congressional staffers were liberals while Stockman was, increasingly as the 1970s went on, a conservative did not hurt his career. On the contrary, it helped, for there were few ahead of him in line; and in the ranks of House Republicans, most of them men of much bonhomie and few ideas, it was easy to gain a monopoly of information and a vast amount of influence. Stockman returned to his home district in Michigan in 1975 and, with his mother's help, managed to bluff the inarticulate incumbent congressman into retirement and get himself elected at age thirty in 1976. In the House he got a seat on what was soon renamed the Energy and Commerce Committee, which with its stewardship of regulatory issues was often the most powerful committee in the House. There he developed intellectually devastating critiques of the measures supported by the Democrats who had a 2–1 margin in the House and by many Republicans who accepted their premises and went along with many of their initiatives. He was part of the group of Republicans who inflicted unexpected defeats on the Democrats in 1978 and 1979, who discredited the arguments for energy price controls and showed how the nominally progressive tax system was inevitably undermined. He became a close ally of Jack Kemp on the Kemp–Roth tax cut and other issues.

Like a staffer and unlike most members, Stockman actually read and mastered the facts, figures, and numbers in the documents Congress and government spewed out. This command of detail and his strong belief in Kemp's supply-side economics recommended him to those who promoted him for director of the Office of Management and Budget in the Reagan administration. Stockman had not supported Reagan in the primaries, and his acquaintance with the president-elect was limited to his portrayal of his old boss John Anderson in practice debate sessions in October 1980. Yet Reagan did appoint him OMB director. To that position he brought a knowledge of facts, a devotion to theory, and a staffer's skill at inside maneuvering[2] to put together a package of some $64 billion in budget cuts, along with the Kemp–Roth 30% tax cut, for Reagan to propose in February 1981. All conventional wisdom said these goals were unattainable, even with the Republican gains in the 1980 elections. Opposition to the spending cuts would cumulate, it was said, as opponents of particular cuts coalesced, while the big current and future deficits which even Stockman's figures showed (he used a "magic asterisk" to indicate that $44 billion in cuts over and above what he was recommending would be necessary to balance the 1984 budget) would stop Republicans as well as Democrats from voting for the tax cuts. But Stockman figured ways around these problems. He used the congressional budget process, developed in the middle 1970s to give Congress bargaining leverage against Richard Nixon's OMB and the executive branch, to package the cuts in a single "reconciliation" resolution; and he tried to rally to its side all of the Republicans together with a sufficient number of southern and other conservative Democrats to make up solid majorities in both houses.

II

The strategy may have been aided by the reaction following the shooting of President Reagan on March 30. Only two months and ten days after he took office, as he was leaving the Washington Hilton after delivering a routine speech, the seventy-year-old Reagan was shot by John W. Hinckley, Jr., who imagined that his deed would impress movie actress Jodie Foster; a Secret Service agent and a Washington policeman were also hit, and presidential Press Secretary James Brady was severely wounded in the head. Reagan underwent surgery at George Washington Hospital—providentially, its top surgical staff were gathered for a routine meeting as he was wheeled in—and for several days he was, unbeknownst to the public,[3] tottering on the edge of disaster. But he showed the grace and charm one would expect only from a 1940s movie hero, telling his wife in the hospital, "Honey, I forgot to duck." He recovered enough to make telephone calls to members of Congress from his hospital bed to ask their support on budget cuts and to return to the White House April 11; there he met ultimately with 467 members, and the coalitions favoring the cuts held together.

In the House, Stockman's vehicle was called Gramm–Latta, for its co-sponsors: Texas Democrat Phil Gramm, a free-market economics professor from Texas A&M

University, and Delbert Latta, one of the hardest-nosed partisans in Republican ranks, from northern Ohio. Gramm had gotten a seat on the Budget Committee with Majority Leader Jim Wright's help and attended Democratic strategy sessions even as he was working with the Republicans. Gramm–Latta passed in early May by 253–176. Much was made of Reagan's support from the "Boll Weevils," conservative southern Democrats whose nominal leader on this issue was Gramm. But what was more striking was that only one Republican voted against the administration. Speaker Tip O'Neill actually suffered fewer Democratic defections than Sam Rayburn had on the Rules Committee vote in January 1961, and then the weight of the White House was on the side of the speaker; but Rayburn had the support of 22 Republicans, most of them were responsive to labor or liberal political forces in their districts, while O'Neill, more partisan, never made any attempt to win Republican votes.[4] By 1981 almost no Republicans felt obliged by convictions or political circumstances to vote with the Democrats. Rather, the solidarity they had gained in opposing the failed economic policies of the Carter administration and backing the Kemp–Roth tax cut in 1978 was strengthened by a desire to see the new Republican administration, and the gallant Republican president recovering from his gunshot wound, score a success.

For at the back of everyone's mind, unstated, was the memory of how the nation's morale had been shaken by the murder of one president; and the feeling was well-nigh universal that this must not happen to the country again. As Richard Darman, then deputy chief of staff and one of the administration's sharpest political operators and most far-sighted thinkers, put it, "Kennedy was shot and died. Reagan was shot and survived. He personifies the restoration of this notion of the possible."[5]

A few days after the triumph of Gramm–Latta, the Senate endorsed the budget cuts by a 72–20 vote. But several old-fashioned Republicans who abhorred deficits, notably Finance Committee Chairman Robert Dole and Budget Committee Chairman Pete Domenici, could not help noticing that Stockman's arithmetic did not add up. Even with his forecasts assuming real economic growth and a decline in the money supply all at once—his "rosy scenario," as it came to be called[6]—they remained edgy about cutting taxes. On the other side of the aisle, Moynihan, in his first term as a Democratic senator from New York after sub-Cabinet or Cabinet service in four consecutive administrations, noticed that the man who had been his house-sitter ten years before was proposing a cut in early-retirement Social Security benefits, effective on people who retired in 1982. In May, Moynihan introduced a resolution opposing it, which passed the Senate 96–0 and abruptly ended any chance to change Social Security entitlements. Tip O'Neill, too, seized on Social Security, marking it down as an election-year issue for Democrats in 1982. And in the House, Stockman's budget-cutting package was coming unstuck. The House committees came back with their versions of a second set of Gramm–Latta cuts, which of course undid Stockman's work considerably; after many concessions and in an atmosphere of pandemonium in which one aide's name and phone numbers scrawled into the margin became part of the bill, the House in

June passed a Gramm—Latta II with fewer savings and reforms in entitlements than Stockman wanted.

For David Stockman, cutting the domestic budget and rationalizing government were the major goals. For Ronald Reagan, the major goal was cutting taxes.[7] Reagan was the only president Americans have had[8] who paid income taxes at or near the marginal rates which rose to 91% in the World War II years and remained in effect through the Kennedy–Johnson tax cut of 1964.[9] Even when his budget-cutting measures seemed in trouble. Reagan never faltered in pushing for his tax cut; and for all the talk of his being manipulated by aides, in this case shrewd aides like White House Chief of Staff James Baker recognized Reagan's steadiness of purpose and deferred to it. The problem was that the across-the-board tax cut, like a number of other reforms enacted in the 1980s, had no strong identifiable political constituency. Presumably most voters would prefer lower tax rates if they were given a choice, but elective politicians knew that they could win crucial support from contributors or groups of voters by supporting spending increases or tax cuts which benefited these contributors or groups particularly. Reagan ended up sacrificing 5 percentage points of the tax cut and adding to it the 10–5–3 depreciation bill sought by business lobbyists. Then the administration got into a bidding war with House Democrats, led by Dan Rostenkowski, the new chairman of the Ways and Means Committee, who was handing out tax breaks even faster than the Reagan strategists could. Perhaps the most cynical agreement resulting from this competition was the administration's agreement not to oppose revival of the sugar import quota system which had been abolished in 1979. When Congressman John Breaux from sugar-producing Louisiana was asked whether his vote on the tax measure was for sale, he responded, "No, but it is available for rent"; the rent-payers were not just U.S. consumers but poor people in the Caribbean and the Philippines who lost their chance to sell their sugar in the United States at the world price, which was far below that of domestically produced sugar. In July 1981, after tough lobbying, the Reagan plan was adopted. The top federal income tax rates would drop from 70% on "unearned" (that is, not wage or salary) income and 50% on "earned" income to 37.5% on all income by 1983.[10]

The Reagan budget and tax cuts were substantial political achievements. The budget cuts by themselves did not reduce government spending drastically, but they signaled that it would no longer be allowed to grow faster than the economy. The annual rates of growth in federal outlays would turn out to be slowed down from 17% and 15% over the period 1979–81 to 10%, 8%, and 5% during 1981–84.[11] The tax cuts represented a real change in American taxation, an implicit recognition that steeply progressive tax rates were no longer sustainable and tended to stifle the economy in a peacetime, increasingly small-unit society. Franklin Roosevelt in the 1930s had been one of the creators of American's big-unit society. He mistrusted unregulated markets and gravitated naturally to solutions which created new big governmental units like NRA, AAA, TVA, and to the never-enacted Brownlow Committee reorganization measures of the Seven TVAs of his abortive Third New Deal. He was comfortable working with the leaders of big business and big labor and the Army and Navy when it came time to prepare for and fight World War II. And he had reason to believe that this big-unit governance worked: it put people back to work and it won the war. Roosevelt adapted government to the demands already put on it by society, demands which it had not addressed under his predecessor. Similarly, Reagan's budget and tax cuts can be seen as an attempt to adapt government to the small-unit economy and society which had been quietly developing for decades, and whose demands had not been met or even much sensed by his predecessors.

With this result Reagan was evidently pleased. But many other Republicans were not, notably Stockman. He felt sick about how much spending had not been cut and how many tax breaks that had been handed out. He quickly became concerned about the prospect of a continuous deficit of more than $100 billion, but he could not get Reagan to focus on the problem. For Stockman this inattention was proof of Reagan's invincible ignorance. But it could also have been like Franklin Roosevelt's inability to focus on the subject at hand when some advisor of his came in with a request he did not want to grant. Roosevelt would make a joke about a Dutchess County farmer or grin at Fala making an indiscretion on the rug; Reagan would tell an old Hollywood story or gaze approvingly at Caspar Weinberger's Defense Department visual aids. The likelier explanation is not that Reagan failed to understand the deficits in the out-years beyond the current budget, but that he decided they represented a tolerable cost for getting the things he wanted: lower tax rates, higher defense spending, some cuts in the domestic budget. If he was, as one reporter says, "gambling with history,"[12] the evidence from the election returns and the economic statistics up through the end of the decade suggested he was winning.

He may have been helped by an event no one connected to American economic policy at the time: the victory of François Mitterrand in the May 1981 election in France. Mitterrand's Socialist government set about fulfilling its campaign promises by reflating the economy and nationalizing several big French banks and industrial companies, whose owners were paid amounts they denounced as unsatisfactorily low or even confiscatory. The macroeconomic policy quickly flopped, and this first big round of nationalizations in Western Europe in years reminded investors there that in almost every country there were parties or factions which could conceivably come to power and, using parliamentary means, seize their property. The one conspicuous exception was the United States. As a result, huge amounts of capital began flowing into the United States, not just from France but from all of Western Europe, from East Asia, and in increasing amounts from Latin America. These capital flows helped to finance the U.S. government's large budget deficits and in time, to some unknown and probably unknowable extent, helped to propel the U.S. economy forward as well. None of this was an intended result of Reagan policies. But Reagan's limited success in turning back the tide of government, and the fact that with the American separation of powers no plan, not even Reagan's seemed likely to be adopted easily or without consideration of its effects on large economic interests, probably helped to convince foreign investors that their money was peculiarly safe in the United States.

III

Just as he was celebrating his tax cut victories, Reagan made another decision which had an effect far out of proportion to the number of people directly affected. This was the decision in August 1981 to dismiss the air traffic controllers who had followed their union, PATCO, out on strike. The conventional wisdom was that firing the controllers would cripple the civil aviation system and that it was better anyhow to mollify people who say they have a grievance. But Reagan evidently understood that any breach in the government's longstanding policy against federal employee strikes—a policy maintained in Democratic as well as Republican administrations, even while teachers and other state and local employees were striking in many states—would result in a series of tumultuous and ruinously expensive walkouts, and he had confidence in Transportation Secretary Drew Lewis's preparations for hiring substitute controllers. The controllers were mostly young men without college educations who believed that they possessed unique skill which the mass of America's air travelers—mostly college-educated, affluent businessmen—could not do without and who believed that they were overworked in their stressful positions. And they knew that in government and out, job security had become a norm in American life, that the big unit of government or business which hired you was likely to keep you on the payroll, regardless of strikes and without regard to productivity, at least until a comfortably early retirement.

But the country was changing, and the controllers' assumptions proved illfounded. The government was able to fill enough controller positions to maintain the flow of air travel, and the only president to have once been a union president had no compunction whatever about firing the strikers. The result was a disaster for PATCO but, much more important, a defeat for unions generally. Reagan's action helped to legitimize the practice of entirely destroying a union (even though PATCO broke rules which most other unions observed), and it showed workers that a union could not necessarily protect and might in fact cost them their jobs. Union membership was declining sharply in the late 1970s and early 1980s, most notably because of the huge layoffs of auto and steel workers: the great CIO unions which had come into existence in a few months in 1937 saw their active membership rolls cut approximately in half in a few years after 1979. Total union membership declined from 22.2 million in 1975 to 20.9 million in 1980, 17.7 million in 1983, and 16.9 million in 1987—in a work force which was greatly expanding. Even more precipitous was the decline in strikes.[13] The number of workers involved in major work stoppages declined from 795,000 in 1980 to 174,000 in 1987, and from an annual average of 1,378,000 for 1973–77 to an average of 841,000 for 1978–82 and an average of 463,000 for 1983–87.[14] Unions were also losing more organizing elections, and the only major growth in union membership in the 1980s came among public employees.

Forty years before unions had been expanding rapidly, and the union movement was becoming one of American society's major institutions. It seemed likely in the years just after World War II that unions would come to represent most workers in collective bargaining and would exert increasing influence in elections and on public officials. In the 1970s the unions in effect priced themselves out of the labor market; and in August 1981 the former president of the Screen Actors Guild, by ostentatiously busting a union, dealt a telling blow to a union movement which was becoming a minor American institution, important in a few metropolitan areas and in certain businesses but no longer capable of setting the norm for the nation on wages or working conditions or even of exerting much upward pressure on wages or prices.

IV

The fall of 1981 saw an economic decline, and a political anticlimax. The stringent monetary policy adopted by Paul Volcker's Federal Reserve Board in October 1979 and adhered to fairly consistently in 1980 and 1981 was contracting the economy, despite current and projected Reagan budget deficits. The coal-steel-auto Great Lakes industrial belt and the Farm Belt centered on Iowa were especially hard hit. "Voluntary" quotas on Japanese car imports and an end to the Soviet grain embargo—both policies adopted by Reagan—came too late, because the Japanese companies used their quotas to import higher-priced models which gave them and cost the Big Three higher profits and the Soviets had moved, pretty much permanently, to other suppliers. As the unemployment numbers and federal deficit projections rose, Reagan's job performance rating plummeted to below 50% by December; for all the talk of his winning personality, he was not rated especially well when things were going badly. But Reagan did not flinch and pursued his policies. The same months which saw sharp rises in unemployment, which most politicians responded to quickly, also saw sharp drops in the rate of inflation, which most politicians hesitated to treat as a meaningful trend. Oil prices, once decontrolled, started to fall. These economic indicators provided both Reagan and his Democratic opponents with evidence that things were going their way, and both acted on the assumption that they were. The Reagan cuts in budget and taxes would prove largely permanent and would provide a battleground on which political conflicts could be played out. The political clashes which were coming in the 1980s would give a sense of whose policies were in line with what voters thought the economy needed in America and what America needed in the world.

The balance of opinion in Washington, however, swung against Reagan, in large part because of an article in the November 1981 *Atlantic* magazine which was written by the *Washington Post*'s William Greider and based on a series of candid breakfast conversations he had held with David Stockman over the preceding year.[15] It proved to be political dynamite.[16] Stockman was quoted as saying that "Kemp–Roth was always a Trojan horse to bring down the top rate" and as referring to the lobbyists competing for tax breaks in July 1981 as "pigs at the trough," an apt enough description. Stockman offered to resign but was instead directed by James Baker to express contrition and have lunch with the president; at lunch Reagan was vaguely sympathetic, but Stockman told reporters that the meeting had been "more in the nature of a trip to the woodshed after supper."[17] Stockman stayed on in the government—evidently his mastery of figures was needed—but he was politically much less potent, intriguing for the major tax increases he believed were necessary to balance the budget, without much credibility either in the White House or on Capitol Hill. The staffer who had gotten the House to pass a bill with his pencil scrawl in the margin was now relegated to the more usual staffer's posture of keeping busy but being largely ignored.

57

→》》 《《←

Correction

For most of Ronald Reagan's first year as president, after the hostages in Iran were released during his first hours in office, foreign policy was mostly obscured by the fights over budget and tax cuts. Iran was quiet, the Middle East was quiet, and Soviet leader Leonid Brezhnev was slowly dying. The most visible foreign policy development occurred in August when U.S. Air Force jets shot down two Libyan jets over the Gulf of Sidra after the Libyan planes had opened fire on them—a confrontation characteristically sought by the Reagan administration rather than avoided as its critics and predecessor would have done, after Libyan dictator Muammar Qaddafi asserted a preposterous claim to the gulf as Libyan waters.

Yet for many Americans, Reagan's assertiveness, his very substantial increase in defense spending, and provocative statements on nuclear war made by some Defense Department appointees stimulated fears that Reagan would lead the nation into war. In Western Europe demonstrators protested the administration's plan to fulfill the Carter administration's commitment to deploy Pershing II missiles in Europe in 1983;[1] in the United States a movement for a "nuclear freeze,"—a freeze on building, testing, or deploying new nuclear weapons—begun in Cambridge, Massachusetts, by veterans of the anti–Vietnam war movement, spread to liberals around the country. Support for a nuclear freeze became required of most northern Democrats by important parts of their constituencies—not so much voters as the activists and fund-raisers they depended on to get reelected or would need to get elected to higher office. On intellectual grounds the freeze was not defensible, as the Democrats found out when they brought it to the House floor in August 1982 and were pummeled in debate and defeated in the vote; keeping nuclear stockpiles and delivery systems precisely the same was more destabilizing and dangerous than making changes and proceeding with routine upgrading, maintenance, and testing. But in emotional terms the freeze obviously struck a chord among the large percentage of Americans who feared that a former movie actor in the White House would prove to be the kind of nuclear maniac they had seen in the 1964 movie *Dr. Strangelove, or How I Learned to Stop Worrying and Love the Bomb,* released at a time when most voters saw Reagan's fellow conservative, Barry Goldwater, as just that kind of figure. The freeze advocates nonetheless proved wrong in their sense that their movement would grow in strength. On the contrary, as Reagan stayed in office without plunging the country into war, the freeze effort would inevitably thaw—as it did, electorally, well before the 1984 election.

II

At home, as deficit projections kept growing, it was Republicans who became alarmed. In the 1980 campaign Reagan had attacked Carter for running $40 billion deficits. By early 1982 there were projections showing a Reagan deficit of $200 billion. As Stockman quickly understood, spending had not been cut enough and taxes had been cut too much to get the budget anywhere close to balance, even in out-years like 1984. The Laffer curve—the theory, supposedly originally sketched out on a napkin by supply-side economist Arthur Laffer, that at some point lower tax rates would produce higher revenues—was an obvious point theoretically, but even Laffer was careful never to say just where this point was, and even the revenue projections of supply-siders did not rely on assumptions that the 1981 tax cuts would produce increased revenues. What the supply-siders and the by now former supply-sider Stockman—and everyone else, for that matter—failed to anticipate was that inflation would come down so rapidly. That sharp drop helped the private economy grow but reduced nominal revenues to far below anyone's estimates.

For many congressional Republicans, like Robert Dole, chairman of the Senate Finance Committee, and Barber Conable, ranking Republican on the House Ways and Means Committee, deficits were alarming. Dole had first been elected to Congress in 1960, Conable in 1964, when almost all congressional Republicans were opposing the Keynesian Kennedy–Johnson tax cuts. The more sophisticated among them admitted that budget deficits might sometimes be useful. But, they went on, requiring a balanced budget was the only way to discipline government over the long run to live within its means and to prevent the public sector from growing so large that it stifled the growth of the private sector. To men from small towns like Russell, Kansas, and Alexander, New York, it was axiomatic that discipline was necessary to an orderly and fair society—the discipline of Protestant prohibitions, of intellectual honesty, of commercial probity, of fair play and sportsmanship. You played by the rules. And one of the rules was that you balance the budget.[2]

Thoughtful and tradition-minded—he furnished his office in antiques rather than government-issue furniture—Conable was always queasy about the tax cut of which he, as a loyal Republican and his party's senior member on Ways and Means, was the lead co-sponsor; his instinctive approach was to lower taxes on business and keep income tax rates high enough to get the budget close to balance. Dole, a shrewd and acidly witty but not at all bookish man, understood even before the supply-siders did that their cuts would generate large deficits; and he understood as well that a simple tax rate cut would make tax shelters and preferences less important and hence tend to diminish the institutional power of the tax-writing committee he had just started to chair. His predecessor, Russell Long, had made himself powerful by dominating the committee and dispensing tax preferences for special interests and occasional rate cuts to protect ordinary voters against bracket creep. Kemp–Roth threatened to upset the game just as Dole was beginning to play. Deficits also threatened the domestic programs like food stamps and aid to the handicapped which Dole, uncharacteristically for an old-line Republican, backed, and the defense buildup, which he favored as strongly as Reagan. But Dole's hatred of supply-side doctrine went further: for him the idea of it purposefully violated some sacred trust. "The good news," he began a joke in 1982, "is that a busload of supply-side economists went over a cliff and everyone was killed. The bad news is that two seats were empty."

Dole believed that Ways and Means had given away far too much in tax concessions in 1981, and in 1982 he went about trying to get some of them back. He worked closely with an assistant secretary and key employees at the Treasury, which had an institutional history of favoring purist tax laws and opposing special breaks and favoritism. He also had some cooperation from Budget Committee Chairman Domenici, who was dismayed over the deficits and felt there was need for additional revenue, and Stockman, by now a fervent deficit-cutter. Although the Constitution requires that revenue measures originate in the House, Dole put together his own tax bill in Senate Finance and attached it to a minor piece of House-passed legislation. It included withholding of taxes for tip income and for interest from bank accounts: Dole the old-fashioned puritan cracking down on cheaters. The son of a Kansas butter-and-egg man enjoyed beating the high-priced lobbyists; when someone told him that everyone in the hall outside the committee room was wearing expensive Italian Gucci shoes, he replied, "They'll all be barefoot by morning." Dole pushed his package through the Senate in July 1982 in a session which lasted till 3 A.M., writing substitutes, twisting arms, and prevailing finally by getting Jesse Helms of the tobacco-producing state of North Carolina—who as chairman of the Agriculture Committee had been rescued on a 1981 farm bill by the more knowledgeable Dole—to vote for a bill which included a tobacco tax increase.[3] The bill, christened with the acronym TEFRA, was passed by the House and signed by a president who appeared to be persuaded it wasn't a tax increase.

III

In June 1982, as the maneuvering on the tax bill continued, a jury in the District of Columbia found the man who had shot President Reagan not guilty by reason of insanity. An almost universal torrent of criticism followed. After President Kennedy was murdered, much articulate comment in those days when the civil rights revolution had been on every television screen had pondered the question of why America was a peculiarly violent nation (Arthur Schlesinger, Jr., even wrote a book on the subject), as though the assassin's act was statistically meaningful. Now the focus was on a would-be murderer who was excused from criminal guilt by rational operation of an insanity defense Americans had long been familiar with and accepted. Instead of seeking to blame their society, Americans were eager to blame—and punish—an individual. In many states the insanity defense, which had been stretched to its farthest limits in the District of Columbia by the Durham rule in 1954, was attacked and weakened.

These changes reflected broader attitudes toward crime and criminals—and a general toughening of attitudes on other issues as well. In 1960, America's prison population had been 212,000, a figure which had declined to the 187,000–199,000 level from 1965 to the early 1970s and risen only to 240,000 in 1975 despite sharply rising crime rates. This refusal to put more people in prisons cannot be explained as the work of a few liberal theorists; it represents the widely decentralized decisions of thousands of prosecutors, judges, jurors, legislators, and voters. Nor can it be explained on racial grounds; about half the prisoners were black, but the large majority of the decision-makers in these years, even in central cities, were white. Then in the middle 1970s, the prison population started to rise sharply, to 294,000 in 1978, 315,000 in 1980, 394,000 in 1982, 445,000 in 1984, 522,000 in 1986, and over 600,000 in 1988.[4] Even though the rise in crime in the dozen years after 1976 was much lower than in the dozen years before (in some years crime actually declined), the prison population *nearly tripled* in this period, again as a result of widely decentralized decision-making, except that by that time many of the decision-makers in the central cities were black.

This change is strong evidence of a swing away from the cultural liberalism of the 1970s. Just as belief in the efficacy of most government programs was growing weaker, so was belief in toleration of criminal behavior. The feeling that society could not legitimately punish a criminal who might have suffered from poverty or discrimination was vanishing, and so was much of the feeling that society owed some positive recompense to people who continued to suffer from poverty and discrimination: these were strong ideas in years of alienation, weak ideas in years of resilience. The trend started before Ronald Reagan came to office, and by no means depended on his acts. He may have strengthened it, but more likely the effect worked the other way around: the trend of feeling among millions of Americans, produced by their view of the world around them and not just by this sound bite or that visual, gave political strength to a politician who had stood for some time where most voters were going. For the first time since the middle 1960s, a president seemed to be in tune rather than out of tune with his times.

IV

To the sleek new politics of young Republicans like David Stockman there could hardly have been a better foil than the figure of Tip O'Neill. White-haired, with the girth and manners of a man who liked a few drinks before his steak and an evening of playing poker, a reflexive dispenser of patronage and supporter of big government programs, he personified old-fashioned Democratic politics. He's "just like the federal budget," said freshman Long Island Congressman John LeBoutillier, author of *Harvard Hates America* and a Vanderbilt and Whitney heir, "fat, bloated, and out of control."[5] But O'Neill's looks were deceiving. He was secure in his position as speaker not becasue he imposed the old ways on the young members of the Democratic caucus, but because he adapted to the new ways and mastered them. "Whaddaya hear?" he would ask friends on the Hill and back home, and he would listen to the answers. He had been the lead sponsor of reforms like the elimination of unrecorded teller votes and had supported the measure to require caucus election of committee chairmen. In his first two terms as speaker, he had deferred to the Democratic president despite insults from Hamilton Jordan; he had expected to serve as Jimmy Carter's loyal lieutenant as Sam Rayburn had served John Kennedy and John McCormack had served Lyndon Johnson. He knew he could not compete with White House staffers or leading Democratic senators for publicity. But with a Republican president and a Republican Senate, O'Neill was suddenly the most visible Democrat in Washington, the major spokesman and strategist for his party. He understood that the political fulcrum of the party had moved south and west, and he didn't try to force on it the whole menu of programs he personally would support. But he determined early on to fight and not compromise on the Reagan budget cuts; and by May 1981 he decided to focus on the issue that he and Reagan, two old New Deal Democrats, both understand was the Republicans' major vulnerability, Social Security: the speaker who usually listened and often deferred to his younger members brusquely swatted down any attempts to compromise on it. O'Neill was banking on a recession to turn voters back to the Democrats, and as the economy sagged in late 1981 and early 1982 he seemed vindicated.

Complementing O'Neill's strategy were the tactics of Democratic Campaign Committee Chairman Tony Coelho.[6] Elected only in 1978 (though he was familiar with the Hill as a longtime staffer), an ebullient flesh-presser and incredibly efficient toucher of bases, Coelho inherited a committee whose treasury was bare, whose mailing lists were well-nigh nonexistent, whose capacity for providing technical support to campaigns was nil, and whose last chairman had himself been defeated for reelection in 1980. Coelho was familiar with big political contributors from his native Central Valley of California, where big growers gave to powerful House Democrats who protected their federally subsidized irrigation water. He was aware that business political action committees, given greater-than-expected leeway under an early Federal Election Commission interpretation of the campaign finance reform laws of 1971 and 1974, had been proliferating in the late 1970s; and he knew that House Republican campaign committee leaders, buoyed by their party's successes in 1980, were telling business PAC operators that 1982 would be their chance to finally elect a Republican House of Representatives, in which they would be able to count on sympathetic Republicans for support rather than have to beg for help from not-very-sympathetic Democrats. Coelho counterattacked. He visited hundreds of PAC offices personally, told their operatives that he expected them to be as non-partisan as the boilerplate language in the law suggested they should be, and presented them with lists of Democratic incumbents and challengers who were right on their issues and deserved contributions. "Remember," he would say, "we have every committee chairmanship and every subcommittee chairmanship in the House, and we keep score." Even while he was building up his committee's fund-raising operation, Coelho broke the back of the Republicans' effort to corner PAC contributions.

The upshot was that the Democrats, instead of losing control of the House made a net gain of 26 seats in November 1982. They gained back many, though not all, of the seats Reagan Republicans had won in 1980; and they picked off some other vulnerable seats Coelho had targeted. They were helped by redistricting, especially in California, where San Francisco Congressman Phillip Burton drew the boundary lines himself not only for the House seats but also for the 40 state Senate and 80 Assembly districts. Smoking Pall Malls and retaining his knowledge of the voting habits of every precinct in California (and in many other states besides) after several tumblers of vodka, Burton camped out in Sacramento; patched up a feud between former Assembly Speaker Leo McCarthy and Assemblyman Howard Berman, who had challenged him (Berman got a new House district); and commanded Democratic legislators, some of whom spent $1 million on their races and were aiming for lifetime careers, to vote for his plans without seeing them. They did. In 1980, California had elected 22 Democrats and 21 Republicans to Congress; in 1982, after a gain of 2 seats in redistricting, it elected 28 Democrats and 17 Republicans even though Democrats led in popular votes by only 50%–47%. Across the country redistricting probably gave the Democrats a net gain of 15 seats in states where they controlled the legislature or were, as in Illinois, the beneficiaries of favorable decisions by the courts.[7]

The Democrats were naturally helped by the recession and the Social Security issue. Claude Pepper, chairman of the special House committee on aging and the most visible advocate of extending rather than cutting back Social Security benefits, was as indefatigable a speaker on the campaign trail in 1982 as he had been in 1940;[8] he had already been a nationally prominent politician over a longer stretch of years than anyone else in American history, and he had more years to go. But the Democrats' victories were not spread evenly across the country. In the Midwest they increased their share of the vote, as compared with the last off-year election, in 1978, from 50% to 54%; and in the non–Atlantic South it went form 57% to 62%. This interior core or Heartland of the country, where unemployment was the highest, did move toward the Democrats; and the movement was larger when measured against the 1980 results. But in the East, where outside of the steel area of western Pennsylvania unemployment had not spiked far upwards, the Democratic percentage increased only marginally, from 55% to 57%. And in two regions where unemployment did not reach the levels of the middle-1970s, the Democratic percentage actually declined as compared with 1978: from 59% to 58% in the South Atlantic states from Virginia to Florida, and from 52% to 50% in the West. An economically troubled Heartland was trending toward the Democrats, while the less troubled coasts were not. The following table shows Democratic percentages by regions in House elections in 1978, 1980, and 1982:[9]

	1978	1980	1982
UNITED STATES	54	50	55
East	55	51	57
South Atlantic	59	54	58
West	52	47	50
Midwest	50	48	54
Non-Atlantic South	57	57	62

The Democrats took great heart from the 1982 results, though they ought to have reflected that the Heartland gains would prove transient if prosperity returned and the cultural issues which tended to work for the Republicans reasserted themselves, and that their failure to make significant gains in the more prosperous coasts, despite the culturally liberal constituencies concentrated in the urban Northeast and Pacific Rim, suggested that in better times the balance of cultural versus economic issues would work against them there, too. Democratic House and statewide candidates in an off year could adapt to the local terrain. Democratic presidential candidates and, to a lesser extent, their ticket-mates in a presidential year would tend to be defined by the issue stands they would be required to take by the culturally liberal and economically parochial interest groups with leverage in their nomination process. The 1982 exit polls[10] showed that the Democrats did not regain substantial numbers of blue-collar votes; their advance did not represent a return of a by now mythical or at least vanished New Deal coalition. Instead, they built on the patterns of support from cultural groups which they had in their losing performance in 1980. Women, risk-averse as always, tended to worry about what they saw as the threat of nuclear war and about the effects of what they saw as the dismantling of the American welfare state, and voted solidly Democratic: the gender gap apparent in 1980 persisted into 1982. The age cohort which had come to political awareness in the Vietnam and Watergate years was definitely Democratic. The elderly, worried about Social Security, became a solid Democratic bloc for the first time in years; it helped that the elderly of the 1980s were the young of Franklin Roosevelt's 1930s and had become solidly Democratic then.

The Republican National Committee in 1982 ran a series of ads saying, "stay the course." The 1982 election results, like the 1982 tax bill, were in the words of Democratic pollster Peter Hart a "mid-course correction."[11] After redistricting is taken into account, the Democrats made only modest gains in the House, not coming close to their 2–1 majorities of 1974 and 1976; and they actually lost seats in the Senate. They noted correctly that they lost most of the close Senate races which could easily have gone the other way.[12] They added, a bit wistfully, that if only the conditions of 1982 could remain in place, if only they could be guaranteed a deep recession and Republicans foolish enough to do things which looked like raids on voters' Social Security, then they could surely win in 1984.[13] But time does not stand still; and the results of the 1982 elections, interpreted in the cold light of day, show that the good news for the Democrats was not that they were the majority party again but that they had prevented Ronald Reagan's Republicans at least for now from becoming the majority.

58

⇥⇥⇥ ⇤⇤⇤

Morning

A merican politicians were busy in the weeks just after the 1982 elections—
busy breaking or at least fudging on their promises. In the lame duck
session of Congress in December 1982, the main business was passage of a gasoline
tax increase recommended by Transportation Secretary Drew Lewis. The Interstate highway system, passed at President Eisenhower's urging in 1956, was financed by proceeds of the gasoline tax; and although almost all the intercity routes
were built, there were still a few expensive missing links in big cities and, more
important, a need for maintenance and rebuilding. Since the oil shock of 1973
political conventional wisdom had held that Americans would not stand any increase
in the gas tax, that they were so traumatized by the sharp increase in the price
of this precious commodity that they would brook nothing higher. But by December
1982 the price of gasoline had already fallen after oil price decontrol and in fact
was lower in real dollars than in the days before 1973. Lewis worked with the
congressional committees which wanted more money to spend and members who
had projects in their states and districts they wanted it spent on. Senate Majority
Leader Howard Baker walked across to Tip O'Neill's office on the south side of
the Capitol and got his support—and the country got and quietly accepted a higher
gas tax. The Republican administration which had vowed it would never raise
taxes had now raised taxes.

As the new Congress assembled in January 1983, the National Commission on
Social Security, deadlocked the month before, issued its report. The problem the
commission was addressing, as in 1977, was that the promises made by politicians
were proving impossible for the taxpayers to fulfull. The commission was chaired
by Alan Greenspan, former head of the Council of Economic Advisers; its members
included Robert Ball, former Social Security administrator and one of the architects
of Social Security almost from its beginning, Senators Dole and Moynihan, and
Congressman Barber Conable. Their essential compromise was to raise Social
Security taxes and at a set date in the future raise the retirement age (the age at
which workers could retire with full Social Security benefits). Agreed on by the
experts, this compromise was passed by both houses of Congress by April. The
only difficult moment came when Claude Pepper, the Democrats' hero of 1982
and always an advocate of increased benefits without much regard to the resources
to pay for them, opposed the rise in the retirement age. Pepper had himself pushed

through the law eliminating mandatory retirement ages for most jobs, so that almost no one could be forced to retire; but he also recognized that most workers, given the choice, preferred to retire sooner than later; and with the clarity of a man who had come to Congress as a New Dealer the year after Social Security was passed, he understood that raising the retirement age was tantamount to cutting future benefits. But O'Neill, who had just finished using the Social Security issue against the Republicans, this time sided against Pepper and with Jake Pickle, the congressman from Lyndon Johnson's old district and chairman of the Social Security subcommittee, who prevailed on the floor. The Democrats who had campaigned on stopping cuts in Social Security now had agreed to a cut in Social Security.

"What this comes down to," Moynihan remembered one participant saying at one of the Social Security Commission meetings, "is whether we can govern." Moynihan himself later wrote in response, "And we can, you know. Americans are pretty good at governing."[1] Already, even before the trough of the recession, confidence in the effectiveness of government at solving problems had been rising in 1982 above the levels of 1974–80.[2] Part of this rise was a tribute to Reagan for getting his program, however imperfect, through Congress; it was a tribute as well to his handling of the PATCO strike, when those trying to hold the government hostage, with the same kinds of non-negotiable demands and lists of grievances as so many other hostage-takers real and figurative of the 1970s, this time failed; it was a tribute to a political process which was finally producing rational and predictable, even if not entirely desirable, results.

It is plain enough in retrospect that the trough of recession was reached in December 1982, and that the rise to recovery was steep in the early months of 1983. The gross national product, almost stagnant for several years, started rising noticeably, as shown in the following table:

Year	GNP[3] $Billion	% Change from Previous Year
1978	3,021	
1979	3,106	+3
1980	3,132	+1
1981	3,175	+1
1982	3,115	−2
1983	3,231	+4
1984	3,446	+7

Unemployment declined rapidly; and, even more important for a country experiencing vast increases in its work force, the number of jobs started to grow. Inflation, once raging so high, had diminished sharply by the end of 1981. By almost every objective measure, things were improving.[4] The economy and the political system were showing resilience, solving old problems and generating new initiatives with a suppleness and a creativity missing in the years just before 1981. Leading politicians, despite differing attitudes and values, compromised in ways which hurt their short-term political interest for almost no other reason than that they thought such compromise was in the national interest. The Republicans agreed to a gas tax and the Democrats, by going along, gave them political cover; the Democrats agreed to a Social Security benefit cut and the Republicans, by going along, gave them political cover.

Yet even as they were looking at the same events and, in some cases, reaching compromises on hitherto uncompromisable issues, politicians of the two parties were seeing the political landscape very differently. For the Democrats, each new development in the 1983–84 political season was a harbinger of the end of what one of the country's shrewdest journalists would call "the Reagan detour"[5] and the rebirth of the Democratic coalition. For the Republicans, each new development was a confirmation of the success of their Reagan revolution and its status as the wave of the future. Many Democrats, with their victories in 1982 and their long years of congressional majorities, were serenely confident, while many Republicans, aware of their party's long weakness and its continuing disadvantage in party identification, not even sure until fall 1983 that Ronald Reagan was going to run again, were edgy and nervous.

II

About the macroeconomy almost everyone in public life was mystified. In the 1970s inflation and stagnation had occurred at the same time, even though Keynesian economics said such "stagflation" was impossible. By the end of the 1970s, Keynesian-trained economists suggested that no policy alternatives could produce the results which the Keynesians claimed credit for in the middle 1960s—sustained growth and low inflation—without producing politically unacceptable side effects.[6] Now in the 1980s Keynesians could not explain why inflation collapsed and why the big Reagan budget deficit did not immediately produce a surge of recovery. On the right, both supply-siders and monetarists were busy producing excuses for why the economy did not behave as they suggested it would: the supply-siders had to explain why revenues sagged after the tax cuts, and monetarists had to show why the Federal Reserve had once again botched what they considered its one task of producing a steady growth in the money supply. Politically, the Republicans were stuck, for better or worse, with the results of the policies decreed by Ronald Reagan. The Democrats, convinced that American politics revolved around economics and that they had a natural advantage on that ground, cast about for a plausible way to frame the issue.

What they came upon in 1982 and 1983 was industrial policy. If they could not plausibly claim to know how to produce prosperity through manipulation of fiscal policy, and if their increasing criticism of the Reagan deficits deterred them from proposing new spending, they still might claim that by providing critical assistance to key industries or companies, government could create jobs and build national productivity. Stimulated by Robert Reich of Harvard, former vice president and 1984 Democratic front-runner Walter Mondale started to advocate "a government–business–labor partnership designed to restructure basic industries and to promote innovation in high technology."[7] The problem with this approach was that it was not clear how the government would pick winners and winnow out losers. Reich was an admirer of the government's rescue of Chrysler; but as he pointed out, it might well not have succeeded except that it was seen by all parties as an extraordinary and distasteful exercise.[8] If government were to routinize and sanction such bailouts, neither the companies nor the government would likely be under such tight discipline, and there might be many bankruptcies. No one could fail to notice that most of the industries—steel, autos, textiles—which came looking for restructuring and protection were older businesses, evidently past their prime years of growth in this country, hoping in many cases to maintain high wages and dividends despite a lack of demand for their products. Such "sunset industries" typically had vocal and effective political constituencies and could squeeze a great deal of money out of government. "Sunrise industries," in contrast, were too busy growing to spend much time lobbying.[9] Almost no one was comfortable with the idea of trusting the government to make not only rational but shrewd investment judgments. So the idea of industrial policy, for a moment so attractive, started to fall of its own weight; in a country where growth seemed to come mostly from robust small units, it did not make sense to subsidize doddering big units. Little was heard of it in the campaign after the late months of 1983.

Education was another issue on which Democrats believed they had an historic advantage. In the argument over whether the federal government should spend more or less on education, the Democrats always came out on the popular side—more. For the 1976 election, the National Education Association, the nation's biggest teacher union, had organized its members to participate in the presidential election process; the NEA's young leaders were from Michigan, home state of Walter Reuther, and they seemed to be modeling their political activity on that of Reuther's United Auto Workers. Their great cause was a separate U.S. Department of Education. They were successful: Jimmy Carter was nominated, with great help from their members, and elected; the Department of Education was created; teachers' salaries continued to rise even as the economy faltered; NEA members helped Carter scotch Edward Kennedy's challenge in 1980. There was one respect in which the NEA's efforts were not successful, however: American schoolchildren were demonstrably learning less than they used to. Scores on the Scholastic Aptitude Test (college boards), which had reached a peak in 1963,[10] were bottoming out in the early 1980s. In the southern states, where political leaders and voters had long understood that local educational levels were below national norms, the middle 1970s had seen a surfacing in the political process of a demand for educational reform—for competency testing of students and teachers, for greater accountability of teachers and administrators, for merit pay for teachers, for greater stress on acquisition of basic skills and maintenance of basic discipline. Elected as educational reformers between 1976 and 1979 were such governors as

Jim Hunt in North Carolina, Richard Riley in South Carolina, Lamar Alexander in Tennessee, Bill Clinton in Arkansas, and William Winter in Mississippi. All except Alexander were, like most successful state politicians in the South, Democrats. But the spirit of their educational reforms did not penetrate to Democratic or governmental circles in Washington.

Then, in April 1983, the National Commission on Excellence in Education issued "A Nation at Risk," a report strongly criticizing public education very much along the lines of the educational reformers in the South; rather than discovering anew the problems it decried, it described for Washington what had been apparent in many of the state capitals for almost a decade. It deplored "a rising tide of mediocrity" and warned that poor education "threatens our very future as a nation and a people." The impulse of the Democrats and of the leaders of the national education establishment, like Terrel Bell, whom Reagan had unaccountably appointed education secretary (for he seemed to share none of Reagan's views) was to call for more spending; and the commission did mention that. But the thrust of its report, in tandem with two other reports issued that spring, was not to raise teachers' salaries but to improve educational policy through such means as more stress on basics, merit pay (opposed fiercely by the NEA), and stimulating reforms by local and state school boards, not the federal government. The report provided a vivid example of the contrasting political atmospheres of the early 1980s and the late 1960s: then, in the wake of the civil rights revolution, there was widespread agreement that the way to improve public policy was to centralize it in the hands of experts in Washington; now, in the wake of the failures of the 1970s, there was widespread agreement that the big unit of the federal government was a clumsy and incompetent policymaker and that it was better to trust the innovations and improvisations of small units closer and more responsive to the people they served. Walter Mondale, on the verge of his presidential candidacy, immediately proposed spending $11 billion more in federal money. But Ronald Reagan, in appearances crafted by White House aide Michael Deaver, emphasized his support for the report's other recommendations and in a few days raised his ratings on education (as measured by his own pollster, Richard Wirthlin) from 42%–48% negative to 52%–41% positive.[11]

III

For Democrats in the 1980s Chicago was still a special city, the home of the party's sturdiest political machine, the site of the party's bloodiest and most divisive convention, the city which works and the city where everybody seems to be on the take. By 1983 the Chicago Democratic machine was more myth than reality. It had been held together for 20 years longer than most other urban machines by the special talents and ascetic abstention from self-enrichment of Richard J. Daley, mayor from April 1955 until December 1976. But once Daley was gone, the Cook County Democratic Committee and the Chicago Board of Aldermen were nothing more than nests of distrustful, ambitious, sometimes venal politicians with little respect for the city's civic institutions and little regard for its history. Daley's designated successor, a lawyer named Michael Bilandic from his own 11th ward,[12] had been elected in April 1977; but after failing to clear the streets after a snowstorm he was beaten in the February 1979 primary by a one-time Daley appointee (and like so many of those, the child of another machine veteran), Jane Byrne.

In office, Byrne was tough-talking and indecisive (a bad combination in any business), switching from Carter to Kennedy in the 1980 presidential race and making enemies at home. In the February 1983 primary she was opposed by the late mayor's son, Cook County State's Attorney Richard M. Daley, and by Congressman Harold Washington, a black from the city's South Side with considerable talents but a checkered political past, who had won only 11% of the vote in the primary four years before. National politicians became involved in the race, with Kennedy backing Byrne, Mondale backing Daley, and Jesse Jackson—a one-time junior associate of Martin Luther King; later head of his own, ultimately insolvent, black self-help organization, Operation PUSH; one of the leaders of the protest delegation which had unseated Daley's organization at the 1972 convention in Miami Beach—backing Washington. As the campaign went on, Byrne and Daley were splitting the white vote, while Washington was making an emotional connection with black voters and an intellectual connection with some small number of liberal whites. With blacks casting about 40% of the primary votes, Washington won the three-way race; on victory night he stood on the podium with Jackson and proclaimed, "It's our turn now!" In the bungalow wards whites were terrified. Some were afraid of losing their city jobs; but more were afraid that blacks would move into their neighborhoods, that black criminals would be roaming their streets, that city government services, including police, would simply stop. Their fears intensified even as Washington went on to win the general election. The Republican nominee was inept, while Washington, a well-educated, articulate, and pleasant man, won as much as half the vote in some of the lakefront wards, full of well-educated professionals, young singles, and Jews.

Among blacks in Chicago and around the country, on the other hand, Washington's victories produced a surge of delight and pride that the biggest machine in the country had been defeated by their candidate and that Mayor Daley's place had been taken by a black, and a sense that anything—even the election of a black president—was possible. Never mind that the machine had already crumbled and that black mayors had been elected in major cities as long as 16 years before: Chicago carried a special emotional charge. And even though Washington had kept him at arm's length since primary night, the immediate beneficiary of this change was Jesse Jackson. He had never sought or held public office; the organization he had long headed had few accomplishments; at forty-one, he made his living by giving speeches. But Jackson did have a political philosophy and some considerable public experience. Too young to have had any major role in the civil rights revolution, he had nevertheless been at King's side just moments before he was shot in Memphis in April 1968; the next day Jackson had appeared on television in Chicago wearing what he said was a shirt stained with King's blood.

On issues Jackson took his lead from King, or at least the side of King which thought that America must embrace socialism because blacks cannot achieve equality under capitalism, and which saw kindred spirits and ideas in the anticolonial movements and new governments in Africa and other parts of the Third World—in Jackson's case, this included Communist Cuba and Nicaragua, the Arab states and the Palestinians, but excluded Israel. Yet on civil rights, Jackson went a step beyond King, as others were doing in the years just after 1968. Whereas King had always stressed equal rights for all, Jackson demanded specific gains for blacks, regardless of the effect on others. While the mainline civil rights organizations advocated racial quotas gingerly and tried to avoid the term, Jackson's PUSH threatened boycotts against big companies which didn't give blacks a certain number of jobs (or give Jackson a public commitment that they would); to some this resembled a shakedown operation, and a *New Republic* cover showed Jackson over the caption, "I have a scheme." Throughout his 1983–84 presidential campaign, Jackson insisted against mountains of evidence that blacks were just as oppressed as they had been 20 years before, as if the movement King led had made no progress. Noting that Washington had won the primary with a minority of the vote in a split field and that black North Carolina legislator Mickey Michaux had lost a runoff for Congress in 1982 after leading in the first primary, Jackson argued that runoff primaries—that is, requiring a party's nominee to have the support of a majority of its voters—were unfair or even unconstitutional. He also complained of the Democrats' threshold rule which prevented candidates for a party's presidential nomination from winning delegates in districts where they got less than 20% of the primary vote. He seems to have gotten the idea that he could somehow get the Democratic nomination with a plurality of the convention vote and then as the candidate of the majority party win the general election and become president of the United States. In October 1983 he declared his candidacy in an interview on CBS's *60 Minutes,* the top-rated program on television.

IV

Jackson's announcement had to share the television spotlight that month with two other major events. American Marines had been landed in Lebanon in August 1982, after partial withdrawal of the Israeli troops who had, despite U.S. disapproval, marched into the riven country and captured its nominal capital in June. The Marines' mission was ill-defined and open-ended. Hostile forces destroyed the U.S. embassy in Beirut in April 1983, killing 67. Then on October 23 an explosive-laden truck crashed into the ill-protected Marine barracks and killed 241 American troops. This seemed a smashing defeat for a Reagan policy. Yet two days later, coming downstairs to his office in the early morning hours in his pajamas, Reagan ordered a U.S. invasion of the Caribbean island nation of Grenada, where one group of Communist leaders had ousted another and were said to be menacing American medical students. That explanation was of course a pretext: Reagan and his advisers wanted to get rid of a Communist government in the Caribbean and were taking advantage of an uprising there to do so. Many congressional Democrats, steeped in the history of the Vietnam conflict, issued vituperative denunciations of the attack until a few days later, after a returning American student kissed the tarmac at the airport, when it became clear the invasion was overwhelmingly popular in the United States (and in Grenada, too). Not long after, the remaining Marines would be withdrawn quietly from Lebanon, their undefined mission unfulfilled. But for most Americans what would continue to matter is that the United States had finally rolled back the tide of Communist conquest, even if it was only in a tiny, backward Caribbean island.

While Reagan was winning the approval of the large majority of Americans by using force, the Democratic presidential contenders, in debates in Cambridge, Massachusetts, and Iowa, were seeking the approval of small numbers of antiwar and antinuclear party activists by renouncing the use of force. Arms control had become a kind of mantra for the Democrats, with positions on the nuclear freeze and negotiating terms with the Soviets repeated as if by rote; it was widely supposed not only by Democrats but by journalists that the Reagan administration's failure to secure an arms control agreement with the Soviets was a political liability. But the arms control arguments were a cynical exercise, for Mondale and most of the others believed that the freeze was at best symbolic and was nonsense as public policy. But Iowa, site of the first contest on the 1984 calendar, had a Democratic caucus electorate which was almost unanimously dovish, and merciless in its repudiation of any candidate who deviated from the mantra.

V

The leading candidate among the Democrats was Walter Mondale, who this time had the ambition and drive he had lacked when he dropped out of the race in December 1974. He brought to the contest a level of experience and maturity seldom seen in a non-incumbent. Carter had given him access to the Oval Office and presidential decision-making which no vice president had ever been given before, and Mondale clearly had made good use of it. In debates and discussions he showed a mastery of facts and a mastery over his rivals which were impressive. His strategy was to win the nomination with the support of the big units of the Democratic party. He began with enthusiastic support from the NEA. By November 1983 he had received the first formal pre-convention endorsement ever issued by the AFL–CIO, many of whose constituent unions had already supported him. Major officeholders and big fund-raisers supported him in large numbers. Mondale had left St. Paul for Washington in December 1964, as a thirty-six-year-old state attorney general appointed to fill Hubert Humphrey's place in the Senate; he had come to the capital at a time when the big units of government, business, and labor were at the peak of their power and effectiveness. Ordinary people in need of help, he believed, were represented by the lobbyists and operatives he knew in the capital; and the endorsements of these insiders, he believed, could be transformed into support from the many individuals they faithfully represented. Mondale had gone to college and been a young lawyer at a time when most articulate opinion in his community was Republican, when his professional peers routinely denounced labor unions and argued that they did not really represent their members. He had resisted those arguments, obeying instead a cardinal rule that the power of unions must never be acknowledged and they must never be criticized in public. So he disregarded advice that most Americans now mistrusted big units and their operatives;[13] and in an Iowa debate he refused to indicate any areas where he disagreed with unions, even though he was well aware of some.

In fall 1983 his strategy was working well. He lost a straw poll in Wisconsin to Alan Cranston, but a seventy-year-old senator with orange-dyed hair was not going to win the nomination. He failed to get the publicity John Glenn reaped from the October release of the film *The Right Stuff*, in which his career as an astronaut was portrayed; but he bested Glenn in a one-on-one exchange in a debate soon after, a blow from which Glenn's candidacy never recovered. His support from big institutions was criticized by Gary Hart, but Hart's fund raising was limited and his organization desultory. The Jackson candidacy was costing Mondale some votes; but he was still winning endorsements from prominent blacks like Detroit Mayor Coleman Young, Philadelphia Mayor Wilson Goode, and Alabama Democratic Conference head Joe Reed. In retrospect it seems plain that Mondale's strategy was crafted for an America which no longer was, and that his basic thrust on issues—from the nuclear freeze to macroeconomics to education—was not in the direction which the public was going or wanted to go. But in fall 1983, when it was not apparent how strong the economic recovery was, when it still seemed plausible to dismiss the Reagan foreign policy as provocative and ineffective, when it seemed possible that Mondale could speedily dispose of his Democratic opposition, when it was by no means certain that a seventy-three-year-old opponent could navigate through a campaign year without serious mistakes, the prospects for the Mondale candidacy seemed as fine as a sunlit fall morning on the Minnesota plains.

VI

Ronald Reagan's campaign was making less news: he was, after all, the first unopposed candidate for a major-party nomination since Dwight Eisenhower in 1956.[14] But his campaign was working hard nonetheless. Commanded by White House Chief of Staff James Baker, run by operatives Ed Rollins, the son of a California blue-collar worker, and Lee Atwater, an upcountry South Carolina blues band veteran, the committee was raising vast sums of money and creating a get-out-the-vote organization unparalleled in recent times. If Jesse Jackson was threatening to register black voters, the Republicans, in cooperation with Jerry Falwell and backers of Jesse Helms, would register white fundamentalist and other evangelical Christians who opposed liberal Democrats and all their works. The Reagan organization was also reading the polls and realizing that as the economy recovered their candidate was rising slowly but steadily as well. The light may have seemed a bit dim to Democrats and many in the press, but the soft, fuzzy light of a movieset morning seemed clearly visible to the Reagan team.

59

-》》 《《-

Celebration

T here was no one magic moment," Nancy Reagan told reporter Laurence
Barrett. Over the fall of 1983 she and her husband talked about, in Barrett's
words, "continuity in office, about the inability to get enough done in four years,
about the prospects for victory. By Thanksgiving, the issue wasn't really in doubt."
It was a personal decision: "the political advisers were kept distant, though they
knew by then what the President would do."[1] This "great communicator" who
had established a bond of cheery intimacy with millions of his fellow citizens was
not on intimate terms with any of his top appointees or with the millionaire
businessmen he socialized with in Palm Springs every New Year's or even with
his own four children; his one intimate colleague was his wife, and it was with
her that he reached his decision to run for a second term in 1984. Administration
insiders have portrayed Reagan as ignorant of basic facts, disconnected from events,
and impervious to their own good advice.[2] But in this as in other big decisions,
in deciding to oppose big tax increases and to send troops into Grenada, in choosing
the words for his summation in the debate with Jimmy Carter or to reassure the
nation after he was shot, it was Ronald Reagan himself who gave the orders and
made the decisions and his aides, however they might snicker at him in chats with
reporters or over Washington dinner tables, who followed them.

In January 1984, Reagan's job performance rating was 55% positive—a good
mark, but not an overpowering one, for a 55%–45% margin does not quite count
as a landslide for an incumbent president. Working more strongly for Reagan were
the underlying feelings of the electorate. For almost the first time since the question
was devised, more Americans felt the nation was going in the right direction than
believed it was pretty seriously off on the wrong track. The fears that nuclear
war was about to break out were dissolving now that Reagan had been in office
three years without starting a war; the fears that the economy would never again
yield significant growth were dissolving amid the plain evidence that it was once
again expanding. The world seemed to be working not as the liberal Democrats
said it did but as the Reagan Republicans said it would. Reagan seemed to have
a solid hold on the 155 electoral votes in the South and on another 70 in the Rocky
Mountains and in odd corners (Alaska, Indiana, Kansas, Nebraska, New Hampshire) elsewhere, leaving him only 45 short of a majority. California alone would
give him 47 votes, and he had always carried California handsomely. The one

637

major threat to his candidacy was his age. He was a seventy-three-year-old man who had suffered a gunshot wound at seventy, who forgot names and got details wrong at times, whose attention span seemed limited and whose capacity to speak extemporaneously with force was not what it had been a few years before. Of course Reagan would not campaign actively; incumbent presidents never do. But a serious mistake in public or any sign that his health was shaky could imperil a candidacy which was otherwise very strong.

Meanwhile, the dynamic of the Democrats' delegate selection process was continuing to drive them away from issue positions and strategies appealing to most voters. In December 1983, Jesse Jackson traveled to Syria to secure the release of an American airman shot down over that country; the Syrian government, with every incentive to elevate the chances of an American politician sympathetic to the Palestinian cause and leftist Third World leaders, turned him over to Jackson. In the Iowa caucuses in February 1984, Walter Mondale, who had been cultivating the state for years from over the border in Minnesota, got 49% of the vote; but that very impressive triumph in an eight-candidate field was given not much more publicity than the 16.5% second-place finish by the theretofore faltering Gary Hart.[3] Suddenly Hart was a serious challenger in New Hampshire, the one state where he had a serious organization, a state which with its aversion to taxes and its market-driven prosperity was perhaps the single most unfavorable venue in the nation for Walter Mondale. Hart was positioning himself as a Democrat more open to market solutions than Mondale, not seeking the endorsements of the old institutions or big units, a bit more skeptical of what government could do by fiat, and at least a little more open to liberal cultural values—a Trend Democrat, in a phrase first used at the time.[4] This was not as new a stance for a Democratic contender as Hart suggested and many observers thought: Eugene McCarthy, Jimmy Carter, and Jerry Brown had run as less interventionist on the economy and more liberation-minded on cultural issues than the Democrats exemplified by Mondale's mentor Hubert Humphrey. Nor was this stance the result of the coaching of former McGovern and Carter pollster Patrick Caddell, as many (most of them prompted by Caddell) claimed.[5] Hart could legitimately claim some original ideas, mostly untranslated into policy; but the stance he took, far from being original and politically daring, was actually derivative and probably better calculated to win the Democratic nomination than the more traditional stance of Mondale.

Between Iowa and New Hampshire, Jackson ran into a problem which removed him as a serious competitor for the nomination if he had ever been one. Jackson's support of the Palestinian cause and hostile attitude toward Israel had created a divide between him and many American Jews; and in a story on that subject printed February 13, the *Washington Post*'s Rick Atkinson wrote, "In private conversations with reporters, Jackson has referred to Jews as 'Hymie' and to New York as 'Hymietown.' " The quotation, in the thirty-seventh paragraph of a fifty-two-paragraph story, was not much noticed. On February 18, however, a *Post* editorial attacked Jackson for using the language;[6] and suddenly, just 10 days before the

New Hampshire primary, he was put on the defensive. The day before the primary, he finally apologized in a Manchester synagogue, but not before Black Muslim minister Louis Farrakhan had made threatening remarks about Jackson's critics while standing by Jackson's side; later in the campaign Farrakhan referred to Judaism as a "gutter religion," but for weeks Jackson allowed him to provide bodyguards for him and introduce him at rallies. In these circumstances it appeared to many voters that the candidate whose race had been the object of the most vicious bigotry in American history was in some smaller but still disturbing way a bigot himself. Before the "Hymietown" remark was publicized, Jackson was receiving the support of 16% of Democrats in the *Boston Globe* poll in almost all-white New Hampshire; on primary day his support was down to 5%. His early appeal was probably greatest to young voters, eager to support the first serious black presidential candidate[7] but repelled by any sign of bigotry; perhaps their votes contributed to Hart's 37%–28% victory—another way in which Jackson hurt Mondale's candidacy. In any case, not until California, on the last day of the primary season, did Jackson receive more than a handful of votes from whites.

Hart had a problem of his own: his campaign organization, though small, was already deeply riven by feuds and rivalries which inevitably produced negative publicity just as the candidate was getting known by the public. Between New Hampshire and the "Super Tuesday" primaries in mid-March there were just nine weeknight newscasts, and there were only four more between Super Tuesday and Illinois a week later. That schedule meant that voters in these primaries would receive only a few bits of information beforehand about candidates like Hart or Jackson, whom they had never heard of or known only a little about before the campaign began. Hart was helped when they saw him in New Hampshire in a lumberjack's shirt throwing an ax into a tree—a shot quickly incorporated into his ads—but he was hurt when he promised the weekend before Illinois to stop running TV spots critical of Cook County Democratic Chairman Edward Vrdolyak and then was unable to do so. Mondale began running an ad showing a red telephone ringing, with an announcer asking ominously which candidate viewers would want to have answering that phone—representing the hotline from the leader of the Soviet Union—when it rang.

The ad's implicit argument that Mondale was more experienced and steadier in crisis than Hart was corroborated by the course of the campaign. Hart's organization feuded openly and spent itself into debt, while Mondale's, aside from a flap over the legality of separate fund raising by committees purporting to support the campaigns of Mondale delegates, rebounded smartly from its sharp defeat in New Hampshire and its totally unexpected loss in the Maine caucuses days later to win the Alabama and, by a narrow margin, the Georgia primaries on Super Tuesday, March 13. Even though Hart won easily the same day in the bigger states of Massachusetts and Florida, the verdict was that Mondale had shown that a Hart victory was not inevitable and had in the process eliminated John Glenn as a candidate and shown he could split the black vote with Jackson. A week later

Mondale beat Hart and Jackson 40%–35%–21% in Illinois. Despite some later Hart victories, including upsets in Ohio and Indiana and a narrow popular vote victory which produced a landslide victory in delegates in California (because Hart narrowly carried many congressional districts), Mondale's victories in Illinois, New York, Pennsylvania, and some smaller states, together with his solid delegate wins in most caucus states, allowed him to stand up in St. Paul at 11:59 A.M. June 6, one day after the final primaries, and make the claim, backed up by United Press International delegate counter David Lawsky, that he had a majority of votes for the nomination. Hart and Jackson nonetheless carried their fights to the July convention in San Francisco.

II

Ronald Reagan spent June 6, 1984, in Normandy, France, commemorating the landings on the beaches 40 years before when American and Allied troops had taken that first risky and bloody step on the road to liberating Western Europe from Hitler and the Nazis. Mondale's campaign manager, watching in St. Paul as Mondale delegate-trackers were getting the last commitments they needed for a majority, noted that Reagan was receiving about 30 minutes' coverage on NBC's *Today* show, an extraordinary figure; "here it was the end of the long primary trail," reporters Jack Germond and Jules Witcover paraphrased his feelings, "and Reagan, who had not had to endure it, was grabbing all the coverage."[8] But this perspective was a myopic one. Gathered before Reagan as he made his speech were veterans who had waded and parachuted onto these beaches when they were young men; 10 years hence, at the next anniversary, many of them would not be there. Reagan read the letter of one daughter of a veteran who had recently died, looking up at her as tears filled many eyes. The camera angles, selected by Michael Deaver, were indeed beautiful; but the Normandy commemoration was moving not because of how it was staged but because of what it recalled. In the ceremonial role he filled so well, Reagan was remembering in behalf of the whole country a moment in history with reverberations greater than any candidate's primary victories.

Reagan's lack of opposition in the primaries maximized his opportunities to look presidential and his campaign managers' chances to build strong fund-raising and voter registration operations. Against Mondale in the polls, he had been running below 50% in January 1984,[9] but he had risen above that magic level in almost all polls in February and March Gallup, which polled most frequently, showed little subsequent movement in the race. Reagan had led Mondale 52%–42% in February, before Iowa and New Hampshire; from then up through D-Day, Reagan had been running in the 50%–54% range (the same range as his job rating in this period) and Mondale in the 41%–45% range[10]—numbers suggesting a final result of about 55%–45%.

III

Though in retrospect the election was over by June 6, the Democratic nominating process was not. Two items of suspense remained: the vice presidential nomination and the performance of the major speakers at the convention. The easy choice for vice president would have been Gary Hart; but Mondale evidently decided that Hart would not be a good president and so, for essentially patriotic reasons, put himself in a difficult spot. He organized a series of visits by vice presidential possibilities to his house in North Oaks, Minnesota, outside St. Paul, just as Jimmy Carter had interviewed potential candidates, including Mondale, eight years before in Plains, Georgia. By declining Mondale's invitation, New York Governor Mario Cuomo and Arkansas Senator Dale Bumpers took themselves out of this process. Of those who went to North Oaks, Texas Senator Lloyd Bentsen was derided by many as a good, gray, white middle-aged man, as was Massachusetts Governor Michael Dukakis; Philadelphia Mayor Wilson Goode and Kentucky Governor Martha Layne Collins, both first elected in November 1983, were interviewed in transparent efforts to include women and minorities; so were two more women of some talent but little national stature, New York Congresswoman Geraldine Ferraro and San Francisco Mayor Dianne Feinstein; so were another black mayor, Thomas Bradley of Los Angeles, and a Hispanic one, thirty-eight-year-old Henry Cisneros of San Antonio. Mondale engaged in this farcical procession because he knew that of the half the delegates who were required by party rules to be women a large majority were feminist, more committed to womanhood than to his candidacy, and that Democratic delegates, overwhelmingly liberal, wanted something other than a "conventional" choice. On July 1 the National Organization for Women demanded a female nominee. Ferraro, asked whether she would let her name be placed in nomination if Mondale selected a white male like Bentsen, refused to say no—and was not cut from the list by the ordinarily loyalty-conscious Mondale.

Finally, in the week before the convention, Ferraro was Mondale's choice. The list of female Democrats with any record in office was thin, and her record in fact would not have gotten her near consideration for national office if she had been a man. She had been elected to Congress in 1978 after a stint as an assistant district attorney in Queens, specializing in domestic relations cases. In the House she had risen as a team player, loyal to the leadership, adept at articulating reasons for supporting positions others decided on, but showing no particular interest in or flair for any substantive issues; she had as limited a background in foreign policy and defense as any member of Congress. Her personal life—Italian-American roots, a successful husband, three attractive children, experience as both a homemaker and a professional—seemed attractive. As a candidate she spoke in the fast tempos and with the sharp sense of humor and the on-target ripostes of the native New Yorker: when the Mississippi commissioner of agriculture asked her if she could bake blueberry muffins, she responded, "Yes. Can you?" Her strengths as well as her sex commended her to her audience in the hall in San Francisco. In

America at large her weaknesses were more apparent; and on balance she contributed no strength to Mondale, who would have been the choice of ideological feminists no matter whom he picked.

IV

By 1984 conventions had long since ceased to be deliberative bodies. The delegates sat in their chairs during sessions, waiting for signals on how to vote to be relayed from their candidate's delegation leader, who received his signals over a special telephone from the candidate's command trailer; television viewers at home had a better idea of what was happening and as much chance to affect it as did rank-and-file delegates. The post-1968 reforms and proliferation of primaries, together with the institutionalization of the delegate count, cheap long-distance telephone rates, and frequent airplane flights, meant that information which used to be communicated and deals which once could only be made at the convention could now be communicated and made much earlier in the process. The conventions by 1984 were simply sets for television programs in which the winning candidate tried to present the best case for his candidacy and the losing candidates and other politicians tried to advance their causes before an audience which, unfortunately for them, was decreasing in numbers.

In fact, in San Francisco both Ferraro and Mondale were overshadowed by the featured speakers at the convention. The first was Cuomo, son of an Italian immigrant who had opened a grocery store in South Jamaica, Queens, in 1933 (displaying optimism worthy of a Ronald Reagan, who graduated from college that year); in 1982, after several political reverses, the younger Cuomo had been elected governor by narrow margins over New York City Mayor Edward Koch in the primary and supply-sider and drugstore millionaire Lewis Lehrman in the general election. The short-term political content of Cuomo's speech was not convincing: he talked of two Americas, concentrating on the one which wasn't doing well economically, when most voters were. But his longer vision, celebrating the achievements of the immigrants like his father, asserting that whatever Americans' achievements they were "standing on the shoulders of giants," struck a responsive chord in a nation more than 50% of whose citizens could trace at least one ancestor from the great immigrations of 1840–1924.

The other stirring speaker at the convention was Jackson, featured in prime time, confessing error and asking forgiveness for his "Hymietown" comment (although he didn't mention it explicitly), sweating profusely on camera and declaring (inaccurately, considering the delegate count) "Our time is come. Our time is come." Jackson's appearance Tuesday actually drew a larger TV audience than Mondale's acceptance speech Thursday. Mondale was behind in the polls; he knew that Reagan was universally known and that he was rather well known and well respected for a challenger, which is to say that there was not much room for change in the standings if all other things remained equal; so he took a gamble. "Mr. Reagan will raise taxes," said Mondale, "and so will I. He won't tell you.

I just did." A fine gamble if the voters believe the conventional wisdom of Keynesian economists that taxes must be raised to cut the deficit; a poor gamble if the voters do not. For the next week the Reagan campaign dithered over whether to declare a tax increase absolutely unthinkable. Finally Ronald Reagan, unworried about what Washington insiders would say and determined to prevent tax rises, did make that commitment; and the Reagan organization started running against Mondale as a tax-raiser.

V

On the six-lane divided El Camino Real, with the Town and Country Shopping Center on one side and the tall regal palms of Stanford University on the other, the crowd was gathering and buzzing with excitement. Ed Zschau, who as a teacher at Stanford Business School and a young computer entrepreneur had been dismayed by the student rebellions of the late 1960s and early 1970s, now was a Republican congressman watching Stanford summer school students and neighbors from heavily Democratic Palo Alto and the culturally liberal suburbs of Los Altos and Menlo Park gather to cheer an athlete carrying a burning torch, which he handed off to others to carry for short distances, on his way to the Summer Olympics in Los Angeles. Palo Alto was part of the 9,100-mile path of the Olympic torch criss-crossing the country, a part of the Olympics celebration which was little noted by the national media at first but attracted spontaneous cheering crowds all over America.[11]

The Soviet Union, in response, it said, to lack of security in Los Angeles, had announced in 1983 that it would not send a team to the games, as the United States had boycotted the Moscow Olympics four years before in protest of the Soviets' 1979 invasion of Afghanistan. The excuse was transparent. The games were being held in what had become the number one immigrant destination in the world, a metropolis rapidly closing in on New York as the largest urban area and largest manufacturing center in the country and the richest and most productive city in the world and the home for almost all of his adult life of the incumbent president of the United States. It was obvious that the Soviets feared mass defections when their athletes got their first glimpse of this paradise. Although the opening ceremonies, broadcast to a midsummer audience far larger than watched either of the political conventions, featured just one sentence from Ronald Reagan, they were a celebration of national pride the likes of which the United States had not seen since the bicentennial of 1976. That celebration had come when the government had just been rid of a criminal president and when confidence in American institutions had been scathingly low; nevertheless, the incumbent Republican president had echoed the pride of the bicentennial celebrations in his acceptance speech and campaign advertising and had nearly won after starting out far behind his Democratic opponent. This celebration (planned and executed by Peter Ueberroth, a former travel agency head and a fraternity brother of Michael Deaver at San Jose State University, with the cooperation of Thomas Bradley, who had himself tried out for the Olympics of 1936) struck a chord in a nation which had a president most of its citizens liked and which had been turning more confident and positive about its institutions even before its economy began to revive and grow. Normandy and the Olympics, more than any purely political events, set the tone for the political year of 1984, honoring the American past and celebrating the American present; and they worked inevitably in favor of a president who himself was a link with that past[12] and who could claim plausibly to have inspired by his acts and his example at least some of the optimist and positive feeling of the present.

VI

The television show which resulted from the Republicans' national convention at Dallas was dominated not by the candidates' rivals and allies, as the Democrats' San Francisco convention had been, but by the candidate himself and the ideas his managers wanted to present. Footage of Normandy was shown even as memories of the Olympics were fresh; the "morning in America" ads aired beginning in May, when the regular television season was finishing up, were echoed in the form and content. Many in the media and among Democrats decried these as mindless appeals to the emotions, but like all poetry they worked only if their minimal words and images evoked the viewer's own genuine experiences and emotions; those who thought that Reagan's ads were manipulating the electorate should have asked whether they would have worked for Jimmy Carter in 1980. The only events with any effect on opinion in the fall campaign were the presidential debates. By now debates had become an expected enough part of the campaign that even a seventy-three-year-old incumbent (or perhaps especially a seventy-three-year-old incumbent) dared not spurn them as Lyndon Johnson had in 1964 and Richard Nixon had in 1968 and 1972; like Ford in 1976 (and unlike Carter, who agreed only late in the game, when he was behind in the polls), Reagan agreed early to debate his opponent, who was, though not theatrical, one of the most articulate and best-informed of American politicians.

In the October 7 debate in Louisville, Reagan was hesitant, stumbling, fuzzy in his recollections; in his summation at the end he told a rambling story about driving up the Pacific Coast Highway which never reached the conclusion. Mondale, in contrast, was not only articulate but magisterial, granting Reagan's strong points respectfully but disagreeing with him forcefully. Public polls did not show much faltering in the president's support; but his campaign's internal polling—the cumulative results of the most recent three days' interviews of 2,000 respondents, which Richard Wirthlin presented to the campaign managers each day—showed his lead dropping to 13 points, putting such major states as New York, Pennsylvania, and California in jeopardy and dropping Reagan perilously close to the magic 50% level.[13] To the outside world, Paul Laxalt, the Nevada senator who was a Reagan friend and general chairman of the Republican party, said that Reagan had been "brutalized by a briefing process" in which David Stockman and other aides tried to pump him full of facts. Inside the campaign, all efforts to help other Republican candidates in Senate and House races by stressing broader themes about the party were abandoned; and attacks on "failed Carter–Mondale policies" were emphasized, in an attempt to shore up the president's support. Marginal losses in congressional races, even loss of control of the Senate, were as nothing to Republican strategists when weighed against the for months unthinkable disaster of losing the White House and control of the whole executive branch of government.

But Reagan rallied in the second debate October 21 in Kansas City, Missouri. His aides fortified him with positive reinforcement, and he was not strained by the light schedule made not only possible but necessary by the central importance of television newscasts in 1980s campaigns. (The goal of the schedule was to give the networks, which were obliged to cover each candidate, a visually attractive "sound bite" which made the point the campaign wanted to emphasize, and to do it early in the day, so that network camera crews, reporters, and editors would have plenty of time to get it on the air and campaign operatives plenty of time to make adjustments for any fluffs which occurred.) But the critical thrust in the second debate came not from any aide but from the candidate himself. When reporter Henry Trewhitt asked Reagan about "the age issue," whether there was "any doubt in your mind that you would be able to function" in crisis, Reagan replied with a trace of a smile, "Not at all, Mr. Trewhitt. And I want you to know that also I will not make age an issue in this campaign. I am not going to exploit, for political purposes, my opponent's youth and inexperience." The questioner, the audience, even Mondale laughed; but the line worked not just because it was funny. Against a less experienced challenger (if Bush had used it against Ferraro in their debate, for example), it would have been too sharp-edged and nasty; Reagan was showing not only that he was still capable of humor but that he still had fine political judgment.

If you had asked almost anyone in November 1976 to forecast the result of a 1984 election between Walter Mondale and Ronald Reagan, between a Mondale just elected vice president after a fine campaign performance as the nominee of what seemed still to be the majority party and a Reagan who even by 1976 had already reached the standard retirement age and represented the extremist wing of what seemed to be the minority party, you might very well have been told that such a contest would be a landslide, perhaps even that one candidate would have won 49 of the 50 states; but you would almost certainly have been told that the winner would be Mondale. Instead Reagan won 49 states and Mondale only his home state of Minnesota, and that by a 3,761–vote margin. Although Mondale as a challenger was rated by voters as equal in experience and competence to the incumbent president, in Gallup polls after D-Day he fluctuated between 38% and 41% of the vote—a clear indication that voters were not interested in his candidacy. In the end Reagan won 59% of the vote and Mondale 41%—not quite as large a margin as in the historic landslides of 1936, 1964, and 1972, but a result devoid of any ambiguity.

It was not devoid of some interest, however. Some interpreted it as a victory for the rich over the poor; and the major exit polls[14] showed clear differences by income, with those over $30,000 voting 2–1 for Reagan. But whites generally voted 2–1 for Reagan: there was negligible difference between whites of different income levels. Bigger differences were apparent between races (blacks were about 90% for Mondale), the sexes (women were 4 to 9 percentage points more for Mondale than were men), and regions (the South was especially strong for Reagan, who got the votes of about three out of four white southern men): splits between different culturally defined groups. Looking microscopically at the electorate makes cultural splits even more apparent. The rich Upper East Side of Manhattan voted heavily for Mondale, while across the East River lower-middle-class Queens neighborhoods represented by Ferraro voted for Reagan; Mondale's highest percentages came in black ghettos and university towns, while Reagan's highest percentages came from not-quite-elite WASP suburbs and religious fundamentalists.

One surprise, to the Democrats at least, was that the youngest voters, those eighteen to twenty-four, gave Reagan about 60% of their votes. When eighteen-year-olds were given the vote in 1972, the youngest voters had split about 50–50 in the Nixon–McGovern race, running 11 points more Democratic than the national average; now the youngest voters were if anything a little more Republican. The strongest Democratic age group were those between twenty-five and forty, who gave Mondale about 44% of their votes. Like the generation who had come of age in the New Deal years, they tended to carry their first political preferences through life; and like so many aging young people, they made the mistake of assuming that the young who came after them would behave as they did. If the youngest voters were protesting, their targets were not "the establishment" or right-wing patriots but the doomsayers of the left and policymakers of the Carter administration. Like Walter Polovchak, the twelve-year-old Ukrainian who in July 1980 had defected from his family when they wanted to go back to the Soviet Union, because he had seen life in what many critics of America would regard as a dreary neighborhood in Chicago and liked it,[15] when these young voters looked about them they saw not a nation of failures and limits and alienation but one of peace and prosperity and resilience; and they voted for the candidates whose words and deeds comported with what they saw.

The contentment registered in the presidential election was not misleading: when all the contests are taken together, 1984 was the number one incumbent year in American electoral history. The Republicans retained control of the Senate despite losing seats in Iowa and Illinois, where the Farm Belt's economic woes hurt, though both incumbents had their particular problems; they also lost Howard Baker's Tennessee seat to Albert Gore, Jr., but won an upset in Kentucky. Altogether, 93 of 100 incumbents returned to the Senate. In the House the Republicans gained a net of 17 seats, wiping out most of the Democrats' gains in 1982 and exceeding the Democrats' gains in that year in seats not won by redistricting. Of the 435 House members 392 were returned to office, just below the all-time high of 396 set in 1968. By 1984, only 13 states elected governors in the presidential year (and Arkansas was doing so for the last time); in those elections only one incumbent was beaten, in anything but barometric North Dakota. There was relatively little turnover in state legislatures, though Republicans raised their share of seats from 39% to 41%.

The most publicized race, and perhaps a harbinger of future political contests, was the North Carolina Senate race between incumbent Jesse Helms and Governor Jim Hunt.[16] Helms was *the* unreconstructed New Right Republican, a crusader with few legislative accomplishments but a huge mailing list of contributors, a segregationist in the 1960s and the leading opponent of the Martin Luther King holiday in the 1980s, a temperamental outsider always afraid that the insiders were giving in to Communists or socialists or cultural liberals. Hunt was a New South Democrat dedicated to more educational spending and tougher educational standards, a proponent of capital punishment and a tougher foreign policy than national Democrats favored, a temperamental doer with support going deep into a decentralized and prospering state's[17] community fabric. Both evoked strong positive feelings from a majority of North Carolina voters. But both spent their large campaign budgets, which added up to the most expensive Senate campaign in history (Helms spent $16.9 million and Hunt $9.5 million), on ads which became increasingly negative. Each started reacting to his opponent's ads within 24 hours by developing a new ad in response: a political argument played out before an otherwise inattentive electorate in commercial time on television entertainment programs. Each also worked closely with his party's candidates for House, governor, and other offices; and North Carolina in 1984 saw a revival of something very close to straight-ticket voting below the presidential level, a kind of convergence of the tops and bottoms of both tickets. Ultimately Helms's negative approach to issues suited this style of campaigning better, and he eked out a 52%–48% victory, though at some cost; he had to promise to continue chairing the Senate Agriculture Committee and not to take over Foreign Relations, as he would have preferred and as he was entitled by seniority after Charles Percy's defeat in Illinois. The negative tone, the thrust-and-parry style, and the trend toward straight-ticket voting were seen later in the 1980s in other contests, though never so intensively or with such fury as in this one.

60

⇥⟫⟫ ⟪⟪⇤

Peace

The major policy initiative of the first half of the second Reagan administration came not from the reelected president, not from the executive
branch, not even from a Republican, but from a former professional basketball
player who was now a Democratic senator from New Jersey, Bill Bradley. Through
what was by this time a long public career, Bradley had always steered by his own
compass. He had grown up in Crystal City, Missouri, the son of a banker, a tall,
brainy boy who trained himself through incredible discipline to play first-rate
basketball. After graduating not from a strong basketball college but from Princeton,
where he had excelled both on the court and in the classroom and been celebrated
in print by the *New Yorker*'s John McPhee,[1] he had decided to forgo two years of
professional basketball to take a Rhodes scholarship at Oxford. Later, as a player
for the New York Knicks, he had declined millions in fees for endorsement ads
and lived not in trendy Manhattan but in New Jersey, where he got involved
quietly in politics. When he decided to run for office, in 1978, he had aimed at
the supposedly safe Senate seat held by liberal Republican Clifford Case, understanding the seventy-four-year-old Case's weakness with the electorate in general
and with Republican voters in particular (he lost the primary to supply-sider Jeffrey
Bell). Despite his victory over Bell in a not very Democratic year, Bradley himself
was fascinated by, though he still did not agree with, his opponent's tax-rate-cut
theory. In the Senate he got a seat on the Finance Committee; but he was out of
sync on all sides there, unsympathetic to Democratic Chairman Russell Long's
personal distribution of tax breaks and shelters, the only member to vote against
the Reagan tax cuts in 1981.

By spring 1982, Bradley had come up with his own "fair tax" bill. He would
eliminate most preferences and deductions, except the sacrosanct deduction for
interest on home mortgages; he would cut rates drastically; he would neither
increase nor decrease revenue, nor shift the burden of taxation from one set of
taxpayers to another, except to ease up on the working poor.[2] It was a reform
admirably suited to a small-unit economy, for it would get government out of the
business of fine-tuning the economy and would treat similarly situated individuals
in the same way. To the enterprise of passing this law Bradley brought both a
piercing mind which cut through a thicket of detail to a conceptually simple yet
intellectually defensible solution and a political skill which drew on the discipline

he had shown in making himself a champion basketball player and on the competitive spark which had made him a leader whose teams almost always seemed to win. He found a House co-sponsor in Richard Gephardt, who was then attuned to similar ideas; he published his ideas in a book;[3] he heard Ronald Reagan announce in his State of the Union message in January 1984 that his secretary of the Treasury would propose a tax reform bill, in December (at the mention of the month Democratic members snickered); he tried and failed to persuade Walter Mondale to back his plan (Mondale thought it was more important to close the deficit, with higher taxes). Then in December 1984, much to the surprise of cynics, Treasury Secretary Donald Regan came in with a plan, soon dubbed Treasury I, which went beyond Bradley–Gephardt and embraced the perennial purist proposals of longtime tax reform advocates.

Treasury I was predictably dead on arrival in Congress. But there were possibilities in Treasury II, concocted in spring 1985 by the new Treasury secretary, James Baker (who had traded positions with Reagan in a bizarre swap passively accepted by Reagan), and Deputy Secretary Richard Darman, than whom there was no shrewder policy-and-politics strategist in 1980s Washington. House Ways and Means Committee Chairman Dan Rostenkowski, in whose institutional interest it was to dispense tax breaks, nonetheless took up the cause; this was his chance to prove that the 32nd ward committeeman of the Cook County Democratic party was also a far-seeing statesman—and a shrewder politician than the neophyte chairman who had gotten rolled in the tax cut fight of July 1981. In May 1985, Reagan went on television to present Treasury II to the people; Rostenkowski followed with the Democratic reply, not opposing Reagan but joining him. In simple language, in his raspy voice with its harsh midwestern accent, drawing on his Polish roots in Chicago, Rostenkowski said, "A Republican president has joined the Democrats in Congress to try to redeem this longstanding commitment to a tax system that's simple and fair. If we work together with good faith and determination, this time the people may win. This time I really think we can get tax reform." He urged viewers to write him: "even if you can't spell Rostenkowski, put down what they used to call my father and grandfather, Rosty. Just address it to R-O-S-T-Y, Washington, D.C."

Some 75,000 people did. For a moment, anyway, there was a demand for a structural reform which had not existed before, with an administration of one party and the key House leader of the other committed to it, not so much in anticipation of great political gains if they succeeded as in contemplation of continual political cynicism if they failed to try, and out of something which resembled more than professional observers like to admit a sense that this reform would be good for the country.

II

The 1st congressional district of Texas in the middle 1980s was one of about forty mostly rural southern districts which held the key to control of the House.

They regularly voted Republican in presidential elections and often voted Republican in seriously contested statewide contests, yet they continued to elect and routinely reelect Democrats to the House. The 1st district, which occupied the northeast corner of Texas, including the border town of Texarkana, was represented in January 1985 by a Democrat named Sam Hall, a sixty-one-year-old lawyer from Marshall with a judicial demeanor and an almost perfectly conservative voting record, the kind of reserved, careful courthouse politician who had been representing such districts through most of the twentieth century. In the House he was typically an ally of Republicans. But as long as there were forty or so Sam Halls there, it seemed unlikely that the Republicans could ever win control.

Or such were the calculations of Texas's incoming Senator Phil Gramm. He had started off as a Democrat himself, when as a thirty-four-year-old he ran against Senator Lloyd Bentsen in the 1976 primary while Bentsen was also running for president. Bentsen won 64%–28%; but Gramm came back two years later when an incumbent retired and ran for the House in the 6th district, which covered many rural and small-town counties and verged also into more metropolitan Houston and the Dallas–Fort Worth Metroplex. In a scrappy race in which Gramm raised and spent almost $500,000, he finished second in the first Democratic primary, making the runoff by 115 votes out of 81,000 cast, then won the runoff 53%–47%, then polished off a Republican by nearly 2–1. In the House, Gramm moved aggressively to put his policy ideas—less government, free markets—into practice. He allied himself with David Stockman on the budget in March 1981, continuing to sit in on the Democrats' negotiations while he was making strategy for the Republicans, and in only his second term, emerging as the lead co-sponsor of the administration's successful budget cut packages. In January 1983, Tip O'Neill moved to strip him of his seat on the Budget Committee because of his duplicity; Gramm responded by resigning his seat and running for reelection as a Republican. "I had to choose between Tip O'Neill and y'all, and I chose y'all," he said on television ads airing in both the Houston and Dallas–Fort Worth markets (and hence about half of Texas), and won the special election as a Republican. In 1984, when John Tower retired from the Senate after having only barely won reelection six years before, Gramm ran for the seat, won the primary with 73%, and then had the good fortune to draw a liberal opponent (rather than a conservative as Tower had), whom he beat 59%–41%. Not six months into his Senate term, he decided to get Sam Hall appointed a federal judge specifically to set up a vacancy which a Republican could win—and to set a precedent, he hoped, which would enable Republicans to sweep House seats in 1986 and 1988.

The political environment was good for such initiatives. By this point in their first terms after landslide victories, Franklin Roosevelt had lost the court-packing fight, Lyndon Johnson had sent American troops in large numbers to Vietnam, and Richard Nixon was fighting Watergate investigators. Ronald Reagan had made no such mistake. His job ratings, rather than sagging, were higher than ever before: 64% positive in Gallup's January 1985 poll, 63% in July. He was especially popular in the South. In the Texas 1st, Gramm had found a good candidate, Edd Hargett, a former pro football quarterback who had returned to his home in Linden and whose campaign was being run by Lee Atwater, the number two man in the 1984 Reagan–Bush campaign. The Democrats, typically, had a gaggle of candidates, with a couple of courthouse lawyers the favorites. But Bentsen and House Campaign Committee Chairman Tony Coelho were as determined to hold the seat as Gramm and Atwater were to capture it. They raised a campaign fund which would go to whoever won the Democratic nomination, and Coelho encouraged a Texas savings and loan operator to raise another $100,000 for a pro-Democratic "independent expenditure" campaign. In Washington Bentsen raised the trade issue in Congress, advancing from his seat on the Finance Committee, a bill to limit foreigners' trade restrictions, and in Texas Coelho ran generic party ads calling for a tough stand on trade. Finally they had some luck. In July 1985, Hargett said he didn't understand what the trade issue had to do with east Texas, even though the Lone Star Steel plant in Morris County had closed. On August 3, Democrat Jim Chapman beat Hargett 51%–49%.

Within a week Gramm, undaunted, had another initiative. It was a bill to require that the federal deficit be cut by specific amounts over the next several years, or else that all programs be cut by equal percentages. In a Congress which was unable to get Ronald Reagan to propose enough cuts to come anywhere near balancing the budget and which was unable to propose such cuts itself, it was an appealing, seemingly automatic device. The Gramm–Rudman bill, as it came to be called, won the support not only of most Republicans, but also of Democrats like Edward Kennedy and Gary Hart.

III

Non-political advertising specialists often take part in presidential campaigns, as in the 1972 Nixon and 1980 and 1984 Reagan campaigns; less often do specialists in political advertising devise ads for commercial products. One time they did came in 1985, and it had lessons for the political analyst as well as the commercial strategist. Patrick Caddell, pollster for Democratic nominees in 1972, 1976, and 1980 and briefly a Mondale adviser in 1984, was brought in by the Coca-Cola Company on its campaign to change the flavor of its chief beverage. Caddell enthusiastically urged the company to launch a "New Coke," to seize on Baby Boom and younger Americans' desire for change and novelty. After satisfying itself from blind taste tests that the new product was considered tastier (it was considerably sweeter, like Pepsi), the company announced in a blaze of publicity in April 1985 that New Coke had replaced the old Coke formula. It was a total bust. Generations of Americans had been reared on the story of how the Coke formula was a secret, held under lock and key, known to only one or two men; all Americans were familiar from childhood with the distinctive shape of the Coke bottle. Whatever people might say in taste tests, almost no one bought the New Coke. By July the company revived the old formula under the name Classic Coke, and it sold so little New Coke that it seems to have kept it on the market only to avoid embarrassment. It was a lesson that in Ronald Reagan's 1980s, even young Americans were not always seeking something new and instead continued to revere many of the American traditions which the young rebels of the late 1960s and early 1970s scoffed at. The new generation of American adults, Reagan voters in 1984 and New Coke rejecters of 1985, were not going to be clones of the campus radicals and antiwar protesters of almost two decades before.

At the same time these young Americans were ready to tolerate diverse life styles which two generations before had been almost universally condemned. In October 1985 movie star Rock Hudson died of AIDS, known officially as acquired immune deficiency syndrome, which had been identified only in 1981 and whose causative virus had been isolated only in 1984. The virus is transmitted through exchange of bodily fluids; and almost all the identified victims in the early years were male homosexuals, drug addicts who had used infected needles, and hospital patients or hemophiliacs inadvertently given blood transfusions or blood products containing the virus; the syndrome impairs the functioning of the body's immune system and up through the end of the 1980s at least seemed invariably to be fatal. There were rumors that Hudson had AIDS before his death, and it was revealed ultimately that he did, but the response to him was one of sympathy, from First Lady Nancy Reagan on down; contributing in a modest way to the climate of toleration of diversity in the 1980s was the fact that the Reagans, for all their championing of traditional values, had been Hollywood figures for decades, where their friends included Jews, blacks, and homosexuals. Acknowledgment of his illness shortly before his death increased the awareness of AIDS among the public generally. Polls showed that only small percentages of Americans expressed punitive attitudes toward AIDS patients, while the large majority favored increased public spending on research and care. There were a few isolated cases of infected persons such as schoolchildren being ostracized. With less publicity but more frequency, small communities as well as large all over the country were setting up programs to care for AIDS patients.

But increasing societal tolerance was accompanied by greater personal restraint. AIDS played some role in this trend, certainly in the apparent large reduction in promiscuous sex which was suggested strongly by responses to surveys and lower rates of venereal disease; but it surely was not the only factor. The number of abortions leveled off and began to decline in 1982, when AIDS was mostly unknown. The divorce rate declined from 1979 to 1982, ending a long upward trend. Use of alcohol, tobacco, and marijuana declined sharply in the 1980s. Sirloin and scotch were no longer the symbols of the good life in America, replaced by chicken and white wine or fish and carbonated water. Crime rates were down notably in the early 1980s, partly no doubt because prison populations were rising very rapidly indeed: a case of restraint imposed by others as well as by oneself. And people were increasingly penalizing what they had been reluctant to regard as misconduct a few years before: laws were being passed to imprison drunk drivers, track down fathers delinquent in child-support payments, ban smoking in public places, and ban or limit pornography. Americans who were liberating themselves from constraints a decade or two before were now restraining themselves and, in a few situations, restraining others, as the excesses and costs of liberation became apparent.[4]

IV

As the news of Rock Hudson's death dominated the headlines and newscasts, the legislative initiatives of Bill Bradley and Phil Gramm continued their seemingly unlikely progress on Capitol Hill. Dan Rostenkowski was superintending the progress of the tax reform bill, dominating the Ways and Means Committee through alliances with his fellow Democrats (although he was beaten on votes occasionally) and dealing with the administration more than Republican members were. Dozens of lobbyists waited in the cramped, dowdy hallway of the Longworth Building— "Guggi gulch"—for news of what was happening inside. In October, Rostenkowski made his key deal, agreeing to retain the deduction for state and local taxes in order to please members from New York and other high-tax states; in December, he had to surmount a challenge from House Republicans, furious at being kept out of the negotiations for months, who voted against the rule to consider the bill. Only in the last days of the session was the passage of the bill assured.

Gramm–Rudman had easier sailing in the Senate, where it originated; but in the House Tip O'Neill was determined to use his Democratic majority to put Republicans on the spot. He noticed that the Senate bill did not require any major cuts until after the 1986 elections, when the twenty-two Republican senators elected in 1980 would be defending their seats. O'Neill enlisted Gephardt, the chairman of the House Democratic caucus, to write a House version to put the Republicans on the spot; something very much like it was passed in December 1985.

V

While Congress was dealing with taxes and budgets, the voters in the few elections of 1985 were approving overwhelmingly the performance of their incumbents. New Jersey Governor Thomas Kean was reelected with 70% of the vote, winning a majority even among blacks—a great achievement for a Republican. In Virginia, where Governor Charles Robb, had he been eligible, would probably have won by a similar margin, his fellow Democrat Gerald Baliles was elected governor with 55%, a black Democrat was elected lieutenant governor, and a woman Democrat, was elected attorney general, despite the state's Republican leanings on national issues. In New York City, Mayor Edward Koch won a third term by a huge margin. A major element of all three victories was an appeal to local pride and patriotism, to a sense that New Jersey, long a butt of jokes, was a place of economic growth and even beauty, that Virginia had overcome the prejudices of its past, that New York City had emerged from near-bankruptcy to become once again the world's richest and most chic city.

Not just these places but the whole country in the middle 1980s seemed at peace with itself—proud of its strengths, accepting of its diversity and tolerant even of those once regarded as deviants, yet more restrained and tradition-minded in its personal life. Its politicians were able to work toward reforming age-encrusted governmental structures and policies and to reach compromises despite the inevitably adversary nature of electoral politics. In the world outside there were threats—perhaps from the Soviet Union, which got a new leader, Mikhail Gorbachev, in March 1985, certainly from the terrorists who hijacked the Mediterranean cruise liner *Achille Lauro* and murdered an elderly American passenger in October 1985. But Ronald Reagan seemed in a position of strength next to the Soviets; and the *Achille Lauro* hijackers, flying in an Egyptian airliner, were forced down and arrested in Italy. At home the alienation of previous years seemed mostly forgotten after several years of resilience and economic growth.

VI

As Ronald Reagan began his sixth year in the presidency, democracy seemed to be breaking out all over the world. In February 1986, Jean-Claude Duvalier, self-styled "president for life," left Haiti for exile in southern France. That same month, Philippines President Ferdinand Marcos left Manila for exile in Hawaii, after being told pointedly by Reagan's emissary, Paul Laxalt, that his sixteen-year dictatorship was over. From the Soviet Union emerged the first news of Gorbachev's policy of *glasnost,* or "openness," and, later, *perestroika,* or "restructuring." In Washington, Congress was prepared to vote for aid to the rebels against the Soviet-backed regime in Afghanistan and for economic sanctions against South Africa in protest of its apartheid policy (sanctions passed over Reagan's veto in October).

But Congress went back and forth over Reagan's proposals for military aid to the Nicaraguan contras, the rebels fighting against the country's leftists Sandinista government. The issue had existed in the first Reagan term, but the president, fighting other battles, had not raised it in any serious and sustained way. In March contra aid was beaten in the House 222–210. In August it was approved. Different restrictions on aid were written into the law in an effort to sway the very small number of votes which made the difference. Many opponents of contra aid were passionate, convinced that it would be only a first step toward U.S. military involvement in Nicaragua, as military aid to the South Vietnamese had been in Vietnam. They charged, clearly correctly, that whatever its rhetoric the Reagan administration wanted to overthrow the Sandinistas; they argued, increasingly unconvincingly, that the Sandinistas were repressive and pro-Communist only because they were being opposed by the United States; they argued that the contras were corrupt, or drug dealers, or backers of the ousted dictator Anastasio Somoza. Some contra aid opponents saw the Sandinistas as progressive reformers, trying to distribute wealth and income from the rich to the poor, though their policies had the effect of stopping the Nicaraguan economy in its tracks, hurting everyone left in the country. Contra aid backers were as confused in their rationales. Tactically, it behooved them to specify ways in which the Sandinistas could demonstrate a commitment to democracy and living peacefully with their neighbors; but they never expected the Sandinistas would do these things. An argument in their favor was that U.S. support for Jose Napoleon Duarte's government in El Salvador against Communist-backed guerrillas had been largely successful, but some contra aid backers were uncomfortable with a social democrat and land reformer like Duarte.

But much of the emotive force in this debate came not from concern over Nicaragua and Central America, but from memories of Vietnam and the years leading up to that conflict. Contra aid opponents seemed to have a vested interest in portraying the United States as allied with repressive regimes, despite the accumulating evidence that the United States was encouraging democracy and human rights all over the world, and with considerable success. Contra aid backers seemed to have a vested interest in portraying Communism as an ever-advancing menace, despite the evidence beginning to accumulate that Communism was receding as a force in world affairs. In making policy toward other parts of the world American politicians were able to move beyond the 1970s into the new world coming into being in the 1980s. They were not able to do this in making policy toward Nicaragua.

VII

At the beginning of 1986 the tax reform bill had gone to the Senate Finance Committee, chaired by Bob Packwood, a cynical, brainy Oregon Republican who favored both business and labor lobbies, whose leadership model was that classic dispenser of tax breaks, Russell Long. In April, Packwood's attempt to patch together a reform bill which would meet some lobbies' complaints and still provide high enough revenues and low enough rates to win approval from the president fell through entirely; facing unfavorable votes on $70 billion in preferences, he announced he wasn't taking scheduled votes on Friday, April 18. Instead he went to lunch with an aide at The Irish Times restaurant, where with the help of two pitchers of beer they came up with an entirely different approach. Packwood was only a month away from his primary in Oregon, where he was opposed by a conservative minister who was pressing him sharply; the disgrace of a tax bill fiasco could end his career (he ultimately won by only 58%–42%, a narrow margin for a veteran senator in a primary). He and his aide decided on a radical shift, to a 25% top rate, at which point they hoped the pressure for deductions and breaks would diminish toward nothing. To almost everyone's surprise, a bill embodying this ultra-simplified approach was approved 20–0 by the committee in May and, after some amendments, 97–3 by the Senate in June. After a perils-of-Pauline conference committee, a cross between the House and Senate versions was approved in September.

Another piece of reform legislation which passed in 1986, much to everyone's surprise, was immigration reform. The chief architect was Wyoming Senator Alan Simpson, who in his third year in the Senate had inherited the chairmanship of the immigration subcommittee in 1981. Tall, humorous, but possessed of a healthy temper, Simpson had worked with his House counterpart, Louisville Congressman Romano Mazzoli, to fashion a bill which would apply sanctions to employers who hired illegal aliens but would also increase the number of legal immigrants allowed into the country and provide an amnesty to many illegal ones already here. It would, in other words, regularize and legalize what had become a large (no one knew exactly how large) flow of illegal immigrants. Simpson had gotten his bill through the Senate easily; but it had foundered in the House in the lame duck session of 1982, under attack from Hispanics who thought it discriminatory and conservatives who were skeptical of its amnesty. In the next Congress it had passed in both houses, but died in conference committee. Starting in 1985, Simpson once more pushed it through the Senate; this time Peter Rodino managed it through the House, and it cleared through the conference committee almost miraculously in the last moments of the session in October 1986. Like tax reform and Gramm–Rudman, this was a bill whose force came less from constituent pressure than from legislators' own sense that something was wrong and needed to be fixed.

The immigration reform was passed the same month as the ceremonies in New York Harbor commemorating the 100th anniversary of the Statue of Liberty. This turned out to be an occasion for the celebration of the achievement of the immigrants who had come steaming into New York Harbor, past the statue, into the entry station at Ellis Island; the station itself was being refurbished and made into a museum by a committee headed by Lee Iacocca, chief executive officer of one of the nation's largest corporations and author of a best-selling memoir. Sixty years before, the flow of immigrants to American had been stopped, by politicians responsive to demographically declining constituencies which had become fearful of the teeming, unfamiliar, fertile, hard-working newcomers. Americans in the 1980s could hardly help noticing the new flow of immigrants, this time not from eastern and southern Europe but from Latin American and East Asia; but this time the impetus for shutting off immigration was much weaker. More than half of all Americans in 1986 could count at least one ancestor from the vast immigrations of 1840–1924, and so at least 50% of voters could be said to be in some metaphorical sense Ellis Islanders: America was now very much their country. In a nation where people tended to identify with the most downtrodden rather than the most elevated of their ancestors, those personal connections—some deeply felt like Mario Cuomo's, many other much more casual—could not help affecting attitudes about the new migrants. Their success undercut the arguments often made in the 1960s and 1970s that the country provided no avenues of upward mobility for the poor; their general acceptance undercut the idea that Americans were bigoted and cruel; their continued arrival helped Americans to think better of themselves and their country, and contributed to the guardedly positive tone of public opinion as the economic recovery and the foreign policy successes of the 1980s continued.

VIII

Gramm-Rudman, tax reform, immigration: the great issues of the 99th Congress had almost no perceptible effect on the elections which chose the members of the 100th. House elections were for the most part not seriously contested. Only 9 House incumbents were defeated, the lowest number in history; 385 were reelected, the highest number up to that point except for 1984 and 1968. As for the Senate, the Democrats gained 8 seats and won control—a big victory. Yet in percentage terms the Democrats' overall majority in voting for the Senate was smaller in 1986 (50%–49%) than it had been the last time these seats were up, in 1980 (52%–47%).[5] The difference is that Democrats won rather than lost most of the close races, winning such contests in 11 states—North Carolina, Georgia, Florida, Alabama, Louisiana, South Dakota, North Dakota, Colorado, Nevada, Washington, and California—while losing in only 4—Oklahoma, Idaho, Missouri, and Wisconsin. Continuing distress in the Farm Belt hurt Republicans, and the capacity of adept southern Democrats to win black votes without antagonizing whites made the difference.

There was some flux in the governors' races in small states, but governors of larger states were reelected by large, often record margins: Michael Dukakis of Massachusetts, Mario Cuomo of New York, Richard Celeste of Ohio, James Blanchard of Michigan, James Thompson of Illinois (though he was helped because his major opponent, Adlai Stevenson III, resigned the Democratic nomination when a follower of a loony conspiracy theorist named Lyndon LaRouche was nominated as his running mate), and George Deukmejian of California. The only big state which turned out a governor was Texas, where Democrat Mark White lost to Republican Bill Clements, whom he had beaten in 1982. Party turnover in state legislative seats was even more minimal than it had been in 1984. Overall, 1986 was almost as good an incumbent's year as 1984; it was a time when most Americans registered, if not contentment, at least a lack of raging dissatisfaction with their elected officials and their government.

61

→》》 《《←

Confirmation

T he day before the off-year elections of November 1986, an obscure newspaper in Beirut revealed that the United States had been selling arms to
Iran in the hopes of securing the release of American hostages held in Lebanon.
Two days after the election U.S. intelligence sources admitted the story was true,
and eight days after the election Ronald Reagan admitted that he had known of
the arms sale. Thus began the disclosure of what came to be known as the Iran–
contra scandal; for it quickly became known that proceeds from the arms sales
had been diverted to the Nicaraguan contras by a White House staffer, Marine
Lieutenant Colonel Oliver North, with the knowledge of Reagan's national security
adviser, Vice Admiral John Poindexter. Before the end of November, Poindexter
resigned, North was fired, and former Texas Senator John Tower was commissioned by Reagan to head a three-member commission to find the facts. As the
commission began its work, the Democratic leaders of both houses of Congress
prepared to conduct their own investigation. Six days before Christmas an independent counsel—the technical term for what in the Watergate period had been
called a special prosecutor—was appointed. In the meantime, Reagan seemed
befuddled at a late November press conference—disquieting behavior in a president
who the month before, at the Reykjavík summit, had been on the verge of accepting
an offer from Mikhail Gorbachev to ban the stationing of nuclear weapons in
Europe, and thus of changing in one session of negotiation the basic Western
military and political strategy which had been maintained for almost forty years.
Were Americans seeing, as a later book title put it, "the unmaking of the president"?[1]

As this story unfolded, the precedent in almost everyone's mind was Watergate.
Once again a Republican chief executive had misused his power and concealed
facts; once again his appointees had lied to Congress and the media; once again
the truth must be established and wrongdoing ferreted out. Both the media and
the Democrats, and critical Republicans as well, glossed quickly over the question
of whether Reagan had followed unwise policies and pursued doggedly the question
of whether he, George Bush, or any of his appointees had violated the law. One
question of policy was easy to gloss over, because it seemed so clear that Reagan
and Bush were wrong politically, as well as in policy: almost no Americans supported
selling arms to the Ayatollah Khomeini's regime in Iran. The idea of dealing with

this government which had held 50 Americans hostage for 444 days seemed preposterous, especially since Reagan had criticized Carter for his restraint in dealing with the Iranians.

Moreover, it quickly became apparent that the government of Israel had been an important intermediary in the arms sales, and almost no American politician wanted to be in the position of attacking Israel. Over the years pro-Israel organizations and individuals had contributed money and support liberally to senators of both parties, building up a pro-Israel majority in the Senate which they believed counterbalanced an inherently anti-Israel bias in the State Department's Middle Eastern bureaucracy. In the 1980s they had also been working hard to support House members, even in districts with very few Jews. An investigation which examined the Israeli connection closely could, many members felt, jeopardize American support of Israel, already threatened by the discovery that Israel had hired two Americans to spy on the U.S. government. On the other hand, most congressional Democrats and some Republicans were strongly opposed to the Reagan policy of military aid to the contras and feared that it could lead to an American military involvement as in Vietnam. So they were inclined to delve into the diversion of money to the contras and efforts to resupply them; at least some of these appeared to have been made in defiance of Congress's express prohibitions, and they arguably threatened to entangle the country in a foreign military involvement through unilateral and unauthorized acts of military officers acting outside the limits of civilian control.

The identities of the investigators underlined the Watergate analogy. The Senate committee was headed by Daniel Inouye, who had served on Sam Ervin's Watergate committee; the House committee included Peter Rodino, who had chaired the Judiciary Committee hearings on the impeachment of Richard Nixon. The committees combined forces and met, every other week, in the same ornate Senate Caucus Room where Ervin's committee, and Joseph McCarthy's before it, had met. The TV network cameras were there to provide live coverage as they had in 1973 and 1974. The difference was that in 1987 committee staffers rather than members did most of the questioning, and the committees found out little more than what the Tower commission had reported in February. Reagan had indeed approved the arms sales, as he admitted; Bush, running for president, admitted that he had been at meetings where they were discussed and had approved them, too. But CIA Director William Casey, who for years had striven to aid the contras, had suffered a disabling stroke in November 1986 and could not testify (he died in May 1987). And Poindexter, a man known for his command of facts, testified that he could not remember many key details and that he had on his own initiative decided not to inform Reagan of the diversion of money to the contras.

The sensation of the hearings was the public testimony in July of North, which turned out to evoke a very different response from what the Watergate analogy suggested. North had lied, had misled Congress and his superiors, had certainly skirted and probably violated some laws; he had even diverted relatively small amounts of money, to build a security fence around his house. The committees' majority probably expected to score points by self-righteously denouncing him. Instead they were surprised when North used their questions to score points off them. He portrayed the contras as men fighting for freedom and democracy, and he proclaimed unashamedly that he had done whatever he could to help them. Since the committees were not much interested in the Iranian end of the deal, he was not forced to defend the politically insupportable; and he made what most members thought was politically unpopular—contra aid—into a popular policy for at least a few weeks in the opinion polls. For a moment, as the hearings ended, North became wildly popular around the country. "Olliemania" soon passed. But North's testimony blunted the thrust of the committee's majority report and strengthened the resolve of its dissenters. Iran–contra, it suddenly appeared, might just not be Watergate; and contra aid might not be Vietnam, after all.

II

Iran–contra did nonetheless alter the political landscape. Ronald Reagan, highly popular in 1985 and 1986, was beleaguered; and his job approval rating, at the 60%–68% level from July 1985 to October 1986, fell to 48% in December 1986 and hovered around the 50% level until early 1988. Other events produced the impression of a president under siege, unable to take reporters' questions because of Iran–contra, on the defensive on other matters. In May 1987, 37 American sailors were killed when an Iraqi missile hit the U.S.S. *Stark* in the Persian Gulf; in July, the United States began putting its own flag on Kuwaiti tankers and escorting them through the gulf to protect them from Iranian attacks. Also in July, Reagan nominated Judge Robert Bork, a former law professor and solicitor general and a critic of activist courts, to the Supreme Court. Unlike previous appointees, he answered detailed questions about his judicial philosophy in Senate hearings. Liberals fearful that he would vote to repeal the *Roe* v. *Wade* decision overturning restrictions on abortion started vocally opposing him early. They won support from nearly all Senate Democrats after Bennett Johnston of Louisiana, running for majority leader, came out against him at a propitious moment and after black leaders urged southern Democrats, to whose narrow 1986 victories black votes had been essential, to oppose him. A few Republicans joined in on similar grounds, and the nomination was beaten in October by a 58–42 margin. The same month the stock market crashed: the Dow Jones average fell 508 points on October 19, a decline of 23% and the largest single drop in history. Nearly twice as many shares were traded as on any previous day; for a week a panic seized Wall Street, as Americans saw billions in equity vanish in hours and wondered whether a depression like that of the 1930s would follow. And Reagan's closest personal aide, Michael Deaver, was convicted of perjury in December, the latest in a number of Reagan administration figures involved in problems with the law.

Yet events did not entirely work against Reagan. In December, Mikhail Gorbachev visited Washington, charmed Americans as he ventured from his limousine at Connecticut Avenue and L Street in front of Washington's highest-rent commercial real estate, and signed a treaty agreeing that the Soviets would disassemble their intermediate-range missiles in return for U.S. removal of the Pershing IIs which had been installed in Western Europe in 1983. Reagan's insistence in 1983 on following through on Jimmy Carter's commitment to install the Pershings, and his general military buildup, seemed vindicated, while the politics of the Democrats and others who had urged a nuclear freeze or who had argued that the United States should unilaterally disarm seemed solidly repudiated. Less immediately apparent in December 1987, but increasingly clear as the months went on, was that the economy did not collapse in the wake of the stock market crash; in fact, for whatever reasons, it resumed growing at a robust rate. For all of Reagan's problems in Iran–contra and the Persian Gulf, for all his mediocre (though by no means disastrous) job ratings, his basic foreign and economic policies were being vindicated.

To these developments the news media, especially the television network newscasts, paid relatively little attention. Journalism has a natural bias toward the negative; it is news if an airplane crashes and not news when thousands of planes land safely. In addition, many journalists in the late 1980s had been conditioned by their own experiences covering or observing the stories of Vietnam and Watergate, the stories which in many cases had given their careers enormous boosts; and those experiences informed their coverage of the Reagan administration. Scandals and charges of scandal were reported with glaring headlines, even if they proved unfounded. Stories about the economic recovery were accompanied usually by reminders that it still was not universal, and that distribution of income had grown somewhat more unequal in the 1980s. The dangers of a provocative military and foreign policy were described in lavish detail while the concessions the Reagan buildup may have forced the Soviets to make were glossed over. Reagan was portrayed as, in Clark Clifford's words, "an amiable dunce," manipulated by aides, unaware of the policies adopted in his name, callous toward the poor and the black. This coverage proceeded not out of partisan motives—journalists often produced critical stories about the Democrats—but rather out of a conviction that it represented a fair picture of the real world. As the foremost political reporter of his generation, David Broder of the *Washington Post,* wrote at the time, "[W]e are constantly devising the scripts that we think are appropriate to the events we are covering."[2] The question for 1988 was whether the script would end as the majority of journalists assumed, with Reagan's Republicanism repudiated and another kind of president in the White House.

III

Such was the backdrop to the 1988 presidential campaign, which had started with the August 1986 election of Republican precinct delegates in Michigan. This was the first election since 1960 and only the second since 1928 in which the incumbent president was at no point considered a candidate.[3] None of the candidates for either party's nomination was known in depth by the voters, and outside their home constituencies most were entirely unknown. The public seemed little interested in politics; it was focused on no one or two or three easily comprehensible issues; it got most of its information about politics from a medium whose 22-minute newscasts' transcripts would take up less than a full front page of the *New York Times*.[4] The machinery for choosing both parties' nominees was creaky and complex, understood by only a few hundred insiders. That the peaceful transfer of leadership in the most powerful and richest country in the world should take place in such a way may be a source of wonderment to those unfamiliar with this system or these times.

The best known of the candidates was George Bush. But his seven years as Reagan's loyal vice president had left him with almost no public record of his own on the issues of the day, and the exception—his admission that he had backed the arms sales to Iran—was no more helpful than the rule. Following the useful precedent that Jimmy Carter had set with Walter Mondale, Reagan gave Bush access to all presidential papers and most White House meetings and met regularly with him alone. Like Carter, Reagan received loyalty in return. But Bush could do little more than hint at any knowledge and understanding he had developed in the White House, and his efforts to do so were hindered by a syntax which seemed the oral equivalent of dyslexia. He could parade the impressive list of jobs which he had held, in each case briefly, between 1971 and 1977 but in which, by his own admission,[5] he had learned relatively little; but he could not parade what he had learned as vice president. Reporters and political opponents were obsessed with Bush's background, the facts that he was the son of an investment banker and senator, that he had attended prep school and belonged to one of the exclusive secret societies at Yale, that he had been staked by some family friends when he went into the oil business in Texas in the 1950s. He was portrayed as an elitist preppie[6] at a time when the one ethnic group which could acceptably be denigrated in public was the one popularly identified with preppie attitudes, white Anglo-Saxon Protestants. These particular associations were important to journalists and politicians who shared some but not all of Bush's background, who from their Washington and New York vantage points saw a country which more closely resembled British than American society, a country with a small elite educated in a small number of secondary schools and colleges, placed at the head of large institutions by virtue of their connections, the privileged occupiers of the top rungs of a ladder in which the vast resentful masses were clustered at the bottom. But America in the 1980s had not just one ladder, but many ladders; it had hundreds of first-rate colleges and thirty-five metropolitan areas with more than 1 million people, thousands of different businesses and scores of different professions. The Americans of 1900, in a country with a few giant industrial firms and a few dozen highly visible millionaires, may have felt ground under the heel of a Wall Street elite, helpless to advance their own economic interests; but the Americans of the 1980s did not seethe with resentment at people with George Bush's background or feel that they enjoyed unfair advantages. So the constant barrage of attacks on him by people who did share those grievances tended to miss the mark.

As his campaign manager, Lee Atwater, maintained throughout 1987 and 1988, Bush was consistently underestimated by his opposition and by the media. He built a superb campaign organization and raised money at a record rate. He concentrated his efforts on the key states—Michigan, with its early caucuses; Iowa, the nation's biggest population loser in the 1980s, where Reagan's policies were arguably more unpopular than anywhere else in the country; New Hampshire, with its first-in-the-nation primary and its aversion to taxes; and the southern states which would be voting simultaneously on Super Tuesday, thanks to Democratic legislators (along with South Carolina, Atwater's home state, which would be voting the weekend before).

Bush was generally deemed a weak debater. But just as he held his own against Geraldine Ferraro in October 1984, so he held his own in the first debate he agreed to participate in with his Republican rivals in November 1987. His most striking confrontation, however, was not with another candidate but with CBS News anchor Dan Rather. Bush refused to submit to a taped interview, which CBS could edit; Rather offered him time live on the *CBS Evening News* and, without informing Bush, prepared a six-minute story questioning whether Bush had told the whole truth about Iran–contra—an unusually long and accusatory story for the newscast. Bush, appearing live immediately afterwards, took Rather's questions and insisted that he had answered all the questions raised by Iran–contra (he had submitted himself to an open-ended questioning session on the subject days earlier on the stump in Iowa. When Rather seemed to hector him, Bush attacked his concentration on this one issue, on which Bush had already admitted an error of judgment, by asking whether Rather would want his whole career to be judged by "those seven minutes you walked off the set in Miami." Like Reagan, Bush had the details wrong (the set was in New York) but got the point right. Rather was visibly shaken and soon afterwards abruptly cut Bush off the air in mid-sentence.

Bush's best-known Republican rival, Senate Minority Leader Robert Dole, for most of 1987 delegated authority to different managers who seldom spoke to one another, spent money lavishly to little purpose, and found himself unprepared in early big contests. Dole's mordant wit and his skill at legislative maneuvering made him a favorite in Washington. But his little-camouflaged desire to raise taxes to bring the budget closer to balance was a severe handicap in Republican contests. He was not a player in Michigan; and while he won in Iowa, a farm state like his native Kansas by proclaiming, "He's one of us," he was not prepared to "take the pledge" not to raise taxes which Republicans in New Hampshire had come to expect of all candidates; and he lost there to Bush 39%–28%. Bush went on to sweep the South, not so much because he was from Texas as because this was the region where approval of the Reagan administration was strongest.

The other Republicans hoped for early breakthrough victories of the sort won by George McGovern in 1972 and Jimmy Carter in 1976. Pat Robertson, the son of a longtime senator from Virginia and the proprietor of a successful religious broadcasting enterprise in Virginia Beach, hoped for an outpouring of fundamentalist and other evangelical Christians; after all, such voters had provided the biggest percentage shift from Carter in 1976 to Reagan in 1980 and then in 1984 of any definable segment of the electorate. In a politics where voters' preferences increasingly hinged on cultural attitudes, the evangelicals were a constituency which could be mobilized in numbers which could inundate the relatively small numbers of Republicans involved in caucuses. So until he was outmaneuvered in the January 1988 state convention, Robertson threatened to be the leader in Michigan; he then surprised almost everyone by finishing second, well ahead of Bush, in Iowa. His problems came with larger electorates and greater exposure. After accusing Bush operatives of engineering the exposure of the scandal surrounding television evangelists and Jim and Tammy Fae Bakker, he made dismal showings in the South on Super Tuesday. Jack Kemp, originator of the Kemp–Roth tax cut, made no headway even in New Hampshire; Pete du Pont's campaign was notable mainly for the fact that a scion of one of the nation's richest families felt the times were market-oriented and anti-government enough to make politically feasible a proposal to phase out the Social Security system.

If the Republican race was decided in anti-tax New Hampshire and the patriotic South, the Democratic race was framed, though not decided in dovish, agriculturally ailing Iowa. From its isolationist days through the Vietnam war and into Ronald Reagan's 1980s, Iowa had been one of the states strongly opposed to an assertive foreign policy, an impulse which helped to make it the sixth most Republican state in the 1940 presidential election and the second most Democratic in the 1988 contest. Iowa's Democratic caucusgoers were almost unanimously opposed to contra aid, and about half of them favored unilateral disarmament. In Iowa debates Democrats were pressed to renounce nuclear testing and various nuclear weapons as well as to embrace expensive programs to aid farmers. Various of the lesser-known candidates enjoyed a surge of popularity, then ebbed back: former Arizona Governor Bruce Babbitt, Illinois Senator Paul Simon, Missouri Congressman Richard Gephardt. With his support of a supply management farm program (which would allocate production to existing farmers and increase food costs to consumers) and his championing of retaliation against trade partners which had a trade surplus with the United States, a theme of "It's your fight too!" and a good field organization, Gephardt ended up in first place, with Simon second and Massachusetts Governor Michael Dukakis, well-financed and well-organized, third.

Dukakis went on to win New Hampshire, where his blocking of a nuclear power plant in Seabrook was popular with Democrats. But with a cluttered field, 1988's primary winners got little coverage on television news and so failed to get the momentum earlier primary winners had gotten from Iowa or New Hampshire. On Super Tuesday, Dukakis's huge advantage in money enabled him to win a four-cornered victory: he finished first in the primaries in Massachusetts and Rhode Island, the caucuses in Washington state, and the primaries in the two biggest southern states, Texas and Florida, where he won absolute majorities among Mexican-Americans and Jews, respectively, in a field of six candidates. Jesse Jackson also made the newscasts Super Tuesday by winning five Deep South states, where large black minorities voted almost unanimously for him. Little noticed amid the clutter were Tennessee Senator Albert Gore's victories in five southern states and his second-place finish behind Jackson in five others. Super Tuesday had produced a southern-based nominee as the southern Democratic legislators who put it together had hoped, but it was not Gore or another Democrat, but a Republican, George Bush.

In effect, Super Tuesday also picked the Democratic nominee: the strongest remaining opponent of Jackson, Dukakis. Jackson's strength was particularly visible on Super Tuesday and the week after in his home state of Illinois, which had a larger percentage of black voters—about 30% in the Democratic primary—than any other large industrial state. But Jackson alienated many white voters, not so much because of his race (for in 1982 about half the whites in the largest state in the nation, California, had been willing to vote for Thomas Bradley for governor) but because of his appeals for racial solidarity, his 1984 association with bigots like Louis Farrakhan and "Hymietown" comments, and his issue positions, symbolized by his physical embrace of Fidel Castro and Yasir Arafat. There was a flutter of interest when he beat Dukakis in the Michigan caucuses, and talk that white auto workers were suddenly voting for Jackson; but when it turned out that about 45% of the turnout in Michigan was black[7] the reason for his victory became clear. Gore made feints at running in several more primaries and finally made an all-out effort in New York; but white and particularly Jewish voters determined to beat Jackson stuck with Dukakis. The winners in both parties were the candidates who were best financed and best organized.

IV

From April until August 1988, Dukakis was leading Bush in the polls, by as much as 54%–38% in mid-May and mid-June and once again in the three weeks following the Democrats' July convention in Atlanta.[8] This lead puzzled many, including both candidates' strategists: Reagan's Gallup job approval rating was running about 50% positive through these months, there was no substantial majority believing that things were pretty seriously off on the wrong track rather than going in the right direction, and only small majorities said they wanted the country to move in a new direction from where it had gone under Reagan. The best explanation seems to be that preferences were very lightly held—an explanation strengthened by the sharp changes in the standings in August and September. When Americans saw Dukakis beating Jackson in a series of primaries or watched his acceptance speech in Atlanta, they found it easy to say they would vote for him. When they saw Bush deliver his acceptance speech in New Orleans, they found it easy to say the same about him. Both candidates carefully staged their conventions as television shows featuring themes which would help their candidacy. Both succeeded in overcoming obstacles to getting their message across—Jackson's insistence on sharing the spotlight with Dukakis and his vice presidential choice, the experienced sixty-seven-year-old Texas senator Lloyd Bentsen; the hubbub over Bush's selection of the little-known forty-one-year-old Indiana Senator Dan Quayle as his running mate.

Both presented their stands on issues, but both of these still not very well known candidates strove especially to color in their personal backgrounds and present themselves as characters in the American story. Dukakis emphasized his immigrant background: his parents had come to the United States from Greece as children, they had succeeded grandly in school, his father had made his fortune as a doctor and sent his son Michael to Swarthmore College and Harvard Law School, and now the immigrant's son was the governor of Massachusetts, running for president. It was a story that had special, personal reverberations for the majority of Americans who were Ellis Islanders; and in the spring primaries and the spring and summer polls Dukakis was running much stronger than other Democrats among Catholics, Jews, and other groups mostly descended from the immigration of 1840–1924. Bush emphasized his background as a pioneer: as the war hero who had moved his young family to the desert of west Texas, working hard to build a new business and to build a new community and its institutions where none had existed before. This was also a story with reverberations for many Americans, for the generation who had pioneered the suburban frontiers of America after World War II and for their children, now adults, who had grown up in the communities they created. And he presented a vision of a Tocquevillian America, a country where people helped one another through voluntary associations—his phrase was "a thousand points of light"—a country which had healed the wounds of the Civil War (for this Yankee's greatest political strength was in the South) and had forgotten the depression (for this investment banker's son ran well among blue-collar workers), a country whose formative experiences had been winning World War II and building the busy, prosperous, tolerant postwar country as Bush had in Texas.

In a contest between the two types, the immigrant had the numerical advantage over the pioneer by 1988; the descendants of Charles F. Murphy's ethnic immigrants outnumbered the descendants of William Howard Taft's Yankee pioneers even in some of the high-income city neighborhoods and suburbs which had been strongholds of the Yankee elite sixty years before. Though it is impossible to prove the point, it seems likely that in the summer of 1988 Dukakis was running several points ahead of what would have been the showing of a son of a midwestern minister, a description that fitted former nominees Mondale and McGovern and 1988 candidate Simon. But Bush gained and seized the advantage of stressing cultural issues and arguing that he was closer than Dukakis to most Americans' values. The issue which turned out to be most useful to him in demonstrating this claim was one which had little directly to do with the presidency, but revealed much about the way Dukakis governed: prison furloughs. In the 1980s it was common practice in most states to release prisoners for limited periods before their terms were up, to accustom them to the outside world and to give those still unfurloughed an incentive for good behavior. But Massachusetts was the only state which granted furloughs to prisoners sentenced to a life term without possibility of parole—its severest penalty, since Dukakis vetoed the death penalty—and Dukakis had specifically endorsed this policy as long before as 1976, when he vetoed a bill which would have changed it. The policy had become an issue in Massachusetts in 1987 when the *Lawrence Eagle-Tribune* discovered that a local murderer, Willie Horton, had escaped while on such a furlough; in April 1987, Horton was caught after beating a couple and committing a rape in Maryland. Although the Dukakis administration had tried to cover up the facts, refusing to respond honestly to questions, the *Eagle-Tribune* had uncovered them, producing a petition drive to overturn the furlough law, large majorities in the legislature for repeal, and a Pulitzer Prize for the newspaper in March 1988. But Dukakis stubbornly continued to endorse the policy of furloughs for life-without-parole prisoners; and when he finally agreed to sign the repeal bill in April 1988, he pointedly refused to agree that it was good policy, conceding only that the legislators and the voters wanted it. In a debate in New York that month he declined to take credit for the repeal and said his critics didn't know what they were talking about. The major newspapers, magazines, and television networks did little investigation into the Horton case or the furlough issue. They failed to recognize that Horton and not Iran–contra or stock market insider trading, would be the story of executive wrongdoing and cover-up which would help determine the outcome of the election. But the July 1988 *Reader's Digest,* still the magazine with the largest circulation in the nation after *TV Guide,* ran an article on the issue which was devastating to Dukakis. His campaign's response was a disingenuous attempt to blame the furlough policy on a previous Republican governor and to charge that the Bush campaign's use of the issue was racist, even though the Bush campaign was careful never to point out that Horton was black and the issue would have cut deep if he had been white.[9]

In his acceptance speech Dukakis said the issue in the campaign was "competence, not ideology"; and later he advanced programs to help financially strapped families pay for child care, housing down payments, and college loans. These proposals were an attempt to shift the ground of the election from cultural to economic issues. But Bush hammered relentlessly on the furlough issue, especially in a television ad which showed prisoners going through a revolving door, and argued that the Republican policy of "peace through strength" had been proved superior to Dukakis's opposition to many weapons systems. Reagan's job rating and voters' satisfaction levels went up several points in August, for no apparent exogenous reason; the Republican convention broadcasts may have helped, or voters may simply have been stepping back and looking not at how Reagan had done in the last week or month but at how he had performed over the whole eight-year period. In this year of volatile opinions, as voters finally learned more about the candidates, Bush's support rose from 37% in a July Gallup poll to 53% in the election, whereas Dukakis's fell from 54% in the same poll to 46% in the election. In all but a few stray polls taken after the Republican convention in August, Bush led Dukakis. By mid-September 1988 his lead rose to as much as 49%–38%, as Dukakis's negative ratings rose and Bush's fell. After each of the two debates in October, Bush's leads ratcheted up a little higher; by late October preferences had become pretty solid.[10]

Bush's final 53%–46% margin enabled him to carry forty of the fifty states.

The regional patterns of his support were much the same as those for Franklin Roosevelt in 1940 and 1944, when he won 55%–45% and 53%–46%. Both Roosevelt and Bush were nominees of the party long thought to be the minority in presidential elections, and both were seeking third consecutive victories for their party despite historical precedents and in the face of their opponents' sense that they lacked solid majority support. Both won solid national majorities, even though their party continued to fail to win control of most big-state governorships and legislatures and their views failed to command working majorities in either house of Congress. Both Roosevelt and Bush, supporters of an assertive foreign policy, won big in the hawkish South and failed to carry the dovish Farm Belt. Both Roosevelt and Bush, who despite their supposedly aristocratic backgrounds turned out to speak the language of ordinary Americans better than their opponents, carried the big industrial states of the East and the Midwest as a group by 52%–48% and won in the West by slightly wider margins.[11]

Of course there was not perfect symmetry in the results. In 1940, Roosevelt was supported by most poor Americans (though not, for instance, poor Yankee Farmers in Maine or mountaineers in Kentucky) and opposed by most rich Americans. In 1988, Bush's support came disproportionately from higher-income voters. But as in 1980 and 1984, the difference in voters' response by income was not as marked as in many regions of the country in the late 1930s and early 1940s: only among the top quarter and the bottom eighth of the income scale did either candidate win more than 60% of the vote. In the vast $12,500–$50,000 range which included 60% of the voters, the responses were not much different from those of voters generally.[12] The elderly, concerned perhaps about Social Security, were about evenly split; young voters, as in 1984, tended to be at least as Republican as the electorate generally, if not more so; the most pro-Dukakis age group, like the most pro-Mondale group in 1984, tended to be those in their thirties who had started following politics in the era of Vietnam and Watergate. The gender gap between men and women was between 7 and 10 percentage points. The gap between southern white men and single urban women was much, much wider—as big a difference as any in the electorate, and one symbolic, as the gap between the banker and the factory worker had been in the days of the New Deal's economic politics, of the basic divisions in this electorate.

V

No election settles everything in American politics even in the short term, and the election of 1988 will not necessarily settle the question of whether the policies followed by the Reagan administration set a new norm for America or whether they were an accident or aberration. If the gross national product should fall 50% from 1989 to 1992 as it did from 1929 to 1932, then it is safe to predict that the America which sang George Bush's favorite 1988 hit, "Don't Worry, Be Happy," as it elected him president will disappear as utterly as the America which whistled the theme song of the Roaring Twenties, "Ain't We Got Fun?," as it elected

Herbert Hoover. And less dire events could change the political outlook as well. The 1988 outcome is regarded as anything but inevitable by many analysts, especially Democrats who were quick to criticize Dukakis's strategy and tactics once it became apparent he was falling in the polls. And it is possible that the election could have been won by another kind of Democrat—Lloyd Bentsen, for example, whose calm experience and cool performances under pressure made a fine impression on voters and even on those liberal Democrats who had barred him from previous consideration for a spot on the national ticket. But it should be remembered that Bush gained his lead just as voters were focusing hard for the first time on the choice before them, and that in American politics, where both parties start out with about 40% of the electorate in almost any presidential contest, the 53%–46% win by Bush in 1988 will probably look no more accidental or contingent in the long run of history than does Franklin Roosevelt's 53%–46% defeat of Thomas Dewey in 1944. Even though the polls oscillated wildly until voters had focused closely on the candidates and the issues, opinion on the fundamental issues of foreign and economic policy favored Bush; and so did the balance of opinion on cultural issues and attitudes. For much of the campaign season in 1987 and 1988, experienced observers believed that the country was losing the resilience it had shown through most of the 1980s and falling back toward the alienation it had experienced during the previous two decades. The 1988 election result suggested that it was not, that it was not about to relive its immediate past.

The world was moving ahead, too, and rapidly. In December 1988, Mikhail Gorbachev came to New York and in an extraordinary speech at the United Nations, where Soviet–Third World majorities for years had condemned America as the imperialist power of the past and hailed Soviet and Third World socialism as the wave of the future, announced a 10% cut in Soviet conventional military forces and conceded that the Soviet economic system had failed while the Western system worked. In the same hall where Nikita Khrushchev had pounded his shoe and predicted that the Soviet economy would overtake America's by 1970, Gorbachev seemed to be conceding that the Soviets had lost the Cold War. Later, on Governor's Island in New York Harbor, Gorbachev met with President Reagan and Vice President Bush. With the three standing in overcoats in the chilly, clear December air, the classic 1920s and shimmering 1980s towers of Wall Street, the very symbol of the continuing strength of market capitalism, in the background, the Soviet leader in effect proferred his surrender to a president-elect who had been an Eisenhower Republican and the son of an investment banker and to a president who had been a Roosevelt Democrat and the son of a WPA worker: to a representative of the Yankees who had guided the American government and extended American power around the world earlier in the twentieth century and to a member of that American majority of Ellis Islanders, the descendants of the immigrants so many of whom had sailed past that very spot on Governor's Island toward the packed streets of New York, where they would make their way upward through hard work and with help on occasion from the voluntary organizations and political machines which were on their way to inventing the American version of the welfare state. The country so many different brands of Americans had built, a country that emerged confident from years of turmoil and stayed resilient after years of alienation, seemed increasingly to be a model others wanted to follow, a country that belonged not just to the many different kinds of Americans but to peoples all over the world.

⇶ ⇜

Notes

Introduction

1. Harold D. Lasswell, *Politics: Who Gets What, When, How* (New York: P. Smith, 1936).
2. See David M. Potter, *People of Plenty* (Chicago: Univ. of Chicago, 1954).
3. Greg J. Duncan, *Years of Poverty, Years of Plenty: The Changing Fortunes of American Workers and Families* (Ann Arbor: Survey Research Center, Univ. of Michigan, 1984).
4. Nathan Glazer and Daniel Patrick Moynihan, "Ethnicity," in Alan Bullock, Oliver Stallybrass, and Stephen Trombley, eds., *The Harper Dictionary of Modern Thought* (New York: Harper & Row, 1988) 285. Glazer and Moynihan also note that "In the Communist Manifesto, Marx and Engels forecast that all preindustrial distinctions of an ethnic character would disappear with the emergence of a world-wide industrial proletariat united by a perceived common condition and shared interest. The Workers of the World belief, central to Marxism, is increasingly presented as central to the falsification of Marxist prediction."
5. One historian describes "the twin processes that constitute a distinctive hallmark of the twentieth century: the industrialization of war and the politicization of economics." William H. McNeill, *The Pursuit of Power* (Chicago: Univ. of Chicago, 1982) 294. That is, as the mass production of armaments increased the size and powers of governments, so those governments also asserted control over and even gained ownership of large parts of their private economies.
6. The phrase is from David Riesman et al., *The Lonely Crowd* (New Haven: Yale Univ., 1950).
7. Robert H. Wiebe, *The Segmented Society* (New York: Oxford Univ., 1975).
8. For the classic statement, see Arthur M. Schlesinger, Jr., *The Cycles of American History* (Boston: Houghton Mifflin, 1987) 3–48.

671

9. See, e.g., William Manchester, *The Glory and the Dream: A Narrative History of America 1932–1972* (Boston: Little, Brown, 1974); Godfrey Hodgson, *America in Our Time: From World War II to Nixon, What Happened and Why* (New York: Random House, 1976); Theodore H. White, *America in Search of Itself: The Making of the President 1956–1980* (New York: Harper & Row, 1982). Many books on America in the 1960s are, not too surprisingly, negative and pessimistic: they seek to explain how things went wrong. See, e.g., William L. O'Neill, *Coming Apart: An Informal History of America in the 1960s* (New York: Quadrangle, 1971); Allen J. Matusow, *A History of Liberalism in the 1960s* (New York: Harper & Row, 1984); Charles R. Morris, *A Time of Passion: America 1960–1980* (New York: Harper & Row, 1984); Milton Viorst, *Fire in the Streets: America in the 1960's* (New York: Simon & Schuster, 1979). Other recent books celebrate the successes of the 1940s and 1950s and, at least implicitly, suggest things went sour after 1960. See, e.g., William L. O'Neill, *American High: The Years of Confidence, 1945–1960* (New York: The Free Press, 1986); John Patrick Diggins, *The Proud Decades: America in War and Peace, 1941–1960* (New York: Norton, 1988); Jeffrey Hart, *When the Going Was Good! American Life in the Fifties* (Westport: Arlington House, 1982).

10. Isaiah Berlin, *The Hedgehog and the Fox: An Essay on Tolstoy's View of History* (New York: Simon & Schuster, 1986) 36–37.

11. Joseph Alsop, *FDR: A Centenary Remembrance* (New York: Viking, 1982) 11, 254.

12. Both voted for him four times, as did Truman. On Reagan, see William E. Leuchtenberg, *In the Shadow of FDR from Harry Truman to Ronald Reagan* (Ithaca: Cornell Univ., 1985) 212–15.

13. Michael Barone, Grant Ujifusa, and Douglas Matthews, *The Almanac of American Politics 1972* (Boston: Gambit, 1971), *The Almanac of American Politics 1974* (Boston: Gambit, 1973), *The Almanac of American Politics 1976* (New York: Dutton, 1975), *The Almanac of American Politics 1978* (New York: Dutton, 1977), *The Almanac of American Politics 1980* (New York: Dutton, 1979); Michael Barone and Grant Ujifusa, *The Almanac of American Politics 1982* (Washington: Barone, 1981), *The Almanac of American Politics 1984* (Washington: National Journal, 1983), *The Almanac of American Politics 1986* (Washington: National Journal, 1985), *The Almanac of American Politics 1988* (Washington: National Journal, 1987), *The Almanac of American Politics 1990* (Washington: National Journal, 1989).

Chapter 1
Republican Chief

1. Michael Barnes, letter to the editor, *Washington Post,* 13 Apr. 1985.

2. At that time the United States, with its republican horror of monarchy, had ministers instead of ambassadors, who were traditionally considered the personal representatives of a sovereign.

3. The case was United States v. Addyston Pipe & Steel Co., 85 Fed. 270 (1898). Henry F. Pringle, *The Life and Times of William Howard Taft,* 2 vols. (New York: Farrar & Rinehart, 1939) 143–47.

4. Henry J. Abraham, *Justices and Presidents: A Political History of Appointments to the Supreme Court* (New York: Penguin, 1975) 175.

5. Pringle 1: 535.

6. *Historical Statistics of the United States, Colonial Times to 1970,* 2 vols. (Washington: U.S. Bureau of the Census, 1975) 1: 178.

7. Pringle 2: 1055. The legality of secondary boycotts was one of the most bitterly fought battles in the labor bill crafted by the chief justice's son, Senator Robert Taft, in 1947.

8. Pringle 2: 1030–34.

Chapter 2
Democratic Chief

1. See Nathan Silver, *Lost New York* (New York: American Legacy Press, 1967) 54–55, and Seymour Mandelbaum, *Boss Tweed's New York* (New York: Wiley, 1965) 92–93.

2. Nancy Joan Weiss, *Charles Francis Murphy, 1858–1924: Respectability and Responsibility in Tammany Politics* (Northampton, Mass.: Smith College, 1968) 8.

3. This was and is the official name, but soon almost everyone referred to the five-borough unit as New York City, even though in Queens and many parts of Brooklyn to this day "the city" means Manhattan.

4. The lines were extended to Brooklyn and Queens by 1918.

5. On Murphy generally, See Weiss; John M. Allswang, *Bosses, Machines, and Urban Voters* (Baltimore: Johns Hopkins, 1986) 60–90; Gustavus Myers, *The History of Tammany Hall* (New York: Boni & Livwright, 1917); J. Joseph Huthmacher, *Senator Robert F. Wagner and the Rise of Urban Liberalism* (New York: Atheneum, 1971) 12–38; *Dictionary of American Biography* 346–47.

6. Edward J. Flynn, the Democratic leader of the Bronx, remembered how he suggested for a vacancy on the Board of Education "a man whom I had known all my life, a man who had been an intimate friend of my family's. He was not politically well known, but he had been successful in business. When I put his name forward, Mr. Murphy said, 'He is not good.' I urged him. I said I knew him well and felt that I could guarantee him. 'Very well,' Mr. Murphy said quietly, 'if you want him, take him. The responsibility is yours.' A year or so later, when a situation developed where I needed the man's help in the Board of Education, I was turned down definitely and completely. Next time I met Mr. Murphy he asked me very formally, 'How is your friend So-and-so?' I was, of course, nonplused, and kept discreetly quiet. . . . I find that the choice of men is more important, perhaps, than policies." Ed Flynn, *You're the Boss* (New York: Harcourt, Brace, 1947) 132.

7. Frances Perkins, *The Roosevelt I Knew* (New York: Viking, 1946) 24–25.

8. Huthmacher 35.

9. David C. Hammack, *Power and Society: Greater New York at the Turn of the Century* (New York: Columbia Univ., 1987) 170–72. Seeking to be elected district leader when the incumbent died in 1892, Murphy made his case against a rival thus: "I don't believe he will do and feel that if he is named leader it won't be a year before the Republicans will control the district. The boys want me as leader." Weiss 21.

10. His power seems to have come solely from personal character. Ed Flynn describes how in 1922 he vetoed one candidate for Democratic leader of the Bronx with the single sentence "Mr. Brown will not do" and then broke a deadlock in favor of the thirty-

one-year-old Flynn by responding to his furious complaint with the simple statement, "There will be a meeting of the committee tomorrow, and you will be elected chairman." Flynn 27–33.

11. Murphy prefaced this statement by saying, "I don't like Roosevelt." Frank Friedel, *Franklin D. Roosevelt: The Ordeal* (Boston: Little, Brown, 1954) 66. James MacGregor Burns, *Roosevelt, the Lion and the Fox, 1882–1940* (New York: Harcourt, Brace, 1956) 73.

12. Robert K. Murray, *The 103rd Ballot* (New York: Harper & Row, 1976) 95–96.

Chapter 3
Madison Square Garden 1924

1. I define "culture" not in the technical sense of the anthropologist, but as indicating ethnic or regional or racial groups (more recently it might include groups based on gender, generation, or lifestyle) which share religious and personal values and mores and whose members see themselves, and are seen within the national society, as distinctive.

2. *Dictionary of American Biography* 347.

3. Henry F. Pringle, *The Life and Times of William Howard Taft* (New York: Farrar & Rinehart, 1939) 2: 1061.

4. The Democratic and Republican national conventions of 1988 still appointed such committees, though their proceedings were utterly controlled by appointees of the nominees.

5. *Dictionary of American Biography,* Supp. 3, 1941–45.

6. William H. Harbaugh, *Lawyer's Lawyer: The Life of John W. Davis* (New York: Oxford Univ., 1973).

7. A map of the counties where Coolidge received 60% or more of the vote is made up primarily of the New England Yankee diaspora, plus a bloc of counties around the historically Republican city of Philadelphia and the Civil War Republican counties of the mountain South from West Virginia to Tennessee.

8. Robert Rhodes James, *The British Revolution, 1880–1939* (New York: Knopf, 1977) 466.

9. Arthur M. Schlesinger, Jr., *The Age of Roosevelt: The Crisis of the Old Order* (Boston: Houghton Mifflin, 1957) 60.

10. Letter to William Saulsbury, 9 Dec. 1924, qtd. in Nathan Miller, *FDR: An Intimate History* (New York: Doubleday, 1983) 207.

Chapter 4
Our Country 1930

1. Stephen Saunders Webb, *1676: The End of American Independence* (New York: Knopf, 1984). Those who wonder at the American stereotype of hostile Indians should remember that there was warfare on the frontier for more than 200 years; the Comanches were attacking settlers within 50 miles of the capital of Texas in 1875. Robert A. Caro, *The Years of Lyndon Johnson: The Path to Power* (New York: Random House, 1981) 21.

2. Theodore Roosevelt, *The Winning of the West* (New York: Current Publishing, 1905) 1: 179–80.

3. David Hackett Fischer, *Albion's Seed: Four British Folkways in America* (New York: Oxford Univ., 1989). Fischer, in a book published just as this one was going to press, describes four major streams of settlement in the colonial period: from the east of England to Massachusetts, 1629–1640; from the south of England to Virginia, 1642–1675; from the North Midlands of England and Wales to the Delaware Valley, 1675–1725; and from the borders of north Britain and northern Ireland to the Piedmont and Appalachian highlands, 1718–1775. The cultures typical of these four streams of migration were transferred westward over the years: "Strong echoes of four British folkways may still be heard in the major dialects of American speech, in the regional patterns of American life, in the complex dynamics of American politics, and in the continuing conflict between four different ideas of freedom in the United States. For vivid illustrations of the westward transmission of such folkways, see Gerald McFarlane, *A Scattered People* (New York: Pantheon, 1985).

4. Bernard Bailyn, *The Peopling of British North America* (New York: Knopf, 1986) 59, 45–111.

5. John F. Rooney, Jr., et al., eds., *This Remarkable Continent* (College Station, Texas: Texas A&M, 1982) 46.

6. Robert H. Wiebe, *The Segmented Society: An Introduction to the Meaning of America* (New York: Oxford Univ., 1975) 21.

7. James M. McPherson, *Battle Cry of Freedom* (New York: Oxford Univ., 1988) 31, citing Henry B. Hubbart, *The Older Middle West, 1840–1880* (New York: Appleton-Century, 1936), and Richard Lyle Power, *Planting Corn Belt Culture: The Impress of the Upland Southerner and Yankee in the Old Northwest* (Indianapolis: Bobbs, Merrill, 1953).

8. Cf. Wiebe 22–23.

9. This I think is the clear teaching of McPherson's brilliant new definitive history.

10. Morton Keller, lecture, Harvard University, 1966.

11. Edmund Morris, *The Rise of Theodore Roosevelt* (New York: Coward, McCann, 1979) passim.

12. Gavin Wright, *Old South, New South: Revolutions in the Southern Economy Since the Civil War* (New York: Basic Books, 1986).

13. Frederick Jackson Turner, *The Frontier in American History* (Tucson: Univ. of Arizona, 1986) 1.

14. John Higham, *Send These to Me: Immigrants in Urban America* (Baltimore: Johns Hopkins Univ., 1984) 15.

15. These figures are derived from census data in the following way. I have assumed that Americans of native stock under age forty in 1930 were descended from native stock and foreign stock in proportion to those groups' share of the population in 1890. These assumptions yield the following results for 1930: whites descended from 1890 native stock, 51 million; whites of foreign stock or descended from 1890 foreign stock, 58 million; blacks and members of other races, 14 million. Given the rough-and-ready nature of the assumptions, rounding off is appropriate; greater precision or use of percentages would imply a degree of reliability the data do not have. Nonetheless, the overall picture is interesting. Most Americans in 1930 assumed that the majority of

their nation's population was white Protestant native stock. Yet this stock had, by some reasonable definitions, already become a minority. Cf. Richard A. Easterlin, "Immigration: Economic and Social Characteristics," in Stephan Thernstrom, ed., *Harvard Encyclopedia of American Ethnic Groups* (Cambridge: Harvard Univ., 1980) 485: "In the late 1840s, however, a major influx began which, if one includes descendants as well as immigrants, doubled the American population by 1920."

16. McPherson 130–44.

17. Most immigrants from Russia and a great many from other parts of eastern Europe were Jewish.

18. The following table shows, in thousands, the total number of immigrants from each source by decade.

Years	Germany	Scandinavia	Italy	Eastern and Central Europe	Russia
1860–69	723	96	10	5	2
1870–79	752	207	47	71	35
1880–89	1476	674	268	366	183
1890–99	578	389	603	652	450
1900–09	330	488	1930	2156	1501
1910–24	323	360	1692	1709	1181

Immigration is low from less developed countries, increases as they advance, then may taper off drastically when, as in Germany after 1890, they develop advanced economies themselves.

19. John Bodnar, *The Transplanted* (Bloomington: Indiana Univ., 1985) 23, 54–56, 55. Bodnar compiles evidence from hundreds of studies of immigrants and where they came from to revise the standard account of "millions of helpless, bewildered people" from "the peasant heart of Europe" in Oscar Handlin's brilliant, impressionistic *The Uprooted* (Boston: Little, Brown, 1985).

20. *The World Almanac 1930,* 322, from figures supplied by the American Jewish Committee for 1917 and 1927. According to the committee, Jews accounted for 45% of the residents of the Bronx, 35% of those of Brooklyn, and 26% of those of Manhattan in 1927.

21. Jews made up roughly 22% of Harvard's class of 1926 and 10% of Harvard's class of 1937. Stephen Thernstrom, "Poor But Hopeful Scholars," *Harvard Magazine,* Sept.–Oct. 1986, 120.

22. This was the highest such figure for native-born whites in American history; never before or after in American history did so many of them stick so close to home. The figure for blacks had been 90% in 1890–1910, the years when the system of southern segregation was established in law.

23. Wright, qtd. in Michael P. Johnson, "The Stagnant South," *New York Review of Books* 8 May 1986, 38–41.

24. For Catholics, see *Historical Statistics of the United States, Colonial Times to 1970,* 2 vols. (Washington: U.S. Bureau of the Census, 1975) 1: 391–92; for Jews, see *The*

World Almanac 1930, 322. A very large percentage of the immigrants of 1920–24 were Jewish.

25. Higham 158.

26. Geoffrey Perrett, *America in the Twenties* (New York: Simon & Schuster, 1982) 192–93.

27. Wiebe 29.

Chapter 5
American Politics 1930

1. D. W. Brogan, *The American Character* (New York: Knopf, 1944) 18.

2. For a dazzling view of how the different cultures of the four major streams of migration to colonial America continued into the 1980s, see David Hackett Fischer, *Albion's Seed: Four British Folkways in America* (New York: Oxford Univ., 1989) 783–898.

3. My father's aunt, born in West Virginia and eligible to cast her first vote in 1930, likes to tell how her father always voted Republican because Confederate soldiers, before he was born, overran his family's farm and burned their barn. Next to this ancestral memory, the tariff and free silver, the League of Nations and Prohibition and the business cycle were of minor importance. His wife, of Virginia stock, was always a Democrat and shocked him by announcing in 1920, when women got the vote, that she was going to vote the Democratic ticket. The daughter, who moved to Detroit, has voted Socialist, Democratic, and Republican over the years for reasons having nothing, so far as I can tell, to do with the Civil War.

4. See Harold Ickes, *Autobiography of a Curmudgeon* (New York: Reynal & Hitchcock, 1943) 74–257.

5. Robert Dahl, *Who Governs?* (New Haven: Yale Univ., 1961) 32–51.

6. *Historical Statistics of the United States, Colonial Times to 1970,* 2 vols. (Washington: U.S. Bureau of the Census, 1975) 2: 1071–72.

7. See Michael McGerr, *The Decline of Popular Politics: The American North, 1865–1928* (New York: Oxford Univ., 1986), for a survey of this subject.

8. In 1930, in a nation of 130 million people, *weekly* movie attendance was 90 million. *Historical Statistics* 1: 400. Leave aside invalids, sharecroppers, and subsistence farmers, and essentially everybody went to the movies every week.

9. Blacks were not barred from voting in the South during or immediately after Reconstruction, which ended in 1877, but rather in the two decades after 1890. C. Vann Woodward, *The Strange Career of Jim Crow* (New York: Oxford Univ., 1955).

10. Control of the Republican party in southern states was fought for by blacks and segregationist whites, neither of whom could deliver (outside Civil War Republican enclaves) any significant number of votes in general election. But they did control key convention votes, much to the chagrin and embarrassment of Republicans like Roosevelt and Taft.

11. David Burner, *Herbert Hoover: A Public Life* (New York: Atheneum, 1984) 194–96.

12. André Siegfried, *America Comes of Age* (London: Jonathan Cape, 1972) 1, 3.

13. Richard Franklin Bensel, *Sectionalism and American Political Development: 1880–1980* (Madison: Univ. of Wisconsin, 1984) 142–46.

14. Figures are not available for calendar year 1930 for state and local government spending. See *Historical Statistics* 1: 224; 2: 1100–1134.

15. *Historical Statistics* 2: 1100–1134.

16. By function, this spending included $2.2 billion on education, $1.8 billion on highways, $1.2 billion on defense, $700 million on postal service, $431 million on hospitals and health, $290 million on police, and $161 million on welfare.

17. Robert A. Caro, *The Years of Lyndon B. Johnson: The Path to Power* (New York: Random House, 1981) 306. In the 1922 primary, running against a member of the Ku Klux Klan, Rayburn celebrated the war in lurid terms: "By the Eternal God, my ancestors' blood has been spilled on nearly every hill in this land, that this should be a white man's country." D. B. Hardeman and Donald Bacon, *Rayburn* (Austin: Texas Monthly, 1987) 113.

Chapter 6
New Era

1. Made more conspicuous by his construction of the huge Commerce Department Building, which dwarfs the Treasury a block away and is now named after him.

2. David Burner, *Herbert Hoover: A Public Life* (New York: Atheneum, 1984) 13.

3. Burner 27, 47.

4. Burner 51.

5. See, e.g., Richard Hofstadter's uncharacteristically wrongheaded portrait, which is based more on Hoover's often disingenuous writings than on the facts of his career. *The American Political Tradition and the Men Who Made It* (New York: Vintage, 1974) 385, 407. Compare Herbert Stein, *The Revolution in Fiscal Policy*.

6. Qtd. in Burner 167.

7. Richard Franklin Bensel, *Sectionalism and American Political Development: 1880–1980* 139–46.

8. David Burner 84–106.

9. E. E. Schattschneider, *Politics, Pressures and Tariffs: A Study of Free Private Enterprise in Pressure Politics as Shown by the 1929–30 Revision of the Tariff* (New York: Prentice-Hall, 1935) 283–84.

10. William Starr Myers and Walter H. Newton, *The Hoover Administration, A Documented Narrative* (New York: Scribner's, 1936) 425 and 424–41 generally.

11. The arithmetic was this. Solidly on the pro-tariff side in 1929 were 41 Republicans (plus a Republican vacancy in Pennsylvania that was later filled by Joseph Grundy, head of the Pennsylvania Manufacturers Association) and 4 Democrats (both senators from Louisiana and Florida). Tending to oppose the tariff were 35 Democrats, 14 Republicans, and Farmer-Laborite Shipstead. The Republicans were Johnson of California, Borah of Idaho, Brookhart of Iowa, Schall of Minnesota, Norris and Howell of Nebraska, Cutting of New Mexico, Frazier and Nye of North Dakota, Pine of Oklahoma, Norbeck and McMaster of South Dakota, and LaFollette and Blaine of Wisconsin—none from east of Madison, Wisconsin. Potentially the anti-tariff group was the larger bloc, but it was not solid. Anti-tariff senators could be pared off to support higher rates for locally important products; pro-tariff senators could seldom be detached from their cause.

12. Jude Wanniski, in *The Way the World Works* (New York: Simon & Schuster, 1978) 127–41, argues that Smoot-Hawley produced the 1929 stock market crash; he provides an elaborate timetable showing turning points in the course of the legislation and contends that they resulted in sharp rises and falls on the stock market. Who can say for sure whether he is right? His book does not attempt to explain why macroeconomic events occurred, but to describe what happened to the extent it has a bearing on politics.

13. Charles P. Kindleberger, *The World in Depression 1929–39* (Berkeley: Univ. of California, 1973) 132.

14. The refusal to reapportion after the 1920 census was deliberate and reflected the same fears and hatreds that produced the 1921 and 1924 immigration restriction acts. Political self-interest, nostalgia for a rural past, hostility to immigrants, and the difficulty of moving any legislative proposal forward all contributed to Congress's refusal to reapportion in the 1920s. The 1929 law froze the membership of the House at 435, a number that had no historical significance but was simply the one set after the 1910 census. There were proposals in the 1920s to increase it to 460 or 483, but it has stayed at 435 ever since, except when the admission of Alaska and Hawaii as states briefly raised it to 437. *Congressional Quarterly's Guide to U. S. Elections* (Washington: Congressional Quarterly, 1975) 530–34.

Chapter 7
Depression

1. Joseph A. Schumpeter, *Business Cycles: A Theoretical, Historical and Statistical Analysis of the Capitalistic Process* (New York: McGraw Hill, 1939) 2: 911, qtd. in Charles P. Kindleberger, *The World in Depression 1929–39* (Berkeley: Univ. of California, 1973) 137.

2. For a definitive description of the state of the polling art in 1932, see Claude E. Robinson, *Straw Votes: A Study of Political Prediction* (New York: Columbia Univ., 1932). As the title indicates, the focus was on predicting results (which, of course, a poll cannot do: it can only tell the state of opinion at the time the poll is taken). In the chapter "Straw Polls on Issues" the only issue treated is Prohibition.

3. The Civil War did not produce, as is often thought, a reliable Republican majority. The Republicans did win all but two of the seven presidential elections in the three decades after the war, but they won most of them by narrow electoral college margins; they ran behind the Democrats in popular votes in four out of the seven, and they won their biggest percentages in years when large numbers of blacks voted in the South. They held majorities in the Senate for most of these years, but in only two elections between 1872 and 1894 did they win a majority in the House.

4. The years between 1894 and 1930 were the one period in the country's history when it had a solid Republican majority, beginning with the depression of the 1890s and ending with the depression of the 1930s. Republicans won a huge majority in the House elections of 1894, won four successive presidential elections with solid majorities starting in 1896, and did not lose control of the White House again until they split in 1912. Democrats won congressional elections only in 1910, 1912, 1914, and 1916. Woodrow Wilson's victory in 1912 was made possible only by the Republican split. He won by the narrowest of margins in 1916 after his Republican opponent, Charles Evans Hughes, while staying at a hotel in Long Beach, California, neglected to call

on Governor Hiram Johnson, who was staying at another room at the time. Hughes apologized for this apparent snub and said he didn't know Johnson was there until it was almost time to leave; but Johnson and his progressives did not work hard for Hughes, and he lost California by 3,000 votes in an election so close that this then medium-sized state's electoral votes would have made him president.

5. *Historical Statistics of the United States, Colonial Times to 1970,* 2 vols. (Washington: U.S. Bureau of the Census, 1975) 1: 135.

6. See Paul Starr, *The Social Transformation of American Medicine* (New York: Basic Books, 1982) 184–94.

7. Geoffrey Perrett, *America in the Twenties* (New York: Simon & Schuster, 1982) 432–33.

8. The fertility rate remained in the 76 to 80 range even as the economy began to recover in the 1930s; it then climbed to 83 in 1941, as war production began, to 91 in 1942, and to 93 in 1943. It would not fall again to the 1930s levels until the early 1970s. *Historical Statistics* 1: 49; *Statistical Abstract of the United States: 1984* (Washington: GPO, 1984) 64.

9. If American women had continued bearing children at the 1930 rate, there would have been 3.2 million additional births between 1931 and 1940. Assume that most of those unborn children were wanted and would have been conceived and born if the economy had not collapsed, and you get some idea of the human impact of the depression.

10. The following table shows the drop in total national income and in employees' compensation, farm income, business and professional proprietors' income, and rental income. *Historical Statistics of the United States,* 1: 235–36.

National Income ($ billions)

Year	Total	Employees' Compensation	Farm Income	Business Proprietors' Income	Rental Income
1929	86.8	51.1	6.2	9.0	5.4
1930	75.4	46.8	4.3	7.6	4.8
1931	59.7	39.8	3.4	5.8	3.8
1932	42.8	31.1	2.1	3.6	2.7
1933	40.3	29.5	2.6	3.3	2.0
1934	49.5	34.3	3.0	4.7	1.7
1935	57.2	37.3	5.3	5.5	1.7
1936	65.0	42.9	4.3	6.7	1.8
1937	73.7	47.9	6.0	7.2	2.1
1938	67.4	45.0	4.4	6.9	2.6
1939	72.6	48.1	4.4	7.4	2.7
1940	81.1	52.1	4.5	8.6	2.9
1941	104.2	64.8	6.4	11.1	3.5

11. "Keynes could not have done better," one economist wrote in the 1960s. Maurice Niveau, *Histoire des faits économiques contemporains* (Paris: Presses Universitaires de France, 1969), qtd. in Kindleberger 135.

12. Hoover's policy now is attacked by some free market enthusiasts, who say he should have let wages fall and then watched as the economy bounced back as it had in 1922 or 1908. But the other precedent—the 1980s—undercuts their argument, for wages were cut savagely then and the downturn was prolonged nonetheless.

13. This was a terrible misjudgment in retrospect but was widely shared at the time. Even liberal writer Stuart Chase (New York Times, Nov. 4, 1929), a critic of the economic order of the 1920s who foresaw "a cyclic tailspin," thought "we probably have three more years of prosperity ahead of us" before it began. Arthur M. Schlesinger, Jr., *The Age of Roosevelt: The Crisis of the Old Order* (Boston: Houghton Mifflin, 1957) 162–65.

14. Richard Neustadt and Ernest May gave their graduate students the economic statistics from the 1929 crash up through early 1930 with a brief history of the previous four decades. "The financial panics of 1907 and 1921, even the depression of 1893–97, yield them—along with Herbert Hoover—no solid footing to predict what they, unlike him, know is coming," they report. *Thinking in Time* (New York: The Free Press, 1986) 262.

15. John Bright, *Hizzoner Big Bill Thompson, An Idyll of Chicago* (New York: Jonathan Cape & Harrison Smith, 1930) 293.

16. By my definition, 33 of the seats the Democrats gained came in the Borderlands, and 25 of these districts had been captured by the Republicans only in 1928. They were Illinois 21; Indiana 3; Kentucky 3, 4, 6, 7, 8, 9; Maryland 2; Missouri 5, 6, 7, 13, 14, 16; Nebraska 4, 5; New Mexico at-large; North Carolina 9, 10; Oklahoma 1, 5; Virginia 7, 9; and West Virginia 3. With no Catholic at the head of the ticket, the Democrats had been generally expected to gain all or most of those seats in 1930; in fact, only one Borderlands district picked up by the Republicans in 1928 was held by them in 1930: Virginia 2, including the Navy's port of Norfolk. Other Borderlands districts picked up by Democrats were Illinois 22, 23, 24, 25; Indiana 1; Kentucky 10; Maryland 6; and Ohio 6.

17. By my count, with a generous definition, they amount to 15: Connecticut 1, 4; Illinois 3, 7; Indiana 5, 6, 11, 13; Massachusetts 2; New Jersey 3; Ohio 3, 12; and Pennsylvania 11, 14. The Indiana districts might easily be classified as Borderlands, since their voting had followed Borderlands patterns since the Civil War era. The Democrats lost 2 seats in 1930, one of them the industrial Pennsylvania 12, the other Texas 14. Both had substantial Catholic populations and had been carried by Smith in 1928 despite historic Republican trends.

18. Richard B. Cheney and Lynne V. Cheney, *Kings of the Hill* (New York: Continuum, 1983) 159.

19. See Robert A. Caro, *The Years of Lyndon Johnson: The Path to Power* (New York: Random House, 1981) 218–19.

20. Starting in 1922, Senator George Norris had campaigned to change the constitutional calendar so that Congress would not assemble in December of election years, after many members, to whom the old Wall Street and political term "lame duck" had been attached, had not sought reelection or been defeated. See Hans Sperber and Travis Trittschuh, *Dictionary of American Political Terms* 233–34.

21. Kindleberger 172. His graph "The contracting spiral of world trade, January 1929 to March 1933" is a gem.

Chapter 8
Disorder

1. Evan Anders, *Boss Rule in South Texas: The Progressive Era* (Austin: Univ. of Texas, 1982) 122. Note that Garner characteristically defined the opposition not as Republicans but as Yankees: the Civil War influence remained strong.

2. William "Fishbait" Miller, *Fishbait: The Memoirs of the Congressional Doorkeeper* (New York: Warner, 1978) 219.

3. Garner's admiring biographer glosses over the sales tax episode in a few sentences. Bascom N. Timmons, *Garner of Texas: A Personal History* (New York: Harper, 1948) 141.

4. James MacGregor Burns, *Roosevelt, the Lion and the Fox 1882–1940* (New York: Harcourt, Brace, 1956) 129.

5. Allan A. Michie and Frank Ryhlick, *Dixie Demagogues* (New York: Vanguard, 1939) 37–40.

6. Frank Friedel, *Franklin D. Roosevelt: The Ordeal* (Boston: Little, Brown, 1954) 242–44. Freidel quotes a letter from Roosevelt to Walter Lippmann, the writer of *Public Opinion,* in August 1928: "I tried the finite experiment this year of writing and delivering my speech wholly for the benefit of the radio audience and press rather than for any forensic effect it might have on the delegates and audience in the convention hall." See also Burns 99. " 'It seems to me,' Roosevelt said in 1929, 'that radio is gradually bringing to the ears of our people matters of interest concerning their country which they refused to consider in the daily press with their eyes.' " Arthur M. Schlesinger, Jr., *The Age of Roosevelt: The Crisis of the Old Order* (Boston: Little, Brown, 1956) 393.

7. Farley had tried to get the rule changed—an ill-advised maneuver that Roosevelt had to issue a statement in Albany to renounce. Farley was often hailed as a political wizard and shrewd maneuverer, but his judgment was fallible, and his chief assets seem to have been a friendly personality, a capacity for hard work, integrity, and a remarkable lack of guile.

8. And he may have been persuaded to do so by Joseph P. Kennedy, son-in-law of former Boston mayor John F. Fitzgerald and a millionaire banker and movie maker in his own right. Kennedy, who always cultivated media moguls, was a friend of Hearst; and in July 1932 he peppered him with calls urging him to support Roosevelt, to whose campaign Kennedy gave $50,000 and assistance in raising another $150,000. Twenty-eight years later, when the Democratic convention met in Los Angeles and nominated his son for president, Joseph Kennedy stayed in the Beverly Hills villa of Marion Davies, Hearst's longtime mistress. Doris Kearns Goodwin, *The Fitzgeralds and the Kennedys* (New York: Simon & Schuster, 1987) 428–29, 800–801.

9. H. L. Mencken, *A Carnival of Buncombe: Writings on Politics* (Chicago: Univ. of Chicago, 1984) 256, 259.

10. Even a Columbia University sociologist writing in 1932 suggested with astonishing naiveté that polls are supposed to provide "political prediction." Claude E. Robinson, *Straw Votes: A Study of Political Prediction* (New York: Columbia Univ., 1932) 180–84.

11. Qtd. in William Starr Myers and Walter H. Newton, *The Hoover Administration: A Documented Narrative* (New York: Scribner's, 1936) 516–21.

12. Qtd. in Myers and Newton 514.

13. The National coalition won 554 seats to Labour's 52 in 1931.

14. Here are the percentages of the popular vote won by the Communist, Social Democratic, and Nazi parties in the German elections of May 1928, September 1930, July 1932, November 1932, and March 1933.

	1928	*1930*	*1932*	*1932*	*1933*
Communist	11	13	14	17	12
Social Democratic	30	24.5	22	20	18
Nazi	3	18	37	33	42

The Communist percentage did rise slightly. But the total on the left declined from 41% to 30% between 1928 and 1933, while the Nazi percentage rose from 3% to 42%.

15. Kenneth McNaught, *The Pelican History of Canada* (New York: Penguin, 1969) 252–55. "The major Acts of the Bennett New Deal provided for unemployment and social insurance, a natural products marketing board, minimum wages and maximum hours in industry and extension of federally supported farm credit." King, who is sometimes depicted as a counterpart of Franklin Roosevelt, actually took positions similar to those of Roosevelt's Republican opponents—but with political success like Roosevelt's (the Liberals won 171 seats to 39 for the Conservatives in 1935 and held power until 1957). "Noting the Liberal slogan: 'It's King or Chaos,' one historian has written that 'Liberalism, as it emerged in Canada after 1935, was the counterpart of Baldwin conservatism in Great Britain, of Le Front Populaire in France, and of Rooseveltian democracy:—it represented the huddling together of frightened people uncertain of their way in a chaotic world.' " McNaught 255, quoting A. R. M. Lower, *Colony to Nation* (Toronto: Longman's, Green, 1936) 519.

16. The Social Democrats won parliamentary majorities in Denmark in 1929, in Norway in 1935, and in Sweden in 1936. "Their financial and economic programme was without originality, and was not even oriented toward Socialism. . . . They concentrated on promoting full employment, public works and increased wages, and on improving the peasants' lot with guaranteed prices and premiums on exports." *The Cambridge Modern History* (Cambridge: Cambridge Univ., 1988) 12: 537.

17. William E. Leuchtenberg, *Franklin D. Roosevelt and the New Deal 1932–1940* (New York: Harper & Row, 1963) 25–27.

Chapter 9
New Deal

1. See Kenneth S. Davis, *FDR: The New York Years* (New York: Random House, 1985) 3–4, and *FDR: The New Deal Years, 1933–1937* (New York: Random House, 1986)

19–21, 381–83; Barry D. Karl, *The Uneasy State: The United States from 1915 to 1945* (Chicago: Univ. of Chicago, 1983) 165–67.

2. This is true whether the Democratic showing is measured against that in the last previous Democratic victory (Woodrow Wilson's 49%–46% win in 1916) or against the better of the two most recent anti-Republican showings, the combined Davis-LaFollette vote of 1924 or the Smith vote in 1928:

	% Democratic 1916	% Democratic Progressive 1924	% Democratic 1928	% Democratic 1932	Change, 1916–1932	Change, 1924–1932 or 1928–1932
UNITED STATES	49	46	41	58	+ 9	+12
Deep South	80	79	56	88	+ 8	+ 9
Borderlands	53	54	42	64	+11	+10
Northeast	45	38	40	52	+ 7	+12
Northwest	48	48	38	61	+13	+13

3. D.B. Hardeman and Donald Bacon, *Rayburn* (Austin: Texas Monthly, 1987) 105–20.

Chapter 10
Hundred Days

1. See Hugh Gregory Gallagher, *FDR's Splendid Deception* (New York: Dodd, Mead, 1985) 65–67, 200.

2. William E. Leuchtenberg, *Franklin D. Roosevelt and the New Deal, 1932–1940* (New York: Harper & Row, 1963) 41; Arthur M. Schlesinger, Jr., *The Coming of the New Deal* (Boston: Houghton Mifflin, 1958) 1–2.

3. The committee was chaired by Peter Norbeck of South Dakota when the Republicans controlled the Senate and by Duncan Fletcher of Florida after the Democrats took control. Neither was a commanding presence.

4. Indeed, the word *depression* historically referred not to a diminished level of economic activity but to the depressed level of prices.

5. Rexford G. Tugwell, *The Battle for Democracy* 213, qtd. in Leuchtenberg 34.

6. Leuchtenberg 58.

Chapter 11
Blue Eagle

1. James MacGregor Burns, *Roosevelt, the Lion and the Fox, 1882–1940* (New York: Harcourt, Brace, 1956) 192.

2. Arthur M. Schlesinger, Jr., *The Age of Roosevelt: The Coming of the New Deal* (Boston: Houghton Mifflin, 1959) 132.

3. Schlesinger 473, 500.

4. Kenneth S. Davis, *FDR: The Beckoning of Destiny* 779–85, and *FDR: The New Deal Years, 1933–1937* (New York: Random House, 1986) 629.

5. Frank Kent, *Without Grease: Political Behavior 1934–36* (New York: Morrow, 1936) 10–11.

6. Roosevelt had "an unwontedly irritable uncertainty" about where the center of the electorate was. Davis, *New Deal* 416.

7. So brilliantly that his words were echoed by Ronald Reagan during his summation in his debate with Jimmy Carter in October 1980.

8. E. Digby Baltzell, *Puritan Boston and Quaker Philadelphia* (New York: The Free Press, 1979) 386–87.

9. The districts where the Democrats gained at least 5 percentage points (based on rounded-off percentages) were Alabama 7; California 7, 11–13, 15, 17; Colorado 3; Connecticut 1; Idaho 1, 2; Illinois 1–4, 7–10 (i.e., almost all of Cook County); Iowa 2, 6, 9; Kansas 1, 3; Massachusetts 8, 9, 12; Michigan 11, 12, 14, 15; Montana 1, 2; Nebraska 4; Nevada at-large; New Jersey 2, 9; New York 28, 38–41; Ohio 9, 12, 16, 18, 22; Oklahoma 5; Pennsylvania 1–8, 10, 14, 16–21, 23, 26, 27, 30; South Dakota 1; Tennessee 1; Utah 1, 2; Vermont at-large; Washington 2, 3, 6; West Virginia 2, 5, 6; Wyoming at-large.

  Districts where the Democrats lost at least 5 percentage points (based on rounded-off percentages) were Connecticut 4; Illinois 16–18, 20–25; Indiana 2, 7–9; Iowa 3, 4; Kansas 5, 6; Maryland 2–6; Michigan 4, 8; Nebraska 1, 3; New Mexico at-large; New York 3, 4, 11–14, 18, 20, 22, 23, 31, 32, 37; North Carolina 3, 4, 8–10; Ohio 11, 13, 14; Oklahoma 2–4, 6; Oregon 2; Tennessee 2, 4; Wisconsin 1–10 (the Progressive showing hurt the Democrats here).

  The following districts had incommensurate results because of redistricting or no two-party contest in one or both elections: Alabama 1–3, 6, 8, 9; Arkansas 1–7; California 1, 4–6, 8, 9, 16, 19; Florida 1–4, at-large; Georgia 1–10; Kentucky 1–9; Louisiana 1–8; Massachusetts 6, 10, 11; Minnesota 1–9; Mississippi 1–7; Missouri 1–13; North Carolina 2, 5; Ohio 20; Pennsylvania 11, 13, 15, 28, 31–34; South Carolina 1–6; Tennessee 3, 5–9; Texas 1–21; Virginia 1–9; Washington 5.

10. The lines are not easy to draw, and some may disagree with my characterization of 172 of the 1934 districts as industrial/immigrant and 153 as rural/Yankee. This division excludes the 102 seats in the South and the 8 at-large seats of Connecticut, Illinois, New York, Ohio, and Oklahoma, which are not used for this analysis because some voters would be counted twice.

  The industrial immigrant districts are California 4–7, 11–18; Colorado 1; Connecticut 1–5; Delaware at-large; Illinois 1–10; Indiana 1, 3, 10–12; Kentucky 3; Maryland 2–4; Massachusetts 1–15; Michigan 1, 5, 6, 11–17; Minnesota 3–5, 8; New Hampshire 1, 2; New Jersey 1–14; New York 1–25, 28, 30, 33, 35, 38, 40–42; Ohio 1–3, 9, 12 14, 16, 18–22; Oregon 3; Pennsylvania 1–9, 11–14, 17, 19, 21, 23–34; Rhode Island 1, 2; Washington 1, 6; West Virginia 1, 5, 6; Wisconsin 1, 4, 5.

  The rural/Yankee districts are Arizona at-large; California 1–3, 8–10, 19, 20; Colorado 2–4; Idaho 1, 2; Illinois 11–25; Indiana 2, 4–9; Iowa 1–9; Kansas 1–7; Kentucky 1, 2, 4–9; Maine 1–3; Maryland 1, 5, 6; Michigan 2–4, 7–10; Minnesota 1, 2, 6, 7, 9; Missouri 1–3, 6–10; Montana 1, 2; Nebraska 1–5; Nevada at-large; New Mexico at-large; New York 26, 27, 29, 31, 32, 34, 36, 37, 39, 43; North Dakota at-large; Ohio 4–8, 10, 11, 13, 15, 17; Oklahoma 1–8; Oregon 1, 2; Pennsylvania 10, 15, 16,

18, 20, 22; South Dakota 1, 2; Utah 1, 2; Vermont at-large; Washington 2–5; West Virginia 2–4; Wisconsin 2, 3, 6–10; Wyoming at-large.

11. These percentages are of what I call the non-trivial vote. They are calculated from returns in *Congressional Quarterly's Guide to U.S. Elections,* which includes results only for candidates who received 5% or more of the vote. The exclusion of minor candidates mildly inflates the percentages for both major parties, but not, I think, in a way that affects my analysis. *Congressional Quarterly's Guide to U.S. Elections* (Washington: Congressional Quarterly, 1975).

12. The classic statement of this thesis is by Samuel Lubell in *The Future of American Politics* (New York: Harper, 1952) 44. Professor David Schoenbaum of the University of Iowa was kind enough to present me with a copy of the first edition of this work, inscribed by Lubell "For Arthur Krock—the best political reporter in the country."

13. Again, these are percentages of the non-trivial vote (see note 11).

14. George McJimsey, *Harry Hopkins* (Cambridge: Harvard Univ., 1987) 58–59.

15. Robert E. Sherwood, *Roosevelt and Hopkins* (New York: Harper, 1950) 2–3.

16. McJimsey 106, 15.

17. "The *Fortune* Survey," *Fortune,* Jan. 1937, 86–87.

18. William E. Leuchtenberg, *Franklin D. Roosevelt and the New Deal, 1932–1940* (New York: Harper, 1963) 340.

Chapter 12
Economic Politics

1. For example, Harry Hopkins had thought in 1933 that NIRA would produce 6 million jobs, ending the need for federal relief. It produced only a fraction of that number, and Hopkins had millions on his public payrolls for most of the rest of the 1930s. See George McJimsey, *Harry Hopkins* (Cambridge: Harvard Univ., 1987) 56.

2. Arthur M. Schlesinger, Jr., *The Age of Roosevelt: The Coming of the New Deal* (Boston: Houghton Mifflin, 1959) 174.

3. Schlesinger 165–67.

4. See T. Harry Williams, *Huey Long* (New York: Random House, 1981) 420–553; Alan Brinkley, *Voices of Protest: Huey Long, Father Coughlin & The Great Depression* (New York: Random House, 1983) 30–32.

5. Williams 682.

6. Williams 692–93.

7. Kenneth S. Davis, *FDR: The New Deal Years, 1933–1937* (New York: Random House, 1986) 401–5; Williams, 693–98; Arthur M. Schlesinger, Jr., *The Politics of Upheaval* (Boston: Houghton Mifflin, 1960) 15–68.

8. "The *Fortune* Survey," *Fortune,* July 1935, 67.

9. "The *Fortune* Survey," *Fortune,* Oct. 1936, 210.

10. See Russell Baker, *Growing Up* (New York: Congdon & Weed, 1982), for an account of how the death of a husband could destroy a family's way of life.

11. Frances Perkins, *The Roosevelt I Knew* (New York: Viking, 1946) 292.

12. All the experts except Altmyer lived on and remained concerned with Social Security into the 1980s. Richard Neustadt and Ernest May note that Altmyer, the first commissioner of the Social Security Administration, and Ball, whom he chose as his successor, "dominated the agency from 1935 to 1973, along with [Altmyer's] onetime assistant, Wilbur Cohen, later (1965–69) HEW Secretary, who was still actively advising the congressional committees [in the 1980s]." *Thinking in Time* (New York: The Free Press, 1986) 226. Ball played a key role in fashioning the Social Security rescue packages of 1977 and 1983.

13. Neustadt and May 102.

14. Brinkley 4–7; Davis 497, 501–3.

15. Brinkley 245.

16. Williams 814–18; Davis 501–3; *Des Moines Register,* 28 Apr. 1935.

17. Williams 802–7. Farley always had a reputation as a brilliant wheeler-dealer. Actually he was scrupulously honest, never asking fellow Cabinet members for any jobs for political appointees, and politically naive, nearly losing the 1932 convention for Roosevelt by trying to kill the two-thirds rule and pretty much ending his political effectiveness by insisting on having his name placed in nomination against Roosevelt in 1940.

18. James A. Farley, *Behind the Ballots* (New York: Harcourt, Brace, 1938) 323.

19. Farley 324–25.

20. James A. Farley, memorandum, 15 May 1935, ts., Franklin D. Roosevelt Library.

21. Farley often dictated memoranda after his working day. His May 15 memo says that a "poll has been taken." The May 24 memo says "an extensive poll was being prepared," and a June 18 memo mentions a Hurja poll "made prior to the Supreme Court decision" on NRA, which was handed down May 27. None of the memoranda mentions Huey Long; only in *Behind the Ballots,* published in 1938, does Farley mention the Long results. Farley, memoranda, 15 May, 24 May, 18 June 1935, ts.

22. Farley, *Behind the Ballots* 249–50. This account is followed by Williams 845, and Harold Ickes, *The Diaries of Harold L. Ickes,* 3 vols. (New York: Simon & Schuster, 1953), 1: 462, and appears to be the only source for the Long poll.

23. That evening Farley had dinner with Roosevelt; also present were Will Hays, the movie industry czar and former postmaster general and Republican national chairman, and Joseph P. Kennedy. After dinner they watched a movie about work relief in Los Angeles. "After the picture was finished," Farley recorded, "the President, Emil Hurja and I went over the poll which Hurja had prepared. The poll was made prior to the Supreme Court decision [invalidating NRA] after whch, in my judgment, the situation changed in favor of the President. The President was greatly interested in the poll. . . . The poll showed that he would carry without difficulty all of the western states with the possible exception of Colorado, including Wisconsin and Minnesota, of course. It showed that in the Eastern states he had lost some ground which, of course, does not worry us because that condition can be corrected in due course." Farley, memorandum, 18 June 1935. The poll result suggests an electoral vote base of 250, without counting any of the big industrial states—a very good start toward the 266 needed for a majority.

24. Farley, *Behind the Ballots* 251.

25. "Convention Here of U.S. Chamber May Hit New Deal," *Washington Star,* 28 Apr. 1935, 1.

26. Robert F. Wagner III, personal interview, 21 Nov. 1986. He is referred to invariably as Mr. Murphy in Ed Flynn's memoir, in which every other man, including Franklin Roosevelt, is referred to by just his last name. Edward J. Flynn, *You're the Boss* (New York: Harcourt, Brace, 1947).

27. J. Joseph Huthmacher, *Senator Robert F. Wagner and the Rise of Urban Liberalism* (New York: Atheneum, 1971) 12.

28. If there was such a thing. The theory of an inner club running the Senate was popularized by *New York Times* reporter William S. White in *The Citadel* (New York: Harper, 1950), describing the Senate he covered in the 1950s, and was attested to by Dean Acheson, who placed Wagner in it and named as its "beaux ideals" Alben Barkley, Walter George, and Arthur Vandenberg. Dean Acheson, *Sketches from Life* (New York: Harper, 1961) 132. But "was there an inner club at all?" asks Nelson Polsby, after noting tartly that "it is difficult, without an exhaustive set of identifications from those in the know, to say who was and who was not in the inner club at a given time." Nelson W. Polsby, *Congress and the Presidency* (Englewood Cliffs: Prentice-Hall, 1986) 93; see also pages 88–93. Perhaps the most that can be said is that some senators were mutually recognized as having weight and reliability, and that the resulting web of mutual respect tended to make it easier for all of them to accomplish their legislative and political goals.

29. See Huthmacher for a highly useful biography of this brilliant politician.

30. Huthmacher 112–13. One example of Wagner's astuteness came later in his career, in 1944, when Treasury Secretary Henry Morgenthau wanted to omit New Hampshire Republican Senator Charles Tobey from the delegation to the conference being held at Bretton Woods in his home state. Wagner went to Dean Acheson and protested that the exclusion would not only "strike at the whole oligarchical structure of Senate committees, but it would be regarded as a particularly mean partisan attack on Tobey, who was a very decent man even though overinclined to somewhat florid oratory." Acheson 137–38. Tobey turned out to be a staunch supporter of the measures agreed on at the conference.

31. Leon H. Keyserling, qtd. in Katie Louchheim, *The Making of the New Deal: The Insiders Speak* (Cambridge: Harvard Univ., 1983) 199–200.

32. Davis 510–13.

33. Thomas I. Emerson, qtd. in Louchheim 211.

34. On the delegation issue, see Barry D. Karl, *The Uneasy State: The United States from 1915 to 1945* (Chicago: Univ. of Chicago, 1983) 143–45.

35. Willkie lobbied Roosevelt personally against the bill and essentially lost his job because of it. Steve Neal, *Dark Horse* (Garden City: Doubleday, 1984) 29–36.

36. During World War II, when White House staffers were housed in the Vanderbilt mansion during presidential trips to Hyde Park, Roosevelt teased White House telephone operator Louise Hachmeister by saying she must stay in Mrs. Vanderbilt's Marie Antoinette (or was it Madame du Barry or Empress Josephine?) bedroom and told the Vanderbilt heiress whom he persuaded to donate the house to the government that it

was "God awful." William D. Hassett, *Off the Record with FDR, 1942–1945* (New Brunswick: Rutgers Univ., 1958), 4, 8–9, 13.

37. See Harold Ickes, *The Secret Diary of Harold Ickes,* 3 vols. (New Brunswick: Rutgers Univ., 1958) 1: 248–51. "I am not very fussy about my food," writes Ickes, who mentions food constantly in his diary and himself set a sumptuous table to which other New Dealers, including Roosevelt, often repaired for a good meal, "and I suppose one ought to be satisfied with dining on and with a solid-gold service, but it does seem a little out of proportion to use a solid-gold knife and fork on ordinary roast mutton. Besides which, I never did like carrots. Wine was served officially at dinner for the first time since prohibition went into effect back in President Wilson's administration. Mrs. Roosevelt announced that she would serve one glass each of two domestic wines and she kept her word. The sherry was passable, but the champagne was undrinkable. I hopefully took one drink and then set my glass down with a final gesture. Mrs. Farley almost made a face when she tasted the champagne." Ickes added that three days later, after a group gathered late at night in the White House, Roosevelt "asked me whether I had ever tasted worse champagne and I frankly told him that I never had. He said that about fifteen minutes before dinner he had asked Mrs. Roosevelt about the wine and she said she was going to serve domestic champagne from New York State, recommended by Rex Tugwell. The President told her that she ought not to serve domestic champagne, but she replied that it had been on the ice and that it was too late to change. The President said that he has been apologizing ever since to dinner guests for this champagne."

38. In 1941, even before Pearl Harbor, Roosevelt "astonished the [Treasury] Department by averring that he favored taxing all personal income above $100,000 a year at $99^{1}/_{2}$ or 100 percent. 'Why not?' he asked. 'None of us is ever going to make $100,000 a year. How many people report on that much income?' But he did not press this confiscatory idea." James MacGregor Burns, *Roosevelt, the Soldier of Freedom* (New York: Harcourt Brace Jovanovich, 1970) 121.

39. Several years later pollster Elmo Roper asked Americans whether "our government" ought to do various things. There was broad support for providing "for all people who have no other means of subsistence" (69%–23%) and "seeing to it that everyone who wants to work has a job" (61%–32%). But majorities opposed redistributing "wealth by heavy taxes on the rich" (35%–54%) and did not want to "confiscate wealth over what people need to live on decently" (15%–76%). "The *Fortune* Survey," June 1939, 69.

40. Frank R. Kent, *Without Grease: Political Behavior 1934–1936* (New York: Morrow, 1936) 10.

Chapter 13
Rendezvous

1. Arthur M. Schlesinger, Jr., *The Age of Roosevelt: The Coming of the New Deal* (Boston: Houghton Mifflin, 1959) 575,576. Roosevelt's iron self-discipline seems to have continued to the end. "He looked at me, his forehead furrowed with pain, and tried to smile," his cousin Daisy Suckley recalled his final collapse in Warm Springs. "He put his left hand up to the back of his head and said, "I have a terrific pain in the back

of my head." Nathan Miller, *FDR: An Intimate History* (New York: Doubleday, 1983) 510.

2. Franklin D. Roosevelt to James P. Warburg, 23 May 1934, qtd. in Schlesinger 502.

3. "The *Fortune* Survey," *Fortune,* July 1936, 83–84.

4. "The *Fortune* Survey," Jan. 1936, 47, 141–43. The figures were statistically indistinguishable several months later. "The *Fortune* Survey," Apr. 1936, 105, 208; July 1936, 84–85, 148. Ironically, support for Roosevelt was lowest among the upscale voters who tended to believe that the economy was reviving, and greatest among the downscale voters who tended to be skeptical of any improvement but felt themselves in need of protection. "The *Fortune* Survey," July 1936, 83–84. *Fortune* reported accurately in October 1936 that Roosevelt's support was still high—though this was far from the desired result of the magazine's proprietors or managers. "The *Fortune* Survey," Oct. 1936, 130–32.

5. Clinton Rossiter, *Conservatism in America: The Thankless Persuasion,* 2nd ed. (New York: Knopf, 1962) 165. For Rossiter "the American Right" consists only of a reaction to Roosevelt and the New Deal. See pages 163–96.

6. The otherwise wonderfully sensitive Kenneth S. Davis calls it "a psychological phenomenon difficult to understand" and makes no effort to set out the arguments of Roosevelt's detractors; he suggests they were furious because "Roosevelt dared laugh *at them!"* Kenneth S. Davis, *FDR: The New Deal Years, 1933–1937* (New York: Random House, 1986) 504–55.

7. Schlesinger 475.

8. "Smilin' Through!" *Saturday Evening Post,* 22 Sept. 1934, qtd. in Schlesinger 473–74.

9. These figures are those of the Bureau of Labor Statistics. *Historical Statistics of the United States, Colonial Times to 1970,* 2 vols. (Washington: U.S. Bureau of the Census, 1975) 1: 176–77.

10. Robert H. Zieger, *American Workers, American Unions, 1920–1985* (Baltimore: Johns Hopkins Univ., 1986) 35–46; Melvyn Dubofsky and Warren Van Tine, *John L. Lewis: A Biography* (Urbana: Univ. of Illinois, 1986) 181–87.

11. Hugh Gregory Gallagher, *FDR's Splendid Deception* (New York: Dodd, Mead, 1985) 102–5. Roosevelt spoke only to his closest attendants about the incident, saying "I was the damnedest, maddest white man at that moment you ever saw; it was the most frightful five minutes of my life." Michael Reilly, *Reilly of the White House* 98–101, and Grace Tully, *F.D.R.* 202, qtd. in Schlesinger 584.

12. When *Fortune's* polling reports showed that a large majority (54%–13%) of those surveyed thought WPA was doing a good job in their own community, the writer advised Landon not to criticize the program but to "keep your powder dry for other issues." "The *Fortune* Survey," Oct. 1936, 130, 210, 215.

13. Gallup's surveys were conducted on random principles, but with quotas for certain subgroups. See *The Gallup Poll* (New York: Random House, 1972) 1: v–viii. In my opinion, these quotas do not vitiate the validity of the sample. See also "The *Fortune* Survey," July 1935, 66, which describes the randomness of Elmo Roper's surveys for Henry Luce's young business magazine.

14. *The Gallup Poll* 1: 1–40.

15. Some had their suspicions, however. Government statistician Louis Bean, who relied

on election results rather than polls, noted that Democrat candidates averaged 45% of the vote in the Maine state elections September 15 and concluded that the country would go about 60% Democratic. An early *Fortune* poll and a *Baltimore Sun* poll in Maryland pointed toward the same result. Louis H. Bean, *Ballot Behavior* (Washington: American Council on Public Affairs, 1940) 77–80.

16. *Fortune,* Oct. 1936, 47, 141–44. Roosevelt's standing was not much changed in the *Fortune* surveys reported in April, July, and October 1936.

17. It purported to prohibit volume discounts—an impossible goal, given the necessary complexity of commercial transactions—and its chief effect over fifty years was to spawn shakedown suits brought by private lawyers.

18. Samuel Lubell, *The Future of American Politics* (New York: Harper, 1952) 51.

19. These percentages, like those given for the 1934 election in chapter 11, are of the "non-trivial" vote: they are calculated from results which exclude candidates who received less than 5% of the total vote in their district. This exclusion tends to overstate slightly the major party percentages: in the total vote, Democrats led Republicans 56%–39%, with 5% for other parties.

20. Zieger 46.

21. Frances Perkins quotes Lewis as saying, disappointedly, in January 1937, "when J. P. Morgan was the principal contributor to the Republican party he certainly had constant access to the President and told him exactly what he wanted done. The tables are reversed now, and I expected to be consulted the same way." Perkins said she sensibly responded that "it was ridiculous to believe that J. P. Morgan or any large contributor had ever dictated to a President." Frances Perkins, *The Roosevelt I Knew* (New York: Viking, 1946) 159.

22. "The *Fortune* Survey," Oct. 1937, 109.

23. Elmo Roper found that only 23% of those he polled in July 1936 thought "the present state of affairs is due to" government, while 39% thought it was "in spite of government." He concluded that many well-off Roosevelt opponents were refusing to concede that his policies worked, while many of his lower-income supporters voted for him despite a resigned sense that government action was to no avail. "Survey returns show that 63.1 percent of the people who believe the present state of affairs—good or bad—is *in spite* of the government favor Roosevelt, [but he has] the approval of only 54.0 percent of those who think the government has caused the present conditions." The *Fortune* Survey," July 1936, 84.

Chapter 14
Recession

1. Victor Reuther, *The Brothers Reuther* (Boston: Houghton Mifflin, 1976). Robert Conot, *American Tragedy* (New York: Bantam, 1965) 436–50. Alfred P. Sloan, Jr., *My Years with General Motors* (New York: MacFadden-Bartell, 1965) 393.

2. Robert Conot, *American Odyssey* (New York: Morrow, 1974) 450–53.

3. Studs Terkel, *Chicago* (New York: Pantheon, 1986) 36–38.

4. Robert H. Zieger, *American Workers, American Unions, 1920–1985* (Baltimore: Johns Hopkins Univ., 1984) 46–51.

5. Studs Terkel, *Hard Times: An Oral History of the Great Depression* (New York: Pocket, 1978) 163.

6. Overall, 47% said labor was being treated fairly and 42% unfairly. The balance of feeling was more negative, though by no means unanimous, among factory labor (39%–50%), farm labor (24%–63%), and the poor (32%–58%). Those not in blue-collar occupations tended to believe that labor was being treated fairly. "The *Fortune* Survey," *Fortune,* Oct. 1935, 164.

7. "The *Fortune* Survey," Jan. 1937, 153.

8. *The Gallup Poll* (New York: Random House, 1972) 1: 41, 48–49; "The *Fortune* Survey," July 1937, 98–100.

9. Terkel, *Hard Times* 312.

10. *The Gallup Poll* 1: 43, 50–52; "The *Fortune* Survey," Apr. 1936, 210, 215.

11. Robert E. Sherwood, *Roosevelt and Hopkins* (New York: Harper, 1950) 105.

12. Roper's findings were similar: 37% favored the plan and 38% opposed it, with 19% favoring some alternate method of reform. "The *Fortune* Survey," July 1937, 96–98.

13. Weeks before, the Court had upheld Washington State's minimum wage, a ruling whose guiding principle seemed to point toward the result in the Wagner Act case. Nonetheless, there were still widespread fears—and hopes—that the federal law would be declared unconstitutional.

14. Gallup asked the third-term question in a poll conducted November 6–11, 1936, just after the election. *The Gallup Poll* 1: 42. *Fortune* waited to ask the third-term question until the poll it reported in its April 1937 issue.

15. Moreover, these numbers, if anything, understate the gap between the president and the issues he was identified with. The 44% and 47% are the Gallup numbers that represent responses to specific questions and those responses which are the most favorable to Roosevelt's positions; responses to other questions would suggest much lower popularity for the CIO organizing campaign and the court-packing bill. Moreover, these percentages should probably be reduced further to reflect the larger percentage of respondents likely to have had no opinion on these issues, as compared with the number with no opinion on whether they would vote for the incumbent president.

16. Just as *depression* was used as a euphemism for the scarier *panic* after the Panic of 1907, so *recession* was used as a euphemism for *depression* after the depression of 1929. The fact that by the late 1980s *recession* was still in use may be taken as evidence that no post-1929 downturn in the economy has so deeply shaken the American people.

17. Earlier in 1937 Elmo Roper had found that 78% of those he polled thought the depression was over or almost over. "The *Fortune* Survey," Apr. 1937, 185–86.

18. James MacGregor Burns, *Roosevelt, the Lion and the Fox 1882–1940* (New York: Harcourt, Brace, 1956) 316–36.

19. See the poll results compiled in Hadley Cantril, *Public Opinion 1935–1946* (Princeton: Princeton Univ., 1951) 62–64.

20. J. Joseph Huthmacher, *Robert F. Wagner* (New York: Atheneum, 1971) 224–28.

21. Gavin Wright, *Old South, New South* (New York: Basic Books, 1986) 216–23.

22. Wright, 223–26.

23. Barry Karl, *The Uneasy State: The United States from 1915 to 1945* (Chicago: Univ. of Chicago, 1983) 167.

24. "The *Fortune* Survey," July 1938, 74, 76.

25. Karl 156–58, 161–71.

26. Sherwood 102–4; George McJimsey, *Harry Hopkins* (Cambridge: Harvard Univ., 1987) 123–24.

27. McJimsey 84, 122.

28. McJimsey 123.

29. Cf. Karl 161. Roosevelt himself, according to James Farley, believed that the example of European dictators made American voters suspicious of his bill. James A. Farley, *Jim Farley's Story, The Roosevelt Years* (New York: McGraw-Hill, 1948) 129.

30. Burns 362.

31. Thomas H. Eliot, qtd. in Katie Louchheim, *The Making of the New Deal: The Insiders Speak* (Cambridge: Harvard Univ., 1983) 161.

32. These included Boston (4), New York City (23, including 2 in New Jersey), Philadelphia (5), the northeast Pennsylvania anthracite country (4), Pittsburgh (6), Cleveland and northeast Ohio (4), Detroit (4), Chicago (10, including 1 in Indiana), St. Louis (4, including 1 in Illinois), and Los Angeles (5).

33. Connecticut, 1, 2, 3, at-large; Delaware at-large; Ohio 3, 16; Pennsylvania 5; and West Virginia 1 all changed hands three times. Changing hands two of three times were California 4, 13; Connecticut 3, 4; Illinois 3, 9, 22; Maryland 4; Michigan 12; Missouri 8, 11; New Jersey 2; New York 16 (Manhattan East Side); Ohio 14, 18; Pennsylvania 1, 11/12 (Wilkes-Barre), 22 (York-Adams-Franklin); Washington 3; West Virginia 3; Wisconsin 2, 8; and Wyoming at-large. Of the 9 districts that changed hands three times, 8 were industrial/immigrant districts, as were 15 of the 23 that changed hands twice.

34. Karl 159.

35. See Richard Neustadt and Ernest May, *Thinking in Time* (New York: The Free Press, 1986) 253.

Chapter 15
"America Hates War"

1. These figures are totals of merchandise exports and imports, excluding gold and silver, which accounted for a substantial percentage of U.S. foreign trade in the 1930s. *Historical Statistics of the United States, Colonial Times to 1970,* 2 vols. (Washington: U.S. Bureau of the Census, 1975) 2: 884.

2. Robert Dallek, *Franklin D. Roosevelt and American Foreign Policy 1932–1945* (New York: Oxford Univ., 1979) 91.

3. Kenneth S. Davis, *FDR: The New Deal Years 1933–1937* (New York: Random House, 1986) 551–53; Ralph B. Levering, *Public Opinion and American Foreign Policy 1918–1978* (New York: Morrow, 1978) 57.

4. On Nye's staff was Alger Hiss, a young lawyer who along with others—some of them, like Lee Pressman, Communists—had recently been purged from AAA. Allen Weinstein, *Perjury: The Hiss-Chambers Case* (New York: Knopf, 1978) 142–45.

5. James MacGregor Burns, *Roosevelt, the Lion and the Fox 1882–1940* (New York: Harcourt, Brace, 1956) 253–55.

6. "The *Fortune* Survey," *Fortune,* Jan. 1936, 46–47; Jan. 1939, 66–67, 93–94.

7. See Claude G. Bowers, *My Mission to Spain* (New York: Simon & Schuster, 1954). Bowers was known as author of *The Tragic Era,* then the best-known work on Reconstruction, which argued that federal enforcement of blacks' civil rights constituted oppression of southern whites. That this position was widely seen as entirely consistent with his reputation as a liberal tells much about attitudes toward civil rights at the time.

8. "The *Fortune* Survey," Jan. 1939, 66–67.

9. Some 28% of those surveyed by *Fortune* in early 1939 approved of the United States selling weapons to democratic countries, and 20% to anyone, for a total of 48%—not much more than the 40% who opposed all foreign arms sales. Opposition was higher (53%) in the Great Plains states from Minnesota and the Dakotas to Missouri and Kansas, states which (with Wisconsin) included the nation's highest concentrations of German- and Scandinavian-American residents. "The *Fortune* Survey," May 1939, 107.

10. Dallek 181.

Chapter 16
Third Term

1. James MacGregor Burns, *Roosevelt, the Lion and the Fox 1882–1940* (New York: Harcourt, Brace, 1956) 409.

2. Robert E. Sherwood, *Roosevelt and Hopkins* (New York: Harper, 1950) 172.

3. James A. Farley, *Jim Farley's Story: The Roosevelt Years* (New York: McGraw-Hill, 1948) 249.

4. Ted Morgan, *FDR* (New York: Simon & Schuster, 1985) 528.

5. Joseph P. Lash, *Eleanor and Franklin* (New York: Norton, 1971) 615–18.

6. Harold Ickes, *The Secret Diary of Harold Ickes,* 3 vols. (New York: Simon & Schuster, 1953–55) 3: 235, 265.

7. "With almost fanatical single-mindedness," reported his one-time subordinate Dean Acheson, "he devoted himself to getting legislative authority, and then acting upon it, to negotiate 'mutually beneficial reciprocal trade agreements to reduce tariffs' on a basis of equal application to all nations, a thoroughly Jeffersonian policy. These often enunciated words, due to a speech impediment, emerged as 'wecipwocal twade agweement pwogam to weduce tawiffs.' " Dean Acheson, *Present at the Creation* (New York: Norton, 1969) 31.

8. Candidates' strength is distorted if, as was common at the time, the poll results are given in the form of percentages of those with a preference. Among all voters, including those with no preference, Garner consistently had the support of only 40%–44% in pairings against various Republicans, and Farley 32%–36%. Hull varied between 39% and 51%. Roosevelt, in contrast, was in the 46%–52% range. Consider this example: an April 1940 poll showed Roosevelt with 58% against Taft, and Hull with 63% against him. But taking account of the undecideds, the results were Roosevelt over Taft 52%–38%, with 10% undecided, and Hull over Taft 49%–29%, with 22% undecided. *The Gallup Poll* (New York: Random House, 1972), 1–5 Dec. 1939; 27 Mar.–1 Apr., 19–24 Apr., 5–10 May 1940.

9. "Indeed, from 1938 on, it became evident that if Roosevelt should run again on purely domestic issues he would be none too sure of winning the election," concedes as great an admirer as his 1940 speechwriter Robert E. Sherwood. Sherwood 169–70.

10. *The Gallup Poll,* 13–18 Sept., 5–10 Oct., 26–31 Oct., 2–7 Dec., 24–29 Dec. 1939; 13–18 Jan., 8–13 Feb., 27 Mar.–1 Apr., 19–24 Apr., 5–10 May, 18–23 May, 9–14 June 1940.

11. "The *Fortune* Survey," *Fortune,* July 1940.

12. *The Gallup Poll,* 5–10 July 1940.

13. Hadley Cantril, *Public Opinion 1935–46* (Princeton: Princeton Univ., 1951) 617. See also polls on page 618, which make the same point: foreign policy issues buoyed Roosevelt upward, putting him above the 50% mark; and see *The Gallup Poll* 1: 247–48.

14. Sherwood 165.

15. James MacGregor Burns, *Roosevelt, the Soldier of Freedom* (New York: Harcourt Brace Jovanovich, 1970) 46; James T. Patterson, *Mr. Republican: A Biography of Robert A. Taft* (Boston: Houghton Mifflin, 1972) 240; William S. White, *The Taft Story* (New York: Harper, 1954) 150. Michael R. Beschloss, *Kennedy and Roosevelt: The Uneasy Alliance* (New York: Norton, 1980) 206–8.

16. Steve Neal, *Dark Horse: A Biography of Wendell Willkie* (Garden City, NY: Doubleday, 1984) 56.

17. Neal 106.

18. Neal 96.

19. This is the movie in which Spencer Tracy, playing the citizen-candidate, foils the professional politicians by declaring "I paid for this microphone" and then saying what he really believes rather than delivering his canned speech. Ronald Reagan echoed those words at the Nashua debate in the February 1980 New Hampshire primary.

20. Neal 120.

21. Ickes 2: 569.

22. *WPA Guide, Illinois* (Chicago: A. C. McClurg, 1939) 94.

23. Harold Ickes, *Autobiography of a Curmudgeon* (New York: Reynal & Hitchcock, 1943) 255–56; John Gunther, *Inside U.S.A.* (New York: Harper, 1947) 368. "Another young engineer who got his start on the Evanston canal came to McCormick's attention when he punched a recalcitrant worker in the jaw." This was Kelly, whom McCormick promoted and later recommended as chief engineer. Joseph Gies, *The Colonel of Chicago: A Biography of the Chicago Tribune's Legendary Publisher, Colonel Robert McCormick* (New York: Dutton, 1979) 25.

24. Len O'Connor, *Clout: Mayor Daley and His City* (New York: Avon, 1976) 54; Bill and Lori Granger, *Lords of the Last Machine: The Story of Politics in Chicago* (New York: Random House, 1987) 106.

25. O'Connor 50–55.

26. Bronx Democratic boss Ed Flynn later wrote, "The persons in the forefront in support of the President's ambition for a third term were largely drawn from the political machines of the country. Again I say they did not support Roosevelt out of any motive of affection or because of any political issues involved, but rather they knew that opposing him would be harmful to their local organizations. The Roosevelt name would help more than it could hurt, and for that reason these city leaders went along on the

third-term candidacy." Edward J. Flynn, *You're the Boss* (New York: Harcourt, Brace, 1947) 156.

27. Gunther 372.

28. Ickes, *Diaries* 1: 439.

29. Sherwood 173.

30. James F. Byrnes, *All in One Lifetime* (New York: Harper, 1958) 117–18.

31. One Massachusetts delegate who stuck to his commitment to vote for Farley was Joseph P. Kennedy, Jr., whose father was still ambassador to Britain. This was the one political office this Kennedy ever held; his father got it for him even though the family had lived in New York since 1927 and had only its summer vacation house in Massachusetts.

32. Did Lyndon Johnson, who based many of his own decisions about the Vietnam war on what Roosevelt had done in 1940 and 1941, decide to have the 1968 Democratic convention in Chicago in the hope that Mayor Richard Daley could manage the galleries as Kelly had for Roosevelt in 1940? See Chapter 42.

33. A title Roosevelt loved. When Cordell Hull was to propose a toast for him in January 1942, "Roosevelt told Hull beforehand that he preferred to be addressed not as President but as Commander in Chief." Cordell Hull, *Memoirs* 1111, cited in Eric Larrabee, *Commander in Chief* (New York: Harper & Row, 1987) 13.

34. "The *Fortune* Survey," May 1940, 169–70.

35. Burns, *Lion and Fox* 449.

36. Joseph Alsop, *FDR: A Centenary Remembrance* (New York: Viking, 1982) 10, 11.

37. Gunther 523, 524.

38. Qtd. in Frances Perkins, *The Roosevelt I Knew* (New York: Viking, 1946) 113.

39. Mrs. Willkie lived there, but Willkie spent much of his time with his mistress, *New York Herald Tribune* book reviewer Irita Van Doren, in her West Side apartment or her weekend home in West Cornwall, Connecticut. Neal 41–44.

40. Gallup's state-by-state figures were probably extrapolated by reducing the percentage he won in each state in 1936 by the number of percentage points his national vote was projected to drop.

41. Burns, *Lion and Fox* 452; Sherwood 199–200.

42. This figure includes sixteen counties containing the nation's twelve largest cities: the five boroughs of New York City; Philadelphia; Baltimore City; St. Louis City; San Francisco; Suffolk, Massachusetts; Erie, New York; Allegheny, Pennsylvania, Cuyahoga, Ohio; Wayne, Michigan; Cook, Illinois; and Los Angeles. The last seven of these include some suburbs.

43. Each side had some basis for claiming it represented the country and for questioning whether its opponents did. Similarly, in eighteenth-century Britain both the Whigs, who supported William of Orange and the Hanovers, and the Tories, who doubted the legitimacy of these monarchs and leaned toward supporting James II and his heirs (the Old and Young Pretenders), had clouds on their title to represent the nation: the Whigs because they were supporting foreign kings, the Tories because they were suspected of supporting Catholics. But in vivid contrast to the previous century, when both sides admitted no doubts about their positions and proceeded to slaughter each other periodically, in the eighteenth-century both were prudent in prosecuting their

claims; and in time both came to recognize the legitimacy of political opposition. See Bernard Bailyn, *The Ideological Origins of the American Revolution* (Cambridge: Harvard Univ., 1967); Edmund S. Morgan, *Inventing the People* (New York: Norton, 1988).

Chapter 17
Deadlock

1. Robert A. Caro, *The Years of Lyndon Johnson: The Path to Power* (New York: Random House, 1981) 621–22.

2. In the South, Roosevelt led 78%–22%, while Democratic congressional candidates led 88%–11%. The discrepancy is without significance, since the Republicans seriously contested only a few southern districts; its main effect is to understate the degree to which Roosevelt ran ahead of the Democratic ticket nationwide.

3. Alan Brinkley, "The New Deal and the Idea of the State," in Steve Fraser and Gary Gerstle, eds., *The Rise and Fall of the New Deal Order, 1930–1980* (Princeton: Princeton Univ., 1989) 91–92.

4. As late as the early 1960s, a leading liberal thinker, James MacGregor Burns, wrote a widely heralded book, *The Deadlock of Democracy* (Englewood Cliffs: Prentice-Hall, 1963), tracing the antagonism between Democratic and Republican advocates of executive action and Democratic and Republican legislators opposed to it as the organizing principle behind the American politics of the preceding quarter-century. Burns's argument that a similar conflict explains all of post-1789 American political history is unpersuasive, for executives have not always favored increased government control over the economy and legislators have not always opposed it (in the Jacksonian era it was just the other way around); more often than not, American politics has not been much concerned with the issue of government control over the economy. That was true in the nineteenth century, when issues of expansion, slavery, and race were paramount and when no one thought the government capable of controlling the economy; and it has been true of the period after which Burns wrote, in which major issues have been civil rights and foreign wars.

5. Robert Dallek, *Franklin D. Roosevelt and American Foreign Policy, 1932–1945* (New York: Oxford Univ., 1979) 256–58.

6. *The Gallup Poll* (New York: Random House, 1972) 1: 259–60, 262.

7. James T. Patterson, *Mr. Republican: A Biography of Robert A. Taft* (Boston: Houghton Mifflin, 1972) 243–44.

8. James MacGregor Burns, *Roosevelt, the Soldier of Freedom, 1940–1945* (New York: Harcourt Brace Jovanovich, 1970) 48–49; James F. Byrnes, *All in One Lifetime* (New York: Harper, 1958) 115.

9. "The *Fortune* Survey," *Fortune*, August 1941; Dallek 266–67.

10. Richard Cheney and Lynne Cheney, *Kings of the Hill* (New York: Continuum, 1983) 161–62. For a vivid account, see D. B. Hardeman and Donald Bacon, *Rayburn: A Biography* (Austin: Texas Monthly, 1987) 266–70.

11. See Richard Lawrence Miller, *Truman: The Rise to Power* (New York: McGraw-Hill, 1986) 296–334.

12. See Nathan Miller, *F.D.R.* (New York: McGraw-Hill, 1983) 467.

13. She was replaced in 1942 by an internationalist college professor named Mike Mansfield.

14. H. G. Nicholas, ed., *Washington Despatches 1941–45* (London: Weidenfeld and Nicolson, 1981) 8, 14, 613; Richard Norton Smith, *Thomas E. Dewey and His Times* (New York: Simon & Schuster, 1982) 425–30. Roberta Wohlstetter, in *Pearl Harbor: Warning and Decision* (Palo Alto: Stanford Univ., 1982) establishes as conclusively as these things can be established that Roosevelt and his top advisers did not know the Japanese were heading to Pearl Harbor: "We failed to anticipate Pearl Harbor not for want of the relevant materials, but because of a plethora of irrelevant ones." Wohlstetter, 387. This position is supported by the most recent authoritative account: Ronald H. Spector, *Eagle Against the Sun* (New York: The Free Press, 1985) 95–100.

Chapter 18
Mobilization

1. James MacGregor Burns. *Roosevelt, the Soldier of Freedom, 1940–1945* (New York: Harcourt Brace Jovanovich, 1970) 268–71.

2. John Gunther. *Inside U.S.A.* (New York: Harper, 1950) 64–75; David Halberstam, *The Reckoning* (New York: Morrow, 1986) 328–33. Gunther is uncritical, even adoring, of Kaiser.

3. *Historical Statistics of the United States, Colonial Times to 1970, 2 vols.* (Washington: U.S. Bureau of the Census, 1975) 1105.

4. *Historical Statistics* 2: 1105.

5. *Historical Statistics* 2: 1114.

6. For a good statement of this thesis, see Geoffrey Perrett, *Days of Sadness, Years of Triumph: The American People, 1939–1945* (Madison: Univ. of Wisconsin, 1985) 9–12.

7. *Historical Statistics* 1: 126.

8. *Historical Statistics* 2: 1141.

9. *Historical Statistics* 1: 133.

10. Richard R. Lingeman. *Dont You Know There's a War On?* (New York: Putnam, 1970) 66–68.

11. Daniel M. Johnson and Rex R. Campbell, *Black Migration in America, A Social Demographic History* (Durham: Duke Univ., 1981) 101–13; *Historical Statistics* 1: 95.

12. This was Victor Berger, a Socialist elected to the House from a Milwaukee district in 1910 and again in 1918. Three times the House declined to seat him, declaring him the first time "not entitled to take the oath of office as a Representative or to hold a seat as such; having been opposed to the entrance of the United States in the First World War and having written articles expressing his opinion on that question, he was indicted in various places in the Federal courts, tried at Chicago, found guilty, and sentenced by Judge Kenesaw M. Landis [the longtime commissioner of baseball] to serve twenty years in the Federal penitentiary; this judgment was reversed by the United States Supreme Court in 1921, whereupon the Government withdrew all cases against him in 1922." *Biographical Directory of the American Congress, 1774–1989* Washington: U.S. Government Printing Office, 1989) 613. Berger was again elected

to the House as a Socialist in 1922, 1924, and 1926 and was seated each time; he was defeated in 1928 and died in August 1929.

13. John Morton Blum. *V Was for Victory* (New York: Harcourt Brace Jovanovich, 1976) 11.

14. Blum 8, 19, 21.

15. H. G. Nicholas, ed., *Washington Despatches, 1941–1945* (London: Weidenfeld and Nicolson, 1981) 2–3, 24, 30, 34–35, 53, 54–56, 81.

16. Blum agrees. Blum 226.

17. Nicholas 71, 83–84.

18. Blum 235–37.

19. Blum 238–39.

20. Gunther 337; Arthur M. Schlesinger, Jr., *The Age of Roosevelt: The Crisis of the Old Order* (Boston: Houghton Mifflin, 1957) 107–8.

21. Marilyn Bender and Selig Altschul, *The Chosen Instrument, Juan Trippe & Pan Am* (New York: Simon & Schuster, 1982) 375–76.

22. Blum 279–88.

23. Robert Conquest, *Kolyma: The Arctic Death Camps* (New York: Viking, 1978) 204–12.

24. Blum 281–84; Nicholas 214–15, 217, 219–21; James F. Byrnes, *All in One Lifetime* (New York: Harper, 1958) 192–93.

25. Juan Williams, *Eyes on the Prize* (New York: Viking, 1987) 197; William H. Harris, A. Philip Randolph, Black Workers, and the Labor Movement," in Melvin Dubofsky and Warren Van Tine, eds., *Labor Leaders in America* (Urbana: Univ. of Illinois, 1987) 258–73.

26. Nancy J. Weiss, *Farewell to the Party of Lincoln: Black Politics in the Age of FDR* (Princeton: Princeton Univ., 1983).

27. Weiss shows how assiduously Roosevelt sought black votes in 1940: meeting often with black leaders, naming Benjamin O. Davis, Sr., as the first black Army general, issuing a Booker T. Washington stamp. Weiss 267–95.

28. Weiss 275.

29. Burns 123–24.

30. Nicholas 141.

31. John Dollard's *Caste and Class in a Southern Town,* published in the 1930s, presented so elaborate and painstaking a picture of the formal and informal rules of segregation as to suggest that the author expected these to be unfamiliar and indeed surprising to his mostly highly educated readers.

32. Gavin Wright, *Old South, New South* (New York: Basic Books, 1986) 236–37.

33. *Historical Statistics* 1: 127, 177.

34. Burns 117, 194–96, 263–64.

35. Nicholas 209.

36. Blum credits the maintenance of membership policy for this growth—and in effect refutes those who claimed the Roosevelt administration was treating management and unions evenhandedly. Blum 140–41.

37. The bonus seems not to have been given any consideration in either the administration or Congress. See Blum 248–50; Burns 362; Perrett 338–39.

38. Perrett 362; William "Fishbait" Miller, *Fishbait: The Memoirs of the Congressional Doorkeeper* (New York: Warner, 1978) 222–23.

39. Blum 248–49.

40. *Historical Statistics* 1: 383.

41. James Fallows, *More Like Us: Making America Great Again* (Boston: Houghton Mifflin, 1989) 158–60; Burns 465, 509; William L. O'Neill, *American High* (New York: The Free Press, 1986) 9–12.

42. *Historical Statistics* 2: 1105.

43. *Historical Statistics* 2: 1105.

44. *Historical Statistics* 2: 1110, 1095.

45. Burns 363–64; Blum 241–45.

46. Accounts of the conflict over the tax bill appear in Burns 433–35; Blum 243–45; Nicholas 319–21; and Byrnes 210–12.

47. *Historical Statistics* 1: 297, 301.

Chapter 19
Victory

1. His chief backers were John J. Pershing, the American commander in World War I, and Harry Hopkins.

2. See Eric Larrabee, *Commander-in-Chief* (New York: Simon & Schuster, 1987) 106–9.

3. Joseph Alsop, *FDR 1882–1945: A Centenary Remembrance* (New York: Viking, 1982) 254.

4. David S. Wyman, *The Abandonment of the Jews: America and the Holocaust, 1941–1945* (New York: Pantheon, 1984) xv.

5. See James M. McPherson, *Battle Cry of Freedom* (New York: Oxford Univ., 1988) 771, 790–91, 803–6, 858.

6. As one of his successors put it in December 1981, "I think he was a great war leader. I think there were less of the great tragic blunders that have characterized many wars in the past than this one. . . . Our war effort was just absolutely magnificent, and we succeeded literally in saving the . . . world and probably achieved the greatest victory in . . . the history of war, in . . . the total surrender of . . . the principal enemy." Ronald Reagan, qtd. in William E. Leuchtenberg, *In the Shadow of FDR: From Harry Truman to Ronald Reagan* (Ithaca: Cornell Univ., 1985) 214–15.

7. William D. Hassett, *Off the Record with FDR 1942–1945* (New Brunswick: Rutgers Univ., 1958) 242, 244.

8. See Matthew Josephson, *Sidney Hillman: Statesman of American Labor* (Garden City: Doubleday, 1952) 600–606; and L. H. Whittemore, *The Man Who Ran the Subways: The Story of Mike Quill* (New York: Holt, Rinehart & Winston, 1968) 82ff.

9. Josephson 597–98.

10. These countries are listed in note 42 of Chapter 16.

11. The Democratic vote was down 1.7 million nationally—in the South, it was down 600,000; down 1.3 million outside the counties containing the twelve big cities, but up more than 200,000 in these counties.

12. Josephson 611.

13. Steve Neal, *Dark Horse: A Biography of Wendell Willkie* (Garden City: Doubleday, 1984) 220–76.

14. Qtd. in John Gunther, *Inside U.S.A.* (New York: Harper, 1950) 523, 528.

15. Rockefeller was a freer spender: Dewey once told him, "Nelson, I don't think I can afford you."

16. James MacGregor Burns, *Roosevelt, the Soldier of Freedom, 1940–1945* (New York: Harcourt Brace Jovanovich, 1970) 510–13.

17. "As was usual when we visited" the Roosevelts in the White House, Flynn reports, "it was a family party, for he knew I was not particularly interested in meeting anyone other than himself and Mrs. Roosevelt and their own immediate family." Edward J. Flynn, *You're the Boss* (New York: Harcourt, Brace, 1947) 179.

18. Flynn 180; Josephson 614–15.

19. Josephson 624.

20. Richard Rhodes, *The Making of the Atomic Bomb* (New York: Simon & Schuster, 1986) 537–48; Robert Dallek, *Franklin D. Roosevelt and American Foreign Policy 1932–1945* (New York: Oxford Univ., 1979) 470, 476; Martin J. Sherwin, *A World Destroyed* (New York: Random House, 1977) 109–10; Burns 458, 521.

21. Steven Fraser, "Sidney Hillman: Labor's Machiavelli," in Melvyn Dubofsky and Warren Van Tine, eds., *Labor Leaders in America* (Urbana: Univ. of Illinois, 1987) 229.

22. These counties are listed in note 42 of Chapter 16.

23. See, for example, Burns's *The Deadlock of Democracy* (Englewood Cliffs: Prentice-Hall, 1963).

24. Richard Norton Smith, *Thomas E. Dewey and His Times* (New York: Simon & Schuster, 1982) 425–30. With characteristic bitterness, "Dewey went to his grave believing that Roosevelt shared in the culpability of a high command that displayed a fine gift for confusion and self-inflicted disaster in the very hours when it should have been taking steps to ward off the worst military defeat in the nation's history." Smith 430.

Chapter 20
Demobilization

1. Richard Lawrence Miller, *Truman: The Rise to Power* (New York: McGraw-Hill, 1986) 57.

2. Miller 56–68.

3. William M. Reddig, *Tom's Town: Kansas City and the Pendergast Legend* (Columbia: Univ. of Missouri, 1986) 49–67, 374–82.

4. Miller 246–47.

5. Miller 174–175.

6. Miller 257.

7. Miller 297.

8. Four senators—Barkley, Hatch, Minton, and Schwellenbach—campaigned for Truman in Missouri in the 1940 primary campaign. Barkley became his vice president, and he made Minton a Supreme Court justice, Schwellenbach secretary of labor, and Hutch a federal judge. John Snyder, a St. Louis banker and fellow veteran who supported Truman strongly, became his secretary of the treasury. Miller 323–24.

9. Samuel Lubell, *The Future of American Politics* (New York: Harper, 1952) 10, 12.

10. Speakers Longworth and Garner used to hold "bureau of education" meetings in which carefully picked congressmen and others were invited to share stories and bourbon and branch. Rayburn's meetings were confined mostly to Democrats and were referred to as the "board of education." D. B. Hardeman and Donald Bacon, *Rayburn* (Austin: Texas Monthly, 1987) 303.

11. They were deadlocked 42%–42% on whether "business firms in this country would be able to provide enough jobs for nearly everyone" or government would have to step in with something like the WPA; and when asked to cite a problem facing the country, more (42%) volunteered "jobs" than any other issue. *The Gallup Poll* (New York: Random House, 1972), 24–29 Aug., 5–10 Oct. 1945.

12. Stephen K. Bailey, *Congress Makes a Law* (New York: Random House, 1964).

13. *Historical Statistics of the United States, Colonial Times to 1970,* 2 vols. (Washington: U.S. Bureau of the Census, 1975) 1: 179.

14. See Fraser J. Harbutt, *The Iron Curtain: Churchill, America, and the Origins of the Cold War* (New York: Oxford Univ., 1986), which explores this episode exhaustively.

15. *The Gallup Poll* 598, 604, 589, 600.

16. Richard R. Lingeman, *Don't You Know There's a War On?* (New York: Putnam, 1970) 82–84.

17. Kenneth T. Jackson, *Crabgrass Frontier: The Suburbanization of the United States* (New York: Oxford Univ., 1985) 196–97, 204–5.

18. J. Joseph Huthmacher, *Senator Robert F. Wagner and the Rise of Urban Liberalism* (New York: Atheneum, 1971) 322–25.

19. *Historical Statistics* 1: 126–27, 177.

20. Crockett declined to vote to condemn the Soviet Union for the shooting down of Korean Air Lines Flight 007 in September 1983.

21. "In theory," writes one biographer of the 1939–41 period, "the Communists planned to use strikes to capture basic American industries in order to interfere with the normal economic life of the country if this were necessary to carry out the foreign policy of Russia." L. H. Whittemore, *The Man Who Ran the Subways: The Story of Mike Quill* (New York: Holt, Rinehart & Winston, 1968) 97.

Chapter 21
The Hinge: From Turmoil to Confidence

1. *Historical Statistics of the United States, Colonial Times to 1970,* 2 vols. (Washington: U.S. Bureau of the Census, 1975) 1: 226–27, 229.

2. *Historical Statistics* 1: 225. I have rounded off the dollar figures for clarity.

3. See Greg J. Duncan's *Years of Poverty, Years of Plenty* (Ann Arbor: Institute for Social Research, 1984), based on the University of Michigan Survey Research Center's

longitudinal study of incomes over 16 years which found "a remarkable amount of change at all income levels." Greg J. Duncan, *Years of Poverty, Years of Plenty* 10.

4. *Historical Statistics* 2: 19.

5. Both fertility rates and number of births are from *Historical Statistics* 1: 49. Note that fertility rates rose during the Korean war period and the years just afterwards but fell sharply during the Vietnam war period and, although the numbers are not presented here, in the years just afterwards also. This contrast suggests the huge difference in American response to two conflicts which were in many respects similar.

6. *Historical Statistics* 2: 646; *Statistical Abstract of the United States: 1986* (Washington: GPO, 1986) 731.

7. *Historical Statistics* 2: 645.

8. Jane Jacobs, *The Economy of Cities* (New York: Random House, 1970) 151–54; Michael Barone and Grant Ujifusa, *The Almanac of American Politics 1986* (Washington: National Journal, 1985) 82.

9. Jacobs 152.

10. The evidence, however, is that prejudice was not increased in the course of military service. Samuel Stouffer, *Studies in Social Pschology in World War II,* 4 vols. (Princeton: Princeton Univ., 1949–50). Each generation of Americans, it seems, is less prejudiced than the last.

11. See Herbert McClosky and Alida Brill, *Dimensions of Tolerance* (New York: Russell Sage, 1983).

12. John Kenneth Galbraith, *American Capitalism: The Theory of Countervailing Power* (Boston: Houghton Mifflin, 1952).

Chapter 22
Cold War

1. Even the rapid demobilization announced by Truman was too slow for one in four Americans. *The Gallup Poll* (New York: Random House, 1972) 24–29 Aug. 1945.

2. Fully 71% favored taking an active part, while only 19% said stay out. *The Gallup Poll,* 5–10 Oct. 1945. Very large majorities agreed with Truman and Marshall in approving compulsory military training—70% favored such training and only 24% opposed it in October 1945, for example—though the proposal was never adopted. *The Gallup Poll,* 19–24 Oct. 1945.

3. Fully 69% thought the United States would be drawn into another war in the next twenty-five years, and only 19% disagreed. *The Gallup Poll* 15–20 Mar. 1946.

4. In March 1946 only 35% thought "Russia will cooperate with us in world affairs," while 52% disagreed. *The Gallup Poll,* 28 Feb.–5 Mar. 1946. Only 7% approved of Soviet Russia's foreign policy while 71% disapproved. *The Gallup Poll,* 15–20 Mar. 1946.

5. There is debate over this point, but the weight of opinion seems to be on the side of the view that Roosevelt was becoming disenchanted with what he considered Stalin's refusal to meet commitments made at Yalta in February 1945. See Robert Dallek, *Franklin D. Roosevelt and American Foreign Policy, 1932–1945* (New York: Oxford Univ., 1979) 521–27.

6. Dean Acheson, *Present at the Creation* (New York: Norton, 1969) 293.

7. On Vandenberg's early career, see C. David Tompkins, *Senator Arthur H. Vandenberg: The Evolution of a Modern Republican; 1884–1945* (East Lansing: Michigan State Univ., 1970) 6–33.

8. Arthur Vandenberg, editorial, *Grand Rapids Herald,* 18 Oct. 1925, qtd. in Tompkins 25.

9. Arthur Vandenberg, letter to constituent, 16 Apr. 1940, qtd. in Tompkins 177.

10. His best run. He was eliminated after losing the Wisconsin and Nebraska primaries in April to Thomas E. Dewey.

11. Dean Acheson, *Sketches from Life* (New York: Harper, 1961) 126–27.

12. *The Economist,* 12 Sept. 1987, p. 12.

13. *Historical Statistics of the United States, Colonial Times to 1970,* 2 vols. (Washington: U.S. Bureau of the Census, 1975) 1105.

14. "In the last 185 years the Chinese people have traveled a rocky road, beset by forces of change from both within and without. From outside have come four wars of foreign aggression, from the Anglo-Chinese War of 1839–42 to the eight years of Japanese invasion, 1937–45. Though gradually mounting in intensity, these attacks (except the Japanese) were largely superficial compared with the five revolutionary civil wars within China during the same era: the massive Taiping Rebellion of 1850–64 and attendant risings, all failures; the Republican Revolution of 1911, a change of polity; the part-way Nationalist Revolution of 1925–28 for unity against foreign imperialism; the Kuomintang-Communist civil war of 1945–49; and finally the ten years of Mao Tse-tung's Cultural Revolution, 1966–76, which was a climax both of revolutionary aspiration and of self-created national disaster." John King Fairbank, *The Great Chinese Revolution 1800–1985* (New York: Harper, 1986) x. Fairbank, an admirer of the "old China hands" in the State Department, betrays here an equivocation; admiration for the "revolutionary aspiration" that he says was behind the cultural revolution as well as disgust for it as a "self-created political disaster." Fairbanks, throughout his long and distinguished career, has seemed to regard the Communist victory in China in 1949 as regrettable but probably the least bad alternative—an odd attitude toward a totalitarian regime that unleashed what amounted to civil war on its own people. What this century of war has meant to the ordinary people of China is suggested by the population estimates of the *Atlas of World Population History.* China is estimated to have accounted for 40% of the world's population in 1800, just after the long, peaceful regime of the Chien Lung emperor. In the 1980s China's share of world population was about 20%.

15. The definitive account based on Stilwell's papers is Barbara W. Tuchman, *Joseph Stilwell and the American Experience in China* (New York: Macmillan, 1970). Strongly sympathetic to Stilwell, who excoriated Chiang, it nonetheless presents facts which can support conclusions to the contrary.

16. William S. White, *The Taft Story* (New York: Harper, 1954) 167, 168.

17. C. Vann Woodward, *Thinking Back* (Baton Rouge: Louisiana State Univ., 1986) 87. See generally Woodward 85–99 and Woodward's *The Strange Career of Jim Crow* (New York: Oxford Univ., 1955).

18. Richard Lawrence Miller, *Truman: The Rise to Power* (New York: McGraw-Hill, 1986) 325.

19. See Chris Mead, *Champion: Joe Louis, Black Hero in White America* (New York: Scribner's, 1985) 103–7, 138–62.
20. Qtd. in John Morton Blum, *V Was for Victory* (New York: Harcourt Brace Jovanovich, 1986) 195.
21. Jules Tygiel, *Baseball's Great Experiment: Jackie Robinson and His Legacy* (New York: Random House, 1984) 48, 74.
22. Robert J. Donovan, *Conflict and Crisis: The Presidency of Harry S. Truman, 1945–1948* (New York: Norton, 1977) 332–37.
23. Donovan 391–92.
24. But not Strom Thurmond, who remained at the Democratic convention and supported Senator Richard Russell of Georgia for president. Interview with Strom Thurmond, August 16, 1988, on the floor of the Republican National Convention in New Orleans.
25. Miller 325–29.

Chapter 23
Whistlestop

1. Bean used the system in his book *Ballot Behavior: A Study of Presidential Elections* (Washington: American Council on Public Affairs, 1940).
2. *The Gallup Poll* (New York: Random House, 1972), 6–11 June 1947. The result was not published, however, until June 29, after Truman's veto of Taft-Hartley.
3. For example, he led Dewey 46%–44% in July 1947, and he led Taft 55%–33% in early December 1947. *The Gallup Poll,* 4–9 July, 28 Nov.–2 Dec. 1947.
4. *The Gallup Poll,* 14–19 Mar. 1947.
5. *The Gallup Poll,* 20–25 June 1947.
6. The classic report on polling in the 1948 election is Frederick Mosteller et al., "The Pre-Election Polls of 1948," *Social Science Research Council Bulletin* 60.
7. For the young Roosevelts it may have made some sense. Two were trying to establish their own political base: James in California, where he was state Democratic chairman, and Franklin, Jr., in New York, where he was looking for something to run for (he eventually ran for and in May 1949 won the House seat on New York City's Upper West Side which was vacated by the death of Foreign Affairs Committee Chairman Sol Bloom). Their father's history had been one of opposing political machines— blocking Billy Sheehan's election to the Senate in 1911, running against party designee James Gerard for the Senate in 1914; they evidently concluded that bucking the powers that be was the way to rise. But their visible and unsuccessful opposition to Truman gave them a reputation for flakiness. James was elected to the House in 1954 but retired in 1965 for an appointive job and was one of the top executives in Bernard Cornfeld's scandal-ridden Investors' Overseas Service in the late 1960s; Franklin, Jr., was beaten by Jacob Javits for attorney general of New York in 1954. Both lost races for governor, James to Earl Warren in 1950; Franklin, Jr., to Averell Harriman at the 1954 Democratic state convention and, as the hapless Liberal nominee, to Nelson Rockefeller in 1966. Elliott Roosevelt, reminding us of Marx's adage that history tends to repeat itself, the first time as tragedy, the second as farce, was later elected mayor of Miami Beach.

8. Richard Lawrence Miller, *Truman: The Rise to Power* (New York: McGraw-Hill, 1986) 55.

9. Richard Norton Smith, *Thomas E. Dewey and His Times* (New York: Simon & Schuster, 1982) 481.

10. The classic interpretation of how opposition from some Democrats sparked support from others is in Samuel Lubell, *The Future of American Politics* (New York: Harper, 1952) 198–205.

11. Robert J. Donovan, *Conflict and Crisis* (New York: Norton, 1977) 351–52.

12. Donovan 395–400.

13. General William Tecumseh Sherman responded to an attempted political draft; "If nominated I will not run, if elected I will not serve."

14. Donovan 406–8.

15. Donovan believes this law was crucial in determining the 1948 result. Donovan 402–3, 422–23.

16. Smith 544.

17. As one prominent Wallace supporter put it, in the tough-guy prose favored by many on the left in those days: "Turn off the white lights and lay off the hotfoot. I admit everything. The Communists are doing a major part of the work of the Wallace movement, from ringing doorbells to framing platforms. Okay if you want it that way, they 'dominate' the party. So what?" I. F. Stone, *The Truman Era* (New York: Random House, 1973) 67–68. Wallace twisted his foreign policy views to suit Communist doctrine, reversing his position on the Marshall Plan after Soviet Foreign Minister Molotov denounced it and claiming the Communist takeover in Czechoslovakia was a defensive response to provocations by the U.S. ambassador in Prague. Donovan 342–43, 360–61.

18. Donovan 423.

19. Richard Bolling interview, 1981.

20. The phrase is Margaret Truman's, quoted in Roy Jenkins, *Truman* (New York: Harper, 1986) 160.

21. See J. Joseph Huthmacher, *Senator Robert F. Wagner* (New York: Atheneum, 1971) 336–40.

22. See Raymond F. Wolfinger, *The Politics of Progress* (Englewood Cliffs: Prentice-Hall, 1974); Martin Anderson, *The Federal Bulldozer* (Cambridge: M.I.T., 1964), the first book by the future Nixon and Reagan administration theorist. I lived between 1969 and 1972 in an urban renewal area in Detroit, where land was cleared (under an earlier law) in 1947 and the first housing completed in 1961.

23. Robert J. Donovan, *Tumultuous Years* (New York: Norton, 1982) 127.

24. Neil MacNeil, *Forge of Democracy* (New York: David McKay, 1963) 106–7; William "Fishbait" Miller, *Fishbait: The Memoirs of the Congressional Doorkeeper* (New York: Warner, 1978) 206.

25. MacNeil 103.

26. Diane Ravitch, *The Troubled Crusade: American Education 1945–1980* (New York: Basic Books, 1983) 33–37.

27. Or even experience of Washington. "In Minneapolis," Humphrey later recalled, "I was mayor, *the* mayor—and I had done a good job. Everybody, it seemed, knew me. I was the center of the political universe. In Washington, I not only did not have a

driver or an official car, I didn't even know the streets. I had to struggle to find my way to work, to seek out meeting rooms in strange hotels where no one knew me." Hubert Humphrey, *The Education of a Public Man* (Garden City: Doubleday, 1976) 122.

28. Humphrey 129–31.

29. Oddly, to my knowledge no one then or later suggested that the one-person-one-vote standard was foreshadowed by the census clause in the Constitution. For the Framers had mandated a decennial federal census precisely for the purpose of allocating representation among the states. This was a startling innovation at a time when no other nation conducted regular censuses (Britain's first decennial census was in 1801). The use of a census for representational purposes implies a belief that something like arithmetic equality in the size of districts is an element of fair representation. Equality of population of congressional districts was regarded as important by state legislatures early on. Rosemarie Zagarri, *The Politics of Size: Representation in the United States, 1776–1850* (Ithaca: Cornell Univ., 1987) 121. On the importance of numeracy to early Americans, see Patricia Cline Cohen, *A Calculating People: The Spread of Numeracy in Early America* (Chicago: Univ. of Chicago, 1982).

Chapter 24
Thunder

1. These are not identical with the Department of Defense budget, but provide a useful index of military spending. *Historical Statistics of the United States, Colonial Times to 1970*, 2 vols. (Washington: U.S. Bureau of the Census, 1975) 2: 1116.

2. *Historical Statistics* 2: 1141.

3. *The Gallup Poll* (New York: Random House, 1972), 14–19 Aug. 1949.

4. *The Gallup Poll,* June, Sept. 1949; Jan., May 1950.

5. Robert J. Donovan, *Tumultuous Years* (New York: Norton, 1982) 53–55, 62–65.

6. Donovan 105–13.

7. See Samuel P. Huntington, *The Common Defense* (New York: Columbia Univ., 1961).

8. Richard H. Rovere, *Senator Joe McCarthy* (New York: Harcourt, Brace, 1959) 125–26.

9. He claimed to have been born in November 1909, but birth records in Outgamie County, Wisconsin, show him to have been born in November 1908. Like a later American politician, Gary Hart, McCarthy systematically lied about his age, but McCarthy was more audacious, winning his first election not only by claiming to be thirty rather than thirty-one but also by charging that his sixty-six-year-old opponent was seventy-three. Rovere 79, 87–88.

10. Stassen called for outlawing the Communist party, and Dewey challenged him to debate this issue during the Oregon primary campaign. By general consent, Dewey won the debate; he beat Stassen 52%–48% in Oregon and thereby effectively eliminated his strongest rival for the 1948 Republican nomination. There is no evidence that McCarthy inspired Stassen's proposal (he showed no particular interest in the Communist issue until January 1950), and one might suppose that he concluded it was not, at least in the climate of May 1948, a politically useful one. Richard Norton Smith, *Thomas E. Dewey and His Times* (New York: Simon & Schuster, 1982) 491–

92. McCarthy later called Stassen "one of the most contemptible politicians of our era." Rovere 240–41.

11. Allen Weinstein, *Perjury: The Hiss-Chambers Case* (New York: Knopf, 1978).

12. David Caute, *The Great Purge,* qtd. in William L. O'Neill, *American High* (New York: The Free Press, 1986) 162.

13. Weinstein 384–86.

14. Dean Acheson, *Present at the Creation* (New York: Norton, 1969) 469–71. In the King James Version of the Bible, Matthew 25: 34–36 reads, "Then shall the King say unto them on his right hand, Come, ye blessed of my Father, inherit the kingdom prepared for you from the foundation of the world; for I was an hungered, and ye gave me meat: I was thirsty, and ye gave me drink: I was a stranger, and ye took me in: naked, and ye clothed me: I was sick, and ye visited me: I was in prison, and ye came unto me." The sentiment of Acheson's remarks is not far from E. M. Forster's statement that he hoped that if he had to choose he would betray his country rather than his friend.

15. Actually, Hiss was convicted of perjury for denying such allegations.

16. This is the conclusion of Nelson Polsby, who demolishes overelaborate theories social scientists developed to explain McCarthy's appeal. Nelson W. Polsby, "Toward an Explanation of McCarthyism," *Political Studies* 8, no. 3 (1960); "Down Memory Lane with Joe McCarthy," *Commentary,* Feb. 1983.

17. Acheson 476.

18. See Polsby, "Toward an Explanation."

19. Acheson 465–67.

20. Donovan 192–203. Donovan has an excellent analysis of Truman's character on page 202.

21. Donovan 176.

22. *Historical Statistics* 2: 1116.

23. Three districts switched to the Democrats, but all four were special cases. Republican Kingsland Macy lost the eastern Long Island district because of personal political problems (he had been accused of getting the Republican Senate nominee to run in return for paying off personal debts); Republicans recaptured the seat in 1952. Communist party-liner Vito Marcantonio, running on the American Labor Party line, lost his East Harlem district—not surprisingly now that American troops were being killed by Communists. Democrats gained a seat in San Francisco after the death in 1949 of the eighty-year-old Republican incumbent, who had usually won both parties' nominations in California's cross-filing system.

24. Pepper, a senior member of the Foreign Relations Committee, considered Truman's foreign policy unwisely provocative to the Soviets, and he conspicuously backed Dwight Eisenhower against him in 1948. See Claude Denson Pepper with Hays Gorey, *Pepper: Eyewitness to a Century* (New York: Harcourt Brace Jovanovich, 1987) 126–68.

25. Samuel Lubell, *The Future of American Politics* (New York: Harper, 1952) 100–112. On the staff of Graham's opponent, Willis Smith, was a young journalist named Jesse Helms.

26. Pepper 197–214. Smathers always denied making these remarks, which were widely circulated in an article in *Time*. Pepper remained bitter at Smathers for years; but in 1986, Smathers, by then a Washington lawyer for eighteen years, contributed to Pepper's campaign for reelection to the House.

27. Lubell 129–57.

28. O'Dwyer was of course not reappointed by President Eisenhower, but he stayed in Mexico long after 1953.

29. *The Gallup Poll,* 26–31 Mar. 1951.

30. *The Gallup Poll,* 16–21 Apr. 1951.

31. *The Gallup Poll,* 26–31 Mar., 14 May 1951.

32. It was well known that Jews had strongly backed Roosevelt in 1940 and 1944 and Truman in 1948, that they were inclined to favor left-wing economic programs, that they formed a large share of Communist party membership and had cast perhaps half the votes that the Communist-backed Henry Wallace was able to win in 1948. But both sides of this "betrayal" argument took some pains not to tar all Jews with the left-wing brush. The Truman administration took care to see that the Rosenbergs were prosecuted by a team headed by Irving Saypol, who was rewarded with a federal judgeship, and tried and sentenced to death by Judge Irving Kaufman, who was (after some lobbying) awarded the Medal of Freedom by President Reagan in 1987. As for the administration's opponents, Taft was a staunch backer of Israel and in close touch with Cincinnati Jews on all major issues; and McCarthy hired as his chief aide Roy Cohn, a young New York Jew whose parents had good Democratic connections in the Bronx. Obviously both sides were protecting themselves against charges that they were anti-Jewish. Yet such a course was certainly preferable to erring in the opposite direction, and it suggests that political actors felt an incentive to show they were not bigoted against Jews—a benign incentive indeed when viewed in the light of recent political developments in Europe.

33. Rovere 173.

34. Rovere 178–79.

35. Donovan 359.

36. William S. White, *The Taft Story* (New York: Harper, 1954) 85.

Chapter 25
Crusade

1. The others, both in the opposite direction, were by William of Normandy in 1066 and by William of Orange in 1688. Both Williams became kings of England.

2. Stephen Ambrose, *Eisenhower,* 2 vols. (New York: Simon & Schuster, 1983–84) 1: 512–23.

3. Ambrose 523–28.

4. Wisdom presented on television the case for the fair play amendment challenge to southern delegations; Tuttle was the chairman of Eisenhower's Georgia delegation. For an account of their work at the convention, see Jack Bass, *Unlikely Heroes: The Dramatic Story of the Southern Judges Who Translated the Supreme Court's Brown Decision into a Revolution for Equality* (New York: Simon & Schuster, 1981) 26–29.

5. Ambrose 542.

6. Kenneth S. Davis, *The Politics of Honor* (New York: Putnam's, 1967) 187. My own view is that Stevenson lacked the characteristic hard R's and flat A's of midwestern speech not only because he traveled widely and attended high-toned schools, but also because he learned to talk in California: he was born in Los Angeles in 1900 and lived

there and in Berkeley before his parents moved back to their family home of Bloomington, Illinois, in 1906.

7. This is the conclusion of his definitive biographer. John Bartlow Martin, *Adlai Stevenson of Illinois* (Garden City: Doubleday, 1977) 267.

8. According to Mike Royko, Arvey's "first major step was to convince Kelly that he couldn't win and had to step aside. Arvey, Al Horan, a West Side war boss, and Joe Gill went to his office to tell him. Kelly wouldn't believe it, so right there in City Hall they ran a phone survey for him, calling random names from the phone book and asking them if they would vote for Kelly again. Kelly was unlucky—the random calls didn't turn up any bookies or pimps. He grudgingly agreed to step aside. Next came the problem of finding a candidate. At first, they thought of running one of the other ward leaders, but Kelly said, 'If you're going to run one of them, you might as well run me again.' The Republicans were expected to run a blue-ribbon reformer, so the Democrats decided to do the same." Mike Royko, *Boss: Richard J. Daley of Chicago* (New York: Dutton, 1971) 49–50.

9. Davis 180.

10. But the offer was not a complete surprise: the combination had been suggested by Milburn Akers, a *Chicago Sun* political writer, in early November 1947. Martin 273.

11. This is the version in Davis 185. Martin quotes Arvey "many years later" as recalling, "I said, 'I will tell you the same thing I told Kennelly in 1947. The only thing I can ask of you is that you help the Democratic Party as much as you can in a decent way. We want the patronage when a Democrat can fill the job. I am not talking about cabinet appointments or your own personal appointments. Get the best men you can for those. We want you to get the best. That's the way you can help the party most. You're our showcase. If you do well, we'll look good. All I ask is that you be loyal to the party—don't make an alliance with the Republicans.' " Martin 279.

12. Harry S Truman, *Years of Trial and Hope* (Garden City: Doubleday, 1956) 492.

13. Martin describes Stevenson as genuinely ambivalent about running—and as assuming that the nomination would not be worth much with Eisenhower as the Republican nominee. Martin 521–28.

14. The headline in the next day's *Times* was "HST Offers Stevenson Nomination: Vinson Out." Martin 524–25.

15. Walter Johnson, *How We Drafted Adlai Stevenson* (New York: Knopf, 1955); Martin 533–34.

16. Martin 537–38, 548–49; Davis 261–64.

17. This was the interpretation of Stevenson's longtime aide and speechwriter, Carl McGowan, at the time. Martin 562.

18. This was also Carl McGowan's theory at the time, based on his observations but not on anything Stevenson said. McGowan discounted the draft efforts. Martin 558–59.

19. Martin 575.

20. Robert J. Donovan, *Tumultuous Years* (New York: Norton, 1982) 397.

21. Martin 540; John Frederick Martin, *Civil Rights and the Crisis of Liberalism: The Democratic Party 1945–1976* (Boulder: Westview, 1979) 94–100. John Bartlow Martin, one of the Democrats' most gifted speechwriters and John Kennedy's ambassador to

the Dominican Republic, was the father of John Frederick Martin, a speechwriter for Walter Mondale in 1984 and Albert Gore's campaign manager in 1988.

22. This optimism may have been a brave front, but "most of those close to Stevenson thought he believed he would win." John Bartlow Martin 755. Another biographer says his bet was on 381 electoral votes. Davis 290.

23. John Bartlow Martin vii.

24. Angus Campbell et al., *The American Voter: An Abridgment* (New York: John Wiley, 1964) 269–74.

25. Stephen E. Ambrose, *Nixon: The Education of a Politician, 1913–1962* (New York: Simon & Schuster, 1987) 297.

Chapter 26
Republicans

1. Republicans gained House seats in Virginia (6) and North Carolina (10) in 1952 and in Florida (1) and Texas (5) in 1954 (they got 49% in the Florida seat in 1952 and fielded no candidate in the Texas seat that year).

2. Doris Kearns Goodwin, *The Fitzgeralds and the Kennedys* (New York: Simon & Schuster, 1987) 758.

3. See Joseph W. Martin, *My First Fifty Years in Politics* (New York: McGraw-Hill, 1960). Martin was ousted from the Republican leadership after the 1958 elections and ended up as one of the few Republicans supporting Rayburn in his last major fight, to increase the size of the Rules Committee, in January 1961. Richard Cheney and Lynne Cheney, *Kings of the Hill: Power and Personality in the House of Representatives* (New York: Continuum, 1983) 184. He was defeated for renomination in September 1966 by Margaret Heckler, who was later Ronald Reagan's secretary of health and human services and ambassador to Ireland.

4. "Once in a debate he roared with such power that he restored hearing in the deaf ear of Representative Leonard W. Schuetz of Illinois, who had been afflicted since birth. Schuetz thanked Taber." Joseph Goulden, *The Best Years* 236, cited in Robert J. Donovan, *Conflict and Crisis* (New York: Norton, 1977) 259.

5. Major metropolitan areas are defined as those with populations over 1,000,000 and smaller metropolitan areas as those with populations between 300,000 and 1,000,000. The table below shows the composition of the House of Representatives elected in 1952:

	Democrats		Republicans	
Non-South				
Major metropolitan areas	65	31%	72	33%
Smaller metropolitan areas	7	3%	24	11%
Non-metropolitan areas	29	14%	117	53%
South	111	52%	7	3%

6. Neal Pierce and Michael Barone, *The Mid-Atlantic States of America* (New York: Norton, 1977) 142.

7. Stephen Ambrose, *Eisenhower,* 2 vols. (New York: Simon & Schuster, 1983–84) 2: 86–87.

8. Ambrose 2: 137–40; Allen Weinstein, *Perjury* (New York: Knopf, 1978) 237–40.

9. Richard H. Rovere, *Senator Joe McCarthy* (New York: Harcourt Brace Jovanovich, 1959) 218.

10. *Historical Statistics of the United States, Colonial Times to 1970,* 2 vols. (Washington: U.S. Bureau of the Census, 1975) 2: 796. Note that the rise continues through the recession year of 1954 and was halted only slightly by the deeper recession of 1957–58. The percentage crossed 90% in 1963 and 95% in 1970, but for all practical purposes television was a universal medium by 1956.

11. Nelson W. Polsby effectively refutes the theory, widely accepted at the time by Washington observers and frightened academics, that McCarthy had a major public following. Nelson W. Polsby, "Toward an Explanation of McCarthyism," *Political Studies* 8, no. 3. See also Polsby's "Down Memory Lane with Joe McCarthy," *Commentary,* Feb. 1983.

12. Two were staunch McCarthyites, Barry Goldwater of Arizona (51% to Eisenhower's 58%) and George Malone of Nevada (52% to Eisenhower's 61%). The other was Frank Barrett of Wyoming (52% to Eisenhower's 63%). Stephen Ambrose and Fred Greenstein have argued that Eisenhower worked behind the scenes to undermine McCarthy and have documented his distaste for the man. Stephen E. Ambrose 162–68; Fred I. Greenstein, *The Hidden-Hand Presidency: Eisenhower as Leader* (New York: Basic Books, 1982) 155–227. But any exoneration of Eisenhower's handshake with McCarthy and his deletion of his defense of George Marshall in Milwaukee in the 1952 campaign must address the possibility that these gestures reelected McCarthy. It may be argued that McCarthy's victory had the important advantage for Eisenhower of clinching Republican control of the Senate. But before the election no one could be sure of that, and afterwards Republican control would probably have been maintained since it was Eisenhower's attitude toward McCarthy that prompted Senator Wayne Morse, who was not up for reelection until 1956, to leave the Republican party.

13. Gallup's interviews were conducted from April 8 to April 13; the hearings began April 22.

14. Ironically, Watkins, not the senators supporting McCarthy, ended up paying a political price. J. Bracken Lee, the right-wing mayor of Salt Lake City, ran as an independent when Watkins's seat came up in 1958 and got 26% of the vote, enabling Democrat Frank Moss to defeat Watkins by a 39%–35% margin. But Lee had his own reasons for running, and McCarthy had died in May 1957 at age forty-eight after several years of heavy drinking.

15. Ambrose 229.

Chapter 27
Desegregation

1. Jules Tygiel, *Baseball's Great Experiment* (New York: Random House, 1984) 54. Rickey maintained that a New York law passed to encourage the hiring of black players played no part in his decision to hire Jackie Robinson, but his denial is not entirely convincing.

2. Daniel M. Johnson and Rex R. Campbell, *Black Migration in America* (Durham: Duke Univ., 1981) 131.

3. The South here is defined as the eleven states which made up the Confederacy, though adding the other states counted as southern in other calculations in this paragraph (West Virginia, Kentucky, Oklahoma) would not make much difference because they had small black populations, below the national average, throughout the period. The numbers are figured using what the Census Bureau calls the components of change method; an alternative, the survivals method, gives the black out-migration from the South as 1.26 million in the 1940s and 1.21 million in the 1950s.

4. *Historical Statistics of the United States, Colonial Times to 1970,* 2 vols. (Washington: U.S. Bureau of the Census, 1975) 22, 25–26, 29: *1986 Statistical Abstract of the United States* (Washington: U.S. Bureau of the Census, 1985) 29. I have recalculated the data to exclude Delaware, Maryland, and the District of Columbia from the South; these had an in-migration and not an out-migration of blacks during the three decades beginning in 1940. From 1940 to 1970 the black population of the South rose only from 9.3 million to 10.7 million, a rise of 14%, while the rest of the southern population, almost all of it white, rose from 29.5 million to 46.9 million, a rise of 59%, and the black population outside the South rose from just under 3 million to 10.6 million, a rise of 258%.

5. The classic description is John Dollard, *Caste and Class in a Southern Town* (Madison: Univ. of Wisconsin, 1988), originally published in 1937.

6. See the vivid and moving account of this case in Juan Williams. *Eyes on the Prize* (New York: Viking, 1987) 38–57.

7. Eisenhower carried the following districts: Arkansas 3; Florida 1, 4, 5, 6, 7; Kentucky 3, 5, 8; Louisiana 1, 4; Mississippi 4; North Carolina 9, 10, 11, 12; Oklahoma 1, 2, 4, 5, 6; South Carolina 1, 2, 6; Tennessee 1, 2, 3; Texas 3, 5, 8, 9, 12, 14, 15, 16, 17, 18, 19, 20, 21, and the at-large seat; Virginia 1, 3, 5, 6, 7, 8, 9, 10; and West Virginia 2, 4.

Chapter 28
Split Ticket

1. The United States was not the only democratic nation with a demographic dividend for the parties of the left, although in most it did not become noticeable until in the 1960s. Similar shifts helped the Labour party win in Britain in 1964 and the Social Democrats in West Germany in 1969; they increased the votes of the leftist parties in Italy in the middle 1970s and nearly elected François Mitterrand president of France in 1974, when he ran just a few points lower than when he won in 1981 and 1988.

2. New York still nominated candidates by convention, and a majority of votes at the Democratic convention were cast by the four party leaders of the four large boroughs of New York City. They selected the sixty-three-year-old Harriman over forty-year-old Franklin D. Roosevelt, Jr., more famous and glamorous but far less knowledgeable and hard-working, who was persuaded to accept the consolation prize of the nomination for attorney general. Harriman won in the fall, but Roosevelt lost to liberal Republican Congressman Jacob Javits, who went on in 1956 to beat Robert Wagner, Jr., mayor of New York City, for the Senate seat occupied then by Herbert Lehman and formerly by Wagner's father. Javits thus ended the statewide careers of two political dynasts.

Roosevelt's dreams are not hard to imagine: governor in 1954, reelection in 1958, and then in 1960. . . . Instead, he campaigned for John Kennedy in the West Virginia primary and served as undersecretary of commerce and head of the Equal Employment Opportunities Commission in the Democratic administrations that followed. He died in October 1988.

3. The Democratic percentage in this northern tier was above the party's national percentage in every presidential election after 1960, except for 1976 and 1980, when southerner Jimmy Carter ran 1 percentage point behind his national percentage. The Republican percentage in this northern tier was below the party's national percentage in every presidential election after 1968, except for 1976, when northern tier native Gerald Ford ran .1% ahead of his national percentage.

4. Stephen E. Ambrose, *Eisenhower,* 2 vols. (New York: Simon & Schuster, 1983–84) 2: 218–20.

5. Ambrose 199.

6. Ambrose 118.

7. Ambrose 282.

8. *The Gallup Poll* (New York: Random House, 1972), 6–11 Oct., 27 Oct–1 Nov., 17–22 Nov., 8–13 Dec. 1955.

9. *The Gallup Poll,* 27 Oct.–1 Nov., 17–22 Nov., 8–13 Dec. 1955; 6–11 Jan. 1956.

Chapter 29
Peace and Prosperity

1. Stephen E. Ambrose, *Eisenhower the President* (New York: Simon & Schuster, 1984) 294, 348.

2. Less than 55% Democratic were the following districts: Virginia 3, 9; North Carolina 9, 12; Florida 5, 6; Tennessee 3; Kentucky 2, 6, 7; Missouri 4, 6, 7 (this was actually a Democratic gain, the defeat of veteran isolationist Dewey Short), 8, 11.

3. *The Gallup Poll* (New York: Random House, 1972), 8–13 Dec. 1955; 16–21 Feb., 19–21 Apr., 10–15 May 1956.

4. Although Franklin Roosevelt made efforts in the off-year campaign of 1934 to appear a man above party—at a time when it was by no means clear that the Democrats were or would be a majority party.

5. "Somewhere in every public school room in America, there is a little boy who throws and throws his hand up before the teacher, before the child she has called upon has had a chance to think of the answer. He knows the answer at once; his soul cries for the chance to give it, perhaps because he needs to be praised, or because he must hear the orderly 'click' when the right answer fits onto the question. He is oblivious to the scorn of his fellow students; the information is the thing. Francis Case was that little boy grown up, pale, square, and deadly dull." Harry McPherson, *A Political Education: A Washington Memoir* (Boston: Houghton Mifflin, 1988) 71.

6. John Bartlow Martin, *Adlai Stevenson of Illinois* (Garden City: Doubleday, 1977) 585–86.

7. Kenneth S. Davis, *Adlai Stevenson* (New York: Putnam's, 1967) 269, 313.

8. Martin 765. On Stevenson's growing disdain for the American public, see John Bartlow Martin, *Adlai Stevenson and the World* (Garden City: Doubleday, 1978) 393–94.

9. John Alsop wrote Arthur Schlesinger, Jr., an egghead if there ever was one, in December 1952, "As far as I know, the term 'egghead' is not local, nor is it my own invention (as I feel sure I must have heard it somewhere) but its application to the nation's intellectuals is probably my responsibility. As he probably told you, Stewart happened to be in Connecticut with Mr. Stevenson during the early part of the campaign and he called me on the telephone to discuss the situation here. During the course of the conversation, he pointed out that certain intellectuals who tended to support Eisenhower up to the Convention were deserting him. This made me rather angry because I knew that it was true, so I dredged up the derogatory term from my subconscious." Hans Sperber and Travis Trittschuh, *Dictionary of American Political Terms* 139.

10. James Q. Wilson, *The Amateur Democrat* (Chicago: Univ. of Chicago, 1966) 53–54. For an analysis of Stevenson's crucial impact on "reform Democrats" in New York, Chicago, and Los Angeles, see Wilson 52–58.

11. Martin, *Adlai Stevenson of Illinois* vii.

12. John Frederick Martin, *Civil Rights and the Crisis of Liberalism: The Democratic Party 1945–1976* (Boulder, Westview, 1979) 117–36. This is a brilliant, lively, and original account by a writer who later became Senator Albert Gore, Jr.'s campaign manager in the 1988 presidential race.

13. John Bartlow Martin, *Adlai Stevenson and the World* 46.

14. *The Gallup Poll,* 27 Oct.–1 Nov., 17–22 Nov. 1955; 6–11 Jan. 1956.

15. The Democrats were delighted when Nebraska delegate Terry Carpenter rose at the Republican convention to nominate "Joe Smith" for vice president—a symbolic protest against Nixon. Carpenter actually was a former and future Democrat: he was elected to the House as a Democrat in 1932, served for many years in Nebraska's non-partisan single-chamber Senate, and as a Democrat won a surprisingly high 47% of the vote in a race against Senator Carl Curtis in 1972. But his "Joe Smith" prank did not hurt the Republicans in 1956.

16. On the "rally round the flag" effect, see Nelson W. Polsby, *Congress and the Presidency* (Englewood Cliffs: Prentice-Hall, 1986) 73.

17. The exception, 1964, proves the rule. The Catholic percentage for John Kennedy in 1960 was so high (78%) that it could not have been exceeded by any later candidate, probably including Kennedy himself, and even including the popular Johnson with his very weak opposition.

18. Connecticut 1; New Jersey 6, 13, 14; Delaware at-large; West Virginia 1, 4; Michigan 6; Illinois 3.

19. Iowa 6; Missouri 7; Kansas 5; South Dakota 1; Montana 2; Oregon 2, 4; California 11, 29.

Chapter 30
Erosion

1. Richard Neustadt, *Presidential Power* (New York: Wiley, 1962) 66.

2. See Stephen E. Ambrose, *Eisenhower the President* (New York: Simon & Schuster, 1984) 388–91; Neustadt 64–80.

3. See Rowland Evans and Robert Novak, *Lyndon Johnson: The Exercise of Power* (New York: New American Library, 1966) 125–40. This book is a brilliant account of Johnson's career up to June 1966, based on aggressive reporting and insightful analysis, and gracefully written to boot. It stands up very well against the excellent works on Johnson by Harry McPherson, Doris Kearns, and Robert Caro which have appeared since.

4. Ambrose 406–10.

5. Robert A. Caro, *The Years of Lyndon Johnson: The Path to Power* (New York: Random House, 1981) 4–25. This wonderful passage is worth reading even by those who have no interest in Lyndon Johnson or the Hill Country.

6. Evans and Novak 43.

7. Nelson W. Polsby, *Congress and the Presidency,* 4th ed. (Englewood Cliffs: Prentice-Hall, 1986) 111.

8. See Diane Ravitch, *The Troubled Crusade: American Education 1945–1980* (New York: Basic Books, 1983) 228–32.

Chapter 31
Setback

1. *Historical Statistics of the United States, Colonial Times to 1970,* 2 vols. (Washington: U.S. Bureau of the Census, 1975) 1: 135, 224.

2. Young won reelection in 1964 against none other than Robert Taft, Jr., and served till the age of eighty. His campaign manager both times was Howard Metzenbaum, a millionaire Cleveland businessman who ran for the seat himself in 1970, when Young retired, and nearly beat Taft. Metzenbaum was appointed to the other Ohio Senate seat in January 1974 but lost the 1974 primary for it to John Glenn; he then beat Taft in a 1976 rematch and won the seat again in 1982 and 1988. Metzenbaum thus held this seat in person or by proxy for twenty-four of the thirty years after 1958, and was entitled to hold it for six more.

Chapter 32
Candidates

1. A leading role in this fight was played by columnist Drew Pearson. Drew Pearson, *Diaries 1949–1959* (New York, Holt, Rinehart & Winston, 1974) 520–24. "I suppose I should register as a lobbyist," Pearson wrote at a time when press ethics were not what they would become.

2. Edward Kennedy, the ninth, was born in February 1932.

3. Doris Kearns Goodwin, *The Fitzgeralds and the Kennedys* (New York: Simon & Schuster, 1987) 428–29.

4. Michael R. Beschloss, *Kennedy and Roosevelt* (New York: Norton, 1980) 213–20; Goodwin 609–13.

5. Harry McPherson, *A Political Education: A Washington Memoir* (Boston: Houghton Mifflin, 1988) 41.

6. Theodore H. White notes one estimate that 41% of the total American population growth in the 1950s was Catholic. Theodore H. White, *The Making of the President*

1960 (New York: New American Library, 1962) 273. Of course, that figure reflects the significantly higher number of children Catholic families had in those days when almost all American Catholics obeyed the church's edict against birth control. Catholics would have accounted for a similarly high share of American population growth in the 1930s and 1940s—something which both Joseph Kennedy and the many Americans who were wary of increasing Catholic influence on American political and cultural life were aware of.

7. This is Rose Kennedy's version of the meeting presented in Goodwin 787–88.

8. Beschloss 215.

9. "Lyndon Johnson and Joseph Kennedy understood each other as kindred souls," observed Ann Gargan, a Kennedy cousin close to the ambassador. Goodwin 802.

10. Richard M. Valelly, *Radicalism in the States: The Minnesota Farmer-Labor Party and the American Political Economy* (Chicago: Univ. of Chicago, 1989).

11. Kenneth S. Davis, *Adlai Stevenson* (New York: Putnam's, 1967) 303.

12. See James Q. Wilson, *The Amateur Democrat* (Chicago: Univ. of Chicago, 1966), the definitive book on "reform" politics.

13. The Bronx, Manhattan, Brooklyn, and Queens together cast 58% of the state's Democratic presidential votes in 1956 and 61% in 1944, the last election before 1956 in which the Democratic nominee carried New York.

14. Richard Norton Smith, *Thomas E. Dewey and His Times* (New York: Simon & Schuster, 1982) 624.

15. Theodore H. White, *The Making of the President 1964* (New York: New American Library, 1966) 112.

16. Stephen E. Ambrose, *The Education of a Politician 1913–1962,* vol. 1 of *Nixon* (New York: Simon & Schuster, 1987) 34–116. On Nixon's career as a young Republican, see pages 91–92.

Chapter 33
Debate

1. *Gallup Poll* (New York: Random House, 1972). But Theodore H. White reports a private Nixon poll, taken in spring 1959, which showed Rockefeller ahead of Nixon 40%–38%. Theodore H. White, *The Making of the President 1960* (New York: New American Library, 1962) 80. This seems an improbable result.

2. "He was vulnerable to attack as moving too fast and too soon," White writes of Rockefeller's situation in 1959 (although in contrast to Nixon, who had held no executive responsibilities, Rockefeller had held high-level foreign and domestic policy positions in the Roosevelt, Truman, and Eisenhower administrations. "But he was 51 years old, and in 1960 he would be 52; if he did not move in 1960, and if the succeeding Republican President held a normal two terms, he would be 60 in 1968, too old." White 83. Rockefeller died at 71, in January 1979; his only full-fledged race for the presidency came in 1964, a year when the Republicans were doomed to fail.

3. The Gallup Poll, Jan. 1959–Nov. 1960. Eisenhower's job rating never fell below 57% in 1959 or 1960, and from August 1959, just before Khrushchev visited the United States, until May 1960, when the Paris summit collapsed after Khrushchev denounced Eisenhower for the downed U-2 flight, his rating was never below 64%.

4. For example, by 35%–27% on keeping the country out of World War III. *The Gallup Poll,* 4–9 Feb. 1960.

5. By margins approaching 3–2 through all this period except in March 1960; a Democratic vote at this level is a historical high for the party. Although trends toward increased ticket-splitting were noted throughout the 1960s and 1970s, by November 1958 it was already a clearly established pattern or, to be more precise, coexisting preferences for a Republican president and a Democratic Congress were clearly established. This fact should not be too surprising: Americans had a government with just this pattern, a Republican president and a wholly or partially Democratic Congress, for twenty-two of the thirty-four years following the November 1954 election. *The Gallup Poll,* Jan. 1959–Oct. 1960.

6. At the same time, Eisenhower did not want it to appear that Nixon, rather than the president himself, was making decisions. Nixon "did not want Eisenhower to campaign on the basis of the record of his administration, but to cite Nixon's great contributions and describe Nixon as 'indispensable,' 'statesmanlike,' 'judicious,' and so forth. But Eisenhower nevertheless spent the campaign defending his own record." Stephen E. Ambrose, *Eisenhower the President* (New York: Simon & Schuster, 1984) 594.

7. This pattern is known among political insiders as Donilon's law, after Thomas Donilon, an aide to Jimmy Carter in 1980 and Walter Mondale in 1984, while among political scientists Martin P. Wattenberg is credited. The early clinchers after 1960 were Lyndon Johnson in 1964, Richard Nixon in 1968 and 1972, Carter in 1976, Ronald Reagan in 1980, and George Bush in 1988—winners all. In 1980 both Carter and Reagan had their nominations effectively won after the Illinois primary, though both continued to have opposition and in fact lost some later primaries.

8. *The Gallup Poll,* 2–7 Apr. 1959.

9. See Joseph Lieberman, *The Power Broker: A Biography of John M. Bailey, Modern Political Boss* (Boston: Houghton Mifflin, 1966). Lieberman was elected attorney general of Connecticut in 1982 and 1986 and U.S. senator in 1988.

10. Benjamin C. Bradlee, *Conversations with Kennedy* (New York: Norton, 1975) 26.

11. While Humphrey scribbled out a $750 check to keep the campaign going, Kennedy was spending the supposedly huge sum of $34,000 on television alone in West Virginia. White 130–31.

12. My paternal grandmother's Buchanan ancestors were recorded in Bath County, Virginia, just across the border from what would become West Virginia, in the 1770s; they reached Tucker County, West Virginia, 60 miles directly north but over a couple of rugged mountain ridges, by the time my grandmother was born there in 1896.

13. White 126, 125.

14. Astonishingly, no recording or transcript of this broadcast was made; we have only White's recollection of it. White 128.

15. Johnson's count was 602 ½ for Kennedy and 502 ½ for himself. White 157–58. For as astute a politician as Johnson to be off as much as 100 delegates shows how conventions worked in those days: the first ballot or ballots were actually delegate counts, in which candidates could gauge how many votes they and their rivals really had. By 1968 the television networks had developed accurate delegate counts long before anyone got to the convention city, and so the communications function of the early ballots was rendered obsolete. In 1960, however, the old politics still prevailed.

16. Michael R. Beschloss, *Mayday: The U-2 Affair* (New York: Harper & Row, 1986) 200.

17. Franklin Roosevelt had developed it in Maryland's Catoctin Mountains and named it Shangri-La. Eisenhower refurbished it and renamed it after his grandson (and biographer) Dwight David Eisenhower II.

18. The only election years in the twentieth century when it was clear from the beginning that the incumbent president was not running were 1908 (Theodore Roosevelt announced just after his victory in 1904 that he wouldn't run), 1920 (Wilson was an invalid), 1928 (Coolidge made his "I do not choose to run for president in 1928" announcement in the summer of 1927), and 1960 and 1988 (incumbents Eisenhower and Reagan were barred from running for a third term). Some suspect that Eisenhower, dismayed with the quality of potential replacements, would have run if he could have; "he had no choice but to turn over the government," Stephen Ambrose concludes, "but he still could not think of anyone to succeed him." Ambrose 593.

19. Gallup also reports a 54%–46% Kennedy lead in a 30 Mar.–4 Apr. 1960 survey. Assuming 5% were undecided, the same as in the previous and successive Gallup surveys, the Kennedy lead was actually 51%–44%—a record 7 points.

20. *The Gallup Poll,* 28 Apr.–3 May 1960.

21. See Graham's fascinating memorandum, reprinted after his tragic death, in Theodore H. White, *The Making of the President 1964,* 483–91. This amplifies the useful account given by the same author in *President 1960,* 199–204.

22. This is the view taken by one of Johnson's most astute and sensitive aides. Harry McPherson, *A Political Education: A Washington Memoir* (Boston: Houghton Mifflin, 1988) 178–79.

23. Herbert S. Parmet, *JFK: The Presidency of John F. Kennedy* (New York: Penguin, 1984) 29. Parmet says that Robert Kennedy was acting in line with the wishes of his brother, who found it hard to make up his mind about the Johnson nomination.

24. New Frontier, he said, "sums up not what I intend to offer the American people but what I intend to ask of them. It appeals to their pride, not to their pocketbook; it holds out the promise of more sacrifice instead of more security. But I tell you the New Frontier is here whether we seek it or not . . . uncharted areas of science and space, unsolved problems of peace and war, unconquered pockets of ignorance and prejudice, unanswered questions of poverty and surplus." This is quoted, with obvious pride, by his speechwriter Theodore Sorenson in *Kennedy* (New York: Bantam, 1968) 188–89.

25. Abigail McCarthy, *Private Faces, Public Places* (New York: Curtis, 1972) 223.

26. "Kennedy exerts over Nixon the same charm that a snake charmer exerts over a snake. . . . Nixon liked Kennedy, which was not reciprocally true." White, *President 1960,* 337–38. Nixon's preoccupation with the Kennedys was apparent as late as May 1987, in the note Nixon sent Gary Hart on May 11, after his withdrawal from the presidential race. *New York Times,* 15 July 1987.

27. This tally counts Alabama for Kennedy. Alabamians voted for each of the state's eleven electors separately, not as part of a state; the winners had been chosen separately in Alabama's Democratic primary. Five of them were pledged to Kennedy and six to Harry Byrd, who also took Mississippi's electoral votes in a three-way race. Yet almost identical numbers of voters voted for all eleven, leaving the tantalizing question: should all or

some or none of those votes be counted for Kennedy? The usual procedure is to count all the popular votes cast for the top Kennedy elector as cast for Kennedy. But if Kennedy is given only 5/11 of the average number of votes cast for a Democratic elector, then Nixon would lead in the total national popular vote.

28. Alaska and Hawaii were each given one representative when they were admitted to the Union, but in accordance with the 1911 apportionment law the total number of representatives was reduced to 435 again for the 1962 election.

29. Even among the then self-consciously Democratic union members, Kennedy got the votes of 85% of the Catholics but only 52% of the Protestants, according to Gallup.

Chapter 34
Frontier

1. Theodore Sorenson, *Kennedy* (New York: Bantam, 1966) 272.

2. After one briefing, President-elect Kennedy asked CIA Director Allen Dulles if he had any good news. Well, said Dulles, things were going pretty well in Iran.

3. These were the six title characters in Walter Isaacson and Evan Thomas, *The Wise Men: Six Friends and the World They Made* (New York: Simon & Schuster, 1986). Harriman became an assistant secretary of state, a lowly post for a man who had negotiated with Churchill and Stalin; Bohlen was named ambassador to France, and Kennan ambassador to Yugoslavia.

4. Each recognized this but recommended him nonetheless. Isaacson and Thomas 589–96. Unlike all other recent presidents, Kennedy relied on veterans of a previous administration, men of his father's generation, like Acheson and Lovett to staff his administration and advise him in crises.

5. As head of the Ford Foundation, Bundy superintended such projects as the Ocean Hill–Brownsville local school board experiment, a quintessential example of the politicizing of ghetto schools which helped to produce a totally uneducated underclass for a generation, and the recommendation that universities place more of their endowments in common stocks, a recommendation made at just the time that the stock market reached a peak it would not exceed in real dollars for the next twenty years.

6. It had been Hubert Humphrey's idea, advanced in the 1960 campaign—one of the very few instances of a campaign promise which came to useful fruition in government policy. It worked so well partly because it tapped the idealism of thousands of Americans and partly because the Kennedy brother-in-law put in charge of it, Sargent Shriver, insisted that it be separated completely from U.S. intelligence and diplomacy and, understanding how people on the bottom of an organization always work to prevent bad news from moving upward, kept himself closely informed of how the Peace Corps was actually working in the field.

7. See Herbert Parmet, *JFK: The Presidency of John F. Kennedy* (New York: Penguin, 1984) 316–20.

8. See Norman Gelb, *The Berlin Wall* (New York: Simon & Schuster, 1986).

9. *Historical Statistics of the United States, Colonial Times to 1970,* 2 vols. (Washington: U.S. Bureau of the Census, 1975) 2: 1114.

10. See Richard Cheney and Lynne Cheney, *Kings of the Hill* 182–89, for a revisionist

account which persuasively differs from the standard accounts of admirers of Rayburn like Richard Bolling, *House Out of Order* (New York: Dutton, 1966) 208–20, and D. B. Hardeman and Donald C. Bacon, *Rayburn* (Austin: Texas Monthly, 1987) 447–65.

11. Rowland Evans and Robert Novak, *Lyndon B. Johnson: The Exercise of Power* (New York: New American Library, 1966) 305–13.

12. Robert J. Donovan, *Tumultous Years: The Presidency of Harry S. Truman, 1949–1953* (New York: Norton, 1982) 360.

13. Stewart Alsop, *The Center* (New York: Harper & Row, 1968) 288.

14. Harry McPherson, *A Political Education: A Memoir* (Boston: Houghton Mifflin, 1988) 42.

15. Evans and Novak 28.

16. Bobby Baker, *Wheeling and Dealing* (New York: Norton, 1978).

17. Parmet 208–9.

Chapter 35
Confrontation

1. See Theodore Sorensen, *Kennedy* (New York: Bantam, 1966) 460–62.

2. The fact that trade adjustment assistance survived through Congress is a good illustration of the strength of the labor lobby; and the surprise at its survival on the part of Sorensen, who had been Kennedy's chief assistant in the Senate, is evidence of the newness of labor's clout.

3. Stephen K. Bailey, *Congress Makes a Law* (New York: Random House, 1964).

4. Here the reference was to the national productivity level, which is to say total output divided by total hours worked. But an intellectually respectable argument could be made that workers in industries which had greater increases in productivity should have higher wage increases, and when that argument was made by one as well-placed as United Auto Workers president Walter Reuther its merit was quickly recognized by the administration.

5. *The Gallup Poll* (New York: Random House, 1972), 8–13 Mar., 3–8 May 1962. His job approval rating was 73% in the later survey.

6. One fierce critic of these high tax rates was the only president the nation has had who actually paid taxes at those rates, Ronald Reagan. He was understandably dismayed that he was losing most of his income at a time when it was painfully obvious that his earning capacity was about to decline and before the law provided for income averaging. Lou Cannon, *Reagan* (New York: Putnam's, 1982) 91.

7. *The Gallup Poll,* 3–8 May 1962.

8. This was the origin of these terms which were later used in the debate over Vietnam. They were made public in a December 1962 article in the *Saturday Evening Post* by Stewart Alsop and Charles Bartlett.

9. Elie Abel, *The Missile Crisis* (New York: Bantam, 1966) 32.

10. *The Gallup Poll,* 16–21 Nov. 1962.

11. *The Gallup Poll,* 28 June–3 July, 1–7 Oct., 29 Oct.–2 Nov. 1962.

12. Turnout as a percentage of eligible voters was 45.4%. Although this figure was equaled in the next off-year contest, 1966, the Voting Rights Act had by that time expanded the number of southern blacks actually able to vote far beyond that of 1962. The previous highs for off-year turnout since 1920, when women won the right to vote, had been 1938 (44%) and 1958 (43%). Beginning in 1974, off-year turnout was well below 40%.

13. The problem was that Morgenthau was a stiff campaigner. Harris left political polling and became an exceedingly successful private and syndicated pollster in 1963; Morgenthau was reappointed United States attorney for the Southern District of New York and later was elected as Manhattan district attorney in the 1970s and 1980s.

14. The result was "better than we hoped" in Kennedy's view. Sorenseon 396–97.

15. Reapportionment accounted for the following gains and losses. Democratic gains: Arizona 3; California 4, 9, 21, 29, 31, 34, 37; Florida 3, 9, 10; Hawaii at-large; Maryland at-large; Michigan at-large; New Jersey 15. Republican gains: California 12; Florida 11; Illinois 12; New York 2, 4; Ohio at-large. Democratic losses: Alabama (Boykin), Arkansas (Norrell, Alford), Illinois (Yates, Mack), Iowa (Coad), Kansas (Breeding), Kentucky (Spence), Massachusetts (Lane), Mississippi (Smith), New York (Anfuso, Santangelo, Zelenko), North Carolina (Kitchin), Pennsylvania (Granahan), West Virginia (Bailey). Republican losses: Maine (Garland) Massachusetts (Curtis), Minnesota (Andresen), Nebraska (Weaver), New York (Taber), Pennsylvania (Fenton, Van Zandt).

    As for seats where reapportionment was not the major factor, Democrats gained California 25, 27, 30; Connecticut 2; New York 16; Ohio 15; and Oregon 4 and lost California 38; Kentucky 3; Maryland 1; North Carolina 9; Ohio 10, 11; Tennessee 3; Texas 16; Utah 1, 2; and Washington 7. Some of these results hinged on such random factors as scandal or the incumbent's health.

Chapter 36
Rights

1. See, among many other works, Harris Wofford, *Of Kennedys and Kings* (New York: Farrar, Straus, 1980); David Garrow, *Bearing the Cross: Martin Luther King, Jr., and the Southern Christian Leadership Conference* (New York: Random House, 1986).

2. Theodore H. White, *The Making of the President 1960* (New York: New American Library, 1962) 355–56.

3. Herbert S. Parmet, *JFK: The Presidency of John F. Kennedy* (New York: Penguin, 1984) 255.

4. Juan Williams, *Eyes on the Prize* (New York: Viking, 1987) 149–61.

5. Parmet 254; Williams 159.

6. C. Vann Woodward, *Looking Back* (Baton Rouge: Louisiana State Univ., 1966) 81–99; C. Vann Woodward, *The Strange Career of Jim Crow* (New York: Oxford Univ., 1986).

7. There was much more violence attendant on the creation of legal segregation around the turn of the century than there was related to the effort to preserve it in the 1950s and 1960s, at least as measured by number and severity of incidents. See Douglas

MacAdam, *Political Process and the Development of Black Insurgency, 1930–1970* (Chicago: Univ. of Chicago, 1982).

8. So far as I know, no one suggested that the experience of integration in the military had any relevance to American civilian life. But in 1965, Daniel Patrick Moynihan, far ahead of his time as usual, noted the following in a report much reviled by most of those who saw themselves as the most fervent supporters of civil rights: "Service in the United States Armed Forces is the only experience open to the Negro American in which he is truly treated as an equal: not as a Negro equal to a white, but as one man equal to any other man in a world where the categories 'Negro' and 'white' do not exist. If this is the statement of the ideal rather than reality, it is an ideal that is close to realization. In food, dress, housing, pay, work—the Negro in the Armed Forces is equal and is treated that way." Daniel Patrick Moynihan, "The Negro Family: The Case for National Action," qtd. in Lee Rainwater and William L. Yancey, *The Moynihan Report and the Politics of Controversy* (Cambridge: M.I.T., 1967) 88.

9. James Silver, *Mississippi: The Closed Society* (New York: Harcourt, Brace, 1964).

10. Williams 213–18.

11. Gary Paul Gates, *Air Time: The Inside Story of CBS News* (New York: Harper & Row, 1978) 291.

12. See Dan Rather, *The Camera Never Blinks* (New York: Morrow, 1977) 73–75.

13. Barbara Matusow, *The Evening Stars: The Making of the Network News Anchor* (Boston: Houghton Mifflin, 1983) 70–81.

14. Matusow 82.

15. At ABC, it did not happen until 1967. Gates 93. For a vivid description of the change, see David Halberstam, *The Powers That Be* (New York: Knopf, 1979) 408–9.

16. Marshall McLuhan, *Understanding Media* (New York: Signet, 1966) 261.

17. By 1962 the number of households with television sets (48.9 million) was only marginally lower than the number with radios (51.3 million). *Historical Statistics of the United States, Colonial Times to 1970,* 2 vols. (Washington: U.S. Bureau of the Census, 1975) 2: 796.

18. It is fitting that King has been the subject of two biographies which see him as a central figure of his time. Garrow's *Bearing the Cross* spans his entire career. Taylor Branch's *Parting the Waters: America in the King Years 1954–1963* (New York: Simon & Schuster, 1988) is the first volume of an even richer and more intensively researched biography, of which the second volume is eagerly awaited.

19. Richard Gid Powers, *Secrecy and Power: The Life of J. Edgar Hoover* (New York: The Free Press, 1987) 369–73.

20. Garrow 382.

21. Williams 179–95.

22. Williams 191.

23. Dan Rather, personal interview, 20 July 1988.

24. Stanley Karnow, *Vietnam: A History* (New York: Viking, 1983) 279–81.

25. Qtd. in Parmet 271.

26. *The Gallup Poll* (New York: Random House, 1972), 21–26 June 1963.

27. The totals were not significantly different when Kennedy was paired against George

Romney, and Kennedy ran stronger against Nelson Rockefeller, who by this time had been weakened by the announcement in November 1961 of his divorce and his marriage in May 1963 to a woman who gave up custody of her children to her first husband in order to marry him. Lou Harris's results were similar: in August he showed Kennedy leading Romney 52%–39%, Goldwater 54%–40%, and Rockefeller 56%–36%.

28. Lou Harris survey, *Washington Post,* 1 July 1963.

29. *The Gallup Poll,* 12–17 Sept. 1963.

30. Parmet 275.

31. Parmet 328.

32. Or so Henry Cabot Lodge, then U.S. ambassador to South Vietnam, reported. Parmet 330.

33. Parmet 331.

34. Qtd. in Parmet 332.

35. Qtd. in Parmet 333.

36. Qtd. in Parmet 328.

37. This was the scathing conclusion of David Halberstam's contemporary *The Making of a Quagmire* (New York: Knopf, 1965), a book anything but dovish in its approach, and Neil Sheehan's recent *A Bright Shining Lie* (New York: Random House, 1988); Vann, an American military officer, was a principal source for Halberstam and Sheehan when, as young reporters in 1963, they reported that the Diem regime was prosecuting the war against the Viet Cong ineffectively. Their conclusion was that the United States should take a more active role—a conclusion that both men, and many others, renounced some time between November 1963 and February 1968. Stephen S. Rosenfeld, *Washington Post,* 21 Oct. 1988. They seem to have seen Diem as the same kind of leader—a corrupt despot, insensitive to events on the ground, unwilling to fight vigorously against an enemy which Americans wanted him to beat—as Chiang Kai-shek, at least as portrayed by General Joseph Stilwell and the Old China hands. See Barbara Tuchman, *Stilwell and the American Experience in China* (New York: Macmillan, 1970); Theodore H. White, *Fire in the Ashes* (New York: Sloane, 1953).

38. Qtd. in Garrow 271–72.

39. This meeting is recounted in Branch 835–41 and in Garrow 271–74.

40. At this writing, Mills is alive and well; and but for the personal scandal which struck him in October 1974 he might now have celebrated his thirtieth anniversary as chairman.

41. Rowland Evans and Robert D. Novak, *Lyndon B. Johnson: The Exercise of Power* (New York: New American Library, 1966) 374. Their account of Johnson's handling of this issue in the first three days of his presidency appears on pages 368–76.

42. Celler had been chairman since January 1949, except for the two years during which Republicans controlled the House. Liberal big-city Democratic veterans like Celler as well as conservative southerners depended for their chairmanships on absolute observance of the seniority rule. Quite contrary to general belief, seniority had not always been the determinant of chairmanships; it had been ignored often in the first three decades of the twentieth century, and sometimes in the 1930s. It was only under Speaker Sam Rayburn, supposedly an example of a strong speaker, and his successor

John McCormack that seniority was observed more scrupulously than it ever had been before or was after.

43. Why did Halleck cooperate with an administration he mostly loathed? "They couldn't understand that once in a while a guy does something because it's right. I had a few experiences. I had a black driver. We used to go down to Warm Springs, Virginia, to see friends. We'd stop at a little bit of a restaurant. I'd go in and ask if he could go in with the Hallecks. They said no but they would be glad to serve him in the car. The goddamned thing just didn't look right to me. Hell, I didn't do it for political advantage. The colored vote in my district didn't amount to a bottle of cold pee." Charles and Barbara Whalen, *The Longest Debate: A Legislative History of the 1964 Civil Rights Act* (New York: New American Library, 1986) 54–55.

44. Whalen 29–71. "The myth that Johnson saved the civil rights bill from slow death has little relation to reality." Evans and Novak 378.

45. This was the conclusion of Democratic and Republican congressional leaders at the time. Arthur M. Schlesinger, Jr., *A Thousand Days: John F. Kennedy in the White House* (Boston: Houghton Mifflin, 1965) 1030.

Chapter 37
Continue

1. Rowland Evans and Robert D. Novak, *Lyndon B. Johnson: The Exercise of Power* (New American Library, 1966) 301–2.

2. Kenneth S. Davis, *The Politics of Honor* (New York: Putnam's, 1967) 487.

3. There will be no attempt here to assess the various conspiracy theories about the assassination.

4. As vice president, Johnson had sought the appointment of Hughes as a federal judge but was rebuffed by the White House on the grounds that she was too old; she was approved when Speaker Sam Rayburn, with his independent power base in Congress, told Robert Kennedy, "That bill of yours will pass as soon as Sarah Hughes becomes a federal judge." Evans and Novak 314–15.

5. The fact that the assassination occurred in Texas cast a pall of illegitimacy over Johnson's presidency in the minds of many. In the spring of 1965 a Berkeley, California, writer named Barbara Garson wrote a play called *Macbird,* a pastiche of *Macbeth,* in which an explicitly named Lyndon Johnson murders his predecessor. *Macbird* had a considerable run in New York during the Johnson presidency.

6. Theodore H. White, *The Making of the President 1964* (New York: New American Library, 1966) 24 n. 1.

7. He led Nelson Rockefeller, who later campaigned as the most electable Republican, 74%–15% and Henry Cabot Lodge 66%–23%. *The Gallup Poll* (New York: Random House, 1972) 12–17 Dec. 1963.

8. See Stephen Hess and David Broder, *The Republican Establishment* (New York: Harper & Row, 1967).

9. Morgenthau held Rockefeller to a 53%–44% margin, slightly smaller than the 55%–45% by which Rockefeller had beaten Averell Harriman. This election saw the emergence on the ballot of New York's Conservative Party, aimed at punishing Rockefeller-

like Republicans by siphoning votes away from them and at giving the Republicans an incentive to nominate more conservative candidates. It thus illustrated the waning efficacy of the liberal Republican strategy. The Conservative party increased its share of vote until it elected, on its own line, Senator James Buckley in 1970.

10. Gallup polled for the Republican preference every month in 1963 except January, and twice in May, despite his own evidence that the nomination wasn't likely to be worth much. Then, in the busy primary season of 1964, he did no national Republican polls at all between February 5 and March 13 and between April 29 and June 4.

11. Stephen E. Ambrose, *Eisenhower the President* (New York: Simon & Schuster, 1984) 651.

12. One was the California 1st, whose largest voting bloc was in affluent Marin County, north of the Golden Gate Bridge; incumbent Democrat Clement Miller, killed in a plane crash, was reelected posthumously in November 1962 but replaced in January 1963 by Republican Don Clausen. The other two were the 23rd, in the Los Angeles basin, captured by Republican Del Clawson in the June 1963 special election to replace deceased Democrat Clyde Doyle, and the 27th, in the San Fernando Valley, where Democrat Everett Burkhalter retired in 1964 and was replaced by Republican Ed Reinecke, later Ronald Reagan's second lieutenant governor. Based on these results, I wrote an article in the *Harvard Crimson* in 1965 suggesting that Ronald Reagan could be elected governor of California.

13. White 151–52.

14. This is not an unusual phenomenon. See Gertrude Himmelfarb, *The Idea of Poverty: England in the Early Industrial Age* (New York: Knopf, 1984), especially pages 3–19. Societies, it seems, tend to notice poverty and decide they must end it only when they feel they can afford to do so.

15. Arthur M. Schlesinger, Jr., argues that he did in *A Thousand Days* (Boston: Houghton Mifflin, 1965) 1005–14. But Nicholas Lemann quotes Walter Heller's notes on his conversation with Kennedy three days before his death: "His attitude was, 'No, I'm still very much in favor of doing something on the poverty theme if we can get a good program, but I also think it's important to make clear that we're doing something for the middle-income man in the suburbs, etc.' " Nicholas Lemann, "The Unfinished War," *The Atlantic,* Dec. 1988, 39–40. Kennedy showed a surer political instinct on this issue than his successor did.

16. For the genesis and development of such ideas, see Daniel Patrick Moynihan, *Maximum Feasible Misunderstanding: Community Action in the War on Poverty* (New York: The Free Press, 1969); see also Lemann 37–56.

17. One northern Democratic congressman voted against the Civil Rights Act: John Lesinski of the 16th district of Michigan, whose home was in militantly all-white Dearborn, home of the Ford Motor Company. Lesinski was the son of a Democratic congressman first elected in a newly created district in 1932; so was John Dingell, congressman from the 15th District, who voted for the Civil Rights Act. Redistricting in 1964 put them both in the same district, most of which had been represented by Lesinski. But Dingell campaigned aggressively and with the strong support of the United Auto Workers and won the September 1964 primary. He continued representing the industrial suburbs of southwest Wayne County for decades and became chairman of the House Committee on Energy and Commerce in 1981; he was voted "the best congressman" by *Washington Monthly* magazine in 1984.

18. Schwartz, an agoraphobic, for many years would not leave Manhattan Island.

19. Edwin Diamond and Stephen Bates, *The Spot: The Rise of Political Advertising on Television* (Cambridge: M.I.T., 1984) 127–33; Kathleen Hall Jamieson, *Packaging the Presidency: A History and Criticism of Presidential Campaign Advertising* (New York: Oxford Univ., 1984) 198–201.

20. Mississippi in 1975 and Louisiana in 1986 came close to electing Republicans to those offices.

21. Of these losses, 7 were in the Deep South: 5 in Alabama, 1 in Georgia, and 1 in Mississippi. The Democrats would have surely lost far more seats there if the Republicans had nominated candidates: Representative W. Arthur Winstead of Philadelphia, Mississippi, for example, lost after 22 years in the House to a chicken farmer named Prentiss Walker; Alabama, where Republicans did contest most seats, lost eighty-seven years of House seniority. Michael Barone, Grant Ujifusa, and Douglas Matthews, *The Almanac of American Politics 1974* (Boston: Gambit, 1973) 2.

    Elsewhere the Democrats lost 1 seat in redistricting in Wisconsin, 1 seat in Idaho to right-winger George Hansen, and 3 seats in California, counting the 2 which had been lost in 1963 special elections.

22. I wrote an article in the *Harvard Crimson* arguing this thesis in 1975. The 1962 gubernatorial results show how discontent was channeled into state and even local politics, while satisfaction was widely expressed with the performance of the Kennedy administration and the federal government generally. Cf. public opinion figures. So the 1964 results represent a sizable shift.

Chapter 38
From Confidence to Alienation

1. Conrad Mallett, an assistant to Detroit's Mayor Jerome Cavanagh in July 1967, had been a Detroit policeman a decade earlier. The white patrolman assigned to share a scout car with him said not a single word to him all day—standard operating procedure, Mallett believed, for dealing with black recruits.

2. Theodore H. White, *The Making of the President 1964* (New York: New American Library, 1966) 279 n. 3.

3. White 281.

4. Milton Viorst, *Fire in the Streets* (New York: Simon & Schuster, 1979) 275–97.

5. Savio goes on and on, echoing knowingly or not the complaints of the few embattled cultural liberals of the 1950s: "Society provides no challenge. It is a bleak scene, but it is all a lot of us have to look forward to. . . . American society is simply no longer exciting. . . . America is becoming ever more the utopia of sterilized, automated contentment. . . . This chrome-plated consumers' paradise would have us grow up to be well-behaved children." Qtd. in Viorst 304–5.

6. Taylor Branch, interview, *New York Times Book Review,* 11 Nov. 1988, 30.

7. The trends are carefully summarized and analyzed in Seymour Martin Lipset and William Schneider, *The Confidence Gap: Business, Labor, and Government in the Public Mind* (New York: The Free Press, 1983) 13–66. This book has no data after 1983 and so does not show much recovery in confidence.

8. *Historical Statistics of the United States, Colonial Times to 1970,* 2 vols. (Washington: U.S. Bureau of the Census, 1972) 1: 224, 229.

9. These economists, like the president they served until his death in November 1963, were "of a new generation of Americans who saw the world differently from their fathers. [They were] brought up to believe, either at home or abroad, that whatever Americans wished to make happen, would happen." Theodore H. White, *In Search of History* 492–93, (qtd. in) Charles R. Morris, *A Time of Passion* (New York: Harper & Row, 1984) 3.

10. By, among others, the "supply-siders" of the late 1970s and early 1980s. See Jude Wanniski, *The Way the World Works* (New York: Simon & Schuster, 1978).

11. Except in Maryland, where black migration from Washington, D.C., to Prince Georges County in the 1960s and 1970s changed the balance of partisan preference statewide and made what had been a national bellwether into one of the nation's most Democratic states.

12. See Everett Carll Ladd, Jr., with Charles D. Hadley, *Transformations of the American Party System: Political Coalitions from the New Deal to the 1990s* (New York: Norton, 1975) 191–211. Almost no Americans identify themselves as upper class, although many (many more than anyone would ever classify as upper class) would admit to being upper middle class. The author Shana Alexander, who grew up on Park Avenue and summered in Southampton, identified herself as a product of the "middle class." If she is right, there is no upper class in America.

13. Percentages are calculated from *Historical Statistics* 1: 139 and *Statistical Abstract of the United States: 1986* (Washington: GPO, 1986) 400. Percentages for 1950, 1960, and 1970 vary according to which definition is used, but never by more than 2 percentage points.

14. The high point was in 1977 and 1978, when it was 74%. *Historical Statistics* 379; *Statistical Abstract: 1986,* 149.

15. *Historical Statistics* 1: 379; *Statistical Abstract: 1986,* 149.

16. *Historical Statistics* 1: 49; *Statistical Abstract: 1986,* 56–57.

17. Even before the U.S. Supreme Court effectively legalized abortion nationwide in January 1973, abortion laws—which until 1968 made abortion illegal everywhere in the nation under practically any circumstances—had been liberalized in sixteen states with 41% of the nation's population; some 74% of all Americans lived within 100 miles, an easy drive, of a state in which abortion was legally available. Michael Barone, op-ed piece, *Washington Post,* September 1, 1983.

18. *Historical Statistics* 1: 225; *Statistical Abstract: 1986,* 433. I have rounded off the figures for clarity.

19. See, e.g., Walter Lippmann, "In Praise of the Parties," a Today and Tomorrow column, 4 Apr. 1936, in Clinton Rossiter and James Love, eds., *The Essential Lippmann* (New York: Random House, 1963) 300–302; Clinton Rossiter, *Parties and Politics in America* (Ithaca: Cornell Univ., 1960); D. W. Brogan, *Government of the People* (New York: Harper, 1933).

Chapter 39
Great Society

1. Rowland Evans and Robert Novak, *Lyndon B. Johnson: The Exercise of Power* (New York: New American Library, 1966) 490.

2. Pathetically low numbers voted in elections held for posts in city antipoverty agencies; these were of course easily manipulated by local activists with organizational competence which would have enabled them easily to succeed in other lines of work. Daniel Patrick Moynihan mercilessly dissects the flawed assumptions and operations of the antipoverty program in his *Maximum Feasible Misunderstanding* (New York: The Free Press, 1969). A fine treatment of the impractical and ludicrous results of the Community Action programs is Allen J. Matusow, *The Unraveling of America: Liberalism in the 1960s* (New York: Harper & Row, 1984) 243–71.

3. Richard Neustadt and Ernest May, *Thinking in Time: The Uses of History for Decision Makers* (New York: The Free Press, 1986) 103–4.

4. Stanley Karnow, *Vietnam: A History* (New York: Viking, 1983) 411–15.

5. Karnow 415.

6. "Taylor and Rusk . . . were probably influenced—and Johnson too—by loose analogizing with 1962, when, it was believed, 'gradual escalation' had been one key to success in the missile crisis." Neustadt and May 78.

7. Doris Kearns Goodwin, *Lyndon Johnson and the American Dream* (New York: Harper & Row, 1976) 252–53.

8. Later, leftist critics made the preposterous argument that U.S. interest in Vietnam was prompted by American oil companies who were interested in offshore oil drilling there. This claim is obviously absurd, even if the geology were favorable for drilling: in these same years American policymakers refused to send even a single American soldier or sailor to the Persian Gulf as the British were withdrawing from it.

9. Johnson expected to reach "crossover" by December 1966, but as early as December 1965 McNamara said that was impossible. Larry Berman, *Lyndon Johnson's War* (New York: Norton, 1989) 9–13.

10. Karnow 415.

11. Townsend Hoopes, *The Limits of Intervention* (New York: Norton, 1969).

12. A vivid and subtle account by a participant in the march, who spent time in jail with King, is Chuck Fager, *Selma 1965: The March That Changed the South* (New York: Scribner, 1974; Boston: Beacon, 1985). See also David J. Garrow, *Bearing the Cross: Martin Luther King, Jr., and the Southern Christian Leadership Conference* (New York: Random House, 1986) 357–430.

13. Fager 7–8; Garrow 372–78; Richard Gid Powers, *Secrecy and Power: The Life of J. Edgar Hoover* (New York: The Free Press, 1987) 415–22.

14. The definitive account is John Bartlow Martin, *Overtaken by Events* (Garden City: Doubleday, 1966). Martin was Kennedy's ambassador to the Dominican Republic and later served as Johnson's envoy; though his initial sympathies were with Johnson's liberal critics, he mostly supports Johnson's version of the facts and his policy.

15. Qtd. in Evans and Novak 511.

16. Evans and Novak 515.

17. The definitive work on Fulbright is Haynes Johnson and Bernard M. Gwertzman, *Fulbright the Dissenter* (Garden City: Doubleday, 1968). Fulbright's arguments for inaction on civil rights were based on the "ancient and melancholy history" of southern race relations, as he called it in an intellectually interesting but ultimately unpersuasive

amicus curiae brief filed in the Little Rock case. See Harry McPherson, *A Political Education: A Washington Memoir* (Boston: Houghton Mifflin, 1988) 148–51.

18. So much so that when Dan Quayle was nominated for vice president in August 1988, it was impossible to argue that his enlistment in the Indiana National Guard in May 1969 was not an attempt to avoid service in Vietnam.

19. See Lawrence Baskir and William Strauss, *Chance and Circumstance: The Draft, the War, and the Vietnam Generation* (New York: Knopf, 1978) 1–11, for a discussion of the percentage of draft-age males who served in the military, in Vietnam, and in combat, between 1965 and 1972.

   Their findings indicate that high school graduates had the highest levels of service (45%) compared to high school dropouts (42%) and college graduates (23%): they were unable to qualify for college deferments but were too bright to fail the mental examination in large numbers, as dropouts did. This intellectual middle of the age cohort—the kind of people who in the 1950s had been honored as average citizens and had quickly become fathers and breadwinners—were now singled out as those most expendable in war.

20. Baskir and Strauss 14–17, 21–28. Interestingly, one of the features of the Selective Service System which made it acceptable to Americans in the 1940s made it widely unacceptable in the 1960s: the wide discretion given to local draft boards. In the 1940s, when most Americans resisted the nationalizing policies of Franklin Roosevelt, local discretion seemed a reasonable way to accommodate local situations. In the 1960s, local discretion seemed to produce a bizarre system in which similarly situated persons were treated very differently.

21. Student deferments were "one of the most damaging aggravations" of the war for the military, writes Colonel Harry Summers, Jr., in *On Strategy: A Critical Analysis of the Vietnam War* (New York: Dell, 1984) 62.

22. See Robert Novak, *The Agony of the G.O.P. 1964* (New York: Macmillan, 1965). Later Novak abandoned the politics of the hard-nosed "center" for the more idealistic and "extremist" politics of the supply-side and tradition-minded right of the Reagan years. When asked why, in November 1983, he said, "That other stuff didn't work out very well." Robert Novak, personal conversation.

23. Karnow, 405. Another example of the use of the golden mean was the use by presidential advisors like McGeorge Bundy of the "Goldilocks principle. By including one choice 'too soft' and one 'too hard,' he could plausibly expect the upper-echelon 'principals' to go for the 'just right' option—in this case the third, which he himself favored." Karnow 404.

24. Evans and Novak 489.

Chapter 40
Guns and Butter

1. *The Gallup Poll* (New York: Random House, 1972), 16–21 June, 29 July–4 Aug. 1966. By January 1967, Johnson was trailing Kennedy among Democrats 39%–48% and Romney among all voters 42%–50%. *The Gallup Poll,* 7–12 Jan., 26–31 Jan. 1967.

2. See, for example, The Harris Poll, 25 July, 11, 17, 26 Oct. 1966.

3. Allen J. Matusow, *The Unraveling of America* (New York: Harper & Row, 1984) 243–71.

4. The wackiness of community action is suggested by Nicholas Lemann's pithy summary. "In retrospect, there was a glaring flaw in community action. Past experience suggested that the best way for the federal government to increase opportunity for the poor was through major national efforts: lowering the unemployment rate, improving schools, undertaking public works, and eliminating discrimination. Sometimes the programs that turned out to be the most effective at reducing poverty—like the Homestead Act, the Erie Canal, universal public education, and the GI Bill—weren't planned for that purpose but nonetheless changed social and economic conditions in some important way. Community action, however, was based on the idea that only through local efforts—in fact, only through efforts inside the poorest neighborhoods—could the government increase opportunity. How, it now seems fair to ask, could there have been so much faith in the ability of a program *inside* the ghettos to increase the amount of opportunity available to the people living there?" Nicholas Lemann, "The Unfinished War," *The Atlantic,* Dec. 1988, 46. The answer to this question was that the framers of the program doubted that macroeconomic measures could help the very poor move up (despite abundant historical evidence that they had done so) and they were dubious about the moral legitimacy of the larger society's teaching ghetto residents how to work their way up.

5. Larry Berman, *Lyndon Johnson's War* (New York: Norton, 1989) 19.

6. *The Gallup Poll,* 5–10 May, 19–24 May 1966.

7. *The Gallup Poll,* 27 Aug.–1 Sept., 29 Oct.–2 Nov. 1965; 25 July–3 Aug., 8–13 Sept., 4 Nov. 1966.

8. *The Gallup Poll,* 2–7 Apr., 23–28 Apr., 13–18 May 1965.

9. These figures count Maryland, West Virginia, and Missouri as northern states, Oklahoma and Kentucky as southern. Reasonable arguments can be made about these classifications, but the overall picture is not much affected.

10. Hale Champion, *Washington Post,* 15 Aug. 1980, A16.

11. The definitive writer on Ronald Reagan is Lou Cannon, who as a reporter covered him from his first campaign through his retirement from the White House. On the 1966 campaign, see Lou Cannon, *Ronnie and Jesse: A Political Odyssey* (Garden City: Doubleday, 1969) 75–88; Lou Cannon, *Reagan* (New York: Putnam's, 1982) 98–118.

Chapter 41
Upheavals

1. Robert Conot, *American Odyssey* (New York: Bantam, 1975) 679–82. This book not only contains the definitive account of the Detroit riot but is also a fine history of the city from the nineteenth century to the 1970s.

2. Qtd. in Milton Viorst, *Fire in the Streets* (New York: Simon & Schuster, 1979) 337–38.

3. I was the only other person present in the police commissioner's office when this exchange took place in the early hours of Monday.

4. Conot 691–706.

5. Later declared unconstitutional by the Supreme Court. Congress cannot exclude a member who has been legally elected, though it can expel him once he takes his seat. Members were so eager to be seen punishing Powell that they refused to wait to apply the sanction which was clearly within their powers.

6. David J. Garrow, *Bearing the Cross: Martin Luther King, Jr., and the Southern Christian Leadership Conference* (New York: Random House, 1986) 367, 382, 427.

7. Except in Kentucky and Georgia, Alaska, and Hawaii, which allowed people to vote at eighteen, nineteen, and twenty, respectively.

8. For fine summaries of the impact of rock music on American life, see Allen J. Matusow, *The Unraveling of America* (New York: Harper & Row, 1984) 293–97, and Charles Kaiser, *1968 in America: Music, Politics, Chaos, Counterculture, and the Shaping of a Generation* (New York: Weidenfeld & Nicolson, 1988) 190–214.

9. They were in 1966, as I know. I graduated from college in 1966 and promptly received a deferment for going to graduate school—in my case, law school. That school year graduate student deferments were abolished, but those who already held them were allowed to complete their degrees. When I graduated from law school in 1969, I became a law clerk for a federal judge and applied for and received an occupational deferment. In the course of that year occupational deferments, at least for such positions, were abolished, but those who already held them were allowed to renew them if they remained in that occupation, which I did. By the time my deferments ended I was twenty-six and therefore too old to be drafted. Even at the time, these deferment policies struck me as absurd: why was it in the national interest that I complete law school or complete my clerkship? But I took advantage of the law as it existed, and I will leave it to others to decide, as I have not yet been able to, whether I should be ashamed of having done so.

10. James Miller, *"Democracy Is in the Streets": From Port Huron to the Siege of Chicago* (New York: Simon & Schuster, 1987). My own view, on reading Miller's definitive work, is that the SDS organizers, inspired to some extent by progressive unions like the UAW and by the Kennedy victory in 1960, were seeking the power to reshape society as they thought best and, sensing that they were not about to gain such power quickly through traditional politics, sought to create new or, as some put it, parallel structures to allow them to govern.

11. Norman Mailer, *The Armies of the Night* (New York: New American Library, 1968).

12. See, for example, I. F. Stone, *The Hidden History of the Korean War, 1950–1951* (Boston: Little, Brown, 1988), which makes arguments against U.S. policy rather similar to those made against the Vietnam war. In the Korea years Stone was a discredited outcast, a supporter of Henry Wallace's candidacy in 1948 who started his own newsletter because no journalistic proprietor would hire someone who was (by his own admission) sympathetic to the Communist party. In the Vietnam years Stone was lionized; subscriptions to his newsletter ballooned, and he sold out to the *New York Review of Books;* he was invited to Walter Lippmann's annual garden party.

13. His posture as a "consumer advocate" was ironic, considering that he himself was the least robust of consumers: Ralph Nader insisted that he lived in modest rooms in Washington (though sometimes he slept in his brother's high-priced town house), that he worked perhaps 16 hours a day seven days a week, and that he purchased almost nothing for his own pleasure and enjoyment.

14. Cannon, *Reagan* (New York: Putnam's, 1982) 134–38.

15. On Romney and his wing of the party, see Stephen Hess and David S. Broder, *The Republican Establishment: The Present and Future of the G.O.P.* (New York: Harper & Row, 1967) 91–140. The authors show their prescience by devoting to Ronald Reagan, in 1967 generally thought a nationally unacceptable extremist, as many pages as to Romney and Charles Percy and only slightly fewer than to the 1960 and 1968 nominee, Nixon.

16. Theodore H. White, *The Making of the President 1968* (New York: Pocket Books, 1970) 70–75; *The Gallup Poll* (New York: Random House, 1972), 14–19 Sept. 1967.

17. Howard Schuman et al., *Racial Attitudes in America* (Cambridge: Harvard Univ., 1988).

18. *The Gallup Poll,* 3–8 Aug., 27 Oct.–1 Nov. 1967.

19. And not just, as Johnson and the Republicans insisted, on Johnson's anti-Goldwater coattails. Kennedy did run behind usual Democratic showings among Jews and reform liberals in New York City, but he ran even farther ahead of the norm among Catholics in the outer boroughs, suburbs, and upstate—almost carrying upstate against the liberal Republican incumbent from upstate, Kenneth Keating.

20. On the transformations of Robert Kennedy, see David Halberstam, *The Unfinished Odyssey of Robert Kennedy* (New York: Random House, 1968); Jack Newfield, *Robert Kennedy: A Memoir* (New York: Dutton, 1969); Jules Witcover, *85 Days: The Last Campaign of Robert Kennedy* (New York: Morrow, 1969). Arthur M. Schlesinger, Jr.'s two-volume *Robert Kennedy and His Times* (Boston: Houghton Mifflin, 1978) is, like his other work, beautifully written and faithful to his vision of liberalism in which the Kennedys were lineal descendants of Franklin Roosevelt.

21. Qtd. in Edwin O. Guthman and Jeffrey Shulman, eds., *Robert Kennedy: In His Own Words* (New York: Bantam, 1988).

22. Some contests had already begun: the Michigan precinct delegates elected in August 1966 (of which I was one, elected by my single write-in vote) would choose state convention delegates in May 1968 who would choose national convention delegates in early June, the weekend before the California primary.

23. Turnout in nine major central-city jurisdictions (Cook County, Illinois; Baltimore City, Maryland; Suffolk County, Massachusetts; Wayne County, Michigan; St. Louis City, Missouri; New York City; Cuyahoga County, Ohio; Allegheny and Philadelphia Counties, Pennsylvania) fell from 10.0 million in 1960 to 9.0 million in 1968, 8.7 million in 1972, 7.5 million in 1980, and 7.0 million in 1988. These central-city constituencies produced 15% of the nation's votes in 1960, 12% in 1968, and 8% in 1988.

24. Edward Koch, *Mayor: An Autobiography* (New York: Simon & Schuster, 1984) 15–17.

25. Albert Eisele, *Almost to the Presidency: A Biography of Two American Politicians* (Blue Earth, Minn.: Piper, 1972) 119–24.

26. Qtd. in Eisele 113.

27. Eisele 124–27;

28. Abigail McCarthy, his former wife, complains about the misattribution in *Private Faces, Public Places* (Garden City: Doubleday, 1972) 236.

29. Lou Harris showed Kennedy leading Johnson 48%–39% in October and 52%–32% in November—a stunning result, with two of three members of his own party ready to reject an incumbent president. *Washington Post,* 27 Nov. 1967.

Chapter 42
Bullets

1. Stanley Karnow, *Vietnam* (New York: Viking, 1983) 523–35.
2. Peter Braestrup, *Big Story* (Boulder: Westview, 1977). See also Don Oberdorfer, *Tet!* (Garden City: Doubleday, 1971).
3. Charles Kaiser, *1968 in America: Music, Politics, Chaos, Counterculture, and the Shaping of a Generation* (New York: Weidenfeld & Nicolson, 1988) 102–3; personal recollection.
4. For the exciting story of this conversion, see Townsend Hoopes, *The Limits of Intervention* (New York: David McKay, 1973) 159–201. This book itself had a major effect on the Washington elite's view of the war, confirming the idea that it was always unwinnable and validating the (not entirely consistent) criticisms by doves at each stage.
5. Some analysts have argued that McCarthy's showing does not represent opposition to Johnson's war policy. Richard M. Scammon and Ben Wattenberg, *The Real Majority* (New York: Coward-McCann, 1970) 90–93, 118–21. This argument, in a book whose analysis has otherwise stood up very well, is based on a one-dimensional spectrum analysis: strong hawks are assumed to prefer Johnson to McCarthy, or to be acting irrationally if they voted for the latter. (Some have even suggested that New Hampshire voters thought they were voting for Joseph McCarthy, who had been dead and out of the headlines for more than a decade in March 1968.) But opinion on Vietnam did not move laterally on a one-dimensional spectrum, with voters at position A always preferring position B to position C. On the contrary, since the beginning of the war a sizable number of Americans had gravitated to one extreme and preferred as their second choice not the center choice but the other extreme: "win or get out." It makes sense that many such voters, given the choice of Johnson and McCarthy, preferred McCarthy, not just as a protest vote but as president.
6. Larry Berman, *Lyndon Johnson's War* (New York: Norton, 1989) 178–79; Karnow 559; Theodore H. White, *The Making of the President 1968* (New York: Pocket Books, 1980) 136–37.
7. *The Gallup Poll* (New York: Random House, 1972), 15–20 Mar., 4–9 April 1968.
8. White 288; Richard M. Cohen and Jules Witcover, *A Heartbeat Away* (New York: Viking, 1974) xx.
9. He eventually succeeded, cracking the last nut—Ohio—with the help of a decision from the Supreme Court whose edicts he liked to excoriate.
10. Even Jimmy Carter won only a minority, albeit a near-majority, of southern whites' votes in 1976. He carried southern states because of near-unanimous support from blacks.
11. *The Gallup Poll,* 2–7 June, 16–21 Nov. 1967.
12. Les Aspin, personal interview, June 1985. Congressman since 1971 and chairman of the House Armed Services Committee since January 1985, Aspin was an Army officer assigned to the Pentagon when he was sent in to manage Johnson's campaign in Wisconsin in March 1968.
13. *Report of the National Advisory Commission on Civil Disorders* (New York: Bantam, 1968) 1.
14. It was the habit of liberals at that time to attribute the reported rise in crime rates to

better reporting and increased cooperation by blacks with law enforcement officials; I remember making this argument myself. And probably such factors do explain part of the rise. But its continuation through the 1970s, the continuing pattern of much higher crime rates among blacks than among any other defined group, and the attendant destruction of so many black neighborhoods push one with the advantage of two decades of hindsight to say that the statistics weren't entirely lying. See James O. Wilson and Richard J. Herrnstein, *Crime and Human Nature* (New York: Simon & Schuster, 1985) 459–86. The melancholy conclusion to which I am forced is that there turned out to be something to the argument that when young blacks were freed from the terroristic restraints of southern segregation and the bullying restraints of (not misnamed) northern police brutality, they would respond by committing many more violent crimes. I should add that it doesn't follow that those restraints should have been kept in force; they were out of line with the traditions of our country. But I do have more sympathy today than I did twenty years ago with the idea that government needed to crack down more vigorously on crime—an argument made most vigorously in the 1988 campaign by none other than Jesse Jackson.

15. White 169 n. 3.

16. See Kaiser 150–66; Ronald Fraser, ed., *1968: A Student Generation in Revolt* (New York: Pantheon, 1988) 203–84.

17. *The Gallup Poll,* 2–7 May 1968. Lou Harris, who had consistently shown Kennedy running stronger than Humphrey and McCarthy against the Republicans, in his May surveys showed Kennedy as the only Democrat trailing Nixon. *Washington Post,* 6 May 1968.

18. McCarthy claimed a moral victory in his third-place finish, to which this most competitive of the Kennedy brothers replied with delicious understatement perhaps unparalleled in the history of American politics: "My father always told me that it was better to win than finish second or third."

19. Jules Witcover, *85 Days: The Last Campaign of Robert Kennedy* (New York: Morrow, 1969) 202.

20. Tip O'Neill, *Man of the House* (New York: Random House, 1987) 83.

21. An exciting account of the Silverman candidacy appears in Jack Newfield, *Robert Kennedy: A Memoir* (New York: Dutton, 1969) 167–71. Silverman won but eventually got bored by the intellectual tedium of the Surrogate's Court and quit.

22. For those who thought at the time (as I did) that a Kennedy victory in California would propel him to the nomination, any hard look at the delegate numbers is sobering. It provides no realistic basis for supposing that Kennedy could have been nominated had he lived.

23. Had Robert Kennedy "lived and not gotten the nomination," Humphrey wrote in his autobiography, "I believe he would have been a willing and effective supporter [of the Humphrey candidacy]. Had he lived and I won the nomination, I would have seemed still stronger, less the candidate of bosses, more my own man. With his support, I think I would have been elected President of the United States." Hubert Humphrey, *The Education of a Public Man* (Garden City: Doubleday, 1976) 374–75. The scenario seems plausible, though not assured.

24. At least judging from his account in his autobiography.

25. White 164–65. Haldeman and Nixon's other media advisors have been portrayed as

cynical manipulators, notably in Joe McGiniss's *The Selling of the President 1968* (New York: Trident, 1969), but in this instance they were simply farsighted and brilliant, well in advance of McCarthy strategists who talked about field organization (usually in primaries, but not in general elections) and Kennedy operatives who talked about the critical role of the advance man.

26. *The Gallup Poll,* 18–23 July 1968.

27. But not an elderly-minded sixty-five. Thurmond, a childless widower, in 1968 married a woman more than forty years younger; the first of their four children was born when he was sixty-nine; in 1986 he set up a committee to seek reelection to the Senate in 1990.

28. In a 1985 interview, Dan Rostenkowski, chairman of the House Ways and Means Committee, asserted in pungent language that Daley did not want the convention. Dan Rostenkowski, personal interview. Len O'Connor seems to follow Rostenkowski's account: " 'Mr. Mayor,' President Johnson said, in a congratulatory tone, 'I've decided the best place for the '68 convention is Chicago! You are the one who can handle it!' Stunned, Daley ceased struggling to get to his feet. Instead, Daley gave Johnson a sickly smile; all others at the table blanched." Len O'Connor, *Clout: Mayor Daley and His City* (New York: Avon, 1976) 197–98. But other accounts say that Daley wanted the convention and worked hard to get it. See David Farber, *Chicago '68* (Chicago: Univ. of Chicago, 1988) 116–17.

29. On *Yippie,* see the exhaustive treatment in Farber 3–99.

30. See James Miller, *"Democracy Is in the Streets": From Port Huron to the Siege of Chicago* (New York: Simon & Schuster, 1987); Fraser 57–141.

31. I know: I had one of those passes myself.

32. White 354.

33. For Humphrey's version of how he caved in and accepted Johnson's position, ditching the plank he had agreed on with the Kennedy forces and cleared with Dean Rusk and Walt Rostow—a move Humphrey, looking back, characterized as "a mistake"—see Humphrey 389–90.

34. White 339.

35. White 366.

36. Nelson W. Polsby, *Consequences of Party Reform* (New York: Oxford Univ., 1983) 33–36; Byron Shafer, *The Quiet Revolution: Reform Politics in the Democratic Party* (New York: Russell Sage Foundation, 1983) 13–40.

37. Farber 165–66.

38. Published as *Rights in Conflict: "The Chicago Police Riot"* (New York: New American Library, 1968).

39. White 419.

40. *The Gallup Poll,* 7–12 Aug., 1–6 Sept., 19–24 Sept. 1968.

41. The record was broken in 1988, when 402 members won reelection.

42. The University of Michigan Survey Research Center's longitudinal study of American incomes makes it clear that there is much more economic mobility, upward and downward ("a remarkable amount of change at all income levels"), than is implied by those economic studies of how each fifth of the income scale does. Europeans may feel imprisoned in a social class and economic status; Americans keep jumping from

one income group to another. See Greg J. Duncan, *Years of Poverty, Years of Plenty* (Ann Arbor: Institute for Social Research, 1984) 10.

43. Lewis Chester et al., *American Melodrama: The Presidential Election of 1968* (New York: Viking, 1969) 150.

44. This was noted in a prescient letter to Nixon's campaign manager, John Mitchell, from Republican campaign consultant Walter DeVries. "This race is by no means in the bag for Nixon," DeVries noted, recommending that Nixon should emphasize "the chance to make things different" and "add the programmatic specifics to back it up." Chester et al. 630–31.

45. He had scheduled a major speech on Vietnam for March 31, but canceled it on learning that Johnson had reserved television time that same night—for the speech in which he withdrew as a candidate.

46. Kevin Phillips, *The Emerging Republican Majority* (Garden City: Doubleday, 1970) 21–23. The book was published after Nixon was in office, but Phillips emphasizes that he wrote it before the campaign.

47. In November 1967, Nixon trailed Johnson 43%–47%, but with Wallace in the picture he trailed 36%–44%–12%. But note that in February 1968, just as the Tet offensive was going on, Nixon–Johnson was 42%–42% as a two-man race and 39%–39%–11% with Wallace in. *The Gallup Poll*, 16–21 Nov. 1967, 1–6 Feb. 1968.

48. The Gallup Poll, 13–18 June, 26 June–1 July, 18–23 July, 7–12 Aug., 1–6, 19–24 Sept. 1968. Lou Harris showed him rising from 13% in June 11–16 to 21% in September 11–13.

49. Chester et al. 282–83. He included "Wild Bill Scranton" and "that radical Jacob Javits of New York" in his list, but omitted Barry Goldwater and Ronald Reagan.

50. The four states are Florida, North Carolina, South Carolina, and Tennessee. This showing would also have given Wallace Virginia if all his additional votes there came from Nixon. Increasing Wallace's popular votes by a factor of 1.5 in other southern states—Kentucky, Oklahoma, Texas—leaves him with less than 33%, not enough to win a three-way race.

51. White 450–59.

52. *The Gallup Poll*, 17–22 Oct. 1968. Lou Harris almost always showed Humphrey doing better.

53. *The Selling of the President, 1968* (New York: Trident, 1969), written by a young journalist who lied to the Nixon managers and penetrated their campaign, has been taken for years as the definitive work showing the perfidy, insincerity, and lack of candor of the Nixon campaign. Actually it shows Nixon's media advisor, Roger Ailes, and other campaign officials trying to take advantage of Nixon's considerable abilities—his ability to respond fluently and knowledgeably to friendly questions, for example—and to minimize his negative qualities. The ideas that this strategy is somehow illegitimate, that it amounts to selling the candidate like soap, that it is intellectually dishonest, are ridiculous. There is a case to be made against Nixon that he failed to specify clearly what he would do in office, and another case to be made that he was insufficiently venturesome in his campaign and that as a result he presided over an administration which ratified and even initiated many policies of which both he and most American voters disapproved. But this is not the case which McGiniss and so many of those who have cited his book with approval have made.

54. All year Humphrey's standing was in tandem with the progress toward peace. He was doing well in the polls in the spring when Johnson was doing well, sagged in the summer with Johnson's job rating, and revived in October as Johnson gained approval for getting the peace talks going.

55. The biggest movement was among women, who as always were more peace-minded and risk-averse than men. Alas for the propounders of the gender gap theory which says that women's preferences drive elections—if only women voted, Nixon would have beaten Kennedy in 1960, Humphrey would have beaten Nixon in 1968, and Gerald Ford would have beaten Jimmy Carter in 1976. As a group, women are not necessarily more leftist than men, as was argued by feminists in the 1980s, but they are always more risk-averse and in each of these elections favored the incumbent party.

Chapter 43
Polarization

1. In early 1988, Nixon predicted that the Democrats would nominate Edward Kennedy for president and that he would be a strong candidate—notions considered utterly fanciful by virtually every other serious observer of American politics.

2. Richard Nixon, *RN* (New York: Warner, 1978) 440–41. But Nixon makes a point of this vow only to justify the otherwise bizarre exercise he indulged in after being reelected in 1972, that of requiring the resignation of every Cabinet officer and preparing purge lists. Here, as elsewhere, the selection and presentation of events in Nixon's memoirs is designed to provide some justification for the acts which he was criticized for during the Watergate period; and so the memoirs should not be considered to be entirely reliable indications of Nixon's intentions or frame of mind at the time.

3. Ken Auletta, *The Streets Were Paved with Gold* (New York: Harper & Row, 1980) 52–53. In February 1975 the state Urban Development Corporation defaulted on its "moral authority" bonds, and within a month the New York City government was unable to borrow money. But by that time Mitchell was facing much more serious problems than the collapse of his borrowing device.

4. Nixon 436.

5. In fact, 1968 was arguably the peak year of all time for the seniority system in the House. Fully 396 House members—the second largest number to date, after 1988—had been returned to office in a chaotic year; John McCormack, at seventy-seven an even more devout believer in seniority than he was a Democratic partisan at home and a foreign policy bipartisan abroad, was still speaker; and the tradition, only fully realized during Sam Rayburn's speakership, of assigning all committee and subcommittee chairmanships and even, after men had been placed on the bottom rung of the ladder, leadership positions by seniority was still observed in every instance, with the single and rather shameful exception of the expulsion of Adam Clayton Powell in February 1967. Nelson W. Polsby, Miriam Gallaher, and Barry Spencer Rundquist, "The Growth of the Seniority System in the U.S. House of Representatives," *American Political Science Review* 63 (Sept. 1969): 787–807.

6. An impressionistic list includes: Frank Church (D-Idaho), Charles Percy (R-Illinois), Vance Hartke (D-Indiana), Birch Bayh (D-Indiana), Harold Hughes (D-Iowa), Robert Dole (R-Kansas), Edmund Muskie (D-Maine), Joseph Tydings (D-Maryland), Edward Kennedy (D-Massachusetts), Eugene McCarthy (D-Minnesota), Walter Mondale (D-

Minnesota), Thomas Eagleton (D-Missouri), Fred Harris (D-Oklahoma), Bob Pack-wood (R-Oregon), Ernest Hollings (D-South Carolina), George McGovern (D-South Dakota), Howard Baker (R-Tennessee), Henry Jackson (D-Washington), William Proxmire (D-Wisconsin).

7. See Eric Redman, *The Dance of Legislation* (New York: Simon & Schuster, 1973); James A. Miller, *Running in Place* (New York: Simon & Schuster, 1986), especially the Introduction by George F. Will on pages 12–13.

8. The key blow may have been struck by Nebraska Senator Roman Hruska, by the workings of seniority the ranking Republican on the Judiciary Committee. When Carswell was attacked as "mediocre," Hruska responded, "Even if he were mediocre, there are a lot of mediocre judges and people and lawyers. They are entitled to a little representation, aren't they, and a little chance? We can't have all Brandeises and Frankfurters and Cardozos and stuff like that there." Michael Barone, Grant Ujifusa, and Douglas Matthews, *The Almanac of American Politics 1972* (Boston: Gambit, 1971) 452. The Democratic staffers especially must have snickered at Hruska—and at the unwisdom of a senator speaking without the aid of a text or talking paper from his staff.

9. See Lou Cannon, *Reagan* (New York: Putnam's, 1982) 182–93.

10. See Charles Peters, *How Washington Really Works* (Reading: Addison-Wesley, 1980). His magazine, the *Washington Monthly,* provided a sounding board for these movements but was capable of turning a critical eye on them in turn.

11. Cf. Robert Wiebe, *The Segmented Society* (New York: Oxford Univ., 1975).

12. For an exhaustive contemporary review, see Lee Rainwater and William L. Yancey, *The Moynihan Report and the Politics of Controversy* (Cambridge: M.I.T., 1967).

13. Ironically, the acknowledgment came in the "workfare" bill passed by Congress in 1988 and sponsored, in the last year of his second term as senator from New York, by Daniel Patrick Moynihan.

14. The definitive work on Fortas and his resignation is Robert Shogan, *A Question of Judgment* (Indianapolis: Bobbs-Merrill, 1972).

15. *The Gallup Poll* (New York: Random House, 1972), 23–28 Jan., 20–25 Feb., 10–15 May 1969.

16. *The Gallup Poll,* 11–16 Sept., 17–22 Oct. 1969.

17. Charles A. Reich, *The Greening of America* (New York: Random House, 1976) 4. The book goes on in great length in this vein.

18. See James Miller, *"Democracy Is in the Streets": From Port Huron to the Siege of Chicago* (New York: Simon & Schuster, 1987), for the definitive account of the Port Huron Statement and the history of Hayden and SDS up through the Chicago convention of August 1968 and the group's degeneration into violent terrorism thereafter.

19. Reich lived out his prediction. He resigned his tenured chair at Yale, declared his homosexuality, moved to San Francisco, and faded into obscurity.

Chapter 44
Incursion

1. Stanley Karnow, *Vietnam* (New York: Viking, 1983) 591–92. William Beecher's report of this secret bombing in the *New York Times* in May 1969 led to the first Nixon

wiretaps on journalists. J. Anthony Lukas, *Nightmare: The Underside of the Nixon Years* (New York: Viking, 1976) 47–62.

2. Richard Nixon, *RN* (New York: Warner, 1978) 499.

3. The Gallup Poll (New York: Random House, 1972), 4 Nov., 12–17 Nov. 1969.

4. Telford Taylor, *Nuremberg and Vietnam: An American Tragedy* (Chicago: Quadrangle, 1970). But he was careful to show how the situations were not precisely analogous.

5. Daniel Patrick Moynihan, *The Politics of a Guaranteed Income: The Nixon Administration and the Family Assistance Plan* (New York: Random House, 1973) 420–21.

6. Moynihan 191.

7. Moynihan 215.

8. Moynihan 249–50.

9. Moynihan 456.

10. "A central fact about American politics at this time was that the educated, affluent business and professional class of the nation was probably the most disposed of any identifiable group to reformist policies in government. Intellectuals, now for the most part academic, had been in part immobilized by their intense distrust and dislike of first Johnson and now Nixon. The labor movement had no great demands to make of society, while increasingly it found itself in the unfamiliar and uncomfortable position of having demands made of it, principally on issues of racial equality. The Civil Rights movement had exhausted its earlier agenda, and had not developed a new one. (The Urban League would periodically call for a Marshall Plan for the cities, but could not produce one.) The Southern-Midwestern coalition that helped elect Nixon had presumably done so under the impression that he would *not* be proposing 'radical' new programs." Moynihan 251.

11. Moynihan 333–35.

12. Qtd. in Moynihan 416–17.

13. Moynihan 425.

14. Moynihan 455.

15. Karnow 602–12.

16. Christopher Matthews, *Hardball: How Politics Is Played—Told by One Who Knows the Game* (New York: Summit, 1988) 46.

17. A confession of personal interest is in order. The prospect of thousands of students lobbying their congressman to oppose the invasion of Cambodia and working to defeat him if he refused prompted Grant Ujifusa to suggesting to me that we write what became the first *Almanac of American Politics*. But it took longer than we expected to write, appearing in November 1971; and among its bulk purchasers was the Committee to Re-elect the President.

18. Theo Lippman, Jr., and Donald C. Hansen, *Muskie* (New York: Norton, 1971) 143, 147–50.

19. Moynihan 444.

20. Though the union is criticized for not getting more by *Detroit Free Press* and *New York Times* reporter William Serrin in his book *The Company and the Union*. Like most other observers at the time, Serrin took the economic strength of the Big Three automakers for granted: "it is vacuous to think that the corporations will become

extinct," he wrote in 1973, not too many years before Chrysler nearly went bankrupt and Ford was threatened with severe financial problems. William Serrin, *The Company and the Union* (New York: Random House, 1974) 310–11.

21. This was not a gentle race. Nixon's political forces secretly funneled some $400,000 into Brewer's campaign in an attempt to remove Wallace from politics forever. The tone of Wallace's campaign is suggested by the text of one of his ads:
"IF YOU WANT TO SAVE
Alabama as we know Alabama
Remember!
The bloc vote (negroes and their
white friends) nearly nominated
Gov. Brewer on May 65th. This
black and white
social-political alliance
MUST NOT DOMINATE
THE PEOPLE OF ALABAMA!
This spotted alliance must be defeated!
This may be your last chance.
VOTE RIGHT—
VOTE WALLACE"
Neal Pierce, *The Deep South States of America* (New York: Norton, 1974) 255, 256.

22. Father John McLaughlin of Rhode Island worked for Nixon, left the priesthood, and hosted a prominent television political talk show; his wife became secretary of labor. Joseph Duffey of Connecticut became head of the National Endowment for the Humanities and chancellor of the University of Massachusetts; his wife became a top White House aide and successful lobbyist. Albert Gore, Sr., of Tennessee had the satisfaction of seeing his son Albert Gore, Jr., elected to the House in 1976 and the Senate in 1984 and run a strong race for the Democratic nomination for president in 1988. Howard Metzenbaum of Ohio was appointed to the Senate in 1974, defeated in the primary that year, then elected to the Senate in 1976, 1982, and 1988. John Danforth of Missouri was elected to the Senate in 1976, 1982, and 1988. George Bush of Texas was appointed ambassador to the United Nations in 1971, Republican national chairman in 1973, American envoy to China in 1975, and CIA director in 1976; he was elected vice president in 1980 and 1984 and president in 1988.

23. The name of a woman who had been a man before having a sex-change operation some years before—a well-known reference in 1970.

24. The argument over the nature of the American electorate was waged most vociferously among Democrats. In 1970, Richard Scammon and Ben Wattenberg's *The Real Majority* argued that Democrats needed to stay close to the center, a course which they defined as paying respectful attention to ordinary Americans who wanted protection from crime, decent schools, and a respect for traditional moral values and patriotism. Their abstract argument for centrism could be faulted, on the ground that centrism in the person of Lyndon Johnson had not worked very well. But Scammon and Wattenberg's specific prescriptions, based on a longstanding knowledge of the electorate, almost all made good sense; in most times they would have been common sense. A counterpoint

to their argument was Fred Dutton's 1971 book *Changing Sources of Power* (New York: McGraw-Hill, 1971), which argued that young voters, changing demographics, and changing attitudes would create new opportunities for liberal Democrats to win elections. Dutton's book has been derided as a recipe for George McGovern's forty-nine–state loss in 1972, but if one looks at congressional elections in the nearly two decades since it was written, it seems prescient: it shows the electoral basis which made the drowsy, tradition-bound House of 1970 into the activist, left-leaning House of the later 1970s and 1980s. Scammon and Wattenberg and Dutton could both be largely right while saying seemingly opposite things, because they were looking at them from different angles: Scammon and Wattenberg wanted to show how the electorate mostly stays the same, while Dutton was focusing on how it might change.

Chapter 45
Shock

1. Neal Pierce and Michael Barone, *The Middle Atlantic States of America* (New York: Norton, 1977) 24.
2. *Historical Statistics of the United States, Colonial Times to 1970,* 2 vols. (Washington: U.S. Bureau of the Census, 1975) 2: 1100; *Statistical Abstract of the United States: 1986* (Washington: GPO, 1986) 294.
3. *Historical Statistics* 2: 1105.
4. Elizabeth Drew, *Washington Journal: The Events of 1973–74* (New York: Random House, 1975) 22.
5. Changes in CPI calculated from *Historical Statistics* 210.
6. Richard Nixon, *RN* (New York: Warner, 1978) 1: 640.
7. Marvin Kalb and Bernard Kalb, *Kissinger* (Boston: Little, Brown, 1974) 217.
8. The Kalbs are definitive on this point. Kalb and Kalb 216–39.
9. Lou Harris showed a favorable–unfavorable ratio of 68%–19% in August 1971, 62%–24% in October 1971, and 73%–5% in February 1972. Nixon's own polling, conducted by Opinion Research Corporation, showed a 68%–20% favorable reaction to his July 1971 announcement that he would go to China and a 74%–16% favorable response to his March 1972 visit there. Poll results from the Roper Center.
10. It was at this juncture that the Nixon administration made a thinly veiled threat to take away the *Post*'s valuable broadcast licenses, at a time when the company was just about to sell stock to the public. *Post* publisher Katherine Graham decided to go ahead and publish, even at some risk of losing her considerable fortune. Sanford J. Ungar, *The Papers and the Papers* (New York: Dutton, 1972) 138–47.
11. *The Gallup Poll* (New York: Random House, 1972) 25–28 June 1971.
12. His political ally Lloyd Bentsen, not Connally, challenged their mutual enemy, the liberal Senator Ralph Yarborough, in the 1970 primary, beat him, and then went on to beat George Bush in the general election. The odds against Bentsen in both races were long, and the swashbuckling Connally probably disdained serving as just one member in the slow-paced Senate. But by 1987 Bentsen was chairman of the Senate Finance Committee and Connally had gone bankrupt—with characteristic flair auctioning off all his possessions in a much-publicized gala event in Houston.

13. *The Gallup Poll,* 25–28 June 1971.

14. *The Gallup Poll,* 14–17 May 1971.

15. *The Gallup Poll,* 25–28 June 1971.

16. Nixon's own memoirs make it clear that the confident, aggressive Connally took utter command here; Nixon makes himself appear a cipher in these matters, easily manipulated by this magnetic personality. Nixon 1: 638–47.

17. *The Gallup Poll,* 16–18 Aug. 1971.

18. J. B. Kelly, *Arabia, the Gulf, and the West* (New York: Basic Books, 1980) 97–98.

19. Kelly 50. Henry Kissinger, *Years of Upheaval* (Boston: Little, Brown, 1982) 669.

20. *The Gallup Poll,* 29 Oct.–2 Nov., 19–22 Nov., 16–19 Dec. 1971.

Chapter 46
Majority

1. Theodore H. White, *The Making of the President 1972* (New York: Bantam, 1973) 12. Nixon was similarly relieved when Wallace told his emissary, John Connally, after the Democratic convention that he would not run on a third-party ticket. Richard Nixon, *RN* (New York: Warner, 1978) 2: 148–49. In fact, by that time it would have been difficult for Wallace to get on the ballot in many states.

2. From Opinion Research Corporation. Roper Center.

3. As early as December 1971, Wallace told Lester Maddox, the Atlanta restauranteur who had gained fame by chasing blacks from his establishment with an ax handle and who was elected governor of Georgia in 1966 and lieutenant governor in 1970, that he had decided to run as a Democrat. Neal Pierce, *The Deep South States of America* (New York: Norton, 1974) 256–57.

4. According to Humphrey, "By the fall of 1971 . . . I was coming close to a decision to run." In order to file to run in Pennsylvania, where he was confident of victory, he had to declare by January 1972, forcing him to enter all but the first primary in New Hampshire and the Illinois "beauty contest." Hubert Humphrey, *The Education of a Public Man* (Garden City: Doubleday, 1976) 434–45, 495.

5. Or united in most cases in their hostility to a politics of economic redistribution. McGovern's issues researchers came up with a perfectly logical plan to increase federal estate and gift taxes, and his political people urged him to use it because it would affect only a minimal number of voters while the benefits would presumably accrue to many. But it turned out to be one of the most unpopular issue positions of an unpopular candidate.

6. Theo Lippman, Jr., and Donald C. Hansen, *Muskie* (New York: Norton, 1971) 12–19; Theodore H. White, *America in Search of Itself* (New York: Harper & Row, 1982) 430.

7. Lippman and Hansen 147–50.

8. Qtd. in Lippman and Hansen 152.

9. White, *President 1972,* 105–6. David Broder, who covered the incident for the *Washington Post,* in retrospect questions whether Muskie cried or whether falling snow was melting on his cheeks; he says that the reason reporters covered the story as they did was that they had observed Muskie's temper in private and felt that what they saw

and attempted to describe accurately reflected a character trait voters ought to know about. The irony, Broder notes, is that the "Canuck letter" was a forgery, written by a paid staffer and "dirty trickster" for the Nixon campaign. David S. Broder, *Behind the Front Page* (New York: Simon & Schuster, 1987) 23–39.

10. Donald Riegle, *O Congress* (Garden City: Doubleday, 1972) 296–97.

11. In the late 1950s, when Humphrey was a senator from Minnesota and McGovern a congressman from Humphrey's native district in South Dakota, these two men who would be rivals in 1972 lived on the same block of Coquelin Terrace in Chevy Chase, Maryland.

12. White, *President 1972,* 167–70.

13. For a sensitive account of White's end of these negotiations, see J. Anthony Lukas, *Common Ground: A Turbulent Decade in the Lives of Three American Families* (New York: Knopf, 1985).

14. White, *President 1972,* 275–78.

15. The delegate allocation formula in New Mexico required splitting the delegation proportionately between the top two finishers, so Pete McCloskey's 6% netted him 1 delegate. This was Congressman Manuel Lujan, who made it clear he really favored Nixon.

16. Lou Harris polls.

17. Seymour Martin Lipset and William Schneider, *The Confidence Gap: Business, Labor, and Government in the Public Mind* (New York: The Free Press, 1983) 41–66.

18. In a November 1972 referendum, 33% of California voters voted to legalize marijuana completely—only 9 percentage points fewer than voted for McGovern! This proved to be a high-water mark, electorally at least, for the drive to legalize this drug. But all the states in the early 1970s were busy reducing the penalties for possession and casual use of marijuana toward the misdemeanor level.

19. Washington had a large black majority, but McGovern carried the white vote there as he did in Massachusetts.

20. See Michael Barone, "The Gains of Landslide Losers," *Washington Post,* March 1973.

21. The House seats changing hands can be categorized as follows:

REAPPORTIONMENT
Democratic gains: California 11, 37, 38, 42, Florida 4, 13, Texas 18, 24. Democratic losses: Alabama, New York (2), North Dakota, Pennsylvania, Tennessee, Texas, West Virginia. Republican gains: Arizona 4, California 36, Colorado 5, Florida 10. Republican losses: Iowa, Ohio, Pennsylvania, Wisconsin.

REPUBLICAN POLITICAL GAINS
Incumbent retirement: Maine 2. Fluke incumbent beaten: New York 26. Minority-party candidate: Mississippi 4, Virginia 4. Incumbent beaten by liberal Democrat in primary: Colorado 4, Nevada at-large. Suburbanization: Illinois 3, 10, Louisiana 3, Maryland 4, New Jersey 13. Nixon coattails: Connecticut 5, Indiana 11, Mississippi 5, South Carolina 6, Tennessee 6, Texas 5.

DEMOCRATIC POLITICAL GAINS
Party switch: New York 24. Reprise of serious 1970 race: Colorado 1, Iowa 1, Massachusetts 12, Oklahoma 1, Utah 2.

22. Bob Woodward and Scott Armstrong, *The Brethren* (New York: Simon & Schuster, 1979) 279–80.

23. In "massage parlors" and through "escort services" which in the late 1960s scarcely existed but which by the middle 1970s were advertised in their own sections of the Yellow Pages across the country.

Chapter 47
Watergate

1. Richard Nixon, *RN* (New York: Warner, 1978) 2: 285.

2. Nixon 2: 275.

3. One of many possible examples, told by Nixon himself: "I took off the gloves in the January 31 [1973] press conference when I announced the peace settlement in Vietnam. I said that we had done the best we could against great obstacles and had finally achieved a peace with honor. 'I know it gags some of you to write that phrase,' I said, 'but it is true, and most Americans realize it is true.'" Nixon 2: 277.

4. John J. Sirica, *To Set the Record Straight* (New York: Norton, 1979) 92–98.

5. And also, understandably, the last, which is a shame for historians. From the time the telephone took over from the letter its basic function of intragovernmental and political communication (as it did sometime during the Roosevelt administration, perhaps) until the time the personal computer takes over that function (as it did for National Security Council Director John Poindexter in the Iran-contra affair uncovered in November 1986) most such communications are vanishing literally into thin air, unrecoverable by historians.

6. Richard M. Cohen and Jules Witcover, *A Heartbeat Away* (New York: Viking, 1974).

7. The vice presidency had been vacant for many years in American history, with the succession varied by statute between Cabinet secretaries and congressional leaders. Vacancies included 1812–13, 1814–17, 1832–33, 1841–45, 1850–53, 1853–57, 1865–69, 1875–77, 1881–85, 1885–89, 1899–1901, 1901–05, 1912–13, 1923–25, 1945–49, and 1963–65.

8. Nixon 2: 481–82.

9. The popularity of consumer advocate Ralph Nader would be sharply diminished a few years later when Congress voted to require an ignition interlock on new cars, preventing the engine from being started until all seat belts were buckled. Nader protested that Congress had rejected less bothersome means, which he preferred, of encouraging seat belt use, but to little avail. Americans resented anything which interfered with their enjoyment of their automobiles. The next year Congress voted to repeal the ignition interlock.

10. By my count approximately 100, of whom about half won. My rule of thumb is that in a year which is not clearly unfavorable for a party, about half its serious challengers will win; in an unfavorable year about one tenth will. The validity of the rule depends, however, on an assessment of what a serious candidate is, something which reasonable people will argue over endlessly. I believe that campaign spending, which became fully reported for the first time for the 1974 election, provides an almost always reliable indicator: candidates who spent less than $100,000 in 1974 or less than $250,000 in 1982 should not be counted as serious. The objection may be made that a self-fulfilling

prophecy is involved here, for not many candidates who are not considered serious by a small network of politicians, political contributors, political consultants, and journalists (a network of which I have been part since the 1972–74 cycle) can usually raise that much money.

11. Tip O'Neill, *Man of the House* (New York: Random House, 1987) 194–201.

12. O'Neill 157–58.

Chapter 48
Impeachment

1. Robert S. Lynd and Helen Merrell Lynd, *Middletown: A Study in Modern American Culture* (New York: Harcourt, Brace, 1929); *Middletown in Transition* (New York: Harcourt, Brace, 1937). For a look at Muncie in the 1970s, see Theodore Caplow et al., *Middletown Families: Fifty Years of Change and Community* (Minneapolis: Univ. of Minnesota, 1982).

2. The 1974 election marked the first time that the campaign finance law of 1971 required disclosure of contributions and expenditures for the entire biennial cycle, since it did not go into effect until April 7, 1972. In the 1974 election, Sharp spent $74,199 and Dennis $79,840. Michael Barone, Grant Ujifusa, and Douglas Matthews, *The Almanac of American Politics 1976* (New York: Dutton, 1975) 283.

3. *The Gallup Poll*, qtd. in *Public Opinion*, Sept./Oct. 1987, 40.

4. The question "Do you think the country generally is going in the right direction, or is it pretty seriously off on the wrong track?" was invented by Burns Roper in 1969. It provided a standard measure, used by pollsters of both parties in the 1970s and 1980s, for the basic underlying mood of the electorate and was typically the first question asked in any poll.

5. See Caplow 32–33, 128–33, 182–86.

6. The Democrats ended up gaining 53 seats and losing 6 in November 1974 (as compared with November 1972), for a net gain of 47. The Democratic gains were California 5, 13, 17, 24, 34, 35, Colorado 2, Connecticut 2, Georgia 4, Illinois 3, 10, 15, Indiana 2, 6, 8, 10, 11, Iowa 5, 6, Maryland 5, Massachusetts 5, Michigan 5, 6, 7, 8, 18, Minnesota 6, Montana 1, Nevada at-large, New Hampshire 1, New Jersey 1, 2, 7, 13, New York 2, 3, 27, 29, 36, North Carolina 5, 8, Ohio 23, Oklahoma 6, Oregon 1, 4, Pennsylvania 7, South Carolina 6, Tennessee 8, Texas 13, Virginia 8, 10, Wisconsin 3, 8. The Republican gains, three of which were accounted for by special circumstances, were Alaska at-large (the incumbent died in October 1972), Florida 5 (the incumbent ran for the Senate), Louisiana 6 (the incumbent, a far-right-wing Democrat, was defeated in the primary; the general election had to be rerun because of incomplete returns, but the Democrat was probably actually ahead and lost only in the rematch), Maine 1, Pennsylvania 25, South Dakota 1. Democrats made serious challenges (in my opinion) but fell short in the following 52 districts: Alabama 6, Arizona 1, 3, 4, Arkansas 3, California 2, 16, 18, 19, Colorado 4, Connecticut 4, 5, Florida 12, Illinois 6, 13, 17, 18, 20, Iowa 3, Kansas 5, Kentucky 4, Maryland 1, Michigan 2, 3, 10, Minnesota 2, Missouri 7, Nebraska 1, 2, 3, New Jersey 5, 6, New York 4, 5, 30, 35, North Carolina 9, 10, North Dakota at-large, Ohio 1, 2, Ohio 12,

17, Pennsylvania 17, 19, 23, South Carolina 2, Texas 5, Virginia 4, 7, 9, Wisconsin 9.

7. Elizabeth Drew, *Washington Journal: The Events of 1973–1974* (New York: Random House, 1975) 224.

8. Johnson's actual comment was earthier and less printable.

9. Rockefeller was dyslexic and, although no one liked to put it this way in his lifetime, could hardly read. When he was speaking from a written text his delivery was wooden, though he was capable of great animation otherwise; and he seems to have absorbed information from oral briefings by experts who were always eager to be received in audience by a Rockefeller. He was certainly capable of absorbing large amounts of information and of assimilating complex arguments. Michael Kramer and Sam Roberts, *"I Never Wanted to Be Vice-President of Anything!"* (New York: Basic Books, 1976) 39.

10. "Even the right-wingers saw some merit in selecting Rockefeller over George Bush, the other finalist. Everyone knowledgeable in Republican politics considered Bush incompetent to be president. . . ." Jules Witcover, *Marathon: The Pursuit of the Presidency 1972–1976* (New York: Viking, 1977) 504. At the UN, Bush had unsuccessfully argued that the Nationalist government on Taiwan should not be expelled from the organization—without realizing that Kissinger was undercutting that policy in Washington. George Bush, *Looking Forward* (New York: Doubleday, 1987) 114–16.

11. See, for example, James MacGregor Burns, *The Deadlock of Democracy: Four-Party Politics in America* (Englewood Cliffs: Prentice-Hall, 1963).

12. The Gallup Poll (New York: Random House, 1975), 16–19 Aug., 6–9 Sept., 27–30 Sept. 1974. The pardon occurred while Gallup's interviewers were in the field.

13. Democrats gained 3 seats in the Carolinas, 2 in the suburbs of Washington, D.C., 1 each in metropolitan Atlanta and Memphis, and 1 in the Texas High Plains district adjacent to a similar Oklahoma district the Democrats also picked up.

Chapter 49
Limits

1. Writers like Robert Kuttner, *The Life of the Party: Democratic Prospects in 1988 and Beyond* (New York: Viking, 1988) would later celebrate the America of 1947–73 as a country where all good things could be had. Yet earlier many writers were harshly critical of the America around them, and others, such as Marty Jezer, *The Dark Ages* (Boston: South End, 1982), were writing about the 1950s or were writing self-pitying books like Jerry Farber's *The Student as Nigger* (North Hollywood: Series/Contact, 1969), about upwardly mobile young people in the most widely tolerant country in the world.

2. See Lou Cannon, *Reagan* (New York: Putnam's, 1982) 119–86.

3. Gary Hart, personal interview, April 1983.

4. The non-college segment of this age cohort, in the late 1960s hostile to the college segment's values, by the middle 1970s had come to embrace them—sporting beards, smoking marijuana, and voting for Democrats like Jerry Brown.

5. The crucial move here was Burton's. The new rule required a certain number of

signatures to provoke a secret roll call on a committee chairmanship. Burton rounded up enough signatures to force a roll call on every chairmanship, at which point a rule was adopted to make this automatic.

6. See Nelson W. Polsby, Miriam Gallaher, and Barry Spencer Rundquist, "The Growth of the Seniority System in the U.S. House of Representatives," *American Political Science Review* 63 (Sept. 1969): 787–807.

7. The quotas came into the rules almost serendipitously, as the result of an interchange between Professor Austin Ranney and Senator Birch Bayh. Byron E. Shafer, *Quiet Revolution: The Struggle for the Democratic Party and the Shaping of Post-Reform Politics* (New York: Russell Sage Foundation, 1983) 163–76. See also the definitive study, Nelson W. Polsby, *Consequences of Party Reform* (New York: Oxford Univ., 1983).

8. The book was published in 1973. By way of reconciling his contradictory views, Schlesinger says, "The book argues that the Constitution intends a strong presidency within an equally strong system of accountability." Arthur M. Schlesinger, Jr., *The Cycles of American History* (Boston: Houghton Mifflin, 1983) 277.

9. *The Gallup Poll* (New York: Random House, 1976), 18–21 April, 30 May–2 June, 27–30 June, 1–4 Aug. 1975. In early June Ford was running about even in pairings with Edward Kennedy (44%–45%); by mid-July he was behind 43%–50%. *The Gallup Poll,* 18–21 July 1975.

Chapter 50
Bicentennial

1. The margin was 44%–40%. *The Gallup Poll* (New York: Random House, 1976), 1–4 Aug. 1975.

2. Jules Witcover, *Marathon* (New York: Viking, 1977) 92.

3. He trailed Ford 48%–25% in a multicandidate poll (but no other candidate had more than 7%) and was behind Ford 58%–36% among Republicans and 51%–40% among independents in a two-candidate pairing. *The Gallup Poll,* 17–20 Oct. 1975. Reagan's greater strength among independents contrasts with the showings of earlier conservatives, who were stronger among self-identified Republicans. It is partial evidence that the decisive group of voters not strongly moored to either party was no longer the bloc typified by New York Jews and Upper Midwest Progressives, liberal on both economic and cultural issues, but had become the bloc typified by southern whites and urban ethnics, possibly liberal on economics but outspokenly anti-liberal on cultural issues.

4. *The Gallup Poll,* 2–5 Jan. 1976.

5. Witcover 126–27; Elizabeth B. Drew, *American Journal: The Events of 1976* (New York: Random House, 1977) 309; Finlay Lewis, *Mondale* (New York: Harper & Row, 1980) 205–14.

6. Hugh Winebrenner, *The Iowa Precinct Caucuses: The Making of a Media Event* (Ames: Iowa State Univ., 1987) 41–66.

7. Jimmy Carter, *Why Not the Best?* (Nashville: Broadman, 1975) 36–37.

8. "Carter adapted his political alliances as his political circumstances changed. He showed a genius at capitalizing on the particular position he held at any one time. As a relative

unknown, he had run against Atlanta and its establishment—emphasizing his own qualities as an outsider, as one of the people, as six years later he would do in his campaign for the White House. But having won office as governor, he then became an insider, utilizing the resources of his own tentative relationships with the 'establishment' to advance his programs. He effectively used the symbols and backdrops of office to enhance his personal authority and public support, and took advantage of his multiple roles to gain politically important information and make contact with other influentials outside of the state. He was a politician plying his trade." Betty Glad, *Jimmy Carter in Search of the Great White House* (New York: Norton, 1980) 160.

9. Witcover 110–15.

10. Thomas Donilon, personal interview, December 1988.

11. "Perhaps the strongest feeling in this country today," he wrote in the memo, "is the general distrust of government and politicians at all levels. The desire and thirst for strong moral leadership in this nation was not satisfied with the election of Richard Nixon. It is my contention that this desire will grow in four more years of the Nixon administration. For this reason I believe it would be very difficult for Senator Kennedy to win a national election, as the unanswered questions of Chappaquiddick run contrary to this national desire for trust and morality in government." Witcover 111.

12. He listed 18 reporters and columnists for Carter to court, and wrote, "Like it or not, there exists an Eastern liberal news establishment which has tremendous influence in this country all out of proportion to its actual audience. The views of this small group of opinion-makers and the papers they represent are noted and imitated by other columnists and newspapers throughout the country and the world. Their recognition and acceptance of your candidacy as a viable force with some chance of success could establish you as a serious contender worthy of the support of party contributors. They could have an equally adverse effect, dismissing your effort as being regional or an attempt to secure the second spot on the ticket." Witcover 113–14.

13. The total popular vote in the primaries was 53% for Ford and 46% for Reagan. The delegate vote was 1187 to 1070.

14. Its presidential primaries usually produced routine wins for organization leaders; and for statewide contests Nelson Rockefeller had several times vetoed primary bills on the theory that Republican primary electorates might not favor big-spending candidates like himself and that Democratic primary contests might produce candidates who, unlike the nominees of the state party conventions, could not be depicted as the candidates of the New York City bosses. In fact, Rockefeller was proved correct. The three Republican gubernatorial nominees after him—Malcolm Wilson, Perry Duryea, and Lewis Lehrman—were not from the big-spending branch of the party, and the Democratic nominees—Hugh Carey and Mario Cuomo—did not suffer from the taint of bossism and were elected in November.

15. Including scandal-ridden Governor Marvin Mandel, who later went to jail. A key intermediary here was Nancy Pelosi, later California Democratic chairman and congresswoman from San Francisco, who was the daughter and sister of former Baltimore mayors Thomas d'Alessandro, Sr. and Jr. Pelosi made the phone calls and the introductions which sealed an alliance of convenience between the diffident trend Democrats of the West and the garrulous traditional Democrats of the East.

16. Carter led 48%–46% and 47%–46% in March, 49%–43% in April, 52%–43% in early

May, and 55%–37% and 53%–36% after he clinched the nomination in June. *The Gallup Poll,* 19–22 Mar., 26–29 Mar., 9–12 Apr., 30 Apr.–3 May, 11–14 June, 25–28 June, 16–19 July 1976.

17. Schweiker and Lewis were both members of the tiny Schwenkenfelder Church, a sect established in Pennsylvania since the eighteenth century. Both served in Reagan's Cabinet, Schweiker at Health and Human Services and Lewis at Transportation.

18. This state of affairs contrasted vividly with earlier times: after the 1946 election Congress had been filled with dozens of veterans of World War II, and men who had not served in the war, such as Hubert Humphrey, were put on the political defensive for that reason as late as 1960.

19. Hamilton Jordan, *Crisis: The Last Year of the Carter Presidency* (New York: Putnam's, 1982) 337.

20. It took longer for Ford's percentage to rise than for Carter's to fall. The Gallup figures are 29% (July 16–19), 32% (August 6–9), 37% (August 20–23), 36% (August 27–30), 40% (September 24–27), 42% (October 8–11), 41% (October 15–18), 44% (October 22), and 47% (October 28–30). This last poll showed Ford leading Carter 47%–46%, a result which (assuming that some undecideds did not vote) was well within the statistical margin of error of the final 50%–48% Carter victory.

21. The prison population fell from 210,000 in 1960 to 196,000 in 1970 and was at 240,000 in 1975, despite vast increases in crime rates. It then increases as shown in the following table. *Statistical Abstract of the United States: 1981,* 191; *Statistical Abstract of the United States: 1988,* 175.

1975	240,000
1980	315,000
1988	481,000

22. Except for Humphrey's home state of Minnesota, these are states where McGovern had run ahead of or even with Humphrey: places where the cultural issues of the early 1970s produced a national Democratic trend.

23. Many Mormons seem to have identified with Kennedy, as a fellow victim of religious prejudice, and to have voted for him in 1960: he came close to carrying Utah, with its 70%–80% Mormon population. But as both Catholics and Mormons became accepted as normal Americans, and as Mormons began regarding themselves as *echt* Americans, Utah ended up as the number one Republican state in the nation.

24. In most of these 24 districts there were special circumstances. In 5 the incumbent was tarred by local scandal (California 4, Georgia 6, Louisiana 1, New Jersey 9, Pennsylvania 24), in 4 the incumbent was handicapped by split opposition or a local party schism (Massachusetts 4, New Jersey 14, Oregon 4, West Virginia 4), in 3 the incumbent was a black unpopular with local whites (Georgia 4, Ohio 21, Tennessee 8), and in 4 the incumbent had personal political liabilities, as demonstrated by a loss then or later or in one case by extremist associations (Georgia 7, Iowa 1, Ohio 9, Texas 8).

That leaves 8 cases of what might be called real coattails. Of these, 3 were non-incumbents running in heavily Democratic northern open seats (Hawaii 1, Ohio 19, Pennsylvania 22), who had every reason to expect their percentages to rise later regardless of Carter. Of the others, 2 won by overwhelming margins (Arkansas 1, Georgia 8). That leaves 3 real coattails districts (North Carolina 11, South Carolina 5, 6)—not much of a base for legislative loyalty to the president.

25. Democrats beat incumbents in New York, Maryland, Ohio, and Tennessee and won open seats in Nebraska and Arizona. Republicans beat incumbents in Indiana, Utah, Wyoming, and California and won open seats in Rhode Island, Missouri, and New Mexico. In close elections for open seats, the Democrat held on in Michigan and the Republican in Pennsylvania. Personal factors and local issues explain these results; no national trend can.

Chapter 51
Democrats

1. By his own account. Jimmy Carter, *Keeping Faith: Memoirs of a President* (New York: Bantam, 1982) 66–73. He came to Washington less knowledgeable about the capital over which he was to preside and the politicians whom he intended to lead than any president probably since Grover Cleveland in 1885.

2. "The next morning," wrote O'Neill, "I called Hamilton Jordan and said, 'Listen, you son of a bitch. When a guy is the Speaker of the House and his family gets the worst seats in the room, he figures there's a reason behind it. I have to believe that you did that deliberately.' 'If that's the way you feel about it,' he replied, 'we'll give you back the three hundred dollars.' 'Don't be a wise guy,' I said. 'I'll ream your ass before I'm through.' " Tip O'Neill, *Man of the House* (New York: Random House, 1987) 310–11.

3. Betty Glad, *Jimmy Carter in Search of the Great White House* (New York: Norton, 1980) 413.

4. In the West as a whole Carter trailed Ford 46%–51%; four years later he trailed Reagan 34%–54%, with 9% for John Anderson.

5. See *Congressional Quarterly 1977 Almanac* (Washington: Congressional Quarterly, 1978) 122–26, especially the table on page 125 which shows switches on the issue. The AFL–CIO's longtime reliance on Republicans yielded only 14 votes of 143 cast, while 23 northern Democrats voted against labor. They were split about evenly between suburban districts (Arizona 3, California 11, Maryland 2, Nevada at-large, New Hampshire 1, New Jersey 2, Pennsylvania 7, Utah 1) and rural and small-town districts (California 17, Colorado 3, Indiana 9, Iowa 6, Maryland 6, Missouri 4, 9, New Mexico 2, New York 30, Oregon 2, Pennsylvania 17, 23, Washington 4), with only two in central-city districts (California 23, Nebraska 2).

6. Glad 420.

7. Wage levels in real dollars tended to decline, but total compensation tended to rise because of fringe benefits and government programs, and so did per capita income because of the rise in number of wage-earners.

8. The following table shows, in thousands, the number of new jobs in the indicated periods, and the annual average gains. *Statistical Abstract of the United States: 1987* (Washington: GPO, 1987) 374; *Statistical Abstract of the United States: 1989* (Washington: GPO, 1989) 377.

Years	Gain	Annual
1971–73	5,498	2,749
1973–75	686	343
1975–79	12,897	3,224
1979–83	2,089	522
1983–87	11,636	2,909

9. The fertility rate fell from 123 in 1958 (the highest since 1916) and 112 in 1962 to 97 in 1965, 88 in 1970, and 66 in 1975. This number seems to have reached bottom, dropping to 65 only in 1978 and 1984. *Statistical Abstract: 1987*, 59; *Historical Statistics of the United States, Colonial Times to 1970*, 2 vols. (Washington: U.S. Bureau of the Census, 1975) 1: 49.

10. *Statistical Abstract: 1987*, 382.

11. The figures are for women 18 and over. *Statistical Abstract: 1987*, 38.

12. Qtd. in Ken Auletta, *The Streets Were Paved with Gold* (New York: Random House, 1979) 30.

13. Edward Koch, *Mayor: An Autobiography* (New York: Simon & Schuster, 1984) 31.

14. For a contemporary account that has held up over time, see Auletta 273–330.

15. It is ironic that this man, who seems to have been a poor businessman but a fine politician, was forced to leave government and politics and go back into the private sector not only in September 1977 but again in July 1984, when his appointment as Democratic national chairman was hooted down.

Chapter 52
Camp David

1. See Ralph B. Levering, *The Public and American Foreign Policy 1918–1978* (New York: Morrow, 1978) 136–39, 145–48.

2. See George Bush, *Looking Forward* (New York: Doubleday, 1987) 135–49.

3. The department's Near East Division has been staffed almost entirely by Arabists since World War II, because the Arab countries would not accept American diplomats who had served in Israel and because there were many more places in Arab countries than in Israel to staff. Hence almost all the experience and the training of Middle Eastern hands was Arab-oriented, and the natural tendency of diplomats to "go native" and sympathize with points of view they were acquainted with worked powerfully, and could be expected always to work powerfully, against Israel in its disputes with Arab countries. Politically, the counterweight to this orientation has been the influence of pro-Israel American Jews as fund-raisers for U.S. senators, especially Democrats, and, after the campaign finance laws of 1971 and 1974 reduced the influence of big contributors by limiting contributions to $1,000, the very large and usually bloc-voting Jewish minority in the New York Democratic presidential primary.

4. Jules Witcover, *Marathon* (New York: Viking, 1977) 402. Witcover quotes Reagan as

saying "built," while Lou Cannon, *Reagan* (New York: Putnam's, 1982) 215, quotes him as saying "bought." Given a discrepancy between these two brilliant reporters, I opt for "built," since "bought" is redundant and crass, while "built" evokes the American know-how and competence which I have come to think was one of the great attractions of the canal and the reason it had a special place in the hearts of so many voters.

5. Jimmy Carter, *Keeping Faith: Memoirs of a President* (New York: Bantam, 1982) 155.

6. *The Gallup Poll* (Wilmington: Scholarly Resources, 1978), 30 Sept.–3 Oct. 1977. Gallup was obviously trying to suggest what the treaties' support would be—or should be—when more information about them was communicated. But only minor progress was made in building treaty support by January 1978. *The Gallup Poll* (Wilmington: Scholarly Resources, 1979), 6–9 Jan. 1978.

7. As a practicing Democratic pollster then, I know I was. I calculated entirely incorrectly that once the treaties were ratified Americans would accept them, as they were accepting the fall of Vietnam to the Communists. I and these other Democrats failed utterly to realize that the Panama Canal loomed much larger in the minds of the majority of Americans older than me than Vietnam ever had.

8. Donald Stewart of Alabama, Floyd Haskell of Colorado, Dick Clark of Iowa, William Hathaway of Maine, Edward Brooke of Massachusetts, Robert Griffin of Michigan, Wendell Anderson of Minnesota, Thomas McIntyre of New Hampshire, and Clifford Case of New Jersey. No senators who voted against the treaty lost. It should be added that the treaty was by no means a prominent issue in every one of these campaigns, but in some where it was not much mentioned it may have had a subliminal effect.

9. *The Gallup Poll,* 21–24 July, 19 Sept. 1978.

10. See, for example, Robert Shogan, *Why Presidents Fail—And What Can Be Done about It* (New York: New American Library, 1982), and Haynes Johnson, *In the Absence of Power: Governing America* (New York: Viking, 1980), who make their case with specifics and subtlety.

11. Michael Barone, Grant Ujifusa, and Douglas Matthews, *The Almanac of American Politics 1980* (New York: Dutton, 1979) 832–33.

Chapter 53
Malaise

1. *The Gallup Poll* (Wilmington: Scholarly Resources, 1980), 6–9 April, 1–4 June, 13–16 July 1979.

2. The inflation figures represent the change in the Bureau of Labor Statistics' Consumer Price Index from the same month one year before (by my own calculations), while the job ratings are Gallup's approval–disapproval figures.

3. *The Gallup Poll,* 5–8 Jan., 19–22 Jan., 23–31 Mar., 6–9 Apr., 4–7 May, 1–4 June, 22–25 June 1979.

4. Jimmy Carter, *Keeping Faith: Memoirs of a President* (New York: Doubleday, 1982) 116.

5. Carter 118.

6. Carter 120.

7. "The truth no one (apparently including Welker) knew was that he was suffering from a blood sugar disorder and a brain tumor, which killed him in 1958. But in 1956 people assumed that Welker was alcoholic." Randy Stapilus, *Paradox Politics: People and Power in Idaho* (Boise: Ridenbaugh, 1988) 88.

8. Church and Jackson had much in common temperamentally: both were hard workers with middle-American tastes and little use for Washington's fancy entertaining, devoted to family and a few friends; both were easy to get along with and deal with legislatively— just regular guys from America's far Northwest, with a flair for geopolitics.

Chapter 54
Hostage

1. See James Stockdale, "I Saw Us Invent the Pretext for Our Vietnam War," *Washington Post*, 7 Oct. 1984.

2. Hamilton Jordan, *Crisis: The Last Year of the Carter Presidency* (New York: Putnam's, 1982) 19–21. Jordan's book shows the same intellectual honesty and acuity as his memorandum to Carter after the 1972 election. In vivid contrast to almost every Washington memoir of the period, it does not always present its author in an effulgently favorable light, it shows his foolish misperceptions more often than his wise premonitions, and it therefore has the ring of truth.

3. *The Gallup Poll* (Wilmington: Scholarly Resources, 1980), 2–5 Nov., 7–9 Dec. 1979.

4. *The Gallup Poll*, 5–8 Oct., 2–5 Nov. 1979.

5. William Greider, *Secrets of the Temple: How the Federal Reserve Runs the Country* (New York: Simon & Schuster, 1987) is a sensitive though mostly hostile account of this policy change; in the face of history and common sense, he persists in believing that inflation is good public policy.

6. *The Gallup Poll*, 16–19 Nov., 30 Nov.–3 Dec., 5–6 Dec. 1979.

7. George Bush, *Looking Forward* (New York: Doubleday, 1987) 139–56.

8. Elizabeth B. Drew, *Portrait of an Election* (New York: Simon & Schuster, 1981) 89.

9. Qtd. in Drew, Portrait of a Campaign, 112.

10. *The Gallup Poll* (Wilmington: Scholarly Resources, 1981), 11–14, 25–27 April 1980. It was perhaps significant that there was no rally-round-the-flag effect to this president after his military failure as there had been to President Kennedy after the Bay of Pigs in April 1961.

11. William Leuchtenberg, *In the Shadow of FDR: From Harry Truman to Ronald Reagan* (Ithaca: Cornell Univ., 1985) 211, quoting David McCullough, "The Legacy: The President They Can't Forget," *Parade*.

12. Lou Cannon, *Reagan* (New York: Putnam's, 1982) 99.

13. Hamilton Jordan quotes Patrick Caddell as explaining at the time: "All these last-minute developments about the hostages and all the anniversary stuff served as a strong reminder that those people were still over there and Jimmy Carter hadn't been able to do anything about it. The hostage crisis symbolizes our impotence. Ronald Reagan's message is, 'Elect me and you won't have to take that anymore.' " Jordan 366.

14. Few people even bothered to argue that Carter lost because of Anderson's candidacy. Reagan's victory margin exceeded Anderson's percentage, and if Anderson had not run his votes would probably have been split roughly equally between Reagan and Carter

and certainly would not have substantially reduced Reagan's popular vote majority. Ironically, Anderson made the arithmetic difference in several southern states where he ran weaker than anywhere else: Carter lost eight southern states by 1 or 2 percentage points, and Anderson typically got 2% or 3% in each.

Chapter 55
From Alienation to Resilience

1. Actually, the meter had stopped before Christmas because the U.S. Big Three automakers shut down their assembly lines and offices between Christmas and New Year's.

2. United States, Dept. of Commerce, Bureau of the Census, *Statistical Abstract of the United States: 1987* (Washington: GPO, 1987) 584; *Statistical Abstract of the United States: 1980* (Washington: GPO, 1980) 650.

3. The story of Chrysler's collapse, the loan guarantee, and the company's recovery is told by Robert B. Reich and John D. Donahue, *New Deals: The Chrysler Revival and the American System* (New York: Times Books, 1985). Their assurance that this rescue shows the viability of joint government–business–labor action is undercut, however, by the evidence they present that the loan guarantee worked largely because it was perceived by the government and the company as irregular, temporary, and unpleasant. If such deals became routinized, the authors give reason to believe, they wouldn't work.

4. David Halberstam, *The Reckoning* (New York: Morrow, 1986) 592.

5. John Kenneth Galbraith, *The New Industrial State* (Boston: Houghton Mifflin, 1967) 87. The thesis of the book had much support in the economic history of the years before 1967 but less in the years after.

6. Alfred P. Sloan of General Motors originated the idea of this progression in the 1920s, reasoning that consumers would want to climb the automotive heights as their economic status improved. See Alfred P. Sloan, *My Years with General Motors* (Garden City: Doubleday, 1963). Much criticized now, it was a good strategy for about 50 years— which is a long time for any business strategy to last.

7. Except, it seems, to people in show business who like to fancy themselves more sophisticated than ordinary Americans yet show a psychological dependency, which they would mock in a factory worker or accountant, on driving exactly the kind of automobile (typically a Mercedes) that sends the right cultural signal, whether they can afford it or not.

8. See Mancur Olson, *The Rise and Decline of Nations* (New Haven: Yale Univ., 1982): James Fallows, *More Like Us: Making America Great Again* (Boston: Houghton Mifflin, 1989) 133–34.

9. *Statistical Abstract: 1987,* 375; *Historical Statistics of the United States, Colonial Times to 1970,* 2 vols. (Washington: U.S. Bureau of the Census, 1975) 1: 127.

10. "During the past decade, businesses on *Fortune's* list of the one thousand largest companies have experienced virtually no job growth at all. . . . Between 1969 and 1976 smaller firms created 7.4 million new jobs, nearly four times as many as the government." George Gilder, *Wealth and Poverty* (New York: Basic Books, 1981) 83, citing David E. Gumpert, "Future of Small Business May Be Brighter Than Portrayed," *Harvard Business Review.*

11. The epitome of quantitative management in both cases was Robert NcNamara, whose careers have been described mercilessly by David Halberstam. Halberstam's *The Best and the Brightest* (New York: Random House, 1972) 214–50 covers McNamara's role in the Vietnam war; and *The Reckoning* 207–15, 236–44, covers his earlier work at the Ford Motor Company.

12. Daniel Yankelovich, *New Rules* (New York: Random House, 1981) 22.

13. *Historical Statistics* 1: 49; *Statistical Abstract of the United States: 1986* (Washington: GPO, 1986) 56–57; *Statistical Abstract: 1987*, 59.

14. As mentioned earlier, by the time the *Roe* v. *Wade* decision was issued, about 70% of the nation's population lived within 100 miles—an easy two hours' drive—of a state with a legalized abortion law. And just as the Supreme Court was speaking, legislatures in almost all of the states were going into session; many would probably have liberalized their abortion laws if the court had not acted.

    The number of recorded abortions increased rapidly from 586,000 in 1972 and 744,000 in 1973 to 1.0 million in 1975 and over 1.5 million in 1980. *Statistical Abstract: 1987*, 67. Since some women started using abortion as a form of birth control, and some of these aborted pregnancies would have been prevented by other means in the absence of legalization, it's reasonable to assume that the impact of legalized abortion on the fertility rate was pretty fully registered by the middle 1970s.

15. *Historical Statistics* 64; *Statistical Abstract: 1980*, 83; *Statistical Abstract: 1987*, 80; *Statistical Abstract of the United States: 1989* (Washington: GPO, 1989) 85.

16. *Statistical Abstract: 1987*, 382; *Statistical Abstract: 1989*, 386.

17. With the introduction of no fault divorce in California in 1970, divorce reform spread rapidly, with almost all of the fifty states having some form of no fault divorce by the early 80s.

18. The key work here is Lenore J. Weitzman, *The Divorce Revolution: The Unexpected Social and Economic Consequences for Women and Children in America* (New York: The Free Press, 1985).

19. The groups are defined by nine "dimensions," of which four are primarily economic (degree of personal financial pressure, degree of belief in social justice, attitudes toward size of government, and attitudes toward business) and five measure cultural values and attitudes (degree of religious faith, of alienation, of tolerance, of militant anti-Communism, and of belief in American exceptionalism).

20. See, for example, Thomas Byrne Edsall, *Power and Money* (New York: Norton, 1989) 296–304, citing Martin P. Wattenberg, "The Hollow Realignment: Partisan Change in a Candidate-centered Era," American Political Science Association Convention, 1985.

Chapter 56
Cuts

1. David Stockman, *The Triumph of Politics: Why the Reagan Revolution Failed* (New York: Harper & Row, 1986) 26–29.

2. All three of these characteristics are amply evidenced in his memoir *The Triumph of Politics*. Stockman's history, as he presents it, is a story of devotions to one theory after another, together with bitter repudiations of the theory just renounced. His scorn

for almost all his past true beliefs extends to his work in the Reagan administration. His book is one long lament that Reagan "chose not to be a leader but a politician," as if the function of a president were to put a single intellectual's abstract ideals into effect rather than to make policy within the limits set by democratic institutions, which include electoral politics.

3. Donald T. Regan, *For the Record: From Wall Street to Washington* (New York: St. Martin's, 1989) 189.

4. Michael Barone and Grant Ujifusa, *The Almanac of American Politics 1984* (Washington: National Journal, 1983) xli.

5. Qtd. in Jeffrey H. Birnbaum and Alan S. Murray, *Showdown at Gucci Gulch: Lawmakers, Lobbyists, and the Unlikely Triumph of Tax Reform* (New York: Random House, 1987) 74.

6. Because it implied that the circulation of increasingly scarce money would have to accelerate greatly. See William Greider, *Secrets of the Temple: How the Federal Reserve Runs the Country* (New York: Simon & Schuster, 1987) 367.

7. "But a drastic shrinking of the welfare state was not his conception of the Reagan revolution. It was mine." Stockman 276.

8. Neither Roosevelt nor Truman had incomes which reached the top bracket of $300,000. Eisenhower got a bill through Congress providing for capital gains treatment of his advance for *Crusade in Europe,* which otherwise would have put him in the top bracket. Kennedy never really paid taxes at all: that task was taken care of by his father and his minions. Johnson, it can readily be assumed, managed to keep himself out of the top bracket. Nixon's income started to rise toward the top bracket only after he left government in 1961. Ford and Carter and Bush don't seem to have come anywhere close to the $300,000 level in the years up to 1964. Neither did any of the candidates for president in 1984 or 1988. Vice President Dan Quayle turned seventeen in 1964.

9. "Reagan's first conservative issue was a personal one—reduction of the progressive income tax. But he gave it something of a liberal twist, saying that actors and others whose productive earning period was limited should be allowed a personal depreciation allowance just like the oil companies." Lou Cannon, *Reagan* (New York: Putnam's, 1982) 91. Income averaging, a later reform entirely consistent with progressive tax principles, would have addressed Reagan's problems—and if adopted in time to affect him might have prevented his successful assault on the progressive income tax.

10. The reduction in rates on "unearned" income was proposed not by the Reagan administration, which never dared to, but by William Brodhead, a liberal Democrat from Michigan and a member of the Ways and Means Committee, who retired from Congress at age forty-one in 1982.

11. These figures are not adjusted for inflation; the corresponding figures in constant dollars are 6% and 4% in 1979–81 and 3%, 4%, and 2% in 1981–84. *Statistical Abstract of the United States: 1987* (Washington: GPO, 1987) 295.

12. Laurence I. Barrett, *Gambling with History: Reagan in the White House* (New York: Doubleday, 1983).

13. *Statistical Abstract of the United States: 1989* (Washington: GPO, 1989) 415–16.

14. *Statistical Abstract: 1989,* 413.

15. The article and more material appear in William Greider, *The Education of David Stockman and Other Americans* (New York: Dutton, 1982).

16. I had a small part in breaking the story. At home sick one day, I started reading the *Atlantic,* which had arrived a few days before, earlier in the month than usual. I thought the Stockman quotes in the Greider article were extraordinary and, in talking on the telephone with CBS News White House correspondent Lesley Stahl, told her so. Stahl sent a messenger for my copy of the article, and her report on the *CBS Evening News* made it big news. Of course, it would have become big news a day or so later anyway if I had gone to work that day; but it is an interesting illustration of how so many busy people in Washington, unlike Stockman, don't read original texts and fine print. For surely the *Atlantic* had arrived earlier than usual to other homes and news organization in Washington, but evidently no one had taken the trouble to read the fine print of the article.

17. Greider xv.

Chapter 57
Correction

1. See Robert Scheer, *With Enough Shovels* (New York: Random House, 1982), a title based on Defense Department appointee T. K. Jones's assertion that in a nuclear war "everyone's going to make it if there are enough shovels to go around." As 1981 went on, increasing majorities in polls believed that a war was likely within a few years, and by a 55%–31% margin thought the Pershing deployment would increase the risk of war. Laurence I. Barrett, *Gambling with History* (New York: Doubleday, 1983) 308.

2. "The imperative to balance the budget is, at bottom, a rule, like any other. People can and do argue all day about what rule is best on economic grounds. . . . But whatever we decide, what we are finally talking about is a rule of social behavior, like the rules of property—a rule defining the nature of what it is people are doing together and how they agree to treat each other, today and over time. . . . For Americans, a balanced budget is like the rainbow of Genesis—the sign of a covenant. 'The bow shall be seen in the cloud, and I will remember my covenant.' " Jonathan Rauch, "Is the Deficit Really So Bad?" *The Atlantic,* Feb. 1989, 42.

3. Bob and Elizabeth Dole with Richard Norton Smith, *The Doles: Unlimited Partners* (New York: Simon & Schuster, 1988) 203–9. Smith is the author of the fine biography *Thomas E. Dewey and His Times* (New York: Simon & Schuster, 1982).

4. *Historical Statistics of the Unites States, Colonial Times to 1970,* 2 vols. (Washington: U.S. Bureau of the Census, 1975) 1: 420; United States, Dept. of Commerce, Bureau of the Census, *Statistical Abstract of the United States: 1980* (Washington: GPO, 1980) 200; *Statistical Abstract of the United States: 1987* (Washington: GPO, 1987) 172; *Statistical Abstract of the United States: 1989* (Washington: GPO, 1989) 183.

5. Qtd. in Michael Barone and Grant Ujifusa, *The Almanac of American Politics 1984* (Washington: National Journal, 1983) 792–93.

6. The classic description of Coelho and his operation is Brooks Jackson's *Honest Graft* (New York: Knopf, 1988). Coelho, one of the most open of politicians, gave Jackson, the *Wall Street Journal*'s specialist on campaign finance, total access to his staff and operations. Also highly instructive are Thomas Byrne Edsall's *The Politics of Inequality* (New York: Norton, 1984) and *Power and Money* (New York: Norton, 1989).

7. Many authorities accept the Republicans' complaints that their net redistricting losses were greater. But the question is an imponderable which produces an impressionistic rather than a statistically verifiable answer, and my own figure is offered in that spirit.

8. See Robert A. Caro, *The Years of Lyndon Johnson: The Path to Power* (New York: Random House, 1981) 638–39.

9. The census definitions of the regions are used, except that the East here includes Delaware, Maryland, and the District of Columbia, and the South Atlantic states are Virginia, the Carolinas, Georgia, and Florida.

10. See *Public Opinion,* Dec. 1982/Jan. 1983, 27–29.

11. Qtd. in Albert R. Hunt, "National Politics and the 1982 Campaign," in Thomas E. Mann and Norman J. Ornstein, eds., *The American Elections of 1982* (Washington: American Enterprise Institute, 1983) 18.

12. A good argument can be made that the Republican campaign committee's constant polling and capacity to channel money quickly into races helped Republicans win most of the close contests in 1980 and 1982. The narrow 1982 wins included those of John Danforth in Missouri (where his opponent Harriett Woods ran out of money and took her commercials off the air for a crucial week in October), Chic Hecht in Nevada, John Chafee in Rhode Island, Robert Stafford in Vermont, and Paul Trible in Virginia; no such close races were won by Democrats. Narrow Republican winners in 1980 included Jeremiah Denton in Alabama, Barry Goldwater in Arizona, Paula Hawkins in Florida, Mack Mattingly in Georgia, Steven Symms in Idaho, Dan Quayle in Indiana, Charles Grassley in Iowa, Warren Rudman in New Hampshire, Alfonse D'Amato in New York, John East in North Carolina, Arlen Specter in Pennsylvania, and Robert Kasten in Wisconsin; the only Democrats who won close races that year were Gary Hart in Colorado and Patrick Leahy in Vermont. In other words, in the two election cycles, Republicans won sixteen of eighteen close races; if they had won only half of them, they would not have controlled the Senate in the 1980s any more than they did in the 1970s or 1960s. But if such an advantage existed, it vanished by 1986, when the Democrats won most of the close contests and regained control of their Senate.

13. "The Democrats in search of the 1984 presidential nomination were in no temper, however, to pore over the fine print looking for bad news. After Reagan's remarkable triumph in 1980, the central question had been whether that result was an aberration or the first step in a transformation of American politics. And the answer in the returns of 1982 suggested the former rather than the latter—and that Ronald Reagan might be vulnerable indeed. The opinion polls seemed to support that optimism. A Gallup poll in December of 1982 found Glenn leading Reagan 54 to 39 percent and Mondale ahead of the President, 52–40. Reagan's approval rating dropped to 41 percent, his lowest and a point lower even than that reached by Jimmy Carter at the same juncture in his presidency." Jack W. Germond and Jules Witcover, *Wake Us When It's Over: Presidential Politics of 1984* (New York: Macmillan, 1985) 42. See also pages 86–87.

Chapter 58
Morning

1. Daniel Patrick Moynihan, *Came the Revolution* (New York: Harcourt Brace Jovanovich, 1988) 131.

2. Arthur Miller, "Is Confidence Rebounding?" *Public Opinion,* June/July 1983, 16–20. "It is evident that the [Reagan] administration's actions have helped stem the tide of a continuing decline in public confidence. They have bolstered the public's faith in government's ability to act with a decisive approach to legislation and the economy."

Miller 20. He might better have said that the political system's ability to cut back government increased confidence in government—the great paradox of the Reagan years.

3. In constant (1982) dollars. United States, Dept. of Commerce, Bureau of the Census, *Statistical Abstract of the United States: 1987* (Washington: GPO, 1987) 418. *Statistical Abstract of the United States: 1985* (Washington: GPO, 1985) 432.

4. The following table shows the month-by-month changes from mid-1981 through 1983 in the unemployment rate, the Consumer Price Index, and Reagan's Gallup job approval rating:

Year	Month	Unemployment %	CPI %	Reagan's Gallup Rating
1981	Aug.	7.2	9.6	60
	Sept.	7.5	14.4	52
	Oct.	8.0	4.8	56
	Nov.	8.4	6.0	54
	Dec.	8.9	8.9	49
1982	Jan.	8.5	2.4	47
	Feb.	8.8	2.4	47
	March	9.0	3.6	46
	April	9.4	2.4	44
	May	9.5	12.0	45
	June	9.5	12.0	44
	July	9.8	7.2	41
	Aug.	9.8	3.6	42
	Sept.	10.1	2.4	42
	Oct.	10.4	6.0	42
	Nov.	10.8	1.2	43
	Dec.	9.7	3.6	41
1983	Jan.	10.2	2.4	35
	Feb.	10.2	−2.4	40
	March	10.1	1.2	41
	April	10.1	7.2	41
	May	10.0	6.0	46
	June	9.8	2.4	47
	July	9.3	4.8	42
	Aug.	9.5	4.8	43
	Sept.	9.1	6.0	48
	Oct.	8.7	3.6	46
	Nov.	8.2	3.6	53
	Dec.	8.2	3.6	54

5. Richard Reeves, *The Reagan Detour* (New York: Simon & Schuster, 1985).
6. See Lester Thurow, *The Zero Sum Society* (New York: Basic Books, 1980); Ben Heine-

man, Jr., and Curtis Hessler, *Memorandum for the President* (New York: Random House, 1980).

7. Finlay Lewis, *Mondale* (New York: Harper & Row, 1984) 249.

8. Robert B. Reich and John D. Donahue, *New Deals: The Chrysler Revival and the American System* (New York: Times Books, 1985).

9. Mancur Olson, *The Rise and Decline of Nations: Economic Growth, Stagflation, and Social Rigidities* (New Haven: Yale Univ., 1982.

10. The high school class of 1963 registered the all-time high SAT scores of 978; they declined to 890 in 1980. These are not a precise indicator of the achievement of all students, but it is generally agreed that such achievement declined over this period. See Diane Ravitch, *The Schools We Deserve: Reflections on the Educational Crises of Our Time* (New York: Basic Books, 1985) 36–37; David Boaz, "Educational Schizophrenia," in David Boaz, ed., *Assessing the Reagan Years* (Washington: Cato Institute, 1988) 291.

11. Hedrick Smith, *The Power Game: How Washington Works* (New York: Random House, 1988) 416–19.

12. The 11th ward, including Daley's home neighborhood of Bridgeport, was also the home of Mayors Ed Kelly and Martin Kennelly (though Kennelly moved to a swank lakefront apartment) and thus was home to the mayors of Chicago from January 1933 to April 1979.

13. Mondale's advisor Richard Moe wrote in a January 1983 memo: "People simply don't want their president to be wholly owned by any group or special interest, and they inevitably react negatively to any candidate who is perceived to be so owned. . . . Most people see special interests as part of the problem, not part of the solution. It follows that they see candidates who pander to these groups for support—saying everything they want to hear, giving them everything they want—as very un-presidential." Qtd. in Jack W. Germond and Jules Witcover, *Wake Us When It's Over: Presidential Politics of 1984* (New York: Macmillan, 1985) 47.

14. Intervening landslide winners had competition: Lyndon Johnson was opposed by George Wallace in 1964, Richard Nixon by Pete McCloskey and John Ashbrook in 1972.

Chapter 59
Celebration

1. Laurence I. Barrett, *Gambling with History: Reagan in the White House* (New York: Penguin, 1985) 488.

2. For example, David A. Stockman, *The Triumph of Politics: Why the Reagan Revolution Failed* (New York: Harper & Row, 1986); Donald T. Regan, *For the Record: From Wall Street to Washington* (New York: Harcourt Brace Jovanovich, 1988).

3. These figures are and always will be imprecise, because the votes in Iowa are never precisely computed. The Democrats elect delegates to county conventions in each precinct caucus, but to add up either just the number of votes cast for delegates backing each presidential candidate or just the number of elected delegates backing each candidate would be misleading, because a small precinct or county may have a large turnout or number of county convention delegates, or vice versa. The state Democratic party prepares a count of state-convention-delegate-equivalents, to provide a measure of presidential candidates' strength commensurate with the state's population of Dem-

ocrats; but the figure is necessarily imprecise. Hugh Winebrenner, *The Iowa Precinct Caucuses* (Ames: Iowa State Univ., 1987) 144–48. To put it more harshly: one of the key numbers on which the American presidential delegate selection system depends is a guess.

4. Michael Barone, "He's a Trend Democrat," *Washington Post,* 1 March 1984.

5. I attended a dinner at Hart's house in Bethesda, Maryland, with five other members of the press and Mrs. Hart in the last week of December 1983, at which the candidate laid out the strategy he would follow and the reasons he believed it would be successful. His first meeting with Caddell was not until December 31. Jack W. Germond and Jules Witcover, *Wake Us When It's Over: Presidential Politics of 1984* (New York: Macmillan, 1985) 151. This was not the first time Caddell has been given more credit for a candidate's strategy than he deserves. He was widely credited with Joseph Biden's winning themes in his upset victory in the 1972 Senate race. But in a May 1972 interview, Biden, then a twenty-nine-year-old member of the New Castle County (Delaware) Council, described the arguments he was making and the tactics he was using to beat Senator Caleb Boggs. The interview took place before he ever met Caddell, whom he says he hired to get credibility with Washington-based fund-raisers.

6. I prepared the first draft of the editorial, though the sequence was not precisely as described by Bob Faw and Nancy Skelton, *Thunder in America* (Austin: Texas Monthly, 1986) 49–50, or Elizabeth O. Colton, *The Jackson Phenomenon: The Man, the Power, the Message* (New York: Doubleday, 1989) 83–86.

7. Congresswoman Shirley Chisholm had run in 1972, winning 3% of total votes cast; and Channing Phillips, a Washington, D.C. minister, had been nominated and received votes at the 1968 convention.

8. Germond and Witcover 319.

9. The polls showed the following Reagan leads: Gallup, 48%–47% (January 13–16); ABC/*Washington Post,* 49%–46% (January 12–17); CBS/*New York Times,* 48%–32% (January 14–21).

10. The results are collected in *Public Opinion,* Oct./Nov. 1984, 38–39.

11. Ed Zschau, personal interview, August 1984.

12. Ronald Reagan has voted for a larger number and a larger percentage of winning presidential candidates than any other president in American history: for twelve winners (Roosevelt four times, Truman, Eisenhower twice, Nixon in 1968 and 1972, himself twice, and Bush) and for only three losers (Nixon in 1960, Goldwater, and Ford).

13. Elizabeth Drew, *Campaign Journal: The Political Events of 1983–1984* (New York: Macmillan, 1985) 693–94.

14. CBS/*New York Times, Los Angeles Times,* NBC, and ABC, conveniently collected in *Public Opinion,* Dec. 1984/Jan. 1985, 28–29.

15. Walter Polovchak with Kevin Klose, *Freedom's Child: A Courageous Teenager's Story of Fleeing His Parents—and the Soviet Union—to Live in America* (New York: Random House, 1988). See also Michael Barone, "Why the Young Are Going for Reagan," *Washington Post,* 21 October 1984.

16. The key works on this race are William D. Snider, *Helms & Hunt: The North Carolina Senate Race, 1984* (Chapel Hill: Univ. of North Carolina, 1985), and Ernest B. Furgurson, *Hard Right: The Rise of Jesse Helms* (New York: Norton, 1986).

17. One analyst describes North Carolina as the prototypical "new American" state, with its small cities and relatively small business units and state government. John Herbers, *The New American Heartland* (New York: Times Books, 1986) 28–38.

Chapter 60
Peace

1. John McPhee, *A Sense of Where You Are: A Profile of Bill Bradley at Princeton* (New York: Farrar, Straus & Giroux, 1965). The title comes from Bradley's description of how he routinely made a certain shot while looking in the other direction. " 'When you have played basketball for a while, you don't need to look at the basket when you are close in like this,' he said, throwing it over his shoulder again and right through the hoop. 'You develop a sense of where you are.' " McPhee 22.
2. On the development of Bradley's thinking the definitive work is Jeffrey H. Birnbaum and Alan S. Murray, *Showdown at Gucci Gulch: Lawmakers, Lobbyists and the Unlikely Triumph of Tax Reform* (New York: Random House, 1987) 23–33.
3. *The Fair Tax* (New York: Pocket Books, 1984). His *Life on the Run* (New York: Quadrangle, 1976), a description of his days as a New York Knick, is first-rate.
4. See Michael Barone, "The Age of Restraint," *Washington Post*, 15 Sept. 1985.
5. A major part of the reason is that in California, which cast one out of seven votes in these Senate races, Democrat Alan Cranston won big in 1980 and only narrowly in 1986.

Chapter 61
Confirmation

1. Jane Mayer and Doyle McManus, *Landslide: The Unmaking of the President* (Boston: Houghton Mifflin, 1988).
2. David S. Broder, *Behind the Front Page* (New York: Simon & Schuster, 1987) 28. The full passage reads: "It is not an accident that we refer to 'news stories' as the basic ingredient of news. Reporters are essentially storytellers, heirs to a narrative tradition as old as mankind. Stories have settings and characters and plot lines. Whether we acknowledge it or not, we are constantly devising the scripts we think are appropriate to the events we are covering."
3. Harry Truman and Lyndon Johnson bowed out after setbacks in primaries in March 1952 and March 1968. Herbert Hoover in 1932, Franklin Roosevelt in 1936, 1940, and 1944, Truman in 1948, Dwight Eisenhower in 1956, Johnson in 1964, Richard Nixon in 1972, Gerald Ford in 1976, Jimmy Carter in 1980, and Ronald Reagan in 1984 all ran for reelection.
4. "In an entire half-hour news broadcast we speak only as many words as there are on two-thirds of one page of a standard newspaper." Walter Cronkite, *The Challenges of Change* (Washington: Public Affairs Press, 1971) 103–4.
5. See George Bush, *Looking Forward* (New York: Doubleday, 1987), for amazingly modest claims about his previous experience.
6. This was a particular obsession of Garry Trudeau, author of the syndicated comic

strip *Doonesbury,* a barometer of Baby Boom attitudes since its first national appearance in 1970. Trudeau graduated from the St. Paul's School in Concord, New Hampshire, and Yale.

7. This was one contest in which none of the networks conducted an exit poll, so the precise percentage is uncertain.

8. The figures are collected in *Public Opinion,* Sept./Oct. 1988, 36–37.

9. An independent committee did run a national television spot showing Horton's face. But neither that ad nor Horton's southern-style name was needed to cue voters that he was black. In the middle 1980s, 46% of American prison inmates were black—a fact which intellectuals and journalists might not want the public to know, but which would not have come as a surprise to most ordinary Americans.

10. The results are collected in *Public Opinion,* Nov./Dec. 1988, 36–39.

11. Michael Barone and Grant Ujifusa, *The Almanac of American Politics, 1990* (Washington: National Journal, 1989) xxvi–xxviii.

12. The figures are from exit polls collected in *Public Opinion,* Jan./Feb. 1989, 24–32.